THEORIES OF
BEHAVIOR
THERAPY

Exploring Behavior Change

Edited by

WILLIAM O'DONOHUE &
LEONARD KRASNER

American Psychological Association
Washington, DC

Published by
American Psychological Association
750 First Street, NE
Washington, DC 20002

Copies may be ordered from
APA Order Department
P.O. Box 2710
Hyattsville, MD 20784

In the UK and Europe, copies may be ordered from
American Psychological Association
3 Henrietta Street
Covent Garden, London
WC2E 8LU England

Typeset in Goudy by PRO-Image Corporation, Techna-Type Div., York, PA

Printer: Data Reproductions Corp., Rochester Hills, MI
Cover and Jacket Designer: Paul Perlow Design, New York, NY
Technical/Production Editor: Kathryn Lynch

Library of Congress Cataloging-in-Publication Data
Theories of behavior therapy : exploring behavior change / edited by
  William O'Donohue & Leonard Krasner.
    p.   cm.
  Includes bibliographical references and index.
  ISBN 1-55798-265-1
  1. Behavior therapy—Philosophy. I. O'Donohue, William T.
II. Krasner, Leonard, 1924–
RC489.B4T525   1995
616.89'142—dc20   94-48476
                                                                        CIP

British Library Cataloguing-in-Publication Data
A CIP record is available from the British Library.

Printed in the United States of America
First edition

CONTENTS

CONTRIBUTORS

Felicity C. Allen, La Trobe University, Bundoora, Victoria, Australia

David H. Barlow, University at Albany, State University of New York

Michele M. Carter, University at Albany, State University of New York

Daniel Cervone, University of Illinois at Chicago

James V. Corwin, Northern Illinois University

Carol M. Dahlquist, Educational Research and Services Center

Dennis Delprato, Eastern Michigan University

David J. Drobes, University of Florida

Barbara Hawk, Pediatric Psychology, Chapel Hill Pediatrics, Chapel Hill, North Carolina

Pamela M. Heck, Lawrence University

Thomas E. Joiner, Jr., University of Texas Medical Branch at Galveston

Paul Karoly, Arizona State University

Kathryn G. Karsh, Educational Research and Services Center

Leonard Krasner, Stanford University

Robert J. Kohlenberg, University of Washington

Rebecca S. Laird, Appleton, Wisconsin

Peter J. Lang, University of Florida

D. R. Laws, Alberta Hospital, Edmonton, Alberta, Canada[1]

Donald J. Levis, State University of New York at Binghamton

Marsha M. Linehan, University of Washington

M. Christine Lovejoy, Northern Illinois University

Dorothy E. McAllister, Northern Illinois University

Wallace R. McAllister, Northern Illinois University

Elizabeth C. McDonel, Indiana University

Gerald I. Metalsky, Lawrence University

Dennis Munk, Educational Research and Services Center

James P. Noll, Department of Veterans Affairs, Lexington, Kentucky

William O'Donohue, Northern Illinois University

Alan C. Repp, Northern Illinois University

Henry Schmidt III, University of Washington

Walter D. Scott, University of Illinois at Chicago

James J. Snyder, Wichita State University

Arthur W. Staats, University of Hawaii at Manoa

---

[1]Now at Adult Forensic Services, Victoria, British Columbia, Canada

Kevin J. Tierney, University of Ulster at Jordanstown, Northern Ireland

William Timberlake, Indiana University

Mavis Tsai, Seattle, Washington

Jerome D. Ulman, Ball State University

Joseph Wolpe, Pepperdine University

INTRODUCTION

Future historians of psychotherapy will likely regard the twentieth century as pivotal in the development of psychotherapy for several reasons:

1. Although medicine historically held a hegemony over legitimized "healing," in the twentieth century nonphysiological (psychological) therapies were developed and were accepted by both professionals and consumers. At least some nonmedical practices were no longer widely regarded by either professionals or the general public as quackery. An important contributor to the increased acceptance and status of nonmedical therapies was their enhanced relationship with science.

2. Physiological and nonphysiological therapies began to be considered complementary rather than antithetical. Medical and nonmedical therapies were each thought to be necessary components in the treatment of problems such as depression, attention deficit disorder, schizophrenia, and many of the anxiety disorders. This development eased some of the animus and competition between medical and nonmedical professionals.

3. Models and theories of psychotherapy proliferated greatly. Although it is difficult to enumerate these models because it is sometimes difficult to determine when a deviation from some paradigm is of sufficient magnitude to constitute a new model (O'Donohue & McKelvie, 1993) or whether some form of therapist behavior is sufficiently systematized to constitute a model, some have claimed that there are over 400 schools of psychotherapy as of the later part of the twentieth century (Beitman, Goldfried, & Norcross, 1989).

4. There were significant shifts in ascendancy among the various competing schools of psychotherapy. The most influential therapy of the first half of the twentieth century was psychoanalysis and its offshoots, and

the most influential therapy of the second half of the twentieth century is behavior therapy.[1]

5. In the middle of the century, increased concern was expressed over evaluating the effectiveness of therapy. Individuals began to argue that the standards of evidence for indicating that therapy was effective needed to be raised. In the 1950s, many serious doubts were raised about the effectiveness of the standard therapies.

6. Intimately associated with the previous development was the notion that science and clinical pursuits should be closer. One of the first ways that this was raised was through the notion that science should be used to evaluate the effectiveness of psychotherapy. Rogerian therapy and behavior therapy were among the leaders in advocating and practicing this position (Eysenck, 1964; Rogers, 1961).

7. In the middle of the century, another position concerning the relation between science and psychotherapy became more popular: the view that the results of basic sciences relevant to human behavior could form the basis of extrapolations to clinical interventions. The relationship of experimental psychology to clinical psychology would have important parallels to the relationship of basic physiology to medicine, or chemistry and physics to engineering.

8. The influence of ideas associated with psychotherapy was not confined to psychotherapy alone. Rather, these ideas had a widespread influence, extending to such diverse areas as literary interpretation, political science, and historiography (in the case of psychoanalysis) and to industry, ecology, athletics, and architecture, to name a few examples (in the case of behavior therapy). Parts of the psychological idiom became so widespread that it was no longer regarded as professional jargon. Phrases and words such as *positive reinforcement, negative reinforcement, time out,* and *assertiveness* were used by more and more nonprofessionals. Psychotherapeutic practice and theory began to become part of the larger culture.

9. However, there was a mistrust of theory on the part of both professionals and nonprofessionals. This was largely due to the fact that many schools of psychotherapy have a disproportionate relationship between their claims and data that can corroborate or falsify their claims.

10. Although behavior therapy was never a homogeneous movement, in that even in its beginning it had Wolpean (reciprocal inhibition and systematic desensitization) and Skinnerian (operant behavior and applied behavioral analysis) branches, as behavior therapy developed, more streams of thought developed. To be sure, most of these streams had certain commonalities or at least some broad family resemblances. However, clearly,

---

[1]We also want to avoid the reification of behavior therapy. Although for the sake of economy we have spoken of behavior therapy as if it is a thing or an actor, it clearly is not. Behavior therapy consists of the behavior of behavior therapists and their clients.

behavior therapy toward the end of the twentieth century contained a number of distinct sets of ideas.

These broad developments set some of the context for the creation of behavior therapy. Krasner (1980, p. 7) listed some of the more specific influences:

- The concept of *behaviorism* in experimental psychology (e.g., J. R. Kantor, 1924, 1963)
- The instrumental (operant) conditioning concepts of Thorndike (1931) and Skinner (1938)
- The technique of reciprocal inhibition as developed by Wolpe (1958)
- The studies of the group of investigators at Maudsely Hospital in London under the direction of H. J. Eysenck (1960, 1964)
- The investigations (from the 1920s through the 1940s) applying *conditioning* concepts to human behavior problems in the United States (e.g., Mowrer & Mowrer, 1938; Watson & Rayner, 1920)
- Interpretations of psychoanalysis in learning theory terms (e.g., Dollard & Miller, 1950), enhancing learning theory as a respectable base for clinical work
- Classical conditioning as the basis for explaining and changing normal and deviant behavior (Pavlov, 1928)
- Theoretical concepts and research studies of social role learning and interactionism, social psychology, and sociology
- Research in developmental and child psychology, which emphasized vicarious learning and modeling (Bandura, 1970; Jones, 1924)
- Social influence studies of demand characteristics, experimenter bias, hypnosis, and placebo (Frank, 1961)
- An environmental social learning model as an alternative to a disease model of human behavior (Bandura, 1969; Ullmann & Krasner, 1965)
- Dissatisfaction with psychotherapy and the psychoanalytic model
- The development of the clinical psychologist as scientist–practitioner
- A group of psychiatrists emphasizing human interaction (e.g., Adolph Meyer, 1948; Harry Stack Sullivan, 1953)
- A utopian stream emphasizing the planning of social environments to elicit and maintain the best of man's behavior (e.g., Skinner's, 1976, *Walden Two*)

Behavior therapy has always been controversial. From its beginning, it provided a strong challenge to many received ideas and practices. It questioned the extent to which the then current forms of psychotherapy were effective (Eysenck, 1952). It pointed to the absence of evidence for many forms of "psychotherapy" and questioned the evidential value of some commonly accepted methodologies, such as the case study. It proposed a set of historically quite stringent criteria for therapy evaluation (Paul, 1969). It questioned the medical model of psychological problems as inner mental illnesses (Ullmann & Krasner, 1969). It criticized the worth of existing taxonomies of problems in living and existing assessment methods (Cone & Hawkins, 1977; Kanfer & Saslow, 1969). It called into question nearly all aspects of accepted psychodynamic theory, from its testability to its assertions regarding psychosexual development, to its hydraulic model of pathology, to its mental anatomy, to its specific claims regarding the etiology of the neuroses. On another front, it criticized the possibility of a "nondirective" therapist (Krasner, 1962). It questioned the value of treasured notions such as personality (Krasner & Ullmann, 1973) and traits (Mischel, 1973). It challenged the usual role of cognition in explaining and causing human behavior (Skinner, 1953).

Thus, from the beginning, behavior therapy was very much the *enfant terrible*, radically challenging the status quo. Moreover, note that behavior therapists were not critics of the established order who had nothing to replace what they found so problematic: They offered replacement taxonomies, measurement methods, therapy methods, standards of evidence, research methods, theories of the cause of psychological problems, and so on. And despite the fact that its challenges were carried out on many fronts and were quite sophisticated and despite the qualities of proffered replacements, behavior therapy somehow gained a reputation among its many detractors as a simpleminded, superficial therapy movement. If Archimedes thought that he could move the world if only given a fulcrum, behavior therapists were characterized as clinicians who believed that they could change the world if only given enough M&Ms. But despite the claims of its detractors, behavior therapy has always been and continues to be much more than the application of reinforcement.

This book is a compendium of some of the major sets of ideas contained in behavior therapy. The reader can judge to what extent these ideas are *simpleminded, superficial,* or deserving of any other pejorative label. What is clear to us, however, is that behavior therapy is a diverse, complex set of values, theories, research methods, assessment procedures, therapy techniques, institutional entities, and social relationships.

Part of the diversity of behavior therapy comes from the diversity of the many streams of influence that affected behavior therapy in its origins. Part of the continued diversity of the behavior therapy movement comes from the continued evolution of these different influences. As a case in point, implosion therapy (see Levis, chapter 7) had different roots (Hullian learning theory, two-factor theory of fear, Pavlovian conditioning, and psychoanalysis) than, say, the more operant-based coercion theory; as implosion theory evolved, it continued to be influenced by different developments than did coercion theory (see Snyder, chapter 12). Why are both considered to be a part of behavior therapy? Largely because both share the commonality of being heavily influenced by conditioning research and theory.

However, another important influence on the diversity of the behavior therapy movement comes from the wide variety of contexts of inquiry that behavior therapists have addressed. As we have discussed previously, behavior therapy had many positions regarding many different issues: It was not a "single-idea" phenomenon. Within behavior therapy, it is common to find that behavior therapists take different positions on these issues. Implosion theorists are less rejecting of psychoanalysis than are applied behavior analysts. Some prominent behavior therapists are less critical of the medical model than are others. Behavior therapists draw on different aspects of the also nonmonolithic experimental psychology. Some exclusively rely on conditioning research, others on cognitive psychology, and others on both. And even when drawing on the same general topic area, behavior therapists focus on different aspects of the topic area. For example, some behavior therapists are influenced by Skinner's original empirical definition of reinforcement; some by Premack's theory; others by response deprivation; and others by a matching law analysis.

Finally, behavior therapists have been concerned with a wide variety of problems. Some focus on treating fears, some on depression, some on conduct problems of children, some on teaching the mentally retarded academic or daily living skills, some on decreasing resource consumption, some on changing personality disorders, some on sexual problems, and so on. Moreover, some behavior therapists are more concerned with assessment, others with treatment, others with prevention, and others with understanding the causal nexus of the changeworthy behavior. It is reasonable to assume not that these problems will yield to a single solution, but rather that their resolutions will require a wide variety of research methodologies, theories, assessment instruments, and therapeutic strategies.

Thus, we see this diversity as understandable, given the variety of influences on the origins of behavior therapy, on the diversity of the continuing evolution of these influences, on the diversity contained in the influences themselves, and on the diversity of problems on which behavior therapists have focused. Behavior therapy is not a single-idea, single-problem phenomenon.

There are no necessary or sufficient criteria for defining behavior therapy. Rather, in our view, the different theories of behavior therapy hold a family resemblance to one another. As Wittgenstein (1958) illustrated in the case of games:

Consider for example the proceedings that we call "games". I mean board-games, card-games, ball-games, Olympic games, and so on. What is common to them all—Don't say: "There *must* be something common, or they would not be called 'games' "—but *look and see* whether there is anything common to all—For if you look at them you will not see something that is common to *all*, but similarities, relationships, and a whole series of them at that. . . . Are they all "amusing"? Compare chess with naughts and crosses. Or is there always winning and losing, or competition between players? Think of patience. In ball games there is winning and losing; but when a child throws his ball at the wall and catches it again, this feature has disappeared. Look at the parts played by skill and luck; and at the difference between skill in chess and skill in tennis. Think now of games like ring-aring-aroses; here is the element of amusement, but how many other characteristic features have disappeared! And we can go through the many, many other groups of games in the same way; can see how similarities crop up and disappear. And the result of this examination is: we see a complicated network of similarities overlapping and criss-crossing: sometimes overall similarities, sometimes similarities of detail. (pp. 31–32)

Although themes such as experimentalism; extrapolations of experimental psychology, particularly conditioning research; and environmentalism may exist in behavior theories, these themes are not definitive. Therefore we see the theories contained in this book, to borrow Wittgenstein's (1958) felicitous phrase, as also consisting of a "complicated network of similarities overlapping and criss-crossing: sometimes overall similarities, sometimes similarities of detail" (p. 32).

ORGANIZATION OF THIS VOLUME

The order of appearance of chapters in a book such as this is always a tough issue. Some systematic scheme that does justice to some inherent themes or developments across chapters is desired. However, the ordering should do justice to exactly how much order is inherent in chapters. At all costs, no artificial order should be constructed for editorial convenience.

The heuristic we used for ordering the chapters was as follows: We wanted both to give the reader some appreciation of the historical development of behavior therapy and simultaneously to provide some contiguity regarding the particular problems or topics being covered. Because Wolpe's theory of reciprocal inhibition and Skinner's theory of positive reinforcement were clearly the two major pillars on which behavior therapy developed in the 1950s, the book begins with chapters covering reciprocal inhibition theory (Wolpe) and reinforcement theory (Timberlake). The next two chapters, on molar regulation (Tierny) and the matching law (Noll), continue with the theme of the influence of the experimental analysis of behavior on behavior therapy by depicting some major developments in an operant/reinforcement analysis. Continuing with the theme of conditioning as a critical factor in the development and treatment of change-worthy behavior, the next two chapters cover two-factor fear theory (McAllister & McAllister) and a therapy that is heavily influenced by this theory, implosion theory (Levis). Completing the theme of behavior therapies whose major focus is on fear and anxiety, the next two chapters cover Barlow's theory of learned alarms (Carter & Barlow) and Lang's bioinformational theory (Drobes & Lang).

The three chapters just mentioned begin to illustrate another important development in behavior therapy: the role of cognition and its interrelationship with conditioning. This theme is then followed by the next seven chapters, with an increased emphasis on cognition in the chapters on self-control (Karoly), self-efficacy (Cervone & Scott), attribution (Metalsky et al.), relapse prevention (Laws), and social information processing (McDonel & McFall). Two chapters (on developmental theories [Lovejoy & Hawk] and on coercion [Snyder]) in this group cover another important theme in behavior therapy: the behavior problems of children. The chapter on coercion theory, which clearly was most heavily influenced by conditioning research and theory, was placed in this group because we thought that it should follow the broad context provided by the chapter on developmental perspectives.

The next three chapters cover some of the ideas that were developed outside of the traditional influences of behavior therapy, which because of their large influence on our culture, influenced behavior therapy: evolution (Corwin & O'Donohue), feminism (Allen), and Marxism (Ulman). Because Marxism emphasizes dialectics, Linehan's theory of dialectical behavior therapy follows this chapter. Finally, the next four chapters provide either broad models of how behavior therapy should be implemented or an explication of a philosophy of science on which behavior therapy, in the authors' view, should be based. The chapters on interbehavioral psychology (Delprato) and paradigmatic behaviorism (Staats) do the latter, whereas the chapters on hypothesis-based interventions (Repp et al.) and functional analytic therapy (Kohlenberg & Tsai) do the former. We (O'Donohue & Krasner) conclude the book with a chapter on the role of theories in the progression of behavior therapy.

Are there any theories that should have been included that were omitted from this book? The answer, unfortunately, is yes. A chapter on multimodal therapy was to be included, but it is not, owing to the press of commitments of its intended author. In retrospect, we also think that chapters on generalizability theory and behavioral community psychology would have added greatly to this book. Unfortunately, these (and other chapters) would have increased the size (and cost) of an already large book. Perhaps in another edition.

A word on the title of this book. We chose to use the preposition *of* in the title in its possessive sense that these are all theories that belong to the behavior therapy movement. Note that the theories described in the following chapters differ greatly in their scope. Some are broad theories of behavior therapy, and these in another sense of *of* are theories of behavior therapy. Others have a more narrow focus (e.g., a theory of fear acquisition, maintenance, and extinction). Because these are commonly thought of, for a variety of reasons, as behavioral theories, they are included in this book.

This book was the product of the efforts of many people. We would first of all like to thank all the chapter authors. It was an honor to work with such an outstanding group of scholars. We also hold a large debt of gratitude to the staff of APA Books: Theodore Baroody, Julia Frank-McNeil, Kathy Lynch, and Susan Reynolds. The staff at Northern Illinois University—Judy Atherton, Cindy Buck, and Cheryl Ross—were always there to provide assistance as needed.

Finally, we would like to thank the members of our families—Jane, Katie, Miriam, Wendy, David, Charles, and Stefanie—for their kindness, patience, and support during this project.

REFERENCES

Bandura, A. (1969). *Principles of behavior modification.* New York: Holt, Rinehart & Winston.

Bandura, A. (1970). Modeling theory. In W. S. Sahakian (Ed.), *Psychology of learning systems, models, and theories.* Chicago: Markham.

Beitman, B. D., Goldfried, M. R., & Norcross, J. C. (1989). The movement toward integrating the psychotherapies: An overview. *American Journal of Psychiatry, 146,* 138–147.

Cone, J. D., & Hawkins, R. P. (Eds.). (1977). *Behavioral assessment: New directions in clinical psychology.* New York: Brunner/Mazel.

Dollard, J., & Miller, N. E. (1950). *Personality and psychotherapy: An analysis in terms of learning, thinking, and culture.* New York: McGraw-Hill.

Eysenck, H. J. (1952). The effects of psychotherapy: An evaluation. *Journal of Consulting Psychology, 16,* 319–324.

Eysenck, H. J. (1960). *Behavior therapy and the neuroses.* London: Pergamon Press.

Eysenck, H. J. (Ed.). (1964). *Experiments in behavior therapy.* New York: Pergamon Press.

Frank, J. D. (1961). *Persuasion and healing.* Baltimore: Johns Hopkins Press.

Jones, M. C. (1924). A laboratory study of fear: The case of Peter. *Pedagogical Seminary and Journal of Genetic Psychology, 31,* 308–315.

Kanfer, F. H., & Saslow, G. (1969). Behavioral diagnosis. In C. M. Franks (Ed.), *Behavior therapy: Appraisal and status* (pp. 417–444). New York: McGraw-Hill.

Kantor, J. R. (1924). *Principles of psychology*. New York: Knopf.

Kantor, J. R. (1963). *The scientific evolution of psychology*. Chicago: Principia Press.

Krasner, L. (1962). The therapist as a social reinforcement machine. In H. H. Strupp & L. Luborsky (Eds.), *Research in psychotherapy* (Vol. 2, 61–94). Washington, DC: American Psychological Assocaition.

Krasner, L. (1980). Introduction. In L. Krasner (Ed.), *Environmental design and human behavior*. Elmsford, NY: Pergamon Press.

Krasner, L., & Ullmann, L. P. (1973). *Behavior influence and personality: The social matrix of human action*. New York: Holt, Rinehart & Winston.

Meyer, A. (1948–1952). *Collected papers of Adolf Meyer* (Vols. 1–4). Baltimore: Johns Hopkins Press.

Mischel, W. (1973). Toward a cognitive social learning reconceptualization of personality. *Psychological Review, 80,* 252–283.

Mowrer, O. H., & Mowrer, W. M. (1938). Enuresis—A method of its study and treatment. *American Journal of Orthopsychiatry, 8,* 436–459.

O'Donohue, W. T., & McKelvie, M. (1993). Problems in the case for psychotherapeutic integration. *Journal of Behavior Therapy and Experimental Psychiatry, 24,* 161–170.

Paul, G. L. (1969). Behavior modification research: Design and tactics. In C. M. Franks (Ed.), *Behavior therapy: Appraisal and status* (pp. 29–62). New York: McGraw-Hill.

Pavlov, I. P. (1928). *Lectures on conditioned reflexes* (W. H. Gantt, Trans.). New York: International Publishers.

Rogers, C. (1961). *On becoming a person*. Boston: Houghton Mifflin.

Skinner, B. F. (1938). *The behavior of organisms*. New York: Appleton-Century-Crofts.

Skinner, B. F. (1953). *Science and human behavior*. New York: Macmillan.

Skinner, B. F. (1976). *Walden two*. New York: Macmillan.

Sullivan, H. S. (1953). *The interpersonal theory of psychiatry*. New York: Norton.

Thorndike, E. L. (1931). *Human learning*. New York: Century.

Ullmann, L. P., & Krasner, L. (Eds.). (1965). *Case studies in behavior modification*. New York: Holt, Rinehart & Winston.

Ullmann, L. P., & Krasner, L. (1969). *A psychological approach to abnormal behavior*. Englewood Cliffs, NJ: Prentice-Hall.

Watson, J. B., & Rayner, R. (1920). Conditioned emotional reactions. *Journal of Experimental Psychology, 3,* 1–14.

Wittgenstein, L. (1958). *Philosophical investigations* (G. E. M. Anscombe, Trans.). New York: Macmillan.

Wolpe, J. (1958). *Psychotherapy by reciprocal inhibition*. Stanford, CA: Stanford University Press.

1

THEORIES IN BEHAVIOR THERAPY: PHILOSOPHICAL AND HISTORICAL CONTEXTS

WILLIAM O'DONOHUE and LEONARD KRASNER

The word *theory* is sometimes used in a pejorative manner. For example, in debates about evolution, detractors claim that evolution is "just a theory." Or one hears that a good, hard-headed scientist is only interested in facts (i.e., empirical observations) as opposed to the unfortunate, woolly-minded, armchair speculator who is preoccupied with theories.

However, we must hasten to add that this is a bit simplistic because in other instances theories are taken to be paradigmatic (and fairly uncontroversial) examples of important scientific achievements. Einstein's theories of relativity, Pasteur's germ theory of disease, and Kepler's heliocentric theory of the planets are cases in point.

William James (1890) once suggested that psychologists could be sorted into two groups: the "hard-headed" and the "soft-hearted." The first group are data-oriented, conservative in the inferences they make from these data, and highly skeptical, at least until the force of meticulously collected and overwhelming data sways them. The soft-hearted, on the other hand, are concerned that methodological strictness may miss something essential in the phenomenon of interest, and therefore they are less methodologically rigorous, interested more in thought experiments than empirical ones, and more interested in generating abstract general accounts.

Behavior therapists have generally been thought of as being the hard-headed type. (Although admittedly detractors have probably thought of them as a hybrid, third type: soft-headed and hard-hearted!) As hard-headed, behavior therapists have been thought of as not valuing theory. In this view, Skinner's cumulative record data are seen in stark contrast to Freud's "theoretical" interpretations of his clients. In fact, Krasner and Houts (1984) found, in a survey of the value positions of therapists, evidence that a group of behavior therapists who were influential in launching the behavior therapy movement in the 30 years after World War II valued theory significantly less than a comparison group consisting of nonbehavioral psychologists of the same period.

These general reflections bring up questions such as, Is a theory a good thing or a bad thing?; What exactly is a theory?; What roles do theories play in science?; and What is the relationship between theory and fact? In this chapter we examine the role of theories in science and in applied science. First, we examine what some influential historians and philosophers of science have said regarding the roles of theory in science. In doing this we find that there is strong agreement that theories—at least certain types of theory—play essential roles in science, and in playing these roles, are "good things." In examining the arguments of these historians and philosophers we define *theory* as well as attempt to help clarify the relationships among theory, experimentation, and fact.

These questions are examined to pave the way for a fuller appreciation of the legitimate role of theory in behavior therapy. Thus, a second section of this chapter is devoted to a brief history of the role of theory in behavior therapy. We see that theory was critical to the beginnings of behavior therapy (i.e., in Wolpe's reciprocal inhibition and in Skinner's operant account of abnormal behavior) and continues to be important in contemporary behavior therapy. The following chapters, in fact, are a demonstration of the importance of theory to contemporary behavior therapy.

THEORIES IN SCIENCE: PERSPECTIVES FROM THE PHILOSOPHY OF SCIENCE

Logical Positivism

The logical positivists provided three key claims regarding the role of theories in science: (a) A theory's relationship to empirical observations is particularly important because this observational basis bestows a special kind of warrant on more general, theoretical statements. (b) Theories are essential because they are the linguistic repositories for representing and summarizing particular empirical observations. (c) Theories have a critical role in explanation and prediction—two key goals of science.

The logical positivists argued that all knowledge is derived from empirical observations and, therefore, all meaningful statements must be verifiable by observation. The positivists thought that many problems arose because some propositions seem meaningful (because they appear to be syntactically correct), but a proper examination would reveal that they are actually unverifiable and hence meaningless. Therefore, the sentence, "God is good," is meaningless because no empirical state of affairs can confirm this proposition. Thus, empirical observations are the touchstone of all meaningful utterances and the foundation of all knowledge.

Despite the primacy placed on observation sentences, the logical positivists thought that theories had an essential role in science because some linguistic entity was necessary to serve as a repository for individual empirical observations. Scientific research does not seek as an end to record data about particulars, but seeks to discover general regularities, laws, and relationships that can be used for prediction and explanation. Moreover, the logical positivists thought that theories were essential in depicting the relationships between diverse sets of empirical observations. Thus, sentences in a theory pick out and summarize the order that becomes evident across numerous and disparate observations.

However, in order to perform these legitimate roles, the theories must be clearly and formally connected to empirical observations. The ideal theory for the logical positivists was viewed as a deductive axiomatic system in which scientific laws served as the axioms, and correspondence rules connected these axioms with empirical observations. An example of a correspondence rule is the following: The mean kinetic energy of a gas's molecules (an unobservable, theoretical term) is proportional to the temperature of the gas (an observable phenomenon). As another example, the positivists agreed with Hume that the concept of causation, which is critical to science, is not directly observable. Thus, theoretical talk about causes is legitimized by observations of constant concomitant variation or functional relationships.

Therefore, according to the logical positivists, a theory is a formal axiomatic system in which the connections between scientific laws and observables are explicit. Theories, if they are properly constructed, are good things because they provide general statements about many particular observations, and they represent other abstract relations (e.g., causal) between observables. However, the positivists thought that many theories had terms that were not properly tied to observables and as such were metaphysical and meaningless. Thus, although the positivists thought that, in principle, theories were essential, it is probably fair to say that they thought that many existing theories were fundamentally flawed and contained meaning-less elements.

The prominent logical empiricist, Carl Hempel (1967), depicted the manner in which theories are used in scientific explanation and prediction. According to Hempel's covering law model of scientific explanation, explanations have the form of valid deductive arguments. The premises of the argument contain statements of initial conditions that may be relevant to the theory, as well as statements of laws contained in the theory. Thus, when asked, Why did the apple fall to the earth? one can give an explanation in terms of Newton's law of universal gravitation (i.e., any two bodies exert forces on each other that are proportional to the product of their masses divided by the square of the distance between them), as well as by statements of the values of variables needed for the law (i.e., the initial conditions of distance between the two masses, as well as the magnitude of the two masses).

Hempel (1967) also pointed out that there was an important symmetry between explanation and prediction. Prediction uses the same form as explanation; however, in prediction the conclusion is about a future event, in contrast with explanation, which is concerned with a past event. Thus, the question might have been, What will happen if this apple is released from my hand? Again, the prediction would use Newton's law and statements of the initial conditions as premises of a valid deductive argument. Therefore, theories play a central role in two key activities of science, explanation and prediction, by specifying relevant laws and variables to be used.

Popper

Popper (1963), too, thought that theories were essential in science, although for different reasons than the positivists. Popper thought that human beings in response to the problems that they inevitably encounter naturally hold a number of theories about the world and that scientific theories initially grow out of correcting the errors in these folk theories. He also maintained that theories suggest methodologies and lines of research, and, therefore, actually logically precede empirical observations. Thus, for Popper, theories drive observations whereas, for the logical positivists, observations drive theories.

Popper (1963) thought that the logical positivist account of theory was flawed in two major ways: (a) Theories contain universal laws (e.g., all copper conducts electricity), and universal laws are not completely grounded in sense experience (because every piece of copper has not been examined). Thus, Popper pointed out that claims can be meaningful and have surplus content to their observational base. (b) Theories logically precede sense observations and, therefore, are not derived or constructed from sense observations. Popper (1963) stated,

> The belief that we can start with pure observations alone, without anything in the nature of a theory is absurd . . . . Twenty five years ago I tried to bring home the same point to a group of physics students in Vienna by beginning a lecture with the following instructions: Take pencil and paper; carefully observe, and write down what you have observed. They asked of course, *what* I wanted them to observe . . . . Observation is always selection. It needs a chosen object, a definite task, an interest, a point of view, a problem. (p. 46)

Popper thought that science begins with problems (not sense observations as the positivists claimed), and in response to problems a tentative theory is proposed. These problems and theories can be highly related. For example, Koertge (1980) stated,

> Scientific problems arise when our expectations are violated, when what we consider to be regularities call for a deeper explanation, when two previously disparate fields look as if they could be united, or when a good scientific theory clashes with our familiar metaphysical framework. (p. 347)

What distinguishes science from nonscience is that in science these tentative theories are tested in an attempt to eliminate their errors. Popper (1963) suggested that good theory testing relied on the valid logical inference rule of *modus tollens*:

1. If the theory is true, then this observational statement should be true.
2. But the research shows that this observational statement is not true.
3. Therefore, the theory is not true.

Thus, three key questions for Popper's falsificationist view of theory appraisal were as follows: (a) What is the set of potential falsifiers of this theory (e.g., the observable states of affairs that the theory rules out)? In general, better theories are more falsifiable. For example, theories that make point predictions are better (i.e., more falsifiable because they rule out all points except one) than theories that make only directional predictions. (b) Is experimentation actually seeking to determine if these potential falsifiers obtain? If this is the case, then this is good research; if it is not, then the research is trivial because it provides no real test of the theory. (c) Are there any falsifiers that have been found to actually be true? If there are, then these anomalies count against the theory, and the theory needs to be revised in a non-ad hoc manner to become consistent with the data. The non-ad hoc way of revising theories is that the new theory must have excess empirical content, that is, have a larger class of falsifiers than the old theory. For Popper, the present version of a theory is approximately true, and observation and experimentation are used to refute and improve the theory. For Popper, the process of science proceeds as follows:

Problem $\longrightarrow$ Theory $\longrightarrow$ Error Elimination $\longrightarrow$ Problem$_2$ $\longrightarrow$ Theory$_2$ $\longrightarrow$ ...

Lakatos

Lakatos's (1978) three major insights regarding the role of theories in science were the following: (a) Science evolves by theories succeeding one another, and this succession of theories often has important core, continuing elements that animate the research program. Whether science is progressive or degenerative can be judged by comparing the common and distinct elements in successive theories. Of particular importance is whether the new theory predicted or subsumed new phenomena. (b) Theories suggest research programs. (c) Observation is theory laden. Thus, theories are important because they permeate all of science, even the observational level.

Lakatos (1978) was a student of Popper's and suggested that in science a series of theories is appraised rather than a single theory. Of particular interest is what sort of change occurs in a theory in light of new, anomalous findings. Lakatos's unit of analysis is a series of theories in which each subsequent theory is a revision of the previous theory in that auxiliary clauses have been added to accommodate some anomaly. Lakatos suggested that a series of theories should be considered scientific and progressive if subsequent theories in the series have excess empirical content (i.e., they predict some novel facts) and if some of these new predictions are corroborated. If either of these criteria is not met, then the series of theories should be considered to be degenerating.

Lakatos (1978) thought that theories within a series tended to share certain core ideas. He suggested that research programs contain a hard core that contains certain key animating ideas for the research program that cannot be given up without discarding the research program. For example, a core idea behind evolving theories in behavior therapy may be that experimental psychology (particularly animal learning and cognitive psychology) has vast implications for understanding and treating psychological problems. In addition to these central propositions, a research program also contains a positive heuristic that sets out the research plan. The positive heuristic consists of sets of suggestions on how to change and develop the hard core in light of anomalous findings.

Lakatos (1978) called into question the theory/observation distinction of the logical positivists. Lakatos argued that there is no theory-neutral observation language. Instead, a theoretically influenced problem definition and a theoretically influenced methodology influence what will ultimately be theoretically influenced empirical observations.

> Galileo claimed that he could 'observe' mountains on the moon and spots on the sun and that these 'observations' refuted the time-honoured theory that celestial bodies are faultless crystal balls. But his 'observations' were not 'observational' in the sense of being observed by the—unaided—senses: Their reliability depended on the reliability of his telescope—and of the optical theory of the telescope—which was violently questioned by his contemporaries. It was not Galileo's pure, untheoretical—*observations* that confronted Aristotelian *theory* but rather Galileo's 'observations' in the light of his optical theory that confronted the Aristotelians' 'observations' in the light of their theory of the heavens. (Lakatos, 1978, p. 98)

Laudan

It is fair to say that Laudan's (1977) views have recently had an enormous influence on the contemporary philosophy of science, so it is apt that he is the last philosopher of science that we discuss. Laudan provided four key insights into the role of theory in science: (a) Science involves both empirical and theoretical problems, and appraising theories involves considering both kinds of problems. (b) In the actual practice of science, theories are not evaluated in isolation, but rather, theory appraisal is a comparative activity in which a theory is evaluated with respect to its competitors. (c) The most important criterion on which to base this comparison is not the degree of empirical confirmation (contra the logical positivists) or the degree to which theories have survived attempts at refutation (contra Popper), but the theory's problem-solving effectiveness (compared with that of its competitors). (d) Another important criterion for comparing theories is the methodological well-foundedness of the theories.

Regarding the role of conceptual problems in science, Laudan (1977) pointed out the following:

> Even the briefest glance at the history of science makes it clear that the key debates between scientists have centered as much on nonempirical issues as on empirical ones . . . . When . . . Newton announced his 'system of the world,' it encountered almost universal applause for its capacity to solve many crucial empirical problems. What troubled many of Newton's contemporaries (including Locke, Berkeley, Huygens, and Leibniz) were several conceptual ambiguities and confusions about its foundational assumptions. What was absolute space and why was it needed to do physics? How could bodies conceivably act on one

another at-a-distance? What was the source of the new energy which, on Newton's theory, had to be continuously super-added to the world order? How, Leibniz would ask, could Newton's theory be reconciled with an intelligent deity who designed the world? In none of these cases was a critic pointing to an unsolved anomalous empirical problem. They were rather raising acute difficulties of a *nonempirical kind.* (p. 46)

For Laudan, scientific progress could occur when a conceptual problem is solved without an increase in the number of empirical problems solved. Laudan (1977) suggested that conceptual problems arise when a theory appears to be internally inconsistent, when its concepts are vague, or when the theory conflicts with other theories that are also believed to be true. An example of a conceptual problem in behavior therapy might be resolving the possible circularity of Skinner's empirical definition of reinforcement (Meehl, 1950; Timberlake, this volume).

Laudan (1977) suggested that science aims at maximizing the number of solved empirical problems, while minimizing the number of conceptual and anomalous problems. Moreover, a rational scientist chooses to conduct research within a particular theory not merely because of the individual merits of the theory, but because of a favorable comparison of the problem-solving effectiveness of the theory with that of its rivals. Thus, a better theory has solved more problems, solved problems of higher priority, and solved problems at a faster rate than its rivals and has achieved these diserdata without generating more serious theoretical problems than its rivals.

Finally, Laudan (1977) argued that theories contain regulative images of science in that they define sets of norms and methodological rules that the good scientist is expected to follow. These methodological criteria are used to evaluate a theory and its competitors. Laudan (1977) stated that, "if a scientist has good grounds for accepting some methodology and if some scientific theory violates that methodology, then it is entirely rational for him to have grave reservations about the theory" (p. 61). For example, Grunbaum (1984) critiqued the methodological well-foundedness of Freudian psychoanalysis by asserting that the psychoanalyst's observations in the clinical setting do not constitute reliable data, and even if they did, they are not the proper type of data that can constitute valid evidence for Freud's causal claims about intrapsychic conflict. Thus, psychologists who accept the methodological stricture that causal claims can only be properly inferred from experiments in which controls isolate extraneous influences and in which only one variable is manipulated at a time have rational reason to reject Freud's reliance on uncontrolled case studies for evidence for his causal assertions.

Skinner

Many behavior therapists have been influenced by the work of B. F. Skinner; therefore, his views on meta-science and, more specifically, the proper role of theories in science need to be considered. For example, Skinner (1972) stated,

> Certain basic assumptions, essential to any scientific activity, are some-times called theories . . . . Certain statements are also theories simply to the extent that they are not yet facts . . . . No empirical statement is wholly nontheoretical in this sense because evidence is never complete, nor is any prediction probably ever made wholly without evidence. The term *theory* will not refer here to statements of these sorts but rather to any explanation of an observed fact which appeals to events taking place somewhere else, at some other level of observation, described in different terms, and measured, if at all, in different dimensions. (p. 39)

Skinner gave mentalistic and physiological theories of learning as examples of undesirable theories. As a result, it seems from the above quote that Skinner criticized only a certain type of theory and not theories in general. For example, in another place Skinner (1972) stated that "whether particular experimental psychologists like it or not, experimental psychology is properly and inevitably committed to the construction of a theory of behavior" (p. 302).

In fact, Skinner (1969) made a positive reference to theory in the title of one of his books, *Contingencies of Reinforcement: A Theoretical Analysis.*

Kitchener (in press) suggested that Skinner recognized six kinds of theory and that it is only the last type that Skinner rejected:

1. Theory as a set of basic assumptions
2. Theory as a proposition yet to be verified
3. Theory as conceptual analysis[1]
4. Theory as the interpretation of behavior[2]
5. Theory as a convenient summary of empirical data[3]

---

[1]For example, in *Verbal Behavior* (Skinner, 1957), he provided conceptual analyses of language and meaning.

[2]For example, in "Why I Am Not a Cognitive Psychologist" (Skinner, 1977), he provided interpretations of problem solving and creativity. Skinner (1969) also appeared to recognize the impact that theory has on the interpretation of empirical observations: "It is only when we have analyzed behavior under known contingencies of reinforcement that we can begin to see what is happening in daily life. Things we once overlooked then begin to command our attention, and things which once attracted our attention we learn to discount or ignore" (p. 10).

[3]Skinner (1972) showed agreement with the logical positivists: "This does not exclude the possibility of theory in another sense. Beyond the collection of uniform relationships lies the need for a formal representation of the data reduced to a minimal number of terms. A theoretical construction may yield greater generality than any assemblage of facts . . . . It will not stand in the way of our search for functional relationships because it will arise only after relevant variables have been found and identified" (p. 69).

6. Theory as a hypothetical mechanism

The first quote of this section indicates that Skinner rejected the sixth kind of theory because it attempts to account for some phenomenon by an appeal to "events taking place somewhere else, at some other level of observation, described in different terms, and measured, if at all, in different dimensions" (Skinner, 1972, p. 39). Unfortunately, Skinner was unclear on exactly what is meant by whether a term, dimensional level, or level of observation is "different" from the observed fact. Is using genetic similarities in explaining higher concordance rates of monozygotic twins for schizophrenia than the rates among adopted siblings an appeal to a "different" term, dimensional level, or level of observation? Is attributing a cause of a heart attack to a high cholesterol level and sedentary lifestyle a violation of this rule? If so, do these examples not show that the rule can be violated in science and that, therefore, it is not a sound rule?

Skinner (1972) stated further:

> Perhaps to do without theories altogether is a *tour de force* which is too much to expect as a general practice. Theories are fun. But it is possible that the most rapid progress toward an understanding of learning may be made by research which is not designed to test theories. An adequate impetus is supplied by the inclination to obtain data showing orderly changes characteristic of the learning process. An acceptable scientific program is to collect data of this sort and to relate them to manipulable variables, selected for study through a common sense exploration of the field. (p. 69)

Skinner (unsurprisingly) recommended behavioral theories to account for behavioral data. However, again, Skinner was vague in indicating how this is to be done. In the preceding quote he stated that "a common sense exploration of the field" can identify relevant variables for initial study. But this is, again, very vague. The nebulous notion of "common sense" seems to be doing a lot of work in Skinner's account. What, substantively, is "common sense"? What is to be done when one person's common sense differs from that of another? Skinner repeatedly criticized explanatory fictions that would allay curiosity with an appearance but not a substance of an explanation. He thought that explanations that themselves immediately called for explanations were paradigmatic examples of these explanatory fictions. But Skinner in this instance seemed to be indulging in just this sort of mistake. When invoking common sense as a guide for identifying relevant variables, the immediate question becomes, And what determines common sense? An answer to this question would seem to inevitably involve some previously held theory. That is, a perhaps implicitly held, informally articulated, and likely inchoate, account of the phenomena.

The Importance of Theory Development in Behavior Therapy

We began this section by asking several fundamental questions about the nature of theory and its roles in science. We conclude this section by presenting some conclusions drawn from the review of meta-scientific considerations:

1. Following the logical positivists, theories play a critical role in two major functions in science: explanation and prediction.
2. Also following the positivists, theories are inevitably involved in science because science does not seek to record particular observations, but seeks to abstract meaning from these for as wide of range of phenomena as possible. Thus, theories "tell the story" of, and behind, these particular observations.
3. As was also suggested by the logical positivists, theories need to be evaluated according to their relationship to empirical observations. Theories can be bad when they have empirical consequences and these go untested, particularly when adherents take the theory in this state to be well-founded.
4. Following Popper, theories precede scientific observations and suggest to the scientist at what, and for what, he or she should look.
5. Also following Popper, the good scientist constantly seeks to improve theories by exposing them to criticism, especially empirical criticism.
6. Popper also pointed out that scientists need to be aware of confirmation biases with respect to their favored theories by looking for observable consequences that the theory excludes, and a good way of overcoming this bias is to attempt to falsify favored theories and by modifying them when anomalies are found in a non-ad hoc manner.
7. Following Lakatos, theories are evolving entities. However, this evolution is not always progressive. The quality (progressive or degenerating) of a theory's evolution can be judged by whether the new theory has excess empirical content and whether some of this new content is corroborated.
8. Also following Lakatos, theories permeate observational data as theories are involved in the interpretation of data.
9. Following Laudan, theories are evaluated with respect to their competitors, their rivals in their domains. Three central evaluative criteria are the theory's problem-solving effectiveness, number and seriousness of conceptual problems,

and its methodological adequacy, compared with its competitors.

10. Also following Laudan, science produces conceptual problems, and legitimate work in science involves progress on theoretical as well as empirical problems.

11. Finally, following Skinner, it is important to beware of superfluous content in theories, especially content that is influenced by some intellectual fad or prejudice (e.g., premature physiologizing or mathematical treatment).

Therefore, it is clear that theories play important roles in science. As a result, it becomes important to understand the major theories in behavior therapy.

THEORIES IN BEHAVIOR THERAPY

In this section we trace the historical development of "behavioral" theories. There are, of course, a number of labels for "behavioral": behaviorism, behavior modification, behavior therapy, behavior influence. In our review we use all of these terms with emphasis on the historical contexts and influences on terminology.

Since the original publication of Kuhn's book on *The Structure of Scientific Revolutions* in 1962, there has been a deluge of citations of his work on the concept of "paradigms" to justify a wide range of theories, models, and historical interpretations. Kuhn's own views were affected by a then obscure monograph written in 1935 by Fleck (1979) that had examined the impact of the social basis of knowledge on the scientific study of syphilis. Fleck stressed the impact of the community "thinking" about the nature of and solution to specific scientific problems. He stressed the dialectic between what was known about a particular problem and the act of knowing it.

Kuhn's (1970) approach is that of social historian placing the behavior and belief systems of scientists of the era in the context of the social, political, and economic developments of the era. Thus, a major element of Kuhn's approach involved an analysis of the scientific community at any given time. This includes the education and origins of the members of the community, their professional initiation, and the type of working consensus they bring to bear in approaching their subject matter.

Kuhn, himself influenced by Fleck's (1935/1979) classic book, came to stress two usages of the term *paradigm*. "On the one hand, it stands for the entire constellation of beliefs, values, techniques, and so on shared by the members of a given community. On the other, it denotes one sort of element in the constellation, the concrete puzzle solutions which, employed as models or examples, can replace explicit rules as a basis for the solutions of the remaining puzzles of normal science" (Kuhn, 1970, p. 23). These interrelated aspects were encompassed by the term *disciplinary matrix*, which incorporated symbolic generalizations, beliefs in models, shared values (e.g., accuracy, quantification), and "exemplars" or recognized puzzle solutions.

Paradigms can be oversimplified into two basic categories: *inner* and *outer*. The inner model (sometimes bearing the label of "medical") explains behavior in terms of such concepts as personality, mind, feelings, genes, and various biological functions, in contrast with the outer model, which uses concepts and procedures such as environmental consequences, reinforcement, verbal behavior, modeling, token economy, social learning, and behavior influence.

Implicit in the outer model is, of course, the notion that change in human behavior is possible because human nature is plastic and not fixed and immutable as implied by the inner model. Not only is change possible, it is quite desirable according to this model. Each of the two most influential behaviorists of this century, Watson (1929) and Skinner (1948), has offered his version of a "utopian" society.

In the introduction to his paper on "Why I Am Not a Cognitive Psychologist," Skinner (1977) cogently summarized the outer or environmental model with its implicit learning base:

> The variables of which behavior is a function lie in the environment. We distinguish between (1) the selective action of that environment during the evolution of the species, (2) its effect in shaping and maintaining the repertoire of behavior which converts each member of the species into a person, and (3) its role as the occasion upon which behavior occurs. Cognitive psychologists study these relations between organism and environment, but they seldom deal with them directly. Instead they invent internal surrogates which become the subject matter of their science. (p. 1)

The broad concept of behaviorism touches on most of the theoretical issues in the study of human behavior—philosophical, psychological, sociological, moral, social, intellectual—that have stirred and plagued mankind not only in our era but at least back to the ancient Greeks, if not the Biblical times. These include the nature of man and of consciousness, free will versus determinism, nature versus nurture, evolution versus creationism, and the impact of value and ethical systems. Behaviorism as a paradigmatic view of human life has been integrally related to every aspect of the science of psychology as well as every aspect of American life in the 20th century. This view would at first imply an imperial grandiosity, but it merely illustrates the point that there is a mutual influence between theoretical views of human nature and the society in which the purveyors of the theories function. In recent years, the issues dealt with by using the behavioral approach have become more sophisticated. The big issues have not been resolved, but they are being fought over at more subtle levels. Current behavior therapy cannot be divorced from these controversial roots. Unfortunately, there is little awareness of the existence of these roots among many current practitioners of behavior therapy.

Skinner (1983), who has, of course, had enormous impact on behaviorism in America, offered a useful, influential, and theoretical/practical definition of the term *behavior*:

> The word *behavior* was first used five centuries ago, and since then it has taken on and discarded many special meanings. In *The Behavior of Organisms* (1938) I offered this definition: "Behavior is what the organism is doing." That would be more helpful if the *Oxford English Dictionary* did not need six large three-column pages to record the history of the forms and significations of the word *do*. From the beginning, however, *do* has meant "achieve some kind of effect," and that is the central meaning of the word *behavior* in modern scientific usage. Whether innate or acquired, behavior is selected by its consequences. In natural selection the consequences are the contribution the behavior makes to the survival of the species. In operant conditioning the effective consequence is called a reinforcer. It strengthens the behavior in the sense of making it more likely to occur again in a similar setting. Operant conditioning is studied in the laboratory by arranging complex and subtle relations among setting, behavior, and consequences. (pp. 155–156)

On Behavior Modification

The term *behavior modification*, which was to represent the pop behaviorism of the 1970s and 1980s, has been used interchangeably with behavior therapy or to refer solely to the application of *operant conditioning* to distinguish it from the behavior therapy derived from the work of Wolpe. It initially was used to describe research studies of those investigators who were approaching the modification of behavior via the systematic application of social learning principles derived from sociopsychological research (Ayllon & Azrin, 1965; Bandura, 1969; Franks, 1969; Kanfer & Phillips, 1970; Skinner, 1953).

The two 1965 volumes of collected papers on theory research and case studies in behavior modification (Krasner & Ullmann, 1965; Ullmann & Krasner, 1965) represented the first use of that term in a book title. The introduction to the research collection placed the work of the investigators involved (e.g., Ferster, Staats, Bijou, Salzinger, Goldiamond, Patterson, Krasner, Sarason, Kanfer, Hastorf, Saslow, Colby, Bandura, and Sarbin) within the context of the broader field of *behavior influence* (Krasner, 1962; Krasner & Ullmann, 1973), which included the following:

> investigations of the ways in which human behavior is modified, changed, or influenced. It includes research on operant conditioning, psychotherapy, placebo, attitude change, hypnosis, sensory deprivation, brainwashing, drugs, modeling, and education. We conceive of a broad psychology of behavior influence that concerns itself with the basic variables determining the alteration of human behavior in both laboratory and "real life" situations. On the other hand, the term *behavior modification* refers to a very specific type of *behavior influence*. (Krasner & Ullmann, 1965, pp. 1–2)

We then adopted the description of *behavior modification* offered by Watson (1962).[4] In presenting a historical introduction to Bachrach's (1962) collection of research on the experimental foundations of clinical psychology, Watson used the term *behavior modification* to cover a multitude of theoretical approaches:

> It includes behavioral modification as shown in the structured interview, in verbal conditioning, in the production of experimental neuroses, and in patient-doctor relationships. In a broader sense, the topic of behavior modification is related to the whole field of learning. (Watson, 1962, p. 19)

The field of behavior modification itself was a major illustration of learning theory applied in the environment. In their introduction to this field, Ullmann and Krasner (1965) defined the then emerging field in the framework of applied learning theory: "In defining behavior modification we follow the work of Robert Watson . . . who noted that behavior modification included many different techniques, all broadly related to the field of learning, *but learning with a particular intent; namely; clinical treatment and change*" (p. 1).

There were two important aspects of this definition. The first is the contention that the basis of treatment stems from learning theory, which deals with the effect of experience on behavior. Subsequently, the basis of behavior modification was a body of experimental work dealing with the relationship between changes in the environment and the changes in a subject's responses. The most immediate consequence that distinguished these behavioral approaches was a difference between the methods by which behavioral therapies and evocative therapies were developed. Instead of starting with a treatment procedure and bringing in learning theory after the fact, it seemed much more effective to start with concepts of

---

[4]It should be noted that this reference is to Robert I. Watson, the historian of psychology, not John B. Watson, the behaviorist (e.g., Watson & Rayner, 1920).

learning and develop a program for behavior change based on these concepts before the fact.

Bandura (1969), in a most influential and widely cited book, placed "the principles of behavior modification" within the

> conceptual framework of social learning . . . . By requiring clear specification of treatment conditions and objective assessment of outcomes, the social learning approach . . . contains a self-corrective feature that distinguishes it from change enterprises in which interventions remain ill-defined and their psychological effects are seldom objectively evaluated. (p. v)

Bandura integrated the investigations, by then greatly expanded, that were derived from the influence of Skinner, Wolpe, and the British group (e.g., Eysenck).

The postwar behavior modification movement followed a two-step approach. Psychology clearly identified itself as a basic laboratory science, and the early behavior modification applications grew out of the labs at university settings, such as Harvard, Indiana, Columbia, Southern Illinois, Stanford, Washington, and Illinois. It was this two-step notion that was the basis of the growth and success of behaviorism in its behavior modification format of the 1960s and 1970s.

A later development was the shifting away from this model, in the late 1970s and 1980s, when applications in the form of technology really became divorced from the original theoretical model. This shift was analogous to developments in the broader fields of science in America in which applied work took off on its own paths independent of the theoretical framework from which it developed.

Franks and Rosenbaum (1983) posed what may well be the major question for behaviorism, in the form of behavior therapy, in the 1980s (and on into the 1990s). "Will the coming years see behavior therapy fragmented into numerous self-contained fields? Or will some common underlying behavioral theme be found to encompass them all?" (p. 9).

On Behavior Therapy

Here we examine the current behavior therapy scene to determine ways in which its ancient theoretical paradigm has changed, the impact of newer paradigms (e.g., cognitive behavior therapy), and the implications of returning to roots (if such return is desirable or even possible in a continually changing world), and we speculate about the future.

• The first use of the term *behavior therapy* in the literature was in a 1953 status report by Lindsley, Skinner, and Solomon, referring to their application of the operant conditioning learning model (of a plunger pulling response) research with psychotic patients. Lindsley suggested the term to Skinner, based on its simplicity and linkage to other treatment procedures.

Independent of this early usage, Lazarus (1958) used the term to refer to Wolpe's (1958) application of reciprocal inhibition techniques to neurotic patients, and Eysenck (1959, 1960) used the term to refer to the application of what he termed "modern learning theory" to the behavior of neurotic patients based in large part on the procedures of a group of investigators then working at the Maudsley Hospital in London. Franks (1964) brought together the works of investigators who were working with human problems influenced by Pavlov along with a brief section on operant techniques (e.g., Ferster, 1958; Ferster & Skinner, 1957; Lindsley, Skinner, & Solomon, 1953) under the general rubric of "conditioning techniques." These were referred to as behavioral techniques or behavior therapy. In the same early period, Wolpe, Salter, and Reyna (1964) edited a series of papers on "The Conditioning Therapies," which combined the work of investigators spanning Pavlovian, Hullian, and Skinnerian learning theories. The term *behavior therapy* was used interchangeably with *conditioning therapy* as the general rubric. The first issues (in 1963) of the journal *Behaviour Research and Therapy*, edited by Eysenck and Rachman, were landmarks in bringing together, conceptually, the laboratory studies of learning within the behavior therapy framework.

We briefly trace the history of behavior therapy in terms of its theoretical and the social, historical, economic, conceptual, and practical contexts in which it developed, and the community of scholars and scientists that developed it. Our view is that behavior therapy, as it developed in the post-World War II period, did indeed represent a paradigmatic shift (using the term in the disciplinary matrix context) in terms of the model, shared values, and exemplars of the community involved. Even the name of the major organization in the field (Association for Advancement of Behavior Therapy) is a strong point for arguing that a paradigmatic state in the behavioral community existed, at least in the 1960s.

It is especially crucial to determine the scope and limitation of the field of behavior therapy because too comprehensive a view (e.g., equating it with all of psychology) renders it meaningless, and too narrow a view (e.g., equating it with a specific technique such as desensitization) renders it useless.

Behavior therapy was a human creation and a very significant one. It is not possible to discuss it out of the context of its creators or the societal context in which they functioned. The behavioral movement in American psychology and society can be approached as a scientific and social movement influenced by, and in turn influencing, the broader society in which it developed. Behaviorism, from which behavior therapy developed, evolved in the context of the social, political, cultural, educational, economic, and intellectual history of 20th century America. Conversely, as the pragmatic philosophy of the behavioral movement spread beyond the bounds of the psychology laboratory, it influenced virtually every aspect of American life. Perhaps no other systematic approach to human behavior has been as vilified, praised, used, and misused as behaviorism (except, perhaps, psychoanalysis!).

As it developed in the 1960s, behavior therapy represented a clear alternative in the mental health industry to the then predominant paradigm with its focus on inner processes. This is, of course, not to say that there was no usage of inner concepts and terminology in behavioral thinking, such as awareness, self, anxiety, phobia, conditioning, bias, expectancy, and so on. However, the major focus was on outer environmental influences and consequences and not on hypothesized inner processes.

In interpreting behavior therapy in the context of broader conceptual helping models, Ullmann and Krasner (1965) described behavior therapy as "treatment deducible from the sociopsychological model that aims to alter a person's behavior directly through application of general psychological principles." This was contrasted with "evocative psychotherapy," which is "treatment deducible from a medical or psychoanalytic model that aims to alter a person's behavior indirectly by first altering intrapsychic organizations" (p. 244).

The breadth and need for an integrative theoretical model was illustrated by Kanfer and Phillips (1970), who classified four types of behavior therapy: *interactive therapy*, methods requiring an extended series of personal interviews using the therapist's verbal behavior to catalyze changes in the patient; *instigation therapy*, use of suggestions and tasks to teach the patient to become his or her own therapist; *replication therapy*, method of changing behavior by replicating a critical segment of the patient's life within the therapy setting; and *intervention therapy*, disruption by the therapist of narrow response classes as they appear in the patient's interactions with her or his natural environment. They called for establishing a well-integrated framework from which practitioners could derive new techniques with clearly stated rationales, predictable effects, and well-defined criteria for examining their efficacy. They argued that a consistent behavioristic view requires an understanding of the entire range of psychological principles that can be brought to bear on the problems of an individual client.

In the first *Annual Review of Psychology* chapter on behavior therapy, in 1971, Krasner noted that there were 15 streams of development that were coming together in the late 1960s "to form a distinctive approach to helping individuals with behavior socially labeled as 'deviant' " (p. 488). In effect, these were the roots of the behavior therapy paradigm. They included behaviorism in experimental psychology; the research and philosophical view of Skinner (and the Skinnerians); the research and clinical work of Wolpe (as influenced by Taylor, Reyna, and Hull); Eysenck and the Maudsley group; investigators in educational institutions influenced by

Watson, Mowrer, Guthrie, and others; developmental and child psychology research such as that of Bijou and Baer (1961, 1965); the Boulder model of clinical psychology; critiques of the then predominant psychodynamic treatment procedures; the Sullivan model of participant–observer; and, perhaps most important, the utopian stream with its emphasis on planning the social environment to elicit and maintain the best of man's behavior.

The philosophical roots of behavior therapy are generally traced to the positivistic philosophy system founded by Comte (1896), which radically rejected all metaphysics, the inquiry into the ultimate causes and nature of things. The objective of science was to discover facts, their relations, and the laws governing them. Positivism strongly reinforced the antimentalistic and anti-introspectionist tendencies in psychology. The behaviorist tenets in American psychology seemed very much in agreement with positivistic views. The controversy as to whether science is value-free or value-laden has been an integral part of the history of behavior therapy (Krasner & Houts, 1984).

"Behavior therapy derives its impetus from experimental psychology and is essentially an attempt to apply the findings and methods of this discipline to disorders of human behavior" (Rachman, 1963, p. 3). Combined under this general heading were aspects of learning theory such as operant conditioning, aversion conditioning, and training in assertive behavior.

Franks (1969) pointed up the disagreements among self-identified behavior therapists as to the definition of behavior therapy. He emphasized that responses alone are the data available to the student of human behavior, and all else is a matter of inference and construct. He noted that at that point most behavior therapists linked their work with the learning theories that were then called stimulus-response, those of Pavlov, Skinner, Guthrie, and Hull. Franks attributed theoretical importance to the base of a multitude of variations of meaning that were attached to behavior therapy after these early approaches.

A more encompassing framework comes from those who viewed behavior therapy in the broader context of social learning (Bandura, 1969) or behavior influence (Krasner & Ullmann, 1973).

A recent development in the behavior therapy field has been the growth of a new term, *cognitive–behavior therapy*, which is going the usual route of new terms, (e.g., journals, organizations, publications galore).

The concept of *cognitive–behavior therapy*, a term that has appeared frequently in recent publications and research, is a puzzle. It is, in effect, a symptom of the loss of the sacred paradigm of the founding community of scholars. We are tempted to label this label the "oxymoron of the year." Lest the reader feel that we are somehow denigrating the label by giving it a category, we are doing nothing of the sort. Oxymoron is a perfectly good English word. The dictionary definition follows:

Oxymoron—"A rhetorical figure by which contradictory terms are co-joined so as to give point to the statement or expression . . . a contradiction in terms" (*The Oxford Universal Dictionary*, 1955, p. 1411).

For example, a mournful optimist. You can have fun developing other oxymorons. Thus, if cognitive–behavior therapy means an integration of cognitive inner concepts with outer concepts, such as behavior, one should have objections from two set of purists: Those who view behavior therapy as an outer alternative paradigm to the old inner paradigm would argue that the term is indeed an oxymoron, two antithetical concepts that are genuine alternatives, hence, not combinable. Others would argue, as we have, that behavior therapy in its original paradigm included variables that are now labeled as "cognitive," such as feelings, thoughts, and so on; hence, to add this new adjective is redundant, misleading, and unnecessary. (See O'Donohue & Szymanski, in press.)

A PERSPECTIVE ON THEORIES IN BEHAVIOR THERAPY

We have introduced this volume by discussing and examining the role and function of the concept of "theory" in science, in general, and specifically in an approach to conceptualizing and influencing a human behavior that has been labeled *behavior therapy*. Theories play a major role in two key factors in science: explanation and function. However, theories in any aspect of science, especially in understanding and using behavior therapy, must be placed within the context of the social, political, and economic influences of the era in which they are developed and applied.

We have presented a brief overview of the behavioral theories (e.g., behavior therapy, behavior modification, behavior influence, and cognitive behavior therapy), and we now proceed with presenting specific theories within this broader context.

REFERENCES

Ayllon, T., & Azrin, N. H. (1965). The measurement and reinforcement of behavior of psychotics. *Journal of Experimental Analysis of Behavior, 8,* 357–383.

Bachrach, A. J. (Ed.). (1962). *Experimental foundations of clinical psychology.* New York: Basic Books.

Bandura, A. (1969). *Principles of behavior modification.* New York: Holt, Rinehart & Winston.

Bijou, S. W., & Baer, D. M. (1961). *Child development* (Vol. 1). New York: Appleton-Century-Crofts.

Bijou, S. W., & Baer, D. M. (1965). *Child development* (Vol. 2). New York: Appleton-Century-Crofts.

Comte, A. (1896). *The positive philosophy*. London: Bell.

Eysenck, H. J. (1959). Learning theory and behavior therapy. *Journal of Mental Science, 195*, 61–75.

Eysenck, H. J. (1960). *Behavior therapy and the neuroses*. Oxford: Pergamon Press.

Ferster, C. B. (1958). Reinforcement and punishment in the control of human behavior by social agencies. *Psychiatric Research Reports, 10*, 101–118.

Ferster, C. B., & Skinner, B. F. (1957). *Schedules of reinforcement*. New York: Appleton-Century-Crofts.

Fleck, L. (1979). *Genesis and development of a scientific fact*. Chicago: University of Chicago Press. (Original work published 1935)

Franks, C. M. (Ed.). (1964). *Conditioning techniques in clinical practice and research*. New York: Springer.

Franks, C. M. (Ed.). (1969). *Behavior therapy: Appraisal and status*. New York: McGraw-Hill.

Franks, C. M., & Rosenbaum, M. (1983). Behavior therapy: Overview and personal reflections. In M. Rosenbaum, C. M. Franks, & Y. Jaffe (Eds.), *Perspectives on behavior therapy in the eighties* (pp. 3–16). New York: Springer.

Grunbaum, A. (1984). *The foundations of psychoanalysis: A philosophical critique*. Berkeley: University of California Press.

Hempel, C. G. (1967). *Aspects of scientific explanation*. New York: Free Press.

James, W. (1890). *The principles of psychology*. New York: Dover.

Kanfer, F. H., & Phillips, J. S. (1970). *Learning foundations of behavior therapy*. New York: Wiley.

Kitchener, R. (in press). Skinner's theories of theories. In W. O'Donohue & R. Kitchener (Eds.), *Psychology and philosophy: Interdisciplinary problems responses*. New York: Allyn & Bacon.

Koertge, N. (1980). Methodology, ideology, and feminist critiques of science. *Philosophy of Science Association, 2*, 246–259.

Krasner, L. (1962). The therapist as a social reinforcement machine. In H. H. Strupp & L. Luborsky (Eds.), *Research in psychotherapy* (Vol. 2, pp. 61–94). Washington, DC: American Psychological Association.

Krasner, L. (1971). Behavior therapy. In P. H. Mussen (Ed.), *Annual review of psychology* (Vol. 22, pp. 483–532). Palo Alto, CA: Annual Reviews.

Krasner, L., & Houts, A. C. (1984). A study of the "value" systems of behavioral scientists. *American Psychologist, 39*, 840–850.

Krasner, L., & Ullmann, L. P. (Eds.). (1965). *Research in behavior modification: New developments and implications*. New York: Holt, Rinehart & Winston.

Krasner, L., & Ullmann, L. P. (1973). *Behavior influence and personality: The social matrix of human action*. New York: Holt, Rinehart & Winston.

Kuhn, T. S. (1970). *The structure of scientific revolutions* (2nd ed.). Chicago: University of Chicago Press.

Lakatos, I. (1978). *The methodology of scientific research programmes.* Cambridge, England: University of Cambridge Press.

Laudan, L. (1977). *Progress and its problems.* Berkeley: University of California Press.

Lazarus, A. A. (1958). New methods in psychotherapy: A case study. *South African Medical Journal, 33,* 660–664.

Lindsley, O. R., Skinner, B. F., & Solomon, H. C. (1953). *Studies in behavior therapy* (Status Report I). Waltham, MA: Metropolitan State Hospital.

Meehl, P. E. (1950). On the circularity of the law of effect. *Psychological Bulletin, 47,* 52–75.

O'Donohue, W., & Szymanski, J. (in press). Skinner on cognition. *Journal of Behavioral Education.*

Popper, K. R. (1963). *Conjectures and refutations.* New York: Harper & Row.

Rachman, S. (1963). Introduction to behavior therapy. *Behaviour Research and Therapy, 1,* 3–15.

Skinner, B. F. (1938). *The behavior of organisms.* New York: Appleton-Century-Crofts.

Skinner, B. F. (1948). *Walden two.* New York: Macmillan.

Skinner, B. F. (1953). *Science and human behavior.* New York: Macmillan.

Skinner, B. F. (1957). *Verbal behavior.* Englewood Cliffs, NJ: Prentice-Hall.

Skinner, B. F. (1969). *Contingencies of reinforcement: A theoretical analysis.* New York: Appleton-Century-Crofts.

Skinner, B. F. (1972). *Cumulative record.* New York: Appleton-Century-Crofts.

Skinner, B. F. (1977). Why I am not a cognitive psychologist. *Behaviorism, 5,* 1–10.

Skinner, B. F. (1983). *A matter of consequences.* New York: Knopf.

Ullmann, L. P., & Krasner, L. (1965). *Case studies in behavior modification.* New York: Holt, Rinehart & Winston.

Watson, J. B. (1929, June 29). Should a child have more than one mother? *Liberty* 31–35.

Watson, J. B., & Rayner, R. (1920). Conditioned emotional reactions. *Journal of Experimental Psychology, 3,* 1–14.

Watson, R. I. (1962). The experimental tradition and clinical psychology. In A. J. Bachrach (Ed.), *Experimental foundations of clinical psychology* (pp. 3–25). New York: Basic Books.

Wolpe, J. (1958). *Psychotherapy by reciprocal inhibition.* Stanford, CA: Stanford University Press.

Wolpe, J., Salter, A., & Reyna, L. J. (Eds.). (1964). *The conditioning therapies: The challenge to psychotherapy.* New York: Holt, Rinehart & Winston.

2

RECIPROCAL INHIBITION: MAJOR AGENT OF BEHAVIOR CHANGE

JOSEPH WOLPE

CONCEPTUAL AND HISTORICAL BACKGROUND

Some maladaptive behaviors are based not on maldevelopment or organic pathology, but on learning. The restoration of adaptive functioning in these cases requires the unlearning of the maladaptive behaviors that learning has produced. Behavior therapy has established itself as the preeminent resource for procuring such unlearning, although other modes of psychotherapy also have varying degrees of success. The most common maladaptive learned behaviors are the neuroses (anxiety disorders), and in these it is maladaptive anxiety (fear) that has to be unlearned. Behavioral methods whose efficacy in this context has been demonstrated include systematic desensitization, flooding, and cognitive correction. The method that is chosen depends on characteristics of the individual and on details of the particular anxiety response habit.

Until midcentury, it was generally regarded as settled that neuroses had their origin in painful events of early childhood, as laid down by Freud (1916). It was thought that because the memories of these events were too painful to bear, they were repressed—pushed "incommunicado" into the unconscious mind—and that neurosis was the manifestation of the repression. A logical corollary of the theory was that recovery from neuroses would follow "derepression," bringing the repressed memories back into consciousness. This theory, in an array of variations, still dominates thinking in the clinical practice of psychiatry and psychology.

However, in the 1950s, an alternative theory began to claim attention: the theory that neuroses are maladaptive anxiety responses that have been acquired by learning and that that learning can occur at any time in a person's life. The therapeutic strategy to overcome a neurosis that emerges from this theory is to bring about the unlearning of the maladaptive anxiety response habit or habits.

This new theory was not plucked from the air, but stemmed in the first place from a series of experiments I reported (Wolpe, 1952a). Following the example of Pavlov and others, I had used an unconditioned source of fear to condition in animals an intense fear of the experimental cage and other stimuli. Fears so produced had been labeled "experimental neuroses" by Pavlov, and once established they are ordinarily almost impossible to eliminate. However, starting from the observation that an animal fearful of the experimental cage would not eat inside it even after 48 hr's starvation, I investigated what would happen if food were available in the presence of less intense anxiety elicited by related stimuli. I found that when the elicited fear was weak enough, eating would occur and that with repetition would occur more and more readily. In other words, at a certain low level of fear, the impulse to eat was no longer inhibited; eating took place and apparently *reciprocally inhibited the fear*, weakening it further. Applying this observation to progressively "stronger" stimuli led to total elimination of the maladaptive fear (see pp. 31–32 of this chapter).

The reciprocal inhibition principle in the context of the treatment of maladaptive anxiety was given this general formulation: When a response antagonistic to anxiety can be made to occur in the presence of anxiety-evoking stimuli, and in consequence effects a complete or partial suppression of the anxiety response, the bond between these stimuli and the anxiety response is weakened.

From 1948 onward, this principle was used in a variety of ways (described later in this chapter) with gratifying success (Wolpe, 1952c, 1954, 1958). A considerable number of psychotherapists applied these methods to their own patients with comparable success (e.g., Hain, Butcher, & Stevenson, 1966; Lazarus, 1963; Paul, 1969); during the next 20 years, there was a growing interest and increasing adoption of the methods, which had meanwhile increased in number and been collectively labeled *behavior therapy*.

At the same time, behind the scenes, some curious things were happening. A number of supporters of behavior therapy were losing sight of the fact that the strength of behavior therapy was its foundation of principles of learning; they were "eclectically" adopting methods that had nothing to do with learning principles. Increasingly, in many places, behavior therapy took on the appearance of an eclectic smorgasbord. Increasingly, the reciprocal inhibition principle faded from view and was mentioned, if at all, as a matter of historical interest, as though long superseded and no longer of practical relevance.

But before a demonstrably useful theory can be superseded, it must be falsified (Popper, 1959). I know of no credible effort at the falsification of reciprocal inhibition theory ever having been undertaken. At best there have been ill-thought-out and perfunctory criticisms, usually emanating from observing, in the context of weak fears, that desensitization may proceed equally well with or without relaxation (Kazdin & Wilcoxon, 1976; Yates, 1975). The critics have not realized that relaxation is not the only source of reciprocal inhibition of fear and that a widely present source is the subject's emotional reaction to the therapist (see pp. 42–43 in this chapter).

In any case, as I show in the final section of this chapter, there is no viable substitute for reciprocal inhibition theory. Nobody has proposed a theory that even begins to explain the wide variety of therapeutic options that reciprocal inhibition theory has generated. Meanwhile, those who reject reciprocal inhibition deprive themselves of a conceptual resource that could yield new solutions for some of their own difficult cases.

Theories of psychotherapeutic change are important, because when they are empirically validated, they not only increase the therapist's confidence in the therapeutic methods that embody them, but they are also a fountainhead of innovations. I provide grounds for the proposition that reciprocal inhibition enters in a major way into practically all instances of psychotherapeutic change and exemplify how reciprocal inhibition theory has directly generated new methods.

DEFINITION AND NEUROPHYSIOLOGY
OF RECIPROCAL INHIBITION

Reciprocal inhibition is the label for a physiological phenomenon that was first described by Sherrington (1906/1961). The evocation of a response is generally accompanied by the inhibition of other responses, particularly those that are functionally opposed to the one being evoked. The excitation of a muscle group, for example, automatically sets off the inhibition of antagonistic groups. The knee-jerk illustrates this. A sharp tap on the patellar tendon elicits a reflex extension of the leg, with simultaneous inhibition (relaxation) of the leg's flexor muscles.

The occurrence of reciprocal inhibition is in a sense built into the structure of the nervous system. There is a neuronal arrangement that neuroanatomists call "reciprocal innervation" (Bosma & Gellhorn, 1946; Gellhorn, 1947; Sherrington, 1906/1961, pp. 83–107, 280–282). The afferent neuron that leads to a motor neuron whose excitation produces a particular movement also leads to another neuron whose excitation *inhibits the opposing movement.* The implication of this is that the extension of the leg in a knee-jerk will always automatically be accompanied by inhibition of the flexor muscles and vice versa.

However, it is important to realize that reciprocal inhibition is not the only relationship that can exist between simultaneous responses. Some responses are mutually facilitative, and others are mutually independent. A firm handshake facilitates the knee-jerk. Eating a hamburger neither increases nor diminishes the attention one pays to a baseball game.

RECIPROCAL INHIBITION IN EVERYDAY LIFE

Reciprocal inhibition occurs at all levels of neural organization. Although its extent was long ago recognized and described by Wendt (1936), it received little attention from psychologists at that time. Wendt (1936) noted that "anything an animal may be doing at the moment, be it sleeping, playing, grooming or vocalizing . . . it is reciprocally related to anything else it might otherwise be doing at the same moment" (p. 278). In the behavior of human beings, this generally extends to language and other complex functions. In the articulation of a word, for example, there is inhibition of the articulation of all other words. Similarly, imaginal rehearsing of a tune blocks the rehearsal of all other tunes, and an imagined visual scene "pushes aside" all other imaginings. The reciprocal interrelations of autonomic reactions were extensively documented by Gellhorn (1967). He found, for example, that when stimulation of the vagus nerve decreases the heart rate, the effect is augmented by simultaneous inhibition of the accelerator nerve to the heart.

Reciprocal inhibition operates in all human behavior, voluntary or involuntary. When an arm is bent, the contraction of the biceps is accompanied by inhibition of the triceps. In complex coordinated acts such as walking, there are serial alternations of excitations and their reciprocal inhibitions. Breathing is an example of alternating reciprocal responses that are involuntary.

People's awareness of their own emotions provides subjective evidence of the reciprocal relations between autonomic responses. Laughter is inhibited by sadness, anger, or anxiety and can in turn inhibit them. People also, though, sometimes have mixed feelings. For example, anger may be interfused with sadness or pity. When this happens, there may be mutual inhibition of some elements of the autonomic responses involved and facilitation of others. This was demonstrated in Simonov's (1967) psychophysiological studies of the emotions of actors. An actor trained in the Stanislavsky method, which focuses on the actor attempting to live the part, will have, to the extent that his or her portrayal is successful, autonomic responses much like those that would arise in the corresponding situation in real life. However, favorable audience response during a performance evokes intercurrent pleasurable responses, at least some of whose autonomic elements are likely to be opposed in direction to those of the portrayed emotion.

THE CONTRIBUTION OF RECIPROCAL INHIBITION TO LEARNING

Reciprocal inhibition has consequences for learning that are not usually noticed. In reinforcing a response, people inevitably also reinforce inhibition of contrary responses. It is almost exclusively in the context of behavior therapy that this fact has received practical application. Reciprocal inhibition is the physiological basis for the therapeutic exploitation of responses that are inhibitory of a response whose habit strength one wishes to diminish.

However, the phenomenon is quite general, extending also to motor conditioning, where it is almost universally ignored. An illustration can be found in Pavlov's (1927) description of the development of a salivary conditioned response to a bell. The bell initially evoked listening movements (i.e., turning of the head and pricking up of the ears). When the sound of the bell was repeatedly followed by food, the dog came to respond to its unaccompanied sound by licking its chops and turning toward the food pan. In the course of the repetitions, the listening movements gradually disappeared. In other words, the listening habit underwent conditioned inhibition, presumably as a consequence of its repeated reciprocal inhibition by the repeatedly reinforced feeding responses.

An experiment by Hilgard and Marquis (1940) showed that conditioned inhibition develops in this way even when the newly conditioned response has been part of the original response complex. Applying puffs of air to the eyes of dogs, the experimenters conditioned a bilateral eye closure response in dogs to a tone of 200 cycles. They then proceeded to condition a *unilateral* eye blink to this tone by administering the airpuff to only one eye. The bilateral closure gave way to a unilateral closure habit of similar latency. The evocation of the one-eye blink evidently inhibited the two-eye blink, so a conditioned inhibition of the latter developed in tandem with the conditioning of the former.

Inhibitory conditioning of antagonistic responses is similarly discernible in the conditioning of complex operant sequences. Consider an animal that has developed the habit of turning right in an alley because the response was consistently followed by food. If food ceases to follow right turning, the right-turn habit will weaken by the process of extinction, but it will weaken more rapidly if at the same time left turning begins to be rewarded. Presumably, with each left turn there is then an inhibition of the right-turning tendency, which summates with the similar consequence of nonreinforcement.

The same relations hold in the realm of cognitive habits. Ordinary forgetting depends on retroactive inhibition. That is, a verbal response is inhibited and its probability diminished when a different verbal response is evoked in the presence of the stimulus to the original one. Osgood (1946) was the first to recognize this as an instance of conditioned inhibition based on reciprocal inhibition.

From the foregoing, one can see that reciprocal inhibition is a simple fact of life, a constant and inevitable part of the central nervous system's functional integrations. It is strange that experimental psychologists have so long ignored it.

RECIPROCAL INHIBITION IN THE TREATMENT OF NEUROSIS

Salient Animal Experiments

The role of reciprocal inhibition in the breaking of emotional (i.e., predominantly autonomic) habits was first clearly revealed in the context of experimentally induced neurotic behavior in the cat (Wolpe, 1952a, 1958). Experimental neuroses were originally reported from Pavlov's (1927, 1941) laboratories and repeated with variations by many other experimenters (e.g., Gantt, 1944; Liddell, 1944; Masserman, 1943; Wolpe, 1952a; see Wolpe, 1958, pp. 37–48 for a detailed review). When anxiety is induced repeatedly in an animal in a constant environment, a rising level of anxiety is progressively conditioned to that environment.

The original method of inducing anxiety to generate experimental neuroses was by conflict based on difficult discrimination (Pavlov, 1927). It was later found to be more convenient to induce the anxiety by means of painful, but physically harmless, electrical stimulation of the animal's feet (Masserman, 1943; Pavlov, 1927; Wolpe, 1952a). Stimuli in contiguity with the evoked anxiety—especially those of the experimental cage—become conditioned stimuli to anxiety and with repetition are able to elicit it at high intensity. The animal then refuses easily available food in the experimental cage even after a day or more of starvation. The anxiety response and the eating inhibition are not diminished by repeated or prolonged visits to the cage even though no further electrical stimulation is administered.

Masserman (1943) described wide-ranging experiments on neuroses in cats. In a cage 40 × 20 × 20 inches (101.6 × 50.8 × 50.8 cm) in size, he used food reinforcement to train an animal to open the lid of a food box in response to a light-and-bell signal. One day, either at the feeding signal or at the moment of food taking, a blast of air would be applied across the food box, or a grid on the floor of the cage would be electrically charged. The usual reaction to an air blast was a rush to crouch at the far side of the cage. The usual reaction to a grid shock was "a startled jump as each impulse was felt, followed by a slow dignified stalking away from the food after the shock ended" (Masserman, 1943, p. 68). In either event, after several repetitions, neurotic behavior would be unremittingly present in the experimental cage, characterized by agitation or immobility, vocalization, sensitivity to extraneous stimuli, trembling, pupillary dilatation, and invariable refusal of food in the cage even after prolonged food deprivation. Outside the experimental cage, some animals became notably more timid. Others became aggressive toward their cagemates or toward humans.

In experiments patterned on those of Masserman (1943), I studied experimental neuroses in 12 cats between June 1947 and July 1948 in the Department of Pharmacology of the University of Witwatersrand (Wolpe, 1952a). The experimental cage was almost identical to that of Masserman. An important observation was that grid shocks alone could produce the neuroses—without feeding responses being in any way involved. I noted that the experimental room, and the experimenter himself, also became conditioned stimuli to anxiety. Anxiety responses of lower intensity were observed in four other rooms. I called the experimental room A and the other rooms B, C, D, and E, respectively, in decreasing order both of resemblance to Room A and, as it happened, in magnitude of manifest anxiety.

My neurotic cats, like those of Masserman (1943), displayed in the experimental cage continuous pupillary dilatation, trembling, sensitivity to extraneous stimuli, and absolute refusal to eat. The last was presumably a function of the strength of the anxiety response over the food-seeking drive. Because there was no apparent way to increase the latter, beyond several days' starvation, the only recourse was to decrease the level of anxiety when food was presented so that eating might take place and reciprocally inhibit the anxiety. To do this, I made use of the series of rooms noted earlier. A neurotic animal would first be offered pellets of meat on the floor of Room A, and then if it did not eat them, in the other rooms in descending order, until one was found, perhaps Room E, where the anxiety was weak enough not to inhibit eating. The animal snatched fearfully at the first meat pellet but ate subsequent ones with progressive alacrity and was eventually looking around expectantly for more. The next day the animal was offered meat pellets in Room D, and again would at first eat hesitantly and afterward with increasing ease. Going up the hierarchy of rooms, the animal eventually ate in the experimental room (Room A) and finally in the experimental cage within it. There, the eating of numerous pellets, widely distributed, led to the elimination of all anxiety.

This therapeutic sequence was successful in all 12 animals. It seemed strongly to support the potency of reciprocal inhibition for overcoming maladaptive anxiety-response habits. Apparently, the greater the relative strength of the alimentary response, the more markedly anxiety was inhibited and the greater was the ensuing measure of conditioned inhibition of anxiety. Repetition of the feeding eventually effected total elimination of the anxiety response.

However, at this point, a challenging question arose. Had we achieved an *extinction* of the anxiety habit, or had we merely overwhelmed the anxiety by the magnitude of the repeatedly reinforced feeding response? The following supplementary experiment was undertaken to test this. At the time of the induction of the experimental neurosis, a particular sound, usually a buzzer, routinely preceded each shock, so that an anxiety response was also conditioned to it. This auditory conditioning was subsequently eliminated in each animal by using a feeding procedure parallel to that used for the visual stimuli. In the process, food seeking became, not surprisingly, a conditioned response to the buzzer. So here, too, it was conceivable that food seeking was suppressing anxiety. If that were the case, the anxiety would reappear if we extinguished the food-seeking response to the buzzer. Each animal was given 30 irregularly massed unreinforced presentations of the buzzer on each of 3 successive days (i.e., a total of 90 extinction trials). After this, no trace of food seeking in response to the buzzer was discernible. A day or two later, the following critical test was performed on each animal. A meat pellet was dropped on the floor about 2 ft away from the animal, and as it began to approach the pellet, the buzzer was sounded close by, repeatedly. In no instance was there inhibition of eating or any other sign of resurgence of anxiety. Clearly, the anxiety had truly been extinguished, not just suppressed.

RECIPROCAL INHIBITION IN HUMAN NEUROSES

Some time after concluding the foregoing experiments, I completed a dissertation based on them and went into clinical practice. The possibility that feeding might be a generally effective agent for deconditioning in human subjects was, naturally, suggested by the animal experiments and encouraged by the successful use of feeding in Mary Cover Jones's (1924a, 1924b) treatment of children's fears. In Watson and Rayner's (1920) discussion of their experiment on Little Albert, in whom they had conditioned a fear of white rats, they had proposed four possible strategies for overcoming the fear, one of which was "reconditioning by having the child eat candy in the presence of the feared object" (p. 11).

Jones, who had been a student of Watson, used this strategy in the treatment of a number of children's phobias. Her procedure (Jones, 1924a) was as follows:

> During a period of craving for food, the child is placed in a high chair and given something to eat. The feared object is brought in, starting a negative response. It is then moved away gradually until it is at a sufficient distance not to interfere with the child's eating. The relative strength of the fear impulse and the hunger impulse may be gauged by the distance to which it is necessary to remove the feared object. While the child is eating, the object is slowly brought nearer to the table, then placed upon the table and, finally, as the tolerance increases, it is brought close enough to be touched. Since we could not interfere with the regular schedule of meals, we chose the time of the mid-morning lunch for the experiment. This usually assured some degree of interest in the food and corresponding success in our treatment. (p. 382)

Jones (1924b) gave a detailed example of this method in the treatment of Peter, a 3-year-old boy with a fear of rabbits—"one of our most serious problem cases." Peter had sessions over a period of 2 months, at the end of which he was able to handle rabbits fearlessly. Jones found that Peter made greater progress in sessions in which hunger was greater. By contrast, if the feared object was repeatedly presented without eating, it seemed more likely to produce an increase of fear than an adaptation.

Although the successful treatment of maladaptive fears in animals and children made it natural to entertain the idea of using feeding for treating the fears of human adults, I was discouraged by two considerations. The first was the widely known results of an enthusiastically promoted treatment for anxiety disorders: the injection of subcoma doses of insulin. It had been expected that improvement would occur in subjects whom the insulin caused to eat more and gain weight. However, a controlled study by Teitelbaum et al. (1946) showed that only a small percentage of patients benefited. The second consideration was the practical difficulty of arranging for eating to coincide with the arousal of social anxiety, the usual adult problem. Therefore, I gave up on feeding responses for adults.

THERAPEUTIC PROCEDURES MEDIATED
BY RECIPROCAL INHIBITION

All of the procedures under this heading are evidently mediated by reciprocal inhibition. With the exception of the first procedure—assertiveness training—they were specifically developed as ways of using reciprocal inhibition to overcome maladaptive anxiety-response habits. It should be noted that they are all used to overcome clinically conditioned fears. About one third of maladaptive clinical fears are based on misconceptions and require cognitive correction (see Wolpe, 1990, pp. xii, 345), which also is achieved through the occurrence of reciprocal inhibition (see pp. 35–36 in this chapter).

Assertiveness Training

Having despaired of the practicality of exploiting feeding for the treatment of human adults, I began to look for alternatives. Anger gave the impression of being inherently opposed to anxiety, and in tentative explorations of its therapeutic possibilities, I sometimes took advantage of its spontaneous presence to encourage its overt expression in cases of interpersonal inadequacy and sometimes tried to induce it for covert practice when there was anxiety at being rejected. Some success emerged from these measures. Before long, I received great encouragement from reading Salter's (1949) *Conditioned Reflex Therapy*, which described the author's extensive experience in the therapeutic promotion of the outward expression of anger and other feelings.

Assertiveness training is directed basically at overcoming interpersonal timidity. The person is shown how to express, in all reasonable circumstances, legitimate anger, affection, and other appropriate feelings. In actions such as standing up for his or her rights and protesting unfair criticism, the person gives motor expression to feelings that maladaptive fear has habitually inhibited. As a result, two kinds of behavior change occur. The fear is inhibited and weakened by the expression of the anger, and new habits of motor expression are learned, reinforced by social success.

There has been surprisingly little psychophysiological research on the effects on anxiety of the expression of anger and other emotions. Arnold (1945, 1960) marshaled evidence of physiological antagonism between anger and anxiety. Ax (1953) expressed doubts about this, although his own data to some extent supported it. Soviet research (e.g., Simonov, 1967) has yielded impressive evidence of the existence of separate and reciprocally inhibitory centers for anger and anxiety in the midbrain. When either of these sources of emotional responses is put out of action by drugs or by ablations, the other is facilitated.

Relaxation-Based Treatment of Anxiety Disorders

Deep muscle relaxation has automatic accompaniments that are the opposite of those of anxiety (Jacobson, 1938; Paul, 1969). Connor (1974) showed that even when the decrease in muscle tension is insufficient to lower autonomic baseline levels, it can still diminish the anxiety responses to conditioned stimuli. Jacobson (1938) was the first to demonstrate directly the therapeutic utility of relaxation. He directed the patients he trained to try to be as relaxed as possible at all times, including, by implication, in disturbing situations that might arise in the normal course of events. The ability to remain calm in those situations is usually possible only after a great deal of training and practice. One hundred or more training sessions were the rule with Jacobson. Even then, beneficial change was uncertain, because the unpredictability of fear in life often finds the person unready to counter it; in any case, even very good relaxation may not suffice when fear is great. Interestingly, Jacobson did not relate the lasting effects of relaxation to the learning process.

Relaxation-Based Treatment Using Imagined Stimuli: Systematic Desensitization

The first therapeutic procedure directly derived from the reciprocal inhibition idea was systematic desensitization (Wolpe, 1954, 1990), which pits the calmness of relaxation against imagined anxiety situations. This usage usually requires about an hour of relaxation training beforehand, spread over several sessions, with practice at home in between. At the same sessions, assorted situations from an area of unadaptive fear have been listed and then arranged in rank order of their fear-evoking power. The ranked list is called a *hierarchy*. An individual case may have one or several hierarchies. The simplest hierarchies are those of the "classical" phobias. For example, in a phobia against heights, the hierarchy may consist of looking out of windows at levels ranging from the 2nd to the 50th floor (e.g., 2, 3, 4, 5, 7, 9, 12, 15, 20, 25, 30, 40, 50). However, the subject matter of a fear may be complex and require careful analysis (see the case of Jane, presented shortly). When the patient can relax well enough and the hierarchies have been formulated, the actual desensitization procedure begins. The patient is made to relax deeply and is then asked to imagine the hierarchy's weakest item—looking out of a 2nd-floor window, whose clear imaging he or she signals by raising a finger. After a few seconds, the scene is terminated and followed by renewed relaxation. The sequence is repeated about once per minute until the imagined item no longer evokes any anxiety. Subsequent items are similarly handled until fear is eliminated from the whole hierarchy. Almost invariably, parallel deconditioning of anxiety is found to have occurred in the corresponding real situation. The imagination-based technique does not succeed in about 15% of participants, people who do not experience anxiety when they imagine situations that in reality make them anxious. In many of them, relaxation can be successfully used with real stimuli (see the section on in vivo desensitization).

Borkovec and Sides (1979) found in a review of 25 studies that adequate relaxation training (in contrast to inadequate training) significantly enhanced the reduction of autonomic responses in desensitization, and McGlynn, Moore, Rose, and Lazarte (1995) showed that relaxed subjects repeatedly exposed to an in vivo fear stimulus displayed significantly greater diminution of fear than subjects not relaxed.

Although there is a widespread belief that systematic desensitization has its main value in the treatment of phobias, this is not true. Its most important application is with social anxieties. In a statistical study of fears treated by systematic desensitization (Wolpe, 1961), only 14 of 68 were phobias, and the remainder were social anxieties. In some of the latter, accurate identification of therapeutically viable configurations of anxiety-evoking stimuli entails considerable thought and effort. The following case (Wolpe, 1989) illustrates this.

> Jane, a single woman of 27, complained of lack of confidence and low self-esteem. Merely to walk in the street made her anxious, feeling that everybody was looking at her critically. This sensitivity dated from a sharply negative evaluation from a teacher in the twelfth grade. Thereafter, she was almost always fearful among people because of their supposed negative attitudes, and later also became uncomfortable at admiration. Despite being very attractive she had little social life and hardly ever dated. Notable anxiety arousing contexts were disapproval, rejection and being ignored.
>
> Two years earlier Jane had seen a behavior therapist who had first adopted a cognitive strategy. He had tried to convince her that the derogatory thoughts she imputed to others were a fiction. Finding that her sensitivity was undiminished by his arguments, he had switched to flooding—having her go out of her way to expose herself for prolonged periods in the company of individuals in whose minds she "inserted" critical thoughts. With no improvement in four months, she had terminated therapy.
>
> Careful examination of the facts she presented revealed that she reacted with anxiety to criticisms of herself that she introjected into the minds of others. The strategy indicated was to desensitize her to the full range of relevant thoughts in the minds of others. It was first necessary to specify the thoughts, subdivide them into themes, rank them in their themes in order of the distress they produced, and finally construct a two-dimensional hierarchy, in which the ranked thoughts were systematically interlinked with individuals ranked according to the importance of their opinions [see Wolpe, 1993, p. 170].

In the actual desensitization, with Jane deeply relaxed, she was made to imagine herself overhearing statements from the two-dimensional hierarchy in ascending order, each until anxiety was eliminated. There was almost complete transfer of change to all real situations. At a follow-up 10 months later, Jane reported that her improvement had consolidated. (p. 15)

Jane's original therapist had based his therapeutic decisions on a fuzzy conception of her problem. Many therapists "do" cognitive correction and "do" flooding, as if they were alternative solutions to the same problem—much as a physician might decide between radiation and surgery in an unambiguously diagnosed carcinoma. Clarity of diagnostic formulation is indispensable to appropriate choice of treatment. That Jane feared what people thought was not a precise formulation of the stimuli antecedent to her anxiety, but only a general statement of her complaint. A treatment performed on anything so amorphous could hardly effect much change. For appropriate treatment, there had to be clear specification of her problem, drawing on knowledge of the range of thoughts she feared and of the channels by which they affected her. The next required step was to decide whether the fears were cognitively based or classically conditioned.

If Jane's therapist had obtained the requisite information, he would have seen in advance the futility of his attempt at cognitive correction. To begin with, there was no way in which he could vindicate the assertion that people in Jane's life did not have the thoughts Jane feared. But even if he had managed to convince her with respect to particular people, her anxious vulnerability to such thoughts would have remained intact.

The "flooding" treatment was also predictably futile. It was left to Jane to perform the flooding in life situations. She found it difficult to sustain constant levels of "exposure," and in any case, from one exposure experience to the next the variation of content would have undermined consolidation of any gains. Above all, it is noteworthy that the efficacy of flooding procedures in complex social fears is very much in question. Desensitization, too, would have failed without correctly formulated hierarchies.

Desensitization in Vivo

Desensitization in vivo differs from standard systematic desensitization in that real instead of imagined hierarchical stimuli are used. The groundbreaking therapeutic experiments of Mary Cover Jones (1924a, 1924b), described earlier, were technically desensitization in vivo. The next reported use of graduated exposure in vivo was by Terhune (1948), for whom it was a purely empirical strategy. Meyer (1957) formally introduced in vivo desensitization as a treatment for agoraphobia. In 1960, Freeman and Kendrick reported the overcoming of a cat phobia by getting the patient to handle pieces of material progressively similar to cat fur, then exposing her to pictures of cats, followed by a toy kitten, a real kitten, and eventually grown cats. A phobia for earthworms was treated in a similar way by Murphy (1964). Goldberg and D'Zurilla (1968) reported systematic desensitization of a fear of receiving injections, using a slide-projected hierarchy.

An agoraphobic woman I treated, whose anxiety level was related to distance from a "reliable" person, was repeatedly brought by her husband to meet me in a public park in the quiet of the morning. She was instructed to relax at these times, but the contribution of relaxation to anxiety inhibition was almost certainly augmented by her emotional response to the therapist (see Therapist-Evoked Responses section). In about 10 meetings, she learned to tolerate increasingly distant and prolonged separations.

In contrast to the limitless availability of imagined stimuli, appropriate in vivo stimuli are not always readily available. Artifices often have to be devised. For example, in treating patients with fear of humiliation, I have had them intentionally give wrong answers to simple arithmetical problems. The anxiety this produces diminishes with repetition. I then introduce more difficult problems until reaching some beyond their capacity, and then I increasingly criticize them, finally introducing witnesses to magnify the "humiliations." By this sequence of experiences people become less and less vulnerable to humiliation.

Alternatives to Muscle Relaxation for Producing Calmness

The autonomic effects characteristic of deep muscle relaxation can also be produced by other interventions: autogenic training, transcendental meditation, and biofeedback. If a person is well practiced in any of these, that skill can replace muscle relaxation for purposes of systematic desensitization. Calmness for desensitization can also be procured by chemical agents, such as the benzodiazepines.

Autogenic training, widely used in Europe, was developed by Schultz and Luthe (1959). It makes use of suggestions of heaviness and warmth. To begin with, heaviness suggestions are repeated five times by the therapist, and then the subject repeats them several times to himself or herself. Warmth suggestions are added later, but it appears that it is the heaviness suggestions that produce the calmness. Nicassio and Bootzin (1974) found that autogenic training and relaxation were equally effective in the treatment of insomnia and superior to controls.

The technique of transcendental meditation consists of giving the patient a meaningless word (called a "mantra") to attend to continuously while seated in a quiet room with eyes closed. If other thoughts intrude, the patient must repel them and return to the word. Wallace (1970) reported that transcendental meditation produced all of the physiological changes found with muscle relaxation.

Budzinski and Stoyva (1969) observed that biofeedback was effective in accelerating and possibly deepening muscle relaxation. Comparative studies of relaxation and biofeedback have yielded conflicting results. Chesney and Shelton (1976) found progressive relaxation to be superior in tension headaches, but Reinking and Kohl (1975) achieved lower tension levels with biofeedback. In a survey of comparative studies, Qualls and Sheehan (1981) found that electromyographic biofeedback compared favorably. More important than which is "better" is the fact that electromyographic feedback is an additional resource and a reasonably convenient one.

Pharmacological inhibition of anxiety—the induction of calmness by tranquilizing medications—has been extensively documented (e.g., Usdin, Skolnik, Tallman, Greenblatt, & Paul, 1982), and lasting diminution of anxiety responses not infrequently follows systematic exposure to anxiety-evoking stimuli during the action of these substances. Miller, Murphy, and Mirsky (1957), in a controlled experiment, demonstrated the anxiety-deconditioning value of adding a tranquilizing drug to exposure to an anxiety-conditioned stimulus. With electric shock as the unconditioned stimulus, they conditioned in four groups of rats an avoidance response to the sound of a buzzer. To study the effect of the tranquilizing drug on extinction of the avoidance response, they injected two of the groups with saline and the other two with chlorpromazine on each of 4 consecutive days. A chlorpromazine group and a saline group were each exposed daily to the buzzer. During subsequent trials without injections, the chlorpromazine group had far fewer avoidance reactions than did the saline group, showing that the drug had facilitated deconditioning. A chlorpromazine group that was not exposed to the buzzer showed no deconditioning.

I have sometimes used tranquilizers for clinical deconditioning in a way that parallels the Miller et al. (1957) experiment. The patient takes the drug in advance of exposure to a disturbing situation in a dose large enough to ensure that no substantial anxiety is ever elicited. For example, finding that the severe classroom anxiety experienced by a graduate student was markedly ameliorated by meprobamate, I kept him on an adequate dosage of the drug on every school day for 6 weeks. In 12 weeks, his anxiety without the drug was diminished by about 70%. Marked and lasting improvements by such means were reported by Maxwell and Paterson (1958) and by Miller (personal communication, 1967).

Other Clinically Effective Anxiety Inhibitors

Sexual arousal. The long-known fact that anxiety is a common cause of male sexual inadequacy, especially premature ejaculation, suggested to me at an early stage of the practice of behavior therapy that sexual arousal might, reciprocally, inhibit relatively weak anxiety in sexual situations and in consequence diminish its evocation, as feeding had done in the neurotic cats. Thus, a man's sexual response might be the vehicle for a kind of in vivo desensitization for the anxiety evoked by the sexual encounter, leading to recovery in cases in which anxiety was the reason for inadequacy of performance. This turned out to be a highly successful basic strategy, although adjuvants were profitably used in some cases. A survey of 18 cases showed 14 to have recovered and 3 others to be much improved after treatment that usually spanned a few weeks (Wolpe, 1990, p. 305).

The success of this procedure, which I first reported in 1954, was the largely unacknowledged starting point for the development that came to be known as the "new sex therapy," whose main early protagonists were Masters and Johnson (1970) and Kaplan (1974). Although many of their procedures obtained improvement in sexual function through diminishing anxiety on the basis of gradually increasing exposure, they did not recognize that reciprocal inhibition was at work. Because the influence of these authors on current psychiatric treatment of sexual disorders has been considerable, their incognizance left their followers unaware of reciprocal inhibition. None of 15 chapters on sexual disorders in the American Psychiatric Association's (1989) authoritative compendium, *Treatments of Psychiatric Disorders*, make any reference to the anxiety-inhibiting effects of sexual responses, although two of the authors do refer to standard systematic desensitization.

It is noteworthy that the anxiety-inhibiting effects of sexual arousal can be successfully applied to anxieties that are not sexual. Napalkov and Karas (1957) reported that nonsexual anxieties in dogs were overcome by counterposed sexual excitation. The same effect is occasionally noted in human cases; the development of a loving relationship may provide an ongoing source of inhibition of maladaptive anxieties.

Verbally induced emotions inhibiting anxiety. There are three modes of verbally induced inhibition of anxiety: emotive imagery, induced anger, and direct suggestion. In emotive imagery, a situation known to be pleasantly exciting to the subject is the verbally painted setting for the imaging of graded anxiety-evoking stimuli; in the latter two, the counteractive emotion is induced by verbal cues.

In emotive imagery (Lazarus & Abramovitz, 1962), anxiety-eliciting stimuli are presented to the subject's imagination against a verbally evoked competing emotion. In the case of a 12-year-old boy who feared darkness, Lazarus and Abramovitz made use of the fact that the boy was greatly interested in Superman and Captain Silver. He was asked to imagine that these characters had made him their agent and that he was, at their behest, traversing dark passages of increasing length. By careful coordination of darkness stimuli with the boy's counteractive emotional responses, the boy overcame his fear in three sessions, a recovery that endured at an 11-month follow-up.

Induced anger (Goldstein, Serber, & Piaget, 1970) consists of getting the patient to pair anger-arousing imagery with fear-evoking scenes. Later, the patient uses the images to arouse anger in spontaneously occurring fear-producing, real-life situations. Goldstein et al. reported benefit in 6 of 10 cases. Although I have rarely used this method, it was the therapeutic turning point in a very obstinate case of agoraphobia (Wolpe, 1990, p. 200).

Rubin (1972) initiated a behavior therapy usage of emotional reactions induced by suggestions in the manner of traditional hypnotists. Where Rubin departed from the traditional practice was in bringing the patient's maladaptive anxiety reactions into opposition with the induced emotion. In a case of my own (Wolpe, 1990, p. 202), marked improvement occurred in a single session in a man's fear of flying by having him imagine a hierarchical succession of flight-related events in a plane in the context of strongly suggested arousal of pleasurable feelings by aspects of planes he positively enjoyed.

Inhibition of anxiety by motor response competition. A variety of methods were described many years ago, and there is a very intriguing new method: eye movement desensitization (EMD).

The older methods include reading aloud (Everaerd, 1970; Stoffel-mayr, 1970) and Asian defense exercises (Gershman & Stedman, 1971) in the context of hierarchically ordered real or imagined anxiety-evoking situations. In some of the cases, standard desensitization had previously failed. An illuminating example was an exceptionally severe case of agoraphobia (Wolpe, 1958, p. 174) in a woman who was unable to be calmed by relaxation and in whom pure repetitions of anxiety-evoking stimuli did not work. Imagining of hierarchically ordered anxiety-arousing situations, paired with arm flexions, produced slow but steady diminution of fearfulness, finally to full recovery.

Eye movement desensitization (Shapiro, 1989) is a recently discovered, often very effective, use of motor responses for overcoming maladaptive anxiety-response habits. Its most impressive results have been in the treatment of posttraumatic stress disorder, in which a number of authors have replicated Shapiro's findings (Kleinknecht & Morgan, 1992; Marquis, 1991; McCann, 1992; Puk, 1992; Spector & Huthwaite, 1993; Wolpe & Abrams, 1991). There is also evidence of its efficacy in treating other anxiety disorders (Marquis, 1991).

The procedure is as follows: After preliminary analysis has defined the anxiety constellations, the patient is asked to imagine a particular anxiety-eliciting situation and to maintain the image while visually tracking the side-to-side movements of the clinician's finger (or a hand-held object such as a pen). Twenty to 30 lateral movements (1 per second) make up a set, and sets are repeated as necessary. The client's anxiety level is elicited before and after each set, using a subjective units of disturbance (*sud*) scale

(Wolpe, 1990, pp. 91–92). The procedure usually results in rapid decrease of the anxiety elicited by the image, with characteristically correlated diminution of secondary symptoms such as nightmares and flashbacks. Several sessions are, however, often required. There is practically no tendency to relapse.

Eye movement desensitization awaits controlled studies in several areas. It is especially necessary to tease out what is essential in the procedure. For example, it may be that certain other rhythmic movements are as effective as eye movements in diminishing maladaptive anxieties. In a controlled comparison, students with test anxiety did as well with alternate tapping of their forefingers as with eye movements (Bauman & Melnick, 1994). Outcome studies comparing EMD with older methods are also necessary, even though, impressionistically, for posttraumatic stress disorder at least, EMD seems to work better than flooding and desensitization (cf. Keane & Kaloupek, 1982; Scrignar, 1984). Another major question relates to the mechanism of change in EMD. Dyck (1994) has persuasively argued on the strength of experimental data that it facilitates extinction by competitively reducing the magnitude of evoked fear.

The treatment of maladaptive motor habits by reciprocal inhibition. Although they do not label it *reciprocal inhibition*, it is clearly the mechanism that accounts for the success of Azrin and his colleagues in the treatment of a variety of maladaptive habits by means of "habit reversal." Precursors of these programs were Taylor's (1963) treatment of compulsive eyebrow plucking and Wolpe's (1958, p. 188) procedure for overcoming compulsive mimicry.

Among the syndromes that Azrin's group have successfully treated by the use of counteractive responses are tics (Azrin & Nunn, 1973), trichotillomania (Azrin, Nunn, & Frantz, 1980), self-destructive oral habits (Azrin, Nunn, & Frantz-Renshaw, 1980), and stuttering (Azrin & Nunn, 1974). The application to stuttering was substantially corroborated by Waterloo and Gotestam (1988).

THERAPEUTIC PROCEDURES WHOSE MECHANISMS ARE UNCERTAIN

Therapist-Evoked Responses: "Nonspecific Effects"

From reviews of the literature by Bergin (1971) and Bergin and Lambert (1978), it is apparent that many anxious patients who receive psychotherapy of any kind experience positive consequences, in contrast to those who have no therapeutic contact. Outside of behavior therapy, the effects of the various psychotherapies are very much the same. This was noted early on by Wilder (1945) and has in recent years generated the "equivalence of therapies hypothesis" (e.g., Bergin & Lambert, 1978; Garfield, 1980; Stiles, Shapiro, & Elliott, 1986). Because therapeutic techniques differ widely, it is reasonable to infer that the similar percentages of favorable results that different therapies obtain are attributable to something that all of them share. The common process is called *nonspecific effects*.

The operation that is common to all therapies is an interview in which the patient confidentially talks about his or her difficulties to a person he or she believes to have the knowledge, skill, and desire to help him or her. This encounter undoubtedly excites in many patients emotional responses, which are the likely mediators of any therapeutic consequences that may ensue. The character and the strength of these responses must vary with many factors, among which the personality and behavior of the therapist and the reactive repertoire of the patient are clearly important. If an emotional response that the interview induces is (a) antagonistic to anxiety and (b) sufficiently strong, it may be expected to inhibit some of the anxiety responses that may be evoked by some contents of the interview and thus promote weakening of underlying anxiety-response habits.

This explanation, attributing the therapeutic benefits of nonspecific processes to reciprocal inhibition, is feasible but speculative. Systematic psychophysiological studies are lacking. It is remarkable that none have ever been undertaken. Some straws in the wind come from studies involving biofeedback. Taub (1977) found that an impersonal and skeptical experimenter succeeded in training only 2 of 22 subjects in self-regulation of tissue temperature, whereas a warmer and more involved one succeeded with 19 of 21 subjects. Borgeat, Hade, Larcouche, and Gauthier (1984) reported that in patients with tension headaches who were treated by electromyographic biofeedback, the mere presence of the therapist had beneficial emotional effects, which varied in magnitude with the individual therapist and with his or her behavior.

Flooding Therapy

Flooding involves the prolonged exposure of a patient to fear-eliciting stimuli of relatively high intensity (see chapter 7 in this book). Its systematic use began with the work of Malleson (1959) and Stampfl (cited in London, 1964), both of whom treated cases by deliberately exposing them to continuous high-level anxiety, with the expectation that experimental extinction would occur. Both achieved many successes.

The method was later adopted by Marks, who named it "exposure therapy." It has been widely adopted in behavior therapy to the extent that "exposure" is today regarded by many as the most viable method for overcoming classically conditioned anxiety. A review by Barlow (1988, p. 486) found its comparative efficacy in simple phobia to be equivocal. Exceptionally favorable outcomes have, however, been reported by Ost (1989) in the treatment of specific phobias, mainly animal phobias, in single sessions lasting about 2 hr.

A signal success of flooding has been in the treatment of obsessive–compulsive neuroses that are characterized by fear and avoidance of contamination. It has markedly improved such patients' prognosis. Meyer (1966) was the first to treat them by prolonged exposure to "contamination," interdicting washing and, when necessary, rituals. Subsequently, the method was applied to a wide range of cases (see Hodgson, Rachman, & Marks, 1972; Marks, 1972; Rainey, 1972).

For any procedure to diminish fear conditioning, it must somehow reduce evoked fear. How does flooding reduce fear? One straw in the wind is the observation that the therapist's presence facilitates fear reduction by flooding. Only one study has provided data on this point: Sherry and Levine (1980) found, in speech-anxious subjects, that in those with whom the therapist was present during flooding, the outcome was significantly better than when the therapist was absent. To the same effect are observations of Butler, Cullington, Munby, Amies, and Gelder (1984). A group of social phobics to whom they gave standard flooding did less well than a second group who also received cognitive and distractive strategies and some relaxation training.

The Mechanism of Flooding

The common view is that flooding weakens fear on the basis of experimental extinction and the fact that the fear weakens as a function of its elicitation without reinforcement conforms to the standard definition of extinction. But what is missing is any explanation for the weakening. One may start from the observations noted earlier indicating that various distracting events facilitate extinction and add them to the general finding that when anxiety is relatively weak, repeated elicitation extinguishes it relatively easily (e.g., Berkun, 1957; Black, 1958); when its arousal is strong, little or no extinction may result. Experimental neuroses (see the previous section), characterized by severe fear, are uniformly resistant to extinction even with prolonged exposure to maximal stimulation. The clinical failures of flooding—such as the aerophobias that do not improve in the course of repeated fear-filled flights—are other examples. It is in line with this that competitive attenuation of elicited anxiety has been put forward as the explanation for the success of eye movement desensitization (Dyck, 1994; see p. 42 of this chapter), the attenuation here being attributed to the eye movements lessening the impact of the stimulus to anxiety. Their effect is apparently to facilitate inhibition of the anxiety response at that time. But what is the source of that inhibition? Conceivably, in both

EMD and flooding it is the emotional response to the therapist (see pp. 42–43 in this chapter), so presumably reciprocal inhibition is at play.

Another possible mechanism is transmarginal inhibition (Gray, 1964; Pavlov, 1927). If a conditioned stimulus is administered to an animal at increasing intensities, the strength of the response increases until it reaches asymptote. In some instances, after the response has reached this maximum, its evocation paradoxically becomes weaker as the intensity of stimulation continues to rise, and this is called *transmarginal inhibition*. It has prima facie credibility as a basis for the effects of flooding. Unfortunately, no research has been done to examine this possibility.

THE SUCCESS OF BEHAVIOR THERAPY SUPPORTS RECIPROCAL INHIBITION THEORY

If the clinical results of behavior therapy, whose methods largely invoke reciprocal inhibition, had been no better than those of the common run of therapies, in which reciprocal inhibition is inadvertent, it could be regarded as a falsification of the reciprocal inhibition theory of psychotherapeutic effects. However, the evidence speaks otherwise.

Since the 1950s there has been a steady stream of reports of the successful treatment of individual cases or small groups by behavior therapy with effects that are usually both marked and lasting. Many of the early studies were conveniently brought together in two books edited by Eysenck (1960, 1964). Two features of these studies, unusual in the literature of psychotherapy, were evidence of clear temporal relationships between specific interventions and therapeutic change, and the economy of time (usually weeks) to procure substantial change. This contrasted impressively with the long duration and inconclusiveness characteristic of psychodynamically treated cases. A seeming negation of this favorable contrast appeared in the meta-analytic study of psychotherapy reported by Smith, Glass, and Miller (1980). Their findings were presented as indicating no significant difference between the effectiveness of behavior therapy and that of psychoanalytically oriented brief psychotherapy; their results were greeted with acclaim by the psychoanalytically disposed (Garfield & Bergin, 1978; Strupp, 1978) because they seemed to dispel a serious threat to the long-vaunted superiority of the psychodynamic approach.

However, it subsequently emerged that the similarity of effectiveness that Smith et al. (1980) had portrayed was the result of the confounding of data of different diagnostic groups. Andrews and Harvey (1981) made a separate analysis of Smith and Glass's neurotic patients and found that in them the effects of behavior therapy were superior to those of psychodynamic therapy ($p < .001$). Searles (1985) found that Andrews and Harvey had also underestimated the superiority of behavior therapy because they, too, had failed to exclude a large number of cases that had nothing to do with neuroses.

Wolpe, Craske, Reyna, and Pascotto (1994) made a broad survey of the outcome literature to compare psychodynamic and behavioral methods in the treatment of anxiety disorders. This survey differed from all its predecessors in accepting as successes only cases rated "apparently recovered" or "much improved" on the criteria laid down by the noted psychoanalyst, Robert P. Knight (1941). In the psychodynamically treated series, the percentages of cases much improved ranged from 21% to 25%, while those of behavior therapy ranged from 65% to 89%. The mean numbers of treatment sessions were in excess of 700 in two reports on psychoanalytic therapy (Kernberg et al., 1972; Masserman, 1962) and 289 for psychodynamic psychotherapy (Kernberg et al., 1972). By contrast, there was a mean of 45.6 sessions in an early behavior therapy study (Wolpe, 1958) and 31 or fewer in contemporary behavioral series of separate syndromes—agoraphobia, panic disorder, simple phobia, obsessive–compulsive disorder, social phobia.

COMMENTS ON OTHER THEORIES

Several rival theories purport to explain how classically conditioned anxiety is weakened by therapy. These theories constitute extinction, and "exposure," and cognitive theories, including changed expectancy and raised self-efficacy. All are untenable, as will be seen.

Extinction

Extinction is the name for the standard procedure that is used in laboratories to weaken a conditioned response—by evoking it repeatedly without reinforcement. With respect to neurotic fears, the original protagonist of extinction was Malleson (1959). He was followed by Stampfl and Levis and their collaborators (Levis & Boyd, 1979; Levis & Hare, 1977; Stampfl & Levis, 1967) and by Eysenck (1976, 1979). They all postulated that the weakening of conditioned maladaptive anxiety results from presenting the conditioned stimulus alone, sometimes at high intensity. Weakening does follow prolonged exposure to relatively strong anxiety-evoking stimulation, but not invariably. It seems never to have been reported in experimental neuroses and often does not occur in clinical neuroses. Clearly, something additional to unreinforced evocation must be present when weakening of the conditioned response does occur.

Absent from the accounts of Stampfl, Levis and Eysenck is any proposed mechanism for this weakening. Eysenck appeals to the observation that response enhancement can sometimes occur when anxiety is strongly and briefly elicited. But he does not explicate what happens in the topography of arousal to make the difference between the strengthening and the weakening of a habit.

Lader and Wing (1966) expressed the view that the response decrements of systematic desensitization were better explained by habituation than by reciprocal inhibition, a position that was enlarged upon by Lader and Mathews (1968). The definition of habituation is the diminution of a response to a stimulus that is repeatedly presented. This is indistinguishable from the definition of extinction. Actually, the word *habituation* was originally applied to the response decrements of repeatedly elicited unconditioned responses, and, as noted by Evans (1973), in that context the response that has disappeared reappears after rest (Sokolov, 1963). Thus, the habituation theory really does not seem to qualify for serious attention.

Exposure

"Exposure" has been vigorously promoted by Marks (1969, 1975, 1976, 1981) and Agras (1985) as the basis for the success of flooding therapy. The way that exposure is supposed to work is by enabling the patient to become "accustomed" to the stimulus. How this happens is not specified, so it is a theory without content. Classical conditioning and deconditioning both entail the organism's exposure to the conditioned stimulus. Marks recognized that not all exposure is therapeutic and that sometimes sensitization is its result, but he had no explanation for this either. He also failed to explain why, in the histories of many neuroses, there is repeated exposure to maladaptive anxiety-evoking stimuli, yet the anxiety-response habit does not weaken.

Cognitive Theories

People's perceptions and thoughts are involved in all psychotherapeutic operations, from communications about presenting complaints to the performance of change procedures such as systematic desensitization. The information the therapist obtains enables him or her to shape the details of instructions to the patient, enhancing cooperation in the measures designed to weaken conditioned anxiety habits. Diminution of conditioned anxiety is the expected consequence of these measures. Change in beliefs may occur secondary to the experience of emotional change. By contrast, in the overcoming of fears based on misconceptions, which constitute about 30% of cases, the correcting of the misconceptions (Ost & Hugdahl, 1981; Wolpe, 1981) is primary and indispensable.

But cognitive theorists such as Beck (Beck & Emery, 1985) and Ellis (1962, 1974) regard changes in thinking as the one and only way to overcome classically conditioned fears as well—which is consistent with their dogmatic assertion that there is no such thing as emotional learning unmediated by beliefs—a position incompatible with a variety of facts (Wolpe, 1990, pp. 132–136). Nevertheless, both Beck and Ellis frequently resort to deconditioning procedures such as assertiveness training and desensitization on the frequent occasions when their pure cognitive methods prove inadequate (see especially Ellis, 1985). They present these practices as trifling digressions whose efficacy they do not explain in cognitive terms, but quietly include under the cognitivistic roof anyway.

More often than not, careful examination of maladaptive fears turns up no evidence of relevant misconceptions. But because it is vital for Ellis and Beck always to find grounds for cognitive doctoring, they routinely impose on their clients thoughts that, according to their theories, they "must" have. Ellis routinely assumes the existence of absolutist "musts" and "shoulds," "awfulizing," and "self-damning" (e.g., Dryden, 1990, pp. 145–183). Beck assumes "automatic thoughts" (Beck & Emery, 1985).

The inefficacy of rational–emotive therapy was displayed in a wide review of outcomes by Gossette and O'Brien (1992). Surveys by Latimer and Sweet (1984) and Sweet and Loiseaux (1991) showed that the addition of Beck's characteristic techniques to standard behavior therapy confers little or no benefit. The only comparative outcome study in which Beck's methodology has had essentially "pure" application is in the Collaborative Research Program for the treatment of nonpsychotic depression. The fact that in that program, cognitive therapy fared less well than psychodynamically based "interpersonal therapy" is at first glance surprising, in view of the fact that most nonpsychotic depressions are a function of maladaptive anxiety (Wolpe, 1990), and in view of the markedly superior outcomes of behavior therapy in the anxiety disorders (see previous section, The Success of Behavior Therapy Supports Reciprocal Inhibition Theory). However, because only a minority of anxiety disorders are cognitively based, the majority of cases of depression would not be amenable to cognitive corrections (pp. 47–48).

As noted previously, nonspecific interview effects are frequently the real reason for the beneficial effects of psychotherapeutic procedures. Whenever fear diminishes following cognitive inputs, cognitive therapists assume that these inputs are the basis for the unlearning of fear; in fact, however, in many instances, the real cause of the diminution is that classically conditioned fear has been overcome by the concurrent inadvertent evocation of nonspecific emotional effects (see pp. 42–43 in this chapter). It was Beck's insistence on the sole relevance of cognitive correction in the treatment of nonpsychiatric depression that led to behavior therapy's poor showing in the collaborative study (noted earlier; see also Wolpe,

1993). Other cognitive theories of elimination of conditioned fear that I consider are expectancy theory and self-efficacy theory, whose advocates, unlike Ellis and Beck, have proposed specific mechanisms of change.

Expectancy

Kazdin and Wilcoxon (1976) advanced the proposition that the basis of anxiety reduction is changed expectancy, but they proffered no evidence that expectancy per se is ever therapeutically beneficial. They based their view on Rosenthal and Frank's (1958) empirically unsupported statement that behavior change can be "due to faith in the efficacy of the therapist and his or her techniques" (p. 53). The expectancy theory has recently been more assertively promoted by Kirsch (1978) and Reiss (1980). Reiss's position has been presented in detail by Reiss and McNally (1985). When fear has been conditioned to a stimulus, and when the subject has experienced the sequence several times, the subject expects the conditioned stimulus to be followed by fear. The authors state, quite correctly, that when fears are based on cognitive learning, they are reducible by cognitive relearning, which can often be said to imply changing expectations. But not content with this, Reiss and McNally argue that even fears that are classically conditioned are reducible by changing expectations. This would need to be demonstrated, but is not. In any case, if expectancy is based on the experience of a demonstrated cause–effect relationship between a stimulus and the arousal of fear, it is difficult to see how the expectancy can be removed except by the subject learning that the cause–effect relationship no longer exists. This would happen through deconditioning the fear, and the expectancy would then change after the fact. Anybody who claims that expectancy can change otherwise has the onus of demonstrating it.

Raised Expectations of Self-Efficacy

"Raised expectations of self-efficacy" is basically a more elaborate form of expectancy theory. According to Bandura (1977), treatments that succeed in eliminating neurotic anxiety do so not by deconditioning anxiety response habits, but through raising expectations of self-efficacy. This proposition could be true in certain cognitively based fears. But Bandura contends that it is true of all fears. In his view, there are no classically conditioned fears, no fears that are automatic responses to a particular perception unmediated by beliefs of any kind.

Bandura was encouraged in this view by experiments (Bandura, Blanchard, & Ritter, 1969; Bandura, Grusec, & Menlove, 1967) in which systematic desensitization, symbolic modeling, and modeling with guided participation were compared for their effectiveness in overcoming people's fears of harmless snakes or other small animals. Symbolic modeling consisted of observing a film of a fearless person handling the animal; in modeling with guided participation, the subject witnessed the therapist handling the animal and then was helped by him or her to make progressive approaches to it. Guided participation was significantly the most successful of the three methods, which Bandura ascribed to its superior ability to induce self-efficacy. He paid no attention to the fact that guided participation is also the only method that includes closeness with another human being in a functional way during exposure to the object of fear. Such closeness is a highly credible source of nonspecific therapeutic effects, as noted earlier.

Bandura later conducted a much more definitive series of experiments (Bandura, Reese, & Adams, 1982). Young women with severe fears of snakes or spiders were tested with regard to how close to the creatures they would approach, and their self-efficacy was correlatively measured. Then by such means as having the subject witness a fearless model handling a spider, she was enabled to make closer and closer approaches, so that she could ultimately approach the animal fearlessly, even to the point of imperturbably permitting it to crawl on her gloved or bare hand. At each stage of the progression self-efficacy was measured and was found to increase with the subject's progress. Bandura saw the growth of self-efficacy as the basis of recovery. However, he did not notice that something else was also happening, that he was doing a kind of graduated flooding, quite in the manner of a behavior therapist. He did not take into account that this by itself could achieve, perhaps more rapidly, a progressive diminution of classically conditioned fear, as demonstrated by Ost (1989), without the example of a model. Clearly, if the implications of the foregoing were confirmed in a controlled experiment, it would decisively falsify the proposition that self-efficacy has therapeutic effects. The conclusion would then be inescapable that the cognitive inputs from a model add nothing to the process of weakening the anxiety response habit.

CONCLUSION

This lengthy tract, traversing a large amount of evidence and a wide range of issues, reveals that reciprocal inhibition has a role in the great majority of methods that have been successfully used to overcome persistent maladaptive reactions of anxiety (fear). Its function is to inhibit fear, an indispensable element of the process of overcoming fear habits. It is, however, quite likely that under some circumstances other modes of fear inhibition, such as transmarginal inhibition, may have the same effect.

I have examined the claims of other theories that have been proposed for the overcoming of unadaptive fears and have found substantiation for none of them. Even in respect to maladaptive fears that arise from misinformation and need to be overcome by corrective information, the cognitive correction achieves change through reciprocal inhibition (see p. 30). Experimental extinction, i.e., the weakening of fear through its nonreinforced evocation undoubtedly occurs, but saying this does not furnish a mechanism. The most credible mechanism for extinction is Amsel's (1972) frustrative nonreward theory, which entails a mode of reciprocal inhibition. For the moment, at least, reciprocal inhibition appears to have pride of place as the best established agent for overcoming maladaptive anxiety.

REFERENCES

Agras, W. S. (1985). *Panic: Facing fears, phobias and anxiety.* San Francisco: Freeman.

American Psychiatric Association. (1989). *Treatments of psychiatric disorders.* Washington, DC: Author.

Amsel, A. (1972). Inhibition and mediation in classical, Pavlovian and instrumental conditioning. In R. A. Boakes & M. S. Halliday (Eds.), *Inhibition and learning.* London: Academic Press.

Andrews, G., & Harvey, R. (1981). Does psychotherapy benefit neurotic patients? A reanalysis of the Smith, Glass, and Miller data. *Archives of General Psychiatry, 38,* 1203–1208.

Arnold, M. B. (1945). The physiological differentiation of emotional states. *Psychology Review, 52,* 35–48.

Arnold, M. B. (1960). *Emotion and personality* (Vol. 1). New York: Columbia University Press.

Ax, A. F. (1953). The physiological differentiation of anger and fear in humans. *Psychosomatic Medicine, 15,* 433–442.

Azrin, N. H., & Nunn, R. G. (1973). Habit-reversal: A method of eliminating nervous habits and tics. *Behavior Research and Therapy, 11,* 619–628.

Azrin, N. H., & Nunn, R. G. (1974). A rapid method of elimination of stuttering by a regulated breathing approach. *Behavior Research and Therapy, 8,* 330.

Azrin, N. H., Nunn, R. G., & Frantz, S. E. (1980). Habit reversal vs. negative practice treatment of nervous tics. *Behavior Therapy, 11,* 169–178.

Azrin, N. H., Nunn, R. G., & Frantz-Renshaw, S. E. (1980). Habit reversal treatment of thumbsucking. *Behavior Research and Therapy, 18,* 395–399.

Bandura, A. (1977). Self-efficacy: Toward a unifying theory of behavioral change. *Psychology Review, 84,* 191–215.

Bandura, A., Blanchard, E. D., & Ritter, B. (1969). Relative efficacy of desensitization and modeling approaches for inducing behavioral, affective and attitudinal changes. *Journal of Personality and Social Psychology, 13,* 173.

Bandura, A., Grusec, J., & Menlove, F. (1967). Vicarious extinction of avoidance behavior. *Journal of Personality and Social Psychology, 5,* 16–23.

Bandura, A., Reese, L., & Adams, N. E. (1982). Microanalysis of action and fear arousal as a function of differential levels of perceived self-efficacy. *Journal of Personality and Social Psychology, 43,* 5–21.

Barlow, D.H. (1988). *Anxiety and its disorders.* New York: Guilford Press.

Bauman, W., & Melnick, W. T. (1994). A controlled comparison of eye movements and finger tapping in the treatment of test anxiety. *Journal of Behavior Therapy and Experimental Psychiatry, 25,* 29–33.

Beck, A. T., & Emery, G. (1985). *Anxiety disorders and phobias: A cognitive perspective.* New York: Basic Books.

Bergin, A. E. (1971). The evaluation of therapeutic outcomes. In A. E. Bergin & S. L. Garfield (Eds.), *Handbook of psychotherapy and behavior change: An empirical analysis* (pp. 299–344). New York: Wiley.

Bergin, A. E., & Lambert, M. J. (1978). The evaluation of therapeutic outcomes. In S. L. Garfield & A. E. Bergin (Eds.), *Handbook of psychotherapy and behavior change* (2nd ed.). New York: Wiley.

Berkun, M. M. (1957). Factors in the recovery from approach–avoidance conflict. *Journal of Experimental Psychology, 54,* 65.

Black, A. H. (1958). The extinction of avoidance responses under curare. *Journal of Comparative and Physiological Psychiatry, 51,* 519.

Borgeat, F., Hade, B., Larcouche, L. M., & Gauthier, B. (1984). Psychophysiological effects of therapist's active presence during biofeedback. *Psychiatry Journal, University of Ottawa, 9,* 132–137.

Borkovec, T. D., & Sides, J. K. (1979). Critical procedural variables related to the physiological effects of progressive relaxation: A review. *Behavior Research and Therapy, 17,* 119–125.

Bosma, J. F., & Gellhorn, E. (1946). Electromyographic studies of muscular coordination on stimulation of motor cortex. *Journal of Neurophysiology, 9,* 263–274.

Budzinski, T. H., & Stoyva, J. M. (1969). An instrument for producing deep muscle relaxation by means of analog information feedback. *Journal of Applied Behavior Analysis, 2,* 231–237.

Butler, G., Cullington, A., Munby, M., Amies, P., & Gelder, M. (1984). Exposure and anxiety management in the treatment of social phobia. *Journal of Consulting Clinical Psychology, 52,* 642–650.

Chesney, M. A., & Shelton, J. L. (1976). A comparison of muscle relaxation and electromyogram biofeedback treatments for muscle contraction headache. *Journal of Behavior Therapy and Experimental Psychiatry, 7,* 221–226.

Connor, W. H. (1974). Effects of brief relaxation training on autonomic response to anxiety provoking stimuli. *Psychophysiology, 11,* 591–596.

Dryden, W. (1990). The basic practice of RET. In W. Dryden (Ed.), *The essential Albert Ellis* (pp. 145–183). New York: Springer.

Dyck, M. (1994). A proposal for a conditioning model of eye movement desensitization treatment for posttraumatic stress disorder. *Journal of Behavior Therapy and Experimental Psychiatry, 24,* 3–13.

Ellis, A. (1962). *Reason and emotion in psychotherapy*. New York: Lyle Stuart.

Ellis, A. (1974). *Humanistic psychotherapy: The rational-emotive approach*. New York: Julian Press.

Ellis, A. (1985). *Overcoming resistance*. New York: Springer.

Evans, I. M. (1973). The logical requirements for explanations of systematic desensitization. *Behavior Therapy, 4*, 506–514.

Everaerd, W. (1970). Reading as the counterconditioning agent in a cardiac neurosis. *Journal of Behavior Therapy and Experimental Psychiatry, 1*, 165–167.

Eysenck, H. J. (1960). *Behavior therapy and the neuroses*. Elmsford, NY: Pergamon Press.

Eysenck, H. J. (1964). *Experiments in behavior therapy*. Elmsford, NY: Pergamon Press.

Eysenck, H. J. (1976). The learning theory model of neurosis: A new approach. *Behavior Research and Therapy, 14*, 251–267.

Eysenck, H. J. (1979). The conditioning model of neurosis. *Behavioral and Brain Sciences, 2*, 155–199.

Freeman, H. L., & Kendrick, D. C. (1960). A case of cat phobia: Treatment by a method derived from experimental psychology. *British Medical Journal, 1*, 497–499.

Freud, S. (1916). The history of the psychoanalytic movement: I. A. A. Brill (Trans.), *Psychoanalytic Review, 3*, 406–454.

Gantt, W. H. (1944). Experimental basis for neurotic behavior. *Psychosomatic Medicine Monographs, 3*(3 and 4).

Garfield, S. L. (1980). *Psychotherapy: An eclectic approach*. New York: Wiley.

Garfield, S. L., & Bergin, A. (1978). (Eds.). *Handbook of psychotherapy and behavior change* (2nd ed.). New York: Wiley.

Gellhorn, E. (1947). Patterns of muscular activity in man. *Archives of Physical Medicine, 28*, 568–574.

Gellhorn, E. (1967). *Principles of autonomic-somatic integrations*. Minneapolis: University of Minnesota Press.

Gershman, L., & Stedman, J. (1971). Oriental defense exercises as reciprocal inhibition of anxiety. *Journal of Behavior Therapy and Experimental Psychiatry, 2*, 117–119.

Goldberg, J., & D'Zurilla, T. J. (1968). A demonstration of slide projection as an alternative to imaginal stimulus presentation in systematic desensitization therapy. *Psychology Reports, 23*, 527.

Goldstein, A. J., Serber, M., & Piaget, J. (1970). Induced anger as a reciprocal inhibition of fear. *Journal of Behavior Therapy and Experimental Psychiatry, 1*, 67–70.

Gossette, R. L., & O'Brien, R. M. (1992). The efficacy of rational emotive therapy with adults. *Journal of Behavior Therapy and Experimental Psychiatry, 23*, 9–24.

Gray, J. A. (1964). *Pavlov's typology*. Elmsford, NY: Pergamon Press.

Hain, J. D., Butcher, R. H. J., & Stevenson, I. (1966). Systematic desensitization therapy: An analysis of results in 27 patients. *British Journal of Psychiatry, 112*, 295–307.

Hilgard, E. R., & Marquis, D. G. (1940). *Conditioning and learning.* New York: Appleton-Century.

Hodgson, R., Rachman, S., & Marks, I. M. (1972). The treatment of chronic obsessive-compulsive neuroses: Follow-up and further findings. *Behavior Research and Therapy, 10*, 181–189.

Jacobson, E. (1938). *Progressive relaxation.* Chicago: University of Chicago Press.

Jones, M. C. (1924a). Elimination of children's fears. *Journal of Experimental Psychology, 7*, 382–390.

Jones, M. C. (1924b). A laboratory study of fear: The case of Peter. *Journal of General Psychology, 31*, 308–315.

Kaplan, H. S. (1974). *The new sex therapy.* New York: Brunner/Mazel.

Kazdin, A. E., & Wilcoxon, L. A. (1976). Systematic desensitization and nonspecific treatment effects: A methodological evaluation. *Psychological Bulletin, 83*, 729–758.

Keane, T. M., & Kaloupek, D. G. (1982). Imaginal flooding in the treatment of posttraumatic stress disorder. *Journal of Consulting and Clinical Psychology, 50*, 138–140.

Kernberg, O., Burnstein, E., Coyne, L., Applebaum, A., Horowitz, L. H., & Voth, H. (1972). Psychotherapy and psychoanalysis: Final report of the Menninger Foundation Psychotherapy Research Project. *Bulletin of the Menninger Clinic, 36*, 1–276.

Kirsch, I. (1978). The placebo effect and the cognitive–behavioral revolution. *Cognitive Therapy and Research, 2*, 255–264.

Kleinknecht, R. A., & Morgan, M. P. (1992). Treatment of posttraumatic stress disorder with eye movement desensitization. *Journal of Behavior Therapy and Experimental Psychiatry, 23*, 43–49.

Knight, R. P. (1941). Evaluation of the results of psychoanalytic therapy. *American Journal of Psychiatry, 98*, 434–446.

Lader, M. H., & Mathews, A. M. (1968). A physiological model of phobic anxiety and desensitization. *Behavior Research and Therapy, 6*, 411–421.

Lader, M. H., & Wing, L. (1966). *Physiological measures, sedative drugs and morbid anxiety.* London: Oxford University Press.

Latimer, P. R., & Sweet, A. A. (1984). Cognitive versus behavioral procedures in cognitive behavior therapy: A critical review of the evidence. *Journal of Behavior Therapy and Experimental Psychiatry, 15*, 9–21.

Lazarus, A. A. (1963). The results of behavior therapy in 126 cases of severe neurosis. *Behavior Research and Therapy, 1*, 69–80.

Lazarus, A. A., & Abramovitz, A. (1962). The use of "emotive imagery" in the treatment of children's phobias. *Journal of Mental Sciences, 108*, 191–195.

Levis, D. J., & Boyd, T. L. (1979). Symptom maintenance: An infrahuman analysis and extension of the conservation of anxiety principle. *Journal of Abnormal Psychology, 88,* 107–120.

Levis, D. J., & Hare, N. (1977). A review of the theoretical and rational and empirical support for the extinction approach of implosive (flooding) therapy. In M. Hersen, R. M. Eisler, & P. M. Miller (Eds.), *Progress in behavior modification.* San Diego, CA: Academic Press.

Liddell, H. S. (1944). Conditioned reflex method and experimental neurosis. In J. McV. Hunt (Ed.), *Personality and disorders* (pp. 389–412). New York: Ronald Press.

London, P. (1964). *The modes and morals of psychotherapy.* New York: Holt, Rinehart & Winston.

Malleson, N. (1959). Panic and phobia. *Lancet, 1,* 225–227.

Marks, I. M. (1969). *Fears and phobias.* London: Heinemann.

Marks, I. M. (1972). Flooding (implosion) and allied treatments. In W. S. Agras (Ed.), *Learning theory application of principles and procedures to psychiatry.* New York: Little, Brown.

Marks, I. M. (1975). Behavioral treatments of phobic and obsessive-compulsive disorders: A critical appraisal. In M. Hersen, R. M. Eisler, & P. M. Miller (Eds.), *Progress in behavior modification.* San Diego, CA: Academic Press.

Marks, I. M. (1976). Current status of behavioral psychotherapy: Theory and practice. *American Journal of Psychiatry, 133,* 253–261.

Marks, I. M. (1981). *Cure and care of the neuroses.* New York: Wiley.

Marquis, J. N. (1991). A report on seventy-eight cases treated by eye movement desensitization. *Journal of Behavior Therapy and Experimental Psychiatry, 22,* 187–192.

Masserman, J. H. (1943). *Behavior and neurosis.* Chicago: University of Chicago Press.

Masserman, J. H. (1962). Ethology, comparative biodynamics, and psychoanalytic research. In J. Scher (Ed.), *Theories of the mind* (pp. 15–64). New York: Free Press.

Masters, W. H., & Johnson, V. E. (1970). *Human sexual inadequacy.* Boston: Little, Brown.

Maxwell, R. D. H., & Paterson, J. W. (1958). Meprobamate in the treatment of stuttering. *British Medical Journal, 1,* 873.

McCann, D. L. (1992). Post-traumatic stress disorder due to devastating burns overcome by a single session of eye movement desensitization. *Journal of Behavior Therapy and Experimental Psychiatry, 23,* 319–323.

McGlynn, F. D., Moore, P. M., Rose, M. P., & Lazarte, A. (1995). Effects of relaxation training on fear and arousal during *in vivo* exposure to a caged snake among snake phobics. *Journal of Behavior Therapy and Experimental Psychiatry, 26.*

Meyer, V. (1957). The treatment of two phobic patients on the basis of learning principles. *Journal of Abnormal Social Psychology, 58,* 259.

Meyer, V. (1966). Modification of expectations in cases with obsessional rituals. *Behavior Research and Therapy, 4,* 273–280.

Miller, R. E., Murphy, J. V., & Mirsky, I. A. (1957). Persistent effects of chlorpromazine on extinction of an avoidance response. *Archives of Neurology and Psychiatry, 78,* 526.

Murphy, I. C. (1964). Extinction of an incapacitating fear of earthworms. *Journal of Clinical Psychology, 20,* 386–398.

Napalkov, A. V., & Karas, A. Y. (1957). Elimination of pathological conditioned reflex connections in experimental hypertensive states. *Zhurnal Vysshei Nervnoi Deiatelnosti, 7,* 402–409.

Nicassio, P., & Bootzin, R. (1974). A comparison of progressive relaxation and autogenic training as treatments for insomnia. *Journal of Abnormal Psychology, 83,* 253–260.

Osgood, C. E. (1946). Meaningful similarity and interference in learning. *Journal of Experimental Psychology, 36,* 277–301.

Ost, L. (1989). One session treatment for specific phobias. *Behavior Research and Therapy, 27,* 1–7.

Ost, L., & Hugdahl, K. (1981). Acquisition of phobias and anxiety response patterns in clinical patients. *Behaviour Research and Therapy, 19,* 439–447.

Paul, G. L. (1969). Behavior modification research. In C. M. Franks (Ed.), *Behavior therapy: Appraisal and status.* New York: McGraw-Hill.

Pavlov, I. P. (1927). *Conditioned reflexes* (G. V. Anrep, Trans.). New York: Liveright.

Pavlov, I. P. (1941). *Conditioned reflexes and psychiatry* (W. H. Gantt, Trans.). New York: International.

Popper, K. (1959). *The logic of scientific discovery.* New York: Harper & Row.

Puk, G. (1992). Treating traumatic memories: A case report on the eye movement desensitization procedure. *Journal of Behavior Therapy and Experimental Psychiatry, 20,* 211–217.

Qualls, P. J., & Sheehan, P. W. (1981). Electromyograph biofeedback as a relaxation technique: A critical appraisal and reassessment. *Psychological Bulletin, 90,* 21–42.

Rainey, C. A. (1972). An obsessive-compulsive neurosis treated by flooding in vivo. *Journal of Behavior Therapy and Experimental Psychiatry, 3,* 117–128.

Reinking, R. H., & Kohl, M. L. (1975). Effects of various forms of relaxation training on physiological and self-report measures of relaxation. *Journal of Consulting and Clinical Psychology, 43,* 595–600.

Reiss, S. (1980). Pavlovian conditioning and human fear: An expectancy model. *Behavior Therapy, 11,* 380–396.

Reiss, S., & McNally, R. J. (1985). Expectancy model of fear. In S. Reiss & R. R. Bootzin (Eds.), *Theoretical issues in behavior therapy*. San Diego, CA: Academic Press.

Rosenthal, D., & Frank, J. D. (1958). Psychotherapy and the placebo effect. In C. F. Reed, I. E. Alexander, & S. S. Tomkins (Eds.), *Psychopathology: A sourcebook*. Cambridge, MA: Harvard University Press.

Rubin, M. (1972). Verbally suggested responses as reciprocal inhibition of anxiety. *Journal of Behavior Therapy and Experimental Psychiatry, 3*, 273–278.

Salter, A. (1949). *Conditioned reflex therapy*. New York: Creative Age.

Schultz, J. H., & Luthe, W. (1959). *Autogenic training: A psychophysiological approach in psychotherapy*. New York: Grune & Stratton.

Scrignar, C. G. (1984). *Post-traumatic stress disorder: Diagnosis, treatment, and legal issues*. New York: Praeger.

Searles, J. S. (1985). A methodological and empirical critique of psychotherapy outcome meta-analysis. *Behavior Research and Therapy, 23*, 453–463.

Shapiro, F. (1989). Eye movement desensitization: A new treatment for post-traumatic stress disorder. *Journal of Behavior Therapy and Experimental Psychiatry, 20*, 211–217.

Sherrington, C. S. (1961). *The integrative action of the nervous system*. New Haven, CT: Yale University Press. (Original work published 1906)

Sherry, G. S., & Levine, G. A. (1980). An evaluation of procedural variables in flooding therapy. *Behavior Therapy, 11*, 148–155.

Simonov, P. V. (1967). *Studies of emotional behavior of humans and animals*. Paper presented at a conference on experimental approaches to the study of behavior, by Soviet physiologists. New York.

Smith, M. L., Glass, G. V., & Miller, T. I. (1980). *The benefit of psychotherapy*. Baltimore: Johns Hopkins University Press.

Sokolov, Y. N. (1963). *Perception and the conditioned reflex* (S. W. Wayedenfeld, Trans.). Elmsford, NY: Pergamon Press.

Spector, J., & Huthwaite, M. (1993). Eye movement desensitization to overcome post-traumatic stress disorder. *British Journal of Psychiatry, 163*, 106–108.

Stampfl, T. G., & Levis, D. J. (1967). Essentials of implosive therapy: A learning-theory-based psychodynamic behavior therapy. *Journal of Abnormal Psychology, 72*, 496–503.

Stiles, W., Shapiro, D., & Elliott, R. (1986). Are all psychotherapies equivalent? *American Psychologist, 41*, 165–180.

Stoffelmayr, B. E. (1970). The treatment of a retching response to dentures by a counteractive reading aloud. *Journal of Behavior Therapy and Experimental Psychiatry, 1*, 163–164.

Strupp, H. (1978). Psychotherapy research and practice: An overview. In S. Garfield & A. Bergin (Eds.), *Handbook of psychotherapy and behavior change* (2nd ed.). New York: Wiley.

Sweet, A. A., & Loiseaux, A. L. (1991). Behavioral and cognitive treatment methods: A critical comparative review. *Journal of Behavior Therapy and Experimental Psychiatry, 22,* 159–185.

Taub, E. (1977). Self-regulation and human tissue temperature. In G. E. Schwartz & J. Beatty (Eds.), *Biofeedback: Theory and research.* San Diego, CA: Academic Press.

Taylor, J. G. (1963). A behavioral interpretation of obsessive-compulsive neurosis. *Behavior Research and Therapy, 1,* 237–244.

Teitelbaum, H. A., Hoekstra, C. S., Goldstein, D. N., Harris, I. D., Woods, R. M., & Cohen, D. (1946). Treatment of psychiatric disorders due to combat by means of a group therapy program and insulin in sub-shock doses. *Journal of Nervous and Mental Disorders, 104,* 123.

Terhune, W. S. (1948). The phobic syndrome: A study of eighty-six patients with phobic reactions. *Archives of Neurology and Psychiatry, 62,* 162–172.

Usdin, E., Skolnik, P., Tallman, J. F., Greenblatt, D., & Paul, S. M. (1982). *Pharmacology of benzodiazepine.* London: Macmillan.

Wallace, R. K. (1970). Physiological effects of transcendental meditation. *Science, 167,* 1751.

Waterloo, K. K., & Gotestam, K. G. (1988). The regulated breathing method for stuttering: An experimental evaluation. *Journal of Behavior Therapy and Experimental Psychiatry, 19,* 11–19.

Watson, J. B., & Rayner, P. (1920). Conditioned emotional reactions. *Journal of Experimental Psychology, 3,* 1–14.

Wendt, G. R. (1936). An interpretation of inhibition of conditioned reflexes as competition between reaction systems. *Psychological Review, 43,* 258–281.

Wilder, J. (1945). Facts and figures on psychotherapy. *Journal of Clinical Psychopathology, 7,* 311–347.

Wolpe, J. (1952a). Experimental neurosis as learned behavior. *British Journal of Psychology, 43,* 243–268.

Wolpe, J. (1952b). The formation of negative habits: A neurophysiological view. *Psychology Review, 59,* 290–299.

Wolpe, J. (1952c). Objective psychotherapy of the neuroses. *South African Medical Journal, 26,* 825–829.

Wolpe, J. (1954). Reciprocal inhibition as the main basis of psychotherapeutic effects. *Archives of Neurological Psychiatry, 72,* 205–226.

Wolpe, J. (1958). *Psychotherapy by reciprocal inhibition.* Stanford, CA: Stanford University Press.

Wolpe, J. (1961). The systematic desensitization treatment of neuroses. *Journal of Nervous and Mental Disorders, 112,* 189–203.

Wolpe, J. (1981). The dichotomy between classically conditioned and cognitively learned anxiety. *Journal of Behavior Therapy and Experimental Psychiatry, 12,* 35–42.

Wolpe, J. (1989). The derailment of behavior therapy. *Journal of Behavior Therapy and Experimental Psychiatry, 20,* 3–15.

Wolpe, J. (1990). *The practice of behavior therapy.* Elmsford, NY: Pergamon Press.

Wolpe, J. (1993). The cognitivist oversell and comments on the symposium contributions. *Journal of Behavior Therapy and Experimental Psychiatry, 24,* 141–147.

Wolpe, J., & Abrams, J. (1991). Post-traumatic stress disorder overcome by eye-movement desensitization: A case report. *Journal of Behavior Therapy and Experimental Psychiatry, 22,* 39–43.

Wolpe, J., Craske, M. G., Reyna, L. J., & Pascotto, V. (1994). Comparative outcomes of behavior therapy and psychodynamic therapy in anxiety disorders: Implications for psychiatric training. *Proceedings of the Ninth World Congress of Psychiatry.*

Wolpe, J., & Wolpe, D. (1981). *Our useless fears.* Boston: Houghton Mifflin.

Yates, A. J. (1975). *Theory and practice in behavior therapy.* New York: Wiley.

3

RECONCEPTUALIZING REINFORCEMENT: A CAUSAL-SYSTEM APPROACH TO REINFORCEMENT AND BEHAVIOR CHANGE

WILLIAM TIMBERLAKE

Laboratory research on response-contingent reinforcement has made a major contribution to the reliable control and modification of behavior in applied settings (e.g., Kazdin, 1980; Martin & Pear, 1992; Timberlake & Farmer-Dougan, 1991). As a means of changing behavior, the procedure of presenting a reinforcer contingent on a target response has superseded aphorisms, homilies, folktales, and fables. A host of specialized techniques for behavior change have been developed on the basis of the experimental

Preparation of this chapter was supported in part by National Institute of Mental Health Grant MH 37892 and National Science Foundation Grant IBN 91-21647. I am most grateful to Fran Silva for comments and conversation and for his work on the figures. I also thank Dick McFall and Rick Viken for comments.

analysis of reinforcement in the laboratory, including token economies (Kazdin, 1982), behavioral contracting (Kelly & Stokes, 1982; Medland & Stachnik, 1982), feedback-based conditioning of autonomic responses (Hatch, Fisher, & Rugh, 1987), and incidental learning (Hart & Risley, 1975; McGee, Krantz, & McClannahan, 1985).

The concepts and technology of response-contingent reinforcement have become so embedded in the fabric of fields such as education, child-rearing, pet training, social work, and business management that each area has assumed a degree of ownership. At the same time, psychology has abandoned ownership by focusing on topics such as consciousness, sensory processing, cognition, and memory without much attendant interest in the continued interchange between laboratory and applied research on reinforcement. Recently, I had the strange experience of listening to a social work student patiently explain to me the novel advances her field was making in the use of high-probability responses as reinforcers. She assumed that psychologists did not know about this work yet because her experience in psychology courses had revealed little interest in reinforcement.

Without question, the methods of response-contingent reinforcement deserve attention. They represent a significant advance over commonsense mentalism in controlling and modifying behavior, but I believe there is still room for improvement. I argue in this chapter that the traditional analysis of reinforcement is not only an incomplete guide to the conditions that produce reinforcement, but also an inadequate framework for dealing with other important determinants of behavior change. The incompleteness can be seen in the inability of traditional analyses to accurately identify the circumstances of reinforcement or the ease of conditioning ahead of time (Timberlake & Farmer-Dougan, 1991; Timberlake & Lucas, 1989). The inadequacy of the reinforcement approach as a general framework for behavior change can be seen in the power of techniques not based on reinforcement methods to modify behavior (e.g., Martin & Pear, 1992; Wahler & Fox, 1981).

The purpose of this chapter is to outline a more complete and inclusive approach to behavior change that clarifies the conditions for reinforcement and provides a useful general framework for conceptualizing different forms of behavior change. The first section examines incomplete aspects of the traditional simple-causal approach to response-contingent reinforcement. The second section proposes upgrading the simple-causal model to a causal-system approach—which adds explicit concern with regulation of behavior, complex initial conditions, and stimulus processing. The third section illustrates how a causal system can provide a general framework for other forms of behavior change as well as for response-contingent reinforcement.

THE SIMPLE-CAUSAL MODEL OF REINFORCEMENT

Learning researchers have a long history of viewing inexperienced organisms as relatively unformed reflexive entities that develop the greater part of their response characteristics through training. In 1896, Lloyd Morgan wrote, "Just as a sculptor carves a statue out of a block of marble, so does acquisition carve an activity out of a mass of random movements" (p. 23). Skinner (1953) identified the sculptor as differential reinforcement: "Learned behavior is constructed by a continual process of differential reinforcement from undifferentiated behavior, just as the sculptor shapes his figure from a lump of clay" (p. 92). The "sculpting tool" most often used by researchers and practitioners is the presentation of a reinforcer contingent on a target response. Presenting the reinforcer is assumed to initiate a simple, straightforward causal chain that differentially increases the probability of the target response in the current stimulus conditions. I refer to this package of concepts and manipulations as the *simple-causal model of reinforcement* (Timberlake, 1993). In the present section, I clarify the simple-causal model and consider some drawbacks to it.

Figure 1a shows the general form of the simple-causal model. Reinforcement of a target response in a particular stimulus context is presumed to be caused in a straightforward, direct fashion by response-contingent presentation of a reinforcer. Support for the model comes from functional laws (see Figure 1b) established by relating changes in the target response to manipulations of contingency characteristics (e.g., reliability, temporal delay, and physical distance) and reinforcer characteristics (e.g., frequency, amount, duration, or quality). Implicit in this model is a condition of extrasession deprivation, which is assumed to establish a stimulus as a reinforcer (Meehl, 1950; Michael, 1993).

Figure 1c shows an instrumental version of the simple-causal model drawn as a temporal sequence, beginning with a stimulus and ending with the reinforcer. The stimulus activates a habit, which produces a response, which leads to a reinforcer. As shown by the causal return line, the reinforcer strengthens and differentiates the original habit so that the next time that the stimulus circumstance occurs, the response also will be more likely to occur. Figure 1d shows a similar picture of the simple-causal model, using the nomenclature of operant conditioning. The stimulus in the context of the reinforcement history of the organism produces a response that, under the terms of the contingency schedule, leads to a reinforcer. The reinforcer initiates a simple-causal chain, updating the reinforcement history of the organism and increasing the future probability of the target response in the stimulus conditions. The result is the strengthening of particular target responses.

(a) Basic Form of the Simple Causal Model

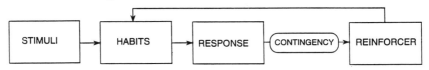

(b) Functional Laws of Learned Behavior

(c) Instrumental Learning Version

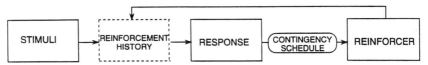

(d) Operant Conditioning Version

Figure I. Different aspects of the simple-causal model of reinforcement. (a) The basic form of the causal model; (b) functional laws established by manipulating the characteristics of the reinforcer and the contingency in a particular stimulus context and observing the change in the target response; (c) the version of the simple-causal model used in traditional instrumental learning (the sequence of events reads left to right, and the simple-causal effect is represented by the arrow from the reinforcer back to habits); (d) the version of the simple-causal model used in operant conditioning. (Again, the sequence of events reads left to right, and the simple-causal effect is represented by the arrow from the reinforcer back to reinforcement history. I inserted dotted lines around reinforcement history to acknowledge that operant theorists distinguish it from intervening variables such as habits.)

Note that the simple-causal model represents a streamlined common denominator of the ways in which experimenters and practitioners treat reinforcement. As a result, it is not a complete account of the subtleties of a particular theory. For instance, it might be argued that the model does not adequately represent Skinner's selectionist theory of reinforcement or his interdependent definition of the circumstances of reinforcement conditional on an effect (Timberlake, 1988). One answer to this objection is that no matter what their conceptual approach, most researchers use a simple-causal model in at least a portion of their thinking and procedures. For Skinner, the simple-causal model emerges clearly in his accounts of shaping and superstition (Skinner, 1948, 1956). A second answer is that the issue here is not one of representing or even evaluating a particular theory of reinforcement, but one of trying to clarify how reinforcement procedures are thought about and used so that researchers and practitioners can work toward changing behavior more effectively. The simple-causal model has proved surprisingly robust as a model of reinforcement. It is the procedural approach that is taught to undergraduates in laboratories as they try to shape rats to leverpress. We also communicate this model to adults in self-help groups to help them better manage their behavior. The simple-causal model also has been applied to pet behavior, childrearing, education, management of business personnel, and efforts to forge contact with autistic children and schizophrenic adults.

Powerful and wide-ranging as it is, though, the simple-causal model has several important drawbacks as a general model of reinforcement. First, it has great difficulty in identifying the conditions of reinforcement ahead of time (Timberlake & Allison, 1974; Timberlake & Farmer-Dougan, 1991). Another problem is its inability to predict the emergence of phenomena such as misbehavior, superstition, and ecological constraints on learning (Breland & Breland, 1966; Timberlake & Lucas, 1989). Still another area of concern is its relation to the emerging importance of stimulus processing and memory in determining what is reinforced (Gallistel, 1990; Roitblat, 1987). The simple-causal model has specific difficulties in applied settings (e.g., Wahler & Fox, 1981). Timberlake and Farmer-Dougan (1991), following Kazdin (1980), pointed out the frustration of practitioners in dealing with a reinforcer that works only sometimes. Despite careful instruction in how to train a rat to leverpress for food, a sizable proportion of undergraduates in applied-learning laboratories produce a "stupid" rat, one over which they have little control. Finally, consider how many well-educated first-time parents worry acutely over whether to pick up a crying baby out of a concern that they will reinforce crying.

It might be argued that difficulties in applied settings are caused by inexperienced "practitioners," who are unable to arrange appropriate response-reinforcer contingencies. But most practitioners have a lot of experience in multiple contexts, yet control of responding by reinforcement remains a sometimes tenuous target. Breland and Breland (1961, 1966) were certainly expert at training animals, and yet they reported examples of the gravest difficulty in implementing response-contingent reinforcement. For example, although they were able to train a pig to carry a token a short distance to a container and deposit it for food, when that distance was increased, the pig began to drop and root the token rather than carrying it in a straightforward fashion to the "bank." Finally, we have all heard (often with some relish, I fear) stories of well-known behaviorists who, despite their vast knowledge and experience with principles of reinforcement, are unable to control the behavior of their own children, or do so only in limited ways.

In summary, a simple-causal model unquestionably can be a successful guide in producing reinforcement of a target response. However, what is equally important is that this model can be surprisingly limited in its application. At times, it is a narrow, bumpy road, which requires an experienced driver, when both experimenters and practitioners would be happier with an easily traveled thoroughfare. One common reaction to the limitations of the simple-causal model is the *road repair* method. In this method, the predictability of reinforcement is improved by repairs that clarify traditional procedures (e.g., establishing operations; Michael, 1993) or that add conceptual development (e.g., rule-governed behavior—Catania, 1992; or phylogenetic history—Skinner, 1966). Because of pressures for immediate change, practitioners frequently use the alternative *convoy method*, that is, marshal all available vehicles (procedures) and keep sending them until one gets through (e.g., Azrin, 1977). In the next section, I suggest the alternative causal-system approach, which attempts to embed the rigor and analytic manipulations of the simple-causal model within a more inclusive framework of behavior.

RECONCEPTUALIZING THE DETERMINANTS OF REINFORCEMENT: A CAUSAL-SYSTEM MODEL

A more general model of reinforcement and behavior change should explicitly include a wider range of causal sequences—especially those related to the regulation of behavior, the initial conditions of the organism, and stimulus and response processing. Attention to these causal sequences points toward reconceptualizing the simple-causal model as a causal system. Such a system can incorporate solutions to present limitations in prediction and control by reinforcement into the basic form of a more general model rather than repairing and patching the simple-causal approach. A potential drawback of system views is that they are often conceptually more appealing than simple-causal models simply because they include more variables and complexity (Ford, 1992). System approaches tend to be empirically useful only as they are made specific. The remainder of this chapter attempts to present a system view of reinforcement that refers to specific determinants.

Figure 2 shows a system model of reinforcement that adds three interrelated components to the simple-causal model (Timberlake, 1993): Specific *initial conditions* reflect the evolutionary and reinforcement history the subject brings to the situation, *stimulus processing* relates environmental stimuli to initial conditions as well as dealing with the stimuli accompanying and resulting from responding, and *response processing* includes the regulatory underpinnings of both the target response and the contingent response (the response related to the reinforcer). These two responses are related by the contingency schedule that links their levels of expression (Hanson & Timberlake, 1983).

Note that the temporal sequence of elements in the simple-causal model of reinforcement (shown in Figures 1c and 1d) can still be traced in the causal-system model in Figure 2. Environmental stimuli impinge on initial conditions (a combination of memories, habits, reinforcement history, and evolution), which affect response processing and ultimate performance of the target response. There is also a feedback loop between the presentation of the reinforcer (access to the contingent response) and an update of the initial conditions. However, in the causal-system view, these sequences are embedded in and depend on the functioning of the entire system. Thus, a response contingency is viewed as a constraint on functioning rather than as the initiator of a simple-causal reinforcement sequence. This important difference is amplified in the next section by showing that depending on its relation to the initial conditions, a given contingency schedule can produce reinforcement of, punishment of, or no effect on a target response.

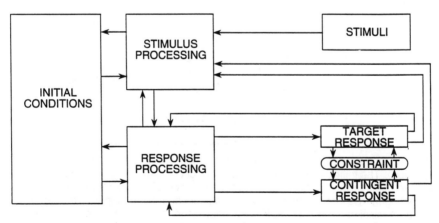

Figure 2. A causal-system model of reinforcement consisting of stimulus processing that combines stimuli and *initial conditions*, which refer to the structure and processes the animal brings to the reinforcement situation; and a regulatory component in which response processing integrates initial conditions of the system with the schedule constraints relating the target and contingent responses.

Regulation of Behavior

Figure 3 amplifies the regulatory aspects of the causal-system model by specifying comparators, feedback loops, and schedule constraints. Each response is assigned its own feedback loop that is regulated around a *settling point* particular to the current stimulus conditions, the subject, and the timing of the session. This settling point represents an initial condition that acts as a set point input to the primary comparator for each response (the larger circles in the diagram). The other input to these comparators is the feedback from expression of the response. Note that feedback is designated as only negative in this diagram, though it can also be facilitatory (Gawley, Timberlake, & Lucas, 1987; Timberlake & Silva, in press). Given Figure 3, each response will continue during the session until the positive input to the comparator is balanced by the cumulative negative feedback from responding.

It follows from a regulatory account that a critical aspect of predicting responding in a particular circumstance for a specific subject is knowledge of the appropriate settling point for responding in the absence of the constraint of a contingency schedule. A reasonable way to discover this information is to measure the free-baseline level of system functioning before

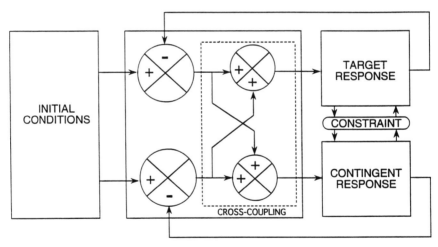

Figure 3. An amplification of the regulatory component of Figure 2 (behavior regulation). The initial conditions in the present circumstances provide settling points to comparators that monitor the response level of the target response and the contingent response. Under a contingency schedule, the output (error signal) from each initial comparator (the larger circles) is fed into a second comparator for each response (the smaller circles). These cross-coupled comparators combine the two outputs to produce the error signal expressed in each response. The error signals from the initial comparators are usually weighted and are usually in a nonlinear fashion.

the schedule is imposed. Premack (1959, 1965) was the first to routinely assess system functioning beforehand by means of a paired baseline in which both the instrumental (target) and the contingent (reward) response were freely and simultaneously available. The paired baseline was usually summarized in terms of the overall totals of the target and contingent responses. However, the regulatory approach is not limited to overall response totals, and, in fact, the temporal patterning of responding has also been treated as a characteristic of responding (a settling point) that may be regulated (Gawley, Timberlake, & Lucas, 1986).

That a paired baseline represents a settling point for the system can be seen in its general reliability from day to day during a particular baseline and its repeatability in subsequent baselines. The typical practice of measuring only the baseline level of the target response is entirely insufficient to establish a system baseline (although see Timberlake & Farmer-Dougan, 1991, for alternate methods of estimating the baseline of the contingent response). As a related aside, considerable concern is often expressed about how to apply a regulatory approach when there is no easily measured contingent response related to a reinforcing stimulus (e.g., when the reinforcer stimulus is assumed to be seconds without shock). The pragmatic solution is to link a flexible and easily measured response to the reinforcer in the free baseline and continue using it as part of the contingency schedule (see Timberlake & Allison, 1974).

Although Premack (1959, 1965) saw clearly the need for an initial paired-baseline assessment of responding, he still frequently appeared to view reinforcement as the result of a simple-causal chain, one in which the response of higher baseline probability reinforced the response of lower probability. However, Premack did argue that although a baseline-probability differential between the target and contingent response can produce reinforcement, it is not the critical condition (Allison, 1989; Premack, 1965, 1971; Timberlake, 1980; Timberlake & Allison, 1974). The key to reinforcement is not at the level of individual or even pairs of stimuli or responses, but at the system level. The key is a constraint (disequilibrium) imposed on the functioning system by the schedule (Timberlake & Allison, 1974; Timberlake & Farmer-Dougan, 1991).

Figure 3 shows how a schedule constrains behavior by linking together (cross-coupling) the separate regulatory loops for the target and contingent responses so that the amount of a response is determined not only by the deviation from its own set point, but also by the deviation of the other response from its set point. Inspection of the dynamics of Figure 3 shows that when both responses are below their baseline levels, the two inputs to the coupled comparator for either response will combine to increase responding. When one response is above its baseline and the other is below, the coupled system will settle at a compromise between the negative input from the response above its set point and the positive input for the response below its baseline. If both responses are at baseline, the system will settle there. These dynamics result in the following reinforcement predictions: If the ratio of target to contingent responding imposed by the schedule is the same as their ratio in baseline, no reinforcement effect will occur; if the schedule ratio is greater than in baseline, reinforcement of the instrumental response will occur; if the ratio is less than in baseline (and the contingent response or stimulus is inescapable), punishment of the instrumental response will occur.

These predictions may be made clearer by an analogy. Assume that the baseline rate of responding corresponds to the rate of flow of a river. Also assume that inserting a stick into the river corresponds to imposing a schedule on responding and that the turbulence in flow created by the stick corresponds to a reinforcement effect. If the stick is inserted into the river by someone walking along the bank in the same direction and at the same rate as the river is flowing, there are no ripples (and, thus, no reinforcement effect). In contrast, if the stick is held by someone moving more slowly than the river (e.g., someone standing still or walking upstream), turbulence will occur on the upstream side of the stick, corresponding to the phenomenon of positive reinforcement. Finally, if the stick is held by someone moving downstream faster than the river is flowing, turbulence will occur on the downstream side of the stick, corresponding to punishment. Note that the relative rates of movement of the person holding the stick and the river determine the result, not the absolute rate of flow of the river or the absolute rate of movement of the person holding the stick.

In short, reinforcement effects are produced when a contingency schedule imposes a constraint on an already functioning system. The result of the constraint is an output that balances simultaneously the relevant regulatory loops in the system, producing either reinforcement, punishment, or no effect, depending on the relation of the schedule and the baseline.

An additional bit of evidence that schedules are appropriately viewed as constraints on regulatory processes has to do with the distinction between a *programmed* and a *realized* contingency schedule. Rarely is the realized linkage between the target and contingent responses exactly what the experimenter programmed. As would be expected from a system constraint view, the behavior of the subject often modifies the schedule in complex and unexpected ways (Gannon, Smith, & Tierney, 1983). For example, the efficiency with which pigeons use a given access time to a hopper is a curvilinear function of access time and responding required for access (e.g., Rashotte & Henderson, 1988).

Another example of an unexpected outcome was reported by Timberlake and Lucas (1989), who programmed a random relation between presentation of a moving ball bearing and delivery of food to a rat. Under the random presentation schedule, the rat produced pairings between the ball bearing and food by grabbing, holding, gnawing, and retrieving the bearing until the food was presented. Then it ate the food and gnawed the bearing at the same time.

The concept of the schedule as a constraint on a functioning system also has proved a powerful empirical tool for clarifying that individual reinforcers have *no fixed value*, either intrinsic or relative. Indeed, the concept of reinforcer value frequently appears to be an ill-defined intervening causal variable used to account intuitively for reinforcement effects. Both laboratory and applied researchers have shown that simply changing the terms of the schedule can change the effect of the response contingency from positive reinforcement to punishment or vice versa (see Konarski, Johnson, Crowell, & Whitman, 1981; Timberlake, 1980; Timberlake & Farmer-Dougan, 1991). This means that contingencies of high-probability responses on low-probability responses can produce punishment as well as positive reinforcement and that contingencies of low-probability responses on high-probability responses also can produce positive reinforcement as well as punishment.

Thus, not only is there no unique class of events called reinforcers, there is no unique class of pairs of events in which the higher probability response is a reinforcer. In fact, there is no hierarchy of reinforcers or reinforcer value without specifying the schedule (Premack, 1959). In short, the intervening causal variable of reinforcer value, even relative reinforcer value, should be discarded. The more appropriate intervening variable is the degree of constraint or disequilibrium, and it is a product of the interaction of the schedule constraint with the regulatory elements of the system.

Perhaps the greatest long-term advantage of a system approach to reinforcement may occur in applied settings. The causal-system view markedly increases the flexibility and power with which response contingencies can be used to modify behavior (Timberlake & Farmer-Dougan, 1991). In comparison with the disruptive effects of creating reinforcers by setting up overall deprivation conditions or by using special treats, a system approach is simpler and more accurate. Rewards are not restricted to universal incentives, like candy, or to high-probability responses, like watching television. Neither is the imposition of long-term deprivation a necessary or sufficient condition for reinforcement. Instead, response contingencies can be imposed on everyday behavior that should affect the target response to the extent that they constrain the system.

Furthermore, the system approach provides a means of conceptually integrating and clarifying effective empirical techniques, such as incidental teaching and overcorrection (Timberlake & Farmer-Dougan, 1991). In essence, with a bit of thought and experience, the practitioner in many cases should be able to take the behavior of the client as it exists in the circumstance and, by means of schedule constraint, guide it into a different distribution without introducing either massive technology or externally based rewards or punishments. For example, Konarski, Crowell, and Duggan (1985), after assessing the free baseline of working arithmetic problems and writing, showed it was possible to increase either response simply by imposing an appropriate disequilibrium schedule linking their performance.

The view of schedules as constraints on functioning also provides guidance in anticipating the results of particular schedule values on overall levels of responding. The fundamental function relating response requirement and responding appears bitonic (Hanson & Timberlake, 1983; Staddon, 1979; Timberlake & Peden, 1987). As the schedule ratio exceeds the baseline ratio, the initial response to the disequilibrium is to increase total target responding (the traditional reinforcement effect), but as the schedule moves ever further from the baseline, the cost of the required amount of target responding apparently increasingly outweighs the small payoff of contingent responding, and the subject decreases total target responding. The turndown is clearest on a ratio schedule, but the trend is present in other schedules as well.

Viken and McFall (1994) used the shape of the response function relating target and contingent responding to explain why schedules recommended by family therapists to increase children's prosocial behaviors often have the reverse or no effect. Because the therapist does not take into consideration the child's free baseline of producing prosocial behavior and receiving parental reward, a recommended schedule relating the two may easily move the child in the direction of less prosocial behavior rather than more. Measuring the current balance of prosocial and parental reward in a home is not a baseline; it is a particular instance of performance under schedule constraint. To effectively control behavior, a paired baseline must be measured, or inferred, in conditions where parental reward is freely available.

Finally, there may be an interesting relation between a regulatory-system approach and operant theories of choice related to the matching law (Herrnstein, 1970; McDowell, 1982). To account for responding in choice situations, theorists have been forced to add free parameters and assumptions to a simple-causal model of reinforcement. One free parameter designates the total amount of responding; the second refers to the reinforcement value of background responses. One assumption is that organisms distribute behavior on a relative basis; the other is that they integrate the effects of reinforcement over each daily session.

These parameters and assumptions basically relate to regulatory issues and would quite likely fit easily with a regulatory model expanded to deal with the simultaneous balancing of deviations from baselines of multiple instrumental and contingent (reward) responses. In fact, the extension of the coupled regulation model proposed by Hanson and Timberlake (1983) might relate well to accounts of matching by both overall-optimality models (Rachlin, Battalio, Kagel, & Green, 1981) and the melioration approach (Herrnstein & Vaughan, 1980). The emphasis of such a model on the separate regulation of each response would also make clear that the typical matching-law experiment, involving pecking one of two keys for a single type of food, is a limited case of the universe of potential responses and rewards that could be tested.

Initial Conditions (Behavior Systems)

The *initial conditions* of a system refer to those processes, response components, and stimulus filters present when the subject enters the reinforcement situation. One sort of initial condition has been introduced in the form of regulatory set points based on the fit of the organism and a particular set of stimulus conditions. A second and equally important set of initial conditions is revealed in the ease with which some responses and discriminative stimuli can be trained, but not others. This phenomenon was initially described by the concept of *belongingness* (Thorndike, 1911) but subsequently became known as *constraints on learning* (Seligman, 1970; Shettleworth, 1972). For example, Sevenster (1973) reported that presenting a reproductive male stickleback with visual access to a receptive female contingent on biting a glass rod failed to increase the rate of biting, while requiring rod biting for the opportunity to display to a rival male produced large increases in rate. The reverse was true when the required response was swimming through a ring. Male sticklebacks readily increased swimming through the ring when the reward was visual access to a female, but not when the reward was visual access to a male.

A more sophisticated version of the constraints concept was advanced by workers who attempted to connect the effectiveness of different contingencies with adaptive specializations related to the animal's ecology (Rozin & Schull, 1988). Such specializations were argued to have evolved to serve a particular adaptive function that increased the individual's relative likelihood of survival and reproduction. For example, many animals are differentially sensitive to the relation between ingesting a novel taste and subsequent illness. Even if the illness is delayed by up to 12 hr, animals still will decrease subsequent ingestion of the novel taste after a single experience (Garcia & Garcia y Robertson, 1985; Garcia & Koelling, 1966).

A frequent response of researchers using the traditional simple-causal model of reinforcement has been to argue that learning constraints and predispositions are compatible with the general form of the simple-causal model. Constraints simply require the addition of time constants, or more complex processing and encoding of stimuli and responses (Domjan & Galef, 1983; Logue, 1979; Revusky, 1977). Skinner (1966) argued that it was no surprise that there were phylogenetic contributions that affected the rate of learning, although he neglected to specify how they should be treated.

In the causal-system view, constraints and predispositions are not entities but are the results of the fit between the current environment and the initial condition of the subject. Reinforcement is assumed to occur in the service of regulating some aspect of the organism-environment fit. This fit is assumed to have been selected to serve some functional end—such as feeding, reproducing, exploring, or defense of territory. Examination of constraints and specializations reveals that they often can be viewed as part of a functional behavior system of structures and processes (Fanselow & Lester, 1988; Timberlake, 1983a, 1983b, 1993; Timberlake & Lucas, 1989).

Some constraints and predispositions related to a behavior system appear to take place at the level of the *perceptual-motor modules* that organisms bring to the environment. This is the level of processing stimuli, forming responses, and relating particular stimuli to particular responses. Part of the effects of any response contingency relate to how the imposed constraint impinges on the set of perceptual-motor modules relevant to obtaining the reward. If relevant modules are not present, they must be trained individually and often slowly.

It is probably not surprising that the most common target responses in laboratory research, namely, running in mazes and leverpressing by rats and keypecking by pigeons, appear related to such perceptual-motor units (Timberlake & Lucas, 1989). For example, Stokes and Balsam (1991) used an analytic-observation approach to show that reinforced leverpressing is made up of components already present in the operant behavior of the rat. In motor skill learning, many integrated acts appear to reflect stimulus-response organization already present, such as the tendency to track and grab moving stimuli. On the other hand, some of the most difficult responses to acquire involve unlearning perceptual-motor organization that is already present, such as teaching humans driving cars to turn their wheels in the direction of a skid.

Other constraints and predispositions appear to arise at the level of motivational *modes* related to the temporal and physical proximity of controlling stimuli to the reinforcer. Traditionally, researchers have highlighted the chained nature of goal-directed behavior. One stimulus elicits a response that produces the next stimulus, eliciting the next response, and so on. More recent research has argued for an important role of a sequence of underlying motivational states in controlling behavior (e.g., Matthews & Lerer, 1987). For example, requiring a rat to contact a moving stimulus followed approximately 6 s later by food produces intense predatory behavior directed to the moving stimulus. In contrast, requiring a rat to contact a moving stimulus that is followed approximately 2 s later by food produces perfunctory contact followed by a dash toward the food hopper (Timberlake, Wahl, & King, 1982). It is as though the rat is in a different motivational mode when food is proximate, a mode that supports immediate food handling rather than chase-and-capture responses.

In applied settings, presenting the reward too close to the target response can be a way to lose control of responding in the situation. For example, in training the chimpanzee Washoe to make hand signs, Gardner and Gardner (1988) reported that presenting immediate food reward contingent on an accurate sign was extremely disruptive to the signing process. The chimpanzee began to produce food-related vocalizations and behavior instead of signing. In a possibly related vein, schoolteachers know how difficult it is to achieve teaching goals with the hint of lunchtime in the air. To accomplish instructional goals, the teacher must minimize the tendency of students to enter a mode based on immediate proximity to being dismissed to go eat or play.

Finally, some control and adaptation issues arise at the level of a behavior system, a level of organization that includes modes and related perceptual-motor modules appropriate to the function of a system. This level of organization can markedly constrain what is readily learned and how it is performed. A classic example of mixing behavior systems was created by Thorndike (1911), who reported that it was most difficult to increase grooming in a cat by rewarding it with food. The work by Sevenster (1973) reported above illustrated the effects of aggression versus courtship motivation in controlling particular perceptual–motor modules.

Although humans appear to have more flexible interrelations of systems, modes, and modules than cats or sticklebacks, it is still possible to observe difficulties in using response contingencies when the responses required are not suitable to the behavior system that is currently engaged. For example, for teenagers, the pursuit of peer approval—especially that of the opposite sex—may interfere markedly with the pursuit of teacher or parental approval. The behavioral repertoire and stimulus sensitivities are quite different in the two circumstances. Thus, it seems likely that trying to reward a teenage boy for doing a complex mathematics assignment by the opportunity to see immediately the current all-consuming love of his life will quite likely lead to a reduced level of performance on mathematics. Finally, as a general rule, grave fear or hunger interferes with careful consideration of alternative response strategies.

Any attempt to specify a behavior system related to human activities is a risky endeavor because of the importance of cultural experience and the common presence of artificial stimuli, responses, and environments. However, the principles should be similar to those used in outlining behavior systems in other animals, and I believe the task to be important in reconceptualizing our treatment of reinforcement.

Figure 4 illustrates an initial attempt to apply a behavior-system approach to the hierarchical and sequential organization of feeding behavior in postindustrial humans. Specifically, Figure 4 hypothesizes a set of initial modes and modules that could influence the outcome of response contingencies related to eating dinner.[1] The hierarchical aspects of the system begin with the system or subsystem level on the left and continue to the perceptual-motor modules and stimuli and responses on the right. In terms of sequences of responding, those aspects of the system that are furthest from reward are at the top of the diagram, and those closest to reward are at the bottom of the diagram.

A brief consideration of Figure 4 may clarify how a behavior system can be used to generate predictions, tests, and further improvements in the way it is represented. One important point is the lack of implication that the hypothesized structures and processes are either learned or innate; they are simply present. General motivational modes are probably not culturally specific; for example, the odor of cooking food is likely to produce focal search-related behaviors in hungry humans in most cultures. On the other hand, there should be examples of cultural specificity in the stimulus control of particular modes. Similarly, the stimuli and responses associated with available perceptual-motor modules should show considerable cultural specificity, though some generalities are probably present as well.

Another important point about a behavior system is that in the absence of any experimenter-imposed response contingency, a system frequently produces a "ready-made" sequence of behavior leading to reward. Thus, in Figure 4, the available modules and modes fit readily together in a sequence of responding. Adding a response contingency compatible with this sequence should work very well, but adding a response contingency that required cooking the food, then driving to work and back, should be more difficult. Similarly, presenting a cue signaling the imminent delivery of food early in the ready-made sequence—for example, while the subject is driving home—would be very disruptive and produce unusual behavior such as speeding or, if the food is delivered to the car, pulling off the road to eat. On the other hand, presenting a cue while the subject is driving home that predicts that food will arrive in ½ hr might facilitate safe driving and subsequent puttering about the kitchen. In contrast, presenting a cue at the end of cooking that predicted food in 1 hr would probably invoke leaving the kitchen or reinitiating general search responses related to finding food.

On a related point, Timberlake and Lucas (1989) argued that the key to the phenomenon of misbehavior in animals (Breland & Breland, 1966) was the emergence of species-typical appetitive behaviors in the presence

---

[1]To see a better developed and more general example of a feeding system, consult Timberlake and Lucas (1989) or Timberlake and Silva (in press).

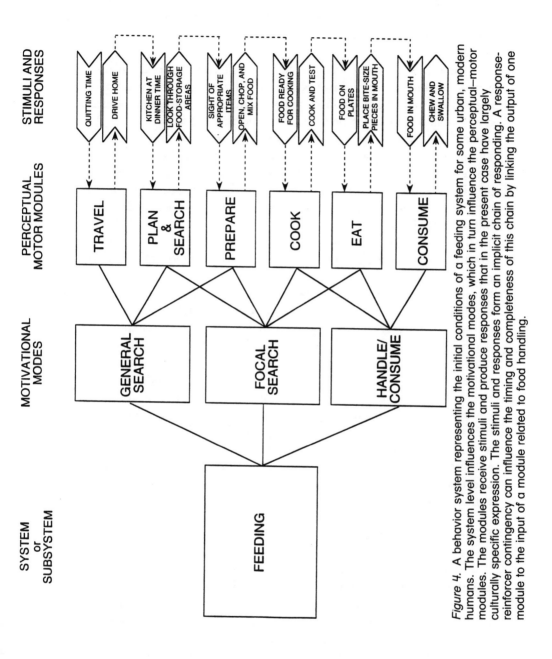

Figure 4. A behavior system representing the initial conditions of a feeding system for some urban, modern humans. The system level influences the motivational modes, which in turn influence the perceptual–motor modules. The modules receive stimuli and produce responses that in the present case have largely culturally specific expression. The stimuli and responses form an implicit chain of responding. A response-reinforcer contingency can influence the timing and completeness of this chain by linking the output of one module to the input of a module related to food handling.

of cues predicting delayed delivery of reward. For example, requiring a raccoon to deposit two coins instead of one to receive food increased the delay to eat and provided the opportunity for the emergence of "washing" movements directed toward the coin. Washing responses typically form a part of the appetitive chain related to searching for fresh water crustaceans as food.

Finally, the present analysis suggests that cooking food (in humans) is, in several respects, a strange behavior. It disrupts the instrumental chain near what would be the end of the sequence except for the requirement of cooking. This poses a problem from the point of view of motivational modes. The cook is required to go from a focal search and handling state to a delay. Receiving a burn from trying to sample cooking food will form a deterrent that encourages preserving this delay. But one still might expect people to engage in responses that lower the instigation for eating the cooking food, such as leaving the kitchen, handling other foods, or snacking on other foods.

Many of us, despite years of reciting principles of reinforcement, have trouble teaching our children to wash their hands before they come to the table half an hour late. I suggest that this is, at least in part, because we have not developed an adequate representation of the behavior systems involved. I believe most successful researchers and practitioners have worked out a model of their subjects that includes many of the elements of a behavior system: stimulus-processing filters, perceptual–motor modules, motivational modes related to goal proximity, and overall organization of these elements with respect to a goal. They use this model in imposing response contingencies and otherwise manipulating stimulus conditions to control behavior. To the extent that a practitioner or researcher implicitly uses such a model, writing it down explicitly should help clarify it as well as facilitate its communication to others. To the extent that researchers and practitioners use only the simple-causal model of reinforcement, their effectiveness should be improved by trying to construct a system of initial conditions.

Stimulus Processing and Memory

The final element in our reconceptualization of the classic simple-causal model of reinforcement is clearer acknowledgment of the roles of stimulus processing and memory in determining how the organism adjusts to the constraint of the schedule. Conditional response contingencies always have been a powerful tool for establishing new discriminative control of responding. However, it has become evident that aspects of stimulus processing and memory already do not require specific training by the time adult organisms encounter experimenters or practitioners (e.g., Gallistel, 1990; Roitblat, 1987). In many cases, response contingencies are not critical in producing learned behavior. The initial conditions of stimulus processing and memory related to regulation are all that is necessary. For example, Timberlake and White (1990) showed that the performance of deprived rats run on an eight-arm radial maze without any baited arms was almost indistinguishable in all respects from the performance of rats run with food at the end of each arm.

In operant psychology, recent work on the formation of equivalence classes and the importance of rule-governed behavior in controlling human behavior has shown the importance of specific processing capabilities (Hayes, 1989; Sidman, Wynne, Maguire, & Barnes, 1989). In instrumental contingencies, Colwill and Rescorla (1985) have shown particularly clearly that what is remembered of a response contingency is far more than the increase in probability of the operant response. The nature of the reward also is retained by the subject, as well as the relation between specific discriminative stimuli or instrumental responses and the nature of the reward. Radial arm maze research from its inception has required a differentiation between forms of memory, separating local (working) memory and longer term (reference) memory (Olton, 1978).

In terms of everyday behavior, ethologists have clarified that animals behave as if their perceptual systems had filters that differentially sharpened and passed stimuli relevant to the organism. Thus, gull chicks peck differentially at contrasting areas of bill-like stimuli moved back and forth in front of them (Hailman, 1967). Small objects elicit pecking in newly hatched chickens (Hogan, 1988). Moving stimuli gate attention and engage predatory behavior in many felid species (Leyhausen, 1973; Turner & Bateson, 1988). Such gating is relevant to what is learned and how readily it is learned.

Studies of food storing in families of seed-caching birds (Balda & Kamil, 1989; Krebs, Healy, & Shettleworth, 1990) have shown important species differences in memory capacities relevant to their feeding ecology. These differences shrink in standardized laboratory tests of memory (such as delayed matching to sample; Olson, 1991), but still are present. Furthermore, species differences in remembering the locations of stored food appear to be related to the size of the hippocampus (Sherry, Vaccarino, Buckenham, & Herz, 1989) and may also be related to specialized forms of memory rather than a single, general memory system (Sherry & Schachter, 1987).

Finally, research has indicated that animals vary in the time interval over which they integrate alternatives. For rats, this interval can be rather short. Alternatives that lie in the future more than 16 min must be very attractive to compete with an alternative currently present (Timberlake, Gawley, & Lucas, 1987, 1988). Yet, within this interval, animals can learn response contingencies separated from reward by intervals ranging up to 5 min (Lattal & Gleeson, 1990; Lattal & Metzger, 1994). Although humans seem able to anticipate arbitrarily timed events much better than many other animals, the contribution of a limited time horizon to the effectiveness of reinforcement contingencies must be considered. Certainly, humans have been shown to steeply discount rewards available at later points in time (e.g., Logue, 1988).

As to the relevance of stimulus processing and memory to response-contingent reinforcement in applied settings, many practitioners, especially those working with humans, already use implicit assumptions about processing and memory as well as about mental states and feelings. For example, self-help groups often include assumptions about the importance of feelings and self-awareness as a critical aspect of their therapy. However, this is not to suggest abandonment of a behaviorally grounded approach. Although the self-reported mental state of a human subject most often bears a relation to his or her behavior (Bernstein, 1986), the predictiveness for future responses, including further self-report, is not consistently better than the variable relation between heart rate or galvanic skin response and behavior. At the least, such information should be combined with other information the practitioner possesses.

I realize that cognitive terms and concepts necessarily remain in some disfavor because they have been thrown about with inappropriate abandon over the history of psychology. Consideration of these issues is beyond the scope of this chapter. What seems clear, though, is that there is a baby in the bathwater of cognition and mentalism that we must take care to rescue so that it can grow up. For the present, I do not intend my diagrams to invoke an entity that processes or memorizes, but I do think that the evidence for stimulus filtering, the relation between processing abilities and functional behavior, and the notion of time horizons suggest that some headway might be made in dealing with human subjects as evolved biological systems. Though always controversial (e.g., Alexander, 1979), a start has been made in that direction by researchers such as Cosmides and Tooby (1987) and Beer (1992), who view humans as possessing evolved, domain-specific processing capabilities.

A CAUSAL-SYSTEM FRAMEWORK FOR BEHAVIOR CHANGE

The traditional assumption that response-contingent reinforcement provides the fundamental cornerstone of behavior appears less related to the biological realities of evolution or the pragmatic realities of behavior change than to some combination of the philosophies of seventeenth-century empiricists, eighteenth-century rationalists, nineteenth-century associationists, and twentieth-century social reformers. Nonetheless, laboratory researchers influenced by the goal of developing a science of behavior have worked hard to establish general functional laws of response-contingent reinforcement that hold across species and circumstances (Timberlake & Silva, 1994).

To establish functional laws of reinforcement, researchers have carefully manipulated the environment and procedures of the laboratory to facilitate and isolate reinforcement effects. Other types of behavior change have been considered primarily when they need to be controlled or distinguished from reinforcement effects. In contrast, the more pragmatic goal of practitioners is to produce results rather than distinguish types of effect (Azrin, 1977). The extent to which behavior change is produced by response-contingent reinforcement versus other determinants is not a critical issue. In fact, experienced practitioners typically use a number of strategies for behavior change that bear little relation to response-contingent reinforcement (Azrin, 1977; Wahler & Fox, 1981).

However, this distinction between laboratory researchers and practitioners may be less obvious than has been realized. Because of their training, many practitioners are heavily invested in at least beginning treatment with response-contingent reinforcement technology. There are many circumstances in which it has been an exceptionally powerful technique for changing behavior. Furthermore, response-contingent reinforcement procedures have been codified in a well-organized, easily communicated form. Other methods may be idiosyncratic to individual practitioners or groups working at a particular location. Finally, possession of a familiar "hammer" such as the technology of reinforcement makes everything look at least a little like a nail.

For their part, laboratory researchers regularly use practitionerlike "tricks of the trade" to get animals to behave appropriately. They hold a surprising amount of their knowledge of how to change behavior in the form of procedural refinements, apparatus design, and general laboratory lore, so as not to clutter up reinforcement principles. Improvement in one's ability to shape a rat to leverpress is based not on a better conceptual grasp of the principles of reinforcement, but on a better appreciation of the rat as a functioning system. Some of this information is included in the Method section of the experiment report, but a good deal of it is passed down as lore. Some of this lore is critical for experimental results, but there has been little systematic attempt to evaluate the contribution of these procedures to reinforcement or, more generally, to behavior change.

The problem then is to develop a conceptual framework that clarifies the functional laws of response-contingent reinforcement and combines them with the pragmatics of applied behavior change and the procedures and lore that underlie the study of reinforcement in the laboratory. This problem seems to be a part of the continuing debate between mechanists and contextualists (e.g., Morris, 1993). Because the causal-system view of reinforcement embeds the study of reinforcement within the context of a relatively specific picture of a functioning organism, the causal-system view seems to be a good initial candidate for an inclusive framework. We have already shown that it is an improvement on the simple-causal model in handling reinforcement. My goal in this section is to illustrate how the causal-system approach can facilitate analysis of the laboratory lore and procedures that accompany the study of reinforcement and to suggest that this analysis can have ramifications for understanding and producing behavior change in applied settings. The techniques and procedures briefly reviewed here are deprivation schedules, adaptation, tuning, presenting stimuli, and complex environments.

Deprivation Schedules

Nearly all researchers have assumed that extra-session deprivation of the reinforcing stimulus is an important setting or establishing condition for reinforcement (Hull, 1943; Michael, 1993). The regulatory component of the causal-system model contradicts this assumption and replaces it with the hypothesis that the important determinant of reinforcement is that the response contingency produce a condition of disequilibrium in relation to what the animal would be doing given a free-behavior baseline (Timberlake, 1980; Timberlake & Farmer-Dougan, 1991). Depriving the animal will affect reinforcement only indirectly at best. If extra-session deprivation increases local baseline levels of eating, it will ensure that a wider range of schedule values will satisfy the disequilibrium condition and produce reinforcement. Data and theory are both clear that long-term restriction of access is not a critical condition for response-contingent reinforcement.

However, the practice of putting animals on deprivation schedules affects more than the probability of eating. Shettleworth (1975) called attention to the role of deprivation in changing the probability of responses related to feeding. She argued and provided evidence that those responses that increased under extra-session deprivation were likely to be easy to reinforce, but those that were not increased in probability by deprivation would not be easy to reinforce. Part of the effect of deprivation on responding may well have been related to another important outcome of a cyclic deprivation schedule: the entrainment of a feeding rhythm by regular daily access to food. There are considerable nonhuman animal data indicating that a regular daily feeding time entrains a specific 24-hr rhythm of food anticipatory activity (Bolles & Moot, 1973; Stephan, Swann, & Sisk, 1979; White & Timberlake, 1994).

In short, although extra-session deprivation is not a critical condition for reinforcement, the cyclic-feeding procedure used to produce extra-session deprivation has potent behavior-change effects by itself, as well as interacting with response contingencies to influence reinforcement effects. Specifically, deprivation may change the probability of responses other than feeding, and the procedure of cyclic food deprivation entrains a circadian food anticipatory state that facilitates changes in both the potential and expressed repertoire of the animal and its sensitivity to stimuli. The cyclic food anticipation rhythm is sufficiently powerful that it supports anticipatory activity in the rat (a nocturnal animal) during the light part of its rest-activity cycle.

Such a circadian effect might well generalize beyond food and be of considerable relevance in applied settings. For example, Mrosovsky (1988) has shown that presentation of social stimuli entrains an anticipatory cyclic rhythm in rats, and we presume that such an anticipatory rhythm would contribute to changes in the repertoire of animals and their sensitivity to response-contingent reinforcement. Thus, given that humans are also a social species, it may be that daily meetings with a client, especially at the same time each day, may be a particularly effective way to facilitate some forms of reinforcement and behavior change.

Adaptation

There is usually a sentence in the Procedure section of laboratory studies that mentions gentling the subjects and adapting them to the procedures and apparatus. The passing nature of this reference bears little relation to the importance of this phase of the study to the eventual results. In the case of some motor activities, adaptation to the environment through repeated exposure and interaction may constitute the primary behavior change—a change to which response-contingent reinforcement adds only a little. Timberlake (1983a) showed that learning to run a straight alley was related to two phases of adaptation to the maze environment: an initial phase in which the rat overcame its fear sufficiently to begin to investigate thoroughly the local cues in the alley and an asymptotic phase in which the animal stopped exploring the immediate local cues in favor of moving rapidly about the environment, stopping to investigate primarily at the beginning and end of the alley. Thus, acquisition of maze running may relate mainly to adaptation rather than to food reinforcement. Data compatible with this view were produced by Brant and Kavanau (1965), using complex mazes instead of a straight alley, and Timberlake and White (1990), using a radial arm maze.

In general, the process of adapting subjects to procedures and apparatus reduces the control of behavior by the system of behavior related to predator avoidance (Fanselow & Lester, 1988) and creates a memory of the apparatus against which changes will stand out. The process of shaping the subject to eat rapidly and reliably from the food hopper quite likely entrains a portion of the feeding-system organization to the environment and location of the hopper. The components of the feeding system that are expressed will vary with the type and timing of stimulus support in the environment. These behavior changes will occur before the imposition of the reinforcement schedule and will affect what subsequently occurs.

Practitioners often have a better grasp of the importance of adaptation than laboratory researchers because they work on it more directly. Practitioners frequently closely monitor the behavior and words of their subjects for indications of stress and take steps either to counteract it or to use it as part of their treatment. Decreasing novelty and fear responses is essential to gaining an indication of the subject's task-related response repertoire and potential for discriminating and remembering stimuli. For example, if a child with a salient repertoire of fear or aggressive responses will soon begin school for the first time, counselors may recommend taking the child to the classroom to meet the teacher before the first day or letting the child meet other children who will also be there. With older children, it may be sufficient to pretend (role play) the important transitions of the first day. Though it seems self-evident that children will be helped by providing them experience with the procedures and environment of school, similar procedures are equally useful for a human adult entering novel situations such as a new job or a therapy situation or for a dog entering an obedience class.

In addition, part of the adaptation process in applied settings may involve establishing the authority of the practitioner. Several professional dog trainers have argued that large male dogs tend to stand on the trainer's foot as a display of dominance. Although I can think of alternative hypotheses, I can also report a supporting case history of a dominant male dog that consistently and with unerring aim stood on my feet during training in marked contrast to the behavior of a female of the same breed and similar size who never did so. A similar story is told by Roger Fouts about trying without success to train a juvenile male chimpanzee to sign the word *hat*. After an hour of carefully shaping the ape's fingers into the sign, rewarding it, and repeating, Dr. Fouts's patience finally deserted him, and he gave what could be termed an *anger display* to the ape. The chimpanzee immediately and repeatedly gave the sign for hat.

Tuning

Most laboratory researchers at one time or another have modified their apparatus or their training and testing procedures to produce a clearer and more vigorous result. For example, if an experimenter wants to measure barpressing in a rat, but the rat keeps chewing on the bar, the answer is to move the bar further into the wall, making it thicker and rounded on the end. I have referred to this time-honored technique as *tuning* (Timberlake, 1983a, 1990). Skinner (1938, 1956), although he attributed it to laziness, gave a particularly clear account of tuning in terms of the extensive manipulations he went through to establish the leverpress as an operant. His manipulations included changing the size, shape, and placement of the lever, as well as the configuration of the chamber surrounding it. Other experimenters have not been so clear about their behavior, but the process is clearly ongoing in most research.

In my estimation, every apparatus and procedure extensively used in the study of reinforcement has been tuned to control the speed and vigor of reinforcement, as well as to facilitate the production of effects related to important independent variables. As Timberlake and Lucas (1989) noted, it seems no accident that the major instrumental responses, leverpressing and maze running in rats and keypecking in pigeons, can be acquired through simple exposure to cues. In the case of leverpressing, a simple exposure to a moving lever predicting food is sufficient to produce interaction with the lever and closing of the microswitch. Illuminating a key as a predictor of food very rapidly produces extensive pecking of the key by naive pigeons, pecking that is acquired and continues even when it omits food delivery. As noted above, placing a rat in a straight alley or a radial arm maze produces acquisition of maze running even when the maze is never baited with food (Timberlake, 1983a; Timberlake & White, 1990).

From a causal-system view, what is occurring in tuning is the modification of the environment and the procedures to make better contact with the processing and structure constituting the initial conditions of the organism. The process of tuning is such a pervasive part of laboratory research that researchers no longer notice how effective and simple it is. In many circumstances, major tuning already has been done by the person who designed the apparatus. In contrast, with humans there is some tendency to expect them to understand what they should do rather than changing the eliciting qualities of the environment. Wahler and Fox (1981) cover a variety of instances in which redesigning the setting can be an important contributor to behavior change. As compared with response-contingent reinforcement, this approach is simpler, requires less training, is less confrontive and overtly manipulative, and produces less resistance on the part of the subject.

Finally, tuning may involve restriction of the stimuli present to prevent competition among them for control of modules, modes, and systems. A famous example of behavior control by restriction was the technique Skinner used to gain control of his writing. He recommended working in a barren room containing adequate tools for writing, but lacking instigating stimuli for competing behavior. He recommended not doing anything except writing while in the room and writing always at the same time each day. This procedure allowed for strong instigation for writing and minimal instigation for other responses.

The Effects of Presenting Significant Stimuli

Of all the ways to change behavior, the simplest method in both the laboratory and applied settings is presenting stimuli that attract behavior. For example, anyone who has attempted to take an object away from an avid toddler finds it much easier to remove the object after first replacing it with something else attractive. If your daughter does not take her music lessons seriously, engage a teacher who has an attractive teenage son. If your dog will not take a pill, put it inside a morsel of meat. If your son is cranky when you pick him up at 5:00, try picking him up at 4:30, taking along something to eat, or providing something to do in the car that is more interesting than complaining. From a causal-system view, presenting an attention-getting stimulus is a way of entraining and organizing responding around temporal or environmental cues. No response contingency is needed. A presented stimulus may elicit its own behavior, or behavior that is based on its predictive relation to another stimulus, such as food. In the next paragraphs, I discuss several behavior-change effects related to presenting stimuli that occur regularly in laboratory research: filling in, conditioning of modes, and changing systems.

Filling In

When food is predictable either on the basis of an explicit stimulus or its correlation with time, organisms tend to fill in instrumental chains of responses leading up to the food. For example, when food is presented periodically at intervals of up to 8 min, animals engage in responses that lead from after-food search focused around the food tray through more general search of the chamber and back to food-tray search before the next item (Lucas, Timberlake, & Gawley, 1988; Staddon, 1977). Hollis (1990) showed that a male gourami exposed to a light predicting exposure to a conspecific competitor developed a variety of aggressive responses preparatory to the exposure. Even though there was no response contingency present, the animal's behavior was engaged by an organized behavior system related to territorial defense and reproduction.

The tendency of humans to fill in instrumental chains under conditions of irregular and unpredictable reinforcement is legendary. Individuals in intense social relations, such as couples or families, often have very unclear notions about the rules for reinforcement. For years, individuals will repeat a particular response sequence with little or no evidence that it is effective. One of the things practitioners may be best at is helping individuals and social units sort out what the actual response contingencies are and what they want them to be. It also may be worthwhile to sort out which stimuli are controlling behavior, because simply removing those stimuli or adding others may change behavior markedly in the absence of a schedule manipulation.

Conditioning Modes

In the laboratory, predictive stimuli of different lengths appear to condition different motivational modes (see also Konorski, 1967). The reader is reminded that simply presenting a rolling ball bearing to a rat followed in 6 s by the delivery of food engages a string of responses related to the ball bearing (Timberlake et al., 1982). The initial responses to the bearing involve search and capture. Subsequent responses involve focal search and handling; the rat turns, gnaws, and retrieves the bearing until food arrives. In contrast, if the same bearing is followed by food after 2 s, the rat does not engage the bearing, but goes directly to the location where food will arrive and there engages in focal search-and-handling-related behaviors of digging and gnawing. The small time difference is apparently sufficient to condition different modes with different stimulus sensitivities and prepotent behaviors. Other examples are discussed in Timberlake and Silva (in press).

In applied settings, many practitioners are quite aware of the differences in response repertoires and stimulus sensitivities as a function of proximity to reward. A coach can inspire an athletic team to new levels of effort by invoking cues proximate to victory (or defeat). Students doing poorly sometimes can be inspired by a single instance of personal attention and encouragement by the teacher that is contingent only on trying. To shape a duck to play the piano, the reward must be neither too close nor too distant. Response-contingent reward can condition different modes, but response contingencies are not essential to the process (see Matthews & Lerer, 1987). In many cases, the conditioning of modes is produced simply by pairing the stimulus situation with food.

Changing Systems

Presenting unconditional stimuli often can change the repertoire of an animal suddenly. Thus, the behaviors available to a thirsty animal drinking are altered radically by the presentation of a single shock. The shock does not have to be contingent on any behavior to have an effect. In fact, perhaps the most interesting aspect of functional systems is that they can take precedence over response contingencies. Recall Sevenster's (1973) stickleback fish, which had difficulty when the response and the reward came from different functional systems. For example, territorial males had no problem biting a rod when the result was presentation of another male, but great difficulty when the reward was presentation of an egg-filled female.

In a related example from an applied setting, Peter Borchelt, a practitioner dealing with pets, told me his experience with changing systems by using response contingencies. The problem was a dog that barked incessantly at any person who was not a resident of the apartment in which the dog lived, thereby making it difficult to have dinner guests. Peter solved the problem by visiting the apartment and seating himself alone in the front room with the barking dog and a piece of cheese. He then began to feed pieces of the cheese to the dog until gradually its barking subsided and it sat begging next to his chair.

As Peter smugly neared the end of yet another successful treatment, his operant training returned to him in a sudden flash. He realized with consternation that he had been reliably rewarding the dog for barking. Every time the dog barked, Peter fed it a piece of cheese. This should have reinforced barking, and yet the treatment had been a success. The barking had stopped, and the dog had treated him as a group member, begging food. This mystery does not exist within a causal-system approach. By feeding the dog, he altered the prepotent system from defense to feeding. The cheese entrained the feeding system, and the dog treated Peter as a conspecific and filled in begging behavior directed to Peter.

Distinguishing Sources of Behavior Change

The failure of laboratory researchers to distinguish how response-contingent reinforcement fits into a more general framework of behavior change in the laboratory probably influences the lack of clarity about reinforcement in applied settings. One example of this is found in the strongly held belief of many educators and theorists that was recently summarized in my local newspaper in the headlines, "Reinforcement Destroys Intrinsic Motivation." A frequently cited example of this "fact" is the study done by Greene and Lepper (1974) on drawing by nursery school children. After a 1-day assessment of baseline levels of drawing, the experimenters increased drawing by making gold stars and teacher approval contingent on it.

The key finding was that when the approval and gold stars were withdrawn the next day, the level of drawing sank below its baseline, producing the conclusion that intrinsic motivation had been lost permanently because of response-contingent reinforcement. This is an exceptionally important conclusion for applied settings, but it seems to have been accepted uncritically by many professional educators. Leaving aside the numerous conceptual issues involved in the question of intrinsic and extrinsic reward, a causal-system view of behavior change suggests the importance of examining several determinants of responding other than the response contingency. Given greater understanding of the determinants, researchers should be able to select the effect of extrinsic reward that they want (M. Morgan, 1984).

First, there appeared to be no control, at least in initial studies, for the possibility that the children were simply adapting to drawing as they adapted to any new task. In other words, the instigation for drawing with crayons probably decreased with expression, presumably recovering later with absence of expression. Response-contingent reinforcement might have accelerated this adaptation by increasing the amount of drawing. A key test would be to examine much longer term effects on drawing.

Second, the sudden and brief introduction of gold stars and teacher attention into the situation may have altered the response potentials of the environment by informing the children that reward was available. When reward was withdrawn without warning, the subjects may have engaged in other behaviors potentially relevant to searching for gold stars or teacher approval, or they may have shown emotional reactions to the withdrawal of an attractive stimulus.

Third, there may have been a question of behaviors related to teacher praise directly interfering with drawing. Remember that in training Washoe to sign, the Gardners first used response-contingent delivery of food (Gardner & Gardner, 1988). The food, though, brought along its own motivation and repertoire of behavior that interfered markedly with signing. The use of ongoing small social interactions with delayed larger rewards worked much more effectively. Perhaps social encouragement and delayed stars would be equally as effective with drawing. In short, statements such as "extrinsic reward destroys intrinsic reward" should be shelved in favor of a clearer analysis of the determinants of behavior change.

Complex Environments

A last reason for the simple-reinforcement effects that have been generated in the laboratory is that to clarify the determinants of reinforcement effects, researchers typically engage only a small part of the functioning of a single system. The drawback to these restrictions is that the simple-causal model of reinforcement then appears lost in complex environments with interacting motivations and multiple responses and reward alternatives. Even the relative complexity of the present causal-system model still leaves many things out, for example, substitution effects among alternative responses and stimuli (Bernstein & Ebbesen, 1978; Green & Freed, 1993). A profitable approach for melding the study of behavior change in the laboratory and in applied settings is the study of behavior in a 24-hr environment. Bernstein and Brady (1986) recently reviewed the attempts to examine human behavior in such controlled settings.

The increasing work with animals in 24-hr environments may also have relevance to the complexity of applied settings. For years, Collier (1983) has shown that the rules determining responding vary with the costs and pattern of access to reward. Animals adjust to high cost for access to a meal by decreasing the frequency and increasing the size of each meal. They adjust to high costs for bites within a meal by increasing their rate of working. Such data make clear that the determinants of choice may differ as a function of whether one is choosing within a particular motivational state, such as a meal, or across motivational states, such as between eating and some other behavior (e.g., nesting). In related work, Lucas et al. (1988) and Timberlake and Lucas (1991) studied how animals redistributed their behavior in time as a function of restricting the maximum rate of ingestion of food or water. A surprising result was the maintenance of meal size and time in nest during severe restrictions on the rate of eating and drinking.

Perhaps the most interesting laboratory data combine questions of interaction and regulation. Helmstetter and Fanselow (1993) studied the effects of pitting fear of predation against feeding in a 24-hr environment. The effect was similar in many ways to the results of increasing the cost of gaining access to meals (Collier, 1983). As predation risk increased, animals decreased the number of meals, but increased the size of each one. Similar effects have been shown in the selection of diet items and patches in research on foraging in more natural settings (Stephens & Krebs, 1986). Finally, Timberlake and Lucas (1991) showed that the effect of restricting the rate of eating and drinking had rather different effects on how rats filled in responding between rewards. Restricting eating rate increased restless activity markedly, whereas restricting drinking rate decreased gross motor activity. Continuing such work should help to clarify the organization present in initial conditions and its influence on behavior-change manipulations.

CONCLUSION

The simple-causal model of response-contingent reinforcement, although providing a set of procedures that can produce behavior change, is neither a complete model of reinforcement nor an adequate model of behavior change. Among its limitations are an inability to identify reinforcers ahead of time, an incomplete specification of the conditions affecting reinforcement, and a failure to deal systematically with behavior change that does not involve reinforcement procedures. Experienced researchers and practitioners have developed techniques of behavior change that work reliably, but the simple-causal model does not provide a common framework for integrating them.

A causal-system model focuses on the role of the response-contingent presentation of a reinforcer in constraining a functioning system. The results of schedule-based constraints depend on the regulatory components, initial structure, and stimulus processing of the system. A causal-system analysis also considers how typical laboratory procedures contribute to reinforcement effects in particular and behavior change in general. Thus, a causal-system model potentially can serve as a general framework for dealing with more than one type of behavior change.

The causal-system model in no way argues that traditional reinforcement procedures cannot be used effectively to change behavior. Practitioners and researchers identified with the simple-causal approach have been exceptionally successful. Personally, I would have been unwilling to enter a contest with the late Dr. Skinner to see who could best shape a pigeon to feed peanuts to an elephant or communicate with a parrot. But I suspect that his marvelous ability to control and change behavior did not come primarily from his understanding of the general principles of reinforcement (otherwise many people would be as expert at shaping responses). Rather, his control came from experience-based hypotheses about the response repertoire and processing capabilities of his subjects (their initial conditions) and how they would interact with response-contingent reinforcement.

I would like to argue for the continuation of a behaviorally grounded approach to behavior change that restructures and amplifies the traditional simple-causal model of reinforcement, thereby improving its procedures for controlling behavior. Classic alternatives, such as exclusively cognitive or physiological theories, give up the obvious power and hard-won experience of a behavior-based approach. What is needed is a more inclusive system framework that better accounts for the specific conditions of response-contingent reinforcement and the general conditions of behavior change. Such a framework would prove useful for both laboratory research and practice.

SUMMARY

Despite difficulties in identifying reinforcers ahead of time and reliably predicting the speed and robustness of reinforcement effects, reinforcement is typically viewed as caused in a simple way by the presentation of a reinforcer contingent on a response. The focus on response-contingent reinforcement has established general laws in laboratory research and helped develop the effective reinforcement technology used in applied settings. However, this simple-causal model has proved an incomplete guide to reinforcement and to behavior change in general. The alternative causal-system approach, which views the response contingency as a constraint on a functioning system, appears to hold several advantages. A causal system includes regulatory principles, complex initial conditions, and the role of stimulus processing and memory in determining reinforcement effects. In addition, a causal-system analysis provides a potential framework for understanding the many types of behavior change not produced by response-contingent reinforcement.

REFERENCES

Alexander, R. D. (1979). *Darwinism and human affairs*. Seattle: University of Washington Press.

Allison, J. (1989). The nature of reinforcement. In S. B. Klein & R. R. Mowrer (Eds.), *Contemporary learning theories: Instrumental conditioning theory and the impact of biological constraints on learning* (pp. 13–39). Hillsdale, NJ: Erlbaum.

Azrin, N. (1977). A strategy for applied research: Learning based but outcome oriented. *American Psychologist, 32*, 140–149.

Balda, R. P., & Kamil, A. C. (1989). A comparative study of cache recovery in three corvid species. *Animal Behaviour, 38*, 486–495.

Beer, C. G. (1992). Conceptual issues in cognitive ethology. *Advances in the Study of Behavior, 21*, 69–110.

Bernstein, D. J. (1986). Correspondence between verbal and observed estimates of reinforcement value. In P. N. Chase & L. W. Parrott (Eds.), *Psychological aspects of language: The West Virginia lectures* (pp. 187–205). Springfield, IL: Charles C Thomas.

Bernstein, D. J., & Brady, J. V. (1986). The utility of continuous programmed environments in the experimental analysis of human behavior. In H. W. Reese & L. J. Parrott (Eds.), *Behavior science: Philosophical, methodological and empirical advances* (pp. 229–243). Hillsdale, NJ: Erlbaum.

Bernstein, D. J., & Ebbesen, E. B. (1978). Reinforcement and substitution in humans: A multiple-response analysis. *Journal of the Experimental Analysis of Behavior, 30*, 243–253.

Bolles, R. C., & Moot, S. (1973). The rat's anticipation of two meals a day. *Journal of Comparative and Physiological Psychology, 83*, 510–514.

Brant, D. H., & Kavanau, J. L. (1965). "Unrewarded" exploration and learning of complex mazes by wild and domestic mice. *Nature, 204*, 267–269.

Breland, K., & Breland, M. (1961). The misbehavior of organisms. *American Psychologist, 16*, 681–684.

Breland, K., & Breland, M. (1966). *Animal behavior*. San Diego, CA: Academic Press.

Catania, A. C. (1992). *Learning*. Englewood Cliffs, NJ: Prentice Hall.

Collier, G. (1983). Life in a closed economy: The ecology of learning and motivation. In M. D. Zeiler & P. Harzem (Eds.), *Advances in analysis of behaviour: Vol. 3. Biological factors in learning* (pp. 223–274). Chichester, England: Wiley.

Colwill, R. M., & Rescorla, R. A. (1985). Postconditioning devaluation of a reinforcer affects instrumental responding. *Journal of Experimental Psychology: Animal Behavior Processes, 11*, 120–132.

Cosmides, L., & Tooby, J. (1987). From evolution to behavior: Evolutionary psychology as the missing link. In J. Dupre (Ed.), *The latest on the best* (pp. 279–306). Cambridge, MA: MIT Press.

Domjan, M., & Galef, B. G. (1983). Biological constraints on instrumental and classical conditioning: Retrospect and prospect. *Animal Learning & Behavior, 11*, 151–161.

Fanselow, M. S., & Lester, L. S. (1988). A functional behavioristic approach to aversively motivated behavior: Predatory imminence as a determinant of the topography of defensive behavior. In R. C. Bolles & M. D. Beecher (Eds.), *Evolution and learning* (pp. 185–212). Hillsdale, NJ: Erlbaum.

Ford, M. E. (1992). *Motivating humans: Goals, emotions, and personal agency beliefs.* Newbury Park, CA: Sage.

Gallistel, C. R. (1990). *The organization of learning.* London: MIT Press.

Gannon, K. N., Smith, H. V., & Tierney, K. J. (1983). Effects of procurement cost on food consumption in rats. *Physiology and Behavior, 31*, 331–337.

Garcia, J., & Garcia y Robertson, R. (1985). Evolution of learning mechanisms. In B. L. Hammonds (Ed.), *Psychology and learning: The master lecture series* (Vol. 4, pp. 187–243). Washington, DC: American Psychological Association.

Garcia, J., & Koelling, R. (1966). Learning with prolonged delay of reinforcement. *Psychonomic Science, 4*, 123–124.

Gardner, R. A., & Gardner, B. T. (1988). Feedforward versus feedbackward: An ethological alternative to the law of effect. *Behavioral and Brain Sciences, 11*, 429–446.

Gawley, D. J., Timberlake, W., & Lucas, G. A. (1986). Schedule constraint of average drink burst length and regulation of wheel running and drinking in rats. *Journal of Experimental Psychology: Animal Behavior Processes, 12*, 78–94.

Gawley, D. J., Timberlake, W., & Lucas, G. A. (1987). System-specific differences in behavior regulation: Overrunning and underdrinking in molar nondepriving schedules. *Journal of Experimental Psychology: Animal Behavior Processes, 13*, 354–365.

Green, L., & Freed, D. E. (1993). The substitutability of reinforcers. *Journal of the Experimental Analysis of Behavior, 60*, 141–158.

Greene, D., & Lepper, M. R. (1974). Effects of extrinsic rewards on children's subsequent intrinsic interest. *Child Development, 45*, 1141–1145.

Hailman, J. P. (1967). The ontogeny of an instinct. *Behaviour* (Suppl. 15), 1–159.

Hanson, S. J., & Timberlake, W. (1983). Regulation during challenge: A general model of learned performance under schedule constraint. *Psychological Review, 90*, 261–282.

Hart, B. M., & Risley, T. R. (1975). Incidental teaching of language in the preschool. *Journal of Applied Behavior Analysis, 8*, 411–420.

Hatch, J. P., Fisher, J. G., & Rugh, J. D. (1987). *Biofeedback: Studies in clinical efficacy*. New York: Plenum.

Hayes, S. C. (1989). *Rule-governed behavior: Cognition, contingencies, and instructional control*. New York: Plenum.

Helmstetter, F. J., & Fanselow, M. S. (1993). Aversively motivated changes in meal patterns of rats in a closed economy: The effects of shock density. *Animal Learning & Behavior, 21*, 168–175.

Herrnstein, R. J. (1970). On the law of effect. *Journal of the Experimental Analysis of Behavior, 13*, 243–266.

Herrnstein, R. J., & Vaughan, W., Jr. (1980). Melioration and behavioral allocation. In J. E. R. Staddon (Ed.), *Limits to action* (pp. 143–176). San Diego, CA: Academic Press.

Hogan, J. A. (1988). Cause and function in the development of behavior systems. In E. M. Blass (Ed.), *Handbook of behavioral neurobiology: Vol. 9. Developmental psychobiology and behavioral ecology* (pp. 63–106). New York: Plenum.

Hollis, K. L. (1990). The role of Pavlovian conditioning in territorial aggression and reproduction. In D. A. Dewsbury (Ed.), *Contemporary issues in comparative psychology* (pp. 197–219). Sunderland, MA: Sinauer Associates.

Hull, C. L. (1943). *Principles of behavior*. New York: Appleton-Century-Crofts.

Kazdin, A. E. (1980). *Behavior modification in applied settings*. Homewood, IL: Dorsey Press.

Kazdin, A. E. (1982). The token economy: A decade later. *Journal of Applied Behavior Analysis, 15*, 431–445.

Kelly, M. L., & Stokes, T. F. (1982). Contingency contracting with disadvantaged youths: Improving classroom performance. *Journal of Applied Behavior Analysis, 15*, 447–454.

Konarski, E. A., Jr., Johnson, M. R., Crowell, C. R., & Whitman, T. L. (1981). An alternative approach to reinforcement for applied researchers: Response deprivation. *Behavior Therapy, 12*, 653–666.

Konarski, E. A., Crowell, C. R., & Duggan, L. M. (1985). The use of response deprivation to increase the academic performance of EMR students. *Applied Research in Mental Retardation, 6*, 15–31.

Konorski, J. (1967). *Integrative activity of the brain: An interdisciplinary approach*. Chicago: University of Chicago Press.

Krebs, J. R., Healy, S. D., & Shettleworth, S. J. (1990). Spatial memory of *Paridae*: Comparison of a storing and a nonstoring species, the coal tit, *Parus ater*, and the great tit, *P. major. Animal Behaviour, 39*, 1127–1137.

Lattal, K. A., & Gleeson, S. (1990). Response acquisition with delayed reinforcement. *Journal of Experimental Psychology: Animal Behavior Processes, 16*, 27–39.

Lattal, K. A., & Metzger, B. (1994). Response acquisition by Siamese fighting fish (*Betta splendens*) with delayed visual reinforcement. *Journal of the Experimental Analysis of Behavior, 61*, 35–44.

Leyhausen, P. (1973). *Cat behavior: The predatory and social behavior of domestic and wild cats.* New York: Garland.

Logue, A. (1979). Taste aversion and the generality of the laws of learning. *Psychological Bulletin, 86,* 276–296.

Logue, A. (1988). Research on self-control: An integrating framework. *Behavioral and Brain Sciences, 11,* 665–679.

Lucas, G. A., Timberlake, W., & Gawley, D. J. (1988). Adjunctive behavior in the rat under periodic food delivery in a 24-hr environment. *Animal Learning & Behavior, 16,* 19–30.

Martin, G. L., & Pear, J. J. (1992). *Behavior modification: What it is and how to do it* (4th ed.). Englewood Cliffs, NJ: Prentice Hall.

Matthews, T. J., & Lerer, B. E. (1987). Behavior patterns in pigeons during autoshaping with an incremental conditioned stimulus. *Animal Learning & Behavior, 15,* 69–75.

McDowell, J. J. (1982). The importance of Herrnstein's mathematical statement of the law of effect for behavioral therapy. *American Psychologist, 37,* 771–779.

McGee, G. G., Krantz, P. J., & McClannahan, L. E. (1985). The facilitative effects of incidental teaching on preposition use by autistic children. *Journal of Applied Behavior Analysis, 18,* 17–31.

Medland, M. B., & Stachnik, T. J. (1982). Good behavior game: A replication and systematic analysis. *Journal of Applied Behavior Analysis, 5,* 45–51.

Meehl, P. E. (1950). On the circularity of the law of effect. *Psychological Bulletin, 47,* 52–75.

Michael, J. (1993). Establishing operations. *The Behavior Analyst, 16,* 191–206.

Morgan, C. L. (1896). *Habit and instinct.* London: Arnold.

Morgan, M. (1984). Reward-induced decrements and increments in intrinsic motivation. *Review of Educational Research, 54,* 5–30.

Morris, E. K. (1993). Mechanism and contextualism in behavior analysis: Just some observations. *The Behavior Analyst, 16,* 255–268.

Mrosovsky, N. (1988). Phase response curves for social entrainment. *Journal of Comparative Physiology A, 162,* 35–46.

Olson, D. J. (1991). Species differences in spatial memory among Clark's nutcrackers, scrub jays, and pigeons. *Journal of Experimental Psychology: Animal Behavior Processes, 17,* 363–376.

Olton, D. S. (1978). Characteristics of spatial memory. In S. H. Hulse, H. Fowler, & W. K. Honig (Eds.), *Cognitive processes in animal behavior.* Hillsdale, NJ: Erlbaum.

Premack, D. (1959). Toward empirical behavioral laws: Instrumental positive reinforcement. *Psychological Review, 66,* 219–233.

Premack, D. (1965). Reinforcement theory. In D. Levine (Ed.), *Nebraska symposium on motivation* (Vol. 13, pp. 123–180). Lincoln: University of Nebraska Press.

Premack, D. (1971). Catching up with common sense or two sides of a generalization: Reinforcement and punishment. In R. Glaser (Ed.), *The nature of reinforcement* (pp. 121–150). San Diego, CA: Academic Press.

Rachlin, H. C., Battalio, R., Kagel, J., & Green, L. (1981). Maximization theory in behavioral psychology. *Behavioral and Brain Sciences, 4,* 371–417.

Rashotte, M. E., & Henderson, D. (1988). Coping with rising food costs in a closed economy: Feeding behavior and nocturnal hypothermia in pigeons. *Journal of the Experimental Analysis of Behavior, 50,* 441–456.

Revusky, S. H. (1977). Learning as a general process with an emphasis on data from feeding experiments. In N. W. Milgram, L. Krames, & T. M. Alloway (Eds.), *Food aversion learning* (pp. 1–51). New York: Plenum.

Roitblat, H. L. (1987). *Introduction to comparative cognition.* New York: Freeman.

Rozin, P., & Schull, J. (1988). The adaptive-evolutionary point of view in experimental psychology. In R. C. Atkinson, R. J. Herrnstein, G. Lindzey, & R. D. Luce (Eds.), *Steven's handbook of experimental psychology* (pp. 503–546). New York: Wiley.

Seligman, M. E. P. (1970). On the generality of the laws of learning. *Psychological Review, 77,* 406–418.

Sevenster, P. (1973). Incompatibility of response and reward. In R. A. Hinde & J. Stevenson-Hinde (Eds.), *Constraints on learning: Limitations and predispositions* (pp. 265–283). San Diego, CA: Academic Press.

Sherry, D. F., & Schachter, D. L. (1987). The evolution of multiple memory systems. *Psychological Review, 94,* 439–454.

Sherry, D. F., Vaccarino, A. L., Buckenham, K., & Herz, R. S. (1989). The hippocampal complex of food-storing birds. *Brain, Behavior, and Evolution, 34,* 308–317.

Shettleworth, S. J. (1972). Constraints on learning. *Advances in the Study of Behavior 4,* 1–68.

Shettleworth, S. J. (1975). Reinforcement and the organization of behavior in golden hamsters: Hunger, environment, and food reinforcement. *Journal of Experimental Psychology: Animal Behavior Processes, 1,* 56–87.

Sidman, M., Wynne, C. K., Maguire, R. W., & Barnes, T. (1989). Functional classes and equivalence relations. *Journal of the Experimental Analysis of Behavior, 52,* 261–274.

Skinner, B. F. (1938). *The behavior of organisms: An experimental analysis.* New York: Appleton-Century-Crofts.

Skinner, B. F. (1948). "Superstition" in the pigeon. *Journal of Experimental Psychology, 38,* 168–172.

Skinner, B. F. (1953). *Science and human behavior.* New York: Macmillan.

Skinner, B. F. (1956). A case history in scientific method. *American Psychologist, 11,* 221–233.

Skinner, B. F. (1966). The phylogeny and ontogeny of behavior. *Science, 153,* 1205–1213.

Staddon, J. E. R. (1977). Schedule-induced behavior. In W. K. Honig & J. E. R. Staddon (Eds.), *Handbook of operant behavior* (pp. 125–152). New York: Prentice Hall.

Staddon, J. E. R. (1979). Operant behavior as adaptation to constraint. *Journal of Experimental Psychology: General, 108,* 48–67.

Stephan, F. K., Swann, J. M., & Sisk, C. L. (1979). Anticipation of 24-hr feeding schedules in rats with lesions of the suprachiasmatic nucleus. *Behavioral and Neural Biology, 25,* 346–363.

Stephens, D. W., & Krebs, J. R. (1986). *Foraging theory.* Princeton, NJ: Princeton University Press.

Stokes, P. D., & Balsam, P. D. (1991). Effects of reinforcing preselected approximations on the topography of the rat's bar press. *Journal of the Experimental Analysis of Behavior, 55,* 213–231.

Thorndike, E. L. (1911). *Animal intelligence: Experimental studies.* San Diego, CA: Academic Press.

Timberlake, W. (1980). A molar equilibrium theory of learned performance. In G. H. Bower (Ed.), *The psychology of learning and motivation* (Vol. 14, pp. 1–58). San Diego, CA: Academic Press.

Timberlake, W. (1983a). Appetitive structure and straight alley running. In R. Mellgren (Ed.), *Animal cognition and behaviour.* Amsterdam: North-Holland.

Timberlake, W. (1983b). The functional organization of appetitive behavior: Behavior systems and learning. In M. D. Zeiler & P. Harzem (Eds.), *Advances in analysis of behaviour: Vol. 3. Biological factors in learning.* Chichester, England: Wiley.

Timberlake, W. (1988). The behavior of organisms: Purposive behavior as a type of reflex. *Journal of the Experimental Analysis of Behavior, 50,* 305–317.

Timberlake, W. (1990). Natural learning in laboratory paradigms. In D. A. Dewsbury (Ed.), *Contemporary issues in comparative psychology* (pp. 31–54). Sunderland, MA: Sinauer Associates.

Timberlake, W. (1993). Behavior systems and reinforcement: An integrative approach. *Journal of the Experimental Analysis of Behavior, 60,* 105–128.

Timberlake, W., & Allison, J. (1974). Response deprivation: An empirical approach to instrumental performance. *Psychological Review, 81,* 146–164.

Timberlake, W., & Farmer-Dougan, V. (1991). Reinforcement in applied settings: Figuring out ahead of time what will work. *Psychological Bulletin, 110,* 379–391.

Timberlake, W., Gawley, D., & Lucas, G. A. (1987). Time horizons in rats foraging for food in temporally separated patches. *Journal of Experimental Psychology: Animal Behavior Processes, 13,* 302–309.

The first variation assumes that there is a set of known reinforcers for human beings that may be obtained from the empirical literature. Applied behavior analysts need only refer to this list to identify effective reinforcers. Occasionally, the list of potential reinforcers is extended by new empirical research.

The second variation of this theme is that each individual has his or her own pool of potential reinforcers. The task of the therapist is to systematically identify these through empirical investigation for future use. This latter variation would seem to be the more prevalent approach (e.g., Kazdin, 1984). Similar approaches may be used to identify effective punishment procedures.

The first major departure from this approach stems from the work of David Premack. Premack (1965) pointed out that the empirical law of effect was based on three assumptions (two explicit and one implicit) that gave the impression of being empirically based, but that had never been explicitly tested.

The first of these assumptions was that some stimuli change the frequency of responses they follow, whereas others do not (e.g., Skinner, 1938, p. 62). The second was that reinforcers are transituational in their effects (Meehl, 1950). A third assumption was that there are two classes of stimuli, one that is reinforcing, but not reinforceable, and another that is reinforceable, but not reinforcing. Although no one, to my knowledge, had ever explicitly claimed that two such distinct categories existed, such an assumption appears to have guided research when Premack was writing. For example, food and water were used exclusively as reinforcers (nobody attempted to reinforce eating or drinking), whereas responses such as leverpressing were never used as reinforcers but exclusively as responses to be reinforced.

Premack (1965) tested these fundamental assumptions and showed them to be unfounded; he went on to propose his probability differential hypothesis as an alternative account of the reinforcing process.

The first assumption ceased to be tenable when it became apparent that many stimuli that had not been previously considered reinforcing could be used to increase the frequency of the response that led to them. The new range of reinforcing stimuli included lights, sounds, puzzles, and so on (Premack, 1965). The reaction of those working within the context of the empirical law of effect was simply to ignore their former assumption and allow new stimuli into the class of reinforcing stimuli.

The first problem for the second assumption of the empirical law of effect was the simple observation that food ceased to be reinforcing for satiated animals (i.e., even the strongest reinforcer was not transituational in its effects). Instead of changing the assumptions of the law of effect to accommodate this observation, its range of application was restricted to situations in which animals were deprived (i.e., to situations in which the

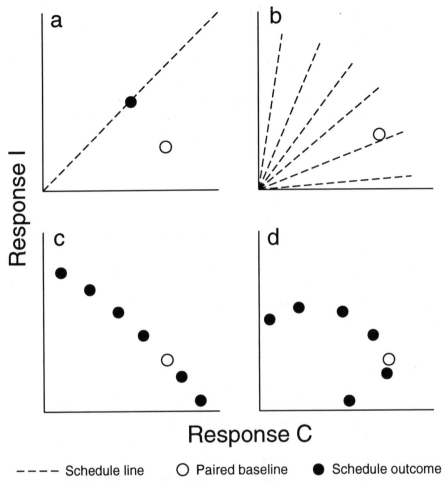

---- Schedule line   O Paired baseline   ● Schedule outcome

Figure 1. Hypothetical schedule constraints and outcomes in two-dimensional space representing instrumental (Response I) and contingent (Response C) responding: (a) a fixed-ratio schedule causing a disequilibrium condition; (b) a series of fixed-ratio constraints; (c) a linear response function; and (d) a bitonic response function.

above the line passing through the origin with slope I/C. In the case of a reciprocal schedule (Allison, 1971), one that requires an amount of the instrumental response to be performed for access to the contingent response and an amount of the contingent response to be performed to regain access to the instrumental response, the animal's behavior is constrained to fall on the line. It is apparent from Figure 1A that all reciprocal schedules, except for the one on which $O_i/O_c = I/C$, prevent access to the paired baseline levels of the two responses. In the case of the schedule line in Figure 1A, if the subject performed its baseline level of the instrumental response (i) it would receive less of the contingent response (c) than in the baseline condition. To obtain its baseline level of c, the subject would have to perform an amount of i in excess of its baseline level. The usual outcome of such schedules is that subjects perform an amount of i in excess of the paired baseline level, but the increase in i is usually not sufficient to gain access to the baseline level of c. This outcome is viewed by optimality theorists as an attempt to minimize the disequilibrium between the preferred baseline package of behaviors and the outcomes permitted by the schedule constraints.

Quantitative Predictions

In addition to making qualitative predictions (i.e., predicting whether an increase, a decrease, or no change in the level of instrumental responding will occur) for the effects of a schedule, many of the optimality models, and indeed other functional models, also attempt to make quantitative predictions. This task can most easily be described by reference to a diagram. In the behavioral space represented in Figure 1B, the constraints of a series of reciprocal fixed-ratio schedules are represented. The outcome of each of these schedules will be a point somewhere along the line, and the task of the models is to predict those points and to account for the shape of the function (referred to as a response function) formed by joining the series of points. Figures 1C and 1D show two possible response functions: The former is a straight line passing through the point representing the paired baseline (the paired basepoint), and the latter is a line that is concave to the origin passing through the paired basepoint. Functions of both of these general shapes have been obtained in experiments that varied the terms of contingency schedules (Staddon, 1979).

The types of "quantitative" evidence cited to support the various models have included (a) demonstrating that the general shape of an empirical response function is permitted by the model; (b) demonstrating that the predicted levels of instrumental responding correlate well with the empirical data; and (c) showing that there is no significant difference across the range of schedules in the predicted and obtained levels of instrumental responding.

In the next sections, I briefly describe some optimality models and the derivation of the mathematical expressions used to make quantitative predictions. This is followed by highly selective reviews of the qualitative and quantitative evidence cited by each model's proponents to support the model.

The Relative Response Deprivation Model

The relative response deprivation model, proposed by Timberlake and Wozny (1979) and discussed in more general terms by Timberlake (1980,

1984), represented an attempt to express in a quantitative form the predictions of the response deprivation hypothesis (Allison & Timberlake, 1974; Timberlake & Allison, 1974) and is perhaps the simplest of the optimality models.

The model assumes that the paired baseline represents an ideal distribution of time among behaviors and that the instrumental response will be facilitated by the schedule to a degree that is determined by the amount to which the contingent response would be deprived relative to its baseline if the instrumental response was performed at its baseline level. These assumptions can be expressed in a mathematical form (Equation 3), which leads to quantitative predictions about the outcome of a schedule:

$$ NI = \frac{k}{O_c} \left(O_i - \frac{O_i C}{I} \right) + O_i, \tag{3} $$

where N is the number of cycles of $I + C$ and k is a fitted empirical constant obtained using the following equation:

$$ k = IO_c \left(\frac{S_i - O_i}{IO_c - O_i C} \right), \tag{4} $$

where S is the obtained amount of instrumental responding on the schedule.

To make predictions about the effects of a schedule, the constant k is calculated using the known outcome of a number of schedules. The estimates of k are averaged and the average used for subsequent predictions.

Timberlake and Wozny (1979) reported data that supported the predictions of the relative response deprivation model. Their experiments required rats to perform an instrumental running response to gain access to food and, in another condition, to perform an instrumental eating response to gain access to a running wheel. For both the run-to-eat and the eat-to-run contingencies, the predictions of this model, but not those of other quantitative models tested, did not differ significantly from the data. The authors attributed this success to the fact that the assumptions on which the model was based were correct. However, in another experiment by Allison, Miller, and Wozny (1979), the predictions of the model were less accurate in accounting for the data obtained, but they were not sufficiently inaccurate to warrant rejection.

The Minimum Distance Model

The minimum distance model proposed by Staddon (1979) is similar in its assumptions to the relative response deprivation model. However, instead of restricting itself to the two responses involved in the contingency relation, the model considers other responses to be important in the function to be optimized. Theoretically, the model could be extended to take into account any number of response categories, but in practice it has considered just two or three: the two responses involved in the contingency relation and all other behaviors.

The response categories involved in the function to be optimized are represented in a multidimensional behavioral space, the axes of which represent the levels of performance of the responses. The model's predictions are then generated by assuming that the outcome of a schedule will be the point on the schedule line that minimizes the weighted algebraic distance to the paired basepoint. The weightings are necessary because it is unlikely that the cost of deviations would be weighted equally along all of the axes. The weightings are empirical constants calculated from data.

These assumptions give rise to a set of predictive mathematical expressions that Staddon (1979) argued are capable of explaining many different response functions, including those obtained on interval and ratio schedules. The simplest of these predictive equations is given in Equation 5, which gives the predicted level of instrumental responding on a fixed-ratio schedule as the point on the schedule function that minimizes the algebraic distance along two dimensions (the instrumental response axis and the contingent response axis) to the paired basepoint.

$$NI = \frac{k^2 IO_i + CO_c}{k^2 I^2 + C^2},\tag{5}$$

where

$$k = \frac{C(O_c - S_c)}{I(S_i - O_i)}\tag{6}$$

and S is the obtained level of contingent responding.

Staddon (1979) supported this model by showing that the response functions predicted by the model for the outcome of a variety of schedule types were consistent with empirical functions in the literature. For example, the model could explain the bitonic response functions observed in approximately half of the experiments that varied ratio requirements (e.g., Barofsky & Hurwitz, 1968; Greenwood, Quartermain, Johnson, Cruce, & Hirsch, 1974; Kelsey & Allison, 1976) and for the linear response functions obtained in other ratio studies (e.g., Allison et al., 1979; Collier, Hirsch, & Hamlin, 1972; Hirsch & Collier, 1974). Furthermore, the model could accommodate the response functions obtained in experiments that manipulated the parameters of interval schedules (e.g., Catania & Reynolds, 1968; Porter, Allen, & Arazie, 1974).

The Value Maximizing Model

The value maximizing model proposed by Rachlin (1978) and Rachlin and Burkhard (1978)—and subsequently developed in articles by Burkhard, Rachlin, and Schroder (1978); Rachlin, Battalio, Kagel, and Green (1981); Rachlin, Kagel, and Battalio (1980); and Rachlin and Krasnoff (1983)—is another functional account of reinforcement that is based on optimality assumptions. The model shares many of the features of the models already discussed.

The basic assumptions of this model are that animals choose from all available packages of responding the package with the highest value and that the baseline package represents the package of the highest possible value or utility. The value of a package of responding is assumed to be a function of the duration of each response in the set. Thus, for example, in a situation in which the three response categories i, c, and n are considered to be relevant, the value of the package of behaviors V would be given by the following expression: $V = f(i, c, n)$. An increase in time spent on any of the response categories, other responses remaining constant, is assumed to increase the value of V. In addition, the value of V is assumed to be independent of the sequence of responses making up the package. For example, a package of 40 min of i and 40 min of c, which is made up by performing 10 cycles of the sequence, 4 min of i followed by 4 min of c, would be assumed to be equal in value to a package of 40 min of i and 40 min of c made up of 20 cycles of the sequence of 2 min of i followed by 2 min of c.

The model's predictions for the effects of a contingency schedule are generated by assuming that the outcome of a schedule is the point on the contingency restriction line that maximizes V. The exact form of the function V is assumed to depend on the degree to which the responses can substitute for each other, and many possible shapes have been considered in the articles by Rachlin and his colleagues. In any given situation, the eventual decision on the exact form of V has been based on the goodness of fit of the function's predictions with empirical data.

I have demonstrated that the value maximizing model can explain such varied phenomena as the bitonic response function observed with increasing fixed-ratio values, schedule-induced behaviors, and several assumed biological constraints on learning (Rachlin, 1981).

The Coupled Regulation Model

The coupled regulation model of schedule performance proposed by Hanson and Timberlake (1983) is another model that is based on optimality assumptions and can be considered a development of the relative response deprivation model that preceded it. However, whereas the relative response deprivation model assumed that schedule performance was controlled by the organism's need to maintain contingent responding at its baseline level in the face of environmental constraints that forced a relative deprivation of that response, the coupled regulation model assumes that the regulatory systems for both the instrumental response and the contingent response are important determinants of schedule performance. The model assumes that the outcome of a schedule that requires an amount of response i in excess of the paired baseline level for access to the baseline level of response c, is the result of a compromise between keeping the excess of response i to a minimum and the deficit of response c to a minimum.

Hanson and Timberlake (1983) translated these assumptions into a set of coupled differential equations, describing the two regulatory systems related by the schedule, and derived from these an equation that describes the function relating instrumental with contingent responding. The basic equation of the model (adapted from Equation 6 of Hanson & Timberlake, 1983) is as follows:

$$\left[bO_c - \frac{1}{O_i a_1} l \, nX - bX \right] + \left[\frac{O_i}{b} + \frac{1}{O_c a_2} l \, nY - \frac{Y}{b} \right] = c, \quad (7)$$

where X and Y are the amounts of time spent on the schedule performing the contingent and instrumental responses, respectively, and a, b, and c are empirical constants. Hanson and Timberlake (1983) described a_1 and a_2 as parameters that "scale the resistance of the two responses to increase" (p. 263) and b as "at least partly an index of the motivated association between the responses" (p. 263); c is a constant of integration.

Hanson and Timberlake (1983) were able to show that their model was capable of explaining many results usually explained by using the more traditional response strengthening theories, including experiments by Catania and Reynolds (1968), and Timberlake and Peden (described by Timberlake, 1980). Furthermore, they were able to show that both the conservation model (Allison, 1976) and the minimum distance model (Staddon, 1979) were special cases of the coupled regulation model; for this reason, the data quoted to support those two models could also be considered as supporting the coupled regulation model.

The Conservation Model

Like the optimality models previously discussed, the conservation model proposed by Allison (1976) attempts to predict the amounts of responding that occur when behaviors are constrained by a contingency schedule from the amounts that occur in the noncontingent baseline condition. However, unlike the optimality models, the conservation model does not assume that the baseline package of behaviors is an ideal state that animals attempt to maintain under schedule constraints. It merely assumes that different types of responding contribute to the total of a dimension and that this total is preserved across different types of sessions of the same duration.

Allison and his colleagues have proposed many different versions of the conservation model to explain situations of varying degrees of complexity. I describe these three versions and the evidence cited to support them.

The simplest version of conservation theory is the original one proposed by Allison (1976). This version proposed that each unit of instrumental and contingent responding contributes to the total of a dimension and that this total is the same in the baseline session in which both responses are freely and independently available as it is in sessions of the same duration involving contingencies between the two responses. By estimating the amount of the dimension attributable to each response type from empirical data, it is possible to predict the effects of a contingency by reallocating the total of the dimension used in the baseline session according to the constraints of the schedule. Thus,

$$kO_i + O_c = N(k1 + C),\qquad(8)$$

where k is a fitted constant representing the amount of the dimension used by one unit of response c relative to one unit of response i, calculated in the following way:

$$k = \frac{O_c - NC}{NI - O_i}.\qquad(9)$$

The model's prediction for the amount of instrumental responding that will be performed on a schedule requiring I units of one response to be performed to gain access to C units of another response is given as

$$NI = I\left(\frac{kO_i + O_c}{kI + C}\right).\qquad(10)$$

This version of the conservation model was shown by Allison et al. (1979) to be capable of accounting for the qualitative effects of schedules involving conditions of disequilibrium (response deprivation and response satiation) using a wide range of species and responses (e.g., Barofsky & Hurwitz, 1968; Bernstein & Ebbesen, 1978; Downs & Woods, 1975; Findlay, 1966; Heth & Warren, 1978; Logan, 1964; Marmaroff, 1971; Premack, Schaeffer, & Hundt, 1964; Rozin & Mayer, 1964; Teitelbaum, 1957; Timberlake & Allison, 1974) and to be capable of making accurate quantitative predictions for the effects of a variety of reciprocal fixed-ratio schedules (Allison, 1976).

However, the model's predictions for the effects of a number of reciprocal schedules, in experiments involving running and drinking by rats reported by Mazur (1975, 1977), were found to be too high. To overcome this problem, Allison et al. (1979) identified a feature of Mazur's experiments, the relatively large distance his animals had to traverse to switch between the two responses involved in the contingency, which they believed was responsible for the lower than predicted levels of schedule performance observed. They then proposed a modified version of the conservation model that assumed that the response of switching between the schedule responses should be considered as contributing to the total to be conserved of the unspecified dimension when predicting the outcome of a schedule.

The modified model's prediction for the amount of responding that would be performed by an animal on a schedule requiring I units of response i to be performed to gain access to C units of response c is given by the equation:

$$NI = \frac{I(kO_i + nj + O_c)}{kI + 2j + C},\qquad(11)$$

where n is the number of switches the animal makes between i and c in the paired baseline and j is a fitted constant representing the amount of the dimension used by one switch relative to a unit of response i. The constant j is calculated as follows:

$$j = \frac{k(O_i - NI) + O_c - NC}{2N - n}.\qquad(12)$$

This modified version of the conservation model was capable of explaining the problematic data reported in the studies by Mazur (1975, 1977).

The versions of the conservation model described predict a linear relationship between the level of instrumental and contingent responding produced by a schedule. However, many studies, including those of Barofsky and Hurwitz (1968), Greenwood et al. (1974), and Kelsey and Allison (1976), have reported bitonic functions. In order to explain these findings, Allison and Moore (1985) proposed that the conservation model be modified by including a term in the model for an unmeasured response that is assumed to be substituted for the contingent response as that response becomes less accessible owing to the high I/C ratio. This third response is also assumed to use the dimension to be conserved, but is assumed not to be performed in the baseline sessions. For example, Allison and Moore (1985) suggested that rats (at 80% of their free-feeding body weight) might substitute body fat for food pellets as the leverpressing requirement becomes demanding. Equation 13 expresses the revised conservation model in mathematical form:

$$J\left(\frac{I}{C}\right) + N(kI + C) = kO_i + O_c,\qquad(13)$$

where J is a constant representing the animal's readiness to substitute the third source of the dimension to be conserved. (No equation is given for

J because the constants in this version of the model were found by multiple regression.)

This equation implies that as *I/C* increases, the subject will be less prepared to work for the contingent response and will be more likely to use the substitutable alternative. This version of the conservation model has been fitted successfully to the data that presented problems for the original version of the conservation model.

Allison and Mack (1982) argued that the various forms of conservation theory have been successful in explaining instrumental responding under a wide range of schedule contingency conditions (Allison, 1976; Allison et al., 1979; Shapiro & Allison, 1978) and two kinds of excessive responding under noncontingent arrangements: schedule-induced polydipsia and autoshaped leverpressing.

Summary of Molar Regulatory Assumptions

I have considered six quantitative models that are based on molar regulatory assumptions and outlined some of the supporting evidence. It is clear from this brief summary that the models have many assumptions in common and might be readily considered to be variations on a theme rather than separate models. For example, all of the models adopt a response-based, as opposed to a stimulus-based, approach to the issue of reinforcement. That is, reinforcers are described as activities rather than as stimuli. For example, rather than describing a reinforcer as access to a running wheel, all of the models allow the opportunity to run for a specified period of time. This is not a trivial issue because the use of an activity- or response-based approach provides a metric for calibrating the value assigned to stimuli. Another assumption shared by all of these models is that animals and humans respond to molar features of the environment. That is, rather than considering single stimulus events to be the determinants of behavior, molar regulatory theories suggest that the rates (or relative rates) of events in the environment are the determinants of behavior and that these rates are perceived directly by the behaving organism. For example, consider the case of a schedule specifying a ratio of 1 min of running for access to 1 min of drinking; this specifies an overall ratio of 1:1 for these behaviors. Molar regulatory theorists assume that this ratio is perceived directly and that behavior is adjusted accordingly to optimize some aspect of responding. The alternative molecular approach is to assume that each 1-min bout of running is reinforced by each 1-min bout of drinking until stable levels of responding are achieved. The final feature that these models share is the view that some aspect of baseline responding is preferred and that subjects adjust their behavior under schedule constraints to approximate as closely as possible this preferred aspect of the paired baseline. For example, the relative response deprivation model (Timberlake & Wozny, 1979) assumes that it is the overall rates of both the instrumental and contingent responses that are the preferred aspect of responding and that subjects attempt to preserve this under schedule constraints. The conservation model (Allison et al., 1979) assumes that the two responses contribute to some unspecified dimension and that it is this dimension that is preserved under different constraints. Clearly, other features of paired baseline responding could be added to the various models. For example, a subject might not just have a preferred amount of the contingent response but might also have a preferred pattern of responding. For example, access to an uninterrupted 30 s of running might be more highly valued than access to 10 opportunities to run for 3 s, even though the total access time might be similar. Under some circumstances it might be necessary to include this additional feature of baseline responding in the model (but not always). The important point is not that different models consider different features of the paired baseline responding to be the determinant of schedule responding, but that they all share the assumption that some feature of the baseline is preferred and that this guides behavior under schedule constraints.

Despite the fact that these various models share at least three important features, in the literature on molar regulatory theories the emphasis has been on attempting to demonstrate that one particular variation on the common theme is superior to all others and not on demonstrating the utility of the general approach. This has resulted in the growth in complexity of the mathematical expressions used to generate predictions and, to some extent, an undermining of the overall approach. It must be said that to some extent the approach of attempting to demonstrate the superiority of one molar regulatory approach over all others is somewhat disingenuous, because this is usually achieved by evaluating a modified model specifically tailored to deal with a particular experimental situation and comparing this favored model's predictions with those of an unmodified alternative framework (e.g., Allison et al., 1979).

Although some of the evidence I have cited is derived from experiments that used human participants (e.g., Eisenberger et al., 1967), the bulk of it is derived from animal studies. This imbalance in the evidence has not hindered the application of molar regulatory principles to clinical situations. However, these clinical applications have usually been based on the simple response deprivation hypothesis rather than the more sophisticated quantitative elaborations of the approach. Nevertheless, the results of these clinical applications can perhaps be better understood using the more elaborate framework.

THE CURRENT STATUS OF MOLAR REGULATORY MODES

I have considered only the evidence that has been generally supportive of molar regulatory models. More recently, there has been an accumulation of evidence that, at face value, seems less than supportive. However, I argue that this evidence does not require an abandonment of the
entire molar regulatory approach, but merely a refinement and a clear specification of the range of application of particular models.

Baseline Maintenance

According to most of the models outlined earlier, the paired baseline
provides an adequate measure of the regulated aspect of responding. For
example, if a schedule is to be imposed for 1 hr, the overall levels of
instrumental and contingent responding during an unrestricted baseline
period of 1 hr is assumed to provide an adequate measure of the regulated
set point. However, some studies suggest that this may not always be the
case. Tierney, Smith, and Gannon (1983, 1987) reported three experiments
that tested, in different ways, the assumption that the total levels of instrumental and contingent responses represent an ideal that subjects attempt to defend under schedule constraints.

Tierney et al. (1983, 1987, Experiment 1) exposed rats to a reciprocal
fixed ratio for which $1/c = O_i/O_c$. Thus, these schedules permitted subjects
access to their paired baseline levels of the instrumental and contingent
responses, which were running in a wheel and drinking a saccharin or
sucrose solution. These schedules are referred to as either nondepriving or
equilibrium schedules. In both experiments, subjects performed less of both
responses than was observed in the paired baseline. Gawley, Timberlake,
and Lucas (1986) cast doubts on the results of the study described by
Tierney et al. (1983) by arguing that the baseline levels of responding were
too low for the subjects to make adequate contact with the schedule and
that because the schedules were specified in terms of times spent responding, the subjects could have achieved the amounts of responding observed
in the baseline by adjusting their rates of responding. However, neither of
these criticisms can be leveled at the Tierney et al. (1987) Experiment 1,
because female rats with high levels of baseline responding were used and
the schedules for two rats were specified in terms of the amounts of responding (i.e., number of licks and wheel turns).

Gawley et al. (1986) carried out an experiment similar to that of
Tierney et al. (1983, 1987, Experiment 1) and found that their subjects
did achieve baseline levels of responding on a nondepriving schedule. Unlike the subjects used by Tierney et al. (1983, 1987), those employed by
Gawley et al. (1986) were water deprived. On a priori grounds, water-
deprived rats might be expected to defend their fluid intake more vigor-

ously than nondeprived rats. However, molar regulatory theories have always been based on the assumption that baseline levels of responding are regulated and do not specify the condition under which such regulation takes place. If the models are to be applied to clinical situations, in which for ethical and legal reasons clients may not be deprived of commodities essential for survival, it will be necessary to specify the conditions under which totals of responding measured under unrestricted baseline conditions are regulated.

In the experiments just described, subjects had only to repeat sufficient repetitions of the instrumental response contingent response cycle to achieve their baseline level of responding. They could not deviate from the ratio of 1:C specified by the schedule. In Experiment 3 of Tierney et al. (1987), the responding of rats on a nondepriving schedule was allowed to deviate from the ratio specified by the schedule by allowing the subjects to overshoot the response requirements. The responses were drinking a sweetened solution and running in a wheel. One of the schedules allowed continuous access to the drinking tube throughout the session. When the schedule was imposed, the subject had to perform the drinking response for the required time to gain access to the running wheel, which remained unlocked until the response requirement had been completed. During the period of access to the wheel, the drinking tube remained available, but any drinking that occurred did not contribute to the next schedule requirement for drinking and therefore caused unnecessary deviation from the paired baseline ratio. The other schedule was similar, except that only the running wheel remained available throughout, allowing overshooting of the running response requirement. On both of these schedules, subjects deviated unnecessarily from their paired baseline levels of responding by overshooting the freely available response and obtaining less of the restricted response than they could have obtained for the amount of time spent on the unrestricted response. In a similar experiment (Allison, Buxton, & Moore, 1987) in which rats performed two different drinking responses, similar deviations from paired baseline responding were observed.

These experiments demonstrate that the total levels of the instrumental and contingent responses measured during a paired baseline session may not always be sufficient to capture the aspects of responding that are regulated under schedule constraints.

Temporal and Sequential Preferences

There is evidence that in addition to defending overall amounts of the instrumental and contingent responses on a schedule, subjects may also have preferred temporal and sequential distribution of bout sizes that are defended. For example, Tierney et al. (1987, Experiment 4) found that male rats responding on schedules that caused deprivation of drinking emit more overall responding on a schedule for which the ratio of running to drinking was 4:4 than when the ratio was 64:64. In a similar experiment (Tierney, 1986) involving female rats, who had much higher total baseline levels and average bout sizes of running, no such effect was found. Similar results were obtained by Kelsey and Allison (1976). Thus, despite the fact that these schedules specified the same run-to-drink ratio and hence at a molar level deviated similarly from the defended set point, they produced different outcomes. Furthermore, the outcome seemed to be related to the extent to which the pattern of responding in the baseline is disrupted by the schedule. Gawley et al. (1986) tested rats deprived of water for 23 hr on five versions of a nondepriving schedule involving running and drinking. They varied the size of the terms of the schedule while keeping the results constant. The results suggested that the total amounts of running and drinking (as opposed to time spent on these activities) are defended. However, there was also evidence of an attempt to regulate the baseline temporal distribution of responding.

From these studies it is clear that animals attempt to defend overall amounts of responding emitted in paired baseline conditions. However, they also appear to defend the local structure of responding. In some cases, such as the experiments described by Tierney et al. (1983, 1987) and Allison et al. (1987), the attempt to defend the molecular features of responding seems to compete with the attempt to defend overall amounts, whereas in others this effect is not so strong (e.g., Gawley et al., 1986). In this latter case, molar regulatory theory provides an adequate prediction of schedule responding, but in the former, the models may need to be modified to incorporate other aspects of responding along the lines indicated by Gawley et al. (1986). It does not seem possible to decide on a priori grounds whether predictions that are based on molar features of responding will be adequate, and it will be necessary to provide rules to guide such decisions. A possible candidate is the total amount of the response emitted in the baseline condition. It would seem reasonable to assume that a response that is emitted at a high rate in the baseline will be defended more vigorously than a low-frequency response and that in such an instance, the defense of molecular aspects of responding will be overridden. However, even this assumption is not always supported (Allison et al., 1987).

Time Frames

Timberlake, Gawley and Lucas (1987) have highlighted a related issue. In applying molar regulatory models of schedule responding, experimenters typically observe behavior during an operant baseline condition lasting between 30 and 60 min. The total amounts of the two responses during this period of time are then taken as the preferred levels that are defended while responding on a schedule over a similar period of time.

However, the arbitrary choice by an experimenter of a 30-min session does not compel the subjects to regulate behavior over this time frame. There is evidence that rats are capable of regulating behavior over 15-min periods under some circumstances but that they are incapable of regulating over longer periods.

Timberlake et al. (1987) used an anticipatory contrast experimental paradigm to study this issue. Essentially, this paradigm involves allowing animals access to two solutions, a less preferred one (saccharin) followed by a preferred one (sucrose). Given sufficient exposure to such a situation, it is observed that subjects will learn to suppress their consumption of the less preferred solution in anticipation of the preferred one. If the preferred solution follows the less preferred one after a brief temporal interval of, say, 5 min, consumption of the less preferred solution is considerably suppressed compared with a baseline condition in which the preferred solution is never presented. However, if the preferred solution is presented after 30 min, consumption of the less preferred solution is at the level observed in the baseline. This suggests that the time frame over which rats can integrate information about the availability of resources in the environment is between 15 and 30 min. There is clearly a need for similar work using human participants of different ability levels.

Sensitivity to Molar Variables

Ettinger, Reid, and Staddon (1987) argued that animals may be insensitive to molar features of schedules. Baum (1973) made the case that what he termed the *molar feedback function* provides an adequate description of the relationship between average response rates and average reinforcement rates enforced by a schedule. For ratio schedules, this relationship is very simple, and the feedback function is a straight line through the origin. For interval schedules, the feedback function also passes through the origin and is positively accelerated, with an asymptote at the scheduled maximum value. Many of the regulatory models incorporate the molar feedback function as a constraint on responding. Ettinger et al. (1987) argued that animals are insensitive to changes in the slopes of the functions describing some schedules and, on the basis of this, rejected the entire molar regulatory approach. They carried out two experiments. In Experiment 1, the schedules used were versions of an interlocking schedule. This is a fixed-ratio schedule that is decremented linearly as a function of postfood interval, generating positively sloped molar feedback functions. In Experiment 2, versions of a negatively sloped linear variable interval schedule (Vaughan & Miller, 1984) were used. These are variable interval schedules in which a reinforcement counter is incremented when each interval is completed and decremented after the completion of a fixed number of responses, generating a negatively sloped molar feedback function. It was observed in both experiments that animals were insensitive to the changes in the slope of these functions. Ettinger et al. (1987) proceeded to the general conclusion that animals in general are insensitive to such functions and that the molar regulatory approach is untenable. However, given the complex nature of the schedules used, it is perhaps not surprising that the feedback functions proved inadequate as descriptions. The study of visual perception has many examples of complex contrived stimuli producing visual illusions. However, it would be inappropriate to infer from these that people are incapable of responding appropriately to visual stimuli in their natural environments. Similarly, it would be inappropriate to infer that subjects in other situations are incapable of responding appropriately to changes in the slope of molar feedback functions on the basis of the results reported by Ettinger et al. (1987).

APPLICATIONS OF THE MOLAR REGULATORY APPROACH

Most of the applications derived from molar regulatory theory have been derived not from the quantitative models described earlier in this chapter, but from the response deprivation hypothesis itself. However, as I make clear later, these applications are entirely consistent with the molar regulatory approach, and the use of the more complex quantitative models would help to anticipate some of the problems encountered in using the simple response deprivation hypothesis in applied settings. Konarski and his colleagues have been largely responsible for pioneering the use of a regulatory approach to reinforcement in applied settings.

Educational Settings

In an early study, Konarski, Johnson, Crowell, and Whitman (1980) demonstrated that the response deprivation hypothesis may be used to predict accurately the effect of reinforcement contingencies for first graders performing academic tasks. In their study, the instrumental task increased in frequency when it followed the contingent task on a schedule that satisfied the response deprivation condition. These findings were replicated in a later study in which educable mentally retarded (EMR) children served as participants (Konarski, Crowell, Johnson, & Whitman, 1982). The responses used were performing math and reading tasks. For 3 children, reading served as the instrumental response; for the remaining child, performing math did so. For 2 children, the instrumental response had a higher probability than the contingent response, and for the remaining children, the probabilities were reversed. Using a reversal design, it was demonstrated that instrumental responding was increased by the contingency when the response deprivation condition was present but not when it was absent (i.e., for an equilibrium schedule). The increase in responding obtained for the children for whom the instrumental response was more probable than the contingent response was not consistent with predictions derived from Premack's (1965, 1971) probability differential hypothesis. These results suggest that educators do not need to rely on "known reinforcers" with EMR children but could potentially use any activity engaged in by the client, providing that appropriate contingency values are used.

In another study, Konarski, Crowell, and Duggan (1985) found that feedback on correct performance and reinforcement that was based on the response deprivation condition was superior to feedback alone in improving the writing skills of EMR children.

Konarski (1987) reported a study in which 20 adults with mental retardation served as participants. The experiment was laboratory based and was similar to the one reported by Heth and Warren (1978). Participants wer² allowed to engage in two activities: watching slides and listening to music. Two schedule requirements were established independently for each participant. One satisfied the response deprivation condition, and the other was a nondepriving, or equilibrium, schedule. Overall, the results supported the contention that instrumental responding is increased on schedules that satisfy the response deprivation condition and not on nondepriving schedules. Facilitation on schedules that satisfied the response deprivation condition was obtained even when the instrumental response was more probable than the contingent response. Although this study was laboratory based and used responses that were somewhat artificial, the relatively large number of participants used provides support for the view that the approach to reinforcement that is based on molar regulatory assumptions is promising.

In the studies just described, only a limited number of response alternatives were available to the participants. This is unlike the circumstances under which people with mental retardation are usually taught. In response to this consideration, Aeschleman and Williams (1989a) attempted to demonstrate that the response deprivation hypothesis may be used to develop effective contingencies for participants with mental retardation in multiple response environments. They used responses that occur in real-life settings and are therefore more ecologically valid than those employed by Konarski and his colleagues. The responses used included playing electronic games, coloring, doing puzzles, and playing with a toy truck. Contingencies were arranged between two activities that satisfied the response condition ($1/c > O_I/O_c$). In Phase 1, a high-probability alternative game was freely available throughout the session, whereas in Phase 2, a low-probability alternative response was available throughout. In general, the results supported the response deprivation hypothesis. Schedules that satisfied the response deprivation condition produced an increase in instrumental responding. However, the effect was attenuated in

Phase 1 when a high-probability alternative response was freely available. These results extended the application of the response deprivation condition to a multiple response environment using ecologically valid responses, but the effect of the freely available alternative response cannot be anticipated from the response deprivation hypothesis. However, this effect is entirely consistent with the general molar regulatory approach. Two of the models described earlier explicitly take into account the availability of alternative responses to the restricted contingent one: the maximization model (Rachlin, 1978) and the conservation model (Allison & Moore, 1985). According to the modified conservation model, the alternative substitutable response will be substituted for the schedule response in direct proportion to the degree to which the schedule ratio of the instrumental and contingent responses deviate from the baseline ratio and as a function of the substitutability of the response alternative. This model anticipated perfectly the results obtained by Aeschleman and Williams (1989a) and enables one to make additional predictions that may be evaluated empirically. For example, is the degree of substitution a function of the disequilibrium caused by the schedule? This model would also lead to the conclusion that Aeschleman and Williams (1989b) reached—that it makes sense to make a highly substitutable alternative to the instrumental response available during punishment conditions (response satiation) and unavailable during reinforcement schedules (response deprivation). Similar findings were reported by Dorio and Konarski (1989).

Clinical Settings

Dougher (1983) has pioneered the application of the response deprivation hypothesis in psychiatric settings. Two adults with diagnoses of schizophrenia participated in the study. In one condition, contingencies were arranged between appropriate verbalizations and coffee drinking that satisfied the response deprivation condition, with verbalizations as the instrumental response and coffee drinking as the contingent response. The result was an increase in appropriate verbalization. In a second condition, a contingency was arranged between inappropriate verbalizations and coffee drinking that satisfied the response satiation condition. Thus, the performance of baseline levels of inappropriate verbalizations led to a requirement that the subjects drink coffee in excess of the baseline levels. This contingency led to a decrease in the target verbalization. A punishment effect therefore may be obtained without the use of noxious stimuli, overcoming some of the objections to the use of punishment in applied settings.

More recently, O'Donohue, Plaud, and Hecker (1992) demonstrated that a positive reinforcement regimen consistent with the molar regulatory approach was effective in increasing time spent outside the home in a woman who had been agoraphobic and housebound for years.

The utility of the general molar regulatory approach in applied settings is hampered to some extent by the need to gather extensive baseline
data prior to deciding on contingency values. Working with intellectually
challenged people in institutional settings does not pose an insurmountable
problem, although it may be somewhat tedious. However, the problem of
gathering extensive baseline data in other settings could render the molar
disequilibrium approach unfeasible. Bernstein and Michael (1990) demonstrated that it is possible to develop a methodology for obtaining accurate verbal estimates of time spent in various activities, at least under laboratory conditions. In their study, 5 participants lived in a laboratory
apartment for up to 30 days and were given an opportunity to engage in
a range of recreational activities. It was observed that there was a reasonable correspondence between self-reports of time spent in the various activities and estimates that were based on experimenter observations. The
self-reports were obtained using a sliding scale mounted on a wooden frame
45 cm long. The scale was 20 cm long and labeled *none of the time* at the
left end and *all of the time* at the right. The verbal estimates corresponded
well to behavioral recordings, especially after participants had been given
an opportunity to engage in the activities. However, when there were discrepancies between the two measurements, the effects of contingencies
were better predicted using the response deprivation hypotheses and the
behavioral measures than using the verbal estimates. If this methodology
can be refined and transferred from the laboratory to real-life settings, it
will provide a convenient method of obtaining estimates of time spent in
various activities from which effective contingencies may be devised using
a molar regulatory approach.

Molar Regulation and Drug Effects

In addition to specifying conditions under which effective reinforcement conditioning may be devised, the molar regulatory approach draws
attention to the ecological context under which reinforcement occurs. Use
of the molar regulatory approach may provide a framework for understanding complex behavioral interactions in the natural environment. One example of this is the application of a simple regulatory model of feeding to
the study of pharmacological effects on feeding.

Ettinger and Staddon (1983) argued that responding on ratio schedules for food reinforcement is regulatory. As the work requirement increases, response rates typically increase to keep the food rate close to the
rate observed when food is freely available. A plot of response rate main-

tained by different schedules as a function of the resulting food rate is called a *response function*. These are usually bitonic with a long approximately linear segment of negative slope (Staddon, 1979). Over a limited range of schedule values they are entirely linear. Thus, feeding is regulated up to some value, after which the attempt to regulate breaks down. Ettinger and Staddon argued that a simple static regulatory model can explain the linear or regulated segment of the response function.

The static regulatory model is of the form, $X = G(Ro - Rx) + K$, which can be written as $X = GRo + K - GRx$. The equation is a straight line relating X and Rx, where X is response rate, Rx is the food rate, Ro is a constant representing the preferred food rate, G is the slope of the line representing the tendency to defend Ro, and K is a constant. Thus, response rate is assumed to be determined by the difference between Rx and Ro plus a constant. Changes in the slope of this function are assumed to reflect a change in motivation to defend the set point (regulatory gain); changes in the y-intercept, changes in the set point itself. Ettinger and Staddon (1983) found that manipulating body weight alters the slope of the function. Decreasing body weight increases the negative value of the slope, whereas decreasing palatability of the food decreases the y-intercept of such functions. This supports the contention that slope reflects regulatory gain, whereas y-intercept represents the incentive value of the food. A number of studies have shown that this model provides a useful paradigm for evaluating the effects of drugs (e.g., O'Hare, Shephard, & Tierney, 1991).

A study that is relevant to present considerations was reported by O'Hare (1993, Experiment 9). He evaluated the effects of the antidepressant desiprimine on the performance of animals responding on ratio schedules. The outcome of this study is presented in Figure 2. It can be seen that desiprimine elevated response rates at low schedule values, thus increasing the y-intercept, but suppressed the response ratio at higher schedule values. Thus, desiprimine increased the incentive value of food, thereby increasing the defended set point. However, desiprimine also decreased the tendency to defend that set point. These findings may shed light on the frequent observation that tricyclic antidepressants increase consumption and body weight in some patients, but not all (Paykel, Meuller, & de la Vergne, 1973). Traditionally, it has been assumed that such effects reflect individual differences. However, the results of O'Hare's study suggest that the effect of drugs depends on the context in which they are administered. In the case of rats, desiprimine increases food consumption when food is readily and cheaply available, but not when it is expensive. Although caution is required in extrapolating from laboratory studies of animals to humans in real-life settings, it may be safely concluded that to understand the effects of drugs and other variables on behavior in the natural environment, the ecological context in which such interactions take place must

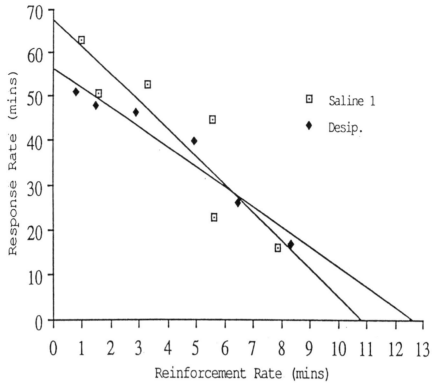

Figure 2. Response functions following exposure to saline and 1.0 mg/kg desiprimine. The mantissa is scaled in responses per minute and the abscissa in reinforcers per minute. Multiple correlations, slopes, and reinforcement rate intercepts were obtained from least squares linear regressions of the data points representing the means of subjects responding on each schedule value. For saline, these were 0.80, −6.16, and 10.87, respectively; for desiprimine, they were 0.94, −4.49, and 12.57, respectively. From *A Psychopharmacological Evaluation of the Cyclic-Ratio Schedule Methodology* by E. O'Hare, 1993, Unpublished doctoral dissertation. Reprinted with permission.

be taken into account. Molar regulatory theories specifically draw attention to this issue and provide a framework that may be used to anticipate and evaluate such interactions.

SUMMARY

Molar regulatory theory is a recent and promising alternative to the empirical law of effect. Models derived from this approach deal with data that cannot adequately be explained using either the empirical law of effect or the forerunner to the molar regulatory approach, Premack's (1965, 1971) probability differential hypothesis. There are a number of outstanding issues or problems that remain to be resolved. These include the extent to which sequential and molecular features of baseline responding are regulated, the nature of the response interactions in multiple response environments, and the time frame over which regulation takes place. It is unlikely that a model will ever be developed that can accommodate all of these issues, and if one were to be developed, it would be too complex and unwieldy to be of use in clinical settings. A more pragmatic objective would be to develop a set of guidelines that indicate when these issues need to be taken into account and the development of specific models to deal with these issues.

It has been demonstrated that the regulatory approach to reinforcement has made some useful and novel contributions to clinical work. Reinforcement and punishment are dealt with within a single framework in a manner that overcomes ethical objections to the use of conventional deprivation procedures and the use of noxious stimuli. The approach can be used in a predictive sense and can be specifically tailored to the needs of the individual. There has been an increasing awareness of the context in which behavior occurs. The regulatory approach specifically explains the context and provides a model for understanding and evaluating behavioral interactions in multiple response environments.

REFERENCES

Aeschleman, S. R., & Williams, M. L. (1989a). A test of the response deprivation hypothesis in a multiple-response context. *American Journal on Mental Retardation, 93,* 345–353.

Aeschleman, S. R., & Williams, M. L. (1989b). Rebuilding burned bridges: Analysis returns to applied behavior analysis. *American Journal on Mental Retardation, 93,* 367–372.

Allison, J. (1971). Microbehavioral features of nutritive and non-nutritive drinking in rats. *Journal of Comparative and Physiological Psychology, 76,* 408–417.

Allison, J. (1976). Contrast, induction, facilitation, suppression and conservation. *Journal of the Experimental Analysis of Behavior, 25,* 185–199.

Allison, J. (1979). Demand economics and experimental psychology. *Behavioral Science, 24,* 403–417.

Allison, J. (1981). Economics and operant conditioning. In P. Harzem & M. Zeiler (Eds.), *Advances in the study of behavior* (Vol. 2, pp. 321–353). New York: Wiley.

Allison, J., Buxton, A., & Moore, K. E. (1987). Bliss points, stop lines and performance under schedule constraints. *Journal of Experimental Psychology: Animal Behavior Processes, 4,* 331–340.

Allison, J., & Mack, R. (1982). Polydipsia and autoshaping: Drinking and lever-pressing as substitutes for eating. *Animal Learning and Behavior, 10,* 465–475.

Allison, J., Miller, M., & Wozny, M. (1979). Conservation in behavior. *Journal of Experimental Psychology: General, 108,* 4–34.

Allison, J., & Moore, K. E. (1985). Lick-trading by rats: On the substitutability of dry, water and saccharin tubes. *Journal of the Experimental Analysis of Behavior, 43,* 195–213.

Allison, J., & Timberlake, W. (1974). Instrumental and contingent saccharin licking in rats: Response deprivation and reinforcement. *Learning and Motivation, 5,* 231–247.

Barofsky, I., & Hurwitz, D. (1968). Within ratio responding during fixed ratio performance. *Psychonomic Science, 11,* 263–264.

Baum, W. M. (1973). The correlational based law of effect. *Journal of the Experimental Analysis of Behavior, 20,* 137–153.

Bernstein, D. J., & Ebbesen, E. B. (1978). Reinforcement and substitution in humans: A multiple response analysis. *Journal of the Experimental Analysis of Behavior, 30,* 243–253.

Bernstein, D. J., & Michael, R. L. (1990). The utility of verbal and behavioral assessments of value. *Journal of the Experimental Analysis of Behavior, 54,* 173–184.

Burkhard, B., Rachlin, H., & Schrader, S. (1978). Reinforcement and punishment in a closed system. *Learning and Motivation, 9,* 392–410.

Catania, A. C., & Reynolds, G. S. (1968). A quantitative analysis of the responding maintained by interval schedules of reinforcement. *Journal of the Experimental Analysis of Behavior, 11,* 327–383.

Collier, G., Hirsch, E., & Hamlin, P. H. (1972). The ecological determinants of reinforcement in the rat. *Physiology and Behavior, 9,* 705–716.

Dorio, M. S., & Konarski, E. A., Jr. (1989). Effects of a freely available response on the schedule performance of mentally retarded persons. *American Journal on Mental Retardation, 93,* 373–379.

Dougher, M. J. (1983). Clinical effects of response deprivation and response satiation procedures. *Behavior Therapy, 14,* 286–298.

Downs, D. A., & Woods, J. H. (1975). Fixed ratio escape and avoidance from naloxone in morphine dependent monkeys. *Journal of the Experimental Analysis of Behavior, 23,* 415–427.

Dunham, P. (1977). The nature of reinforcing stimuli. In W. K. Honig & J. E. R. Staddon (Eds.), *Handbook of operant behavior* (pp. 98–124). Englewood Cliffs, NJ: Prentice Hall.

Eisenberger, R., Karpman, M., & Trattner, J. (1967). What is the necessary and sufficient condition for reinforcement in the contingency situation? *Journal of Experimental Psychology, 74,* 342–350.

Ettinger, R. H., Reid, A. K., & Staddon, J. E. R. (1987). Sensitivity to molar feedback functions: A test of molar optimality theory. *Journal of Experimental Psychology: Animal Behavior Processes*, *4*, 366–375.

Ettinger, R. H., & Staddon, J. E. R. (1983). Operant regulation of feeding: A static analysis. *Behavioral Neuroscience*, *97*, 639–653.

Findley, J. D. (1966). Programmed environments for the experimental analysis of human behavior. In W. K. Honig (Ed.), *Operant behavior: Areas of research and application*. New York: Appleton-Century-Crofts.

Gawley, D. J., Timberlake, W., & Lucas, G. A. (1986). Schedule constraint on the average drink burst and the regulation of wheel running and drinking in rats. *Journal of Experimental Psychology: Animal Behavior Processes*, *12*, 78–94.

Greenwood, M. R. C., Quartermain, D., Johnson, P. R., Cruce, J. A. F., & Hirsch, J. (1974). Food motivated behavior in genetically obese and hypothalamic hyperphagic rats. *Physiology and Behavior*, *13*, 687–692.

Hanson, S. J., & Timberlake, W. (1983). Regulation during challenge: A general model of learned performance under schedule constraint. *Psychological Review*, *90*, 261–282.

Heth, C. D., & Warren, A. G. (1978). Response deprivation and response satiation as determinants of instrumental performance. *Animal Learning and Behavior*, *6*, 294–300.

Hirsch, E., & Collier, G. (1974). The ecological determinants of reinforcement in the guinea pig. *Physiology and Behavior*, *12*, 239–249.

Holstein, S. B., & Hunt, A. (1965). Reinforcement of intracranial brain stimulation by licking. *Psychonomic Science*, *3*, 17–18.

Hundt, A. G., & Premack, D. (1963). Running as both a positive and negative reinforcer. *Science*, *142*, 1087–1088.

Kazdin, A. E. (1984). *Behavior modification in applied settings* (3rd ed.). Homewood, IL: Dorsey Press.

Kelsey, J. E., & Allison, J. (1976). Fixed-ratio lever pressing by VMH rats: Work vs. accessibility of sucrose reward. *Physiology and Behavior*, *17*, 749–754.

Konarski, E. A., Jr. (1987). Effects of response deprivation on the instrumental performance of mentally retarded persons. *American Journal of Mental Deficiency*, *5*, 537–542.

Konarski, E. A., Jr., Crowell, C. R., & Duggan, L. M. (1985). The use of response deprivation to increase the academic performance of EMR students. *Applied Research in Mental Retardation*, *6*, 15–31.

Konarski, E. A., Crowell, C. R., Johnson, M. R., & Whitman, T. L. (1982). Response deprivation, reinforcement and instrumental academic performance in an EMR classroom. *Behavior Therapy*, *13*, 94–102.

Konarski, E. A., Jr., Johnson, M. R., Crowell, C. R., & Whitman, T. L. (1980). Response deprivation and reinforcement in applied settings: A preliminary analysis. *Journal of Applied Behavior Analysis*, *13*, 595–609.

Logan, F. A. (1964). The free behavior situation. In D. Levine (Ed.), *Nebraska Symposium on Motivation* (Vol. 12, pp. 99–128). Lincoln: University of Nebraska Press.

Marmaroff, S. (1971). *Reinforcement: A test of Premack's differential probability rules.* Unpublished master's thesis, Dalhousie University, Halifax, Nova Scotia, Canada.

Mazur, J. E. (1975). The matching law and quantifications related to the Premack principle. *Journal of Experimental Psychology: Animal Behavior Processes, 11,* 374–386.

Mazur, J. E. (1977). Quantitative studies of reinforcement relativity. *Journal of the Experimental Analysis of Behavior, 25,* 137–149.

Meehl, P. E. (1950). On the circularity of the law of effect. *Psychological Bulletin, 45,* 52–75.

O'Donohue, W., Plaud, J. J., & Hecker, J. E. (1992). The possible function of positive reinforcement in home-bound agoraphobia: A case study. *Journal of Behavior Therapy and Experimental Psychiatry, 23,* 303–312.

O'Hare, E. (1993). *A psychopharmacological evaluation of the cyclic-ratio schedule methodology.* Unpublished doctoral dissertation, University of Ulster, Jordanstown, Ireland.

O'Hare, E., Shephard, R. A., & Tierney, K. J. (1991). Cyclic-ratio analysis of a serotonin agonist and depletor on consummatory behavior. *Physiology and Behavior, 49,* 331–334.

Paykel, E. S., Meuller, P. S., & de la Vergne, P. M. (1973). Amitriptyline, weight gain and carbohydrate craving: A side effect. *British Journal of Psychiatry, 3,* 501–507.

Porter, J. H., Allen, J. D., & Arazie, R. (1974). Reinforcement frequency and body weight as determinants of motivational performance in hypothalamic hyperphasic rats. *Physiology and Behavior, 13,* 627–632.

Postman, L. (1947). The history and present status of the law of effect. *Psychological Bulletin, 44,* 489–563.

Premack, D. (1959). Towards empirical behavior laws: 1. Positive reinforcement. *Psychological Review, 66,* 219–233.

Premack, D. (1962). Reversibility of the reinforcement relation. *Science, 136,* 255–257.

Premack, D. (1963). Rate-differential reinforcement in monkey manipulation. *Journal of the Experimental Analysis of Behavior, 6,* 81–89.

Premack, D. (1965). Reinforcement theory. In D. Levine (Ed.), *Nebraska Symposium on Motivation* (Vol. 13, pp. 123–180). Lincoln: University of Nebraska Press.

Premack, D. (1971). Catching up with common sense, or two sides of a generalisation: Reinforcement and punishment. In R. Glaser (Ed.), *The nature of reinforcement.* San Diego, CA: Academic Press.

Premack, D., Schaeffer, R. W., & Hundt, A. (1964). Reinforcement of drinking by running: Effect of fixed ratio and reinforcement time. *Journal of the Experimental Analysis of Behavior, 6,* 91–96.

Rachlin, H. (1978). A molar theory of reinforcement schedules. *Journal of the Experimental Analysis of Behavior, 30,* 345–360.

Rachlin, H. (1981). Learning theory in its niche. *Behavioral and Brain Sciences, 4,* 155–156.

Rachlin, H., Battalio, R., Kage, J., & Green, L. (1981). Maximization theory in behavioral psychology. *Behavioral and Brain Sciences, 4,* 371–388.

Rachlin, H., & Burkhard, B. (1978). The temporal triangle: Response substitution in instrumental conditioning. *Psychological Review, 85,* 22–47.

Rachlin, H., Kagel, J. H., & Battalio, R. C. (1980). Substitutability in time allocation. *Psychological Review, 87,* 355–374.

Rachlin, H., & Krasnoff, J. (1983). Eating and drinking: An economic analysis. *Journal of the Experimental Analysis of Behavior, 39,* 385–404.

Rozin, P., & Mayer, J. (1964). Some factors influencing short-term intake of the goldfish. *American Journal of Physiology, 206,* 1430–1436.

Schaeffer, R. W., Hanna, B., & Rousso, P. (1966). Positive reinforcement: A test of the Premack theory. *Psychonomic Science, 4,* 7–8.

Shapiro, N., & Allison, J. (1978). Conservation, choice, and the concurrent fixed-ratio schedule. *Journal of the Experimental Analysis of Behavior, 29,* 211–223.

Skinner, B. F. (1938). *The behavior of organisms.* New York: Appleton-Century Crofts.

Spence, K. W. (1956). *Behavior theory and conditioning.* New Haven, CT: Yale University Press.

Staddon, J. E. R. (1979). Operant behavior as adaptation to constraint. *Journal of Experimental Psychology: General, 108,* 48–67.

Teitelbaum, P. (1957). Random and food-directed activity in hyperphagic and normal rats. *Journal of Comparative and Physiological Psychology, 50,* 486–490.

Tierney, K. J. (1986). *Some tests of molar regulatory models of instrumental performance.* Unpublished doctoral dissertation, Trinity College, Dublin, Ireland.

Tierney, K. J., Smith, H. V., & Gannon, K. N. (1983). Effects of switching rate and change-over requirement on performance on nondepriving schedules. *Journal of Experimental Psychology: Animal Behavior Processes, 9,* 281–291.

Tierney, K. J., Smith, H. V., & Gannon, K. N. (1987). Some tests of molar models of instrumental performance. *Journal of Experimental Psychology: Animal Behavior Processes, 13,* 341–353.

Timberlake, W. (1980). A molar equilibrium theory of learned performance. In G. H. Bower (Ed.), *The psychology of learning and motivation* (Vol. 14, pp. 1–58). San Diego, CA: Academic Press.

Timberlake, W. (1984). Behavior regulation and learned performance: Some misapprehensions and disagreements. *Journal of the Experimental Analysis of Behavior, 41,* 355–374.

Timberlake, W., & Allison, J. (1974). Response deprivation: An empirical approach to instrumental performance. *Psychological Review, 81,* 146–164.

Timberlake, W., Gawley, D. J., & Lucas, G. A. (1987). Anticipatory contrast as a measure of time horizons in the rat. *Animal Learning and Behavior, 16,* 377–382.

Timberlake, W., & Wozny, M. (1979). Reversibility of reinforcement between eating and running by schedule changes: A comparison of modules. *Animal Learning and Behavior, 7,* 461–469.

Vaughan, W., Jr., & Miller, H. L. (1984). Optimization or response-strength accounts of behavior. *Journal of the Experimental Analysis of Behavior, 42,* 337–348.

5

THE MATCHING LAW
AS A THEORY OF CHOICE
IN BEHAVIOR THERAPY

JAMES P. NOLL

Although the definition of behavior therapy has been debated for nearly 40 years, most definitions concur that behavior therapy concentrates on the current determinants of behavior (e.g., O'Leary & Wilson, 1987). Moreover, Skinner (1974, p. 125) stated that "to exercise a choice is simply to act." One may argue by extrapolation that behavior therapy concerns the current determinants of choice behavior. Many have conceded that reinforcers are available concurrently in applied settings (e.g., Fuqua, 1984; Myerson & Hale, 1984). However, consider the choice situation: A person may have a variety of behaviors that he or she may choose to perform, which in turn may produce qualitatively different reinforcers with different associated magnitudes and delays. Furthermore, each possible behavior may have a different schedule of reinforcement associated with it. How then do behavior therapists begin to unravel this complex interaction of the determinants of choice behavior in the applied setting? Operant research conducted from the 1960s to the present may help the behavior therapist clarify the determinants of choice behavior.

Although Tolman (1932, 1938) began to systematically study instrumental choice behavior in the 1930s, Skinner conducted the initial operant studies of choice behavior approximately 15 years later. Skinner (1950) exposed pigeons to two keys in a standard operant conditioning chamber. He found that when responding to both keys was occasionally reinforced, response rates were equal on both keys and that subjects generally alternated rapidly from key to key. When reinforcement was given only for responding to one of the keys, the response rate to the key associated with reinforcement increased, while the response rate to the key associated with no reinforcement decreased. Moreover, the rate of alternating between the keys decreased. Skinner then switched the keys in terms of which one was associated with reinforcement and which one was not. The same pattern of results was obtained. This indicated that an inverse proportionality in responding was present, in that responding to one key was a function of reinforcement associated with the other key. This finding is significant because Skinner (1938) found earlier that, in single-key procedures, increases in response rates following extinction were greater than decreases in response rates during extinction; that is, no inverse proportionality existed. Thus, the behavior of subjects in a choice situation may be fundamentally different from behavior observed in a single-choice situation. This finding also implies that the allocation of behavior changes as a function of alternative sources of reinforcement. However, the exact nature of the way in which the allocation of behavior changes remains elusive.

THE MATCHING LAW

The Strict Matching Law

Herrnstein (1961) began to elucidate the nature of operant choice behavior. In Herrnstein's study, two keys were concurrently available to pigeon subjects in an operant conditioning chamber. Changes in response frequency were observed to be a function of changes in reinforcement frequency. Herrnstein found that the relative response frequencies approximately equalled, or "matched," the relative reinforcement frequencies. In other words, the percentage of responding matched the percentage of reinforcement. This relationship is described in Equation 1,

$$\frac{R_1}{R_1 + R_2} = \frac{r_1}{r_1 + r_2}, \tag{1}$$

where R is the frequency of response and r is the frequency of reinforcement for response alternatives 1 and 2. If the relative response frequency is plotted against the relative reinforcement frequency (see Figure 1), a theoret-

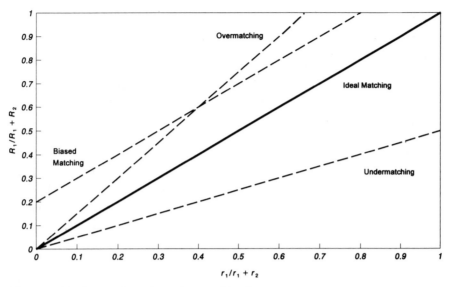

Figure 1. Deviations from the strict matching law.

ical line (or matching line) with an intercept of 0 and a slope of 1 would indicate that the relative frequency of response equals or matches the relative frequency of reinforcement. Undermatching occurs when the value of the slope estimate is less than 1 (Baum, 1974, 1979). Undermatching indicates that the subject is responding more to the leaner alternative. Likewise, overmatching occurs when the value of the slope is greater than 1 (Baum, 1974, 1979). Overmatching indicates that the subject is responding more to the richer alternative. Bias is indicated when the value of the intercept deviates from 0 (Baum, 1974, 1979). Bias is unaccounted for preference where there is an asymmetry in responding that leads to one alternative's being preferred over others independently of reinforcement. Thus, when reinforcement rates are equal, bias indicates the magnitude of preference (Baum, 1974). Herrnstein found that with the three pigeons studied, there was, in the worst case, an 8% deviation from Equation 1 (or the *strict matching law*, as it is often called).

Consider what Equation 1 implies. First, the allocation of behavior may be quantitatively described. Thus, more precise predictions regarding the actual magnitude of change can be made, as compared with simple qualitative predictions. Second, the relation shows how behavior in the choice situation is different from behavior in a single-choice situation. Third, and perhaps most importantly for behavior therapists, the allocation of a given behavior may be a function of reinforcement associated with other behaviors. Thus, relative rather than absolute rates of reinforcement are important. For example, the frequency of smoking may be decreased by increasing the frequency of reinforcement associated with other behaviors. Likewise, the frequency of exercising may be increased by decreasing the frequency of reinforcement associated with other behaviors. Clinically speaking, generalization of changes obtained during treatment may occur because of the potential for optimizing the behavior of interest across settings and time (Martens & Houk, 1989; McDowell, 1982).

Herrnstein's Hyperbola

Behavior therapists may be concerned with the frequency of only one behavior. Moreover, the measurement of the myriad of potential alternative sources of reinforcement may be pragmatically limiting (Fuqua, 1984). Fortunately, Equation 1 may be algebraically derived for the single-alternative case (Herrnstein, 1970). This derivation is described in Equation 2 (often termed *Herrnstein's hyperbola*),

$$R_1 = \frac{kr_1}{r_1 + r_e},\qquad(2)$$

where R_1 is the rate of responding for the behavior of interest, r_1 is the rate of reinforcement for the behavior of interest, r_e is the rate of reinforcement for extraneous (free or noncontingent) sources of reinforcement, and k is an empirically derived constant, usually interpreted as the maximal rate of responding (e.g., McDowell, 1982, 1988). The parameter k indicates the maximal amount of responding an individual can exhibit. The parameter r_e indicates the rapidity at which an individual reaches the maximal level of responding. Thus, r_e determines the shape of the hyperbola (see Figure 2).

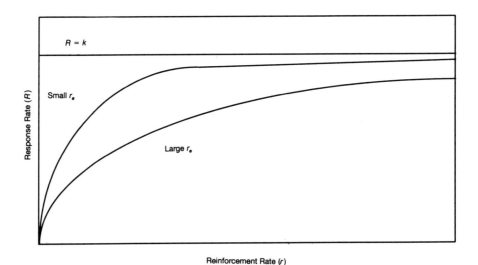

Figure 2. Herrnstein's hyperbola.

With small values of r_e relative to r_1, maximal responding will be reached quickly, and r_1 will have much more impact on the behavior of interest as compared to other sources of reinforcement (a "lean" environment). On the other hand, with large values of r_e relative to r_1, maximal responding will be reached more slowly and r_1 will have much less impact on the behavior of interest as compared to other sources of reinforcement (a "rich" environment). In addition, Equation 2 predicts two treatments for increasing desired behavior or decreasing problem behavior that the law of effect cannot (McDowell, 1981): (a) increasing extraneous reinforcement and (b) increasing the reinforcement rate for an alternative behavior. (Note that this is not necessarily differential reinforcement of incompatible behavior or differential reinforcement of other behavior; see next section.)

RESEARCH

Although there is some research examining concurrent schedules performance with human subjects in the laboratory (for reviews and bibliographies, see Bradshaw & Szabadi, 1988; Bukist & Miller, 1982; Dougherty, Nedelmann, & Alfred, 1993; Pierce & Epling, 1983), studies that have been conducted in applied settings will be described in this section. Studies involving the use of differential reinforcement of other behavior (DRO) schedules in applied settings will not be examined. Although some have considered DRO schedules to approximate concurrent schedules and the matching relation (e.g., Martens & Houk, 1989), concurrent and DRO schedules are fundamentally different (McDowell, 1988). With DRO schedules, a reinforcer is delivered after some specified interval in the absence of the target behavior. However, when reinforcement occurs under concurrent schedules, a contingency is constructed for the nontarget behavior: Reinforcers are delivered, regardless of the status of the target behavior. In this case, the target behavior is affected by altering the context in which the behavior results, as the matching law predicts (McDowell, 1988). In addition, applied studies using differential reinforcement of incompatible behavior (DRI) procedures will not be reviewed. Response alternatives may be incompatible, but that point is not what is at issue here (McDowell, 1981). What is important is that choice is a function of relative reinforcement rates rather than the compatibility of responses. A pigeon may choose to peck one key or another. Pecking both keys at the same time is incompatible. Similarly, working on math problems is incompatible with out-of-seat behavior. Both the pigeon and the child have the choice to respond to either response alternative, but the allocation of behavior is a function of relative reinforcement rates rather than the pragmatic compatibility of response alternatives.

The first description of the matching law in an applied setting was conducted by McDowell (1981) using Carr and McDowell's (1980) data. The subject was an 11-year-old boy who exhibited self-injurious scratching. The rates of scratching and contingent verbal reprimands were recorded by observers in the boy's living room while he was watching television. Using the data from this study, McDowell (1981) examined the fit of Equation 2 to the scratching behavior of the boy (R_1) and verbal reprimands (r_1). Equation 2 demonstrated a very good fit of the data, with 99.67% of the variance accounted for, k being equal to 256.35 scratches per hour and r_e equal to 50.04 reprimands per hour. The analysis of percentage of variance accounted for is usually conducted in order to estimate the fit of the observed data to the data path as predicted by the matching law. Thus, percentage of variance accounted for gives a suggestion of how well the observed data conform to the matching law. (However, as Davison and McCarthy, 1988, have indicated, percentage of variance accounted for may not be a good measure of the matching law because this statistic varies with the slope estimate.) These results were taken to indicate that the matching law is capable of describing human behavior in an applied setting. Moreover, the large value of r_e indicates that the living room constituted a "rich" environment and, thus, that extraneous sources of reinforcement may have been affecting the boy's scratching behavior as compared to verbal reprimands. However, it should be emphasized that McDowell's (1981) analysis did not involve the manipulation of reinforcement contingencies. More definitive statements regarding the applicability of the matching law to human behavior in the applied setting require experimental manipulation.

Martens and Houk (1989) conducted a study in which an 18-year-old woman who was developmentally disabled displayed disruptive and autisticlike movements (e.g., repetitive hand flapping). The behavioral observation system consisted of mutually exclusive and exhaustive categories for the subject (on-task, disruptive) and for the teaching staff or peers (instruction, praise, reprimand, proximity, attention to others, nonassigned contact). After a baseline condition was determined, conditions in which the teacher was present and in which the teacher's aide was present were assessed. Reinforcement was defined as "any staff or peer behavior that (a) was directed toward the subject, (b) occurred while the subject was engaged in an activity, and (c) was significantly and positively correlated with total duration of that activity" (Martens & Houk, 1989, p. 20). The researchers recognized that this definition of reinforcement approximated a functional relationship and may have included other behavior–environment interactions (e.g., staff behavior becoming a discriminative stimulus for the subject's behavior). However, the inclusion of staff behavior that overlapped with the subject's behavior may have precluded the inclusion of some of these potential interactions. Analyses of zero-order correlations then allowed for the identification of reinforcers.

The results indicated that instruction and proximity (r) were reinforcing disruptive and on-task behavior (R) in the teacher condition. In addition, instruction, praise, and proximity (r) were reinforcing disruptive behavior (R), and instruction (r) was reinforcing on-task behavior (R) in the aide condition. Because the category for subject behavior consisted of two mutually exclusive and exhaustive components, r_1 served as an estimate of r_e for the other response class. The results were mixed in terms of the degree of fit of Herrnstein's hyperbola (Equation 2) to the data. For disruptive behavior, an average of 83% of the variance was accounted for. Examination of slope and intercept values of logarithmic transformed data (Baum, 1974) indicated that these values did not differ significantly from 1 and 0, respectively. Obtained values of r_e were somewhat large, indicative of a rich environment for disruptive behavior. However, for on-task behavior, an average of 44% of the variance was accounted for. Values of r_e were small, indicative of a lean environment for on-task behavior. In addition, bias and undermatching were observed in the teacher condition.

Martens and Houk (1989) concluded that Herrnstein's hyperbola was capable of describing human behavior occurring in an applied setting. However, they attempted to reconcile the results of the on-task data. First, because of the leanness of the on-task environment, estimates of extraneous reinforcement may have been poor and therefore affected the ability of Equation 2 to fit the data accordingly. Thus, percentage of variance accounted for may have been limited because of the small variability in behavior observed in the on-task environment. Second, perceptual or self-reinforcement (e.g., Lovaas, Newsom, & Hickman, 1987) may have affected estimated values of r_e and the fit of Equation 2. Moreover, the researchers cautioned that, because of the correlational nature of the definition of reinforcement, some behavior–environment interactions that were not reinforcing may have been included in the analyses. The researchers did not comment on the undermatching observed in the on-task environment. Some have concluded that undermatching is more descriptive of human concurrent behavior compared to animal behavior (e.g., Bradshaw & Szabadi, 1988). Although the reasons for this discrepancy are unclear, Navarick and Chellsen (1983) noted that undermatching observed with humans may result from exposure to a limited range of schedule values. This appears to be the case in the Martens and Houk (1989) study, as evidenced by the small values of r_e in the on-task environment. Thus, a poor fit of the data may have resulted from exposure to a limited range of schedule values rather than from perceptual or self-reinforcement.

Martens, Lochner, and Kelly (1992, Experiment 1) conducted a study with experimental manipulation of reinforcement contingencies to assess the matching law in a classroom setting. In this study, two boys, aged 9 and 10, served as subjects. Both subjects were of average to above average intelligence, although they were identified by their teacher as being off-task for a majority of independent seat-work time and as exhibiting inappropriate behavior. A 10-s partial-interval sampling procedure was used to observe adult and peer behavior (i.e., teacher approval, teacher disapproval, individual instruction, group instruction, peer approach, experimenter approval) and subject behavior (i.e., out of seat, noise, vocalization, touching, playing, inactivity). Engagement of the subjects was assessed by means of a momentary time sampling procedure. A reinforcer consisted of the delivery of verbal praise by the experimenter on a variable interval basis. The variable interval schedule values were 2, 3, 4, and 5 min. Thus, the study constituted an ABCDE design across subjects (Martens et al., 1992). The logic behind this design is that changes observed in the dependent variable (behavior) will be a function of the introduction of the independent variable (treatment condition). In general, when behavior changes, it is assumed to be a function of the treatment procedure (Barlow & Hersen, 1984).

The results of the Martens et al. (1992) study indicated that Equation 2 accounted for the data well, with 99.1% of the variance accounted for in the behavior of one subject and 87.6% for in that of the other subject. Obtained values for r_e were small (6.9 and 1.0, respectively), indicative of a lean environment. However, as indicated by the researchers, there are limitations to the study. First, there was a small number of sessions per condition. Second, there were downward trends during the experimental conditions. Third, the ABCDE design is a quasiexperimental design, and definitive statements about the effectiveness of the reinforcement procedure cannot be made. In addition, it does not appear that the intervention phases were staggered across subjects. Thus, the generality of the results may be limited (Barlow & Hersen, 1984; Cooper, Heron, & Heward, 1987).

SUMMARY FOR THE CLINICAL APPLICATION OF THE MATCHING LAW

The first step in the application of the matching law to behavior in the applied setting is to identify the target behavior and what consequent event is reinforcing the target behavior. The identification of the reinforcing event may be difficult, but some applied researchers have used a correlational technique to identify reinforcers (Martens & Houk, 1989). Techniques that use the sequential analysis of contingent events may be useful also in the identification of operants (Gottman & Roy, 1990). Once the target behavior and associated reinforcer have been identified, the behavior and reinforcer may be observed in the applied setting. Response and reinforcement rates are then calculated for each observation session. The fit of the observed data to Equation 2 may be accomplished with the use of a hand calculator (Davison & McCarthy, 1988). The values of k and r_e are estimated by a reiterative process developed by Wilkinson (1961). With Wilkinson's method, the values of k and r_e are modified with a weighted least-squares method of variance reduction. Wilkinson's method also gives standard errors for k and r_e. In addition to percentage of variance accounted for, the standard errors of the parameter estimates give an indication of the degree of fit (Davison & McCarthy, 1988).

CRITICISMS

The primary criticism of the matching law in applied settings has been that behavior observed in the laboratory is not generally comparable with behavior observed in applied settings (Fuqua, 1984). The study of concurrent schedules in the laboratory has generally involved the use of a changeover delay (COD; de Villiers, 1977). A COD of 5 s means that if a subject were responding on the left key and then switched to the right key, responses to the right key would not satisfy the schedule requirement for reinforcement (if a reinforcer had been set up) until the first and second responses to the right key were separated by at least 5 s. Herrnstein (1961) used a concurrent procedure with a COD that has subsequently become used as a method for reducing rapid alternation between response alternatives (de Villiers, 1977). It has been argued that CODs are rarely explicit in applied settings (Fuqua, 1984). Thus, because the COD has been required, in general, to produce matching in the laboratory and because the COD is not explicit in applied settings, the utility of the matching relation has been questioned in the applied setting. It also has been argued that the existence of "naturally occurring" CODs would be "difficult to gather" (Fuqua, 1984, p. 382).

However, the role of the COD has been equivocal in terms of human choice behavior (Bradshaw & Szabadi, 1988; Horne & Lowe, 1993). Recent research involving the COD using human subjects has revealed some potential determinants of the COD on human choice behavior. Noll and Fisher (1993) exposed five adult subjects to symmetrical and asymmetrical CODs under concurrent variable-interval, 30-s schedules. The researchers found that through exposure to the CODs, the subjects began to switch among the alternatives after receiving reinforcement. For example, after receiving reinforcement associated with the left manipulandum, subjects switched to the right manipulandum. By the end of the experiment, subjects were switching between alternatives within 1 s after obtaining a reinforcer. These results suggest that reinforcement may serve as a discriminative stimulus for changing over in humans. It may be that, although reinforcement is commonly considered to be a consequent event, reinforcement is also an antecedent event in the flow of behavior. Likewise, when the temporal properties of the concurrent reinforcement schedules become discriminative stimuli for changing over, matching is expected. Therefore, the COD may not be required for producing matching in humans (e.g., Bradshaw & Szabadi, 1988). However, the idea that the COD may not be required for matching because reinforcement serves as a discriminative stimulus needs to be replicated in laboratory and applied settings.

Another criticism has been that topographically different responses would be difficult to measure by the matching law (Fuqua, 1984). According to this criticism, for example, how are smoking and exercising equated? Simply because of topography, the behaviors may have different values of the parameter k, or the maximal amount of responding. However, the response classes may be equated by creating a scaling factor (k') defined as the ratio of k associated with smoking to k associated with exercising. Thus, Equation 1 may be transformed into the following equation (Davison & McCarthy, 1988):

$$\frac{R_1}{R_1 + R_2} = \frac{k'r_1}{k'r_1 + r_2},\tag{3}$$

where R and r are as defined in Equation 1. In this manner, the scaling factor in Equation 3 allows smoking and exercising to be measured on the same scale by relating the measurement of smoking to the measurement of exercising. Therefore, the measurement of topographically different responses may be quantitatively handled by the matching law. In addition, research with animal subjects demonstrates that matching can be obtained with topographically different response classes (e.g., Davison & Ferguson, 1978). Furthermore, applied researchers have handled topographically different response classes by measuring time spent responding (duration) rather than response frequency (Martens & Houk, 1989). Although there is some debate on this issue (e.g., Bradshaw & Szabadi, 1988; de Villiers, 1977), response and time measures may be interchangeable under concurrent schedules of reinforcement (Baum & Rachlin, 1969; Herrnstein, 1979).

Similarly, asymmetry in responding (bias) may exist when response or reinforcer parameters are not equivalent. For example, responding may be biased toward smoking rather than exercising. As indicated earlier, the matching law affords equating asymmetries. The applied relevance of asymmetry is that bias is likely to be the rule rather than the exception in the applied setting (McDowell, 1989). However, the matching law is capable of describing such asymmetries.

Perhaps a more difficult criticism concerns the identification of reinforcers in the applied setting (Fuqua, 1984). Reinforcers in the applied setting may be conditioned, nondiscrete, or socially mediated. Although it is true that the matching law does not afford the clinician the specification of effective reinforcers before implementation, it does allow for the determination of behavioral allocation once effective reinforcers have been specified (Timberlake & Farmer-Dougan, 1991). As indicated above, qualitative or quantitative differences in reinforcers may be accounted for by the matching law (McDowell, 1989). The difficulty lies in the identification of reinforcers. As Martens and Houk (1989) demonstrated, reinforcers at least may be defined as a correlation between behavior and environmental events. Although this definition is not perfect, as it may include events that are not reinforcers (e.g., discriminative stimuli), it does provide a method for identifying potential reinforcers.

Another method for identifying reinforcers relies on the analysis of conditional probabilities (e.g., Gottman & Roy, 1990). In this manner, the direction of the relationship and the delay of reinforcement (i.e., lags) may be specified. Thus, the behavior and reinforcing event constitute a contingent event among sequential data. Moreover, for the analysis of contingent relationships in sequential data, several statistics have been proposed to account for observation sample size and base rates of behavior (Allison & Liker, 1982; Gottman, 1980).

Some have argued that the clinician is unconcerned with mathematical treatments of behavior and that they are too difficult (Cullen, 1981). Even basic researchers have questioned whether researchers are becoming bored with behavior and are becoming more interested in mathematical treatments (Ferster, 1978). This contrary attitude toward mathematical treatments of behavioral phenomena may reflect Skinner's criticisms (Marr, 1989). Mathematical analyses of behavior are not impeding research on socially relevant phenomena (Bradshaw & Szabadi, 1988; McDowell, 1988). Indeed, mathematical models of behavior, such as the matching law, are leading to the discovery of functional relationships.

DIRECTIONS FOR FUTURE RESEARCH

Symptom substitution (Kazdin, 1982) and side effects of reinforcement (McDowell, 1981; Sajwaj, Twardosz, & Burke, 1972) may be explained by the matching law. Symptom substitution implies that the elimination of a given problem or symptom without treating the underlying cause may produce a substitute problem or symptom (Kazdin, 1982). Although earlier debate on this issue produced extreme positions, most now agree that new behaviors or symptoms may result after treatment (Kazdin, 1982). However, these new behaviors may be negative or positive (Kazdin, 1982). New negative problems are what has traditionally been termed *symptom substitution*. New positive symptoms are what has constituted *treat-*

ment generalization. During treatment, changes in behavior, cognition, affect, and physiology may induce other changes in behavior, cognition, affect, and physiology. Thus, responses covary. Response covariation implies that responses are related in some way (Kazdin, 1982).

Response covariation may be explained by the matching law if all covarying responses are included in the analysis (i.e., all covarying responses are contained in the denominator of Equation 2). But herein lies the difficulty. How can clinicians determine which responses cluster together or covary? The symptom substitution and generalizability problem appears to imply that the matching law may be limited with respect to response clusters. For example, smoking may be a function of the physiological reinforcement of nicotine, peer approval, group identification, and so on. However, an unrelated behavior such as working on math problems may be a function of academic achievement, teacher approval, parent approval, and so on. In this manner, each behavior constitutes a different response class or cluster that will have a different matching relation associated with it. This relationship may be described in the equations,

$$R_1 = \frac{k_1 r_1}{r_1 + (r_a + r_b + \ldots + r_g) + r_e}, \text{ and} \tag{4}$$

$$R_2 = \frac{k_2 r_2}{r_2 + (r_s + r_t + \ldots + r_z) + r_{e'}}, \tag{5}$$

where R and r are as defined in Equation 2. Variables in parentheses are reinforcement rates associated with covarying responses. Equations 4 and 5 are derivatives of Herrnstein's (1970) equation for an environment containing n sources of reinforcement,

$$R_1 = \frac{k r_2}{\sum_{i=0}^{n} r_i},$$

where R and r are as defined in Equation 2. Notice that the denominators of Equations 4 and 5 contain different covarying responses. Moreover, extraneous reinforcement will differ between the two equations (r_e and $r_{e'}$). This property implies that increasing extraneous reinforcement would not necessarily decrease the response rate of a target behavior unless the reinforcement were reliably associated with a behavior within the response cluster. The formal properties of the matching law may not differ between the response clusters (i.e., each target behavior will still be a function of relative reinforcement rates); however, the constituent events will differ. Thus, altering the reinforcement rates for a behavior not within a cluster will not affect the response rate of the target behavior. Likewise, altering the reinforcement rates for a behavior within a cluster will affect the response rate of the target behavior. In this respect, lean and rich environments may have a different number of behaviors within their respective response clusters. This may explain poor fits of data in applied settings and good fits of data in laboratory settings: Applied settings probably are richer environments compared with laboratory settings. Furthermore, extraneous sources of reinforcement may be inadequately sampled in applied settings. Because applied settings are likely to be richer environments, more sources of extraneous reinforcement are likely to affect the target behavior. As it concerns the matching law, it would be beneficial to know what responses tend to cluster together or covary. If the potential number of constituent behaviors may be delimited, then the task of identifying associated reinforcers may become easier. As a result, better experimental control and fits of data would be expected.

The applied relevance of the matching law may rest on defining an appropriate taxonomy of covarying responses. In lean environments where values of r_e are small, the delimiting of the covariation taxonomy may not be as difficult as it is in rich environments. Thus, research is required to determine which responses covary in applied settings. If clusters of covarying responses can be identified in applied settings, the matching law may prove to be more relevant than some have determined (Fuqua, 1984). The determination of the applied relevance of the matching is an empirical matter rather than a logical matter. It would be most beneficial to determine phenomena with which the matching law is compatible and incompatible, rather than condemning laboratory research as irrelevant (Fuqua, 1984) or lamenting the schism between laboratory and applied settings (Hayes, Rincover, & Solnick, 1980; Michael, 1980; Pierce & Epling, 1980).

CONCLUSION

In this chapter, I have endeavored to make the applied relevance of the matching law apparent. It should also now be clear to the behavior therapist that all behavior is choice behavior. According to the matching law, this conclusion is true. The allocation of behavior among alternatives is a function of relative reinforcement rates. This implies that the efficacy of behavior therapy is a function of altering relative reinforcement rates. Thus, client behavior changes because behavior therapists alter relative reinforcement rates such that the richer alternative is chosen. However, *richer* is a relative term and requires the analysis of other sources of reinforcement. The matching law affords the behavior therapist a method for quantitatively analyzing the impact of extraneous sources of reinforcement. Without assessing the impact of extraneous sources of reinforcement, especially in rich environments, the target behavior may not be affected by direct manipulation of reinforcers, and changes in behavior may not be evidenced.

REFERENCES

Allison, P. D., & Liker, J. K. (1982). Analyzing sequential categorical data on dyadic interaction. *Psychological Bulletin, 91,* 393–403.

Barlow, D. H., & Hersen, M. (1984). *Single case experimental designs* (2nd ed.). New York: Pergamon Press.

Baum, W. M. (1974). On two types of deviation from the matching law: Bias and undermatching. *Journal of the Experimental Analysis of Behavior, 22,* 231–242.

Baum, W. M. (1979). Matching, undermatching and overmatching in studies of choice. *Journal of the Experimental Analysis of Behavior, 32,* 269–281.

Baum, W. M., & Rachlin, H. C. (1969). Choice as time allocation. *Journal of the Experimental Analysis of Behavior, 12,* 861–874.

Bradshaw, C. M., & Szabadi, E. (1988). Quantitative analysis of human operant behavior. In G. Davey & C. Cullen (Eds.), *Human operant conditioning and behavior modification* (pp. 225–259). New York: Wiley.

Bukist, W. F., & Miller, H. L. (1982). The study of human operant behavior, 1958–1981: A topical bibliography. *Psychological Record, 32,* 249–268.

Carr, E. G., & McDowell, J. J. (1980). Social control of self-injurious behavior of organic etiology. *Behavior Therapy, 11,* 402–409.

Cooper, J. O., Heron, T. E., & Heward, W. L. (1987). *Applied behavior analysis.* Columbus, OH: Merrill.

Cullen, C. (1981). The flight to the laboratory. *The Behavior Analyst, 4,* 81–83.

Davison, M., & Ferguson, A. (1978). The effects of different component response requirements in multiple and concurrent schedules. *Journal of the Experimental Analysis of Behavior, 29,* 283–295.

Davison, M., & McCarthy, D. (1988). *The matching law: A research review.* Hillsdale, NJ: Erlbaum.

de Villiers, P. A. (1977). Choice in concurrent schedules and a quantitative formulation of the law of effect. In W. K. Honig & J. E. R. Staddon (Eds.), *Handbook of operant behavior* (pp. 233–287). Englewood Cliffs, NJ: Prentice Hall.

Dougherty, D. M., Nedelmann, M., & Alfred, M. (1993). An analysis and topical bibliography of the last ten years of human operant behavior: From minority to near majority (1982–1992). *Psychological Record, 43,* 501–530.

Ferster, C. B. (1978). Is operant conditioning getting bored with behavior? *Journal of the Experimental Analysis of Behavior, 29,* 347–349.

Fuqua, R. W. (1984). Comments on the applied relevance of the matching law. *Journal of Applied Behavior Analysis, 17,* 381–386.

Gottman, J. M. (1980). On analyzing for sequential connection and assessing interobserver reliability for the sequential analysis of observational data. *Behavioral Assessment, 2,* 361–368.

Gottman, J. M., & Roy, A. K. (1990). *Sequential analysis: A guide for behavioral researchers.* Cambridge, England: Cambridge University Press.

Hayes, S. C., Rincover, A., & Solnick, J. V. (1980). The technical drift in applied behavior analysis. *Journal of Applied Behavior Analysis, 13,* 275–284.

Herrnstein, R. J. (1961). Relative and absolute strength of response as a function of frequency of reinforcement. *Journal of the Experimental Analysis of Behavior, 4,* 267–272.

Herrnstein, R. J. (1970). On the law of effect. *Journal of the Experimental Analysis of Behavior, 13,* 243–266.

Herrnstein, R. J. (1979). Derivatives of matching. *Psychological Review, 86,* 486–495.

Horne, P. J., & Lowe, C. F. (1993). Determinants of human performance on concurrent schedules. *Journal of the Experimental Analysis of Behavior, 59,* 29–60.

Kazdin, A. E. (1982). Symptom substitution, generalization, and response covariation: Implications for psychotherapy outcome. *Psychological Bulletin, 91,* 349–365.

Lovaas, I., Newsom, C., & Hickman, C. (1987). Self-stimulatory behavior and perceptual reinforcement. *Journal of Applied Behavior Analysis, 20,* 45–68.

Marr, M. J. (1989). Some remarks on the quantitative analysis of behavior. *The Behavior Analyst, 12,* 143–151.

Martens, B. K., & Houk, J. L. (1989). The application of Herrnstein's law of effect to disruptive and on-task behavior of a retarded adolescent girl. *Journal of the Experimental Analysis of Behavior, 51,* 17–27.

Martens, B. K., Lochner, D. G., & Kelly, S. Q. (1992). The effects of variable-interval reinforcement on academic engagement: A demonstration of matching theory. *Journal of Applied Behavior Analysis, 25,* 143–151.

McDowell, J. J. (1981). On the validity and utility of Herrnstein's hyperbola in applied behavior analysis. In C. M. Bradshaw, E. Szabadi, & C. F. Lowe (Eds.), *Quantification of steady-state operant behaviour* (pp. 311–324). Amsterdam: Elsevier.

McDowell, J. J. (1982). The importance of Herrnstein's mathematical statement of the law of effect for behavior therapy. *American Psychologist, 37,* 771–779.

McDowell, J. J. (1988). Matching theory in natural human environments. *The Behavior Analyst, 11,* 95–109.

McDowell, J. J. (1989). Two modern developments in matching theory. *The Behavior Analyst, 12,* 153–166.

Michael, J. L. (1980). Flight from behavior analysis. *The Behavior Analyst, 3,* 1–21.

Myerson, J., & Hale, S. (1984). Practical implications of the matching law. *Journal of Applied Behavior Analysis, 17,* 367–380.

Navarick, D. J., & Chellsen, J. (1983). Matching versus undermatching in the choice behavior of humans. *Behaviour Analysis Letters, 3,* 325–335.

Noll, J. P., & Fisher, J. E. (1993, May). *Symmetrical and asymmetrical changeover delay durations: An analysis of changeover responses and distributions.* Paper presented at the 19th Annual Convention of the Association for Behavior Analysis, Chicago, IL.

O'Leary, K. D., & Wilson, G. T. (1987). *Behavior therapy: Application and outcome* (2nd ed.). Englewood Cliffs, NJ: Prentice Hall.

Pierce, W. D., & Epling, W. F. (1980). What happened to analysis in applied behavior analysis? *The Behavior Analyst, 3,* 1–9.

Pierce, W. D., & Epling, W. F. (1983). Choice, matching, and human behavior: A review of the literature. *The Behavior Analyst, 6,* 57–76.

Sajwaj, T., Twardosz, S., & Burke, M. (1972). Side effects of extinction procedures in a remedial preschool. *Journal of Applied Behavior Analysis, 5,* 163–175.

Skinner, B. F. (1938). *The behavior of organisms: An experimental analysis.* New York: Appleton-Century-Crofts.

Skinner, B. F. (1950). Are theories of learning necessary? *Psychological Review, 57,* 193–216.

Skinner, B. F. (1974). *About behaviorism.* New York: Vintage Books.

Timberlake, W., & Farmer-Dougan, V. A. (1991). Reinforcement in applied settings: Figuring out ahead of time what will work. *Psychological Bulletin, 110,* 379–391.

Tolman, E. C. (1932). *Purposive behavior in animals and men.* New York: Appleton-Century-Crofts.

Tolman, E. C. (1938). Determiners of behavior at a choice point. *Psychological Review, 45,* 1–41.

Wilkinson, G. N. (1961). Statistical estimation in enzyme kinetics. *Biochemical Journal, 80,* 324–332.

6

TWO-FACTOR FEAR THEORY: IMPLICATIONS FOR UNDERSTANDING ANXIETY-BASED CLINICAL PHENOMENA

WALLACE R. McALLISTER and DOROTHY E. McALLISTER

Although the terms *two-factor theory* and *two-process theory* are frequently used interchangeably in the learning literature, a distinction between them may serve a salutary purpose. The two *factors* will be considered here to refer to two learning procedures, classical or Pavlovian conditioning and instrumental learning. Frequently, both factors are involved in the same learning situation. The two *processes* will refer to the theoretical explanation, either contiguity or reinforcement, for the learning that occurs in a given procedure. These distinctions apply to situations in which the primary motivation is appetitive (e.g., hunger), as well as to those in which it is aversive (e.g., pain).

The two-factor, two-process learning theory proposed by Mowrer in 1947 has been most influential in its application to learning situations involving pain and fear, the aspect of the theory of interest here. In this case, the theory holds that classical conditioning is solely dependent on the contiguity of a neutral stimulus (conditioned stimulus: CS) and an aversive or noxious stimulus (unconditioned stimulus: UCS), such as shock, that reliably produces a response of pain (unconditioned response: UCR). As a result of this pairing, the CS comes to elicit a conditioned response (CR) of fear or anxiety that antedates the UCS and can be considered to be an anticipation or expectation of the painful event. Conditioned fear is assumed to have motivational and reinforcing properties. As such, it is held that fear motivates instrumental responding, which is then reinforced by fear reduction occurring after the response. Such reinforcement is, of course, dependent on the removal after the response of some or all of the fear-eliciting stimuli or on whatever other means can be devised to accomplish a similar reduction in fear.

Additional theoretical assumptions were made by Mowrer (1947). He postulated that only emotional (visceral and vascular) responses, mediated by the autonomic nervous system, could be classically conditioned and that only skeletal responses, mediated by the central nervous system, could be learned instrumentally. Although these latter assumptions were an integral part of Mowrer's learning theory, they are not relevant to the two-factor, two-process portion of his theory as it applies to the understanding of aversively motivated behavior. Therefore, whether or not these added assumptions are correct, they need not be considered in assessing the worth of two-factor theory.

Actually, those aspects of two-factor theory that are most influential in the application of the theory to clinical problems were first introduced by Mowrer in 1939. There he assumed that maladaptive behavior resulted from an attempt by the individual to deal with anxiety or fear that had been classically conditioned. Thus, if some response, motivated by fear, was made that was instrumental in alleviating fear to some degree, that response would be reinforced by fear reduction and, hence, learned. Such instrumental or symptomatic behavior—for example, repetitive counting in a compulsive individual—might appear to the observer to be maladaptive because it persisted even when it seemed to serve no purpose. However, for the individual, such symptomatic behavior would be adaptive because of the reduction of fear that would accompany the response. In passing, note that although these tenets of the theory have most frequently been used to explain anxiety disorders such as phobias and compulsions, they have also been applied to other areas of human dysfunction. For example, Beck (1993, p. 386) interpreted the onset and maintenance of vaginismus in terms of two-factor theory. Also, Stasiewicz and Maisto (1993) applied the theory to account for problems of substance abuse.

One impetus for Mowrer's 1947 article was to resolve a paradox that was posed by the results of avoidance-learning experiments using animal subjects. In avoidance tasks, a response is learned to a CS (warning signal) even though that response prevents (avoids) the presentation of the aversive UCS, for example, shock. A question is raised by such learning. As stated by Mowrer (1947), "How can a shock which is *not experienced*, i.e., which is avoided, be said to provide either a source of motivation or of satisfaction?" (p. 108). The resolution, according to Mowrer (1947), was that "*avoidance* of shock, or any other painful experience, is never, in and of itself, rewarding. The reward comes when the fear of such an experience is reduced or, still better, eliminated" (p. 109).

Probably because of the important contribution of the 1947 article in accounting for avoidance learning, the theory presented there is frequently called the *two-factor theory of avoidance learning*. Furthermore, the learned instrumental responses are called *avoidance responses*. This terminology is regrettable because, as indicated above, the learned instrumental response offers escape from fear and only incidentally avoids the aversive stimulus that was involved in the fear conditioning. That is, the instrumental response is made not *to* avoid the aversive event, but the response is made *and* the event is avoided. *Avoidance* is descriptive; *escape* is explanatory. In short, avoidance is an epiphenomenon of escape.

When the interest in classical conditioning is limited to the acquisition of fear and the interest in instrumental learning is limited to the acquisition of responses that are based on fear, we suggest that the term *fear theory* be used rather than *two-factor theory*. This usage circumvents problems associated with that part of two-factor theory that makes assumptions regarding the types of responses that can be learned through classical or instrumental procedures, assumptions that have not been upheld. For example, visceral responses may be learned instrumentally (e.g., Miller, 1985, p. 266). Such considerations serve only to distract attention from the essence of the theory. The preference for the term *fear theory* in no way alters Mowrer's fundamental conception of two-factor theory with respect to the relationship between classically conditioned fear and instrumental learning based on fear.

Because fear theory is embedded in general learning theory, all of the laws of classical conditioning—such as those dealing with acquisition, extinction, generalization, intensity of the stimuli, and so on—can be assumed to apply to fear just as they do to any other classically conditioned response. Similarly, all of the laws of instrumental learning—such as those dealing with acquisition, extinction, magnitude of reward, and so on—can be assumed to apply to such learning based on fear just as they do when other sources of motivation and reinforcement are involved.

As psychological research continues, it is to be expected that new discoveries will be made that will modify the understanding of classical conditioning and instrumental learning. Such refinements and amplifications, once established, would enrich general learning theory and would, of course, also apply to fear theory. In this way, fear theory would remain current.

That there is a parallel between fear theory and frustration theory (Amsel, 1992) is of theoretical importance. In each case, a classically conditioned response (fear or frustration) has motivational properties, and the termination of each is reinforcing. Furthermore, as responses, both fear (Miller, 1951) and frustration (Amsel, 1992) can produce stimuli to which other responses may be learned or that may elicit innately associated responses (e.g., freezing, fleeing, or fighting). The response-produced stimuli (i.e., from fear and from frustration) also are sufficiently similar so that a response learned to one stimulus may transfer to the other. A study by Fonberg (1958), to be presented later, illustrates this relationship. (A discussion of the functional similarities between frustration and fear is provided by W. R. McAllister & McAllister, 1971, pp. 164–168.)

Knowledge that an instrumental response may be learned to stimuli produced by fear or frustration has important practical consequences. When maladaptive behavior is learned to the fear or to the frustration stimulus in one situation, it could be expected to be exhibited whenever one or the other of these stimuli occurs, regardless of the situation. Richardson and Riccio (1991, p. 12) discussed empirical evidence for this type of transfer. Thus, an explanation is provided for what might seem, on the surface, to be a puzzling spread of symptomatic behavior.

ACQUISITION OF FEAR AND FEAR-BASED INSTRUMENTAL BEHAVIOR

Classical Conditioning of Fear

According to fear theory, the pairing of a CS with a noxious UCS leads to the conditioning of fear to the CS. Phrased in this way, the implication is that the CS is a simple, elemental entity. This usage, however, serves only as a matter of convenience in exposition. Actually, aside from the discrete CS, conditioning may occur to a multitude of stimuli that include the ever present contextual or situational cues. Mowrer (1947, p. 142) specifically indicated that the CS, as well as the total experimental situation, is associated with the UCS. Hull (1943, pp. 205–208) also pointed to the importance of considering these static situational cues. In addition, he provided a long list of other internal and external stimuli that were potentially conditionable to various degrees in a simple conditioning situation where a buzzer was the ostensible CS.

In discussing psychopathology, Levis (1991) emphasized the importance of fears conditioned to internal cues, such as images, thoughts, and memories. Evidence reported by Holzman and Levis (1991) indicated convincingly that fear could be conditioned to an imagined CS and that the level of conditioning equaled that obtained with the "same" CS presented externally. Differences between the stimuli to which fear is typically conditioned in the laboratory and those usually present in a natural setting were discussed by Stampfl (1991). He stressed the importance of considering the sequential nature of the stimuli that constitute the CS complex and the changing nature of the CS and context cues that are typical of natural settings. As an example of these complexities, consider the case of physical child abuse, in which the pain inflicted would seldom occur in a single stimulus situation. Rather, the victim would probably attempt to escape the initial painful event by running away, with the perpetrator following and administering abuse as the victim moved from one location to another. The aversive UCS could vary in kind and in intensity in the several locations, so different amounts of fear would be conditioned in each. These fear-eliciting stimulus complexes would become ordered sequentially in terms of their aversiveness. In addition, the stimuli constituting the CS complex would be dynamic (i.e., moving) in contradistinction to the static stimuli usually used in the typical laboratory experiment. According to Stampfl (1991), these complexities found in natural settings should not be construed as reasons for negating the use of principles developed in the less complex laboratory setting. What is required is a detailed analysis of the complexities, so that laboratory analogs may be developed. These requirements were met by an innovative experimental preparation devised by Stampfl (1987). Other laboratory studies that attempted to duplicate a characteristic of natural settings by studying the effect of sequential CSs were summarized by Levis (1991, p. 409).

Instrumental Learning Based on Fear

Thus far, the reinforcement for the learning of instrumental, symptomatic behavior has been specified simply as fear reduction. The most obvious way to achieve a reduction of fear after a response is to remove some or all of the stimuli that elicit fear. However, even if the fear-eliciting stimuli remain, fear reduction may be accomplished by other means, for example, the occurrence, after the response, of some neutral stimulus. Such a stimulus, called a *feedback stimulus*, would alter the stimulus complex and produce a stimulus generalization decrement of fear (W. R. McAllister & McAllister, 1992). Feedback stimuli may be internal, such as those produced by the instrumental response, or external. This reinforcing (fear-reducing) role of a feedback stimulus is not based on previous learning. However, with continued occurrences, the feedback stimulus can acquire an additional reinforcing capacity. This learned capacity is based on the assumption that whenever fear is reduced, a response of relaxation (or relief) occurs (Denny, 1971, 1991; Denny & Adelman, 1955; Miller, 1951; Miller & Dollard, 1941; Mowrer, 1960). Relaxation may be considered to be fear reduction conceptualized as having the functional properties of a response. As a response, relaxation would be expected, after a number of trials, to become classically conditioned to the feedback stimulus. Eventually, the occurrence of the feedback stimulus after a response would provide for secondary (learned) reinforcement by eliciting the relaxation response, which is assumed to be antagonistic to the fear response. Neutral stimuli that acquire secondary reinforcing properties are frequently called *safety signals*.

A neutral stimulus need not occur as a feedback stimulus contingent on a response, as described above, for it to become a safety signal. As proposed here, all that is necessary is that a neutral stimulus be presented contiguously with the elicitation of relaxation. Another view holds that a neutral stimulus becomes a safety signal when it precedes a long, shock-free period in a situation where shock occurs. In this case, the safety signal is often called a *Pavlovian inhibitor of fear*. Evidence supporting the relaxation interpretation was provided by Grelle and James (1981). They demonstrated that a neutral stimulus could become a safety signal when it was presented in a nonaversive environment, but one in which relaxation was occurring. For more detailed discussions of these matters, see D. E. McAllister and McAllister (1991, pp. 145–147) and W. R. McAllister and McAllister (1992).

There is general agreement that neutral stimuli can become safety signals or secondary reinforcers. However, there is disagreement about the manner in which safety signals serve to support the learning of instrumental behavior in situations where fear remains after the response. The position taken here is that safety signals reinforce the learning of fear-motivated instrumental responses by eliciting relaxation. In contrast, others hold that safety signals are positive reinforcers and that instrumental responses are learned as an approach to safety. According to Mineka (1985, p. 227), safety signals serve as fear inhibitors (fear reducers) early in instrumental training, but later become positive reinforcers. A problem inherent in considering that an instrumental response is an approach to a positive reinforcer or safety, rather than an escape from fear, is that as long as the safety signal continues to occur, the approach response should never cease. For example, if the safety signal is provided by response-produced proprioceptive cues, every response will be reinforced, and responding should continue indefinitely. Yet, it is known that with continued trials, in the absence of a UCS contingency, instrumental responses will eventually cease to be made (e.g., W. R. McAllister, McAllister, Scoles, & Hampton, 1986). Such a result is understandable if it is held that instrumental responses are reinforced by fear reduction because reinforcement ends when fear is extinguished.

The notion that an instrumental response is an approach to a safety signal, rather than an escape from fear, is here discounted. It does not follow from this position, however, that an approach component in instrumental responding is precluded. When relaxation is elicited after a response, it can, through stimulus generalization or higher order conditioning, come to be elicited in fractional form (anticipatory relaxation) by the stimuli present before the response and thereby increase the motivation to respond. This process of incentive motivation can, in addition, account for response decrements that emerge when the reduction in fear after a response is less than anticipated. Such disconfirmation of anticipated reward would lead to frustration with its ensuing disruption of instrumental responding. Corroborating evidence for such a negative contrast effect was obtained by D. E. McAllister, McAllister, Brooks, and Goldman (1972). A more detailed discussion of this process is included in D. E. McAllister and McAllister (1991, pp. 156–159).

ELIMINATION OF FEAR AND FEAR-BASED INSTRUMENTAL BEHAVIOR

Fear theory makes an important contribution to clinical psychology by providing a basis for understanding how both fear and symptomatic behavior are acquired. However, the important practical consideration for clinical practice is how fear and undesirable behavior based on fear can be alleviated or eliminated. To accomplish this end, the therapist can take advantage of the fact that fear theory is part of general learning theory and, therefore, can use or devise procedures based on the principles or laws of learning. As Stampfl (1983) pointed out, the ability to meet this challenge has been compromised by "the growing neglect of general-experimental courses in learning and conditioning in our clinical training programs" (p. 528). (See Levis, 1991, pp. 397–400, for further discussion.)

There seems to be wide agreement that fear can be reduced or eliminated by exposing the individual to the eliciting stimuli (e.g., a CS) in the absence of aversive stimulation (UCS). The amount of such extinction of fear is directly related to the amount of exposure (Shipley, 1974; Shipley, Mock, & Levis, 1971; Wilson, 1973). In the exposure treatment, the actual fear-arousing stimulus (e.g., a snake) can be used, or exposure can be to a representation of that stimulus, for example, to a picture, an image, or a verbal description. To achieve an adequate therapeutic intervention leading to the elimination of fear, it would be necessary to identify the fear-eliciting stimuli, so that appropriate exposure treatments could be administered. Such identification can be a time-consuming task for the therapist, particularly if the stimuli are internal, such as images, thoughts, or memories (Dollard & Miller, 1950, p. 67; Levis, 1991, pp. 411–413).

In keeping with this discussion, prevention of exposure would, of course, lead to the persistence of fear. Thus, if a person with an anxiety-based disorder performed a symptomatic (instrumental) response with a short latency and escaped incipient fear, little exposure and, hence, little extinction could occur. Such rapid responding would be particularly effective in preventing extinction if the feared stimuli were sequentially ordered. That is, a response made to the first stimulus in the sequence would prevent exposure to later segments and thereby preserve the fear conditioned to them. Although escape responses can be overt movements, such as withdrawal from the feared stimuli, they can also be, as pointed out by Borkovec (1985, pp. 465–466), imaginal or attentional responses that minimize functional exposure to the fear-arousing stimulus.

Therapeutic techniques, such as flooding or response prevention or those used in implosive therapy, have been successful, presumably because they ensure prolonged exposure to the phobic stimulus and thereby extinguish fear. They also prevent symptomatic escape responses that otherwise might occur and be strengthened (reinforced) by fear reduction. A complicating feature of procedures that block a response that previously had led to reinforcement is that frustration would be expected to ensue (Brown & Farber, 1951). On this basis, an increase in emotionality from frustration would occur initially during exposure therapy even as fear was being extinguished. However, as the motivation (fear) supporting the symptomatic behavior decreases, frustration should diminish.

Although the various exposure therapies reduce the occurrence of maladaptive behavior by extinguishing the fear that supports it, unless the effective associative strength of that behavior is also diminished, it would be expected to reoccur if fear is reintroduced (D. E. McAllister & McAllister, 1994). A permanent therapeutic solution would, therefore, require that in addition to extinguishing fear, maladaptive behavior be replaced by more acceptable behavior. A recent article by Stasiewicz and Maisto (1993), in discussing the treatment of substance abuse, likewise emphasized the importance of including in treatment the elimination both of fear and of the undesirable symptomatic behavior.

Despite the fact that symptomatic or instrumental behavior is held to depend on the presence of fear, theoretically, it is not necessary for the strength of fear and that of the behavior it supports to covary, a fact not always recognized in the literature. A clear illustration of this separability is provided by the results of so-called "acquired-drive" experiments. For example, in one such study (W. R. McAllister et al., 1986), fear was first classically conditioned by pairing a CS with inescapable shock in the grid side of a two-compartment apparatus. Subsequently, in the absence of shock, subjects were allowed to escape the fear of the CS and situational cues in the grid compartment by jumping a hurdle to an adjacent, distinctively different, safe compartment. The mean speed of hurdle jumping increased for about 50 trials, reflecting a growth in the associative strength of the instrumental response even as fear was presumably extinguishing on each trial because of the absence of shock. As the extinction of fear proceeded with continuing escape-from-fear trials, the speed of hurdle jumping gradually decreased, and responding eventually ceased, presumably because it was no longer reinforced by sufficient fear reduction. (Similar data are presented and discussed in Dollard & Miller, 1950, pp. 71–73.) Then, after a single fear-conditioning trial, there was an immediate reappearance of hurdle-jumping responding at a level comparable to the maximum originally reached. This result indicates clearly that the instrumental response strength had not been lost, despite the decline and subsequent cessation of performance. Rather, the loss of instrumental performance and the ensuing recovery may be attributed, respectively, to the extinction of fear and to the reconditioning of fear.

In summary, these findings demonstrate two facets of the separability of fear and instrumental responding. First, the strength of fear can be decreasing while the strength of the instrumental response is increasing, as long as sufficient fear is present to provide motivation and reinforcement. Second, despite the cessation of performance, the associative strength of the instrumental response can remain high when the strength of fear is below threshold. A further contribution provided by this study is the indication that reconditioning of fear occurs more rapidly than original conditioning.

On the basis of the previous discussion, a frequently stated criticism of fear theory may be repudiated. The argument is that fear theory should predict a parallelism between the level of fear and the strength of the avoidance behavior that it supports (e.g., Mineka & Gino, 1980). Because an avoidance response is an escape-from-fear response, the same considerations mentioned earlier would hold. Therefore, fear would be expected to decrease on each nonshock trial even as the avoidance response increased in strength. Thus, a negative correlation between the strengths of fear and of avoidance behavior is not inconsistent with the tenets of fear theory. Further discussion of these matters may be found in Levis (1989) and in D. E. McAllister and McAllister (1991).

Thus far, the concern has been with the procedure for eliminating fear, namely, the nonreinforced exposure of fear-eliciting stimuli. A likely mechanism underlying this effect is the counterconditioning of fear by relaxation. As pointed out previously, whenever pain or fear is reduced, a relaxation response is assumed to occur and to become conditioned to the concurrent stimuli. Therefore, the termination of a fear-eliciting CS during nonreinforced exposure would allow for relaxation to occur and to become conditioned to the traces of the CS and, through stimulus generalization, to the CS itself. Because relaxation is antagonistic to fear (Denny, 1971; Solomon & Corbit, 1974; Wolpe, 1958), the amount of fear elicitable by the CS would be decremented. In keeping with this contention is the finding that the amount of fear of a CS was less after 200 than after 50 shuttlebox avoidance trials (Cook, Mineka, & Trumble, 1987). During these trials, of course, relaxation would occur and become conditioned to the CS on every trial, some shock (escape) and some nonshock (avoidance) trials. It follows that if training had been continued in this experiment with CS presentations, but without the UCS contingency (shock), conditioning of relaxation would proceed, but conditioning of fear would not. Hence, according to theory, relaxation would eventually countercondition fear, and the instrumental response would cease. Empirical evidence consistent with the described role of relaxation in facilitating extinction is discussed in Denny (1991) and in Hawk and Riccio (1977).

The relaxation analysis of the extinction of fear also provides an explanation of instances when, in the process of being extinguished, an instrumental response based on fear becomes more persistent. This effect may be observed if an aversive event occurs when a relaxation response is being made. As a result, fear would become conditioned to the stimuli produced by the relaxation response. Subsequently, whenever relaxation occurred, fear would be elicited, and instrumental responding would be supported. Experimental data consistent with this analysis may be found in Denny (1971, pp. 285–289; 1976; 1991, p. 207) and Baum (1968). Also, see Miller (1951, p. 450). This process, whereby relaxation elicits fear, can account for the fact that avoidance responses sometimes show a marked resistance to extinction. Similarly, it can account for the difficulty in eliminating some maladaptive behaviors. In addition, it suggests a mechanism for understanding generalized anxiety disorders in which no obvious external conditions can account for the chronic elicitation of fear or anxiety. (See Borkovec, 1985, pp. 475–477, for further discussion.)

SOME LEARNING PRINCIPLES RELEVANT TO UNDERSTANDING FEAR AND SYMPTOMATIC BEHAVIOR

Certain of the laws or principles of learning seem to be particularly pertinent to clinical observations. Knowledge of such principles, some of which are discussed in the following sections, may aid the therapist in interpreting behavior that on the surface might seem puzzling.

Increase in the Stimulus Generalization of Fear With Time

One of the fundamental principles of learning is that when a response is learned to one stimulus, that response will generalize to (that is, will be elicited by) other similar stimuli. The more similar the generalized stimulus is to the original stimulus, the stronger will be the response.

Immediately after a traumatic event, an individual may show a sizable amount of fear or anxiety to the stimuli associated with that event and a much lesser amount to generalized stimuli. Yet at a later time, both the generalized stimuli and the original stimuli may elicit the same large amount of fear. This observation indicates that an addendum to the principle of stimulus generalization is required, namely, that there is an increase in the stimulus generalization of fear with time.

The first experiment demonstrating the importance of the temporal interval after the classical conditioning of fear in determining the amount of fear elicitable by generalized stimuli was reported by W. R. McAllister and McAllister in 1963. In that study, four groups of rats received a series of conditioning trials in which a light CS was paired with inescapable shock either in the grid side of a two-compartment apparatus or in a different, but highly similar, grid compartment. Either 3 min or 24 hr after conditioning, subjects in all groups were allowed to escape from the grid compartment of the two-compartment apparatus to the adjacent, distinctively different, safe compartment. Thus, one group at each temporal interval escaped from the fear-eliciting stimuli (CS and situational cues) in the grid compartment that was the *same* as the one used for conditioning (3-min-same and 24-hr-same). The other two groups, conditioned in the *different* grid compartment (3-min-different and 24-hr-different), escaped fear of generalized stimuli.

Learning of the escape response was equal for the two groups under the *same* condition, indicating that the temporal interval played no role under this condition. Under the *different* condition, the 24-hr group performed as well as the two same groups. However, the learning shown by the 3-min-different group was markedly inferior to that of the 3-min-same group, indicating a stimulus-generalization decrement of fear immediately after conditioning. The increase in performance from 3 min to 24 hr in the *different* condition, but not in the *same* condition, demonstrates an increase in the stimulus generalization of fear over time. These findings rule out an interpretation based on a spontaneous increase in fear with time (incubation), because that notion requires an increase in fear over time in response to both the original and generalized stimuli (D. E. McAllister & McAllister, 1967). Other studies using procedures comparable to those described above, but with a larger number of temporal intervals, reported a progressive increase in generalized fear, and hence an increase in performance, for up to 24 hr (see W. R. McAllister & McAllister, 1971, p. 147n).

In certain situations, an opposite effect on escape-from-fear performance may be predicted on the basis of an increase in the stimulus generalization of fear with time. That is, degraded, rather than enhanced, performance may be manifest with a long, as compared with a short, delay interval after conditioning. Such a result was obtained in a series of experiments in which the generalization could occur not between two similar conditioning (grid) compartments, as in the previous study, but rather between a conditioning compartment and a safe compartment that were similar (W. R. McAllister & McAllister, 1965). Because the reinforcement for learning the escape response is fear reduction, any circumstance that makes the safe compartment more similar to the conditioning compartment should decrease reinforcement and interfere with learning. Presumably, the long delay degraded performance, in comparison with the short delay, because it allowed for an increase in the stimulus generalization of fear. Therefore, the amount of fear in the safe compartment was greater, and consequently, the amount of reinforcement for the instrumental response was less with the longer delay. When the possibility of stimulus generalization between the conditioning and safe compartments was minimized by making them distinctive, the delay variable was ineffective, as would be expected.

An increase in response strength over time to generalized stimuli seems to be a phenomenon with general applicability. It was first reported in appetitively motivated tasks by Perkins and Weyant in 1958 and by Thomas and Lopez in 1962. More recently, confirming evidence for this principle has been demonstrated in a number of studies using a variety of preparations, species (including humans), and longer temporal delays between conditioning and testing. A number of these studies have been conducted by Riccio and his colleagues, who have also provided excellent reviews and discussions of the literature in this area of research (Riccio, Ackil, & Burch-Vernon, 1992; Riccio, Richardson, & Ebner, 1984; Riccio & Spear, 1991, pp. 245–249).

The gradual spread of fear or anxiety from an original situation in which some traumatic event occurred to an increasing number of other situations is characteristic of agoraphobia and post-traumatic stress disorder. This observation may be explained by an increase over time in the stimulus generalization of fear. Symptomatic or instrumental behavior, probably withdrawal, that would reduce fear would be learned to the stimuli associated with the initial traumatic event. The expectation would be that over time, along with the spread of fear or anxiety to other situations that were similar on some dimension, there would also be a concomitant spread of the fear-reducing symptomatic behavior. Verbal or symbolic processes (see below) may play a role in mediating the similarity of the stimulus situations. With agoraphobia, the spread of anxiety and the consequent spread of the symptomatic withdrawal behavior make it understandable that the person could become immobilized.

Symbolic Processes

Verbal processes constitute a ubiquitous aspect of human behavior. It is unlikely that any human endeavor is free from some linguistic accompaniment. Thus, whenever fear or anxiety is conditioned to a given stimulus situation, overt or covert verbal stimuli probably constitute part of the stimulus complex. If some behavior instrumental in reducing conditioned fear is learned, it will quite likely be learned to all of the stimuli present, including the verbal stimuli. As a consequence, anxiety—and hence the instrumental, symptomatic behavior—might subsequently be elicited in a novel situation if the verbal stimuli present are shared with those of the original situation. Fear and symptomatic behavior may also be elicited in a novel situation by verbal stimuli that bear some semantic similarity (e.g., synonyms or homonyms) to those present in the original situation.

A study by Mednick (1957) provided support for the notion that a spread of anxiety could occur through a mediational process involving verbal stimuli. The galvanic skin response (GSR) was conditioned to a CS, the word *light*, by pairing it with a raucous buzzer. Then, the GSR to several test words (*dark*, *lamp*, *heavy*, and *soft*), which had been found to be associated with the word *light*, was measured. The GSR to each of these test words was less than that to the CS, but greater than that to a nonassociated control word, *square*. These results may be interpreted to indicate that the test words elicited the CS word, which in turn elicited the GSR, which presumably was a measure of anxiety. Thus, a mechanism is provided by mediated generalization for the spread of fear or anxiety to a novel situation.

Eifert (1987) contributed an extensive discussion of language conditioning and the role of symbolic processes in psychotherapy, as did Dollard and Miller (1950).

Vicious-Circle Behavior

According to Horney (1937; cited in Mowrer, 1950), "a vicious circle . . . is one of the most important processes in neuroses" (p. 512). As an example of behavior characterizing a vicious circle, consider a university football player who, fearful of failing and losing his eligibility to play, begins to drink excessively so as to alleviate his fear. As a consequence, his ability to study becomes compromised, his academic performance becomes increasingly degraded, his fear increases, and as a result, his drinking increases: a vicious circle. Mowrer considered this type of compulsive behavior to be an exemplar of the "neurotic paradox," which refers to the observation that "neurotic behavior is at one and the same time *self-defeating and yet self-perpetuating*, instead of self-eliminating" (Mowrer, 1950, p. 351).

In 1947, Mowrer noted the similarity between vicious-circle behavior in humans and behavior in animals that was observed and described to him by Judson S. Brown. Brown reported that rats readily learned to escape shock in a straight runway by running to a nonshock, safe compartment at its end. When shock was removed from all but an intermediate section of the runway, the rats continued to traverse the runway for many trials even though shock was received en route to the safe compartment on each trial. This persistence of responding in the face of punishment is paradoxical because typically a punished response ceases to be made. Mowrer offered an explanation of this unusual behavior in terms of his two-factor theory. Specifically, during the escape-from-shock training, fear would become classically conditioned to the stimuli in the runway. The instrumental running response would be reinforced by the reduction of both shock and fear when the safe compartment was reached. Subsequently, when shock was restricted to an intermediate segment of the runway, the running response would be motivated by fear conditioned to the initial part of the runway, and because of the receipt of shock on each trial, such fear would continue to be conditioned. The instrumental response would be reinforced by shock reduction when the shocked segment of the runway was crossed and by fear reduction when the safe compartment was reached. Thus, the animal behavior reported by Brown was amenable to Mowrer's (1947) theoretical explanation. On this basis, Mowrer suggested that similar vicious-circle behavior in humans, such as that described earlier, might be accounted for in a like manner. He speculated that "perhaps the two-factor theory of learning will turn out to have important clinical significance" (Mowrer, 1947, p. 134), a statement showing considerable foresight.

In the ensuing years, a large number of investigations of vicious-circle behavior using rats as subjects have been conducted, many of them by Brown and his colleagues. The terms *self-punitive behavior* or *masochisticlike behavior* have often been used to refer to the vicious-circle phenomenon. A thorough review of the empirical evidence and a discussion of the methodological and theoretical issues involved in this research area were provided by Brown in 1969 and, more recently, by Dean and Pittman in 1991. In general, the animal research on vicious-circle behavior has been supportive of Mowrer's explanation.

CRITICISMS OF FEAR THEORY AS IT RELATES TO CLINICAL APPLICATIONS

It is a given that rejection of theoretical positions should be based on reliable data, on impeccable logic, or on both. In some instances, it is difficult to apply this dictum to psychological propositions because of the imprecision of theories and the unreliability of some of the available data. In the case of two-factor fear theory, however, it seems that the theory has been stated in sufficiently unambiguous terms and that adequate reliable data pertaining to the theory are available. Therefore, the theory should be easily understood, and faulty evaluations should be precluded. Nevertheless, a number of criticisms have been made that can be considered to be unjustified. This problem is exacerbated by the tendency for writers to cite sources of criticisms, or to repeat criticisms of fear theory made by others, apparently without considering the adequacy of the arguments that were used initially as a basis for the negative judgment. A case in point is that Herrnstein (1969) is frequently cited as having provided a devastating critique of fear theory; yet his criticisms seem to be based on misinterpretations of it. For example, he claimed that fear theory held that the reinforcement for learning an avoidance response was the termination of the CS. He then pointed out that learning occurred when the CS was not terminated in a situation in which a distinctive feedback stimulus was presented after the response. This circumstance was cited as evidence contrary to fear theory. In fact, however, it is exactly what the theory would predict, as has been indicated in the discussion regarding feedback stimuli. All that is required for reinforcement to occur is that there be less fear after than before the response. The basis for the reduction in fear is irrelevant; CS termination is only one means to this end (Mackintosh, 1974, pp. 315, 319; D. E. McAllister & McAllister, 1991, p. 146).

Note that mediational concepts, such as fear, that are accepted by neobehaviorists (e.g., Mowrer) are anathema to radical (Skinnerian) behaviorists (e.g., Herrnstein), although, as pointed out by Amsel (1989), some softening of this latter position is evident in some quarters. Herrnstein (1969) denied that fear or fear reduction played any role in avoidance learning and proposed an alternative theory. However, his proposal, that the learning of an avoidance response occurred because it reduced the frequency of shock, came under severe criticism from many sources on both empirical and logical grounds (e.g., Dinsmoor, 1977; Seligman & Johnston, 1973, pp. 72–75). This theory currently cannot be considered a viable alternative to two-factor fear theory.

The message for therapists who may be interested in basing their treatments on fear theory is that they should not be dissuaded by any critique of it before examining carefully the accuracy of the arguments presented.

In the next sections, other criticisms that bear on the adequacy of fear theory as a basis for understanding anxiety-based maladaptive behavior will be examined. Additional evaluations of the appropriateness of various criticisms of fear theory have been published elsewhere (e.g., Levis, 1989, 1991; D. E. McAllister & McAllister, 1991; Plaud & Vogeltanz, 1991; Seligman & Johnston, 1973; Wolpe, 1986).

Do Humans, but Not Animals, Avoid Warning Signals (CSs)?

In discussing whether the features of conditioned avoidance responses found in laboratory experiments were like those shown with human phobias, Mineka (1985, p. 204), following Seligman (1971), argued that one major difference was that humans respond to avoid the CS (phobic stimulus), whereas animals do not. Rather, it is held that animals are trained to respond to avoid the UCS. This ostensible difference was felt to weaken the relevance of fear theory based on animal research for understanding human phobias. Such an analysis about avoidance behavior may misrepresent the reality for both animals and humans. If the phobic stimulus (CS) that humans are said to avoid is not present in some way (physically, imaginally, or as an expectation), on what grounds could one ever assume that a response would be made to avoid that stimulus? It would surely require prescience to make an avoidance response in the absence of any referent to the CS to be avoided. As was pointed out in 1940 by Hilgard and Marquis, "absence of stimulation can obviously have an influence on behavior only if there exists some sort of preparation for or expectation of the stimulation" (p. 59). It is more reasonable to assume that with both humans and animals, the presence of some aspect of the fear-eliciting CS precedes the occurrence of the response that escapes fear. The UCS, if it is scheduled to occur (animals) or if it could occur (humans), would be avoided only incidentally when the escape-from-fear response was made.

Hineline (1977), in his critique of two-factor theory—either Mowrer's (1947) or Anger's (1963) version—has correctly pointed out (pp. 364–365) that according to these theories, the avoidance response is simply a by-product of an escape response from a conditioned aversive stimulus (CS or warning signal). Nevertheless, he then proceeded to argue against such theories on the basis that CSs are not always aversive. In this regard, he stated that "the most telling evidence against the traditional two-factor formulation comes from procedures in which preshock cues, often called 'warning stimuli,' are introduced into shock-delay procedures" (p. 393), the so-called "Sidman avoidance task." This task involves presenting a noxious stimulus (e.g., shock) after a fixed interval of time unless the subject makes a specified response (e.g., a barpress) before the onset of shock. Such a response delays the presentation of the shock for a fixed interval of time. This training does not involve the presentation of a stimulus signaling the imminent delivery of the shock. However, in some experiments, once the subject has learned to delay the receipt of the shock by barpressing, a warning signal (CS) is introduced and is presented just before the shock. As a result, on those occasions when shock is not delayed by a barpress, the CS would be paired with shock. With these procedures, it is found that the subjects make the majority of their barpress responses during the CS and not before its presentation. That is, the subject does not avoid the CS, but rather makes a response during the CS that terminates that stimulus. In discussing such results, Hineline (1981, p. 208) argued that the CS did not become a conditioned aversive stimulus, as two-factor theory would predict, because the subject failed to avoid the stimulus. Hence, he concluded that "the results . . . soundly contradict standard, traditional two-process avoidance theory" (p. 212). Actually, the results are precisely what two-factor fear theory would predict. Presentation of the CS in the Sidman avoidance task would allow a discrimination to be formed by the subject between the CS plus apparatus cues, which are fear arousing based on their pairing with shock, and the apparatus cues alone, which are never paired with shock after the CS is introduced. Thus, responses would be expected to be made during the CS because they would be reinforced by fear reduction. However, little fear would be present before the onset of the CS, so responses made at that time would not be reinforced and, thus, would seldom occur. A similar interpretation of these experiments has been made by Mackintosh (1974, p. 313).

The implication of this discussion for the therapist is that in the treatment of anxiety disorders, symptomatic behavior should *not* be considered an attempt to avoid an event that could arouse fear but rather an attempt to escape from fear already aroused to some extent by that event.

Are Precipitating Events Underlying Anxiety Disorders Identifiable?

A frequent criticism of a conditioning account of phobias or obsessive–compulsive disorders is that often it is not possible to identify a traumatic experience that could serve as the basis for their acquisition (e.g., Marks, 1982, p. 19; Rachman, 1977). Data are available, however, indicating that this conclusion may be an overstatement. Öst and Hugdahl (1981) studied a clinical population of patients with animal or social phobias or with claustrophobia. They found that overall, "a large majority (58%) of the patients attributed their phobias to conditioning experiences" (p. 439). It was also reported that some patients acquired their phobias indirectly; 17% recalled vicarious experiences, and 10% attributed their phobias to instructions or information. Only 15% could not recollect any specific event that led to the phobia. In a later study of agoraphobics, Öst and Hugdahl (1983) found that 81% of their patients "attributed their phobias to conditioning experiences, while 9% recalled vicarious learning, none recalled instruction/information and 10% could not recall any specific onset circumstances" (p. 623).

The failure of phobic patients to recall a precipitating event (15% and 10% in the studies discussed in the previous paragraph) does not necessarily mean that there was none. Such failures should not be surprising in the light of the data reported by Loftus (1993, p. 522), which showed that traumatic events known to have occurred are sometimes forgotten. She indicated that of 590 individuals interviewed in a U.S. government study, approximately 14% did not remember having been in an injury-producing accident known to have occurred a year earlier. Another study involved 1,500 individuals who had been hospitalized and discharged within the previous year. A year later, more than 25% did not recall the hospitalization. The findings of the Öst and Hugdahl (1981, 1983) studies regarding the percentage of patients failing to recall a circumstance leading to the onset of their phobia seem to be quite consistent with these results.

An argument has been made (Rachman, 1977) that conditioning theory cannot account for phobias that are acquired indirectly, that is, through vicarious or observational learning or learning based on information or instruction. Presumably, these indirect processes are not considered to be conditioning events, so the theory is held to be inadequate. However, such indirect learning can easily be interpreted as classical conditioning. For instance, on the basis of their research, Mineka (1987), and Cook and Mineka (1990, p. 380), suggested that the mechanisms involved in observational learning of fear in monkeys were the same as those of direct conditioning. Support for this position concerning such indirect learning is based on the principles of classical conditioning. Specifically, a prerequisite for the acquisition of a classically conditioned fear response is that the response be consistently elicited, under appropriate conditions, by some stimulus (UCS), so that it may become associated with some neutral stimulus (CS), internal or external, that is present. There is no restriction made concerning the nature of the UCS that elicits fear. Thus, it could be a painful or noxious stimulus (e.g., an electric shock, a loud noise, a bite, or a blow), observation of emotion being expressed by another individual, or, in humans, a fear-arousing verbal event (spoken or written). Any fear-arousing CS can serve as a functional UCS for further, higher order, conditioning. It has also been suggested (Borkovec, 1985, p. 466; Eifert, 1987, p. 170; W. R. McAllister & McAllister, 1979) that classical fear-conditioning trials may be self-administered. That is, a person may supply an effective UCS and, hence, a UCR through symbolic processes such as implicit verbalizations or images. Likewise, Seligman (1971) stated that "people sometimes talk themselves into phobias" (p. 317), such as phobias about airplanes or electric shock.

An emotional response that supports maladaptive behavior need not depend on the occurrence of aversive events but, rather, can be aroused by appetitive events presented in a situation that leads to conflict. Supporting evidence is provided by Fonberg (1958), who demonstrated that a response learned in an avoidance task was elicited at a later time in an appetitively motivated discrimination task. This occurred when the discrimination between a cue that was reinforced by food and a cue that was not reinforced was made sufficiently difficult so as to produce experimental neurosis. Presumably, the conflict engendered by the difficult discrimination led to frustration (Brown & Farber, 1951). As documented in the introductory section of this chapter, the stimuli produced by frustration and by fear are similar. Therefore, it is understandable that the response learned to the fear stimulus in the avoidance task was elicited later in the appetitive task by the frustration stimulus. This evidence that an emotional response akin to fear can be elicited in a situation that involves only positive rewards may provide a basis for the observation that in some cases, a traumatic event underlying maladaptive behavior cannot be recalled. In planning treatment, it would seem to be important for the therapist to understand that an anxiety disorder may be based on frustration rather than fear.

Should a Preparedness Model Supplant General Process Learning Theory?

Seligman (1971) argued that because of evolutionary processes, certain stimuli were more likely to acquire phobic properties through classical conditioning than were others. In addition to this selectivity of association, it was also assumed that phobias are quickly learned, often in one trial; are highly resistant to extinction; and are irrational or noncognitive (not easily subject to modification by information). Because of these characteristics, the classical conditioning of phobias was considered to be an instance of prepared learning. Taste aversions were likewise regarded as examples of prepared classical conditioning. In contrast, according to Seligman (1971), the classical conditioning of fear in the laboratory is nonselective with respect to the stimuli that may be conditioned, requires a number of trials for acquisition, and extinguishes readily. Therefore, such fear conditioning was considered to be an instance of unprepared learning. These considerations, as well as other observations involving instrumental learning, led Seligman (1970) to conclude that the central assumption of general process learning theory that "all events are equally associable and obey common laws" (p. 406) does not hold. On this basis, he suggested that general process learning theory be replaced by a preparedness model of learning.

The assumed uniqueness of the conditioning of phobias as compared to fears conditioned in the laboratory has not been established. Data are available to indicate that some of the characteristics ascribed to prepared learning can be found also with unprepared learning, as long as appropriate parameters and preparations are used. In both cases, acquisition may occur quickly (e.g., Levis, 1979; W. R. McAllister & McAllister, 1979). Fears conditioned in the laboratory can be highly resistant to extinction in animals (e.g., Levis & Boyd, 1979; W. R. McAllister et al., 1986; Mineka & Gino, 1980; Stampfl, 1987; Starr & Mineka, 1977) and in humans (e.g., Malloy & Levis, 1988; Williams & Levis, 1991) just as phobias are held to be, and phobias can be extinguished with sufficient exposure to the feared stimulus (e.g., Barlow, 1988, pp. 407–409, 484–485; Marks, 1987, pp. 457–460; McNally, 1987, p. 298; Mineka, 1985, p. 209) just as is the case with laboratory fears. In addition, a difference between prepared and unprepared associations with respect to their cognitive nature has not been convincingly demonstrated (McNally, 1987, pp. 286–287). The indication from these comparisons that prepared and unprepared learning possess similar, rather than dissimilar, characteristics suggests that on this basis, there is little reason for substituting a preparedness theory for general process learning theory.

Whether selective associations can be unequivocally demonstrated remains a question. A major problem in coming to a resolution of this issue is the difficulty in designing experiments that demonstrate selectivity of association while also ruling out alternative interpretations. LoLordo (1979a, 1979b), McNally (1987, p. 289), and LoLordo and Droungas (1989) discussed experimental designs that purported to solve this problem. Even so, LoLordo (1979b, p. 380) pointed out weaknesses in these designs with respect to controlling the effects of pseudoconditioning and sensitization. It would also seem important when these designs are used to consider that the ease of conditioning, or whether conditioning occurred at all, would depend not only on the CSs and UCSs involved but also on the values of the parameters and the constant conditions used (Bitterman, 1975; LoLordo, 1979a).

A recent study by Cook and Mineka (1990), which seemed to overcome some of the difficulties mentioned above, provided evidence that fear may be conditioned vicariously in monkeys to fear-relevant but not to fear-irrelevant stimuli. Note, however, that demonstrating that certain combinations of conditioned and unconditioned stimuli may be associated more easily than other combinations does not deny the applicability in both cases of the established general laws and mechanisms of learning. Logue (1979) concluded, with respect to taste aversion learning, that "in no instance are different principles required to describe taste aversion and traditional learning" (p. 276), a view shared in general by others (e.g., Bitterman, 1975, 1976; Domjan & Galef, 1983). In comparing species, research has shown many similarities in learning between widely diverse species (Domjan & Galef, 1983) despite various obvious differences among them. After all, "fish got to swim and birds got to fly" (Hammerstein, 1927). Nevertheless, except for variations in parametric values, the variables and the laws relating these variables to classical conditioning performance are remarkably alike throughout most, if not all, of the phylogenetic scale. (For further discussion, see Amsel, 1989, pp. 76n; Rescorla & Holland, 1982, pp. 277–280.)

The major import of this discussion for the present essay is how the controversy concerning preparedness and general process learning theory affects the evaluation of two-factor fear theory. The acceptance of Seligman's (1970) arguments in support of the preparedness model led some investigators to reject fear theory, presumably because it was part of general process learning theory (e.g., Marks, 1977; Rachman, 1977). However, for now, the conventional wisdom, as indicated in the preceding discussion, is that the characteristics ascribed by Seligman to the learning of certain (prepared) associations are not unique and do not place an explanatory burden on general process learning theory.

CONCLUSION

Despite all of the controversies discussed in this chapter, it has not been necessary to modify the fundamental principles of two-factor fear theory. That is, it seems unquestionable that fears and phobias can be classically conditioned, perhaps more easily to some stimuli than to others. And once conditioned, they can be extinguished by appropriate exposure conditions. It also seems unquestionable that instrumental (symptomatic) behavior that allows escape from fears or phobias can be learned.

REFERENCES

Amsel, A. (1989). *Behaviorism, neobehaviorism, and cognitivism in learning theory: Historical and contemporary perspectives.* Hillsdale, NJ: Erlbaum.

Amsel, A. (1992). *Frustration theory: An analysis of dispositional learning and memory.* New York: Cambridge University Press.

Anger, D. (1963). The role of temporal discriminations in the reinforcement of Sidman avoidance behavior. *Journal of the Experimental Analysis of Behavior, 6,* 477–506.

Barlow, D. H. (1988). *Anxiety and its disorders: The nature and treatment of anxiety and panic.* New York: Guilford Press.

Baum, M. (1968). Efficacy of response prevention (flooding) in facilitating the extinction of an avoidance response in rats: The effect of overtraining the response. *Behaviour Research and Therapy, 6,* 197–203.

Beck, J. G. (1993). Vaginismus. In W. O'Donohue & J. H. Geer (Eds.), *Handbook of sexual dysfunctions: Assessment and treatment* (pp. 381–397). Boston: Allyn & Bacon.

Bitterman, M. E. (1975). The comparative analysis of learning. *Science, 188,* 699–709.

Bitterman, M. E. (1976). Flavor aversion studies. *Science, 192,* 266–267.

Borkovec, T. D. (1985). The role of cognitive and somatic cues in anxiety and anxiety disorders: Worry and relaxation-induced anxiety. In A. H. Tuma & J. D. Maser (Eds.), *Anxiety and the anxiety disorders* (pp. 463–478). Hillsdale, NJ: Erlbaum.

Brown, J. S. (1969). Factors affecting self-punitive locomotor behavior. In B. A. Campbell & R. M. Church (Eds.), *Punishment and aversive behavior* (pp. 467–514). New York: Appleton-Century-Crofts.

Brown, J. S., & Farber, I. E. (1951). Emotions conceptualized as intervening variables—With suggestions toward a theory of frustration. *Psychological Bulletin*, 48, 465–495.

Cook, M., & Mineka, S. (1990). Selective associations in the observational conditioning of fear in rhesus monkeys. *Journal of Experimental Psychology: Animal Behavior Processes*, 16, 372–389.

Cook, M., Mineka, S., & Trumble, D. (1987). The role of response-produced and exteroceptive feedback in the attenuation of fear over the course of avoidance learning. *Journal of Experimental Psychology: Animal Behavior Processes*, 13, 239–249.

Dean, S. J., & Pittman, C. M. (1991). Self-punitive behavior: A revised analysis. In M. R. Denny (Ed.), *Fear, avoidance, and phobias: A fundamental analysis* (pp. 259–284). Hillsdale, NJ: Erlbaum.

Denny, M. R. (1971). Relaxation theory and experiments. In F. R. Brush (Ed.), *Aversive conditioning and learning* (pp. 235–295). San Diego, CA: Academic Press.

Denny, M. R. (1976). Post-aversive relief and relaxation and their implications for behavior therapy. *Journal of Behavior Therapy and Experimental Psychiatry*, 7, 315–321.

Denny, M. R. (1991). Relaxation/relief: The effect of removing, postponing, or terminating aversive stimuli. In M. R. Denny (Ed.), *Fear, avoidance, and phobias: A fundamental analysis* (pp. 199–229). Hillsdale, NJ: Erlbaum.

Denny, M. R., & Adelman, H. M. (1955). Elicitation theory: I. An analysis of two typical learning situations. *Psychological Review*, 62, 290–296.

Dinsmoor, J. A. (1977). Escape, avoidance, punishment: Where do we stand? *Journal of the Experimental Analysis of Behavior*, 28, 83–95.

Dollard, J., & Miller, N. E. (1950). *Personality and psychotherapy*. New York: McGraw-Hill.

Domjan, M., & Galef, B. G., Jr. (1983). Biological constraints on instrumental and classical conditioning: Retrospect and prospect. *Animal Learning & Behavior*, 11, 151-161.

Eifert, G. H. (1987). Language conditioning: Clinical issues and applications in behavior therapy. In H. J. Eysenck & I. Martin (Eds.), *Theoretical foundations of behavior therapy* (pp. 167–193). New York: Plenum.

Fonberg, E. (1958). The manifestation of the defensive reactions in neurotic states. *Acta Biologiae Experimentalis*, 18, 89–116.

Grelle, M. J., & James, J. H. (1981). Conditioned inhibition of fear: Evidence for a competing response mechanism. *Learning and Motivation*, 12, 300–320.

Hammerstein, O., II. (1927). Can't help lovin' dat man. In J. Kern & O. Hammerstein II, *Show Boat: Vocal Score*. New York: T. B. Harms Company.

Hawk, G., & Riccio, D. C. (1977). The effect of a conditioned fear inhibitor (C − S) during response prevention upon extinction of an avoidance response. *Behaviour Research and Therapy*, 15, 97–101.

Herrnstein, R. J. (1969). Method and theory in the study of avoidance. *Psychological Review, 76*, 49–69.

Hilgard, E. R., & Marquis, D. G. (1940). *Conditioning and learning.* New York: Appleton-Century.

Hineline, P. N. (1977). Negative reinforcement and avoidance. In W. K. Honig & J. E. R. Staddon (Eds.), *Handbook of operant behavior* (pp. 364–414). Englewood Cliffs, NJ: Prentice Hall.

Hineline, P. N. (1981). The several roles of stimuli in negative reinforcement. In P. Harzem & M. D. Zeiler (Eds.), *Advances in analysis of behaviour: Vol. 2. Predictability, correlation, and contiguity* (pp. 203–246). Chichester, England: Wiley.

Holzman, A. D., & Levis, D. J. (1991). Differential aversive conditioning of an external (visual) and internal (imaginal) CS: Effects of transfer between and within CS modalities. *Journal of Mental Imagery, 15*, 77–90.

Hull, C. L. (1943). *Principles of behavior.* New York: Appleton-Century-Crofts.

Levis, D. J. (1979). A reconsideration of Eysenck's conditioning model of neurosis. *The Behavioral and Brain Sciences, 2*, 172–174.

Levis, D. J. (1989). The case for a return to a two-factor theory of avoidance: The failure of non-fear interpretations. In S. B. Klein & R. R. Mowrer (Eds.), *Contemporary learning theories: Pavlovian conditioning and the status of traditional learning theory* (pp. 227–277). Hillsdale, NJ: Erlbaum.

Levis, D. J. (1991). A clinician's plea for a return to the development of nonhuman models of psychopathology: New clinical observations in need of laboratory study. In M. R. Denny (Ed.), *Fear, avoidance, and phobias: A fundamental analysis* (pp. 395–427). Hillsdale, NJ: Erlbaum.

Levis, D. J., & Boyd, T. L. (1979). Symptom maintenance: An infrahuman analysis and extension of the conservation of anxiety principle. *Journal of Abnormal Psychology, 88*, 107–120.

Loftus, E. F. (1993). The reality of repressed memories. *American Psychologist, 48*, 518–537.

Logue, A. W. (1979). Taste aversion and the generality of the laws of learning. *Psychological Bulletin, 86*, 276–296.

LoLordo, V. M. (1979a). Constraints on learning. In M. E. Bitterman, V. M. LoLordo, J. B. Overmier, & M. E. Rashotte (Eds.), *Animal learning: Survey and analysis* (pp. 473–504). New York: Plenum.

LoLordo, V. M. (1979b). Selective associations. In A. Dickinson & R. A. Boakes (Eds.), *Mechanisms of learning and motivation: A memorial volume to Jerzy Konorski* (pp. 367–398). Hillsdale, NJ: Erlbaum.

LoLordo, V. M., & Droungas, A. (1989). Selective associations and adaptive specializations: Taste aversions and phobias. In S. B. Klein & R. R. Mowrer (Eds.), *Contemporary learning theories: Instrumental conditioning theory and the impact of biological constraints on learning* (pp. 145–179). Hillsdale, NJ: Erlbaum.

Mackintosh, N. J. (1974). *The psychology of animal learning*. San Diego, CA: Academic Press.

Malloy, P., & Levis, D. J. (1988). A laboratory demonstration of persistent human avoidance. *Behavior Therapy, 19,* 229–241.

Marks, I. (1977). Phobias and obsessions: Clinical phenomena in search of laboratory models. In J. D. Maser & M. E. P. Seligman (Eds.), *Psychopathology: Experimental models* (pp. 174–213). San Francisco: W. J. Freeman.

Marks, I. (1982). Is conditioning relevant to behaviour therapy? In J. C. Boulougouris (Ed.), *Learning theory approaches to psychiatry* (pp. 19–31). Chichester, England: Wiley.

Marks, I. M. (1987). *Fears, phobias, and rituals: Panic, anxiety, and their disorders*. New York: Oxford University Press.

McAllister, D. E., & McAllister, W. R. (1967). Incubation of fear: An examination of the concept. *Journal of Experimental Research in Personality, 2,* 180–190.

McAllister, D. E., & McAllister, W. R. (1991). Fear theory and aversively motivated behavior: Some controversial issues. In M. R. Denny (Ed.), *Fear, avoidance, and phobias: A fundamental analysis* (pp. 135–163). Hillsdale, NJ: Erlbaum.

McAllister, D. E., & McAllister, W. R. (1994). Extinction and reconditioning of classically conditioned fear before and after instrumental learning: Effects of depth of fear extinction. *Learning and Motivation, 25,* 339–367.

McAllister, D. E., McAllister, W. R., Brooks, C. I., & Goldman, J. A. (1972). Magnitude and shift of reward in instrumental aversive learning in rats. *Journal of Comparative and Physiological Psychology, 80,* 490–501.

McAllister, W. R., & McAllister, D. E. (1963). Increase over time in the stimulus generalization of acquired fear. *Journal of Experimental Psychology, 65,* 576–582.

McAllister, W. R., & McAllister, D. E. (1965). Variables influencing the conditioning and the measurement of acquired fear. In W. F. Prokasy (Ed.), *Classical conditioning: A symposium* (pp. 172–191). New York: Appleton-Century-Crofts.

McAllister, W. R., & McAllister, D. E. (1971). Behavioral measurement of conditioned fear. In F. R. Brush (Ed.), *Aversive conditioning and learning* (pp. 105–179). San Diego, CA: Academic Press.

McAllister, W. R., & McAllister, D. E. (1979). Are the concepts of enhancement and preparedness necessary? *The Behavioral and Brain Sciences, 2,* 177–178.

McAllister, W. R., & McAllister, D. E. (1992). Fear determines the effectiveness of a feedback stimulus in aversively motivated instrumental learning. *Learning and Motivation, 23,* 99–115.

McAllister, W. R., McAllister, D. E., Scoles, M. T., & Hampton, S. R. (1986). Persistence of fear-reducing behavior: Relevance for the conditioning theory of neurosis. *Journal of Abnormal Psychology, 95,* 365–372.

McNally, R. J. (1987). Preparedness and phobias: A review. *Psychological Bulletin, 101,* 283–303.

Mednick, M. T. (1957). Mediated generalization and the incubation effect as a function of manifest anxiety. *Journal of Abnormal and Social Psychology*, 55, 315–321.

Miller, N. E. (1951). Learnable drives and rewards. In S. S. Stevens (Ed.), *Handbook of experimental psychology* (pp. 435–472). New York: Wiley.

Miller, N. E. (1985). Theoretical models relating animal experiments on fear to clinical phenomena. In A. H. Tuma & J. D. Maser (Eds.), *Anxiety and the anxiety disorders* (pp. 261–272). Hillsdale, NJ: Erlbaum.

Miller, N. E., & Dollard, J. (1941). *Social learning and imitation.* New Haven, CT: Yale University Press.

Mineka, S. (1985). Animal models of anxiety-based disorders: Their usefulness and limitations. In A. H. Tuma & J. D. Maser (Eds.), *Anxiety and the anxiety disorders* (pp. 199–244). Hillsdale, NJ: Erlbaum.

Mineka, S. (1987). A primate model of phobic fears. In H. J. Eysenck & I. Martin (Eds.), *Theoretical foundations of behavior therapy* (pp. 81–111). New York: Plenum.

Mineka, S., & Gino, A. (1980). Dissociation between conditioned emotional response and extended avoidance performance. *Learning and Motivation*, 11, 476–502.

Mowrer, O. H. (1939). A stimulus–response analysis of anxiety and its role as a reinforcing agent. *Psychological Review*, 46, 553–565.

Mowrer, O. H. (1947). On the dual nature of learning—A re-interpretation of "conditioning" and "problem-solving." *Harvard Educational Review*, 17, 102–148.

Mowrer, O. H. (1950). *Learning theory and personality dynamics: Selected papers.* New York: Ronald Press.

Mowrer, O. H. (1960). *Learning theory and behavior.* New York: Wiley.

Öst, L.-G., & Hugdahl, K. (1981). Acquisition of phobias and anxiety response patterns in clinical patients. *Behaviour Research and Therapy*, 19, 439–447.

Öst, L.-G., & Hugdahl, K. (1983). Acquisition of agoraphobia, mode of onset and anxiety response patterns. *Behaviour Research and Therapy*, 21, 623–631.

Perkins, C. C., Jr., & Weyant, R. G. (1958). The interval between training and test trials as a determiner of the slope of generalization gradients. *Journal of Comparative and Physiological Psychology*, 51, 596–600.

Plaud, J. J., & Vogeltanz, N. (1991). Behavior therapy: Lost ties to animal research? *The Behavior Therapist*, 14, 89–93, 115.

Rachman, S. (1977). The conditioning theory of fear-acquisition: A critical examination. *Behaviour Research and Therapy*, 15, 375–387.

Rescorla, R. A., & Holland, P. C. (1982). Behavioral studies of associative learning in animals. *Annual Review of Psychology*, 33, 265–308.

Riccio, D. C., Ackil, J., & Burch-Vernon, A. (1992). Forgetting of stimulus attributes: Methodological implications for assessing associative phenomena. *Psychological Bulletin*, 112, 433–445.

Riccio, D. C., Richardson, R., & Ebner, D. L. (1984). Memory retrieval deficits based upon altered contextual cues: A paradox. *Psychological Bulletin, 96*, 152–165.

Riccio, D. C., & Spear, N. E. (1991). Changes in memory for aversively motivated learning. In M. R. Denny (Ed.), *Fear, avoidance, and phobias: A fundamental analysis* (pp. 231–257). Hillsdale, NJ: Erlbaum.

Richardson, R., & Riccio, D. C. (1991). Memory processes, ACTH, and extinction phenomena. In L. Dachowski & C. F. Flaherty (Eds.), *Current topics in animal learning: Brain, emotion, and cognition* (pp. 1–23). Hillsdale, NJ: Erlbaum.

Seligman, M. E. P. (1970). On the generality of the laws of learning. *Psychological Review, 77*, 406–418.

Seligman, M. E. P. (1971). Phobias and preparedness. *Behavior Therapy, 2*, 307–320.

Seligman, M. E. P., & Johnston, J. C. (1973). A cognitive theory of avoidance learning. In F. J. McGuigan & D. B. Lumsden (Eds.), *Contemporary approaches to conditioning and learning* (pp. 69–110). Washington, DC: Winston.

Shipley, R. H. (1974). Extinction of conditioned fear in rats as a function of several parameters of CS exposure. *Journal of Comparative and Physiological Psychology, 87*, 699–707.

Shipley, R. H., Mock, L. A., & Levis, D. J. (1971). Effects of several response prevention procedures on activity, avoidance responding, and conditioned fear in rats. *Journal of Comparative and Physiological Psychology, 77*, 256–270.

Solomon, R. L., & Corbit, J. D. (1974). An opponent-process theory of motivation: I. Temporal dynamics of affect. *Psychological Review, 81*, 119–145.

Stampfl, T. G. (1983). Exposure treatment for psychiatrists? [Review of *Learning theory approaches to psychiatry*]. *Contemporary Psychology, 28*, 527–529.

Stampfl, T. G. (1987). Theoretical implications of the neurotic paradox as a problem in behavior theory: An experimental resolution. *The Behavior Analyst, 10*, 161–173.

Stampfl, T. G. (1991). Analysis of aversive events in human psychopathology: Fear and avoidance. In M. R. Denny (Ed.), *Fear, avoidance, and phobias: A fundamental analysis* (pp. 363–393). Hillsdale, NJ: Erlbaum.

Starr, M. D., & Mineka, S. (1977). Determinants of fear over the course of avoidance learning. *Learning and Motivation, 8*, 332–350.

Stasiewicz, P. R., & Maisto, S. A. (1993). Two-factor avoidance theory: The role of negative affect in the maintenance of substance use and substance use disorder. *Behavior Therapy, 24*, 337–356.

Thomas, D. R., & Lopez, L. J. (1962). The effects of delayed testing on generalization slope. *Journal of Comparative and Physiological Psychology, 55*, 541–544.

Williams, R. W., & Levis, D. J. (1991). A demonstration of persistent human avoidance in extinction. *Bulletin of the Psychonomic Society, 29*, 125–127.

Wilson, G. T. (1973). Counterconditioning versus forced exposure in extinction of avoidance responding and conditioned fear in rats. *Journal of Comparative and Physiological Psychology, 82*, 105–114.

Wolpe, J. (1958). *Psychotherapy by reciprocal inhibition.* Stanford, CA: Stanford University Press.

Wolpe, J. (1986). Retreat from principles [A critical review of the *Annual review of behavior therapy: Theory and practice,* Volume 10]. *Journal of Behavior Therapy and Experimental Psychiatry, 17,* 215–218.

7

DECODING TRAUMATIC MEMORY: IMPLOSIVE THEORY OF PSYCHOPATHOLOGY

DONALD J. LEVIS

The quest of psychology to explain the diversity and range of unusual and puzzling behaviors displayed by persons labeled neurotic and psychotic has created conceptual disunity in the mental health field. Critical issues related to assessment and treatment of human psychological disturbances have been repeatedly addressed in a vast and extensive literature. Yet despite these efforts, the scholarly search to establish integrative lawful statements about psychopathology continues. This attempt to functionally enhance precision in assessment and treatment is an ongoing process. The goal to identify, experimentally establish, and develop comprehensive treatment models has been retarded, inhibited by conceptual diversity, training inadequacies, and a lack of agreement among mental health professionals on the need to objectify and validate a given theoretical model and treatment approach. This disarray has been fostered largely by the lack of consensus among scholars on issues of etiology, symptom maintenance, and treatment. The central problem in resolving these issues is the inherent difficulty in isolating the conditions that determine the etiology of psychopathology.

The primary purpose of this chapter is to outline the comprehensive theory and treatment approach of implosive therapy (IT). Recent advances in theory and treatment purport to achieve the aforementioned objectives by removing many of the mysteries and the complexity associated with the field of psychopathology. Minor alterations in the therapy have resulted in opening a "memorial window" to the past that for the first time isolates the key principles responsible for a wide range of clinical nosologies. Numerous new observations have been made that challenge many current beliefs.

The theory and treatment technique of IT were conceptualized and developed by Thomas G. Stampfl in 1959 (Stampfl & Levis, 1967). He was influenced by his extensive therapeutic experience with emotionally disturbed children and by his attempt to integrate principles from psychoanalytic theory and the experimental learning literature (Stampfl & Levis, 1969). In his work with emotionally disturbed children, he observed, using nondirective play therapy, that children would frequently confront their conflicts and most dreaded fears in play activity. This in turn would result in the elicitation of intense emotional responding, which would weaken with repetitive play behavior and lead to positive behavioral changes. Stampfl rejected the analytic notion that "insight" was the corrective therapeutic change agent. Instead, he adopted the Pavlovian principle of direct experimental extinction. This principle states that the repeated presentation of an emotionally conditioned stimulus (CS) in the absence of a biologically unconditioned stimulus (UCS) will lead to extinction of the conditioned response (CR; the symptom). He became convinced that Maslow and Mittleman (1951) were correct in their insistence that the neurotic's symptoms, defense mechanisms, and general maladaptive behavior resulted from a state that has anticipation or expectation of some catastrophe as one of its primary features. Although it appeared that this anticipation provided the motivating force for symptom development, the catastrophe anticipated usually remained unspecifiable by the client. Maslow and Mittleman concluded that what was feared involved the anticipation of abandonment, injury, annihilation, condemnation and disapproval, humiliation, enslavement, loss of love, and utter deprivation. Stampfl (1966) reasoned that for therapy to succeed, these anticipatory fears needed to be confronted directly in order for unlearning of the emotional response attached to them to take place.

He then set out to develop a new theory and treatment approach designed to meet these objectives. Borrowing a term from physics, he called his new exposure technique "implosion" to reflect the inwardly bursting (dynamic) energy process inherent in the release of affectively loaded memorial cues encoded in the brain. Once the process of cue release begins, an internal chain reaction occurs in which the first set of cues leads to elicitation of another set that, in turn, generates another set, and so on. Each new set of cues is associated with a higher level of emotional responding. The process reflects the reintegration of anxiety-arousing associations that leads to memory recovery of a given traumatic event (Stampfl & Levis, 1967).

Stampfl delayed publishing his new theory and clinical technique for 10 years until he was convinced of the technique's safety and its applicability to a wide range of neurotic and psychotic nosologies and until experimental support was obtained (Stampfl & Levis, 1967). Finally, note that the terms *implosion* and *flooding* are often used interchangeably. Both terms refer to the therapist's attempt to repeatedly and continually expose the patient to avoided fear cues to maximize the level of emotional responding and the subsequent extinction effect. Some writers, however, reserve the term *flooding* for those therapists who use the implosive procedure but restrict themselves only to the *in vivo* or imagined presentation of those cues correlated with symptom onset (Levis & Hare, 1977). Implosive therapists, especially in treating severe pathology, have found the necessity to go beyond the symptom-contingent cues and to incorporate "hypothesized" cues. This point will be clarified once the theoretical foundation underlying the technique is more fully described.

IMPLOSIVE THEORY: AN OVERVIEW

Stampfl's approach can be characterized as a stimulus–response (S-R) dynamic cognitive–behavioral approach to the treatment of psychopathology. The resulting theory is unique in its ability to integrate areas of psychology, in its resolution of the neurotic paradox, and in its ability to define complex behavior according to basic principles of experimental psychology.

Because the theory and treatment technique of IT have been described in detail elsewhere (Levis 1980a, 1991b; Stampfl, 1970, 1991; Stampfl & Levis, 1967, 1969, 1976), only a cursory review of the model will be provided here. (See Levis, 1985 for a comprehensive presentation.) In developing the theory, Stampfl was influenced by his extensive clinical experience with a wide range of psychopathological disorders and by the animal learning literature dealing with the acquisition and maintenance of fear and avoidance behavior. Maladaptive behavior was conceptualized as learned behavior resulting from the organism's exposure to past, specific aversive conditioning experiences of considerable intensity. To explain theoretically the development and maintenance of psychopathology, Stampfl adopted Mowrer's (1947) two-factor theory of avoidance learning.

Two-Factor Theory of Avoidance

Mowrer (1939, 1947, 1960; see also McAllister & McAllister, 1991) concluded that the development of human and animal avoidance behavior comprises the learning of two response classes. The first involves the conditioning of an aversive emotional state that is based on the well-established laws of classical conditioning. Fear and other emotional conditioning result from the simple contiguity of pairing this nonemotional stimulation in space or time with an inherent primary aversive event producing pain, fear, frustration, or severe deprivation. The biologically reactive, pain-producing stimulus is the UCS. Following sufficient repetition of the neutral stimulus with the UCS, the nonemotional stimulus is able to elicit an emotional response in the absence of the UCS. Following this process, the previous neutral stimulus is the CS, and the resulting emotional response is the CR. Most important, Stampfl believes the conditioning events of humans to be multiple, involving a complex set of stimuli comprising both external and internal CSs. Such conditioning events are believed to be encoded in long-term memory.

From this analysis, it is possible for central state constructs such as images, thoughts, and memories to function as conditioned cues, and these have been found to represent frequently the major part of the controlling stimulation maintaining psychopathology. Although the traumatic conditioning initially involves the presence of a primary UCS, considerable human emotional learning becomes conditioned through pairings with other aversive CSs. The learning principles involved in this transfer include the process of secondary conditioning, higher order conditioning, primary stimulus generalization, response-mediated generalization (e.g., shortness of breath elicits feelings of being choked), semantic and symbol-mediated conditioning (e.g., snake is a symbol for penis), and memory reactivation or reintegration of past aversive events (e.g., being burned by a cigarette). These principles are needed to account for children's fear of ghosts and skeletons or many adults' fear of spiders, rats, snakes, or flying, when such stimuli have never been directly paired with bodily injury or physical pain (Levis, 1985; Stampfl, 1991).

In the same vein, these principles also provide an explanation for the development of symbolism and displacement (Miller & Kraeling, 1952). For example, if conditioned fear is elicited by the sight of a knife, then the fear associated with this stimulus may generalize to all sharp objects or to other stimuli capable of producing bodily injury, such as cars, guns, unprotected high places, and so on. Similarly, if the sight of feces is associatively linked to the fear of disease, transference to such items as dirt, money, water fountains, and public toilets may occur. Likewise, fear elicited by the sight of a penis may be displaced to other objects, such as snakes, telephone poles, and knives, which have similar stimulus characteristics

(Dollard & Miller, 1950; Freud, 1936; Kimble, 1961; Stampfl & Levis, 1969).

Mowrer's (1939) theory of avoidance was greatly influenced by Freud's (1936) conclusion that human symptoms reflecting psychopathology result from the patient's attempts to escape the anxiety elicited by stimuli ("danger signals") associated with previous traumatic experiences. Maslow and Mittleman (1951) suggested that they represent an attempt to ward off the occurrence of a catastrophic event. The concept of symptoms and maladaptive behaviors as avoidance behavior is a central component of Mowrer's (1947, 1950) two-factor theory of avoidance and is an idea commonly accepted today by the vast majority of behavioral theorists (e.g., Stampfl & Levis, 1967; Wolpe, 1958).

As stated earlier, Mowrer's first factor of this two-process theory states that fear (emotional) learning is governed by the laws of classical conditioning. According to Mowrer, the resulting conditioned fear response can also be viewed as a secondary source of drive, possessing motivational or energizing properties (Amsel & Maltzman, 1950; Brown, Kalish, & Farber, 1951) as well as reinforcing effects (Brown & Jacobs, 1949; Kalish, 1954; Miller, 1948). The drive or motivating properties of the fear response set the stage for the learning of the second class of responses, referred to as avoidance behavior. Avoidance behavior, Mowrer's second factor, is considered to be governed by the laws of instrumental learning, which include both a contiguity and drive reduction notion of reinforcement. Avoidance behavior is learned because the response results in a termination or reduction of fear or anxiety. It is this reduction in fear that serves as the reinforcing mechanism for the learning of the avoidance behavior (see Levis, 1989).

Human psychological symptoms in this case of maladaptive behavior comprise response topographies that involve the skeletal nervous system and can be classified as external, overt, or behavioral; the higher mental processes of the central nervous system (cognitive processes) that can be classified as internal or covert; and the autonomic nervous system. Overt symptomatic behaviors involving the skeletal nervous system can be seen in patient's flight responses, aggressive acts, phobic behavior, compulsive rituals, and passive avoidance behavior (e.g., agoraphobia, depression). Covert avoidance behavior involves primarily the classic cognitive defenses of repression (not thinking or remembering), denial, rationalization, intellectualization, suppression, and projection. Avoidance behavior associated with autonomic responding occurs when the patient focuses on the emotional consequences of autonomic responding (e.g., anxiety, guilt, or anger) in order to avoid exposure to the stimulus situation eliciting the emotion, thereby reducing the overall fear level; this behavior can be seen in cases of pervasive anxiety, depression, and hysterical reactions. In the same vein, by focusing on one's emotional reactivity, one can avoid or block full exposure to the eliciting stimulus complex that, if exposed, would heighten the level of emotional reactivity. For example, feeling guilty can help reduce feelings of anger or fear, or feeling anger can mitigate feelings of fear or guilt (Levis, 1985, 1991b). Although the avoidance model is central to conceptualizing psychopathology, it should be understood that maladaptive behavior frequently reflects a conflict situation involving the pitting of more than one primary and secondary drive states (see Levis, 1985; Levis & Hare, 1977).

As noted earlier, a central feature of IT theory is the premise that symptomatic behavior involves the avoidance of multiple CS complexes comprising both external and internal stimuli and is usually associated with the presence of more than one drive state. Nevertheless, the apparent complexity associated with psychopathology can be reduced to a few basic, established learning principles operating independently or in combination with each other. These laws have been the subject of extensive controlled laboratory research conducted at both the human and animal level of analysis (Levis, 1989; McAllister & McAllister, 1991). The assumption that the emotional conditioning of internal states follows the same laws as those established with external stimuli helps simplify the complexity issue and appears to be supported at the clinical and experimental levels (Holzman & Levis, 1989, 1991; Levis, 1991b).

At first, the empirical finding that humans and animals could learn a response that prevented the presentation of an aversive event (e.g., electric shock) did not appear to be theoretically important. The finding that avoidance responses were learned seemed to reflect everyday experience. For example, does not a child learn to avoid a hot stove after touching it? The explanation seemed obvious: The child keeps away from the stove so he or she will not get burned. Similarly, the laboratory rat responds to the CS in order to avoid the shock (Hilgard & Marquis, 1940). This commonsense, cognitive explanation did not sit well with behaviorists, who strove to rid psychology of teleological concepts.

However, unlike appetitive learning, where the removal of the reinforcement leads to a weakening of the CR, avoidance behavior increases in strength if the aversive stimulus is avoided. Mowrer (1939) and Schoenfeld (1950) asked the critical question: How can the nonoccurrence of the UCS (e.g., shock) act as a reinforcement?

It soon became apparent to theorists that the area of avoidance responding was more problematic for the field of learning than was first realized. Unlike appetitive learning, once the UCS (e.g., food) is removed, "unlearning" or extinction takes place. In avoidance learning, the acquisition of the response occurs in the absence of the UCS (e.g., shock), a condition well established as producing extinction, not acquisition. This theoretical puzzle became even more difficult when the question was raised as to how the first avoidance response was made. Prior to the occurrence of the first avoidance response, no exposure had occurred to the contingency that an avoidance response terminated the CS and prevented the occurrence of the UCS. A simple random response occurrence explanation for the first response seemed unlikely, given the finding that avoidance learning can occur following the first CS–UCS pairing (Levis, 1971; Stampfl, 1987). Finally, how could the removal of the UCS following the learning of the avoidance response continue to produce an acquisition and maintenance function (faster response latencies and continued responding), which was then followed at some point by an extinction function (slower response latencies and no responding)?

Although other theorists (e.g., Miller, 1948; Sheffield, 1948) made significant contributions to resolving these paradoxes, it was Mowrer's (1947) rather simple yet ingenious theoretical solution that attracted the most attention. Mowrer realized that to resolve the existing paradoxes adequately, the introduction of the theoretical construct of fear or anxiety was necessary in order to reflect some internal process within the organism. Alternative theoretical accounts designed to explain these paradoxes without a fear construct (Dinsmoor, 1950, 1954; Sidman & Boren, 1957) or by substituting a cognitive construct for fear (Herrnstein, 1969; Seligman & Johnston, 1973) failed at either the conceptual or empirical level (Levis, 1989). As a result, two-factor fear theory became the dominant theory of avoidance, a position it still holds today. For a thorough review of this position, including a discussion of critical viewpoints, see Levis (1989) and McAllister and McAllister (1991).

Avoidance Maintenance and the Neurotic Paradox

In 1926, Freud (1926, 1936), in discussing human psychopathology, raised a theoretical problem, the resolution of which has defied repeated attempts. Freud's (1936) words follow:

> We consider it entirely normal that a little girl should weep bitterly at the age of four if her doll is broken, at the age of six if her teacher reprimands her, at the age of sixteen if her sweetheart neglects her, at the age of twenty-five, perhaps, if she buries her child. Each of these grief-occasioning situations has its proper time and vanishes with its passing; but the later and more definite one remains operative throughout life. We should be rather surprised, in fact, if this girl, after she had become a wife and mother, should weep over some knick-knack getting broken. Yet this is how neurotics behave. Although in their mental apparatus there have long since developed all the agencies necessary for dealing with a wide range of stimuli, although they are mature enough to be able to gratify the greater part of their needs them-

selves ... they nevertheless behave as though the old danger situation still existed, they remain under the spell of all the old causes of anxiety.... But how does this situation come about? Why are not all neuroses merely episodes in the individual's development which become a closed chapter when the next stage of development is reached? Whence comes the element of permanency in these reactions to danger? ... In other words, we find ourselves abruptly confronted once again by the oft-repeated riddle: What is the source of neurosis, what is its ultimate, its specific, underlying principle? After decades of analytic effort this problem rises up before us, as untouched as at the beginning. (pp. 89–92)

Eysenck (1976) also reached the conclusion that because neurotic behavior does not follow Thorndike's law of effect or Skinner's law of reinforcement, a special theory is required to account for these departures.

It was Mowrer (1948, 1950, 1952) who labeled the phenomenon described by Freud the "neurotic paradox." As Stampfl (1987) noted, Mowrer acknowledged the paradox as posing severe difficulties for learning-based explanations of neurotic behavior: "It is the question as to why so-called neurotic behavior is at one and the same time *self-defeating and yet self-perpetuating,* instead of self-eliminating" (Mowrer, 1950, p. 351). Mowrer, as did Freud, questioned, "Why is it, then, that in neuroses we have fears which appear to have long outlived any real justification but which stubbornly persist or which may even augment to the point of seriously incapacitating the individual?" (Mowrer, 1952, p. 679).

It is the neurotic paradox and its resolution that have become the major nemesis of all theories of psychopathology, present and past. Unless this issue is fully addressed and at least theoretically resolved, the merits of a given theory can be seriously questioned. Once the neurotic paradox is fully resolved, advances in the areas of conceptualization and treatment should be forthcoming, moving the area of psychopathology substantially forward. As Eglash (1952) concluded, "We stand today where Freud stood, with the problem unsolved" (p. 378).

As is the case with theories of psychopathology, critics of two-factor theory (Gray, 1971; Rachman, 1976; Seligman & Johnston, 1973) have suggested that the laboratory demonstration of extreme resistance to extinction of avoidance behavior represents the Achilles heel of most contemporary avoidance theories. In the words of Seligman and Johnston (1973), "Even the more flexible versions [of fear theory], however, cannot be reconciled with the great resistance to extinction of avoidance and the concomitant absence of fear" (p. 69). They go on to state that animals will commonly respond for hundreds of trials without receiving a shock. Actually, at the time of their publication, laboratory examples of extreme resistance to extinction of avoidance behavior were rare (see Mackintosh, 1974). However, recent evidence at the animal level (e.g., Levis & Boyd,

1979; McAllister, McAllister, Scoles, & Hampton, 1986; Stampfl, 1987) and the human level (Malloy & Levis, 1988; Williams & Levis, 1991) indicates extreme resistance to extinction can now be obtained reliably.

Conservation of Anxiety Hypothesis

Solomon and Wynne (1954) attempted to address the issue of extreme avoidance maintenance within a two-factor theory framework. In previously reported studies (Solomon, Kamin, & Wynne, 1953; Solomon & Wynne, 1953) that had demonstrated extreme resistance to extinction, they noted four observations that required theoretical explanations. First, the avoidance latencies of their dogs shortened considerably with training. Second, they reported that overt signs of anxiety disappeared with training and seemed nonexistent in extinction when short-latency responses occurred. Third, they noted that if a dog happened to produce a long-latency response on a particular extinction trial, the reappearance of behavioral signs of fear on that trial was followed by a return of short-latency responses for the next few trials. Fourth, they observed apparent failure of extinction following 200 trials. It should be noted that the observations about the absence or presence of fear were independent of any objective measurement.

The development of short-latency responses during acquisition would be expected from a fear position and simply reflects the process of avoidance acquisition that fear conditioned to the CS backs up to the onset of the CS. However, the observation that overt signs of anxiety rapidly disappeared during training with the occurrence of short-latency avoidance responses would not be expected because fear must be present for avoidance behavior to occur. Solomon and Wynne (1954) postulated that overt signs of anxiety rapidly disappeared because the short exposure of the CS resulting from a quick avoidance response did not permit the time required for the full elicitation of the classically conditioned fear reaction. The observation of long-latency responses during extinction and the subsequent return of fear and short-latency avoidance responses sets the stage for the introduction of the conservation hypothesis. Longer latency avoidance responses periodically occurred during extinction because of fear extinction to the first part of the CS–UCS interval. The longer latency responses permitted sufficient time for the full elicitation of the fear response, resulting in the observation of the fear response. The return to a short-latency response was explained by the resulting strengthening of the avoidance response by the increased fear level and fear reduction following long-latency avoidance responses. To account for their final observation—the absence of avoidance extinction following 200 trials—Solomon and Wynne (1954) felt compelled to introduce yet another principle, which they labeled *partial irreversibility*. This principle is based on the assumption that a very intense pain–fear reaction produced by the use of traumatic shock in their studies became associated to the CS, resulting in a permanent fear reaction.

Solomon and Wynne (1954) attempted to amend two-factor theory by including the principles of conservation of anxiety and partial irreversibility. Their theory as stated became problematic for fear theory. First, if a short CS exposure does not provide sufficient time for the fear response to occur, how can the avoidance response be elicited (a critical point raised also by Seligman & Johnston, 1973)? Fear stimuli must be present in sufficient strength to elicit avoidance behavior. Second, the principle of partial irreversibility suggests a kind of functional autonomy for avoidance behavior that is inconsistent with the Pavlovian laws of extinction. Solomon and Wynne (1954) used traumatic shock in their attempt to mirror human symptoms' etiology and maintenance. If the avoidance maintenance is irreversible, however, how can therapy be successful?

For fear theory to be consistent, it must maintain that fear is present if the CS elicits avoidance responding. Solomon and Wynne (1954) suggested that behavioral signs of fear to a short CS exposure are noted only early in training and appear to dissipate over trials. Levis and Boyd (1979) argued that the avoidance response, when rapidly learned, reaches asymptote quickly. Once at asymptote, only a fractional level of fear activation is needed to elicit the avoidance behavior, and such small levels of fear may not be easily observable. Levis and Boyd (1979) made a critical test of this position and found that following a large number of short-latency responses, fear was indeed present, a finding replicated by Smith and Levis (1991). Fear theory also maintains that the laws of Pavlovian extinction were operating in the Solomon and Wynne (1953) study and that their dogs would have extinguished completely (some did) if a sufficient number of trials had been administered (see Levis & Boyd, 1979; Malloy & Levis, 1988). Concerning the partial irreversibility hypothesis, Solomon and Wynne failed to demonstrate that the extreme avoidance behavior reported was a function of traumatic shock as they suggested. No control nontraumatic shock level was used for a comparison. Brush (1957) conducted the appropriate study in Solomon's laboratory and found that traumatic shock level was not responsible for the sustained avoidance behavior. This seriously questioned the merits of the partial irreversibility hypothesis. According to my knowledge, there is no evidence to suggest that the law of Pavlovian extinction is not operating in persistent avoidance behavior.

To provide two-factor theory with a more consistent S-R interpretation of avoidance maintenance, Stampfl reinterpreted the conservation of anxiety hypothesis in an attempt to provide a resolution of the neurotic paradox.

Stampfl's Avoidance Maintenance Resolution

To understand the IT technique fully, it is essential that the therapists comprehend Stampfl's theoretical explanation of symptom maintenance (Stampfl, 1970, 1987; Stampfl & Levis, 1967, 1969). Clinical observations revealed that although some human symptoms do appear to last for lengthy periods, the cues initially reported for eliciting symptom onset frequently undergo a change over time, with the earlier fear-eliciting cues failing to trigger the symptom. Theoretically, it follows that because of repeated CS exposure, the fear-eliciting properties associated with these cues produce an extinction effect and are replaced from memory with a new set of cues with fear-motivating properties that have not previously received much CS exposure. These new cues and their emotional reactivity can be observed when symptom occurrence is prevented. This observation led Stampfl to conclude that a network of cues was involved in motivating a given symptom and that these cues, which represent past conditioning events involving pain, were stored in memory and ordered in a sequential or serial arrangement in terms of their accessibility. Furthermore, it appeared that these cue patterns were ordered along a dimension of stimulus intensity, with the more aversive cue patterns being least accessible. It was hypothesized that these memorial encoded cues are activated by a stimulus situation in the patient's current life that is similar on a generalization dimension to those cues associated with previous traumatic conditioning events. The patient's symptoms block the release of such cues and avoid the intense emotional properties attached to them. However, because these generalized cues are eventually exposed, the fear of them undergoes an extinction effect, which in turn reactivates the next set of cues in the serial chain. Stampfl (1970; Stampfl & Levis, 1967) translated this observation into S–R terminology by extending and modifying the now classic conservation of anxiety hypothesis suggested by Solomon and Wynne (1954).

The laboratory avoidance conditioning paradigm is arranged in such a manner that if an animal makes the appropriate response to the CS (e.g., jumps out of the conditioning box) prior to UCS onset, the CS immediately terminates and the UCS is prevented on that trial. In extinction, the UCS is removed. The conservation part of Solomon and Wynne's hypothesis is based on the observation that in avoidance learning, the occurrence of a short-latency avoidance response prevents the full exposure of the CS on that trial. Therefore, that part of the CS that is unexposed will be conserved from fear extinction because exposure is a requirement for extinction. Stampfl reasoned from his observations of human symptom maintenance that the neurotic paradox could be conceptually understood by extending the conservation of anxiety hypothesis. As stated earlier, the traumatic conditioning events maintaining human symptomatology are assumed to be elicited by a complex set of cues that are encoded in long-term memory. These various CS complexes are believed to be sequenced in order of their aversive loading and in terms of their accessibility to reactivation. It therefore follows that if short-latency avoidance responses conserved the fear to longer CS segments by preventing their exposure, then the process of conservation could be maximized even further in the laboratory by dividing the CS–UCS interval into distinctive stimulus components. This procedure in turn should enhance the conservation of anxiety effects by reducing the generalization of extinction effects from a short CS exposure to a long CS exposure. For example, consider the presentation of an 18-s CS–UCS interval in which the first 6 s of the CS involve the presentation of a buzzer (S1), the next 6 s involve the presentation of flashing lights (S2), and the last segment involves the presentation of a tone (S3). Once avoidance responding is firmly established to the S1 component, S2 and S3 are prevented from exposure. The conservation of anxiety to the S2 and S3 components should be maximized because any extinction effects from exposure to the S1 component would be unlikely to produce much generalization of extinction effects to the remaining unexposed segments of the CS–UCS interval. This is because the remaining cues in the segment are highly dissimilar to the exposed part of the interval. Thus, the greater the reduction in generalization of extinction from the early exposed part of the CS–UCS interval to the unexposed portions, the greater the degree of anxiety conservation to the components closer to UCS onset.

In principle, the use of a serial CS presentation should maximize the conservation effect and retard the extinction process in the following manner. Eventually, exposure to the S1 component will result in sufficient extinction to produce longer avoidance response latencies. At some point, the S2 component will be exposed. When this occurs, the level of fear activation will change from a relatively low level elicited by the S1 component to a high state elicited by the S2 component. The S2 component is more fearful because much of the original fear level has been conserved and because the initial conditioning effects were stronger because of the closer proximity of this stimulus during conditioning to the UCS. Upon exposure of the S2 component, behavioral signs of fear should be observed. Once exposed, the S2 component functions as a second-order conditioning stimulus, strengthening the fear level to the S2 component (see Rescorla, 1980). This reconditioning effect (S1–S2) should result in a return of short-latency responses to the S1 component, which in turn preserves any further extinction of the S2 component. The reconditioning effect of S1 associated with the S2 exposure should continue to occur until the S2 component's fear level has undergone a sufficient extinction effect. Responding should then be mainly under the control of the S2 component. When S2 is extinguished, S3 will be exposed, and the process of reconditioning S2 and S1 reoccurs. Thus, by adding components in a serial fashion, one maximizes both the conservation of anxiety hypothesis and the process of secondary intermittent reinforcement, which should produce extreme avoidance maintenance. The overall effect results in a distribution of avoidance latencies in extinction that produces a kind of see-saw effect. These theories have received strong empirical support in laboratory studies using animals (e.g., Levis, 1966, 1979; Levis & Boyd, 1979; Levis & Stampfl, 1972) and in humans (Malloy & Levis, 1988). It is these principles that are believed to be operating in humans and that are responsible for retarding the unlearning of fear. (For clinical examples of this effect, see Levis, 1980a, 1988; Stampfl, 1970; Stampfl & Levis, 1969, 1976.)

Fear and Symptom Unlearning

As can be deduced from the preceding analysis of symptom maintenance, the principles of fear extinction are operating with each occurrence of the patient's symptom but are retarded by the ability of the defense system to prevent any lengthy CS exposure, by the ability of newly exposed cues to recondition the previously extinguished cues, and by the complexity of the network of cues and defense system previously conditioned. Thus, it would logically follow that extinction of both the emotional eliciting cues and the resulting behavior motivated to avoid these cues could be facilitated by somehow exposing the patient to as many of the avoided cues as possible. This would result in the elicitation of a strong emotional response in the absence of any primary aversive stimulus (UCS), which in turn should produce an equally strong extinction effect. In the laboratory, this strategy has been achieved by directly preventing or blocking the occurrence of the avoidance response, by permitting the response to occur but removing the CS termination contingency arrangement, or by delaying the occurrence of the response until after full CS exposure. Each of these forced-exposure CS procedural manipulations has been shown in the laboratory to facilitate both fear and avoidance extinction (Baum, 1970; Shipley, 1974; Shipley, Mock, & Levis, 1971). The strategy has been adopted by IT therapists to treat human fears by using an *in vivo* exposure approach or by presenting the avoided cue via an imagery extinction technique.

IMPLOSIVE THERAPY: AN OVERVIEW

Because emotional unlearning is a function of repeated CS exposure, it follows that the established laboratory procedures for facilitating this effect may be effective in the treatment of human psychopathology. CS exposure is a common link binding all psychotherapeutic procedures. What makes IT unique is the theoretical assumption that CS exposure and sub-sequent emotional extinction is the key variable in producing symptom removal. As noted earlier, it follows from this orientation that with each occurrence of a patient's symptom, some unlearning is taking place because of partial CS exposure. This leads to the prediction that remission of symptoms would be especially notable in those cases in which the patient's avoidance is only partially effective in reducing CS exposure. This appears to be the case in depression and pervasive anxiety (see Boyd & Levis, 1980; Hare & Levis, 1981; Levis, 1980b, 1987). A change in the stimuli-eliciting symptom onset should also occur over time and reflect the process of CS extinction. Similarly, changes in the patient's response pattern should occur when new conflicts emerge and when the existing symptom ceases to function as an effective CS terminator.

To obtain substantial symptom reduction, repeated exposure may be needed not only to the CS cues directly correlated with symptom onset but also to the cues reactivated by the exposure procedure and associated with the traumatic conditioning events. However, for symptom reduction or removal to occur, it is not essential that all the conditioned stimuli comprising the total CS complex motivating a given symptom be presented by the therapist or that their presentation be completely accurate. Extinction effects occurring from exposure to a given set of cues should generalize to other CS cues not exposed as a function of stimulus similarity. This is the reverse process to that taking place during fear acquisition. However, it is important that extinction effects are obtained to those cues with the greatest affective loading. Finally, it follows that the stronger the emotional responses are to the exposed CS complex, the greater the degree of emotional extinction (see Levis, 1980b, 1985).

Implosive theory technique is based primarily on a single principle, that of direct extinction. The task of the therapist is to extinguish the conditioned aversive CS complexes that provide the motivation for symptom occurrence and maintenance. This can be achieved by representing, reinstating, or symbolically reproducing in the absence of physical pain (UCS) the previously conditioned cues motivating the patient's symptomatology (Stampfl & Levis, 1976). In those cases where the CS patterns being avoided involve discrete external stimuli, in vivo exposure to those cues has been found to be very effective (Levis & Boyd, 1985; Levis & Hare, 1977). Such in vivo CS exposure should function as an activation of other connected, internally coded cues. If pathology is not severe, generalization of extinction effects from exposure to the in vivo cue may be sufficient to reduce symptom behavior. However, in those cases where the conditioning history is severe or the cues eliciting symptom onset are primarily internal, the therapist can introduce these avoided cues by using an imagery technique.

The use of an imagery procedure is especially needed for the presentation of those internal cues associated with the neural representation of specific past conditioning events involving pain and punishment. Through verbal instruction to imagine, scenes incorporating various stimuli (visual, auditory, tactile) hypothesized to be linked to the original conditioning events are represented to the patient. The technique is an *operational procedure* in that confirmation of a suspected cue area is determined by whether the presentation of the material elicits a strong emotional response. According to theory, cues that elicit negative affect in imagery do so because of previous learning and thus are extinguishable through repetition. Images function solely as CSs; the same is true for all thoughts or memories.

The technique used is a feedback approach and, as Stampfl (1970) noted, is analogous to the situation in which an experimenter is given the task of extinguishing a rat's avoidance behavior but is not told what CS the rat was conditioned to (e.g., a 4-KHz tone). Although there is an infinite number of possible CSs that could have been used to condition the rat, knowledge of the avoidance literature should increase the probability of finding the right CS. A careful experimenter would start to introduce in a systematic way a variety of stimuli known to be used with rats, such as lights, buzzers, and tones. If signs of fear or avoidance behavior occur when the probe stimulus is introduced, support for the preconditioning of this stimulus is obtained. The stronger the overt response, the greater the support. Let us assume by a process of elimination that the experimenter finds that an 8-KHz tone elicits a strong emotional response. By presenting this tone selected over and over, the experimenter is now able to extinguish the emotional response to the tone. Note that because of the generalization of extinction effects, precise accuracy is not necessary. Repeated presentation of an 8-KHz tone should effectively weaken the eliciting tendencies of a 4-KHz tone.

This strategy is essentially the same as that employed by the IT therapist. The therapist has the added advantage in reconstructing the avoided cues to be dealing with a verbally communicating organism. By focusing on the patient's reported associations to the stimuli presented and incorporating them into additional imagery scenes, the therapist produces a chain of associations that not only adds new unexposed fear cues but also appears to reflect the decoding of an actual traumatic memory. With this overview in mind, I now turn to a more detailed presentation of the technique.

One of the primary tasks of the therapist in administering the IT technique is to determine what aversive cues are triggering the symptomatic behavior of the patient. Assessment represents an important ingredient in using the technique successfully. To facilitate this objective, the following discussion of stimulus cue categories may prove helpful.

Classification of Avoided-Stimulus Cue Categories

Although Levis (1980b) outlined seven different cue categories to be considered for research investigation, Stampfl's (1970) suggestion of a four-category system is sufficient for clinical purposes. These cues can be thought of in terms of a progression along a continuum that ranges from extremely concrete and physical cues at one end to more hypothetical, dynamic cues at the other. The first category encompasses what are referred to as *symptom-contingent cues*, or those environmental cues that initially serve to elicit a given symptom. Symptom-contingent cues can include seeing an icepick, riding in an elevator, eating in public, touching the keys to a rental car, smelling of smoke, hearing the sound of thunder, and so forth. Such cues are generally the least complex and are most accessible to the patient and, hence, to the therapist.

The second cue category consists of *reportable, internally elicited cues.* This refers to the thoughts, feelings, and physical sensations that the patient reports experiencing while engaging in his or her problematic behavior. For example, a man with an obsessive–compulsive hand-washing symptom reports to his therapist that, among other problems, he finds it extremely difficult, at times impossible, to enter his living room. Despite his desire to watch television and spend time with his family, he is unable to bring himself to set foot in the living room. Here, the sight of the living room serves as the symptom-contingent cue that leads to the symptom, the uncontrollable desire to wash his hands, and the subsequent avoidance of the living room.

When asked to describe his thoughts and feelings, the patient explains that, as a result of a work-related accident in which he was exposed to a radioactive compound, he is convinced that the placement of his briefcase and jacket on a living room chair has resulted in radioactive contamination of his entire home, most especially the living room. He further reports that he experiences feelings of great anxiety when he is in or near the living room and that his anxiety is accompanied by a racing heart, rapid and shallow breathing, dizziness, and a dry mouth.

Given this report, the therapist proceeds to form hypotheses regarding the next cue category, namely, *unreportable cues hypothesized to be related to reportable, internally related cues.* Given that the physical symptoms that the patient reports are similar to those that accompany panic attacks, the therapist might consider the possibility that the patient also experiences feelings of loss of control and might fear that he is going insane. Further unreported cues might include fear of death and damnation and the experience of anger, muscle tension, sweaty palms, and feelings of suffocation.

Finally, the therapist, from information obtained during a detailed interview, will attempt, when warranted, to generate a fourth category of cues, which Stampfl labeled *hypothesized dynamic cues*. In this case, interview material regarding the patient's childhood—his parents' divorce when he was young and his overenmeshed relationship with his mother, accompanied by information regarding the troubled nature of his marriage—suggested, among other things, an unresolved oedipal complex. In addition to oedipal cues, dynamic cues involved oral, anal, primal scene, and death wish impulses; castration; and a variety of primary process cues. These types of cues are then reduced to their stimulus equivalents. Dynamic cues have been found to be especially useful in the treatment of more severely disturbed patients.

Progression from the category of symptom-contingent cues to that of hypothesized dynamic cues is roughly consistent with a progression along the serial CS continuum. The cues in the former category lie farthest from the hypothesized UCS, whereas those in the latter category lie relatively closer along the chain. This is not, however, by any means a linear relationship. As I stated earlier, human beings possess extremely complex learning histories. No therapist can ever expect to find a neat conditioning chain in which cues will hold membership in a single cue category. Rather, it is far more likely that cues will warrant membership in two or more categories simultaneously. Despite such complexity, the proposed cue categories are useful in assisting the therapist in developing a conceptualization of the case.

An important factor to consider in developing hypothesized cues is the attention given to critical features of the conditioning process. Because the original conditioning events required the presence of a UCS, the assumption is made that cues associated with tissue injury and pain (e.g., enduring physical punishment, being cut, falling) have been encoded in the brain as a memory and function as a CS activator. Therefore, stimuli immediately associated with bodily injury (e.g., sight of blood) are assumed to be integral elements of the aversive stimulus complex, even though not reported by the patient. Stampfl (1970) emphasized this point and provided a number of illustrative examples. Consider a patient who is abnormally afraid of falling from high places. It would logically follow that the patient also fears the bodily consequences of the impact following the fall. In reconstructing the fear, the falling sequence of aversive stimuli is assumed to be related to the phobia: S1 (cues associated with being in a higher place—symptom-contingent cues); S2 (cues associated with falling—reportable cues); S3 (stimuli associated with the impact, such as a mangled body—hypothesis-related cues); and if the patient fears afterlife, S4 (suffering in hell—dynamic cues).

Once the therapy process is under way, confirmation for the validity of the cues introduced is determined by the degree of the patient's emotional reactivity to the scenes. Frequently the therapeutic process will release actual memories of the traumatic conditioning event, resulting in the incorporation by the therapist of these reportable cues and reducing the need for continual use of hypothesized cues.

The IT technique has been used successfully to treat a wide range of clinical symptoms, including phobic behavior, obsessive–compulsive disorders, depression, pervasive anxiety, hysteria, psychosomatic problems, hypochondriasis, psychopathology, posttraumatic stress disorder, multiple personalities, hallucinations and delusions, and other types of maladaptive behavior labeled neurotic or psychotic. Its "safety" has been firmly established (Boudewyns & Levis, 1975; Boudewyns & Shipley, 1983; Levis, 1985; Shipley & Boudewyns, 1980). Details of the treatment procedure and its implementation can be found in the following references: Boudewyns and Shipley, 1983; Levis, 1980a, 1985; Stampfl, 1970, 1991; and Stampfl and Levis, 1967, 1969, 1973, 1976. For a formal statement of the theoretical model, see Levis, 1985; for supporting evidence for the underlying principles of the theory, see Levis, 1985, 1989, 1991; Levis and Boyd, 1979; and Smith and Levis, 1991; and for treatment outcome evaluation research, see Boudewyns and Shipley, 1983; Levis and Boyd, 1985; Levis and Hare, 1977, and Levis and Malloy, 1982.

Enhancement of the Memory Reactivating Properties of Implosive Therapy

A major premise of implosive theory, as well as numerous other theories of psychopathology, centers on the assumption that the origin of psychopathology stems from past, specific traumatic experience encoded in long-term memory. Freud (1959) was the first major theorist to recognize the therapeutic importance of both reactivating these memories and discharging them through repetition. He reached this conclusion in 1893, a discovery unfortunately since forgotten by a large segment of the therapeutic community. Freud (1959) stated the following:

> The discovery that we made, at first to our own surprise, was that when we had succeeded in bringing the exciting events to clear recollection, the patient had also succeeded in arousing with it the accompanying effect, and when the patient had related the occurrence in as detailed a manner as possible and had expressed his feeling in regard to it in words, the various hysterical symptoms disappeared at once, never to return. *Recollection without affect is nearly always quite ineffective; the original physical process must be repeated as vividly as possible*, brought into *statum noscendi* [state of awareness] and then "talked out." (p. 28; italics added)

Recognizing the importance of Freud's discovery, Stampfl (Stampfl & Levis, 1967) attempted to maximize the memory-reactivation component of IT by emphasizing the presentation in imagery of context cues (e.g., providing a detailed description of the patient's childhood bedroom) and by incorporating multiple stimulus sensations (e.g., visual, auditory, tactile) into scene presentations. Both of these variables have been shown to play a role in memory reactivation (Spear, 1978).

Although memory recovery does play a critical role in exposing significant CS cues in need of extinction, the cognitive defense structure of most patients inhibits the full recovery of all the stored memories controlling the patient's behavior. In an attempt to circumvent this problem, IT relies heavily for its effectiveness on the principle of stimulus generalization of extinction (see Dubin & Levis, 1973a, 1973b). By using an imagery technique, Stampfl provides a vehicle for introducing those "horrific" cues that the therapist hypothesizes are still being avoided. Thus, this approach makes it possible for the therapist to follow the lead of Maslow and Mittleman (1951) to expose the patient to those catastrophic events being anticipated, such as abandonment, bodily injury, annihilation, condemnation, disapproval, humiliation, loss of love, and utter deprivation. According to the model, complete accuracy in reproducing the critical cues controlling symptomatology is not necessary, nor is it necessary to recall fully the actual controlling memories. One would expect that if the affective loading of the cues extinguished only approach the real event, considerable symptom reduction would occur as a result of generalization of extinction effects (Levis, 1980a, 1985; Stampfl & Levis, 1967).

However, for a full understanding of the etiology and maintenance of psychopathology, as well as the governing principles involved, it would be necessary to develop a procedure that was capable of eliciting complete recovery of all the traumatic encoded memories responsible for producing and maintaining symptomatology, a goal frequently attempted, but one that has, as yet, eluded discovery.

As a result of 25 years of experience in using the implosive procedure with a wide range of psychopathological behaviors, I have become convinced that Stampfl's technique represents a major step in reaching this objective. However, because of the technique's speed (usually within 1 to 30 treatment sessions) in reducing or eliminating the patient's presenting symptoms, long-term use of the approach with a given patient rarely occurs. Fortunately, approximately 10 years ago I stumbled upon a procedure that has greatly enhanced the memory-activation component of the implosive technique. Continual use of this new procedure with a number of patients for a long period of time has convinced me that, for the first time, a technique is available that is capable of completely decoding *all* stored traumatic memories. As a result of completing the decoding process with a number of patients, a host of new discoveries have emerged that challenge many of the recently held beliefs in the field (Levis, 1988, 1989, 1991a, 1991b). The purpose of this section is to outline briefly these new findings and the procedure that produced them. The recent enhancement of the memory-reactivating properties of the IT technique (Levis, 1988) suggests a common feature linking together most clinical nosologies in the presence of a history of both physical and sexual abuse. Support for this observation comes from the reported frequency of sexual abuse and published clinical literature. Following a careful literature review, Demouse (1991) concluded that in the United States, the best estimates we have for reported memories of childhood sexual abuse are 40% for girls and 30% for boys, with almost half being directly incestuous for girls and with about a quarter being directly incestuous for boys. Estimates of the incidents of sexual abuse in the general population range from 4% to 14%, with the incidents among psychiatric patients thought to be higher (Finkelhor, 1984). These statistics do not take into account the large number of documented court and verified medical cases or the increasing number of individuals who initially deny the presence of such memories only to later find compelling evidence for the historical presence of such abuse. Even a cursory review of the abundance of clinical literature on the topic attests to the presence of childhood sexual abuse in every major diagnostic category (e.g., see Bemporod & Romano, 1992).

The mental health field has been—and I believe still is—in a clinical state of denial when it comes to acknowledging the importance of childhood physical and sexual abuse in maintaining and treating psychopathology. However, it should be clearly understood from the start that my intent is not to convince anyone of the scientific validity of the observations and conclusions to be presented. *Case material does not represent, nor can it be a substitute for, experimental validation.* My professional career has primarily been devoted to establishing the scientific validity of the principles associated with implosive theory. Rather, the intent here is to draw the attention of the reader to the importance that such clinical observations play in advancing theory and research, developing new testable hypotheses, and facilitating new discoveries. Aware of the dangers of generalizing from clinical cases, I remained silent for the first few years after discovering this new approach until I was personally convinced of the validity of these discoveries by obtaining independent confirmation, ensuring the absence of any suggestive effects, and establishing that the findings were reproducible over a wide range of nosologies and by other therapists. Although clinical observations of psychological phenomena do not represent scientifically established facts, their importance should not be underestimated. Paul Meehl (1978) stated: "There is not a single experiment reported in my 23 volume set of the standard edition of Freud nor is there a *t* test. But I would take Freud's clinical observations over most people's *t* test any time" (p. 817).

The resulting modification in the implosive procedure was developed as a result of two patients' in-session behavior. While in the process of describing a scene, one patient reported seeing only a field of white. I was unable to alter her visual field by repeating the scene I wanted her to visualize. In frustration, I attempted to extinguish what I considered a defense (seeing the white field) by having the patient increase her focusing on the white field. Eventually this procedure produced a white table, which was followed by a white hallway and, finally, by a brown bottle on the table. Continuing this approach led to the recovery of a traumatic memory involving an alcoholic uncle who, after fondling the patient, inserted a beer bottle into her vagina. This event apparently took place when the patient was 4 or 5 years old, in a summer cottage that she visited for many years. The patient reported having no conscious memory of the cottage prior to recovering the memory. The white field represented the color of the walls, table and flooring in the hallway of the cottage. This memory led to other associations that resulted in the recovery of another memory, and so on (Levis, 1991b). A second patient, who was successfully treated for a series of anxiety attacks elicited by entering certain rooms within her home (Levis, 1987), requested to continue therapy despite the fact that she was completely symptom-free following 30 sessions of IT. She wanted to work on her lack of sexual feelings, which she had not viewed as a major problem in need of treatment at the time that she entered therapy. The importance of this case is that it provided me with an opportunity of extending the use of the technique beyond the presenting problem.

As a result of the cases, modifications in the technique were made. The most important change in the procedure involved shifting the responsibility for producing the content of the material exposed over to the patient. The procedure is simple in that all the therapist is required to do is to select a relevant, previously reported partial aversive memory and to present it as an implosive imagery scene, instructing the patient to report all associations elicited by the procedure. By focusing on the self-generated association, the patient will report new associations. Continuing this process produces more content, and eventually, a traumatic memory will surface. Repeating the memory until it is fully decoded sets the stage for the releasing of the next memory, and so forth. It is as if the brain takes over the decoding process, with the therapist becoming relatively inactive except to record the material elicited. The affect released is intense beyond anything previously experienced by this therapist. The willingness and ability of the therapist to listen to the content elicited and to be exposed to the high levels of affect elicited also play a role in the continual releasing of such aversive content. Additional repetition and extinction are obtained by having the patient repeat the recovered memory for homework. Once this process is started, the decoding appears complete in that all stimuli—internal and external—associated with the beginning, middle, and end of the traumatic event are reproduced in great and unbelievable detail. This includes (a) the reactivation of *all sensory systems* involved in the original conditioning event, including visual, tactile, auditory, kinesthetic, and odoriferous systems; (b) *all cognitive components*, including words spoken, internal thoughts and fear elicited; and, most important, (c) the release of *all autonomic responses* conditioned, including the reexperience of intense physical and psychological pain.

The content of these encoded traumatic memories includes intense psychological and physical pain associated with vile, sadistic acts imposed by the abuser. Examples include memories associated with long-term confinement involving primary deprivation states; intense beatings producing bodily damage; systematic burning and cutting of various parts of the body, including the genital area; genital insertion of knives, guns, and other foreign objects, such as a shoehorn, pole, coat hanger, statue, soldering iron, and electrified lamp bulb. Memories of repeated, forced oral, vaginal, and anal sex are common, frequently occurring under the age of 5 years, along with group sex or inclusion in satanic ritual abuse. Each of my patients has been brought to the point of death. For all female patients so far treated, adolescent pregnancy occurred, with horrible memories being uncovered of abortion, birth of a dead baby, or birth of a live baby who was then killed and mutilated.

It is the avoidance of memories with this type of content that represents the motivational origin for later development of clinical symptomatology. *Diagnostic and Statistical Manual of Mental Disorders* (American Psychiatric Association, 1994) clinical symptoms are not created by simple verbal rejection, coldness, spankings, marital conflict, or other forms of emotional pain. These kinds of secondary learned stimuli clearly affect personality development and feelings of self-worth, but I believe that for the formation of most clinical symptoms, the kind of trauma previously illustrated exists. I have treated a wide range of clinical symptomatology and so far have uncovered this kind of trauma in most patients who initially have no memory of the presence of any physical or sexual abuse. Many of my patients have moderate or mild clinical symptoms, yet they produce memories that rival those reported for cases diagnosed as being psychotic or as having multiple personalities. Until I better understood how the brain functioned, I had difficulty understanding why each of my patients did not have a history of long-term hospitalization in a mental ward. Patients we see in part have developed clinical symptoms to protect themselves from becoming abusers. Research on those who are doing the abuse supports the contention that they may present only mild symptoms, because they are frequently found to be nonpsychotic or to appear normal.

At first, these self-generated images of the patient were difficult for me to believe as factual representations. However, when they repeatedly occurred within and across a variety of different diagnosed symptoms, in cases in which I would never have suspected such material, they became harder to dismiss as fantasy. Symptom reduction or elimination under the control of a given encoded memory, as well as significant positive personality changes, usually follows the affective decoding of a given memory.

Once the patient is fully involved in the decoding process, the therapist's participation is minimal. What material is forthcoming appears to be completely under the control of the patient.

Brain Decoding of Trauma

The manner in which the brain decodes or releases the traumatic memories is a very complicated and integrated process, although lawful and systematic. The various neural engrams that make up each memory or set of memories associated temporally are interconnected with other traumatic memories along a dimension of both stimulus and response similarity. The cues encoded within a given neural engram or within a given network of engrams are ordered sequentially in terms of accessibility from least to most aversive. In most patients treated, there are a number of these interconnected neural networks that can also be cross-connected with each other. The associative linkage within a given network may be interconnected in the following manner: (a) by the encoding of *extroceptive stimulus cues* involving an object (e.g., knives, guns, and clothes hangers), people (e.g., family friends, neighbors, siblings, mother, father), or places (e.g., bedroom, basement, hospitals); (b) by *response-produced stimulation* involving behavior (e.g., taking a shower, participating in sexual activity, eating, drinking); (c) by *cognitive stimuli* (e.g., thoughts of dying, suicide, murder, or revenge; dream content); and (d) by *interoceptive emotional stimuli* (e.g., fear, guilt, anger, loneliness, shame, loss of control, pain).

It has been well established that the human brain regularly attempts through a variety of cognitive mechanisms to avoid or inhibit unpleasant emotion-eliciting thoughts and experiences. The brain, on the other hand, also appears to be striving to discharge the affective component in its quest to return the neural engram to a homeostatic level of functioning. The more intense the emotional experience, the greater the need for discharge and the stronger the defense needed to suppress it. Generalized stimuli within the environment repeatedly release some of the emotional component of the avoided memory, which in turn results in the emitting of defenses to block the further release of memory. Thus, the brain engages in a series of excitatory and inhibitory clashes until the affective component is extinguished to the point that the threshold level for eliciting the neural engram falls below that of the eliciting stimuli.

Following a given trauma, the abused child attempts to block out or avoid conscious memory of the conditioning event. He or she appears to be reasonably successful in avoiding those components of the neural engram representing high levels of emotionality. However, as long as the abuser remains abusive and the stimulus situation in which the abuse occurs remains the same, partial memory recovery repeatedly occurs. Complete memory avoidance is not maintained until the abuse stops.

Within a given traumatically encoded engram, there are a number of intense emotion-eliciting cues surrounded by a strong, protective inhibitory mechanism. I have referred to these cues as "hidden," because they remain avoided following the completion of the initial stages of memory recovery. The most avoided of these emotions is the encoded memory of very high levels of intense pain (e.g., protopathic pain; see Stampfl, 1991). When the pain reaches a protopathic level of intensity during the traumatic experience, patients frequently report having a "mind-out-of-body" experience that has the effect of immediately eliminating the pain response from consciousness. Although pain is reportedly not experienced when the child is "out of his or her body," it still appears to be encoded in the neural engram representing that memory. Further, the mind-out-of-body experience appears to be a learned operant. Patients have reported fading into lights, curtains, colors, wallpaper, or cracks in the wall or hallucinating a peaceful experience far removed from the traumatic situation. Patients also report returning to their bodies when the abuser stops producing the pain or if the intense pain is repeated or increased. When the latter situation occurs, the only avoidance behavior left is a state of unconsciousness or death.

Central to complete removal of psychopathology is the necessity for the patient to reexperience these memory cues of pain. Throughout the patient's life it appears that the brain is attempting to release this component of the stored memory and may well directly affect the immune system in order to produce the physical symptom historically experienced. This possibility conceptually presented itself when I observed the appearance of a painful physical symptom concurrent with the reactivation of each traumatic memory. These memory-reactivated symptoms are physical in nature, such as the feeling of a weight on the chest, pain in various bodily areas, the appearance of black and blue marks and burns on the body, bumps and cuts on the genital area, burning sensations or blood discharge from the vagina or anus, involuntary body spasms, choking, breathing difficulties, or excessive mucus and salivation. These symptoms represent that part of the body injured during the trauma and quickly disappear once the stimulus properties of the memory are recovered and the affective component extinguished. They frequently are released prior to the uncovering of the memory and are symptoms reported to occur periodically throughout the patient's adult life. It is conceivable that a very large percentage of medical problems have their origin in encoded traumatic memories.

It is the avoidance of the pain component of memory and its periodic release that provides the primary motivational factor in maintaining psychopathology. Memory pain (a CR) differs from real pain (a UCR) in that, following its release to the original stimulus complex, memory pain undergoes an extinction effect that in turn produces a corresponding reduction in the drive state eliciting symptom behavior. Real pain produced by a UCS does not disappear upon exposure and repetition.

With the cessation of the abuse, blockage of the memories, either complete or partial, occurs. In either case, the nervous system is in a state of imbalance between the need to discharge the affective loading of the encoded memories and the need to protect the individual from reexperiencing the painful memories. Inhibition of those emotions most directly associated with pain, usually the expression of anger and rage, is particularly strong. It appears that the inhibitory defensive mechanisms are developed and maintained to protect the abused child from further bodily injury. I have been amazed at the level of pain that a child can endure while still actively resisting and fighting the abuser. There appears to be a constant ongoing battle between the abuser and the abused to control the situation. At the end, the abused child's willingness to resist is lost.

Despite the absence of conscious memory, the excitatory–inhibitory conflict continues, with the nervous system constantly pushing to release the affective component of each encoded memory. The defense pattern designed to hold the memories in check has to be modified constantly to remain effective. This occurs because life situations are constantly presenting the abused person with generalized cues that activate a given avoided traumatic memory. Each time this happens, affect is released to the generalized cues, resulting in an extinction effect that in turn releases the next set of cues ordered in the sequence of encoded memories. This process repeats itself, reducing the effectiveness of old defenses. The abused person's cognitive defenses of suppression and denial start to weaken, resulting in the development of two general patterns of avoidance. In the first pattern, the abused person cannot control the release of affective feelings, especially those associated with rage. In an attempt to prevent the release of the content of his or her own memories and to regain the feeling of being in control, the victim releases his or her anger onto others, thus actually becoming an abuser. In a sense, the abuser's behavior serves as an avoidance response to prevent his or her own memories of being abused from surfacing. If the abuser's history were known, it is possible that there exists a direct correlation between the method of abuse engaged in and the abuse historically experienced.

The second general pattern is demonstrated in most therapeutic cases. The dominant emotions being released for the patients are feelings of fear, guilt, shame, abandonment, and "being out of control." To keep the content of their memories from surfacing, they develop clinical symptoms to cue areas represented in their avoided memories. Their lives are a constant replay, at a reduced affective level, of the emotional conflicts experienced in childhood. The extent of the pathology manifested is not necessarily related to the overall degree of trauma experienced but rather to the degree that their cognitive defense mechanisms failed.

Stages of Memory Recovery

The process of brain decoding can be organized into a number of distinctive stages of memory recovery. Because many of these have been outlined elsewhere (see Levis, 1988, 1991a, 1991b), I will provide only a cursory overview here. As noted earlier, memory release appears to be ordered sequentially in terms of level of affect release and aversiveness of the material being decoded, with the least aversive content being released first. In the initial stages, the memory release appears fragmented and disjointed. With repetition, new information is released. This process is continued until a complete memory is decoded, including the beginning, middle, and end. Once this objective is achieved, it appears that the brain takes over the remaining decoding process, reducing the role of the therapist to one of note taking and support. At this point the patient appears to be reliving the event as if it were happening. Voice and language changes are common and appear to reflect the childhood period of the memory. Strong affective responding occurs, including the reporting of actual physical pain in the body area injured in the memory. This pain response usually precedes the recovery of the events that occurred to produce the pain and, in many cases, is experienced weeks before the memory is decoded.

Each new memory appears to be triggered by a stimulus component elicited in the preceding memory. It should also be noted that the brain releases the posttraumatic cues before or at the time that the patient is working on decoding the traumatic content. The posttraumatic cues may involve body pains in the area injured during the trauma; feelings of fatigue, depression, or hopelessness; suicide ideation; or behavior such as excessive eating, drinking, or sleeping. These cues occur during and between sessions and represent emotions, thoughts, or behaviors that were historically engaged in following the trauma being activated. Techniques have been developed to reduce or eliminate these cues between sessions.

If a particularly high level of emotion is encoded in a given memory, it is common for the brain to stop releasing new material by refocusing the patient to an earlier memory in historical time that appears, upon decoding, to prepare the patient for the emotional content of the previous uncompleted memory. Each memory decoded is followed by a new memory involving a greater intensity of encoded trauma.

This process of decoding continues until the patient reaches the "end" memory. The release of the end memory usually represents events experienced by the patient between the ages of 10 and 14. The end memory is not one memory, but rather a sequence of traumatic memories leading to the point where the child finally completely gives up and stops fighting the abuser. In this stage, the complete etiology of all the patient's pathology is revealed, as are the circumstances and methods used by the patient to suppress all memory of the physical or sexual abuse. Following the completion of the decoding of the end memory—which takes months—full recovery of memory occurs, as well as complete integration and assimilation of all previously encoded memory. Incredible positive changes in personality occur, with the complete removal of all psychopathology and full acceptance of the reality of the memories decoded. All patients treated until they reach this point deny the reality of the memories recovered throughout therapy, maintaining that they are "unbelievable" and, therefore, they must be "making them up." Their only justification for staying in therapy is that following the complete decoding of a given traumatic memory, they report being reinforced by significant positive changes in personality structure and symptom relief. If it had not been for these positive changes in behavior, I doubt that I also would have had the motivation to continue witnessing the horrors and pain experienced by these patients and to continue experiencing my own pain at repeatedly listening to the horrible, sadistic descriptions—descriptions that I also found initially difficult to believe.

To my knowledge, no other observer has taken therapy this far or decoded memories in such complete detail. This journey through many patients' historical time not only has given me remarkable insight into how psychopathology develops and is maintained but also has permitted me to observe a host of new psychological principles, many of which were discovered only with the completion of the end memory—including the development of the "false memory" syndrome. Although this journey has had its personal liabilities for me, it has provided me with a brief look into the protective and healing properties of the most remarkable organ in existence, the human brain.

EPILOGUE

The findings reported from my use of the modified implosive procedure are based on the extinction of hundreds of traumatic memories and on the completion of this process throughout the lives of a number of patients. Finishing the decoding process is essential, not only for the removal of all the negative effects produced by the original trauma but also for the understanding of a given psychopathology to be complete. The range of memories recovered span from around the age of 2 years to the teenage period. The number of memories recovered also seems infinite, with one being followed by another and with each succeeding memory appearing more traumatic than the preceding one. Unfortunately, the process of decoding takes years of therapy to complete, but once completed, major personality changes occur, producing what can only be described as a "super-healthy" individual. Fortunately, these changes in personality and psychopathology appear throughout the decoding process, following the emotional release of each traumatic memory.

One cannot fully appreciate the level of detail decoded, the degree of affective intensity released, and the lawfulness and orderliness of the decoding process within and across patients without inspecting the verbatim transcripts of these therapy sessions. Reliability of the content of a given traumatic memory has been documented by these transcripts even if the reelicitation of a given memory occurs over a year later. Finally, similar findings, as described earlier, have been replicated by other therapists trained in the technique.

Because I had difficulty accepting the content produced, I realized that so would most other therapists. Therefore, I set out to develop a systematic strategy for validating the content being elicited. As Loftus (1993) recently concluded, memory validation has become a major issue today for therapists dealing with sexual abuse cases. Validation of memory content representing historical material is a difficult, if not impossible, task. My first approach was to determine whether documented cases of such sadistic torturing behavior could be found. I quickly realized how naive I was, after contacting local social workers and reviewing court proceedings in the community in which I lived. Not only did such horrific events occur, but they appeared to be the general rule in the vast majority of documented child abuse cases. I next reviewed the historical literature and found that the type of abusive activity that I was obtaining from patients' memory had been reported to have occurred from ancient times to the present in all cultures (Radbill, 1987).

It became clear to me that the human brain regularly denies the reality of the extensive inhumanity that surrounds us daily. My first objective was to refrain from reporting my findings until I was personally sure of the validity of the content being released. This objective took some 6 years, until I had treated a sufficient number of cases and attempted to rule out other possible explanations. The first alternative hypothesis that I entertained was that the content of the memories resulted from a suggestive effect. Because the new approach did not require any therapist's input other than starting the process, I remained silent throughout each therapy session, simply recording the content being presented. Because the vast majority of patients treated denied the reality of what they produced, I refrained from agreeing or disagreeing. (In fact, I have since concluded that if a patient shows no tendency to deny the reality of the memories produced, I should seriously question whether they are real.) I next systematically attempted to alter the content by having the patient imagine content that I suggested or that could not have occurred. For example, a patient was reporting seeing her sister being raped by her father. At the time, she reported being in a closet viewing the event through a keyhole. I described in detail the rape as occurring in front of the closet door at an angle that logically could not have been viewed by the patient through a keyhole. When I asked the patient to open her eyes and describe what she saw, she reported that she did not see what I described. She saw herself huddled in the corner of the closet with her hands over her face. She then proceeded to describe what the father said to her sister, content that I did not even think of suggesting. Every attempt I have made in similar cases to alter the content of what is being reported always resulted in the patient's saying that is not what happened while going on to describe what apparently did. To date, I have been unable to alter any content via attempts at direct suggestion. Furthermore, I tried to manipulate expectations by verbalizing what I thought happened next, without success. My own expectation of what happened next also proved to be wrong on many occasions. I even tried telepathy without success. I am now personally convinced that once the decoding process starts, it has a life of its own and is not easily modifiable.

Another source of validating evidence relates to the intensity of affect generated and the corresponding behavioral indications of pain that occur and correspond perfectly to the content of the memory being decoded. I am convinced that even a gifted actress or actor could not feign the behavior elicited by the patient.

Perhaps the strongest clinical evidence for the validity of what is being reproduced is the occurrence of what I call "memory-reactivated physical symptoms." These usually occur in the weeks preceding the decoding of the controlling memory. They involve the reporting of a physical symptom, usually a severe body pain or changes in body activity, such as continual vaginal blood flow or the sudden appearance of bumps on the vagina or bruises on the body. Frequently, the patient seeks medical treatment, with a report that reflects a failure to find a physical cause or a treatment approach that fails to produce any changes. Shortly following the reporting of physical symptoms, a memory is decoded in which that part of the body where the pain is felt was severely injured (e.g., a knife or other foreign object being jammed into the vagina). Once the affect of the decoded memory is released, the physical symptom disappears.

Finally, the validity of these reported memories has been supported empirically in a number of cases by reports from significant others, hospital records, medical reports, and existing body scars. Given my failure to alter the content of the memories; the extreme level of emotional reactivity elicited by the material; the obtained correlation of the current behavior, including the development of physical symptoms to the content of the past traumatic memory; and the substantial positive changes in symptom behavior and personality structure following the emotional deconditioning of the trauma, my original doubts about the accuracy of the reports have been reduced considerably. Nevertheless, it should be clearly understood: Clinical evidence cannot serve as a substitute for experimental validation.

In closing, note that many of the discoveries and operating principles developed from observing this decoding process have yet to be put into print. I believe that once this is achieved and fully understood, the length of treatment can be reduced significantly. However, the evidence to date supports the contention that the recovery of memory in itself does not change symptom behavior. Self-understanding and insight, which are partly correlated with emotional extinction and memory recovery, are in and of themselves also insufficient factors in altering symptom behavior. Support or empathy from the therapist, although important in providing motivation for the patient to continue the process of memory recovery, is also by itself unable to produce symptom elimination. Rather, the overwhelming evidence suggests that symptom reduction occurs only when the intense affect associated with the controlling memory cues undergo extinction via exposure or release from memory. That is to say, the laboratory principle of Pavlovian extinction (Pavlov, 1927) appears to be the corrective therapeutic change agent.

REFERENCES

American Psychiatric Association. (1994). *Diagnostic and statistical manual of mental disorders* (4th ed.). Washington, DC: Author.

Amsel, A., & Maltzman, I. (1950). The effect upon generalized drive strength of emotionality as inferred from the level of consummatory response. *Journal of Experimental Psychology, 40,* 563–569.

Baum, M. (1970). Extinction of avoidance responding through response prevention (flooding). *Psychological Bulletin, 74,* 276–284.

Bemporod, J. R., & Romano, S. J. (1992). Childhood maltreatment and adult depression: A review of research. In D. Cicchetti & S. Toth (Eds.), *Rochester Symposium on Developmental Psychopathology series: Vol. IV. Developmental perspectives on depression* (pp. 351–375). Rochester, NY: University of Rochester Press.

Boudewyns, P. A., & Levis, D. J. (1975). Autonomic reactivity of high and low ego-strength subjects to repeated anxiety eliciting scenes. *Journal of Abnormal Psychology, 84,* 682–692.

Boudewyns, P. A., & Shipley, R. H. (1983). *Flooding and implosive therapy.* New York: Plenum Press.

Boyd, T. L., & Levis, D. J. (1980). Depression. In R. J. Daitzman (Ed.), *Clinical behavior therapy and behavior modification* (Vol. 1, pp. 301–350). New York: Garland STPM Press.

Brown, J. S., & Jacobs, A. (1949). The role of fear in the motivation and acquisition of responses. *Journal of Experimental Psychology, 39*, 747–759.

Brown, J. S., Kalish, H. I., & Farber, I. E. (1951). Conditioned fear as revealed by magnitude of startle response to an auditory stimulus. *Journal of Experimental Psychology, 41*, 317–328.

Brush, F. R. (1957). The effect of shock intensity on the acquisition and extinction of an avoidance response in dogs. *Journal of Comparative and Physiological Psychology, 50*, 547–552.

Demouse, L. (1991). The universality of incest. *The Journal of Psychohistory, 19*, 123–164.

Dinsmoor, J. A. (1950). A quantitative comparison of the discriminative and reinforcing functions of a stimulus. *Journal of Experimental Psychology, 41*, 458–472.

Dinsmoor, J. A. (1954). Punishment: I. The avoidance hypothesis. *Psychological Review, 61*, 34–36.

Dollard, J., & Miller, N. E. (1950). *Personality and psychotherapy.* New York: McGraw-Hill.

Dubin, W. J., & Levis, D. J. (1973a). Generalization of extinction gradients: A systematic analysis. *Journal of Experimental Psychology, 100*, 403–412.

Dubin, W. J., & Levis, D. J. (1973b). Influence of similarity of components of a serial CS on conditioned fear in the rat. *Journal of Comparative and Physiological Psychology, 85*, 305–312.

Eglash, A. (1952). The dilemma of fear as a motivating force. *Psychological Review, 59*, 376–379.

Eysenck, H. J. (1976). The learning theory model of neurosis—A new approach. *Behaviour Research and Therapy, 14*, 251–267.

Finkelhor, D. (1984). *Child sexual abuse: New theory and research.* New York: Free Press.

Freud, S. (1936). *The problem of anxiety* (H. A. Bunker, Trans.). New York: Psychoanalytic Quarterly Press and W. W. Norton.

Freud, S. (1959). *Collected papers* (Vol. 1; J. Riviere, Trans.). New York: Basic Books.

Gray, J. A. (1971). *The psychology of fear and stress.* New York: McGraw-Hill.

Hare, N., & Levis, D. J. (1981). Pervasive ("free-floating") anxiety: A search for a cause and treatment approach. In S. Turner, K. Calhoun, & H. Adams (Eds.), *Handbook of clinical behavior therapy* (pp. 41–66). New York: Wiley.

Herrnstein, R. (1969). Method and theory in the study of avoidance. *Psychological Review, 76*, 49–69.

Hilgard, E. R., & Marquis, P. G. (1940). *Conditioning and learning.* New York: Appleton-Century-Crofts.

Holzman, A. D., & Levis, D. J. (1989). The effects of increasing the number of stimulus modalities included in a fear-eliciting imagery scene on reported imagery clarity, scene repetition and sympathetic (fear) arousal. *Cognitive Therapy and Research, 13,* 389–405.

Holzman, A. D., & Levis, D. J. (1991). Differential aversive conditioning of an external (visual) and internal (imaginal) CS: Effects of transfer between and within CS modalities. *Journal of Mental Imagery, 15,* 77–90.

Kalish, H. I. (1954). Strength of fear as a function of the number of acquisition and extinction trials. *Journal of Experimental Psychology, 47,* 1–9.

Kimble, G. A. (1961). *Hilgard and Marquis' Conditioning and Learning.* New York: Appleton-Century-Crofts.

Levis, D. J. (1966). Effects of serial CS presentation and other characteristics of the CS on the conditioned avoidance response. *Psychological Reports, 18,* 755–766.

Levis, D. J. (1971). One-trial-a-day avoidance learning. *Behavioral Research Methods and Instrumentation, 3,* 65–67.

Levis, D. J. (1980a). Implementing the technique of implosive therapy. In A. Goldstein & E. B. Foa (Eds.), *Handbook of behavioral interventions: A clinical guide* (pp. 92–151). New York: Wiley.

Levis, D. J. (1980b). The learned helplessness effect: An expectancy, discrimination deficit or motivational-induced persistence? *Journal of Research in Personality, 14,* 158–169.

Levis, D. J. (1985). Implosive theory: A comprehensive extension of conditioning theory of fear/anxiety to psychopathology. In S. Reiss & R. R. Bootzin (Eds.), *Theoretical issues in behavior therapy* (pp. 49–82). New York: Academic Press.

Levis, D. J. (1987). Treating anxiety and panic attacks: The conflict model of implosive therapy. *Journal of Integrative and Eclectic Psychotherapy, 6,* 450–461.

Levis, D. J. (1988). Observation and experience from clinical practice: A critical ingredient for advancing behavioral theory and therapy. *The Behavior Therapist, 11*(5), 95–99.

Levis, D. J. (1989). The case for a return to a two-factor theory of avoidance: The failure of man–fear interpretations. In S. B. Klein & R. R. Mowrer (Eds.), *Contemporary learning theories, Pavlovian conditioning and the status of traditional learning theory* (pp. 227–277). Hillsdale, NJ: Erlbaum.

Levis, D. J. (1991a). A clinician's pleas for a return to the development of non-human models of psychopathology: New clinical observations in need of laboratory study. In M. R. Denny (Ed.), *Fear, avoidance, and phobias: A fundamental analysis* (pp. 395–427). Hillsdale, NJ: Erlbaum.

Levis, D. J. (1991b). The recovery of traumatic memories: The etiological source of psychopathology. In R. G. Kunzendorf (Ed.), *Mental imagery* (pp. 233–240). New York: Plenum Press.

Levis, D. J., & Boyd, T. L. (1979). Symptom maintenance: An infrahuman analysis and extension of the conservation of anxiety principle. *Journal of Abnormal Psychology, 88,* 107–120.

Levis, D. J., & Boyd, T. L. (1985). The CS exposure approach of implosive therapy. In R. M. Turner & L. M. Ascher (Eds.), *Evaluation of behavior therapy outcome* (pp. 59–94). New York: Springer.

Levis, D. J., & Hare, N. (1977). A review of the theoretical rationale and empirical support for the extinction approach of implosive (flooding) therapy. In M. Hersen, R. M. Eisler, & P. M. Miller (Eds.), *Progress in behavior modification* (Vol. IV, pp. 300–376). New York: Academic Press.

Levis, D. J., & Malloy, P. F. (1982). Research in infrahuman and human conditioning. In C. M. Franks & G. T. Wilson (Eds.), *Handbook of behavior therapy* (pp. 65–118). New York: Guilford Press.

Loftus, E. F. (1993). Psychologists in the eyewitness world. *American Psychologist, 48*, 550–552.

Mackintosh, N. J. (1974). *The psychology of animal learning.* New York: Academic Press.

Malloy, P., & Levis, D. J. (1988). A laboratory demonstration of persistent human avoidance. *Behavior Therapy, 19*, 229–241.

Maslow, A. H., & Mittleman, B. (1951). *Principles of abnormal psychology: The dynamics of psychic illness.* New York: Harper & Brothers.

McAllister, D. E., & McAllister, W. R. (1991). Fear theory and aversively motivated behavior: Some controversial issues. In M. R. Denny (Ed.), *Fear, avoidance, and phobias: A fundamental analysis* (pp. 35–163). Hillsdale, NJ: Erlbaum.

McAllister, W. R., McAllister, D. E., Scoles, M. T., & Hampton, S. R. (1986). Persistence of fear-reducing behavior: Relevance for conditioning theory of neurosis. *Journal of Abnormal Psychology, 93*, 365–372.

Meehl, P. E. (1978). Theoretical risks and tabular asterisks: Sir Karl, Sir Ronald, and the slow process of soft psychology. *Journal of Consulting and Clinical Psychology, 46*, 806–834.

Miller, N. E. (1948). Studies of fear as an acquirable drive: I. Fear as motivation and fear-reduction as reinforcement in the learning of a new response. *Journal of Experimental Psychology, 38*, 89–101.

Miller, N. E., & Kraeling, D. (1952). Displacement: Greater generalization of approach than avoidance in generalized approach–avoidance conflict. *Journal of Experimental Psychology, 43*, 217–221.

Mowrer, O. H. (1939). A stimulus–response analysis and its role as a reinforcing agent. *Psychological Review, 46*, 553–565.

Mowrer, O. H. (1947). On the dual nature of learning—A re-interpretation of "conditioning" and "problem-solving." *Harvard Educational Review, 17*, 102–148.

Mowrer, O. H. (1948). Learning theory and the neurotic paradox. *American Journal of Orthopsychiatry, 18*, 571–610.

Mowrer, O. H. (1950). *Learning theory and personality dynamics: Selected papers.* New York: Ronald Press.

Mowrer, O. H. (1952). Learning theory and the neurotic fallacy. *American Journal of Orthopsychiatry, 22,* 679–689.

Mowrer, O. H. (1960). *Learning theory and behavior.* New York: Wiley.

Pavlov, I. P. (1927). *Conditioned reflexes: An investigation of the physiological activity of the cerebral cortex* (G. V. Anrep, Ed.). London: Oxford University Press.

Rachman, S. (1976). The passing of the two-stage theory of fear and avoidance: Fresh possibilities. *Behavior, Research and Therapy, 14,* 125–131.

Radbill, S. (1987). Children in a world of violence: A history of child abuse. In R. R. Helfer & R. S. Kempe (Eds.), *The battered child* (4th ed., pp. 3–22). Chicago: University of Chicago Press.

Rescorla, R. A. (1980). *Pavlovian second-order conditioning: Studies in associative learning.* Hillsdale, NJ: Erlbaum.

Schoenfeld, W. N. (1950). An experimental approach to anxiety, escape and avoidance behavior. In P. H. Hoch & J. Zubin (Eds.), *Anxiety.* New York: Grune & Stratton.

Seligman, M. E. P., & Johnston, J. C. (1973). A cognitive theory of avoidance learning. In F. J. McGuigan & D. B. Lumsden (Eds.), *Contemporary approaches to conditioning and learning* (pp. 69–110). Washington, DC: Winston.

Sheffield, F. D. (1948). Avoidance training and the contiguity principle. *Journal of Comparative and Physiological Psychology, 47,* 97–100.

Shipley, R. H. (1974). Extinction of conditioned fear in rats as a function of several parameters of CS exposure. *Journal of Comparative and Physiological Psychology, 87,* 699–707.

Shipley, R. H., & Boudewyns, P. A. (1980). Flooding and implosive therapy: Are they harmful? *Behavior Therapy, 11,* 503–508.

Shipley, R. H., Mock, L. A., & Levis, D. J. (1971). Effects of several response prevention procedures on activity, avoidance responding, and conditioned fear in rats. *Journal of Comparative and Physiological Psychology, 77,* 256–270.

Sidman, M., & Boren, J. J. (1957). A comparison of two types of warning stimulus in an avoidance situation. *Journal of Comparative and Physiological Psychology, 50,* 282–287.

Smith, J. E., & Levis, D. J. (1991). Is fear present following sustained asymptotic avoidance responding? *Behavioural Processes, 24,* 37–47.

Solomon, R. L., Kamin, L. J., & Wynne, L. C. (1953). Traumatic avoidance learning: The outcomes of several extinction procedures with dogs. *Journal of Abnormal and Social Psychology, 48,* 291–302.

Solomon, R. L., & Wynne, L. C. (1953). Traumatic avoidance learning: Acquisition in normal dogs. *Psychological Monographs, 67,* No. 354, 1–19.

Solomon, R. L., & Wynne, L. C. (1954). Traumatic avoidance learning: The principle of anxiety conservation and partial irreversibility. *Psychological Review, 61,* 353–385.

Spear, N. E. (1978). *The processing of memories, forgetting and retention.* Hillsdale, NJ: Erlbaum.

Stampfl, T. G. (1966). Implosive therapy, part I: The theory. In S. G. Armitage (Ed.), *Behavioral modification techniques in the treatment of emotional disorders* (pp. 12–21). Battle Creek, MI: VA Hospital.

Stampfl, T. G. (1970). Implosive therapy: An emphasis on covert stimulation. In D. J. Levis (Ed.), *Learning approaches to therapeutic behavior change* (pp. 182–204). Chicago: Aldine.

Stampfl, T. G. (1987). Theoretical implications of the neurotic paradox as a problem in behavior theory: An experimental resolution. *The Behavior Analyst, 10,* 161–173.

Stampfl, T. G. (1991). Analysis of aversive events in human psychopathology: Fear and avoidance. In M. R. Denny (Ed.), *Fear, avoidance, and phobias: A fundamental analysis* (pp. 363–393). Hillsdale, NJ: Erlbaum.

Stampfl, T. G., & Levis, D. J. (1967). The essentials of implosive therapy: A learning-theory based on psychodynamic behavioral therapy. *Journal of Abnormal Psychology, 72,* 496–503.

Stampfl, T. G., & Levis, D. J. (1969). Learning theory: An aid to dynamic therapeutic practice. In L. D. Eron & R. Callahan (Eds.), *Relationship of theory to practice in psychotherapy* (pp. 85–114). Chicago: Aldine.

Stampfl, T. G., & Levis, D. J. (1973). Implosive therapy. In R. M. Jurjevich (Ed.), *The international handbook of direct psychotherapy: Vol. 1 Twenty-eight American originals* (pp. 83–105). Coral Gables, FL: University of Miami Press.

Stampfl, T. G., & Levis, D. J. (1976). Implosive therapy: A behavioral therapy. In J. T. Spence, R. C. Carson, & J. W. Thibault (Eds.), *Behavioral approaches to therapy* (pp. 89–110). Morristown, NJ: General Learning Press.

Williams, R. W., & Levis, D. J. (1991). A demonstration of persistent human avoidance in extinction. *Bulletin of the Psychonomic Society, 24,* 125–127.

Wolpe, J. (1958). *Psychotherapy and reciprocal inhibition.* Stanford, CA: Stanford University Press.

8

LEARNED ALARMS: THE ORIGINS OF PANIC

MICHELE M. CARTER and DAVID H. BARLOW

Disorders involving panic and anxiety are among the most extensively investigated emotional disorders (Barlow, 1988). During the past two decades, numerous researchers from a variety of theoretical orientations have attempted to unravel the nature and origins of these phenomena. Such explanations, however, have tended toward linearity, specifying one causal variable that has a unidirectional relationship with the target disorder, and may be too simplistic to capture the true origins of panic and anxiety. A more theoretically, empirically, and clinically accurate model may necessarily encompass several of the current theories.

In this chapter, we discuss the concept of "learned alarms" and how it can account for the development of panic, noting differences and similarities between our conceptualization and those of several other prominent theories. We also address differences between panic and anxiety and the role of alarms in the development of pathology. Finally, we discuss the directions for future theoretical and research undertakings designed to test the major tenets of the theory outlined in this chapter.

THE ORIGINS OF PANIC

A major emphasis in research over the past decade has been to discover the origins of panic. The prominent contemporary models have proposed either biological or cognitive causes of panic.

Biological Model

This conceptualization assumes a biological dysfunction as the causal mechanism in the origin of panic. Theorists such as Klein (1981, 1993) contend that panic attacks are the result of the "misfiring" of a physiological mechanism (Klein & Gorman, 1987). Although the *locus coeruleus* is thought to be involved in the genesis of panic, the specific pathophysiological mechanism or mechanisms remain unclear. In this model, the biological mechanism is considered to be both *necessary* and *sufficient* to account for the development of panic attacks and panic disorder.

In efforts to provide evidence of biological causation, these theorists have pointed to the laboratory provocation of panic. There is abundant evidence that many pharmacological procedures can reliably produce panic attacks. Substances such as yohimbine (Charney, Woods, Goodman, & Heninger, 1987), carbon dioxide (Sanderson & Wetzler, 1990), sodium lactate (Gorman et al., 1988), and caffeine (Shear, 1986) have all been used to provoke panic attacks, with varying degrees of success. Although supportive of the involvement of biological processes in panic, the results from such procedures alone cannot shed light on causation. It seems plausible, and has been demonstrated, that the physiological triggering of panic may be moderated by other factors such as a sense of control (Sanderson, Rapee, & Barlow, 1989) or the presence of a safe person (Carter, Hollon, Carson, & Shelton, in press). There is also evidence that psychological provocation procedures such as relaxation can induce panic in individuals with panic disorder (Adler, Craske, & Barlow, 1987). Such results indicate that a purely biological model of panic disorder may not be entirely tenable.

Cognitive Model

Alternatively, the cognitive model hypothesizes that the catastrophic misattribution of otherwise normal somatic sensations is the cause of panic (Beck & Emery, 1985; Clark, 1986). There seems to be ample evidence in the literature that cognitive factors are a part of the phenomenon of panic (Clark, 1988; Sanderson et al., 1989). What remains unclear is whether these cognitive variables are necessary *and* sufficient for the development of panic.

Most cognitive theorists would argue that negative cognitions are necessary in that the misattribution must be present for panic to occur. Such cognitions, however, may not be sufficient in that physiological sensations of some type must also be present to trigger a panic attack (Beck & Emery, 1985). Catastrophic cognitions, in fact, typically occur following the detection of specific somatic sensations (Hibbert, 1984; Ley, 1985). The presence of such cognitions alone, therefore, does not guarantee panic.

It is becoming increasingly clear that any model of panic disorder that is expected to fully describe and account for its etiology will necessarily be multidetermined. The current linear causal models are clearly not adequate in that such models will necessarily miss some important aspects of panic disorder. It is more likely that there is a complex interaction between the biological and psychological variables that accounts for the development of panic (Barlow, 1988, 1991). We now describe how such an interaction can be ascribed to the model in development at our clinic.

ALARM THEORY AND PANIC DISORDER

Accumulating evidence indicates that panic is a complex biopsychosocial process involving the interaction of an ancient alarm system crucial for survival with maladaptive learning (Barlow, 1988). The most common of the alarms is what we label a "true" alarm.

True Alarms

True alarms, more commonly referred to as *fear*, occur when one is directly threatened with a dangerous event or situation. Examples of situations triggering such reactions include being held at gunpoint, being in the path of a speeding vehicle, and seeing one's child in danger. Few would disagree that such situations would and should produce a fear reaction in most people. In addition to these modern-day alarms, there also seem to be alarms that were more common to our ancestors (e.g., being threatened with attack by wild animals) but to which we may show a susceptibility (e.g., being in the presence of lions or snakes) to becoming alarmed (Seligman, 1971).

The alarm is associated with intense neurobiological reactions (e.g., increased blood flow, increased oxygen intake) and specific, action-oriented cognitions (e.g., "I've got to get out of here"). The emotion itself mobilizes one to take quick action, either by running away, escaping, or attacking the threatening object or situation. These actions have been characterized as the "fight or flight" mechanism or the "emergency reaction" (Cannon, 1929). Evolutionarily, to be effective, the response must be immediate in order to help ensure the organism's survival. In the face of real danger, it would not do to exhibit a delayed reaction. Succinctly, then, a true alarm is the intense, immediate, biopsychological process triggered when an organism is threatened. If fear is a true alarm, what constitutes a false alarm?

False Alarms

False alarms are what we observe clinically as panic. Unlike true alarms, false alarms often occur in the absence of any identifiable threat. In nearly all other respects, panic and fear seem nearly identical phenomenologically (Barlow, 1988).

Panic attacks, or false alarms, are typically described as sudden bursts of intense anxiety characterized by the occurrence of somatic symptoms such as heart palpitations, dizziness, and shortness of breath and cognitions such as thoughts of dying, being trapped, or losing control (American Psychiatric Association, 1987). These attacks are typically short-lived, lasting on average about 5–10 min at their peak level. The symptoms of panic seem to be relatively consistent across individuals, but individual attacks may vary in terms of the number or the intensity of symptoms (Barlow, 1991). For example, certain attacks may consist of several somatic symptoms, while others may be associated with only two or three.

The occurrence of these attacks is often described by the client as "unexpected" or "out of the blue," particularly initially. It is not uncommon for patients with panic to report that one of their greatest concerns is that they feel a panic attack can happen at virtually any moment and that the panics are entirely unpredictable. The unexpected nature of panic attacks, however, seems to be a construct of the client in that systematic examination often uncovers cues (Barlow, 1988). Therefore, the attacks can at times be predictable, although the cues are frequently subtle such as cognitions (e.g., "What if I pass out?") or certain somatic sensations (e.g., heart palpitations) and need not be tied to specific environmental triggers (Barlow, 1988; Barlow & Cerny, 1988).

Panic attacks can also be cued by external environmental stimuli, as in the case of the specific phobic who is afraid to venture close to dogs and experiences a panic attack nearly each time he or she does. Another example is the case of the social phobic who expects to panic whenever he or she must give a presentation in front of others. These cued panic attacks are similar in composition to the unexpected panic attacks described above (Barlow, 1991).

PREVALENCE OF PANIC

Remarkably, the occurrence of panic attacks appears to be relatively common. Evidence from early empirical investigations suggests that as many as 35% of normals sampled have experienced at least one panic attack in the previous year (Norton, Dorward, & Cox, 1986; Norton, Harrison, Hauch, & Rhodes, 1985). The attacks reported, however, appear to have been largely those associated with a particular environmental trigger such as public speaking or taking an exam. Later empirical studies examining the occurrence of uncued panic attacks indicate that considerably fewer individuals experience these types of attacks. It has been estimated that between 9% and 15% of the population have experienced unexpected panic attacks (Brown & Cash, 1990; Rapee, Ancis, & Barlow, 1987; Selge, Beck, & Logan, 1988). These estimates, however, are based on results from studies using self-report questionnaires. Brown and Deagle (1992) examined the rate of unexpected panic attacks using a structured clinical interview in a large college sample. They found that only 2.9% of the sample had experienced an unexpected attack (Brown & Deagle, 1992). The lifetime prevalence rate for the full clinical syndrome (the occurrence of four attacks within a 1-month period) has been estimated to be 1.6% (Regier, Narrow, & Rae, 1990).

Although research has converged on a fairly detailed description of panic and suggests that panic is fairly common, theories addressing the origins of panic have until recently been relatively narrow. The model outlined in this chapter is an attempt to integrate key biological and psychological findings into the context of learned alarms.

A MODEL OF THE ETIOLOGY OF PANIC DISORDER

If panic is in essence a false alarm, what accounts for its development? That is, how does one first experience a false alarm? Because the nature of a false alarm suggests no easily identifiable antecedent, it seems that some type of biological vulnerability underlies the false alarm (see Figure 1). Thus far, however, no specific biological mechanism responsible for panic has been discovered. It may be that by the time the patient presents clinically, the panic attacks are no longer pure false alarms but instead are learned alarms with additional emotional complications and, therefore, present differently than would a pure false alarm (Barlow, 1988). This would make it difficult to study and discover unique biological mechanisms operating in a relatively pure false alarm.

One avenue deserving further exploration is the occurrence of panic in the general population. As noted earlier, it seems that a substantial percentage of the population has experienced a panic attack but has not sought help. These individuals show little concern over the panic or the possibility of experiencing an attack in the future and may serve as a better sample in which to search for specific biological markers. Nonetheless, we believe that there is a biological vulnerability predisposing one to experi-

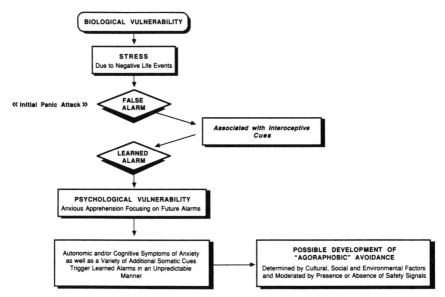

Figure 1. A model of the etiology of panic disorder. From *Anxiety and Its Disorders: The Nature and Treatment of Anxiety and Panic*, by D. H. Barlow, 1988, New York: Guilford Press. Copyright 1988 by Guilford Press. Reprinted with permission.

ence a false alarm. Both family (Crowe, Noyes, Pauls, & Slymen, 1983) and twin (Torgersen, 1983) studies have provided evidence that panic disorder has a genetic component. What may be inherited is a hyperresponsive autonomic nervous system, so vulnerable individuals may be more prone to experience somatic sensations (Barlow, 1988; Eysenck, 1967).

In and of itself, however, the biological vulnerability is not sufficient for such an alarm reaction to be triggered. Thus, the vulnerability is seen as necessary but not sufficient. For the false alarm to be triggered, at least initially, the experience of stress is also required.

The Role of Stress

There is extensive evidence that negative life events precede the initial panic attack in individuals who react with panic disorder (Barlow, 1988). In several investigations, systematic retrospective questioning has revealed that approximately 80% of panic patients report the occurrence of negative life events prior to the onset of their first panic (Doctor, 1982; Mathews, Gelder, & Johnston, 1981; Uhde et al., 1985). For example, Last, Barlow, and O'Brien (1984) administered a structured interview to 58 agoraphobic patients. They found that 81% of their sample reported one or more stressful life events prior to the development of agoraphobia. Of that sample, more than 50% reported interpersonal conflict or stress prior to the development of the disorder (Last et al., 1984).

In a more recent investigation, however, Rapee, Litwin, and Barlow (1990) found evidence that the number of stressful life events preceding the onset of the disorder did not differ between panic subjects and non-anxious subjects. Panic subjects did, however, rate the events as having a significantly greater negative impact than did the nonanxious subjects, indicating that the interpretation of the stressor may be of import (Rapee et al., 1990).

These findings have led some to conclude that the experience of stress, or the interpretation of that experience, plays a major role in the development of panic (e.g., Mathews et al., 1981). However, studies showing a strong association between stress and panic have been largely retrospective and, as such, cannot rule out the possibility that panic patients may somehow be predisposed to recall negative life events (Barlow, 1988). Furthermore, the experience of stress alone cannot account for the occurrence of a false alarm. There seems to be only a modest correlation between stress and psychopathology. That is, there are a substantial number of people who experience similar stressors but do not manifest panic or some other disorder, and vice versa (Barlow, 1988). One's threshold for experiencing an event as stressful may, in part, be biologically determined.

As shown in Figure 1, the combination of stressful life events and a biological vulnerability may predispose one to experience a false alarm. It should be noted, however, that various factors such as cognitive and personality characteristics and social support may moderate the effect of the stressor on the individual. Such moderator variables may explain why, under seemingly similar conditions, some will develop a particular disorder whereas others will not and why the reaction of some may be delayed until the moderator variable is removed or altered. Consider, for example, the 34-year-old patient who moved in with his partner immediately after high school. One of his siblings has difficulty managing anxiety, perhaps suggesting some biological predisposition. The patient is somewhat dependent, has never really lived alone, and has come to rely on his partner's support. Recently, his partner changed occupations and now is away from him 3–4 days each week. As a result, he and his partner begin to argue more frequently and have, on occasion, discussed separating. Contending with the possibility of being alone for the first time is upsetting, and he finds that he experiences his first false alarm. Although such a late onset is atypical, one can see how a change in a potential moderator of stress (the availability of social or interpersonal support) could increase the chance of experiencing a false alarm. The diathesis–stress model of panic previously outlined predicts that infrequent or nonclinical panickers will continue to have occasional false alarms, depending on their biological reactivity, stressful life events, and ability to cope with the stressors. What, then, accounts for the development of more frequent attacks or full-blown panic disorder? We consider the occurrence of additional alarms to be attributable to learning. Returning to Figure 1, we now describe the process by which false alarms become learned alarms.

Learned Alarms

As stated earlier, the occurrence of a false alarm is very common. The overwhelming experience of panic in some individuals, however, seems to ensure that learning will take place. How, then, do these alarms come to be learned? In classical conditioning terminology, if a neutral stimulus (conditioned stimulus [CS]) is paired with a fear-arousing stimulus (unconditioned stimulus [UCS]), the previously neutral stimulus can acquire the capacity to elicit the feared response (conditioned response [CR]) in the absence of the original fear-arousing stimulus (Mowrer, 1960; Wolpe, 1952).

However, it has become clear that traditional classical conditioning theory cannot account for several features of clinical phobias. It does not, for example, explain the selectivity of phobias (Marks, 1969), the reason that repeated exposure to the CS fails to extinguish some phobias (Rachman, 1977), or the vicarious or informational acquisition of phobias (Bandura, 1969; Rachman, 1978).

Several alternatives to strict classical conditioning theory have been proposed to account for the development of phobias. Seligman (1971), for example, proposed that individuals have been highly "prepared" to fear certain objects or situations. This type of learning is hypothesized to facilitate the survival of the species. The evolutionary preparedness theory integrates biological with classical conditioning models (Barlow, 1988). Such modifications, however, have led some to abandon "strict" conditioning theory altogether and to incorporate more cognitive variables such as attention and information processing to account for the development of phobias (Rescorla, 1988).

We believe that in the case of panic disorder, the repeated experience of false alarms can result in learned alarms. The majority of patients with panic disorder are often unable to clearly demarcate a conditioning experience for their alarms. We contend that what is learned is an association between a false alarm and a specific, albeit subtle, cue. The cues are internal physiological sensations, or "interoceptive" cues (Barlow, 1988). The label *interoceptive* was first applied to internal somatic sensations by a Russian investigator who slightly stimulated the colon of a dog while simultaneously administering an electric shock (Razran, 1961). In this study, the dog became conditioned to respond with anxiety during the natural passage of feces. Furthermore, the observed learning was quite resistant to extinction (Razran, 1961).

The concept of interoceptive conditioning as a mechanism underlying panic has, however, received criticism. Theorists such as McNally (1990) contend that conceptually, panic is difficult to describe in terms of interoceptive conditioning. He states that if, for example, certain physiological sensations are considered the CS, what constitutes the CR? Because panic is indexed by the occurrence of physiological sensations, it becomes unclear what the CS is and what the CR is. As such, interoceptive conditioning is seen as a misleading metaphor for panic (McNally, 1990).

We contend, however, that it is possible to learn an association between internal cues and false alarms. In the case of patients with panic disorder (with or without agoraphobia), the internal cues signal the possibility of another false alarm occurring. As shown in Figure 1, the association of false alarms with interoceptive cues results in the phenomena we term *learned alarms*. Consider, for example, the individual who has experienced several false alarms, each accompanied by an increase in heart rate. One morning he or she ingests 2 cups of coffee and notices an elevated heart rate. Failing to recognize the causal chain of events, he or she may think, "I'm going to have a heart attack" and consequently experience a panic attack. This example depicts a common scenario for patients with panic disorder. That is, recognition of certain interoceptive cues (e.g., elevated heart rate), despite their true origin (e.g., caffeine consumption), may produce a false alarm. The individual may then form a strong association between the experience of certain interoceptive cues (e.g., changes in heart rate) and the occurrence of a false alarm. This explanation accounts for the difficulty in identifying specific external events that may have triggered an alarm reaction and addresses the seemingly "spontaneous" nature of panic attacks.

There are two important factors in the process of developing learned alarms. First, of course, is the experience of false alarms. Second is the interpretation of the false alarm as dangerous. It may be that what separates nonclinical panickers from those who continue on to develop more frequent and intense alarms is the occurrence of what cognitive theorists label *misattributions*. The individual who associates the occurrence of an alarm with an impending catastrophe may be more likely to relate specific interoceptive cues to the alarm and consequently be more likely to learn to react with an alarm when such sensations are experienced.

Similarly, phenomena such as nocturnal panic attacks (attacks when one is awakened from a sleep) and relaxation-induced panic attacks can be explained by interoceptive conditioning. Both of these occurrences are associated with certain physiological sensations, such as a slowed breathing rate during periods of relaxation. Although these sensations occur naturally in most people, the panic-prone individual may have become conditioned to respond to them in a fearful manner (Adler, Craske, & Barlow, 1987). Therefore, the naturally occurring somatic cues during these periods may produce an alarm reaction.

From our perspective, then, biological factors (vulnerability to experience alarms), cognitive factors (misinterpretation of alarms and physiological sensations), and behavioral factors (conditioning of interoceptive cues with alarm reactions) are important in the genesis of learned alarms (Barlow, 1988, 1991). We recognize, of course, that conditioning may also be a fundamental cognitive process.

One consequence of this learning can be the development of a psychological vulnerability or a pathological tendency to focus on the possibility of future alarms (see Figure 1). Before explicating the specific vulnerability, it will be useful to illustrate the process of what we term *anxious apprehension*.

ANXIOUS APPREHENSION

The term *anxious apprehension* is used to describe what is more commonly referred to as *anxiety*. Although perhaps the most universal of all human emotions, anxiety has been difficult for theorists to define. Contrary to the popular misconception of anxiety as "fear without a cue," put forth in many general psychology texts, an alternative description of anxiety is a cognitive–affective structure comprised of high negative affect, a sense of uncontrollability, and an attentional shift to self-preoccupation (Barlow, 1991). The anxious individual experiences a sense of uncontrollability and is focused on possible future threat or danger. An example of common anxious thoughts would be "If that terrible event were to happen again, I might not be able to manage it." For this reason we believe the term *anxious apprehension* better conveys the notion that anxiety is a future-oriented mood state in which one is preparing to manage upcoming negative events (Barlow, 1991). The process of anxious apprehension is depicted in Figure 2.

In this diagram, a variety of cues (or anxious propositions) are sufficient to evoke anxious apprehension without the necessity of rational appraisal. These cues can be situational (e.g., test anxiety) or physiological in nature (e.g., unexplained arousal) and may be very broadly or very narrowly based (Barlow, 1991). The negative affect produced by the anxious propositions is associated with distortions in cognitive processing. Such distortions typically take the form of an attentional shift to self-evaluation or a rapid shift in attention from external to internal sources. The result of the distortion in information processing is a further increase in arousal, which forms its own positive feedback loop with negative affect (see Figure

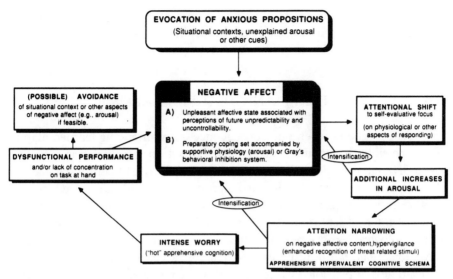

Figure 2. The process of anxious apprehension. From *Anxiety and Its Disorders: The Nature and Treatment of Anxiety and Panic*, by D. H. Barlow, 1988, New York: Guilford Press. Copyright 1988 by Guilford Press. Reprinted with permission.

2). The individual's attention then narrows toward possible sources of threat or danger and becomes hypervigilant to cues associated with sources of apprehension, resulting in an arousal-driven worry that is difficult to control at intense levels. This process results in a decrement in performance and possibly avoidance of sources of apprehension (Barlow, 1988, 1991).

An example here would be a client with erectile dysfunction. He is working at home when his partner expresses an interest in sexual activity. The mere mention of sexual activity produces negative affect characterized by physiological arousal (e.g., heart palpitations, sweating) and is associated with unpredictable performance. The client may think, "I'm going to be asked to perform sexually, and I won't be able to obtain an erection." The negative thoughts concerning his sexual functioning produce further arousal, and his attention shifts from working and begins to focus on his sexual performance. The process then generates such intense worry that he can no longer concentrate on work (an example of performance impairment). When his partner approaches him, he is unable to focus on sexual activity and is overwhelmed by thoughts of obtaining an erection. He may be so focused on the consequences of not performing (e.g., "My partner will find someone else to be intimate with") that he cannot achieve an erection, resulting in additional increases in negative affect and, possibly, avoidance of sexual intimacy. This example illustrates the process of anxious apprehension but is not intended as a description of the etiology of anxiety. With an understanding of the process of anxious apprehension, we return now to the discussion of the psychological vulnerability to experience a learned alarm.

ANXIETY AND FUTURE ALARMS

As described earlier, one consequence of experiencing learned alarms is the possible development of anxiety focused on future alarms. That is, the individual is anxious about or fears the occurrence of additional alarms. As a result of experiencing learned alarms, replete with associated interoceptive cues, the panic patient may become hypervigilant for the occurrence of internal sensations (Barlow, 1988). The resulting attentional shift to physiological sensations will increase the probability of noticing somatic sensations (e.g., while walking briskly across a parking lot). The increase in awareness of physiological sensations will consequently increase arousal, thereby increasing the likelihood of experiencing the feared physiological sensations. Associated with the learned alarms are the catastrophic types of cognitions commonly reported by panic patients (e.g., "I will have a heart attack and die"). Such cognitions further shift one's attention to internal sensations and, consequently, increase the already elevated sense of uncontrollability and alarm.

At this point, the stage is set for the recurrence of learned alarms triggered by either negative thoughts, physiological sensations, or both. The anxious apprehension focusing on future alarms can trigger alarms in an unpredictable manner. For example, a patient who is hypersensitive to changes in heart rate may be raking leaves and suddenly experience a panic attack for no apparent reason. He or she may report the attack as "spontaneous" and consequently become even more fearful that another attack, which may result in death, will happen at any moment. What has happened in this case is that the patient has become so hypersensitive to any physiological changes that even small changes (e.g., increased heart rate while raking leaves) that others would not perceive, or would not be able to correctly assign causal responsibility for, produce an intense fear reaction. As there is no real threat in the environment to which the fear can be attached, the focus becomes internal. The attack may seem "spontaneous" but was actually triggered by the occurrence of a physiological sensation and the reaction to that sensation.

After repeated experiences of false alarms, the individual may become so conditioned (pairing of certain sensations with learned alarm responses) that even the occurrence of very mild physiological sensations may produce an alarm reaction (Barlow & Cerny, 1988). Examples of such conditioned hypersensitivity to certain somatic cues would be the experience of nocturnal panic attacks or relaxation-induced panic (Barlow & Craske, 1988).

Both states may be associated with a reduction in heart rate and with natural changes in respiration to which a panic patient is sensitive, thus having the potential to trigger a panic attack (Barlow, 1988).

Following the experience of learned alarms and the development of anxiety focused on future alarms, the individual may exhibit agoraphobic avoidance. As indicated in Figure 1, the development of avoidance will depend on several associated factors, including cultural, social, and environmental constraints. For a complete review of the developmental process of agoraphobia, see Craske and Barlow (1988).

SUMMARY OF THE MODEL

The model we have described to account for the development of panic is an attempt at integrating some of the empirical evidence from biological, cognitive, and behavioral theories (Barlow, 1988). Consistent with biologically oriented theory, we have depicted the first attack as occurring during times of stress and as a result of an underlying biological vulnerability. However, we have described a process by which additional attacks can occur despite the absence of a stressor and how such attacks can appear to be "spontaneous" and unpredictable. In line with cognitive theory, we have incorporated the occurrence of catastrophic cognitions in the maintenance of panic. Also, we have discussed how conditioning theory can still be applied to the development of learned alarms.

This model, however, may have distinct advantages over existing linear models in its depiction of the development of panic and panic disorder. First, we have accounted for various facets of panic (i.e., the occurrence of nonclinical, nocturnal, and relaxation-induced panic) that have been difficult for simple linear models to address. Second, we have attempted to bridge the gap between the first attack and the occurrence of subsequent attacks via interoceptive conditioning. Third, we have described the process by which anxiety develops and have explicated the consequences of such anxiety. In this manner, we have attempted to incorporate the major theoretical contributions in this area into a comprehensive model of the development of panic and panic disorder.

A central component of the model we have outlined is the development of anxious apprehension. Alarms, in and of themselves, whether learned, false, or true, are generally not problematic unless they become associated with anxious apprehension (Barlow, 1988). That is, if the alarms become predictable because *access* to the cue can be controlled (as in the case of the simple phobic who avoids dogs), or the *alarm* itself can be controlled because specific coping mechanisms have been developed (e.g., avoidance of the cue), then the alarms may produce little distress. In the absence of anxious apprehension, learned alarms become associated with predictability, and false alarms seem to cause minimal distress (Barlow, 1988). Therefore, it is really the occurrence of chronic, severe anxious apprehension that is at the root of the development of panic disorder and not simply the occurrence of alarms. Considering the importance assigned to anxious apprehension, we turn now to the etiology of anxious apprehension and discuss its contribution to anxiety disorders not directly linked to the experience of alarms.

PATHOLOGICAL ANXIETY AND ALARM THEORY

Thus far, we have described the development of panic disorder, an anxiety disorder characterized by alarms and anxious apprehension about future alarms. There are disorders (e.g., generalized anxiety disorder) that are, instead, characterized by anxious apprehension focusing on situations or objects other than an alarm (e.g., intense, chronic worry across a number of life circumstances). In such cases, the occurrence of an alarm reaction is not uncommon, but the focus of concern is not the alarm (Barlow, 1988). For example, it is common for socially phobic individuals to experience an alarm when faced with social situations. The focus of their concern, however, is not on the alarm, but on the possibility of saying or doing something that might embarrass them in front of others. The development of anxious apprehension is presented in Figure 3.

At the core of the model is a biological vulnerability most probably transmitted genetically (Barlow, 1988; Weissman, 1990). In line with the model of panic presented in Figure 1, the vulnerability coupled with stressful life events results in a diffuse response characterized by the occurrence

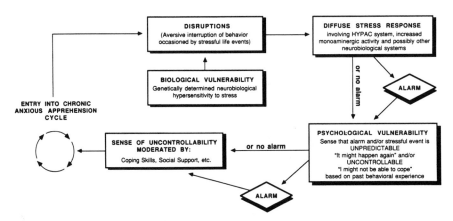

Figure 3. The origins of anxious apprehension. From *Anxiety and Its Disorders: The Nature and Treatment of Anxiety and Panic*, by D. H. Barlow, 1988, New York: Guilford Press. Copyright 1988 by Guilford Press. Reprinted with permission.

of physiological sensations. The intense stress-produced response often results in false alarms. Although the alarm itself is identical to those described earlier, the individual does not focus on the consequences of experiencing the alarm but instead remains focused on the stressor. Whether the alarm is a false alarm or a true alarm is determined by the context of the situation or negative event—that is, whether there is a perceived life-threatening danger (e.g., a dog) in the situation (Barlow, 1988).

As shown in Figure 3, some individuals will not experience an alarm (Barlow, 1988). Whether or not an actual alarm occurs, the stressor is experienced as uncontrollable ("I may not be able to manage it effectively") and unpredictable ("It might happen again"). The overwhelming sense of uncontrollability and unpredictability is associated with negative affect and may subsequently lower the threshold for alarms, if an alarm has not yet been experienced (Barlow, 1988). It would make sense ethologically for alarm reactions to fire more readily if one has sensed an environmental threat. Nonetheless, these are different, but related, responses. Consider, for example, the individual who is under a great deal of stress at work and is attempting to meet several deadlines. As the stress of the impending deadline approaches, he or she may begin to experience many of the neurobiological symptoms of anxiety, including trembling, a flushed feeling, muscle tension, irritability, and restlessness. Associated with the manifestation of these symptoms may be negative cognitions such as, "I won't be able to make the deadline, and I'm going to end up losing my job." Thoughts of an inability to control the situation produce additional symptoms of anxiety, which, in turn, may trigger an initial alarm (Barlow, 1988).

Whether one enters into a chronic state of anxious apprehension will, in part, be determined by various moderator variables (see Figure 3). The presence of adequate coping skills and social support, for example, may help protect one against the onset of anxious apprehension (Barlow, 1988).

Most important in the genesis of anxious apprehension as outlined herein are the biological and psychological vulnerabilities. Both vulnerabilities are assigned equal significance and are seen as necessary, although not sufficient, in this model. Once the cycle begins, these vulnerabilities interact to increase one's sense of uncontrollability and emotionality, and, consequently, the probability of learned alarms (Barlow, 1988).

As in the process of, for example, learning how to drive a manual transmission automobile, the cycle becomes automatic and no longer requires each of the phases to be consciously experienced for the intense reaction to occur. When one first learns manual transmission, each of the steps is meticulously thought out, from depressing the clutch to gradually releasing it, to applying the correct amount of pressure to the accelerator, and so on. Once the basic skills have been mastered, however, the entire process becomes smooth and automatic, and no longer requires awareness to be performed efficiently and correctly. The same is true for the development of pathological anxiety. In the early stages, each of the phases must be passed through to experience anxious apprehension. Once the cycle is set in motion, however, the individual can enter the cycle even without his or her awareness. It is its cyclical nature that makes it difficult for one to disrupt and manage anxious apprehension effectively.

PANIC VERSUS ANXIETY

In the models we have described, panic and anxiety are related, but qualitatively separate, clinical manifestations (Barlow, 1991). Several researchers have, however, suggested that panic and anxiety are quantitatively different, but qualitatively similar (Clark, 1986; Ley, 1987). It has been noted by these theorists that panic and anxiety share symptomatology, and it has been further suggested that the difference in severity between panic and anxiety may not be as large as previously thought (Ehlers & Margraf, 1989).

There are, however, several reasons to maintain the distinction between panic and anxiety. First, panic and anxiety are presented differently and seem to be described differently by patients with these disorders (Barlow, 1991). Second, there seems to be a strong functional relationship between panic attacks and anticipatory anxiety (Barlow, 1991). Third, a review of the basic theories of emotion suggests that fear or panic are tightly organized action tendencies toward fight or flight (Gray, 1982, 1987, 1991), whereas anxiety is more a diffuse blend of several emotions, or a loose, future-oriented action tendency (Antony & Barlow, in press; Barlow, 1988, 1991).

FUTURE DIRECTIONS

Although panic and anxiety have been the focus of increased empirical investigations over the past two decades, many of the current theories are causally unidimensional. The biopsychosocial model outlined in this chapter (explained in greater detail in Barlow, 1988, 1991) provides a comprehensive framework within which to view the etiology of panic and anxiety. Although the model is based on the results of current empirical investigations, there are several directions for future research that will ultimately confirm or disconfirm the major tenets of this model.

First, there is a need for longitudinal investigations of panic and anxiety. These types of studies can gather prospective information about the mode of transmission of each pathological state and speak more directly about the relationship between the two. Second is the need to examine further the phenomenon of nonclinical panic. Investigations in this area would allow further specification of the variables moderating the development of a full clinical syndrome. Third is the need to examine cross-sections of panic patients with differing onsets. Such study would provide additional information regarding possible moderator variables, as well as increase the ability to identify additional possible risk factors. Finally, further research is needed to address the occurrence of alarms in other types of anxious syndromes. Similar lines of research would add greatly to the understanding of these pathological states and would provide further evidence of the validity and utility of the model outlined in this chapter.

REFERENCES

Adler, C. M., Craske, M. G., & Barlow, D. H. (1987). Relaxation-induced panic (RIP): When resting isn't peaceful. *Integrative Psychiatry*, 5, 94–112.

American Psychiatric Association. (1987). *Diagnostic and statistical manual of mental disorders* (3rd ed., rev.). Washington, DC: American Psychiatric Press.

Antony, M. A., & Barlow, D. H. (in press). Emotion theory as a framework for explaining panic attacks and panic disorder. In R. M. Rapee (Ed.), *Current controversies in the anxiety disorders*. New York: Guilford Press.

Bandura, A. (1969). *Principles of behavior modification*. New York: Holt, Rinehart & Winston.

Barlow, D. H. (1988). *Anxiety and its disorders: The nature and treatment of anxiety and panic*. New York: Guilford Press.

Barlow, D. H. (1991). Disorders of emotion. *Psychological Inquiry*, 2(1), 58–71.

Barlow, D. H., & Cerny, J. A. (1988). *Psychological treatment of panic*. New York: Guilford Press.

Barlow, D. H., & Craske, M. G. (1988). The phenomenology of panic. In S. Rachman & J. D. Maser (Eds.), *Panic: Psychological perspectives* (pp. 11–35). Hillsdale, NJ: Erlbaum.

Beck, A. T., & Emery, G. (1985). *Anxiety disorders and phobias: A cognitive perspective*. New York: Basic Books.

Brown, T. A., & Cash, T. F. (1990). The phenomenon of nonclinical panic: Parameters of panic, fear, and avoidance. *Journal of Anxiety Disorders*, 4, 15–29.

Brown, T. A., & Deagle, E. A. (1992). Structured interview assessment of nonclinical panic. *Behavior Therapy*, 23, 75–85.

Cannon, W. B. (1929). *Bodily changes in pain, hunger, fear and rage* (2nd ed.). New York: Appleton-Century-Crofts.

Carter, M. M., Hollon, S. D., Carson, R., & Shelton, R. C. (in press). Effects of a safe-person on induced distress following a biological challenge in panic disorder with agoraphobia. *Journal of Abnormal Psychology*.

Charney, D. S., Woods, S. W., Goodman, W. K., & Heninger, G. R. (1987). Neurobiological mechanisms of panic anxiety: Biochemical and behavioral correlates of yohimbine-induced panic attacks. *American Journal of Psychiatry*, *144*, 1030–1036.

Clark, D. M. (1986). A cognitive approach to panic. *Behavior Research and Therapy*, *24*(4), 461–470.

Clark, D. M. (1988). A cognitive model of panic attacks. In S. Rachman & J. D. Maser (Eds.), *Panic: Psychological perspectives* (pp. 71–89). Hillsdale, NJ: Erlbaum.

Craske, M. G., & Barlow, D. H. (1988). A review of the relationship between panic and avoidance. *Clinical Psychology Review*, *8*, 667–685.

Crowe, R. R., Noyes, R., Pauls, D. L., & Slymen, D. J. (1983). A family study of panic disorder. *Archives of General Psychiatry*, *40*, 1065–1069.

Doctor, R. M. (1982). Major results of a large-scale pretreatment survey of agoraphobics. In R. L. DuPont (Ed.), *Phobia: A comprehensive summary of modern treatment*. New York: Brunner/Mazel.

Ehlers, A., & Margraf, J. (1989). The psychophysiological model of panic attacks. In P. M. G. Emmelkamp, W. T. A. M. Everaerd, F. W. Kraaimaat, & M. J. M. Van Son (Eds.), *Fresh perspectives on anxiety disorders*. Amsterdam: Swets & Zeitlinger.

Eysenck, H. J. (1967). *The biological basis of personality* Springfield, IL: Charles C Thomas.

Gorman, J. M., Goetz, R. R., Uy, J., Ross, D., Martinez, J., Fyer, A. J., Liebowitz, M. R., & Klein, D. F. (1988). Hyperventilation occurs during lactate-induced panic. *Journal of Anxiety Disorders*, *2*, 193–202.

Gray, J. A. (1982). *The neuropsychology of anxiety*. New York: Oxford University Press.

Gray, J. A. (1987). *The psychology of fear and stress* (2nd ed.). Cambridge , England: Cambridge University Press.

Gray, J. A. (1991). Fear, panic, and anxiety: What's in a name? *Psychological Inquiry*, *2*, 77–78.

Hibbert, G. A. (1984). Ideational components of anxiety: Their origin and content. *British Journal of Psychiatry*, *144*, 618–624.

Klein, D. F. (1981). Anxiety reconceptualized. In D. F. Klein & J. G. Rabkin (Eds.), *Anxiety: New research and changing concepts*. New York: Raven Press.

Klein, D. F. (1993). False suffocation alarms, spontaneous panics, and related conditions. *Archives of General Psychiatry*, *50*, 306–317.

Klein, D. F., & Gorman, J. M. (1987). A model of panic and agoraphobic development. *Acta Psychiatrica Scandinavica*, *76*, 87–95.

Last, C. G., Barlow, D. H., & O'Brien, G. T. (1984). Precipitants of agoraphobia: Role of stressful life events. *Psychological Reports*, *54*, 567–570.

Ley, R. (1985). Agoraphobia, the panic attack, and the hyperventilation syndrome. *Behaviour Research and Therapy*, *23*, 79–81.

Ley, R. (1987). Panic disorder: A hyperventilation interpretation. In L. Michelson & L. M. Ascher (Eds.), *Anxiety and stress disorders: Cognitive–behavioral assessment and treatment* (pp. 191–212). New York: Guilford Press.

Marks, I. M. (1969). *Fears and phobias*. London: Heinemann.

Mathews, A. M., Gelder, M. G., & Johnston, D. W. (1981). *Agoraphobia: Nature and treatment*. New York: Guilford Press.

McNally, R. J. (1990). Psychological approaches to panic disorder: A review. *Psychological Bulletin, 108*, 403–419.

Mowrer, O. H. (1960). *Learning theory and behavior*. New York: Wiley.

Norton, G. R., Dorward, J., & Cox, B. J. (1986). Factors associated with panic attacks in nonclinical subjects. *Behavior Therapy, 17*, 239–252.

Norton, G. R., Harrison, B., Hauch, J., & Rhodes, L. (1985). Characteristics of people with infrequent panic attacks. *Journal of Abnormal Psychology, 94*, 216–221.

Rachman, S. J. (1977). The conditioning theory of fear acquisition: A critical examination. *Behaviour Research and Therapy, 15*, 375–387.

Rachman, S. J. (1978). *Fear and courage*. New York: W. H. Freeman.

Rapee, R., Ancis, J., & Barlow, D. H. (1987). Emotional reactions to physiological sensations: Comparison of panic disorder and non-clinical subjects. *Behavior Research and Therapy, 26*, 265–269.

Rapee, R. M., Litwin, E. M., & Barlow, D. H. (1990). Impact of life events on subjects with panic disorder and on comparison subjects. *American Journal of Psychiatry, 147*, 640–644.

Razran, G. (1961). The observable unconscious and the inferable conscious in current Soviet psychophysiology: Interoceptive conditioning, semantic conditioning, and the orienting reflex. *Psychological Review, 68*, 81–150.

Regier, D. A., Narrow, W. E., & Rae, D. S. (1990). The epidemiology of anxiety disorders: The epidemiological catchment area (ECA) experience. *Journal of Psychiatric Research, 24*, 3–14.

Rescorla, R. A. (1988). Pavlovian conditioning: It's not what you think it is. *American Psychologist, 43*, 151–160.

Sanderson, W. C., Rapee, R. M., & Barlow, D. H. (1989). The influence of an illusion of control on panic attacks induced via inhalation of 5.5% carbon dioxide-enriched air. *Archives of General Psychiatry, 46*, 157–164.

Sanderson, W. C., & Wetzler, S. (1990). Five percent carbon dioxide challenge: Valid analogue and marker of panic disorder? *Biological Psychiatry, 27*, 689–701.

Selge, R. A., Beck, J. G., & Logan, A. C. (1988). A community survey of panic. *Journal of Anxiety Disorders, 2*, 157–167.

Seligman, M. E. P. (1971). Phobias and preparedness. *Behavior Therapy, 2*, 307–320.

Shear, K. M. (1986). Pathophysiology of panic: A review of pharmacologic provocative tests and naturalistic monitoring data. *Journal of Clinical Psychiatry, 47*, 18–26.

Torgersen, S. (1983). Genetic factors in anxiety disorders. *Archives of General Psychiatry, 40*, 1085–1089.

Uhde, T. W., Boulenger, J. P., Roy-Byrne, P. P., Geraci, M. P., Vittone, B. J., & Post, R. M. (1985). Longitudinal course of panic disorder: Clinical and biological considerations. *Progressive Neuro-Psychopharmacology and Biological Psychiatry, 9*, 39–51.

Weissman, M. M. (1990). Panic and generalized anxiety: Are they separate disorders? *Journal of Psychiatric Research, 24*, 157–162.

Wolpe, J. (1952). Experimental neurosis as learned behavior. *British Journal of Psychology, 43*, 243–268.

9

BIOINFORMATIONAL THEORY AND BEHAVIOR THERAPY

DAVID J. DROBES and PETER J. LANG

Since its introduction as a biologically oriented information-processing account of emotional behavior in the late 1970s (e.g., Lang, 1977, 1979), bioinformational theory has received broad applications in the understanding and modification of behavioral pathology. This chapter explores the roots of the theory from earlier analyses of behavior therapy, tracing its development and evaluation as an information-processing view of emotional imagery, and then describes its more recent development as a general theory of emotional–motivational organization, integrating cognitive and psychophysiological levels of analysis. An overview is provided of current applications in psychological research, considering its import for behavioral and cognitive therapies. The description necessarily extends beyond the therapeutic enterprise, as the bioinformational approach uses ideas and data from diverse fields, including cognitive psychology, psychophysiology, reflexology, animal behavior, and the neurosciences.[1]

---

[1] For more detailed explications of this view, please refer to previous papers (Lang, 1977, 1979, 1984, 1985, 1987, 1993, 1994; Lang, Bradley, & Cuthbert, 1990, 1992; Lang & Cuthbert, 1984).

THREE SYSTEMS OF FEAR

Lang (1964, 1968, 1971) was an early promoter of the "three-systems" view of fear analysis. That is, he suggested that fear was not the unitary internal state suggested by dynamic theories. Noting that different fear measures were poorly correlated, he proposed that fear should be thought of as a construct defined by coincident assessment of three loosely related response systems: verbal report, overt behavior, and expressive physiology (e.g., autonomic, cortical, and somatic). This conception developed from the need for an objective approach to emotional measurement that would substantiate several highly successful behavior therapy techniques in the early 1960s, such as systematic desensitization, flooding, implosion therapy, and exposure. Of the three hypothesized response systems, the most obvious in clinical settings was the verbal report made by patients about their subjective experience of fear—for instance, its intensity, frequency, and duration. Also fairly evident was the overt behavior associated with fear, such as the extent to which a feared object or situation would be confronted or avoided, or what specific actions were elicited when the person was confronted with a fear stimulus (e.g., shake, freeze, or fight/flight). The least observable system, except at high intensity, was the expressive physiology associated with fear, such as increased autonomic activity (e.g., heart rate and sweating responses).[2] As originally introduced, this three-systems approach was not an articulated theoretical model, but an effort to define the appropriate targets for behavioral assessment and intervention. Additionally, this view provided a core focus on responding that would eventually become a defining feature of bioinformational theory.

Behavioral researchers and theorists quickly became engrossed with the "grist for the mill" provided by the three-systems view. As a result, the gathering empirical data refuted the long-held assumption that fear was a unitary state within the individual, which, once activated, would be evidenced by concordant changes across response systems (e.g., Himadi, Boice, & Barlow, 1985; Hodgson & Rachman, 1974; Michelson, 1986; Öst, Jerremalm, & Jansson, 1984; Vermilyea, Boice, & Barlow, 1984). For instance, a common observation was that a person who reported a high level of fear when confronted with a particular object or situation might show little or no avoidance and little appreciable physiological changes in this situation. Alternatively, a person might report little discomfort or fear, yet exhibit substantial autonomic or behavioral reactivity when confronted with a fear-eliciting stimulus. In response to such observations, Rachman (1976) described eight separate possibilities in which verbal, behavioral, and soma-

---

[2]Increasing technological sophistication, together with an ever growing appreciation for the importance of multisystem assessment, continues to make psychophysiological measurement a more integral response domain in behavioral research and clinic settings.

tovisceral systems could be combined. The challenge for researchers became the elucidation of circumstances under which three-systems covariation would occur, as well as the determinants of responding in each of the relevant systems.

Lang (1971), among others, argued that an important benefit of a multisystem approach to fear measurement was that it would allow clinicians to tailor their treatments according to individual response patterns. For instance, a patient who reacts primarily with strong physiological responses in a fear-eliciting situation may benefit most from procedures geared directly at reducing physiological responding (e.g., progressive muscle relaxation). Conversely, a patient who primarily avoids fearful stimuli may receive the greatest benefit from exposure-based treatment. Although system-specific changes have certainly been observed as a function of multicomponent treatment programs, only a few studies have explicitly attempted to demonstrate improved effectiveness when therapy techniques were geared toward individual response profiles, with mixed results (e.g., Michelson, 1986; Öst et al., 1984; Öst, Jerremalm, & Johansson, 1981; Öst, Johansson, & Jerremalm, 1982). For instance, Öst and his colleagues demonstrated improved treatment effectiveness when social phobics or claustrophobics classified as behavioral or physiological responders were matched to a behavioral (in vivo exposure) or physiological (applied relaxation) treatment, but this was not observed for agoraphobics. The bioinformational conceptualization of anxiety described below addresses how these differences may be related to fundamental differences in the way that response systems are organized across disorders.

DESENSITIZATION AND THE PSYCHOPATHOLOGY OF FEAR

Before the wide proliferation of three-systems methodology into assessment and research protocols, Lang and his colleagues embarked on a program of treatment-outcome research that clearly demonstrated the relevance of multidimensional fear measurement. These studies were designed to clarify some of the mechanisms through which treatment benefits were derived during systematic desensitization (Wolpe, 1958; see chapter 2 of this volume). In the first studies (Lang & Lazovik, 1963; Lang, Lazovik, & Reynolds, 1965), imaginal systematic desensitization was found to be highly effective at reducing fear among snake phobics, with changes indexed along the dimensions of subjective report and avoidance behavior. In one of the first experiments in which physiological recordings were taken during systematic desensitization, a "device for automated desensitization" (DAD) was developed and compared with a standard desensitization treatment and a no-treatment control group (Lang, Melamed, & Hart, 1970). Although both desensitization methods led to impressive rates of improvement, measured by performance on a behavioral avoidance test and verbal report, the automated procedure actually resulted in slightly better outcomes than the live therapists. More important, DAD-treated subjects who showed greater fear reduction across treatment had higher heart rates during those trials during which fear was signaled. Furthermore, although all patients described similar, intense fear reactions when imagining fearful material, there was a positive correlation between heart rate change and fear reports only for patients who responded well to treatment. In addition, successful subjects were more likely to report being highly fearful during sessions in which their base heart rate was high, indicating that subjective fear and general physiological arousal were concordant for these subjects. Thus, therapeutic gain appeared to be related to synchronous verbal and physiological responding. Finally, this research demonstrated consistently stronger relationships between various autonomic indicators and imagined fear content for spider phobics than for social phobics. Although verbal reports of fear and heart rate increased systematically with increasing hierarchy items for both phobic groups, there was a positive relationship between verbal report and skin conductance among spider phobics only.

These findings generated a number of important questions with respect to the mechanisms underlying imaginal systematic desensitization and the interrelationships among fear response systems. For instance, why did some people evidence higher heart rates during imagery of high-fear material, and why did these people have better outcomes in therapy? Also, why should different fear/anxiety disorders show different response patterns across fear hierarchies, and why were there differential success rates of imagery-based treatments across anxiety disorders? We now turn to a description of bioinformational theory, which attempts to address some of these questions within an information-processing framework.

BIOINFORMATIONAL THEORY

Bioinformational theory was initially developed as an attempt to organize many of the findings discussed above within an adaptive, organized nervous system, one that could account for complex human emotions as subsidiary to human beings' basic survival instincts. The model was originally forwarded as a theory of emotional imagery (Lang, 1977, 1979) and was developed largely in conjunction with an ongoing program of research on fear and anxiety. The theory has subsequently been extended into a more general theory of emotion (Lang, 1984, 1985, 1993; Lang et al., 1990, 1992), and it has received diverse applications across a variety of behavioral and emotional phenomena.

Emotion as Action Disposition

Bioinformational theory applies several concepts from modern cognitive psychology, regarding the structure and processing of information in memory, toward the realm of emotion. Thus, information about emotions is contained in associative memory networks. These emotion representations are similar to nonemotional memory networks, with the difference that they include action information (motor programs) and connections to subcortical motivation circuits. Emotions are viewed as context-specific action or response dispositions. They are activated by input that matches concepts in the emotion network. When sufficient informational units are active in working memory, the whole network is engaged, with its efferent elements resulting in the variety of response phenomena labeled as emotion.

There are three basic types of information contained in emotional memory networks: stimulus, response, and meaning concepts. The stimulus elements of the network (e.g., sensory or perceptual inputs and text information) are largely responsible for cuing the rest of the network. Once the network becomes activated, response outputs may be elicited in any of the three previously described response systems. Finally, meaning concepts represent mental elaborations pertaining to the stimulus and response components. These components may refer to connections between stimulus and response components, or they may add information to the network that may augment or modify the motivational significance of a situation. Thus, they represent information that is not part of the objective context.

Emotional networks can be described linguistically as linked sets of propositions. For example, the contents of a network representing a phobic fear of driving may be represented as follows:

> *Fear episode. Stimulus:* You are driving home from work. There is a lot of traffic on the highway, and the road is slippery because it has been raining. A truck passes you on the left and suddenly swerves back into your lane. *Meaning:* Truck drivers are erratic and dangerous. You have heard that there have been numerous accidents on this highway lately and that several people have been seriously injured. *Response:* Scream, "Oh no! We're going to crash and die!" (verbal); heart rate, blood pressure, and palmar sweating increase (physiological); muscles tense. You swerve and slam on your brakes, almost driving off the road (behavioral).

This set of logically linked statements offers a convenient description of an affective network, although the theory does not suppose that specific elements or their associations are necessarily linguistic. That is, network elements have more fundamental neuroconceptual representation in memory that is activated primarily by the external events and actions they represent. Indeed, there is considerable debate among cognitive psychologists as to how units of information are stored and organized in memory (e.g., Johnson-Laird, Herrmann, & Chaffin, 1984; McClelland & Rumelhart, 1988), and bioinformational theory does not depend on an ultimate resolution of these issues. A critical assumption is that an affective informational network can enter working memory through a variety of cues other than exposure to the actual stimulus conditions, including language or text descriptions, pictures, and other symbolic stimuli remote from the actual event. Given a vast literature showing that instructionally evoked action images prompt activity in the appropriate muscle systems (see Cuthbert, Vrana, & Bradley, 1991; McGuigan, 1973), a central hypothesis is that processing of text descriptions of relevant situations is associated with efferent output that varies according to the emotional content being processed. We now describe a program of imagery research that was designed specifically to test several predictions related to this hypothesis, first with normal subjects and then within clinical studies of fear.

An Imagery Research Program

Several predictions derived from bioinformational theory have been tested with imagery procedures developed by Lang and his colleagues, largely within studies of fear behavior. Because the original imagery paradigm has subsequently been used by several other researchers, it is described here in some detail. The procedure involved prerecorded imagery scripts of varying content, with each trial involving 30 s for the baseline period, 50 s for listening to the imagery script, 30 s of active imagery, and 30 s for the recovery period (cued by a tone at the end of the imagery period). Subjects were instructed to imagine the scene while it was being described to them and then to continue vividly imagining the scene until the beginning of the recovery period was signaled. Physiological measures were taken throughout the imagery trials. After the recovery period, subjective ratings were made, including imagery vividness and the experience of the imagery trial on affective dimensions, such as pleasant–unpleasant, aroused–calm, and dominant–controlled.

One of the first predictions to be evaluated with this paradigm was that processing of imagery scripts that included response-oriented propositions (e.g., "fist clenched" and "heart racing"), in addition to the typical stimulus descriptions, would be associated with enhanced physiological responding. This prediction was based on two assumptions of bioinformational theory: (a) Textual scripts that contained response information would better match the relevant emotional network, thereby increasing the likelihood that an emotional response would be elicited, and (b) cued processing of response information in imagery would lead directly to appreciable efferent activity. As part of this research, a procedure was developed in which subjects were trained to actively attend to and process different aspects of the imagery script content (Lang, Kozak, Miller, Levin, & McLean, 1980). Specifically, groups of subjects were reinforced for verbally elaborating either stimulus or response aspects of the image. By the end of training, subjects all reported more vivid images, but with an emphasis on the content to which they were trained to process. The following imagery sessions for these subjects involved imagery of fear, action, and neutral scripts; in addition to the presence of stimulus elements for all subjects, half of the subjects in each of the stimulus and response training groups received imagery scripts that contained response propositions. As predicted, subjects who received response training and who received response information in the scripts showed significantly enhanced heart rate and muscle tension responses compared with the other subject groups. These effects were specific to the action and fear scripts, which was expected on the basis of the relevance of this script material for response activation. Stimulus-trained subjects showed responses in the same direction, but they were not statistically significant.

The next phase of this research focused on highly fearful subjects, namely, groups of undergraduate snake phobics and socially anxious subjects (Lang, Levin, Miller, & Kozak, 1983). In the first study, both of these groups were exposed to their own and the other group's fear imagery situations, as well as nonfear control situations (i.e., exercise and neutral). In addition, subjects imagined snake situations and public speaking both before and after actual exposure to these situations. The results for the actual exposure situations demonstrated that heart rate and skin conductance responses were greater for snake phobics than for socially anxious subjects during snake exposure, whereas there were no group differences in physiological responding during the speech test. The lack of physiological differentiation among groups during the speech test was interpreted as a function of the increased metabolic demands of speaking for both groups, irrespective of level of fear. Indeed, there were differences in reported levels of fear in the actual situations that were consistent with group membership, and only speech phobics demonstrated elevated skin conductance level in anticipation of speech exposure. Finally, the imagery results of this experiment resembled those from the stimulus-trained subjects in the previous study (Lang et al., 1980), in that they were in the predicted direction but nonsignificant.

Next, a new sample of snake phobics and socially anxious subjects was selected; half of the subjects in each of these groups received response-oriented training, as in the first study, whereas the remaining half received stimulus-oriented training. All subjects then imagined fear, action, and neutral scenes, with all scripts containing both stimulus and response elements. The results were now highly similar to the actual exposure situation.

For response-trained subjects, heart rate increases during snake imagery discriminated the two fear groups, but responding during speech imagery did not. Stimulus training led to nonsignificant effects in the same direction. Further specificity in the physiological responses elicited during imagery was revealed by electromyogram (EMG) measurements, in which there was greater muscle tension (forehead and neck) during imagination of exercise than of fear.

Several findings from these studies supported the major predictions of bioinformational theory. First, physiological responses elicited during imagery were similar to those elicited by actual exposure, supporting the hypothesis that imagery activates the same emotional memory structures and associated response elements as actual experience. The inclusion of response elements in imagery scripts, with response-training procedures, served to amplify physiological response patterns, but only for preexisting response dispositions (i.e., there was a lack of differentiation during neutral and speech imagery scripts). Finally, the results showed that the intrinsic metabolic demands of tasks, whether actual or imagined, might be critical in determining physiological activity in the absence of any indication of fear.

Another prediction that was evaluated in this series of imagery studies was that individual differences in imagery ability would be associated with different patterns of emotional response evoked during imagery. More specifically, individuals who can generate vivid, coherent images should produce a more consistent content-relevant physiological response during imagery. This prediction was supported by a study (Miller et al., 1987) in which college students were classified as good or poor imagers on the basis of their responses to a self-report measure of imagery ability (Questionnaire Upon Mental Imagery; Sheehan, 1967). Good imagers exhibited greater physiological activity to standard affective and action scenes than poor imagers, and these differences were particularly strong after response training. Response-training procedures also enhanced reactivity to personally relevant fear images among initially poor imagers. This has potentially important implications for the clinical treatment of fear, in that it may be possible to elicit autonomic responding in persons who do not initially respond, with corresponding improvements in clinical outcome.

Schwartz (1971) first described a different imagery procedure, which used self-initiated processing of images. This approach was later refined by G. E. Jones and Johnson (1978, 1980) and May (1977a, 1977b) and has recently been adapted for use in our studies of fear imagery. In this research, single sentences are used as emotional prompts, rather than the lengthier text descriptions used in the studies described above. Either subjects self-initiated when they processed and created an image to a target sentence (Vrana, Cuthbert, & Lang, 1986), or they were instructed to process fearful or neutral sentences on hearing a tone cue within a repetitive series of nonsignal tones (Vrana, Cuthbert, & Lang, 1989; Vrana & Lang, 1990). In keeping with the earlier studies, sentences containing fear-relevant information were associated with greater heart rate acceleration than were neutral sentences. Furthermore, although this difference was apparent during recall tasks that quite likely involved less semantic processing (i.e., silent articulation of the imagery script or null sentence processing), the differences were greatest during active imagery. These results were interpreted as an indication that language propositions served as effective prompts for response components within relevant fear-informational networks and that the level of language processing was positively related to the degree of spread to response properties.

Clinical Fear Research

Over the past several years, the basic imagery research paradigms described above have been applied, with some additions and modifications, within a program of research at the University of Florida Fear and Anxiety Disorders Clinic. These procedures were deemed useful for providing comprehensive patient assessments, as well as for advancing an understanding of the psychopathology of fear and anxiety. The emphasis of this work has been on differentiating subtypes of anxiety disorders, and differentiating these from normal response patterns, from a bioinformational perspective.

In the initial stage of this research (e.g., Cook, Melamed, Cuthbert, McNeil, & Lang, 1988), patients who were diagnosed as simple phobic, social phobic, or agoraphobic participated in an imagery assessment in which physiological responding and subjective reports were obtained during standardized and personally relevant clinical fear scripts. The most notable finding was that simple phobics displayed significantly greater heart rate and skin conductance change during imagery of personalized phobic material, as compared with the other groups. Another interesting finding was that although social phobics showed smaller responses to their personalized clinical fear scenes than simple phobics, they showed larger responses to a standardized "speech fear" scene than simple phobics or agoraphobics. Cook et al. (1988) speculated that the personalized social phobic scenes had been experienced many times by these patients and thus were associated with a relatively diminished, perhaps naturally desensitized, response when these cues were presented during imagery. The standardized speech scene, on the other hand, presented these subjects with specific, highly salient, fear cues to which they had not yet been exposed.

The primary conclusion from this research was that the associative memory networks mediating phobic behavior differ among patient groups. Specifically, simple phobia networks involve highly coherent, organized structures that are high in associative strength among elements. Accordingly, processing of specific stimuli that are part of a simple phobia fear network will reliably evoke fear responding, which can be manifest across response systems. Indeed, simple phobics are the patient group most likely to display a strong behavioral disposition toward avoidance or escape, and they reliably showed enhanced autonomic responding to fear-relevant images. Agoraphobia, on the other hand, is characterized by memory structures much lower in associative strength and considerably less reliable in their activation. The informational networks involved with this disorder are far less coherent, with relevant response components only loosely woven to specific eliciting stimuli. In relation to simple phobia and agoraphobia, social phobia is an intermediate condition, mediated by a network marked by vigilance and evaluative concerns. Although responding among social phobics is generally less reliably evoked by discrete stimuli than it is among those with simple phobia, some forms of this disorder may resemble focal phobias (e.g., speech phobia). More generalized forms of social phobia, however, may resemble agoraphobia more closely. According to this schematization, all anxiety disorders may be arranged on this continuum of network coherence. In the [Diagnostic and Statistical Manual of Mental Disorders (DSM–IV; American Psychiatric Association, 1994), the ordering of anxiety disorders from most to least coherent is as follows: posttraumatic stress disorder, simple phobia, obsessive–compulsive disorder, social phobia, panic disorder, and generalized anxiety disorder.

In these clinical studies, simple phobics have generally yielded a positive relationship between imagery vividness and physiological responding during personalized fear imagery (e.g., Cook et al., 1988; McNeil, Vrana, Melamed, Cuthbert, & Lang, 1993). Good imagers in other diagnostic groups, as well, have responded more physiologically to standard aversive scenes, such as receiving a dental examination (e.g., Cook et al., 1988). As noted above, simple phobics show the most consistent physiological response to relevant phobic material presented during imagery. This suggests that imagery ability, for these patients, may mediate the enhanced physiological responding observed during imagery, as well as the relationship between imagery vividness and responding. To the extent that physiological responding during imagery may provide a more direct indication of imagery ability than self-report, the results showing better treatment outcome among imagery responders suggest that response training may have utility in improving treatment-outcome rates.

Other Fear Imagery Research

A variety of researchers using different imagery procedures have generally supported the major predictions of bioinformational theory. For instance, in early research involving autonomic measurement during imaginal treatment for phobia, Marks and his colleagues (Marks & Huson, 1973; Marks, Marset, Boulougouris, & Huson, 1971) reported that both physiological and subjective responses discriminated between neutral and phobic imagery during treatment and that physiological responses were useful indicators of treatment-initiated change. These researchers also reported a general lack of correspondence among these two response systems. Robinson and Reading (1985) reported that response training increased the correlation between physiological responding and subjective ratings of arousal and image vividness. May (1977b) reported that fearful students showed larger autonomic responses during imagery of their own fears than to other images. Bauer and Craighead (1979) conducted a study with undergraduates that examined the effects of imagery instructions on responding during imagery of four fearful and four neutral situations. In keeping with previous findings, fear scenes produced larger heart rate and skin conductance responses than did neutral scenes, and subjects who were instructed to focus directly on responses during the imagery scenes showed greater heart rate increases. Several other research groups have demonstrated that increased response processing during imagery, achieved either by manipulating imagery content or through explicit response training and instructions, enhances physiological responding (e.g., Carroll, Marzillier, & Merian, 1982; Hirota & Hirai, 1986). More recently, Zander and McNally (1988) attempted to introduce increasing amounts of information into imagery scripts for agoraphobics (i.e., fear scripts included stimulus content only; stimulus and response content; or stimulus, response, and meaning content). In keeping with the findings of Lang and his colleagues (e.g., Cook et al., 1988), agoraphobics were not physiologically reactive during these fear scripts, nor were there any differences in responding on the basis of the amount of information contained in the scripts.

MOTIVATION AND EMOTION

Bioinformational theory has recently been expanded to incorporate a view of motivational–emotional organization that is similar to Konorski's (1967) classification of mammalian exteroceptive reflexes (Lang et al., 1990, 1992). Specifically, emotional behaviors—from complex affects to primitive reflexes—are seen as response dispositions that are categorized according to reciprocal drive states. Emotional behavior is thought to be organized along a basic appetitive–aversive (i.e., valence) dimension, with the central motivational state at any given time being dominated by a behavioral set favoring appetitive responding (e.g., approach, attachment, and consumption) or a reciprocal aversive set (e.g., avoidance, escape, and defense). Furthermore, the appetitive–aversive systems are mutually inhibitory and self-priming; thus, the affective valence of the current motivational state can be inferred through the enhancement of a broad range of other responses from the same system.

Although this formulation substantially broadens the scope of bioinformational theory, in many ways this expansion represents a logical extension of the theory. The core focus of the theory remains on how response elements are primed through activation of informational networks, with the added feature that responses become primed or inhibited by concurrent activation of compatible or opposing systems, respectively. Furthermore, through its supposition of a broad generality in response effects, the theory now incorporates an explicit formulation of cortical-reflex connections. For example, when a foreground affective stimulus is aversive (e.g., an unpleasant picture or image), an aversive probe (e.g., a sudden, loud acoustic stimulus) delivered concurrently will be primed, producing an augmentation of an aversive reflex (e.g., startle eyeblink reflex). Conversely, a reflex elicited from a system other than the one that is dominant will be diminished, because of the mismatch of the foreground stimuli and the reflex probe (e.g., an appetitive salivary reflex will be inhibited during ongoing processing of aversive material).

The Startle Reflex Probe

A program of research that has been under way for the past several years has attempted to evaluate predictions of the expanded bioinformational theory by studying the elicitation and modulation of the defensive startle reflex. The startle reflex is a progressive flexor movement that is evoked by onset of a sudden stimulus, with a positive relationship between stimulus intensity and the reliability of the response. In recent studies of the startle reflex in humans, the primary measure of startle is the eyeblink component, as this is the first and most stable element in the reflex sequence. Several recent investigations have examined the role of affect in modulating startle responses within a picture-viewing paradigm by manipulating the affective categorization of slides. These studies have reliably demonstrated an enhanced startle blink response occurring while viewing unpleasant pictures and relatively inhibited responding during viewing of pleasant pictures (e.g., Bradley, Cuthbert, & Lang, 1990, 1991; Hamm, Stark, & Vaitl, 1990; Vrana, Spence, & Lang, 1988). This *affect–startle effect* is in keeping with the bioinformational view in which emotions are organized biphasically and with the prediction that responses from corresponding systems will be mutually primed (e.g., Lang et al., 1990).

A promising aspect of the startle probe as a measure of motivational–emotional state is that it appears to have effects that are relatively independent of the modality of the affective stimulus. Whereas other physiological effects can depend largely on the mode of stimuli used (e.g., see Vrana & Lang, 1990), fear material presented either through imagery or through the visual domain is associated with enhanced startle responding (e.g., Cook, Hawk, Davis, & Stevenson, 1991; Vrana et al., 1989). Another advantage of the startle reflex is its potential as an unbiased measure of fear change. Because the eyeblink reflex is obligatory and probes can be presented randomly, there is little chance for volitional control of the response.

Two recent studies used the startle reflex as a measure of treatment outcome after behavior therapy for phobia. Vrana and his colleagues (Vrana, Constantine, & Westman, 1992) reported that two animal phobics treated with systematic desensitization displayed a marked reduction in startle responding during phobic imagery after treatment, and these changes were accompanied by verbal and behavioral indexes of reduced fear. In another study (de Jong, Arntz, & Merckelbach, 1993), a group of spider phobics demonstrated the expected linear trend in startle responding when confronted with positive, neutral, and negative behavioral avoidance test conditions after treatment, but not before treatment, although startles were generally larger during all test conditions before treatment. Additionally, investigation with pharmacological anxiety-reduction agents has shown that these drugs also reduce fear-potentiated startle responses in animals (e.g., Berg & Davis, 1984).

DEVELOPMENTS AND ADAPTATIONS OF BIOINFORMATIONAL THEORY

Bioinformational theory currently stands as a broad, general theory of motivational–emotional organization that has been well supported through a program of basic and clinical research. To portray the scope of bioinformational theory and to further understand its relevance for the behavior therapy enterprise from which it was derived, we briefly consider a sampling of empirical research and theoretical development within studies of aversive or appetitive motivational systems.

The Aversive System

Criminal Psychopathy

A deficit in emotional processing is considered a classic feature of psychopathy (e.g., Cleckley, 1955; Fowles, 1980; Hare, 1985; Lykken, 1957). The general pattern of findings across this area of research suggests that psychopaths have a fundamental deficit in aversive affect and motivation. For instance, psychopaths tend to show reduced physiological responding to aversive events and are generally deficient in their ability to learn as a consequence of negative outcomes or conditioning (e.g., Newman, Widom, & Nathan, 1985). In a recent imagery study, Patrick, Cuthbert, and Lang (1994) reported a general, diminished autonomic response in psychopaths, in relation to nonpsychopathic controls, during fearful imagery.

Given this conceptualization of an aversive processing deficit in psychopaths, bioinformational theory would predict that psychopaths should show diminished startle potentiation during processing of unpleasant materials. This hypothesis was recently tested in a picture-viewing study (Patrick, Bradley, & Lang, 1993). Patrick et al. (1993) studied 54 members of a prison treatment program for sexual offenders and divided this sample into psychopathic and nonpsychopathic groups. Nonpsychopathic prisoners demonstrated subjective and physiological responses while viewing affective pictures, similar to normal college students, in which pleasant material was associated with inhibited startle eyeblink reflexes and unpleasant material prompted enhanced blinks. Psychopaths, on the other hand, exhibited a normal pattern of inhibited startle responding to positive material, yet they did not show the typical enhancement in startle magnitude in response to the negative slides. As with the positive slides, their responses to negative slides were inhibited, in relation to neutral slides. This is in keeping with the perspective of psychopaths as being cold and callous individuals, and with the hypothesis that psychopaths have an abnormal pattern of responding to aversive material. The psychopaths showed normal patterns of self-report and autonomic responding to the negative slides. This suggests that although they orient normally to the stimuli and know the proper response at a verbal level, psychopaths may have a more fundamental deficit in the response components of the emotional response to negative material.

Posttraumatic Stress Disorder

The bioinformational conceptualization of anxiety disorders states that these disorders can be arranged on a continuum related to the coherence among network elements. The more closely associated informational elements become, the higher the likelihood of eliciting response components on exposure to relevant stimulus inputs and the stronger the association among various channels of responding. From this conceptualization, it would appear that posttraumatic stress disorder (PTSD) involves highly coherent fear networks, because responding is reliably elicited by trauma-associated cues and is often multisystemic (DSM–IV; American Psychiatric Association, 1994).[3]

Research has demonstrated that PTSD patients are indeed reactive physiologically to relevant cues. In one series of studies (e.g., Blanchard,

---

[3]Although a wide range of stimuli may elicit substantial fear responding in PTSD patients, this should not be construed as a lack of network coherence. Given the highly salient nature of most trauma associated with PTSD, it is not surprising that both stimulus and response generalization would occur over time. This may be conceived as a highly elaborated fear-informational network, with many stimulus and meaning connections.

Kolb, Gerardi, Ryan, & Pallmeyer, 1986; Pallmeyer, Blanchard, & Kolb, 1986), Vietnam era veterans were successfully discriminated from other groups on the basis of heart rate responding to combat sounds. In another series of studies, imagery methodology borrowed from Lang's earlier fear research was used, and results supported the notion that PTSD involved a highly coherent fear-response network (Orr, Pitman, Lasko, & Herz, 1993; Pitman et al., 1990; Pitman, Orr, Forgue, de Jong, & Claiborn, 1987). In this research, only combat veterans with PTSD demonstrated a positive relationship between physiological responding and imagery of combat-relevant cues.

Approximately 20 PTSD patients have participated in the current research protocol at the University of Florida Fear and Anxiety Disorders Clinic. These patients had experienced a diverse range of traumatic incidents (e.g., combat, rape, vehicle accidents, industrial accidents, attempted strangulation, and kidnapping). Preliminary analyses suggest that contrary to the *DSM–III–R* (American Psychiatric Association, 1987) definition of the disorder, these patients do not exhibit stronger, exaggerated responses relative to other groups of anxiety patients (Cuthbert, Drobes, Patrick, & Lang, 1994). However, it appears that these patients show a potentiated startle response during imaginal processing of fear material, similar to results found with simple phobics. Autonomic responding among these patients is also highly similar to that of the simple phobics, suggesting that the relevant emotional network that becomes activated during imagery among PTSD patients is highly coherent. Further research will be important for determining the extent to which response dispositions within PTSD are related to the range of trauma experienced.

Stress, Type A Behavior, and Imagery

A great deal of research has explored relationships between physiological reactivity to laboratory stressors and real-life responding, as well as between acute physiological reactivity and long-term physical functioning (see van Doornen & Turner, 1992, for a recent review). A wide range of cognitive and physical tasks have been used as laboratory stressors in this research, including aversive imagery. Research has demonstrated a clear correspondence between elicited during imagery physiology and that elicited during actual participation in the imagined events; this relationship appears to be particularly strong for good imagers or after explicit training in response processing (e.g., Lang et al., 1983).

If aversive imagery can elicit bodily responses associated with stress, then it follows that ongoing stress reactions may occur if stress-relevant images are ubiquitous. It seems that certain individuals may experience chronic stress as a result of unremitting stressful imagery. Baum (1990) discussed the relationship between chronic stress and intrusive imagery, suggesting that chronic stress was a result of frequently thinking about past "bad" events. He suggested that ongoing stress resulted specifically from the activation of physiological components during frequent negative imagery. An important implication of this perspective is that stress-related physical problems may occur with increased frequency when recollections of previous events substitute for the events themselves. We later distinguish this type of recollection from the stress-reducing forms of imaginal processing within systematic desensitization.

The relationship between stress and physical disorder has received a great deal of attention in the study of type A, or coronary-prone, behavior patterns. This behavioral pattern, related to a hard-driving, time-pressured, achievement-oriented, and aggressive or hostile personality style, has been clearly linked to an increased incidence of coronary heart disease. A number of studies have examined physiological responses to discrete stressors among type A individuals, and these studies have generally shown enhanced autonomic stress reactivity among these subjects. A recent study used an imagery paradigm that was based on bioinformational theory to study physiological reactions to complex, emotional situations among type A individuals (L. J. Baker, Hastings, & Hart, 1984). In this study, cardiac patients engaged in guided and self-guided imagery of type A (e.g., driving in traffic or work responsibilities piling up) and neutral imagery scripts. Subjects classified as type A, on the basis of questionnaire and interview methods, exhibited greater heart rate and neck EMG during type A scripts, in relation to neutral scripts, whereas type B subjects did not show differences between script types. On the basis of these results, it appears that type A individuals may have more elaborate informational networks related to type A cues, or more connections between these stimulus and response components. Because the physiological responses displayed during type A imagery for these subjects were in keeping with those that are presumed to be related to coronary heart disease, the imagery procedure appeared to be useful for studying these response patterns more carefully in the laboratory situation. Furthermore, it would be highly valuable to determine whether physiological responders during type A imagery were, indeed, more likely to develop coronary heart disease and whether these individuals would benefit from desensitization treatment designed to reduce type A responding (e.g., Suinn & Bloom, 1978).

Pain and Illness

Increasing awareness of the role of emotional and psychological factors in physical functioning has led to several applications of bioinformational theory toward pain and illness (e.g., Lang, Cuthbert, & Melamed, 1986). McNeil and Brunetti (1992) recently attempted to differentiate fear and pain information networks by means of Lang's earlier imagery paradigm

(Lang et al., 1980, 1983; Miller et al., 1987). Undergraduates first received training in response processing, then they imagined either fear, pain, or pain-plus-fear scripts, as well as control (neutral and action) scripts. Verbal and heart rate responding was enhanced during each of the experimental script types, in relation to neutral and action scripts. However, although subjects rated pain scripts more negatively, they demonstrated greater heart rate acceleration to fear scripts. To the extent that both types of networks were accessed equally, these findings suggest that fear networks may prompt more action-oriented response networks than pain networks. This explanation is in keeping with the relatively passive nature of many pain situations (i.e., pain often occurs after injury has occurred, when preventive action is no longer viable), in comparison with the strong escape–avoidance tendencies associated with fear.

Another recent study used a similar imagery procedure to study responding among people who were extremely sensitive to their own physical sensations and likely to report vague somatic symptoms (hypervigilants), in comparison with extensive users of the health care system and normal subjects (Brownlee, Leventhal, & Balaban, 1992). In this study, subjects were presented imagery scenes in which the content was either neutral, action related, or illness related (e.g., discovering cancer, receiving a nose examination, or surgical incision). Hypervigilants were significantly more reactive physiologically (i.e., accelerated heart rate) during imagery of illness scenes, as compared with the other groups, suggesting that these scripts activated coherent informational networks for these subjects.

The Appetitive System

Although considerably more research has been concerned with aversive emotional states, largely because of the palpable clinical significance of these states, the generality of bioinformational theory depends as much on its applicability within appetitive systems. Appetitive motivational systems, such as those activated during approach, consumption, or pleasurable activity or during anticipation of positive outcomes, have received more attention in recent years.

Drug Urges and Appetitive Motivation

Within studies of addictive behavior and drug-dependence processes, the study of drug urges as an appetitive motivational construct has occupied a role, relative to approach behavior, similar to the role ascribed to fear as the motivational substrate of avoidance. Several recent theoretical models have discussed urges in a three-systems context. In an extension of bioinformational theory, T. B. Baker, Morse, and Sherman (1987) forwarded a dual-affect motivational model of drug urges in which mutually inhibitory, positive- or negative-affect urge systems are activated to the extent that matching affective, situational, and internal cues are present. The positive-affect urge system is elicited by cues such as a priming drug dose, or cues that have previously been associated with drug use. The negative-affect urge system is elicited by drug withdrawal, and factors that have become associated with withdrawal. Both systems can be indexed through behavioral, verbal, and physiological measures, and the coherence among these response systems is thought to vary according to the extent of urge cues present and the level of drug withdrawal.

Niaura and his colleagues (Niaura, Goldstein, & Abrams, 1991) also proposed a bioinformational account of drug dependence. Similar to the T. B. Baker et al. (1987) model, these authors emphasized a multiple-response-system approach for understanding aspects of drug addiction. Establishing "bioinformational maps" was seen as a primary task, with important implications for understanding individual differences in drug-usage patterns and how these patterns change over time. From Niaura et al.'s perspective, cognitive propositional elements (i.e., expected drug effects) are seen as the primary determinants of drug use, and drug dependence is thought to be related to the coherence among these and other network elements, as well as the degree of automaticity developed in drug-use behavior.

Tiffany (1990) used the cognitive concepts of automatic and non-automatic processing to account for the common lack of coherence across behavioral, self-report, and physiological components of drug urges. Rather than a central motivational urge state that is associated with particular patterns of somatovisceral activity, this theory proposes that physiological responding in an urge-eliciting situation depends on two primary factors: (a) cognitive and metabolic demands of the situation (e.g., problem solving) and (b) imagined or anticipated motor actions. Although drug use normally occurs with little or no intentional or controlled processing, the theory states that urges represent nonautomatic, or controlled, processing that is invoked in parallel with automatized drug-use action schemata. This can occur either in support of drug use, as in the ongoing addict who must engage in problem-solving activity to obtain drugs, or in support of drug abstinence.

Tiffany and his colleagues conducted a series of studies using imagery as a procedure for the induction of smoking urges (e.g., Burton, Drobes, & Tiffany, 1992; Drobes & Tiffany, 1993; Tiffany & Drobes, 1990; Tiffany & Hakenewerth, 1991). Borrowing the original imagery paradigm used in Lang et al.'s (1980, 1983) earlier fear research, standardized imagery scripts were developed that included explicit descriptions of smoking-urge situations, including response components, or that contained no urge content. Positive- and negative-affect content was also explicitly manipulated across urge and nonurge scripts. Inclusion of urge material was highly effective in generating strong self-reported urges, and scripts associated with the highest levels of urge report were associated with enhanced physiological reactivity. In particular, strong-urge scripts resulted in enhanced heart rate and skin conductance activity, as well as in decreases in finger temperature. Facial EMG measures were also sensitive to the affective content manipulation embedded within the urge and nonurge imagery scripts. Finally, although the levels of physiological reactivity were clearly related to the content of imagery scripts, there was little concordance between these responses and self-reported urge strength.

A critical assumption of bioinformational theory is that imagined affective cues should elicit psychophysiological responses resembling those observed in the actual affective context. In these imagery studies, each of the significant autonomic responses observed during smoking-urge imagery was consistent with the agonistic effects of nicotine. In addition, Drobes and Tiffany (1993) observed increased zygomatic muscle activity on exposure to live or imaginal smoking urge cues, and this responding was significantly correlated with verbal urge report. In the light of the fact that the overt act of smoking generally involves the zygomatic muscle region, this finding is in keeping with the theory.

Sexual Response

Another appetitive domain in which bioinformational concepts have been applied is in the study of human sexual response. For instance, J. C. Jones and Barlow (1989) used Lang's original fear imagery paradigm (e.g., Lang et al., 1980, 1983; Miller et al., 1987) to study responding among sexually functional and dysfunctional males while they imagined fear, erotic, and neutral scenarios, both before and after a response-oriented training procedure. The fear and erotic scenes contained either stimulus information only or stimulus and response information. Whereas the results demonstrated increased penile tumescence specifically during erotic imagery, these changes occurred for dysfunctional as well as functional subjects, and they were independent of response information and response training. It seems that the highly salient nature of sexual images, together with the adaptive importance of elaborate and coherent sexual bioinformational networks, was highly efficient at engaging a physiological response closely associated with male sexual activity. In addition, tumescence during the erotic images closely followed the expected pattern in which there was a significant increase during script presentation, an even larger response during active imagery, and then a reduction during the recovery period. Finally, normal subjects exhibited significant heart rate and skin conductance increases during both fear and erotic images, though the pattern of increased responding was not as closely aligned with the predicted inverted-V pattern.

Bioinformational theory is concerned with how emotions are organized: how they are elicited, how they are displayed, and how they interact. Thus, the primary value of the theory within the broad field of behavior therapy has been through its understanding of basic processes involved in normal and abnormal forms of emotional behavior. Bioinformational theory can also address the process of change that occurs as a function of behavior therapy. The present discussion focuses on fear reduction, but the concepts may be applied within many of the domains discussed above.

Most behavior therapists would agree that an important goal is the generation of more adaptive responses within relevant contexts. From the view presented here, simple exposure to fear-eliciting stimuli is neither sufficient nor required for these adaptive changes to occur. Rather, the necessary feature of any attempt at emotional behavior change is that the relevant emotional information structure must be actively processed, including response components (i.e., verbal report, behavioral acts, and somatovisceral events). Various forms of imaginal and actual cue exposure may activate network processing, and particular behavior therapy techniques are thought to differ primarily in the methods and extent to which processing of response components of the network are emphasized. A practical implication of this analysis is that emotional response activation during therapeutic intervention should be confirmed, and physiological measurement is considered to be particularly useful in this respect.

According to the bioinformational approach, processing an emotional network is requisite for therapeutic change to occur. Extensions of the theory have attempted to clarify various aspects of this emotional processing. Rachman (1980) agreed that emotional processing was a necessary aspect of behavior therapy and that autonomic activity was a useful indicator of this processing. He outlined several conditions that would facilitate complete emotional processing—such as exposure, vivid and long presentations, repeated practice, habituation and extinction, calm rehearsals of coping, and autonomic reactivity. Processing would be impeded by avoidance, inadequate practice and coping rehearsals, fatigue, excessively brief presentations, and a lack of autonomic reactivity. Rachman (1980, pp. 54–55) advocated the use of autonomic "test probes" to determine whether processing had occurred, though there was no attempt to explain the processes through which this processing yielded its beneficial effects.

In another extension of the bioinformational processing approach toward fear and anxiety reduction, Foa and Kozak (1986) proposed that exposure-based treatments were effective to the extent that patients were provided with "response corrective information" while relevant emotional networks were activated. Foa and Kozak proposed that by gradually introducing new information while emotional networks were being processed, they would integrate more adaptive response elements into the network, thereby replacing maladaptive responses. The primary emphasis was placed on meaning components as the focal point of change, and it was hypothesized that maladaptive responses would diminish as patients incorporated new information about appropriate stimulus–response associations. Although the formation of new response tendencies during network activation is in keeping with bioinformational theory, there is little empirical evidence to date that suggests that corrective meaning input is necessary to effectively reduce fear responding.

What, then, determines whether activation of an emotional information network will be associated with modification of the network into a more functional form? A partial answer to this question can be obtained by first recognizing that an emotional network necessarily changes on its activation. As with increments in learning that occur with experience, associative connections among emotional network elements should become strengthened or weakened each time the network is activated. The nature, or direction, of these changes should depend entirely on the context of network activation. If network activation is accompanied by reduced responding (e.g., counterconditioning, extinction, or habituation), then the maladaptive response component within the network should become weakened. In general, therapy involves emotional elicitation in a supportive, calming, response-reducing environment; therefore, the stimulus representations that are evoked in behavior therapy, either imaginally or in vivo, tend to become associated with diminished responding. These new response tendencies will eventually become generalized to the nontherapy environment. On the other hand, exposure to a phobic stimulus in a nontherapeutic context is often aversive and may be associated with increased responding; the association between the stimulus and the maladaptive response may even become strengthened. Furthermore, to the extent that behavioral avoidance is a prominent feature of fear-based disorders, there are few opportunities for fear response networks to be modified outside of therapy.

On the basis of this analysis, the critical feature in behavior therapy is the activation of relevant emotional networks in a context in which reduced emotional responding can become associated with relevant stimulus features. Further research may provide information as to what specific processes of response reduction are involved in different forms of therapy. Given the large differences in individual response and degradation patterns, we are compelled to restate the importance of multisystem measurement as a regular part of research and clinical practice. Finally, because increased physiological activation during processing of relevant affective informational networks has been positively related to treatment success, further research should explore the potential benefit of response training as a precursor to various forms of behavioral treatment.

FUTURE DIRECTIONS

We finally describe several areas of basic and applied research that should assist in the ongoing evaluation, refinement, and application of bioinformational theory:

1. Startle-probe methodology has already proven to be a valuable research tool for studying emotional responding among normal and disordered populations within a bioinformational framework (e.g., Cuthbert et al., 1994; Cuthbert, Strauss, & Lang, 1992; Patrick et al., 1993). Given the relative immunity of the startle reflex to volitional control, this methodology should be highly useful for advancing our understanding of various forms of emotional disorder. For instance, because increased startle responding is one of the diagnostic criteria for PTSD (American Psychiatric Association, 1987), the startle methodology used in studies of affective responding may be particularly useful for exploring the nature of enhanced startle reactivity in these patients. This measure should also prove to be highly useful in clinical assessment and diagnosis (e.g., as a measure of treatment outcome).

2. A full evaluation of the biphasic response properties hypothesized by the theory will depend greatly on the elicitation of reflex systems other than the defensive eyeblink response in a variety of emotional–motivational states. For example, an appetitive reflex such as salivation in response to taste or olfactory cues may provide a more direct test of the response-matching hypothesis within the appetitive system. The development of a suitable appetitive probe could also be a useful research tool for studying appetitively oriented forms of behavioral pathology, such as drug addiction and eating disorders.

3. Recent findings suggest that the unilateral classification of various forms of psychopathology as pure aversive or appetitive syndromes may be overly simplistic. In a recent study involving affective picture viewing among anxiety disorder patients, the primary deficit observed was a diminished reporting of pleasure while viewing standardized positive material (e.g., Cuthbert et al., 1992). In another study (Drobes, Miller, & Lang, 1993), binge eaters and food-deprived subjects exhibited enhanced startle reactivity while viewing appetizing pictures of food, a response that is typically associated with an aversive state. Bioinformational theory provides a framework from which fundamental issues with respect to

the correspondence and interaction of emotional–motivational states can be addressed.

4. Much of the research discussed in this chapter involves exposure to text-prompted or pictorial affective material. Bioinformational theory, though, suggests that emotional networks can be prompted by any variety of sensory, perceptual, or semantic forms of information that matches the network. Further evaluation of the theory should involve an expansion of the types of media used to prompt emotional networks (e.g., sounds, smells, moving pictures, or cue combinations). These stimuli would ideally be standardized, similar to the approach taken with recent studies on emotional picture viewing (e.g., Bradley, Greenwald, & Hamm, 1993; Center for Psychophysiological Study of Emotion and Attention, 1994). Recent work has begun to investigate affective modulation of the startle reflex during presentation of a standardized set of affective sounds (Bradley, Zack, & Lang, 1994), as well as during olfactory stimulation (Miltner, Matjak, Braun, Diekmann, & Brody, 1994), with early results resembling the affect–startle effect observed during picture viewing and imagery paradigms. Extension of these standardized forms of assessment into clinical practice will increase the flexibility of therapists, both for collecting useful assessment data and for providing patients with realistic and diverse emotional prompts for exposure-based treatments.

REFERENCES

American Psychiatric Association. (1987). *Diagnostic and statistical manual of mental disorders* (3rd ed., rev.). Washington, DC: Author.

American Psychiatric Association. (1994). *Diagnostic and statistical manual of mental disorders* (4th ed.). Washington, DC: Author.

Baker, L. J., Hastings, J. E., & Hart, J. D. (1984). Enhanced psychophysiological responses of Type A coronary patients during Type A-relevant imagery. *Journal of Behavioral Medicine, 7,* 287–306.

Baker, T. B., Morse, E., & Sherman, J. E. (1987). The motivation to use drugs: A psychobiological analysis of urges. In P. C. Rivers (Ed.), *The Nebraska Symposium on Motivation: Alcohol use and abuse* (pp. 257–323). Lincoln: University of Nebraska Press.

Bauer, R. M., & Craighead, W. E. (1979). Psychophysiological responses to the imagination of fearful and neutral situations: The effects of imagery instructions. *Behavior Therapy, 10,* 389–403.

Baum, A. (1990). Stress, intrusive imagery, and chronic distress. *Health Psychology*, *9*, 653–675.

Berg, W. K., & Davis, M. (1984). Diazepam blocks fear-enhanced startle elicited electrically from the brainstem. *Physiology and Behavior*, *32*, 333–336.

Blanchard, E. B., Kolb, L. C., Gerardi, R. J., Ryan, P., & Pallmeyer, T. P. (1986). Cardiac response to relevant stimuli as an adjunctive tool for diagnosing post-traumatic stress disorder in Vietnam veterans. *Behavior Therapy*, *17*, 592–606.

Bradley, M. M., Cuthbert, B. N., & Lang, P. J. (1990). Startle reflex modulation: Emotion or attention? *Psychophysiology*, *27*, 513–523.

Bradley, M. M., Cuthbert, B. N., & Lang, P. J. (1991). Startle and emotion: Lateral acoustic stimuli and the bilateral blink. *Psychophysiology*, *28*, 285–295.

Bradley, M. M., Greenwald, M. K., & Hamm, A. O. (1993). Affective picture processing. In N. Birbaumer & A. Östhman (Eds.), *The organization of emotion* (pp. 48–65). Toronto, Ontario, Canada: Hogrefe-Huber.

Bradley, M. M., Zack, J., & Lang, P. J. (1994). Cries, screams, and shouts of joy: Affective responses to environmental sounds [Abstract]. *Psychophysiology*, *31*, S29.

Brownlee, S., Leventhal, H., & Balaban, M. (1992). Autonomic correlates of illness imagery. *Psychophysiology*, *29*, 142–153.

Burton, S. M., Drobes, D. J., & Tiffany, S. T. (1992, May). *The manipulation of mood and smoking urges through imagery: Evaluation of facial EMG activity.* Paper presented at the 64th Annual Meeting of the Midwestern Psychological Association, Chicago.

Carroll, D., Marzillier, J. S., & Merian, S. (1982). Psychophysiological changes accompanying different types of arousing and relaxing imagery. *Psychophysiology*, *19*, 75–82.

Center for Psychophysiological Study of Emotion and Attention [CPSEA-NIMH] (1994). *The International Affective Picture System* [photographic slides]. The Center for Research in Psychophysiology, University of Florida, Gainesville, FL.

Cleckley, H. (1955). *The mask of sanity* (3rd ed.). St. Louis, MO: Mosby.

Cook, E. W., Hawk, L. W., Davis, T. L., & Stevenson, V. E. (1991). Affective individual differences and startle reflex modulation. *Journal of Abnormal Psychology*, *100*, 5–13.

Cook, E. W., Melamed, B. G., Cuthbert, B. N., McNeil, D. W., & Lang, P. J. (1988). Emotional imagery and the differential diagnosis of anxiety. *Journal of Consulting and Clinical Psychology*, *56*, 734–740.

Cuthbert, B. N., Drobes, D. J., Patrick, C. J., & Lang, P. J. (1994). Autonomic and startle responding during affective imagery among anxious patients [Abstract]. *Psychophysiology*, *31*, S18.

Cuthbert, B. N., Strauss, C. C., & Lang, P. J. (1992). Psychophysiological responses to slides in anxiety disorder patients. *Psychophysiology*, *29*, S26.

Cuthbert, B. N., Vrana, S. R., & Bradley, M. M. (1991). Imagery: Function and physiology. In P. K. Ackles, J. R. Jennings, & M. G. H. Coles (Eds.), *Advances in psychophysiology* (Vol. 4, pp. 1–42). Greenwich, CT: JAI Press.

de Jong, P. J., Arntz, A., & Merckelbach, H. (1993). The startle probe response as an instrument for evaluating exposure effects in spider phobia. *Advances in Behaviour Research and Therapy, 15,* 301–316.

Drobes, D. J., Miller, E. J., & Lang, P. J. (1993). Effects of food deprivation and eating patterns of psychophysiological responses to slides [Abstract]. *Psychophysiology, 30,* S23.

Drobes, D. J., & Tiffany, S. T. (1993). Imaginal and in vivo inductions of smoking urge: Physiological and self-report manifestations [Abstract]. *Psychophysiology, 30,* S23.

Foa, E. B., & Kozak, M. J. (1986). Emotional processing of fear: Exposure to corrective information. *Psychological Bulletin, 99,* 20–35.

Fowles, D. C. (1980). The three arousal model: Implications of Gray's two-factor learning theory for heart rate, electrodermal activity, and psychopathy. *Psychophysiology, 17,* 87–104.

Hamm, A. O., Stark, R., & Vaitl, D. (1990). Startle reflex potentiation and electrodermal response differentiation: Two indicators of two different processes in Pavlovian conditioning [Abstract]. *Psychophysiology, 27,* S37.

Hare, R. D. (1985). Comparison of procedures for the assessment of psychopathy. *Journal of Consulting and Clinical Psychology, 53,* 7–16.

Himadi, W. G., Boice, R., & Barlow, D. H. (1985). Assessment of agoraphobia: Triple response measurement. *Behaviour Research and Therapy, 23,* 311–323.

Hirota, A., & Hirai, H. (1986). Effects of stimulus- or response-oriented training on psychophysiological responses and the propositional structure of imagery. *Japanese Psychological Research, 28,* 186–195.

Hodgson, R. I., & Rachman, S. J. (1974). Desynchrony in measures of fear. *Behaviour Research and Therapy, 12,* 319–326.

Johnson-Laird, P. N., Herrmann, D. J., & Chaffin, R. (1984). Only connections: A critique of semantic networks. *Psychological Bulletin, 96,* 292–315.

Jones, G. E., & Johnson, H. J. (1978). Physiological responding during self generated imagery of contextually complete stimuli. *Psychophysiology, 15,* 439–446.

Jones, G. E., & Johnson, H. J. (1980). Heart rate and somatic concomitants of mental imagery. *Psychophysiology, 17,* 339–348.

Jones, J. C., & Barlow, D. H. (1989). An investigation of Lang's bioinformational approach with sexually functional and dysfunctional men. *Journal of Psychopathology and Behavioral Assessment, 11,* 81–97.

Konorski, J. (1967). *Integrative activity of the brain: An interdisciplinary approach.* Chicago: University of Chicago Press.

Lang, P. J. (1964). Experimental studies of desensitization psychotherapy. In J. Wolpe (Ed.), *The conditioning therapies*. New York: Holt, Rinehart & Winston.

Lang, P. J. (1968). Fear reduction and fear behavior: Problems in treating a construct. In J. M. Shlien (Ed.), *Research in psychotherapy* (Vol. 3, pp. 90–103). Washington, DC: American Psychological Association.

Lang, P. J. (1971). The application of psychophysiological methods to the study of psychotherapy and behavior modification. In A. E. Bergin & S. L. Garfield (Eds.), *Handbook of psychotherapy and behavior change* (pp. 75-125). New York: Wiley.

Lang, P. J. (1977). Imagery in therapy: An information processing analysis. *Behavior Therapy*, 8, 862–886.

Lang, P. J. (1978). Anxiety: Toward a psychophysiological definition. In H. S. Akiskal & W. L. Webb (Eds.), *Psychiatric diagnosis: Exploration of biological criteria*. New York: Spectrum.

Lang, P. J. (1979). A bio-informational theory of emotional imagery. *Psychophysiology*, 16, 495–512.

Lang, P. J. (1984). Cognition in emotion: Concept and action. In C. Izard, J. Kagan, & R. Zajonc (Eds.), *Emotion, cognition, and behavior* (pp. 193-226). New York: Cambridge University Press.

Lang, P. J. (1985). The cognitive psychophysiology of emotion: Fear and anxiety. In A. H. Tuma & J. D. Maser (Eds.), *Anxiety and the anxiety disorders* (pp. 131–170). Hillsdale, NJ: Erlbaum.

Lang, P. J. (1987). Image as action: A reply to Watts and Blackstock. *Cognition and Emotion*, 1, 407–426.

Lang, P. J. (1993). The network model of emotion: Motivational connections. In R. S. Wyer & T. K. Srull (Eds.), *Perspectives on Anger and Emotion: Advances in Social Cognition* (Vol. 6, pp. 109–133). Hillsdale, NJ: Erlbaum.

Lang, P. J. (1994). The motivational organization of emotion: Affect–reflex connections. In S. Van Goozen, N. E. Van de Poll, & J. A. Sergeant (Eds.), *Emotions: Essays on emotion theory* (pp. 61–93). Hillsdale, NJ: Erlbaum.

Lang, P. J., Bradley, M. M., & Cuthbert, B. N. (1990). Emotion, attention, and the startle reflex. *Psychological Review*, 97, 377–398.

Lang, P. J., Bradley, M. M., & Cuthbert, B. N. (1992). A motivational analysis of emotion: Reflex–cortex connections. *Psychological Science*, 3, 44–49.

Lang, P. J., & Cuthbert, B. N. (1984). Affective information processing and the assessment of anxiety. *Journal of Behavioral Assessment*, 6, 369–395.

Lang, P. J., Cuthbert, B. N., & Melamed, B. (1986). Cognition, emotion, and illness. In S. McHugh & T. M. Vallis (Eds.), *Illness behavior: A multidisciplinary model* (pp. 239–252). New York: Plenum.

Lang, P. J., Kozak, M. J., Miller, G. A., Levin, D. N., & McLean, A. Jr. (1980). Emotional imagery: Conceptual structure and pattern of somatovisceral response. *Psychophysiology*, 17, 179–192.

Lang, P. J., & Lazovik, A. D. (1963). Experimental desensitization of a phobia. *Journal of Abnormal and Social Psychology, 66*, 519–525.

Lang, P. J., Lazovik, A. D., & Reynolds, D. J. (1965). Desensitization, suggestibility and pseudotherapy. *Journal of Abnormal Psychology, 70*, 395–402.

Lang, P. J., Levin, D. N., Miller, G. A., & Kozak, M. J. (1983). Fear behavior, fear imagery, and the psychophysiology of emotion: The problem of affective response integration. *Journal of Abnormal Psychology, 92*, 276–306.

Lang, P. J., Melamed, B. G., & Hart, J. D. (1970). A psychophysiological analysis of fear modification using an automated desensitization procedure. *Journal of Abnormal Psychology, 31*, 220–234.

Lykken, D. T. (1957). A study of anxiety in the sociopathic personality. *Journal of Abnormal and Clinical Psychology, 55*, 6–10.

Marks, I. M., & Huson, J. (1973). Physiological aspects of neutral and phobic imagery: Further observations. *British Journal of Psychiatry, 122*, 567–572.

Marks, I. M., Marset, P., Boulougouris, J., & Huson, J. (1971). Physiological accompaniments of neutral and phobic imagery. *Psychological Medicine, 1*, 299–307.

May, J. R. (1977a). A psychophysiological study of self and externally regulated phobic thoughts. *Behavior Therapy, 8*, 849–861.

May, J. R. (1977b). Psychophysiology of self regulated phobic thoughts. *Behavior Therapy, 8*, 150–159.

McClelland, J. L., & Rumelhart, D. E. (1988). *Explorations in parallel distributed processing: A handbook of models, programs, and exercises.* Cambridge, MA: MIT Press/Bradford Books.

McGuigan, F. J. (1973). Electrical measurement of covert processes as an explication of "higher mental events." In F. J. McGuigan & R. A. Schoonover (Eds.), *The psychophysiology of thinking* (pp. 343–376). San Diego, CA: Academic Press.

McNeil, D. W., & Brunetti, D. G. (1992). Pain and fear: A bioinformational perspective on responsivity to imagery. *Behaviour Research and Therapy, 30*, 513–520.

McNeil, D. W., Vrana, S. R., Melamed, B. G., Cuthbert, B. N., & Lang, P. J. (1993). Emotional imagery in simple and social phobia: Fear versus anxiety. *Journal of Abnormal Psychology, 102*, 212–225.

Michelson, L. (1986). Treatment consonance and response profiles in agoraphobia: The role of individual differences in cognitive, behavioral, and physiological treatments. *Behavior Research and Therapy, 24*, 263–275.

Miller, G. A., Levin, D. N., Kozak, M. J., Cook, E. W., McLean, A., & Lang, P. J. (1987). Individual differences in imagery and the psychophysiology of emotion. *Cognition and Emotion, 1*, 367–390.

Miltner, W., Matjak, M., Braun, C., Diekmann, H., & Brody, S. (1994). Emotional qualities of odors and their influence on the startle reflex in humans. *Psychophysiology, 31*, 107–110.

Newman, J. P., Widom, C. S., & Nathan, S. (1985). Passive avoidance in syndromes of disinhibition: Psychopathy and extraversion. *Journal of Personality and Social Psychology, 48,* 1316–1327.

Niaura, R., Goldstein, M., & Abrams, D. (1991). A bioinformational systems perspective on tobacco dependence. *British Journal of Addiction, 86,* 593–597.

Orr, S. P., Pitman, R. K., Lasko, N. B., & Herz, L. R. (1993). Psychophysiological assessment of posttraumatic stress disorder imagery in World War II and Korean combat veterans. *Journal of Abnormal Psychology, 102,* 152–159.

Öst, L., Jerremalm, A., & Jansson, L. (1984). Individual response patterns and the effects of different behavioral methods in the treatment of agoraphobia. *Behaviour Research and Therapy, 22,* 697–707.

Öst, L., Jerremalm, A., & Johansson, J. (1981). Individual response patterns and the effects of different behavioral methods in the treatment of social phobia. *Behaviour Research and Therapy, 19,* 1–16.

Öst, L., Johansson, J., & Jerremalm, A. (1982). Individual response patterns and the effects of different behavioral methods in the treatment of claustrophobia. *Behaviour Research and Therapy, 20,* 445–460.

Pallmeyer, T. P., Blanchard, E. B., & Kolb, L. C. (1986). The psychophysiology of combat-induced post-traumatic stress disorder in Vietnam veterans. *Behaviour Research and Therapy, 24,* 645–652.

Patrick, C. J., Bradley, M. M., & Lang, P. J. (1993). Emotion in the criminal psychopath: Startle reflex modulation. *Journal of Abnormal Psychology, 102,* 82–92.

Patrick, C. J., Cuthbert, B. N., & Lang, P. J. (1994). Emotion in the criminal psychopath: Fear image processing. *Journal of Abnormal Psychology, 103,* 523–534.

Pitman, R. K., Orr, S. P., Forgue, D. F., Altman, B., de Jong, J. B., & Herz, L. R. (1990). Psychophysiologic responses to combat imagery of Vietnam veterans with posttraumatic stress disorder versus other anxiety disorders. *Journal of Abnormal Psychology, 99,* 49–54.

Pitman, R. K., Orr, S. P., Forgue, D. F., de Jong, J. B., & Claiborn, J. M. (1987). Psychophysiologic assessment of posttraumatic stress disorder imagery in Vietnam combat veterans. *Archives of General Psychiatry, 44,* 970–975.

Rachman, S. (1976). The passing of two-stage theory for fear and avoidance: Fresh possibilities. *Behavioural Research and Therapy, 14,* 125–131.

Rachman, S. (1980). Emotional processing. *Behavior Research and Therapy, 18,* 51–60.

Robinson, A., & Reading, C. (1985). Imagery in phobic subjects: A psychophysiological study. *Behaviour Research and Therapy, 23,* 247–253.

Schwartz, G. E. (1971). Cardiac responses to self-induced thoughts. *Psychophysiology, 8,* 462–466.

Sheehan, P. W. (1967). A shortened form of Betts' Questionnaire Upon Mental Imagery. *Journal of Clinical Psychology, 223,* 380–389.

Suinn, R. M., & Bloom, L. J. (1978). Anxiety management training for pattern A behavior. *Journal of Behavioral Medicine, 1,* 25–35.

Tiffany, S. T. (1990). A cognitive model of drug urges and drug-use behavior: Role of automatic and nonautomatic processes. *Psychological Review, 97,* 147–168.

Tiffany, S. T., & Drobes, D. J. (1990). Imagery and smoking urges: The manipulation of affective content. *Addictive Behaviors, 15,* 531–539.

Tiffany, S. T., & Hakenewerth, D. M. (1991). The production of smoking urges through an imagery manipulation: Psychophysiological and verbal manifestations. *Addictive Behaviors, 16,* 389–400.

van Doornen, L. J. P., & Turner, J. R. (1992). The ecological validity of laboratory stress testing. In J. R. Turner, A. Sherwood, & K. C. Light (Eds.), *Individual differences in cardiovascular response to stress* (pp. 63–83). New York: Plenum.

Vermilyea, J. A., Boice, R., & Barlow, D. H. (1984). Rachman and Hodgson (1974) a decade later: How do desynchronous response systems relate to the treatment of agoraphobia? *Behaviour Research and Therapy, 22,* 615–621.

Vrana, S. R., Constantine, J. A., & Westman, J. S. (1992). Startle reflex modulation as an outcome measure in the treatment of phobia: Two case studies. *Behavioral Assessment, 14,* 279–291.

Vrana, S. R., Cuthbert, B. N., & Lang, P. J. (1986). Fear imagery and text processing. *Psychophysiology, 23,* 247–253.

Vrana, S. R., Cuthbert, B. N., & Lang, P. J. (1989). Processing fearful and neutral sentences: Memory and heart rate change. *Cognition and Emotion, 3,* 179–195.

Vrana, S. R., & Lang, P. J. (1990). Fear imagery and the startle probe reflex. *Journal of Abnormal Psychology, 99,* 189–197.

Vrana, S. R., Spence, E. L., & Lang, P. J. (1988). The startle probe response: A new measure of emotion? *Journal of Abnormal Psychology, 97,* 487–491.

Wolpe, J. (1958). *Psychotherapy by reciprocal inhibition.* Stanford, CA: Stanford University Press.

Zander, J. R., & McNally, R. J. (1988). Bio-informational processing in agoraphobia. *Behaviour Research and Therapy, 26,* 421–429.

10

SELF-CONTROL THEORY

PAUL KAROLY

The applied science of behavior therapy is much like an immense tree with many branches, one that is fed by an intricate and often arcane root system. A distinct purpose of the present volume is to reveal how roots with diverse origins can nourish and uphold the central structure as well as its far-reaching offshoots. Unfortunately, this integrative objective varies in its achievability, as some root structures are more easily unearthed than others. In the case of self-control theory, for example, boundary marking and even philosophical issues arise that challenge the best ecumenical intentions of textbook authors and editors.

Before considering issues and sticking points, however, I sketch the basic premises that historically gave rise to the self-control movement within contemporary behavior therapy.

The foundational assumption of traditional (externally managed) learning-based approaches to clinical problems is that the principles of operant and classical conditioning are sufficient to explain the etiology of deviant behavior and to provide a set of conceptual guidelines for the

I am indebted to Peter Killeen and Richard I. Lanyon for their helpful comments on an earlier version of this manuscript.

design of interventive strategies. Dysfunctional habits can be deconditioned or extinguished by experimenter (clinician)-mediated procedures, setting the stage for the acquisition of adaptive habits. This arrangement can be diagrammed as follows:

1. Externally guided learning/conditioning (EGLC)→

   old habit eliminated/new habit established and automated

This simple and elegant model did not always yield the expected results, however. The newly acquired adaptive habit often disappeared with the removal of powerful, externally mediated cues and contingencies. Thus, a second approach emerged:

2. EGLC → fading of EGLC → new habit acquired/automated

Unfortunately, some observers found that Models 1 and 2 were still not satisfying, particularly because of the failure of the new habit to persist over time. In addition, the target problem to be modified was often hidden from view (i.e., urges or forbidden thoughts) or occurred too infrequently to be systematically shaped or extinguished by behavior therapists. The emergence of self-directed learning and conditioning led to a third model:

3. EGLC + self-directed treatment → fading of EGLC →

   new habit/automated/a capacity for future self-modification acquired

In self-directed treatment, or self-control, the patient takes on much of the responsibility for program execution that previously fell to the clinician. The patient, rather than the intervention agent, "alters the probability of occurrence of a behavior by changing the variables that have controlled the behavior in the past" (Kanfer & Phillips, 1970, p. 453). In addition, the self-directive client ostensibly acquires the generalized skills to serve as his or her own change agent in the future.

Of course, not all behavioral clinicians and researchers accepted the premises of Model 3. To many, it seemed to fall outside the range of conditioning theory, being mentalistic and lacking in parsimony. Even for those who deemed Model 3 worth trying, questions remained: What were the essential ingredients of self-directed therapy? Did Model 3 lead to the promised long-term maintenance of change? What theory or theories underlay self-control therapies? How did one establish that self-directed learning was, in fact, taking place? What factors (internal or external) accounted for adherence to self-mediated contingencies? Despite these and other unanswered questions about self-mediated change, enthusiasm for the potential of a "humanistic," or noncoercive, model of behavior influence abounded in the 1970s. Applications in psychology, education, business, industry, and health care appeared, despite the paucity of systematic experimental evidence supporting the viability of self-control as either a rival to or an ally of Pavlovian, operant, or observational learning-based procedures. As we move into the twenty-first century, self-directed, or client-mediated, intervention models and methods are so well integrated into the cognitive–behavioral zeitgeist that their unique identity has become obscured. Indeed, success has made self-control a somewhat elusive topic from a conceptual standpoint (cf. Karoly & Kanfer, 1982; Mahoney, 1991).

Multiple models and definitional ambiguities represent the first layer of problems that arise as we endeavor to trace a clear path from theory to person-centered intervention. No singular conceptual approach exists today under the heading of self-control theory. In fact, the term *self-control* is not applied uniformly in the clinical literature: Labels such as *self-regulation, self-intervention, self-management, independence training, volitional control, self-directed change, self-help,* and *relapse prevention* are frequent and confusing substitutes. Moreover, for an apparent minority of behavior therapists, self-control is a hypothetical construct derived from an evolving analytic framework that seeks to explain the features, mechanisms, and the developmental emergence of the capacity for goal-governed habit modification in an ever changing, experimenter-free environment. For many others, however, self-control reflects not a working conceptual stance at all, but a shorthand for the technical procedures that purportedly enable behavior therapists (and others) to facilitate their clients' use of mainly externally mediated interventions (e.g., self-directed desensitization, self-hypnosis, and self-administration of rewards and punishers) to facilitate treatment maintenance and generalization. I suggest that both uses of the term *self-control,* the hypothetical and the pragmatic, are reasonable, so long as one remains cognizant of the distinction.

Beyond definitions, a second layer of problems is philosophical or metatheoretic. Debates still revolve around the acceptability in the natural sciences of person-centered mediation in contrast to explanation through stimulus–response connections and conditioned perceptions. To many, the *self* in self-control denotes a ghost in the machine: a nonverifiable, reified entity that inevitably invokes dualistic and circular reasoning along with the presumption of free will or the seemingly inexpressible quality of agency (cf. Bruner, 1990; Williams, 1992). Inferential accounts, furthermore, rely on verbal or questionnaire-based reports that, although treated as explanatory constructs or independent variables by cognitivists, are believed by most behaviorists to be "merely one class of correlated behaviors, no one of which causes any other" (Zuriff, 1985, p. 154).

Debates over the nature of self-control are similar to, if not as old as, debates over the nature of human consciousness. In both instances, empiricists and philosophers have moved along parallel as well as independent tracks, sometimes prodding each other toward improved formulations, sometimes talking at cross-purposes. As is the case for consciousness, there is no single best way to conceptualize self-control. However, if self-control is to be a viable construct for practical clinical application, then some ways of articulating it are likely to be better than others. Because this chapter is not the venue for resolving questions of definition or philosophy of science, I offer only a brief rationale for the conceptual approach to be taken here. Particularly because much of contemporary (Skinnerian) learning theory is predicated on the disavowal or minimization of mediational constructs and because much of contemporary behavior therapy is built on learning theory, a brief defense of the social–cognitive/goal systems/control theory viewpoint to be articulated here would seem warranted.

A PHILOSOPHY OF SCIENCE FOR COGNITIVE–BEHAVIORAL MODELS OF SELF-CONTROL

Several key assumptions or metatheoretic commitments form the bedrock of the present conceptual rendering of self-control. First, it is assumed that consciousness plays a functional role in human adaptation. It is by means of a reflective awareness of our inner and outer experiences that we are presumably able to traverse a continually changing and often challenging set of external life contexts. Automatic or nonconscious control is likewise an important feature of human adaptation, along with control by powerful environmental forces; yet these are typically backstage processes that on occasion share the spotlight with person-centered, limited-capacity, decisional determinants, but are infrequently the principal protagonists of life's directional drama. Furthermore, although the causes and correlates of various forms of self- and world awareness may someday be articulated at the biochemical or neurophysiological levels, such an account will not explain away subjective experience or symbolic processing. Of course, once an adaptive pattern is established (through external or internal guidance or both), it should be capable of subsymbolic maintenance.

Second, among the important functions of conscious mentation are the selective scanning of the environment; the ability to construct, model, or simulate actual and hypothetical events; and the comparison of sensed events to internal representations (simulations) of desired future states (goals). *Volition* refers to the capacity to deliberately and consistently recruit motor systems to bring performance in line with multiple, self-set goals, particularly when the goals conflict with one another, are associated with minimal external rewards, or possess differential (conflicting) payoffs over time.

The complexity of volitional processes cannot be overstated (cf. Baars, 1988; Sappington, 1990). Clearly, if a person's actions automatically or naturally matched her or his intentions, there would be little need for a process model of volition. Similarly, there would be scant need for a clinical science aimed at assessing and training the components of voluntary action management, if individuals were always sensitive to potential and actual conflicts between the short- and long-term consequences of their habitual behaviors and could act effectively to eliminate any self-defeating patterns.

Finally, meaningful self-directive action is believed to occur in social (interpersonal), biologic, and temporal contexts. Thus, despite linguistic conventions that seem to elevate the person above environmental and somatic influences (terms such as *self-control, independence, free will,* and *autonomy*), neither environment nor body transcendence is a necessary assumption of a cognitive–behavioral framework. Or, put slightly differently, the cognitive–behavioral model deals in interactions as opposed to main effects. Similarly, it is unreasonable to seek to declare individual acts or brief episodes of behavior to be examples of self-control. Rather, we must look to extended patterns of volitional action across settings to feel confident that the behavior changes observed are more than simple, steady state fluctuations. In summary, cognitive, environmental, temporal, and biologic features must share the explanatory stage, and the drama of self-control cannot be enacted without all the principal players in attendance.

Viewed within the radical behaviorist tradition, on the other hand, self-control has been defined operationally as behavior that leads to alterations in the probability of selecting one outcome, or end state, over another. In this context, there is ample reason to focus empirical analysis solely on contingency patterns that can be shown, particularly in animal research, to influence choice among temporally conflicting reinforcers (Logue, 1988; Rachlin, 1974; Rachlin & Logue, 1991). Indeed, self-control (as opposed to impulsivity) can be modeled by a variant of the well-known *matching law,* that is, by a discount function wherein the choice of a larger, but temporally delayed, reward over a smaller, but immediately available, reinforcer can be mathematically specified on an a priori basis. However, quite aside from debating whether so-called *delay of gratification* is the paradigm case of self-control, we can conclude the following, as did Kalish (1981):

> The factors that can influence the making of a choice for humans are considerably more complex than they are for pigeons. Apart from organismic variables—genetic and constitutional differences about which very little is known at present—humans have language and the ability to contemplate future events. (pp. 291–292)

More specifically, it is asserted that not only are humans choice makers, they are meaning makers as well. The amount of reward associated with a particular object or activity is not fixed or invariant but is a provisional construction, subject to individual interpretation and social validation. The rate of delivery of rewards (particularly subtle or idiosyncratic ones) is likewise neither precise nor predictable. Hence, preference for one outcome versus another is inevitably a "moving target," influenced in the extra-laboratory world by a host of situational, organismic, and intrapsychic variables—including the other goals in a person's hierarchy and their manner of representation. Bringing action into compliance with an ideal, rational, or evolutionarily prescriptive (biologically useful) model laid out with mathematical precision by an all-powerful experimenter is not what clinicians have to contend with when attempting to conduct self-control interventions. A critical adaptive task of free-ranging humans is the management of a largely covert, complexly organized, and changing preference system, not the discovery of a method for maximizing hedonic gain (cf. Logue, 1988, for an alternative view). Hence, for a self-control model to be useful for clinical work, it must attempt to account for both the observable and internal mechanisms by which humans select and then guide their life trajectories against the pressures of immediate contingencies over extended periods of time and across variable circumstances. Accounting for individual differences in feelings of *voluntariness*, or decisional freedom, and in people's willingness to expend effort or risk discomfort in the interest of long-term outcomes is yet another explanatory target. A mediational perspective is deemed essential for the accomplishment of this purpose (Karoly, 1981).

An additional important conceptual presupposition often associated with mediational models is the so-called *continuity assumption*. That is, a functional identity is posited between overt learning (conditioning) principles and their covert counterparts. In the early days, when cognitive (person-centered) models were struggling for acceptance, the assumption of continuity provided an elegantly simple and convenient bridge between the world of stimulus–response (S-R) learning and that of stimulus–organism–response (S-O-R) learning. The conceptual stretch was meager. If individual A could monitor animal B, differentially reward or punish B, and thereby gain stimulus and contingency control over it, then why not assume that the process could be interiorized (internalized) so that person A comes to control himself or herself in the same manner (using the identical principles). As Mahoney (1974) noted, "the skull becomes a rather crowded Skinner box" (p. 61). Likewise, if person A could hypnotize, desensitize, persuade, or contract with person B, then A could do these things to and for himself or herself. Assuming, as did Luria (1961), that human speech (and imagination) afforded a special means of self-cuing and self-consequation, early self-control theorists could speak the language of their S-R brethren and develop new behavioral technologies (like covert conditioning and self-instructional training), while requiring their colleagues to merely tolerate the premise of continuity unless or until it was proven false. Of course, few psychologists ever seek to falsify their premises (or their hypotheses, for that matter); thus, the new covert techniques soon won a place alongside their exteriorized counterparts (Kendall, Vitousek, & Kane, 1991; Mahoney, 1974). Although the logical status of the continuity assumption is suspect, and it contributes little to the discovery of new or nonparallel principles of covert regulation, it still serves the field well, justifying the importation of models from domains such as cybernetics, computer science, and contemporary learning and memory. Thus, owing to its heuristic value, it remains a vital part of the cognitive–behavioral metatheory.

SYSTEMS THEORY AND SELF-CONTROL: SOME CONTEMPORARY WORKING MODELS

Many current textbook accounts of self-control appear to be written from a purely descriptive rather than an explanatory vantage. First, self-control problems are defined in terms of behavioral excesses or deficiencies. A behavior such as excessive alcohol consumption is considered problematic because, although it brings short-term pleasure, it often eventuates in sickness and premature death. There exists an essential conflict between its immediate and its long-range consequences. Alternatively, participating in potentially embarrassing, time-consuming, costly, and sometimes painful medical/dental examinations is unpleasant in the short term but can (when reckoned over the long haul) prolong life and enhance its quality. The clinical objective, then, is to assist clients to effectively reverse the seemingly natural approach–avoidance gradients in each case. Self-control therapy, again stated in descriptive terms, is defined as involving training that can help people "control their own behavior through the systematic use of behavior technology" (Gross, 1985, p. 192).

Despite the considerable value of descriptive accounts, they are noncommittal in the realm of theory. Gross's (1985) definition is not atheoretical, but rather pantheoretic, inasmuch as almost any behavioral method might be adopted to assist the client in gaining effective control over self-defeating action patterns. The only requirement would be that the client would eventually be able to independently, reliably, and correctly use the procedure taught by the therapist. Later in his discussion, Gross (1985) pointed out that, in its "most common form," self-control therapy tends to involve the components of *self-monitoring, self-evaluation,* and *self-consequation* (self-administered reward and punishment).

These widely identified components are features of a three-stage sequential model of person-mediated control articulated over 20 years ago by F. H. Kanfer and his colleagues (Kanfer, 1971, 1977; Kanfer & Karoly, 1972) and subsequently revised and elaborated (e.g., Bandura, 1977; Kanfer & Gaelick-Buys, 1991; Kanfer & Hagerman, 1981; Kanfer & Schefft, 1988; Karoly, 1977, 1981, 1985; Thoresen & Coates, 1976). Thus, a broad descriptive model does seem to underlie the practice of self-control intervention, but only implicitly. By this I mean that many discussions of the three phases of self-control in the contemporary literature treat the hypothesized components as if they were established facts. In journal articles, books, and book chapters, in recent years, the topic of self-control has often been orchestrated around these three phases, but without any direct acknowledgment of the presumptive or rudimentary nature of the constructs being used. This practice is troubling because further conceptual advancement or clarification is precluded by a widespread disregard for the epistemic status of the concepts at hand. The three-stage model is actually part of a family of conceptualizations, whose ability to describe and explain individual differences in self-guidance is taken up next.

Control Theory: Themes and Variations

In lieu of elevating action to a preeminent place in explanatory accounts of human adaptation, contemporary cognitive theorists emphasize information as the basic unit of analysis. The pivotal informational unit in a supposedly self-directive system is that which reflects the system's current purpose, reference value, or goal. This information is contained in what control theorists call a *feed-forward* (command or directive) function (Bandura, 1986; Carver & Scheier, 1981; Ford, 1987; Powers, 1973). More familiar terms for this hypothetical mechanism of self-determination include *forethought, standard setting, intentionality, mental simulation, anticipation, value/expectancy, purpose,* and *goal cognition* (Karoly, 1993b). As Ford (1987) noted, people are guided (their motor behavior is targeted) by their varied cognitive representations of desired (and undesired) future states (as if asking themselves, "What outcome or results do I want to produce?"). In an intelligent machine, such as a guided missile, the feed-forward function is programmed or hard-wired into the system. In humans, goals and values are learned, and their causal influence is, at best, probabilistic.

A second, equally important, function of a self-directive system is knowledge of results, or feedback. Although self-control is often contrasted with control by external contingencies, both are dependent on feedback and differ only in who (the actor or the experimenter) is keeping track of and underscoring critical movement toward a goal. In fact, more than 30 years ago, Mowrer (1960) extolled the virtues of feedback by noting that learning involves the strengthening not of a connection between an act and a drive, but of the connection between action and the "emotion of hope":

> The assumption here is that learning is related, exclusively, to the connections involved in the *informational feedback* from a response or

response "intention" (i.e., a partial or perhaps symbolic occurrence of the response), and that it involves no change in what may be called the "executive" (brain-to-muscle) pathways in the nervous system. (Mowrer, 1960, p. 220)

If instrumental learning includes (among other things) the process of knowing that one is getting closer to his or her goal(s), the twin operations of feed-forward (having a goal) and feedback sensitivity (knowing where one is; also called *self-monitoring*) are essential mechanisms in a closed-loop model, aided by the additional ability to compare the goal (the reference value or standard) with the perception of one's current status. This third self-evaluative component is called a *comparator* or *regulatory* process (Carver & Scheier, 1981; Ford, 1987; Kanfer & Karoly, 1972; Powers, 1973).

Although feed-forward, feedback, and comparator (regulatory) processes are the most often discussed elements of human self-direction, several other mechanisms are nonetheless pivotal. As outlined by Ford (1987), a control system requires a means of correcting sensed discrepancies between the goal or standard and the information being fed back to the comparator. In human systems, these are called *instrumental, problem-solving, self-instructional,* or *coping* skills. In control theory language, these are summarized as the *control function*. A person would indeed be adrift in her or his own head if all she or he had to work with were the sensory, perceptual, and cognitive functions heretofore discussed; one needs an effector or motor system as well (not an unreasonable view in the context of behavior therapy).

Furthermore, the organism must be able to collect information about all person–environment exchanges relevant to the purpose(s) at hand. That is, before any information can be fed back to the individual, that information must be noticed and properly tagged as relevant. Task-relevant information is capable of detection through different modalities (e.g., visual, tactile, and auditory); not everyone is capable of using available modalities with equal facility to accomplish this so-called *information collection function*.

Finally, Ford (1987) noted that a control system requires an energy source and the ability to vary the amount, rate, and intensity of its transactions with the world. Three types of *arousal functions*, as Ford called them, include the following: activation or energization of physical activity, emotional arousal, and attention. Clearly, this is a domain within which individual differences can complicate the assessment, display, and manipulation of human self-control. Furthermore, by including affect regulation as a component skill of a self-directive system, the self-control of emotion, often discussed as an important and neglected target of clinical intervention, emerges also as a possible determinant of action (a potential means whereby instrumental or expressive behavior is modulated by the deliberate exhibition or inhibition of emotion).

Having addressed some of the main control system themes, I now introduce the variations (or qualifying conditions). For example, the important comparator mechanism, described above, does not tend to operate in a logical, dispassionate, machinelike fashion. First, goals or standards (e.g., to cut back on cigarettes smoked, to refrain from between-meal snacking, and to exercise regularly) are not always in the center of one's awareness. Situational cues and performance-based feedback are needed to activate a person's self-control directives; both of these potential goal-activating mechanisms can be overridden by ongoing thought processes and their related attentional foci (Bandura, 1986). Kanfer and Hagerman (1981) illustrated the importance of attributional factors in determining whether relevant standards are accessed in situations that might seem to call for self-controlling behavior. They show how the would-be dieter, generally aware of the "dangers" of an impending meal, might nonetheless consume all the fattening food presented over several courses if he or she felt that eating was the "socially correct" thing to do (e.g.,"How could I insult the boss's wife?"). Another potentially dysregulating type of attribution occurs when the would-be self-controller encounters problems or obstacles on the road to self-improvement and concludes that the process of bringing action in line with goals or standards is simply too difficult given his or her current level of skill or knowledge (Carver & Scheier, 1990). Indeed, one of the most studied mechanisms in modern cognitive social research is the *self-efficacy attribution* (Bandura, 1977, 1986; Karoly, 1993b).

It is not uncommon for an aspiring self-controller to disengage his or her efforts, owing to low-efficacy expectations that are completely justified by virtue of the setting of *patently unrealistic standards*. In this way, goal-setting mistakes lead to appropriately low estimates of future success.

Furthermore, focusing on the wrong standards can be problematic. In many instances, a person trying to change a dysfunctional habit (like smoking cigarettes) focuses too narrowly on an instrumental act or chain of behaviors (e.g., the sequential acts of reaching for a cigarette, lighting it, and inhaling) and fails to appreciate that there are affective precipitants and affective correlates of extended efforts at self-control. Failure to manage emotional antecedents and side-effects in the pursuit of a restrictively defined self-improvement goal is another reason for untimely program abandonment. Likewise, the social (interpersonal) implications of protracted self-control efforts must be taken into account (cf. Marlatt & Gordon, 1985) so as to forestall premature disengagement. Of course, there is also a considerable price to pay for remaining rigidly committed to a self-change goal that is unrealistic or functionally unattainable, but whose importance is so great that even frequent failure and low-efficacy expectations cannot foster a "healthy disengagement." In this latter case, the person becomes caught up in "defensive" maneuvers designed to preserve self-esteem, but at the cost of self-deception, nonplanful rumination, heightened arousal, and unpreparedness to reengage in more achievable self-change projects (Curtis, 1991).

In summary, models of the self-change process can be considered to be idealized to the extent that they suggest that A leads to B leads to C, and so on, with all other things being equal. Trying to determine exactly what the other things are, and why they are not always equal, is essential to a clinically complete and useful approach to self-control.

Representational Dimensions

Earlier, I noted the importance of the distinction between theoretical and technical conceptions of self-control—conceptions that are the intellectual concerns of the researcher or interventionist, respectively. I now contend that a workable theory of self-direction must concern itself as well with the conceptual model(s) that are part of the knowledge system of the would-be self-controller. Cognitions about oneself, the world, and self–world relations are important as potential sources of phenomenologic mediation, occupying explanatory space in the ubiquitous gaps between idealized models and real-life outcomes.

Consider, for example, a person who has been on a diet for 2 weeks. He or she has engaged in hundreds of separate acts that might be construed as self-control relevant. If asked, "What have you been doing for the last few weeks?", this person might answer, "I've been counting calories," "I've been eating fewer fattening foods," or simply "I've been on a diet." Likewise, the person might answer that she or he has been trying to change her or his life or has "been in treatment with a behavior therapist who is helping me lose weight." The exact treatment goal may have been to lose 5 lb, but the client's construal reveals the *conscious representational underpinnings* of 2 weeks' worth of complex action and may bear as much on the eventual success of the self-control program as the client's skill at implementing specific treatment techniques (cf. Vallacher & Wegner, 1985). In recent years, interest in the nature of schematic processing of control-relevant action has increased, providing a rich source of data that have helped the field transcend the simplified or mechanistic models of self-control derived largely from learning or engineering paradigms.

It has long been recognized that individuals are not "one-goal-at-a-time" creatures but are constantly managing a variety of personal objectives of varying incentive strength. Presumably, the causal organization of goals is a *hierarchical structure* (Carver & Scheier, 1981; Hyland, 1988; Powers, 1973). Although it is not necessary that all goals in the latticelike structure be represented at a propositional, if–then declarative level (indeed, pre-verbal children and animals cannot be expected to do so), most important adaptive purposes eventually become propositionally specified. Whether a goal such as staying on one's diet is pursued in the face of minimal external guidance, immediate pressures to avail oneself of immediate rewards, or internal goal competition is then taken to be a function of the representational characteristics of the intention.

European action theory has had a number of interesting things to say about the cognitive organizational features of motivational systems that facilitate or impede the translation of an intention into a pattern of instrumental activity in pursuit of a goal. Kuhl and his colleagues (e.g., Kuhl, 1985, 1986; Kuhl & Beckmann, 1985) have, for example, argued that an *intention* is distinct from a *motivational tendency* because the former possesses a specific propositional (memory) structure (i.e., under certain contextual conditions, an actor [agent] specifies a commitment to bring about a future desired state by taking action in relation to an object), whereas the latter (the motivational tendency) refers to the selection of one directional path over another. Kuhl's distinction relates to a dichotomy, in German theorizing, between goal setting/selection versus goal striving or implementation (cf. also Gollwitzer, 1990). Goal striving can be undercut by what Kuhl terms *degenerated intentions*, defined as, "cognitive representations in which one or more elements of an intention are ill-defined, weakly activated, or not specified at all" (Kuhl, 1985, p. 108). Depending on what element of the propositional cognitive structure representing an intention happens to be "degenerated," the person is expected to develop a specific form of *state orientation*, that is, a mode of thinking (as well as a personality predisposition) that tends to impede implementation of goals by perseverating on past, present, or future states and thereby deemphasizing action or movement toward the goal (which is supposedly facilitated by what Kuhl calls an "action orientation").

In recent years, my colleagues and I have concentrated on explicitly mapping the representational terrain associated with both maintenance goals (*self-regulation*) and change goals (*self-control*). Our approach, termed *goal systems analysis* (Karoly, 1993a, 1993b; Karoly & Ruehlman, 1993), presumes that there are multiple, interacting dimensions of human goals. Likening goal pursuit to a planned journey, we assume that one of several key determinants of success is the manner in which a goal is cognitively represented. Representation is seen as

> the traveller's subjective map or mental model of what the trip is likely to entail both behaviorally and emotionally. The individual's schematic or scriptlike knowledge of how his or her goal-seeking enterprise is expected to unfold and how it will be evaluated and managed (especially under difficult or unforeseen circumstances) is arguably the most

critical cognitive determinant of emotional well-being and adaptive success. (Karoly, 1993a, p. 275)

A mental model is much more than a static propositional statement encoded in memory, however; it is, in a dynamic sense, a simulation of the person's anticipated and remembered realities (cf. Taylor & Schneider's, 1989, discussion of mental simulation as "the cognitive construction of hypothetical scenarios or the reconstruction of real scenarios" [p. 175] and the writings of Johnson-Laird, 1983.) People think about where they are going, how they are going to get there, their emotional connection to the trip, and what they may have given up or negotiated along the way. Obviously, a standardized index is needed to assess such intentional construc-tions, one capable of differentiating the *degenerated* from the *enriched* (my term). The measurement approach that I and my colleagues have taken to address this need is embodied in what we call the Goal Systems Assessment Battery (GSAB).

Briefly, the GSAB is an evolving set of questionnaire and real time experience-sampling procedures currently being tested to gauge the *how* as well as the *what* of goal cognition. Our approach is not the first attempt to capture goal construals (see Cantor & Zirkel, 1990; Emmons, 1986; Karoly, 1993a; Little, 1983; and Pervin, 1989, for discussions of forerun-ners), but it is unique in its use of a self-regulatory model as the conceptual scaffold. Four of Ford's (1987) key functional capabilities believed to be essential to a self-regulating organism are assessed by means of a Directive (feed-forward or command) Function Questionnaire (tapping goal value and self-efficacy), a Regulatory Function Questionnaire (assessing self-monitoring and social comparison [the comparator]), a Control Function Questionnaire (measuring planning, self-reward, and self-criticism [self-corrective strategies]), and an Arousal Function Questionnaire (gauging positive and negative arousal associated with goal pursuit). The four brief questionnaires, all with good psychometric properties, give us a glimpse into people's stored schematic understandings of how they typically traverse the intentional landscape and provide a useful methodology for predicting and differentiating among successful and unsuccessful self-control efforts. For example, in a concurrent validation effort, we have shown (Karoly & Ruehlman, 1993) that individuals with high versus low scores on Rosen-baum's (1983) measure of self-control (or, as he now calls it, *learned re-sourcefulness*), yield very distinct profiles of scores on the GSAB (the two groups differing significantly on 7 of 9 subscales and scoring in the expected direction on all 9).

Microprocess Analysis

Describing, in real time, the dynamic connections among control-related cognitions, emotions, physiological reactions, and tangible goal-directed or expressive behaviors constitutes self-control modeling at the microprocess level. Such analysis can be considered distinct from (albeit related to) the episodic study of functional (systems) components and their qualifiers and from the study of metamotivational/representational dimensions, as discussed above. Mounting a dynamic microprocess analysis in the extralaboratory world would require a combination of diary keeping, ambulatory physiological monitoring, and behavioral observation, along with the capacity to change time-series or conditional probability analyses of the data (cf. Haynes, Spain, & Oliveira, 1993). Controlled laboratory designs should also prove useful.

Comparatively little theorizing at the microprocess level has yet taken place, and there are many basic questions in need of answers. When and how does a thought influence a physiochemical system (and vice versa)? What motivates a person to seek to alter his or her moods or emotions either through cognition, action, or the generation of other feelings? How does a person's thoughts about her or his thoughts influence those thoughts? How does a person's thoughts about his or her feelings influence those feelings? What role does the setting play in successful behavioral and affective regulation? Can relatively stable dispositions (acquired or physiologically prewired) predict the direction of thought and behavior streams? How does one intentionally create or turn off a mental state? Why do people ruminate, and why is rumination so hard to suppress? What role does attention deployment, selective memory, fantasy, imagery, thought suppression, or physical arousal/relaxation play in the self-control of action and affect? How does one negotiate multiple goals in a world of limited resources and limited time? For some intriguing preliminary discussions of questions such as these, see Wegner and Pennebaker (1993).

To attempt to summarize this section on control theory in its idealized and naturalized versions would be difficult. However, one needs to come away with the understanding that simple, lockstep accounts of volitional control are neither realistic nor comprehensive enough to serve as guides to clinical intervention. Furthermore, the task of providing a comprehensive model of self-control that cuts across the functional, representational, and microprocess levels is far from complete.

APPLICATION AND EVALUATION OF SELF-CONTROL/SELF-REGULATION MODELS IN BEHAVIOR THERAPY

The terrain of behavior therapy/behavior modification has widened considerably over the past 10–15 years, growing from a seemingly manageable and pristine applied learning theory base to an eclectic and often controversial mix of perspectives, but with unmistakable cognitive contours. As noted by Craighead (1990), 70% of the membership of the Association for the Advancement of Behavior Therapy (AABT) consider themselves to be cognitive–behavioral in orientation as compared with 27% pure behaviorists (and only 2% strict cognitivists). Starting in 1990, the masthead of the flagship journal in the field, *Behavior Therapy*, declared its mission to be the "application of behavioral and cognitive sciences to clinical problems." One consequence of this conceptual expansion, as noted at the beginning of this chapter, has been the absorption of self-control constructs into the larger corpus of cognitive–behavioral therapy. Interest in self-control as a specific and flexible mode of intervention has been replaced (although not entirely) by interest in specific clinical target domains (not surprisingly those that previously served as vehicles for demonstrating the power and relevance of self-control) such as obesity, cigarette smoking, alcoholism, anxiety, depression, and the like. Self-control interventions have become health psychology interventions, as well as practical mechanisms of relapse prevention. Behavior therapists are interested less in the power of individualized, client-managed, or participant models of intervention and more in seeking to combine the most powerful change ingredients (usually an eclectic mix) into multicomponent programs that can make the biggest difference in the least amount of time.

The incorporation of control theory conceptualizations into the mainstream of behavior therapy should be taken as a positive growth sign. It is clearly out of respect that modern change agents merge control theory concepts with rational emotive theory, stress managment, skills training, and the philosophy of the self-help movement. The only potential downside to this newly blended family of treatments and rationales may be the tendencies (a) to draw on only the most prominent and easily defined self-control procedures (thus ignoring potentially useful concepts), (b) to assume, without adequate testing, the empirical necessity or sufficiency of these procedures, (c) to assume that self-control methods and external control methods can be reliably and meaningfully separated, (d) to ignore both the complexity and boundedness of the self-control process (i.e. to expect too much from too little), (e) to oversimplify the assessment of self-control skills and deficits, and (f) to prematurely limit or inadvertently discourage theory testing and theory development in self-control psychology.

Theory Into Practice

In truth, most of the extant techniques used to facilitate self-control were not derived from any formal theory. The Bible, Koran, Talmud, and other holy books contain much of the essential wisdom that occasionally appears in the pages of our learned journals. Common sense, as exemplified in *Poor Richard's Almanac* or the pages of newspaper advice columns, is another ready source of ideas (both good and bad). Many of the practical self-control methods now in use were detailed 40 years ago by Skinner (1953).

The list of all procedures currently available to aid in the self-control process is actually quite extensive. Consider that at one time or another, each of the following has been put forward as a strategy to enhance the individual's ability to alter or modulate patterns of thought, feeling, or action: progressive muscle relaxation, self-instruction (self-cuing), mental rehearsal, meditation, biofeedback, covert modeling, journal keeping, information acquisition, thought stopping/thought starting, goal setting or resetting, stimulus control (stimulus narrowing), imagery and visualization, deep breathing, planning, training in perspective taking, correspondence training, mental distraction, problem-solving (problem analysis) training, yoga, self-hypnosis, environmental restructuring, task decomposition, expressive (writing) techniques, attribution (and reattribution) training, contingency contracting, self-generated reward and punishment, flooding, alternate- (incompatible-) response training, bibliotherapy, physical exercise, transcendental meditation, covert modeling, behavioral rehearsal, self-medication, autogenic training, cognitive restructuring, use of decisional balance sheets, social skills training, reinforcer sampling, positive thinking, labeling and relabeling of feelings, systematic practice in concentrating and remembering, acceptance of thoughts and feelings, differential self-observation and recording (i.e., recording only successes), assertiveness training, self-shaping, and role playing (Kanfer & Schefft, 1988; Karoly, 1991; Karoly & Kanfer, 1982; Watson & Tharp, 1993).

Reviewing each of these procedures, as applied to a host of self-control problems, is not possible here (nor is it the best way to appreciate the current translations of theory into practice). Nevertheless, in the decade of the 1970s, individual (isolated) techniques were indeed scrutinized and their effects discussed within the framework of minimodels, such as Kanfer's three-stage approach, Mischel's (1974) delay-of-gratification paradigm, and Cautela's (Cautela & Baron, 1977; Upper & Cautela, 1979) covert conditioning perspective. However, many of the first demonstrations of feasibility were uncontrolled case studies (Epstein & Peterson, 1973; Maletzky, 1974); externally managed interventions with presumed, but not empirically demonstrated, self-directive implications (Sherman & Plummer, 1973); examinations of putative correlates of self-control, but without a means for determining causal direction (Schallow, 1975); post hoc analyses (retrospective designs) aimed at ferreting out the factors that might distinguish successful from unsuccessful self-controllers (Perri, Richards, & Schultheis, 1977); and occasional theory-driven studies of nonclinical populations (Karoly & Kanfer, 1974; Spates & Kanfer, 1977).

Over the years (from the late 1970s onward), almost all of the supposed self-change procedures listed eventually found their way into the clinician's armamentarium—typically included as members of an integrative, multicomponent cognitive–behavioral treatment package and evaluated usually through controlled, pretest, posttest, and follow-up group designs. Individual self-control components dictated by the dominant three-stage model and other systems (elements such as self-monitoring, self-reward, and the self-selection of standards), became but a portion of the active ingredients in what were expected to be highly effective, synergistic treatment and maintenance packages.

To discuss the application of self-control theory to clinical work, therefore, I organize the presentation around the combination of putative self-control mechanisms as applied to distinct (but overlapping) types (or levels) of intervention. The discussion is necessarily illustrative rather than exhaustive and draws heavily on the control systems model.

A number of useful systems for parsing the self-control process have been put forward over the years. Thoresen and Mahoney (1974), for example, discussed the distinctions among increasing problem awareness, altering the environmental cues, and programming new and different contingencies. Marlatt and Gordon (1985) noted that the "journey of habit change" could be broken down into predeparture preparation (goal clarification and efficacy enhancement), the departure proper (control techniques used and social support elicited), and postdeparture maintenance (coping with lapses). Therapeutic change consists of alliance building, commitment promotion, goal assessment, goal negotiation, change implementation proper, progress monitoring, and the phase of maintenance/generalization, according to Kanfer and Schefft (1988). A category system that I suggested (Karoly, 1991) maps on to each of these previous schemes; hence, I will use it in conjunction with a consideration of Ford's (1987) exegesis of self-regulating functions. Except for the initial category (early-phase motivation enhancement), no linear sequencing is implied; that is, the levels are cyclical and interactive rather than stagelike.

Early-phase motivation enhancement. "I can't resolve, and I can't concentrate, and I can't clench my teeth and make up my mind. And, if I do make a sort of start, it's a failure after the first day. And this goes on year after year" was the complaint heard by turn-of-the-century philosopher and lecturer Arnold Bennett and quoted in his collection of essays *Self and Self-Management* (1918/1975, p. 54). Insofar as the difficulties in getting started with a self-change program are concerned, nothing much is experientially new after 75 years. However, modern clinicians can do more than merely lecture their clients.

Before activating and maintaining a client's desire to alter a self-defeating pattern, the clinician must seek to assess the nature and integrity of his or her motivational system. The GSAB, as noted previously, can be used to examine the strength of the client's desire to work toward a "therapeutic goal" (the feed-forward function). The perceived value of the treatment goal and self-efficacy expectations may be low on an absolute basis, or they may be low in relation to the feed-forward functions associated with other (perhaps incompatible) goals in the client's life. In addition to incorporating the four function questionnaires, the GSAB assesses the person's perceptions of the costs associated with change. Perhaps a self-change intention "degenerates" because of apprehensions about potential losses or sacrifices that such change might entail. Ambivalence is also assessed on the GSAB, along with perceived social support for and obstacles to change. Furthermore, the person's desire for change may be quite strong, but he or she might tend to pursue goals in either a "lone wolf" or strongly dependent fashion—either one presaging failure (owing to potential social isolation or social rejection). Other goal-setting and goal-pursuit proclivities are likewise assessed.

Among the methods available to remediate motivational deficiencies or excesses are the following: goal clarification; realistic goal selection; division of a goal into manageable subgoals; reinforcer sampling to discover incentives capable of offsetting current (deviant) objectives; short-term change assignments under the guidance of the intervention agent in order to assist the patient in trying out new, and perhaps difficult, control strategies in a low-risk setting; imagery exercises; training in self-recording of successes, especially when the program is new and challenging; reattribution exercises (role play); and use of gradually escalating commitments for patient adherence to the change program. At this stage, it is most critical that clients have a strong directive and arousal function and are adequately skilled in information collection. Weaknesses in the regulatory and control function are targeted later.

Behavioral enactment. Having been helped to adopt the right mindset for prolonged efforts at self-change, the client must be taught the instrumental behaviors needed to alter a high-probability response (such as cigarette smoking, overeating, or overdieting). Among the most used skills-training approaches aimed at strengthening what Ford (1987) called the *control function* is self-instructional training. For example, Kendall and Braswell (1985) taught so-called "impulsive" children to make five types of self-cuing statements designed to enhance rational problem solving. These included statements on problem definition, problem approach, attentional focusing, choosing an answer, and finally a self-reinforcing self-statement. The therapist modeled the requisite verbal behaviors aloud, encouraged the child to practice aloud, and then gradually faded into whispered statements and the eventual reliance on child covert self-cuing (cf. also Meichenbaum & Goodman, 1971).

Development of cognitive comparators. Just as an individual can learn about the game of chess by memorizing the moves and learning to execute them in isolation, so too can the acquisition of self-control skills be rote and unintegrated. The results for would-be chess champions and patients are likely to be a similar brand of disappointment at less-than-adequate real-world performance. I suspect, in fact, that the frequent failure of packaged self-control programs to effect long-term change is due, in large part, to the neglect of subtle, higher order dimensions of procedural knowledge (Karoly, 1991). To avoid the charge of superficiality, interventionists should focus on the following: clients' attitudes about change over the course of training, their emergent models of self-control, their ongoing attributions, and the other qualifiers noted earlier in the section detailing variations on the control system theme. Clinicians also need to be aware of the operational boundaries associated with any self-modification project, including the nature of the environment (i.e., home, family, work, school, and so on) that is expected to support self-control efforts as well as the physical requirements of the task. Sometimes family therapy or a program of physical exercise is needed to supplement the typical course of intervention. Likewise, certain metaskills underlie complex self-regulatory performance (Karoly, 1993b), and they should not be overlooked in the assessment and treatment of self-control disorders. Among the key metaskills are the following: memory, attention, interpersonal communication, imaginal capacity, forethought, affect regulation, and language. In control theory terms, a system's functional components may each be intact, but their coordination may be limited. Attention to the so-called *cognitive comparators* over the course of therapy (e.g., testing to see if instructions are recalled or if the client can vividly imagine a new and desired end state) can help ensure the durability and flexibility of treatment and the integrity of the client's self-directive repertoire.

Pre- and postperformance monitoring and evaluation. The information collection, feedback, and comparator functions detailed in Ford's (1987) scheme are critical and should not take a back seat to the feed-forward (goal cognition) and control (motor skill) functions. As it turns out, self-monitoring may be the single most studied dimension of self-control, explored as a unitary intervention and as a coacting element in multimodal treatment packages. Sometimes self-monitoring (self-recording) has therapeutic (reactive) effects. Sometimes it does not. Frequently, a self-evaluative and self-reward component, when added to self-monitoring, yields a superior outcome in relation to self-monitoring alone. The combination almost always does better than a no-treatment control condition (Kanfer & Gaelick-Buys, 1991). Teaching self-monitoring involves tutoring in systematic self-observation and in the use of convenient recording devices. Modeling and role play are also used to assist clients in acquiring the skill of self-observation.

Environmental manipulation. Among the oldest of the control function strategies in the behavioral literature is the prearrangement of cues in the environment so as to constrain maladaptive action, and the prearrangement of response contingencies (cf. Goldiamond, 1965). These procedures seem to work best when used in conjunction with operant interventions designed to reward behavior incompatible with the to-be-controlled response.

Affect management. In a control system, emotion serves as a source of general activation and as a strategic means whereby specific behaviors may be facilitated or inhibited. Training individuals in the recognition of emotion may be a necessary first step, along with training in identifying the antecedents of emotional reactivity. When the situation calls for emotional dampening, relaxation training or some self-directed variant (cue-controlled relaxation) may prove useful. Similarly, yoga, meditation, self-hypnosis, and anger control methods are available to help eliminate maladaptive reaction tendencies (e.g., fear, depression, or hostility) often implicated in the etiology or maintenance of self-defeating patterns such as alcoholism, obesity, bulimia, cigarette smoking, and the like (Rudestam, 1980).

Persistence training. In recent years, self-control has come to be seen as practically synonymous with relapse prevention and efforts to enhance therapeutic maintenance and generalization. It is often assumed that the more powerful and intrusive the behavioral intervention (externally managed), the less likely the behavior to persist after the withdrawal of the contingencies. Likewise, the more the client attributes change to internal (self-relevant) factors, the greater the likelihood of maintenance. The ultimate test of a self-control intervention (or of a cognitive–behavioral one with strong self-management components) is that it can be shown to have established the conditions for long-term gain and maintenance (Karoly & Steffen, 1980). Persistence training draws on all of the control theory components to the degree that a fully operational and integrated set of Fordian functions needs to be in place.

Whereas operant investigators may view self-control as a special case of contingency fading (Kazdin, 1989), cognitive–behavioral modelers like Marlatt and Gordon (1985) emphasized the role of instrumental coping and cognitive restructuring in relapse prevention. Marlatt and Gordon sought to build their clients' feedback sensitivity and ability to modulate their affective displays so as to equip them to avoid (prevent) the kinds of interpersonal strife that have been found to precipitate relapse (particularly among persons with addictive disorders).

Evaluating Effectiveness and Looking Ahead

The empirical evaluation of self-control and self-regulatory interventions is difficult and frustrating. When therapy-induced change is evidenced, it is not always clear that the change is meaningful (i.e., often effect sizes are small, and the measured change is not clinically interpretable). Sometimes (although not often) self-control programs yield no appreciable change in the targeted response patterns (Peterson, 1983;

Romanczyk, 1974; Wing, Epstein, Nowalk, & Scott, 1988). Unfortunately, when the no-change verdict is rendered, one is usually unable to determine whether failure stemmed from the fact that clients did not learn or did not use the self-control procedures or from the actual clinical ineffectiveness of the methods. At still other times, programs of self-administered consequences (reward or punishment) are eventually discontinued or are applied noncontingently by clients (Kazdin, 1989). Furthermore, when several self-control components are used together in a program, their individual contributions cannot readily be disentangled (assuming that there is an effect to explain). Most important, even when change does occur at clinically significant levels, as it has in recent years with smoking cessation (Lichtenstein & Glasgow, 1992) and weight loss programs (Brownell & Wadden, 1992), there appears to be scant evidence that self-control programs can produce long-term maintenance or generalization of learning (Hall, 1980; Kendall, 1989; Masters, Burish, Hollon, & Rimm, 1987). If self-control programs are to be considered completely successful in the light of the theoretical model that engenders them, they must not only "cure," they must facilitate independent (minimally assisted) management of problems to the point of new habit automatization. The apparent failure of self-control programs to achieve such an admittedly lofty goal prompted one writer (Runck, 1982) to comment that "collectively, the literature on behavioral self-control is full of theoretical gumption and clinical hum-drum" (p. 47).

If, as it appears, theory has outpaced clinical application, there would appear to be at least two courses to take. The first would be to seek to more fully capture the complexities of the functional, representational, and microprocess levels of self-control in our interventions (something I would like to see). The other is to concentrate first on improving the long-term potency of our clinical interventions through the continued refinement of combined externally and internally managed intervention programs. Although there is no reason why both of these tracks cannot be pursued simultaneously, the current trend (which I expect to continue) is to omit from Model 3 (discussed at the beginning of this chapter) the notion of timely fading of the externally guided program elements (including the provision of external rewards for client adherence to the schedule of self-administered consequences). Contemporary clinical investigators with some allegiance to a self-control philosophy are knowingly hedging their bets by introducing longer programs of therapy, booster sessions, support groups, aftercare, family involvement, and expanded use of powerful technologies capable of achieving better results sooner (cf. Brownell & Wadden, 1992; Connors, Tarbox, & Faillace, 1992; Kirschenbaum et al., 1992).

If self-control-based interventions cannot yet stand alone (or are not being allowed to), one can nevertheless be pleased at their role in cognitive–behavioral programs that are yielding impressive short- and long-term results with traditionally hard-to-treat clinical disorders. On the other hand, a new generation of clinical researchers and interventionists can work toward tapping the deep well of theoretical material associated with a control systems framework. To do so would first require greater recognition that self-control models are just that—idealized and incomplete accounts that are meant to reflect a dynamic process. Second, future investigators will need to attend to cognitive comparators, to representational elements, and to real time interactions across multiple levels (thoughts, feelings, and behaviors). Finally, the withdrawal of powerful external cues and incentives should eventually be included within cognitive–behavioral interventive models. After all, if externally guided treatment goes on indefinitely, the maintenance problem is not solved; it is merely put on hold.

REFERENCES

Baars, B. J. (1988). *A cognitive theory of consciousness*. New York: Cambridge University Press.

Bandura, A. (1977). *Social learning theory*. Englewood Cliffs, NJ: Prentice Hall.

Bandura, A. (1986). *Social foundations of thought and action: A social–cognitive theory*. Englewood Cliffs, NJ: Prentice Hall.

Bennett, A. (1975). *Self and self-management: Essays about existing*. Plainview, NY: Books for Libraries Press. (Original work published 1918)

Brownell, K. D., & Wadden, T. A. (1992). Etiology and treatment of obesity: Understanding a serious, prevalent, and refractory disorder. *Journal of Consulting and Clinical Psychology, 60*, 505–517.

Bruner, J. (1990). *Acts of meaning*. Cambridge, MA: Harvard University Press.

Cantor, N., & Zirkel, S. (1990). Personality, cognition, and purposive behavior. In L. A. Pervin (Ed.), *Handbook of personality: Theory and research* (pp. 135–164). New York: Guilford Press.

Carver, C. S., & Scheier, M. F. (1981). *Attention and self-regulation: A control-theory approach to human behavior*. New York: Springer-Verlag.

Carver, C. S., & Scheier, M. F. (1990). Principles of self-regulation: Action and emotion. In E.T. Higgins & R. M. Sorrentino (Eds.), *Handbook of motivation and cognition* (Vol. 2, pp. 3–52). New York: Guilford Press.

Cautela, J. R., & Baron, M. G. (1977). Covert conditioning: A theoretical analysis. *Behavior Modification, 1*, 351–368.

Connors, G. J., Tarbox, A. R., & Faillace, L. A. (1992). Achieving and maintaining gains among problem drinkers: Process and outcome results. *Behavior Therapy, 23*, 449–474.

Craighead, W. E. (1990). There's a place for us: All of us. *Behavior Therapy, 21*, 3–23.

Curtis, R. (1991). Toward an integrative theory of psychological change in individuals and organizations: A cognitive–affective regulation model. In R. C. Curtis & G. Stricker (Eds.), *How people change: Inside and outside therapy* (pp. 191–210). New York: Plenum.

Emmons, R. A. (1986). Personal strivings: An approach to personality and subjective well-being. *Journal of Personality and Social Psychology, 51,* 1058–1068.

Epstein, L. H., & Peterson, G. L. (1973). The control of undesired behavior by self-imposed contingencies. *Behavior Therapy, 4,* 91–95.

Ford, D. H. (1987). *Humans as self-constructing living systems: A developmental perspective on behavior and personality.* Hillsdale, NJ: Erlbaum.

Goldiamond, I. (1965). Self-control procedures in personal behavior problems. *Psychological Reports, 17,* 851–868.

Gollwitzer, P. M. (1990). Action phases and mind-sets. In E. T. Higgins & R. M. Sorrentino (Eds.), *Handbook of motivation and cognition* (Vol. 2, pp. 53–92). New York: Guilford Press.

Gross, A. M. (1985). Self-control therapy. In A. S. Bellack & M. Hersen (Eds.), *Dictionary of behavior therapy techniques* (pp. 192–195). New York: Pergamon Press.

Hall, S. M. (1980). Self-management and therapeutic maintenance: Theory and research. In P. Karoly & J. J. Steffen (Eds.), *Improving the long-term effects of psychotherapy* (pp. 263–300). New York: Gardner Press.

Haynes, S. N., Spain, E. H., & Oliveira, J. (1993). Identifying causal relationships in clinical assessment. *Psychological Assessment, 5,* 281–291.

Hyland, M. E. (1988). Motivational control theory: An integrative framework. *Journal of Personality and Social Psychology, 55,* 642–651.

Johnson-Laird, P. N. (1983). *Mental models.* Cambridge, MA: Harvard University Press.

Kalish, H. I. (1981). *From behavioral science to behavior modification.* New York: McGraw-Hill.

Kanfer, F. H. (1971). The maintenance of behavior by self-generated stimuli and reinforcement. In A. Jacob & L. B. Sachs (Eds.), *The psychology of private events* (pp. 39–57). San Diego, CA: Academic Press.

Kanfer, F. H. (1977). The many faces of self-control, or behavior modification changes its focus. In R. B. Stuart (Ed.), *Behavioral self-management* (pp. 1–48). New York: Brunner/Mazel.

Kanfer, F. H., & Gaelick-Buys, L. (1991). Self-management methods. In F. H. Kanfer & A. P. Goldstein (Eds.), *Helping people change* (4th ed., pp. 305–360). New York: Pergamon Press.

Kanfer, F. H., & Hagerman, S. (1981). The role of self-regulation. In L. P. Rehm (Ed.), *Behavior therapy for depression* (pp. 143–179). San Diego, CA: Academic Press.

Kanfer, F. H., & Karoly, P. (1972). Self-control: A behavioristic excursion into the lion's den. *Behavior Therapy, 3,* 398–416.

Kanfer, F. H., & Phillips, J. S. (1970). *Learning foundations of behavior therapy*. New York: Wiley.

Kanfer, F. H., & Schefft, B. K. (1988). *Guiding the process of therapeutic change*. Champaign, IL: Research Press.

Karoly, P. (1977). Behavioral self-management in children: Concepts, methods, issues, and directions. In M. Hersen, R. M. Eisler, & P. M. Miller (Eds.), *Progress in behavior modification* (Vol. 5, pp. 197–262). San Diego, CA: Academic Press.

Karoly, P. (1981). Self-management problems in children. In E. J. Mash & L. G. Terdal (Eds.), *Behavioral assessment of childhood disorders* (pp. 79–126). New York: Guilford Press.

Karoly, P. (1985). The logic and character of assessment in health psychology: Perspectives and possibilities. In P. Karoly (Ed.), *Measurement strategies in health psychology* (pp. 3–45). New York: Wiley.

Karoly, P. (1991). Self-management in health-care and illness prevention. In C. R. Snyder & D. R. Forsyth (Eds.), *Handbook of social and clinical psychology: The health perspective* (pp. 579–606). New York: Pergamon Press.

Karoly, P. (1993a). Goal systems: An organizing framework for clinical assessment and treatment planning. *Psychological Assessment, 5*, 273–280.

Karoly, P. (1993b). Mechanisms of self-regulation: A systems view. *Annual Review of Psychology, 44*, 23–52.

Karoly, P., & Kanfer, F. H. (1974). Situational and historical determinants of self-reinforcement. *Behavior Therapy, 5*, 381–390.

Karoly, P., & Kanfer, F. H. (Eds.). (1982). *Self-management and behavior change: From theory to practice*. New York: Pergamon Press.

Karoly, P., & Ruehlman, L. S. (1993). *Development and preliminary validation of the Goal Systems Assessment Battery (GSAB): Toward a self-regulatory perspective on goal cognition*. Manuscript submitted for publication.

Karoly, P., & Steffen, J. J. (Eds.). (1980). *Improving the long-term effects of psychotherapy: Models of durable outcome*. New York: Gardner Press.

Kazdin, A. E. (1989). *Behavior modification in applied settings* (4th ed). Pacific Grove, CA: Brooks/Cole.

Kendall, P. C. (1989). The generalization and maintenance of behavior change: Comments, considerations, and the "no-cure" criticism. *Behavior Therapy, 20*, 357–364.

Kendall, P. C., & Braswell, L. (1985). *Cognitive–behavioral therapy for impulsive children*. New York: Guilford Press.

Kendall, P. C., Vitousek, K.B., & Kane, M. (1991). Thought and action in psychotherapy: Cognitive–behavioral approaches. In M. Hersen, A. E. Kazdin, & A. S. Bellack (Eds.), *The clinical psychology handbook* (2nd ed., pp. 596–626). New York: Pergamon Press.

Kirschenbaum, D. S., Fitzgibbon, M. L., Martino, S., Conviser, J. H., Rosendahl, E. H., & Laatsch, L. (1992). Stages of change in successful weight control: A clinically-derived model. *Behavior Therapy, 23*, 623–635.

Kuhl, J. (1985). Volitional mediators of cognition–behavior consistency: Self-regulatory processes and action versus state orientation. In J. Kuhl & J. Beckmann (Eds.), *Action control: From cognition to behavior* (pp. 101–128). Berlin: Springer-Verlag.

Kuhl, J. (1986). Motivation and information processing: A new look at decision-making, dynamic change, and action control. In R. M. Sorrentino & E. T. Higgins (Eds.), *Handbook of motivation and cognition* (Vol. 1, pp. 404–434). New York: Guilford Press.

Kuhl, J., & Beckmann, J. (Eds.). (1985). *Action control: From cognition to behavior.* Berlin: Springer-Verlag.

Lichtenstein, E., & Glasgow, R. E. (1992). Smoking cessation: What have we learned over the past decade? *Journal of Consulting and Clinical Psychology, 60,* 518–527.

Little, B. R. (1983). Personal projects: A rationale and method for investigation. *Environment and Behavior, 15,* 273–309.

Logue, A. W. (1988). Research on self-control: An integrative framework. *Behavioral and Brain Sciences, 11,* 665–679.

Luria, A. (1961). *The role of speech in the regulation of normal and abnormal behaviors.* New York: Liveright.

Mahoney, M. J. (1974). *Cognition and behavior modification.* Cambridge, MA: Ballinger.

Mahoney, M. J. (1991). *Human change processes.* New York: Basic Books.

Maletzky, B. M. (1974). Behavior recording as treatment: A brief note. *Behavior Therapy, 5,* 107–111.

Marlatt, G. A., & Gordon, J. R. (1985). *Relapse prevention: Maintenance strategies in the treatment of addictive behaviors.* New York: Guilford Press.

Masters, J. C., Burish, T. G., Hollon, S. D., & Rimm, D. C. (1987). *Behavior therapy.* San Diego, CA: Harcourt Brace Jovanovich.

Meichenbaum, D., & Goodman, J. (1971). Training impulsive children to talk to themselves: A means of developing self-control. *Journal of Abnormal Psychology, 77,* 115–126.

Mischel, W. (1974). Processes in delay of gratification. In L. Berkowitz (Ed.), *Advances in experimental social psychology* (Vol. 7). San Diego, CA: Academic Press.

Mowrer, O. H. (1960). *Learning theory and behavior.* New York: Wiley.

Perri, M. G., Richards, C. S., & Schultheis, K. R. (1977). Behavioral self-control and smoking reduction: A study of self-initiated attempts to reduce smoking. *Behavior Therapy, 8,* 360–365.

Pervin, L. A. (Ed.). (1989). *Goal concepts in personality and social psychology.* Hillsdale, NJ: Erlbaum.

Peterson, L. (1983). Failures in self-control. In E. B. Foa & P. M. G. Emmelkamp (Eds.), *Failures in behavior therapy* (pp. 172–196). New York: Wiley.

Powers, W. T. (1973). *Behavior: The control of perception.* Chicago: Aldine.

Rachlin, H. (1974). Self-control. *Behaviorism, 2*, 94–107.

Rachlin, H., & Logue, A. W. (1991). Learning. In A. E. Kazdin & A. S. Bellack (Eds.), *The clinical psychology handbook* (2nd ed., pp. 170–184). New York: Pergamon Press.

Romanczyk, R. G. (1974). Self-monitoring in the treatment of obesity: Parameters of reactivity. *Behavior Therapy, 5*, 531–540.

Rosenbaum, M. (1983). Learned resourcefulness as a behavioral repertoire for the self-regulation of internal events: Issues and speculations. In M. Rosenbaum, C. M. Franks, & Y. Jaffe (Eds.), *Perspectives on behavior therapy in the eighties* (pp. 54–73). New York: Springer.

Rudestam, K. E. (1980). *Methods of self-change: An abc primer*. Monterey, CA: Brooks/Cole.

Runck, B. (1982). *Behavioral self-control: Issues in treatment assessment*. (DHHS Publication No. ADM 82–1207). Rockville, MD: National Institute of Mental Health.

Sappington, A. A. (1990). Recent psychological approaches to the free will versus determinism issue. *Psychological Bulletin, 108*, 19–29.

Schallow, J. R. (1975). Locus of control and success at self-modification. *Behavior Therapy, 6*, 667–671.

Sherman, A. R., & Plummer, I. L. (1973). Training in relaxation as a behavioral self-management skill: An exploratory investigation. *Behavior Therapy, 4*, 543–550.

Skinner, B. F. (1953). *Science and human behavior*. New York: Macmillan.

Spates, C. R., & Kanfer, F. H. (1977). Self-monitoring, self-evaluation, and self-reinforcement in children's learning: A test of a multistage self-regulation model. *Behavior Therapy, 8*, 9–16.

Taylor, S. E., & Schneider, S. K. (1989). Coping and the simulation of events. *Social Cognition, 7*, 174–194.

Thoresen, C. E., & Coates, T. J. (1976). Behavioral self-control: Some clinical concerns. In M. Hersen, R. M. Eisler, & P. M. Miller (Eds.), *Progress in behavior modification* (Vol. 2, pp. 307–352). San Diego, CA: Academic Press.

Thoresen, C. E., & Mahoney, M. J. (1974). *Behavioral self-control*. New York: Holt, Rinehart & Winston.

Upper, D., & Cautela, J. R. (Eds.). (1979). *Covert conditioning*. New York: Pergamon Press.

Vallacher, R. R., & Wegner, D. M. (1985). *A theory of action identification*. Hillsdale, NJ: Erlbaum.

Watson, D. L., & Tharp, R. G. (1993). *Self-directed behavior* (6th ed.). Pacific Grove, CA: Brooks/Cole.

Wegner, D. M., & Pennebaker, J. W. (Eds.). (1993). *Handbook of mental control*. Englewood Cliffs, NJ: Prentice Hall.

Williams, R. N. (1992). The human context of agency. *American Psychologist, 47*, 752–760.

Wing, R. R., Epstein, L. H., Nowalk, M. P., & Scott, N. (1988). Self-regulation in the treatment of Type II diabetes. *Behavior Therapy, 19*, 11–23.

Zuriff, G. E. (1985). *Behaviorism: A conceptual reconstruction*. New York: Columbia University Press.

11

A DEVELOPMENTAL PERSPECTIVE ON BEHAVIOR THERAPY

M. CHRISTINE LOVEJOY and BARBARA HAWK

Developmental psychology focuses on the "description, explanation, and modification of intraindividual change in behavior across the life span, as well as interindividual differences in such change" (Baltes & Reese, 1984, p. 493). Developmental theories serve to organize our thoughts about the nature and process of change within the individual and to guide empirical research (P. H. Miller, 1983). A vastly diverse group of theories, unified by their focus on the processes of change and continuity, fall under the rubric of developmental theory (Cowan, 1988; Dixon & Lerner, 1988; P. H. Miller, 1983). These include (but are not limited to) Piaget's (1970) theory of cognitive development, Werner's (1957) general theory of development, social learning theory (Bandura, 1986), the psychoanalytic theories of Freud (1955) and Erikson (1963), modern contextualism (R. M. Lerner & Kauffman, 1985), and Riegel's (1975) dialectic theory of development. This group of theories has stimulated massive quantities of empirical research and writing; unfortunately, however, there is a tendency for both developmental theory and empirical work to be fractured along lines defined by content (e.g., cognitive, emotional, social, and perceptual domains) and age and developmental levels (e.g., infancy, childhood, and adulthood).

Because of the volume of the empirical work, and the sometimes contradictory nature of developmental theories (Reese & Overton, 1970), even developmental psychologists face a difficult task in trying to integrate the different theories within their discipline. For those with primary interests outside the discipline of developmental psychology, the task of organizing the developmental literature so that it can be integrated with other fields of psychology becomes a truly formidable one. The size and difficulty of this task probably contribute to the frequent failure of clinical psychologists to do more than "pay lip service" to the importance of developmental issues.

Despite the difficulty of consolidating developmental "facts" and theories into a form that is conducive to clinical applications, an understanding of developmental issues is essential to the conduct of therapy with children and adolescents. R. M. Lerner, Hess, and Nitz (1991) argued that because therapeutic change is influenced by the development of the individual, *all* therapies or interventions should address developmental issues. However, developmental issues are particularly relevant for any therapeutic interventions conducted during childhood, when change occurs at a very rapid rate. In keeping with this notion, there have been increasingly frequent attempts by behavior therapists over the past 20 years to explore how applications of developmental theory and knowledge might enhance the effectiveness of behavioral treatments (e.g., Forehand & Wierson, 1993; Furman, 1980; Holmbeck & Kendall, 1991; Kendall, Lerner, & Craighead, 1984). However, the integration of developmental theory and child behavior therapy is difficult in that some of the assumptions of the two areas are seemingly incompatible (Reese & Overton, 1970).

The purpose of this chapter is twofold. First, we describe the assumptions and principles that characterize a general developmental perspective. This developmental perspective is not tied to any specific developmental theory but instead provides a broad framework for studying and interpreting diverse developmental processes. The assumptions that underlie the developmental perspective generally reflect the organismic worldview (Overton & Horowitz, 1991). These assumptions form the foundation for the newly emerging interdisciplinary field of developmental psychopathology and have influenced current thinking about the nature, prevention, and treatment of childhood disorders (Cicchetti, 1990; Overton & Horowitz, 1991; Sroufe & Rutter, 1984).

The mechanistic view of development is discussed only to the extent that it provides contrast with the organismic perspective. Although mechanistic views have had a strong influence on conceptualizations of psychopathology and treatment, they have been less prominent in developmental psychology and have also been less influential in the emerging field of developmental psychopathology (Overton & Horowitz, 1991). This has certainly been true in the case of learning theories, where the influence of these theories on child and developmental psychology has been relatively small compared with their important contributions in the establishment of treatment programs for children (White, 1970).

The second purpose of this chapter is to discuss the implications of the developmental perspective and, more specifically, developmental psychopathology for child behavior therapy. We focus on the compatibility of the behavioral and developmental perspectives and attempt to evaluate the strengths and limitations of a developmental approach to assessment and treatment.[1]

ASSUMPTIONS OF THE DEVELOPMENTAL PERSPECTIVE

Many of the major developmental theories, including those of Piaget (1970), Werner (1957), and Bowlby (1969), are based on an organismic model (Dixon & Lerner, 1988; Overton & Horowitz, 1991). In their now classic essays, Overton and Reese (Overton & Reese, 1973; Reese & Overton, 1970) contrast the organismic and mechanistic views on development and discuss the implications of the organismic view for developmental theories and research. They argue that organismic developmental theories are characterized by common assumptions (at a metatheoretical level) regarding the nature of the phenomenon to be explained, as well as the types of explanatory processes that are acceptable (Overton & Horowitz, 1991; Reese & Overton, 1970). These assumptions include *holism*, the *structure–function relationship*, *constructivism*, and *reciprocal influences* between the organism and the environment.

Because Piaget's cognitive–developmental theory is probably the most familiar of all developmental theories and is an excellent example of an organismic theory, it is used to illustrate these assumptions in the discussion that follows.

As noted by Reese and Overton (1970), organismic theories are based on the principle of holism, which emphasizes the essential interrelatedness and organization of the parts of the organism. Accordingly, any behavior, structure, or activity of the organism takes its meaning from the context in which it occurs. For example, in Piaget's theory, the meaning of a child's behavior is influenced by his or her stage of development and the cognitive schema he or she is using. Therefore, "identical" behaviors occurring at the different stages of development (e.g., sensorimotor and formal operations) would be construed to have different meanings because they serve

---

[1]Because of the extensive literatures pertaining to both developmental theory and child behavior therapy, our discussion does not provide an exhaustive review of all of the work in these areas.

different goals for the individual. Similarly, holism implies that behaviors within one domain of development (e.g., cognitive) must be evaluated within the context of other domains (e.g., affective and social). In contrast, from the mechanistic perspective, any phenomenon can be reduced to its component parts.

Second, organismic developmental theories focus on the relationship between structure and function. Basic psychological functions or goals are presumed to exist, and the task of a theory is to identify these functions and explicate how they are served by hypothesized psychological structures (Reese & Overton, 1970). In other words, the first question for the theory is "the functional question of what is the system for" (Overton & Horowitz, 1991, p. 28), and the second question relates to the "nature of the design or organization that serves this function" (Overton & Horowitz, 1991, p. 28). Piaget, for example, identified adaptation and organization as two basic psychological functions and proposed cognitive structures (e.g., sensorimotor, symbolic, and operational schemas) that allow the function of adaptation to be performed. Reese and Overton (1970) contrast this focus on structure and function with the emphasis on antecedents and consequences that characterizes a mechanistic model.

Third, organismic developmental theories are constructivistic (Overton & Horowitz, 1991). The meaning of experience is created through the activity and internal organization of the person as he or she interacts with the environment. As noted by several authors (Overton & Horowitz, 1991; Rosen, 1985), Piaget's cognitive–developmental theory provides an excellent example of a constructivist perspective in that he argued that even the basic biological structures that guide learning and understanding are constructed by the organism through its interaction with the environment.

A fourth and related assumption shared by organismic theories is that there are bidirectional influences between the organism and the environment (Overton & Reese, 1973). This has been characterized as a "strong" interactionist model by Overton and Reese (1973) and as a reciprocal action–transaction model by Pervin and Lewis (1978). In these models, the term *interaction* refers to more than either additive or multiplicative effects of organismic and environmental factors (i.e., statistical interactions; Sameroff & Chandler, 1975) and implies instead that there are continuous reciprocal interactions between the person and his or her environment. Note that the organismic perspective does not dictate the relative importance of person and environment factors and that their balance may differ over the course of development and with characteristics of the person. Overton and Reese (1973) described how this interactionist assumption was translated into Piaget's cognitive–developmental theory: For Piaget, the interaction between the organism and the environment occurs through the complementary processes of assimilation and accommodation.

Environmental stimuli are adapted to the existing structure of the organism through assimilation, and the organism adapts to the characteristics of the environment through accommodation.

The organismic view also leads to shared assumptions regarding the nature of developmental change, the process(es) through which it occurs, and the legitimacy of different types of explanations for change (Overton & Reese, 1973; Reese & Overton, 1970). From the organismic perspective, development involves reorganization and alteration of structures within the individual. As a result, later behaviors are qualitatively different from earlier forms of behavior. In other words, there are discontinuities in behavior. Werner (1957) argues that discontinuity is characterized by two features: *emergence* (later behavior cannot be reduced to the components of earlier forms) and *gappiness* (an absence of intermediate stages between earlier and later forms of behavior). As noted by Reese and Overton (1970), these assumptions about change are very different from those that characterize the mechanistic worldview, in which development is seen as a continuous additive process. The organismic assumptions regarding the nature of change are evident in Piaget's theory, in which development is associated with changes in cognitive structures (i.e., schemas).

From the organismic perspective, development involves a dialectic process (Overton & Horowitz, 1991), in which imbalances or asynchronies form the basis for change (Riegel, 1975). Riegel (1975) championed the importance of dialectics in understanding human development and argued that development involved the coordination of progression along four dimensions (inner–biological, individual–psychological, cultural–sociological, and outer–physical). Important developmental change occurs in response to conflicts and tensions that exist either internal to the individual or between the individual and the external world.

Finally, organismic models share assumptions regarding the legitimacy of different scientific explanations. Overton and Reese (1973) stated that in organismic theories, all of Aristotle's causal determinants (i.e., material, efficient, formal, and final causes) are viewed as legitimate explanations for development. Material and efficient causes involve genetic, physiological, and neurological influences and environmental factors, respectively (Overton & Reese, 1973), and are observable. In contrast, formal and final causes are pattern explanations involving the form (i.e., structures) and goals of development (Overton & Horowitz, 1991). Organismic models make an a priori assumption that development involves a directional process in which there is progress toward an ideal or mature end state. Development is ultimately explained by movement toward this end state (final cause), as well as by changes in the structure of the organism (formal cause). The acceptance of all four levels of causation in organismic theories contrasts with the exclusive reliance on material and efficient causes that characterizes mechanistic models.

Many of the "grand" organismic theories have attempted to describe and explain the universal sequences that appear in normal growth and development (Scarr, 1992). Other developmentalists have applied the general principles of the organismic approach to the study of individual differences (e.g., Magnusson & Allen, 1983a; Pervin & Lewis, 1978). This interactional perspective on development, with its focus on individual differences, has particular relevance for clinical psychology. Within the context of the normal developmental progression, interactional perspectives on development attempt to describe the different pathways or trajectories that individual lives may follow. Magnusson and Allen (1983a) described the interactional perspective to have a "focus on the continuously ongoing, bidirectional interaction between an individual and his or her environment (especially the situation in which the individual appears)" (p. 7). Furthermore, "from a developmental point of view, the person–environment interaction is regarded as a continuously emerging and ever-changing process over time—as symbolized not by a circle but by a helix or spiral" (Magnusson & Allen, 1983a, p. 7).

Magnusson and Allen (1983b) highlighted several important implications of an interactional perspective for the conceptualization and study of the developmental process. First, they noted that the appropriate unit of analysis is the relationship between systems (i.e., between the child and the parent or between biological and psychological systems within the individual) rather than any individual system in isolation. This relational focus is well illustrated in goodness-of-fit models of adjustment (J. V. Lerner, Baker, & Lerner, 1985; Thomas & Chess, 1977). Goodness-of-fit models propose that child behavior problems occur or are exacerbated when there is a poor match between the needs and characteristics of the child and the expectations and demands of the environment. For example, Thomas and Chess (1977) argued that child temperament is associated with the development of behavior problems when it is dissonant with parental expectations and demands. Thus, in keeping with a relational focus, they contended that it is the relationship between parent and child, rather than the child or the parent in isolation, that is the appropriate focus of study.

The timing of events is one important parameter of the interaction between organismic and environmental systems that may affect the developmental process. Rutter (1989), for example, described three ways in which the timing of an experience might affect its influence on development. Experiences may have different effects, depending on the neural development of the organism at the time of the event (i.e., the effects of a teratogen or injury). Similarly, the psychological functioning of the individual will moderate the effects of environmental events. For example, Rutter (1989) noted that separation experiences are more disruptive for preschool children than for infants (who have not developed any specific attachments) or for older children (who can use cognitive strategies to cope with the physical absence of an attachment figure). Finally, if experiences take place at nonnormative times, both the affective experience of the individual and societal reactions may differ from those that accompany more normative timing. For example, although sexual maturation is a nearly universal event in the course of physical development, early or late onset of puberty appears to affect developmental course (Magnusson, 1988).

Second, an interactional perspective focuses on patterns of competency and adjustment within persons rather than on single variables (Magnusson & Allen, 1983b), and common patterns form the basis for categorizing or grouping individuals for study. For example, psychological structures, defined as "relatively stable organizational properties or patterns of specific behavioral systems" (Reese & Overton, 1970, p. 137) are used to classify people according to cognitive level (i.e., sensorimotor, preoperational, or concrete operational) or attachment quality (i.e., secure, anxious–resistant, anxious–avoidant, or disorganized). Patterns of behavior can also be based on symptoms or problematic behaviors (e.g., Magnusson, 1988).

Finally, from an interactional perspective, emphasis is placed on understanding and explaining the "lawfulness of the processes underlying individual functioning and the continuous change taking place in these processes" (Magnusson & Allen, 1983b, p. 374) rather than on the prediction of specific variables or behaviors. The focus is thus on understanding continuities and discontinuities in individual functioning and on understanding the ways in which early patterns of behavior are related to later patterns. The study of continuity of normal and problem behaviors does not imply that there is isomorphism in behavior across the life span but rather that there is a meaningful and lawful progression of behavior across development.

The assumptions of the organismic and interactional views on development are an integral part of the newly emerging field of developmental psychopathology. Developmental psychopathology is an interdisciplinary field that integrates academic developmental psychology, clinical psychology, and psychiatry (Cicchetti, 1984, 1990). As a discipline, developmental psychopathology deals with both normal and abnormal behavior, with the assumption that processes that influence the development of normal behavior are also important in understanding abnormal behavior and vice versa. However, in contrast to traditional developmental psychology, with its focus on nomothetic principles of species-normal development, developmental psychopathology has its focus on individual patterns of adaptation and maladaptation. Emphasis is placed on description and explanation of deviations from the normal or "average" developmental path. There is also a strong emphasis on identifying the patterns and processes of both continuity and change in behavior, and accordingly, there is heavy reliance on longitudinal studies.

As psychologists and psychiatrists attempted to integrate their disciplines and define the field of developmental psychopathology, efforts were made to identify the assumptive bases of the new field. These assumptions and principles characterized many developmental theories but were not tied to the specific content of any of these theories (Santostefano, 1978; Sroufe & Rutter, 1984). In an important 1984 article that helped define the field of developmental psychopathology, Sroufe and Rutter (based on Santostefano, 1978) identified four characteristics of what they termed a *developmental perspective*. These included (a) *holism*, (b) *directedness*, (c) *differentiation of goals and modes*, and (d) *mobility of behavioral functioning*.

Sroufe and Rutter (1984) described *holism* in terms of the meaning of behaviors, stating that from a holistic perspective, a given behavior could only be understood within the context of the individual's total experience. Holism also implies that different domains of functioning (e.g., cognitive, emotional, physical, and social) and their interdependence must be considered in understanding the current and future functioning of the child. *Directedness* (Sroufe & Rutter, 1984) implies that people do not respond passively to their environments; rather, they "selectively perceive, respond to, and create experience" (p. 20). As a consequence, both the subjective environments (the components and meaning of events) and the objective environments (different events and experiences) of individuals will differ depending on their developmental level, genetic makeup, and previous experiences. People become increasingly active in selecting their environments as they mature (Scarr & McCartney, 1983), and development occurs by active reorganization of old and new elements (Sroufe, 1979).

Differentiation of goals and modes refers to the principle that development involves both increased flexibility and organization (Sroufe & Rutter, 1984). It is assumed that these changes are adaptive in that they provide the individual with a wider repertoire of behaviors to meet her or his goals. Furthermore, the decreased reliance on physical aspects of a situation and increased ability to deal with events in the abstract are assumed to reflect adaptive changes (Santostefano, 1978). This notion is in keeping with Werner's (1957) *orthogenetic principle*, which claims that "wherever development occurs it proceeds from a state of relative globability and lack of differentiation to a state of increasing differentiation, articulation, and hierarchic integration" (Werner, 1957, p. 126). Sroufe and Rutter (1984) suggested that developmental deviations may be conceptualized in terms of failure to use or to acquire a wider and more flexible repertoire of behavioral choices. *Mobility of behavioral functioning* refers to an assumed developmental process in which "earlier forms of behavior become hierarchically integrated within more complex forms of behavior" (Sroufe &

Rutter, 1984, p. 21). The nature and quality of early experience and the resulting behavioral competencies thereby affect the quality of later development. Earlier forms of behavior also remain potentially active and may be manifest during periods of stress. Thus, old behaviors are not necessarily transformed (and thereby lost) through the process of development or interaction with the environment, but remain available to the individual.

IMPLICATIONS FOR CHILD BEHAVIOR THERAPY

In contrast to the developmental perspective, with its roots in organismic interactive models, behavioral formulations of psychopathology and treatment are generally categorized as mechanistic models (Overton & Horowitz, 1991). There are obvious points of strain between the mechanistic assumptions that underlie contingency or reinforcement models of child behavior therapy and the organismic/interactive assumptions of the developmental perspective. Specifically, in contingency models the child is seen as a relatively passive recipient of environmental input, and change is viewed as linear and additive. Cognitive–behavioral approaches have also generally taken a mechanistic view (Mahoney & Nezworski, 1985): Cognitive mediators have been conceptualized as internal stimuli that are part of a causal chain rather than (as would be true in an organismic developmental perspective) one component of a dynamically interacting system. Although cognitive–behavioral treatments are not by necessity mechanistic (Bandura, 1986) and several authors have pleaded for a more developmental, interactionist approach to cognitive treatments for children (e.g., Craighead, Meyers, & Craighead, 1985; Mahoney & Nezworski, 1985), treatments have nonetheless generally continued to be based on mechanistic premises.

The challenge of integrating developmental principles and child behavior therapy is thus to identify points of compatibility between these sometimes contradictory views on human nature (Reese & Overton, 1970). In the remainder of this chapter, we discuss the implications of each of the four characteristics of the developmental perspective (Sroufe & Rutter, 1984) for the conduct of child behavior therapy.

Holism

The holistic assumption of the developmental perspective has implications for both assessment and treatment. With regard to assessment, holism implies that any child behavior must be evaluated in terms of the total context in which it occurs, with *context* being broadly defined to include the child's age and developmental level, the pattern of his or her adaptation, and family and cultural factors.

That behavior should be evaluated in relation to the child's age is a commonly accepted principle in the assessment of children. For instance, the descriptive data generated by Gessell and his colleagues (e.g., Gessell, Ames, & Ilg, 1977; Gessell et al., 1940) provide a fund of normative information on physical, cognitive, language, social, and emotional development. This descriptive knowledge provides a very basic framework for assessing the normalcy of a child's development in these areas, and when difficulties are suspected, more detailed assessment can be conducted with a variety of age-normed scales (Sattler, 1992; Schroeder & Gordon, 1991).

The meaning of problem behaviors is also influenced by the child's age and developmental level. The same behavior (e.g., crying) can have very different meaning when exhibited by a toddler or by an adolescent. Conversely, of course, different behaviors can have the same meaning or serve the same function at different ages, as when the toddler has tantrums and the adolescent refuses to talk, both to signal their disapproval and get attention from the parent. It is especially difficult, however, to judge the meaning of behavior that is age-appropriate but may be occurring at a deviant rate. For this reason, many authors have argued for the importance of a normative approach in evaluating child behavior disorders (Achenbach, 1991; Furman, 1980; Mash & Terdal, 1988).

The work of Achenbach (1991) exemplifies the use of normative data in child assessment. Using a behavioral checklist, Achenbach and his colleagues have collected data on parent- and teacher-rated frequencies of over 100 child behaviors, and these data suggest that even normal, nonreferred children exhibit quite high rates of disruptive behavior at some ages. This finding is in keeping with other studies of nonreferred children (Costello, 1990) and highlights the importance of knowing and using age norms in evaluating child behavior.

Although Achenbach (1991) presented data on the ratings of individual behaviors, his overriding purpose was to develop a dimensional system of classification on the basis of empirical data. Starting with the ratings of individual behaviors, he identified first-order factors of child behavior for children of different ages and genders and attempted to develop a taxonomy that is based on factor profiles at different ages. This approach, which explicitly recognized the importance of patterns of behavior, is more consistent with the holistic assumptions of the developmental perspective than are traditional categorical diagnostic systems. Nonetheless, the empirical approach to classification has been criticized as lacking a developmental perspective because of its failure to focus on the context of child behaviors, underlying coping or adaptive strategies, and developmental issues (Sroufe, 1989).

Sroufe (Sroufe, 1989; Sroufe & Rutter, 1984) and others (Cicchetti, Toth, Bush, & Gillespie, 1988; Garber, 1984; Ollendick & Hersen, 1984) argued that assessment of child disorders must address the developmental context of the child, that is, the developmental issues or tasks that the child is facing. In infancy, these tasks include regulating biological functions and establishing an attachment relationship and smooth dyadic interactions; in early childhood, they include exploring the material world, learning to cope with external control of impulses, and developing individuality; in later childhood, they include becoming self-reliant, establishing satisfactory peer relationships, and achieving a sense of competence (Sroufe & Rutter, 1984). The focus of assessment thus shifts from the frequency of behavior to the potential effectiveness of the child's behavior in successfully dealing with specific developmental tasks.

From a developmental perspective, these stage-salient issues must be considered in evaluating the behavior of children. However, contrary to the traditional behavioral emphasis on excesses and deficits, it is frequently qualitative differences in behavior that are considered important from the developmental perspective. For example, the influential work of Ainsworth (Ainsworth, Blehar, Waters, & Wall, 1978) on attachment and more recently developed typologies of social relationships (Coie, Dodge, & Coppotelli, 1982) focus primarily on qualitative rather than quantitative individual differences.

Mash and Terdal (1988) noted that a focus on child behavior within the context of a specific developmental task is in keeping with the emphasis on situational assessment that characterizes child behavior assessment. In addition, focus on developmental level and age of the child is in keeping with the SORKC (i.e., prior Stimulation–Organism–Response– Contingency–Consequence) model of assessment if these factors are considered organism variables. A developmental approach to assessment adds several dimensions to traditional behavioral assessment. Assessment of developmentally relevant variables such as relationship quality, affect, and cognitive development are in keeping with the idiographic approach of traditional behavior therapy, but in new behavioral domains. In contrast, the use of normative–developmental comparisons introduces a nomothetic element into assessment. As Ollendick and King (1991) pointed out, however, the idiographic and nomothetic approaches are not necessarily inconsistent and may augment each other. The holistic developmental assumption thus stretches the definition of context for child behavior therapists but does not conflict with the basic principles of behavioral assessment.

Normative data of another type can be used to evaluate the stability of behavior problems in children and guide decisions about treatment. As Furman (1980) pointed out, even when the rate of behavior is statistically deviant, consideration should be given to the stability and typical continuity of that behavior at different ages when making treatment decisions. Of course, this requires both the existence of longitudinal data that speak to the stability of patterns of behavior over the course of development, (e.g., Caspi, Elder, & Bem, 1987, 1988) and awareness of these data on the part of clinicians.

To this point, only the intrapersonal context of the child's behavior has been discussed, but of course, the ecological or environmental context of behavior is also important in evaluating its meaning and significance. Developmental psychologists, especially those who hold contextual views, define the environment broadly so as to include cultural, community, and family influences (R. M. Lerner, Hess, & Nitz, 1990). Furthermore, the developmental perspective emphasizes the interrelatedness of the different levels and components of the environment and dictates that the relationship between environmental systems be assessed as well as the individual systems themselves.

This view of the context suggests the need for broad-based assessment of the environment, a position that contrasts with the more narrow focus on proximal environmental influences that has characterized the traditional behavioral approach. However, child behavior therapists have increasingly come to recognize the importance of distal causes of behavior (Mash & Terdal, 1988) and to include wider aspects of the child's ecology in their assessment procedures. Because environmental conditions that elicit and maintain behavior have always been a focus of behavioral assessment, the inclusion of a broader range of environmental influences appears to be in keeping with basic principles of this approach.

Note that although the assessment of a multilevel, interrelated context is appealing from a conceptual standpoint, its application is problematic. First, there are problems with measurement of the environment. Although we are beginning to have reliable and valid measures of some components of the child's environment (e.g., Holden, 1990, noted progress in the measurement of parenting and the family environment), measures of other aspects of the environment are lacking or inadequate, and many of the measures that are available are impractical for clinical use. Second, when the environment is conceptualized as a complex, multilevel, interacting system, the task of integrating data on different aspects of the environment (and their interrelationships) also becomes very difficult and complex. Research psychologists deal with these complexities by testing simplified models and using statistics to elucidate multivariate relationships. Models can also be simplified in clinical situations, using either empirical findings or clinical judgment as the basis for simplification. Unfortunately, even with a simplified model, the information-processing demands of integrating large quantities of data may exceed human capabilities. As a result, interpretations of these data become highly susceptible to the biases and judgment errors that afflict clinical decision making in general.

Behavior therapists, thus, face a dilemma in the assessment of children. If simple operant models are adopted as the basis for assessment, it is highly likely that many important contextual variables will be ignored;

however, the data in hand will require less inference for interpretation and will be potentially less subject to bias. In contrast, a more contextual approach will most certainly be more inclusive but may threaten some of the objectivity traditionally associated with behavioral assessment.

The holistic position also has implications for the goals of treatment and the means by which these goals may be met. From a holistic perspective, a primary goal of treatment is to improve the fit between the child and the environment. Obviously, this can be accomplished by changing the child's behavior, the demands and expectations of the environment, or both. There are, thus, many possible points of intervention, including the child, his or her peer and family networks, the school, and the community. J. V. Lerner et al. (1985) suggested that decisions about where to intervene may be guided by data on the plasticity of the child and the environment, with the assumption that interventions directed toward more malleable systems will potentially be more effective. For example, in situations where there are clear biological constraints on the child's behavior, as is the case with Down's syndrome, interventions aimed at educating parents and modifying their expectations would seem most appropriate (e.g., Cicchetti, Toth, Bush, & Gillespie, 1988).

Holism also suggests that indirect approaches to treatment may be effective. Because of the interrelatedness of biological, psychological, and cultural factors, changes in any area may indirectly affect others. For example, relief of marital distress may indirectly result in improvements in child behavior and affect, even in the absence of direct treatment. Similarly, because cognitive, affective, behavioral, and physiological processes are interrelated within the individual, indirect effects of treatment may occur at this level as well.

The holistic assumption is in keeping with social learning and cognitive–behavioral approaches to child treatment. However, just as holism requires behavior therapists to stretch their definition of assessment, it also forces them to take a broader view of what constitutes appropriate targets for intervention. As child behavior therapists increasingly come to recognize and assess distal causes of behavior, these have also become targets for intervention (Mash & Terdal, 1988). For example, in the area of conduct disorders there is substantial evidence to support the utility of parent-training programs in which parents are taught more effective child management strategies (Kazdin, 1987). However, despite the general effectiveness of this approach, not all families respond to treatment, and there is limited maintenance of treatment gains. Furthermore, treatment failure appears to be associated with identifiable family and environmental factors—including poverty, marital discord, social isolation, and parental psychopathology (G. E. Miller & Prinz, 1990). Recent research in this area has therefore been directed toward identifying adjunctive treatments (e.g., marital therapy or stress management) and multisystem approaches (e.g., child, family, and ecological) that may enhance the overall effectiveness of parent-training programs (G. E. Miller & Prinz, 1990).

Activity and Goal Directedness

This assumption of the developmental perspective has primary implications for our understanding of psychopathology and for the design and implementation of appropriate intervention strategies with children. As noted above, this assumption implies that children actively process the environment around them, selectively attending to certain components of the environment and organizing and interpreting environmental stimuli, and that this process changes as the child develops. It is assumed that the child's past experiences, genetic predispositions, and cognitive, social, and physical development will all affect the processing of environmental input.

In terms of psychopathology, this assumption implies individual and developmental differences in reactions to both normative and nonnormative experiences. The importance of individual differences in children's reactions to their environment is well explicated in the literature (Kagan, 1989; Thomas & Chess, 1977); however, developmental factors affecting reactions to environmental events have received less attention. For example, the bulk of the literature on stress reactivity in children simply examines the degree to which maladjustment correlates with the number of stressful events, and there has been less effort directed toward identifying how interpretation of those events changes with development (Compas, 1987). Developmental perspectives on stress and coping are, however, emerging in several areas, including stress associated with illness and medical procedures (LaGreca, Siegel, Wallander, & Walker, 1992), family conflicts (Grych & Fincham, 1990), and family disruptions (Allison & Furstenberg, 1989).

The activity assumption also has implications for the way in which children experience psychological interventions. Children of different developmental levels are expected to differ in the ways they organize and interpret therapeutic events, and developmental differences in processing therapeutic interventions may affect the effectiveness of treatment. Despite their potential importance, there has been surprisingly little effort by child behavior therapists to investigate how developmental factors affect the process and outcome of treatment.

Most of the literature on developmental factors and child behavior therapy focuses on levels of cognitive development. In the early 1980s, cognitive–behavior therapists began to acknowledge the child as an active processor of information and to recognize the importance of matching the child's level of cognitive development with the demands of treatment (Craighead et al., 1985; Kendall et al., 1984; Mahoney & Nezworski, 1985). It was assumed that the child's ability to benefit from training or instruction, even within the narrow confines of a training task, was influenced by her or his level of cognitive development. It was further assumed that more mature levels of cognitive processing might be necessary for generalization and that the lack of these skills might account for poor generalization effects.

Unfortunately, there have been few formal attempts to identify the cognitive abilities that are involved in different cognitive–behavioral procedures. Wasserman (1983) performed an informal analysis of the cognitive operations involved in different interventions with children and proposed a developmental continuum of cognitive–behavioral interventions. He considered modeling interventions to require the lowest level of cognitive development, followed by self-instructional training, imagery techniques, and semantic-based interventions (e.g., RET; Beck's cognitive therapy).

Kendall (1993b) also discussed how the cognitive strategies available to children of different ages or developmental levels may affect their response to treatment. For example, he suggested that for children younger than 6 or 7 years of age, verbal cues tend to be excitatory rather than inhibitory. He, therefore, suggested that both adult instructions and self-instructional training with very young children should provide cues for what to do, rather than either cues for what not to do or cautionary cues (e.g., "stop and think"). Traditional self-instructional training, which often uses inhibitory statements, may work best for children who are 7 to 10 years of age, because they generally have the skills to benefit from this intervention and are more amenable to "being told what to do" than older children and adolescents (Kendall, 1993b).

There is some evidence from meta-analyses to support the hypothesis that older children are better able to benefit from cognitive–behavioral interventions. Cognitive–behavioral interventions in general (Durlak, Fuhrman, & Lampman, 1991), specifically self-statement modification programs (Dush, Hirt, & Schroeder, 1989), show greater effectiveness with older children who presumably have reached the level of formal operations. Unfortunately, age is an imprecise index of cognitive development, leaving the effects of specific cognitive operations on the effectiveness of specific therapeutic interventions unclear.

Cohen and his colleagues conducted a series of studies investigating the effectiveness of self-instructional training for children at different levels of cognitive development (Meyers & Cohen, 1990). They conceptualized the intervention situation to be composed of four components: cognitive status of the child, the nature of the learning activities (procedures such as role playing or modeling), the nature of the materials (props or learning aids), and the criterial tasks for assessing learning and generalization (Cohen & Meyers, 1984). Furthermore, they proposed that generalization of training is enhanced when there is optimal discrepancy between the components of the learning situation. That is, generalization occurs when training involves tasks that are challenging to the child, yet not so demanding as to interfere with his or her ability to integrate the information and to extract important principles from it. Research in this area has demonstrated that children at the stage of concrete operations, as compared with pre-operational children of the same age, are generally superior on a number of tasks after self-instructional training (e.g., Fastove, Glenwick, & Wasserman, 1991; Schleser, Cohen, Meyers, & Rodick, 1984; Schleser, Meyers, & Cohen, 1981). There is also some support for their optimal discrepancy hypothesis (e.g., Schleser et al., 1984); however, evidence in support of this hypothesis has been inconsistent (Cohen & Meyers, 1984).

It is safe to conclude that there has been much more theorizing than action with respect to the need for developmentally appropriate forms of treatment. Reaching this same conclusion, Holmbeck and Kendall (1991) have suggested three ways in which knowledge of developmental level can guide treatment strategies. These include identifying appropriate treatment goals, creating alternate versions of therapies for children at different developmental levels, and delivering treatments that mimic normal developmental stages.

Differentiation of Modes and Goals

This assumption of the developmental perspective is clearly compatible with the goals and techniques of some cognitive–behavioral interventions (Kendall, 1993a). Santostefano (1978) described the importance of this concept:

> The availability of multiple means and alternative ends frees the individual from the demands of the immediate situation, enabling him to express behavior in more delayed, planned, indirect, organized, stage-appropriate terms and to search for detours that acknowledge opportunities and limitations of the environment while permitting successful adaptation. (p. 23)

The application of this assumption in child behavior therapy is well illustrated by social problem-solving approaches to treatment. In their seminal article on problem solving in behavior modification, D'Zurilla and Goldfried defined problem solving as a process that "makes available a variety of potentially effective response alternatives for dealing with the problematic situation" and "increases the probability of selecting the most effective response from among these various alternatives" (D'Zurilla & Goldfried, 1971, p. 108). A basic assumption of problem-solving training is that it will result in an increasingly flexible and effective approach to problem situations.

When cognitive problem-solving strategies are used with children, however, it is important to recognize the limits of their abilities, focus on problems associated with their current developmental tasks, help them acquire skills consistent with their developmental level, and avoid expecting them to use problem-solving strategies that exceed their abilities (and those of their age mates). Problem-solving training with adults and adolescents often focuses on teaching the client a set of cognitive activities (e.g., problem orientation, problem definition, and generation of alternatives); however, when working with children, some of these activities can be appropriately delegated to the adults in the environment or structured so that the child learns to use concrete, external rules. For example, caretaking adults can be taught to provide very young children with choices between two acceptable behaviors (e.g., between rocking or a story before napping) rather than between one acceptable and another unacceptable behavior (taking a nap vs. having a tantrum). The young child who is clearly unable to generate and evaluate alternatives thus participates in the decision process but is led indirectly into "choosing" between appropriate behaviors that will enhance competency and skill mastery. Similarly, somewhat older children who can generate alternative solutions but are unable to engage in the complex and abstract task of weighing outcomes may be taught to use concrete rules when faced with difficult decisions.

Mobility of Behavioral Functions

This proposition, which states that early behaviors are integrated into later and more complex behaviors (Sroufe & Rutter, 1984), has primary implications for the nature and timing of interventions. Because the quality of the resolution of early developmental tasks (e.g., establishing feelings of security or developing early forms of autonomy) affects the development of later forms of competency, it follows that early intervention and interventions directed specifically toward helping the child achieve a healthy resolution of stage-salient developmental issues are viewed as the most appropriate forms of treatment (Cicchetti, Toth, & Bush, 1988; Cicchetti, Toth, Bush, & Gillespie, 1988).

Using a variety of developmental stage theories as the basis for intervention, several authors have suggested general guidelines for treatments aimed at enhancing the resolution of early developmental tasks (Booth, Spieker, Barnard, & Morisset, 1992; Cicchetti, Toth, Bush, & Gillespie, 1988; Lieberman, Weston, & Pawl, 1991). These programs focus primarily on the relational needs of very young children and suggest ways to enhance the qualities of attachment, provide a greater sense of trust and security, and enable children to approach relationships outside the family in more successful ways. These therapies include child-focused treatments (e.g., development of affective regulation and social skills) as well as more ecologically focused interventions (e.g., reduction of parental stress or adaptation of caregiver expectations to the developmental level of the child and his or her temperamental characteristics).

Although these interventions are often derived from psychoanalytic developmental theories (object relations theory and attachment theory provide the most common rationales for treatment), the techniques that are advocated overlap considerably with those used by behaviorists. For example, Lieberman and her associates (Lieberman, 1991; Lieberman et al., 1991) conducted a study of preventive intervention with a group of anxiously attached, physically healthy toddlers and their mothers. Infants were initially assessed at age 12 months using Ainsworth et al.'s (1978) categories of secure, avoidant, resistant, and disorganized attachment, and treatment was provided to half of the anxiously attached dyads. Interventions focused specifically on improving the mothers' responsiveness to the children (especially contingent responding to child signals) and the "tactful negotiation of conflict and competing agendas between mother and child" (Lieberman, 1991, p. 277). The intervention also targeted the provision of a safe environment for the child and opportunities for exploration that were appropriate for the child's developmental level. Even though Lieberman couched her program in the language and assumptions of object relations theory and attachment theory, her approach contained many elements that were in keeping with the behavioral perspective: A careful assessment with a well-validated instrument was conducted; intervention focused on defined objectives or target areas; and the interventions included behavioral components of education, contingent response to behaviors (child signals), and positive interactions skills (tactful negotiation of conflict).

Although some of the techniques of early relational interventions (e.g., Booth et al., 1992; Lieberman et al., 1991) are consistent with those used in behavior therapy, these relational therapies (as currently described and practiced) also conflict with some of the assumptions that underlie the behavioral approach. First, there are little published data to support the effectiveness of these interventions, although some of the steps necessary for developing relational treatment programs and validating their effectiveness are in progress. This approach to treatment rests on the identification of relational difficulties that are predictive of later adjustment problems. It is at this initial step where the most progress has been made: There is increasing evidence that poorly resolved issues of attachment and poor peer relationships are associated with later adjustment difficulties (Bretherton & Waters, 1985; Parker & Asher, 1987), although note that these continuities may be due to consistency in the child's environment rather than consistency in working models of relationships (e.g., Lamb, 1987). Much less progress has been made in identifying the maladaptive processes that occur in relationships and specifying clinical change strategies to ameliorate these dysfunctional processes. Finally, there are very few data available that demonstrate immediate changes in the quality of relationships after intervention or the long-term effectiveness of these programs for reducing levels of maladjustment.

Second, there is an inherent assumption in this model that successful treatment not only changes behavior but also changes underlying, deep structures and psychological organization. Child behavior change is considered to be reflective of change within those underlying structures, and it is the deep, underlying structures that are the focus of concern. The behavioral view, on the other hand, focuses on the same external behaviors while not making an assumption that these behaviors reflect an organized competency or deep structure within the individual. Furthermore, from a behavioral perspective, the importance of these interventions may rest on their effectiveness in making meaningful changes in the child's current and future environment.

There are also some practical problems with relational therapies. These therapies are somewhat inconsistent with the exigencies of current delivery systems. Increasing demands for accountability associated with third-party payments and managed care systems (Mash & Hunsley, 1993) necessitate both well-documented and brief treatment strategies. Additionally, infants and preschool children are underrepresented in child referrals, yet it is during those very early years when developmental treatment approaches may be most useful.

Despite some difficulties with current relational interventions for early childhood, they nonetheless highlight the importance of considering developmental tasks in the design of treatment programs. Although children are often referred for specific bothersome behaviors, successful interventions should not only reduce the problem behaviors but also help the children successfully negotiate solutions to the developmental challenges that they face.

CONCLUSION

The principles of the developmental perspective discussed in this chapter provide a useful organizational framework for the assessment and treatment of child behavior problems. The developmental perspective provides a more comprehensive context within which to evaluate the "normalcy" of child behaviors and can also guide decisions about both the need for treatment and the appropriateness of treatment goals. Similarly, developmental principles have implications for the choice of therapy techniques.

Although it seems logical to look toward developmental principles for help in conducting child treatment, behavior therapists have been latecomers in terms of adopting a developmental perspective (Holmbeck & Kendall, 1991; Rutter, 1983). The different assumptive bases of early contingency-based treatment approaches and the organismic/developmental view (Overton & Horowitz, 1991; Reese & Overton, 1970) may have contributed to child behavior therapists' reticence to make use of developmental principles. In recent years, however, there has been an increasing acceptance of an interactionist perspective among child behavior therapists, and this has been reflected in some changes in assessment and treatment strategies.

Note that acceptance of developmental principles does not deny the importance of the environmental and educational approaches to treatment that have characterized child behavior therapy. Rather, it requires that both types of interventions be viewed as events that occur in a dynamic system (Delprato, 1987). Thus, the effects of these interventions can only be understood when other environmental influences and the child's active processing of the interventions are also simultaneously considered. Interventions cannot be viewed as something done "to" the child; rather, the child's active involvement in treatment must always be recognized. Mutual benefits may accrue for both developmental psychopathology and child behavior therapy when there is more open exchange between the two disciplines. Child behavior therapists should be able to use the growing body of literature in developmental psychopathology to enhance the effectiveness of their treatments. Likewise, to the extent that changes resulting from therapeutic interventions speak to the plasticity of development, treatment data generated by child behavior therapists may further the understanding of developmental processes. Through a process of mutual exchange, both disciplines should see advances in their fields that will ultimately promote the welfare of children.

REFERENCES

Achenbach, T. M. (1991). The derivation of taxonomic constructs: A necessary stage in the development of developmental psychopathology. In D. Cicchetti & S. L. Toth (Eds.), *Rochester Symposium on Developmental Psychopathology: Vol. 3. Models and integrations* (pp. 43–74). Hillsdale, NJ: Erlbaum.

Ainsworth, M. D. S., Blehar, M., Waters, E., & Wall, S. (1978). *Patterns of attachment.* Hillsdale, NJ: Erlbaum.

Allison, P. D., & Furstenberg, F. F., Jr. (1989). How marital dissolution affects children: Variations by age and sex. *Developmental Psychology, 25,* 540–549.

Baltes, P. B., & Reese, H. W. (1984). The life span perspective in developmental psychology. In M. H. Bornstein & M. E. Lamb (Eds.), *Developmental psychology: An advanced textbook* (pp. 493–531). Hillsdale, NJ: Erlbaum.

Bandura, A. (1986). *Social foundations of thought and action: A social cognitive theory.* Englewood Cliffs, NJ: Prentice Hall.

Booth, C. L., Spieker, S. J., Barnard, K. E., & Morisset, C. E. (1992). Infants at risk: The role of preventive intervention in deflecting a maladaptive trajectory. In J. McCord & R. E. Tremblay (Eds.), *Preventing antisocial behavior: Interventions from birth to adolescence* (pp. 21–42). New York: Guilford Press.

Bowlby, J. (1969). *Attachment and loss. Vol. 1: Attachment.* London: Hogarth Press.

Bretherton, I., & Waters, E. (Eds.). (1985). Growing points in attachment theory and research. *Monographs of the Society for Research in Child Development, 50,* (Nos. 1 and 2). Chicago: University of Chicago Press.

Caspi, A., Elder, G. H., Jr., & Bem, D. J. (1987). Moving against the world: Life-course patterns of explosive children. *Developmental Psychology, 23,* 308–313.

Caspi, A., Elder, G. H., Jr., & Bem, D. J. (1988). Moving away from the world: Life-course patterns of shy children. *Developmental Psychology, 24,* 824–831.

Cicchetti, D. (1984). The emergence of developmental psychopathology. *Child Development, 55,* 1–7.

Cicchetti, D. (1990). A historical perspective on the discipline of developmental psychopathology. In J. Rolf, A. S. Masten, D. Cicchetti, K. H. Nuechterlein, & S. Weintraub (Eds.), *Risk and protective factors in the development of psychopathology* (pp. 2–28). New York: Cambridge University Press.

Cicchetti, D., Toth, S. L., & Bush, M. A. (1988). Developmental psychopathology and incompetence in childhood: Suggestions for intervention. In B. B. Lahey & A. E. Kazdin (Eds.), *Advances in clinical child psychology* (Vol. 11, pp. 1–71). New York: Plenum.

Cicchetti, D., Toth, S. L., Bush, M. A., & Gillespie, J. F. (1988). Stage-salient issues: A transactional model of intervention. In E. D. Nannis & P. A. Cowan (Eds.), *Developmental psychopathology and its treatment: New directions for child development* (No. 39, pp. 123–146). San Francisco: Jossey-Bass.

Cohen, R., & Meyers, A. W. (1984). The generalization of self-instructions. In B. Gholson & T. L. Rosenthal (Eds.), *Applications of cognitive–developmental theory* (pp. 95–112). San Diego, CA: Academic Press.

Coie, J. D., Dodge, K. A., & Coppotelli, H. (1982). Dimensions and types of social status: A cross-age perspective. *Developmental Psychology, 18,* 557–570.

Compas, B. E. (1987). Coping with stress during childhood and adolescence. *Psychological Bulletin, 101,* 393–403.

Costello, E. J. (1990). Child psychiatric epidemiology: Implications for clinical research and practice. In B. B. Lahey & A. E. Kazdin (Eds.), *Advances in clinical child psychology* (Vol. 13, pp. 53–90). New York: Plenum.

Cowan, P. A. (1988). Developmental psychopathology: A nine-cell map of the territory. In E. D. Nannis & P. A. Cowan (Eds.), *Developmental psychopathology and its treatment: New directions for child development* (No. 39, pp. 5–29). San Francisco: Jossey-Bass.

Craighead, W. E., Meyers, A. W., & Craighead, L. W. (1985). A conceptual model for cognitive–behavioral therapy with children. *Journal of Abnormal Child Psychology, 13,* 331–342.

Delprato, D. J. (1987). Developmental interactionism: An integrative framework for behavior therapy. *Advances in Behavioral Research and Therapy, 9,* 173–205.

Dixon, R. A., & Lerner, R. M. (1988). A history of the systems in developmental psychology. In M. H. Bornstein & M. E. Lamb (Eds.), *Developmental psychology: An advanced textbook* (2nd ed., pp. 3–50). Hillsdale, NJ: Erlbaum.

Durlak, J. A., Fuhrman, T., & Lampman, C. (1991). Effectiveness of cognitive–behavioral therapy for maladapting children: A meta-analysis. *Psychological Bulletin, 110,* 204–214.

Dush, D. M., Hirt, M. L., & Schroeder, H. E. (1989). Self-statement modification in the treatment of child behavior disorders: A meta-analysis. *Psychological Bulletin, 106,* 97–106.

D'Zurilla, T. J., & Goldfried, M. R. (1971). Problem-solving and behavior modification. *Journal of Abnormal Psychology, 78,* 107–126.

Erikson, E. H. (1963). *Childhood and society* (2nd ed.). New York: Norton.

Fastove, M. E., Glenwick, D. S., & Wasserman, T. H. (1991). The relationship of cognitive developmental level to outcome of self-instructional training in behaviorally disordered children. *Child and Family Behavior Therapy, 13,* 15–28.

Forehand, R., & Wierson, M. (1993). The role of developmental factors in planning behavioral interventions for children: Disruptive behavior as an example. *Behavior Therapy, 24,* 117–141.

Freud, S. (1955). *Complete psychological works, standard edition.* London: Hogarth Press.

Furman, W. (1980). Promoting social development: Developmental implications for treatment. In B. B. Lahey & A. E. Kazdin (Eds.), *Advances in clinical child psychology* (Vol. 3, pp. 1–40). New York: Plenum.

Garber, J. (1984). Classification of child psychopathology: A developmental perspective. *Child Development, 55,* 30–48.

Gessell, A., Ames, L. B., & Ilg, F. L. (1977). *The child from five to ten.* New York: Harper & Row.

Gessell, A., Halverson, H. M., Thompson, H., Ilg, F. L., Costner, B. M., Ames, L. B., & Amatruda, C. S. (1940). *The first five years of life: A guide to the study of the preschool child.* New York: Harper & Row.

Grych, J. H., & Fincham, F. D. (1990). Marital conflict and children's adjustment: A cognitive–contextual framework. *Psychological Bulletin, 108,* 276–290.

Holden, G. W. (1990). Parenthood. In J. Touliatos, B. F. Perlmutter, & M. A. Strauss (Eds.), *Handbook of family measurement techniques* (pp. 285–308). Newbury Park, CA: Sage.

Holmbeck, G. N., & Kendall, P. C. (1991). Clinical–childhood–developmental interface: Implications for treatment. In P. R. Martin (Ed.), *Handbook of behavior therapy and psychological science: An integrative approach* (pp. 73–99). New York: Pergamon Press.

Kagan, J. (1989). The concept of behavioral inhibition to the unfamiliar. In J. S. Reznick (Ed.), *Perspectives in behavioral inhibition* (pp. 1–23). Chicago: University of Chicago Press.

Kazdin, A. E. (1987). Treatment of antisocial behavior in children: Current status and future directions. *Psychological Bulletin, 102,* 187–203.

Kendall, P. C. (1993a). Cognitive–behavioral therapies with youth: Guiding theory, current status, and emerging developments. *Journal of Consulting and Clinical Psychology, 61,* 235–247.

Kendall, P. C. (1993b, March). *Cognitive–behavioural procedures in child and adolescent therapy.* Paper presented at the XXV Banff International Conference on Behavioural Science, Banff, Alberta, Canada.

Kendall, P. C., Lerner, R. M., & Craighead, W. E. (1984). Human development and intervention in childhood psychopathology. *Child Development, 55,* 71–82.

LaGreca, A. M., Siegel, L. J., Wallander, J. L., & Walker, C. E. (1992). *Stress and coping in child health.* New York: Guilford Press.

Lamb, M. (1987). Predictive implications of individual differences in attachment. *Journal of Consulting and Clinical Psychology, 55,* 817–824.

Lerner, J. V., Baker, N., & Lerner, R. M. (1985). A person–context goodness of fit model of adjustment. In P. C. Kendall (Ed.), *Advances in cognitive–behavioral research and therapy* (Vol. 4, pp. 112–136). San Diego, CA: Academic Press.

Lerner, R. M., Hess, L. E., & Nitz, K. (1990). A developmental perspective on psychopathology. In M. Hersen & C. G. Last (Eds.), *Handbook of child and adult psychopathology* (pp. 9–32). New York: Pergamon Press.

Lerner, R. M., Hess, L. E., & Nitz, K. (1991). Toward the integration of human developmental and therapeutic change. In P. R. Martin (Ed.), *Handbook of behavior therapy and psychological science: An integrative approach* (pp. 13–34). New York: Pergamon Press.

Lerner, R. M., & Kauffman, M. B. (1985). The concept of development in contextualism. *Developmental Review, 5,* 309–333.

Lieberman, A. F. (1991). Attachment theory and infant–parent psychotherapy: Some conceptual, clinical, and research considerations. In D. Cicchetti & S. L. Toth (Eds.), *Rochester Symposium on Developmental Psychopathology: Vol. 3. Models and integrations* (pp. 261–287). Rochester, NY: University of Rochester Press.

Lieberman, A. F., Weston, D. R., & Pawl, J. H. (1991). Preventive intervention and outcome with anxiously attached dyads. *Child Development, 62,* 199–209.

Magnusson, D. (1988). *Individual development from an interactional perspective: A longitudinal study.* New York: Erlbaum.

Magnusson, D., & Allen, V. L. (1983a). An interactional perspective for human development. In D. Magnusson & V. L. Allen (Eds.), *Human development: An interactional perspective* (pp. 3–31). San Diego, CA: Academic Press.

Magnusson, D., & Allen, V. L. (1983b). Implications and applications of an interactional perspective for human development. In D. Magnusson & V. L. Allen (Eds.), *Human development: An interactional perspective* (pp. 369–387). San Diego, CA: Academic Press.

Mahoney, M. J., & Nezworski, M. T. (1985). Cognitive–behavioral approaches to children's problems. *Journal of Abnormal Child Psychology, 13*, 467–476.

Mash, E. J., & Hunsley, J. (1993). Behavior therapy and managed mental health care: Integrating effectiveness and economics in mental health practice. *Behavior Therapy, 24*, 67–90.

Mash, E. J., & Terdal, L. G. (1988). Behavioral assessment of child and family disturbance. In E. J. Mash & L. G. Terdal (Eds.), *Behavioral assessment of childhood disorders* (2nd ed., pp. 3–65). New York: Guilford Press.

Meyers, A. W., & Cohen, R. (1990). Cognitive–behavioral approaches to child psychopathology: Present status and future directions. In M. Lewis & S. M. Miller (Eds.), *Handbook of developmental psychopathology* (pp. 475–485). New York: Plenum.

Miller, G. E., & Prinz, R. J. (1990). Enhancement of social learning family interventions for childhood conduct disorder. *Psychological Bulletin, 108*, 291–307.

Miller, P. H. (1983). *Theories of developmental psychology*. San Francisco: W. H. Freeman.

Ollendick, T. H., & Hersen, M. (1984). An overview of child behavioral assessment. In T. H. Ollendick & M. Hersen (Eds.), *Child behavioral assessment: Principles and procedures* (pp. 3–19). Elmsford, NY: Pergamon Press.

Ollendick, T. H., & King, N. J. (1991). Developmental factors in child behavioral assessment. In P. R. Martin (Ed.), *Handbook of behavior therapy and psychological science: An integrative approach* (pp. 57–72). New York: Pergamon Press.

Overton, W. F., & Horowitz, H. A. (1991). Developmental psychopathology: Integrations and differentiations. In D. Cicchetti & S. L. Toth (Eds.), *Rochester Symposium of Developmental Psychopathology: Vol. 3. Models and integrations* (pp. 1–42). Rochester, NY: University of Rochester Press.

Overton, W. F., & Reese, H. W. (1973). Models of development: Methodological implications. In J. R. Nesselroade & H. W. Reese (Eds.), *Life-span developmental psychology: Methodological issues* (pp. 65–86). San Diego, CA: Academic Press.

Parker, T. G., & Asher, S. R. (1987). Peer relations and later personal adjustment: Are low accepted children at risk? *Psychological Bulletin, 102*, 357–389.

Pervin, L. A., & Lewis, M. (1978). Overview of the internal–external issue. In L. A. Pervin & M. Lewis (Eds.), *Perspectives in interactional psychology* (pp. 1–22). New York: Plenum.

Piaget, J. (1970). Piaget's theory. In P. H. Mussen (Ed.), *Carmichael's manual of child psychology* (Vol. 1, pp. 703–732). New York: Wiley.

Reese, H. W., & Overton, W. F. (1970). Models of development and theories of development. In L. R. Goulet & P. B. Baltes (Eds.), *Life-span developmental psychology: Research and theory*. San Diego, CA: Academic Press.

Riegel, K. F. (1975). Toward a dialectical theory of development. *Human Development, 18*, 50–64.

Rosen, H. (1985). *Piagetian dimensions of clinical relevance*. New York: Columbia University Press.

Rutter, M. (1983). Psychological therapies: Issues and prospects. In S. B. Guze, F. J. Earls, & J. E. Barrett (Eds.), *Childhood psychopathology and development* (pp. 139–164). New York: Raven Press.

Rutter, M. (1989). Pathways from childhood to adult life. *Journal of Child Psychology and Psychiatry, 30*, 23–51.

Sameroff, A. J., & Chandler, M. J. (1975). Reproductive risk and the continuum of caretaking casualty. *Review of Child Development Research, 4*, 187–244.

Santostefano, S. (1978). *A biodevelopmental approach to clinical child psychology: Cognitive controls and cognitive control therapy.* New York: Wiley.

Sattler, J. M. (1992). *Assessment of children* (3rd ed., rev.). San Diego, CA: Sattler.

Scarr, S. (1992). Developmental theories for the 1990s: Development and individual differences. *Child Development, 63*, 1–19.

Scarr, S., & McCartney, K. (1983). How people make their own environments: A theory of genotype → environment effects. *Child Development, 54*, 424–435.

Schleser, R., Cohen, R., Meyers, A., & Rodick, J. D. (1984). The effects of cognitive level and training procedures on the generalization of self-instructions. *Cognitive Therapy and Research, 8*, 187–200.

Schleser, R., Meyers, A., & Cohen, R. (1981). Generalization of self-instruction: Effects of general versus specific content, active rehearsal, and cognitive level. *Child Development, 52*, 335–340.

Schroeder, C. S., & Gordon, B. N. (1991). *Assessment and treatment of childhood problems: A clinician's guide.* New York: Guilford Press.

Sroufe, L. A. (1979). The coherence of individual development. *American Psychologist, 34*, 834–841.

Sroufe, L. A. (1989). Pathways to adaptation and maladaptation: Psychopathology as developmental deviation. In D. Cicchetti & S. L. Toth (Eds.), *Rochester Symposium on Developmental Psychopathology: Vol. 1. The emergence of a discipline* (pp. 13–40). Hillsdale, NJ: Erlbaum.

Sroufe, L. A., & Rutter, M. (1984). The domain of developmental psychopathology. *Child Development, 55*, 17–29.

Thomas, A. T., & Chess, S. (1977). *Temperament and development.* New York: Brunner/Mazel.

Wasserman, T. H. (1983). The effects of cognitive development on the use of cognitive behavioral techniques with children. *Child and Family Behavior Therapy, 5*, 37–50.

Werner, H. (1957). The concept of development from a comparative and organismic point of view. In D. B. Harris (Ed.), *The concept of development* (pp. 125–148). Minneapolis: University of Minnesota Press.

White, S. H. (1970). The learning theory tradition and child psychology. In P. H. Mussen (Ed.), *Carmichael's manual of child psychology* (Vol. 1, pp. 657–701). New York: Wiley.

12

COERCION: A TWO-LEVEL THEORY OF ANTISOCIAL BEHAVIOR

JAMES J. SNYDER

The goal of coercion theory is to ascertain the developmental origins and social conditions that account for between-individual variation in the performance of aggressive, antisocial behavior and consequently to provide an empirical basis to formulate and deliver behavioral interventions to prevent and treat that behavior. Coercion theory is characterized by three sets of assumptions about the nature and determinants of aggressive and antisocial behavior. The first set of assumptions is clearly behavioral. It is a performance theory, focusing primarily on variates associated with the frequency at which antisocial behavior is performed rather than the acquisition of that behavior. It is an environmental theory. Antisocial behavior is postulated to be a function of the environmental context in which it occurs. Coercion theory uses an operant learning model to describe how the environment influences behavior. The performance of aggressive and antisocial behavior is governed by antecedent stimuli that serve to evoke the behavior and by the consequences that serve to reinforce or punish its performance. It focuses on aggressive behavior as a public event and uses observation in the natural environment as a primary measurement strategy.

The second set of assumptions emphasizes the social nature of aggression. The primary environmental contexts relevant to understanding the performance of aggressive behavior are social in nature. Aggression is shaped during social interaction in a number of social settings and is performed because of its social effects.

The third set of assumptions of coercion theory is developmental in nature. Coercion theory views antisocial behavior as a failure in socialization. Socialization processes relevant to antisocial behavior occur over time and across settings as parents, siblings, peers, and other agents influence and are influenced by the child in daily interaction. Thus, coercion theory attempts to describe and explain the developmental trajectories of individuals in reference to antisocial behavior.

Research on coercion theory has progressed at two analytical levels that might be termed *microsocial* and *macrosocial* (Chamberlain & Bank, 1989). Microsocial analysis attempts to delineate the developmental trajectory and causes of aggression and antisocial behavior by using observation of moment-by-moment interactions of the developing individual with various socialization agents. Macrosocial analysis attempts to delineate the developmental trajectory and causes of antisocial behavior by using information from multiple informants (e.g., target child, parents, peers, teachers) obtained by multiple methods (e.g., checklists, interviews, nominations, observations) that summarize information over longer periods of time and across a larger number of settings.

In this chapter I describe these assumptions in greater detail and examine the empirical base for the theory at both the microsocial and macrosocial levels. The implications of the theory and associated research for intervention are then examined. Finally, the empirical status of the theory is considered from the perspective of competing theories of aggression and antisocial behavior, followed by an analysis of how coercion theory might be further developed to enhance its empirical status and its utility for prevention and treatment.

COERCION THEORY: THE BASIC MICROSOCIAL PARADIGM

The term *coercion*, in reference to aggression and antisocial behavior, was originally coined by Patterson and Reid (1970). Coercion theory, put simply, hypothesizes that aggressive behavior is performed insofar as it forces other people to give in to the aversive demands that make up that behavior. For example, hitting a sibling in response to sibling teasing will be performed insofar as hitting effectively terminates teasing. A child's tantrum in a store in response to parental refusal to buy candy will promote similar responses to parental refusals in the future insofar as tantrums lead to termination of the parent's refusal and getting the candy. The basic paradigm involves negative reinforcement and may also involve positive reinforcement. When a behavior stops an aversive stimulus or acquires a desired outcome, the likelihood of its subsequent performance under similar stimulus conditions will be increased.

As described in these examples, this seems like a mundane, innocuous process. It occurs with some frequency in most families and social settings and would not seem to have very powerful or lasting effects. However, this is not the case. Under certain conditions, reinforcement of coercion may lead to a developmental progression characterized by the performance of increasingly varied and serious aggressive behavior. The danger lies in the behavioral trap inherent in negative reinforcement. The trap is that coercion is functional in the short run but leads to maladaptive long-term outcomes. In the short run, a coercive response effectively terminates conflict. In the long run, the likelihood of coercive behavior in subsequent conflicts is increased. Both the "victim" and the "perpetrator" of the coercion are reinforced. The perpetrator's aggression is reinforced by the victim's acquiescence. The victim's acquiescence is reinforced by the perpetrator's termination of coercion contingent on acquiescence.

Patterson and Reid (1970) also emphasized a second characteristic of social interaction: The effects of behavior are reciprocal. Not only is the child's behavior influenced by socialization agents, but the child also influences the behavior of those agents. This is inferred in the notion of the behavior trap. Children shape and reinforce their parents', siblings', and peers' coercion, as well as being shaped and reinforced by them.

A basic implication of coercion theory is that the determinants of aggressive behavior are located in the moment-by-moment social interchanges of children with other people and that such behavior is governed by temporally proximate events. Methodologically, this requires the observation of social interaction in the natural environment and a microsocial level of analysis. The first step in a test of coercion theory entails searching for structure or patterns in parent–child, sibling–child, and peer–child interactions that account for individual differences in children's aggressive behavior (Patterson, 1982). As used in coercion theory, the term *structure* (or *pattern*) refers to a probabilistic connection between two observed events in social interaction or to reliable action–reaction sequences. What does one person do that is systematically associated with aggressive behavior by another?

Once structural characteristics of interaction that explain individual differences in aggression are identified, a second step in testing coercion theory is needed. A pattern or functional relationship between two people's behavior is not immutable across individuals or over time. This requires a search for variables that account for temporal change or individual differences in the structure of interaction (Patterson, 1982). Why is the behavior of one individual reliably connected to that of another, and under what conditions is this probabilistic association likely to change?

EVIDENCE FOR COERCION THEORY: MICROSOCIAL LEVEL

Patterns of Social Interaction Associated With Aggression

One method of searching for structure in social interaction is to determine how well the occurrence of a specific target response of one person can be predicted from antecedent actions of a second person. A structure or pattern in social interaction can be identified insofar as the conditional probability of the target response of one person, given the antecedent action of another person, is reliably different from the unconditional probability of the target response. The presence of reliable associations between individuals' behavior, or structure in social interaction, directly reflects interpersonal influence. The behavior of one person has communication, influence, or teaching value when it reduces uncertainty in the behavior of another (Gottman, 1979). Presumably, individual differences in children's aggressive behavior should be associated with systematic variations in the pattern or structure of their interaction with socialization agents. Furthermore, the exact nature of this structure changes systematically over time as the socialization process unfolds.

In a series of studies, it has been clearly demonstrated that there is an increased probability of aggressive behavior relative to its base rate by children, siblings, and parents, given the occurrence of an aversive antecedent action by another family member (e.g., Patterson, 1977, 1979a; Patterson & Cobb, 1973). Social interaction in the family is clearly structured: Coercion begets coercion. The causal status of these antecedent variables in controlling the performance of aggression has been demonstrated through experimental manipulation of the antecedents (Patterson, 1982). These aversive antecedent–aggressive response (or coercive) patterns are found both in families with and without aggressive children. What, then, differentiates these families?

Additional studies have demonstrated that, although coercive patterns are observed in both types of families, these patterns are significantly more robust in families with aggressive children than in those with non-aggressive children. Members in families with aggressive children are 2–5 times more likely to initiate aggression (make an aggressive response, given a nonaversive antecedent action by another member), are 1.5–3 times more likely to reciprocate in kind (make an aggressive response, given an aversive antecedent action by another member), and are 1.5–4 times more likely to persist in the response (make another aggressive response, given that their own previous response was aggressive (e.g., Patterson, 1979a, 1979b, 1982; Reid, 1978; Snyder, 1977). These aversive action–aggressive reaction exchanges tend to cluster together during interaction (Stoolmiller, 1992), and they make up the minutiae of parent–child and sibling–child conflicts. Members in families with an aggressive child, compared with those without an aggressive child, are more likely to initiate conflict and to persist in that conflict once initiated.

These data represent a static "snapshot" of the coercive process. However, coercion theory is also developmental in focus. How does the process change over time? How does the process influence the performance of aggressive behavior? The model hypothesizes that, over time, there will be a progressive shaping of aggressive behavior to more varied and extreme forms insofar as that behavior has continuing functional utility (Cairns & Cairns, 1986; Patterson, 1982).

A modest amount of data is available to support this developmental hypothesis. As conflicts between family members become frequent and of long duration, there is an escalation in the intensity of aggressive behavior used during those conflicts. Physical aggression is most likely to occur at the end of long-duration conflict. Furthermore, the occurrence of physical aggression toward a target is strongly correlated with the rate of performance of milder aversive behavior toward that target by the aggressor (Reid, 1986). A mean increase in the intensity of aversive behavior is found at every transition during conflict (Loeber, 1980). Conflicts in aggressive compared with nonaggressive mother–child dyads are characterized by shorter latency and more frequent escalation, even in response to bids to de-escalate or end the conflict by the other party (Snyder, Edwards, McGraw, Kilgore, & Holton, 1994). What begins as a seemingly banal process involving exchanges of mildly aversive behavior leads slowly, over time, to the development of a widening repertoire of high-amplitude coercive responses. This suggests a transitive developmental progression from less to more serious aggressive child behavior. The data are consistent with such a progression that typically begins with noncompliance and moves through temper tantrums and fighting to stealing (Patterson & Dawes, 1975; Patterson, Reid, & Dishion, 1992).

Once this coercive pattern of dealing with other people is well established in the family, it is likely to generalize to the playground and the school. Observation of the interaction of aggressive and nonaggressive children with peers results in a picture very similar to that found in the home. Aggressive children instigate and receive more aversive behavior than their nonaggressive counterparts and are more likely to persist in aversive behavior once it is initiated (Shinn, Ramsey, Walker, Strieber, & O'Neill, 1987; Snyder & Brown, 1983). Peers are also more likely to direct aversive behavior at aggressive children and to persist in that aversive behavior, regardless of the aggressive child's actions (Shinn et al., 1987; Snyder &

Brown, 1983). Escalation in the aversiveness of behavior during peer conflict has also been documented (Cairns & Cairns, 1986). Children who are frequently and intensively aggressive in the home are at substantial risk for carrying their coercive social repertoire into the peer and school settings (Loeber & Dishion, 1984; Patterson et al., 1992), where there is exposure to conditions that may promote the continued shaping of aggressive behavior toward more serious forms.

Both aggressive children and the socialization agents with whom they interact contribute to this coercion–countercoercion process. The children exist in a highly irritable, noxious environment and, thus, are frequently faced with coercive actions of others, but the children also contribute in that they irritate those agents (Patterson, 1976, 1985). Given that the social interaction of aggressive children with family members and peers differs reliably from that of nonaggressive children, the second question is, Why? What explains the individual differences in the structure or patterning of social interaction? Why do some children move along a developmental trajectory that involves the performance of an expanding repertoire of increasingly noxious behaviors?

The Role of Reinforcement in Coercion

Coercion theory hypothesizes that the action–reaction patterns observed during interaction are established, maintained, and shaped as the result of reinforcement. Reliable associations between the antecedent action of one person and the response of a second person depends on the functional value of that response relative to other responses that could be made to that antecedent (Patterson, 1982). Family members engage in aggressive responses because such behavior relative to its more constructive alternatives results in getting others' attention, gaining access to desired activities, or obtaining desired materials (positive reinforcement); it also terminates the aversive, controlling behavior of others (negative reinforcement). Aversive reactions to aggression should decrease its reoccurrence (punishment). It is also assumed that the effects of reinforcement often occur without awareness.

Early studies did not appear to provide strong support for this crucial hypothesis. Individual differences in children's rate of aggression were not reliably correlated with the positive reinforcement that they received from other family members for that aggression (Johnson, Wahl, Martin, & Johansson, 1973; Taplin, 1974). There were no reliable differences between samples of normal children and those who were clinic referred for conduct problems in the rate of parental positive reinforcement for aggressive behavior (Patterson, 1982). The aggressive behavior of clinic-referred relative to that of nonreferred children was more likely to be punished by parents, with the paradoxical effect of increasing the immediate recurrence of aggressive behavior (Patterson, 1979b).

Similarly, the role of negative reinforcement in maintaining and shaping coercive responding did not appear to be clearly supported by research. Individual differences in children's rate of aggressive behavior were not reliably correlated with the proportion of that behavior that was negatively reinforced by family members (Patterson, 1979b). Although aggressive children showed a higher probability of responding to other family members' aversive behavior with coercion, a significant but small difference in the rate of negative reinforcement for such countercoercion was observed when comparing the family interactions of aggressive and nonaggressive children (Patterson, 1982). This empirical state of affairs led reviewers in both the developmental (Maccoby & Martin, 1983) and behavioral (Robinson, 1985) literature to conclude that the role of positive and negative reinforcement in shaping and maintaining child aggression had not been unambiguously established and that cognitive processing of events was of critical importance.

However, the seemingly negative implications of these data for coercion theory and the conclusions drawn in these reviews are based on a misunderstanding of coercion theory specifically and of reinforcement theory more generally. In fact, coercion and reinforcement theory do not predict that positive or negative reinforcement will explain these known-group and between-individual differences in aggressive behavior. The common, but erroneous, assumption is that the relationship between the frequency with which a response is performed and the frequency with which it is reinforced is linear and direct: A child who receives frequent positive or negative reinforcement for aggression should be aggressive more often than a child who is less frequently reinforced for aggression. Reinforcement somehow strengthens behavior. The assumption is that the absolute frequency or probability of reinforcement is a meaningful between-individual difference when, in fact, it is not.

Following the matching law (Herrnstein, 1974; Noll, chapter 5 in this book; Williams, 1986), reinforcement contingencies operate on an intra- rather than interindividual level. According to the matching law, there is a positive linear relationship between the relative probability of an array of responses in a given situation and the relative probability of the reinforcement of those responses in that situation. Reinforcement does not mechanically increase the "strength" of a particular response independent of other responses, but it does provide information about the functional or adaptive value of each of the multiple responses that could be made in a particular situation. Responses are selected rather than strengthened.

Translating this formulation of reinforcement to the natural social environment, action–reaction patterns (or structure) in social interactions reflect reliable response choices made by an individual. As a result of previous experience, each response or reaction in a person's repertoire has an associated functional value specific to the antecedent social conditions (i.e., action of others). A target person codes which response relative to other responses in a repertoire "work best" for him or her in a given situation (an intraindividual effect), not how well the response works for him or her relative to how well it works for others (an interindividual effect). Reinforcement makes an indirect contribution to the frequency of aggressive behavior by influencing the probability of a response to an antecedent. The frequency with which a particular response is performed depends on two pieces of information: the degree to which that response has accumulated a selective utility (reinforcement) in a given antecedent situation and the frequency with which that situation occurs in the individual's environment. An interesting implication of this behavioral choice formulation is that aggressive children will necessarily also display a deficit in the performance of constructive, skilled behavior.

There are several studies that support the role of reinforcement in coercion using this matching law approach. Patterson (1979b) demonstrated that there was a reliable rank order correlation between the relative rate of various coercive child responses and the relative utility of those responses in terminating maternal aversive behavior in a conduct problem sample, but not in a normal sample. Additionally, there was a negative correlation between the relative rate of an array of child coercive behaviors and the relative probability with which they were punished by mothers. Those coercive responses that were most effective in terminating aversive intrusions and least likely to be punished were performed the most often.

These findings have been replicated and extended in two more recent studies. Snyder and Patterson (1986) assessed the impact of maternal consequences for two coercive mother action–child reaction patterns at one point in time on the reoccurrence of those patterns at a later point in time. Positive maternal reinforcement was associated with an increased maternal punishment with a decreased probability of the child reaction on the next temporal occurrence of the maternal action. This suggests that consequences effect momentary shifts in the probability of interaction patterns around their base rate probabilities. In a more direct test of the matching law, Snyder and Patterson (1992) found a reliable rank order correlation, replicated across children from both problem and nonproblem dyads, between the relative probability with which a mother negatively reinforced an array of coercive and constructive child conflict tactics during one time period and the relative probability with which her child used those tactics during conflict with the mother during a later period. Furthermore, coercive child tactics (commands, disapproval, refusal, hitting) were more strongly associated with negative reinforcement in problem dyads, whereas constructive child tactics (agreement, talking, withdrawal) were more strongly associated with negative reinforcement in nonproblem dyads. This suggests that negative reinforcement serves as a powerful mechanism for the development of constructive as well as coercive behavior.

These studies have focused on one dimension of coercive behavior: its relative rate of performance. Another important dimension is its intensity. Developmentally, it is hypothesized that there is a gradual shaping of coercive behaviors toward more intense, noxious forms as these behaviors aggregate into extended aversive exchanges in which each person attempts to "outcoerce" the other family member. Insofar as more intense coercive responses (e.g., threatening and hitting) are more effective than less intense coercive responses (e.g., whining and disapproving) in terminating conflict, coercive behavior is slowly shaped into a sharper and more dangerous interpersonal tool. In an intensive study of two mother–child dyads, Patterson (1982) found that when the mother gave in to the child contingent on the child's escalation during conflict, the child was more likely to escalate the aversive behavior in the subsequent conflict. Snyder et al. (1994) replicated this finding. In both aggressive and nonaggressive mother–child dyads, the cessation of conflict contingent on the escalation of one dyad member's behavior was reliably associated with an increased likelihood of escalation and escalation to a higher level of aversiveness by that member in the subsequent conflict. Mothers and their sons shape each other's escalation. The likelihood of escalation, its intensity, and the likelihood of its negative reinforcement was greater in aggressive than in nonaggressive dyads.

The causal status of reinforcement in the shaping and maintenance of coercive behavior can be more strongly documented by experimental manipulation of contingencies during social interaction in the natural environment. Patterson (1982) reported several single-subject experimental studies that demonstrate that making maternal attention (positive reinforcement) or the withdrawal of maternal aversive behavior (negative reinforcement) contingent on child coercive behavior resulted in reliable increases in the probability of that behavior.

The role of reinforcement in coercive interaction in peer settings has received less attention. Patterson, Littman, and Bricker (1967) found that successful aggressive attacks (positive reinforcement) by a child toward a peer were associated with an increased probability that the same peer would be targeted by the child using the same aggressive strategy and that unsuccessful attacks (punishment) were associated with a shift in the targeted peer or in the aggressive strategy the next time the child was aggressive. Snyder and Brown (1983) found that the oppositional behavior of conduct problem children to peer-aversive behavior was associated with an increased, and the constructive behavior of conduct problem children to those antecedents was associated with a decreased, likelihood of conflict termination (i.e., negative reinforcement). Obversely, the oppositional behavior of nonproblem children to peer-aversive behavior was associated with a decreased, and constructive behavior with an increased, probability of conflict termination. Finally, Dishion and Patterson (1993) found that delinquent adolescents and their (typically delinquent) best friends selectively responded to each other's antisocial talk with laughter and encouragement, whereas nondelinquent adolescents and their (typically nondelinquent) best friends selectively reinforced normative talk.

In summary, research using microsocial analyses of family interaction is consistent with the coercion theory of aggressive behavior. Coercive interactional sequences reliably differentiate the interaction of families with children who have conduct problems from those with children who do not have significant conduct problems. However, the role of reinforcement in shaping and maintaining this coercive structure has been less convincingly supported. One weakness of this research is its correlational, cross-sectional nature. This leaves open the possibility that there are other third-variable causes that explain the findings and other reasonable theoretical explanations for coercive behavior.

COERCION THEORY: THE MACROSOCIAL LEVEL

A thorough understanding of the origins and sequelae of coercion cannot be attained solely at a microsocial level. Microsocial analyses that are based on observation of moment-by-moment interaction in family and peer settings may be critical to understanding the socialization processes by which specific developmental outcomes are engendered, but are limited in the description of those outcomes and of the broader socialization contexts in which that socialization process occurs. There are two reasons for this. First, the measurement strategies (which focus on immediate, situational determinants of behavior in a highly restricted time frame) characterizing the observation of social interaction are not designed to capture broad contextual factors in the parents' or the child's experience outside of that immediate interaction (e.g., stress, social support, personality, school, mood, economic resources, and marital and other social relationships), nor are they capable of capturing more enduring, transsituational developmental processes and outcomes both inside (e.g., parent discipline and monitoring) and outside (e.g., peer sociometric status, selective peer association, and delinquent activity) of the family. The measurement of contexts and outcomes requires macrosocial measurement strategies (e.g., ratings, structured interviews, self-report, tests, school grades, and police contacts) that maximally capture more molar, enduring, and transsituational characteristics of developmental contexts and outcomes (Cairns & Green, 1979).

Second, from a theoretical perspective, microsocial structure and process serve as vehicles or mechanisms that mediate the interplay among socialization contexts, experiences, and developmental outcomes. Microsocial structure and process serve several mediational roles. They serve as transducers by which broad contextual variables affect developmental outcomes. They serve to facilitate or disrupt social interactional sequences (e.g., problem solving, monitoring, discipline) that become, as a result of accumulated experience and increasing developmental sophistication of the child, increasingly organized, rule driven, and abbreviated. They result in the shaping of a stable repertoire of child social behaviors or traits that is applied in the family setting and new developmental environments (e.g., school, peers, neighborhood). The interactional expression of those traits affects how others treat the child and facilitates or constrains the child's choices of and access to environments (contexts) that amplify or modify that repertoire of responses (traits; Patterson & Dishion, 1988).

As applied to aggression, coercion is a core mechanism that serves to move an individual along a deviant developmental trajectory as the individual is exposed to the temporally unfolding contexts and agents constituting socialization. Research using macrosocial methodological and theoretical perspectives allows the delineation of how coercion affects and is affected by broader developmental contexts and outcomes.

Contextual Effects on Coercive Family Interaction

Family interaction does not occur in a vacuum. How one family member acts toward or reacts to another member is not determined solely by momentary stimuli, but is also influenced by the broader experiential contexts and stable, generalized dispositions of family members (Bronfenbrenner, 1979; Wahler & Dumas, 1987). From the perspective of coercion theory, these contextual and dispositional variables contribute to the development of child antisocial behavior insofar as they increase family members' irritability and alter the contingencies family members provide for each other's behavior.

The traits characterizing family members constrain their interaction. Data suggest, for example, a correlation between a parent's antisocial trait and parental irritability during parent–child interaction: Antisocial parents are more likely to direct unprovoked aversive behavior toward their children and to escalate that aversive behavior to threats and hitting (Patterson & Dishion, 1988). Depressed mothers are highly irritable toward their children, and expression of their depression has functional value in stopping other family members' aversive behavior (Hops et al., 1987). Child traits provide a reciprocal influence. Lee and Bates (1985), for example, found that temperamentally difficult children, compared with "easy" children, were more likely to engage in aversive behavior and to resist maternal efforts at controlling that behavior.

Stress experienced by parents is also associated with irritable and non-contingent responses to children. For example, daily variations in maternal self-reported mood and stress are reliably associated with same-day variations in the likelihood with which the mother initiates, reciprocates, and persists in aversive behavior during interactions with her child and in the likelihood that she will negatively reinforce her child's aversive behavior (Patterson, 1983; Snyder, 1991; Snyder & Huntley, 1990). The lack of socially supportive relationships also appears to be associated with the co-ercion process. Negative social contacts with other people in- and outside of the nuclear family are associated with an increased likelihood of mater-nal initiation of aversive behavior and reciprocation of her child's aversive behavior during family interaction (Wahler, 1980; Wahler & Dumas, 1987).

The Development of Antisocial Behavior

The emphasis of coercion theory on the moment-by-moment, shifting social interactional processes as the mechanism for the development of aggressive behavior seems paradoxical to research indicating that such be-havior is highly stable over time and across settings, giving it a traitlike status. More specifically, there is substantial evidence for continuity in an-tisocial behavior from early childhood through adulthood (Loeber, 1982; Olweus, 1979), and for intergenerational transmission of that behavior (Huesmann, Eron, Lefkowitz, & Walder, 1984). Antisocial behavior also appears to have some stability across environmental settings (Loeber & Dishion, 1984).

According to coercion theory, the antisocial trait is a disposition to respond in a patterned manner that is stable over time and across settings and that is characterized by the contingent use of aversive behavior to manipulate the social environment (Patterson et al., 1992). The antisocial trait is the result of a developmental progression in which there is a gradual expansion in the variety of antisocial behaviors toward increasingly serious forms. Frequent but seemingly trivial aversive behaviors such as noncom-pliance and temper tantrums in the home, if left unchecked, act as pre-cursors to more serious aversive behavior such as fighting, stealing, drug use, and delinquency in peer, school, and neighborhood settings. The risk of progression to serious and persistent antisocial behavior until it achieves a traitlike status increases when that behavior has an early developmental onset and is performed at high frequencies in multiple settings.

Coercion is at the core of this developmental progression. The dis-position develops as the use of aversive behavioral strategies in dealing with other people are applied and meet with success over time and across settings. This progression occurs in three steps. In the first step, ineffective parenting leads to a failure to inhibit child coercion and to teach needed skills. In the second step, continued child coercion and lack of skills lead to school failure and rejection by normal peers. In the third step, there is a drift toward peer groups and settings compatible with the child's deviant repertoire that provide the models and reinforcement requisite to advanced training in antisocial behavior (Patterson & Bank, 1985; Patterson, De-Baryshe, & Ramsey, 1989). Several longitudinal studies using a multi-method, multi-informant measurement strategy and structural equation modeling (Patterson & Bank, 1985) support this three-step developmental model of antisocial behavior.

Step 1: Parent Training Model

The development of antisocial behavior often begins in the home during the preschool years when the acquisition of behavioral and emotional self-control is a critical developmental task (Maccoby & Martin, 1983). According to coercion theory, the degree to which children exercise self-control depends on two critical family management practices: discipline and monitoring (Patterson, 1982; Patterson et al., 1992). The term *discipline* refers to parents' ability to track and accurately classify child behavior as problematic or nonproblematic, to ignore trivial child misbehavior, and to contingently use effective means (e.g., clear directives, limit setting, time-out, and loss of privileges) of discouraging more serious misbehavior. Such disciplinary practices also serve as a prerequisite to teaching social and work skills in the home setting.

As the child moves into school and other social settings as a result of normative transitions and increasing maturation, parental monitoring of the child's behavior outside of the home takes on increasing importance. Effective monitoring entails knowledge by the parent of where the child is, who the child is with, and what the child is doing in school, peer, and neighborhood settings. Monitoring entails an extension of discipline to child behavior in out-of-home settings.

Data from several longitudinal studies of families with children who are at risk for the development of antisocial behavior are consistent with this hypothesized model. Discipline and monitoring make significant and independent contributions to variance in child antisocial behavior measured both concurrently and later in childhood and adolescence. Together, discipline and monitoring have been found to account for 30%–80% of the variance in antisocial behavior from the preschool years through early adolescence. These findings are robust. They have been replicated across a range of samples differing in child age, ethnicity, and gender, and in family socioeconomic status and composition. Discipline predicts future antisocial behavior even after its indirect effects mediated by concurrent child antisocial behavior are statistically controlled (Forgatch, 1991; Patterson, 1990; Patterson et al., 1992).

Discipline and monitoring are necessary, but not sufficient, conditions for teaching social and work skills in the home. Fostering a reasonable degree of compliance to parental directives and noncoercive means of conflict resolution are a prerequisite to teaching such skills. Given that self-control has been achieved, several other "positive" family management practices are needed to foster child social and work skills, including problem solving, positive reinforcement, and parental involvement with the child. Effective problem solving in the family entails (a) stating the problem in neutral, nonblaming terms; (b) communicating an understanding of the problem by the parties involved; (c) generating possible solutions; and (d) selecting a reasonable solution using compromise and negotiation (Forgatch & Patterson, 1989). Positive reinforcement entails accurate parental tracking of desirable child behavior and reacting in a contingent manner to that behavior with praise, attention, and access to activity and material reinforcers. Involvement is the degree to which the parents and children spend time together in joint activities that are mutually enjoyable (Patterson, 1982; Patterson et al., 1992).

The data from longitudinal studies do not strongly or consistently support the hypotheses concerning the relationship between these positive family management practices and child skills. With a few exceptions, bivariate and multivariate correlations of problem solving, positive reinforcement and involvement with child academic skills, peer relationships, and self-esteem are either modest (accounting for 0%–20% of the variance) or are not replicable (Patterson et al., 1992). In fact, multivariate analyses indicate that discipline and monitoring account for more variance in measures of child skillfulness than do the positive parenting constructs (Patterson, 1986; Patterson et al., 1992).

Although using as criteria that the hypothesized models must account for significant variance and replicate across samples is stringent, the data on the role of positive parenting in the development of child skills do not meet these criteria. There are several potential reasons for this failure. First, it may be that positive parenting constructs were not clearly conceptualized or measured. Second, families with youth who are at risk for antisocial behavior may simply not provide a very good sample to assess the role of positive parenting. Third, positive parenting may play a more critical role in the development of children who are younger than those sampled in these studies.

Step 2: Parent and Peer Rejection, and Academic Failure

The failure by the child to acquire adequate self-control and skills in the home has a number of effects as the child makes transitions to other environments. According to coercion theory, high-level child coercive behavior and associated skills deficits are hypothesized to evoke two types of reactions in the social environment. First, antisocial children are at high risk for poor school performance. Their noncompliance, undercontrolled behavior, and inability to sustain attention and to accept feedback represent a deficit in skills requisite to good academic performance. Second, the antisocial child is at high risk for being rejected by normal peers. A frequent and intense aversive style quickly turns off peers and engenders a peer environment characterized by a high density of aversive social stimuli that tends to sustain and amplify aggressive behavior (Patterson & Bank, 1989; Patterson et al., 1992).

Longitudinal research supports the hypotheses concerning the Step 2 sequelae of antisocial behavior. Models assessing the association of child antisocial behavior during earlier childhood with peer rejection and academic difficulties during later childhood and early adolescence fit the data. Antisocial behavior accounts for 20–25% of the variance in academic difficulties, and academic difficulties and antisocial behavior account for 25–60% of the variance in peer rejection. These findings have been replicated across samples (Dishion, 1990a; Patterson, 1986; Patterson & Dishion, 1985; Patterson et al., 1992).

Step 3: Association with Deviant Peers: Transition to Delinquent Behavior and Drug Use

Antisocial behavior, peer rejection, and academic failure, along with ineffective parental monitoring, serve as critical antecedents to association with deviant peers and increasing unsupervised "street time." This provides the antisocial child with advanced training in antisocial behavior. Deviant peers model and reinforce negative attitudes and behavior, and provide the opportunity for a variety of delinquent acts. Peers also serve as potent agents promoting the use of a progression of licit and illicit drugs (Patterson, 1993; Patterson et al., 1992). The antisocial child's association with deviant peers is not solely the result of rejection by normal peers but also entails an active selection of settings and agents that are congruent with the child's coercive repertoire and that maximize reinforcement. Deviant peers maintain and amplify antisocial behavior resulting from ineffective parenting in the home toward increasingly varied and extreme forms. As children move farther into the trajectory defined as the antisocial trait, their options in selecting normative social settings and agents become increasingly limited.

Longitudinal research provides considerable support for the hypotheses concerning this Step 3 transition. Earlier antisocial behavior and its Step 2 products—rejection by normal peers and academic failure—are clearly related to increased risk for association with deviant peers. Poor parental monitoring makes a continuing, independent contribution to this risk. Antisocial behavior, peer rejection, and monitoring account for 40%–80% of the variance in deviant peer association. These findings have been replicated in several samples (Dishion, 1990b; Dishion, Patterson, Stoolmiller, & Skinner, 1991; Patterson & Dishion, 1985; Snyder, Dishion, & Patterson, 1986).

Rejection by normal peers does not mean that aggressive children are socially isolated but that they tend to form peer groups with other antisocial children (Cairns, Cairns, Neckerman, Gest, & Gariepy, 1988). Macrosocial studies suggest that children distribute their time among peers according to the ratio of positive-to-negative payoffs accrued from those peers (Snyder, Stockemer, & West, 1993). What is different in normative versus deviant peer groups is what is reinforced. In the normative peer group, it is prosocial and normative talk and behavior. By contrast, there is considerable reinforcement for antisocial talk and behavior within the antisocial group (Buehler, Patterson, & Furniss, 1966; Dishion & Patterson, 1993).

Data from longitudinal studies confirm the critical role of peers in the development of antisocial behavior. The association of antisocial children with deviant peers is clearly related to an earlier onset of delinquency and to recidivism, especially in the absence of effective parental monitoring (Dishion, 1990a; Patterson, Capaldi, & Bank, 1991; Patterson, Crosby, & Vuchinich, 1993; Patterson & Dishion, 1985). In these studies, child antisocial behavior, poor parental monitoring and discipline, and association with antisocial peers accounted for 40%–60% of the variance in delinquency across several samples. There is similar support for these Step 3 hypotheses in terms of experimentation and progression of drug use during adolescence. The association of antisocial children with deviant peers under conditions of poor parental supervision (and parental modeling of drug use) places those children at increased risk for earlier experimentation with drugs and for progression to more routine use and the use of a wider variety of drugs (Dishion & Loeber, 1985; Dishion, Reid, & Patterson, 1988; Patterson & Yoerger, 1993). Early antisocial behavior, parental supervision, and association with deviant peers account for 20%–50% of the variance in adolescent drug use.

Early Starters, Late Starters, and Dropouts in the Antisocial Developmental Process

The macrosocial research just reviewed focuses on a progression toward antisocial behavior that starts early and persists over time with accumulating developmental products that maintain and amplify deviant behavior toward a stable, transsituational, traitlike status. However, the continuity of antisocial behavior, although high, is certainly not perfect.

There are individuals who as children are not particularly antisocial, but who commit delinquent acts and use drugs as adolescents—"late starters." There are also individuals who are aggressive as children, but who do not go on to become delinquent or to use drugs during adolescence—"de-sisters." The causal models hypothesized by coercion theory should reflect these variations in the developmental trajectory of antisocial behavior.

The data comparing early starters, late starters, and desisters on family management variables, family contextual variables, and peer relationships are consistent with coercion theory. Late starters evidence an increase in deviant peer association over the 10–14-year-old age range, but desisters show a reduction in peer rejection over the same age range (Dishion, 1990b). Family problem solving, discipline, family socioeconomic status, and marital adjustment of the parents predict the timing of first arrest and individual growth curves of antisocial behavior (Forgatch & Ray, cited in Patterson et al., 1993; Patterson, 1993). The parents of desisters appear to "get their act together" to interrupt their children's early antisocial behavior. The parents of late starters experience stressors that disrupt effective parenting, fail to adjust their parenting to changes in their child's developmental and social status, or both. However, the long-term risk for continued social and work failure, and for continued criminal activity, is considerably less for late than for early starters (Patterson et al., 1992).

Summary of Macrosocial Research on Coercion Theory

In general, the data from longitudinal studies focusing on a macrosocial level of analysis are consistent with coercion theory. The three-step progression hypothesized by that theory accurately describes the development of chronic antisocial behavior. To some extent, the theory has evolved over time into the form presented here on the basis of empirical findings. This data-sensitive approach may appear post hoc, but insistence on replication across samples and on accounting for substantial variance in antisocial behavior obviates these concerns. Two characteristics of coercion theory provide the potential for a rich practical yield. First, the core microsocial and macrosocial variables accounting for the development of antisocial behavior are also relatively malleable, thereby having direct application in efforts to prevent and treat antisocial behavior. Second, its emphasis on explaining substantial variance in antisocial behavior implies that manipulation of these malleable variables potentially has a substantial impact in the applied setting.

PREVENTIVE AND CLINICAL INTERVENTIONS

The development of preventive and clinical interventions to address antisocial behavior, as well as being the ultimate goal of coercion theory, has played two other important roles. First, it has served as a source of hypotheses about the familial, contextual, and peer conditions that explain the development of antisocial behavior. Second, these interventions serve as field experimental manipulations to provide strong tests of the causal status of variables identified in correlational-longitudinal research as being associated with the development of antisocial behavior (Forgatch, 1991).

In this section, research on clinical interventions derived from coercion theory is reviewed and evaluated. The review is organized around a series of specific questions that must be answered to unambiguously establish the efficacy of clinical and preventive interventions: (a) Does the intervention bring about change? (b) Is the change attributable to the intervention? (c) Is the change clinically significant, and does it generalize over time, clients, and settings? (d) Is the change mediated by alteration of variables specified by the theory on which the intervention is based? At the most basic level, coercion theory would suggest that child aggressive and antisocial behavior will change insofar as intervention is successful in enhancing parenting practices, especially discipline and monitoring.

Does Parent Training Effect Change in Child Antisocial Behavior?

Initially, parent training was applied to families of relatively young children whose presenting problems could be best described diagnostically as oppositional–defiant. The major focus of intervention was to alter parental discipline with the assumption that a reprogramming of the contingencies applied in the home environment would lead to a reduction in children's noncompliance and aggression, and to increases in prosocial, skilled behaviors. Using instruction, modeling, role playing, and homework, parents were taught a set of skills requisite to this environmental reprogramming: (a) identification of the coercive behaviors to be reduced (e.g., noncompliance, hitting) and of the skillful behaviors to be increased (e.g., compliance, doing chores, completing homework) in observable terms; (b) systematic tracking and recording of the occurrence of target behaviors in the home; (c) contingent reinforcement of skilled behaviors using social attention and praise, and tokens exchanged for backup reinforcers; and (d) systematic and contingent use of mild, but effective, punishment of target coercive behaviors using time-out and response cost (Patterson & Forgatch, 1987; Patterson, Reid, Jones, & Conger, 1975).

A series of case studies and quasi-experimental pre–post design studies has demonstrated the feasibility and potential utility of teaching parents to use reinforcement contingencies to alter the aggressive behavior of young children (see Patterson, 1979c, for a summary). Parent training led to sizable and reliable changes in child aggressive behavior as measured both by direct observation (total aversive behavior [TAB]) and by parent daily reports (PDRs) of concrete target behaviors. These findings were replicated by a number of researchers. It appeared that the aggressive behavior of relatively young children could be reliably reduced by teaching parents to alter the contingencies they applied to that behavior.

Are Changes in Child Antisocial Behavior Attributable to the Intervention?

These initial successes led to a series of controlled clinical trials in which families were randomly assigned to parent training or to a control group. Three group-comparison studies in which the families of preadolescent, aggressive children were randomly assigned to parent training or to a waiting-list control group (Wiltz & Patterson, 1974), a leaderless discussion (placebo) group (Walter & Gilmore, 1973), or a nonbehavioral intervention group (Patterson, Chamberlain, & Reid, 1982) clearly established that parent training led to reductions in child aggressive behavior as measured by TAB and PDRs, whereas there was no change in behavior of children assigned to the control conditions. These findings were replicated in a large number of other controlled, programmatic studies of parent training carried out by other investigators, so that parent training is currently considered one of the most effective treatments for child aggressive behavior (Kazdin, 1987).

Are the Changes Clinically Significant, and Do They Generalize Over Time, Settings, and Clients?

Given the continuity of antisocial behavior, its progression toward more varied and serious forms, and its generalization to settings other than the home, the clinical significance and generalization of treatment effects engendered by parent training are of critical importance. Research suggests that the antisocial behavior (as measured by TAB and PDRs) is within normative limits at the termination of treatment for 70%–80% of young children whose families received parent training and that these changes are maintained at follow-up (Patterson & Fleischman, 1979). These findings have been replicated by other researchers (Forehand & Long, 1986). Data also suggest that the effects of parent training generalize to the behavior of nontargeted children in the family. However, it does not appear that treatment effects generalize from the home to other settings (McMahon & Wells, 1989).

The results of several outcome studies suggest that parent training is not equally effective for all children and families. Standard parent training, with its primary focus on enhancement of discipline in the home setting, appears to be less effective as target children get older and display covert (e.g., stealing, fire setting) as well as overt (e.g., noncompliance, tantrums, hitting) antisocial behavior (McMahon & Wells, 1989; Reid & Hendricks,

1973). These variables reflect the child's further developmental progression into antisocial behavior and its generalization beyond the home setting. This led to the expansion of coercion theory to include parental monitoring as a second critical variable in understanding and treating antisocial behavior (Patterson, 1982; Reid & Patterson, 1976).

Research also suggests that family characteristics influence the completion of treatment, the amount of change effected by treatment, and the maintenance of treatment effects. These characteristics include marital distress, maternal depression, lack of parental social support, poverty, and single-parent households (McMahon & Wells, 1989). These characteristics reflect a high level of stress and chaos in the family, along with diminished resources that interfere with sustained efforts at effective family management practices that are the primary focus of intervention. This led to an increased emphasis on the role of family contextual factors and parental characteristics in understanding the development of antisocial behavior and to an expansion of parent training intervention to include problem-solving and other "adjunctive" interventions.

Two recent efforts to treat children who are more seriously antisocial and who come from highly disorganized, chaotic home environments confirm these findings. Marlowe, Reid, Patterson, and Weinrott (1992) tested the efficacy of an expanded, intensive form of parent training to families of chronic juvenile offenders, a group that is markedly resistant to treatment. The intervention focused on parental discipline and monitoring, behavioral contracting, and problem solving to remediate child behavior and to enhance parent resourcefulness. Offenders were randomly assigned to this expanded parent training format or to a community treatment control group. No change was found in child TAB scores after intervention, but there was improvement in PDR scores (especially stealing) in the parent training group. Parent training, but not the community intervention, led to a reduction in offending and in institutional time at follow-up. Rather than attempting to focus solely on altering antisocial children's family of origin, Chamberlain (1988) developed and assessed a therapeutic foster home program for seriously antisocial youth. The foster families selected were characterized by effective family management practices and then received intensive training in discipline, monitoring, contracting, and problem solving prior to and during the child's placement. Individual behavioral intervention was used to enhance child skills, complemented by intensive home–school consultation. Compared with matched controls, the children in the foster home program were more likely to successfully complete their community placement and were less likely to be institutionalized over a 2-year follow-up. Neither of these interventions normalized the children. Both programs were able to engender reliable but modest changes in the children's behavior that became apparent only over longer time periods.

The data from the treatment studies of highly antisocial adolescents have two implications. First, a sole focus of intervention on the family environment is insufficient as the child progresses toward more serious and varied forms of antisocial behavior. Second, change becomes increasingly difficult as the child moves further into the antisocial progression. This has led to recent efforts to develop and implement programs to prevent antisocial behavior of younger at-risk children using interventions with multiple agents (parents, peers, teachers) in multiple settings (home, school).

Is Change Mediated by an Alteration of Variables Specified by the Theory on Which the Intervention Is Based?

Although clinical trials demonstrate that parent training is more effective than comparison interventions, this is not sufficient to clearly delineate that the alteration of parenting practices is the unambiguous cause of the observed changes in child antisocial behavior. To answer this question, it is necessary to assess changes in family management practices, as well as in child antisocial behavior, before and after intervention. To support coercion theory, there should be some correlation between improvements in family management and reductions in child antisocial behavior (Patterson & Chamberlain, 1988).

At the microsocial level, coercion theory would posit that successful treatment should be associated with two changes in family interaction. First, there should be a reduction in the likelihood that family members would initiate conflict and persist and escalate the intensity of the conflict once it occurs. Second, these reductions in aversive behavior should be accompanied by reductions in the reinforcement of that behavior by family members. There is a modest amount of support for the first hypothesis. Taplin and Reid (1977) found a reduction in mothers' likelihood of initiating aversive behavior toward the target child and reciprocating her child's aversive behavior in families receiving parent training, but not in families assigned to a waiting-list or placebo control group. Dumas (1984) found similar changes after treatment and at 1-year follow-up in families successfully treated by parent training. I could not find data on changes in reinforcement during family interaction that result from treatment.

At a macrosocial level, coercion theory would hypothesize that changes in child antisocial behavior should occur only insofar as intervention changes family management practices. Using multiple indicators of family management practices and child antisocial behavior before and after treatment, Patterson and Chamberlain (1988) and Forgatch (1991) showed that enhanced monitoring, problem solving, and discipline were associated with reductions in observed child TAB and in child antisocial behavior at termination. Both microsocial and macrosocial data are consistent with the coercion hypothesis that family management practices and family interaction are the proximate mediators of change in child aggression and antisocial behavior. Furthermore, these experimental data provide strong support of the causal status of variables identified as correlates of antisocial behavior in cross-sectional and longitudinal research.

COMPETING THEORIES OF ANTISOCIAL BEHAVIOR

There are a variety of competing theoretical explanations of antisocial behavior. These theories are of two types: those that focus on microsocial interaction processes and those that focus on macrosocial developmental models of antisocial behavior. These competing theories will be briefly described and used to provide a context for an evaluation and description of potential modifications of coercion theory.

Competing Microsocial Theories

There is relatively wide agreement that coercive patterns of social interaction are associated with antisocial behavior. However, the mechanisms by which these patterns are shaped and maintained are a matter of lively debate. The coercion theory hypothesis that these patterns are shaped and maintained by negative reinforcement of family members and peers has not been clearly established. Several alternative explanations are available.

Within the behavioral tradition, Wahler and Dumas (1986) offered an alternate account called the *predictability hypothesis*. They suggested that the mothers of antisocial children, as a result of chronic and pervasive stress and negative social contacts, are noncontingent or unpredictable toward their children. Such lack of contingency is aversive to the child. In response, the child is coercive toward the mother, reliably evoking aversive maternal reactions and leading to highly predictable patterns of aversive interaction. This high predictability removes the former uncertainty and serves as a negative reinforcer for the child's behavior. Wahler and Dumas did not dispute the role of negative reinforcement but simply suggested an alternate manner by which it should be conceptualized and operationalized.

Other theorists suggest that the establishment and maintenance of coercive patterns of interaction can be understood without recourse to the construct of reinforcement. Cairns (1979) suggested that social interaction patterns become increasingly consolidated and generalized over time in a Markov type of process (i.e., the occurrence of a specific event is predicted by the occurrence of preceding events) as a result of social experience. There is an inherent, organismic matching of behavior (i.e., aggression begets aggression, prosocial behavior begets prosocial behavior) that is replicated over time and across settings. The structure of interaction is a product of the quality of a child's repeated social contacts with others over time. There is a mutual shaping of behavior, resulting in stable changes in the child's repertoire that is carried to new social environments in which the consolidation of interaction patterns continues. Reinforcement is required as a mechanism only insofar as there is observed deviation from this accumulating Markovian process.

Gottman (1991) offered an explanation for the shaping and maintenance of coercive interaction patterns on the basis of emotion. The strong negative affect accompanying coercive interaction leads to diffuse physiological arousal. This arousal results in an emotional flooding of the participants with a number of adverse effects. It reduces cognitive processing and promotes a reliance on overlearned behavioral responding. There is likely to be escalation in negative affect and behavior, and a narrowing of attention that results in a hypervigilance to negative events and misattribution of other individuals' behavior. The aversive nature of this escalation and flooding is likely to lead to the capitulation by one party, and the reduction in negative affect serves to reinforce this process. These affect-driven coercive patterns are more likely to occur in families in which members have not learned to soothe themselves or other family members.

Social cognitive theory is the most widely held microsocial alternative to coercion theory. The basic premise offered by social cognitive theory is that the child actively extracts information and gives meaning to social environmental events and acts on this information rather than being an object whose behavior is passively controlled and shaped by external contingencies. A large part of the impetus for the development of social cognitive theory came from the work of Lepper (1981) on intrinsic motivation and overjustification. This work has been interpreted to show that children make attributions about the causes of their behavior and show reactance to external control. In other words, reinforcement does not have a specific, automatic effect on behavior. The social cognitive perspective has been endorsed by a large number of developmental (e.g., Maccoby, 1992) and cognitive–behavioral clinical (e.g., Robinson, 1985) researchers.

These alternate microsocial approaches to patterns of social interaction share some common characteristics. First, children are active agents in understanding and creating their own environment. The flow of influence in parent–child relationships is bidirectional and not a "top-down" process. Second, socialization agents do not provide direct contingencies that control the behavior of children. Rather, the behavior of socialization agents sets a social context that more or less successfully scaffolds experience in a manner that facilitates or inhibits the development of child aggressive behavior. Third, there is an emphasis on organismic variables. As the child matures, new "tools" are brought to bear that influence the nature of the socialization process. Phylogenetically and ontologically, operant principles that may describe learning in lower species and in human infants do not apply as the developing child's linguistic and cognitive capacities expand. Fourth, even if contingencies do influence behaviors, other processes mediate their effect on social interaction patterns, specifically attributions and affect.

Competing Macrosocial Theories of Antisocial Behavior

Description and explanation of the development of antisocial behavior has a long and active history in criminology and sociology, as well as psychology. Two types of theories have been offered: those that focus on the environment and those that focus on genetic, biological, or temperamental determinants of behavior. Exemplars of each of these types are briefly described, beginning with environmentally focused theories.

Strain theory (Elliot & Voss, 1974) suggests that deviance results when there is a discrepancy between aspirations and opportunity for achievement. Individuals normatively learn and internalize conventional social goals for success and expectations of its accompanying rewards. When access to such goals and rewards are limited by class, socioeconomic, or ethnic conditions, people experience frustration over the discrepancy between aspirations and opportunities. This frustration results in antisocial behavior that represents an alternate means of satisfying needs. Thus, prevailing socioeconomic and cultural conditions are hypothesized to play a major role in the genesis of antisocial behavior.

Differential association theory (Sutherland & Cressy, 1974) suggests that individuals naturally establish peer networks with individuals with whom they share values, aspirations, and interests. Insofar as this peer group is made up of people who endorse an antisocial way of life, the attitudes and behaviors of the developing child will be shaped toward a similar antisocial style. A more specific variant of this approach is labeled *subcultural deviance*. Antisocial behavior resulting from membership in a specific subculture does not represent a failure in socialization, but an alternate form of socialization in that there is conformity to local norms, values, and behaviors even if they conflict with those of conventional society.

The macrosocial theories considered to this point emphasize the importance of larger cultural, economic, and geographical contexts on socialization. These forces result in a failure to identify with normative activities, agents, values, and aspirations. To a great extent, causes of antisocial behavior are outside the person. A contrasting perspective more closely associated with psychology uses a trait approach to antisocial behavior. Recall that antisocial behavior shows a good deal of developmental continuity, situational generality, and intergenerational transmission. The basic premise of the trait approach is that the source of this continuity and stability in antisocial behavior is in the individual rather than the environment.

There are a number of theories that attempt to explain this stable antisocial trait. *Behavioral genetics* offers one explanation (Plomin, Nitz, & Rowe, 1990). Although data from coercion and other socialization theories show correlations between family environmental variables and child antisocial behavior, these correlations are confounded by shared genes as well as shared environments. It simply may be that genetically transmitted temperamental differences place the child at risk for antisocial behavior. In addition to this gene–environment correlation, there are also gene–environment interactions such that at-risk children evoke reactions from the social environment, respond selectively to that environment, and select environments that foster a progression in antisocial behavior toward increasingly stable and extreme forms.

Other trait theorists have focused on describing and tracking those personality characteristics associated with antisocial behavior at different points during development. Children who evidence a "difficult" temperament during early childhood are at increased risk for later antisocial behavior (Loeber, Stouthamer-Loeber, & Green, 1987). Later, during adolescence and adulthood, a number of personality dimensions (e.g., harm avoidance, reward dependence, and novelty seeking; Cloninger, Christiansen, Reich, & Gottesman, 1978) and individual differences in neurophysiology (e.g., insensitivity to environmental contingencies attributable to variation in nervous system substrates for approach and avoidance learning; Gray, 1982; Quay, Routh, & Shapiro, 1987) have been identified that are potentially compatible with learning theory. Other theories emphasize additional organismic variables. Cairns and Cairns (1986) pointed out that an adequate theory must explain why there are consistent gender differences in antisocial behavior and why there is an exponential growth in that behavior during adolescence followed by a reduction in early adulthood.

These alternative macrosocial theories "stretch" the determinants of aggressive and antisocial behavior in several ways. Environmental theories suggest that immediate socialization environments (family, peers) involved in the development of antisocial behavior reside in even larger contexts (neighborhoods, socioeconomic conditions). A full understanding of antisocial behavior may require even more of a macrolevel analysis than that addressed by coercion theory (Bronfenbrenner, 1979). On the other side, trait theories suggest that genes, biology, and temperament may create individual differences in vulnerability to antisocial behavior. This vulnerability can then be modified by the environment such that it increases or decreases the liability for the development of antisocial behavior (Lytton, 1990).

Microlevel Analysis

Coercion theory has made a substantial contribution to the description and understanding of social interactional processes associated with antisocial behavior in children. The patterns of mutual aggression and escalation describing parent–child and peer–child conflict offer a clear window into the daily social experiences of children experiencing conduct problems and provide substantial support for coercion theory (Patterson, 1982; Patterson et al., 1992).

There is currently less evidence to support the keystone assumption of coercion theory about the role of reinforcement in shaping and maintaining coercive patterns of family and peer interaction. This is the result of two factors. First, much of the effort from 1980 to the present has gone into specifying and testing a macrolevel model of the development of antisocial behavior. In this work, microanalysis became a measurement strategy to define macrolevel constructs rather than an important process in and of itself.

Second, there is an inherent difficulty in defining and operationalizing reinforcement as it occurs in the natural social environment. Compared with the experimental settings in which there is control of antecedent stimuli and contingent delivery of reinforcers, the natural environment is characterized by a matrix consisting of an array of responses to a shifting stimulus context in which each response has its associated contingent payoffs. This leads to a series of questions that must be answered to assess the role of reinforcement in shaping patterns of social interaction in the natural environment: What is the unit of analysis in social interaction that is to be used as the dependent variable? What social events serve as reinforcers? Are these events functionally equivalent across families? How can reinforcement contingencies be defined without experimental control? How can the causal status of variables identified as potential reinforcers in correlational studies be confirmed experimentally?

Some initial progress in answering these questions and in supporting coercion theory has been made by applying the matching law to transition probability matrices that describe the patterns of interaction (Snyder & Patterson, 1986, 1992), but this work has not answered these questions in a definitive manner. There is a clear need for additional theoretical, methodological, and empirical work if the reinforcement hypotheses espoused by coercion theory are to remain viable explanations of microsocial processes associated with the development of aggressive behavior (see chapter 3 in this book).

It is likely that coercion theory must be modified to take into account cognitive processing of environmental information. Developmental research from an operant perspective has demonstrated that the behavioral effects of environmental contingencies shift as children develop language. In addition to being shaped by external contingencies, responding also becomes increasingly rule governed or language mediated during the preschool years (e.g., Bentall, Lowe, & Beatty, 1985). The importance of active information processing as a central determinant of behavior is emphasized even more by the social cognitive perspective. However, it is unlikely that all environmental information is effortfully processed. Rather than viewing social cognitive and reinforcement explanations as mutually exclusive, it may be more useful to see these processes as operating in a tandem, complementary manner. The task then becomes to clarify the environmental and organismic conditions that influence the operation and interplay between these processes, to operationalize both during ongoing social interaction in the natural environment, and to assess whether their combination explains more variance in behavior relative to either alone. Modern cognitive theory would suggest that both effortful and automatic processing of information occur and influence behavior (e.g., Ellis & Hunt, 1989). The issue should be empirical rather than polemical.

In a similar manner, emotions may serve as a third process in shaping coercive patterns of social interaction. The methodology for measuring affect during ongoing interaction has been developed and been shown to be a powerful predictor of social interaction patterns and long-term outcomes (Gottman & Levenson, 1984). There is also a substantial literature on the interplay between affect and cognitive processes. A similar linkage may clarify the role of reinforcement in social interaction. Formulations about individual differences in sensitivity to reinforcement and, in neural substrates for approach and avoidance conditioning closely tied to emotional responding (Gray, 1982; Quay et al., 1987), may serve as the basis for such a linkage.

Macrolevel Analysis

Coercion theory has made a substantial contribution to the description and understanding of antisocial behavior. It has offered a simple yet elegant theory concerning the contribution of family and peers to the development of antisocial behavior in males during the elementary and secondary school years. Furthermore, the theory explains substantial variance in antisocial behavior, and the findings have been replicated in independent samples. Clinical trials have been used to demonstrate the causal status of family management variables in the etiology of antisocial behavior. Together with research at the microsocial level, coercion theory has successfully identified malleable environmental variables that explain substantial variance in antisocial behavior and has led to the formulation of effective clinical interventions for antisocial behavior during preadolescence. It holds additional promise in the design of preventive interventions.

Given its validity and utility, there are a number of ways in which coercion theory may be extended. First, it has focused almost exclusively on antisocial behavior in males; it awaits an extension to females. Second, research indicates that the development of aggressive and antisocial behavior begins during the preschool years. Coercion theory has primarily focused on children beginning at ages 8–10; its extension to earlier periods would provide a more complete picture of the development of antisocial behavior. Third, major tests of coercion theory and its clinical applications have used geographically (including international) and ethnically homogeneous samples. It is important that the findings be replicated in other geographical areas and other ethnic groups. Fourth, the practical implications and applications of coercion theory in efforts to prevent and treat antisocial behavior in children (the real payoffs) need further specification and empirical testing.

Although there is some inherent danger in extending a theory too broadly, coercion theory may be enhanced by incorporating a more organismic focus. This is evident in several ways. First, there are clear gender differences in antisocial behavior. What is it about being male or female that explains these differences? Is it all a product of socialization? Second, the onset and timing of puberty has been shown to play an important role in other facets of development. Does puberty play a similar role in altering the developmental trajectory of antisocial behavior? Third, arguments are increasing that the strong continuity of antisocial behavior is a reflection of fundamental temperamental, biological, or genetic characteristics of the developing individual and that the social environment plays a less powerful or singular role than that postulated by coercion theory. Such arguments need to be put to empirical test in a manner similar to that elegantly done by Vuchinich, Bank, and Patterson (1992). They demonstrated that parent and peer influences made a contribution to the prediction of later antisocial behavior above that of early antisocial behavior.

Finally, the hypothesis made by other environmental, macrosocial theories that socioeconomic conditions, neighborhood characteristics, and cultural contexts play a role in antisocial behavior is an important one. To a degree, these influences have been incorporated into coercion theory by using the proxies of parental stress and mood, and then ascertaining how these variables affect child antisocial behavior as mediated by disruptions in discipline and monitoring. However, broader epidemiological studies assessing systematic variation in these broad contextual conditions would provide a more direct empirical integration of coercion and broader sociological theories. This is important because it addresses the issue concerning the degree to which enhancement of family management practices can compensate for the vagaries of rearing children in high-risk, highly disadvantaged environments.

Integration of Microsocial and Macrosocial Levels of Explanation

The interplay between microsocial and macrosocial levels of explanation and analysis are not well delineated or thoroughly tested in current coercion theory. The primary manner in which they are related is methodological rather than theoretical. The interplay of an antisocial child's day-to-day social experiences (coercive microsocial processes) with the increasing stable and cross-situational expression of antisocial behavior and lack of skills, with the reduction in contacts with normative socialization agents and activities, and with the increasing drift toward deviant socialization agents and activities has not been clearly specified or empirically tested. Until this is done, the theory has something of a "split personality."

There are several ways in which microsocial and macrosocial processes may influence one another. For example, it may be that the child's early development of a highly coercive repertoire during the preschool years effectively disrupts parents' discipline and monitoring of the child during later childhood and adolescence. Every time the parent attempts to track or correct the child, or to provide a consequence, the child uses coercion to subvert the process. Similarly, highly coercive behavior may turn off normal peers and lead to a selective association with other deviant, rejected children. This selection may be made at the level of microsocial payoffs for association with different peers. The lack of social and work skills may lead to frequent conflict with teachers and employers. Antisocial children, because of their coercive means of dealing with such conflict, are ill-equipped to resolve conflict constructively.

As shown by these examples, microsocial and macrosocial processes are likely to have mutual effects. Microsocial interaction may mediate macrosocial effects, and macrosocial events may constrain or amplify microsocial processes. The distinctive contribution of each to the development of antisocial behavior provides a richer, more complete picture than a view of them as simply different but complementary levels of measurement.

SUMMARY OF COERCION THEORY

Coercion theory has provided a rich source of testable hypotheses concerning the development of aggression and antisocial behavior. It has received extensive empirical support and made a substantial contribution to understanding antisocial behavior. It is a "live" theory in the sense that it is data sensitive and has been expanded to incorporate empirical work from other perspectives.

Coercion theory has also made important methodological contributions both in terms of the observation and analysis of social interaction in the natural environment and in terms of the development and analysis of theoretical relationships among constructs defined by multiple methods and informants. It has served as a benchmark for design and assessment in clinical trials of parent management approaches to child aggression.

Finally, and perhaps most important, coercion theory has contributed to the development of parent training interventions that are highly effective in changing antisocial behavior, and it holds substantial promise for the development of effective preventive interventions. The interplay among clinical and preventive interventions, theory-driven basic research, and cutting-edge methodology has contributed significantly to the ongoing validity and utility of coercion theory.

REFERENCES

Bentall, R. P., Lowe, C. E., & Beatty, A. (1985). The role of verbal behavior in human learning: II. Developmental differences. *Journal of the Experimental Analysis of Behavior, 43,* 165–181.

Bronfenbrenner, U. (1979). *The ecology of human development.* Cambridge, MA: Harvard University Press.

Buehler, R. E., Patterson, G. R., & Furniss, J. M. (1966). The reinforcement of behavior in institutional settings. *Behavior Research and Therapy, 4,* 157–167.

Cairns, R. B. (1979). *Social development: The plasticity and origins of interchanges.* San Francisco: W. H. Freeman.

Cairns, R. B., & Cairns, B. D. (1986). The developmental-interactional view of social behavior: Four issues in adolescent aggression. In D. Olweus, J. Block, & M. Radke-Yarrow (Eds.), *Development of antisocial and prosocial behavior: Research, theories, and issues* (pp. 315–342). San Diego, CA: Academic Press.

Cairns, R. B., Cairns, B. D., Neckerman, H. J., Gest, S. D., & Gariepy, J. L. (1988). Social networks and aggressive behavior: Peer support or rejection? *Developmental Psychology, 24,* 815–823.

Cairns, R. B., & Green, J. A. (1979). How to assess personality and social patterns: Observations or ratings? In R. B. Cairns (Ed.), *The analysis of social interactions: Methods, issues, and illustrations* (pp. 209–226). Hillsdale, NJ: Erlbaum.

Chamberlain, P. C. (1988). *The use of trained nonprofessionals in providing therapeutic foster homes for state hospital mentally and emotionally disturbed youth.* Unpublished manuscript, Oregon Social Learning Center, Eugene, OR.

Chamberlain, P., & Bank, L. (1989). Toward an integration of macro and micro measurement systems for the researcher and clinician. *Journal of Family Psychology, 3,* 199–205.

Cloninger, C. R., Christiansen, K. O., Reich, T., & Gottesman, I. I. (1978). Implications of sex differences in the prevalences of antisocial personality, alcoholism and criminality for familial transmission. *Archives of General Psychiatry, 35,* 941–951.

Dishion, T. (1990a). The family ecology of boys' peer relations in middle childhood. *Child Development, 61,* 874–892.

Dishion, T. (1990b). The peer context of troublesome child and adolescent behavior. In P. E. Leone (Ed.), *Understanding troubled and troubling youth* (pp. 128–153). Newbury Park, CA: Sage.

Dishion, T. J., & Loeber, R. (1985). Adolescent marijuana and alcohol use: The role of parents and peers revisited. *American Journal of Drug and Alcohol Abuse, 11,* 11–25.

Dishion, T., & Patterson, G. R. (1993, March). *The geography of boys' early adolescent friendships: The indirect effect of parenting on social development.* Paper presented at the annual meeting of the Society for Research in Child Development, New Orleans, LA.

Dishion, T., Patterson, G. R., Stoolmiller, M., & Skinner, M. (1991). Family, school, and behavioral antecedents to early adolescent involvement with antisocial peers. *Developmental Psychology, 27,* 172–180.

Dishion, T. J., Reid, J. B., & Patterson, G. R. (1988). Empirical guidelines for a family intervention for adolescent drug use. *Journal of Chemical Dependency Treatment, 1,* 189–224.

Dumas, J. E. (1984). Interactional correlates of treatment outcome in behavioral parent training. *Journal of Consulting and Clinical Psychology, 52,* 946–954.

Elliot, D. S., & Voss, N. L. (1974). *Delinquency and dropout.* Lexington, MA: Heath.

Ellis, H. C., & Hunt, R. R. (1989). *Fundamentals of human memory and cognition.* Dubuque, IA: W. C. Brown.

Forehand, R., & Long, N. (1986, November). *A long term follow-up of parent training participants.* Paper presented at the meeting of the Association for the Advancement of Behavior Therapy, Chicago.

Forgatch, M. S. (1991). The clinical science vortex: A developing theory of antisocial behavior. In D. Pepler & K. H. Rubin (Eds.), *The development and treatment of childhood aggression* (pp. 291–316). Hillsdale, NJ: Erlbaum.

Forgatch, M. S., & Patterson, G. R. (1989). *Parents and adolescents living together: 2. Family problem solving.* Eugene, OR: Castilia.

Gottman, J. M. (1979). *Marital interaction: Experimental investigations.* San Diego, CA: Academic Press.

Gottman, J. M. (1991). Chaos and regulated change in families: A metaphor for the study of transitions. In P. A. Cowan & E. M. Hetherington (Eds.), *Family transitions* (pp. 247–272). Hillsdale, NJ: Erlbaum.

Gottman, J. M., & Levenson, R. W. (1984). Why marriages fail: Affective and physiological patterns in marital interaction. In J. C. Masters & K. Yarkin-Levin (Eds.), *Boundary areas in social and developmental psychology* (pp. 67–106). Hillsdale, NJ: Erlbaum.

Gray, J. A. (1982). *The neurophysiology of anxiety: An inquiry into the functions of the septohippocampal system.* New York: Oxford University Press.

Herrnstein, R. J. (1974). Formal properties of the matching law. *Journal of the Experimental Analysis of Behavior, 21,* 159–164.

Hops, H., Biglan, A., Sherman, L., Arthur, J., Friedman, L., & Osteen, V. (1987). Home observations of family interactions of depressed women. *Journal of Consulting and Clinical Psychology, 55,* 341–346.

Huesmann, L. R., Eron, L. D., Lefkowitz, M. M., & Walder, L. O. (1984). Stability of aggression over time and generations. *Developmental Psychology, 20,* 1120–1134.

Johnson, S. M., Wahl, G., Martin, S., & Johansson, S. (1973). How deviant is the normal child: A behavioral analysis of the preschool child and his family. In R. D. Rubin, J. P. Brady, & J. D. Henderson (Eds.), *Advances in behavior therapy* (Vol. 4, pp. 37–54). San Diego, CA: Academic Press.

Kazdin, A. E. (1987). Treatment of antisocial behavior in children: Current status and future directions. *Psychological Bulletin, 102,* 187–203.

Lee, C. L., & Bates, J. E. (1985). Mother-child interaction at age two years and perceived difficult temperament. *Child Development, 56,* 1314–1325.

Lepper, M. R. (1981). Intrinsic and extrinsic motivation in children: Detrimental effects of superfluous social controls. In W. A. Collins (Ed.), *Aspects of the development of competence: The Minnesota Symposium on Child Psychology* (Vol. 14, pp. 107–143). Hillsdale, NJ: Erlbaum.

Loeber, R. (1980). *Child precursors of assaultive behavior.* Unpublished manuscript, Oregon Social Learning Center, Eugene, OR.

Loeber, R. (1982). The stability of antisocial and delinquent behavior: A review. *Child Development, 53,* 1431–1446.

Loeber, R., & Dishion, T. (1984). Boys who fight at home and school: Family conditions influencing cross-setting consistency. *Journal of Consulting and Clinical Psychology, 52,* 759–768.

Loeber, R., Stouthamer-Loeber, M., & Green, S. M. (1987, April). *Age of onset of conduct problems, different developmental trajectories, and unique contributing factors.* Paper presented at the meeting of the Society for Research in Child Development, Baltimore.

Lytton, H. (1990). Child and parent effects in boys' conduct disorder: A reinterpretation. *Developmental Psychology, 26,* 683–697.

Maccoby, E. E. (1992). The role of parents in the socialization of children: A historical overview. *Developmental Psychology, 28,* 1006–1017.

Maccoby, E. E., & Martin, J. A. (1983). Socialization in the context of the family: Parent-child interaction. In E. M. Hetherington (Ed.), *Handbook of child psy-*

chology: Vol. 4. *Socialization, personality, and social development* (pp. 1–102). New York: Wiley.

Marlowe, H., Reid, J. B., Patterson, G. R., & Weinrott, M. R. (1992). *Treating adolescent multiple offenders: A comparison and follow-up of parent training for families of chronic delinquents*. Unpublished manuscript, Oregon Social Learning Center, Eugene, OR.

McMahon, R. J., & Wells, K. C. (1989). Conduct disorders. In E. J. Mash & R. A. Barkley (Eds.), *Treatment of childhood disorders* (pp. 73–134). New York: Guilford Press.

Olweus, D. (1979). Stability of aggressive reaction patterns in males. *Psychological Bulletin, 86*, 852–875.

Patterson, G. R. (1976). The aggressive child: Victim and architect of a coercive system. In L. A. Hamerlynck, L. C. Handy, & E. J. Mash (Eds.), *Behavior modification and families: Vol. 1. Theory and research* (pp. 267–316). New York: Brunner/Mazel.

Patterson, G. R. (1977). Accelerating stimuli for two classes of coercive behaviors. *Journal of Abnormal Child Psychology, 5*, 334–350.

Patterson, G. R. (1979a). Siblings: Fellow travelers in coercive family process. In R. J. Blanchard (Ed.), *Advances in the study of aggression* (pp. 173–215). San Diego, CA: Academic Press.

Patterson, G. R. (1979b). A performance theory for coercive family interaction. In R. B. Cairns (Ed.), *Social interaction: Methods, analysis, and illustrations* (pp. 119–162). Hillsdale, NJ: Erlbaum.

Patterson, G. R. (1979c). Treatment of children with conduct problems: A review of outcome studies. In S. Feshbach & A. Fraczek (Eds.), *Aggression and behavior change: Biological and social processes* (pp. 83–132). New York: Praeger.

Patterson, G. R. (1982). *Coercive family process*. Eugene, OR: Castilia.

Patterson, G. R. (1983). Stress as a change agent for family process. In N. Garmezy & M. Rutter (Eds.), *Stress, coping, and development in children* (pp. 235–264). New York: McGraw-Hill.

Patterson, G. R. (1985). A microsocial analysis of anger and irritable behavior. In M. A. Chesney & R. H. Rosenman (Eds.), *Anger and hostility in cardiovascular and behavioral disorders* (pp. 83–100). Washington, DC: Hemisphere.

Patterson, G. R. (1986). Performance models for antisocial boys. *American Psychologist, 41*, 432–444.

Patterson, G. R. (1990, March). *Developmental changes in antisocial behavior*. Paper presentation at the 22nd Banff International Conference on Behavioral Sciences, Banff, Alberta, Canada.

Patterson, G. R. (1993). Orderly change in a stable world, or the trait as a chimera. *Journal of Consulting and Clinical Psychology, 61*, 911–919.

Patterson, G. R., & Bank, L. (1985). Bootstrapping your way in the nomological thicket. *Behavioral Assessment, 8*, 49–73.

Patterson, G. R., & Bank, L. (1989). Some amplifying mechanisms for pathologic processes in families. In M. R. Gunnar & E. Thelen (Eds.), *Systems and development: The Minnesota Symposium on Child Psychology* (Vol. 22, pp. 167–209). Hillsdale, NJ: Erlbaum.

Patterson, G. R., Capaldi, D., & Bank, L. (1991). An early starter model for predicting delinquency. In D. J. Pepler & K. H. Rubin (Eds.), *The development and treatment of childhood aggression* (pp. 139–168). Hillsdale, NJ: Erlbaum.

Patterson, G. R., & Chamberlain, P. C. (1988). Treatment process: A problem at three levels. In L. C. Wynne (Ed.), *The state of the art in family therapy research: Controversies and recommendations* (pp. 189–223). New York: Family Process Press.

Patterson, G. R., Chamberlain, P. C., & Reid, J. B. (1982). A comparative evaluation of parent training procedures. *Behavior Therapy, 13,* 638–650.

Patterson, G. R., & Cobb, J. A. (1973). Stimulus control for classes of noxious behaviors. In J. F. Knutson (Ed.), *The control of aggression: Implications from basic research* (pp. 223–256). Chicago: Aldine.

Patterson, G. R., Crosby, L., & Vuchinich, S. (1993). Predicting risk for early police arrest. *Journal of Quantitative Criminology, 8,* 335–355.

Patterson, G. R., & Dawes, R. M. (1975). A Guttman scale of children's coercive behaviors. *Journal of Consulting and Clinical Psychology, 43,* 594.

Patterson, G. R., DeBaryshe, B. D., & Ramsey, E. (1989). A developmental perspective on antisocial behavior. *American Psychologist, 44,* 329–335.

Patterson, G. R., & Dishion, T. (1985). Contributions of families and peers to delinquency. *Criminology, 23,* 63–79.

Patterson, G. R., & Dishion, T. (1988). Multilevel family process models: Traits, interaction, and relationships. In R. Hinde & J. Stevenson-Hinde (Eds.), *Relationships within families: Mutual influences* (pp. 283–310). Oxford, England: Clarendon Press.

Patterson, G. R., & Fleischman, M. J. (1979). Maintenance of treatment effects: Some considerations concerning family systems and follow-up data. *Behavior Therapy, 10,* 168–185.

Patterson, G. R., & Forgatch, M. S. (1987). *Parents and adolescents living together: The basics.* Eugene, OR: Castilia.

Patterson, G. R., Littman, R. A., & Bricker, W. (1967). Assertive behavior in children: A step toward a theory of aggression. *Monographs of the Society for Research in Child Development, 32*(5, Serial No. 113).

Patterson, G. R., & Reid, J. B. (1970). Reciprocity and coercion: Two facets of social systems. In C. Neuringer & J. L. Michael (Eds.), *Behavior modification in clinical psychology* (pp. 133–177). New York: Appleton-Century-Crofts.

Patterson, G. R., Reid, J. B., & Dishion, T. (1992). *Antisocial boys.* Eugene, OR: Castilia.

Patterson, G. R., Reid, J. B., Jones, R. R., & Conger, R. E. (1975). *A social learning approach to family intervention: Vol. 1. Families with aggressive children.* Eugene, OR: Castilia.

Patterson, G. R., & Yoerger, K. (1993). Developmental models for delinquent behavior. In S. Hodgins (Ed.), *Crime and mental disorder* (pp. 140–172). Newbury Park, CA: Sage.

Plomin, R., Nitz, K., & Rowe, D. C. (1990). Behavioral genetics and aggression in childhood. In M. Lewis & S. M. Miller (Eds.), *Handbook of developmental psychopathology* (pp. 119–134). New York: Plenum.

Quay, D. C., Routh, D. K., & Shapiro, S. K. (1987). Psychopathology of childhood: From description to validation. *Annual Review of Psychology, 38,* 491–532.

Reid, J. B. (1978). *A social learning approach to family intervention: Vol. 2. Observation in the home setting.* Eugene, OR: Castilia.

Reid, J. B. (1986). Social-interactional patterns in the families of abused and nonabused children. In C. Zahn-Waxler, E. M. Cummings, & R. Iannotti (Eds.), *Altruism and aggression: Biological and social origins* (pp. 238–255). Cambridge, England: Cambridge University Press.

Reid, J. B., & Hendricks, A. (1973). Preliminary analysis of the effectiveness of direct home intervention for the treatment of predelinquent boys who steal. In L. A. Hamerlynck, L. C. Handy, & E. J. Mash (Eds.), *Behavior change: Methodology, concepts and practice* (pp. 209–220). Champaign, IL: Research Press.

Reid, J. B., & Patterson, G. R. (1976). The modification of aggression and stealing behavior of boys. In E. Ribes-Inesta & A. Bandura (Eds.), *Analysis of delinquency and aggression* (pp. 123–146). Hillsdale, NJ: Erlbaum.

Robinson, E. A. (1985). Coercion theory revisited: Toward a new theoretical perspective on the etiology of conduct disorders. *Clinical Psychology Review, 5,* 1–29.

Shinn, M. R., Ramsey, E., Walker, H., Strieber, S., & O'Neill, R. E. (1987). Antisocial behavior in school settings: Initial differences in an at risk and normal population. *Journal of Special Education, 21,* 69–84.

Snyder, J. J. (1977). A reinforcement analysis of interaction in problem and nonproblem families. *Journal of Abnormal Psychology, 86,* 528–535.

Snyder, J. (1991). Discipline as a mediator of the impact of maternal stress and mood on child conduct problems. *Development and Psychopathology, 3,* 263–276.

Snyder, J. J., & Brown, K. (1983). Oppositional behavior and noncompliance in preschool children: Environmental correlates and skills deficits. *Behavioral Assessment, 5,* 333–348.

Snyder, J., Dishion, T., & Patterson, G. R. (1986). Determinants and consequences of associating with deviant peers during preadolescence and adolescence. *Journal of Early Adolescence, 6,* 29–43.

Snyder, J., Edwards, P., McGraw, K., Kilgore, K., & Holton, A. (1994). Escalation and reinforcement in mother–child conflict: Social processes associated with physical aggression. *Development and Psychopathology, 6,* 305–321.

Snyder, J., & Huntley, D. (1990). Troubled families and troubled youth: The development of antisocial behavior and depression in children. In P. E. Leone (Ed.), *Understanding troubled and troubling youth* (pp. 194–225). Newbury Park, CA: Sage.

Snyder, J., & Patterson, G. R. (1986). The effects of consequences on patterns of social interaction: A quasi-experimental approach to reinforcement in the natural environment. *Child Development, 57,* 1257–1268.

Snyder, J., & Patterson, G. R. (1992). *Individual differences in social aggression: A reinforcement model of socialization in the natural environment.* Unpublished manuscript, Wichita State University, Wichita, KS.

Snyder, J. J., Stockemer, V., & West, L. (1993). *Selective association with similar peers: A social exchange and reinforcement analysis.* Unpublished manuscript, Wichita State University, Wichita, KS.

Stoolmiller, M. (1992, September). *Contagion models of social interaction.* Paper presented at the Oregon Social Learning Center Symposium on the Social Dynamics of Development and Psychopathology, Eugene, OR.

Sutherland, E. H., & Cressy, D. R. (1974). *Criminology* (9th ed.). Philadelphia: Lippincott.

Taplin, P. S. (1974). *Changes in parental consequation as a function of intervention.* Unpublished doctoral dissertation, University of Wisconsin, Madison.

Taplin, P. S., & Reid, J. B. (1977). Changes in parent consequences as a function of family intervention. *Journal of Consulting and Clinical Psychology, 45,* 973–981.

Vuchinich, S., Bank, L., & Patterson, G. R. (1992). Parenting, peers, and the stability of antisocial behavior in preadolescent boys. *Developmental Psychology, 28,* 510–521.

Wahler, R. G. (1980). The insular mother: Her problems in parent–child treatment. *Journal of Applied Behavior Analysis, 13,* 207–219.

Wahler, R. G., & Dumas, J. (1986). Maintenance factors in coercive mother–child interactions: The compliance and predictability hypotheses. *Journal of Applied Behavior Analysis, 19,* 13–22.

Wahler, R. G., & Dumas, J. (1987). Family factors in childhood psychopathology: Toward a coercion-neglect model. In T. Jacob (Ed.), *Family interaction and psychopathology: Theories, methods, and findings* (pp. 581–627). New York: Plenum.

Walter, H. I., & Gilmore, S. K. (1973). Placebo versus social learning effects in parent training procedures designed to alter the behavior of aggressive boys. *Behavior Research and Therapy, 4,* 361–377.

Williams, B. (1986). Reinforcement, choice and response strength. In R.A. Atkinson, R. Herrnstein, & G. Lindzey (Eds.), *Steven's handbook of experimental psychology* (pp. 167–244). San Diego, CA: Academic Press.

Wiltz, N. A., & Patterson, G. R. (1974). An evaluation of parent training procedures designed to alter inappropriate aggressive behavior of boys. *Behavior Therapy, 5,* 215–221.

13

SELF-EFFICACY THEORY OF BEHAVIORAL CHANGE: FOUNDATIONS, CONCEPTUAL ISSUES, AND THERAPEUTIC IMPLICATIONS

DANIEL CERVONE and WALTER D. SCOTT

Self-efficacy theory (Bandura, 1977; 1986; in press) has attracted great attention. From its outset, the publication of Bandura's theory was hailed as an "important event" (Rachman, 1978, p. 137), one that promised to "sustain and nourish . . . a better understanding and more effective treatment of psychological disorders" (Wilson, 1978, p. 227). The subsequent years witnessed a veritable explosion of research. Indeed, a computerized literature search conducted for this chapter yielded 933 self-efficacy references in the past 5 years alone.

We do not attempt to survey here the vast empirical literature on perceived self-efficacy. Instead, in keeping with the purpose of this volume,

We thank Robin Mermelstein, Suzanna Penningroth, Bill Shadel, and Theresa Schultz for their comments on this chapter.

we focus on a set of theoretical issues that is most defining of self-efficacy theory and most important to its further development. Specifically, our purposes are threefold: to present the basic features of self-efficacy theory; to explore a set of conceptual issues that are critical to understanding the self-efficacy perspective; and to examine the role of perceived self-efficacy in therapeutic behavior change, including the relation between self-efficacy theory and traditional cognitive–behavioral treatment strategies.

BASIC PRINCIPLES OF SELF-EFFICACY THEORY

Self-efficacy theory addresses people's perceptions of their capabilities for performance. The most basic proposition is that perceived self-efficacy is a fundamental element of human agency (Bandura, 1989). People affect their own levels of motivation and achievement through appraisals of their capabilities for coping with life's challenges.

In its analysis of self-perceptions and human agency, self-efficacy theory can be seen as having four parts: (a) a definition of *perceived self-efficacy*, including distinctions between this and other variables; (b) an analysis of the effects of self-efficacy judgment, that is, of psychological processes that are directly affected by efficacy appraisals; (c) an analysis of determinants of perceived self-efficacy, including different sources of information that differentially affect efficacy judgments; and (d) a methodology for analyzing reciprocal links among the environment, self-efficacy perceptions, and behavior. We consider each part of the theory in turn.

Perceived Self-Efficacy

Definition and Distinctions

People do not merely act in the world. They think about their actions, the world, and themselves. They wonder why events turned out as they did and how things might change in the future (Kelley, 1972; Weiner, 1985). They recall past events and use those recollections to evaluate the present (Kahneman & Miller, 1986). They ponder future possibilities, set goals for themselves, and plan strategies for reaching their aims (Lewin, Dembo, Festinger, & Sears, 1944; Locke & Latham, 1990). They evaluate whether past and potential actions are valuable and morally justifiable and whether they themselves are worthy of respect (Baumeister, 1991; Coopersmith, 1967).

Self-efficacy theory focuses on one particular aspect of human thinking, namely, people's thoughts about their capabilities for performance. *Perceived self-efficacy* is defined as a perception of one's capability to attain a specified level or type of performance in a given setting (Bandura, 1986).

Perceptions of one's capability to perform socially skilled behaviors with members of the opposite sex (Hill, 1989), to avoid overeating (Glynn & Ruderman, 1986) or smoking (DiClemente, Prochaska, & Gilbertini, 1985) when feeling tense or depressed, to participate in an exercise program despite experiencing some physical discomfort (McAuley & Jacobsen, 1991), or to engage in normal work or sexual activities after an abortion (Major et al., 1990) illustrate the class of self-referent thinking referred to as perceived self-efficacy.

It is important to distinguish carefully between perceived self-efficacy and other self-referent variables. Perceived self-efficacy does not refer to a generalized, transsituational sense of oneself as being a "capable" or "incapable" person. Rather, it refers to one's perceived capabilities for action within a specified domain of activity. Perceived self-efficacy does not refer to the perceived value or worthiness of a person or act. It refers to judgments of what behaviors one can perform, independent of the value that one attaches to them. To illustrate, an official of the Internal Revenue Service may have a high sense of self-efficacy for performing the legal and interpersonal activities required to foreclose on a mortgage and expel delinquent taxpayers from their family farm, but may draw little self-worth from this action. Combining these two points illuminates the distinction between perceived self-efficacy and self-esteem. The self-esteem construct generally refers to a global sense of self-worth (e.g., Coopersmith, 1967). The perceived self-efficacy construct is not global, nor does it refer to a sense of self-worth.

Perceived self-efficacy also must be differentiated from two task-specific cognitions: goals and outcome expectations. *Goals* refer to one's aims in an activity (Locke & Latham, 1990). Although self-efficacy perceptions are a key determinant of the goals that one adopts (Bandura & Cervone, 1986; Wood, Bandura, & Bailey, 1990), the psychological constructs of "goals" and "self-efficacy perceptions" are conceptually and empirically distinct. If one does not value an activity, then a high sense of efficacy will not foster the adoption of challenging task goals. When both variables are assessed, self-efficacy perceptions and personal goals have been shown to contribute uniquely to performance (e.g., Cervone, Jiwani, & Wood, 1991). Research on affect and cognition has further validated this distinction by revealing that a given emotional state can differentially influence goals and efficacy judgments. Negative mood can induce higher goals and standards while either having no effect on, or lowering, efficacy expectations (Cervone, Kopp, Schaumann, & Scott, 1994; Wright & Mischel, 1982).

Bandura (1977) has emphasized the distinction between self-efficacy perceptions and outcome expectations. Many psychological theorists (e.g., Rotter, 1954; Vroom, 1964) focus on expectations for reward, that is, expectations that one's behavior may be followed by a rewarding outcome.

Bandura distinguished between this expectation and a logically prior one: the expectation that one can perform the behavior in the first place. Self-efficacy perceptions, then, refer to perceptions of being able to accomplish a given type of performance, whereas outcome expectations refer to the consequences that one expects will follow this performance. Peterson and Stunkard (1992) illustrated the distinction with this scenario:

> a basketball coach might believe . . . the Chicago Bulls can be defeated if they are held to fewer than 90 points. Whether he believes that his team can hold the Bulls to fewer than 90 points is of course a different matter. (p. 113)

We consider the distinction between outcome expectations and perceived self-efficacy in detail later in this chapter.

Behavioral, Cognitive, and Affective Consequences

Self-efficacy theory posits that efficacy judgments are proximal determinants of a set of psychological processes that are critical to human adjustment and achievement (Bandura, 1989). One process involves choosing activities to undertake. People boldly engage in activities for which they judge themselves highly efficacious, yet shy away from valued pursuits they judge they cannot handle (Betz & Hackett, 1986; Lent & Hackett, 1987). Such choices can have powerful effects on the course of personality development (Bandura, 1986; Caspi & Bem, 1990; Snyder & Ickes, 1985). Those who avoid situations on the basis of subjective feelings of inefficacy may fail to develop valuable skills that they otherwise might have acquired.

Once one becomes engaged in an activity, self-efficacy perceptions affect one's degree of effort and task persistence. On challenging tasks, people dwell not only on the task, but also on themselves (Sarason, 1975; Sarason, Sarason, & Pierce, 1990; Wine, 1971). Decisions about how long to persevere are based partly on self-assessments of one's capabilities. Those who doubt their efficacy tend to slacken their efforts and give up, whereas those with a strong sense of self-efficacy persevere (Bandura & Cervone, 1983, 1986; Cervone & Peake, 1986; Peake & Cervone, 1989; Stock & Cervone, 1990; Weinberg, Gould, Yukelson, & Jackson, 1981).

Self-efficacy perceptions also influence cognitive processes that are critical to achievement. On cognitively complex activities that require the acquisition of task knowledge and formulation of strategies, people with a higher sense of efficacy develop and test strategies more analytically (Cervone, 1993; Wood & Bandura, 1989b). On stressful memory tasks, robust efficacy perceptions enhance performance (Berry, West, & Dennehey, 1989). Self-efficacy appraisals also can affect cognitive activity prior and subsequent to performance. Those who question their ability to cope with events dwell on potential calamities (Borden, Clum, & Salmon, 1991; Kent & Gibbons, 1987). After an event, efficacy perceptions affect people's attributions for outcomes that have occurred (Alden, 1986; McAuley, Duncan, & McElroy, 1989).

Finally, affective responses are a fourth class of phenomena that are determined, in part, by perceptions of self-efficacy. People with a high sense of efficacy experience less anxiety when facing stressful, threatening events (Bandura, Cioffi, Taylor, & Brouillard, 1988; Bandura, Reese, & Adams, 1982; Bandura, Taylor, Williams, Mefford, & Barchas, 1985). A low sense of efficacy for accomplishing important life tasks engenders depression (Cutrona & Troutman, 1986). Although it has not traditionally been emphasized in self-efficacy research, efficacy perceptions also may play a role in the onset of certain discrete emotional experiences. Lazarus (1991) noted the conceptual overlap between self-efficacy theory and his analysis of cognitive appraisals of "coping potential," that is, appraisals of one's ability to "manage the demands of the encounter or actualize personal commitments" (p. 150). Appraisals of coping potential have been shown to partly differentiate the experiences of sadness, anger, and fear (Ellsworth & Smith, 1988; C. A. Smith & Lazarus, 1990). When an individual is offended, a low appraisal of coping ability generates fear and avoidance, whereas an appraisal of high coping potential may result in anger and assertiveness. The analysis of perceived self-efficacy and discrete emotions is a promising area of expansion for self-efficacy theory.

By detailing mechanisms through which efficacy perceptions affect behavioral outcomes, self-efficacy theory avoids positing a "black box" model of human performance, in which processes linking cognition and achievement are unspecified. Indeed, self-efficacy theory is centrally concerned with cognition–behavior links. The theory's core prediction is not that a higher sense of efficacy inevitably generates superior performance outcomes. Rather, the theory predicts that self-efficacy perceptions influence choice of tasks, motivation, emotion, and the organization of cognitive skills. Through these processes, higher efficacy perceptions generally promote superior achievement. In some exceptional cases, however, extremely high efficacy perceptions may be dysfunctional. Highly self-efficacious persons may be overly persistent on unsolvable tasks (Janoff-Bullman & Brickman, 1982) and may engage in risky actions that they should avoid (Haaga & Stewart, 1992b).

Determinants

Self-efficacy theory examines not only the consequences of perceptions of self-efficacy but also their causes, that is, the determinants of one's level of perceived self-efficacy within a given domain. Two distinct questions arise here. The first concerns the social experiences that influence self-efficacy perceptions. The second concerns the psychological processes involved in appraising one's efficacy on an activity.

Bandura (1977, 1986) outlines four types of experience that influence self-efficacy perceptions. The first and most influential is firsthand, enactive experience. Personal encounters with the world provide the most reliable index of one's capabilities. Enactive psychological treatments generally boost efficacy perceptions more strongly and rapidly than do treatments lacking a performance component (Bandura, 1977; Rosenthal & Bandura, 1978; Williams, 1990). A second influence is vicarious. People partly base assessments of their own capabilities on the performance of others who are similar to themselves (e.g., Brown & Inouye, 1978). A third source of influence is verbal persuasion. People often attempt to instill efficacy beliefs by persuading others of their capabilities. Mere persuasion, however, is less effective than actual commerce with the environment (Biran & Wilson, 1981). Finally, affective and physiological states may provide information about one's efficacy (cf. Schwarz, 1990). Noticing that one is too anxious, fearful, or exhausted to perform optimally may lower assessments of what one can do.

A second issue concerns the cognitive processes through which individuals integrate these diverse sources of information to arrive at a judgment of their performance capabilities. The precise processes involved in gauging one's efficacy are likely to vary, depending on the task. On highly familiar activities, one may develop a firm sense of one's capabilities for performance. Assessing one's efficacy on any given occasion may involve a simple memory-based process in which one accesses knowledge of what one can do (Turk & Salovey, 1985). However, individuals often face situations that contain significant novelty and uncertainty. One may be unsure of the precise skills that are required, the difficulties that may arise, or one's ability to mobilize the requisite effort at a given time. Here, accurate appraisals of one's capabilities may require a more deliberate, or "systematic" processing (Chaiken, Liberman, & Eagly, 1989) of personal and situational information.

Two factors, however, may preclude a systematic weighing of personal and situational information in efficacy appraisals. Because of limited information-processing capacity, people cannot integrate large numbers of factors (Simon, 1983). Even if they could, ongoing interactions often require quick action and thereby inhibit extensive deliberations on one's capabilities. Thus, judgments of personal efficacy often are based on simple, rapid judgmental strategies, or "heuristics" (Tversky & Kahneman, 1974). These judgmental strategies frequently yield efficient and accurate self-appraisals. However, they also leave efficacy judgment open to systematic biases.

Two judgmental strategies and biases have been shown to affect self-efficacy appraisal. *Anchoring-and-adjustment processes* (Tversky & Kahneman, 1974), in which an initial possibility is considered and then adjusted to yield a final judgment, are relevant to activities on which a range of performance outcomes is possible. Anchoring research reveals that self-

efficacy judgments are biased in the direction of whatever potential outcome one considers first (Cervone, 1993). Such biases occur even when
the outcome one considers first is determined by social cues that are completely irrelevant to the performance domain (Cervone & Palmer, 1990;
Cervone & Peake, 1986; Peake & Cervone, 1989). A second heuristic
involves the ease with which performance-related information comes to
mind, or is cognitively "available" (Schwarz et al., 1991; Tversky & Kahneman, 1973). Availability processes are pertinent when a large number of
personal or situational factors can influence one's future performance. Because people generally cannot contemplate large numbers of performance-
related factors, efficacy judgments may be based on the ease with which a
relatively small number of success- or failure-related factors come to mind.
Information that is most important often is the most cognitively available.
However, factors other than objective importance can influence availability. Positive and negative mood may affect the availability of information
that is suggestive of success or failure (Kavanagh & Bower, 1985). Briefly
dwelling on either aids or hindrances to performance may prime these
factors and thereby influence subsequent self-efficacy perceptions (Cervone,
1989).

Gauging Relations Between Efficacy and Action

Self-efficacy researchers generally have used self-report questionnaire
measures to assess perceived self-efficacy. In accord with the theory, these
instruments have not been designed to assess an abstract sense of general
efficacy. Instead, they are tailored to a particular activity or domain of
functioning. Two aspects of perceived self-efficacy generally are assessed:
(a) level of self-efficacy, the absolute level or type of performance that one
judges one can achieve, and (b) strength of self-efficacy, one's subjective
confidence in being able to attain designated levels of performance (Bandura, 1977).

To assess relations between self-efficacy perceptions and absolute levels of performance, Bandura (1977) proposed a microanalytical research
strategy. This method gauges the relation between efficacy judgments and
performance at the level of individual tasks. For each of a series of items
(e.g., a series of tasks in a behavioral avoidance test; Bandura, Adams, &
Beyer, 1977), the subject examines the match between judgments of
whether he or she can perform the task and whether he or she actually
does so. The percentage of tasks for which efficacy and action are congruent
is computed for each subject. Remarkably high congruence rates, ranging
from 80% to 90%, have been found (e.g., Bandura et al., 1977).

A number of writers have raised questions about the microanalytical
congruence index, noting correctly that chance congruence levels may exceed 50%. Unfortunately, the statistical procedures that these commenta-

tors (Kirsch, 1980; Lee, 1985) have suggested are statistically flawed and highly misleading (Cervone, 1985, 1987). Appropriate methods for determining the statistical significance of microanalytical congruence data have revealed that obtained relations between efficacy judgment and action are highly significant (Cervone, 1985; Williams, Dooseman, & Kleifield, 1984).

The self-efficacy assessment strategy can be viewed within a broader strategy of cognitive assessment (Segal & Shaw, 1988). Although cognitive constructs were once viewed with skepticism, they are no longer considered unscientific as long as they are tied to observable measurement procedures (Mahoney, 1977; Parks & Hollon, 1988). Various cognitive assessment procedures, such as recording, production, and sampling methods (Kendall & Hollon, 1981; Parks & Hollon, 1988), have been developed. These procedures provide potentially valuable alternatives to commonly employed questionnaire methods in self-efficacy research (e.g., Haaga & Stewart, 1992b).

CONCEPTUAL ISSUES IN SELF-EFFICACY THEORY

In this section, we address a set of conceptual issues that are critical to an accurate understanding of the self-efficacy perspective. Some of these have generated a degree of confusion and controversy in the literature. Others, we feel, have received inadequate attention.

Not a Single-Factor Theory

Humorist Matt Groening lampooned academicians who propose a "single-theory-to-explain-everything" by depicting a professor who raves, "The country that controls magnesium controls the universe!!!" Fortunately, self-efficacy is not this sort of theory. Perceived self-efficacy must be understood as part of a much broader theoretical perspective, namely, Bandura's (1986) social cognitive theory.

Social cognitive theory (Bandura, 1986) can be seen as based on two key principles (Cervone & Williams, 1992). First, human functioning is understood in terms of reciprocally interacting influences. The environment, behavior, and personal factors—including cognitive, affective, and physiological processes—are viewed as reciprocal determinants (Bandura, 1978) of one another. Second, personality functioning is understood, within this model, in terms of a set of cognitive capabilities through which people learn about, interpret, and anticipate environmental events, and guide and motivate their own actions. According to social cognitive theory, then, self-efficacy perceptions are one of a number of personal factors that, in concert, determine motivation, affect, and performance.

An even broader perspective places self-efficacy theory within a family of contemporary social–cognitive models of personality (Cervone, 1991; Cervone & Williams, 1992). Social–cognitive theories (Bandura, 1986; Cantor & Kihlstrom, 1987; Dweck & Leggett, 1988; Mischel, 1973, 1993; see also Higgins, 1990) place human thinking processes at the center of an analysis of personality. They analyze the cognitive structures and processes that underlie human competencies, preferences, values, and emotions and explore the relations among these cognitive variables, the social environment, and behavior. These perspectives provide a clear alternative to traditional trait theories of personality (Cervone, 1991; Shadel & Cervone, 1993).

Although social–cognitive theory is highly multifaceted, Bandura's (1977) original self-efficacy analysis of avoidant behavior was, in one sense, a single-factor theory. Self-efficacy perceptions were postulated to be the singular mediator of behavior change. Bandura's emphasis on a single causal pathway did not, of course, represent an abandonment of his broader theory. Rather, it reflected the particular problem at hand at the time, namely, identifying cognitive mediators of changes in fearful behavior. A complete explication of other therapeutic problems naturally may invoke social–cognitive processes in addition to perceived self-efficacy. For example, personal standards and goal-setting processes contribute to changes in refractory behaviors, such as eating (Bandura & Simon, 1977) and smoking (Borrelli & Mermelstein, 1994), and may influence the onset and maintenance of dysphoric states (Ahrens, 1987; Rehm, 1977).

Perceived Self-Efficacy as Cause

The most basic postulate of self-efficacy theory (Bandura, 1977) is that efficacy perceptions causally contribute to behavior. Perceived self-efficacy is viewed not as a mere reflection of behavioral change (Borkovec, 1978), but as a proximal determinant of behavior. This proposal has not been accepted uncritically. Commentators on Bandura's (1977) initial statement of self-efficacy theory questioned whether the extant data truly supported a causal role for efficacy judgment (Borkovec, 1978; Eysenck, 1978; Wolpe, 1978). These criticisms generally invoked "third variables" that might explain relations between self-efficacy and action. For example, the finding that efficacy judgments predict approach behavior within and between treatment conditions (Bandura & Adams, 1977; Bandura et al., 1977) might be explained by reference to subjects' knowledge of coping strategies. Modeling treatments that boost efficacy perceptions (Bandura et al., 1977) also may convey knowledge about how to cope with feared stimuli. Enhanced knowledge could, in theory, account for changes in efficacy perceptions and behavior and the relation between these variables.[1]

In the years since these critiques, much research has directly addressed the third variable problem. Two basic strategies have been used. The first assesses relations between self-efficacy and behavior while statistically controlling for other variables that might affect performance. Findings have consistently supported a causal role for efficacy judgment. On skilled motor tasks associated with anxiety and hesitancy in performance, efficacy perceptions significantly predict performance after anxiety arousal and past performance are controlled for (Feltz, 1982, 1988; McAuley, 1985). On complex decision-making tasks, self-efficacy contributes to performance after the effects of prior attainments are controlled for (Bandura & Wood, 1989; Cervone et al., 1991; Cervone & Wood, 1993; Wood & Bandura, 1989a). On mathematical problems, self-efficacy perceptions predict performance after the effects of assessed mathematical aptitude (Collins, 1982) and past experience in mathematics (Sexton & Tuckman, 1991) are controlled for.

The strategy of assessing relations between self-efficacy and action while statistically controlling for other variables does have a limitation. One cannot be certain that all influential third variables have been identified. Existing levels of self-efficacy may covary with other causal factors that have not been assessed. A second strategy, then, has been to manipulate self-efficacy perceptions experimentally. In the most stringent tests of self-efficacy theory, researchers manipulate self-efficacy perceptions while holding constant all other performance-related factors, including information and experiences that might influence subjects' competencies on a task. A particularly useful strategy in this regard has been to alter self-efficacy perceptions by affecting the judgmental processes through which individuals assess their efficacy on a task (Cervone & Peake, 1986).

A number of studies have involved the manipulation of self-efficacy judgments through subtle contextual cues that provide no information about a judgment domain but that nonetheless powerfully influence self-appraisals. Self-efficacy perceptions have been reliably influenced by having subjects consider apparently random values that represent high or low levels of performance (Cervone & Palmer, 1990; Cervone & Peake, 1986), varying the order in which subjects consider hypothetical levels of future performance (Berry et al., 1989; Peake & Cervone, 1989), and having people briefly contemplate personal and situational factors that might help or hinder their efforts (Cervone, 1989). Variations in self-efficacy stemming

---

[1]Commentators (e.g., Eysenck, 1978; Wolpe, 1978) have more commonly cited anxiety-related processes as potential "third variables." However, given the evidence that self-efficacy perceptions are better predictors of therapeutic change than experienced or anticipated anxiety (Bandura, 1988; Williams, 1992), we find knowledge of coping strategies to be a more plausible counterexplanation.

from these judgmental biases have correspondingly affected subsequent motivation (Cervone, 1989; Cervone & Peake, 1986; Peake & Cervone, 1989). In other words, even when people's high or low self-efficacy perceptions stem from trivial factors—such as their having received a high or low anchor value by chance (Cervone & Peake, 1986)—variations in perceived self-efficacy still affect subsequent behavior. These findings directly speak to the causality issue. In this research, experimental conditions vary neither exposure to the tasks nor information about the activities. Subjects differ on self-perceived capabilities but on no other variable that reasonably could be thought to affect their abilities on the tasks. Nonetheless, variations in perceived self-efficacy produce corresponding differences in behavior.

Related evidence derives from research in which efficacy perceptions are altered by presenting bogus or counternormative information. Bogus information about past successes can enhance self-efficacy perceptions and subsequent physical stamina (Weinberg, Gould, & Jackson, 1979). False information about the relation between one's own and others' performance can enhance efficacy perceptions and task persistence (Jacobs, Prentice-Dunn, & Rogers, 1984). False feedback has been shown to alter self-efficacy perceptions and pain tolerance on cold-pressor tasks (Litt, 1988). In highly inventive research, Holroyd and colleagues (Holroyd et al., 1984) induced high and low self-efficacy perceptions for coping with headache pain by varying the direction and accuracy of performance feedback on a biofeedback task. Subjects who performed the task in a potentially deleterious manner, but received feedback indicating that they were performing it beneficially, displayed high levels of self-efficacy and reported low levels of subsequent headache activity.

Self-efficacy research also can address two related arguments. The first questions the causal impact of efficacy perceptions by criticizing research demonstrating that perceived self-efficacy predicts absolute levels of achievement on activities that are under volitional control and that are performed soon after a self-efficacy assessment. As Seligman gibed, "A phobic asserts that she can touch a snake, then touches a snake. Excellent predictive value!" (1992, p. 119). Such a commentary, however, ignores four classes of evidence. The first, of course, is that efficacy judgments retain predictive value even when they are manipulated experimentally (e.g., Peake & Cervone, 1989). Second, self-efficacy measures predict responses that are not under simple voluntary control, such as physiological arousal (Bandura et al., 1982, 1985) or the quality of analytical decision making (Cervone, 1993; Wood & Bandura, 1989b). Third, perceived self-efficacy governs task persistence, even when no subjects attain the absolute level of performance they anticipated (Cervone & Peake, 1986). Finally, self-efficacy measures predict not only immediate performance in therapy but also the long-term maintenance of therapeutic change (Borrelli & Mermelstein, 1994; Condiotte & Lichtenstein, 1981).[2]

A final argument is that the obtained relations between perceived self-efficacy and behavior reflect extraneous methodological features. When self-efficacy questionnaires tap cognitions about the exact class of behavior that subsequently is assessed, one may contend that efficacy–behavior relations result from a mere "overlap" of methods. This argument, however, fails to account for systematic variations in the strength of relations between self-efficacy and performance. For example, perceived self-efficacy most strongly contributes to goal-directed performance when individuals have a clearly specified goal (Bandura & Cervone, 1983; Cervone et al., 1991) and receive specific feedback on their efforts (Bandura & Cervone, 1983; Cervone & Wood, 1993). When these factors are absent, relations between identical measures of self-efficacy and behavior are much weaker and are often nonsignificant—despite the continued presence of the "methods overlap."

Generalizations in Self-Efficacy Perceptions

By definition, *perceived self-efficacy* refers to perceptions of capabilities for performance within a given situation, activity, or domain. This definition recognizes that efficacy perceptions may vary substantially across situations and tasks. Such situational specificity is commonly found. Men and women judge themselves equally efficacious for academic attainments in general, but differ in perceived self-efficacy within subject areas that typically are dominated by members of one gender (Betz & Hackett, 1981). Judgmental cues that bias self-efficacy perceptions for one activity do not generalize to other tasks within the same setting (Cervone, 1989). Adolescents' beliefs in their ability to resist pro-drug pressures are only moderately generalizable across differing social situations (Hays & Ellickson, 1990). Finally, agoraphobics treated within one phobic domain do not show uniform generalized improvements in self-efficacy within other domains; instead, generalizations are variable and idiosyncratic (Williams, Kinney, & Falbo, 1989).

Self-efficacy theorists do not argue that there is no generalizability to self-efficacy perceptions. Indeed, Bandura (1977) explicitly addressed this issue and found that mastery-based treatment gains do generalize (Bandura et al., 1977; see also R. E. Smith, 1989). The situation-based definition and assessment of perceived self-efficacy is best understood as a conceptual strategy, one common to social–cognitive research (Cervone, 1991). In this

---

[2]Seligman (1992) did note the longitudinal predictive power of self-efficacy measures, but then concluded that predicting across time "makes self-efficacy a personality trait" (p. 119). We find this conclusion puzzling in that it blurs the many important distinctions between trait theories and the social–cognitive approach (Bandura, 1991; Cervone, 1991; Mischel, 1993).

approach, generalization is treated as an empirical question. One first assesses self-efficacy perceptions within specific domains and then determines whether perceptions across domains generalize. The exact pattern of generalizations might vary from person to person.

An alternative approach is to treat self-efficacy as a generalized trait. For example, one may assess beliefs about typical behavioral tendencies without regard to the social context in which one is behaving (e.g., Sherer et al., 1982). Social–cognitive theory rejects such trait-based strategies on a number of grounds. They misrepresent the self-efficacy construct, which pertains not to generic self-knowledge, but to perceived capabilities to cope with specified activities and challenges. They sacrifice predictive power, with a concomitant loss in explanatory ability, because of their insensitivity to contextual variation in efficacy judgment. They rank all individuals on a context-free personality dimension by compiling their responses into a set of heterogeneous items assumed to be equally applicable to everyone—precisely the trait-theoretical procedures that social–cognitive theories repudiate (Bandura, 1986; Cantor & Kihlstrom, 1987; Cervone, 1991; Mischel, 1968, 1993).

Self-Efficacy and Outcome Expectations

As noted earlier, self-efficacy theory distinguishes between self-efficacy perceptions and outcome expectations. This theoretical distinction is substantiated by empirical findings indicating that these variables are distinct and have unique predictive value. Some researchers assess naturally occurring levels of perceived self-efficacy and expected outcomes as individuals engage in challenging or aversive tasks. Self-efficacy perceptions uniquely add to the prediction of approach behavior toward feared stimuli (Lee, 1984b), assertive interpersonal behavior (Lee, 1984a), athletic performance (Barling & Abel, 1983), pain tolerance (Baker & Kirsch, 1991; Manning & Wright, 1983; Williams & Kinney, 1991) and the use of coping strategies for chronic pain (Jensen, Turner, & Romano, 1991), and mathematical problem solving (Sexton & Tuckman, 1991; Sexton, Tuckman, & Crehan, 1992). Others experimentally manipulate outcome expectations and perceived self-efficacy. Efficacy judgments uniquely predict cognitive performance (Davis & Yates, 1982) and predict interpersonal behavioral intentions after both outcome expectations and outcome value (Maddux, Norton, & Stoltenberg, 1986) are controlled for. Thus, self-efficacy perceptions clearly contribute to performance beyond the effects of outcome expectations. Indeed, this is a conservative interpretation of these data. Self-efficacy perceptions frequently prove superior to outcome expectations, subjective importance of outcomes, or other outcome-related predictors (e.g., Manning & Wright, 1983).

The extensive investigations of phobic behavior change by Williams and colleagues (reviewed in Williams, 1992; Cervone & Williams, 1992) provide further evidence of the unique impact of self-efficacy perceptions. Various cognitive perspectives on phobic distress (Beck, 1976; Chambless & Gracely, 1989; Reiss, 1991) suggest that anticipated negative outcomes—such as anticipated harm, negative social evaluation, or personal distress—are the key determinants of phobic behavior. These perspectives can be compared with self-efficacy theory by assessment of both efficacy perceptions and anticipated negative outcomes during the course of therapy. Self-efficacy consistently proves to be a superior predictor of therapeutic improvement. Self-efficacy remains a significant predictor after the effects of anticipated danger, anxiety, and panic are considered, whereas anticipated negative outcomes add little or nothing to the prediction of behavior after the effects of self-efficacy are controlled for (Williams, Dooseman, & Kleifield, 1984; Williams, Kinney, & Falbo, 1989; Williams & Rappoport, 1983; Williams, Turner, & Peer, 1985; Williams & Watson, 1985). Contrary to some arguments (Kirsch, 1985), similar findings have been obtained when efficacy assessments explicitly instruct subjects to rate their capability to perform phobic tasks, as opposed to their mere willingness to do so (Palmer & Cervone, 1992). Thus, on the basis of accumulated empirical data, the argument that outcome expectancies and self-efficacy perceptions do not differ (Rotter, 1992) appears untenable.

Despite the consistency of this empirical literature, the theoretical distinction between self-efficacy and outcome expectations has elicited criticism and confusion. Some commentators have suggested that these constructs are not distinct (Eastman & Marzillier, 1984; Kazdin, 1978; Rotter, 1992; Teasdale, 1978). Others have disagreed about their defining properties (Devins, 1992; Haaga & Stewart, 1992a). The continuing debate about the relation between self-efficacy and outcome expectations rests in part on methodological issues (Maddux et al., 1986). However, the enduring concerns about these constructs strongly reflect a set of conceptual confusions that plague this literature.

First, the term *outcome expectancies* has been used in two distinct ways (Baker & Kirsch, 1991; Kirsch, 1985). To some, outcome expectancies refer to "judgments regarding the potential controllability of an outcome in general, regardless of whether a particular individual is able to influence the outcome" (Rodin, 1990, p. 3). Alternatively, outcome expectancy may refer to "people's expectations about the outcomes of *their own* behavior" (Baker & Kirsch, 1991, p. 504, italics added). These definitions differ substantially. The former refers to knowledge of outcome contingencies (e.g., "If a student earns a 3.95 grade point average, will the student be admitted to medical school?"). The latter refers to cognitions concerning outcomes that will accrue to oneself (e.g., "Will I be admitted to medical school?"), cognitions that are partly determined by self-assessments of self-efficacy (Kent

& Gibbons, 1987). Answers to seemingly straightforward questions about the relation between self-efficacy perceptions and outcome expectations obviously hinge on which definition one adopts.

A second point of confusion results from equating self-efficacy theory's distinction between self-efficacy and outcome expectancies with the proposal that "efficacy expectations are arrived at independently of considerations of potential outcomes" (Eastman & Marzillier, 1984, p. 216). The proposition that variables are conceptually distinct does not imply that they cannot affect one another. The process of arriving at an efficacy judgment is a complex one. Affective states (Kavanagh & Bower, 1985) and judgmental processes that underlie self-efficacy judgment (Cervone, 1989) may be affected by differential information about outcome contingencies.

A third source of confusion in the efficacy–outcome literature results from failing to recognize that the contingency between actions and outcomes varies substantially across activities (Bandura, 1991). In many domains, the performance of an action and the desired outcome are clearly distinct and are imperfectly related (e.g., Peterson & Stunkard's [1992, p. 113] example, cited earlier). In such instances, assessing the independent impact of efficacy- and outcome-related cognitions is a straightforward matter. However, in some cases, the performances to be achieved and the outcomes one desires overlap and, in the extreme, may be essentially identical. To the artist unconcerned with critical acclaim or financial gain, successfully completing a work may constitute a challenging act to be performed and an end result that is desired. To the headache sufferer, controlling headache pain is both an act to be achieved and a desired outcome. The difficulty of distinguishing between self-efficacy and outcome cognitions in such instances does not imply that these constructs are identical (cf. Rotter, 1992), but merely that they overlap in the special case in which desired outcomes and performance converge.

Identifying the Behavior

A related question deserving closer attention was summarized well by Haaga and Stewart (1992a): "How do you know an act when you see one?" These investigators asked whether, in a stream of ongoing behavior and cognition, one can unambiguously distinguish "the act" to be performed from "the outcome" one desires (cf. Devins, 1992). In a smoking cessation program, for example, is executing treatment strategies the act to be performed and abstinence the desired outcome, or is abstinence the act that is the target of self-efficacy judgment and enhanced long-term health status the outcome?

This ambiguity stems not from a shortcoming of self-efficacy theory, but from ambiguity inherent in the identification of acts. Any action can be identified, or known, in many different ways. Vallacher and Wegner (1987) specified multiple levels at which one may identify a given act and factors that determine one's level of identification. As authors, we may see ourselves as contributing to science, synthesizing research and theory on self-efficacy, meeting a publishing deadline, or trying to figure out our new-fangled word processor. People shift to lower level identifications (e.g., solve word-processor mysteries) when actions are disrupted (e.g., a block of text vanishes; Wegner, Vallacher, Macomber, Wood, & Arps, 1984).

The implications of action identification theory (Vallacher & Wegner, 1987) for self-efficacy research are considerable. For any given activity, there is no singular cognition that constitutes the one-and-only self-efficacy perception. Instead, perceived self-efficacy is best conceptualized as a class of thinking having to do with one's capability to perform behaviors. The exact nature of people's thoughts about their capabilities may vary from person to person, task to task, and moment to moment, as people grapple with varying task demands. Some may focus on their capability to achieve high-level goals (e.g., abstain from smoking, maintain weight loss, or earn an A in math). Others who are engaged in identical actions may dwell on their efficacy at "lower levels" and reflect on their capability to perform specific actions (e.g., self-monitor smoking, count calories, or solve a particular math problem).

The recognition that people identify and reflect on their actions at varying levels (Vallacher & Wegner, 1987) implies a number of different strategies for assessing self-efficacy. One strategy, adopted implicitly in most self-efficacy research, is to use self-report questionnaires that describe specific performances that constitute relatively high-level identifications that are important to all individuals. For example, one might assess students' perceived efficacy for completing specific college majors (Betz & Hackett, 1981) without also assessing beliefs about lower level component behaviors, such as mastering certain types of material or motivating oneself to study. A second assessment strategy is to use less structured methods, such as think-aloud procedures (e.g., Haaga & Stewart, 1992b), which could assess both the strength of efficacy beliefs and the level at which people are dwelling on their actions. A third strategy is to assess multiple aspects of self-efficacy judgment within a given domain (e.g., Bernier & Avard, 1986; DiClemente et al., 1985; Schneider, O'Leary, & Agras, 1987). In a weight control program, one might separately assess perceived self-efficacy for performing behavioral components of the treatment program, adhering to one's diet, and attaining overall weight loss goals (Stotland & Zuroff, 1991). Participants are likely to consider each of these aspects of self-efficacy at various points in the course of treatment; thus, each may be a valuable predictor of therapeutic gains.

Perceived Self-Efficacy for Strategies and Goals

Assessing multiple aspects, or levels, of perceived self-efficacy raises an analytical concern. The investigator may obtain numerous intercorrelated predictors, each of which seemingly has the same conceptual status— a measure of self-efficacy—and each of which is predictive of behavior. What is needed is a conceptual framework for organizing these multiple aspects of self-efficacy appraisal. One useful heuristic in this regard is a distinction between perceived self-efficacy for strategies and for goals.

Goals are the overall aim of a course of action (Locke & Latham, 1990). *Strategies* (Cantor & Kihlstrom, 1987), or *plans* (Miller, Galanter, & Pribram, 1960), refer to one's tactics for achieving a goal. When gauging one's performance efficacy, one may focus on either the attainment of overall goals or the execution of specific strategies. For example, a participant in a smoking cessation program may dwell on the goal of permanently abstaining from smoking or may be concerned with executing a specific strategy, such as self-monitoring. As people gain experience and confidence in executing treatment strategies, their self-efficacy for achieving overall treatment goals should grow (Borrelli & Mermelstein, 1994). Perceived self-efficacy for strategies, in other words, should influence self-efficacy for goals. Perceived self-efficacy for overall treatment goals, thus, may mediate the behavioral effects of self-efficacy for strategy execution.

A recent study of bulimics in a cognitive–behavioral treatment group illustrates this conceptual strategy (Henry, Ruderman, & Cervone, 1993). Self-efficacy measures included an index of perceived efficacy for performance of treatment strategies (e.g., making a written record of all binge-eating and purging episodes) and a measure of self-efficacy for achieving the treatment goal of controlling binge eating episodes. Both self-efficacy measures significantly predicted posttreatment binge eating. A mediator-variable analysis (Baron & Kenny, 1986) brought further order to the data by revealing that efficacy perceptions for controlling binges mediated the behavioral effects of self-efficacy for executing treatment strategies. In other words, perceived self-efficacy for treatment strategies affected behavior through its influence on self-efficacy for treatment goals.

PERCEIVED SELF-EFFICACY AND THERAPEUTIC CHANGE

Self-efficacy theory is not merely a theory of behavioral change. In other words, work on perceived self-efficacy is not just concerned with explaining changes resulting from psychotherapeutic treatments. It is broadly concerned with the role of self-efficacy appraisals in human emotion, cognition, and action. Applications of self-efficacy theory are found in such diverse areas as educational achievement (Bandura, 1993; Schunk,

1989), athletic performance (Feltz, 1982, 1988), and interpersonal behavior (Hill, 1989). Clinical behavior change, however, is self-efficacy theory's place of origin and remains a fundamental concern of the field.

Perceived Self-Efficacy as a Mediator of Therapeutic Change

Bandura (1977) originally proposed self-efficacy theory as a framework "for analyzing changes achieved in fearful and avoidant behavior" (p. 193). Psychotherapeutic treatments, whatever their form, were posited to reduce avoidant behavior by strengthening people's perceptions of self-efficacy for coping with threatening situations. Self-efficacy thus was a unifying theory, in that any and all behavior-therapeutic treatments were seen as altering avoidant behavior through a common mechanism.

The hypothesis that self-efficacy perceptions mediate the effects of therapeutic treatments has been investigated through extensive lines of research. This work has yielded a consistent set of findings that supports self-efficacy theory (reviewed in Bandura, 1986, 1988, in press; Williams, 1992). First, between-group differences in perceived self-efficacy resulting from alternative therapeutic treatments parallel group differences in posttreatment approach behavior, supporting the position that changes in self-efficacy perceptions mediate changes in behavior. Second, self-efficacy perceptions predict behavior within diverse treatment modalities, including modeling, participant modeling, and systematic desensitization, supporting the proposition that efficacy perceptions mediate the effects of these diverse treatment modalities. Third, self-efficacy perceptions can predict posttreatment behavior more accurately than does past behavior in treatment, which counters the argument that self-efficacy perceptions are merely epiphenomenal reflections of behavioral change. Fourth, self-efficacy perceptions significantly predict approach behavior after alternative cognitive mediators, such as anticipatory anxiety or expected danger, are statistically controlled for. Finally, varying whether subjects explicitly indicate their self-efficacy perceptions to the experimenter does not affect mean levels of performance or the strength of relations between self-efficacy and behavior, indicating that these results do not simply reflect demand characteristics associated with the completion of self-efficacy measures. Although initial self-efficacy research has largely focused on simple phobias (e.g., Bandura et al., 1977), subsequent work has investigated diverse fears and included extensive research on agoraphobia (Bandura, Adams, Hardy, & Howells, 1980; Williams, 1992).

In addition to the treatment of fears and avoidant behavior, investigators have applied self-efficacy theory over the years to numerous other behavior change issues. Self-efficacy perceptions have been found to mediate behavioral change in diverse domains in which an inadequate sense of one's capabilities may limit achievement and generate distress. A survey of these areas is beyond the scope of this chapter. Fortunately, we can refer the reader to valuable reviews of the role of efficacy perceptions in smoking cessation (DiClemente, 1986), cardiac rehabilitation (Lemanski, 1990), and other health-related outcomes that involve the adoption of health-related practices and the reduction of stress (Holden, 1991; O'Leary, 1992).

Enactive Mastery

A notable strength of self-efficacy theory is that it not only analyzes mediators of behavioral change but also provides guidelines for maximizing the effectiveness of psychotherapeutic treatments. For those who seek to foster behavioral change, self-efficacy theory has three fundamental messages. First, efficacy perceptions are the common pathway of behavioral change. To succeed, psychotherapeutic treatments—whatever their form—must bolster clients' beliefs in their capability to handle life's threats, challenges, and obstacles. Second, the most powerful way of strengthening self-efficacy cognitions is through behavior. Enactive mastery experiences, which provide firsthand success on challenging tasks, are the most influential source of efficacy information. Finally, although successful performances are a powerful influence, they alone do not guarantee success. It is the clients' interpretation and cognitive representation of their experiences that are crucial to self-efficacy appraisal.

These three points are most fully realized in "participant modeling" (Bandura et al., 1977; Rosenthal & Bandura, 1978) or "guided mastery" (Williams, 1990) treatments for phobias. In these procedures, the therapist first models the feared activities for the client. The appropriate coping behavior is then broken down into graded, attainable subtasks, which the therapist and client then perform together. If the client experiences difficulty with any of the specific subtasks, the therapist helps the client perform the task by using a variety of aids and techniques, such as "graduated time" procedures in which the client performs the subtask for a shorter and more tolerable time period (Bandura, Jeffrey, & Wright, 1974; Williams, 1990; Williams et al., 1984; see also Bandura, 1986, 1988). When the client feels sufficiently efficacious, however, the therapist gradually withdraws the aids, and the client performs independently. Finally, the therapist and client collaborate on designing additional self-directed mastery experiences to further enhance the strength and generality of the client's self-efficacy for engaging in the feared activities.

The guided mastery approach contrasts with treatment strategies that rely on exposure as the primary vehicle of change. As Bandura (1988) noted, many psychologists still contend that avoidance behavior in anxiety-related disorders is driven primarily by anticipatory anxiety. This view persists despite substantial evidence that perceived self-efficacy, not anticipatory fear, is the key variable in modifying avoidance (Williams, 1992).

The belief that avoidance is fear mediated leads to a heavy reliance on exposure and systematic desensitization treatments for reducing anxiety. In these treatments, clients expose themselves to a hierarchy of phobic situations, with the aim of reducing anxiety arousal at each successive step. It is reasoned that nonaversive exposures to feared stimuli will desensitize the client. By contrast, in the mastery treatments advocated by self-efficacy theory, clients engage in mastery experiences as rapidly as is possible. Performance maximization, not anxiety reduction, guides the interventions (Williams, 1990). Guided mastery treatments routinely have proven to be highly effective and, indeed, more effective than desensitization treatments in alleviating anticipatory anxiety and thoughts of danger and in raising levels of self-efficacy and approach behavior (Williams, 1990).

Perceived Self-Efficacy and Cognitive–Behavioral Treatment Strategies

Given the extensive evidence that self-efficacy perceptions mediate therapeutic change, it is surprising that perceived self-efficacy has not been targeted more explicitly in cognitive–behavioral therapy protocols. Although self-efficacy-based strategies are found in treatments for addictive behaviors (Marlatt & Gordon, 1985) and some approaches to anxiety disorders (Goldfried, 1986; Wilson, 1986), the self-efficacy perspective is somewhat less evident in many commonly used protocols for anxiety and depression (e.g., Barlow & Cerny, 1988; Beck, Rush, Shaw, & Emery, 1979). For example, analyses of cognitive therapy sessions for depression revealed that the behavioral mastery stressed by self-efficacy theory is not a primary component of these interventions (Startup & Shapiro, 1993).

This relative lack of a self-efficacy focus is puzzling in that, conceptually, self-efficacy theory and traditional cognitive–behavioral models are highly compatible. A defining feature of the cognitive–behavioral approach is that it places primary importance on cognitive variables in human dysfunction (Ingram & Scott, 1990). In this approach, both behavioral and cognitive procedures are used to alter target cognitions, with the goal of producing adaptive behavior change. Perhaps no cognitive variable is more critical to behavioral change than perceived self-efficacy. Thus, cognitive–behavioral techniques that explicitly target increases in the level, strength, and generality of self-efficacy perceptions may offer unique therapeutic benefit.

In this section, we consider relations between self-efficacy-based treatment strategies and traditional cognitive–behavioral methods. These approaches may have mutual benefits that have not yet been fully exploited. Specifically, self-efficacy theory suggests a specific class of cognitive activity for the therapist to target. Traditional cognitive strategies may help to maximize the effectiveness of efficacy-based mastery treatments (Mattick & Peters, 1988). In discussing these potential applications, we draw on methods used in well-known cognitive–behavioral treatment protocols (e.g., Barlow & Cerny, 1988; Beck & Emery, 1985; Beck et al., 1979; Meichenbaum, 1985).

Central to this analysis is the process of weighing experiences in forming judgments of personal efficacy. Efficacy perceptions are based on the cognitive processing of one's experiences (Bandura, 1977). Different clients may differentially cognize the same experience. Thus, in addition to providing enactive experiences, it is important that therapists monitor clients' interpretations of their performance (Wilson, 1986). The analysis of cognitive processes in efficacy appraisal is particularly germane to clinical disorders involving anxiety or depression. These disorders involve characteristic "profiles" (Beck & Weishaar, 1988; Ingram & Kendall, 1986), that is, cognitive schemas that are specific to the disorder. These schemas can distort the cognitive processing of self-efficacy information (Bandura, 1986). In the following paragraphs, we consider how cognitive strategies that target the processing of efficacy information might reduce such distortions and thereby help to enhance self-efficacy beliefs and coping efforts.

Self-Efficacy Education

One self-efficacy-based cognitive strategy would be to educate clients about the role of self-efficacy perceptions in human thought and action. Being fully aware of the causes and consequences of self-efficacy appraisals may better equip clients to combat underestimations of their own capabilities and to recognize the limitations they may place on themselves through low self-efficacy estimates. Such a process of self-efficacy education could supplement other cognitive strategies for dealing with anxiety or depression (Beck et al., 1979). The therapist might review, in nontechnical language, how perceived self-efficacy influences physiological arousal, affect, thinking, and action. Guided imagery (Beck et al., 1979), in which clients imagine approaching stimuli with thoughts of low or high self-efficacy, could be used to illustrate these effects of self-efficacy beliefs.

Educating clients about perceived self-efficacy may be most useful with regard to influences on efficacy judgment that are not obvious to the client. For example, self-efficacy perceptions are systematically related to the amount of time that remains before the performance of challenging tasks. As the time for performance draws near, perceived self-efficacy tends to diminish (Gilovich, Kerr, & Medvec, 1993; Kent & Gibbons, 1987). A client who is aware of this nonobvious tendency can better anticipate, recognize, and challenge any preperformance lessening of self-appraisals. Similarly, depressed clients may be unaware that depressed mood itself can lower efficacy judgments (Kavanagh & Bower, 1985; Salovey & Birnbaum, 1989). People who are aware of the potential impact of mood on cognition are less prone to such effects (Schwarz, 1990; Scott & Cervone, 1994).

Another educational tool would be to inform clients about the impact of implicit conceptions of ability on perceived self-efficacy and performance. Dweck and colleagues (Dweck & Leggett, 1988) found that individuals differ in their implicit theories of ability. Some view ability as an acquirable skill and see achievement situations as opportunities to learn. Such people seek challenges, tolerate mistakes, and maintain a strong sense of efficacy (Elliott & Dweck, 1988; Wood & Bandura, 1989a). Others implicitly view ability as a fixed entity and see achievement situations as tests of their ability. They interpret mistakes as failures that are diagnostic of low ability, feel less efficacious, worry about the personal consequences of performance, and perform more poorly (Elliott & Dweck, 1988; Wood & Bandura, 1989a). Clients who are made aware of their implicit beliefs about ability may be better equipped to counter maladaptive interpretations of performance and to maintain an optimistic sense of efficacy despite occasional setbacks.

Identifying Cognitive Errors

A fundamental feature of cognitive therapy is the identification of "cognitive errors" (Beck et al., 1979) that bias information processing. Therapists teach clients to question their potentially erroneous thoughts. The relevance of self-efficacy theory to such efforts is that the self-efficacy perspective identifies a critical aspect of thinking for therapists to target and explains how these cognitions influence coping efforts and achievement (Bandura, 1986).

Cognitive errors in anxiety and depression partly stem from the influence of schemas that are specific to each disorder. Anxious individuals generally possess schemas that overestimate risk and the magnitude of danger, underestimate their own ability to cope, and result in a "what if" catastrophic thinking style (Beck & Emery, 1985; Ingram & Kendall, 1987; Vasey & Borkovec, 1992). In contrast, depressed individuals possess schemas that are characterized by self-deprecatory thoughts, a sense of personal inadequacy, and a pessimistic view of the future (Abramson, Metalsky, & Alloy, 1989; Beck et al., 1979; Robins & Hayes, 1993). These schemas can influence the type of performance information that is most cognitively available (Ingram, 1984). Because self-efficacy judgments often reflect the environmental and personal information that most readily comes to mind (Cervone, 1989), anxiety- and depression-related schemas and associated errors may have a great impact on self-efficacy perceptions.

Various cognitive errors are relevant to a self-efficacy analysis of anxiety. In "overgeneralization" (Beck et al., 1979), clients infer inefficacy to perform an entire class of activities based on one bad performance. Therapists could counter such conclusions by directly questioning their underlying logic (e.g., by asking "Is this situation really the same kind as the one you failed in?"). In "dichotomous thinking" (Beck et al., 1979), clients see only two possibilities for themselves: faultless performance or complete failure. They thereby may overlook the full spectrum of potential outcomes and may fail to recognize that they are capable of at least moderately competent performance. "Temporal causality" beliefs (Beck et al., 1979) involve thoughts that something true in the past will always be true. This error may reflect biased, schema-driven retrieval processes, with clients overlooking recent therapeutic gains and basing their efficacy estimates on recall of long-established failures of the past (Goldfried, 1986). They thus may fail to recognize novel factors, such as newly acquired skills, that might enable them to perform more efficaciously. To combat this tendency, therapists could instruct clients to focus on encounters that were successful. Dwelling on past successes in meeting challenges can boost perceived coping efficacy and reduce anxiety (Rybarczyk & Auerbach, 1990). Combating these cognitive errors may foster more accurate efficacy appraisals in anxious clients (Wilson, 1986).

Many of the cognitive errors that have been cited also are relevant to self-efficacy appraisals in depression. In addition, depressed clients are susceptible to several other cognitive errors. For instance, they often infer excessive personal responsibility (Beck et al., 1979) for negative outcomes, perhaps reflecting more general biased attributional processing (Abramson, Seligman, & Teasdale, 1978; Peterson & Seligman, 1984). "Selective abstraction" (Beck et al., 1979) by depressed clients may lead them to believe that the only events that matter are failures. Both of these biases may generate perceptions of inefficacy that, in turn, could reduce clients' willingness to engage in goal-directed activities that can help to alleviate depressive states (Bandura, 1986; Lewinsohn, Hoberman, Teri, & Hautzinger, 1985). Reattribution techniques that target the process of self-efficacy appraisal may help clients to identify extraneous factors that contribute to failure and personal factors responsible for success (Beck et al., 1979) and thereby enhance perceived self-efficacy and motivation.

Educating the client about self-efficacy perceptions and identifying distortions in self-appraisal should not be the only ingredients in one's therapeutic package. It is essential, whenever possible, to ground treatments in performance-based techniques (Williams, 1990), which are more effective than cognitive procedures alone (Biran & Wilson, 1981). However, with some problems (e.g., social phobias), it may be difficult to create enactive procedures that fully capture aspects of the natural environment, yet ensure that clients experience mastery. Such problems may particularly benefit from a thorough analysis, and modification, of how clients process self-efficacy information.

GENERAL CONCLUSION AND FUTURE DIRECTIONS

A singular theme that emerges from this chapter concerns the interplay of self-efficacy theory and research. In the early days of self-efficacy theory, many commentators raised questions about the nature of self-efficacy perceptions and their role in social behavior and psychological change. These questions arose in a virtual empirical vacuum. Very few studies had directly tested the theory's basic hypotheses at the time of Bandura's initial statement. The times, however, have changed. Theoretical questions about perceived self-efficacy can now be addressed with a wealth of empirical findings. These results have helped to resolve contentious issues, have raised intriguing new questions, and have yielded a detailed picture of the role of self-efficacy perceptions in human functioning.

In considering directions for future research, one would find it useful to delineate the types of questions that have been addressed thoroughly in the past and then to ask whether alternative issues are deserving of greater attention. Much of the work we have reviewed has examined two general questions: (a) Do self-efficacy perceptions influence behavior and mediate the effects of therapeutic interventions? and (b) How do self-efficacy perceptions affect performance; that is, what are the mechanisms linking efficacy judgments and attainments? Much has been learned about both of these issues. Although future work can continue profitably in these same directions, it may be time for the field to expand its theoretical focus. Do they? and How? are not everything we ever wanted to know about perceived self-efficacy. Other basic questions include: When do people make self-efficacy judgments; that is, when are people most likely to dwell on their capabilities for performance? Where do self-efficacy perceptions affect behavior; in other words, do different situations or activities moderate the strength of relations between perceived self-efficacy and behavior? What determines the degree and patterning of generalizations in perceived self-efficacy from one situation to another? What is the relation between self-efficacy perceptions and enduring individual differences, and what processes link broad personality variables to perceived self-efficacy? These questions demand novel conceptualizations and methodologies. Their answers may provide a greatly enhanced understanding of the interrelations among the environment, thought, and behavior.

REFERENCES

Abramson, L. Y., Metalsky, G. I., & Alloy, L. B. (1989). Hopelessness depression: A theory-based subtype of depression. *Psychological Review, 96,* 358–372.

Abramson, L. Y., Seligman, M. E. P., & Teasdale, J. D. (1978). Learned helplessness in humans: Critique and reformulation. *Journal of Abnormal Psychology, 87*, 49–74.

Ahrens, A. H. (1987). Theories of depression: The role of goals and the self-evaluation process. *Cognitive Therapy and Research, 11*, 665–680.

Alden, L. (1986). Self-efficacy and causal attributions for social feedback. *Journal of Research in Personality, 20*, 460–473.

Baker, S. L., & Kirsch, I. (1991). Cognitive mediators of pain perception and tolerance. *Journal of Personality and Social Psychology, 61*, 504–510.

Bandura, A. (1977). Self-efficacy: Toward a unifying theory of behavioral change. *Psychological Review, 84*, 191–215.

Bandura, A. (1978). The self system in reciprocal determinism. *American Psychologist, 33*, 344–358.

Bandura, A. (1986). *Social foundations of thought and action: A social cognitive theory.* Englewood Cliffs, NJ: Prentice Hall.

Bandura, A. (1988). Self-efficacy conception of anxiety. *Anxiety Research, 1*, 77–98.

Bandura, A. (1989). Human agency in social cognitive theory. *American Psychologist, 44*, 1175–1184.

Bandura, A. (1991). The changing icons of personality psychology. In J. H. Cantor (Ed.), *Psychology at Iowa: Centennial essays* (pp. 117–139). Hillsdale, NJ: Erlbaum.

Bandura, A. (1993). Perceived self-efficacy in cognitive development and functioning. *Educational Psychologist, 28*, 117–148.

Bandura, A. (in press). *Self-efficacy: The exercise of control.* San Francisco: W. H. Freeman.

Bandura, A., & Adams, N. E. (1977). Analysis of self-efficacy theory of behavioral change. *Cognitive Therapy and Research, 1*, 287–308.

Bandura, A., Adams, N. E., & Beyer, J. (1977). Cognitive processes mediating behavior change. *Journal of Personality and Social Psychology, 35*, 125–139.

Bandura, A., Adams, N. E., Hardy, A. B., & Howells, G. N. (1980). Tests of the generality of self-efficacy theory. *Cognitive Therapy and Research, 4*, 39–66.

Bandura, A., & Cervone, D. (1983). Self-evaluative and self-efficacy mechanisms governing the motivational effects of goal systems. *Journal of Personality and Social Psychology, 45*, 1017–1028.

Bandura, A., & Cervone, D. (1986). Differential engagement of self-reactive influences in cognitive motivation. *Organizational Behavior and Human Decision Processes, 38*, 92–113.

Bandura, A., Cioffi, D., Taylor, C. B., & Brouillard, M. E. (1988). Perceived self-efficacy in coping with cognitive stressors and opioid activation. *Journal of Personality and Social Psychology, 55*, 479–488.

Bandura, A., Jeffrey, R. W., & Wright, C. L. (1974). Efficacy of participant modeling as a function of response induction aids. *Journal of Abnormal Psychology, 83*, 35–64.

Bandura, A., Reese, L., & Adams, N. E. (1982). Microanalysis of action and fear arousal as a function of differential levels of perceived self-efficacy. *Journal of Personality and Social Psychology, 43*, 5–21.

Bandura, A., & Simon, K. M. (1977). The role of proximal intentions in the self-regulation of refractory behavior. *Cognitive Therapy and Research, 1*, 177–193.

Bandura, A., Taylor, C. B., Williams, S. L., Mefford, I. N., & Barchas, J. D. (1985). Catecholamine secretion as a function of perceived coping self-efficacy. *Journal of Consulting and Clinical Psychology, 53*, 406–414.

Bandura, A., & Wood, R. (1989). Effect of perceived controllability and performance standards on self-regulation of complex decision-making. *Journal of Personality and Social Psychology, 56*, 805–814.

Barling, J., & Abel, M. (1983). Self-efficacy beliefs and performance. *Cognitive Therapy and Research, 7*, 265–272.

Barlow, D. H., & Cerny, J. A. (1988). *Psychological treatment of panic.* New York: Guilford Press.

Baron, R. M., & Kenny, D. A. (1986). The moderator–mediator variable distinction in social psychological research: Conceptual, strategic, and statistical considerations. *Journal of Personality and Social Psychology, 51*, 1173–1182.

Baumeister, R. (1991). *Meanings of life.* New York: Guilford Press.

Beck, A. T. (1976). *Cognitive therapy and the emotional disorders.* New York: International Universities Press.

Beck, A. T., & Emery, G. (1985). *Anxiety disorders and phobias: A cognitive perspective.* New York: Basic Books.

Beck, A. T., Rush, A. J., Shaw, B. F., & Emery, G. (1979). *Cognitive therapy of depression.* New York: Guilford Press.

Beck, A. T., & Weishaar, M. (1988). Cognitive therapy. In A. Freeman, K. M. Simon, L. E. Beutler, & H. Arkowitz (Eds.), *Comprehensive handbook of cognitive therapy* (pp. 21–36). New York: Plenum.

Bernier, M., & Avard, J. (1986). Self-efficacy, outcome, and attrition in a weight-reduction program. *Cognitive Therapy and Research, 10*, 319–338.

Berry, J. M., West, R. L., & Dennehey, D. M. (1989). Reliability and validity of the memory self-efficacy questionnaire. *Developmental Psychology, 25*, 701–713.

Betz, N. E., & Hackett, G. (1981). The relationship of career-related self-efficacy expectations to perceived career options in college men and women. *Journal of Counseling Psychology, 28*, 399–410.

Betz, N. E., & Hackett, G. (1986). Applications of self-efficacy theory to understanding career choice behavior. *Journal of Social and Clinical Psychology, 4*, 279–289.

Biran, M., & Wilson, G. T. (1981). Treatment of phobic disorders using cognitive and exposure methods: A self-efficacy analysis. *Journal of Consulting and Clinical Psychology, 49,* 886–899.

Borden, J. W., Clum, G. A., & Salmon, P. G. (1991). Mechanisms of change in the treatment of panic. *Cognitive Therapy and Research, 15,* 257–272.

Borkovec, T. D. (1978). Self-efficacy: Cause or reflection of behavioral change? In S. Rachman (Ed.), *Advances in behaviour research and therapy* (Vol. 1, pp. 163–170). New York: Pergamon Press.

Borrelli, B., & Mermelstein, R. (1994). Goal setting and behavior change in a smoking cessation program. *Cognitive Therapy and Research, 18,* 69–83.

Brown, I., Jr., & Inouye, D. K. (1978). Learned helplessness through modeling: The role of perceived similarity in competence. *Journal of Personality and Social Psychology, 36,* 900–908.

Cantor, N., & Kihlstrom, J. F. (1987). *Personality and social intelligence.* Englewood Cliffs, NJ: Prentice Hall.

Caspi, A., & Bem, D. J. (1990). Personality continuity and change across the life course. In L. A. Pervin (Ed.), *Handbook of personality: Theory and research* (pp. 549–575). New York: Guilford Press.

Cervone, D. (1985). Randomization tests to determine significance levels for microanalytic congruences between self-efficacy and behavior. *Cognitive Therapy and Research, 9,* 357–365.

Cervone, D. (1987). Chi-square analyses of self-efficacy data: A cautionary note. *Cognitive Therapy and Research, 11,* 709–714.

Cervone, D. (1989). Effects of envisioning future activities on self-efficacy judgments and motivation: An availability heuristic interpretation. *Cognitive Therapy and Research, 13,* 247–261.

Cervone, D. (1991). The two disciplines of personality psychology. *Psychological Science, 2,* 371–377.

Cervone, D. (1993). The role of self-referent cognitions in goal setting, motivation, and performance. In M. Rabinowitz (Ed.), *Cognitive science foundations of instruction* (pp. 57–95). Hillsdale, NJ: Erlbaum.

Cervone, D., Jiwani, N., & Wood, R. (1991). Goal-setting and the differential influence of self-regulatory processes on complex decision-making performance. *Journal of Personality and Social Psychology, 61,* 257–266.

Cervone, D., Kopp, D. A., Schaumann, L., & Scott, W. D. (1994). Mood, self-efficacy, and performance standards: Lower moods induce higher standards for performance. *Journal of Personality and Social Psychology, 67,* 499–512.

Cervone, D., & Palmer, B. W. (1990). Anchoring biases and the perseverance of self-efficacy beliefs. *Cognitive Therapy and Research, 14,* 401–416.

Cervone, D., & Peake, P. K. (1986). Anchoring, efficacy, and action: The influence of judgmental heuristics on self-efficacy judgments and behavior. *Journal of Personality and Social Psychology, 50,* 492–501.

Cervone, D., & Williams, S. L. (1992). Social cognitive theory and personality. In G. Caprara & G. L. Van Heck (Eds.), *Modern personality psychology: Critical reviews and new directions* (pp. 200–252). New York: Harvester Wheatsheaf.

Cervone, D., & Wood, R. (1993). *Goals, feedback, and the differential influence of self-regulatory processes on a complex decision task.* Unpublished manuscript, University of Illinois at Chicago.

Chaiken, S., Liberman, A., & Eagly, A. H. (1989). Heuristic and systematic information processing within and beyond the persuasion context. In J. S. Uleman & J. A. Bargh (Eds.), *Unintended thought* (pp. 212–252). New York: Guilford Press.

Chambless, D. L., & Gracely, E. J. (1989). Fear of fear and the anxiety disorders. *Cognitive Therapy and Research, 13*, 9–20.

Collins, J. L. (1982, March). *Self-efficacy and ability in achievement behavior.* Paper presented at the annual meeting of the American Educational Research Association, New York.

Condiotte, M. M., & Lichtenstein, E. (1981). Self-efficacy and relapse in smoking cessation programs. *Journal of Consulting and Clinical Psychology, 49*, 648–658.

Coopersmith, S. (1967). *The antecedents of self-esteem.* San Francisco: W. H. Freeman.

Cutrona, C. E., & Troutman, B. R. (1986). Social support, infant temperament, and parenting self-efficacy: A mediational model of postpartum depression. *Child Development, 57*, 1507–1518.

Davis, F. W., & Yates, B. T. (1982). Self-efficacy expectancies versus outcome expectancies as determinants of performance deficits and depressive affect. *Cognitive Therapy and Research, 6*, 23–35.

Devins, G. M. (1992). Social cognitive analysis of recovery from a lapse after smoking cessation. *Journal of Consulting and Clinical Psychology, 60*, 29–31.

DiClemente, C. C. (1986). Self-efficacy and the addictive behaviors. *Journal of Social and Clinical Psychology, 4*, 302–315.

DiClemente, C. C., Prochaska, J. O., & Gilbertini, M. (1985). Self-efficacy and the stages of self-change of smoking. *Cognitive Therapy and Research, 9*, 181–200.

Dweck, C. S., & Leggett, E. L. (1988). A social-cognitive approach to motivation and personality. *Psychological Review, 95*, 256–273.

Eastman, C., & Marzillier, J. S. (1984). Theoretical and methodological difficulties in Bandura's self-efficacy theory. *Cognitive Therapy and Research, 8*, 213–229.

Elliott, E. S., & Dweck, C. S. (1988). Goals: An approach to motivation and achievement. *Journal of Personality and Social Psychology, 54*, 5–12.

Ellsworth, P. C., & Smith, C. A. (1988). From appraisal to emotion: Differences among unpleasant feelings. *Motivation and Emotion, 12*, 271–302.

Eysenck, H. J. (1978). Expectations as causal elements in behavioural change. *Advances in Behaviour Research and Therapy, 1*, 171–175.

Feltz, D. L. (1982). Path analysis of the causal elements in Bandura's theory of self-efficacy and an anxiety-based model of avoidance behavior. *Journal of Personality and Social Psychology, 42*, 764–781.

Feltz, D. L. (1988). Gender differences in the causal elements of self-efficacy on a high avoidance motor task. *Journal of Sport and Exercise Psychology, 10*, 151–166.

Gilovich, T., Kerr, M., & Medvec, V. H. (1993). Effect of temporal perspective on subjective confidence. *Journal of Personality and Social Psychology, 64*, 552–560.

Glynn, S. M., & Ruderman, A. J. (1986). The development and validation of an eating self-efficacy scale. *Cognitive Therapy and Research, 10*, 403–420.

Goldfried, M. R. (1986). Self-control skills for the treatment of anxiety disorders. In B. F. Shaw, Z. V. Segal, T. M. Vallis, & F. E. Cashman (Eds.), *Anxiety disorders: Psychological and biological perspectives* (pp. 165–178). New York: Plenum.

Haaga, D. A. F., & Stewart, B. L. (1992a). How do you know an act when you see one? *Journal of Consulting and Clinical Psychology, 60*, 32–33.

Haaga, D. A. F., & Stewart, B. L. (1992b). Self-efficacy for recovery from a lapse after smoking cessation. *Journal of Consulting and Clinical Psychology, 60*, 24–28.

Hays, R. D., & Ellickson, P. L. (1990). How generalizable are adolescents' beliefs about pro-drug pressures and resistance self-efficacy? *Journal of Applied Social Psychology, 20*, 321–340.

Henry, A. E., Ruderman, A. J., & Cervone, D. (1993, May). *Self-efficacy judgments and bulimic-behavior change.* Paper presented at the annual convention of the Midwestern Psychological Association, Chicago.

Higgins, E. T. (1990). Personality, social psychology, and person–situation relations: Standards and knowledge activation as a common language. In L. A. Pervin (Ed.), *Handbook of personality: Theory and research* (pp. 301–338). New York: Guilford Press.

Hill, G. J. (1989). An unwillingness to act: Behavioral appropriateness, situational constraint, and self-efficacy in shyness. *Journal of Personality, 57*, 871–890.

Holden, G. (1991). The relationship of self-efficacy appraisals to subsequent health related outcomes: A meta-analysis. *Social Work in Health Care, 16*, 53–93.

Holroyd, K. A., Penzien, D. B., Hursey, K. G., Tobin, D. L., Rogers, L., Holm, J. E., Marcille, P. J., Hall, J. R., & Chila, A. G. (1984). Change mechanisms in EMG biofeedback training: Cognitive changes underlying improvements in tension headache. *Journal of Consulting and Clinical Psychology, 52*, 1039–1053.

Ingram, R. E. (1984). Toward an information processing analysis of depression. *Cognitive Therapy and Research, 8*, 443–478.

Ingram, R. E., & Kendall, P. C. (1986). Cognitive clinical psychology: Implications of an information processing perspective. In R. E. Ingram (Ed.), *Information processing approaches to clinical psychology* (pp. 3–21). San Diego, CA: Academic Press.

Ingram, R. E., & Kendall, P. C. (1987). The cognitive side of anxiety. *Cognitive Therapy and Research, 11,* 523–536.

Ingram, R., & Scott, W. D. (1990). Cognitive behavior therapy. In A. S. Bellack, M. Hersen, & A. E. Kazdin (Eds.), *International handbook of behavior modification* (2nd ed., pp. 53–65). New York: Plenum.

Jacobs, B., Prentice-Dunn, S., & Rogers, R. W. (1984). Understanding persistence: An interface of control theory and self-efficacy theory. *Basic and Applied Social Psychology, 5,* 333–347.

Janoff-Bullman, R., & Brickman, P. (1982). Expectations and what people learn from failure. In F. H. Kanfer & A. P. Goldstein (Eds.), *Helping people change* (2nd ed., pp. 334–389). New York: Pergamon.

Jensen, M. P., Turner, J. A., & Romano, J. M. (1991). Self-efficacy and outcome expectancies: Relationship to chronic pain coping strategies and adjustment. *Pain, 44,* 263–269.

Kahneman, D., & Miller, D. T. (1986). Norm theory: Comparing reality to its alternatives. *Psychological Review, 93,* 136–153.

Kavanagh, D. J., & Bower, G. H. (1985). Mood and self-efficacy: Impact of joy and sadness on perceived capabilities. *Cognitive Therapy and Research, 9,* 507–525.

Kazdin, A. E. (1978). Covert modeling—Therapeutic application of imagined rehearsal. In J. L. Singer & K. S. Pope (Eds.), *The power of human imagination: New methods in psychotherapy. Emotions, personality, and psychotherapy* (pp. 255–278). New York: Plenum.

Kelley, H. H. (1972). Attribution in social interaction. In E. E. Jones, D. E. Kanouse, H. H. Kelley, R. E. Nisbett, S. Valins, & B. Weiner (Eds.), *Attribution: Perceiving the causes of behavior* (pp. 151–174). Morristown, NJ: General Learning Press.

Kendall, P. C., & Hollon, S. D. (1981). Assessing self-referent speech: Methods in the measurement of self-statements. In P. C. Kendall & S. D. Hollon (Eds.), *Assessment strategies for cognitive-behavioral interventions* (pp. 85–118). San Diego, CA: Academic Press.

Kent, G., & Gibbons, R. (1987). Self-efficacy and the control of anxious cognitions. *Journal of Behavior Therapy and Experimental Psychiatry, 18,* 33–40.

Kirsch, I. (1980). "Microanalytic" analyses of efficacy expectations as predictors of performance. *Cognitive Therapy and Research, 4,* 259–262.

Kirsch, I. (1985). Self-efficacy and expectancy: Old wine with new labels. *Journal of Personality and Social Psychology, 49,* 824–830.

Lazarus, R. S. (1991). *Emotion and adaptation.* New York: Oxford University Press.

Lee, C. (1984a). Accuracy of efficacy and outcome expectations in predicting performance in a simulated assertiveness task. *Cognitive Therapy and Research, 8,* 37–48.

Lee, C. (1984b). Efficacy expectations and outcome expectations as predictors of performance in a snake-handling task. *Cognitive Therapy and Research, 8,* 509–516.

Lee, C. (1985). Efficacy expectations as predictors of performance: Meaningful measures of microanalytic match. *Cognitive Therapy and Research, 9,* 367–370.

Lemanski, K. M. (1990). The use of self-efficacy in cardiac rehabilitation. *Progress in Cardiovascular Nursing, 53,* 114–117.

Lent, R. W., & Hackett, G. (1987). Career self-efficacy: Empirical status and future directions. *Journal of Vocational Behavior, 30,* 347–382.

Lewin, K., Dembo, T., Festinger, L., & Sears, P. S. (1944). Level of aspiration. In J. M. Hunt (Ed.), *Personality and the behavior disorders* (Vol. 1, pp. 333–378). New York: Ronald Press.

Lewinsohn, P. M., Hoberman, H. M., Teri, L., & Hautzinger, M. (1985). An integrative theory of depression. In S. Reiss & R. R. Bootzin (Eds.), *Theoretical issues in behavior therapy* (pp. 331–359). San Diego, CA: Academic Press.

Litt, M. D. (1988). Self-efficacy and perceived control: Cognitive mediators of pain tolerance. *Journal of Personality and Social Psychology, 54,* 149–160.

Locke, E. A., & Latham, G. P. (1990). *A theory of goal setting and task performance.* Englewood Cliffs, NJ: Prentice Hall.

Maddux, J. E., Norton, L. W., & Stoltenberg, C. D. (1986). Self-efficacy expectancy, outcome expectancy, and outcome value: Relative effects on behavioral intentions. *Journal of Personality and Social Psychology, 51,* 783–789.

Mahoney, M. J. (1977). *Cognition and behavior modification.* Cambridge, MA: Ballinger.

Major, B., Cozzarelli, C., Sciacchitano, A. M., Cooper, M. L., Testa, M., & Mueller, P. M. (1990). Perceived social support, self-efficacy, and adjustment to abortion. *Journal of Personality and Social Psychology, 59,* 452–463.

Manning, M. M., & Wright, T. L. (1983). Self-efficacy expectancies, outcome expectancies, and the persistence of pain control in childbirth. *Journal of Personality and Social Psychology, 45,* 421–431.

Marlatt, G. A., & Gordon, J. (Eds.). (1985). *Relapse prevention.* New York: Guilford Press.

Mattick, R. P., & Peters, L. (1988). Treatment of severe social phobia: Effects of guided exposure with and without cognitive restructuring. *Journal of Consulting and Clinical Psychology, 56,* 251–260.

McAuley, E. (1985). Modeling and self-efficacy: A test of Bandura's model. *Journal of Sport Psychology, 7,* 283–295.

McAuley, E., Duncan, T. E., & McElroy, M. (1989). Self-efficacy cognitions and causal attributions for children's motor performance: An exploratory investigation. *The Journal of Genetic Psychology, 150,* 65–73.

McAuley, E., & Jacobsen, L. (1991). Self-efficacy and exercise participation in sedentary adult females. *American Journal of Health Promotion, 5,* 185–207.

Meichenbaum, D. (1985). *Stress inoculation training.* New York: Pergamon Press.

Miller, G. A., Galanter, E., & Pribram, K. H. (1960). *Plans and the structure of behavior.* New York: Holt, Rinehart & Winston.

Mischel, W. (1968). *Personality and assessment.* New York: Wiley.

Mischel, W. (1973). Toward a cognitive social learning reconceptualization of personality. *Psychological Review, 80*, 252–283.

Mischel, W. (1993). *Introduction to personality.* San Diego, CA: Harcourt Brace Jovanovich.

O'Leary, A. (1992). Self-efficacy and health: Behavioral and stress-physiological mediation. *Cognitive Therapy and Research, 16*, 229–245.

Palmer, B. W., & Cervone, D. (1992). *Experience moderates relations among perceived self-efficacy, negative outcome expectations, and avoidance.* Paper presented at the annual convention of the American Psychological Society, San Diego, CA.

Parks, C. W., & Hollon, S. D. (1988). Cognitive assessment. In A. S. Bellack & M. Hersen (Eds.), *Behavioral assessment: A practical handbook* (3rd ed., pp. 161–212). New York: Pergamon Press.

Peake, P. K., & Cervone, D. (1989). Sequence anchoring and self-efficacy: Primacy effects in the consideration of possibilities. *Social Cognition, 7*, 31–50.

Peterson, C., & Seligman, M. E. P. (1984). Causal explanations as a risk factor for depression. *Psychological Review, 91*, 347–374.

Peterson, C., & Stunkard, A. J. (1992). Cognates of personal control: Locus of control, self-efficacy, and explanatory style. *Applied and Preventive Psychology, 1*, 111–117.

Rachman, S. (1978). Perceived self-efficacy: Editorial introduction. *Advances in Behaviour Research and Therapy, 1*, 137.

Rehm, L. P. (1977). A self-control model of depression. *Behavior Therapy, 8*, 787–804.

Reiss, S. (1991). Expectancy model of fear, anxiety, and panic. *Clinical Psychology Review, 11*, 141–153.

Robins, C. J., & Hayes, A. M. (1993). An appraisal of cognitive therapy. *Journal of Consulting and Clinical Psychology, 61,* 205–214.

Rodin, J. (1990). Control by any other name: Definitions, concepts, and processes. In K. W. Schaie, J. Rodin, & C. Schooler (Eds.), *Self-directedness: Causes and effects throughout the life course.* Hillsdale, NJ: Erlbaum.

Rosenthal, T. L., & Bandura, A. (1978). Psychological modeling: Theory and practice. In S. L. Garfield & A. E. Bergin (Eds.), *Handbook of psychotherapy and behavior change* (2nd ed., pp. 621–658). New York: Wiley.

Rotter, J. B. (1954). *Social learning and clinical psychology.* Englewood Cliffs, NJ: Prentice Hall.

Rotter, J. B. (1992). Some comments on the "Cognates of personal control." *Applied and Preventive Psychology, 1*, 127–129.

Rybarczyk, B. D., & Auerbach, S. M. (1990). Reminiscence interviews as stress management interventions for older patients undergoing surgery. *Gerontological Society of America, 30*, 522–528.

Salovey, P., & Birnbaum, D. (1989). Influence of mood on health-relevant cognitions. *Journal of Personality and Social Psychology, 57*, 539–551.

Sarason, I. G. (1975). Anxiety and self-preoccupation. In I. G. Sarason & D. C. Spielberger (Eds.), *Stress and anxiety* (Vol. 2, pp. 27–44). Washington, DC: Hemisphere.

Sarason, I. G., Sarason, B. R., & Pierce, G. R. (1990). Anxiety, cognitive interference, and performance. *Journal of Social Behavior and Personality, 5,* 1–18.

Schneider, J. A., O'Leary, A., & Agras, W. S. (1987). The role of perceived self-efficacy in recovery from bulimia: A preliminary examination. *Behavior Research and Therapy, 25,* 429–432.

Schunk, D. H. (1989). Self-efficacy and academic motivation. *Educational Psychologist, 26,* 207–231.

Schwarz, N. (1990). Feelings as information: Informational and motivational functions of affective states. In E. T. Higgins & R. N. Sorrentino (Eds.), *Handbook of motivation and cognition: Foundations of social behavior* (Vol. 2, pp. 527–561). New York: Guilford Press.

Schwarz, N., Bless, H., Strack, F., Klumpp, G., Rittenauer-Schatka, H., & Simons, A. (1991). Ease of retrieval as information: Another look at the availability heuristic. *Journal of Personality and Social Psychology, 61,* 195–202.

Scott, W. D., & Cervone, D. (1994). *The informative function of negative mood in setting performance standards.* Unpublished manuscript, University of Illinois at Chicago.

Segal, Z. V., & Shaw, B. F. (1988). Cognitive assessment: Issues and methods. In K. S. Dobson (Ed.), *Handbook of cognitive behavioral therapies* (pp. 39–81). New York: Guilford Press.

Seligman, M. E. P. (1992). Power and powerlessness: Comments on "Cognates of personal control." *Applied and Preventive Psychology, 1,* 119–120.

Sexton, T. L., & Tuckman, B. W. (1991). Self-efficacy beliefs and behavior: The role of self-efficacy and outcome expectations over time. *Personality and Individual Differences, 12,* 725–736.

Sexton, T. L., Tuckman, B. W., & Crehan, K. (1992). An investigation of the patterns of self-efficacy, outcome expectations, outcome value, and performance across trials. *Cognitive Therapy and Research, 16,* 329–348.

Shadel, W. G., & Cervone, D. (1993). The Big Five versus nobody? *American Psychologist, 48,* 8–10.

Sherer, M., Maddux, J. E., Mercandante, B., Prentice-Dunn, S., Jacobs, B., & Rogers, R. W. (1982). The self-efficacy scale: Construction and validation. *Psychological Reports, 51,* 663–671.

Simon, H. A. (1983). *Reason and human affairs.* Stanford, CA: Stanford University Press.

Smith, C. A., & Lazarus, R. S. (1990). Emotion and adaptation. In L. A. Pervin (Ed.), *Handbook of personality: Theory and research* (pp. 609–637). New York: Guilford Press.

Smith, R. E. (1989). Effects of coping skills training on generalized self-efficacy and locus of control. *Journal of Personality and Social Psychology, 56,* 228–233.

Snyder, M., & Ickes, W. (1985). Personality and social behavior. In G. Lindzey & E. Aronson (Eds.), *Handbook of social psychology* (pp. 883–947). New York: Random House.

Startup, M., & Shapiro, D. A. (1993). Dimensions of cognitive therapy for depression: A confirmatory analysis of session ratings. *Cognitive Therapy and Research, 17*, 139–152.

Stock, J., & Cervone, D. (1990). Proximal goal-setting and self-regulatory processes. *Cognitive Therapy and Research, 14*, 483–489.

Stotland, S., & Zuroff, D. C. (1991). Relations between multiple measures of dieting self-efficacy and weight change in a behavioral weight control program. *Behavior Therapy, 22*, 47–59.

Teasdale, J. D. (1978). Self-efficacy: Toward a unifying theory of behavioural change? *Advances in Behaviour Research and Therapy, 1*, 211–215.

Turk, D. C., & Salovey, P. (1985). Cognitive structures, cognitive processes, and cognitive–behavior modification: I. Client issues. *Cognitive Therapy and Research, 9*, 1–17.

Tversky, A., & Kahneman, D. (1973). Availability: A heuristic for judging frequency and probability. *Cognitive Psychology, 5*, 207–232.

Tversky, A., & Kahneman, D. (1974). Judgment under uncertainty: Heuristics and biases. *Science, 185*, 1123–1131.

Vallacher, R. R., & Wegner, D. M. (1987). What do people think they're doing? Action identification and human behavior. *Psychological Review, 94*, 3–15.

Vasey, M. W., & Borkovec, T. D. (1992). A catastrophizing assessment of worrisome thoughts. *Cognitive Therapy and Research, 16*, 505–520.

Vroom, V. (1964). *Work and motivation.* New York: Wiley.

Wegner, D. M., Vallacher, R. R., Macomber, G., Wood, R., & Arps, K. (1984). The emergence of action. *Journal of Personality and Social Psychology, 46*, 269–279.

Weinberg, R. S., Gould, D., & Jackson, A. (1979). Expectations and performance: An empirical test of Bandura's self-efficacy theory. *Journal of Sport Psychology, 1*, 320–331.

Weinberg, R. S., Gould, D., Yukelson, D., & Jackson, A. (1981). The effect of preexisting and manipulated self-efficacy on a competitive muscular endurance task. *Journal of Sport Psychology, 4*, 345–354.

Weiner, B. (1985). An attributional theory of achievement motivation and emotion. *Psychological Review, 92*, 548–573.

Williams, S. L. (1990). Guided mastery treatment of agoraphobia: Beyond stimulus exposure. *Progress in Behavior Modification, 26*, 89–121.

Williams, S. L. (1992). Perceived self-efficacy and phobic disability. In R. Schwarzer (Ed.), *Self-efficacy: Thought control of action* (pp. 149–176). New York: Hemisphere.

Williams, S. L., Dooseman, G., & Kleifield, E. (1984). Comparative effectiveness of guided mastery and exposure treatments for intractable phobias. *Journal of Consulting and Clinical Psychology, 52,* 505–518.

Williams, S. L., & Kinney, P. J. (1991). Performance and nonperformance strategies for coping with acute pain: The role of perceived self-efficacy, expected outcomes, and attention. *Cognitive Therapy and Research, 15,* 1–19.

Williams, S. L., Kinney, P. J., & Falbo, J. (1989). Generalization of therapeutic changes in agoraphobia: The role of perceived self-efficacy. *Journal of Consulting and Clinical Psychology, 57,* 436–442.

Williams, S. L., & Rappoport, A. (1983). Cognitive treatment in the natural environment for agoraphobics. *Behavior Therapy, 14,* 299–313.

Williams, S. L., Turner, S. M., & Peer, D. F. (1985). Guided mastery and performance desensitization treatments for severe acrophobia. *Journal of Consulting and Clinical Psychology, 53,* 237–247.

Williams, S. L., & Watson, N. (1985). Perceived danger and perceived self-efficacy as cognitive determinants of acrophobic behavior. *Behavior Therapy, 16,* 136–146.

Wilson, G. T. (1978). The importance of being theoretical: A commentary on Bandura's "Self-efficacy: Towards a unifying theory of behavioral change." *Advances in Behaviour Research and Therapy, 1,* 217–230.

Wilson, G. T. (1986). Psychosocial treatment of anxiety disorders. In B. F. Shaw, Z. V. Segal, T. M. Vallis, & F. E. Cashman (Eds.), *Anxiety disorders: Psychological and biological perspectives* (pp. 149–163). New York: Plenum.

Wine, J. (1971). Test anxiety and direction of attention. *Psychological Bulletin, 76,* 92–104.

Wolpe, J. (1978). Self-efficacy theory and psychotherapeutic change: A square peg for a round hole. *Advances in Behaviour Research and Therapy, 1,* 231–236.

Wood, R., & Bandura, A. (1989a). Impact of conceptions of ability on self-regulatory mechanisms and complex decision making. *Journal of Personality and Social Psychology, 56,* 407–415.

Wood, R., & Bandura, A. (1989b). Social cognitive theory of organizational management. *Academy of Management Review, 14,* 407–415.

Wood, R., Bandura, A., & Bailey, T. (1990). Mechanisms governing organizational productivity in complex decision-making environments. *Organizational Behavior and Human Decision Processes, 46,* 181–201.

Wright, J., & Mischel, W. (1982). Influence of affect on cognitive social learning person variables. *Journal of Personality and Social Psychology, 43,* 901–914.

14

ATTRIBUTION THEORY: CLINICAL APPLICATIONS

GERALD I. METALSKY, REBECCA S. LAIRD, PAMELA M. HECK, and
THOMAS E. JOINER, JR.

In this chapter, we examine attributional theories and their implications for cognitive and behavioral interventions. We first turn to classic
work on *misattribution* theory and therapy (e.g., Davison, Tsujimoto, &
Glaros, 1973; Storms & Nisbett, 1970) and then turn to more recent work
on *reattribution* approaches (e.g., Forsterling, 1988; Ickes & Layden, 1978).
In addition, we consider theory and research that incorporates attributional
therapy as one element of a broader approach to treatment (e.g., Beck,
Rush, Shaw, & Emery, 1979). For each approach, we first discuss the theoretical framework from which the approach was derived and then review
the empirical work in that area. In addition, we examine attribution therapy as it pertains to a variety of behavioral problems and disorders (e.g.,
insomnia, depression, and marital conflict). Throughout, we discuss limitations with current research and implications for future research on attributional approaches to cognitive and behavioral therapy.

Preparation of this chapter was supported by a research grant from Lawrence University to G. I.
Metalsky. We wish to thank Greg Blume for his valuable comments and suggestions.

MISATTRIBUTION VERSUS REATTRIBUTION

We first consider attempts to formulate clinical interventions that focus directly on attributional manipulation and change. These clinical applications have primarily involved theory and research in two areas: misattribution and reattribution training (see Forsterling, 1988).

Misattribution and reattribution training differ in several important respects. Misattribution training attempts to alter a person's causal attributions about his or her own internal physiological states. Reattribution training, in contrast, involves manipulating a person's causal attributions about environmental outcomes (e.g., social rejection) and behavior (e.g., avoiding others). This distinction reflects the difference in the theoretical models and research paradigms out of which misattribution and reattribution training has arisen.

MISATTRIBUTION THEORY AND RESEARCH

Misattribution therapy is based on an attributional reformulation (Ross, Rodin, & Zimbardo, 1969) of Schachter and Singer's (1962; Schachter, 1964) two-factor theory of emotion. This theory asserts that emotional states arise in a person from an interaction between interoceptive peripheral physiological arousal and the cognized external source associated with that arousal. The person's attribution of his or her arousal to the situational source is what gives rise to emotions, motives, and concomitant behaviors. For example, a man begins to give a speech to his colleagues. He becomes aware that his heart is pounding, his skin feels clammy, and his mouth is dry. He attributes these physiological symptoms to the fact that he is worried about how his speech will be received by the audience and that he is afraid that he will not be able to convince them of his points. Thus, his attribution of his internal physical arousal (pounding heart, clammy skin, and dry mouth) to the external situation (giving a speech to his colleagues) results in an emotion (fear). The intensity of the physiological arousal determines the corresponding degree of emotional intensity, and the particular attribution determines the nature or quality of the emotion that is experienced. The attributional process may sometimes be automatic and at other times may result from a conscious causal search initiated by the person.

In his review of the misattribution research, Reisenzein (1983) predicted that unpleasant emotional arousal could be attenuated if interoceptive physiological arousal (and its feedback) was itself attenuated or blocked. One set of studies proceeding from this prediction involved reducing physiological arousal by giving adrenergic-receptor blocking agents to clinical populations, to diminish unpleasant affective experiences (McMillin, 1973; Tyrer & Lader, 1974). Reisenzein (1983) concluded that despite reductions in physiological arousal among nonclinical subjects, investigators did not obtain corresponding amelioration of unpleasant emotional states across a wide variety of situations. However, results were more promising with clinical subjects suffering from moderate to severe anxiety problems. Anxious subjects receiving beta-blocking drugs rather than a placebo reported a significant decrease in subjective feelings of tension and anxiety. Of importance from the misattribution perspective, this effect was most pronounced among subjects for whom physiological symptoms were of primary importance in their experience of anxiety (Lader & Tyrer, 1975). Thus, pharmacotherapy for such people seen in clinical settings may be a useful adjunct in an overall misattribution treatment plan.

An additional class of clinical interventions involves relaxation training techniques in a coping imagery approach to systematic desensitization (Meichenbaum, 1977). In contrast to classical systematic desensitization, clients in the coping imagery procedure are encouraged to continue in the desensitization hierarchy even when feeling anxious. They then use relaxation techniques to reduce physiological arousal as they proceed with the anxiety-arousing imagery. This imagery coping procedure has an advantage over classical systematic desensitization: In naturally occurring fearful situations, an anxiety-prone person is likely to experience and have to cope with anxiety. Studies by Kazdin (1974) and Meichenbaum (1972) showed this coping approach to systematic desensitization to be superior to classical approaches in enabling people to cope more effectively with their own interoceptive physiological arousal in real-life fearful situations and to more easily attenuate their own arousal by means of relaxation techniques.

Another application of Schachter and Singer's (1962) two-factor model in misattribution studies involves arousal states that occur sequentially. In some naturally occurring situations, a person who is already in a state of physiological arousal after exposure to one set of stimuli may in turn experience an increase in the intensity of that arousal when experiencing a second set of stimuli. If the person has not already attributed his or her arousal to the first set of events, he or she may attribute the combined arousal from both situations solely to factors associated with the second situation. For example, imagine a couple who has just viewed a frightening horror film and who then return to the woman's apartment. She feels physiologically aroused and attributes this to the fact that she is alone with her date in the privacy of her apartment. She therefore makes an inference that she is sexually aroused without due consideration to the arousal generated by the frightening movie. Of course, this may be a veridical inference. However, Hoon, Wincze, and Hoon (1977) found that prior exposure to fear-eliciting stimuli was associated with heightened sexual arousal in female subjects. Thus, arousal to fear-eliciting stimuli may be transferred to perceptions of sexual excitation if the appropriate situational cues are present.

Laboratory studies in which this phenomenon is assessed typically use the excitation-transfer paradigm developed by Zillman (1971). Reisenzein and Gattinger (1982) found that antecedent physical exercise increased subjects' negative affective states when the subjects read negative self-referential statements. Rimm, Kennedy, Miller, and Tchida (1971) found that snake phobics' ability to master steps of a graded behavioral approach hierarchy was diminished when these subjects were already in a state of arousal. This phenomenon illustrates the importance of the relaxation component in behavioral interventions of this sort. Cognitive interventions, too, ought to take account of the possibility of excitation-transfer phenomena when processing a person's attributions for events. Individuals might be induced to misattribute arousal from emotional factors to antecedent neutral situational factors.

A third line of misattribution studies yielded by Schachter and Singer's (1962) two-factor model involves examining the impact on emotional arousal when a person is induced to misattribute physiological arousal to a salient neutral source that is not associated with arousal-causing factors. For example, Ross et al. (1969) suggested providing phobic clients with a neutral explanation for physical symptoms when they encountered the phobic stimulus (e.g., convincing an acrophobic that his or her symptoms had actually resulted from an optical effect associated with heights). In a classic study, Storms and Nisbett (1970) used a drug-inducing arousal manipulation in which they attempted to treat insomniacs with a placebo and misattribution therapy. Subjects' attribution of arousal was manipulated by being told either that the pills had an arousing effect or that they had a relaxing effect. Insomniacs fell asleep more quickly in the arousal condition than in the relaxation condition. Thus, insomniacs were able to fall asleep more quickly if they were provided with environmental cues that allowed them to explain their insomnia as being caused by an external neutral stimulus.

The drug-induced arousal paradigm has been used successfully in misattribution interventions in a variety of other clinical conditions, including anxiety (Erdmann & Janke, 1978), anger (Erdmann & Janke, 1978), affective reactions in psychotherapy (Hoehn-Saric et al., 1974) smoking abstinence (Barefoot & Girodo, 1972), and shy behavior (Brodt & Zimbardo, 1981). However, other studies have failed to replicate this effect for many clinical conditions including insomnia (Bootzin, Herman, & Nicassio, 1976; Kellogg & Baron, 1975), anxiety (Holroyd, 1978; Singerman, Borkovek, & Baron, 1976), and smoking abstinence (Chambliss & Murray, 1979).

In our view, one possible explanation for these mixed findings is that the efficacy of misattribution training may vary as a function of the attributions made for initial improvement in symptoms. The classic study by Davison and Valins (1969) may be instructive in this context. Davison and Valins suggested that external attributions for therapeutic change used in misattribution training might not be associated with lasting benefit. They designed an experimental analogue of psychoactive drug therapy to test the hypothesis that a behavioral change that was attributed to one's own internal efforts, rather than to an external cause (e.g., a psychoactive drug), might be maintained for a longer duration posttreatment. In this study, subjects received a placebo after being administered an experimental shock-pain-tolerance test. The test was then administered again but at half the previous intensity. Half of the subjects were subsequently told that they had actually received a placebo, whereas the other half were told that they had received a drug that had helped them tolerate the shock. Subjects in the first condition, who attributed their behavior change in tolerating the second set of shocks to their own efforts, reported that they believed these shocks to be less painful and tolerated significantly more pain at Time 2 than did subjects who were provided with external attribution information.

In a further and more direct test of the hypothesis that internal effort attributions would be associated with greater posttreatment maintenance than external attributions, Davison et al. (1973) manipulated insomniacs' attributions for therapeutic improvement in their sleep disturbance in a controlled field experiment. Subjects were given chloralhydrate and taught relaxation and scheduling procedures. After treatment, half of the subjects, who were in the internal-attribution condition, were told that the sleeping pills were too weak to have caused any of their experienced improvement in sleep behavior. The remaining subjects (in the external-attribution condition) were told that they had been given an "optimal dosage" of the drug. All subjects were then told to discontinue drug usage but to continue the relaxation and scheduling procedures for another week. The greatest posttreatment maintenance of therapeutic gain was found in the subjects who believed that their own efforts in following the relaxation and scheduling program were responsible for their improvement, rather than in subjects who attributed improvement to the drug. Thus, misattribution therapy may be most effective if combined with a clinical intervention that induces an internal effort attribution for initial gains made in treatment.

An important limitation with the misattribution research should be underscored. Most misattribution studies have failed to include manipulation checks to verify the posited theoretical sequence of processes involving subjects' attributions. Thus, the majority of misattribution studies assume but do not directly examine whether subjects' causal inferences proceed in accord with the Schachter and Singer (1962) model. Note also that

Reisenzein (1983) presented a number of alternative theoretical accounts for a variety of misattribution findings (cf. Olson, 1988).

In summary, the research to date on misattribution therapy provides only partial support for predictions generated by the Schachter and Singer (1962) theory of emotion. Nevertheless, we believe that this approach to therapy continues to hold promise, particularly if cognitive–behavior therapists were to create conditions conducive to making internal effort attributions for initial therapy gains. Unfortunately, interest in misattribution therapy appears to have diminished, perhaps due to the mixed findings in this literature. In our view, this decrease in interest is premature, particularly in view of the beneficial effects of this therapy when internal effort attributions are made for initial therapeutic gains.

REATTRIBUTION THEORY AND RESEARCH

Reattribution training involves changing attributions about environmental events and behavioral outcomes, typically through providing attribution-relevant information and through persuasion, although an operant conditioning paradigm has occasionally been used (e.g., Andrews & Debus, 1978). In contrast to misattribution research, reattribution research more carefully considers the stability dimension of causality (Weiner et al., 1971) and, in some cases, adds to this the causal dimension of globality (Abramson, Seligman, & Teasdale, 1978). We use the term *reattribution therapy* broadly, including any procedure that attempts to change behaviors or symptoms by modifying the causal attributions people make for their behavior or for events in their life. Reattribution studies are primarily based on the self-efficacy expectancy-value theory of Bandura (1977, 1982), Weiner's (1972, 1985, 1986) causal analysis of achievement motivation and emotion, the reformulated learned helplessness theory of depression (Abramson et al., 1978), and its recent revision, the hopelessness theory of depression (Abramson, Metalsky, & Alloy, 1989), as well as Kelley's (1967) classic work in social psychology on the attribution process. Reattribution research and clinical applications derived from each of these theoretical perspectives are considered in turn.

Bandura's Self-Efficacy Theory

Self-efficacy expectancies, together with *outcome expectancies* and *outcome values*, are the three basic components of Bandura's (1977, 1982) model. Self-efficacy expectancies are a person's beliefs about the probability that he or she will be able to perform a specific behavior that is instrumental in obtaining a desired outcome (see chapter 13, this volume). An outcome expectancy is the belief about the probability that performing that action will lead to the desired outcome. The outcome value is the perceived value of the outcome to the person. Thus, difficulties arise for a person when he or she believes himself or herself to be incapable of achieving a desired outcome and places too much value on achieving that outcome.

Bandura (1977) suggested that a person would experience an enhanced sense of self-efficacy if, when successes occurred, he or she made attributions to his or her own ability rather than to task difficulty, to luck, or to his or her effort in that particular situation. More research has been done linking self-efficacy expectancies to behavior (Bandura, Reese, & Adams, 1982) and affective states (Kanfer & Zeiss, 1983) than has been investigated regarding the other two components of Bandura's model, so we focus on self-efficacy expectancy studies here.

Several investigators reported an association between self-efficacy expectancies and therapeutic outcome in research on phobics' approach and avoidance behaviors. Williams and Watson (1985) found that subjects' self-efficacy expectancies predicted approach behavior in acrophobics better than outcome expectancies or subjective feelings of anxiety. Other studies have consistently found a strong association between self-efficacy expectations and approach behavior in a variety of other phobias (Bandura, 1982; Bandura, Adams, Hardy, & Howells, 1980; Williams, Dooseman, & Kleinfeld, 1984). Thus, self-efficacy expectancies appear to be a very useful point of intervention in treating phobic disorders. A clinician might assess a person's self-efficacy expectancies at the start of treatment, designing additional interventions as needed to target these expectancies in individuals with a poor sense of self-efficacy in the relevant clinical domain.

Alden (1987) manipulated information about self-efficacy in a study of socially anxious and nonanxious subjects. Subjects received one of four patterns of social feedback across two experimental trials: (a) consistent success, (b) improvement from Time 1 to Time 2, (c) consistent failure, or (d) deterioration from Time 1 to Time 2. She found that socially anxious subjects made the strongest effort attributions for their performance in the improvement condition than in any of the other three feedback conditions. Anxious subjects did not differ across conditions in the extent to which they made ability attributions. Nonanxious subjects, on the other hand, made stronger ability attributions for consistent success, compared with anxious subjects in this condition. Anxious subjects differed from nonanxious subjects across all four feedback conditions in the greater extent to which they attributed outcomes to external factors (luck and task difficulty). Anxious subjects expected to do more poorly on the task both times, even after receiving success feedback at Time 1, whereas nonanxious subjects expected to do well on the task both times, even after receiving failure feedback at Time 1. Alden suggested that treatment might be kept closely in line with a person's self-efficacy expectancies. Specifically, interventions might be offered in a graduated way to increasingly and selectively enhance a person's proclivity to make internal attributions (e.g., to effort) for successes and then to address the stability dimension by building up through repeated successes in a specific domain a sense of stability across time (an ability attribution in the domain of interest). As will be seen, the hopelessness theory of depression (Abramson et al., 1989), taken together with Kelley's (1967) theory of the attribution process, suggests that repeated successes across different domains (low distinctiveness information in Kelley's model; see below) will contribute to a global (e.g., ability across domains) attribution for success, which will further enhance self-efficacy expectations.

Bandura (1986) suggested that individuals are at risk for depression when their self-expectancy is low in a situation of high outcome expectancy and high outcome value. In keeping with this view, Anderson and colleagues (Anderson & Arnoult, 1985; Anderson, Horowitz, & French, 1983) found an association between low self-efficacy expectancies and perceptions of uncontrollability in depressed subjects. This suggests that clinical interventions for depressed clients might be designed to reduce outcome values with a corresponding focus on enhancing self-efficacy and perceived controllability.

Halberstadt, Andrews, Metalsky, and Abramson (1984) suggested another point of intervention with depressed patients that arose from Bandura's self-efficacy model as well as the hopelessness theory of depression (Abramson et al., 1989). Bandura (1971) argued that goal setting played a central role in depression (see also Rehm, 1977). Golin and Terrell (1977) found that depressed students were more apt to set higher goals on laboratory tasks than were nondepressed students. Diggory (1966) also found that depressed inpatients tended to set unrealistically high performance goals for themselves in relation to other inpatients. Thus, Halberstadt et al. suggested that interventions directed toward modifying unrealistic goal-setting tendencies might be of value in working with depressed individuals. Toward this aim, the cognitive–behavioral approach of Beck et al. (1979) involving graded task assignments may be particularly helpful. Patients were given increasingly difficult yet realistically attainable tasks to master in vivo while at the same time they were encouraged to engage in realistic evaluations of task performance. Ellis's approach to modifying unrealistic goal setting also may prove fruitful in setting more realistic goals (e.g., Ellis, 1962; Ellis & Grieger, 1977). In our view, it may be most productive to first use Beck et al.'s graded task assignments because this approach provides an opportunity for the client to have success experiences on increasingly difficult tasks. On the other hand, should the client suffer from particular skills deficits (e.g., social skills), it would be necessary to first work on these behavioral deficiencies. If the client is not responsive to this intervention and, consequently, is likely to experience failure in Beck's graded task assignment, then Ellis's approach may be most beneficial.

Self-efficacy measures have also been used successfully in predicting outcome and relapse rates in a variety of other clinical groups, including smokers (Coehlo, 1984), alcohol abusers (Marlatt & Gordon, 1985), and obese subjects (Weinberg, Hughes, Critelli, England, & Jackson, 1984). These measures might be incorporated in clinical settings to aid therapists in designing individualized programs that emphasize enhancing self-efficacy expectations in the overall treatment plan. Clearly, if self-efficacy expectations moderate whether cognitive and behavioral treatment is effective in these populations, it is critical to examine the extent to which these interventions become more effective when low self-efficacy expectations are targeted for direct intervention.

Goldfried and Robins (1982) suggested four general clinical applications of Bandura's self-efficacy model that involve reattribution training. A person initially can be helped to make internal (e.g., effort) rather than external (e.g., luck or task difficulty) attributions when he or she achieves a desired outcome. The person can then, after repeated success experiences, come to attribute the pattern of success to dispositional factors (e.g., ability). This internal, stable, global attribution should thereby result in enhanced self-efficacy expectancies. In addition, when acquiring a new set of coping or instrumental behaviors, a person can be encouraged to make external, situational rather than internal, dispositional attributions for outcome failures. Finally, Goldfried and Robins suggested that a person be taught to cope with high levels of internal physiological arousal by noting other causal factors implicated in achieving successful outcomes. By developing more complex causal attributions (e.g., "I did not perform well, in part, because of my level of arousal; however, there are other causal pathways through which I can obtain my desired goal, in spite of being overly aroused"), the client may come to deemphasize the importance of the internal arousal in attempting to achieve a desired goal. In our view, an important goal for future research is to develop interventions targeted toward increasing attributional complexity and to examine whether such an approach enhances self-efficacy expectations in the clinic.

Weiner's Attributional Theory

Weiner and associates developed a comprehensive theoretical model detailing the role of attributional processes in the domain of achievement motivation (Weiner et al., 1971). More recently, Weiner extended this attributional model to provide a more general theory of motivation and emotion (Weiner, 1982, 1985, 1986). In his more general theory, Weiner (1985, 1986) suggested that the basic dimensions underlying causal attributions include *internality* (locus; where the cause is located), *stability* (the degree to which the cause is constant or fluctuates over time), and *controllability* (the extent to which the cause is perceived to be controllable).

Weiner (1985, 1986) also raised the possibility that a complete classification of attributional dimensions might require inclusion of *globality* (the extent to which the cause affects many situations or is circumscribed). Nevertheless, as will be seen, the majority of empirical work on Weiner's model conducted to date focuses on the internality and stability dimensions. We therefore focus on this body of research and its implications for reattribution therapy.

Weiner et al.'s (1971) addition of the *stability* dimension to the *internality* dimension, which had been the exclusive focus of early attributional accounts (e.g., Heider, 1958), allowed for four possibilities in the type of attribution that a person makes for an event: *internal, stable* (ability); *internal, unstable* (effort); *external, stable* (task difficulty); and *external, unstable* (chance). Weiner (1979) further detailed the links between the type of attribution made and the emotional and motivational state resulting from that attribution, as well as expectancies for future performance. He suggested that internal, stable attributions for failures led to reductions in a person's self-esteem, motivation, and level of expectancy, whereas external, unstable attributions for failures did not result in a decrement in self-esteem, motivation, or expectancies.

Numerous studies support these theoretical propositions (see Forsterling, 1988, for a review). Weiner and his colleagues (Weiner, Russell, & Lerman, 1978) conducted a series of studies demonstrating links between the two causal dimensions of attributions for positive and negative outcomes and specific emotions associated with each, including pride and shame, happiness and unhappiness, and feelings of competence and incompetence. Metalsky and Abramson (1981) reported that high-test-anxious subjects tended to make internal, stable attributions for negative outcomes, compared with individuals low in test anxiety. Note in this context that Lavelle, Metalsky, and Coyne (1979) found high-test-anxious subjects to be especially prone to performance deficits after experimenter-induced failure, whereas low-test-anxious subjects persisted in performance after the same amount of failure. Similarly, Arkin, Appleman, and Burger (1980) found a greater tendency in socially anxious subjects to make internal, stable attributions for failures and external, unstable attributions for successes, compared with socially nonanxious subjects. Peplau et al. (1979) found that internal, stable attributions for loneliness in college was associated with higher levels of depressive symptoms, compared with students who made unstable attributions for loneliness.

Reattribution techniques growing out of Weiner's work typically target one or both dimensions of causality in attempting to alter a person's attributions for successes and failures, encouraging them to make external, unstable attributions for failures and internal, stable attributions for successes. Andrews and Debus (1978) used operant conditioning procedures to reinforce internal, specific (lack of effort) attributions in response to failures on a laboratory task. They were able to reverse subjects' motivational and performance deficits by altering subjects' attributions, obtaining an increase in internal, unstable (lack of effort) attributions on the same task at a 4–month follow-up. Similarly, Anderson (1983) found that subjects who were induced to attribute failure to internal, unstable causes (lack of effort) exhibited enhanced motivation and performance on an interpersonal persuasion task compared with subjects who were induced to attribute failure to internal, stable causes (lack of ability).

In his review of the reattribution literature arising from Weiner's model, Forsterling (1988; see also 1990) concluded that most of the research that had been conducted had focused on attempts to induce subjects to make effort attributions for success and lack-of-effort attributions for failure, redirecting attributions along the internality and stability dimensions. And still, much of the research in this area has not included an examination of the attributional dimension of globality (Abramson et al., 1978), which may have important implications for the efficacy of reattribution therapy (see Halberstadt et al., 1984; Seligman et al., 1988). Moreover, few of these studies have assessed long-term changes as a function of reattribution therapy; thus, the implications for lasting change in a clinical setting are unclear. Nevertheless, Weiner's model has been instrumental in the development of theories that are tailored more directly to clinical applications.

Helplessness and Hopelessness Theories of Depression

The hopelessness theory of depression (Abramson et al., 1989) and its forerunner, the reformulated theory of learned helplessness (Abramson et al., 1978), posit the existence of individual differences in *attributional styles*. The concept of attributional styles was first introduced by Ickes and Layden (1978) as well as by Abramson et al. (1978). Abramson et al.'s (1978) conceptualization differed from that of Ickes and Layden (1978) in that Ickes and Layden focused on the attributional dimensions of Weiner et al. (1971; *internality and stability*) whereas Abramson et al. (1978) also retained these dimensions but introduced a new dimension as well: *globality*. In keeping with Kelley's (1967) covariation principle, especially that part of the "Kelley cube," that highlights covariation across situations (i.e., *distinctiveness information*), Abramson et al. (1978) suggested that some people have a generalized tendency to attribute negative life events to internal, stable, and global causes (e.g., lack of ability), whereas others have a proclivity toward attributing negative life events to external, unstable, and specific causes (bad luck). In addition, when confronted with an actual negative life stressor, internal attributions were posited to lead to self-esteem deficits, stable attributions were posited to lead to enduring deficits over time in similar situations, and global attributions were posited to lead to generalized deficits across situations. In contrast, self-esteem would remain relatively intact when an external attribution was made, deficits would be short-lived when an unstable attribution was made, and deficits would be circumscribed when a specific casual attribution was made. Abramson et al. (1978) further proposed that an internal, stable, global attributional style for negative outcomes might confer a risk or vulnerability to depression when a person with such a style was confronted with a negative life stressor.

Metalsky, Abramson, Seligman, Semmel, and Peterson (1982) clarified that this aspect of the theory might best be conceptualized in a *diathesis–stress* framework. That is, the style to attribute negative life events to internal, stable, global causes was a cognitive diathesis that would contribute to depressive reactions in the presence, but not in the absence, of negative life events (i.e., attributional style would interact with negative life stressors such that the posited negative attributional style would be more highly associated with onset and maintenance of depressive symptoms under high compared with low levels of stress).

Although the hopelessness theory delineates a causal sequence hypothesized to culminate in hopelessness and, in turn, the hopelessness subtype of depression and although the causal sequence includes nonattributional as well as attributional concepts, we focus on attributional styles in the context of the present chapter (see Abramson et al., 1989, for nonattributional vulnerability factors as well as a description of the posited hopelessness subtype of depression; see Alloy & Clements, 1992; Metalsky, Halberstadt, & Abramson, 1987; Metalsky & Joiner, 1992; Metalsky, Joiner, Hardin, & Abramson, 1993; and Needles & Abramson, 1990, for recent empirical tests of the theory).

The hopelessness theory differs from its predecessor in a variety of ways. In the present context, the most important difference concerns the hopelessness theory's revision of how the attributional dimensions *combine* to confer risk for development and maintenance of the hopelessness subtype of depression. In short, whereas the reformulated theory viewed *each* attributional dimension as playing a distinct role in the development of depression, the hopelessness theory argues that it is the joint influence of making stable *and* global attributions (*generality*; see Metalsky et al., 1987; Metalsky & Joiner, 1992; Metalsky et al., 1993) that confers vulnerability to the hopelessness subtype of depression. Consequently, unstable, global attributions for negative life stressors will not contribute to hopelessness or the hopelessness subtype of depression, nor will stable, specific attributions for negative life stressors (although in the latter case, circumscribed pessimism and mild depressive reactions may ensue). Moreover, internal attributions are viewed as adaptive by the hopelessness theory if they are combined with unstable, specific causal attributions (e.g., lack of effort) for life stressors. In contrast, when stable, global attributions are combined with an internal attribution, then hopelessness (arising from the stable, global attribution) may be accompanied by lowered self-esteem and dependency (see Abramson et al., 1989, for a more complete discussion of the differences between the two theories).

To date, the most common target of intervention arising from the reformulated helplessness theory and hopelessness theory is reattribution training designed to change attributional styles. The goal is to modify an internal, stable, global attributional style for negative outcomes to either an external, unstable, specific attributional style (e.g., negative events are due to a temporary cause located in the outside world, which will not affect many situations) or to an internal, unstable, specific attributional style (e.g., attributing negative events to lack of effort).

Dweck and associates (1973) have conducted some of the earliest work on reattribution training from this theoretical perspective. For example, Dweck (1975) compared the effectiveness of success experiences versus a reattribution training program in the alleviation of learned helplessness among 8- to 13-year-old children. In Dweck's work, helplessness-oriented children are those who give up in the face of failure. In contrast, mastery-oriented children persist in the face of failure. Reattribution training for the helplessness-oriented children consisted of 25 sessions (15 trials per session) in which helplessness children were encouraged to attribute failure to lack of effort rather than lack of ability. Whereas success experiences were not at all effective in reducing performance decrements after failure, children in the reattribution-training condition showed either no impairment or actual improvement in performance after failure.

In another interesting series of studies, Dweck and associates found gender differences in which female children were more likely to exhibit a helplessness orientation than were male children (Dweck & Bush, 1976). In addition, Dweck and Bush reported that among fourth- and fifth-grade children, girls displayed helplessness more readily when they received failure feedback from adults (especially women) than from peers (especially boys), suggesting that girls of this age are most sensitive to negative feedback from adult women and least sensitive to negative feedback from male peers. In contrast, fourth- and fifth-grade boys displayed helplessness more readily when they received failure feedback from peers (especially boys) than from adults (especially women), suggesting that boys of this age are most sensitive to negative feedback from male peers and least sensitive to negative feedback from adult women. These findings raise the possibility that adult females (e.g., mothers, female teachers) may have more impact on inducing helplessness in girls than boys, whereas adult males (e.g., fathers, male teachers) may have more impact on inducing helplessness in boys than girls. In addition, when making causal attributions for failure, boys may be most influenced by information provided to them by same-gender peers (e.g., a boy who is picked last when forming teams for athletic games may infer that he lacks athletic ability), whereas girls' attributions for failure may be influenced most by information provided to them by same-gender adults (e.g., a girl whose female teacher tells her that she may not be cut out to play sports may infer that she lacks athletic ability).

Along these lines, Dweck, Davidson, Nelson, and Enna (1978) examined interactions between female teachers and their students (fourth and fifth grade) when the teacher and students were engaged in academic tasks. Concerning evaluative feedback given to girls versus boys, Dweck et al. (1978) found that female teachers were more likely to focus on intellectual aspects of performance for boys than girls after success (e.g., "You have the ability to do this task") and were less likely to focus on intellectual aspects of performance for boys than girls after failure. In essence, female teachers unwittingly were providing girls with feedback that would promote lack of ability attributions for academic failure while providing boys with feedback that would promote lack-of-effort attributions for failure. Consequently, fourth- and fifth-grade girls were more likely to show a helplessness orientation (and negative attributional style), whereas boys of this age were more likely to show a mastery orientation (and positive attributional style).

In the second phase of their study, Dweck et al. (1978) experimentally manipulated the feedback teachers provided to the students. When both boys and girls received failure feedback that referred exclusively to the intellectual inadequacy of performance (as the girls received in the first phase of the study), boys and girls both made lack-of-ability attributions for failure. In contrast, when failure feedback emphasized both intellectual and nonintellectual aspects of performance, both boys and girls made lack-of-effort attributions for failure. The implications for parenting as well as teaching are clear: Adults can have a profound impact on the attributional styles of children, to the point of inducing an internal, stable, global attributional style for negative events and thereby leaving the child at risk for performance deficits and motivational deficits, as well as depression. On a more positive note, this line of research also suggests that reattribution training is effective in modifying children's attributional styles from a lack of ability (internal, stable, and global) to a lack of effort (internal, unstable, and specific) orientation (see also Chapin & Dyck, 1976).

In devising reattribution therapies for modifying adults' attributional styles, it may be useful to consider basic research on the attribution process (e.g., Kelley, 1967) and to keep in mind the suggestion made by several investigators (e.g., Metalsky & Abramson, 1981; Ross, 1977, 1978) that attributions are determined by both environmental evidence and the cognitive schemas that guide the processing of causally relevant information (see Cantor & Kihlstrom, 1982; Metalsky & Abramson, 1981; see also Halberstadt et al., 1984).

Concerning environmental evidence, Kelley's (1967) model depicts particular configurations of information, which make some attributions more compelling than others and some not compelling at all. Specifically, Kelley's model includes three types of information relevant to a causal analysis: (a) *consensus* (extent to which the outcome occurs only to the attributor [low] or to relevant others as well [high], (b) *consistency* (extent to which the outcome occurs repeatedly over time in similar situations), and (c) *distinctiveness* (extent to which the outcome occurs just in one particular situation [high] or across many situations [low]). In this view, after a failure on a midterm exam in psychology, the attributor will make an internal, stable, global (e.g., lack of ability) attribution if consensus is low (others did well), consistency is high (the attributor typically fails exams in psychology), and distinctiveness is low (the attributor typically fails exams in a variety of subjects, not just psychology). In contrast, the attributor will make an external, unstable, specific attribution for failing the psychology midterm if consensus is high (others also failed), consistency is low (the attributor typically does well on psychology exams), and distinctiveness is high (the attributor typically does well on exams in a variety of subjects).

As we suggested, however, people do not rely solely on "the evidence" in making causal judgments; they also rely on their schemas, typically conceptualized as organized representations of prior experiences, beliefs, and knowledge that guide the processing of current information (Beck, 1967; Kahneman & Tversky, 1972, 1973; Neisser, 1967; Ross, 1978). Considerable work in the area of social cognition as well as cognitive psychology suggests that people readily use current information when it is consistent with their schemas. In contrast, current information that is at odds with one's schemas may be discounted or elaborated on and interpreted in such a way so as to be consistent with one's schemas (e.g, Ajzen, 1977; Bartlett, 1932; Bruner & Postman, 1949; Kuhn, 1970; for reviews, see Cantor & Kihlstrom, 1982; Metalsky & Abramson, 1981).

To the extent that causal judgments are schema driven, people's attributional styles may not be readily changed simply by exposure to contradictory evidence. For example, a person with an internal, stable, global attributional style for negative outcomes may make a lack-of-ability attribution for a failure in spite of the fact that consensus information is high (e.g., most others also failed the exam). Because the information is selectively interpreted in line with the person's schemas, the current "data point" is unlikely to outweigh or override the schemas that are guiding the causal analysis. Thus, simply exposing people to the type of "Kelley information" that should lead to an external, unstable, specific attribution (high consensus, low consistency, and high distinctiveness) may not be a sufficient behavioral intervention to induce a change in attributional style.

Fortunately, Beck's cognitive therapy (Beck, 1976; Beck et al., 1979) operates at both levels, modifying the schemas as well as current information to which patients are exposed. Although this approach to treatment is not limited to reattribution training, it does include an attributional retraining component. For example, in the framework of *collaborative empiricism*, the therapist encourages the client to consider consensus information, comparing himself or herself with appropriate reference groups, because depressives sometimes exhibit a tendency to compare themselves to inappropriate reference groups (e.g., a first-year graduate student comparing himself or herself with a student who is preparing for final dissertation orals).

Beck would encourage the client to observe others who are also first-year graduate students to obtain a more realistic comparison. Therapy in a group setting can provide this function for individuals by providing them with a ready-made reference group of others who are experiencing problems similar to theirs. The client is encouraged to examine his or her causal assumptions according to inductive empirical methods. Evidence for and against a particular causal attribution is collected and evaluated in a more impartial manner than his or her biases have previously allowed. The client is thereby enabled to reattribute causes of a negative event to a more benign factor.

In essence, Beck's approach puts dysfunctional schemas "on hold," thereby allowing the attributor to collect and fairly evaluate "the evidence." Moreover, if skills deficits exist, behavioral interventions are used to increase the chances that the client will obtain positive information about the self, the world, and the future (Beck, 1967). As more and more positive causal information is gathered (e.g., "Some people like me and some people don't; it's not as bad as I thought"; an instance of high-distinctiveness information), the client's schemas eventually may become less dysfunctional. If not, then the therapy would nevertheless serve the purpose of having clients consider positive causal information (consider the "Kelley information") rather than discount it automatically.

In short, the early stages of Beck's approach move clients from being schema driven to evidence driven. As therapy progresses, continued experiences with positive causal information as well as persuasion on the basis of "the evidence" should eventually lead to change in the dysfunctional schemas themselves. Beck et al. (1979) suggested that these reattribution interventions were especially beneficial for clients who were excessive in self-blame (in our terminology, for those with an *internal, stable, and global attributional style for negative events*).

Although there is considerable empirical evidence concerning the effectiveness of Beck et al.'s (1979) therapy in the treatment of clinical depression (see Hollon, Shelton, & Loosen, 1991, for a review), work in this area has not examined whether the reattribution component is partly responsible for the therapy's effectiveness. However, Seligman et al. (1988) examined whether improvements in attributional style may be one of mechanisms of improvement in unipolar depressed outpatients receiving

Beck et al.'s cognitive therapy of depression. The results were in line with the view that improvements in attributional style (i.e., becoming less internal, stable, and global for negative outcomes) mediated recovery. As attributional style became more external, unstable, and specific, patients became less depressed and remained less depressed at therapy termination. Patients with a more external, unstable, specific attributional style at termination were also less depressed at 1-year follow-up compared with those with a more internal, stable, and global attributional style at termination. Note, however, that the design did not allow a definitive evaluation of whether improvement in attributional style preceded improvement in symptoms. Thus, the causal role of attributional style as a principal mechanism of change in cognitive therapy for depression cannot be stated definitively. Nevertheless, the Seligman et al. (1988) results are quite encouraging. Clearly, more work is needed following up on Seligman et al.'s (1988) initial evaluation of this important issue.

ATTRIBUTIONS, MARITAL DISTRESS, AND THERAPY

Recently, investigators have begun to apply attributional principles to an understanding of marital problems and marital therapy. We focus on this exciting area of work in the final section of the chapter.

In our view, spouses' attributions about the nature of one another's behaviors have rich potential as therapeutic targets for change. In what follows, we review basic research on attributional processes and marital satisfaction as well as applied work on cognitive techniques within a marital therapy framework. In addition, we offer suggestions for ways in which attribution theory may be better used in clinical marital work.

In a thorough review of the literature, Bradbury and Fincham (1990) concluded that negative attributions by one spouse regarding his or her spouse's behavior were cross-sectionally (e.g., Baucom, Sayers, & Duhe, 1989) and prospectively (e.g., Fincham & Bradbury, 1987) associated with marital dissatisfaction. The prospective research is important because it suggests that negative attributions temporally precede marital dissatisfaction (see Hollon, Kendall, & Lumry, 1986, for a discussion of causality within nonexperimental, longitudinal psychopathology research). In addition, Fincham, Beach, and Bradbury's (1989) findings that the attributions–marital distress relation remained when depression was controlled, and that the attributions of maritally distressed, depressed, and nondepressed women were similar, suggest that attributions and marital distress are not associated because both covary with depression. Taken together, this work is in keeping with the view that attributional processes play a significant role in contributing to marital dissatisfaction.

Much of the work on attribution in marriage has not been limited to *causal* attributions for a given event but, in addition, has explored inferences concerning *responsibility* and *blame* for an event (e.g., Antaki & Fielding, 1981; Madden & Janoff-Bulman, 1981; Sillars, 1985). Causal attributions pertain to factors that have produced or created an event and therefore are *explanations* as to why an event happened, attribution of responsibility pertains to an individual's accountability for an event, and attribution of blame is an evaluation of an individual's liability for censure (Bradbury & Fincham, 1990). The distinction between attributions of responsibility and blame is subtle but quite important. According to Shaver (1985), responsibility judgments are made before the responsible party has given his or her account (e.g., a husband judges that his wife is responsible for being late, whether or not her explanation relieves her of blame). In contrast, attributions of blame are made after responsibility has been determined and the responsible party has explained the situation (e.g., a husband does not blame his wife for being late, despite believing that she is responsible, after she explains that she did not intend to upset him and was not aware that her being late would upset him). Bradbury and Fincham (1990) suggested that because many spouses readily assign blame without waiting for an explanation from their spouse, the distinction between the *responsibility* and *blame* dimensions may be difficult to demonstrate empirically. Nevertheless, the distinction is valuable for marital therapists, who can teach spouses to defer the assignment of blame until their partner has explained. Similarly, responsibility attributions can be delayed until causality is determined.

Shultz and Schleifer (1983a, 1983b; see also Fincham & Jaspars, 1980) proposed an *entailment model* of attribution in marriage, wherein attributions of cause lead to attributions of responsibility, which, in turn, lead to attributions of blame. Taken together with the attributional dimensions of internality (*stability, globality,* and *controllability*), the differing types of attributions (i.e., for cause, responsibility, and blame) reveal numerous points of intervention for marital therapy. Determination of which attributional dimension is most salient will direct the focus of reattribution techniques. For example, attributing a negative spouse behavior to an internal, stable, global characteristic about the spouse (e.g., he or she is selfish) calls for reattribution to less spouse-centered dispositional causes. Similarly, attributions for negative spouse behavior to uncontrollable factors (e.g., he or she has an extremely bad temper and therefore cannot stop yelling) would be reattributed to controllable causes or to causes that the couple is learning to control through their therapy (e.g., he or she can control his or her verbal attacks).

Determination of which attributional type is most salient will place the couple on the continuum proposed by the entailment model. Couples who are at the "blame node" will need to work toward making reasonable causal attributions, which may or may not entail responsibility and blame attributions. Couples who start with causal attributions will need to detoxify the "downward drift" from causal to responsibility and blame attributions.

Assessment of attributional processes in marital dyads, and some derivative issues, warrants consideration. The most common assessment tool is the Marital Attributional Style Questionnaire (MASQ; e.g., Fincham, Beach, & Nelson, 1987). As with the original Attributional Style Questionnaire (ASQ; Peterson et al., 1982; Seligman, Abramson, Semmel, & von Baeyer, 1979), respondents write down the one major cause for each of six hypothetical negative spouse behaviors and then rate the cause along relevant attributional dimensions. As has been the case with the original ASQ, reliability coefficients have not always been acceptable, a problem that can probably be addressed by increasing the number of negative spouse behaviors rated (cf. Metalsky et al., 1987). Observer ratings have also been used (e.g., Fichten, 1984). Nevertheless, the pattern of results has been consistent regardless of psychometric limitations or assessment strategy.

Although some variations of the MASQ and all observer-rated approaches use actual negative spouse behavior as stimuli, this area of research has not fully capitalized on the diathesis–stress reasoning contained in the hopelessness theory of depression (Abramson et al., 1989; see also Metalsky & Joiner, 1992; Metalsky et al., 1982, 1987, 1993). Although the hopelessness theory pertains to depression and not to marital discord (see Fincham et al., 1989), diathesis–stress logic may nonetheless enhance the degree to which attributional style predicts marital dissatisfaction. Specifically, attributional styles that are "activated" by the recent occurrence of negative marital events are perhaps more potent predictors of marital distress than less activated attributional styles. Note that observer-rating schemes and self-report measures that use previously assessed negative spouse behavior incorporate this approach to some degree, in that attributions for actual negative events are assessed. However, more pointed assessment of the presence and frequency of negative spouse behaviors would allow for tests of whether the interaction between attributional styles and negative spouse behaviors would enhance prediction of marital distress. In addition, from a diathesis–stress perspective, it would be important to obtain a measure of negative spouse behavior that was not highly correlated with attributional styles. Toward this aim, when assessing these behaviors, items should be concrete (e.g., "Spouse told me he or she is unhappy with me" as opposed to items that are subject to interpretation and that already may be "filtered through" the rater's attributional style (e.g., Spouse is often angry with me; see Joiner & Wagner, 1993).

The research on attributions and marital dissatisfaction can perhaps take another cue from the hopelessness theory. The hopelessness theory posits that the relation between the Attributional Style × Stress interaction and increases in depression occurs as a function of increases in hopelessness (see Metalsky & Joiner, 1992; Metalsky et al., 1993, for recent results in keeping with this view). The factors that mediate the relation between attributions and marital distress constitute an open question. Because stable, global attributions are involved, hopelessness is one possible mechanism. Another possibility is that distressed spouses who have made dispositional attributions about negative spouse behavior feel abandoned or betrayed, but not yet hopeless (e.g., "Perhaps he or she will change").

The Fincham et al. (1989) study provides important information about the interrelations among attributions, distress, and depression. Of course, additional work needs to be done. For example, the hopelessness theory would predict that the attribution of negative spouse behavior to stable, global causes would contribute to the development of hopelessness and, in turn, depression (see Heim & Snyder, 1991), whereas the work on marital dyads would predict the development of marital dissatisfaction. Of course, these are not mutually exclusive predictions (i.e., one can independently develop depression and dissatisfaction), and it is important to determine whether depression or dissatisfaction, once developed, contributes to the development of the other.

In view of the fact that research on the efficacy of behavioral marital therapy (BMT; Greer & D'Zurilla, 1975; Jacobson, 1984; Jacobson & Martin, 1976) has been thoroughly reviewed elsewhere (e.g., see, Gurman, Kniskern, & Pinsof, 1986), we focus on cognitive interventions. Three studies that evaluate the efficacy of cognitive techniques in treating marital distress have been reported. Note that no rigorous system of marital reattribution techniques has been developed (but see Berley & Jacobson, 1984; Dobson, Jacobson, & Victor, 1988, for general cognitive approaches to marital therapy), making an empirical analysis of the approach's efficacy difficult. However, each study included a reattribution component to the cognitive intervention.

Margolin and Weiss (1978) compared three groups of distressed couples: a control group receiving nonspecific, supportive counseling; a group receiving communication training; and a group receiving communication training and "cognitive restructuring." Cognitive restructuring entailed helping spouses "to abandon blaming attributions, to accept greater personal responsibility for relationship failure, and to be more accepting of their partner's positive efforts" (Margolin & Weiss, 1978, p. 1485). The group that received cognitive restructuring experienced higher posttreatment marital satisfaction than the remaining two groups.

Epstein, Pretzer, and Fleming (1982) compared distressed couples who received either cognitive therapy focusing on attributional processes or communication skills training. The groups did not differ on measures of marital satisfaction, although the cognitive group did improve somewhat on cognitive and perceptual measures. This study did not support the efficacy of attribution-focused cognitive therapy in comparison with a communication skills building approach.

Baucom and Lester (1986) compared couples receiving behavioral marital therapy (BMT) to those receiving a combination of BMT and cognitive–behavior therapy. The cognitive–behavioral treatment included reattribution training (e.g., changing internal, stable, and global attributions for undesired spouse behavior to external, unstable, and specific attributions). Both groups improved more than wait list controls, but the two treatment groups did not differ from one another. Holtzworth-Munroe and Jacobson (1987) offered an interesting explanation of why this may have occurred. They suggested that reattribution techniques may only be appropriate for couples who function at a relatively abstract level, whereas they may fall flat with couples who are more concrete and only interested in behavioral change without explanation of why behavioral patterns may exist. This speculation suggests an interesting study wherein the Baucom and Lester methodology is altered to include couples who operate at relatively more and less abstract levels.

To date, a detailed system of reattributional therapy for marital dyads has not been developed. Therefore, current reattribution techniques should be viewed as adjuncts to established marital therapies (e.g., BMT). However, in the light of the considerable literature linking attributions to marital distress, development of a complete therapeutic reattribution protocol is clearly warranted. Another important area for future work is to determine whether established therapies, such as BMT, work in part because they influence attributional processes. It would also be important to examine whether BMT leads to renewed hope in distressed couples and whether hope is a critical ingredient for successful treatment.

CONCLUDING COMMENT

In spite of considerable research on the role played by attribution processes in the understanding of a variety of behavioral problems and disorders, attribution therapy typically is conducted as one element of a broader approach to treatment. Therefore, with notable exceptions (e.g., misattribution therapy), it is difficult to evaluate the efficacy of attribution therapy separate from the other aspects to treatment. Thus, in our view, the most pressing goals in this area are to develop an approach to attribution therapy that is versatile enough to be tailored to specific behavioral problems and disorders and, in addition, to compare the efficacy of attribution therapy to other cognitive and behavioral interventions.

REFERENCES

Abramson, L. Y., Metalsky, G. I., & Alloy, L. B. (1989). Hopelessness depression: A theory-based subtype of depression. *Psychological Review, 96,* 358–372.

Abramson, L. Y., Seligman, M. E. P., & Teasdale, J. D. (1978). Learned helplessness in humans: Critique and reformulation. *Journal of Abnormal Psychology, 87,* 49–74.

Ajzen, I. (1977). Intuitive theories of events and the effects of base-rate information on prediction. *Journal of Personality and Social Psychology, 35,* 303–314.

Alden, L. (1987). Attributional responses of anxious individuals to different patterns of social feedback: Nothing succeeds like improvement. *Journal of Personality and Social Psychology, 52,* 100–106.

Alexander, J. F., Waldron, H. B., Barton, C. , & Mas, C. H. (1989). The minimizing of blaming attributions and behaviors in delinquent families. *Journal of Consulting and Clinical Psychology, 57,* 19–24.

Alloy, L. B., & Clements, C. M. (1992). Illusion of control: Invulnerability to negative affect and depressive symptoms after laboratory and natural stressors. *Journal of Abnormal Psychology, 101,* 234–245.

Anderson, C. A. (1983). Motivation and performance deficits in interpersonal settings: The effect of attributional style. *Journal of Personality and Social Psychology, 45,* 1136–1147.

Anderson, C. A., & Arnoult, L. H. (1985). Attributional style and everyday problems in living: Depression, shyness, and loneliness. *Social Cognition, 3,* 16–35.

Anderson, C. A., Horowitz, L. M., & French, R. de S. (1983). Attributional style of lonely and depressed people. *Journal of Personality and Social Psychology, 45,* 127–136.

Andrews, G. R., & Debus, R. L. (1978). Persistence and the causal perception of failure: Modifying cognitive attributions. *Journal of Educational Psychology, 70,* 154–166.

Antaki, C., & Fielding, G. (1981). Research on ordinary explanations. In C. Antaki (Ed.), *The psychology of ordinary explanations of social behavior* (pp. 27–55). San Diego, CA: Academic Press.

Arkin, R. M., Appleman, A. J., & Burger, J. M. (1980). Social anxiety, self-presentation, and the self-serving bias in causal attribution. *Journal of Personality and Social Psychology, 38,* 23–35.

Bandura, A. (1971). Vicarious and self-reinforcement processes. In R. Glaser (Ed.), *The nature of reinforcement* (pp. 228–278). San Diego, CA: Academic Press.

Bandura, A. (1977). Self-efficacy: Toward a unifying theory of behavioral change. *Psychological Review, 2,* 191–215.

Bandura, A. (1982). Self-efficacy mechanism in human agency. *American Psychologist, 37,* 122–147.

Bandura, A. (1986). *Social foundations of thought and action.* New York: Prentice Hall.

Bandura, A., Adams, N. E., Hardy, A. B., & Howells, G. N. (1980). Tests of the generality of self-efficacy theory. *Cognitive Therapy and Research, 4,* 39–66.

Bandura, A., Reese, L., & Adams, N. E. (1982). Microanalysis of action and fear arousal as a function of differential levels of perceived coping self-efficacy. *Journal of Personality and Social Psychology, 43,* 5–21.

Barefoot, J. C., & Girodo, M. (1972). The misattribution of smoking cessation symptoms. *Canadian Journal of Behavioral Science, 4,* 358–363.

Bartlett, F. (1932). *Remembering.* London: Cambridge University Press.

Baucom, D. H., & Lester, G. W. (1986). The usefulness of cognitive restructuring as an adjunct to behavioral marital therapy. *Behavior Therapy, 17,* 385–403.

Baucom, D. H., Sayers, S., & Duhe, A. (1989). Attributional style and attributional patterns among married couples. *Journal of Personality and Social Psychology, 56,* 596–607.

Beck, A. T. (1967). *Depression: Clinical, experimental, and theoretical aspects.* Philadelphia: University of Pennsylvania Press.

Beck, A. T. (1976). *Cognitive therapy and the emotional disorders.* New York: International Universities Press.

Beck, A. T., Rush, A. J., Shaw, B. F., & Emery, G. (1979). *Cognitive therapy of depression.* New York: Guilford Press.

Berley, R. A., & Jacobson, N. S. (1984). Causal attribution in intimate relationships: Toward a model of cognitive–behavioral marital therapy. In P. Kendall (Ed.), *Advances in cognitive–behavioral research* (pp. 168–209). San Diego, CA: Academic Press.

Bootzin, R. R., Herman, C. P., & Nicassio, P. (1976). The power of suggestion: Another examination of attribution and insomnia. *Journal of Personality and Social Psychology, 34,* 673–679.

Bradbury, T. N., & Fincham, F. D. (1990). Attributions in marriage: Review and critique. *Psychological Bulletin, 107,* 3–33.

Brodt, S. E., & Zimbardo, P. G. (1981). Modifying shyness-related social behavior through symptom misattribution. *Journal of Personality and Social Psychology, 41,* 437–449.

Bruner, J. S., & Postman, L. (1949). On the perception of incongruity: A paradigm. *Journal of Personality, 18,* 206–223.

Cantor, N., & Kihlstrom, J. F. (1982). Cognitive and social processes in personality. In G. Wilson and C. Franks (Eds.), *Contemporary behavior therapy* (pp. 142–201). New York: Guilford Press.

Chambliss, C., & Murray, E. J. (1979). Cognitive procedures for smoking reduction: Symptom attribution versus efficacy attribution. *Cognitive Therapy and Research, 3,* 91–95.

Chapin, M., & Dyck, D. G. (1976). Persistence in children's reading behavior as a function of N length and attribution retraining. *Journal of Abnormal Psychology, 85,* 511–515.

Coehlo, R. J. (1984). Self-efficacy and cessation of smoking. *Psychological Reports, 54,* 309–310.

Davison, G. C., Tsujimoto, R. N., & Glaros, A. G. (1973). Attribution and the maintenance of behavior change in falling asleep. *Journal of Abnormal Psychology, 82,* 124–133.

Davison, G. C., & Valins, S. (1969). Maintenance of self-attributed and drug-attributed behavior change. *Journal of Personality and Social Psychology, 11,* 25–33.

Diggory, J. C. (1966). *Self-evaluation: Concepts and studies.* New York: Wiley.

Dobson, K. S., Jacobson, N. S., & Victor, J. (1988). Integration of cognitive therapy and behavioral marital therapy. In J. F. Clarkin, G. L. Haas, & I. D. Glick (Eds.), *Affective disorders and the family: Assessment and treatment* (pp. 53–88). New York: Guilford Press.

Dweck, C. S. (1975). The role of expectations and attributions in the alleviation of learned helplessness. *Journal of Personality and Social Psychology, 31,* 674–685.

Dweck, C. S., & Bush, E. S. (1976). Sex differences in learned helplessness: I. Differential debilitation with peer and adult evaluators. *Developmental Psychology, 12,* 147–156.

Dweck, C. S., Davidson, W., Nelson, S., & Enna, B. (1978). Sex differences in learned helplessness: II. The contingencies of evaluative feedback in the classroom and III. An experimental analysis. *Developmental Psychology, 14,* 268–276.

Dweck, C. S., & Repucci, N. D. (1973). Learned helplessness and reinforcement responsibility in children. *Journal of Personality and Social Psychology, 25,* 109–116.

Ellis, A. (1962). *Reason and emotion in psychotherapy.* New York: Lyle Stuart.

Ellis, A., & Grieger, R. (1977). *Handbook of rational–emotive therapy.* New York: Springer.

Epstein, N., Pretzer, J. L., & Fleming, B. (1982, November). *Cognitive therapy and communication training: Comparison of effects with distressed couples.* Paper presented at the 16th annual meeting of the Association for the Advancement of Behavior Therapy (AABT), Los Angeles.

Erdmann, G., & Janke, W. (1978). Interaction between physiological and cognitive determinants of emotions: Experimental studies on Schachter's theory of emotions. *Biological Psychology, 6,* 61-74.

Fichten, C. S. (1984). See it from my point of view: Videotape and attributions in happy and distressed couples. *Journal of Social and Clinical Psychology, 2,* 125–142.

Fincham, F. D. (1983). Clinical applications of attribution theory: Problems and prospects. In M. Hewstone (Ed.), *Attribution theory: Social and functional extensions* (pp. 187-203). Oxford: Basil Blackwell.

Fincham, F. D., Beach, S. R. H., & Bradbury, T. N. (1989). Marital distress, depression, and attributions: Is the marital distress–attribution association an artifact of depression? *Journal of Consulting and Clinical Psychology, 57*, 768–771.

Fincham, F. D., Beach, S. R. H., & Nelson, G. (1987). Attribution processes in distressed and nondistressed couples: 3. Causal and responsibility attributions for spouse behavior. *Cognitive Therapy and Research, 11*, 71–86.

Fincham, F. D., & Bradbury, T. N. (1987). The impact of attributions in marriage: A longitudinal analysis. *Journal of Personality and Social Psychology, 53*, 510–517.

Fincham, F. D., & Jaspars, J. M. (1980). Attribution of responsibility: From man the scientist to man as lawyer. In L. Berkowitz (Ed.), *Advances in experimental social psychology* (Vol. 13, pp. 81–138). San Diego, CA: Academic Press.

Forsterling, F. (1988). *Attribution theory in clinical psychology.* New York: Wiley.

Forsterling, F. (1990). Attributional therapies. In S. Graham & V. S. Folkes (Eds.), *Attribution theory: Applications to achievement, mental health, and interpersonal conflict* (pp. 123–137). Hillsdale, NJ: Erlbaum.

Goldfried, M., & Robins, C. (1982). On the facilitation of self-efficacy. *Cognitive Therapy and Research, 9*, 583–590.

Golin, S., & Terrell, F. (1977). Motivational and associative aspects of mild depression in skill and chance tasks. *Journal of Abnormal Psychology, 86*, 389–401.

Greer, S. E., & D'Zurilla, T. J. (1975). Behavioral approaches to marital discord and conflict. *Journal of Marriage and Family Counseling, 1*, 299–315.

Gurman, A. S., Kniskern, D. P., & Pinsof, W. M. (1986). Research on the process and outcome of marital and family therapy. In S. L. Garfield & A. E. Bergin (Eds.), *Handbook of psychotherapy and behavior change* (3rd ed., pp. 565–624). New York: Wiley.

Halberstadt, L. J., Andrews, D., Metalsky, G. I., & Abramson, L. Y. (1984). Helplessness, hopelessness, and depression: A review of progress and future directions. In N. S. Endler & J. M. Hunt (Eds.), *Personality and the behavioral disorders* (Vol. 1, pp. 373–411). New York: Wiley.

Heider, F. (1958). *The psychology of interpersonal relations.* New York: Wiley.

Heim, S. C., & Snyder, D. K. (1991). Predicting depression from marital distress and attributional processes. *Journal of Marital and Family Therapy, 17*, 67–72.

Hoehn-Saric, R., Liberman, B., Imber, S., Stone, A., Frank, J., & Ribich, F. (1974). Attitude change and attribution of arousal in psychotherapy. *Journal of Nervous and Mental Disease, 159*, 234–243.

Hollon, S. D., Kendall, P. C., & Lumry, A. (1986). Specificity of depressotypic cognitions in clinical depression. *Journal of Abnormal Psychology, 95*, 52–59.

Hollon, S. D., Shelton, R. C., & Loosen, P. T. (1991). Cognitive therapy and pharmacotherapy for depression. *Journal of Consulting and Clinical Psychology*, 59, 88–99.

Holroyd, K. A. (1978). Effectiveness of an "attribution therapy" manipulation with test anxiety. *Behavior Therapy*, 9, 526–534.

Holtzworth-Munroe, A., & Jacobson, N. S. (1987). An attributional approach to marital dysfunction and therapy. In J. E. Maddux, C. D. Stoltenberg, & R. Rosenwein (Eds.), *Social processes in clinical and counseling psychology* (pp. 153–170). New York: Springer-Verlag.

Hoon, P. W., Wincze, J. P., & Hoon, E. F. (1977). A test of reciprocal inhibition: Are anxiety and sexual arousal in women mutually inhibitory? *Journal of Abnormal Psychology*, 86, 65–74.

Ickes, W., & Layden, M. A. (1978). Attributional styles. In J. H. Harvey, W. Ickes, & R. F. Kidd (Eds.), *New directions in attribution research* (Vol. 2, pp. 119–152). Hillsdale, NJ: Erlbaum.

Jacobson, N. S. (1984). A component analysis of behavioral marital therapy: The relative effectiveness of behavior exchange and communication/problem solving training. *Journal of Consulting and Clinical Psychology*, 52, 295–305.

Jacobson, N. S., & Martin, B. (1976). Behavioral marriage therapy: Current status. *Psychological Bulletin*, 83, 540–556.

Joiner, Jr., T. E., & Wagner, K. D. (1993). *Assessing attributional processes in families of depressed and suicidal children and adolescents*. Manuscript in preparation.

Kahneman, D., & Tversky, A. (1972). Subjective probability: A judgment of representativeness. *Cognitive Psychology*, 3, 430–454.

Kahneman, D., & Tversky, A. (1973). On the psychology of prediction. *Psychological Review*, 80, 237–251.

Kanfer, R., & Zeiss, A. M. (1983). Depression, interpersonal standard-setting, and judgments of self-efficacy. *Journal of Abnormal Psychology*, 92, 319–329.

Kazdin, A. (1974). Covert modeling, model similarity, and reduction of avoidance behavior. *Behavior Therapy*, 5, 624–636.

Kelley, H. H. (1967). Attribution theory in social psychology. In D. Levine (Ed.), *Nebraska Symposium on Motivation: Volume 15. Current theory and research in motivation* (pp. 192–238). Lincoln: University of Nebraska Press.

Kellogg, R., & Baron, R. S. (1975). Attribution theory, insomnia, and the reverse placebo effect: A reversal of Storms and Nisbett's findings. *Journal of Personality and Social Psychology*, 32, 231–236.

Kuhn, T. S. (1970). *The structure of scientific revolutions* (2nd. ed.). Chicago: University of Chicago Press.

Lader, M., & Tyrer, P. (1975). Vegetative system and emotion. In L. Levi (Ed.), *Emotions—their parameters and measurement*. New York: Raven Press.

Lavelle, T. L., Metalsky, G. I., & Coyne, J. C. (1979). Learned helplessness, test anxiety, and acknowledgment of contingencies. *Journal of Abnormal Psychology*, 88, 381–387.

Madden, M. E., & Janoff-Bulman, R. (1981). Blame, control, and marital satisfaction: Wives' attributions for conflict in marriage. *Journal of Marriage and the Family, 43*, 663–674.

Margolin, G., & Weiss, R. L. (1978). Comparative evaluation of therapeutic components associated with behavioral marital treatments. *Journal of Consulting and Clinical Psychology, 46*, 1476–1486.

Marlatt, G. A., & Gordon, J. R. (Eds.). (1985). *Relapse prevention.* New York: Guilford Press.

McMillin, W. P. (1973). Oxprenolol in anxiety. *Lancet, 1*, 1193.

Meichenbaum, D. (1972). Cognitive modification of test anxious college students. *Journal of Consulting and Clinical Psychology, 39*, 370–380.

Meichenbaum, D. (1977). *Cognitive–behavior modification.* New York: Plenum.

Metalsky, G. I., & Abramson, L. Y. (1981). Attributional styles: Toward a framework for conceptualization and assessment. In P. C. Kendall & S. D. Hollon (Eds.), *Assessment strategies for cognitive–behavioral interventions* (pp. 13–58). San Diego, CA: Academic Press.

Metalsky, G. I., Abramson, L. Y., Seligman, M. E. P., Semmel, A., & Peterson, C. R. (1982). Attributional styles and life events in the classroom: Vulnerability and invulnerability to depressive mood reactions. *Journal of Personality and Social Psychology, 43*, 612–617.

Metalsky, G. I., Halberstadt, L. J., & Abramson, L. Y. (1987). Vulnerability to depressive mood reactions: Toward a more powerful test of the diathesis–stress and causal mediation components of the reformulated theory of depression. *Journal of Personality and Social Psychology, 52*, 386–393.

Metalsky, G. I., & Joiner, T. E., Jr. (1992). Vulnerability to depressive symptomatology: A prospective test of the diathesis–stress and causal mediation components of the hopelessness theory of depression. *Journal of Personality and Social Psychology, 63*, 667–675.

Metalsky, G. I., Joiner, T. E., Jr., Hardin, T. S., & Abramson, L. Y. (1993). Depressive reactions to failure in a naturalistic setting: A test of the hopelessness and self-esteem theories of depression. *Journal of Abnormal Psychology, 102*, 101–109.

Needles, D. J., & Abramson, L. Y. (1990). Positive life events, attributional style, and hopefulness: Testing a model of recovery from depression. *Journal of Abnormal Psychology, 99*, 156–165.

Neisser, U. (1967). *Cognitive psychology.* New York: Appleton-Century-Crofts.

Olson, J. M. (1988). Misattribution, preparatory information, and speech anxiety. *Journal of Personality and Social Psychology, 54*, 758–767.

Peplau, A., Russell, D., & Heim, M. (1979). The experience of loneliness. In I. H. Frieze, D. Bar-Tal, & J. Carroll (Eds.), *New approaches to social problems* (pp. 53–78). San Francisco: Jossey-Bass.

Peterson, C. R., Semmel, A., von Baeyer, C., Abramson, L. Y., Metalsky, G. I., & Seligman, M. E. P. (1982). The Attributional Style Questionnaire. *Cognitive Therapy and Research, 6*, 287–299.

Rehm, L. P. (1977). A self-control model of depression. *Behavior Therapy, 8,* 787–804.

Reisenzein, R. (1983). The Schachter theory of emotion: Two decades later. *Psychological Bulletin, 94,* 239–264.

Reisenzein, R., & Gattinger, E. (1982). Salience of arousal as a mediator of misattribution of transferred excitation. *Motivation and Emotion, 6,* 315–328.

Rimm, D. C., Kennedy, T. D., Miller, H. C., & Tchida, G. R. (1971). Experimentally manipulated drive level and avoidance behavior. *Journal of Abnormal Psychology, 78,* 43–48.

Ross, L. (1977). The intuitive psychologist and his shortcomings: Distortions in the attribution process. In L. Berkowitz (Ed.), *Advances in experimental social psychology* (Vol. 10). San Diego, CA: Academic Press.

Ross, L. (1978). Some afterthoughts on the intuitive psychologist. In L. Berkowitz (Ed.), *Cognitive theories in social psychology* (pp. 385–400). New York: Academic Press.

Ross, L., Rodin, J., & Zimbardo, P. G. (1969). Toward an attribution therapy: The reduction of fear through induced cognitive–emotional misattribution. *Journal of Personality and Social Psychology, 12,* 279–288.

Schachter, S. (1964). The interaction of cognitive and physiological determinants of emotional state. In L. Berkowitz (Ed.), *Advances in experimental social psychology* (Vol. 1, pp. 49–80). San Diego, CA: Academic Press.

Schachter, S., & Singer, J. (1962). Cognitive, social and physiological determinants of emotional state. *Psychological Review, 69,* 379–399.

Seligman, M. E. P., Abramson, L. Y., Semmel, A., & von Baeyer, C. (1979). Depressive attributional style. *Journal of Abnormal Psychology, 88,* 242–247.

Seligman, M. E. P., Castellon, C., Cacciola, J., Schulman, P., Luborsky, L., Ollove, M., & Downing, R. (1988). Explanatory style change during cognitive therapy for unipolar depression. *Journal of Abnormal Psychology, 97,* 13–18.

Seligman, M. E. P., & Maier, J. F. (1967). Failure to escape traumatic shock. *Journal of Experimental Psychology, 74,* 1–9.

Shaver, K. G. (1985). *The attribution of blame: Causality, responsibility, and blameworthiness.* New York: Springer-Verlag.

Shultz, T. R., & Schleifer, M. (1983a). Judgements of causation, responsibility and punishment in cases of harm-doing. *Canadian Journal of Behavioral Science, 13,* 238–253.

Shultz, T. R., & Schleifer, M. (1983b). Towards a refinement of attribution concepts. In J. Jaspars, F. D. Fincham, & M. Hewstone (Eds.), *Attribution theory and research: Conceptual, developmental, and social dimensions* (pp. 37–62). San Diego, CA: Academic Press.

Sillars, A. L. (1985). Interpersonal perception in relationships. In W. Ickes (Ed.), *Compatible and incompatible relationships* (pp. 277–305). New York: Springer-Verlag.

Singerman, K. J., Borkovec, T. D., & Baron, R. S. (1976). Failure of a "misattribution therapy" manipulation with a clinically relevant target behavior. *Behavior Therapy, 7*, 306–313.

Storms, M. D., & Nisbett, R. E. (1970). Insomnia and the attribution process. *Journal of Personality and Social Psychology, 16*, 319–328.

Tyrer, P., & Lader, M. H. (1974). Response to propranolol and diazepam in somatic and psychic anxiety. *British Medical Journal, 2*, 4–16.

Weinberg, R. S., Hughes, H. H., Critelli, J. W., England, R., & Jackson, A. (1984). Effects of preexisting and manipulated self-efficacy on weight loss in a self-control program. *Journal of Research in Personality, 18*, 352–358.

Weiner, B. (1972). *Theories of motivation.* Chicago: Markham.

Weiner, B. (1979). A theory of motivation for some classroom experiences. *Journal of Educational Psychology, 72*, 676–681.

Weiner, B. (1982). An attributional based theory of motivation and emotion: Focus, range, and issues. In N. T. Feather (Ed.), *Expectations and actions: Expectancy-value models in psychology* (pp. 163–204). Hillsdale, NJ: Erlbaum.

Weiner, B. (1985). An attributional theory of achievement motivation and emotion. *Psychological Review, 92*, 548–573.

Weiner, B. (1986). *An attributional theory of motivation and emotion.* New York: Springer.

Weiner, B., Frieze, I. H., Kukla, A., Reed, L., Rest, S., & Rosenbaum, R. M. (1971). Perceiving the causes for success and failure. In E. E. Jones, D. E. Kanouse, H. H. Kelley, R. E. Nisbett, S. Valins, & B. Weiner (Eds.), *Attribution: Perceiving the causes of behavior.* Morristown, NJ: General Learning Press.

Weiner, B., Russell, D., & Lerman, D. (1978). Affective consequences of causal ascriptions. In J. H. Harvey, W. J. Ickes, & R. F. Kidd (Eds.), *New directions in attribution research* (Vol. 2, pp. 59–90). Hillsdale, NJ: Erlbaum.

Williams, L. S., Dooseman, G., & Kleinfeld, E. (1984). Comparative effectiveness of guided mastery and exposure treatments for intractable phobias. *Journal of Consulting and Clinical Psychology, 52*, 505–518.

Williams, L. S., & Watson, N. (1985). Perceived danger and perceived self-efficacy as cognitive determinants of acrophobic behaviors. *Behavior Therapy, 16*, 136–146.

Zillman, D. (1971). Excitation transfer in communication-mediated aggressive behavior. *Journal of Experimental Social Psychology, 7*, 419–434.

15

AN INFORMATION-PROCESSING THEORY OF THE MEASUREMENT OF SOCIAL COMPETENCE

ELIZABETH C. McDONEL

A BRIEF HISTORY OF SOCIAL COMPETENCE THEORIES

A social skills approach has been successful in assessment and treatment of a disparate range of psychological problems. The social skills perspective had substantial applications to behavioral problems such as depression,[1] alcoholism,[2] chronic psychiatric disorders and schizophren-

I would like to thank Richard McFall, John McGrew, and Perilou Goddard for their comments and contributions to this manuscript. To those just named, as well as to David Schlundt, Kenneth Dodge, Clyde Peter Donahoe, Robert Levenson, Tom Johnson, David Lipton, Rick Sowder, and Cara Shapiro, I would like to express my deepest appreciation for their support and collaboration in conducting the research discussed in this chapter. I am also deeply grateful to Dolf Zillmann for feedback on my work and for mentorship in the arena of pornography research.

[1] e.g., Lewinsohn, Mischel, Chaplin, & Barton, 1980; Libet & Lewinsohn, 1973
[2] e.g., Chaney, O'Leary, & Marlatt, 1978; Marlatt & Gordon, 1978; Twentyman et al., 1982

ia,[3] childhood behavioral problems,[4] marital and interpersonal relationship problems,[5] and rape and sexual assault.[6]

Strong empirical linkages between social competence and many forms of psychopathology are now clearly established. Yet a theoretical relationship to account for such linkage must await further elaboration and testing of models (Goldfried, 1984; McFall, 1982; McFall, McDonel, Dodge, & Coie, 1986). Social incompetence may yield etiological significance; it may be a primary symptom of a psychopathological state. Alternatively, the negative outcome of social incompetence may enhance risk or relapse of certain behavioral syndromes in predisposed individuals. Although we may know from previous research that persons with certain psychological disorders tend to exhibit certain skills deficits, we know little about how deficits arose or what their continuing role is in maintenance of disordered behavior (McFall et al., 1986).

Earlier work in social skills research (pre-1980s) tended to be atheoretical and fragmented. A social competence investigator faced an extensive menu of skills and behavior sequences of possible relevance to the clinical problem or population of interest, with no logical way of choosing among them as a focus for study. Skills, or the behaviors underlying socially competent performance, were variously defined and unsystematically selected for inclusion in assessment protocols and in treatment programs. No comprehensive conceptual framework was available for integrating findings.

One prominent, early attempt to provide a systematic scheme focused on discrete behaviors that occur during social interaction, such as eye contact/gaze, smiling, head nodding, body fidgeting, self-manipulations, gestures, total talk time, silences/response latencies, total positive or negative verbal content, and so on. These were operationalized as *component social skills* (Trower, 1980). Conger and Conger (1982) elaborated on Trower's *component–process* distinction, in which process skills are seen as abilities such as timing, sequencing, turn taking, social sensitivity, and self-monitoring, which derive from the capacity to generate behavior according

---

[3]e.g., Anthony & Nemec, 1984; Barthell & Holmes, 1968; Bellack, Hersen, & Turner, 1976; Corrigan, Schade, & Liberman, 1992; Finch & Wallace, 1977; Goldsmith & McFall, 1975; Gutride, Goldstein, & Hunter, 1973; Hersen & Bellack, 1976a, 1976b; Jacobs, Muller, Anderson, & Skinner, 1972; Jaffe & Carlson, 1976; Liberman, Massel, Mosk, & Wong, 1985; Liberman, Mueser, & Wallace, 1986; Liberman, Nuechterlein, & Wallace, 1982; Matson & Stephens, 1978; Zigler & Levine, 1981; Zigler & Phillips, 1961, 1962

[4]e.g., Freedman, Rosenthal, Donahoe, Schlundt, & McFall, 1978; Gaffney & McFall, 1981; Garmezy, 1974; Gottman, Gonso, & Rasmussen, 1975; Gottman, Gonso, & Schuler, 1976; Oden & Asher, 1977; Rothenberg, 1970

[5]e.g., Arkowitz, Lichtenstein, McGovern, & Hines, 1975; Bander, Steinke, Allen, & Mosher, 1975; Borkovec, Stone, O'Brien, & Kaloupek, 1974; Curran, Gilbert, & Little, 1976; Gottman, Notarius, Gonso, & Markman, 1976; Kahn, 1970; MacDonald, Lindquist, Kramer, McGrath, & Rhyne, 1975; Pilkonis, 1977; Twentyman, Boland, & McFall, 1981; Twentyman & McFall, 1975

[6]e.g., Abel, Blanchard, & Becker, 1978; Becker, Abel, Blanchard, Murphy, & Coleman, 1978; Laws & Serber, 1975; Lipton, McDonel, & McFall, 1987; McDonel & McFall, 1991; McDonel, McFall, & Sowder, 1994; Murphy, Coleman, & Haynes, 1986

to rules and goals. These microunits of component skills in combination with process skills are theorized to predict global ratings of skilled behavior. Conger and Conger (1982) further explored component skills research and reviewed findings in support of this viewpoint. Corrigan et al. (1992) dubbed this component conceptualization the *topographic behavior model* of social skills and noted its consistency with the behavioristic and operant learning concepts that prevailed during the genesis of the model. Still, this molecular definition of skills failed to identify skills necessary for competent performance in relation to a specific task (Goldfried & D'Zurilla, 1969; McFall, 1982; Trower, 1980, 1982).

The same theoretical deficiency applied to early treatment studies. Training programs were often formulated without a careful analysis of the requisite skills for *effective performance on the particular task of interest*. Skills were chosen by face validity or the researcher's hunch. Thus, a researcher concluding that a social skills treatment package ineffectively addressed a particular behavioral problem was faced with several reasons that could account for this null effect: It could be due to the choice of irrelevant skills, to a true lack of relationship between any skills treatment to the solution of the behavior problem, or to insensitivity of the particular treatment protocol to increase the chosen skills. Further complicating the picture, a social skill that is important or useful for one situation may not be for another. Attention to frequent or appropriate eye contact may be critical to some situations (or cultures) but not to others. This inefficient and haphazard method of conducting skills research threatened the utility of the skills concept and dampened some researchers' enthusiasm for the approach. Investigators began to realize that skill is a relativistic concept, meaningful only in a specified context (e.g., Goldfried & D'Zurilla, 1969; Hersen & Bellack, 1977; McFall, 1976, 1982).

In their classic article, Goldfried and D'Zurilla (1969) set forth a methodology for conducting a systematic analysis of the skills required for a particular behavioral task. This five-step behavior–analytic procedure was validated by Goldfried and D'Zurilla on a set of heterosocial tasks that typically challenge college freshmen. Using the new method, a researcher first generates a problem situation pool and second, generates a sample of potential responses for each item in the problem situation pool. The third and fourth steps are to present the sample responses to a normative criterion group for judgments of appropriateness and then to create a scoring format based on the normative ratings. As the final step, the researcher chooses a subset of scorable items from the pool, thereby creating a competence measure for a given social task.

Subsequently, the behavior–analytic approach has been widely used and validated for a variety of behavioral problems (see McFall et al., 1986 for a review of the scope and success of this technique).

Goldfried and D'Zurilla's procedure advanced an important conceptual shift, reinforcing the concept of skills as situation-specific abilities rather than personality traits or response tendencies persisting across situations (McFall, 1976, 1982; McFall et al., 1986). This conceptual turn had enormous implications. A trait model saw people as consistently skillful across differing situations: Skillful behavior in one situation would be predictive of skillful behavior in other, dissimilar situations. By contrast, if skills are viewed as situationally specific abilities, a person can be thought of as skilled at interpreting social information, but not at problem solving; the relationship between these skills is assumed to be orthogonal, unless otherwise demonstrated in the context of a specific task. For example, in a sample of college males, Muehlenhard, Miller, and Burdick (1983) found no correlation between accuracy in reading heterosocial cues and the self-reported ability to initiate heterosocial interactions. Lanzetta and Kleck (1970) discovered an inverse correlation between a person's ability to decode (interpret) and encode (enact) affective responses. Viewing skills as situationally specific rather than traitlike had far-reaching implications for the enterprise of building assessment instruments: The process was now more complex, difficult, and time-consuming than building trait measures. (See Mischel, 1968 for the classic overview of the limitations of the trait concept; see McFall & McDonel, 1986, for an updated and comprehensive review of the trait concept as a psychological unit of analysis; and see J. Wallace, 1966, 1967, for an early discussion of abilities as an alternative conception of personality.)

Development and validation of the behavior–analytic method of measuring competence represented a productive advance in the field of social skills research. Still, the technique was limited in the types of skills it captured for assessment. This procedure could evaluate a person's ability to choose the best response from a menu of options, whereas other important capacities were not tapped (e.g., identifying problem situations, generating alternative responses, enacting responses, or evaluating the efficacy of responses once enacted). Consequently, this method evolved such that the entire sequence of problem-solving steps was elaborated into new measures (e.g., D'Zurilla & Goldfried, 1971; Platt, Siegel, & Spivack, 1975; Platt & Spivack, 1972a, 1972b, 1975; Spivack, Platt, & Shure, 1976). See Corrigan et al. (1992) for a review on the usefulness of such problem-solving measures with severely psychiatrically disabled patients.

Although the importance of problem-solving and enactment skills had been recognized, the theory and methodology then available for assessing skills had still to incorporate measures of the ability to receive and accurately interpret social information. Several investigators had already identified the importance of social perception skills, and some had made efforts to measure this type of skill.[7] Before 1980, no model fully explicated a method for systematically measuring and integrating into an assessment format all the skills necessary to succeed at a particular social task. Further theoretical and methodological enhancements were needed to complete a comprehensive skills assessment approach.

Concurrent with early efforts to measure social competence, scientific psychology as a discipline was shifting from a strongly behavioral to a cognitive–behavioral paradigm (Dember, 1974). The "cognitive revolution" brought exciting new theoretical templates and metaphors for conceptualizing behavior. Studies of human memory, language, perception, and emotion were challenging the widely embraced behavioristic stimulus–response model (Dember, 1974). Behaviorism began to yield to information-processing psychology in the 1960s, with the cognitive position achieving the status of accepted metatheory among most psychologists by the mid-1980s (Baars, 1986). These theoretical advances in the study of human information processing increased the objectivity and precision of measurement and thus the scientific acceptability of cognitive processes as a target for empirical investigation.

Similarly, the cognitive *zeitgeist* influenced a number of social competence researchers. In parallel, the topographic approaches to skills assessment in the 1970s gave way to cognitive formulations. An information-processing framework begins with the reception, perception, and interpretation of social input or stimuli and then proceeds to a decision-making sequence involving the generation of response alternatives, matching of alternatives to task demands, selection of the optimal response for a task, searching of one's behavioral repertoire for the availability of the chosen response, and the evaluation of the probable consequences of the response. Once a response is selected, it is enacted, and then the situation is monitored to determine the actual consequences of implementing the response.

Trower (1982) contributed heavily to this conceptual transition from the behavioral to the cognitive in the arena of skills research. He synthesized such early voices in the cognitive–behavioral movement as Bandura (1977), Harré and Secord (1972), Mischel (1973), and Schank and Abelson (1977). These theorists viewed the person as an active, information-processing agent—rather than as a passive agent—responding reflexively to stimuli, as in the behavioral model. From this perspective, a person is

---

[7]e.g., Argyle, 1969; Argyle, Laljee, & Cook, 1968; Beck, 1976; Bellack, 1979; Bellack & Hersen, 1978; Conger & Conger, 1982; DePaulo, Stone, & Lassiter, 1985; Ekman & Oster, 1979; Firth & Conger, 1980; Hall, Rosenthal, Archer, DiMatteo, & Rogers, 1978; Hoehn-Hyde, Schlottman, & Rush, 1982; Kahn, 1970; Kendon, 1967; Mischel, 1973; Morrison & Bellack, 1981; Nasby, Hayden, & DePaulo, 1980; O'Sullivan, 1982; Rosenthal, Hall, DiMatteo, Rogers, & Archer, 1979; Trower, 1980, 1982; Trower, Bryant, & Argyle, 1978; Walker, Marwit, & Emory, 1980

goal-oriented and, to that end, actively seeks out information and controls his or her actions to achieve a goal. McFall (1976) also stressed the active, task-oriented and goal-seeking properties of persons in an early conceptual paper on social competence. Trower (1982) connected new cognitive findings to the skills concept. Trower construed facility with social scripts or schemas as a type of skill. For example, when a person uses preexisting knowledge structures, such as social scripts (Schank & Abelson, 1977) or person schemata (Trower, 1982) to guide the choice of action, these cognitive processes can be measured as skills.

By the early 1980s, a critical mass of skills investigators had reenvisioned their various perspectives to include information-processing concepts.[8] For each social task, these models posited needed skills to correspond to stages in an information-processing sequence.

In 1984, Marvin Goldfried and Richard McFall brought together six different social skills research teams for a 3-hr symposium at the 18th Annual Convention of the Association for the Advancement of Behavior Therapy. As its stated purpose, the symposium was to move "toward a unified model of social skills and social competence." Each of the six teams presented research in social competence; five groups used social information-processing concepts in their work (Curran & Faraone, 1984; Dodge, Pettit, & McClaskey, 1984; Donahoe, Boone, Foy, & Liberman, 1984; McFall, McDonel, & Lipton, 1984; Trower, 1984), whereas Gottman and Levenson (1984) spoke about their findings relating psychophysiological processes to social competence. The symposium established the information-processing perspective as being ascendant among skills researchers, as findings were synthesized and ideas cross-fertilized.

Bearing in mind this historical background, I now turn to an elaboration of one of these proposed social information-processing models of social competence with a brief presentation of supporting research conducted to validate that model. Following this is a look at problems and pitfalls in conducting such research, as well as a summary of its contributions toward demonstrating the utility of a social information-processing conceptualization of social competence. Reviews of other similar models and subsequent programmatic research stimulated by those models are available elsewhere.[9] The focus here is on the model of social competence presented by McFall in 1982 and the research conducted by McFall, McDonel, and our colleagues in an attempt to validate that model.

---

[8]e.g., Dodge, 1983; Dodge & Newman, 1981; McFall, 1982; McFall & Dodge, 1982; Schlundt & McFall, 1985; Trower, 1982; C. J. Wallace et al., 1980; C. J. Wallace, 1982
[9]e.g., Coie & Dodge, 1986; Corrigan et al., 1992; Dodge, 1983; Dodge, Murphy, & Buchsbaum, 1984; Dodge, Pettit, McClaskey, & Brown, 1986; C. J. Wallace, 1982; C. J. Wallace, Boone, Donahoe, & Foy, 1985; C. J. Wallace et al., 1980

McFALL'S INFORMATION-PROCESSING MODEL OF
SOCIAL COMPETENCE

McFall (1982) proposed a comprehensive reformulation of the social skills concept grounded in information-processing theory. McFall proposed solutions for the lack of standardization of terms and conceptual precision in the field of social competence research. The basic tenets of the model are summarized here; for in-depth treatment, the reader may refer to McFall (1982), to McFall et al. (1986), or to Schlundt and McFall (1985).

Social competence is defined as an external, relativistic, social judgment one makes about another person's behavior. Competence is a subjective evaluation made by someone and, as such, is subject to error or bias. Consequently, the evaluation of *competence* at a particular task requires a measurement approach that averages global judgments across a large normative group of raters to balance out these distorting influences.

On the other hand, *social skills* are defined as the specific abilities that enable a person to earn the appraisal of competence. This clarification of constructs is important and establishes that they should no longer be used synonymously.

Social skills required for competent performance are hypothesized to correspond to steps in an information-processing sequence. The incoming stimuli, or situational task demands, are the input that pass through a series of steps that eventually lead to the output, or task performance. These steps are outlined in Figure 1, adapted from McFall (1982).

Decoding skills comprise the first portion of the information-processing sequence and involve three distinct steps. Information must be accurately received, perceived, and interpreted. *Reception* of information refers to the sensory registration of stimulus information. Errors in reception could occur if a person is visually or hearing-impaired, is distracted, or is in an affective state that would divert attention away from receiving incoming information. *Perception* involves the active transformation of sensory information into a representation in memory. This perceptual representation is then actively compared against other representations in memory in the *interpretation* step. At the interpretation phase, the incoming information is assigned meaning. It is at the interpretation stage that cognitive *schemas* may be activated to add meaning to perceptual data. A schema is a knowledge structure in memory that represents and organizes information about a concept or sets of concepts (Fiske & Taylor, 1991). Most of us have schemas that organize our knowledge about types of people (e.g., Democrats or Republicans), objects (e.g., scissors or pencils), or events (e.g., football games or church services).

Once information has been decoded, a series of *decision skills* are needed to transform the information into a response choice. These resem-

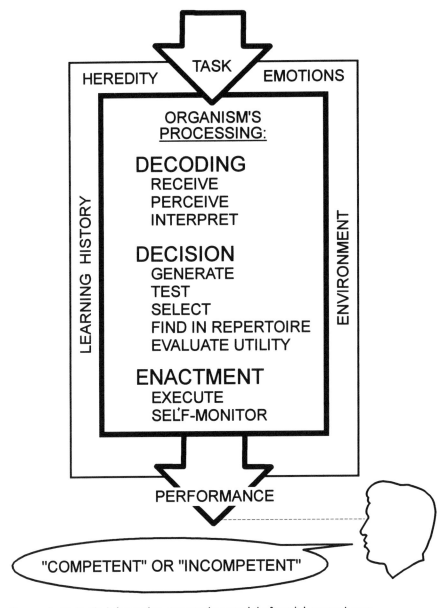

Figure 1. McFall's information-processing model of social competence.

ble the steps in the problem-solving literature discussed earlier. The first decision step involves generating a list of response alternatives. We know this colloquially as "brainstorming." Each alternative must then be evaluated for its probable efficacy against the presenting task demands. The response that best matches the task demands from the pool of alternatives is chosen. This choice is then evaluated against one's own response repertoire: A person may not have the expertise or fortitude to implement the best response choice for the task at hand. In this case, a person may cycle back and choose the second-best response that fits task demands, because it best fits the person's own capabilities. For example, confronting a family member about his or her problem drinking may be the best response in a given situation. Yet that family member may not be facile with a confrontive style of communication and so might choose another response.

Once a response has been selected and it has been determined that the response is within one's capacity to carry it out, the response must be enacted, or *encoded*. (The use of the term *encoding* here is consistent with the usage in the tradition of research in human communication, e.g., Ekman & Oster, 1982, and is distinguished from its very different meaning in the cognitive literature, where encoding refers to the process of creating a mental representation of information in memory.)

Once the response is performed, the person must use *self-monitoring skills*: If a discrepancy occurs between the intended and the actual impact of the enacted response, the individual may have to engage in corrective action and will cycle through these information-processing steps again.

Clearly, a deficit at any step or set of steps can impair performance. Subjects who, as a group, all perform poorly at a particular social task may be quite heterogeneous as to the nature of the deficits responsible for their externally judged incompetence. Poor performance could be a function of decoding, decision, encoding, or monitoring skills deficits, or of some combination of these skills deficits. Skill at each step in the model is seen as *necessary, but not sufficient*, in and of itself, for competent performance. This principle has clear implications for research and training. A profile of skills deficits could be obtained by measuring proficiency at each step in the model. In a sample of subjects defined as incompetent at a particular task, subgroups of subjects with similar patterns of skills deficits could be identified and targeted for treatment that is tailored to their specific deficiencies. The therapeutic utility of skills approaches may have been underestimated in previous investigations because of a failure to custom design treatment to fit the clients. Treatment efforts have often been broad-spectrum in nature to compensate for the imprecision of assessment and the multiplicity of pathways that can lead to incompetent performance. With a more systematic and detailed analysis of the underlying skills deficits, treatment programs can be designed to be more focused and efficiently applied.

VALIDATION OF THE INFORMATION-PROCESSING MODEL

To validate McFall's model, assessment instruments must be developed, psychometrically fine-tuned, and validated for each skill in the model. Further, this process must be implemented with respect to the specific situational task for which one wants to predict competence. The measurement of only one skill will yield limited power in predicting global evaluations of competence; as additional skills are added to an assessment battery, predictive power will increase. However, if a person does demonstrate a deficit in a particular skill, the model dictates that there will necessarily be some decrement in the final outcome; a group of subjects with a known decoding deficit, on average, should receive lower ratings of social competence than a group of subjects who do not exhibit decoding deficits. Therefore, evidence for the validity of a single skill measure using this known-groups method is, by definition, partial and preliminary; the full power of the model can be determined only when decoding skill is measured simultaneously in the context of other requisite skills.

McFall and I believed that the best way to begin validating the model was at the start of the information-processing sequence: We chose to measure the reception, perception, and interpretation of social information combined in the stage called "decoding skills." Decoding of social information is unconfounded by any of the other processing stages. Researchers starting at any other step in the sequence would have to account or control for previous steps in applying the new measure. Also, decoding skill had received relatively less attention in the literature, in contrast to decision and performance skills.

The next section describes the development and validation of three decoding skills measures undertaken by McFall and myself with help from several other graduate and undergraduate assistants. We chose heterosocial competence as the situational task to target for study for several reasons: heterosocial incompetence (i.e., shyness, social anxiety, minimal dating) is a clinically significant research topic. Success or failure at heterosocial relationships is a commonly experienced problem, bringing about considerable distress and anxiety (e.g., Borkovec, Stone, O'Brien, & Kaloupek, 1974; Hersen & Bellack, 1977; Pilkonis, 1977). Heterosocial incompetence is also an important correlate of more serious forms of psychopathology (e.g., Zigler & Levine, 1981; Zigler & Phillips, 1961, 1962).

Development of a Measure of Decoding Ability: The TRAC

In 1980, I was a new graduate student in clinical psychology at Indiana University, under the direction of Dick McFall. Lyle Jaffe had just completed an undergraduate honors thesis with McFall, and David Schlundt was a senior graduate student of McFall's at that time. My program of graduate research, as well as Schlundt's, and Jaffe's honors thesis addressed the validation and elaboration of McFall's model of social competence. Robert Levenson was also a faculty member at Indiana University who was interested in the psychophysiology of emotion. Together, we formed a collaborative research group.

As we began to plan for the development of a decoding measure in 1980, we first searched the literature to determine if there was an already available measure that would suit our purposes. At that time, the concept of social perceptual ability had been established as an area of inquiry within a number of other theoretical frameworks. Similar constructs are social intelligence (Thorndike, 1939), social perception (e.g., Taft, 1955), empathy (see Eisenberg & Miller, 1987, for a review of the construct and related measures), person perception (e.g., Tagiuri, 1969), cognitive appraisals (Mischel, 1973), perceptual social skill (e.g., Morrison & Bellack, 1981), and nonverbal sensitivity (Firth & Conger, 1980; Rosenthal et al., 1979). Decoding ability had been a general interest in the area of emotion (e.g., Ekman & Oster, 1979).

By 1980, measures of the decoding construct had already provided substantial evidence of the link between the inability to decode social information accurately and psychopathology. A dysfunction in the decoding of affective cues had been implicated in schizophrenia,[10] in depression (e.g., Beck, 1976; Lewinsohn et al., 1980; Strack & Coyne, 1983), aggressive behavior in children (Dodge, 1980; Dodge & Newman, 1981), social and emotional adjustment in children (Gottman et al., 1975; Rothenberg, 1970), and heterosocial dating problems (Firth & Conger, 1980; Gottman, Notarius, Gonso, & Markman, 1976).

Many tests had been generated to measure decoding accuracy for different emotions (eight of these tests are well reviewed by O'Sullivan, 1982). For the most part, existing tests focused on the decoding of cues in nonverbal channels, were trait-oriented rather than situationally specific, or were not developed in relation to clinical problems. Although a few tests did have demonstrated clinical utility, they did not meet the criterion of being situationally specific. Thus, no available test was a good fit for testing decoding skill within McFall's formulation.

In 1980, McFall, Levenson, and Jaffe had laid the groundwork for a decoding skill measure in a pilot study, conducted as Jaffe's honors thesis (Jaffe, 1980). An instrument was constructed of nine videotaped segments of opposite-sexed dyadic interactions. The actors were instructed to portray one of three affects in each interaction (i.e., positive, neutral, or negative feelings toward the partner). Subjects viewed this videotape and were asked to guess which affect each actor was portraying. Accuracy scores for raters were constructed. Two extreme groups of subjects who scored either high

---

[10]e.g., Dougherty, Bartlett, & Izard, 1974; Higgins, Mednick, Philip, & Thompson, 1966; Levy, Orr, & Rosenzweig, 1960; Mednick, 1958; Spiegel, Gerard, Grayson, & Gengerelli, 1962; Trower et al., 1978; Walker et al., 1980

or low on the measure were extracted and tested on other measures of competence as an exploratory validation exercise. Validation subjects gave a speech about their interests, special qualities, and about why they would be a good date. Physiological measures were collected before, during, and after the speech. Subjective ratings of these speeches made by another subject group indicated that high accuracy subjects were rated as more appealing and as having made a more positive impression. Striking physiological differences were found: High-accuracy decoders were more reactive on measures of cardiovascular and electrodermal response during portions of the speech than were low-accuracy decoders.

There were several problems with this first pilot study. The fidelity of the measure was poor, the videotapes were black and white, and the actors' profiles were shown at a distance, rather than full-face and close-up. There were too few items to obtain reliability and too few subjects in the study to have confidence in the generalizability of findings. However, this pilot study served as a successful check on the feasibility of investing more time and resources into a better measure. Consequently, a second-generation measure was constructed, psychometrically tuned, and validated: This measure we called the Test of Reading Affective Cues, or the TRAC (McDonel, McFall, Schlundt, & Levenson, 1985).

To develop the TRAC, we first generated a large sample of videotaped segments of more than 200 opposite-sexed dyadic interactions. Actors for these segments were college subjects who interacted in two dating scenarios: a first date, where the actors were fairly unacquainted, and a more intimate relationship scene, where actors were well acquainted. Within each of the two types of scenes, the target actor portrayed one of five different affective sets—romantic, positive, neutral, negative, or bad mood. The affect portrayed by the other person in each dyad, the nontarget actor, was held constant, and was always positive. This sample of videotaped interactions was then processed through two item-selection phases for the development of the final version of the TRAC. In the first step, the research team selected a subset of items to include in the preliminary TRAC; in the second step, this subset was rated by a large sample of college students. A final version of the TRAC was constructed using these normative ratings to eliminate bad items and to construct a scoring format for the remaining items. Good items were considered to be any item that had achieved a 31% to 95% consensus range in the normative rating stage.

In the final TRAC, 40 items were selected for the final first-date portion (TRAC-D), and 32 items were selected for the intimate portion (TRAC-I). Each videotaped item was about 30 s in length; these items were edited onto a single videotape for each of the two scenes, with the scoring scheme for rating the actors presented for 15 s in between each item. A sample item was used at the beginning of each of the two types of date scenes, to familiarize raters with the scoring format. For each item in the TRAC, future raters would be asked to guess the affective state of each of the actors. Raters would be told in advance that one person in each item was portraying a positive affect and that the other person in the item could portray any of the five affective cues. Normative data were again collected for each scene in the TRAC, using large samples of college subjects for the creation of a final scoring protocol. (See McDonel et al., 1985 for a complete analysis of the psychometric properties of the TRAC.) Using these new norms, a validation sample was selected, using the upper ($N = 16$ high-accuracy decoders) and lower ($N = 15$ low-accuracy decoders) quartiles in the distribution of male scores.

TRAC Validation Study 1

Subjects were administered behavioral, self-report, and physiological measures of social skill, similar to those that had been used in the pre-TRAC pilot study. Four self-report measures of heterosocial competence were used: (a) the Survey of Heterosexual Interactions (SHI), a measure of social avoidance (Twentyman & McFall, 1975); (b) the Watson-Friend Social Anxiety and Distress Scale (SAD; Watson & Friend, 1969); (c) the Social Situations Questionnaire (SSQ), which measures competence in dating and assertion situations (Levenson & Gottman, 1978); and (d) a dating frequency questionnaire. Validity and reliability of these measures is discussed in McDonel et al. (1985). Men were asked to make a speech about their interests, special qualities, and potential for being a good date. Behavioral measures of competence were acquired through obtaining global ratings of these audiotaped speeches from female raters. We also obtained ratings of subjects' physical attractiveness from photographs taken at the time of the experiment. Physiological measures were taken throughout pre- and postspeech baselines and during the speech.

The results of this three-tiered validation study were mixed. There were no significant differences between high and low decoding accuracy on any of the four self-report measures or the attractiveness measure. The speeches were rated for global competence and for 10 specific categories of speech quality; the groups did not differ on global competence ratings, but a stepwise discriminant function analysis found that 5 of the 8 reliable specific speech categories could correctly classify 87% of the 31 subjects. Better decoders described more of their own special qualities, gave more information about their background, were less likely to be specific about what they would do on a potential date, sounded less nervous during the speech, and were more likely to mention that the speech was a difficult task, according to the female raters, than the low-accuracy decoding group. Physiological measures taken during the speech task did not yield significant results, failing to replicate the physiological findings in the pilot study.

At this point, our research team wondered if our subject selection criterion had yielded adequately extreme subsamples; we conducted further exploratory, post hoc analyses for a new subset of high- ($N = 11$) and low- ($N = 9$) accuracy decoders selected using more stringent TRAC cutoff scores. New analyses on all the validation measures revealed previously undetected relationships between attractiveness and decoding accuracy (with better cue-readers judged as less physically attractive) and between decoding accuracy and physiological responsiveness (with high-accuracy decoders showing more cardiac reactivity during the initial instructions for the speech, during speech countdown, and during the speech than low-accuracy decoders). Low-accuracy decoders were more electrodermally responsive during speech instructions, countdown, and speech presentation. These findings were interesting, yet perplexing, as the skin conductance results were in the opposite direction from our findings in the pilot study using a different decoding measure. One possible interpretation from these results is that decoding skill is a different skill than that tapped by the SHI, which measured the ability to initiate dates (an enactment skill), by the SSQ, which measured competence in dating and assertion situations (a combination of decision skills and enactment skills), by the SAD, which measured global fear of social situations, (perhaps closest to a self-monitoring skill), and dating frequency, which may not have a direct relationship to heterosocial success. Dating frequency measures may be more directly related to social competence when measured as a ratio to the number of different partners dated. These null findings were not inconsistent with the model, because skills in the information-processing sequence were postulated to be orthogonally related. We speculated that, given the high value society places on physical attractiveness, less attractive persons may have learned to compensate for this social disadvantage by becoming more skilled at decoding others' heterosocial intention cues. Perhaps the consistent heart rate findings were evidence that better decoders of social information were also more physiologically attuned to social stimuli. The results of the specific speech category ratings showed that better decoders were generally more socially appropriate in the content of their speech. In fact, their speeches more closely followed the directions the experimenter had given subjects about the purpose of the speech—another decoding task.

TRAC Validation Study 2

In a different attempt to validate the TRAC, we used the measure with a clinical sample to see if it would discriminate between a sample of subjects theorized to have social perception skill deficits and a control group. In the literature on rapists, there had been some evidence of deficiencies among rapists in heterosocial skills and knowledge (Abel et al., 1978; Becker et al., 1978), and speculation that social skills training would be a useful form of rehabilitation (Boozer, 1975; Pacht, 1975). We investigated the hypothesis that convicted rapists could be discriminated from two control groups: samples of violent and of nonviolent nonrapist controls, also incarcerated for their crimes (Lipton, et al., 1987). David Lipton joined us in this investigation while he was a psychology intern at the U.S. Penitentiary in Terre Haute, Indiana. The TRAC-D and TRAC-I were administered to each of these three groups. Rapists were found to be significantly poorer at reading women's cues on the TRAC-D than violent inmates, and violent inmates were found to be significantly poorer decoders of women's cues on the TRAC-D than nonviolent inmates. The rapist group was especially prone to errors in judging negative information (i.e., lack of romantic interest) emitted by women. In other words, rapists displayed a blind spot with respect to their ability to process negative social information from women. To interpret this result for violent convicts, it would be important for future research to rule out as a confound the possibility that a significant proportion of violent subjects may have had undetected episodes of sexual violence. We know that there is a high base-rate of sex offenses in the general population and that the majority of these go unreported, and of those that are reported, a majority do not reach a conviction (e.g., Koss & Oros, 1982). No group differences were obtained for the TRAC-I or for reading of men's cues on the TRAC-D. The TRAC-I result may be attributable to a true insensitivity of the measure, to measurement artifact—fewer items in the TRAC-I or a situation-specific deficit—with rapists showing decoding impairment in situations in which actors are relatively unacquainted but not in situations where actors are intimately acquainted. The lack of findings for reading of men's cues would be consistent with the view of decoding skills deficits in rape being specific to the reading of women only.

In a substudy with these three samples, we found evidence for excellent test–retest reliability of the TRAC, increasing our confidence in the psychometric adequacy of the measure. Given the very few social and psychological measures that have been identified in the sex offender literature as useful for discriminating sex offenders from nonoffenders (for a review of rape correlates, see Koss & Leonard, 1984; Lipton et al., 1987; McDonel, 1986; McDonel & McFall, 1991; McDonel et al., 1994), we were cautiously excited about the implications of our findings.

TRAC Validation Study 3

McFall and I further tested the construct validity of the TRAC as a measure of rape proclivity. Neil Malamuth and his colleagues (e.g., Malamuth, Haber, & Feshbach, 1980) had created and validated a self-report instrument of rape proclivity or likelihood to rape in male subjects. The rape proclivity scale measured the degree of endorsement of a number of rape-supportive attitudes in the context of the presentation of a written rape vignette, and the man's self-report of likelihood that he would commit a similar rape, given that there would be no chance he would be caught and punished. We hypothesized that there would be a relationship between two of our heterosocial perception instruments and the Malamuth et al. (1980) proclivity measure. Thus, in a new validation study with a large sample of male college students, we examined the correlational relationships between the TRAC-D, a paper-and-pencil measure of heterosocial perception skill we had created (the Heterosocial Perception Survey, or HPS), and Malamuth's rape proclivity measure (McDonel & McFall, 1991). The new HPS measure consisted of three dating scenarios, intended to measure the extent to which subjects accept that a woman means no when she says "no" to a man's sexual advances. Three different situations are depicted: (a) a couple is alone together in her apartment and are newly acquainted; (b) a couple is alone in her apartment and has known each other for 3 months; and (c) a man and woman who have just met at a party are together in the woman's apartment, both have used alcohol, and the woman has accepted an invitation of a ride home and has offered an invitation to the man to come in for a cup of coffee.

Results of this study showed that the tendency to hold rape-supportive attitudes and to self-report rape proclivity on the Malamuth measure was negatively and significantly ($p < .05$) correlated with decoding accuracy on the TRAC-D. Specifically, four rape-supportive attitudes correlated with decoding accuracy on female negative cues, ranging from $r(49) = -.24$ to $r(49) = -.35$. Males' self-reported proclivity to rape on the average of two proclivity items correlated with decoding accuracy of negative female cues, $r(49) = -.48$. Also, better decoders of negative female cues on the TRAC-D as well as those men who expressed fewer rape-supportive beliefs and less rape proclivity were more conservative in their estimates of a man's justification in continuing to make sexual advances in the face of a woman's negative cues on the HPS. To measure the combined utility of the two social perception measures in predicting rape proclivity, a stepwise multiple regression analysis was computed using a measure of dating satisfaction, the HPS, and the Negative Female decoding portion of the TRAC-D as independent variables and rape proclivity as the dependent variable. The multiple R of .67 was significant ($p < .05$), with the beta weights showing that all three independent variables were significantly related to the dependent variable. Together, the three measures accounted for 45% of the variance in rape proclivity scores, with the TRAC-D accounting for 23% of the variance, HPS accounting for an additional 12% of the variance, and dating satisfaction accounting for another 10% of the variance. These findings further reinforced the value of the TRAC-D, as well as a new heterosocial perception measure, the HPS, for use in rape research.

In another attempt to validate the TRAC as a social perception measure useful for rape research, McFall and I, as part of my doctoral dissertation (McDonel, 1986), investigated the influence of nonviolent pornography on the ability to accurately decode women's heterosocial cues. We hypothesized that brief, videotaped presentations of pornographic stimuli would affect men's social perception of women's cues of interest in the opposite sex. We believed that the social information portrayed in the pornographic segments would interfere with, distort, or bias the interpretation of women's negative cues in the TRAC. At the time of this research project, Malamuth and Check (1980, 1981) found that exposure to violent pornography rendered both men and women less sensitive to the plight of the rape victim, fostered belief in rape myths, and encouraged greater tolerance of violence toward women. We were interested in whether nonviolent pornography had a similar influence on the men's perception of women. In a set of two experiments, videotaped segments of nonviolent pornographic material were edited between items of the TRAC-D at four equal intervals and administered to a sample of male college students. Decoding scores from this group were compared to two control conditions: One group viewed a version of the TRAC-D with arousing but nonerotic stimuli, and another group rated a version of the TRAC-D containing nonarousing, neutral stimuli interspersed throughout. Contrary to predictions, subjects in the pornography condition did not perform more poorly at the decoding task than neutral controls; unexpectedly, subjects in the nonerotic arousal control group scored significantly better than the neutral group on the decoding of women's negative cues on the TRAC-D. The study was repeated, moving the locations of the interspersed stimuli. Again, we failed to find significant differences between the pornography and neutral conditions for decoding skill. Subjects in the nonerotic arousal control condition were again significantly better decoders of women's negative cues on the TRAC-D than subjects in the pornography condition or neutral control group. This finding may best be understood in light of previous research relating arousal to attention or vigilance. For any task, there is an optimal level of arousal that results in maximal performance. Presumably, this relationship is mediated by attentional processes. The relationship between arousal and attention is well known to resemble an inverted U-shaped curve. Subjects in our arousal condition may have experienced arousal at a more optimal level compared to the neutral controls for maximizing performance on the decoding task.

We also speculated that the interactions in the TRAC-D may not provide the type of cues that would be most sensitive to a pornography manipulation; we wondered if a new measure that portrayed richer and more varied types of heterosocial information would be a better test of our pornography hypothesis. We decided to construct a new decoding measure, the TRAC-S, that incorporated more cues of a sexual nature (e.g., more looking, touching, intimate and suggestive conversation) and to use this measure in another pornography experiment.

TRAC-S Development and Validation Study

McFall and I developed the TRAC-S using a procedure similar to the development of the TRAC (McDonel, 1986; McDonel et al., 1994). The new measure recorded videotaped vignettes of heterosocial interaction collected "on location" at sites in the community rather than in our university laboratory. Male actors were instructed to convey more cues of a sexual or romantic interest compared to positive portrayals of the male nontarget actors in the TRAC. For the TRAC-S, because we were interested only in measuring men's ability to decode women's cues, all male actors were instructed to portray a positive, romantic interest in the female actor. Female actors were instructed to portray one of five affective sets toward the male characters: very interested, somewhat interested, uncertain, somewhat uninterested, or very uninterested. When the TRAC-S is given to men as a decoding measure, their task is to assess the female actor's receptiveness to the male actor's advances. We created instructions for the rating of the TRAC-S that took inspiration from colloquial language: Subjects were asked to rate female actors as giving a "green," "partly green," "yellow," "partly red," or "red" signal indicating her receptiveness to the man's advances. We reasoned that this system would be simple and intuitive so that it could be used with subjects of diverse levels of intelligence and education. At the outset, we also planned to include a larger sample of items in the TRAC-S than we had in the TRAC-D of women portraying neutral, negative, and bad mood cues. Because of our previous findings that decoding of negative female cues was most predictive of rape status and of other rape correlates, we hypothesized that the inclusion of more items that targeted negative female cues would heighten the difficulty or sensitivity of the new measure, especially for rapists, and for men with high rape proclivity. The TRAC-S could be broken down into two decoding subscores: accuracy on the 14 positive items (those normed at green or partly green) or accuracy on the 16 negative items (those normed at yellow, partly red, or red). Once this measure was developed and normed (see McDonel et al., 1994 for a description of the development, psychometric properties, and validation of the TRAC-S), we repeated the pornography experiment that we had conducted with the TRAC-D. We expanded the subject population to three levels to include a sample of convicted rapists and a sample of nonviolent, nonrapist convicts, in addition to a group of male college students. Following the administration of the TRAC-S, we also gave all subjects in all three experimental conditions the Malamuth rape attitude and rape proclivity measures that we had used previously (McDonel & McFall, 1991). In addition, we included five questions to tap men's endorsement of common rape myths not covered in the Malamuth instrument.

The hypothesized main effect of pornography on decoding performance was obtained; all three subject groups who viewed pornography showed a decrement in performance in reading both positive and negative cues emitted by women, compared to neutral controls and to arousal controls. Unlike the findings in the pornography studies with the TRAC-D, we did not find an enhancement of decoding skill for the arousal control subjects, compared to neutral control. A significant main effect was found for rape status, with rapists showing poorer decoding skill than male college students on each of the positive and negative cue scales of the TRAC-S. However, we were disappointed that an a priori contrast failed to reveal a significant difference in the decoding skill of rapists and nonrapist convicts on either decoding scale. We had also hypothesized an interaction between rape status and arousal condition such that rapists' ability to decode female cues would be disrupted to a greater degree by the pornography manipulation than the performance of the other two subject groups. However, this interaction was not obtained for either scale of the TRAC-S. Upon obtaining these results, we speculated that an interaction effect might emerge in future research that examined exposure to pornographic stimuli that were violent or coercive in nature.

To analyze the questionnaire data, responses of all three subject groups were combined from the two control conditions. For this entire subsample, better decoders on the TRAC-S were less likely to endorse the five rape myth items as true, were less likely to self-report rape proclivity, were more sympathetic in their view of a rape victim, and were less sympathetic toward the actions of a rapist than were poorer decoders. These results were consistent with the pattern of findings in our earlier validation studies with the TRAC-D. We also found that better decoders were less likely to report that they had viewed commercially available pornographic videotapes.

Our work on decoding skill in rapists adds to the growing research literature on the negative effects of nonviolent pornography on heterosocial perception and contributes a new type of dependent variable that may be useful for future research on the problem of rape and on the effects of pornography. The new measure, the TRAC-S, was successful in detecting a pornography effect, and in replicating a pattern of correlations with other self-reported rape attitude and proclivity measures that we had obtained previously with the TRAC-D. Unlike the TRAC-D, the TRAC-S failed to discriminate rapists from nonrapist convict controls.

UTILITY OF INFORMATION-PROCESSING THEORY FOR CONCEPTUALIZING SOCIAL COMPETENCE

We believe that our program of research, as a whole, shows that an information-processing approach to the analysis of social competence is promising. It is clear that further programmatic research and refinement of measures is needed to clarify the role of decoding skill in sex offenses. However, we hope that our findings show that the pursuit of situationally specific measures of social decoding skill is a worthwhile enterprise and that these findings are a partial and preliminary demonstration of the validity and utility of McFall's information-processing approach to the measurement of social competence. McFall's model stipulates that measurement of a single skill will likely yield only moderate associations with the target variable. As other requisite skills are included (i.e., decision, performance, and self-monitoring skills), this information can be combined to yield even greater predictive power. Dodge (1983) successfully used this aggregated skill assessment approach in predicting a child's competence in a peer group entry task and in a peer provocation situation. The assessment of multiple skill deficits in rapists may prove just as valuable, once accomplished. Only after sufficient assessment research has been completed and accurate and comprehensive specification of deficits is obtained can the treatment and remediation of skills deficits be efficiently approached.

As a footnote, it would be unfair not to be candid in describing some of the disadvantages of investing in this type of research, from my own perspective. This process has been tedious, labor-intensive, and time-consuming, with many steps of measure development and analysis and with many versions of the measure created toward the end of evolving progressively more refined measures. These steps do not correspond to many publishable phases that will help to build an academic vita or to earn tenure. Building a new assessment instrument is also not a highly fundable research enterprise in and of itself. Although I am strongly committed to the importance of the model and am pleased with the general trend of the results we have obtained, I have been discouraged about the supports, rewards, and recognition available for performing this research. One needs a strong capacity for delayed gratification. Furthermore, although the TRAC and TRAC-S have been partially validated, I have also watched how such measures that use videotaped segments of social interaction can become dated in appearance, and so they have become obsolete or invalid before they have reaped their full potential (e.g., the clothing, language, and cultural fads current at the time of taping the TRAC are now out of favor; watching some portions of the TRAC is a little like watching reruns of old TV programs—the point comes across, but the outmoded context may detract from the original message). McFall and I feel that we have provided a demonstration that the approach we have taken will work. The methodology has been demonstrated, but we acknowledge that the instruments that are created will require constant updating and refining. Paper-and-pencil measures have not escaped the problem of anachronism, but videotaped behavior samples appear to be even more vulnerable. Video and computer technology is enormously better and more user-friendly now than it was 11–14 years ago when we began our work and would greatly enhance the quality, flexibility, and speed in modifying similar assessment tools if conducted currently. Finally, as we knew at the outset, it is a more grueling process to go about measuring situationally specific abilities than traits. A greater variety of measures for any particular skill is needed to reflect situational variability. We believe that we have made headway in demonstrating the ultimate payoff of this approach—that of achieving better prediction. We take this opportunity to encourage institutions supporting academic researchers to consider their payoff for providing more support for conducting behavioral assessment research. McFall, his colleagues, and current students are continuing the testing of the information-processing model of social competence.

REFERENCES

Abel, G. G., Blanchard, E. B., & Becker, J. V. (1978). An integrated treatment program for rapists. In R. T. Rada (Ed.), *Clinical aspects of the rapist* (pp. 161–214). New York: Grune & Stratton.

Anthony, W. A., & Nemec, P. B. (1984). Psychiatric rehabilitation. In A. S. Bellack (Ed.), *Schizophrenia treatment, management, and rehabilitation* (pp. 375–413). Orlando, FL: Grune & Stratton.

Argyle, M. (1969). *Social interaction.* London: Methuen.

Argyle, M., Laljee, M., & Cook, M. (1968). The effects of visibility on interaction in a dyad. *Human Relations, 21,* 3–77.

Arkowitz, H., Lichtenstein, E., McGovern, K., & Hines, P. (1975). The behavioral assessment of social competence in males. *Behavior Therapy, 6,* 3–13.

Baars, B. J. (1986). *The cognitive revolution in psychology.* New York: Guilford Press.

Bander, K. W., Steinke, G. W., Allen, G. J., & Mosher, D. L. (1975). Evaluation of three dating-specific approaches for heterosexual anxiety. *Journal of Consulting and Clinical Psychology, 43,* 259–265.

Bandura, A. (1977). *Social learning theory.* Englewood Cliffs, NJ: Prentice Hall.

Barthell, C. N., & Holmes, D. S. (1968). High school yearbooks: A nonreactive measure of social isolation in graduates who later became schizophrenic. *Journal of Abnormal Psychology, 73,* 313–316.

Beck, A. T. (1976). *Cognitive therapy and the emotional disorders.* New York: International Universities Press.

Becker, J. V., Abel, G. G., Blanchard, E. B., Murphy, W. D., & Coleman, E. (1978). Evaluating social skills of sexual aggressives. *Criminal Justice and Behavior, 5,* 357–368.

Bellack, A. S. (1979). A critical appraisal of strategies for assessing social skill. *Behavioral Assessment, 1,* 157–176.

Bellack, A. S., & Hersen, M. (1978). Chronic psychiatric patients: Social skills training. In M. Hersen & A. S. Bellack (Eds.), *Behavior therapy in the psychiatric setting* (pp. 169–185). Baltimore: Williams & Wilkins.

Bellack, A. S., Hersen, M., & Turner, S. M. (1976). Generalization effects of social skills training in chronic schizophrenics: An experimental analysis. *Behaviour Research and Therapy, 14,* 391–398.

Boozer, G. (1975). *Offender treatment: Programming.* Proceedings of the Sixth Alabama Symposium on Justice and the Behavioral Sciences, University of Alabama, Tuscaloosa, AL.

Borkovec, T. D., Stone, N. M., O'Brien, G. T., & Kaloupek, D. G. (1974). Identification of a clinically relevant target behavior for analogue outcome research. *Behavior Therapy, 5,* 503–513.

Chaney, E. F., O'Leary, M. R., & Marlatt, G. A. (1978). Skill training with alcoholics. *Journal of Consulting and Clinical Psychology, 46,* 1092–1104.

Coie, J. D., & Dodge, K. A. (1986). A social information-processing approach to distinguishing between hostile and instrumental aggressive behavior problems in rejected children. Paper presented at the annual meeting of the American Psychological Association, Washington, DC.

Conger, J. C., & Conger, A. J. (1982). Components of heterosocial competence. In J. P. Curran & P. Monti (Eds.), *Social skills training* (pp. 313–347). New York: Guilford Press.

Corrigan, P. W., Schade, M. L., & Liberman, R. P. (1992). Social skills training. In R. P. Liberman (Ed.), *Handbook of psychiatric rehabilitation* (pp. 95–126). New York: Macmillan.

Curran, J. P., & Faraone, S. V. (1984). *Schizophrenia as perceived from a social competency model.* Panel presentation at the 18th Annual Convention of the Association for the Advancement of Behavior Therapy, Philadelphia.

Curran, J. P., Gilbert, F. S., & Little, L. M. (1976). A comparison between behavioral replication training and sensitivity training approaches to heterosexual dating anxiety. *Journal of Counseling Psychology, 23,* 190–196.

Dember, W. N. (1974). Motivation and the cognitive revolution. *American Psychologist, 29,* 161–168.

DePaulo, B. M., Stone, J. I., & Lassiter, G. D. (1985). Deceiving and detecting deceit. In B. R. Schlenker (Ed.), *The self and social life* (pp. 323–370). New York: McGraw-Hill.

Dodge, K. A. (1980). Social cognition and children's aggressive behavior. *Child Development, 51,* 162–170.

Dodge, K. A. (1983). *A social information processing model of social competence in children*. Paper presented at the Minnesota Symposium on Child Psychology, Minneapolis.

Dodge, K. A., Murphy, R. M., & Buchsbaum, K. (1984). The assessment of intention-cue detection skills in children: Implications for developmental psychopathology. *Child Development, 55,* 163–173.

Dodge, K. A., & Newman, J. P. (1981). Biased decision-making processes in aggressive boys. *Journal of Abnormal Psychology, 90,* 375–379.

Dodge, K., Pettit, G., & McClasky, C. (1984). *Social information processing components of social competence in children*. Panel presentation of the 18th Annual Convention of the Association for the Advancement of Behavior Therapy, Philadelphia.

Dodge, K., Pettit, G., McClaskey, C., & Brown, M. (1986). Social competence in children. *Monographs of the Society for Research in Child Development, 51* (2, Serial No. 213).

Donahoe, C. P., Boone, S. E., Foy, D. W., & Liberman, R. P. (1984). *Problem-solving with schizophrenics*. Panel presentation at the 18th Annual Convention of the Association for the Advancement of Behavior Therapy, Philadelphia.

Dougherty, F. E., Bartlett, E. S., & Izard, C. E. (1974). Responses of schizophrenics to expressions of the fundamental emotions. *Journal of Clinical Psychology, 30,* 243–246.

D'Zurilla, T. J., & Goldfried, M. R. (1971). Problem solving and behavior modification. *Journal of Abnormal Psychology, 78,* 107–126.

Eisenberg, N., & Miller, P. A. (1987). The relation of empathy to prosocial and related behaviors. *Psychological Bulletin, 101,* 91–119.

Ekman, P., & Oster, H. (1979). Facial expressions of emotion. *Annual Review of Psychology, 30,* 527–554.

Finch, B. E., & Wallace, C. J. (1977). Successful interpersonal skills training with schizophrenic inpatients. *Journal of Consulting and Clinical Psychology, 45,* 885–890.

Firth, E., & Conger, J. C. (1980). *The role of nonverbal sensitivity in social skills*. Paper presented at the 14th Annual Convention of the Association for the Advancement of Behavior Therapy.

Fiske, S. T., & Taylor, S. E. (1991). *Social cognition*. New York: McGraw-Hill.

Freedman, B. J., Rosenthal, L., Donahoe, C. P., Jr., Schlundt, D. G., & McFall, R. M. (1978). A social–behavioral analysis of skill deficits in delinquent and nondelinquent boys. *Journal of Consulting and Clinical Psychology, 46,* 1448–1462.

Gaffney, L. R., & McFall, R. M. (1981). A comparison of social skills in delinquent and nondelinquent adolescent girls. *Journal of Consulting and Clinical Psychology, 49,* 959–967.

Garmezy, N. (1974). The study of competence in children at risk for severe psychopathology. In E. J. Anthony & C. Koupernik (Eds.), *The child in his family: Children at psychiatric risk* (pp. 77–97). New York: Wiley.

Goldfried, M. (1984). *Toward a unified model of social skills and social competence.* Symposium chaired at the 18th Annual Convention of the Association for the Advancement of Behavior Therapy, Philadelphia, PA.

Goldfried, M. R., & D'Zurilla, T. J. (1969). A behavior–analytic model for assessing social competence. In C. D. Spielberger (Ed.), *Current topics in clinical and community psychology* (Vol. 1, pp. 151–196). San Diego, CA: Academic Press.

Goldsmith, J., & McFall, R. (1975). Development and evaluation of an interpersonal skill-training program for psychiatric inpatients. *Journal of Abnormal Psychology, 84,* 51–58.

Gottman, J. M., Gonso, J., & Rasmussen, B. (1975). Social interaction, social competence, and friendship in children. *Child Development, 46,* 709–718.

Gottman, J. M., Gonso, J., & Schuler, P. (1976). Teaching social skills to isolated children. *Journal of Abnormal Psychology, 85,* 179–197.

Gottman, J. M., & Levenson, R. W. (1984). *The social psychophysiology of marriage.* Panel presentation at the 18th Annual Convention of the Association for the Advancement of Behavior Therapy, Philadelphia, PA.

Gottman, J. M., Notarius, C., Gonso, J., & Markman, H. (1976). *A couple's guide to communication.* Champaign, IL: Research Press.

Gutride, M. E., Goldstein, A. P., & Hunter, G. F. (1973). The use of modeling and role playing to increase social interaction among asocial psychiatric patients. *Journal of Consulting and Clinical Psychology, 40,* 408–415.

Hall, J., Rosenthal, R., Archer, D., DiMatteo, M., & Rogers, P. (1978, May). Decoding wordless messages. *Human Nature,* pp. 68–75.

Harré, R., & Secord, P. (1972). *The explanation of social behaviour.* Oxford: Blackwell.

Hersen, M., & Bellack, A. S. (1976a). Social skills training for chronic psychiatric patients: Rationale, research findings, and future directions. *Comprehensive Psychiatry, 17,* 559–580.

Hersen, M., & Bellack, A. S. (1976b). A multiple-baseline analysis of social-skills training in chronic schizophrenics. *Journal of Applied Behavior Analysis, 9,* 239–245.

Hersen, M., & Bellack, A. (1977). Assessment of social skills. In A. R. Ciminero, K. S. Calhoun, & H. E. Adams (Eds.), *Handbook of Behavioral Assessment* (pp. 509–554). New York: Wiley.

Higgins, J., Mednick, S. A., Philip, F. J., & Thompson, R. E. (1966). Associative responses to evaluative and sexual verbal stimuli by process and reactive schizophrenics. *Journal of Nervous and Mental Disease, 142,* 223–227.

Hoehn-Hyde, D., Schlottman, R., & Rush, A. (1982). Perception of social interactions in depressed psychiatric patients. *Journal of Consulting and Clinical Psychology, 50,* 209–212.

Jacobs, M. A., Muller, J. J., Anderson, T., & Skinner, J. C. (1972). Therapeutic expectations, premorbid adjustment, and manifest distress levels as predictors of improvement in hospitalized patients. *Journal of Consulting and Clinical Psychology, 39,* 455–461.

Jaffe, L. B. (1980). The relationship between the ability to read social cues in dating situations and heterosexual competence. Undergraduate honors thesis, Indiana University.

Jaffe, P. G., & Carlson, P. M. (1976). Relative efficacy of modeling and instructions in eliciting social behavior from chronic psychiatric patients. *Journal of Consulting and Clinical Psychology, 44,* 200–207.

Kahn, M. (1970). Non-verbal communication and marital satisfaction. *Family Process, 9,* 449–456.

Kendon, A. (1967). Some functions of gaze direction in social interaction. *Acta Psychologica, 27,* 1–47.

Koss, M. P., & Leonard, K. E. (1984). Sexually aggressive men: Empirical findings and theoretical implications. In N. M. Malamuth (Ed.), *Pornography and sexual aggression.* San Diego, CA: Academic Press.

Koss, M. P., & Oros, C. J. (1982). Sexual experiences survey: A research instrument investigating sexual aggression and victimization. *Journal of Consulting and Clinical Psychology, 50,* 455–457.

Lanzetta, J. T., & Kleck, R. E. (1970). Encoding and decoding of nonverbal affect in humans. *Journal of Personality and Social Psychology, 16,* 12–19.

Laws, D. R., & Serber, M. (1975). Measurement and evaluation of assertive training with sexual offenders. In R. Hosford & C. Moss (Eds.), *The crumbling walls: Treatment and counseling prisoners.* Champaign, IL: University of Illinois Press.

Levenson, R. W., & Gottman, J. M. (1978). Toward the assessment of social competence. *Journal of Consulting and Clinical Psychology, 46,* 453–462.

Levy, L., Orr, T., & Rosenzweig, S. (1960). Judgments of emotion from facial expressions by college students, mental retardates, and mental hospital patients. *Journal of Personality, 28,* 342–349.

Lewinsohn, P. M., Mischel, W., Chaplin, W., & Barton, R. (1980). Social competence and depression: The role of illusory self-perceptions. *Journal of Abnormal Psychology, 89,* 203–212.

Liberman, R. P., Massel, H. K., Mosk, M. D., & Wong, S. E. (1985). Social skills training for chronic mental patients. *Hospital and Community Psychiatry, 36,* 396–403.

Liberman, R. P., Mueser, K. T., & Wallace, C. J. (1986). Social skills training for schizophrenic individuals at risk for relapse. *American Journal of Psychiatry, 143,* 523–526.

Liberman, R. P., Nuechterlein, K. H., & Wallace, C. J. (1982). Social skills training and the nature of schizophrenia. In J. P. Curran & P. M. Monti (Eds.), *Social skills training: A practical handbook for assessment and treatment* (pp. 5–56). New York: Guilford Press.

Libet, J. M., & Lewinsohn, P. M. (1973). Concept of social skill with special reference to the behavior of depressed persons. *Journal of Consulting and Clinical Psychology, 40,* 304–312.

Lipton, D. N., McDonel, E. C., & McFall, R. M. (1987). Heterosocial perception in rapists. *Journal of Consulting and Clinical Psychology, 55,* 17–21.

MacDonald, M. L., Lindquist, C. V., Kramer, J. A., McGrath, R. A., & Rhyne, L. L. (1975). Social skills training: The effects of behavior rehearsal in groups in dating skills. *Journal of Counseling Psychology, 22,* 224–230.

Malamuth, N. M., & Check, J. (1980). Penile tumescence and perceptual responses to rape as a function of victim's perceived reactions. *Journal of Applied Social Psychology, 10,* 528–547.

Malamuth, N. M., & Check, J. (1981). The effects of mass media exposure on acceptance of violence against women: A field experiment. *Journal of Research in Personality, 15,* 436–446.

Malamuth, N. M., Haber, S., & Feshbach, S. (1980). Testing hypotheses regarding rape: Exposure to sexual violence, sex differences, and the "normality" of rapists. *Journal of Research in Personality, 14,* 121–137.

Marlatt, G. A., & Gordon, J. R. (1978). *Determinants of relapse: Implications for the maintenance of behavior change* (Alcoholism and Drug Abuse Tech. Rep. No. 18-07) Seattle: University of Washington.

Matson, J., & Stephens, R. M. (1978). Increasing appropriate behavior of explosive chronic psychiatric patients with a social skills training package. *Behavior Modification, 2,* 61–75.

McDonel, E. C. (1986). Sexual aggression and heterosocial perception: The relationship between decoding accuracy and rape correlates (Doctoral dissertation, Indiana University, Bloomington, 1986) *Dissertation Abstracts International, 47,* 08B.

McDonel, E. C., & McFall, R. M. (1991). Construct validity of two heterosocial perception skill measures for assessing rape proclivity. *Violence and Victims, 6,* 17–29.

McDonel, E. C., McFall, R. M., Schlundt, D. G., & Levenson, R. W. (1985). *Heterosocial perception: Development and validation of a performance measure.* Unpublished manuscript, Indiana University, Bloomington.

McDonel, E. C., McFall, R. M., & Sowder, R. (1994). *Nonviolent pornography, heterosocial decoding skill, and rape proclivity.* Manuscript submitted for publication.

McFall, R. M. (1976). *Behavioral training: A skill acquisition approach to clinical problems.* Morristown, NJ: General Learning Press.

McFall, R. M. (1982). A review and reformulation of the concept of social skills. *Behavioral Assessment, 4,* 1–33.

McFall, R. M., & Dodge, K. A. (1982). Self-monitoring and interpersonal skills learning. In P. Karoly & F. H. Kanfer, (Eds.), *Self-management and behavior change: From theory to practice* (pp. 353–392). New York: Pergamon Press.

McFall, R. M., & McDonel, E. C. (1986). The continuing search for units of analysis in psychology: Beyond persons, situations, and their interactions. In R. Nelson & S. C. Hayes (Eds.), *Conceptual foundations of behavioral assessment* (pp. 201–241). New York: Wiley.

McFall, R. M., McDonel, E. C., Dodge, K. A., & Coie, J. D. (1986, February). *Social information processing and sexual aggression.* Paper presented at NIMH Invitational Meeting on the Assessment and Treatment of Sex Offenders, Florida Mental Health Institute, Tampa, FL.

McFall, R. M., McDonel, E. C., & Lipton, D. (1984). *Heterosocial cue-reading skills in psychopathology.* Panel presentation at the 18th Annual Convention of the Association for the Advancement of Behavior Therapy, Philadelphia.

Mischel, W. (1968). *Personality and assessment.* New York: Wiley.

Mischel, W. (1973). Toward a cognitive social learning reconceptualization of personality. *Psychological Review, 80,* 252–283.

Morrison, R. L., & Bellack, A. S. (1981). The role of social perception in social skill. *Behavior Therapy, 12,* 69–79.

Muehlenhard, C. L., Miller, C. L., Burdick, C. A. (1983). Are high-frequency daters better cue-readers? Men's interpretations of women's cues as a function of dating frequency and SHI scores. *Behavior Therapy, 14,* 626–636.

Murphy, W. D., Coleman, E. M., & Haynes, M. R. (1986). Factors related to coercive sexual behavior in a nonclinical sample of males. *Violence and Victims, 1,* 255–278.

Nasby, W., Hayden, B., & DePaulo, B. M. (1980). Attributional bias among aggressive boys to interpret unambiguous social stimuli as displays of hostility. *Journal of Abnormal Psychology, 89,* 459–468.

Oden, S., & Asher, S. R. (1977). Coaching children in social skills for friendship making. *Child Development, 48,* 495–506.

O'Sullivan, M. (1982). Measuring the ability to recognize facial expressions of emotion. In P. Ekman (Ed.), *Emotion in the human face* (pp. 281–317). Cambridge, England: Cambridge University Press.

Pacht, A. (1975). *The rapist in treatment: Professional myths and psychological realities.* Proceedings of the Sixth Alabama Symposium on Justice and the Behavioral Sciences, University of Alabama, Tuscaloosa, AL.

Pilkonis, P. A. (1977). The behavioral consequences of shyness. *Journal of Personality, 45,* 196–211.

Platt, J. J., Siegel, M. J., & Spivack, G. (1975). Do psychiatric patients and normals see the same solutions as effective in solving interpersonal problems? *Journal of Consulting and Clinical Psychology, 43,* 279.

Platt, J. J., & Spivack, G. (1972a). Problem-solving thinking of psychiatric patients. *Journal of Consulting and Clinical Psychology, 39,* 148–151.

Platt, J. J., & Spivack, G. (1972b). Social competence and effective problem-solving thinking in psychiatric patients. *Journal of Consulting and Clinical Psychology, 28,* 3–5.

Platt, J. J., & Spivack, G. (1975). *The Means Ends Problem Solving Procedure Manual*. Philadelphia: W. B. Saunders.

Rosenthal, R., Hall, J. A., DiMatteo, M. R., Rogers, P. L., & Archer, D. (1979). *Sensitivity to nonverbal communication: The PONS test*. Baltimore: Johns Hopkins University Press.

Rothenberg, B. B. (1970). Children's social sensitivity and the relationship to interpersonal competence, interpersonal comfort, and intellectual level. *Developmental Psychology, 2*, 335–350.

Schank, R. C., & Abelson, R. P. (1977). *Scripts, plans, goals, and understanding*. Hillsdale, NJ: Erlbaum.

Schlundt, D. G., & McFall, R. M. (1985). New directions in the assessment of social competence and social skills. In M. A. Milan & L. L. L'Abate (Eds.), *Handbook of social skills training and research*. New York: Wiley.

Spiegel, D., Gerard, R., Grayson, H., & Gengerelli, J. (1962). Reactions of chronic schizophrenic patients and college students to facial expressions and geometric forms. *Journal of Clinical Psychology, 18*, 396–402.

Spivack, G., & Platt, J. J., & Shure, M. (1976). *The problem-solving approach to adjustment*. San Francisco: Jossey-Bass.

Strack, S., & Coyne, J. C. (1983). Social confirmation of dysphoria: Shared and private reactions to depression. *Journal of Personality and Social Psychology, 44*, 806–814.

Taft, R. (1955). The ability to judge people. *Psychological Bulletin, 52*, 1–23.

Tagiuri, R. (1969). Person perception. In G. Lindzey & E. Aronson (Eds.), *Handbook of social psychology* (Vol. 3, pp. 395–449). Reading, MA: Addison-Wesley.

Trower, P. (1980). Situational analysis of the components and processes in behavior of socially skilled and unskilled patients. *Journal of Consulting and Clinical Psychology, 48*, 327–339.

Trower, P. (1982). Toward a generative model of social skills: A critique and synthesis. In J. P. Curran & P. M. Monti (Eds.), *Social skills training: A practical handbook for assessment and treatment* (pp. 399–427). New York: Guilford Press.

Trower, P. (1984). *A self system model of social competence*. Panel presentation at the 18th Convention of the Association for the Advancement of Behavior Therapy, Philadelphia.

Trower, P., Bryant, B., & Argyle, M. (1978). *Social skills and mental health*. London: Methuen.

Twentyman, C., Boland, T., & McFall, R. M. (1981). Heterosocial avoidance in college males. *Behavior Modification, 5*, 523–552.

Twentyman, C., Greenwald, D., Greenwald, M., Kloss, J., Kovaleski, M., Zibung-Hoffman, P. (1982). An assessment of social skill deficits in alcoholics. *Behavioral Assessment, 4*, 317–326.

Twentyman, C., & McFall, R. M. (1975). Behavioral training of social skills in shy males. *Journal of Consulting and Clinical Psychology, 43*, 384–395.

Walker, E., Marwit, S. J., & Emory, E. (1980). A cross-sectional study of emotion recognition in schizophrenics. *Journal of Abnormal Psychology, 89,* 428–436.

Wallace, C. J. (1982). The Social Skills Training Project of the Mental Health Clinical Research Center for the Study of Schizophrenia. In J. P. Curran & P. M. Monti (Eds.), *Social skills training: A practical handbook for assessment and treatment* (pp. 57–89). New York: Guilford Press.

Wallace, C. J., Boone, S. E., Donahoe, C. P., & Foy, D. (1985). The chronically mentally disabled: Independent living skills training. In D. Barlow (Ed.), *Clinical handbook of psychological disorders: A step-by-step treatment manual* (pp. 462–501). New York: Guilford Press.

Wallace, C. J., Nelson, C. J., Liberman, R. P., Aitchison, R. A., Lukoff, D., Elder, J. P., & Ferris, C. (1980). A review and critique of social skills training for patients with schizophrenia: A controlled clinical trial. *Psychiatry Research, 15,* 239–247.

Wallace, J. (1966). An abilities conception of personality: Some implications for personality measurement. *American Psychologist, 21,* 132–138.

Wallace, J. (1967). What units shall we employ? Allport's question revisited. *Journal of Consulting and Clinical Psychology, 31,* 56–64.

Watson, D., & Friend, R. (1969). Measurement of social–evaluative anxiety. *Journal of Consulting and Clinical Psychology, 33,* 448–457.

Zigler, E., & Levine, J. (1981). Premorbid competence in schizophrenia: What is being measured? *Journal of Consulting and Clinical Psychology, 49,* 96–105.

Zigler, E., & Phillips, L. (1961). Social competence and outcome in psychiatric disorders. *Journal of Abnormal and Social Psychology, 63,* 264–271.

Zigler, E., & Phillips, L. (1962). Social competence and the process–reactive distinction in psychopathology. *Journal of Abnormal and Social Psychology, 65,* 215–222.

16

A THEORY OF RELAPSE PREVENTION

D. R. LAWS

I'm discovering, not recovering (relapse prevention slogan)

Relapse prevention (RP) was a natural outgrowth of the therapy movement that eventually linked early, traditional behavior therapy with cognitive therapy. The original premise of behavior therapy was focused on changing troublesome behavior first, with the expectation that cognitions would eventually become congruent with the altered behavior. This point of view is nicely expressed in the old behaviorist adage, "It's easier to behave your way into thinking differently than it is to think your way in behaving differently." Sometimes it turned out that way, and sometimes it did not. Cognitive–behavior therapy states this premise differently. The altered position asserts that behaviors and cognitions are inextricably linked. These cognitive–behavioral chains are present in most complex behaviors. Some cognitive–behavioral chains produce outcomes that are

Preparation of this chapter was supported in part by Contract No. 21100-0-0818 from Correctional Service Canada and by Alberta Hospital Edmonton.

I wish to thank Alan Marlatt, Janice Marques, and Bill Pithers for their assistance in preparation of this chapter.

potentially positive for the actor and others (socially appropriate or non-deviant behavior), whereas other outcomes may be potentially positive for the actor (at least in the short term) and negative for others (socially inappropriate or deviant behavior). The main focus of RP is on the analysis and restructuring of the various elements of these cognitive–behavioral chains. The chains that result in socially or personally undesirable outcomes represent the targets for treatment.

It is important to understand that RP was not initially intended to serve as a treatment intervention. In its initial formulation (Marlatt, 1980; Marlatt & Gordon, 1985), it was described as a *maintenance strategy* that was intended to follow a more conventional treatment program. Given its early focus on classical addictive behaviors (drugs and alcohol), in public health terms it has been characterized as a *tertiary prevention technique* (i.e., treatment of a developed disorder; Marlatt & Tapert, 1993). With few exceptions, RP procedures continue to be generally construed as a fairly labor-intensive, hands-on follow-up (see selections in Wilson, 1992c). More recent writers (Baer, 1993; Sobell & Sobell, 1993; Wanigaratne, Wallace, Pullin, Keaney, & Farmer, 1990) suggest that RP may be used as both a tertiary prevention technique and a secondary prevention technique (arresting the progress of a potential disorder; e.g., safe sex practices to avoid HIV risk).

ORIGINS

The basic idea of RP (Marlatt, 1980; Marlatt & Gordon, 1985) emerged from the alcohol- and drug-treatment field. Workers in that field observed that a variety of treatments could effectively moderate, if not eliminate, undesired behaviors such as heroin, alcohol, and tobacco addiction (e.g., Hunt, Barnett, & Branch, 1971). At the time that the cessation-oriented treatment ended, they noted, the probability of continued abstinence was highest. However, they also noted that in the absence of further intervention, over the next 12 months, relapse rates would approach 80% and two thirds of all relapses would occur within the first 90 days after treatment termination. Marlatt (1980) and his colleagues reasoned that a follow-up treatment that was specifically designed to *maintain* the effects of the cessation-oriented treatment would thereby prevent relapse. If one could determine which situations or states of mind posed the highest risk for relapse for a client and adequate coping skills (both behavioral and cognitive) could be taught to deal with those threatening situations, then the effects of the original treatment could be maintained. If it is true that the number of available, effective coping skills will discriminate relapsers from survivors, then a method such as this should prevent relapse.

A THEORY OF RELAPSE PREVENTION

It is my position that RP can stand alone as a theory. It may be viewed as a maintenance program following a formal cessation-oriented treatment (Marlatt, 1985d, pp. 3–67; Wanigaratne et al., 1990), or it may be viewed as an overarching concept under which a host of behavioral and cognitive–behavioral treatments may be organized (i.e., the cessation-oriented treatment may be administered within an overall RP framework; George & Marlatt, 1989; Marques, Day, Nelson, & Miner, 1989; Pithers, Martin, & Cumming, 1989; Wanigaratne et al., 1990). It is in either case a theory that has never received an adequate test. Therefore, in this chapter I organize the various statements of RP into a formal theoretical statement of principles, propositions, and hypotheses (stated as *assessment* or *treatment* operations). I use Marlatt's (1985) original statements as the basic framework, adding where necessary other or more recent statements that serve either to clarify or to expand the basic model (Wanigaratne et al., 1990).

DESCRIPTION

Assumptions

Primary Assumptions

The basic assumption of RP as a theory is that there is no reason to expect that the effects of a treatment designed to moderate or to eliminate an undesirable behavior will necessarily persist for very long beyond the termination of that treatment. This assertion would be especially true of what might be called *addictive disorders* (e.g., alcohol or drug addiction, smoking) or *disorders of impulse control* (e.g., compulsive sexual behaviors, compulsive gambling, sexual deviance, problem drinking, compulsive spending, shoplifting, and interpersonal violence). After treatment for any of these disorders, the treated client will experience thoughts and feelings related to the now-terminated behavior and find himself or herself in situations or in the presence of stimuli previously associated with that behavior. To the extent that the client is able to deal effectively with these multiple risks, the effects of the cessation-oriented treatment can be maintained.

A Model of Relapse

The cognitive–behavioral model of the relapse process originally described by Marlatt (1985d) has been revised very little in the intervening years (Emmelkamp, Kloek, & Blaauw, 1992; Pithers, 1991). At the termination of the cessation-oriented treatment, the treated client is confident and certain that he or she will not relapse. He or she is in a state of *abstinence*, has a high sense of *self-efficacy*, and a *positive outcome expectancy* for successfully maintaining abstinence. However, sooner or later the client may begin making a series of minidecisions that, if not recognized and checked, could result in lapses from abstinence. These were originally called *apparently irrelevant decisions* (AIDs). (Because of the unfortunate derived acronym, they are now referred to as either *seemingly irrelevant decisions* (Somers & Marlatt, 1992) or *seemingly unimportant decisions* (Pithers, 1991). I use the former term, abbreviated as SIDs). A SID is a little slip, a minilapse (e.g., "finding" onself in an environment previously associated with the terminated behavior). A SID is a highly risky decision, seen at the time as not terribly important, but one that takes the client one step closer to even larger lapses or a full-blown relapse. SIDs are also referred to as deliberate *setups* (Wanigaratne et al., 1990). This process is exacerbated if the client insists on "testing" him- or herself in dangerous situations to determine if treatment has "worked." If the client does not make a SID, then the probability of relapse will remain low, self-efficacy will remain high, and a positive outcome expectancy will be maintained. If the client does make a SID (or a series of SIDs), he or she will eventually arrive at a *high-risk situation*, which poses a threat to his or her perception of self-control.

These situations are frequently characterized by negative emotional states, interpersonal conflicts, and social pressure from others, all major precursors of relapse. To this point, we assume that in addition to the SIDs, the client has also been making a series of *maladaptive coping responses*, all of which are inexorably leading him or her toward additional lapses. If, at this point, the client can summon an *adaptive coping response* (ACR), abstinence will be maintained along with high self-efficacy and a positive outcome expectancy. If the preceding fails, eventually a lapse will occur (e.g., smoking *one* cigarette, being socially pressured into taking *a* drink or smoking *some* marijuana, or putting *only* the change in one's pocket into a slot machine). Because these behaviors are exactly the ones from which the client is supposedly abstaining, he or she may experience the *abstinence violation effect* (AVE; also called the *rule violation effect* [RVE]; Wanigaratne et al, 1990). The AVE is the recognition by the client that he or she has violated the vow of abstinence and thus that the whole purpose of treatment is being defeated. There are sequelae to the AVE that include *self-deprecation* ("You're worthless! You can't stay away from it!"), *failure expectation* ("Well, I guess treatment didn't work."), the *problem of immediate gratification* (the PIG phenomenon), the desire to reexperience the sensations previously associated with the behavior ("How can one time hurt? And anyhow, I need it!"), and *erroneous self-attributions* ("It's my fault. I'm a failure."). Individually or in combination, these elements of the AVE markedly increase the probability of a full-blown relapse. However, despite the cascading negative feelings associated with the AVE, if the client can once again summon an ACR, he or she can return to abstinence and soberly consider the lessons of the AVE-related episode. If the adaptive coping response cannot be produced, a full relapse is likely.

Although RP was originally presented as a *maintenance strategy*, a careful reading of Marlatt's (1985) original statements shows that little or no mention is ever made of the cessation-oriented treatment that RP is intended to follow. The cessation treatment program appears, rather, to be embodied in the theory, and it could easily stand alone as a series of interventions. The program can be tailored to an individual's needs, as Marlatt and Gordon (1985) suggested, or RP elements can be packaged and delivered to groups as treatment components (e.g., Marques et al., 1989; Marshall, Hudson, & Ward, 1992; Pithers et al., 1989; Wanigaratne et al., 1990).

Scope of the Theory

A Limited Theoretical Scope

Although it was originally developed as a treatment for alcoholism and drug addiction, Marlatt (1985d) suggested that RP could be applied to

> any compulsive habit pattern in which the individual seeks a state of immediate gratification. With many addictive behaviors . . . the immediate experience of gratification (the pleasure, "high," tension reduction, or relief from distress associated with the act itself) is followed by delayed negative consequences such as physical discomfort or disease, social disapproval, financial loss, or decreased self-esteem. (p. 4)

From this point of view, RP is applicable not only to traditional *addictive behaviors*—such as alcoholism, drug dependency, and smoking—but also to *disorders of impulse control*—such as compulsive gambling; shoplifting; weight management; obsessive–compulsive behaviors; interpersonal violence; phobias or panic states in general; some sexual deviations, such as exhibitionism, pedophilia, voyeurism, fetishism, or obscene telephone calling; problem drinking; or compulsive spending. Other sexual targets might include so-called "sexual addiction," or "sexual compulsion," or exposure to HIV risk, where safe sexual practices would be a major coping skill in an RP program.

Given the definition above, all of these behaviors share common elements. All of them appear to be compulsive habit patterns that produce immediate gratification, which are followed by a variety of delayed negative consequences. Successful treatment of any of them requires abstention from the problem behavior. All of them should therefore be amenable to treatment by RP. This is not an exhaustive list, but limiting the scope of application to these types of behaviors initially still provides a fairly broad test of the theory.

Structure of the Theory

The following set of statements is intended to present RP as a structured theory that is amenable to empirical test. These are presented as general principles and propositions derived from or related to them, from which specific hypotheses (i.e., about assessment and treatment interventions) are determined. I have divided the theory statement into three parts: (a) basic RP concepts, (b) covert antecedents of relapse (how people get into high-risk situations), and (c) determinants of relapse (how people can manage high-risk situations). In doing this, I have essentially used the conceptual framework advanced by George and Marlatt (1989, pp. 1–29), although I have reordered their format somewhat. Where necessary, I have noted the relevant pages in the cited text. I have supplemented Marlatt's statements with some more recent statements by Wanigaratne et al. (1990), whose treatment manual describes RP in highly accessible and common-sense clinical terms.

A THEORY OF RELAPSE PREVENTION

Basic Relapse Prevention Concepts: Maladaptive Behavior and Relapse

Principle 1: Relapse Prevention Definition of Maladaptive Behavior

Addictive behaviors and disorders of impulse control consist of overlearned, maladaptive habit patterns. They are usually followed by some form of immediate gratification and are often performed in situations perceived as stressful. When performed during or before stressful or unpleasant situations, they represent maladaptive coping mechanisms, which may lead to delayed negative consequences in terms of health, social status, and self-esteem (Marlatt, 1985d, p. 10).

Proposition 1.1. These maladaptive habit patterns are multiply determined by past learning experiences, situational antecedent influences, prevailing reinforcement contingencies (rewards *and* punishments), cognitive expectations or beliefs, and biological influences (George & Marlatt, 1989, p. 3).

Proposition 1.2. The maladaptive habit pattern is used to cope with life stressors and dissatisfactions. More adaptive coping responses are not used by the individual, and the maladaptive response has developed as a replacement for this deficiency (George & Marlatt, 1989, p. 3).

Proposition 1.3. The maladaptive habit pattern lies on a continuum between nonproblematic expression and addictive or problematic expression (George & Marlatt, 1989, p. 3). It is not an either/or phenomenon. The flexibility of this shifting between the two extremes permits intervention at many points along the continuum.

Hypothesis 1.1. If maladaptive behavior patterns are governed by the same learning principles as adaptive ones, they are therefore open to modification and change. Because cognitions and behaviors are closely related in the process of lapse and relapse, a social learning–based cognitive–behavioral therapy is the best vehicle for promoting behavior change.

Hypothesis 1.2. Irrespective of the fact that an individual's habit pattern has been determined by multiple factors often beyond his control, the changing of habits involves the active participation and responsibility of the person involved (Marlatt, 1985d, p. 11).

Hypothesis 1.3. The exact nature of the maladaptive behavior pattern can be determined through the preparation of *client autobiographies* (Long, Wuesthoff, & Pithers, 1989, pp. 88–94; Marlatt, 1985e, pp. 102–103) and *structured interview.*

Hypothesis 1.4. The *Addiction Severity Index* may also be used to assess overall level of functioning (adapted by Wanigaratne et al., 1990, pp. 193–197).

Principle 2: The Change Process

Overcoming a maladaptive behavior pattern may be viewed as a learning task. The process of changing a habit involves three separate stages: (a) commitment and motivation (preparing for change), (b) the specific behavioral change (cessation of the problem behavior), and (c) maintenance of the behavioral change (prevention of relapse) (Marlatt, 1985d, p. 21).

Proposition 2. To avoid setting up a failure experience, it is necessary to establish the degree of the client's commitment to change his or her behavior as well as the client's determination to carry out the posttreatment maintenance program.

Hypothesis 2. To assess the client's ongoing perception of his or her problem as well as preparedness to continue the change/maintenance process, the *motivational interviewing* technique (Miller & Rollnick, 1991) may be used. This procedure may be used before the inception of each new major treatment component to reinforce continued commitment. This permits a graduated series of interventions called a *stepped-care approach* (Sobell & Sobell, 1993; Somers & Marlatt, 1992, p. 37–38).

Principle 3: Relapse Versus Lapse

It is necessary for any single behavior disorder to carefully distinguish between what is meant by a *lapse* as opposed to a *relapse*. A relapse is a complete violation of a self-imposed rule or set of rules governing abstinence from a particular target behavior (e.g., an ex-smoker who returns to full-time smoking). A lapse is a single instance of violating the rule (e.g., an ex-smoker who smokes a single cigarette) (George & Marlatt, 1989, p. 6).

Proposition 3.1. Although a relapse is a violation of the abstinence rules, it may be viewed as a transitional state: a series of events that may or may not lead to a return to the baseline level of the target behavior (Marlatt, 1985d, p. 32). According to Wanigaratne et al. (1990, p. 9) relapse can simply be viewed as a failure to reach targets/goals set by the individual over a set period of time.

Proposition 3.2. The lapse is viewed as a single mistake or error and is construed as temporary (George & Marlatt, 1989, p. 6). It is an indulgence in the target behavior over a short period of time (Wanigaratne et al., 1990, p. 78).

Hypothesis 3.1. The nature of and distinction between lapse and relapse may be determined by having the client produce *relapse fantasies* (Marlatt, 1985e, pp. 103–104; Sandberg & Marlatt, 1989, pp. 147–151) with reference to situations or conditions under which he or she has lapsed or relapsed in the past. They may also provide information on specific vulnerabilities, coping skills, and self-image (Wanigaratne et al., 1990, p. 27).

Hypothesis 3.2. The covert modeling technique, *relapse rehearsal* (Marlatt, 1985e, pp. 118–119; Hall, 1989, pp. 197–205) may also provide details on lapse and relapse.

Covert Antecedents of Relapse: How People Get Into High-Risk Situations

Principle 4: Lifestyle Imbalance

A *balanced lifestyle* is one in which there is equilibrium between the demands of daily life ("shoulds") and the pleasures that a person enjoys pursuing ("wants"). When the shoulds of life overbalance the wants, the person is likely to feel deprived and develop a desire for self-indulgence and immediate gratification (Marlatt, 1985d, pp. 290–291). Major changes in a person's circumstances, as well as more minor occurrences, can affect lifestyle balance (Wanigaratne et al., 1990, pp. 138–140).

Proposition 4.1. Lifestyle imbalance may produce a hostile reaction to the rules for abstaining from the prohibited behavior (Marlatt, 1985d, p. 48).

Proposition 4.2. This reaction may be instrumental in setting up the necessary conditions for a lapse or relapse (Marlatt, 1985d, p. 48).

Hypothesis 4.1. "(T)he assessment of wants and shoulds requires the individual to provide ... (an) ... accounting ... of daily events and their perceived quality as external demands or self-fulfilling activities" (Marlatt, 1985c, p. 291). The shoulds:wants ratio may be determined by use of the Daily Want–Should Tally Form (Marlatt, 1985c, p. 292) or the Daily Want/Should Record (Wanigaratne et al., 1990, p. 48). This may be used to quantify lifestyle imbalance on an ongoing basis.

Hypothesis 4.2. Lifestyle balance may be restored by encouraging the client to engage in behaviors that may serve as alternatives to the prohibited one. The behavior(s) must be easily learned, readily available, and provide benefits both in the short and long term. These alternative behaviors (e.g., meditation, relaxation, or running), if practiced as "wants," may become *positive addictions* (Glasser, 1976; Marlatt, 1985c, p. 299–300). For an activity to become a positive addiction, it should be one that (a) can be done alone, (b) can be done easily, (c) has some value to the person, (d) produces some improvement over time, and (e) can be done without self-criticism (Wanigaratne et al., 1990, p. 142).

Hypothesis 4.3. Lifestyle imbalances may be restored by having the individual develop *substitute indulgences.* These may be activities that are immediately pleasurable (e.g., reading, gardening, and cooking) but do not necessarily provide long-term benefits (George & Marlatt, 1989, p. 7).

Principle 5: Precursors to Relapse

To develop an understanding of the individual's exact path to lapse and relapse, it is necessary to identify the precursors to relapse.

Proposition 5.1. Knowledge of lapse or relapse precursors can identify points of intervention in lapse or relapse cycle.

Hypothesis 5.1. Use of the Categories for Classification of Relapse Episodes (Marlatt, 1985e, pp. 80–81), modified for the presenting problem, can identify in considerable detail the *intrapersonal–environmental determinants* and *interpersonal determinants* of relapse. More simply, Wanigaratne et al. (1990, pp. 80–82) recommended focusing on "The Big Three" precursors, that is, *negative emotional states* ("downers"), *interpersonal conflict* ("rows"), and *social pressure* ("joining the club").

Hypothesis 5.2. Construction of the *cognitive–behavioral chain* (Nelson & Jackson, 1989, pp. 167–177) may provide the most complete picture of the lapse cycle (i.e., the exact behavioral elements of the chain and their accompanying and reinforcing cognitions). If the individual presents more than one problem (e.g., alcohol *and* drug abuse) chains must be constructed for each.

Hypothesis 5.3. Relapse fantasies (Marlatt, 1985e, pp. 103–104; Sandberg & Marlatt, 1989, pp. 147–151) may also provide information on precursors to relapse, particularly high-risk situations, personal vulnerabilities, and coping skills (Wanigaratne et al., 1990, p. 27).

Hypothesis 5.4. Precursors to relapse in high-risk situations may be most easily identified on an ongoing basis through the use of *daily self-monitoring* (Marlatt, 1985e, pp. 98–101). Ideally, the objectives of self-monitoring are to encourage the client to (a) focus consciously upon the behavior, (b) discover the when, how, and where of maladaptive behavior patterns, (c) identify high-risk situations, (d) identify the consequences to the client, and (e) calculate the cost of the behavior to the client (Wanigaratne et al., 1990, p. 25).

Principle 6: Urges and Craving

Affectively, the desire for indulgence may produce urges and craving to engage in the prohibited activity. *Urge* is defined as the sudden impulse to engage in the forbidden act, whereas *craving* is the desire to experience the consequences of the prohibited behavior. Both are mediated by expectations regarding indulgence (i.e., immediate gratification) (Marlatt, 1985d, pp. 48–49).

Proposition 6.1. Urges and craving can be the result of prior conditioning (craving as a conditioned response associated with past indulgent experiences) (Marlatt, 1985d, p. 49).

Proposition 6.2. Urges and craving, if sufficiently strong, can dispose an individual to set up a high-risk situation, which can permit a lapse (George & Marlatt, 1989, pp. 10–11; Marlatt, 1985d, pp. 48–49).

Hypothesis 6.1. It may be possible to discern trends in situations that stimulate urges and craving by use of the *craving diary* (Wanigaratne et al., 1990, p. 91).

Hypothesis 6.2. Use of the *decision matrix* (George & Marlatt, 1989, p. 22; Jenkins-Hall, 1989b, 159–165; Marlatt, 1985a, p. 217–218) can assist the client in dealing with urges in terms of outcome expectancies. "The client is presented with ... a three-way table (2 × 2 × 2 matrix) with the following factors: the decision to resume the old behavior or maintain abstinence, the immediate versus the delayed effects of either decision, and, within each of the former categories, the positive or negative consequences involved" (Marlatt, 1985d, p. 58). Consultation of the matrix may lead the client to the conclusion that the factors favoring abstinence greatly outweigh indulgence. The matrix must be revised as conditions improve or worsen. A simpler version of the decision matrix, called the *decisional balance sheet*, is used in teaching problem solving (Wanigaratne et al., 1990, pp. 26–27, 127).

Hypothesis 6.3. Coping skills for managing urges and craving can be cognitive or behavioral in emphasis. The following are some suggested techniques (George & Marlatt, 1989, p. 23).

1. *Cognitive urge coping.*

(a) *Labeling and detachment.* Clients are encouraged to experience the urge without yielding to it. The strategy is to observe the urge when it occurs, that is, to assume an attitude of detached awareness without reacting to it (Marlatt, 1985a, p. 241). An urge is a phenomenon that grows in intensity, peaks, and then subsides. By observing this curvilinear function, clients may learn that urges are not irresistible and need not be acted on. This disengaged observation is sometimes called *urge surfing* (Carey & McGrath, 1989, pp. 189–190; George & Marlatt, 1989, p. 23; Marlatt, 1985a, p. 241; see also Wanigaratne et al., 1990, p. 90).

2. *Behavioral urge coping.*

(a) *Stimulus control procedures.* Procedures that minimize exposure to external cues associated with high-risk situations. The client should destroy or remove reminders or paraphernalia associated with the prohibited behavior (George & Marlatt, 1989, p 23).

(b) *Avoidance strategies.* Events or situations associated with the maladaptive behavior pattern must be avoided until adequate coping skills are developed (George & Marlatt, 1989, p. 23).

(c) *Covert sensitization.* The client is instructed to imagine performing the target behavior and then imagine an aversive consequence (Carey & McGrath, 1989, p. 192; Cautela, 1985).

(d) *Thought stopping.* The client produces the thoughts that accompany urges and craving. The client is instructed to identify the beginning of the thought sequence and say "Stop!" aloud or covertly, which interrupts the sequence (Carey & McGrath, 1989, p. 193; Wisocki, 1985).

(e) *Chain breaking.* As an urge sequence (i.e., the initial elements of the cognitive–behavioral chain) begins to unfold, the client may perform a simple behavioral action that breaks the continuity of the sequence (e.g., getting up and moving around) (George & Marlatt, 1989, pp. 23–24).

(f) *Craving pack.* A set of instructions on what to do in a craving attack may assist in self-control (Wanigaratne et al., 1990, p. 91; see *reminder card*, Hypothesis 11.2).

Principle 7: Cognitive Distortions

Urges and craving, coupled with the associated expectancies for immediate gratification, can lead to the use of defense mechanisms to reduce the conflict and guilt that might ensue from deliberately setting up a high-risk situation.

Proposition 7.1. Rationalization provides an apparently legitimate reason for engaging in the prohibited behavior (Marlatt, 1985a, pp. 268–269).

Proposition 7.2. Denial provides the individual with a means of ignoring the negative elements of a situation that ordinarily would be perceived as risky (Marlatt, 1985a, p. 270; 1985b, p. 190).

Hypothesis 7.1. The technique of *cognitive restructuring* is used to challenge and dispute cognitive distortions such as rationalization and denial. A simple, easy to learn, and effective method is *rational–emotive therapy (RET)* (Ellis & Grieger, 1977). In RET, the client is trained to identify certain types of irrational thinking (cognitive distortions), the beliefs supporting them, and how to challenge and dispute those thoughts and beliefs (Jenkins-Hall, 1989, p. 210).

Hypothesis 7.2. The focus of cognitive restructuring should be the common cognitive distortions encountered in doing RP (Wanigaratne et al., 1990, pp. 105–106): (a) absolutistic thinking, (b) overgeneralization, (c) dwelling on the negative, discounting the positive, (d) jumping to conclusions, (e) magnification or minimization, (f) "should" statements, (g) identifying with one's shortcomings, (h) taking things too personally, (i) linking unconnected events, and (j) various irrational beliefs (e.g., "Everyone has to like me").

Principle 8. Seemingly Irrelevant Decisions (SIDs)

Rationalization and denial can provide a convenient cover for the performance of a series of minidecisions over time that bring the individual progressively closer and closer to lapse and relapse (Marlatt, 1985d, p. 49). These are also called *setups*:

> [they] describe the series of everyday decisions, such as where to eat lunch, what route to take home, whether to visit this friend or that, which lead the client into a situation where it was beyond human powers to resist temptation. The client is unaware or only partly aware of this process and often can only see the influence of these decisions in retrospect. . . . (The) client frequently enters the high-risk situation unaware and/or bound by circumstances to continue the course of action. "Seemingly irrelevant decisions" describe this process of self-deception. (Wanigaratne et al., 1990, p. 111)

Proposition 8.1. At each choice point in the cognitive–behavioral chain leading to relapse, cognitive distortions justify the previous link in the chain and set the occasion for the next.

Proposition 8.2. Rationalization and denial neutralize each decision, so that it appears to be "seemingly irrelevant" to the impending lapse (Marlatt, 1985a, p. 271).

Hypothesis 8.1. "The *relapse roadmap* enables the . . . (client) . . . to envision the maintenance phase as a journey from initial cessation to prolonged abstinence" (George & Marlatt, 1989, p. 27). In preparing this "map," which may be a cognitive map or a physical one, the client identifies various choice points along the way, some leading directly to high-risk situations, others to escape routes, and others to relapse (Marlatt,

1985d, p. 46; Wanigaratne et al., 1990, p. 27). Used in conjunction with the decision matrix, the relapse roadmap may assist in the management of HRSs.

Hypothesis 8.2. Reexamination and revision of the *decisional balance sheet* (decision matrix) may result in better understanding and management of SIDs (Wanigaratne et al., 1990, p. 118).

Hypothesis 8.3. Through the use of cognitive restructuring, clients become able to see through the distortions of rationalization and denial. In so doing they can come to identify SIDs as early warning signals, to see them as covert relapse antecedents, and to recognize that in making these minidecisions, they are acting on their urges (George & Marlatt, 1989, p. 27).

Hypothesis 8.4. The most common types of setups to watch out for are the following (Wanigaratne et al., 1990, pp. 117–118): (a) engineering exposure to the target behavior or substance ("I'll just drop by and see John; I don't think he's using [drugs, alcohol] any more"), (b) setting unrealistically high goals so that failure is inevitable ("I know I'll never take another drink!"), (c) testing one's ability to refuse a target behavior or substance ("If I can cope with X, then . . ."), and (d) making abstinence (or control) contingent on someone else's behavior ("As long as Jack doesn't drink, then I . . .").

Principle 9: Entering the High-Risk Situation

Thus—operating separately and in combination—an unbalanced lifestyle, desire for immediate gratification, urges and craving, and use of cognitive distortions to cover up a series of seemingly irrelevant decisions may lead the individual to a high-risk situation.

Determinants of Relapse: How People Can Manage High-Risk Situations

Principle 10: High-Risk Situations

Once an individual accepts the self-imposed set of rules governing abstinence, he or she will experience perceived control until a high-risk situation is encountered. An HRS is any situation that poses a threat to perceived control and increases the probability of lapse or relapse (i.e., a situation for which no coping response is available) (George & Marlatt, 1989, p. 7; Wanigaratne et al., 1990, pp. 79–80).

Hypothesis 10.1. Where the behavior is accessible, the nature and potential threat of high-risk situations can be identified on an ongoing basis through the use of *daily self-monitoring* (Marlatt, 1985e, pp. 98–101; see objectives of self-monitoring, Hypothesis 5.4 above).

Hypothesis 10.2. Where the behavior is inaccessible, the nature and potential threat of high-risk situations can be identified by use of the High-Risk Situations Test (Marques, 1986). Clients are presented with a list of potentially threatening situations and rate each according to its potential to foster lapse or relapse.

Hypothesis 10.3. Construction of the *cognitive–behavioral chain* (Nelson & Jackson, 1989, pp. 167–177) will assist in identifying high-risk situations in the lapse cycle. Chains must be constructed for each presenting problem.

Hypothesis 10.4. The Situational Competency Test (Chaney, O'Leary, & Marlatt, 1978; Miner, Day, & Nafpaktitis, 1989) can be used to evaluate coping skills in high-risk situations. Clients describe cognitive and behavioral responses to high-risk situations presented on audiotape.

Hypothesis 10.5. "Clients . . . (may be) . . . presented with a series of high-risk situations and asked to rate how *confident* they are that they would be able to resist the urge to engage in the . . . (prohibited) . . . activity" (Marlatt, 1985a, p. 221). (These *self-efficacy ratings* [Bandura, 1977] are to be distinguished from the Situational Competency Test, which asks what the person would *do* to cope with a high-risk situation).

Proposition 10.1. If the individual is able to perform an effective coping response in the HRS, his or her sense of self-efficacy will increase, and the probability of relapse will decrease (George & Marlatt, 1989, p. 8).

Proposition 10.2. If no coping response is available, the individual's sense of self-efficacy will decrease: He or she may begin to feel helpless and develop positive outcome expectancies about engaging in the target behavior (i.e., gain immediate gratification), a situation that increases the probability of a lapse.

Hypothesis 10.6. Deficiencies in coping skills: 1. Remedial skill training. Habilitative or remedial training may be required to improve basic interpersonal skills. The following interventions are closely related and should be matched to presenting problem(s):

1. Frustration and anger in interpersonal situations, particularly involving an argument or disagreement with a significant other, has been shown to fuel relapse. "The model of relapse . . . predicts that the performance of an assertive response that enables the individual to cope . . . with this type of high-risk situation will decrease the probability of relapse" (Marlatt, 1985e, p. 105; see also Wanigaratne et al., 1990, p. 122). Standard models of *assertiveness training* (Alberti, 1977; Lange & Jakubowski, 1979) may be used. In doing assertiveness training, attention should be directed to the combination of speech, body language, and cognitive processes (Wanigaratne et al., 1990, pp. 120–122).

2. Clients may be trained to anticipate and cope with potential relapse precursors through the use of *stress-inoculation training* (Resick, 1985). A common model is that of Meichenbaum and Cameron (1983).
3. Improvement of *social and communication skills*, particularly *social decoding skills* (McFall, 1990) may improve ability to cope with potential relapse stressors.

Hypothesis 10.7. Deficiencies in coping skills: 2. Behavior therapy techniques. The following interventions are closely related and should be matched to presenting problem(s):

1. *Behavior rehearsal* is a "specific procedure which aims to replace deficient or inadequate social or interpersonal responses by efficient and effective behavior patterns. . . . The . . . (client) . . . achieves this by practicing the desired forms of behavior under the direction of the therapist" (Lazarus, 1985, p. 22). In RP terms, this is interchangeable with *relapse rehearsal* (Marlatt, 1985e, p. 118).
2. *Modeling* of appropriate social behavior by the therapist (e.g., assertive refusal) may serve to mitigate the effects of major relapse precursors such as social pressure, particularly social modeling of undesirable behavior (Marlatt, 1985e, p. 89).
3. Also related to handling negative social modeling and social pressure is *role playing*. Clients are asked to role play appropriate social behaviors and verbalize their thoughts and reactions during the enactment (Marlatt, 1985e, p. 112). This could be subsumed by *relapse rehearsal.*

Hypothesis 10.8. Deficiencies in coping skills: 3. General problem solving. The notion of *self-efficacy enhancement* complements and cuts across the preceding suggested skill training and behavior therapy interventions. Basically, "employment of the various training techniques is accompanied by instructions to imagine that the . . . (trained) . . . experience is accompanied by mounting feelings of competence and confidence. As a consequence, the person experiences heightened expectations of successful coping in future real-life situations, thereby reducing the probability of relapse" (George & Marlatt, 1989, p. 21).

Self-efficacy may be enhanced by making sure of the following (Wanigaratne et al., 1990, p. 179): (a) Therapeutic assignments are seen as challenging, (b) the task is seen as directly related to the process of controlling the target behavior, (c) only a moderate amount of effort is needed for the task, (d) few external aids are needed so that the client attributes success to himself or herself, and (e) the task is part of an overall pattern of success so that steady improvement may be seen.

Principle 11: Abstinence Violation Effect (Rule Violation Effect)

The occurrence of a lapse followed by the perception that the self-imposed set of rules has been breached may produce the AVE. The AVE is considered to be a cognitive–affective reaction to a lapse that can influence whether an initial lapse will become a relapse (Marlatt, 1985b, p. 179). In general, the greater the AVE, the greater the probability of relapse. Wanigaratne et al. (1990) describe the AVE/RVE as a "psychological trap":

> The trap arises from the prohibition of the addictive behavior when someone elects or is forced *never* to do something ever again. . . . The way the prohibition is interpreted or construed affects the impact. Some people construe the "never again" rule as absolute, with no room for error and with the feeling that dire consequences will transpire should the rule be transgressed. . . . If the rule is interpreted in a harsh, absolute, self-punitive manner, the pressure of this leads to the rule violation effect. (pp. 113–114)

There are two components to the AVE, an *attributive* and an *affective* reaction.

Proposition 11.1: Attribution 1. If the individual attributes the lapse to internal, stable, and global factors thought to be uncontrollable (e.g., lack of willpower), the AVE will increase, and further lapses or relapse is *more* likely (Marlatt, 1985b, p. 179).

Proposition 11.2: Attribution 2. If the individual attributes the lapse to external, unstable (changeable), and specific factors thought to be controllable (e.g., coping is possible), the AVE will decrease, and further lapses or relapse are *less* likely (Marlatt, 1985b, pp. 179–180).

Proposition 11.3: Affective 1. If the individual attributes the lapse to personal factors (e.g., lack of willpower), a sense of *loss of control* will occur (decreased self-efficacy), and the AVE will be increased (Marlatt, 1985b, p. 180).

Proposition 11.4: Affective 2. If the attribution is that the lapse is a momentary failure to cope with a high-risk situation, the AVE will be minimal and the individual will retain a sense of *self-control* (increased or maintained self-efficacy) (Marlatt, 1985b, p. 180).

Hypothesis 11.1. The technique of *cognitive reframing* may be used to deal with attributional and affective reactions following the AVE. General strategies of reattribution would include the following:

> A lapse is similar to a mistake or error in the learning process. . . . (L)apses can be reframed as mistakes, as opportunities for corrective learning, instead of . . . indications of total failure or irreversible relapse. . . . (E)ach mistake contains more "information" than repeated success trials. . . . In the reframing process, clients should be encouraged to make clear distinctions between a lapse as a mistake or error rather than a failure experience. (Marlatt, 1985a, p. 253)

In developing a reframing procedure, the following points should be emphasized to assist clients in managing the AVE and for provision of reassurance (Marlatt, 1985a, pp. 254–255): (a) The lapse can be reattributed to external, specific, and controllable factors. (It is necessary to isolate factors that *are* controllable), (b) a lapse can be turned into a *prolapse* instead of a relapse (i.e., the learning gained from the lapse moves the client forward rather than backward), (c) as long as the person is not engaging in the prohibited behavior after the initial lapse, a state of abstinence exists, and (d) the goal of RP is always the same, irrespective of whether a lapse has occurred: prevention of the next lapse or relapse.

Hypothesis 11.2. The use of the *reminder card* can serve to structure the reframing process and provide information on what to do if a lapse occurs. Variations of the following are suggested (Marlatt, 1985a, pp 255–257; Wanigaratne et al., 1990, p. 89):

1. *Stop, look, and listen.* Stop the ongoing flow of events and look and listen to what is happening. The lapse is a warning that one is in danger.
2. *Keep calm.* The AVE is essentially a normal reaction, unless one gives into it and gives up control. Allow the AVE to occur without evaluating it or oneself negatively. Try not to give in to temptations and urges.
3. *Renew the commitment to abstinence.* Motivation to continue is the problem. Do not give up on progress made to date.
4. *Review the situation surrounding the lapse.* What events led up to the slip? Were there any warning signals? What was the high-risk situation that triggered the slip?
5. *Make an immediate plan for recovery.* Get rid of all materials associated with the prohibited behavior. Get out of the high-risk situation as soon as possible. Plan and execute a substitute activity.
6. *Ask for help.* Contact the support system immediately (see *Principle 12*).

Hypothesis 11.2. A *relapse contract* (Marlatt, 1985a, pp. 257–259) may be drawn up before or during treatment. This is a contingency management contract (Stokes, 1985) between therapist and client that specifies the steps to be followed in the event of a lapse. The relapse contract specifies behaviors to be performed in the situation, in distinction to the reminder card, which is part of the cognitive reframing process.

Principle 12: Support System

One of the possibly negative outcomes of apparently successful treatment is the development of the belief in some clients that they can completely manage the rehabilitation process on their own. This is especially true of programs that inculcate the belief that treatment will "cure" the client's particular addiction or impulse control disorder and that relapse will not occur because he or she has "gotten well."

Proposition 12. As an important part of the behavior management plan, the client should endeavor to establish an external *support system* (Pithers, 1991). The support system is a small group of people known intimately by the client (e.g., family, friends, workmates, clergy, or probation officer) who assist in maintenance of the client's pattern of abstinence. Their function is to support, remind, and confront the client without indulging him or her.

Hypothesis 12.1. The support system will function properly if the client provides to them the following (Pithers, 1991, p. 23):

1. Precise specification of all high-risk situations and precursors to lapse or relapse. This provides the support system with identifiable indicators of potential lapses.
2. Since relapse precursors often appear in a distinct sequence, support system members may then have knowledge of the imminence of a lapse.
3. Support system members may provide the first level of intervention to forestall the lapse, while contacting the client's therapist.

WHAT'S NEW IN RELAPSE PREVENTION?

In the 15 odd years of its existence, there have been very few new additions to RP theory and practice. There have been three global additions, which complement the theory. In addition, there has been one major addition and several minor modifications.

Harm reduction (Marlatt, in press; Marlatt & Tapert, 1993). The concept of harm reduction is conceptually larger but consistent with RP theory as stated above. Marlatt and Tapert (1993, p. 246) conceptualize maladaptive habit patterns as lying on a continuum from excess through moderation to abstinence (see Proposition 1.3 above). The motto underlying harm reduction is that "any steps toward decreased risk are steps in the right direction." Procedurally, and this is consistent with RP, this means moving the client away from excess toward moderation, with the ideal goal being abstinence. Marlatt and Tapert (1993) stated the following:

> How does relapse prevention (RP) . . . fit in with the harm reduction approach? . . . RP represents a tertiary prevention approach to harm reduction, designed to reduce the magnitude of relapse. (p. 267)

Harm reduction represents the movement of RP interventions into the arena of public health and policy. A harm reducing move toward moderation, however, provides a problem for those working with sexual deviants where abstinence must be the goal (J. K. Marques, personal communication, July 7, 1993).

Stepped care (Sobell & Sobell, 1993; Somers & Marlatt, 1992). Stepped, or tiered, care is related to harm reduction. Stepped care envisions a graduated series of interventions that increase in intensity over time. Initial interventions are characterized by being the least intensive, least intrusive, most cost-effective, and having the greatest probability of success. If this fails, the next step is introduced. As the treatment program increases in intensity, fewer and fewer clients in any category will require more and more intensive treatment (Sobell & Sobell, 1993). Primary, secondary, or tertiary RP interventions could be cast in a stepped care format, depending on the initial assessment of the problem.

Motivational interviewing (Baer, 1993; Miller & Rollnick, 1991). This technique fits the harm reduction and stepped care models, as well as the theory statement above (see Hypothesis 2). It is intended to minimize resistance in persons who are ambivalent toward changing self-indulgent behaviors. In a motivational interview, the facts about the particular problem are simply laid before the client: habit patterns, risks, long-term consequences, family history, and previous problems with the behavior. Nothing is labeled as a *problem*. Rather, the assumption is made that given sufficient information about risks and consequences, the client is then able to make an informed choice. Although this is often done as a one-time procedure that may produce therapeutic benefits (Baer, 1993), it may also be used in a harm reduction–stepped care approach, where motivational interviewing is introduced before the initiation of each new component of treatment to increase motivation and continued commitment.

The cognitive–behavioral chain (Nelson & Jackson, 1989). This cognitive–behavioral chain has become a central element in RP programs (Marques et al., 1989; Pithers et al., 1989), a new addition that developed in the sexual deviation field. Indeed, Marques (personal communication, July 7, 1993) called it *the* central element in an RP program for sexual offenders. It is the one important program component to develop from RP practice that was not part of the original theory. Simply stated, the basic purpose of the cognitive–behavioral chain is to put the client in touch with the complete sequence of behaviors that lead from high-risk situations to lapse or relapse (see Hypothesis 10.3). Once this chain is established, the client must provide the cognitions that accompany performance of each behavioral component. When complete, the chain provides a (usually graphic) picture of the cognitive–behavioral model of relapse. The Marques program further requires clients to produce credible cognitive *and* behavioral coping responses to deal with the threat(s) posed by the events in the chain. Marques (personal communication, July 7, 1993) believes that this is one of the more difficult program tasks for clients to complete (an observation that the writer can confirm from his own experience).

Evaluating RP. Note in the theory statement above that there is a great deal of information about assessing problems and suggestions for dealing with them, but there is little or nothing suggested for evaluating success other than clinical judgment. Marques (personal communication, July 7, 1993) developed a simple rating scale to assess the impact of RP. This 7–point scale, completed by program staff, simply assesses the extent to which the client comprehends and uses what he has learned in a given treatment component, where 1 represents *doesn't get it* and 7 represents *complete and adequate understanding.* Marques reported that these ratings were strongly related to successful program completion. However, such a simple scale has its limitations. It is methodologically weak in that a low rating (*doesn't get it*) or, particularly, a midpoint rating is inconclusive and difficult to interpret. Tests of comprehension and use of RP concepts or performance-based tests such as Situational Competency (Miner et al., 1989) represent superior indicators of outcome.

Redefining high-risk. W. D. Pithers (personal communication, July 1, 1993) redefined high-risk situations as high-risk *factors*

> to decrease the offenders' tendencies to externalize responsibility for risk, denying that their own distortions, emotions and fantasies pose risk. We define the lapse as the first experience (of) the first fantasy, thought, emotion, or behavior that creates an urge to engage in an abusive behavior.

Pithers and his colleagues had observed that their clients were defining risk in a highly concrete way (i.e., if they were not in a particular situation, then they were not at risk). This makes the work more difficult, he says, as clients now have to deal with abstractions rather than concrete situations.

Redefining precursors. W. D. Pithers (personal communication, April 20, 1992) also broadened the definition of precursors (risk factors) by breaking them into three parts. *Predisposing* risk factors occur early in life and set the occasion for later difficulties (e.g., family violence or poor social skills). *Precipitating* risk factors are part of the cognitive–behavioral chain described above (e.g., cognitive distortions, defense mechanisms, and SIDs). *Perpetuating* risk factors are those that serve to maintain and reinforce existing maladaptive habit patterns (e.g., alcoholism, drug abuse, or sexualization of relations with children).

Absence of the AVE. Some sex offender treatment programs have found that RP treatments work less well with rapists than with child molesters (e.g., Pithers, 1991). W. D. Pithers (personal communication, July 1, 1993) noted the following:

Concepts such as the abstinence violation effect may not apply to general criminal offenders who find anti-social behaviors to be more ego-syntonic than a pro-social lifestyle. . . . Rather than experiencing distress at the return of criminogenic thinking (as in the abstinence violation effect) . . . (these offenders) . . . actually found comfort in . . . (their lapses). . . . (E)xisting treatment models for sex offenders may require modification for use with a subset of rapists. Alternately, entirely new treatment models need to be devised.

Pithers's report was also confirmed by J. K. Marques (personal communication, July 7, 1993). This is an extremely important observation, which very likely does not apply only to sex offenders. If so, an essential element of the cognitive–behavioral model of relapse must be reconceptualized for some clients.

Commentary on RP as a theory. In reviewing the preceding theoretical structure, it is clear that many of its statements are not unique to Marlatt or other cognitive theorists. The definitions of maladaptive behavior, lapse, and relapse could apply to a wider variety of behavior disorders than are considered here. Assessment and treatment interventions such as autobiographies, self-monitoring, motivational interviewing, positive addictions, the behavioral and cognitive coping strategies, remedial skill training, behavior therapies, cognitive restructuring, self-efficacy ratings, and lifestyle imbalance are common to other treatments. Concepts such as relapse fantasies, relapse rehearsal, relapse roadmap, specification of relapse precursors, high-risk situations, the cognitive–behavioral chain, urges and craving, the decision matrix, labeling and detachment, urge surfing, seemingly irrelevant decisions, the AVE, attributional reframing, situational competency, efficacy enhancement, and use of the reminder card appear to be unique to Marlatt's theorizing in this context. It is obvious that of the specified techniques, the borrowed ones slightly overbalance the original ones. For some clinicians and researchers, RP is to some extent a melange of old techniques and redefinitions of old techniques with a generous proportion of new concepts and procedures. This attitude in large part accounts for the looseness with which the term *relapse prevention* has come to be used.

The most critical contribution of Marlatt and his colleagues as theorists and clinicians has been twofold. First, they have successfully reconceptualized the relapse process as a learning experience rather than as a treatment failure, hence the RP slogan "I'm discovering, not recovering." This is a largely unrecognized victory. This reconceptualization really *is* a new way of thinking as it flies in the face of traditional medical and psychiatric dogma as well as public (primarily US) health policy. Second, they originally designed a forthright intervention, which, *prima facie*, ought to be effective, with minor modification, across a broad spectrum of addictive behaviors and disorders of impulse control. That theory, tentatively specified here, still awaits a full empirical test.

APPLICATION TO BEHAVIOR THERAPY

In the earlier days of the behavior therapy movement, Rimm and Masters (1974) defined the enterprise as

> any of a large number of specific techniques that employ psychological (especially learning) principles to deal with maladaptive behavior. The term, "behavior," is interpreted broadly, encompassing covert respond-ing (for example, emotions and implicit verbalizations), when such can be clearly specified, in addition to overt responding. (Rimm & Masters, 1974, p. 1)

They listed the following as the basic assumptions of behavior therapy (pp. 6–17): (a) Behavior therapy tends to concentrate on the maladaptive be-havior itself as the problem, (b) behavior therapy assumes that maladaptive behaviors are acquired through learning, (c) behavior therapy assumes that principles of learning can be effective in modifying maladaptive behavior, (d) behavior therapy sets specific, clearly defined treatment goals, (e) the behavior therapist adapts his or her method of treatment to the client's problem, (f) behavior therapy concentrates on the here and now, and (g) it is assumed that any techniques used have been subjected to empirical test and have been found to be relatively effective.

Twenty years later, in terms of those assumptions, RP as an avowedly cognitive or cognitive–behavioral therapy fares rather well. For comparison purposes, Marlatt (1985d, pp. 29–30) identified the following elements of an ideal self-control program for maintaining behavior change: (a) It should be effective in maintaining behavior change for clinically significant periods of time, (b) it should enhance and maintain an individual's com-pliance and adherence to program requirements, (c) it should contain a mix of cognitive and behavioral intervention procedures as well as global lifestyle modification, (d) it should facilitate the development of motiva-tion and decision-making skills, (e) it should attempt to replace maladap-tive habit patterns with alternative behaviors and skills, and (f) it should enable the individual to cope effectively with new problem situations as they arise and should have built-in generalization components. It should teach the client new and adaptive ways of dealing with failure experiences. (g) It should make use of client support systems to enhance treatment generalization effects.

Comparing these two statements of assumptions, and allowing for syntactical differences, I believe that we could conclude that RP is, in fact, a behavior therapy.

EVALUATION OF THE THEORY

A review of the some relevant clinical literature (Wilson, 1992) showed that in the past 15 years, RP has become a sort of loose clinical rubric under which a variety of clinical interventions have been housed. Virtually any type of posttreatment planning, or any further intervention after treatment, has been called "relapse prevention." In my point of view, this was never the intention of the primary author of the theory. The major RP theorists, Marlatt and his colleagues, have written extensively on the theory and have tested portions of it, but even they admit that they have yet to test the theory as a complete statement (George & Marlatt, 1989). Only two clinical researchers, Marques (Marques et al., 1989) and Pithers (Pithers, 1991; Pithers et al., 1989), writing on sexual deviance, have come close to an extensive theoretical statement, but these are primarily advanced in the language of treatment operations. Other statements in the areas of, for example, obsessive–compulsive disorder (Emmelkamp et al, 1992), behavioral marital therapy (Truax and Jacobson, 1992), and obesity (Sternberg, 1985), have advanced models and programs that closely resemble the Marlatt original.

Problems in the application of RP. Although it is indisputable that any pretermination or posttreatment intervention designed to avoid a return to the pretreatment status is a method for preventing relapse, the vast majority of the interventions reported in the literature cannot properly be labeled *RP procedures*.

The recent edited volume by Wilson (1992c), *Principles and Practice of Relapse Prevention*, reveals many of the problems that have prevented an adequate test of RP as a theory. Although this volume is an excellent review of limited portions of the clinical literature, most of the selections have little or nothing to do with RP per se, and several do not even mention it at all (Brown & Barlow; Andrews). The chapters on alcohol problems (Somers & Marlatt), smoking (Mermelstein, Karnatz, & Reichman), obesity (Fremouw & Damer), depression (Wilson), obsessive–compulsive disorders (Emmelkamp et al.), and marital distress (Truax & Jacobson) come closest to following an RP model, but none of them represent an extensive test of the theory.

Throughout the work, virtually any intervention, occurring within or after a formal cessation treatment, is considered to be some form of relapse prevention if its intent is to prevent reversion to an undesirable state. Thus, there are many nonspecific or vaguely described terms such as *booster sessions, maintenance sessions, skills training, long-term monitoring, problem solving, cognitive–behavior therapy,* or *cognitive therapy,* to name only a few, which are said to be "consistent with" RP or "RP-like," all gathered under the banner of RP.

In those instances in which true RP interventions à la Marlatt appear, they are often mixed together with other, non-RP treatment components. To be sure, all of these interventions are intended to prevent relapse, but they are not RP as theoretically stated. The problem that produces this unnecessary vagueness and confusion, it seems to me, lies in the attempt to broaden a clinically popular theory and intervention to accommodate more than it should. Perhaps it is more accurate to say that it is premature to attempt this accommodation. If, on the other hand, we now limit the scope of clinical application, as suggested above, then the theory may prove supple enough to be applied across a smaller range of behavioral disorders without major alteration of the theoretical terminology or the nature of the clinical interventions. This would permit a fuller test of the theory over a range of disorders that share common elements.

FUTURE DIRECTIONS

In attempting to suggest directions in which RP theory should move, there are a number of conceptual and methodological issues that need to be considered.

Is Relapse Prevention Really a Theory?

I argued in this chapter that RP is indeed a theory, which can stand alone but which probably has direct application to a limited scope of behavioral disorders, primarily addictive behaviors and disorders of impulse control. I suggested that the model originally proposed by Marlatt and Gordon (1985), and hardly modified since then (e.g., Wanigaratne et al., 1990), is sufficient in itself to deal with this range of disorders, albeit with some fine tuning. It is worth mentioning in this context that this "limited" range of disorders are ones that wreak immense havoc, both personally and socially. Application of a relatively simple, straightforward, and *consistent* model to them would represent a very large step forward.

Evaluation of Relapse Prevention

RP has been empirically tested in a piecemeal fashion, usually one component at a time. Shiffman (1992) noted that adding RP components to existing treatment packages added little or nothing to long-term outcomes. In my judgment, only Marques et al. (1989) and Pithers et al. (1989) made the attempt to empirically test a model that embraced most of Marlatt's theoretical elements. Their results would suggest that a relatively "pure" RP approach works reasonably well with sexual offenders, a clientele notoriously intractable to conventional treatments. The treatment manual by Wanigaratne et al. (1990) offers a rather clear and unambiguous clinical model of RP that would be usable for treatment of the disorders suggested previously. Most of the RP elements are included, and there is considerable advice given on conduct of the treatment. What the manual lacks is a sound evaluation scheme, but it is quite clear where these elements would fit in. Aside from these programs, given the problems with the way RP has been used and misused over the years, we would have to conclude that its present evidentiary status vis à vis its main rivals (i.e., any kind of cognitive–behavior therapy) is not particularly good.

Offering one way to address this problem, Wilson (1992b, p. 368) suggested the following:

> Statistical prediction offers the best solution to many of the problems at this stage of research on relapse. In particular, a *general model* (author emphasis) that can be tested using multiple regression techniques has great appeal. One can consider several different sources that contribute to the occurrence of relapse.

Wilson (1992b, p. 368) suggested that these sources might be the following: (a) pretreatment factors (enduring, permanent characteristics of the person), (b) factors related to the disorder (duration, symptoms, subclassification), (c) factors related to the initial intervention (type and client compliance), (d) outcome of initial intervention (response to treatment, posttreatment severity, overall change, presence of residual symptoms, and self-efficacy regarding therapy tasks), (e) postintervention strategies (use of procedures taught in therapy, use of support system), and (f) variables proposed as relapse-inducing agents (life events or social factors).

Wilson (1992b) proposed that use of multiple regression would assign the proportion of variance in relapse associated with each of these classes of variables. These suggestions seem eminently sensible, particularly with reference to the recommendation that a general (i.e., a relatively "pure" RP) model be the subject of the test. Given the accessibility of RP as theory and practice, one can only wonder why this has never been done.

SUMMARY

The roots of RP as both theory and clinical intervention are anchored in the mainstream development of cognitive–behavioral treatment. Although often unrecognized, what has made RP different, and has retarded its growth, is its emphasis on the lapse–relapse sequence as a learning experience rather than a treatment failure. This chapter argued that RP could be successfully applied not only to the classical addictive disorders from which it originated but also to virtually any disorder of impulse control. In that interest, the chapter outlined a theory of RP in terms of basic principles, derived propositions, and empirically testable hypotheses. What is required now is the test.

REFERENCES

Alberti, R. E. (1977). *Assertiveness: Innovations, applications and issues.* San Luis Obispo, CA: Impact Publications.

Andrews, G. (1992). Stuttering. In P. H. Wilson (Ed.), *Principles and practice of relapse prevention* (pp. 349–365). New York: Guilford Press.

Baer, J. S. (1993). Etiology and secondary prevention of alcohol problems with young adults. In J. S. Baer, G. A. Marlatt, & R. J. McMahon (Eds.), *Addictive behaviors across the life span* (pp. 111–137). Thousand Oaks, CA: Sage.

Bandura, A. (1977). Self-efficacy: Toward a unifying theory of behavior change. *Psychological Review, 84,* 191–215.

Brown, T. A., & Barlow, D. H. (1992). Panic disorder and panic disorder with agoraphobia. In P. H. Wilson (Ed.), *Principles and practice of relapse prevention* (pp. 191–212). New York: Guilford Press.

Carey, C. H., & McGrath, R. J. (1989). Coping with urges and craving. In D. R. Laws (Ed.), *Relapse prevention with sex offenders* (pp. 188–196). New York: Guilford Press.

Cautela, J. R. (1985). Covert sensitization. In A. S. Bellack & M. Hersen (Eds.), *Dictionary of behavior therapy techniques* (pp. 96–100). New York: Pergamon Press.

Chaney, E. F., O'Leary, M. R., & Marlatt, G. A. (1978). Skill training with alcoholics. *Journal of Consulting and Clinical Psychology, 46,* 1092–1104.

Ellis, A., & Grieger, R. (Eds.). (1977). *Handbook of rational–emotive therapy.* New York: Springer.

Emmelkamp, P. M. G., Kloek, J., & Blaauw, E. (1992). Obsessive–compulsive disorders. In P. H. Wilson (Ed.), *Principles and practice of relapse prevention* (pp. 213–234). New York: Guilford Press.

Fremouw, W., & Damer, D. (1992). Obesity. In P. H. Wilson (Ed.), *Principles and practice of relapse prevention* (pp. 69–84). New York: Guilford Press.

George, W. H., & Marlatt, G. A. (1989). Introduction. In D. R. Laws (Ed.), *Relapse prevention with sex offenders* (pp. 1–31). New York: Guilford Press.

Glasser, W. (1976). *Positive addiction.* New York: Harper & Row.

Hall, R. L. (1989). Relapse rehearsal. In D. R. Laws (Ed.), *Relapse prevention with sex offenders* (pp. 197–206). New York: Guilford Press.

Hunt, W. A., Barnett, L. W., & Branch, L. G. (1971). Relapse rates in addiction programs. *Journal of Clinical Psychology, 27,* 455–456.

Jenkins-Hall, K. D. (1989a). Cognitive restructuring. In D. R. Laws (Ed.), *Relapse prevention with sex offenders* (pp. 207–215). New York: Guilford Press.

Jenkins-Hall, K. D. (1989b). The decision matrix. In D. R. Laws (Ed.), *Relapse prevention with sex offenders* (pp. 159–166). New York: Guilford Press.

Lange, A. J., & Jakubowski, P. (1979). *Responsible assertive behavior*. Champaign, IL: Research Press.

Lazarus, A. A. (1985). Rehearsal. In A. S. Bellack & M. Hersen (Eds.), *Dictionary of behavior therapy techniques* (p. 182). New York: Pergamon Press.

Lightfoot, L. O. (1993). The Offender Substance Abuse Pre-Release Program: An empirically based model of treatment for offenders. In J. S. Baer, G. A. Marlatt, & R. J. McMahon (Eds.), *Addictive behaviors across the life span* (pp. 184–201). Thousand Oaks, CA: Sage.

Long, J. D., Wuesthoff, A., & Pithers, W. D. (1989). Use of autobiographies in the assessment and treatment of sex offenders. In D. R. Laws (Ed.), *Relapse prevention with sex offenders* (pp. 88–95). New York: Guilford Press.

Marlatt, G. A. (1980). *Relapse prevention: A self-control program for the treatment of addictive behaviors*. Unpublished manuscript, University of Washington, Department of Psychology, Seattle.

Marlatt, G. A. (1985a). Cognitive assessment and intervention procedures for relapse prevention. In G. A. Marlatt & J. R. Gordon (Eds.), *Relapse prevention* (pp. 201–279). New York: Guilford Press.

Marlatt, G. A. (1985b). Cognitive factors in the relapse process. In G. A. Marlatt & J. R. Gordon (Eds.), *Relapse prevention* (pp. 128–200). New York: Guilford Press.

Marlatt, G. A. (1985c). Lifestyle modification. In G. A. Marlatt & J. R. Gordon (Eds.), *Relapse prevention* (pp. 280–348). New York: Guilford Press.

Marlatt, G. A. (1985d). Relapse prevention: Theoretical rationale and overview of the model. In G. A. Marlatt & J. R. Gordon (Eds.), *Relapse prevention* (pp. 3–70). New York: Guilford Press.

Marlatt, G. A. (1985e). Situational determinants of relapse and skill-training interventions. In G. A. Marlatt & J. R. Gordon (Eds.), *Relapse prevention* (pp. 71–127). New York: Guilford Press.

Marlatt, G. A. (in press). *Harm reduction*. New York: Guilford Press.

Marlatt, G. A., & Gordon, J. R. (Eds.). (1985). *Relapse prevention*. New York: Guilford Press.

Marlatt, G. A., & Tapert, S. F. (1993). Harm reduction: Reducing the risks of addictive behaviors. In J. S. Baer, G. A. Marlatt, & R. J. McMahon (Eds.), *Addictive behaviors across life span* (pp. 243–273). Thousand Oaks, CA: Sage.

Marques, J. K. (1986). *The High-Risk Situations Test*. (Available from J. K. Marques, California State Department of Mental Health, Division of State Hospital Programs, 1600 Ninth Street, Sacramento, CA 95814)

Marques, J. K., Day, D. M., Nelson, C., & Miner, M. H. (1989). The Sex Offender Treatment and Evaluation Project: California's relapse prevention program. In D. R. Laws (Ed.), *Relapse prevention with sex offenders* (pp. 247–267). New York: Guilford Press.

Marshall, W. L., Hudson, S. M., & Ward, T. (1992). Sexual deviance. In P. H. Wilson (Ed.), *Principles and practice of relapse prevention* (pp. 235–254). New York: Guilford Press.

McFall, R. M. (1990). The enhancement of social skills: An information-processing analysis. In W. L. Marshall, D. R. Laws, & H. E. Barbaree (Eds.), *Handbook of sexual assault* (pp. 311–330). New York: Plenum.

Meichenbaum, D., & Cameron, R. (1983). Stress inoculation training: Toward a general paradigm for training coping skills. In D. Meichenbaum & M. E. Jaremko (Eds.), *Stress reduction and prevention* (pp. 115–154). New York: Plenum.

Mermelstein, R. J., Karnatz, T., & Reichman, S. (1992). Smoking. In P. H. Wilson (Ed.), *Principles and practice of relapse prevention* (pp. 43–68). New York: Guilford Press.

Miller, W. R., & Rollnick, S. (Eds.). (1991). *Motivational interviewing.* New York: Guilford Press.

Miner, M. H., Day, D. M., & Nafpaktitis, M. K. (1989). Assessment of coping skills: Development of a situational competency test. In D. R. Laws (Ed.), *Relapse prevention with sex offenders* (pp. 127–136). New York: Guilford Press.

Nelson, C., & Jackson, P. (1989). High-risk recognition: The cognitive–behavioral chain. In D. R. Laws (Ed.), *Relapse prevention with sex offenders* (pp. 167–177). New York: Guilford Press.

Pithers, W. D. (1991). Relapse prevention with sexual aggressors. *Forum on Corrections Research, 3,* 20–23.

Pithers, W. D., Martin, G. R., & Cumming, G. F. (1989). Vermont Treatment Program for Sexual Aggressors. In D. R. Laws (Ed.), *Relapse prevention with sex offenders* (pp. 292–310). New York: Guilford Press.

Resick, P. A. (1985). Stress inoculation. In A. S. Bellack & M. Hersen (Eds.), *Dictionary of behavior therapy techniques* (pp. 210–211). New York: Pergamon Press.

Rimm, D. C., & Masters, J. C. (1974). *Behavior therapy.* San Diego, CA: Academic Press.

Sandberg, G. G., & Marlatt, G. A. (1989). Relapse fantasies. In D. R. Laws (Ed.), *Relapse prevention with sex offenders* (pp. 147–151). New York: Guilford Press.

Shiffman, S. (1992). Relapse process and relapse prevention in addictive behaviors. *The Behavior Therapist, 15,* 9–11.

Sobell, M. B., & Sobell, L. C. (1993). Treatment for problem drinkers: A public health priority. In J. S. Baer, G. A. Marlatt, & R. J. McMahon (Eds.), *Addictive behaviors across the life span* (pp. 138–157). Thousand Oaks, CA: Sage.

Somers, J. M., & Marlatt, G. A. (1992). Alcohol problems. In P. H. Wilson (Ed.), *Principles and practice of relapse prevention* (pp. 23–42). New York: Guilford Press.

Sternberg, B. (1985). Relapse in weight control: Definitions, processes, and prevention strategies. In G. A. Marlatt & J. R. Gordon (Eds.), *Relapse prevention* (pp. 521–545). New York: Guilford Press.

Stokes, T. F. (1985). Contingency management. In A. S. Bellack & M. Hersen (Eds.), *Dictionary of behavior therapy techniques* (pp. 74–78). New York: Pergamon Press.

Truax, P., & Jacobson, N. (1992). Marital distress. In P. H. Wilson (Ed.), *Principles and practice of relapse prevention* (pp. 290–321). New York: Guilford Press.

Wanigaratne, S., Wallace, W., Pullin, J., Keaney, F., & Farmer, R. (1990). *Relapse prevention for addictive behaviours*. Oxford, England: Blackwell Scientific Publications.

Wilson, P. H. (1992a). Depression. In P. H. Wilson (Ed.), *Principles and practice of relapse prevention* (pp. 128–156). New York: Guilford Press.

Wilson, P. H. (1992b). Directions for future research in relapse prevention. In P. H. Wilson (Ed.), *Principles and practice of relapse prevention* (pp. 366–372). New York: Guilford Press.

Wilson, P. H. (1992c). *Principles and practice of relapse prevention*. New York: Guilford Press.

Wisocki, P. (1985). Thought stopping. In A. S. Bellack & M. Hersen (Eds.), *Dictionary of behavior therapy techniques* (pp. 219–221). New York: Pergamon Press.

17

EVOLUTIONARY THEORY AND BEHAVIOR THERAPY

JAMES V. CORWIN and WILLIAM O'DONOHUE

Behavior therapists adhere to the scientist–practitioner model of clinical psychology. Although there are varying interpretations of what this model may entail (O'Donohue & Halsey, 1994), one reasonable interpretation is that the model broadly mandates that clinical psychologists apply the methods and results of science to the problems that they are attempting to solve. In following this mandate, clinical psychologists apply the results of the scientific research of others to their problem situations and generate data through the application of research methods to the problem of interest. This chapter argues that evolutionary theory is relevant to both of these aims. Evolution is relevant in that it is a scientific account of the history of life that helps to explain the current status of life as well as the conditions that result in certain modifications of life. As a part of the web of scientific information, evolution should not be considered as irrelevant to the scientific pursuits of behavior therapists. In brief, the scientist–practitioner model should not be confined to applying only the science of psychologists, but rather behavior therapists should opportunistically use any aspect of science that can help to provide a more comprehensive and consistent understanding of human behavior and its problems. Thus, in this chapter we also examine how evolution can be useful to forming hypotheses about clinical problems and their therapy.

AN OVERVIEW OF EVOLUTION

Evolutionary theory as proposed by Darwin (1859) and subsequent modifications by more recent theorists is perhaps one of most popular and poorly understood of all theories. Darwinian notions of "survival of the fittest," adaptation, and evolution itself are often misused in the popular press and scientific literature. In this chapter we attempt to familiarize the reader with some of the basic concepts of evolutionary theory as a prelude to a better understanding of the implications of evolutionary processes for human behavior both appropriate and problematic.

Evolution is the change in gene frequency over time within a population. Understanding evolution involves accounting for the variables that cause genes to enter, disappear from, or change in frequency within the gene pools of populations. Evolution is based on two factors: genetic variability and natural selection (Mayr, 1976). An important basis of genetic variability within a species is a mutation, a change in the genotype (although gene frequencies may also change because of migration and chance factors). Conversely, natural selection exerts its influence through the environment, determining the survival and reproductive success of members of a species. (Actually, survival is important only to the extent that it affects reproduction.) All living things have four attributes that provide the capacity for them to evolve through natural selection:

1. Inheritance. Offspring resemble their parents. (Alleles [gene sets] can be passed intact, in terms of the information they carry, from generation to generation.)
2. Mutation. (The genetic material changes occasionally, and the changes are heritable, giving rise to heritable variation.)
3. Differential reproduction. (Not all individuals reproduce equally.)
4. Isolation. (Not all genetic lines are able to interbreed freely. External barriers or intrinsic ones stand in the way of genetic recombination between some of them.) (Noonan, 1987, pp. 34–35).

Natural selection determines which of the genetically diverse individuals within a species are best suited to survive and reproduce in a specific environment. Those that are best suited will survive and reproduce, whereas those that are not will perish. Individuals are in competition, particularly reproductive competition, with one another. It is precisely the

476   *CORWIN AND O'DONOHUE*

genetic variability in a species, however, that enhances the probability that some members of that species may survive and proliferate, particularly if selection pressures change. Perhaps one of the best known examples was described by Kettlewell (1973) in which selection pressures for the pigmentation of moths changed as a result of changes in tree coloration that were caused by industrial emissions. In this case, the changes in the moths' local environment occurred quite rapidly. However, because the genotype of the moth was variable enough to produce a wide range of pigmentation, the rapid environmental change, although shifting the selection pressure toward darker moths that were less easily seen on the darker trees, did not produce extinction of the species. Sexual reproduction (as opposed to asexual reproduction) may also be selected for, because it produces more genetically diverse offspring than does asexual reproduction because of the mixing of genes from the male and female. The first message is that environmental change is more likely to be deadly for invariant species. The second is that the selective value of a gene depends on the (often changing) features of the environment in which the species is found.

The result of natural selection is the adaptation of organisms to their environmental niches. Although a casual onlooker may see purposiveness in the way an organism achieves certain ends (e.g., the manner in which a hatchling squawks and presents an open mouth for food). However, a less teleological explanation is that ancestors who did not have effective appetite displays simply were selected out. As Noonan (1987) has stated, "the apparent purposiveness of adaptation merely reflects the accumulation of genes that have been reproductively successful in the past" (p. 38).

Given these two basic factors in modern evolutionary theory a major question has arisen from a number of sources (Gould, 1984; Mayr, 1976). How could these two factors, genetic variability and natural selection, account for the incredible diversity and complexity of all living things? This is a fundamental question because, surely, genetic variation within a species would not explain how qualitatively different species have evolved. For example, how could incredibly complex systems like the human auditory system or the eye have evolved in this way?

This argument has focused on three basic approaches to the evolution of new species and organ systems. The first approach, favored by Darwin (1859) and Mayr (1959), is gradualism. New structures emerge gradually in a series of small steps that are then selected by the environment. The second approach is held by saltationists (Mayr, 1959) and suggests that the dramatic changes seen across species (e.g., the development of the eye, the wings of birds) occurred in a single dramatic change. How else, according to saltationist views, could a new structure originate and function adaptively unless the rest of the organism were already suited for the structure? Further, how or why would a partially developed structure be selected for before it was sufficiently functional to provide some adaptive advantage?

The third approach, formulated by Lamarck (1809/1960), is the theory that acquired characteristics can be passed along in the genotype of a species and inherited by offspring within that species.

Given any cursory examination of the complexity of differences in the structure and behavioral repertoires of species, it seems to strain credulity to suggest that such complexity could emerge gradually. However, the vast majority of evidence on the evolution of structures supports gradualism. Mayr (1959) has reviewed the evidence in support of the gradualist approach. Perhaps the major source of support for the gradualist approach derives from modern genetics. Most mutations of the genotype typically have no discernible effect on the phenotype of the organism, that is, the actual appearance of the organism. This is in contrast to the large number of dramatic and simultaneous changes in structure and function expected by the saltationist approach, which is presumably followed by environmental selection of the dramatically new organism. Mayr (1959) found further support for the gradualist approach from several sources. We briefly mention three of those sources. *Intensification* refers to the finding that what appear to be large evolutionary changes can occur through a variation on a basic theme, for example, the eventual formation of glands from scattered secretory cells. The second source, considered the most important by Mayr, is change in function. This change in function occurs most often when a particular structure can perform two separate functions or when two different organs may perform the same function in an individual. For example, the forelimbs of mammals are capable of many functions: digging, swimming, predation, and so on. All that would be required is that gradually one of these functions comes to predominate over the others. Campbell (1974) and Wachtershauser (1987) have suggested that vision might have evolved in this manner. They suggest that although humans live in a sea of electromagnetic radiation they perceive only a very small range (roughly between 400–700 nanometers). In response to food shortages, primitive organisms developed photosynthesis, the ability to manufacture food through the use of light. This capability was selected because it provided a novel source of food. Photosynthesis occurs only in the 400 to 700 nanometer range because longer wavelengths have insufficient energy to fuel the photochemical reaction and shorter wavelengths destroy proteins and DNA. Phototropisms could then be selected because they allow the organism to orient and therefore maximize the use of light. However, most important is that this "edible radiation" also corresponds to the range in which the transparent coincides with the penetrable. That is, things that cannot be seen through usually cannot be moved through. Therefore, an organism that is photosensitive could use vision as a vicarious substitute for direct movement and have a clear selective advantage because of the increased accuracy and efficiency of its knowledge of its environment.

However, here one can see how one function comes to evolve from other functions and becomes the predominate function.

The final source of support comes from a counterargument to the saltationist belief that new structures could not have evolved gradually because they would not have been selected until they were sufficiently elaborated to provide some selective advantage. Mayr (1959) points out that even incipient structures can provide a selective advantage, for example, the slight lengthening of the neck of the giraffe would have an immediate adaptive advantage by increasing access to food sources at higher elevations and by allowing the animal to view potential predators in high grass at a greater distance.

A third approach to the evolution of new structures and species was formulated by Lamarck (1809/1960), initially as a way to rectify the creationist view of invariance of species and the fact that many species have become extinct and seemed to change (evolve) rather than remaining static. Adaptations to new environments could only occur if animals evolve by some means. Lamarck suggested two causes as the basis for evolutionary change. The first was an inherent tendency for increasing complexity, a tendency toward perfection endowed by the creator. The second cause was based on an ability to adapt to the conditions of the environment. Thus, Lamarck was an evolutionist and his ideas predated those of Darwin; however, there was a crucial difference between the mechanisms of evolution proposed by Lamarck and those proposed by Darwin. Unlike the natural selection proposed by Darwin and the importance of random variation independent of the environment, Lamarck proposed that the environment alone was the cause of variation. The organism has needs that must be satisfied, and the efforts to satisfy those needs in a changing environment modifies the individual. For example, if the environmental conditions require the strengthening of an organ, that organ will enlarge and become stronger. Conversely, if an organ is not used there will be a resultant atrophy and disappearance. Furthermore, the results of the continued use or disuse of an organ could be passed on to future generations.

Lamarck's major contribution was in pointing out, prior to Darwin, that species do evolve and that the response to environmental pressures plays an essential part in evolution. However, the notion of the inheritance of acquired biological characteristics has been thoroughly discredited. As Mayr (1959) pointed out, the development of molecular biology and the discovery of the genetic basis of inheritance—the structure of DNA—have demonstrated that acquired characteristics do not alter DNA, and, thus, the acquired characteristics would not be transmitted to the next generation. For example, the genes of an individual who sustains brain damage during his or her life do not change in a manner that would cause this individual's offspring to be brain damaged. Therefore, it is neither the individual who is changed by the environment nor the individual's genes, but rather it is the population that is modified.

Finally, we want to briefly mention two major criticisms that have been leveled against evolutionary theory. Sometimes, the controversy described above and other controversies within evolution have been used by critics to suggest that evolution is "just a theory" or, even more strongly, that it is false. We believe that Mayr (1982) has said it well:

> For many biologists today, evolution is no longer a theory but simply a fact, documented by the changes in the gene pools of species from generation to generation and by the changes in the fossil biota in accurately dated geological strata. Current resistance is limited entirely to opponents with religious commitments. (p. 507)

The last major criticism is that evolutionary theory explains nothing because it is unfalsifiable: An explanation drawing on adaptation and natural selection can be created for anything that needs explanation. However, Darwin (1859) correctly pointed out that evolution is falsifiable. It excludes the evolution of a trait that benefits a genetic competitor (Noonan, 1987). Moreover, it is not a problem that multiple, competing evolutionary hypotheses can be formed to explain the adaptation of a certain mechanism or trait. A good theory need not only have a very limited, univocal set of implications. Research can evaluate the relative merits of these competing evolutionary hypotheses.

THE RELATIONSHIP BETWEEN BEHAVIOR AND EVOLUTION

As noted previously, a key issue in evolution is that of random variation. Species that are static or invariant are highly susceptible to an inevitable change in the environment, whereas genetic diversity in a species promotes variability that tends to promote survival of some members of that species in the face of a changing environment. The roles of the environment and genetic variability in evolution have led naturally to conceptions of the role of behavior in these processes.

Barash (1977) has given a general rationale for the relevance of evolution to behavior:

> Consider it [the correlation between genes and behavior] from a purely mechanistic viewpoint: the DNA of which genes are composed specifies the production of proteins leading to the various structures constituting an organism. These structures include bone, muscle, blood, and nerve cells. Behavior unquestionably arises as a consequence of the activity of nerve cells, which presumably are susceptible to specification by DNA, much as any other cells. Accordingly, insofar as genes

specify the organization of nerve cells, just as they specify the organization of bone cells, there is every reason to accept a role of genes in producing behavior, just as we accept the role of genes in producing structure. As phenotypes go, behavior may be somewhat more flexible or susceptible to environmental influence than most. But the relevance of genetics to behavior is undeniable, and since evolution is the primary force responsible for the genetic make-up of living things, evolution must also be relevant to behavior. (pp. 47–48)

Barash's point is a good one: Behavioral capacities such as ability to be classically or operantly conditioned must have some physiological basis, and this physiological basis ultimately has genetic and evolutionary roots. However, the relationship between behavior and evolution is particularly complex. Behaviors that are observed are likely to result from the evolutionary pressures favoring structural adaptation, but there is no fossil record of the behavior of species. Also, general attributes associated with the ability to learn may be critical for species' survival, yet not be associated with a specific set of behaviors. Rather, a specified change in capacity for many behaviors may be the result of evolutionary pressures. Such changes in capacity would, in a sense, allow for variation in behavior both within an individual (flexibility and plasticity) and between individuals (systematic variation). A change in capacity (enhanced behavioral flexibility and plasticity) would also necessitate other changes (e.g., protracted development) during which the brain would be easily affected by environmental contingencies as well as the resulting support systems (e.g., maternal behavior, group cohesiveness) that are necessary for the flourishing of such changes in capacity.

Diversity is also reflected in behavioral variability within a species. Wasps, rats, and monkeys can vary widely in intraspecific behaviors, and the view that animal behavior in so-called "lower species" is invariant is clearly incorrect. As Mayr (1958) indicated:

> It is not only wrong to speak of the monkey but even of the behavior of the rhesus monkey. The variability of behavior is evident in the study not only of such a genetically plastic species as man but even of forms with very rigid stereotyped behaviors, such as hunting wasps. (p. 684)

Mayr (1958) further questioned the notion that the term innate reflects invariance in behavior:

> "Innate" is of course only the reaction norm, which has a more or less wide range of phenotypic expression. The term "innate" is meaningful only if it is interpreted epigenetically (rather than preformistically!). This is fully understood by the geneticist, who states that a certain flower color or the presence of wing veins is "inherited." The fact that the tendency to hoard is "innate" in the Norway rat is not negated by

the fact that certain treatments or experiences may reduce this tendency or obliterate it altogether. Most mammals cannot be induced to hoard no matter what treatment they get. The time has come to stress the existence of genetic differences in behavior, in view of the enormous amount of material the students of various forms of learning have accumulated on nongenetic variation in behavior. Striking individual differences have been described for predator–prey relations, for the reaction of birds to mimicking or to warning colorations, for child care among primates, and for maternal behavior in rats. It is generally agreed by observers that much of this individual difference is not affected by experience but remains essentially constant throughout the entire life-time of the individual. Such variability is of the greatest interest to the student of evolution, and it is to be hoped that it will receive more attention from the experimental psychologist than it has in the past. (p. 685)

Great intraspecific variation in behavior raises a very important issue: Is the variability in behavior the result of genetic differences, or have variable environmental influences modified the expression of the behavior?

Mayr (1974) has examined the issue of genetic and environmental influences on behavior and, borrowing from information theory, has suggested that behaviors can be classified phenotypically as being under the control of either *closed genetic programs* or *open genetic programs*. *Closed programs* are genetic programs that cannot be modified based on experience and are characteristic of the behavior of many species. *Open programs* can be modified by environmental influences based on the particular life experiences of an individual. In general, programs for species recognition (with the notable exception of imprinting) are properly considered to be closed programs.

Closed programs tend to dominate the behavioral repertoire of species with very short life spans. Such organisms must be "well-wired" because of the severely limited opportunity for learning and behavioral plasticity during the life span. The organism must be able to behave appropriately in the presence of certain stimuli on the first experience with those stimuli. A second chance may not be forthcoming. Another example is that reflexes such as the startle response, the eyeblink, salivation, and so forth may be closed programs that play a role in the open program of classical conditioning.

Mayr (1974) pointed out that, in organisms with protracted life spans, with extended parental care, there is a dramatic increase in the number of open programs. "The great selective advantage of a capacity for learning is, of course, that it permits storing far more experiences, far more detailed information about the environment, than can be transmitted in the DNA of the fertilized zygote." (p. 699). Open and closed genetic programs have major evolutionary consequences. Mayr (1974) suggested that changes in parental behavior are of great importance because extended parental care may allow for a shift from a reliance on closed to open genetic programs. The increase in open programs increases the evolutionary potential of individuals by allowing for rapid behavioral adjustments to environmental changes that would be impossible for species with less behavioral plasticity. Symons (1979) summarized the advantages and disadvantages of this plasticity nicely:

> [P]lasticity is a double-edged sword: the more flexible an organism is the greater the variety of maladaptive, as well as adaptive, behaviors it can develop; the more teachable it is, the more fully it can profit from the experiences of its ancestors and associates and the more it risks being exploited by ancestors and associates; the greater its capacity for learning morality the more worthless superstitions, as well as traditions of social wisdom, it can acquire; the more cooperatively interdependent the members of a group become the greater is their collective power and the more fulsome are the opportunities for individuals to manipulate one another; the more sophisticated language becomes the more subtle are the lies, as well as the truths, that can be said. (pp. 307–308)

Thus, there is a selective advantage if there are relatively closed mechanisms that channel the plasticity toward adaptive ends.

IMPLICATIONS FOR HUMANS

What are the implications of an evolutionary perspective for a better understanding of human behavior? As a species, it is quite clear that human behavior relies largely on open genetic programs. Is there any use in taking an evolutionary perspective toward specific instances of human behavior? A recent series of articles and reviews suggested that the emerging area of evolutionary psychology has much to contribute to the understanding of human behavior (Buss, 1991; Buss & Schmidt, 1993; DeKay & Buss, 1992; Tooby & Cosmides, 1990).

In their review, DeKay and Buss (1992) suggested that three questions are the foundation of evolutionary psychology: What are the origins of human psychological mechanisms? What adaptive problems selected for their existence? What functions were they designed to serve? Although the evolutionary principles of systematic variation and natural selection are fundamental aspects of the approach, evolutionary psychology attempts to apply the evolutionary approach to an understanding of specific aspects of human behavior. A fundamental assumption is that, as a species, humans possess "specialized psychological mechanisms" that have evolved because of their adaptive usefulness (DeKay & Buss, 1992). According to DeKay and Buss (1992) "the central goal of evolutionary psychology is to identify these evolved psychological mechanisms and to understand their functions" (p. 185). Thus, evolutionary psychology seeks to provide explanations in terms of *ultimate causes* (Why did this come to exist; what are its evolutionary causes?), compared with explanations that involve *proximate causes* (What are the immediate links in the causal chain that account for this phenomenon?).

Buss and Schmidt (1993) proposed a contextual-evolutionary theory as an approach to understanding human mating strategies. The approach begins with the cross-cultural behavioral observation that 90% of all individuals marry. This is characterized as a long-term mating strategy. A second short-term mating strategy is also ubiquitous in human behavior. The behavior of both males and females was examined in the context of the two identified mating strategies because the evolutionary mechanisms for guiding behavior for males and females are likely to differ in these two contexts. Human mating from an evolutionary perspective is strategic and used to solve adaptive problems that arose during the course of human evolution. The authors examined a number of specific hypotheses of mate selection in males and females. The results indicated that mating preferences and strategies differ predictably depending on sex and temporal context. The male–female differences appear to be systematically related to different, historically based, adaptive pressures between males and females.

The evidence strongly supports the contention that many aspects of human behavior, including mate selection, status-striving, and reciprocal alliance formation, have their basis in evolved psychological mechanisms (Buss, 1991). Furthermore, these mechanisms are likely to be manifested in the behavioral strategies necessary to achieve these ends.

EVOLUTIONARY MECHANISMS AND INDIVIDUAL DIFFERENCES

In addition to describing general strategies, a theory of evolutionary psychology must also deal with the origins of human individual differences. Buss (1991) and others (Tooby & Cosmides, 1990) have approached the issue of individual differences from the perspective of evolutionary personality psychology. Buss (1991) suggested that there are at least four evolutionary routes that may lead to individual differences: (a) heritable alternative strategies, in which on the basis of environmental fluctuations, high variation in a strategy has been selected for; (b) heritable calibration of psychological mechanisms, in which different strategies have been selected for within alternative environmental niches; (c) situationally contingent alternative strategies, which refers to a situation in which several strategies may have evolved for dealing with a particular environmental contingency, and the strategy of choice is situation specific; and (d) developmental calibration of psychological mechanisms, which refers to the role of different developmental experiences in affecting the threshold for the evocation of a species-typical behavior.

In conclusion, Buss (1991) suggested that evolutionary theory provides a conceptual framework for many of the central issues in personality psychology, but the suggestion comes with a warning:

> Evolutionary personality psychology, however, is neither simple nor easy. It requires a non-trivial mastery of evolutionary biology. Many attempts to use evolutionary theory have been conceptually sloppy. Some have committed the "sociobiological fallacy" by assuming that humans have as a psychological goal the maximization of inclusive fitness. Others have erred in seeking in evolution a justification of particular political views. Still others err in adopting the view that evolutionary theory implies genetic determinism in the sense of intractability and lack of environmental influence. These misunderstandings must be eliminated before the field can progress. (p. 486)

EVOLUTION AND BEHAVIOR THERAPY

In this section, we examine some of the major implications of evolution for behavior therapy and trace this influence through the work of Skinner. We conclude that evolution provides a context for understanding the proximate causal mechanisms in which behavior therapists are directly concerned. In doing this, evolutionary theory can provide a useful framework for generating and developing theories about human behavior and its difficulties.

What Are Humans?

Behavior therapists, in the language of the politically correct, are specists. That is, behavior therapists confine their interests to humans. But if confronted with the question of what is a human, the clinical psychologist must resort to biological constructs that ultimately are based on an evolutionary account. Humans are members of a biological category of life, the species, *homo sapiens*. However, as we have discussed earlier, speciation—the formation of distinct interbreeding populations—is itself an evolutionary process.

Human beings are an evolved animal species. This may be a surprising statement to practitioners of certain therapeutic paradigms, for example, humanistic or existential therapists, but it should be much less surprising to a behavior therapist. There are a number of interesting implications of this rather simple statement. First, as animals humans share important commonalities with other members of the animal kingdom. Of foremost interest is that all animals—in fact, all life—share some common ancestors and, thus, some common history. The most basic building block of life, DNA, is the same across all life forms. About 4 billion years ago, the ancestor of all current life was a replicating organic molecule. This similarity is exploited by experimental psychologists who study nonhuman animals in order to understand humans. Thus, evolution provides the justification as well as the bridge for behavior therapists' long-standing interest in the animal studies of experimental psychology.

A second implication of the statement explains why the extrapolation from nonhuman animals to humans is never perfect. Evolution produces different species by the continuous process of branching. Human beings have a unique genetic makeup, and, as a result, there are differences as well as similarities between humans and other animals. Behavior therapists need to be aware of the possibilities that some animal research may not be generalizable across that species to the human species or that the generalization requires a good deal of qualification. Cognitively inclined behavior therapists who argue against the relevance of relying on studies of animal species who have poorly developed (relative to humans) cognitive abilities may base their assertions on this implication. These are important empirical questions that must be considered.

Another important implication is that humans have an evolutionary history. It should not be surprising that anything that is so complex that it can produce a human eye or nervous system should also have subtle and complex implications for human behavior and its problems. One major implication is that evolution is a slow process that does not create ex nihilo but instead can only select from what already exists. Thus, evolutionary design is often jury-rigged. It, like what has been said about the Roman Catholic church, "thinks in centuries." That is, evolution has generally prepared the species for problems it consistently found in past environments; however, the present may not be like the past, and the jury-rigged nature of evolution might have problematic vestiges of this history:

> [the] evolutionary past of every species of organism—the ghostly world of time in which animals are forever slipping from one environment to another and changing their forms and features as they go. But the marks of the passage linger, and so we come down to the present bearing the traces of all the curious tables at which our forerunners have sat and played the game of life. Our world, in short, is a marred world, an imperfect world, a never totally adjusted world, for the simple reason that it is not static. The games are still in progress and all of us, in the words of Sir Arthur Keith, bear the wounds of evolution. Our backs hurt, we have muscles which no longer move, we have hair that is not functional. All of this bespeaks another world, another game played far behind us in the past. We are indeed products of "descent with modification." (Eiseley, 1958, p. 197)

It has been said that modern humans are one of the most important relics of early humans. Thus, an important question becomes To what extent are certain behavioral propensities phylogenetic vestiges?

A final implication of the simple statement that humans are an evolved animal species is the effect of viewing a species as a population that has a fair amount of diversity. Mayr (1982) has criticized what he calls an essentalist view of species, that is, the view that species have fixed and relatively invariant characteristics. Mayr noted that this view is not consistent with observations of phenotypes (humans vary dramatically in height, weight, etc.), and genetic homogeneity is usually not a good evolutionary strategy in that variability hedges the species' bets concerning what it might take to survive and reproduce. Populationist thinking suggests that there is a distribution of characteristics within a species. There is both phenotypical variability and genetic variability.

This variability across individuals is important for clinical psychologists to understand for several reasons. First, it explains how selective mechanisms work in an individual's lifetime. Only some win the race, only some are chosen as mates, only some are victims of assaults, and so forth. Some are selected by environmental pressures; some are not. Second, it provides some underpinning for notions such as Kiesler's (1966) client uniformity myth. Clients as individual homo sapiens are not all the same, either genetically or experientially. Moreover, clients do not all have the same capacities to overcome or be the victims of various challenges in life.

Conditioning and Evolution

Although most behavior therapists would not immediately recognize the relevance of Darwin to their problems, many behavior therapists would recognize the relevance of Skinner to their concerns because the conditioning paradigms, and especially operant conditioning, are central to behavior therapy. However, Skinner, especially in his later writings, emphasized the role of evolution in providing comprehensive explanations of human behavior. Skinner (1984) stated:

> Human behavior is the joint product of (i) contingencies of survival responsible for natural selection and (ii) contingencies of reinforcement responsible for the repertoires of individuals, including (iii) the special contingencies maintained by an evolved social environment. Selection by consequences is a causal mode found only in living things, or in machines made by living things. It was first recognized in natural selection. Reproduction, a first consequence led to the evolution of cells, organs, and organisms reproducing themselves under increasingly diverse conditions. The behavior functioned well, however, only under conditions similar to those under which it was selected. Reproduction under a wider range of consequences became possible with the evo-

lution of processes through which organisms acquired behavior appropriate to novel environments. One of these, operant conditioning, is a second kind of selection by consequences. New responses could be strengthened by events which followed them. When the selecting consequences are the same, operant conditioning and natural selection work together redundantly. But because a species which quickly acquires behavior appropriate to an environment has less need for an innate repertoire, operant conditioning could replace as well as supplement the natural selection of behavior. (p. 477)

Therefore, for Skinner what are primary reinforcers and punishers are the biologically manifested products of evolution, and the capacity to be operantly conditioned is homologous to natural selection and is itself a product of natural selection.

Although not mentioned by Skinner, evolution is relevant to classical conditioning also in that all classical conditioning builds on a preexisting reflex (i.e., an unconditional stimulus producing an unconditional response). These reflexes, such as salivation to food, eyeblinks to puffs of air, pupil constriction to bright lights, and so on, are biologically determined and have rather obvious evolutionary advantages. Moreover, the capacity to learn other associations to stimuli that provide information (Rescorla, 1988) about the probability of the unconditional stimulus also appears to be an inherited tendency, which can be explained by its obvious survival value.

But it is too crude to say simply that evolution has produced a biologically mediated capacity to be classically and operantly conditioned as well as providing reflexes and primary reinforcers for these processes. Evolution has struck a compromise between a completely open system and a closed one. Behavior is not indefinitely plastic. Conditioning can occur between many events, but not all, and certain events seem to be more learnable then others. The hypothesis that learning was equipotent, that is, behavior was indefinitely modifiable with no antecedent directness has been shown to be false. The experiments of Garcia and his colleagues (Garcia & Koelling, 1966) as well as those of the Brelands (Breland & Breland, 1961) suggest biological biases for conditioning.

A potential criticism should be addressed at this point. Behavior therapists typically emphasize environmental determinants of behavior, and evolutionary theory as part of biology may be seen as inconsistent with this emphasis. However, this is not the case. First, there are different levels of analysis within biology, and an evolutionary analysis is much different than a physiological one. Skinner (1984) criticized a tendency to regard physiological explanations as somehow more satisfying or superior to environmental ones but had no direct objections to physiological explanations. However, an evolutionary account does not engage in any of the problematic physiologizing criticized by Skinner. Second, as Buss (1990) has pointed out (consistent with Skinner) an evolutionary account is an environmentalist account:

> There is an important sense in which *all* human behavior is the product of the environment. But environments vary on a temporal dimension from distal to proximate. The distal environment is the "environment of evolutionary adaptedness," the ancestral conditions that forged basic human adaptations. A more proximate environment is that of ontogeny—the conditions encountered or created during development. At the most proximate level are immediate environmental contingencies that, through organismic structure created over phylogeny and ontogeny, affect current behavior. (p. 2)

EVOLUTION AND HUMAN SEXUALITY

Finally, we shall illustrate many of the general points made above as well as the relevance of evolutionary theory to the framing of hypothesis by examining some hypotheses concerning the evolutionary roots of human sexuality. Behavior therapists can be concerned about human sexuality and its problems (O'Donohue & Geer, 1993), and we show the extent to which evolutionary theory allows for a deeper understanding of the ultimate causes of sexual behavior.

First, note that evolutionary theory allows social scientists to understand why there is such a thing as sex. Sex itself probably evolved because of its relative efficiency at producing genetic diversity. Humans could have evolved to reproduce asexually (and what a different world it would be if this were the case) but the rather conservatively creative manner (offspring are different than either parent or their siblings, but not all that different) of gaining some genetic diversity would probably win out over the less creative process of asexual reproduction.

Second, evolution allows the understanding that sex is not an activity that is simply one among many equals but that sex is nearly unequaled in importance. It has a special importance in several ways. It is the cornerstone of evolution. As pointed out previously, it is not survival that is actually important, but it is surviving so that one can reproduce fecund offspring. And, of course, reproduction requires sex. Sex is also important because sex is a powerful primary reinforcer. Again, evolution allows us to see that ancestors who found sex unreinforcing or only mildly reinforcing (and this capacity for reinforcement was heritable) would probably place less of these genes in the gene pool than a competing group who found sex highly reinforcing. Sex can then be viewed as important because it has evolved to be an intensely reinforcing act. Because of the magnitude of its reinforcing effects, it can help evoke a lot of behavior that is only indirectly related to sex (acquisitiveness, attraction enhancing activities, etc.). This may help account for the large interest humans have in sex.

A point related to the first two considerations is that humans are not only dimorphic in regard to sexual anatomy, but also in regard to sexual behavior. Differences in primary and secondary sexual anatomy are well-known and will not be repeated here. However, the dimorphic nature of human sexual behavior needs some explication. Trivers (1972) has suggested that males and females have different reproductive strategies because of differing evolutionary pressures on their reproductive roles. Although both sexes are interested in reproducing, because females have a much higher parental investment than males their orientation toward sex and reproduction has evolved to be much different. Because of menopause, significant gestation periods, and increased care of the neonate (e.g., breast feeding), a female can only have a very limited number of offspring in her lifetime. Thus, females became highly selective in their choice of mate (as the mating may tie up a significant percentage of their limited reproductive possibilities) and became highly concerned about care of their offspring. Males, in contrast, have a much lower parental investment in their offspring. In reproducing, males expend only a short amount of time, and a little bit of immediately replenishable sperm. Moreover, males are physically able to have nearly an unlimited number of offspring.

The differential parental investments in offspring have lead evolutionary theorists to suggest the following:

1. Males will be more promiscuous than females, because promiscuity is a reproductive strategy that is consistent with low parental investment. As part of the more promiscuous reproductive strategy, males will have a higher sex drive than females.
2. In contrast, females will be more discriminating in choice of mates, because each mating can be potentially much more costly in terms of limiting reproductive possibilities.
3. Males will be more visually aroused than females, as evolutionarily sound promiscuity suggests mating with many visibly healthy fecund females. Symons (1987) has pointed out that visible signs of health such as clear skin, shiny hair, good muscle tone, some stored fat, and the absence of obvious signs of illness are highly sexually attractive to most males. (Think of the generational viability of a population that found the opposite attractive.)
4. Females will be more concerned about how much and how likely it is that a male will invest time and resources in her offspring. Thus, a female will be concerned with the amount

and quality of resources that a man controls and with signs that he will remain with her and invest in their offspring.

5. However, for males, a good reproductive strategy may be a mixed strategy of pair bonding and philandering. This would give males the best of both worlds: care of some particularly important offspring and promiscuity to increase their genetic bets.

6. Because females know that when they are pregnant the fetus is theirs, but males are not sure if they are the fathers in a pregnancy, and because it is evolutionarily unwise to spend a lot of resources raising offspring that are not theirs (i.e., are genetically unrelated), males should be more jealous, and more troubled by female infidelity.

7. Human females are one of the few primates that do not have periods of estrous but have concealed ovulation. One reason this might have evolved is that because males can never know when ovulation is occurring they must "stick around" to maximize their chances of inseminating and to guard against another male interest.

8. There is intrasexual competition for mates, particularly among males. Because females are the "choosers," males compete for sexual access to females. They do this in a variety of ways, from (true and misleading) resource displays to direct aggression against other males. Darwin (1859) called male competition and female choosiness sexual selection and suggested that sexual selection accounted for many secondary sex characteristics in males (increased size, increased aggressiveness, etc.). But females are also in reproductive competition with one another; females are competing for the best males.

Three caveats must be made at this point: First, these points need to be framed in a population context. We are not saying that every male or female is this way. Instead, we are saying that, although there is so much variability as to produce overlap, on average, males and females form a bimodal distribution on these traits. Second, when we talk about reproductive strategy we do not mean to imply that this is a consciously held plan. It is an organizing framework that serves as a general motivator of diverse behavior. This is similar to discussions of a hedonistic view. When one says humans seek to maximize pleasure and minimize pain, one is not saying that in every decision humans remind themselves of this, nor is one saying that humans are ever aware of this general rule. In both cases, one is simply saying that this rule can be used to help understand the diverse behavior of the organism. Third, because of space limitations, we have not cited the research evidence that supports the empirical claims discussed above. We refer the reader to Symons (1987) and Buss and Schmidt (1993) for summaries of this literature.

Finally, we would like to highlight how each of the above points becomes clinically relevant:

1. Male promiscuity is related to marital dissatisfaction, marital breakup, the spread of sexually transmitted disease, and male guilt and female pain over this inclination. The greater sex drive of a male may cause males to engage in a wider range of sexual behavior (hence their far greater tendency to engage in some paraphilic behaviors) and to be oriented toward sex at the expense of other activities.
2. Females may judge males as underinterested in relationships and as not valuing relationships or being willing to work on them as much as females. Males may judge females as having low sexual desire and as being overly concerned about the minutiae of relationships.
3. Males may become overinvolved in pornography and related visual sexual activities. Males may become problematically interested in young (18–26-year-old) females, because this is when female reproductive viability is maximized.
4. Males who are having difficulty gaining resources may have more problems attracting females and, therefore, may have an increased chance of problems such as loneliness. Relatedly, males may have a higher tendency to be deceptive in acquiring resources or to deceptively display resources.
5. Again, this may explain the higher rate of male marital infidelity.
6. This may explain the tendency of males to be more sexually jealous than females, the greater frequency of males committing homicides that are related to jealousy, and the male creation and propagation of sexist beliefs to limit women's sexual functioning.
8. This mechanism may motivate a lot of intramale competition and hostility that may result in nonharmonious relationships and aggressive events.

In closing we want to point out that identifying possible evolutionary influences on behavior does not justify or "excuse" the behavior. Just as one would not want to say that sickle cell anemia is justified (and therefore should not be changed) because we can understand its adaptive advantages in malaria resistence in the heterogenous genetic expression, we would not want to suggest that we approve of any of these tendencies. However, we do believe that with increased understanding comes an increased likelihood of change. An understanding of the evolutionary influences on behavior can place behavior therapists in a better position to change unwanted behavior.

REFERENCES

Barash, D. P. (1977). *Sociobiology and behavior.* New York: Elsevier Science.

Breland, K., & Breland, M. (1961). The misbehavior of organisms. *American Psychologist, 16,* 681–684.

Buss, D. M. (1990). Toward a biologically informed psychology of personality. *Journal of Personality, 58,* 1–16.

Buss, D. M. (1991). Evolutionary personality psychology. *Annual Review of Psychology, 42,* 459–491.

Buss, D. M., & Schmidt, D. P. (1993). Sexual strategies theory: An evolutionary perspective on human mating. *Psychological Review, 100,* 204–232.

Campbell, D. T. (1974). Evolutionary epistemology. In P. A. Schilpp (Ed.), *The philosophy of Karl Popper* (pp. 413–463). La Salle, IL: Open Court.

Darwin, C. (1859). *The origin of species.* New York: New American Library.

DeKay, W. T., & Buss, D. M. (1992). Human nature, individual differences, and the importance of context: Perspectives from evolutionary psychology. *Current Directions in Psychological Science, 1,* 184–189.

Eiseley, L. (1958). *Darwin's century.* New York: Doubleday.

Garcia, J., & Koelling, R. A. (1966). Relation of cue to consequence in avoidance learning. *Psychonomic Science, 4,* 123–124.

Gould, S. J. (1984). *The flamingo's smile: Reflections in natural history.* New York: Norton.

Kettlewell, H. B. D. (1973). *The evolution of melanism: The study of a recurring necessity, with special reference to industrial melanism in the Lepidopterra.* Oxford, England: Clarendon Press.

Kiesler, D. J. (1966). Some myths of psychotherapy research and the search for a paradigm. *Psychological Bulletin, 65,* 110–136.

Lamarck, J. B. (1960). *Philosophie zoologique.* Forestburgh, NY: Lubrecht & Cramer. (Original work published 1809)

Mayr, E. (1958). Behavior and systematics. In E. Mayr (Ed.), *Evolution and the diversity of life* (pp. 677–693). Cambridge, MA: Harvard University Press.

Mayr, E. (1959). The emergence of evolutionary novelties. In E. Mayr (Ed.), *Evolution and the diversity of life* (pp. 88–113). Cambridge, MA: Harvard University Press.

Mayr, E. (1974). Behavior programs and evolution. In E. Mayr (Ed.), *Evolution and the diversity of life* (pp. 694–711). Cambridge, MA: Harvard University Press.

Mayr, E. (1976). *Evolution and the diversity of life.* Cambridge, MA: Harvard University Press.

Mayr, E. (1982). *The growth of biological thought*. Cambridge, MA: Belknap Press.

Noonan, K. M. (1987). Evolution: A primer for psychologists. In C. Crawford, M. Smith, & D. Krebs (Eds.), *Sociobiology and psychology: Ideas, issues, and applications* (pp. 31–60). Hillsdale, NJ: Erlbaum.

O'Donohue, W., & Geer, J. H. (1993). *Handbook of sexual dysfunctions*. Boston: Allyn & Bacon.

O'Donohue, W., & Halsey, L. (1994). The differing conceptions of science of four psychotherapy theorists. Manuscript submitted for publication.

Skinner, B. F. (1984). Selection by consequences. *Brain and Behavioral Sciences, 7*, 477–510.

Symons, D. (1987). An evolutionary approach: Can Darwin's view of life shed light on human sexuality. In J. Geer & W. O'Donohue (Eds.), *Theories of Human Sexuality* (91–126). New York: Plenum.

Symons, D. (1979). *The evolution of human sexuality*. New York: Oxford University Press.

Tooby, J., & Cosmides, L. (1990). On the universality of human nature and the uniqueness of the individual: The role of genetics and adaptation. *Journal of Personality, 58*, 17–68.

Trivers, R. L. (1972). Parental investment and sexual selection. In B. Campbell (Ed.), *Sexual selection and the descent of man. 1871–1971*. Chicago: Aldine.

Wachtershauser, G. (1987). Light and life: On the nutritional origins of sensory perception. In G. Radnitzky & W. W. Bartley (Eds.), *Evolutionary epistemology, rationality, and the sociology of knowledge* (pp. 121–138). La Salle, IL: Open Court.

18

FEMINIST THEORY AND COGNITIVE BEHAVIORISM

FELICITY ALLEN

Modern feminist ideologies in English-speaking societies can be traced to Wollstonecraft's A *Vindication of the Rights of Woman* (1792/1975). Appearing in the French revolutionary period, when many traditional "givens" were being questioned, her book was a best-seller. The theory of natural rights, as extended by Wollstonecraft, maintained that women had a right to develop their intellects, to pursue their interests, and to enjoy the protection of the law on the basis of their common humanity with men. A cognitive behaviorist would understand these philosophical arguments as cognitions that individuals might activate as behavioral schemata, with varying degrees of success, depending on the opportunities available in the social setting.

As I will show, this formulation of women as human beings whose rights should be considered on a par with those of men has strongly influenced feminist perspectives in both psychology and psychiatry. The role of "structured social interaction" in changing individual beliefs about appropriate roles has interested cognitive behaviorists and will be addressed later in this chapter. Very little is known, however, about either the processes

495

whereby individuals choose among available schemata or the triggers that lead to action. Feminism is an intriguing example of a social movement that took an inexplicably long time to develop from a minority opinion to a mass movement. Although the theoretical basis for a political movement had been available for decades and small numbers of women attempted to improve women's social status, large-scale social movements to change the position of women did not appear until the early 1860s (Bauer & Ritt, 1979; Kraditor, 1981). The Seneca Falls Declaration of 1848 was largely ignored, yet, 20 years later, American women had won limited rights to vote (Klein, 1984).

Why feminism was taken up by women in many countries after 1860, but not before, has never been adequately explained. Kraditor (1981) described how exposure to the ideology of equality in the abolition campaigns and the experience of organizing political pressure against the slavery laws molded the attitudes and developed the skills of the women involved in the American suffrage movement. Clearly, many American women drew parallels between their own civic status and that of the slaves, although why some female abolitionists made the connection and acted on it, but others did not, remains unclear.

Demographic pressures within a monogamous marital system have been suggested as a partial explanation for social change in the relationships between the genders in other countries. In Britain, for example, an improvement in women's life expectancy relative to men's, beginning post-1850, led to a sudden rise in the ratio of single women to single men (72.7% in one 20-year period; Vicinus, 1977). Improved female life expectancy was concentrated in the middle classes—the sector of society committed to female dependency as a male status symbol. Considerable contemporary comment in Britain discussed the problem of "redundant" women. Commentators vacillated between considering lifestyle options for women that might permit a greater variety of acceptable jobs, so that women could support themselves, or advocating the superior attractions of a domestic life, which many women could not attain. In Britain, emigration of women was a third alternative, but this option was not viable in Australia or the United States (Bauer & Ritt, 1979).

Whether the "redundant-woman" problem improved women's social position becomes questionable when the status of women in Britain is compared with that in the United States and Australia. Both of these countries had markedly skewed sex ratios, in favor of men, throughout the 19th century, yet where objective measures of women's status were concerned, such as voting and educational opportunities, the United States and Australia were both ahead of Britain. Although there were only 6 university places for women in England in 1869, Vassar had opened 4 years earlier in 1865, offering 350 university places for women. In that year, the territory of Wyoming entered the Union while retaining women's suffrage—a world first (Kraditor, 1981). A similar pattern was discernible in Australia. All of Australia's 19th-century universities admitted women to degrees; Cambridge held out until 1948, awarding certificates to women until that year (McWilliams-Tullberg, 1977; Summers, 1975). Australian women received the vote when the states joined together in a Federation in 1901; English women had to wait another 18 years. It might therefore be argued that the surplus of women in Britain weakened their bargaining power.

Whatever the reasons for the first wave of feminist activism, it was a remarkably successful political movement. Women's status rose from that of chattels to citizens, albeit second-class citizens, within a very short space of time. These sudden changes placed demands on both sexes. Women could choose between a broader range of opportunities; men had to adjust to a loss of personal power. No longer was it possible, for example, for a man to gain absolute control over large amounts of capital by the time-honored practice of marrying an heiress. Although divorce was difficult and deplored, it became an option for women (McWilliams-Tullberg, 1977; Vicinus, 1977). Better education and the gradual opening of job opportunities in the new technologies in the last part of the 19th century conferred on women a chance to support themselves independently and eased the economic pressure to marry and to stay married. The speed and extent of these changes precipitated gender-role confusion, which may have contributed to the popularity of psychoanalysis (see discussion later in this chapter).

FEMINIST ACTIVITY DURING THE 20TH CENTURY

A complete history of feminist activity during the 20th century is beyond the scope of this chapter. In brief, feminist activism reached a high point during the early 1920s. During that decade, most English-speaking countries passed enabling legislation that spelled out women's rights to enter universities, to practice professions, to retain their own property in marriage, and to enjoy full citizenship, including voting and standing for election. Many women entered the paid workforce in professional or managerial roles or stood for political office. Women's status seemed secure, yet they were unable to build on their achievements to attain full and lasting equality with men. Their status gradually declined after the mid-1920s and suffered a severe blow during the Great Depression. At that time, the scarcity of paid employment was used as an excuse to revive ideologies of men as the natural support of dependents. In almost all English-speaking countries, the "man as breadwinner" ideology was enforced both legally and administratively (Summers, 1975). The American Congress, for example, passed the Federal Economy Act in 1932, which stipulated that wives of government employees could not be appointed to federal jobs, no matter what their competence (Klein, 1984).

More to the point of this chapter, the new legislation was supported by media campaigns disseminating images of feminine helplessness. These ideologies limited women's visions of possibilities for their lives (Friedan, 1963). They also appealed to a view of women as selfless nurturers rather than independent citizens. The more brutal face of this movement was shown to those women who ungratefully rejected the chance to sacrifice themselves. They were publicly attacked as selfish and parasitic (Klein, 1984). The popular concatenation of femininity with self-sacrifice and the use of this image of self-denial to control women and limit their demands led to the development of assertiveness training for women during the 1970s (see discussion later).

The Second World War imposed a sudden demand for labor on the combatant countries, which could only be satisfied by drawing on the reserves of women at home. Women then reentered the paid workforce in large numbers, and many undertook nontraditional jobs in heavy industry (Friedan, 1963; Klein, 1984; Summers, 1975). This short period of socially approved independence and competence for women was followed by a period of relative quiescence and domesticity during the 1950s and 1960s. During this period, women's homemaker role was again valorized, as it had been during the 19th century, but with a modern twist: in the mid-20th century, a homebound mother was found to be essential for the normal development of the child (Bowlby, 1969; Oakley, 1981). Again, the needs of men and children were deemed to take precedence over women's rights to independence. The latest fashions in sex roles were communicated through advertisements, magazines, films, and even songs (e.g., Rodgers and Hammerstein's "I Enjoy Being a Girl," whose lyrics give a detailed set of role expectations and behaviors).

In some countries, notably Britain, reviews of the primary and secondary education systems concluded that girls' opportunities to learn should be limited to domestic skills and basic literacy. For example, a leading English educationalist, Newsom, wrote that secondary school girls should be led "to see that there is more to marriage than feeding the family and bathing the baby, and that they will themselves have a key role in establishing the standards of the home and in educating their children" (1963, p. 136). To achieve this attitude change, girls were to have a separate curriculum that led to the home rather than to the university. Newsom's report, commissioned by the British government, was titled (without apparent irony) *Half Our Future*.

Similar attempts in the United States to limit girls' education and to discourage women from gaining professional qualifications were deplored by Friedan (1963). The discouragement of girls' formal education during these decades has ongoing relevance for therapists because the victims of these ideas, in the form of "displaced homemakers," are still with us. Many girls of the 1960s believed their educators and did not acquire employable skills but, as women, lost their breadwinner and now need support, counseling, and training to enable them to escape the poverty trap. Many not only have an objective lack of qualifications but also suffer from low self-esteem, which, combined with anxiety about achievement, makes it very difficult for them to acquire and practice the skills they need (Friedan, 1981; Worell & Remy, 1992).

Another major feminist revival called the "second wave" then occurred (usually dated to 1968). The reasons for the upsurge in feminist activity at that point are not fully understood, although some writers (e.g., Oakley, 1981) have suggested that it was a reaction to a decline in the status of women that was occurring simultaneously in several English-speaking countries. Klein (1984) pointed to the increasing frustration of American women activists with a Congress that considered a record number of pieces of legislation about women's rights yet failed to act. Others (e.g., Lewis, 1992) have suggested that the availability of oral contraception during the 1960s played a role in helping redefine women's self-image away from that of wife and mother and toward that of career woman.

Women's renewed political activism once more led to a social and legislative change in a relatively short space of time. The history of modern feminism depicts a change from a time when women had a few clearly defined roles to the present, when women are free to choose between many possibilities. The speed and magnitude of the changes pose two problems for the psychologist. The first, assisting women who have been "left behind" by social changes, has already been briefly mentioned. The second problem, however, is harder to solve. Both sexes have become uncertain of what is expected of them, what is the "right" behavior at any given time. This can adversely affect social interactions and make life transition periods (e.g., adolescence, divorce) even more difficult than usual. Men in low-status jobs may be threatened by feminism because they derive much of their sense of personal worth from their breadwinner role. Men in a wide variety of occupations may feel threatened by women as competitors and may unite to exclude them from opportunities for appointment and promotion (see discussion later). In addition to the sense of threat experienced by individual men, the speed of change has generated a response from conservative social groups concerned with maintaining the status quo for women and the family.

MODERN FEMINIST THEORY

There is now a considerable and diverse body of feminist theory (e.g., Dworkin, 1983; Friedan, 1963, 1983; Greer, 1970; Millett, 1972; Oakley,

1981). However, common themes can be discerned. Feminist theories emphasize social justice and the need to develop social conditions and community support systems that would facilitate people's selection of life goals on the basis of their interests and merits rather than on the basis of membership in gender groups. The route to attaining these goals is believed to be through collective action rather than individual solutions. Considerable effort has been devoted to clarifying for both sexes that "women's problems" are not due to an individual failure to adjust but are the logical outcome of a social system that is unsympathetic to women's needs. There is a strong emphasis in feminist theory on the need for women to achieve economic independence. These theories predicate a considerable amount of self-determination for women and an independence of cultural norms, many of which are still limiting for women.

Feminist writers and therapists attempt to increase women's pride in themselves, to empower women, and to expand their range of life choices. They reject theories of society or of human adjustment that depict women as deviations from a male "norm." This aspect of feminism has been taken up in feminist approaches to psychology (see discussion later). The role of cognitions in promoting prescribed feminine behavior, in the form of cognitive schematas about appropriate roles for women and anxiogenic schematas about possible consequences of overstepping limits, has occupied many feminist writers (see discussion later).

In mass communication societies, print and visual media are important sources of cognitions. Both early (e.g., Friedan, 1963) and more recent, second-wave feminist writers (e.g., Wolf, 1991; Worell & Remy, 1992) have objected to media images linking female sexual attractiveness to helplessness and vulnerability. Friedan was largely concerned with the impact of these images in limiting women's ambitions to low-status, low-paid jobs or in excluding them from the paid workforce. Wolf drew attention to the pathogenic aspects of images of female "beauty" that lead to an obsession with physical appearance. She believed that the current epidemic of eating disorders is partly caused by unattainable slimness being presented as beautiful. Worell and Remy commented on the high proportion of films promoting violence against women as sexually attractive. They suggested that this may raise the probability that men would have violent thoughts about women, increasing women's vulnerability to attack. The prevalence of images linking sexuality with violence may "normalize" the experience for women and make them believe that opposing these ideas is futile.

In direct opposition to the depiction of cute-but-helpless women as desirable, feminists have argued the need for women to take control of their lives in many ways. These have included undertaking activities that enhance women's status and capabilities (e.g., achieving goals, improving emotional states, acquiring essential skills, and overcoming irrational fears) and controlling social pressues on women (e.g., setting limits on the demands that they are prepared to meet and resisting prescriptions for perfection).

Recent feminist theory is a prescription for women to deal with social pressures in an active, considered manner, representing a major break from the passivity traditionally ascribed to women. Although many feminists argue for collective action (see earlier discussion) to produce large-scale political change, others (e.g., Steinem, 1984) have stressed the utility of individual action to induce change at the micro level of social interaction. Indeed, this view is inherent in the slogan "The personal is political." The relationship of women to the patriarchal society suggests that changing the roles of women means that change will occur at a more personal level than is usual with other political movements, so that individuals will need to reconsider their actions and possibly alter their interpersonal exchanges. Feminism as a political movement endeavors to make it possible for all women, not just a privileged few, to choose their life goals and achieve them. This ideology has major implications for the usefulness of behaviorism to women, particularly when it is used as a self-directed tool for change (which I will describe later).

THE RELATIONSHIPS BETWEEN PSYCHOLOGY AND FEMINISM

The social sciences, including psychiatry and psychology, have responded variously to the social unrest and role confusion that occurred in the wake of first-wave feminism. There have been demands from social groups, including government-sponsored commissions of enquiry, as well as from patients and clients, for rulings on what is "normal" gender role behavior and for support in dealing with conflicting demands from employers and family. Although psychiatry, particularly in its role of defining normal behavior, has largely attracted criticism from feminists (e.g., Chesler, 1972; Rosewater & Walker, 1985), the relationships between psychology and feminism have varied according to the school of thought. The relationships between feminism and the psychoanalytic schools of psychology will be briefly described as a background to the interaction between feminism and behaviorism.

The psychoanalytic schools, particularly those of Freudian or Jungian orientation, are important to women because of the influence that they have had over recent Western culture. Their beliefs about typical female conflicts and needs and normal female development have dominated psychological and sociological theory, books, and films for over 50 years and show no sign of ceasing to do so. Feminists (e.g., Firestone, 1971; Millett, 1972; Rosewater & Walker, 1985) have criticized the psychoanalytic schools, especially those with a strong Freudian orientation. Firestone

(1971) argued that psychoanalytic tenets supporting traditional roles for women had great appeal when these were threatened but that both the theory and practice became major components of social rationales for women's continuing oppression. Although feminist criticism of psychoanalytic ideas may appear vehement, it is important to recognize what the prevailing attitude toward women was present among the founding analytic writers.

The psychoanalytic group, with some exceptions (usually women; e.g., Horney 1967), has presented the role of women as economically dependent child rearers as a universal, biologically determined given. In addition, many leading psychoanalysts were misogynists, maintaining not only that women's roles were biologically determined but also that women were inferior to men. Freudian theory postulated that little girls are shocked by the discovery of the penis and believe that their own lack of a penis is a deficiency (Freud, 1933). It is less well-known that Freud further argued that the absence of a penis means that the castration complex plays no part in normal female psychosexual development and, therefore, that women are less able to sublimate than are men. Inability to sublimate, Freud concluded, means that women are incapable of contributing to culture by creative thought. Their only contribution, as properly adjusted women, can be as wives and mothers.

Despite being the husband of one practicing analyst and the lover of another, Jung also maintained that a woman's place was ministering to the needs of men. He was fond of arguing that women had no souls. This has been passed off as a "joke" by later apologists (e.g., Douglas, 1990), but his underlying belief in the essential inferiority both of women and of the feminine cannot be denied. Women are faced with a clear choice in this theoretical framework. If they contribute to culture they are defined as neurotic; if they are well-adjusted, they cannot contribute to culture.

Historically, the emphasis of the clinical applications of the psychoanalytic schools has been on using therapeutic techniques to adjust women to fit their social roles, rather than questioning the prescriptions of the roles. The psychoanalytic school of thought influenced Bowlby (1969) in his view that if women entered the paid workforce, they would endanger the mental stability of their infants. Freud's theory that masochism was truly feminine has been absorbed into current beliefs that women somehow invite or enjoy violence against them (Rave, 1985) and has been used to excuse the behavior of rapists and batterers by blaming the victim.

Feminists have argued that the psychoanalysts have given insufficient emphasis to the role of social conditions in their prescriptions of normality, that they have overemphasized the role of intrapsychic conflicts (e.g. Millett, 1972; Rosewater & Walker, 1985), and that they have acted as conservative social forces, preventing the resolution of demands for gender equality (Firestone, 1971; Lerman, 1985).

In contrast, social learning theory has attracted considerable positive interest from feminists, particularly the area dealing with sex role socialization. This may be due to the fact that social psychologists have usually argued against biological determination of gender-typical behavior in humans (e.g., Archer & Lloyd, 1982).

One of the most interesting contributions of social psychology to sex role socialization was the concept of "nonconscious ideology." Bem and Bem (1974) believed that people conform to traditional gender roles partly because of the social reinforcers for doing so but partly because they are exposed to a very limited range of alternatives. Role models simply repeat behaviors that have already been defined as appropriate for a particular gender. Such a rigid definition of appropriate activities might lead to an inability to imagine any other way of life. This absence of imaginable alternatives, as experienced by individuals, is defined as a nonconscious ideology and is a highly effective way of hindering behavioral change, because cognitive structures never reach the conscious level.

The problem of nonconscious ideology has been tackled directly by "consciousness-raising," a technique that attempts to bring previously accepted or ignored shared oppression to full consciousness so that it can be examined and, if possible, changed (Lazarus, 1971). This technique has been widely used by feminist and other political movements, although its success in altering individual behaviors has never been directly evaluated. The possible contributions of cognitive behaviorism to this approach will be discussed later in this chapter.

Students of sex-role socialization in English-speaking countries have pointed out that both sexes lose if they are socialized too rigidly. Women and girls may be limited to a dependent social role, with few opportunities to achieve either psychological or economic independence as adults. As a result of their awareness of this dependency, they may have low self-esteem and limited horizons as adults. Some writers have argued that extreme sex-role socialization reduces women's cognitive capacity (e.g., Maccoby & Jacklin, 1978), increases their likelihood of life-time depression and neurosis, renders them out of touch with negative emotions such as anger (e.g., Major, 1987), raises their chance of suffering postpartum depression (e.g., Tennant, Bebbington, & Hurry, 1982), and renders them too unskilled to adapt to the demands of a rapidly changing workforce (Friedan, 1983).

Men and boys usually gain the benefit of the skills to sustain economic independence and of a self-image as problem solvers. They may, however, lose touch with their emotions, find it difficult to express themselves verbally, and, ironically, have limited problem-solving skills in the social arena—one area where women are expected to excel. It has been argued that the deficits of extreme male sex-role socialization include a tendency to use violent solutions to interpersonal problems (e.g., Formaini, 1989), raised risk of alcoholism, and increased risk of accidental death (e.g., McMichael & Hartshorne, 1982).

In addition to the study of the processes and consequences of sex-role socialization, concepts derived from social learning theory have been used to facilitate important developments of behaviorism, especially in the area of cognitive behaviorism. A key theme in social psychology is that of freedom of choice; this school of thought believes that individuals are free to make their own choices, at least to some extent. To do so, they may need to reconsider their options and to expand their skills, particularly their social skills. An example of this is the approach taken to "modeling" as a contribution to human behavioral repertoires (Bandura, 1971, 1977). Bandura drew attention to the fact that human learning is not always dependent on contingencies; indeed, he argued that this form of learning plays a relatively minor part in human social learning. Although the importance of modeling in human learning of complex motor behaviors (e.g., driving a car) has been questioned (James, 1993), modeling is still accepted as playing a major role in acquiring social skills (e.g., Which knife do I use?).

A person is not limited to the models in his or her immediate vicinity; people are free to choose their role models to some extent and may model their actions on media heroes rather than on people in the environment. This theme corresponds strongly with feminist views that men and women are free to make choices, although they should take responsibility for the impact of these choices on others.

BEHAVIORISM

Behaviorism began as a revolt against the structuralist theories (e.g., psychoanalysis) that dominated the early development of psychology during the late 19th century (Leahey, 1991). Behaviorists emphasized the need to study objectively verifiable behaviors. The radical behaviorists (e.g., Watson, 1919) relegated any consideration of human consciousness to the "black box," or that part of humanity that was inaccessible to scientific study. The implied model of human behavior among the radical behaviorists emphasized the role of the external environment in shaping behavior and deemphasized the role of cognitive structures such as beliefs or attitudes. At the same time, behavior was seen as flexible and responsive to environmental pressures. In seeking explanations for human actions, radical behaviorism directed its gaze outward from the individual toward the environment.

In earlier as well as more recent publications, behaviorist writers (e.g., Skinner, 1938; Wolpe, 1990) have insisted that it is a science in the same sense as the physical sciences and contrasted this feature with the less objective approaches of other areas of psychology. The volume of these publications shows the considerable diversification that has occurred in behaviorist theory. However, the strong early emphasis on objective studies of simple behaviors led to extensive experimental work on rats and other nonhuman animals, which was then generalized to humans, precisely as if people could be viewed as larger, slightly more complex rats. This approach, decried by generations of psychology students as "rats and stats," has also attracted feminist criticism on the grounds of reductionism.

The behaviorists have long been divided into "radical" and "neo" behaviorists. The fault line between the two groups can be traced along the issue of the role of cognition in human behavior. Although Watson rejected the role of the cognitive aspects of human experience in determining human action, Skinner did not, although he is often wrongly considered to be a member of the radical school. In fact, he believed that thought should be included in explaining responses and stated that whenever behaviorists "excluded sensations, images, thought processes and so on, from their deliberations . . . the charge is justified that they have neglected the facts of consciousness. The strategy is, however, quite unwise" (1969, p. 227). Curiously, Skinner's work in this area seems not to have been read.

Just as behaviorism was seen as laying the theoretical foundations for a scientific study of human behavior, behavior therapy was viewed by exponents as an applied science. For example,

> Behavior therapy is an exact science, in every way parallel to other modern techniques. . . . However, the scientifically minded behaviorist need not confine himself [sic] to methods derived from principles. . . . He employs, whenever necessary, methods that have been empirically shown to be effective. (Wolpe, 1973, p. ix)

Despite these assertions, the practice of behavior therapy remains far more of an art than the applied science Wolpe would have us believe that it is. Readers of his introduction cited above are then startled to discover him citing his own subjective experiences as evidence for the usefulness of thought-stopping techniques (see discussion later).

In fact, clinical behaviorists (e.g., Lazarus, 1971; Wolpe, 1973, 1990) urged that each patient be treated as an individual and, in their writings, outlined the principles that should guide a careful exploration of the social and cultural background of each patient's presenting problem. Lazarus referred to the role of language when rejecting the simple generalization of behaviorist findings from animals to humans, commenting that "speech and symbolic processes add an entirely different dimension to man's [sic] otherwise animal behavior" (1971, p. 164). Wolpe prefaced his discussion of behavior analysis by remarking that "people are infinitely varied and so are their complaints and the ways in which these are tied to stimulus conditions" (1990, p. 60). The interest in objectivity and the need for proof has not obliterated the behaviorist clinician's concern with human individuality.

Behaviorism, then, has been, and remains, divided on the role played in human behavior by cognition. Similarly, behavior therapists take a less mechanistic approach to individual patients than some of their theoretical perspectives suggest.

THE PRACTICE OF BEHAVIOR MODIFICATION

Behaviorists usually provide clinical treatment on a one-to-one basis to adults who come to them voluntarily. As a rule, behavior modification is under the control of the therapist, who assesses the presenting problem and the patient's coping resources and then draws up a protocol of treatment. Although attention is given to the cultural background and upbringing of patients, the primary emphasis is on the "here and now" (Lazarus, 1971). The patient contributes more to defining the problem than is usual in the analytic approaches. Written contracts between patient and therapist are quite often drawn up, following the initial assessment, in which each party undertakes to carry out specified actions. It is usual to teach the patient skills (e.g., relaxation) and to point out that these can be generalized to future difficult situations. The patient is expected to take an active role in solving his or her own problems.

Possibly because of the active role usually accorded the patient, behavior modification has rarely been the subject of specifically feminist criticism about its treatment of women. Despite its clinical emphasis, the behaviorist school as a whole has passed little public comment on feminism. There are probably two reasons for this. First, its main interest has been the microbehaviors of individuals rather than social movements. Second, behaviorists usually avoid labeling responses as "normal"; they limit themselves to describing responses as "maladaptive" or "stressful" for a particular individual in a particular environment.

Two aspects of the behaviorist movement have promoted the use of follow-up studies to assess the usefulness of its interventions: the self-image of behavior therapists as applied scientists and criticism from the psychoanalytic schools.

The psychoanalysts maintained that behaviorists merely treated symptoms, not causes, and that psychoanalytic methods were more effective precisely because they addressed causes of neurosis. In fact, follow-up studies (e.g. Dobson & Pusch, 1993) have established that behavior therapy is effective in a wide range of disorders in the "neurosis" group and that it can be useful for people who want to make systematic alterations in their lifestyle (e.g., stopping smoking). Although behavior therapy has not been found to be very useful for the psychotic group of disorders, it can be a helpful adjunct to prevent the development of institutionalized behaviors.

Although there has been a concentration on changing behaviors, direct attempts to change thought patterns have also been a part of behavior therapy since it first appeared. Wolpe described thought stopping as follows: "Perseverating trains of thought that are unrealistic, unproductive, and anxiety-arousing are a common clinical problem. If chronic, they are called obsessions" (1973, p. 211). He reported positively on his own experience of training himself to say "stop" aloud when he was troubled with unpleasant thoughts.

Although most behavior therapy occurs in a clinical setting under the direction of a therapist, the typical involvement of the patient in both the definition of the problem and in therapy means that behaviorists have been open to the idea of self-directed change as a viable alternative to counselor-directed therapy and as a means of increasing life skills outside the therapeutic relationship (e.g., Rosenbaum, 1990). Self-directed techniques have been devised both to modify existing problematic behavior and to sustain new adaptations (Meichenbaum, 1986; Rosenbaum, 1990; Thoreson & Thoreson, 1974). These are discussed in the next section under cognitive behaviorism. The possibility of devising a self-directed approach to enhancing interpersonal skills has considerable relevance to the practice of feminism as a political movement.

COGNITIVE BEHAVIORISM AND COGNITIVE–BEHAVIORIST THERAPY

A third approach to behaviorism—cognitive behaviorism—attempts to retain the earlier emphasis on objectively verifiable aspects of human behavior without giving up the explanatory power of nonverifiable thoughts or beliefs. Indeed, a major tenet of this school of thought is that actions can be changed if beliefs are altered, either by reasoning or disproof. This tradition exerts considerable influence within psychotherapy, with four of the seven most influential psychotherapy writers of history coming from it: Ellis, Beck, Meichenbaum, and Lazarus (Warner, 1991).

Cognitive behaviorism links large-scale social modes of altering opinion and controlling behavior (e.g., formal education, the media, the legal system) to the control of individual actions and decisions. Meichenbaum and Gilmore alluded to the role of structured social interaction in changing cognitive schemata:

> Cognitive structures or schemas about oneself may change without formal psychotherapy. Various consciousness-raising groups such as "Black

Pride" or "Womens Lib" and so forth can be seen as attempts to help individuals appreciate the tacit nature of their already existing schemata and to encourage the development of different schemata, feelings and behaviors. (1984, pp. 284–285)

The potential for change of these interactive groups is believed to be derive from their capacity to act as a means of making the "nonconscious ideology" described by Bem and Bem (1974) available for conscious reevaluation. However, I was unable to locate any systematic study of the impact of consciousness-raising groups on the behavior of their members.

There are now several models of cognitive behavior therapy, although they all share the same three fundamental tenets: (a) cognitive activity affects behavior, (b) cognitive activity may be monitored and altered, and (c) desired behavior change may be effected through cognitive change (Beck & Weishaar, 1989; Dobson & Block, 1988; Dobson & Pusch, 1993). All individuals derive beliefs or cognitive schemata about themselves, or about people like themselves, from the society in which they live. Sources of beliefs about the self include parents, friends, the educational system, and the media. Having derived these schemata, individuals then transform them into courses of action according to the reinforcements available at the time. According to the individual's social position, the beliefs he or she derives may be positive, enhancing choices and building capabilities (e.g., "I can solve mathematical problems," "Women have untapped artistic capacity"), or they may be negative, leading the individual to question his or her abilities to deal with life (e.g., "Women can't deal with mechanical breakdowns," "I am fat and no one will love me until I lose weight"). Positive schemata are believed to underlie effective adjustment; negative schemata lead to maladjustment or neurosis.

The fundamental argument of cognitive behaviorism is that information processing is crucial to the survival of the organism. Without the ability to select relevant information from the environment and synthesize it into a plan of action, the organism would die. In certain psychopathologies of humans, information processing becomes subject to a systematic bias. An individual whose thinking selectively synthesizes themes of inevitable loss and defeat is likely to suffer a depressive reaction (Beck & Weishaar, 1989). This shift in information synthesis is believed to be due to specific attitudes that interact with particular life situations and lead people to start processing information abnormally. The route to therapeutic change is to reverse the cognitive shift. These premises are supported by an impressive array of clinical research findings demonstrating the therapeutic efficacy of this modality, particularly in the areas of depression, anxiety, and pain (e.g., Dobson & Pusch, 1993).

Cognitive behavior therapy is a collaborative process of reality testing between patient and therapist during which the patient's maladaptive beliefs and conclusions are treated as testable hypotheses. The strategies used have been described as guided discovery, in which the therapist guides the patient to discover neutral approaches to information processing that will enable him or her to select and process information in an orderly way. It is the patient who ultimately decides whether to reject, modify, or retain his or her personal beliefs after having become aware of the consequences of these choices during therapy. This process of increasing awareness of the effect of belief structures is termed the *cognitive shift*. Interventions are short and structured. The relationship between counselor and client is typically egalitarian, with the counselor acting as a consultant or, more rarely, a teacher (Worell & Remy, 1992).

Beck and Weishaar (1989) compared the strategies of cognitive–behavioral therapies with those of psychoanalysis, making the distinction that in cognitive therapy, the thoughts causing the patient's distress are believed to be readily accessible to the consciousness. There is also some overlap between the therapeutic approaches of cognitive therapy and rational emotive therapy, with the major distinction being that in cognitive therapy, it is maintained that specific psychopathologies have their own specific cognitive content.

Cognitive behaviorism is particularly adapted to the demands of self-directed behavior change. Just as behaviorists encourage their clients to transfer their new skills to other difficult situations, cognitive behaviorists provide a way of thinking about the world that can be generalized. The accessibility of these techniques means that they can easily be brought under the client's own control. This has been a continuing theme in the development of the area. Beginning with the discovery that people learned to be helpless under specified circumstances (Seligman, 1975), Rosenbaum (1990) argued that they might also learn to be resourceful. The concept of "learned resourcefulness" is new but has already been successfully applied in areas as diverse as the promotion of positive health behaviors and the training of soldiers to undertake hazardous duties. In short, it is maintained that more effective individuals could be developed with the psychological tools available.

USEFULNESS OF THE COGNITIVE COMPONENT OF COGNITIVE–BEHAVIORIST THERAPY

Cognitive models in applied psychology include a range of approaches—for example, the health belief model (Janz & Becker, 1984), attribution theories (Jaspars, Fincham, & Hewstone, 1983), and the self-efficacy and social cognition theories (Bandura, 1977). They also include cognition-centered therapeutic models such as those of Beck (1984) and Ellis (1962). Follow-up studies on cognitive–behaviorist therapy for depression have found that it is equal to, or more effective than, drug treatment (e.g., Beck & Weishaar, 1989; Rush, Beck, Kovacs, & Hollon, 1977), but the relative effectiveness of the different components of therapy remains the subject of dispute.

Most cognitive behaviorists would argue that altering maladaptive belief structures will lead to more constructive behaviors. However, the nature of the causal role of beliefs in behavior has been debated for decades. Lazarus believed that the relationship between belief and behavior was less than clear-cut: "It is fatuous to ask whether a change in cognition leads to a change in behavior or vice versa. 'Insight' may often precede an observable behavior change; at other times insight clearly follows an individual's changed behavior" (1971, p. 165). The unpredictability of the nature or direction of the relationship between cognition and behavior has led to questioning the explanatory power of cognition in the cognitive-behaviorist equation (e.g., Lee, 1990).

Wolpe (1990) listed eight fundamental objections to the cognitivist view of psychotherapy. These included the observation that most phobic patients were afraid of situations that they correctly judged as having no objective danger. The accuracy of their beliefs had no effect on the intensity of their fear of nonthreatening stimuli (e.g., small animals). He also pointed out that there were effective therapeutic techniques (e.g., systematic densensitization) that did not include cognitive correction.

The power of cognitive models to make accurate predictions, either about human activity in everyday settings or about responses to therapeutic intervention, has led to criticism of the models. The exact role played by various beliefs about a problem (e.g., achieving cardiovascular fitness) and the weight given by an individual to different aspects of a problem (e.g., the seriousness of the health threat) have rarely been specified fully in the cognitive models discussed earlier. This lack of specificity means that it is impossible to predict the likely direction of behavior change for any individual or the impact of attempts to change beliefs on the behaviors believed to result from these beliefs (Lee, 1990).

Work on the predictive power of the health behavior model (Cody & Lee, 1990) found that the age and sex of the subjects accounted for more variance in behavior than all of the attitudinal variables measured. They concluded that this finding suggests that more attention should be paid to the sources of attitudes and opinion and to the effects that social, biological, and political factors might exercise on behavior. This conclusion is in line with most feminist thinking, which has often criticized psychology for ignoring the wider social context in which individual behaviors occur and choices are made.

FEMINIST THERAPY AND BEHAVIORISM

Feminist therapists have yet to develop an original set of techniques, but they have modified, adapted, and extended existing techniques. The defining characteristic of feminist therapy is the framework of values within which the techniques are used. Feminist therapists (e.g., Rosewater & Walker, 1985; Smith & Siegel, 1985; Worell & Remy, 1992) have spelled out broad principles to guide the practice of feminist therapy. There are areas of overlap and agreement:

- Sexist social structures are genuinely harmful to women.
- Therapeutic relationships should be egalitarian to demystify power relationships.
- A nonsexist frame of reference is important to the success of therapy.
- Pathologizing concepts should be avoided.
- The validity of feelings is accepted.
- There is a need to include social theory to complete a sex-role analysis of the experience of individuals.

These points can also be used to evaluate other therapies for compatibility with the goals of feminist therapy.

Feminist therapists have responded diversely to the opportunities and tools offered by behaviorism. The most positive response has been toward those approaches that enhance interpersonal skills, such as assertiveness training, especially those that lend themselves to independent practice by people who might otherwise seek the help of a therapist. These forms of therapy meet the goal of empowerment of women (Smith & Siegel, 1985). Other forms of behavior modification, such as positive and negative reinforcement schedules, especially when these have been used in institutional settings, have met with a much more critical response (Worell & Remy, 1992).

The application of feminist principles to cognitive behavior therapy shows that many of its aspects are suited to the practice of feminist therapy. The basic learning theory concepts emphasize that behavior occurs in a context; among humans, this is usually a social context. The determinants of which behaviors are reinforced or punished occur in a micropolitical setting (see Micropolitics of Sexism below). Discovering the determinants of reinforcement allows the therapist to place the woman's behavior in the context of a sexist society. There is a strong emphasis on egalitarian relationships between counselor and client that meshes well with feminist philosophies.

Cognitive–behaviorist therapy, with its emphasis on collaboration between therapist and patient and a gender-neutral and flexible approach to presenting problems, has been favorably rated as "a comfortable choice for feminist therapists" (Worell & Remy, 1992, p. 128). Its derivation from social learning theory means that the language and concepts embedded in it emphasize the capacity for behavior change for both genders. The inherent flexibility of this approach means that it can be applied throughout the life span and to the problems presented by individuals from diverse ethnic groups.

The use of terms like "maladaptive" or "irrational" to describe the patient's self-schemata has, however, been criticized. Research on the accuracy of the perception of depressed people has shown that the clients perceptions of his or her life situation are often more accurate than those of nondepressed people, who often believe that the environment is benign and that outcomes are under their control (e.g., Hammen, 1988; Lee, 1990). In light of the discovery that the systematic cognitive bias is to be found not in the gloomy views of the depressed but in the irrationally expansive beliefs of the nondepressed, Worell and Remy (1992) argued that this should alert the therapist to the need to explore the realities in the lives of their depressed clients. For therapy to succeed it may be necessary to obtain a more accurate understanding of the role of social pressures in the client's dysphoria. Similarly, clients with other disorders (e.g., agoraphobia) may have a more reasonable basis for their anxieties than previously thought.

The role that feelings play in cognitive behaviorism has also been questioned by feminist therapists. Feelings are believed to arise as a result of cognitions, and feelings usually labeled as "maladaptive," such as fear, anxiety, and rage, are believed to be due to faulty or irrational cognitions. Major (1987) pointed out the ways in which traditional gender socialization discourages women from direct confrontation with their negative feelings, particularly rage. Anger and rage may, however, be eminently rational responses to social situations in which women are overworked and ignored. Worell and Remy (1992) suggested that feminist therapists should encourage women to work through legitimate feelings of anger in a safe environment. The appropriate expression of reasonable anger can be seen as empowering for women. Fear and anxiety may also be rational responses to situations in which the client is threatened or powerless. Women may feel afraid to travel, particularly at night or by public transport, because it is objectively dangerous for them to do so.

To practice feminist therapy, it is important to be aware of the larger social-role issues surrounding the problems of a client (Smith & Siegel, 1985). Socialized role expectations and power imbalances influence people's lives and limit the choices open to them. That they may also reduce women's opportunities to develop their talents should not be ignored. Maccoby and Jacklin reported a long-term follow-up of children's intellectual development. They reported that "the more bold, assertive girls continue to show greater intellectual abilities and interests than other girls" (1978,

p. 131). Being bold and assertive is usually considered incompatible with femininity, yet these are the characteristics that appear to promote intellectual growth. Almost all women have been exposed to these role expectations, either in the form of direct inhibition of responses or in the failure to provide opportunities, equipment, or support to develop nonstereotyped behaviors. Knowledge of the limiting nature of feminine role socialization enables feminist therapists to maintain their awareness of the contribution of patriarchal concepts to pathology among women, to analyze certain aspects of roles (e.g., role overload), and to relabel so-called deficit behaviors in terms of over- or undersocialization. It may be appropriate to provide women with opportunities to expand their behavioral repertoires in later life. With these alterations and additions, cognitive behaviorism has been endorsed by feminist therapists as an approach that does not enforce gender bias and has the potential to free clients of both sexes from crippling role expectations.

Given the relative effectiveness of cognitive behaviorism and its acceptability in terms of feminist principles, a particular example of intervention will now be described as a backdrop to considering the possible contributions cognitive behaviorism might make to empowering women in their everyday lives. The example chosen is assertiveness training.

ASSERTIVENESS TRAINING FOR WOMEN

Assertiveness training (AT) began as a behavior modification approach by Wolpe (1973) but has been further developed by cognitive behaviorists. Proponents of AT argue that there are three possible responses to an unreasonable demand or request: compliance, aggression, and assertion. Assertion, seen as the most desirable, represents a set of social skills that can be acquired in the same way as people learn table manners. Wolpe's description of the common upbringing of patients for whom he found assertiveness training useful (e.g., "early teaching that over-emphasised social obligations, engendering the feeling in the patient that the rights of others are more important than his [sic] own" [1973, p. 82]) included typical socialization experiences of women in English-speaking societies. Much of the feminine social repertoire consists of nonassertive behaviors (e.g., yielding, flattering, and avoiding expression of opinion). These responses are vigorously modeled and reinforced by most socializing agents. Girls and women are rewarded for being gentle and helpful and constantly persuaded to defer, nurture, and share in family, education, and work settings (e.g., Kaplan, 1985; Spender & Sarah, 1980). Over a lifetime, this response style can leave women out of touch with their own wants and needs and may lead to unresolved anger and bitterness and symptoms of depression (Weiss, 1985).

AT courses designed for women were an outgrowth of the women's movement (e.g., Jakubowski, 1977). Nonassertion was conceptualized as a "socially conditioned feminine trait associated with passive, submissive, helpless, and altruistic behaviors in women. Assertiveness techniques were utilised in work with women's groups to provide an antidote to the traditional feminine nonassertive social programming" (Goldstein-Fodor & Epstein, 1992, p. 138). Assertiveness was defined as a human right by the pioneers of this technique, and it was believed that women could use AT as a personal power base to confront the male establishment.

Acceptance of this view has never been universal; critics of AT have raised several objections. First, it has been argued that there is an implied philosophy that gives too great a primacy to individual rights and too little to social responsibilities. The importance of cooperation as an inherently feminine value has also been advanced as an argument against both the use of AT and the promotion of beliefs supporting individual striving. Finally, it has been claimed that training individual women to be assertive will be insufficient for them to tackle the entire patriarchal establishment (e.g., Goldstein-Fodor & Epstein, 1992).

Women are still the main consumers of AT, but few studies have been conducted on its long-term efficacy for them. What little is known about members of AT groups suggests that they are mostly young, White, and middle-class. Even in this select group, women who are highly identified with the traditional feminine stereotype were found to be the most likely to drop out of the group (Stere, 1985). A certain amount of disquiet has by now replaced the earlier optimism about the usefulness of these techniques for building women's personal power bases.

Goldstein-Fodor & Epstein (1992) reviewed the assumptions and goals of the AT-for-women packages:

- Women have a deficit in assertiveness that can be replaced by the use of appropriate assertive behaviors.
- Fear of being assertive is irrational and can be dealt with using cognitive restructuring.
- Women will apply their new skills to real situations and will continue to use them over an extended period of time.
- Greater assertiveness will allow women to become more successful in their personal and work lives.

The principles of feminist therapy enunciated by Worell and Remy (1992) should lead to a suspicion of any explanation based on the idea of "women as defective." In fact, there is little evidence for the view that women are deficient in their existing assertiveness behavior as compared with men, largely because little assessment work has been done in measuring these behaviors. However it has been found that women report more difficulty than men refusing requests, expressing negative feelings, and setting limits, although they report that they are more able than men to express approval of others (Chandler, Cook, & Dugovics, 1978). How closely self-report reflects behavior in natural settings is unclear. Lack of behavioral definition means that there is little evidence for the success of interventions (Goldstein-Fodor & Epstein, 1992).

The proposition that women's fear of assertiveness is always irrational is probably untrue, yet Irrational Belief #1 from Bloom, Coburn, and Pearlman (1975) states, "If I assert myself, others will get mad at me." This may be an accurate statement of outcomes for many women; AT has little relevance to women who depend on men who exploit or batter them. Even when power relationships are not an issue, Goldstein-Fodor & Epstein (1992) reported a bias against assertive women. In experimental settings using raters, comparable behaviors are described as assertive when performed by men but aggressive, and unacceptable, when performed by women.

The method of cognitive restructuring used in many AT groups— handing out lists of personal rights and of irrational beliefs—has been criticized by Stere (1985) as likely to induce cognitive dissonance (and hence dropout) in women who adhere to traditional sex-role values. Although she agrees with introducing the concept of personal rights, which is a very powerful action to take, Stere points to the need for recognition of cultural differences in perceived personal rights and suggests deciding them for each group, by discussion and voting.

The reality of women's fears about the reactions of others to their assertiveness constitutes a major barrier to applying these techniques in real situations (Stere, 1985). Attempts to train women to be assertive on the job may encounter additional problems because women in traditional occupations may have different needs for assertiveness from women in non-traditional fields. Women may also expect too much, too soon from their new-found skills and may be discouraged when they do not get what they want after asking for it reasonably. The lack of follow-up of AT clients means that women's use of their new skills is unknown; 53% of published studies of AT groups had no follow-up, and 26% followed their clients for one month or less (Goldstein-Fodor & Epstein, 1992).

Given the bias against assertive behavior in women, the belief that using these skills will promote success in women's personal and work lives seems untenable. Women may find that their bosses or lovers preferred them when they were self-denying. Women may have to choose between behaviors that enhance their self-respect, but elicit negative responses from significant others, on the one hand, and those that do the opposite, on the other. Negative responses from significant others have yet to be seen as signaling a behavior deficit on *their* part. It may be time to focus on the problems leading people to refuse reasonable requests from women and to treat those problems.

Although there is a clear need for better designed follow-up studies of AT groups, and probably for better targeting of AT interventions, AT may have played an important role in the lives of many women, if only by introducing them to the revolutionary notion that they have personal "rights." The full extent of its influence cannot, at present, be judged.

AT courses for women were originally developed by people with a feminist orientation, and the few studies that have been done suggest that AT benefits women with nontraditional gender-role orientations more than other women (Stere, 1985). Goldstein-Fodor and Epstein (1992) pointed out that there is a need to avoid placing the whole burden of change on individual women, who are expected to act assertively in a social system that does not provide reinforcement for assertive women, but sees them as odd or threatening. Goldstein-Fodor and Epstein advocated feminist therapists' entering the business and industrial world as trainers, not only for women seeking promotion, but for the corporate managers who refused it to "pushy" women, while granting it to "ambitious" men. Feminist therapy cannot be practiced in isolation from the social setting in which patients or clients must live (Smith & Siegel, 1985; Worell & Remy, 1992).

It is important to distinguish between descriptions of behavior, which are usually well done by behaviorists, and explanations of human behavior, which are often underemphasized in this area. Sociologists (e.g., Bourdieu & Passeron, 1977) have described the reproduction and transmission of power imbalances between classes and genders across generations and drawn attention to the role of the educational system in this process. Is it possible to use the insights derived from cognitive behaviorism to explain the sociological phenomenon of the conservation and reproduction of group norms? If these behaviors can be explained, can they be changed?

It may be time to take other techniques besides AT out of therapists' rooms and into a broader social setting, using skills as trainers to alter the behaviors of both parties to interactions. Such a move would lead psychologists into the arena of micropolitics. The emphasis in psychology on relatively small groups means that the politics of psychology must be confined to micropolitics. Nevertheless, this is a worthy object of study because it is in this interpersonal arena that most people experience the outcome of large-scale political movements.

MICROPOLITICS OF SEXISM

The power relationships between men and women in all known societies are determined by the relative control over resources available to members of each gender. Compared with women, men control a considerable array of institutional resources. In English-speaking countries, men are more likely to work for wages and to do so full-time than are women.

Men typically work in occupations that enjoy better conditions and higher prestige than those typical of women, and their hourly rates of pay are greater than those that women can command (ABS, 1992).

These pay differentials have proved remarkably resistant to equal-opportunity initiatives. In Australia, for example, the wage differential between the sexes in the full-time, year-round sector of the workforce has only decreased by 3¢ on the dollar over the past 10 years (ABS, 1992). Women in the most privileged section of the Australian workforce still earn only 82¢ for every $1 earned by men. This difference in earning capacity has repercussions for the organization of household work because if one partner is going to give up paid work for any reason, it should not be the one who earns the larger salary, almost invariably the man. Women may put off leaving a threatening domestic situation because they fear, reasonably, that they will be unable to support their children on the wages that they could expect to earn.

Even where both adults in a household work for wages, men typically put in far fewer hours of unpaid household work than do women (ABS, 1992). When men do perform domestic chores, it is seen as "helping" the person who is really responsible, the wife and mother. This domestic imbalance of responsibilities can lead to women becoming sleep deprived and exhausted as they struggle to keep up with all of the responsibilities that pertain to performing on a high level both at work and at home.

In industry and academia, men generally hold more senior ranks than do women. This seniority confers on them the role of gatekeeper to institutional resources. It is more usual for men than women to hold professional positions (e.g., psychiatrist, judge, politician) that give them the power to define behaviors as "desirable," "normal," or "legal." Alternatively, they may define behaviors as pathological. This definitional role of men is so pronounced that nobody thinks it odd when men write about femininity, which they cannot experience, or child rearing, an activity in which they are unlikely to have first-hand experience (e.g., Spock, 1946/ 1985).

As the authors of such texts, men normally appeal to their professional training to legitimize their authority. Whether this is relevant to living as a woman or to rearing children at home, or even is an accurate guide to the problems of either activity, is not an issue that is normally raised. In cognitive-behaviorist terms, these books may be fertile sources of those inaccurate schemata that lead to maladaptive feelings of anxiety and distress (e.g., "a tense mother makes a colicky baby"; although it has been known for decades that the reverse is true [Lennane & Lennane, 1977], many doctors still believe that the mother is the problem).

It is against a background of marked power imbalances between the genders that the micropolitics of daily interactions occur. Women are guided or directed to certain areas of work in employment settings (e.g., personnel, low-level administration) and are praised for compliance. Stepping outside of the self-sacrificing role activates anxiogenic schemata about the consequences of being thought "unfeminine." There is a network of assumptions about what is "right and natural" for women. Many of these beliefs form part of a cultural framework in which men play potent defining roles while women have relatively little input. It may be a consequence of that fact that what is "right and natural" for women in the workplace is frequently monotonous, stressful, and unlikely to lead to promotion. Each woman is in the position of challenging a "well-known fact" if she does not go along with the assumptions of others about what will be best for her.

As Cockburn (1991) put it (describing the English civil service), men create a culture where women do not flourish. Some aspects of these interactions have been analyzed to identify the methods by which the gender power imbalance is maintained at the face-to-face level. Different workplaces use different approaches, and their members are prepared to accept different levels of gender harassment as normative.

Excluding women from shared facilities such as tea rooms or libraries by simple regulation has recently become rare. However, that should not be taken to mean that women now have equal access to all facilities in the workplace. Most blatantly, women may be excluded from shared facilities by sexual harassment (French, 1992) so that they are unable to participate in the informal side of work life. Cockburn (1991) described the systematic undermining of female authority by male criticism of appropriately directive behavior as "mannish."

In academia, Kaplan (1985) described the tactic of information control. She identified a pattern of male-to-male office visiting and chatting in which important information was shared only between men. Although it is usual for staff members to lunch together in this employment setting, women may still be excluded from the information exchange even when present. Kaplan described the process of exclusion as follows:

> One of the most typical tactics of expressing nonverbal hostility consists of turning shoulders away from the intruder . . . or forming a tight circle which cannot be easily broken. Another one . . . is to engage in a super-lively and animated discussion with another male colleague, reestablishing eye contact as often as possible . . . and being so engrossed in conversation that it is made difficult if not impossible for the woman to break into the interaction. (1985, p. 20)

Although Kaplan described this ritual among Australian academics, it can be seen in many other employment settings.

Other tactics to promote personal power in face-to-face interactions include the "pause and continue" response to women's contributions to the conversation, as first described by Bernard (1964). This pattern of response involves a pause in the conversation between men while a woman speaks, but the male conversation then resumes without acknowledgment of her comments. The greater frequencies of male interruptions, particularly of female speakers, has been noted by many linguists, beginning with Lakoff (1975). A refusal to be interrupted, she noted, was often met with hostility if the interrupter was male.

"Helpful explanation" is another form of verbal sexism observed by Allen (1991). This tactic, observable in a wide variety of employment settings, involves a man explaining at great length to a women some simple point. Her efforts to clarify that she is already aware of the facts are met with resistance. Either the man insists on explaining, or injured cries of "I was only trying to help" are heard. The woman is forced to choose between listening to the explanation and tolerating the man's public assessment of her as ignorant of the basics in her field, on the one hand, and seeming ungrateful, on the other. Any one of these incidents, taken individually, is petty, yet daily exposure to this sort of treatment is demoralizing. The first step in counteracting these behaviors is to recognize them for what they are: a face-to-face form of sexism.

There are many ways in which emotions can be manipulated to control behavior. The victim can be allowed to "feel good" when she complies and put in the wrong if she insists on something that those in charge do not support. Women are known to be more vulnerable than men to emotional manipulation, partly because of the typical childrearing methods used on the two sexes (e.g., Harter, 1993). Another contribution to women's vulnerability to emotional blackmail is the systematic attribution of responsibility for things that are outside their control. It is common, for instance, to blame mothers not only for their children's developmental "failures" (e.g., Bowlby, 1969), but even for attacks of others (e.g., sexual abusers) on their children (e.g., Thomas, 1991).

STRATEGIES FOR CHANGE

Although changing individual interactions will not alter the major imbalances of economic and social power between the sexes, having the choice to attempt to control or deflect some of these practices may make life more bearable from day to day for individuals. It may also enable people to adopt more effective strategies for long-term planning. Although it is likely that this movement will be inaugurated by women, it is not my intention to suggest that women are the only ones whose behavioral repertoires might be extended.

Behavior-modification techniques can be used to inaugurate self-directed behavior change or self-management (Karoly, chapter 10, this volume; Mahoney & Thoresen, 1974; Rosenbaum, 1990). This form of change is directly relevant to modern feminism. It is possible to set goals, make independent decisions about the desirable behaviors, and move toward them using these techniques. Self-management offers a way of thinking about problems in skill acquisition, self-presentation, and interpersonal interactions that helps to solve them. The relevant response patterns in paid employment arenas might include attaining membership on a powerful committee, putting items on the agenda for staff meetings, and negotiating a reasonable rate of pay. Important behaviors for full-time homemakers might include arranging with a spouse or partner for some regular personal time for leisure and recreation or reassigning responsibility for household tasks.

Interactions between human adults are largely mediated through complex cognitive symbolic processes—thoughts about anticipated consequences, including self-praise and self-criticisms. Negative thoughts like "I'll never be able to stand up for my rights" may prevent individuals from attempting activities that are within their abilities. Women in a patriarchal society are more likely than men to be inhibited by negative self-talk, because they have lower self-esteem than do men, from an early age (Harter, 1993; Rosenthal & Palthiel, 1982) and are more dependent on the good opinion of others. As a result, many women carry a heavy burden of negative self-talk.

This negative self-talk can be crippling to women's opportunities to put their point of view across. Anyone who wishes to participate fully in public life may, at some time, need to speak in public. My observation of women's self-presentation skills in public settings has largely been confined to academic colleagues. The surprising finding is that years of public speaking to students, in the course of their employment, frequently fails to desensitize women to addressing their peers. Requests of women to undertake more complex aspects of public presentation, such as chairing a meeting, are frequently met with verbalized negative self-talk statements such as "I couldn't possibly do that." These refusals mean that women are rarely seen in powerful, public positions and hence that younger women are left to continue with few role models. It is important to realize that one aspect of the practice of feminism is to suggest to women (and to oneself) that this belief in female incompetence has no basis in fact and that women are perfectly capable of carrying out public representation roles. The main barrier is negative self-talk, which can be changed (Meichenbaum, 1986; Rehm & Rokke, 1988) to allow opportunities for skill acquisition or performance.

When women do agree to address a meeting, they almost invariably begin their speech by apologizing for something, putting themselves into a defensive position immediately. Although awareness of the "apologizing woman" syndrome is usually enough to stop it, nonverbal and paraverbal components of self-presentation can be more difficult to deal with. These include speaking very softly or using a high, childish voice and an inability to deal with electronic equipment such as microphones. These habits probably reflect a reasonable fear of being perceived as "pushy" or even as "assertive" simply as a result of deciding to speak. However, they set women up to experience a vicious circle of anxiety leading to failure. Given that women are more likely to encounter "pause-and-continue" (Bernard, 1964), interruptions (Lakoff, 1975), and exclusion (Kaplan, 1985), if they want to be heard at all, it is essential to take self-presentation seriously and to learn how to do it in the most effective way possible.

Many women find public speaking difficult because of a lack of practice. However, the reluctance among academic women to address peers suggests that something more is involved. One hypothesis is that women are speaking against a background of expecting to be defined and judged by men, who usually undertake this role of definition in English-speaking societies (see discussion earlier). Not unnaturally, members of a weaker social group fear the reactions of a more powerful one. To change this, women need to regain the power to set their own goals and standards and thus become the judges of their own conduct. Once women cease to accept that men have the right to judge them and determine normality, they will change the balance of power in everyday interactions.

Cognitive–behaviorist therapy has developed self-management techniques that may be usefully adapted to meet these goals. *Self-management* can be defined as teaching learning principles to individuals so that they can apply them to themselves. When learned in a therapeutic situation, self-management entails teaching controlling strategies to the individual. Self-management and self-monitoring behavior has been used successfully in the treatment of anxiety, pain, and depression (Beck, Rush, Shaw, & Emery 1979; Rehm & Rokke, 1988). Frederick (1990) found that the capacity to set personal goals can be retained even under extreme conditions, such as a hostage situation. He established that victims who exerted control, even over minor issues, were less likely to suffer posttraumatic stress disorder than those who passively accepted their situation.

Barriers to using these self-management techniques include attribution and efficacy beliefs. The use of self-management techniques to change actions, with the long-term goal of effecting a change in the environment, implies that the individual believes that his or her actions are under personal control (Rehm & Rokke, 1988). There is a gender difference in attribution, with men being more likely to attribute their successes to ability, whereas women are more likely to attribute them to luck (Harter, 1993; Smith & Siegel, 1985). Smith and Siegel (1985) argued that women's attribution of success to luck is partly because they doubt their own capacity to manage their own lives, but also partly because they avoid challenging men. Avoiding responsibility for success prevents women from taking charge of their immediate environment to repeat or extend successful activities. This refusal to acknowledge responsibility for success among women can and should be tackled using the approaches of cognitive behaviorism toward other forms of cognitive bias. Although this can be done relatively easily in one-to-one therapy, further work will be needed in program development if "consciousness-raising" approaches are to be used.

Attempts to change the gender balance of power, even at the level of micropolitics, will almost certainly encounter resistance, as many women believe. Feminist therapists have recently addressed the issue of resistance in the area of family counseling and marital therapy (Lerner, 1990). Realizing that there will be resistance and preparing to deal with it may be enough to assist women to move through to a point of real change in the balance of their relationships with others. Elgin (1980) proposed the use of verbal self-defense techniques to deflect unreasonable attacks from either employers or family members. That there may be interpersonal situations (e.g., domestic violence) in which it is too dangerous for women to attempt change should not be ignored. In these situations, they should consider escape as an option.

The obstacles to women's promotion in the workplace are often relatively obvious and can be contested either on an individual basis or by taking legal or administrative action. Which approach is more effective needs to be determined by women in the particular workplace. However, there are other factors operating to limit women's aspirations, particularly where the demands of the domestic setting interact with the responsibilities of paid work.

In all English-speaking countries, women have entered the paid workforce in large numbers, thus reducing the burden of responsibility on men to support the family (ABS, 1992; Klein, 1984). However, men have not responded by taking over an equal share of housework and childcare responsibilities (ABS, 1992). Women are simply expected to do both, and many are so exhausted by this double load that they do not have the energy or time to plan ahead to enhance their employment skills. Prolonged periods of sleep deprivation are viewed as quite normal for the mothers of small children, yet this is well known to be a risk factor for mental breakdown (Lennane & Lennane, 1977).

An essential first step for women is to gain control of their own time. If they are in the paid workforce, they need to consider ways to make it clear at home that they are not solely responsible for the smooth running of the household. This may entail careful consideration of their own values. If women seek counseling and support in this area, it is vital to avoid foisting the therapist's views onto them. If women decide that they are carrying an unfair burden but cannot get cooperation from family members after several reasonable requests, they may reconsider the approach to household chores or may decide to simplify their activities (e.g., leaving nonessential work undone, refusing to play hostess for their husbands' business acquaintances). Acquiring labor-saving devices, or buying ready-made articles, should be considered. Labor-saving devices are usually acceptable and omnipresent, but one approach that has been underused is paid household help. Some women will find this personally unacceptable, but it does provide employment for people who may have no other avenue to earn money. Another objection to this strategy is that it will leave less money available for other family goals. This consideration may cause other family members to reconsider the value of taking a fair share of the workload. The discovery that housework costs money unless Mum does it may lead to the revelation that it is "real work." Even if this does not happen, the woman has regained some time for her own relaxation and recuperation.

CONCLUSION

One of the criticisms that may reasonably be made of cognitive behaviorism is that there is little information about the processes by which individuals select schemata or determine that the time has come to act on them. In an individual who has recently become depressed, what were the triggers setting off the "cognitive shift" toward a bias to themes of defeat? Conversely, why are some individuals consistently hardy and resourceful? Greater attention to the sources of schemata and the reasons individuals have for selecting and activating them would confer greater explanatory power on this theory. Strengthening this area of cognitive behaviorism would be useful in health psychology as well as in therapy of all kinds. Because all social movements are made up of thousands of individual choices, it might be possible to build a bridge between psychology and sociology if the causes guiding individual choices were more thoroughly understood.

Cognitive behaviorism, particularly in its self-directed form, has a great deal to offer women as a force for personal change. AT groups have been widely used for many years, although little has been done to analyze the possibly problematic nature of the responses of others to women displaying a normal level of assertion. Another recent development is the self-management and self-monitoring techniques that have largely been used in the health psychology area. Self-management techniques offer women an opportunity to make conscious, considered responses to social pressures. There is no need to continue responding along the lines of automatic schemata that may have been acquired in circumstances no longer matching those surrounding women today. Nor are women obliged to continue to accept the explanations and attributions of powerful others.

The promise of specific techniques, such as AT for women, needs to be reconsidered. Although earlier claims for them may have been exaggerated, they should not be dismissed without more extensive follow-up than they have received. AT, which promotes women's independence, is important to feminist therapy as a source of information about the kinds of social pressures experienced by women. The nature of women's relationships to patriarchal power structures means that much of the politics of liberation for women consists of altering power structures in small face-to-face groups of people who know each other well. Very little is known about these processes. Following up the failures and problems of AT groups may lead to new strategies to make AT more relevant or to new approaches to enhancing women's freedom of choice.

If self-management techniques are promoted for groups of women, follow-up should be built into the groups from the start. Participants should be encouraged to record success and failures in order to make the techniques more flexible, appropriate, and responsive to women's needs. An important component of structured change should be dealing with the responses of men to changes in women's behavior. It is important to set up forums in which they can be constructively confronted with their reactions and requested to match women's moves to greater independence and freedom of action with appropriate changes of their own.

REFERENCES

ABS (1992). *Social indicators no. 5* (Australian Bureau of Statistics Cat. No. 4101.0). Canberra, Australia: Australian Government Publishing Service.

Allen, F. C. L. (1991). Feminism and behaviorism in academia: Strategies for change. *Behavior Change, 8*(1), 10–16.

Archer, J., & Lloyd, B. (1982). *Sex and gender*. London: Penguin Books.

Bandura, A. (1971). *Psychological modeling: Conflicting theories*. Chicago: Aldine-Atherton.

Bandura, A. (1977). *Social learning theory*. Englewood Cliffs, NJ: Prentice-Hall.

Bauer, C., & Ritt, L. (1979). *Free and ennobled*. New York: Pergamon Press.

Beck, A. (1984). Cognition and therapy. *Archives of General Psychiatry, 41*, 1112–1114.

Beck, A., Rush, A., Shaw, B., & Emery, G. (1979). *Cognitive therapy of depression*. New York: Guilford Press.

Beck, A., & Weishaar, M. (1989). Cognitive therapy. In R. Corsini & D. Wedding (Eds.), *Current psychotherapies* (4th ed., pp. 285–322. New York: Peacock.

Bem, S., & Bem, D. (1974). Case study of nonconscious ideology: Training the woman to know her place. In M. Garskoff (Ed.), *Roles women play* (pp. 46–54). Monterey, CA: Brooks/Cole.

Bernard, J. (1964). *Academic women*. New York: New American Library.

Bloom, L., Coburn, K., & Pearlman, J. (1975). *The new assertive woman*. New York: Dell.

Bourdieu, P., & Passeron, J. (1977). *Reproduction in education, society and culture.* London: Sage.

Bowlby, J. (1969). *Attachment.* New York: Basic Books.

Chandler, T., Cook, B., & Dugovics, K. (1978). Sex differences in self-reported assertiveness. *Psychological Reports, 43,* 394–402.

Chesler, P. (1972). *Women and madness.* New York: Avon Books.

Cockburn, C. (1991). *In the way of women: Men's resistance to sex equality in organisations.* London: Macmillan.

Cody, R., & Lee, C. (1990). Behaviours, beliefs and intentions in skin cancer prevention. *Journal of Behavioral Medicine, 13,* 373–390.

Dobson, K., & Block, L. (1988). Historical and philosophical bases of the cognitive–behavioral therapies. In K. Dobson (Ed.), *Handbook of cognitive behavioral therapies* (pp. 3–38). New York: Guilford Press.

Dobson, K. S., & Pusch, D. (1993). Towards a definition of the conceptual and empirical boundaries of cognitive therapy. *Australian Psychologist, 28*(3), 138–144.

Douglas, C. (1990). *The woman in the mirror: Analytical psychology and the feminine.* Boston: Sigo Press.

Dworkin, A. (1983). *Right wing women: The politics of domesticated females.* London: The Women's Press.

Elgin, S. (1980). *The gentle art of verbal self-defense.* New York: Prentice-Hall.

Ellis, A. (1962). *Reason and emotion in psychotherapy.* New York: Lyle Stuart Press.

Firestone, S. (1971). *The dialectic of sex: the case for feminist revolution.* New York: Bantam Books.

Formaini, H. (1989). *Men: The darker continent.* London: Mandarin.

Frederick, C. (1990). Resourcefulness in coping with severe trauma: The case of the hostages. In M. Rosenbaum (Ed.), *Learned resourcefulness. On coping skills, self-control and adaptive behavior* (pp. 218–228). New York: Springer.

French, M. (1992). *The war against women.* London: Hamish Hamilton.

Freud, S. (1933). The psychology of women. In J. Sprott (Trans.), *New introductory lectures in psychoanalysis* (pp. 170–191). London: Hogarth Press.

Friedan, B. (1963). *The feminine mystique.* London: Penguin Books.

Friedan, B. (1983). *The second stage.* London: Sphere Books.

Goldstein-Fodor, I., & Epstein, R. (1992). Assertiveness training for women: Where are we failing? In P. Foa & P. Emmelkamp (Eds.), *Failures in behavior therapy* (pp. 137–158). New York: Wiley.

Greer, G. (1970). *The female eunuch.* London: Paladin.

Hammen, C. (1988). Depression and personal cognitions about stressful life events. In L. Alloy (Ed.), *Cognitive processes in depression* (pp. 77–108). New York: Guilford Press.

Harter, S. (1993). Causes and consequences of low self esteem in children and adolescents. In R. Baumeister (Ed.), *Self-esteem: The puzzle of low self regard* (pp. 87–116). New York: Plenum.

Horney, K. (1967). The flight from womanhood: The masculinity complex in women as viewed by men and women. In H. Kelman (Ed.), *Feminine psychology* (pp. 131–158). New York: Norton.

Jakubowski, P. (1977). Self-assertion training procedures for women. In E. Rawlings & D. Carter (Eds.), *Psychotherapy for women* (pp. 168–190). Springfield, IL: Charles C Thomas.

James, J. (1993). Cognitive–behavioural theory: An alternative conception. *Australian Psychologist, 28*(3), 151–155.

Janz, N., & Becker, M. (1984). The health belief model: A decade later. *Health Education Quarterly, 11,* 1–47.

Jaspars, J., Fincham, F., & Hewstone, M. (Eds.). (1983). *Attribution theory and research: Conceptual, developmental and social dimensions.* London: Academic Press.

Kaplan, G. (1985). Coming up with bright ideas: Women in academia. *Vestes, 28,* 25–38.

Klein, E. (1984). *Gender politics.* Cambridge, MA: Harvard University Press.

Kraditor, A. (1981). *The ideas of the women's suffrage movement: 1890–1920.* New York: Norton.

Lakoff, R. (1975). *Language and women's place.* New York: Harper & Row.

Lazarus, A. (1971). *Behavior therapy and beyond.* New York: McGraw-Hill.

Leahey, T. (1991). *A history of modern psychology.* Englewood Cliffs, NJ: Prentice-Hall.

Lee, C. (1990). Theoretical weaknesses: Fundamental flaws in cognitive–behavioural theories are more than a problem of probability. *Journal of Behavior Therapy and Experimental Psychiatry, 21,* 143–145.

Lennane, J., & Lennane, J. (1977). *Hard labor: A realist's guide to having a baby.* London: Gollancz.

Lerman, H. (1985). Some barriers to the development of a feminist theory of personality. In L. Rosewater & L. Walker (Eds.), *Handbook of feminist therapy: Women's issues in psychotherapy* (pp. 5–12). New York: Springer.

Lerner, H. (1990). *The dance of intimacy.* New York: Harper & Row.

Lewis, J. (1992). *Women in Britain since 1945.* London: Institute of Contemporary British History.

Maccoby, E., & Jacklin, C. (1978). *The psychology of sex differences.* Stanford, CA: Stanford University Press.

Mahoney, M., & Thoreson, C. (1974). *Self control: Power to the person.* Monterey, CA: Brooks/Cole.

Major, B. (1987). Gender, justice and the psychology of entitlement. In P. Shaver & C. Hendrick (Eds.), *Sex and gender: Review of personality and social psychology* (Vol. 7, pp. 124–148). Newbury Park, CA: Sage.

McMichael, A., & Hartshorne, J. (1982). Mortality risks in Australian men by occupational groups, 1968–1978: Variations associated with differences in drinking and smoking habits. *Medical Journal of Australia, 1,* 253–256.

McWilliams-Tullberg, R. (1977). Women and degrees at Cambridge University, 1862–1897. In M. Vicinus (Ed.), *A widening sphere: Changing roles of Victorian women* (pp. 117–145). London: Methuen.

Meichenbaum, D. (1986). Cognitive behavior modification. In F. Kanfer & A. Goldstein (Eds.), *Helping people change: A textbook of methods* (3rd ed., pp. 346–380). New York: Pergamon Press.

Meichenbaum, D., & Gilmore, J. (1984). The nature of unconscious processes: A cognitive–behavioral perspective. In K. Bowers & D. Meichenbaum (Eds.), *The unconscious reconsidered* (pp. 273–298). New York: Wiley.

Millett, K. (1972). *Sexual politics.* New York: Abacus.

Newsom, J. (1963). *Half our future* (Report of the Central Advisory Committee on Education: England). London: Her Majesty's Stationery Office.

Oakley, A. (1981). *Subject women.* London: Fontana.

Orbach, S. (1978). *Fat is a feminist issue.* London: Paddington Press.

Rave, E. (1985). Violence against women: An overview. In L. Rosewater & L. Walker (Eds.), *Handbook of feminist therapy: Women's issues in psychotherapy* (pp. 199–201). New York: Springer.

Rehm, L., & Rokke, P. (1988). Self-management therapies. In K. Dobson (Ed.), Handbook of cognitive–behavioral therapies (pp. 136–166). New York: Guilford Press.

Rosenbaum, M. (Ed.). (1990). *Learned resourcefulness: On coping skills, self-control and adaptive behavior.* New York: Springer.

Rosenthal, D., & Palthiel, M. (1982). Children's knowledge and use of gender stereotypes. *Psychological Reports, 51,* 849–850.

Rosewater, L., & Walker, L. (1985). *Handbook of feminist therapy: Women's issues in psychotherapy.* New York: Springer.

Rush, A., Beck, A., Kovacs, M., & Hollon, S. D. (1977). Comparative efficacy of cognitive therapy and pharmacotherapy in the treatment of depressed outpatients. *Cognitive Therapy and Research, 1,* 17–37.

Seligman, M. (1975). *Helplessness: On depression, development and death.* San Francisco: Freeman.

Skinner, B. (1938). *The behavior of organisms: An experimental analysis.* Englewood Cliffs. NJ: Prentice-Hall.

Skinner, B. (1969). *Contingencies of reinforcement: A theoretical analysis.* New York: Appleton-Century-Crofts.

Smith, A., & Siegel, R. (1985). Feminist therapy: Redefining power for the powerless. In L. Rosewater & L. Walker (Eds.), *Handbook of feminist therapy: Women's issues in psychotherapy* (pp. 13–21). New York: Springer.

Spender, D., & Sarah, E. (1980). *Learning to lose: Sexism and education.* London: Women's Press.

Spock, B. (1985). *Baby and childcare.* New York: Pocket Books. (Original work published 1946)

Steinem, G. (1984). *Outrageous acts and everyday rebellions.* London: Flamingo.

Stere, L. (1985). Feminist assertiveness training: Self-esteem groups as skill training for women. In L. Rosewater & L. Walker (Eds.), *Handbook of feminist therapy: Women's issues in psychotherapy* (pp. 51–61). New York: Springer.

Summers, A. (1975). *Damned whores and god's police.* Sydney, Australia: Penguin.

Tennant, C., Bebbington, P., & Hurry, J. (1982). Female vulnerability to neurosis: The influence of social roles. *Australian and New Zealand Journal of Psychiatry, 16,* 135–140.

Thomas, G. (1991). Child sexual abuse. In R. Cochrane & T. Carroll (Eds.), *Psychology and social issues* (pp. 162–171). London: Falmer Press.

Thoreson, C., & Thoreson, R. W. (1974). On developing personally competent individuals: A behavioral perspective. In R. Ulrich, T. Stachnik, & J. Mabry (Eds.), *Control of human behavior: Behavior modification in education* (pp. 210–213). Glenview, IL: Scott, Foresman.

Vicinus, M. (1977). *A widening sphere: Changing roles of Victorian women.* London: Methuen.

Warner, R. (1991). A survey of theoretical orientations of Canadian clinical psychologists. *Canadian Psychology, 32,* 525–528.

Watson, J. B. (1919). *Psychology from the standpoint of a behaviorist.* Philadelphia: Lippincott.

Weiss, L. (1985). Getting to "No" and beyond. In L. Rosewater & L. Walker (Eds.), *Handbook of feminist therapy: Women's issues in psychotherapy* (pp. 62–70). New York: Springer.

Wolf, N. (1991). *The beauty myth.* London: Vintage.

Wollstonecraft, M. (1975). *A vindication of the rights of woman.* London: Penguin Books. (Original work published 1792)

Wolpe, J. (1973). *The practice of behavior therapy.* New York: Pergamon Press.

Wolpe, J. (1990). *The practice of behavior therapy* (4th ed.). New York: Pergamon Press.

Worell, J., & Remy, P. (1992). *Feminist perspectives in therapy: An empowerment model for women.* New York: Wiley.

19

MARXIST THEORY AND BEHAVIOR THERAPY

JEROME D. ULMAN

WHY MARXIST THEORY?

At the start it seems fair to ask, In what way might Marxist theory be relevant in behavior therapy? Behavior therapists work to ameliorate the problems people experience in everyday living. Commonly, behavior therapists work with individuals or family units with the goal of enabling their clients to better cope with the stresses and conflicts arising from their personal environments—their homes, their places of employment, and their communities. To be most effective, behavior therapists need to identify the variables that distress their clients so that effective therapeutic changes can be made. In doing so, behavior therapists face three basic courses of action: (a) They can attempt to change the internal condition of the client (e.g., through systematic desensitization), leaving the client's environment unchanged. (b) They can encourage their clients to remove themselves from the distressing environment (e.g., by changing jobs). (c) They can give their clients new coping skills to deal more effectively with the distressing situation (e.g., by acquiring assertive skills). None of these alternatives involve a wide-ranging alteration of the social environment, however; at most, behavior therapists may become involved in localized, community-based interventions.

When a society as a whole becomes dysfunctional (e.g., when unemployment rates increase sharply, with the attendant rise in the rates of alcoholism and drug abuse, conflict situations in the home, and behavior disorders), more and more people seek help from human service professionals, including behavior therapists. To be effective under these circumstances, behavior therapists need to take into consideration the larger context called *society*. Of course, as the society in which they live and practice becomes increasingly dysfunctional, as the demand for their services increases, it is entirely possible for behavior therapists to continue their business as usual (and, along with the lawyers, quite profitably) and not concern themselves with this larger context.

Behavior therapists live in the same world as the rest of humanity, so what happens on a global scale (wars, economic depressions, social turmoil, ecological disasters, etc.) affects all people regardless of their vocation. However, there is another compelling reason for behavior therapists to endeavor to make sense of society and thus make some headway in dealing with the huge social problems facing people. Behavior therapists who have been thoroughly trained in the science of behavior (i.e., behaviorology), including the philosophy of radical behaviorism, may be uniquely equipped to contribute to the solution.

Malagodi (1986) made this point most cogently in his article, "On Radicalizing Behaviorism: A Call for Cultural Analysis." He was concerned "with certain of those practices of our culture which either continue to evolve along ethnocidal and genocidal pathways or which simply diminish the quality of life for the majority" (Malagodi, 1986, p. 15). To begin to deal with these pressing social problems, Malagodi (1986) suggested two solutions: "First, that radical behaviorism be treated as a comprehensive world view in which epistemological, psychological [i.e., behaviorological], and cultural analyses constitute interdependent components; second, that principles derived from compatible social-science disciplines be incorporated into radical behaviorism" (p. 1). Malagodi's call for cultural analysis provides the point of departure for this chapter, but with one critical amendment to his second suggested solution: that behavior therapists turn not to the principles derived from mainstream (bourgeois) social science disciplines but to those from Marxist theory.

In a follow-up discussion, Malagodi and Jackson (1989) criticized both conventional psychologists and behavior analysts for limiting their concerns to their clients' troubles instead of examining larger issues (a contradistinction they borrowed from C. Wright Mills): "Troubles become issues when troubling conditions such as inadequate reinforcement for . . . desirable behavior, or punishment of those behaviors, contact significant and/or increasing numbers of individuals" (p. 19). Moreover, behavior therapists are not led to question even their immediate situations, let alone the broader social system, "when widespread personal problems that occur within that system are viewed as troubles arising out of common human failings rather than as issues arising out of fundamental failures of the culture's political, economic, legal, religious, educational, mental-health, and other institutions of social control" (Malagodi & Jackson, 1989, p. 27).

To the extent that behavior therapists take individual ("self-contained") contingencies as a given, they "are open to the charge . . . often made in reference to conventional psychology's concentration on 'inner man'. . . of showing a predilection for unfinished causal sequences (e.g., Skinner, 1969)" (Malagodi & Jackson, 1989, p. 21). Instead, I suggest that behavior therapists should become issue oriented and examine Marxist theory as a viable scientific approach to the study of society and then begin to combine their behavior analysis with Marxist class analysis (see Ulman, 1983, 1986a, 1986b).

THE ORIGINS OF MARXIST THEORY

The intellectual turmoil of the 18th century set the stage for the development of Marxist theory. As feudalism, and with it the influence of the Church, began to wane with the rise of industrialization and bourgeois revolutions, a variety of evolutionary theories—both on nature and society—were spawned. Twenty-five years before Marx was born, Charles Darwin's grandfather, Erasmus Darwin (1731–1802), proposed that all living things were originally derived from microscopic ones. Antoine Concorcet in France and William Godwin in England both put forward the concept of social evolution that was similarly governed by certain inherent laws. However, their theories of historical evolution were idealistic, supposing that such evolution was the result of an innate quality of the human mind ("reason"). Somewhat later, a similar but much more intricate and sophisticated idealist evolutionary theory was developed by the German philosopher, Georg Wilhelm Friedrich Hegel (1770–1831). This theory, though, was put in mystical terms: Behind the ideas causing historical development lay the Absolute or God, with history being an unfolding of the nature of God. These early evolutionary theories, along with French utopian socialism and English political economy, were the progenitors of Marxist theory.

Contrary to the Hegelian worldview, the roots of Marxist theory, like that of any body of thought, are not the result of a mystical unfolding of "pure ideas." Rather, they are products of real social relations, and those roots produced a perspective that one can consider properly as Marxist ("proto-Marxist") well before Marx came on the scene. In brief, the movement in history from which Marxism emerged was that of the Industrial Revolution, an economic development that was heralded politically by the French Revolution and was distinguished socially by the rise of a new class, the proletariat, a mass working class which operated the new factories, mines, steel mills, and railways. It was . . . basically out of the struggles, social and ideological, of the young proletariat, particularly in Britain, that Marxism arose. (Cameron, 1993, p. 1)

Although the countryside in Britain and on the Continent remained essentially a feudal society, the situations in the cities—the centers of trade and manufacturing—began to change dramatically. The owners of these tremendous new means of production, the bourgeoisie, became increasingly powerful economically and politically. The inevitable struggle between the bourgeoisie and the landed aristocracy for political power ended in triumph for the bourgeois; parliaments were established throughout western Europe, replacing the authority of the nobility and the Church.

At the same time, workers who once were scattered in light cottage industries (cloth, leather, wood) became concentrated in heavy industry (coal, iron, steel), forming a potentially powerful industrial working class, the proletariat. As it increased in might, the proletariat soon began to push for a share of political power, first in the massive Chartist movement in Britain in the 1830s and 1840s and then in bourgeois revolutions on the Continent. Representing this continental workers' movement was the Communist League, "and it was for the League that two of its members, Karl Marx (1818–1883) and Frederick Engels (1820–1895), wrote the *Manifesto of the Communist Party*, popularly known as *The Communist Manifesto* (1848)" (Cameron, 1993, p. 3).

Marx had discovered the economic base for historical evolution and the structure of the state, but it was Engels's (1845/1973) empirically based study, *Conditions of the Working-Class in England* (completed 3 years prior to *Communist Manifesto*), that enabled Marx to envision the role of the proletariat in the destruction of capitalism and humanity's advance to socialism. It became increasingly clear to Marx and Engels that economic facts are a decisive historical force.

Finally, in tracing the roots of Marxism, one must consider other sources of influence on Marx and Engels, another kind of communist movement that included radical trade unionism and other radical groupings such as the Owenites. These utopian socialists (Robert Owen, Comte de Saint Simon, Francois-Charles Fourier, et al.), however, tended to adhere to the notion that one should abstractly construct a plan for socialism first and then work to achieve it. By contrast, the Chartists favored putting productive forces under worker control for the general good of all, combining mass tactics with the socialist outlook of Robert Owen. Although their immediate aim was to secure the vote for workers, the Chartists' ultimate objectives were militantly socialist (Cameron, 1993).

In short, Marx took the richness of Hegel's analysis of complex sociohistorical relationships—the so-called *dialectical laws*—but put his theory of historical evolution on a firm materialistic footing, drawing from the viewpoints of materialist philosophers: Feuerbach in Germany and the 18th-century French writers, Diderot and Holbach. Subsequently, Marx spent enormous labor on his critique of political economy, concentrating on the works of Adam Smith and David Ricardo. However, the foundation of Marxist theory is not in the texts of Hegel's dialectics, Feuerback's materialism, or the English political economists, but in the experience of the industrial working class, in particular, the British working class of the 1840s. As intellectuals who were part of this working-class movement, Marx and Engels thus set out to "synthesize its world-view and to forward its economic and political interests" (Cameron, 1993, p. 5), and so began the systematic work on Marxist theory.

THE SCIENTIFIC STATUS OF MARXIST THEORY

Marxist and quasi-Marxist theorizing can be found in the various social science disciplines, anthropology, economics, political science, sociology, psychology, as well as in history and philosophy (see Ollman & Vernoff, 1982). What one political scientist, David Easton (1991), said about Marxism in his discipline applies as well to the others:

> Theoretical Marxism, after lying dormant in the U.S. social science since the 1940s (even though very much alive in Europe), was reintroduced in the 1970s. However, no single orthodoxy in the Marxist methods or theories has been adopted. The fragmentation of European Marxism reflected in its American renaissance. We find all schools of Marxism represented—critical theory, humanist, cultural, structural, as well as orthodox.
> What is clear, however, is that in being absorbed into U.S. social research the various schools of Marxism have been attenuated; most inquiry is only quasi-Marxist in character. Even in that form, however, the revival of Marxist thinking has brought . . . a renewed awareness of the importance of history and of the significance of the economy, social classes, and ideology, as well as the total social context. (p. 49)

What, though, is the scientific status of Marxist theory? In an essay entitled "Marx Wasn't All Wrong," Rosenberg (1991) commented that "perhaps we should hesitate before consigning Marx to the dustbin of history" (p. 158). Although the demise of the Soviet Union is being interpreted widely as evidence of the final breakdown of Marxism, Rosenberg questioned such a reading:

> Marx's writings essentially analyze the historical process by which capitalist societies grow and become transformed. Marx needs to be disengaged from the disastrous 20th-century economic experiments with socialism because in his view of history socialism would emerge only out of advanced capitalist societies. Socialism would arise after capitalist societies became wracked by their "internal contradictions." (p. 158)

Thus, the collapse of the socialist economies can be interpreted more correctly as evidence that Marx was right, not wrong, that socialism would emerge only after capitalism has exhausted its potential for growth. Rosenberg (1991) added, "Marx was also right in his analysis of capitalism as a unique system that provided powerful impulses for initiating technological change" (p. 158).

Although capitalism remains the most dynamic force in world development, the historian Erick Hobsbawm (1991a) related, "it will certainly continue to develop, as Marx predicted that it would, by generating internal contradictions leading to periodic eras of crisis and restructuring. These may once again bring it close to breakdown, as happened earlier this century" (p. 122). Hobsbawm (1991b) observed that, in spite of (or more accurately, because of) its dynamics, there are at least three consequences of world capitalist development that it has not been able to control: (a) the ecology—"humanity has now got to the point where it can actually destroy the biosphere" (p. 323); (b) "the appalling way in which the gap between the inhabitants of the rich and developed countries and those of the poor ones is widening" (p. 323); (c) "by subordinating humanity to economics, capitalism undermines and rots away the relations between human beings which constitutes societies, creates a moral vacuum, in which nothing counts except what the individual wants, here and now" (pp. 323–324). To these, one can add a fourth catastrophic consequence of capitalist dynamics: (d) the inevitable "broadening [of] class, national, and inter-imperialist conflicts" (Barnes, 1991, p. 125). Hobsbawm (1991b) concluded "that is why socialism still has an agenda 150 years after Marx and Engels's manifesto" (p. 325). It is why Marxist theory is still on the agenda and remains as relevant than ever.

Of course, to appreciate Marxist theory as a body of scientific thought, it is not enough to assess the accuracy of Marx's predictions. He was no mere prophesier—he was a materialistic social scientist whose primary subject matter was the dynamics of capitalism. In fact, it may be more appropriate to say that Marx's theory of history is not really predictive; rather, like Darwinian evolutionary theory, it is retrodictive. Thus, like evolutionary biology, which can describe how a given species might have evolved but would not be able to demonstrate that only that particular species could have arisen, Marxist theory can describe how a given society evolved but would not argue that it could not have been otherwise. Slightly different initial conditions acting on an organism (society) in a slightly different order could have selected a somewhat different species (social formation).

To evaluate Marx's scientific contributions, one must examine how and on what basis he reached his conclusions. To compound the problem of evaluating Marxist theory, as Marx continued to develop his theory, he changed his emphases on and interpretations of various aspects of socio-historical phenomena that constituted his subject matter. The work of subsequent Marxist theorists must also be evaluated, but in a highly selective manner given the enormous, diverse, and even contradictory body of literature that has come to be called Marxist.

Therefore, the following is an attempt to render an overview of Marxist theory that is commensurate with the natural science of behavior, behaviorology, and the philosophy that guides it, radical behaviorism. My goal in this chapter, then, is to present an interpretation of Marxist theory that will be relevant to the practice of behavior therapy.

MARXIST THEORY VERSUS CULTURAL MATERIALISM

In their efforts to expand their focus to issues, to take into account the larger sociocultural context of social dysfunctions, several authors have suggested that behaviorists should turn to cultural anthropology; in particular, behaviorists should adopt the framework of Harris's *cultural materialism* (Glenn, 1988; Lloyd, 1985; Malagodi, 1986; Malagodi & Jackson, 1989; Malott, 1988; Vargas, 1985). Recently, an entire book was devoted to this topic (Lamal, 1991). Marxist theory, in contrast to cultural materialism, has hardly received notice in the behavioral literature. As I have argued for many years (Ulman, 1979, 1983, 1986a, 1986b, 1986c, 1988, 1990, 1991), however, the time for radical behaviorists to seriously consider Marxist theory as a comprehensive frame of reference for "examining the issues" is long overdue. Hence, it seems fitting to begin by contrasting Marxist theory with cultural materialism. Given the popularity of Harris among behaviorists, it is important to understand that cultural materialism is not a variation of Marxist theory (see Ulman, 1986b).

Harris credited Marx with "anticipating" the kernel of the principles that guided the development of cultural materialism, specifically Marx's (1859/1970) statement that

> the mode of production in material life determines the general character of the social, political, and spiritual processes of life. It is not the consciousness of men that determines their existence, but on the contrary, their social existence determines their consciousness. (p. 21)

On the basis of this statement, Harris (1979) derived what he termed "the principle of infrastructure determinism" (p. 56), where *infrastructure* is composed of variables responsible for the production and reproduction of a given human group (e.g., methods of food production and storage, methods of birth control, etc.).

However, Harris (1979) was not clear about how one is to determine which infrastructural variable is operative in each instance, and therefore his principle of infrastructure determinism might more properly be termed the *principle of infrastructure eclecticism.* Furthermore, when pressed, Harris (1979) conceded that there are occasions in which structural/superstructural variables may play a determining role (e.g., conscious political-ideological struggle is clearly capable of [changing] . . . the direction and pace of the transformational processes initiated within the infrastructure" [p. 73]). Perhaps the most revealing difference between cultural materialism and Marxist theory is found in Harris's book, *America Now* (subsequently titled *Why Things Don't Work*). According to Harris, the problem with the United States is not, as Marxists would argue, the inherent crises of capitalism, but that the means of production have become too huge, centralized, and bureaucratized.

As Legros (1977) made clear, "cultural evolutionism and historical materialism are two fundamentally divergent theories of evolution" (p. 26). Harris's cultural materialism is a form of cultural evolutionism (see Lett, 1987) and thus differs from historical materialism in a crucial way: It fails to grasp the centrality of the concept *mode of production*, which, for Marxists, "constitutes a discriminating criterion for a science of history" (Legros, 1977, p. 79). Legros (1977) pointed out that this concept "allows us to construct an evolutionary sequence in terms of general evolution" (p. 79). That is, by comprehending a given society not as a single structure of interrelated levels (as in Harris, 1979) but as a unique synthesis and articulation of various modes of production, historical materialism not only offers a more scientifically comprehensive view of the human social environment than does cultural evolutionism, it is an opposite view—one that is "closer to the modern conception of biological evolution in which the concept of chance has become as crucial as the concept of necessity (cf. Monod, [1970/]1971)" (p. 79).

Moreover, Lett (1987), a former student of Harris, observed that cultural materialism "is concerned primarily with the general question of cultural causality . . . and not the particular question of dynamic processes" (p. 92). Cultural materialism cannot explain the causes of all sociocultural phenomena, but instead offers explanations for those phenomena (as its proponents duly recognize) that "either benefit or detract from the productive and reproductive efforts of particular sociocultural systems. In effect, the principle of infrastructural determinism is only capable of accounting for those components of sociocultural systems that are affected by infrastructural determinants" (Lett, 1987, p. 92).

Harris's (1979) cultural materialism thus reduces societal phenomena, including that of class struggle, to cultural practices, to structural and superstructural events driven by infrastructural determinants. One net result is that the priority he gave infrastructural determinism obscures the question of political power, which is central to a Marxist analysis (see Isaac, 1987). The point here is not to criticize cultural materialism as much as it is to emphasize that Marx's theory and Harris's theory are concerned with different kinds of questions—respectively, of power and of cultural causality. After all, Harris never claimed to be a Marxist.

In general, behaviorists appear to be attracted by Harris's emphasis on infrastructural determinism combined with his antimentalism. They give little or no credence to Marxism, as is typical among North American academics. The popularity of Harris among radical behaviorists notwithstanding, I argue that there is nothing inherent in the philosophy of radical behaviorism that would necessarily commit one to cultural evolutionism as opposed to historical materialism. To the contrary, what is inherent in radical behaviorism, I think, is a materialistic selectionist viewpoint that, if it is applied consistently in the interpretation of large-scale social change, would lead one toward historical materialism (i.e., toward a version of historical materialism that is conceptualized within the selectionistic explanatory framework and the radical behavioral epistemology).

THE PHILOSOPHY OF MARXIST THEORY: DIALECTICAL MATERIALISM

Marxists distinguish between two modes of reasoning: metaphysical and dialectical. In the metaphysical mode, one thinks in terms of absolutes and imposes exact and unchanging classification systems on natural and social phenomena. Changes in phenomena are either not considered or considered in purely quantitative terms. Dialectical thinking is the exact opposite. Hegel's great philosophical achievement was in ending the total dominance of the absolutist medieval worldview, a static and unchanging world composed of isolated objects. For Hegel, everything is interconnected and in a constant state of flux. Marx's great philosophical achievement was to "turn Hegel upright" by grounding the dialectical perspective on a solid materialist foundation. Characterizing dialectical materialism in a minimum number of words, Cornforth (1980), quoting Engels, stated that materialism "means nothing more 'than to comprehend the real world—nature and history—as it presents itself . . . free from preconceived idealistic fancies' " (p. 55). Cornforth (1980) went on to provide a working definition of dialectics by quoting Lenin: "It consists in the all-sided consideration of relationships in their concrete development" (p. 58).

The assumptions underlying orthodox Marxist theory are putatively those of dialectical materialism, generally considered to be the philosophy of Marxism. This philosophy has been subjected to so many varied and mutually contradictory interpretations and distortions (more so than even the term *behaviorism*) that it becomes difficult to separate the wheat from the chaff (for a reliable guide, see Novack, 1978). I should first note that Marx never used the term; it was probably first used by Georgii Plekhanov in 1891 (Edgerly, 1991), although there is a claim that Josef Dietzgen coined the term (see Sheehan, 1985, p. 115).

In reply to critics who find fault with Marxist theory because of its supposed inherent Hegelian character (e.g., Harris, 1979), Dietzgen's (1828–1888) philosophical writings provide an effective counter. Although rarely recognized today, Dietzgen's early work earned qualified praise from Marx, who called him "our philosopher," and from Engels, who later credited him with the independent discovery of dialectical materialism. "Dietzgen was a strenuous opponent of speculative thought who insisted on the need for an inductive method based on sensory experience" (Fine, 1991, p. 152), a refreshing viewpoint for natural scientists who are curious about what dialectics may have to offer but who are put off by Hegel's idealistic metaphysics. As Fine (1991) observed, Dietzgen "believed that humanity needed to be liberated from traditional religion and from those metaphysical systems that separated mind from matter, fact from value" (p. 152). Thus, to the charge that Marx was a Hegelian—in the pejorative sense—one may reply with equal (but also qualified) validity that Marx was a "Dietzgenian."

In a balanced appraisal of his philosophical contributions, Sheehan (1985) wrote the following:

> Dietzgen's philosophical writings, although irritatingly rambling and repetitious and full of [banal] points . . . were pioneering efforts in their time, efforts of which Marx and Engels were duly appreciative. His ontology was one that saw reality as one, changing and interconnected. He was a forthright critic of both idealism and mechanistic materialism. . . . His epistemology was one which, although it put heavy stress on mental constructivism, was nevertheless firmly realist. He was very explicit in his affirmation of the independent existence of the external world. (p. 104)

Sheehan (1985) added that Dietzgen put great emphasis on the inductive method, had great respect for the methods and achievements of science, and strongly identified the mission of the proletariat with that of science: "The proletariat was the appropriate bearer, not only of science, but of monism. It was in the interest of the enemies of socialism, advocates of a class-divided society, to adhere to dualism" (p. 104). Interestingly, Lenin enlisted Dietzgen's work in his materialistic assault on the empirio-critics—those Bolsheviks inspired by the idealistic, phenomenological view of Mach—"but distinguished between the 'muddleheaded' Dietzgen and the strictly realist contributions of Dietzgen the atheist" (Fine, 1991, p. 153).[1] Dietzgen's (1906) major work was the *Positive Outcome of Philosophy*.[2]

THE STRUCTURE OF MARXIST THEORY

I have now considered some philosophical assumptions underlying Marxist theory. Next, I briefly examine the structure of Marxist theory, that is, the Marx theory of history and analysis of the capitalist economic system.

Historical Materialism

Historical materialism is the materialistic conception of the evolution of social formations (i.e., the Marxist theory of human beings and society). In orthodox Marxist theory, historical materialism is the application of the general precepts of dialectical materialism to the comprehension of human history. The dogmatic (Stalinist) interpretation of this relationship posits that the dialectical laws determine human history, but, in recent times, with the demise of the bureaucratic regimes in Eastern Europe and the former Soviet Union, this view has largely gone by the wayside. Following Cornforth's (1980) description of dialectical materialism, this philosophy would enjoin one to study actual social relations in their real changes and interconnections, thereby enabling one to infer historical materialist conclusions about social affairs, about regularities ("laws") of social development, and what may be necessary to solve the pressing problems of contemporary society. Properly understood, the materialist dialectic guides a Marxist sociohistorical analysis in the same sense that radical behaviorism guides a behaviorological analysis.

Thus, historical materialism is not a theory deduced from certain a priori philosophical principles or from "dialectical laws of human development." Marx and Engels (1932/1965), in *The German Ideology*, their

---

[1]B. F. Skinner was strongly influenced by Mach, but he also came to reject the phenomenological view; see Skinner, 1984.
[2]An adequate treatment of dialectical materialism is precluded here, but one source that I recommend to radical behaviorists is *The Dialectical Biologist* by Richard Levins and Richard Lewontin (1985). Both authors are biological scientists. As stated on its back cover, "the book successfully achieves the authors' goal of demonstrating by example the power and nature of the dialectical method." For a thorough but sympathetic critique of dialectical materialism from the standpoint of scientific realist philosophy, see the chapter "Dialectics, Materialism and Theory of Knowledge" in Bhaskar (1989), as well as several chapters in Mepham and Ruben (1979).

preliminary exposition of the general principles of historical materialism, stated that "the premises from which we begin ... are real individuals, their activity and the material conditions under which they live, both those already existing and those produced by their activity" (p. 42). Humans distinguish themselves most from other animals as soon "as they begin to *produce* their means of subsistence ... [and by doing so they] are indirectly producing their actual material life" (Marx & Engels, 1932/1965, p. 42). What this means is that "the nature of individuals depends upon the material conditions determining their production" (Marx & Engels, 1932/ 1965, p. 42). Although humans have certain inborn capacities, most notably their capacity to think through a plan of action before changing their surroundings (for Marx and Engels, the capacity that distinguishes the worst architect from the bee), how humans produce and under what material conditions determines their actual nature. This observation by Marx and Engels has become a central point of departure for Marxist-oriented anthropologists (e.g., see Bloch, 1983).

Thus, historical materialism focuses on how people go about obtaining their means of subsistence, which Marx termed the *social mode of production*. There are two core concepts in terms of which the social mode of production is defined and together constitute the basic scientific paradigm of historical materialism: the *forces of production* and the *relations of production*. To produce their means of subsistence, humans make tools and acquire the skills and knowledge required for their use, which, taken together, are their forces of production. In using these productive forces, humans enter into social relations of production. As Marx (1849/1933) wrote in *Wage-Labor and Capital*, humans produce only by co-operating with one another, and only within these relations does production take place. Accordingly, the concept of productive relations refers to the nexus of the social relations among individuals as they exchange their activities and take part in the whole action of production. Included in productive relations are those relations that "people enter into in owning the means of production and in appropriating and distributing the products, and define the economic structure of society and the division of society into classes" (Cornforth, 1977, p. 36).

Thus, Marx concluded that in a given mode of production, humans enter into definite relations of production in the use of definite forces of production. From these concepts, one might formulate the central idea of historical materialism (Marx's "guiding thread"), reduced to the simplest possible terms, as follows: The forces of production *select* the relations of production. Class conflicts arise when the productive relations fetter the development of productive forces. Those productive relations are ultimately selected that best accommodate the development of the productive forces. Within this framework, historical materialism includes analysis of the state, ideology (including religion, political theories, philosophy, science, and even art), the repressive apparatus (the military, police, courts, prisons, etc.), and all other social institutions within the context of the mode of production of the society in which they exist. Changes in these institutions are comprehended in relation to changes in the dominant mode of production.[3]

Marxist Analysis of Capitalism

The first volume of Marx's *Capital* was published in 1867. After Marx's death, Engels assumed the task of getting two more volumes published. Marx (1976/1867) began with an analysis of the most basic unit of the capitalist economic system—the commodity. One can define a *commodity* (C) as any useful value (i.e., some reinforcer) that can be exchanged for another commodity. In bartering, for example, exchanging a sack of potatoes for a pair of shoes can be designated as a C–C relation, one commodity is exchanged for another. For this exchange to take place, however, one party needs shoes and the other potatoes. A major problem with bartering, of course, is that parties with complementary needs must somehow find one another. The exchange process becomes qualitatively improved with the introduction of a generalized medium of exchange, *money* (M). Now the producer makes a commodity so that it can be exchanged for money: the C–M relation. After obtaining a given amount of money, that person can then exchange money for some needed commodity: the M–C relation. The location where that transaction takes place is called the *marketplace*. It is here that transactions go on that complete the exchange circuit, the C–M–C relation, selling in order to buy.

The C–M–C relation does not describe the capitalist economic system, however. To understand capitalism, one must turn to another place where money and commodities are exchanged: the *workplace*. The commodity offered in the workplace is *labor power*, the worker's capacity for productive (commodity-producing) behavior. Within the last 400 years of human history, the productive forces—farming, mining, manufacturing, and transportation—have advanced to such an extent that the coordinated labor of thousands of workers may be required to produce a particular product. At the same time, these major means of production came to be owned,

---

[3]This characterization of the basic structure of historical materialism is grossly simplistic, however. At this point, I can only refer the reader to the most incisive treatments of historical materialism I have found: *Karl Marx's Theory of History* by Cohen (1978) and *Reconstructing Marxism: Essays on Explanation and the Theory of History* by Wright, Levine, and Sober (1992). The former is a germinal work in the rigorous style of the analytic Marxists, and the latter is a penetrating, albeit somewhat technical, critique (especially of the former) from a selectionist standpoint. Incidentally, one of the authors, Elliot Sober, has contributed significantly to development of the selectionist perspective in the life sciences (in particular, Sober, 1984), one consistent with Skinner's (1981/1988) *selection by consequences* as a causal mode (see Smith, 1986). Finally, I recommend the recent article by Carling (1993), which offers further refinements in the selectionist interpretation of historical materialism.

not by the direct producers themselves, but by a relatively small group of private owners, the capitalist class. Having no independent means of sustenance, the producers—the workers—had and continue to have only their labor power to offer in exchange for money. Without money, workers face grave deprivations.

The famous discovery Marx made about capitalism is that the source of all profit (value) ultimately derives from labor power. That is, labor power is a commodity having the unique capacity to yield more money in the exchange circuit than the capitalist originally paid for it. The capitalist exchanges money for a commodity, then exchanges that commodity for money, the M–C–M' relation, buying in order to sell. Obviously, there would be no reason for making the exchange unless the capitalist ended up with more money at the end of the exchange than at the onset. Therefore, M' denotes some quantity greater than M; in economic terms, M' minus M equals profit (surplus value). Because the capitalist does not buy a set amount of labor but the workers' potential for producing, the employer is motivated by capitalist competition to coerce as much productive behavior out of the worker as possible. Thus, the capitalist system is inherently exploitative.

Central to the Marxist economic analysis of the modern world is how capitalism has evolved on the basis of competition. Although prominent radical behaviorists such as Sidman (1989) see the devastating effects of competition "in the market place" (p. 178), they take capitalist property relations for granted and fail to understand the dynamics of the world capitalist system. Yet, as Marxist economic theory makes clear, malevolent effects of competition are all-pervasive in capitalist society. Under capitalism, owners of one firm compete with owners of similar firms; workers compete with owners for more wages and owners with workers for more labor time; and workers compete with other workers for jobs. Multinational corporations compete all over the world for raw materials, cheap labor, and new markets. Consequently, the huge imbalance in trade between the advanced Western nations and the Third World has trapped the latter in a condition of debt peonage, unable even to pay interest on the loans, which renders the lives of the millions of people in those poor countries more and more miserable each year. The capitalist economic system requires a free labor market, preferably with a greater supply of workers than available jobs (as Marx called them, "the reserve army of the unemployed"). Additionally, private ownership of the means of production requires a government with sufficient coercive capacity (i.e., laws, police, courts, and jails) to ensure that the laws defining those property rights are obeyed.

In summary, it is important to remember that the term *capital* refers not to some *thing* but to a particular kind of social relation. According to the Marxist perspective, it is the uncontrolled operation of the profit system that has resulted in the massive Third World debt, widening the gap between the rich and the poor; the rampant exploitation of natural resources with the consequent destruction of the biosphere; the triumph of greed at any social cost; the international competition for markets, raw materials, cheap labor, minimal taxes, and unrestricted dumping of industrial waste; and broadening of class, national, and interimperialist conflicts over world domination.

WHAT IS A MARXIST?

I have yet to address the following question: What is a Marxist? The answer, of course, depends on who is asked. Is a Marxist simply a scholar who discusses social phenomena in Marxist terminology? By this measure— in virtue of his discussion of such Marxist concepts as modes of production, superstructure, and so on—Marvin Harris would be a Marxist. What about the neo-Hegelians of the Frankfurt school such as Jurgen Habermas, who reduces Marx to a mere critic of ideology (see Ulman, 1979)? Is he a Marxist? Can one be a Marxist and not be involved in a revolutionary movement or at least to some degree in emancipatory political action?

As stated earlier (Ulman, 1983), "following Lenin's (1917/1932) definition, 'a Marxist is one who *extends* the acceptance of the class struggle to the acceptance of the *dictatorship of the proletariat*' (p. 30, emphasis in the original)" (p. 18). It is crucial to note that Lenin did not state "dictatorship *over* the proletariat" (i.e., the domination of workers by a bureaucratic caste as found in deformed worker states). Since then, the world has seen one after the other of the Stalinist regimes swept away by the democratic movement of toilers in those states. A genuine Marxist can only welcome this world-shaking change. At the same time, however, a genuine Marxist should be able to recognize and defend a worker state that is not deformed, a true dictatorship *of* workers and farmers (and understand that people in the United States live under the dictatorship of profit-motivated employers *over* working people and those without work).

I argue that Cuba continues to be a revolutionary, not deformed, worker state (Ulman, 1983, 1988, 1990, 1991, 1992). Notwithstanding the severe economic hardships the Cuban people have suffered as the result of the U.S. trade embargo of more than 30 years' standing (and continuing into this supposedly post-Cold War period, combined with the recent loss of favorable trade relations with Eastern Europe and the former Soviet Union), Cuba continues on the revolutionary course toward socialism and communism as the founders of Marxist theory had originally envisioned.

Given the crises-ridden world in which we live, when our entire society is becoming increasingly dysfunctional, I believe that Cuba provides a unique and valuable variation for the future of humanity of social organization by design (see Tablada, 1989), one that, for the good of coming generations, should not be dismissed out of ignorance and misinformation (actually, disinformation; see Castro & Guevara, 1993). Ultimately, people need to ask themselves how much longer humankind can afford to endure the anarchy and massive destructiveness of M–C–M′ circuit, the worldwide profit system. Of course, people still have the option of treating problems and ignoring issues, seeking individualistic solutions to societal problems. To paraphrase Skinner (1971), however, if people do choose that alternative, so much the worst for everyone.

IMPLICATIONS OF MARXIST THEORY FOR BEHAVIOR THERAPY

A behavior therapist does not have to be a Marxist to be politically progressive, to be part of the solution rather than part of the problem (see Holland, 1978). However, one must first understand a social system before one can be effective in changing it. Accepting Malagodi and Jackson's (1989) recommendation that behavior therapists extend their concern from clients' problems to social issues is a start, but they still need some kind of frame of reference as a guide for ethical action. Malagodi and Jackson suggested that behavior therapists turn to the social sciences for guidance. I reject their suggestion on the grounds that the mainstream (bourgeois) social sciences lead to piecemeal reform, a program that supports the increasingly destructive capitalist system (see Ollman & Vernoff, 1982), when what is required is a program of revolutionary reform, a program leading to its total replacement by a system that puts human needs before profits, a socialist system. To illustrate, electoral politics (e.g., electing or lobbying a "better" Democrat or Republican politician) supports the system and thus is part of the problem, whereas what is needed is *independent* political action (e.g., supporting striking workers or demonstrating for abortion rights).

Ethical Differences

I next consider these differences in regard to alternative ethical systems. In Western culture, as Engels (1878/1947) noted, there are three major ethical alternatives: Christian-feudal, bourgeois-modern, and proletarian. In contemporary bourgeois society, one finds various combinations of ethical systems, but the predominant system can be characterized as pragmatic, the viewpoint of the political liberal. Perhaps the most advanced form of this mode of thinking is in the philosophy of John Dewey (1859–1952). According to Dewey (1938/1973), the worth of any moral action is to be judged not on the good intentions or motives of the actor but solely on its consequences. What counts is concrete results.

Leon Trotsky (1877–1940), a central organizer of the Red Army during the 1918–1921 Russian Civil War, discussed moral values from the revolutionary Marxist perspective. He argued that ends and means are *dialectically interdependent*:

> A means can be justified only by its ends. But the end in its turn needs to be justified. From the Marxist point of view, which expresses the historical interest of the proletariat, the end is justified if it leads to increasing the power of humanity over nature and to the abolition of the power of one person over another. (Trotsky, 1938/1973, p. 48)

In his debate with Trotsky, Dewey (1938/1973) agreed that the ends justify the means, but insisted that the means and ends are merely *reciprocally interdependent*.

The difference between Trotsky and Dewey on this question reduces to an essential difference in methods. Dewey believed that Trotsky's position was incorrect because he deduced it from a peculiar reading of the course of social development, class struggle, and that Trotsky was not warranted in entrusting the fundamental tasks of progressive social change to the proletariat because it is a common concern of all. According to Dewey, all people of good will, from the topmost level to the lower levels, should be mobilized for this task. Moreover, selecting one means over another can be based only on a tentative guess; again, only concrete results matter.

In Trotsky's view, on the basis of the materialist study of history (historical materialism), only the working class is capable of carrying through with the changes required to eliminate the catastrophic problems facing humanity. Nothing short of worldwide social revolution will do. In achieving this historic task, the choice of means is crucial. One need examine only the history of successes and failures in revolutionary struggles to comprehend this fact. The point is that politically, ethically, and philosophically, pragmatism and Marxism are absolutely irreconcilable (see Novack, 1975). Practically by default, the overwhelming majority of social scientists in modern bourgeois society are pragmatists of one shade or another.

Essentially, the implications of Marxist theory for behavior therapy revolve around the issue of class struggle. In times of social crisis, when workers and farmers begin to organize their own government and advance toward the revolutionary overthrow of capitalism—such as occurred in Russia in 1917 and in Cuba in 1959—the reality of class struggle is not a theoretical question; rather, it is a stupendously palpable fact. However, class struggle is not like a light bulb, either on or off. Most of the time its manifestations are considerably more translucent. Nonetheless, as long as a class-divided society continues to exist, class struggle will continue to some degree, ranging from resistance to employer demands on the shop floor to open class warfare. It is important to understand that whether workers believe that they are engaging in some form of class struggle is not the criterion for judging its reality. The criterion Marxists use is class analysis (see Ulman, 1983).

Developing Class Consciousness

In behavioristic terms, class struggle may be regarded as the outcome of competing *macrocontingencies* (i.e., functionally related but competing constellations of verbal and nonverbal behavioral contingencies). Thus, one could define *class struggle* as agonistic behavior (countercontrolling cultural practices) among people organized by macrocontingencies into conflicting institutions selected by antagonistic *relations of production* within a class-divided society. Stated in ordinary language, class struggle means that

> one class now owns the tools while another class uses them. One class is small and rich and the other large and poor. One wants more profit and the other more wages. One consists of capitalists and the other of workers. These two classes are at war. . . . There can be no peace and good will between these two essentially antagonistic economic classes. Nor can this class conflict be covered up or smothered over. (Debs, quoted in Malapanis, 1994, p. 11)

These words of Eugene Debs, a U.S. labor leader and socialist agitator, hold as true today as when he spoke them at the turn of the century, with one important amendment: In addition to the two major social classes, a large segment of middle layers (for the most part, professionals and managers) has emerged in the latter part of this century: the so-called middle class or, in Marxist terminology, the petty bourgeoisie. What is important to note about this segment is that it is not a coherent social class in itself but is made up of contradictory class locations (see Wright, Levine, & Sober, 1992). Some layers are more closely oriented to the working class, other layers to the capitalist class. With few exceptions, behavior therapists are among the petty bourgeoisie.

The extent to which individuals govern their political behavior with respect to their discrimination of class-struggle macrocontingencies, to that extent they can be said to be *class conscious*. Or, as Marx put it, it is not consciousness that determines one's existence; rather, it is social existence that determines one's consciousness. What they do as a result depends largely on their learning history in the context of their social class position. For example, one can predict that a behavior therapist employed by a large corporation may behave (verbally and nonverbally) politically one way, whereas a behavior therapist who practices in a working-class community may behave politically in a much different and contradictory way. Thus, because of differing positions in the relations of production, class consciousness (as defined earlier) among behavior therapists may differ radically. In times of social crisis and class polarization, there is no escape from class conflict. For example, if one works in a unionized plant during a strike, the choice is clear: One either does or does not cross the picket line.

Understanding that the actions a behavior therapist takes with respect to class struggle are determined largely by his or her class position in society, I can now address the lead question: What bearing does Marxist theory have on the practice of behavior therapy? Does Marxist theory have anything to say about what behavior therapists should do? Not directly, for exactly the same reason that the science of behavior does not. As materialistic scientists, Marxists and radical behaviorists agree that *ought* and *should* are questions of ethical values and therefore unanswerable within the sphere of natural science. However, the variables responsible for ethical conduct can be investigated.

In *Beyond Freedom and Dignity*, Skinner (1971) considered values from the radical behavioral perspective. For Skinner (1971), "to make a value judgment by calling something good or bad is to classify it in terms of its reinforcing effects" (p. 99). He added, " 'should' and 'ought' begin to raise more difficult questions when we turn to the contingencies under which a person is induced to behave for the good of others" (p. 107). Hence, a radical behaviorist might describe what a behavior therapist *ought* to do in light of Marxist theory as follows: If approval by the verbal community of vanguard workers is an important source of reinforcement for you, then you will be reinforced when you engage in revolutionary activities.

E. A. Vargas's (1975) radical behavioral analysis of rights provides a useful way to examine this issue. Ultimately, Vargas argued, it is the ethical verbal community that effectively asserts an individual's rights—where rights are forms of verbal behavior and therefore amenable to Skinner's (1957/1992) analysis. What makes a verbal community an ethical community, according to Vargas, are the contingencies the community shares in common, or what I referred to earlier as *macrocontingencies*.

Marxists conversant in operant terminology (rare birds indeed) would not disagree with Vargas (1975). They would, however, insist that an additional step be taken in this analysis; namely, that the contingencies (macrocontingencies) controlling the practices of the verbal community be explained by reference to the productive relations in which the ethical community exists (i.e., in terms of a class analysis combined with a behaviorological analysis). As I have suggested elsewhere,

> Vargas' (1975) operant analysis of political *rights*—in particular, the verbal behavior and antagonistic macrocontingencies responsible for 'the competitive struggle between ethical communities [or social classes] as they seek solutions to their problems' (189)—points to a new avenue for developing a synthetic Marxist-behaviorological approach for the investigation of ideological control associated with class-struggle social relations. (Ulman, in press, Footnote 23)

This task remains for the future, however.

In my chapter in a recently edited book, *Psychology and Marxism: Coexistence and Contradiction* (Ulman, in press), I attempted to bring to the attention of Marxist theorists the relevance of radical behaviorism and the science of behaviorology. In the current chapter I attempt to bring to the attention of behavior therapists the relevance of Marxist theory. In discussing social issues and social change at the societal level, I have not provided concrete guidelines for the daily practice of behavior therapy. However, with a specific focus on power relations informed by Marxist theory, behavior therapists are in a unique position to make important contributions to this effort. As Isaacs (1987) made clear, Marxist theory is a theory about power relations in capitalist society, from the level of the mode of production to the level of the working person in everyday life.

Although written in psychodynamic language, Michael Learner's (1986) book *Surplus Powerlessness* may prove helpful in exploring the implications of Marxist theory for the daily practice of behavior therapy. If one can sift through his Freudian psychobabble, one will find an acute sensitivity to the distress of working people in their everyday lives, plus many valuable insights on therapeutic practice within the context of capitalist society.

In Learner's (1986) words, surplus powerlessness is "the set of feelings and beliefs that make people think of themselves as even more powerless than the actual power situation requires, and then leads them to act in ways that actually confirm them in their powerlessness" (p. ii). Radical behaviorists, however, know that it is not the feelings or beliefs that cause people to behave in an "even more powerless way than the situation requires." Rather, it is the contingencies and macrocontingencies—controlling variables that can be studied and acted on by all progressive behavior therapists, Marxist or not. In doing so, behavior therapists can appreciate that they are contributing to the real solution to the catastrophic problems now facing humanity. In a class-divided society, empowering the powerless can have a revolutionary dynamic of its own, about which even the participants in the empowerment process may not be immediately or fully aware. That is precisely where Marxist theory comes into play.

REFERENCES

Barnes, J. (1991). Opening guns of World War III: Washington's assault on Iraq. *New International, 7,* 21–133.

Bhaskar, R. (1989). *Reclaiming reality: A critical introduction to contemporary philosophy.* New York: Verso.

Bloch, M. (1983). *Marxism and anthropology.* New York: Oxford University Press.

Cameron, K. N. (1993). *Marxism: A living science* (2nd ed.). New York: International Publishers.

Carling, A. (1993). Analytic Marxism and historical materialism: The debate on social evolution. *Science and Society, 57,* 31–65.

Castro, F., & Guevara, C. (1993). *To speak the truth: Why Washington's "cold war" against Cuba doesn't end.* New York: Pathfinder Press.

Cohen, G. A. (1978). *Karl Marx's theory of history: A defence.* Oxford, England: Oxford University Press.

Cornforth, M. (1977). *Marxism and the linguistic philosophy.* New York: International Publishers.

Cornforth, M. (1980). *Communism and philosophy: Contemporary dogmas and revisions of Marxism.* London: Lawrence & Wishart.

Dewey, J. (1973). Means and ends. In L. Trotsky, J. Dewey, & G. Novack, *Their morals and ours: Marxist vs. liberal views on morality* (5th ed., pp. 67–73). New York: Pathfinder Press. (Original work published 1938)

Dietzgen, J. (1906). *The positive outcome of philosophy.* Chicago: Charles Kerr.

Easton, D. (1991). Political science in the United States: Past and present. In D. Easton & C. S. Schelling (Eds.), *Divided knowledge: Across disciplines, across cultures* (pp. 37–58). Newbury Park, CA: Sage.

Edgerly, R. (1991). Dialectical materialism. In T. Bottomore (Ed.), *A dictionary of Marxist thought* (2nd ed., pp. 142–143). Cambridge, MA: Blackwell.

Engels, F. (1947). *Anti-Dühring* (E. Burns, Trans.). Moscow: Progress Publishers. (Original work published 1878)

Engels, F. (1973). *The conditions of the working-class in England.* Moscow: Progress. (Original work published 1845)

Fine, B. (1991). Dietzgen, Josef. In T. Bottomore (Ed.), *A dictionary of Marxist thought* (2nd ed., pp. 152–153). Cambridge, MA: Blackwell.

Glenn, S. S. (1988). Contingencies and metacontingencies: Toward a synthesis of behavior analysis and cultural materialism. *The Behavior Analyst, 11,* 161–179.

Harris, M. (1979). *Cultural materialism: The struggle for a science of culture.* New York: Vintage Books.

Harris, M. (1981). *America now: The anthropology of a changing culture.* New York: Simon & Schuster.

Hobsbawm, E. (1991a). Goodbye to all that. In R. Blackburn (Ed.), *After the fall: The failure of communism and the future of socialism* (pp. 115–125). London: Verso.

Hobsbawm, E. (1991b). Out of the ashes. In R. Blackburn (Ed.), *After the fall: The failure of communism and the future of socialism* (pp. 315–325). London: Verso.

Holland, J. G. (1978). Behaviorism: Part of the problem or part of the solution? *Journal of Applied Behavior Analysis, 11,* 163–174.

Isaac, J. C. (1987). *Power and Marxist theory.* Ithaca, NY: Cornell University Press.

Lamal, P. A. (Ed.). (1991). *Behavioral analysis of societies and cultural practices*. Washington, DC: Hemisphere.

Lett, J. (1987). *The human enterprise: A critical introduction to anthropological theory*. Boulder, CO: Westview Press.

Learner, M. (1986). *Surplus powerlessness*. Oakland, CA: Institute for Labor and Mental Health.

Legros, D. (1977). Chance, necessity, and mode of production: A Marxist critique of cultural evolutionism. *American Anthropologist, 79*, 26–41.

Lenin, V. I. (1932). *State and revolution*. New York: International Publishers. (Original work published 1917)

Levins, R., & Lewontin, R. (1985). *The dialectical biologist*. Cambridge, MA: Harvard University Press.

Lloyd, K. E. (1985). Behavioral anthropology: A review of Marvin Harris' cultural materialism. *Journal of the Experimental Analysis of Behavior, 43*, 279–287.

Malagodi, E. F. (1986). Radicalizing behaviorism: A call for cultural analysis. *The Behavior Analyst, 9*, 1–17.

Malagodi, E. F., & Jackson, K. (1989). Behavior analysis and cultural analysis: Troubles and issues. *The Behavior Analyst, 12*, 17–33.

Malott, R. W. (1988). Rule-governed behavior and behavioral anthropology. *The Behavior Analyst, 11*, 181–203.

Malapanis, A. (1994, September 5). Eugene Debs: Two classes are at war. *The Militant*, p. 11.

Marx, K. (1933). *Wage-labor and capital* (E. Engels, Ed.). New York: International Publishers. (Original work published 1849)

Marx, K. (1970). *A contribution to the critique of political economy*. New York: International Publishers. (Original work published 1859)

Marx, K. (1976). *Capital: A critique of political economy* (Vol. 1, B. Fowkes, Trans.). New York: Vintage Books. (Original work published 1867)

Marx, K., & Engels, F. (1965). *The German ideology*. London: Lawrence & Wishart. (Original work published 1932)

Mepham, J., & Ruben, D. (1979). *Issues in Marxist philosophy: Materialism* (Vol. 2). Sussex, England: Harvester Press.

Monod, J. (1971). *Chance and necessity: An essay on the natural philosophy of modern biology* (A. Wainhouse, Trans.). New York: Knopf. (Original work published 1970)

Novack, G. (1975). *Pragmatism versus Marxism*. New York: Pathfinder Press.

Novack, G. (1978). *Polemics in Marxist philosophy*. New York: Monad Press.

Ollman, B., & Vernoff, E. (1982). *The left academy: Marxist scholarship on American campuses*. New York: McGraw-Hill.

Rosenberg, N. (1991, December). Essay: Marx wasn't all wrong. *Scientific American*, p. 158.

Sheehan, H. (1985). *Marxism and the philosophy of science: A critical history*. Atlantic Highlands, NJ: Humanities Press.

Sidman, M. (1989). *Coercion and its fallout*. Boston: Authors Cooperative.

Skinner, B. F. (1969). Behaviorism at fifty. In *Contingencies of reinforcement: A theoretical analysis* (pp. 221–268). New York: Appleton-Century-Crofts.

Skinner, B. F. (1971). *Beyond freedom and dignity*. New York: Knopf.

Skinner, B. F. (1984). *The shaping of a behaviorist*. New York: New York University Press.

Skinner, B. F. (1988). Selection by consequences. In A. C. Catania & S. Harnad (Eds.), *The selection of behavior: The operant behaviorism of B. F. Skinner: Comments and consequences* (pp. 11–76), Cambridge, England: Cambridge University Press. (Original work published 1981)

Skinner, B. F. (1992). *Verbal behavior*. Acton, MA: Copley. (Original work published 1957)

Smith, T. L. (1986). Biology as allegory: A review of Elliot Sober's *The Nature of Selection*. *Journal of the Experimental Analysis of Behavior, 46,* 105–112.

Sober, E. (1984). *The nature of selection: Evolutionary theory in philosophical focus*. Cambridge, MA: MIT Press.

Tablada, C. (1989). *Che Guevara: Economics and politics in the transition to socialism* (M. Baumann, Trans.). Sidney: Pathfinder/Pacific and Asia. (Original work published 1987)

Trotsky, L. (1973). Their morals and ours. In L. Trotsky, J. Dewey, & G. Novack, *Their morals and ours: Marxist vs. liberal views on morality* (5th ed., pp. 13–52). New York: Pathfinder Press. (Original work published 1938)

Ulman, J. (1979). A critique of Skinnerism: Materialism minus the dialectic. *Behaviorists for Social Action Journal, 1*(2), 1–8.

Ulman, J. (1983) . Toward a united front: A class analysis of social and political action. *Behaviorists for Social Action Journal, 4*(1), 17–24.

Ulman, J. (1986a). A behavioral-Marxist reply to Schwartz and Lacey. *Behaviorism, 14,* 45–49.

Ulman, J. (1986b). Working class strategies for world peace. *Behavior Analysis and Social Action, 5,* 38–43.

Ulman, J. (1986c, May). *Historical materialism, culture, and the science of human behavior*. Paper presented at the meeting of the Association for Behavior Analysis, Milwaukee, WI.

Ulman, J. (1988). Just say no to commodity fetishism: A reply to Rakos. *Behavior Analysis and Social Action, 6*(2), 25–32.

Ulman, J. D. (1990). Beyond the carrot and the stick: A rejoinder to Rakos. *Behavior Analysis and Social Action, 7,* 30–34.

Ulman, J. D. (1991). Toward a synthesis of Marx and Skinner. *Behavior and Social Issues, 1*(1), 57–70.

Ulman, J. D. (Ed.). (1992). Behavior influence in Cuba [Special series]. *Behavior and Social Issues, 2*(2).

Ulman, J. D. (in press). Radical behaviorism, selectionism, and social action. In I. Parker & R. Spears (Eds.), *Psychology and Marxism: Coexistence and contradiction*. London: Pluto Press.

Vargas, E. A. (1975). Rights: A behavioristic analysis. *Behaviorism, 3,* 178–190.

Vargas, E. A. (1985). Cultural contingencies: A review of Marvin Harris's *Cannibals and Kings. Journal of the Experimental Analysis of Behavior, 43,* 419–428.

Wright, E. O., Levine, A., & Sober, E. (1992). *Reconstructing Marxism: Essays on explanation and the theory of history.* New York: Verso.

20

THE DIALECTICS OF EFFECTIVE TREATMENT OF BORDERLINE PERSONALITY DISORDER

MARSHA M. LINEHAN and HENRY SCHMIDT III

The universe is so constructed that the opposite of a true statement is a false statement, but the opposite of a profound truth is usually another profound truth.

N. Bohr, cited in *The Spectrum of Consciousness*

In this chapter we describe the theoretical bases of dialectical behavioral therapy (DBT). DBT was originally developed to treat suicidal behaviors (Linehan, 1987), was expanded to treat borderline personality disorder (BPD; Linehan, 1993a, 1993b), and is currently being expanded once again to treat substance abusers (Linehan, 1993c). To our knowledge, however, the only empirical investigations of the treatment have been with chronically suicidal BPD clients (Barley et al., 1993; Linehan, Armstrong, Suarez, Allmon, & Heard, 1991; Linehan & Heard, 1993; Linehan, Heard, & Armstrong, 1993; Linehan, Tutek, & Heard, 1992). These studies have demonstrated the effectiveness of DBT when compared with standard "treatment as usual" in the community. As the treatment's name suggests, the concepts of synthesis and integration are important in DBT. The treatment evolved from a tension between an emphasis on change, typical of behavior therapy interventions, and an emphasis on radical acceptance of the client "in the moment," which is seen by Linehan as a requisite stance for treating severely impaired individuals. Although the concept of acceptance is ubiquitous in psychotherapy, the strategies of acceptance in DBT were drawn primarily from Western client-centered approaches (e.g., Rogers & Truax, 1967) and Eastern philosophies, particularly Zen philosophy and practice. The tension inherent in the opposition of acceptance versus change, which Linehan proposed as the core tension in psychotherapy, required a theoretical framework that could both accommodate and ultimately synthesize opposing views. A dialectical theoretical and philosophical position provided such a framework.

The focus in this chapter is on describing the dialectical bases of the treatment. Although the principles of both learning and of Zen practice are extremely important to understanding and applying DBT, we describe them only briefly here. As noted by Heard and Linehan (1994) and described more fully by Linehan (1993a), the behavioral theory underlying DBT is closest to the psychological behaviorism advocated by Staats (1975). Similar to Staats's approach, the biosocial theory of borderline personality disorder offered by Linehan integrates basic theories of emotion and temperament (Cacioppo, Klein, Bernston, & Hatfield, 1993; Derryberry & Rothbart, 1984, 1988; Ekman, Levenson, & Friesen, 1983; Eliasz, 1985; Izard, Kagan, & Zajonc, 1984; Izard & Kobak, 1991; Kagan & Snidman, 1991; Malatesta, 1990; McGuire, 1993; Strelau, 1985), cognitive and social learning theories (e.g., Bernard & Teasdale, 1991), as well as principles of operant and classical conditioning. The integration of Zen within DBT is described in Heard and Linehan (1994) and is not discussed here. The astute reader, however, will note that the dialectical principles of interrelatedness and change are similar to the emphasis on unity and impermanence in Zen; the dialectical notion of opposition can be compared to the "harmony of empty oneness and the world of particulars" (p. 143), which is the definition of Zen given by Zen master Robert Aitken (1982).

DIALECTICS

Dialectics has been referred to as the logic of process. Most often associated with Marx and Marxist socioeconomic principles, the philosophy of dialectics actually dates back thousands of years (Bopp & Weeks, 1984; Kaminstein, 1987). Hegel is generally credited with reviving and elaborating the dialectical position. He discerned that specific forms or arguments come and go in a complex interplay, with each argument creating its own contradiction, and each contradiction in turn being negated by a synthesis that often included or enlarged on both preceding arguments, beginning the entire process anew. What remains consistent, and thus becomes worthy of study and philosophical explication, is the process of change. Hegel wrote that "appearance is the process of arising and being and passing away again, a process that itself does not arise and pass away, but is per se, and constitutes reality and the life-movement of truth" (cited in Weiss, 1974, p. 8). As such, "the truth of the process is not to be found in any of its single phases, but in its totality (which is no mere plurality), the rational rhythm of the organic whole" (cited in Weiss, 1974, p. 8).

Dialectics has been offered as a coherent system of exploring and understanding the world (Basseches, 1984; Kaminstein, 1987; Levins & Lewontin, 1985; Riegel, 1975; Wells, 1972) and has been given often as an alternative to the classificatory logic found in traditional science. After all, "real life operates dialectically, not critically" (Berman, 1981, p. 23). Hegelian dialectics is the philosophy of movement, of processes unfolding in time, and of the interactions among phenomena that make up the beginning, middle, and end of any process. An extensive discussion of dialectical philosophy (in its various incarnations) may be found in Wells (1972) and Reese (1993). A few paragraphs here would not do the philosophy justice, but they are necessary to flesh out the developmental background of DBT and to provide a rationale for some of its tactics and goals.

The Philosophy of Dialectics

One difficulty in presenting the viewpoint of dialectics is the inherent contradiction between a dynamic philosophy and a linear form of communication. Hegel pointed out that within each beginning is necessarily found an endpoint, for the beginning is posited only on the assumption of some process that is unfolding toward an end; there is no beginning without an explicit reference to a process and conclusion. Thus, each beginning also contains its own endpoint and also includes the potential for developing toward that endpoint. Conversely, each endpoint contains its own beginning and developmental history.

> A beginning, Hegel will say, in the sense of something primary and underived, not only makes an assumption but is an assumption, and its fate is to be abolished as such. Any proper, self-respecting beginning, he holds, suffers this fate at its own hands, its negation being the result of an immanent dialectic that abhors the vacuous abstraction of immediacy and converts its promise into a performance. (Weiss, 1974, p. 3)

The process whereby a phenomenon is transformed is the dialectic, which essentially is a three-stage process. The first stage is the beginning (which, of course, is essentially indivisible from the ending). It is the initial proposition, a positive statement, an affirmation (e.g., "life has meaning and possibility"). The second stage involves the negation of the beginning phenomenon and is therefore the contradiction of the initial proposition.

It is the suicidal patient denying that life has possibility or relevance. The contradiction is resolved in its third stage through the negation of the negation. Hegel indicated that the thesis and antithesis are more fully developed by the synthesis; Marxist theory states that the synthesis actually replaces the contradiction or transforms one of the opposites into the other (Reese, 1993). DBT would look for the synthesis that combines the two arguments, thesis and antithesis. It is important to note that the final stage also marks the beginning of a new dialectic at a level higher than the previous, incorporating as it does aspects of both of the former levels. Thus, the task for the suicidal patient is to come to grips with a life that both is inherently meaningful and entirely irrelevant.

The debate concerning what forces actually drive the process of synthesis or resolution is one that divides those espousing the dialectical viewpoint. Dialectical materialism contains a root metaphor that is "a concrete, goal-directed act being performed by a human being in a concrete situation at a specific time" (Reese, 1993, p. 72). (Marxism, which is a particular instantiation of the dialectical materialistic worldview, holds labor, or production, as the root metaphor.) As such, behaviors are grounded within a particular context, with a given history, and are directed at the achievement of a particular goal; the resolution of contradiction requires an active participant. (Reese, 1993, clearly outlined an argument that placed dialectical materialism directly in line with the contextualist viewpoint.) Hegelian dialectics, or dialectical idealism, views the resolution of contradiction as an evolution toward some teleological end (Reese, 1993). "The supreme principle and truth of the universe is *one*, an undivided unity of differences, which is enriched rather than dissipated by the multitude of its manifestations" (Weiss, 1974, p. 5). Thus, each dialectical interplay of contradiction and unity is activated through the force of expression of truth. Reese (1993) pointed to Piaget's genetic epistemology as an example of dialectical idealism instantiated (p. 73). DBT proposes that dialectics describe far more of the universe than can be tied to human intervention and encourages clients to observe the interaction of seeming intangibles such as good–evil, black–white, warmth–coolness, and so on, while nonetheless admitting that it has been humans who have created such distinctions. DBT directs the client's attention to what appears to be a larger natural process in which humans participate rather than place themselves as the creative center of the process.

There are several other essential tenets of dialectics. First, it is assumed that a "whole" is a relation of heterogeneous "parts" that hold no intrinsic or previous significance in and of themselves. The parts are important only in relation to one another and in relation to the whole that they help to define. (To dispense with the distraction of placing quotes around the words *part* and *whole* for the duration of the chapter, we assume that the inherent subjectivity of such a view is noted by the reader. The two are indivisible within the dialectical reasoning.) Levins and Lewontin (1985, p. 278) pointed out that the consideration of phenomena as heterogeneously composed has important implications for scientific inquiry. The fact that parts are not merely diverse but are actually in contradiction or opposition to one another focuses the observer not on a taxonomical identification of the parts but on the relationship or interaction of the two as they move toward resolution. Also, the fact that wholes comprise heterogeneous parts argues that "there is no basement," no fundamental unit or particle. What is fundamental is the pattern of relationship.

Second, the parts acquire properties only as a result of being identified as parts of a particular whole. Thus, the same part may have much different qualities or properties if viewed as an aspect of different wholes. Of course, parts of different wholes will embody different contradictions and dialectical syntheses. Third, parts and wholes are interrelations, not mere collisions of objects with fixed properties and immutable boundaries. As such, the parts cannot participate in creating the whole without being simultaneously affected themselves by the whole. Thus, we argue, for instance, that it is not possible for the inpatients of a particular mental health center not to somehow alter the system within which they interact (and which would not exist without them), and it is certainly the case that they will simultaneously be affected by the system.

Fourth, as mentioned already, dialectics recognizes that change is an aspect of all systems and is present at all levels of a system. Stability is the rare occurrence, not the idealized goal. However, as Levins and Lewontin (1985, pp. 274–282) pointed out, dialectics should not be viewed as some dynamic balance or homeostatic environment; it is neither the careful balance of opposing forces nor the melding of two open currents. Rather, dialectics involves the complex interplay of opposing forces. The white yin and black yang of Eastern philosophies do not combine to form a tepid, gray mush but continue to oppose one another, surging here and receding there as they respond to both internal and external forces. Equilibrium among forces, when found, is discovered at a higher level of observation, namely, by looking at the overall process of affirming, negating, and the formation of a new, more inclusive synthesis of the two (Basseches, 1984, pp. 57–59). What is stable is the continued interplay of forces; there can be no final domination. Thus, change is not the superficial pattern masking some underlying stability; it is the underlying dance of the world, and stasis is one's own imposition of convenience based on societal values (Levins & Lewontin, 1985, p. 275).

Finally, it would be helpful to examine the root metaphors of dialectics to see how they might relate to the therapeutic process and to DBT in particular. As discussed by Reese (1993), dialectical materialism has its base in the concept of *praxis*. Although this term has different levels of meaning, the sense common to all of them is "a concrete, goal-directed act being performed by a human being in a concrete situation at a specific time" (Reese, 1993, p. 72). Praxis is thus the linchpin of dialectical materialism, the central element on which analyses rest. The "energy" in dialectical materialism, the force that ultimately drives the creation and synthesis of opposites, is the efforts of humans to enforce change in their world (see Reese, 1993, for an extended discussion of this). Although some may recoil at this distinctly anthropocentric viewpoint, it is perhaps refreshing to others to note the acknowledgment of human activity inherent in people's understanding of the world around them (see Jaeger & Rosnow, 1988). By contrast, the process of struggle and unity of opposites in dialectical idealism is energized by the universal truth bursting forth in manifold ways. In some way the universe itself is driving the process, delighting in its display of manifest truth (dialectical change). DBT moves back and forth between the two views, using human activity as a motivator in some instances (e.g., pointing out the contradiction between the cultural ideals created and upheld by humans and actual body types of individuals) and larger, natural contradictions in others (e.g., the interplay of chance and skill in the outcome of human interventions). Although the philosophy of dialectical materialism relevant to DBT (corresponding to behavioral theory as a foundation of DBT) views humans as imposing an order on an uncaring world, dialectical idealism (corresponding to the roots of DBT in Zen psychology) believes that people can recognize and experience a unity and pattern inherent in the organization of the universe.

The definition of praxis as human activity unfolding toward a specific goal within a given context is one that naturally lends itself to the therapeutic environment. It contributes both a focus for therapeutic inquiry (behavioral analysis) and a structure for contemplating knowledge and truth (the effectiveness of behavior). Praxis is the fulcrum that supports theory or belief on one end and reality or context on the other; people's theories about how the world works are continually being put to the test in their attempts to modify or effect change within it. Experience gained during one's efforts may then be used to modify knowledge and thus to inform future interventions. Of course, just as one cannot step into the same stream twice, dialectics would acknowledge that people interact with a constantly changing world, albeit one that may have some consistency. Dialectical analysis of actions and theories encourages people to stay awake, to continue to review their beliefs about the world that fuel their interventions, and to remain open to the impact of their actions and to feedback from the environment. Humans are encouraged to engage the world and simultaneously observe its response and effects on them, with their natural inclinations being to maximize the success of their actions.

Therapeutically, the application of behavioral principles to a given client requires just such open experimentation. A basic example is in constructing a contingency plan for behaviors exhibited by the client. Reinforcers and punishers are not universal phenomena. Praise may be either reinforcing or punishing to an individual (see Emotional Vulnerability Versus Self-Invalidation section for the DBT caution concerning praise with BPD individuals), and thus the therapist must be aware of the response of the client, including whether the behavior that the therapist praised occurs more or less frequently in the future, and rely less on his or her own assumptions about whether a given behavior is reinforcing.

Before proceeding, two caveats are important. First, dialectics is an attempt to study movement and change by using a language that has been shaped assuming the fundamental stability of nature. Deitz (1986) discussed the influence of "mental idioms," common words that do not always mean what they seem to mean. Particularly relevant to our discussion is the section devoted to nouns that masquerade as "person, place, or thing." Some of these nouns are the "heuristic concepts" noted in frustration by Bateson (1979), including notables such as *patience*, *length*, and even *mind*. Other nouns are those that, to paraphrase Skinner, "find, or seem to find, things where there are only actions" (cited in Deitz, 1986, p. 163). Of course, Skinner could not phrase the sentence without using one of the nouns that he criticized; *action*, like *activity*, is the noun form of an event occurring in real time. What we are attempting to capture through the noun is the movement of one *acting*, movement that is much more "sensible" in the gerund form (i.e., one has more of a sense of movement when one is discussing "acting" rather than discussing a discrete "act"). In essence, people's language has turned many of their processes into static entities, and these in turn shape their thought to attend to completed events rather than the flowing stream of activity and interaction of forces.

Second, we discuss briefly the issue of dialectics as opposed to other ways of viewing the world. It is important to recognize that arguments between proponents of differing worldviews are, in essence, "illegitimate" and nonresolvable (Hayes, Hayes, & Reese, 1988). Causal and dialectical logic are, in and of themselves, differing worldviews (Wells, 1972). Thus, although both levels of examination may be appropriate when answering different questions, those who are inclined to argue the merits of one system over the other are doomed from the start. Not only is it senseless to use the values of one to criticize another, but to point out the shortcomings of one worldview does nothing to strengthen the position of the second (Hayes et al., 1988). Linehan advocates dialectics because the viewpoint has been extremely helpful in directing treatment with specific populations, and because, as she and her colleagues have devoted more of their efforts to observing "process," they have come to new realizations concerning DBT itself and new ways of looking at therapy in general.

Dialectics and Psychology

Although not the foundation of a formal school of thought within psychology, dialectical methods and inquiry have found a small following. Dialectics has shaped the thinking of articles in topic areas as diverse as development (Basseches, 1984; Riegel, 1975), cognitive development (Kramer & Melchior, 1990), interpersonal communication and creativity (Spitzberg, 1993; Thompson, 1991), and organizational behavior (Schwenk, 1990). We have already pointed out that dialectics have been theoretically tied to contextualism (Reese, 1993), which is itself the root metaphor underlying the application of radical behavioral techniques to therapy (see Hayes, 1987).

Within cognitive developmental theory, Basseches (1984) and Kramer and Melchior (1990) proposed that dialectical thinking is the final stage of cognitive development, superceding Piaget's stage of formal operations. Whereas formal operational thought enables a thinker to deal with closed systems as wholes, those authors proposed that dialectical thinking enables one to organize the interactions of multiple systems over time and thus engages one in thinking about the nature of *systems* rather than about the nature of *parts* in one system. Kramer and Melchior (1990) wrote that a number of cognitive developmental psychologists have now recognized this ability, placing the rudiments of dialectical thinking in adolescence. Furthermore, they noted that females tend to develop dialectical thinking several years earlier than males, perhaps because of the necessity of balancing conflicting role options and demands during adolescent decision-making. These results would seem to indicate that therapy with BPD clients, who appear to demonstrate a marked deficiency in dialectical thinking, should include specific strategies to foster more dialectical approaches to viewing the world and interacting with it. DBT does both.

Dialectics and BPD

DBT is based on a biosocial theory that assumes that BPD is the outcome of a transaction between an individual with a constitutional vulnerability to emotion dysregulation and an environment that is prone to invalidate the expression of private experiences, beliefs, and actions (Linehan, 1993a). In contrast to theories such as the stress–diathesis model (which posits that an inherent debilitating factor resides within the individual, awaiting activation by events within the environment), DBT suggests that the individual and the environment are developmentally coactive in providing conditions for the development of dysfunction. On the one hand, the individual "elicits" the environment that creates dysfunction, and, on the other hand, the environment exacerbates vulnerabilities that, in a more benign environment, might not have developed. In the first case, the individual eliciting the invalidating environment, the theory is similar to Millon's (Millon & Everly, 1985) biosocial learning theory of personality disorders, wherein childhood biological substrates lead to behaviors that elicit particular classes of response from caretakers and begin to establish patterns of interaction that later "crystallize" into personality.

Linehan (1987, 1993a) posited that BPD individuals have a biological predisposition toward emotional dysregulation. As such, emotional responses to environmental stimuli occur more quickly, are more intense, and have a slower return to baseline than responses of non-BPD individuals. This creates the potential for an individual who will not only respond strongly, but one who may be inclined to display increasingly intense levels of responding attributable to continued environmental input before return to baseline has occurred, creating a vicious feedback cycle. As such, babies who are easily subject to overstimulation may withdraw more readily from close contact initiated by their parents, a tendency that is not likely to reinforce parents who are seeking closeness or responsiveness. This withdrawal may prompt a response from the parents, such as intensified efforts to attract the infant or perhaps giving the infant less attention. Either response will elicit yet another response from the infant, until a pattern of interaction begins to emerge that more or less consistently characterizes the relations of the family constellation. (See Scarr & McCartney, 1983, for a further discussion of this point.)

The invalidating environment is one in which actions and communication of private experiences are met by erratic, inappropriate, extreme responses. The fundamental message sent to the individual is that his or her typical responses to events are invalid, incorrect, or inaccurate. In such environments, verbal expressions are not taken as accurate descriptions of private experience. Both verbal and nonverbal expressions and actions are not taken as valid responses to events; are punished, trivialized, dismissed, or disregarded; or are attributed to socially unacceptable characteristics such as overreactivity, inability to see things realistically, lack of motivation, motivation to harm or manipulate, lack of discipline, or failure to adopt a positive (or, conversely, discriminating) attitude. In such environments, escalation of emotional displays or communication efforts are frequently met by erratic, intermittent reinforcement. Restrictions are often placed on the type and degree of demand that the person can put on the environment. The invalidating environment typically produces a need for extreme behaviors in order to have problems recognized. The end result of such an environment for those who are highly responsive and who are not taught emotion coping skills (because problems are essentially denied) is that extreme emotional outbursts may become adaptive behaviors.

Dialectical Dilemmas

Along with the primary dialectic between the emotionally dysregulated individual and the invalidating environment, Linehan (1987, 1993a) proposed three additional dialectical patterns of behavior frequently observed among BPD individuals. All three are not necessarily issues for every person meeting criteria for BPD, but, on the basis of clinical observation, they seem to be typical of the group as a whole.[1] These patterns may be represented as polar positions on three major axes: emotional vulnerability versus self-invalidation, unrelenting crisis versus inhibited grieving, and active passivity versus apparent competence. Neither end is inherently dysfunctional; rather, it is the rapid or wide swings between the two that typifies the borderline individual's process. Although most individuals will recognize these dialectical dilemmas as representative of their own behaviors at certain points in their lives, it is the inability of the BPD individuals to synthesize the poles and transcend the dichotomy that typifies their behavior. BPD individuals are seemingly fixed at a level of observation that is bound too tightly; they are neither able to break free from their vacillations between opposing positions nor are they able to enlarge their contextual framework to allow for a synthesis and resolution of the two poles.

Emotional Vulnerability Versus Self-Invalidation

The term *emotional vulnerability* refers to the extreme sensitivity to emotional arousal and susceptibility to negative emotions, together with the individual's awareness or experience of this vulnerability. Linehan (1993a) hypothesized that individuals with BPD have emotional responses to environmental stimuli that occur more quickly, are more intense, and have a slower return to baseline than the responses of non-BPD individuals. There are consequences of this vulnerability and to the individual's awareness and experience of it. First, emotions are postulated to be primary to experience (e.g., Zajonc, 1984) and are entire-system responses, which is to say that an emotion cannot be separated from the processes of cognition or physiology; it is instead, the substrate or medium within which these systems operate (Malatesta, 1990; see also Smith & Lazarus, 1990). Individuals with BPD often appear to experience difficulty regulating the entire pattern of responses that accompany a particular emotional state (Linehan, 1993a). As such, people with BPD are the prototypical examples of the James-Lange (James, 1884; Lange, 1885) theory of emotion, finding themselves running away from the bear before they have realized that they are

---

[1]DBT encourages practitioners to assess each client individually before drawing any conclusions concerning characteristic patterns of behavior. In this way, it is more similar to the "discovery-oriented philosophy" of science advocated by Follette, Houts, and Hayes (1992) than the medical model advocated by taxonomic categorization of behavior.

fearful. Thus, they may not be able to interrupt obsessive ruminations or block escape behaviors commonly associated with fear. Although Zajonc (1984) would argue that all emotions precede people's cognitive appraisal of a situation, Smith and Lazarus (1990) pointed out that cognitive activity is exceedingly important to their experience of any given emotion. Specifically,

> more complicated species have to stake their security on the capacity to evaluate the significance of what is happening. . . . However, because there is no simple mapping between objective stimulus properties and adaptive significance, the task of detecting significant events becomes quite formidable, and to accomplish it the organism must be able to somehow classify what is being confronted into a relatively small number of categories, corresponding to the various kinds of harm or benefit it may face. Above all, the emotional response is not a reaction to a stimulus, but to an organism (person)-environment *relationship*. (Smith & Lazarus, 1990, p. 614)

Thus, Smith and Lazarus (1990) linked emotional experiencing to a biological substrate in dialectical engagement with cognitive processes, which are in turn shaped by sociocultural learning. Individuals with BPD may find themselves at a disadvantage in all three areas, given that they may have disruption in both biological (reactivity) and cognitive (memory, cognitive development) systems that are further compounded by the poorness of fit with their family system.

In addition to difficulties in regulating emotions, intense emotional arousal interferes with other ongoing behavioral responses. As a result, the most carefully laid plans or well-rehearsed response may be beyond reach as emotional response levels rise. Furthermore, the unpredictable onset and inability to control intense emotional reactions lead to a sense of loss of control and unpredictability about the self. This is not to say that there are not times when control is possible but that the prediction of those times is uncertain. Finally, this sense of being out of control leads to specific fears that increase emotional vulnerability even more. For instance, fears of novel situations or situations in which the individual is out of control are increased, and such situations are either strictly avoided or met with intense efforts to assert control. As such, an entire range of experiences (novel situations) is missed with their concomitant broadening of experience or extension of competencies. Similarly, outcomes that might have been possible were the individual not attempting to dominate the flow of events are blocked off; positive events and outcomes are limited, and negative outcomes that are based on repetition of previously ineffective strategies are increased. Such experiences inevitably would seem to increase one's sense of vulnerability.

In addition to the fear of situations in which there is loss of control, individuals with BPD also demonstrate intense fears surrounding the expectations of individuals with whom they have significant relationships (Linehan, 1993a). The reason is simple: An inability to predict under what circumstances they will perform well leads them to question when they will be able to meet expectations. Additionally, individuals with BPD often have a history of disappointing others who have expected things that they are incapable of delivering (e.g., being unable to simply smile through pain and ignore their emotional discomfort). As such, praise from significant others may be associated with a history of increased expectations, and therefore they may elicit a negative reaction from individuals with BPD. Praise in these instances comes to be associated with expectations that the individual can perform the praised behavior in different situations or at different times. The pairing of praise with expectations, and the subsequent pain of not meeting those expectations, creates an aversion to praise in some BPD individuals and a situation that may increase suffering as they scramble to undo the praise or, conversely, to exceed their current capabilities and please the friend or family member.

At the other end of this dialectic is *self-invalidation*. Self-invalidation is the adoption by individuals with BPD of the attitudes and characteristics of the invalidating environment. This adoption means that these individuals will tend to mistrust their own perceptions of reality and thus lose some sense of their individual identities. Although one might easily imagine such a loss of self occurring in extreme circumstances (such as "brainwashing" prisoners of war), the radical behavioral view of "self" development easily explains such a process. In fact, given the total domination of family over the activities and socialization of some children, it is difficult to imagine how children subjected to such invalidation could help but adopt the prevailing attitudes.

The radical behaviorist view claims that identity, or "self," is a product of one's verbal community and is learned as the "constant" that is referred to by others seeking one's point of view; it is the "you" in sentences and questions addressed to a child (see Kohlenberg & Tsai, 1991). It is fostered through parental (or other) attention to minute changes in behavior on the part of the child and correct labeling of what the new behavior may represent in terms of the child's internal state. For instance, irritability may be caused by fatigue, hunger, or a host of other conditions. Correct identification of the cause of discomfort and communication of this to the child increases the child's ability to identify and report on his or her own internal states. Lack of consistent identification and validation of that viewpoint may therefore interfere with the development of a consistent sense of identity.

Theoretically, there may be multiple adverse consequences of being raised in an invalidating environment (Linehan, 1993a). First, given the enormous pressure to mask negative emotions, a BPD individual's conscious experience of them may be greatly curtailed. Along with this, the ability to recognize and label emotions appropriately is left undeveloped, leaving individuals confused and unable to validate their own emotional experiences or those of others. Third, individuals do not learn to trust their own emotional experiences as valid reflections of individual and situational events. Furthermore, if, as often happens in invalidating environments, communication of negative emotions is punished, then a secondary reaction of guilt and shame begins to be associated with the initial experience of negative emotions, further increasing the avoidance of experiencing them in the first place. In response to such an environment, the individual will need to escalate the intensity of his or her emotional responses or the presentation of environmental circumstances to be validated. Such individuals may also learn to scan the environment for cues of what is appropriate behavior. Both are adaptive measures in a world in which emotions are experienced as highly intrusive, yet something to be feared.

A fourth consequence of living in an invalidating environment may be that individuals learn to apply the behavior change tactics of the environment to themselves. As such, they tend to set unrealistic goals for behavior for themselves and to punish themselves for not attaining their goals, ignoring the possible incremental changes in responding by which they may have progressed. The powerful principles of shaping are never learned; individuals may find themselves trapped in a vicious cycle of attempting to interact with their environments while being unsure of their ability to respond, setting goals that far exceed their capabilities, and inevitably failing to live up to those goals. Furthermore, such individuals may miss behaviors representing approximations toward their goals, thereby failing to profit from any positive increments of change in effectiveness of their behavior that may be built on in responding to future similar situations. Despondency or desperation increase, with concordant emotional reaction and lowering of ability to respond nonemotionally, and the rollercoaster continues.

It is important to note the interconnection of the two ends of the dialectic. Dialectics allow for the juxtaposition of any two aspects of being (in this case, behaviors) that are relevant (see Reese, 1993). This is to say that there must be some intrinsic connection between the two ends of the dialectic and some meaningful movement between the two ends that can end in synthesis and the concurrent creation of a new dialectic that incorporates elements of the prior thesis and antithesis. The dialectic of emotional vulnerability versus self-invalidation may be seen as the substrate of experience that necessarily colors the rest of the BPD individual's life. As noted by Malatesta (1990), "emotions or moods act as selective filters on the world, controlling perception and hence one's interpretation of reality" (p. 10). Furthermore, although basic emotional programs appear to be hard-wired into the mammalian nervous system . . . humans, and possibly other primates, are capable of exerting instrumental control over the behavioral expression of emotion. Most commonly this control takes the form of *intensifying or deintensifying the basic emotional expression or qualifying it in some way.* (Malatesta, 1990, p. 16, italics added)

For individuals with BPD, the experience of attempting to control their emotions has been largely through adopting the environmental biases of denial and invalidation. Such strategies are not only ineffective but may be damaging to the development of what may be considered the second most primary experience, that of self. It is along this continuum from domination by emotional reactivity to domination of environmental control that the individual with BDP moves. It is at this level that interventions must be directed if he or she is to address the dialectic and allow a synthesis to emerge.

Linehan (1993a) noted that the dialectical dilemma for individuals with BPD lies between accepting the environmental evaluations placed on them (i.e., they are able to control their emotional responses, and they are bad or evil for not doing so) and accepting their own subjective experience (i.e., they have little control over their own emotional responses and the world is inherently unfair for subjecting them to such trials). A closely related dilemma revolves on whom to blame for their situation, the environment that makes them feel bad or themselves for their apparent lack of control over their own emotions and experiences. Assisting the client to achieve some synthesis between the two positions also places the therapist in the dilemma of whether to validate the pain of the client (and thus be seen as not attempting to help) or induce change in the client (and thereby invalidate the pain the client is experiencing or overestimate the client's abilities, re-creating his or her environment of origin). Resolution of the therapist's dilemma involves swift movement from validating pain to confronting the client's interpretations and suggesting constructive change. Change is necessary *because* the pain is so intense.

Active Passivity Versus Apparent Competence

"Active passivity" describes the tendency on the part of the patient to approach problems passively, demanding that the environment or persons in the environment offer solutions. Thus, the individual is actively expecting that others solve the problem instead of actively attempting a solution himself or herself. Such behaviors have also been noticed in "high monitors" of medical research (Miller & Mangan, 1983). The learned helplessness model of learning (Seligman, 1975) may help to describe the etiology of some of this behavior. Individuals with BPD often vacillate between the classical learned helplessness of passive apathy and giving up versus active (albeit often indirect) attempts to elicit help from the environment. Given a history of inability to meet behavioral demands of the social environment despite one's best efforts, and an environment in which coping strategies are neither taught nor recognized as necessary steps toward the behaviors demanded, the individual is left in a no-win situation of being asked to respond appropriately without being taught how. The properties of active passivity have been documented in hospitalized parasuicide patients (Linehan, Camper, Chiles, Strosahl, & Shearin, 1987) and have been noted by other researchers to be corollaries of BPD (Perry & Cooper, 1985).

The term *apparent competence* (Linehan, 1987, 1993a) refers to the tendency of individuals with BPD to appear to observers to be more emotionally and behaviorally competent than they in fact are. Such apparent competency is a result of two distinct patterns. First, people with BPD often display effective and appropriate behaviors in a given situation, yet they behave remarkably inappropriately or claim no knowledge of what is appropriate in (seemingly, to the observer) similar situations. For instance, individuals with BPD may demonstrate very good skills in assisting others, but they may not necessarily be able to apply the same skills to similar situations in their own lives. Unfortunately for such people, apparent competence works against them by predisposing others to be resistant to offer assistance, assuming that they possess the skills necessary to solve their own problems and are simply unwilling to use them.

These "apparently competent" behaviors may be the result of a number of factors. First, as Millon (1981) suggested, the defining characteristic of this disorder may be that individuals are "stably unstable." Competencies that are displayed in one context simply do not generalize for individuals with BPD to other situations. This may be due to learning that occurs in one mood state or situation that simply does not generalize to other mood states or situational settings (see Mischel, 1968, 1984). Given the extreme fluctuations and unpredictability of moods in individuals with BPD, it would be most difficult to predict when abilities performed in one setting would be available in another.

A second behavioral pattern that may contribute to the display of apparent competence is the learned pattern of masking negative emotions that was encouraged in the invalidating environment of childhood or family of origin (Linehan, 1993a). The individual may automatically inhibit the display of negative emotions, placing the observer in the position of assuming that nonverbal displays are congruent with inner experiences. Thus, an observer may not even be aware that the individual is in distress. In addition, individuals with BPD also may have adopted some of the expectations of their early environments, namely, that they will be consis-

tently competent across situations. Despite their experience of unpredictability and of discomfort or distress in a given situation, they may communicate assurances that are based on others' expectations.

Finally, clinical observations suggest that individuals with BPD are
able to respond with competence in two specific interpersonal situations:
Either the person is in the presence of a supportive, nurturing individual
or he or she has the perception of being in a secure, supportive, and stable
relationship. For example, in a therapy session discussion of distressing
events may proceed smoothly, given that the client perceives the therapist
as supportive. Hours later, however, the therapist may receive a call from
the same client who is now experiencing great distress in response to the
session. It would appear as though the supportive influence of the therapist
is reduced when she or he is no longer present with the client. It may be
difficult for significant others in the client's life to understand how the
client, in the presence of the painful stimuli, can act competently and then
fall apart later. Again, the client may be punished for reaching out at this
time by those who infer motives of manipulation as a result of their own
confusion as observers.

The dialectical dilemma for individuals with BPD is to resolve their
experiences of moving between the extremes of either communicating effectively to others their need for assistance in coping and, conversely, dealing with the shame of asking for help and the fear of losing significant
others who provide assistance (Linehan, 1993a). Learning to help oneself
involves learning to communicate effectively when one needs assistance
and to predict situations wherein one may find oneself in need. The pattern
of short-term versus long-term gains must be examined. Secondary gains
that reinforce passivity (i.e., reduced performance anxiety, relational benefits, etc.) are poor exchanges for the long-term costs, which may include
lower self-efficacy, a restricted range of skills, and, ultimately, reduced freedom to alter one's own circumstances. The behavioral view of self-control,
which stresses the individual coming more under the control of long-term
contingencies than short-term contingencies, is the dialectical tension that
must be uncovered and addressed. Clients who refuse to acknowledge or
consider long-term effects of their behavior are at the mercy of short-term
payoffs. Thus, communication to others must be improved to combat the
judgments resulting from apparent competencies (change in strategy), and
a realistic assessment of which behaviors the client is actually able to perform (acceptance) is necessary so that the client does not fuel the problem
by asking for help when he or she does not need it.

The dilemma for the therapist is to become more responsive to cues
and patterns that predict difficulty for the client and to recognize the
client's true capabilities so as not to unnecessarily leap in and offer assistance. Emphasizing the difficulty of change (acceptance) and requiring that
clients actively participate in solving their problems (change) is the bal-

ance to achieve: patience combined with exhortation. Therapeutic challenges to change behavior must be surrounded with validation to maintain the client in treatment and to avoid re-creating the invalidating environment of the client's early family experience.

Unrelenting Crises Versus Inhibited Grieving

Many of the BPD individual's characteristic dysfunctional behaviors are in response to a sense of being in a state of chronic, overwhelming crisis (Linehan, 1993a). High reactivity combined with a slow return to baseline create a situation in which successive events continue to drive the emotional response system, never allowing the individual to "catch his or her breath," so to speak. Using Selye's (1956) model of stress response, the client is constantly approaching the "exhaustion" stage of the stress adaptation cycle. Poor episodic memory, a characteristic of parasuicidal individuals (Williams, 1991), may decrease the ability to remember more positive emotional states or to notice the cyclicity of despair and hope. The therapist's understanding of the overwhelming sense of helplessness in the face of the onslaught of minor crises may help in working with the repetitive parasuicidal and self-abusive behaviors exhibited by the individual with BPD. When combined with resistance to helping on the part of others in the environment (often a result of the client's apparent competence), the sense of isolation for the client facing a loss may increase dramatically, leading to a more severe sense of hopelessness and possibly even completed suicide. The postulation of BPD as an emotional disorder leads to interventions to treat emotional hyperreactivity, establishing a dialectical tension within treatment (see next section) that the client must resolve, thereby modifying his or her emotional responding.

The term *inhibited grieving* refers to the repeated occurrence of trauma and loss combined with the inability of individuals with BPD to fully experience and resolve the events. Individuals with BPD have a phobic response to emotions, particularly those associated with trauma and loss. The accumulation of loss without subsequent emotional experiencing and processing may lead to two consequences. First, significant early or unexpected loss may result in sensitization to later loss (Brasted & Callahan, 1984; Callahan, Brasted, & Granados, 1983; Parkes, 1964). Second, a pattern of many losses may ultimately serve to inhibit the process of grieving itself (see "bereavement overload", Kastenbaum, 1969). These patterns also overlap with symptoms displayed in posttraumatic stress disorder. Individuals with BPD have been shown to experience more childhood loss (see Gunderson & Zanarini, 1989) than other psychiatric populations. Moreover, individuals with BPD treated by Linehan and her colleagues often exhibit a pattern that includes brief exposure to the loss through obsessive rumination, followed by an immediate attempt to distract or otherwise avoid the painful emotions associated with the exposure. Such behavioral patterns have been shown elsewhere to contribute to the incubation of distress responses (Gauthier & Marshall, 1977; Napalkov, 1963), in effect heightening the response to the distressing event rather than alleviating it.

The dialectical dilemmas for the client in synthesizing both ends of the spectrum—inhibited grieving and unrelenting crisis—are two-fold. First, it is difficult to do anything that may increase vulnerability, such as allowing oneself to experience grief and mourning, when faced with un-relenting crisis. Second, the behaviors involved in avoiding grieving (drug or alcohol abuse, denial, high-risk behaviors) often lead to further crises. In addition, avoidance behaviors do nothing to elicit social support for the client's loss, nor does it lead to resolution of the trauma. Thus, the client is caught in a pattern of jumping from the trauma of crisis to the complete inhibition of experiences associated with it. Although emotional respond-ing is addressed therapeutically through specific interventions designed to modulate its degree of expression, the grieving process itself must be al-lowed to be expressed more fully. If natural grieving is resolved through a process of moving from intense loss to appreciation of the lost object, resulting in some sense of satisfaction gained by having come into contact with that which is now lost, then the dialectical need for the client is to move toward appreciation. In other instances, grieving may be associated with anger (as in the case of sexual or physical abuse). In this case both emotional experiences are typically avoided or experienced as overwhelm-ing by an individual with BPD, and either anger or pain may elicit sec-ondary responses such as guilt or shame that have been conditioned through the responses to such emotions in childhood. As with crisis states, dialectical treatment will involve exposing the client to the core emotional responses while encouraging more skillful and adaptive responses to them.

The therapist, on the other hand, must attempt to remain focused on the larger pattern of movement within the client and not be drawn into attempting to resolve the unending carousel of crises. The therapist must offer hope that there is resolution to the crises and that grieving is both necessary and will not completely overcome the client. Simultaneously, treatment must involve validation on the part of the therapist of the pain and distress being suffered by the client (acceptance) and a demand that the client alter his or her emotional responding in ways that facilitate the experience of the emotion and modulate its intensity and duration (change).

DBT AND AFFECT DYSREGULATION

DBT is a treatment that developed in response to a specific theory concerning BPD, namely, that individuals with BPD are suffering primarily from a difficulty in affect regulation. Affect, as defined in DBT (see Linehan, 1993a, for a more extended discussion of this), involves not only brain and physiological changes but cognitions (interpretation of events), attention to environmental events, and action urges. As such, DBT has developed strategies to alter affect in any number of ways through an intervention aimed at any of the events contained within the affective response system. This particular formulation of emotion and its role in behavioral dysfunction is congruent with the emerging view (see Greenberg & Safran, 1987, for a review) that places emotion as the core element in the organization of personality (i.e., Malatesta, 1990) and as an evolutionarily important response and motivator in the interaction between organism and environment (see Smith & Lazarus, 1990). Thus, Linehan's drawing of the "boundaries" of emotion to include attending to environmental stimuli, cognitive interpretations, facial expressiveness, and action urges falls directly in line with current thinking on the subject.

DBT works with clients to sharpen their skills in attending to environmental stimuli (specifically, to widen their attentional focus and develop abilities to discriminate between relevant and irrelevant stimuli), alter cognitive patterns (i.e., take the perspective of the other actor and be more cautious in ascribing motives), change facial and body language, and improve on the quality and variety of actions available to the client when experiencing an emotion. Attention to any one of these will improve the client's ability to modulate and regulate emotional experiencing; DBT attempts to move forward in a pincerlike maneuver to work on all aspects of the client's affective experience and response by creating an environment in which the client is forced to develop new affective responses and thereby new emotional experiences. Behavior is not viewed as separable from emotion, and so to change behavior is to change emotion.

One of the more intriguing findings of emotion research involves the connection between facial expression and emotion (i.e., Ekman, Friesen, & Ellsworth, 1972). Emotions have not only motivational properties for the individual, but also may have become adaptive as signaling stimuli for others; the "hardwiring" between facial expressiveness and emotional responding is proposed to be an adaptive advantage by behavioral–expressive theorists (Ekman et al., 1972; Izard, 1977). Likewise, there is an impressive array of literature being gathered that indicates that changes in facial expression may not only be reflective of emotional changes, but may in and of themselves be instrumental in modulating the duration, intensity, or even activation of emotional experience (Duncan & Laird, 1977; Laird, 1974; Rhodewalt & Comer, 1979; Zuckerman, Klorman, Larrance, & Spiegel, 1981). Similarly, Barlow (1988) suggested that exposure-based procedures typically used to target fear-related problems are effective precisely because they block the typical action impulses of the person experiencing the emotion, which is flight, in the case of fear.

DBT uses this information to work with clients with BPD, most of whom demonstrate clearly maladaptive responses to emotion, and negative emotion in particular. The dialectic in treatment that must be maintained is to have the client experience an emotion and to block the client's typical response patterns to that emotion. Both of these are change strategies for clients, and they may be balanced with an acceptance of emotional experience that is modeled by the therapist (emotions are, in fact, inevitable and may be viewed as important guides to people in interaction with their environment; the emotional *experiences* of clients are entirely acceptable) and with acceptance of the clients' previous strategies to regulate their emotions as the best that they could do at the time. Becoming angry, self-abusive, or self-medicating may all be effective short-term strategies in dealing with an emotional system that is otherwise beyond control; they are simply not effective strategies in the long term or as a fixed set of choices.

Therefore, DBT uses contingencies set by the therapist (or contained within the treatment, such as mandatory vacation from treatment for missing four sessions in a row) to restrict the client's ability to respond in typical ways. A commitment to end suicidal and parasuicidal behavior is a prerequisite for entering treatment, and, when combined with requests that the client phone the therapist before committing such acts and restricted access to the therapist following parasuicide, such commitments force the client to dig deeper into his or her response repertoire when faced with highly charged affective responses. DBT does not leave clients to their own devices in this respect, however. While blocking the typical action patterns through contingencies, the therapist is also providing a warm, accepting environment to keep the client in treatment and is directing behavior through skill training homework and phone strategizing. Thus, DBT dialectically moves the client from a (highly maladaptive) homeostasis of dramatic response to severe emotional dysregulation into a new tension between the opposites of blocked responding and emotional experience. The resolution of the new dialectic for the client is the new behaviors coached by the therapist, including physiological change (i.e., changes in facial expressiveness and body language to move the client toward the opposite emotion and shorten the duration of the present emotion); cognitive change (i.e., expanding of interpretive possibilities of environmental events), and modified action repertoires to improve adaptivity of response. Clients are slowly moved from attempts to rigidly control phenomena into a more dialectical manner of interacting with the environment, developing patterns of emotional responding that (a) are flexible, (b) more situation–person specific, and (c) maintain the clients' contact with environmental (including physiological) stimuli while they regulate and modulate their own emotional experience. As such, clients are better able to use important information within their environment that may have been previously lost through poor attending prior to the emotional experience and loss of contact during the experience as clients withdrew or exploded while attempting to eliminate the unwanted emotion. Such flexibility and environmental contact are necessary for the enhancement of a more dialectical lifestyle and are fundamental for the development of long-term adaptive interaction strategies.

THE DIALECTICAL THERAPIST

DBT is based on a biosocial model that holds in dialectical tension two different models of behavioral dysfunction: motivation versus capability. In the motivational model, it is assumed that clients are experiencing difficulties because they lack the motivation to change. This is not to say that they do not have the will, desire, or strength to change. Motivation may include diverse elements such as having adaptive behaviors inhibited by fear, guilt, or shame; being hampered by a reinforcement history that has reinforced maladaptive responses; or operating out of a set of dysfunctional beliefs. The capability model asserts that clients do not have the skills to be effective in their environments or to change their behavior and is a model often held within the drug treatment community as the basis for relapse prevention or harm reduction programs of change. DBT moves forward with both programs simultaneously, working with clients to change their motivation to change and to provide them skills and new behavioral alternatives to use.

In effect, the two poles of motivation versus capability mirror the fundamental dialectic within DBT, that of change versus acceptance. Clinicians must attempt to change the client's motivation while accepting the client as he or she is, regardless of where the client falls on the spectrum of "skillfulness." The tightwire that therapists must walk is placed between the client's history and fear of being invalidated again (by therapist demands to change, which are statements that the client is not "right" as he or she is) and the client's own knowledge that change is necessary to end the misery. The therapist, in essence, is in danger of invalidating clients by either demands to change or acceptance of them as they are. The synthesis of the dialectic is to do both simultaneously, or, failing that, to quickly move from one to another.

This is not to say that therapists should pretend to accept the clients while they wait for their work on change to produce results. Both ends of the dialectic must be played from conviction and communicated in ways that are credible to the client. DBT has no difficulty with this; the dialectical worldview maintains that within every truth is its opposite. It is almost always possible to validate some part of the client's experience, and this is held to be an important aspect of treatment not just because it balances out the change strategies. In fact, clients with BPD are notoriously difficult to keep in treatment (cf. Koenigsberg, Clarkin, Kernberg, Yeomans, & Gutfreund, in press). One possible explanation for the success of DBT in keeping clients in treatment is that the treatment not only demands change, but also provides a therapeutic environment that validates their experience. Clients with BPD are so sensitive to any communication that even smacks of criticism that they must be validated throughout or the therapist stands a good chance of losing them. In addition, a focus on change recreates the environment of the family of origin, which demanded that the clients as children mask their negative emotions and not express or react to negative emotional responses. In a similar vein, a treatment strategy that focused exclusively on the acceptance end of the dialectic would drive clients from therapy because it fails to validate the pain in which clients live and invalidates their own desperation to alter their situation.

A second level of therapeutic attention must be devoted to recognizing the dialectical tensions being displayed by a particular client. Dialectics is not merely the putting together of opposites; any given thing may contain many different aspects to which it is "opposite." For example, a white circle may be considered to be opposite to a black circle, a white square, or a white sphere, depending on the relevant dimension being considered. The definition of dialectical tension is that "any difference that makes a difference for some purpose is a dialectical contradiction; if a difference makes no difference, it is not a difference" (Reese, 1993, p. 84). Thus, for different clients there will be different struggles, and resolution may come quickly to some situations and more slowly to others. Attention needs to be paid to the process and to the content of dialectical tensions in each client and to the dialectics involved in the relationship between client and therapist.

Skills Training

DBT attempts, therefore, to move forward on multiple fronts simultaneously. In standard outpatient DBT, there are four primary modes of treatment: individual therapy (addressing motivational problems); group skills training (addressing skills acquisition); telephone consultation (addressing skills generalization); and the supervision or consultation meetings for therapists (aimed at keeping therapists within the therapeutic frame and balancing clients' behaviors that might pull them out of that frame; see Linehan, 1993a, 1993b). DBT also incorporates therapeutic modes that run the breadth of health care, and Linehan has consulted extensively with inpatient units implementing the program. Typically, inpatient units will contain many more modes of treatment (i.e., milieu, vocational rehabilitation, dance or art therapy, unit meetings, etc.) than are available or used in outpatient work. Group skills training is incorporated as a fundamental aspect of DBT, designed to focus exclusively on working with clients to develop new (or more fully develop existing) approaches to dealing with stressful events or toward increasing interpersonal effectiveness. Participation in skills groups is a prerequisite of individual treatment, and there are strict guidelines surrounding attendance. Skills covered in the training balance skills in accepting life and events as they are in the moment (mindfulness and distress tolerance skills) with skills for changing oneself and the environment (emotion regulation and interpersonal effectiveness skills).

Mindfulness and Tolerance

"Mindfulness" is a set of techniques that Linehan adapted from her study and practice of Zen meditation techniques. They are also found within the Western contemplative tradition. It is considered a core skills set within DBT (Linehan, 1993a, 1993b) and thus is one of the first taught during skills training. Mindfulness training forms the backbone of the set of techniques that teach clients how to observe, describe accurately, and participate while taking a nonjudgmental stance, focusing on one thing in the moment, and being effective. These skills, together with the distress tolerance skills (strategies for tolerating crises and for cultivating a stance of radical or complete acceptance of reality as it is in the moment) directly address the side of the dialectic that deals with observing and participating in one's environment so that one may collect accurate feedback and make predictions about what the consequences of future actions may be; it is the segment of the dialectic that deals with planning actions and observing effects. Reese (1993) noted that, within the contextualist position, action precedes knowledge by providing information about the environment in which the action is performed. Thinking about what a peach might taste like does not provide information; biting into it does. Truth is arrived at, and hence the dialectic is resolved, when actions are successful in the world medium. Viewed from this paradigm, DBT is actually training clients both to engage more fully and to observe more clearly (i.e., improving the ability to do both by removing judgments) in order to act more harmoniously within their environment. As Wilber (1977) noted, "these Eastern disciplines . . . are not theories, philosophies, psychologies, or religions—rather, they are primarily a set of experiments in the strictly scientific sense of that term. They comprise a series of rules or injunctions which, if carried out properly, will result in the discovery of [awareness]" (p. 23). He pointed to traditions that have endured for thousands of years and continue to train young initiates in time-tested and proved techniques of increasing awareness and continues by observing that "to refuse to examine the results of such scientific experiments because one dislikes the data so obtained is in itself a most unscientific gesture" (Wilber, 1977, p. 23).

It is notable that many of the techniques (i.e., breathing) used in meditative practice are common across disciplines. Although DBT does not, during treatment, initiate discussions of the religious or spiritual contexts in which the practices originated, their presence within many spiritual disciplines enables a therapist to allay clients' fears that they may be practicing something beyond the bounds of their own religious doctrines. Conversely, the practices may be couched in strictly behavioral terms to remove any spiritual or religious overtones and to foster compliance among clients who are avowedly antireligion.

The dialectic that is discussed in group skills training when introducing mindfulness is the interplay between "emotion mind" and "reasonable mind" (Linehan, 1993a, 1993b). Resolution of the dialectic involves entering the state of "wise mind," which synthesizes and includes aspects of both arguments. As with all syntheses, wise mind is more than simply the sum of its parts. Along with logic and emotion, wise mind incorporates the sense of knowledge often referred to as intuition; it relies on the deep interaction of all ways of knowing and is evidenced through wisdom. Most clients with BPD must be taught how to access wise mind, and some will need to be convinced that they even have access to such a state. Some clients are able to recall experiences of being centered and operating from "wise mind" including instances following a crisis or perhaps after a very settling conversation with someone with whom they have "connected." Clients who cannot recall such experiences are asked simply to look for such states and are given a series of exercises ("experiments" in the language of Wilber, 1977) to enable them to reach that level of awareness. A more extensive discussion of the presentation of the skill is available in the skills training manual (Linehan, 1993b).

Regulating Emotions and the Interpersonal Environment

Other skills taught within the group training are designed specifically to target what Linehan theorized to be deficiencies in the BPD individual's ability to regulate himself or herself and his or her interpersonal environments (Linehan, 1993a, 1993b). Emotion regulation is taught, including instruction on how to identify and label current emotions, obstacles to changing emotions, reducing vulnerability to "emotion mind," ways to increase the occurrence of positive emotional events, and the use of "opposite action" as a means of regulating emotional response. Interpersonal effectiveness skills are also taught. Although clinical observation has indicated that individuals with BPD frequently possess good interpersonal skills, they often are unable to apply the skills in the appropriate situation. Their belief patterns or intense emotional responding often get in the way of appropriate use of the skills that they have. Distress tolerance and emotion regulation skills are often necessary to ensure successful application of interpersonal skills, and so DBT recognizes the need for interpersonal skills to be advanced only as quickly as other skills improve. The groups skills training modules have been put into manuals (Linehan, 1993b), complete with worksheets for therapists interested in studying the training, and the workbooks are required as a textbook for clients attending the training.

One other point that can be made concerning the development and implementation of groups within DBT demonstrates an example of dialectical theory influencing a therapy decision. The need for group skills training evolved because, despite the best of intentions to train clients in skills that they needed desperately, individual therapy simply could not seem to get beyond dealing with the weekly need to manage crises with clients; there was never the lull in the process into which skills training could be introduced. Linehan's initial inclination was to have groups be closed forums with fixed membership for the duration of the commitment (one year). She and her colleagues, in fact, led several groups under these conditions. However, it became increasingly clear that to teach dialectical principles of change and synthesis within a closed system was contradictory and in some ways worked against the acceptance and accommodation of change that she intended clients to be learning. Thus, the decision was made to allow clients to join at 8-week intervals (between modules) while those who had completed their year dropped out. The "acceptance of change" has also been introduced into individual therapy, and therapy now is more pointedly focused on clients learning to deal with the natural and ongoing fluctuations of events both within therapy and in their home environment.

Dialectics in Treating the Therapist

At the same time that the therapist is treating the client, the therapist is also being treated through consultation with the treatment team (Linehan, 1987, 1993a). The team is composed of other mental health professionals who have committed to working within the DBT framework, some of whom may be working with the client being seen in individual therapy. Many different modes of treatment may be represented on the DBT supervision team. Included may be the psychiatrist or nurse who prescribes medication, social workers, psychiatric nurses and aides providing milieu therapy, individual therapists, skills group trainers, back-up therapists, and so on. Anybody involved in treating the client may be present on the team, and there are often professionals present who are working with different clients. It is not necessary for every mental health worker who deals with a client undergoing DBT treatment to be working from the same orientation. Professionals not working from the DBT framework, however, do not attend the consultation sessions. DBT includes provisions for working with a health care community that may not even be familiar with its principles or strategies.

Consultation to the therapist is a necessary part of doing DBT (Linehan, 1993a). As a regularly scheduled activity it fulfills many functions. Primary is its function as dialectical counterweight to treatment of the client. The team or supervisor applies DBT to the therapist, allowing the therapist to be the recipient of acceptance and change strategies even as he or she is applying these same strategies with the client. A system of treatment is established wherein the transactions between client and therapist are brought into a dialogue among the therapist and individuals on the DBT consultation team. Therapy is thus modified from the client up and from the consultation team down, with both subsystems being affected by the presence of the other. The team works to keep the therapist in therapy with the client and the therapist works to keep the client in therapy. Thus, team members may need to cheerlead and support the therapist in addition to providing a dialectical framework for the therapist to refresh his or her perspective on treatment.

The team is also required to help the therapist maintain balance in the therapeutic relationship. Assuming some dynamic tension among therapist, client, and team, balance may be regained by the consultation team moving closer to the individual therapist and allowing him or her to gain distance from the client, or by backing off and thereby forcing the therapist to move closer to the client. Primarily, however, the consultation team provides a context for DBT, reminding the therapist of important principles that may be overlooked or providing a dialectical balance to the individual, subjective viewpoint. Prerequisites for supervision are regular attendance on the part of all participants and a willingness to engage in open exploration of difficult situations through a nondefensive application of DBT principles. As with individual therapy itself, the group consultation meetings are part education, part support, and part challenge to individuals to widen their perspective or balance their view. Humility is a necessary ingredient for all who participate, for those who instruct today will be taught tomorrow, and those whose sight is clear now will discover their own blindness at some point. The meetings are weekly reminders to remain grounded and supportive.

SUMMARY

This has been a necessarily brief introduction and overview to some of the ways in which dialectics has been incorporated into the therapeutic process in DBT. Note that the understanding and application of the principles of dialectics to treatment processes continues to evolve within DBT. Mahoney (1993) discussed this same process in work currently being done in psychotherapy theoretical integration in which there is an "emphasis on open-ended dialogical process" (p. 7) that has no endpoint, only an ongoing open forum for new views. One key to maintaining the development of DBT has been, and will continue to be, the use of dialectics as a tool to guide the therapist's actions and inquiry. Dialectics also is the process that furthers the theory of behavior change underlying DBT; experiments in the real work of therapy help to further modify the theory, which in turn modifies the strategy used. Interestingly, what began as an attempt to label and identify a treatment has become the process directing and forwarding new innovations within the therapy.

As mentioned earlier, there is no therapist without a client, no beginning of treatment without end goals, and no theory devoid of practice. It remains an empirical question whether therapists need to understand and model dialectics in order to effectively practice DBT. If, as seems possible, clients with BPD are truly deficient in their own ability to think and act dialectically, then explanation and modeling would seem to be important aspects of the treatment; it is not enough to simply "do dialectics" to them. Indeed, within the system we have described, it is not possible. Therapists are consistently engaged in some dialectical process when doing therapy, operating out of theories of behavior change and (hopefully) responding to client responses generated by the past intervention in determining the next move. A focus on dialectics primarily shifts one's attention to the process occurring rather than to the endpoint toward which one is moving.

In this chapter we have discussed the rudiments of philosophical dialectics and touched on the application of this philosophy to therapeutic theory and, more specifically, the dialectical processes for clients and therapists that are the focus of DBT. Of course, there may be similar or vastly different dialectical tensions among clients or among clinical populations. Similarly, the dialectical tensions between client and therapist may vary among pairings or across sessions. What we have intended to demonstrate is the process of using dialectics as a theory to guide therapeutic practice, noting other phenomena within psychology that are currently being viewed dialectically, and touching on the growth of dialectics as a paradigm in other scientific disciplines. The impact of such a shift, we believe, has yet to be realized.

REFERENCES

Aitken, R. (1982). *Taking the path of zen.* San Francisco: North Point Press.

Barley, W. D., Buie, S. E., Peterson, E. W., Hollingsworth, A. S., Griva, M., Hickerson, S. C., Lawson, J. E., & Bailey, B. J. (1993). The development of an inpatient cognitive–behavioral treatment program for borderline personality disorder. *Journal of Personality Disorders, 7*, 232–240.

Barlow, D. H. (1988). *Anxiety and its disorders: The nature and treatment of anxiety and panic.* New York: Guilford Press.

Basseches, M. (1984). *Dialectical thinking and adult development.* Norwood, NJ: Apex.

Bateson, G. (1979). *Mind and nature: A necessary unity.* New York: Bantam Books.

Berman, M. (1981). *The reenchantment of the world.* New York: Bantam Books.

Bernard, P. J., & Teasdale, J. (1991). Interacting cognitive subsystems: A systemic approach to cognitive–affective interaction and change. *Cognition and Emotion, 5,* 1–39.

Bopp, M. J., & Weeks, G. R. (1984). Dialectical metatheory in family therapy. *Family Process, 23,* 49–61.

Brasted, W. S., & Callahan, E. J. (1984). A behavioral analysis of the grief process. *Behavior Therapy, 15,* 529–543.

Caccioppo, J. T., Klein, D. J., Berntson, G. G., & Hatfield, E. (1993). The psychophysiology of emotion. In M. Lewis & J. M. Haviland (Eds.), *Handbook of emotions* (pp. 143–154). New York: Guilford Press.

Callahan, E. J., Brasted, W. S., & Granados, J. L. (1983). Fetal loss and sudden infant death: Grieving and adjustment for families. In E. J. Callahan & K. A. McCluskey (Eds.), *Life-span developmental psychology: Nonnormative life events* (pp. 144–166). San Diego, CA: Academic Press.

Deitz, S. M. (1986). Understanding cognitive language: The mental idioms in children's talk. *The Behavior Analyst, 9,* 161–166.

Derryberry, D., & Rothbart, M. K. (1984). Emotion, attention, and temperament. In C. E. Izard, J. Kagan, & R. B. Zajonc (Eds.), *Emotions, cognition, and behavior* (pp. 132–166). Cambridge, England: Cambridge University Press.

Duncan, J., & Laird, J. D. (1977). Cross-modality consistencies in individual differences in self-attribution. *Journal of Personality, 45,* 191–196.

Ekman, P., Friesen, W. V., & Ellsworth, P. (1972). *Emotion in the human face: Guidelines for research and an integration of findings.* Elmsford, NY: Pergamon Press.

Ekman, P., Levenson, R., & Friesen, W. V. (1983). Autonomic nervous system activity distinguishes among emotions. *Science, 221,* 1208–1210.

Eliasz, A. (1985). Mechanisms of temperament: Basic functions. In J. Strelau, F. H. Farley, & A. Gale (Eds.), *The biological bases of personality and behavior: Theories, measurement techniques, and development* (pp. 45–49). Washington, DC: Hemisphere.

Follette, W. C., Houts, A. C., & Hayes, S. C. (1992). Behavior therapy and the new medical model. *Behavioral Assessment, 14,* 323–343.

Gauthier, J., & Marshall, W. (1977). Grief: A cognitive-behavioral analysis. *Cognitive Therapy and Research, 1,* 39–44.

Greenberg, L. S., & Safran, J. D. (1987). *Emotion in psychotherapy.* New York: Guilford Press.

Gunderson, J. G., & Zanarini, M. C. (1989). Pathogenesis of borderline personality. *Review of Psychiatry 8,* 25–48.

Hayes, S. C. (1987). A contextual approach to therapeutic change. In N. S. Jacobson (Ed.), *Psychotherapists in clinical practice: Cognitive and behavioral perspectives* (pp. 327–387). New York: Guilford Press.

Hayes, S. C., Hayes, L. J., & Reese, H. W. (1988). Finding the philosophical core: A review of Stephen C. Pepper's world hypotheses: A study in evidence. *Journal of the Experimental Analysis of Behavior, 50,* 97–111.

Heard, H. H., & Linehan, M. M. (1994). Dialectical behavior therapy: An integrative approach to the treatment of borderline personality disorder. *Journal of Psychotherapy Integration, 4,* 55–82.

Izard, C. E. (1977). *Human emotions.* New York: Plenum.

Izard, C. E., Kagan, J., & Zajonc, R. B. (Eds.). (1984). *Emotions, cognition, and behavior.* Cambridge, England: Cambridge University Press.

Izard, C. E., & Kobak, R. R. (1991). Emotions systems functioning and emotion regulation. In J. Garber & K. A. Dodge (Eds.), *The development of emotion regulation and dysregulation* (pp. 303–322). Cambridge, England: Cambridge University Press.

Jaeger, M. E., & Rosnow, R. L. (1988). Contextualism and its implications for psychological inquiry. *British Journal of Psychology, 79,* 63–75.

James, W. (1884). What is an emotion? *Mind, 9,* 188–205.

Kagan, J., & Snidman, N. (1991). Temperamental factors in human development. *American Psychologist, 46,* 856–862.

Kaminstein, D. S. (1987). Toward a dialectical metatheory for psychotherapy. *Journal of Contemporary Psychotherapy, 17,* 87–101.

Kastenbaum, R. J. (1969). Death and bereavement in later life. In A. H. Kutscher (Ed.), *Death and bereavement* (pp. 28–54). Springfield, IL: Charles C Thomas.

Koenigsberg, H. W., Clarkin, J., Kernberg, O. F., Yeomans, F., & Gutfreund, J. (in press). Some measures of process and outcome in the psychodynamic psychotherapy of borderline patients. In P. Fonagy & O. F. Kernberg (Eds.), *The integration of research and psychoanalytic practice: The proceedings of the IPA First International Conference on Research.*

Kohlenberg, R. J., & Tsai, M. (1991). *Functional analytic psychotherapy: Creating intense and curative therapeutic relationships.* New York: Plenum.

Kramer, D. A., & Melchior, J. (1990). Gender, role conflict, and the development of relativistic and dialectical thinking. *Sex Roles, 23,* 553–575.

Laird, J. D. (1974). Self-attribution of emotion: The effects of expressive behavior on the quality of emotional experience. *Journal of Personality and Social Psychology, 29,* 475–486.

Lange, K. (1885). *The emotions.* Denmark. I. A. Haupt, Trans., for K. Dunlop (Ed.).

Levins, R., & Lewontin, R. (1985). *The dialectical biologist.* Cambridge, MA: Harvard University Press.

Linehan, M. M. (1987). Dialectical behavioral therapy: A cognitive behavioral approach to parasuicide. *Journal of Personality Disorders, 1,* 328–333.

Linehan, M. M. (1993a). *Cognitive-behavioral treatment of borderline personality disorder.* New York: Guilford Press.

Linehan, M. M. (1993b). *Skills training manual for treating borderline personality disorder.* New York: Guilford Press.

Linehan, M. M. (1993c). Dialectical behavior therapy for treatment of borderline personality disorder: Implications for the treatment of substance abuse. In L. Onken, J. Blaine, & J. Boren (Eds.), *Behavioral treatments for drug abuse and dependence* (NIDA Monograph No. 137). Rockville, MD: National Institute on Drug Abuse.

Linehan, M. M., Armstrong, H. E., Suarez, A., Allmon, D., & Heard, H. L. (1991). Cognitive-behavioral treatment of chronically parasuicidal borderline patients. *Archives of General Psychiatry, 48,* 1060–1064.

Linehan, M. M., Camper, P., Chiles, H. A., Strosahl, K., & Shearin, E. (1987). Interpersonal problem solving and parasuicide. *Cognitive Therapy and Research, 11,* 1–12.

Linehan, M. M., & Heard, H. L. (1993). Impact of treatment accessibility on clinical course of parasuicidal patients: In reply to R. E. Hoffman [Letter to the editor]. *Archives of General Psychiatry, 50,* 157–158.

Linehan, M. M., Heard, H. L., & Armstrong, H. E. (1993). Naturalistic follow-up of a behavioral treatment for chronically parasuicidal borderline patients. *Archives of General Psychiatry, 50,* 971–974.

Linehan, M. M., Tutek, D., & Heard, H. L. (1992, November). *Interpersonal and social treatment outcomes for borderline personality disorder.* Poster presented at the annual meeting of the Association for the Advancement of Behavior Therapy, Boston.

Mahoney, M. J. (1993). Diversity and the dynamics of development in psychotherapy integration. *Journal of Psychotherapy Integration, 3,* 1–13.

Malatesta, C. Z. (1990). The role of emotions in the development and organization of personality. In R. A. Thompson (Ed.), *Socioemotional development: Nebraska Symposium on Motivation, 1988* (pp. 1–56). Lincoln: University of Nebraska Press.

McGuire, T. R. (1993). The neuropsychology of emotion and affective stye. In M. Lewis & J. M. Haviland (Eds.), *Handbook of emotions* (pp. 155–166). New York: Guilford Press.

Miller, S. M., & Mangan, C. E. (1983). Interacting effects of information and coping style in adapting to gynecologic stress: Should the doctor tell all? *Journal of Personality and Social Psychology, 45,* 223–236.

Millon, T., (1981). *Disorders of personality: DSM-III Axis II.* New York: Wiley.

Millon, T., & Everly, G. S., Jr. (1985). *Personality and its disorders: A biosocial learning approach.* New York: Wiley.

Mischel, W. (1968). *Personality and assessment*. New York: Wiley.

Mischel, W. (1984). Convergences and challenges in the search for consistency. *American Psychologist, 39,* 351–364.

Napalkov, A. V. (1963). Information process and the brain. In N. Wiener & J. P. Schade (Eds.), *Progress in brain research* (pp. 59–69). Amsterdam: Elsevier.

Parkes, C. M. (1964). The effects of bereavement on physical and mental health: A study of the case records of widows. *British Medical Journal, 2,* 274–279.

Perry, J. D., & Cooper, S. H. (1985). Psychodynamics, symptoms, and outcome in borderline and antisocial personality disorders and bipolar type II affective disorder. In T. H. McGlashan (Ed.), *The borderline: Current empirical research* (pp. 19–41). Washington, DC: American Psychiatric Press.

Reese, H. W. (1993). Contextualism and dialectical materialism. In S. C. Hayes, L. J. Hayes, H. W. Reese, & T. R. Sarbin (Eds.), *Varieties of scientific contextualism* (pp. 71–105). Reno, NV: Context Press.

Rhodewalt, F., & Comer, R. (1979). Induced compliance attitude change: Once more with feeling. *Journal of Experimental Social Psychology, 15,* 35–47.

Riegel, K. R. (1975). Toward a dialectical theory of development. *Human Development, 18,* 50–64.

Rogers, C. R., & Truax, C. B. (1967). The therapeutic conditions antecedent to change: A theoretical view. In C. R. Rogers (Ed.), *The therapeutic relationship and its impact*. Madison: University of Wisconsin Press.

Scarr, S., & McCartney, K. (1983). How people make their own environments: A theory of genotype-environment effects. *Child Development, 54,* 424–435.

Schwenk, C. R. (1990). Effects of devil's advocacy and dialectical inquiry on decision making: A meta-analysis. *Organizational Behavior and Human Decision Processes, 47,* 161–176.

Seligman, M. E. P. (1975). *Helplessness*. San Francisco: Freeman.

Selye, H. (1956). *The stress of life*. New York: McGraw-Hill.

Smith, C. A., & Lazarus, R. S. (1990). Emotion and adaptation. In L. A. Pervin (Ed.), *Handbook of personality: Theory and research* (pp. 609–637). New York: Guilford Press.

Spitzberg, B. H. (1993). The dialectics of (in)competence. *Journal of Social and Personal Relationships, 10,* 137–158.

Staats, A. W. (1975). *Social behaviorism*. Homewood, IL: Dorsey Press.

Strelau, J. (1985). Temperament and personality: Pavlov and beyond. In J. Strelau, F. Farley, & A. Gale (Eds.), *The biological bases of personality and behavior: Theories, measurement techniques, and development* (pp. 25–44). Washington, DC: Hemisphere.

Thompson, T. N. (1991). Dialectics, communication and exercises for creativity. *Journal of Creative Behavior, 25,* 43–51.

Weiss, F. G. (1974). *Hegel: The essential writings*. New York: Harper & Row.

Wells, H. K. (1972). Alienation and dialectical logic. *Kansas Journal of Sociology, 3,* 7–32.

Wilber, K. (1977). *The spectrum of consciousness.* Wheaton, IL: Theosophical Publishing.

Williams, J. M. G. (1991). Autobiographical memory and emotional disorders. In S. A. Christianson (Ed.), *Handbook of emotion and memory* (pp. 451–477). Hillsdale, NJ: Erlbaum.

Zajonc, R. B. (1984). On the primacy of affect. *American Psychologist, 39,* 117–132.

Zuckerman, M., Klorman, R., Larrance, D., & Spiegel, N. (1981). Facial, autonomic, and subjective components of emotion: The facial feedback hypothesis versus the externalizer–internalizer distinction. *Journal of Personality and Social Psychology, 41,* 929–944.

21

HYPOTHESIS-BASED INTERVENTIONS: A THEORY OF CLINICAL DECISION MAKING

ALAN C. REPP, KATHRYN G. KARSH, DENNIS MUNK, and CAROL M. DAHLQUIST

In the past decade or so, hypothesis-based interventions have been developed to address problem behaviors, primarily of persons with developmental disabilities such as mental retardation and autism. These interventions require a therapist to develop a hypothesis for the reason behavior is occurring and then to implement a treatment on the basis of that hypothesis.

At first thought, hypothesis-based interventions may seem to exemplify most treatments. The opposite, however, has been true, at least with problem behaviors of persons with disabilities. The purpose of this chapter is to explain the theory and background for hypothesis-based interventions. We begin with a discussion of the historical context leading to their de-

This work was supported in part by Grant H023C00092 from the Office of Special Education Programs and Grant H133G20098 from the National Institute on Disability and Rehabilitation Research.

velopment and several ways of deriving the interventions. We then provide examples of the way the interventions have been derived.

The published research on hypothesis-based interventions has been conducted almost exclusively with individuals who have developmental disabilities. The reason for this focus is not that it is suited only to individuals with disabilities; rather, it is because the researchers developing the procedure happen to work with persons with disabilities. Nevertheless, because the published research is in the area of development disabilities, we present this method in that context.

CONTEXT OF THE DEVELOPMENT OF HYPOTHESIS-BASED INTERVENTIONS

Developmental Disabilities

Applied behavior analysis began as an effort to transpose procedures from the operant laboratory to natural settings, generally in the mid-1950s. Many people were involved in that broadening of the field of operant psychology, but some of the more important ones were Bijou and Baer (e.g., Bijou, 1963; Bijou & Baer, 1961, 1963; Bijou & Orlando, 1961), who wrote about child development, mental retardation, education, and the application of operant methods to natural settings (Repp, 1983). At that time, individuals with retardation or autism were often institutionalized and treated in a custodial fashion. However, the 1960s was a period in which the United States was interested in civil rights, an interest that began to extend to those with disabilities. The times provided a setting event for an amalgamation of the hopefulness of social conscience and the hopefulness of the power of operant methods. During this period, the professionals in the field of mental retardation—at least the nonacademics who actually had to deal with the problems of these individuals—welcomed those skilled in behavior analysis, and the treatment, educational programming, and research responsibilities in this field were assumed by behavior analysts.

Although clinicians faced many challenges, one of the most persistent was how to treat behaviors that presented serious problems for the well-being as well as the social and educational integration of these individuals. The challenge was considerable not only because of the behaviors themselves but also because of their incidence and prevalence. The rates of these problem behaviors are simply much higher for persons with developmental disabilities than for those without. For example, several studies have shown that 6–40% of persons with developmental disabilities engage in self-injurious behaviors (SIBs), 40–60% engage in stereotyped behaviors, and 14–38% demonstrate destructive or aggressive behaviors (Borthwick, Myers, & Eyman, 1981; Corbett & Campbell, 1981; Eyman & Call, 1977;

Griffen, Williams, Stark, Altmeyer, & Mason, 1986; Jacobson, 1982; Oliver, Murphy, & Corbett, 1987; Repp & Barton, 1980).

Treatment of Problem Behavior

Beginning in the 1960s, there have been many attempts to treat problem behaviors, and numerous authors have addressed these attempts (e.g., Carr, Robinson, Taylor, & Carlson, 1990; Gorman-Smith & Matson, 1985; LaGrow & Repp, 1984; Lundervold & Bourland, 1988; Matson & Gorman-Smith, 1986; Matson & Taras, 1989; O'Brien & Repp, 1990). Although recognizing that any generalization of this type carries with it errors, we would characterize most of these efforts, particularly until recently, as interventions that were applied independent of an analysis of the reasons the problem behavior was occurring (in the terminology of this chapter, those authors did not base intervention on a hypothesis of the *function* of behavior).

There are many ways to classify previous interventions, but the one provided under the auspices of the National Institutes of Health (1989) may be useful:

1. behavior reduction approaches designed to reduce the rate of behavior by producing an environmental change contingent on the occurrence of the behavior (includes faradic shock, disagreeable solutions, oral hygiene, air or water mist, ammonia salts, overcorrection, contingent restraint, facial screening, time-out, response cost, verbal reprimand, and extinction);
2. behavior enhancement approaches designed to reduce problem behavior by reinforcing competing or alternative behavior rather than by suppressing the problem behavior directly (includes differential reinforcement of alternate behavior, of incompatible behavior, or of other behavior);
3. educational or skills-acquisition training designed to teach new behaviors that are likely to increase a person's social competence and perhaps to displace the function of the problem behavior (includes training to comply with educational instructions, self-management training, training to communicate "needs" in socially acceptable ways, and training a variety of socially useful behaviors that presumably correct deficits triggering problem behaviors); and
4. stimulus-based treatments designed to substitute stimuli that are correlated with low rates of problem behaviors for stimuli that are correlated with high rates.

Another way of categorizing interventions is in terms of their aversiveness. Although there are technical debates about whether positive reinforcement and negative reinforcement are really the same, and whether differential reinforcement is really a punishment procedure because it postpones reinforcement under certain conditions, the general public clearly sees a difference between the behavior reduction procedures and the other three categories of procedures. The first is more aversive.

Aversive Debate

The categorization of some behavior reduction procedures as aversive provided another important context for the development of hypothesis-based interventions. During the 1980s, a bitter controversy developed between two groups of researchers and treatment providers. One felt that punishment procedures should not be used for persons with disabilities because these procedures were generally not used for persons without disabilities and because the procedures violated the constitutional right to freedom from harm (e.g., the American Association on Mental Retardation, the Association for Persons with Severe Handicaps). Another group felt that aversive procedures were necessary, particularly for severe behaviors for which nonaversive procedures had failed, and that prohibiting their use deprived persons with disabilities of their right to effective treatment (e.g., the Association for Behavior Analysis, Division 33 [Mental Retardation and Developmental Disabilities] of the American Psychological Association, the Council for Children with Behavioral Disorders).[1]

Some based their position in this debate only on ethical grounds; tangential was a belief that nonaversive procedures were or could be as effective as or even more effective than aversive procedures. Others based their position on literature showing that aversive procedures were effective in many cases in which nonaversive procedures had been ineffective; theirs was characterized as a belief grounded in data (see Repp & Singh, 1990, for both sides of this controversy).

A third group, with its members from both sides of this issue, took another approach for addressing severe problem behaviors. This approach can be characterized as follows:

1. The researcher concentrated during baseline or a prebaseline period on identifying environmental conditions under which the behaviors did and did not occur;
2. the researcher identified functional relationships between the behaviors and the environmental conditions, and decreased

---

[1]The positions of these organizations as resolutions can be found printed in their entirety in Singh, Lloyd, and Kendall (1990).

those relationships according to hypotheses of positive reinforcement, negative reinforcement, and stimulation; and

3. the researcher prescribed interventions that were based on
   these hypotheses.

This approach emphasizes the identification of the function of the
problem behavior and teaching or reinforcing alternative, socially acceptable behaviors that can perform the same function for the individual (generally more efficiently and with less effort). This approach may include the
behavior reduction procedures listed by the National Institutes of Health;
however, it is unlikely to do so. The approach is more likely to use behavior
enhancement and skills-acquisition procedures while programming reinforcement for behaviors that perform the same function as the aberrant
behavior. This approach may also include stimulus-based treatments, and
does so in combination with these other procedures in an effort to disrupt
the stimulus control exerted by the environment on the aberrant behavior.

In the next section, we discuss the hypotheses for problem behavior
integral to this approach, and in the ensuing section we present some of
the several procedures for developing hypothesis-based interventions.

HYPOTHESES

Central to this approach is the development of hypotheses for the
controlling conditions of problem behavior. The alternative approach has
been an emphasis on cure rather than on understanding the variables of
which behavior is a function (Carr, Robinson, & Palumbo, 1990). The
difference between the two approaches is more than academic, as Carr,
Robinson, and Palumbo (1990) have indicated. In their review of 96 nonaversive treatments, success (reduction of 90% or more) was much higher
for the procedures that were based on an assessment of the functional
relationship between the problem behavior and environmental variables.
Therefore, the question is, What constitutes the set of hypotheses under
which one can place the function of these behaviors?

Because the development of hypothesis-based interventions is relatively new, the field has several sets of hypotheses, with the set depending
on the group of researchers using this approach. For example, Carr (1977),
in the seminal article for this field, posed three: positive reinforcement,
negative reinforcement, and stimulation. This is the set also used by Iwata
and his colleagues, although stimulation has been redefined as *automatic
reinforcement* (Iwata, Vollmer, & Zarcone, 1990).

The positive reinforcement hypothesis states that events that are contingent on the occurrence of behavior will increase the behavior's recur-

rence. Examples of events that have increased problem behaviors for persons with developmental disabilities include delivery of attention (Carr & Durand, 1985) and tangibles (Edelson, Taubman, & Lovaas, 1983). The negative reinforcement hypothesis is also treated traditionally; it suggests that events that are removed, attenuated, or prevented contingent on the occurrence of behavior will increase the behavior's recurrence. Examples of events for this population include difficult tasks (Weeks & Gaylord-Ross, 1981); nonpreferred activities (Dunlap, Kern-Dunlap, Clarke, & Robbins, 1991); and repetitive, boring tasks (Winterling, Dunlap, & O'Neill, 1987).

The third hypothesis is automatic reinforcement, which is used to describe the strengthening of behavior by the consequences the behavior directly produces. We recognize that this construct can be subsumed under positive or negative reinforcement, but some find it useful to describe behaviors such as rocking and other rhythmic, repetitive behaviors that seem to provide reinforcement without the external environment. Several studies have shown that when sensory feedback from these behaviors is interrupted or when other behaviors are targeted to provide the same stimulation, stereotypies (Rincover, 1978) or SIBs (Favell, McGimsey, & Schell, 1982) can be reduced.

In our approach we use several of the hypotheses that others use. However, we follow several steps that may be different from those others follow. First, however, we try to distinguish between behaviors that are environmentally independent and dependent. By the use of the term *environmentally dependent*, we mean behaviors whose rate, duration, magnitude, or topography is affected by the environmental context in which the behaviors occur. Examples of environmental variables that may affect problem behaviors include task difficulty, staff attention, opportunities to make choices, and pace of instruction. For these behaviors, therapists can manipulate the critical variables in the environment during the intervention in order to reduce the problem behavior. Other behaviors may not be affected by the environment and may be considered to be environmentally independent; these may be better treated through means such as psychopharmacology. Because our approach is outside the realm of medicine, we do not address these behaviors; instead, we limit the discussion to environmentally dependent behaviors.

Second, we address the environmentally dependent behaviors within the context of setting events. Setting events are events that change the probability that antecedents will be correlated with target behaviors or the probability that consequences will be reinforcing or punishing. For example, a meal a few minutes earlier would probably lessen the probability that food would reinforce task completion. Vigorous exercise before instruction may lessen the probability that instruction will be correlated with stereotypies (Bachman & Fuqua, 1983; Kern, Koegel, & Dunlap, 1984). A combination of sleeping late in the morning, missing breakfast, being assisted in dressing, and sleeping en route to school may affect the probability that school-based events will be correlated with aggression, running away, and SIBs (Kennedy & Itkonen, 1993).

When we address the hypotheses for environmentally dependent problem behaviors, we treat the positive reinforcement and negative reinforcement hypotheses as others do. However, we use the stimulation hypothesis different from others. Although we agree that stimulation can have automatic consequences that are reinforcing, we tend not to attribute those properties to positive reinforcement. Instead, we use the term *stimulation* to refer to some level of activity that organisms seek to maintain at a particular time or under certain stimulus conditions and attribute the effect more to biological mechanisms. Several studies with persons with developmental disabilities have shown that lack of stimulation (Horner, 1980), lack of play materials (Berkson & Mason, 1965), or lack of social interaction (Moseley, Faust, & Reardon, 1970), can be associated with higher levels of stereotypy. One study has shown that some subjects will decrease stereotypies when the rate at which the learning environment contacts them is increased considerably (Repp & Karsh, 1992); another study (Repp, Karsh, Deitz, & Singh, 1992) showed that individuals sought to maintain a homeostatic level of responding during the school day. Results with 12 individuals studied for 25 hr each showed that (a) 4 subjects were almost invariant across hours with respect to their level of stereotypy; (b) motor movements other than stereotypy were highly variable for 11 subjects; but (c) total movement (stereotypy plus other motor movements) was consistent for each individual subject. In essence, these subjects substituted stereotypies and other motor movements for each other while maintaining a relatively constant level of overall responding. Because many of the individuals with whom we intervene engage in stereotypies and often are in environments that do not facilitate motor movements, we have found this use of the construct of stimulation helpful because it leads directly to the selection of an intervention.

Independent of the set of hypotheses adopted, researchers use several procedures for developing hypothesis-based interventions. These, which we discuss in the next section, include (a) indirect methods, (b) analogue assessments, and (c) descriptive analyses through observations in the natural environment. The important point is that regardless of the procedure used, each intervention is based on hypotheses of the conditions maintaining problem behavior. Borrowing from Carr, Robinson, and Palumbo (1990), we could characterize the differences between hypothesis-based interventions and traditionally selected interventions as those presented in Table 1.

TABLE 1
Differences Between Hypothesis-Based and Traditionally
Selected Interventions

Intervention	
Hypothesis based	Traditional
Treatment selection is explicitly based on hypothesis of the function of behavior. Focus is on understanding conditions maintaining behavior.	Treatment selection is implicitly based on behavior topography (e.g., stereotypy) or type of subject (e.g., autistic). Focus is on use of previously demonstrated technologies (e.g., time-out, DRO).
Treatment is proactive, often taking place when the individual is not engaging in the problem behavior.	Treatment is reactive, generally taking place when the individual is engaging in problem behavior.
Purpose of treatment is to increase the rate of socially acceptable behaviors. Reduction of problem behavior is an important side effect.	Purpose of treatment is to reduce problem behavior, the reduction of which is the main effect.

Note. DRO = differential reinforcement of other behavior. The material in this table was derived from Carr, Robinson, Taylor, and Carlson (1990).

METHODS OF DEVELOPING HYPOTHESES

Although there are often difficulties in making absolute categorizations of procedures, we attempt to do so in this case, discussing three procedures for assessing the function of problem behavior. These three are (a) indirect methods, which generally use interviews rather than direct observation; (b) analogue assessments, in which artificial conditions that relate to the therapist's hypotheses (e.g., positive reinforcement, negative reinforcement, stimulation) are presented; and (c) naturalistic functional assessments, in which direct observations are made in the natural environment during conditions that also relate to the therapist's hypotheses. The degree to which each of the following is considered during an assessment should affect the degree to which the function of the aberrant behavior can be isolated:

1. identifying antecedents that are reliably correlated with the presence and the absence of the behavior;
2. identifying consequences that reliably follow both the problem behavior and socially appropriate, related behaviors;
3. determining whether setting events affect the control exerted by antecedents and consequences related to both the inappropriate and appropriate behaviors;

4. presenting the results in a format that leads to a hypothesis of the maintaining conditions; and

5. identifying alternative, socially appropriate behaviors that can perform the same function as the inappropriate behaviors.

Indirect Method

The indirect method does not rely on direct observation of the problem behavior but on the recall by an informed observer of the events surrounding the behavior's occurrence and nonoccurrence. These interviews can, of course, be of considerably different depth. There are several interviews that have been used. One is in the form of an antecedent behavior–consequence questionnaire and provides a 16-item rating scale. Developed by Durand and Crimmins (1988), the questionnaire is called the Motivation Assessment Scale (MAS), and it seeks to isolate one of four hypotheses for possible functions of SIBs: positive reinforcement through access to materials, positive reinforcement through attention, automatic reinforcement through sensory stimulation, and negative reinforcement through escape from tasks.

Although the MAS has been found useful by Durand (e.g., Durand & Kishi, 1987), it has been criticized by others, particularly Iwata and his associates. Some of the criticisms are as follows: (a) Reliability calculations by Durand and Crimmins (1988) were based on correlational analyses rather than on an item-by-item comparison of the raters' scores (Iwata, Vollmer, et al., 1990); (b) reliability data were less consistent than originally reported, with only 31 of 48 correlations of rank order being significant at the .05 level (Crawford, Brockel, Schauss, & Miltenberger, 1992) and with none of the reliability scores based on the percentage agreement between observers above 80% (Zarcone, Rodgers, Iwata, Rourke, & Dorsey, 1991); and (c) a factor analysis failed to identify the four hypotheses with data from a sample of 96 students with developmental disabilities who engaged in problem behaviors less than 15 times per hour (Singh et al., 1993).

Another interview has been developed by O'Neill, Horner, Albin, Storey, and Sprague (1990), and it consists of nine pages of questions. Unlike the MAS, this interview is part of a system that includes three strategies for collecting information: the interview, direct observation, and systematic manipulation of the environmental variables. The purpose of the interview is to review a large number of potential variables, narrow the focus to a smaller number, and identify variables to be coded during the direct observation phase. Also unlike the MAS, this interview is not intended to document functional relations but to set the occasion for the therapist to do so. We have found this approach to be useful in our work (e.g., Karsh & Repp, 1994; Repp & Karsh, 1994), as have others (e.g., Flannery & Horner, in press; Kennedy & Itkonen, 1993).

Analogue Assessments

An entirely different procedure, which is based on using experimental methods, has also been used to identify functional relationships within the hypotheses of positive reinforcement, negative reinforcement, and stimulation. This procedure analyzes behavior before the baseline period in order to identify its function. Often, such functional analyses are conducted using analogue conditions, which approximate those in the natural environment and which test one or more possible functions of the target behavior. For example, Carr and colleagues conducted a series of studies demonstrating the relationship between demands and either aggression, tantrums, or SIBs (Carr & Durand, 1985; Carr & Newsom, 1985; Carr, Newsom, & Binkoff, 1980; Durand & Carr, 1987). A hallmark of this work has been that assessments were experimental in nature. That is, through contrasting both the absence and presence of independent variables (e.g., by comparing demand and no-demand conditions), the authors identified functional relationships.

Iwata and his associates have also conducted a series of analogue studies in which they used the presence and absence of independent variables to test the function of behavior. On the basis of Carr's (1977) hypotheses of the motivation of SIB, Iwata, Dorsey, Slifer, Bauman, and Richman (1982) conducted one of the first systematic analyses of the functions of aberrant behavior. Iwata et al. exposed subjects who engaged in SIBs to three experimental conditions and one control condition to test whether SIBs were maintained by negative reinforcement, positive reinforcement, or automatic stimulation. Results showed that a specific condition was associated with higher rates of SIBs for 6 of 9 subjects. This study, although not an intervention study, was important because it showed that a system of analysis could be designed to correlate problem behavior and associated conditions with hypothesized causes of the behavior. Similar analogue assessments provide evidence of the method's considerable utility (e.g., Day, Rea, Schussler, Larsen, & Johnson, 1988; Derby et al., 1992; Iwata, Pace, Kalsher, Cowdery, & Cataldo, 1990; Northup et al., 1991; Steege, Wacker, Berg, Cigrand, & Cooper, 1989).

Analogue assessment procedures may have advantages over traditional assessments, including brevity (e.g., Northup et al., 1991), a quantifiable demonstration of the contingencies between behavior and the environment (Iwata, et al., 1982), and the development of a treatment program based on the maintaining variables (e.g., Day et al., 1988). However, such assessments may also have a few possible weaknesses including an absence of the variables found in the natural environment and establishment of a new relationship by exposing a current problem behavior to different reinforcement contingencies (Day et al., 1988; Iwata et al., 1990). In addition, it may be problematic in nonclinical settings. For example, analogue assessments cannot be used in some schools or residential settings because the approach intentionally presents conditions designed to produce the problem behavior. Although we agree with the experimental rationale that the condition is usually short-lived, personnel have been hesitant to present such an approach to school review boards and to parents. As a result, other procedures need to be developed for these settings.

One such approach, which is based entirely on Iwata's and Carr's work, has been the development of hypothesis-based interventions in which a hypothesis is developed in the natural setting during baseline and an intervention is based on that hypothesis (Repp, Felce, & Barton, 1988). This form of assessment is discussed in the following section.

Naturalistic Assessments

Another approach has been developed wherein individuals are observed in their natural settings rather than in analogue representations of these conditions (Karsh & Repp, 1994; Kern, Childs, Dunlap, Clarke, & Falk, 1994; Lalli, Browder, Mace, & Brown, 1993; Repp & Karsh, 1994). In the procedure that we have developed, teachers, other staff, or parents are asked not to change anything in the way they interact with the target individual. Baseline data on behaviors and environmental conditions are collected, and the data on behaviors are nested under the naturally occurring conditions (e.g., easy vs. hard tasks, active vs. passive tasks, staff presence vs. staff absence). Hypotheses are then generated for the conditions maintaining the aberrant behaviors, and interventions are based on manipulating those conditions already in the environment. The hypotheses, in general, have been positive reinforcement, negative reinforcement, or stimulation.

We have used naturalistic assessment to select hypothesis-based interventions for many individuals exhibiting serious problem behaviors (Karsh & Repp, 1994; Karsh, Repp, Dahlquist, & Munk, in press; Munk & Repp, 1994; Repp & Karsh, 1994; Repp, Karsh, & Dahlquist, 1994). Because the methodology for implementing this procedure and subsequent treatment is consistent across all cases, we describe the procedure in detail with three case examples. One individual was a 9-year-old boy with severe mental retardation who screamed, self-injured, threw objects, spit, mouthed objects, rocked, and was aggressive. A second individual was an 11-year-old boy with severe mental retardation who fell to the floor, kicked or hit staff members, threw objects, and destroyed property. A third individual was a 10-year-old boy with severe mental retardation, autisticlike behaviors, and hyperactivity who ran from staff, threw things, and was severely aggressive toward staff (e.g., kicked staff).

Individual topographies of behavior and environmental variables for each child were identified in two ways. First, we interviewed teachers to obtain descriptive information about the individual child (e.g., age, diagnosis, medical history, adaptive behavior, language skills). Problem behaviors were identified, and the teaching staff were asked questions about the conditions under which the problem behaviors did and did not occur. Second, the classroom inventory presented in Table 2 was used as a guide to conduct informal observations of classroom activities, teacher behaviors, peer behaviors, and other variables that may be functionally related to the problem behavior. These informal observations were used to identify the target behavior as well as specific environmental conditions, antecedents, and consequences for formal data collection during baseline. The topographies of behavior and environmental variables identified for each child are presented in Table 3.

Baseline data were collected for two purposes. The first was to indicate the extent to which each of the codes occurred, the second was to develop the hypotheses on which the interventions were to be based. The latter purpose was addressed by developing contingency tables that were based on the hypotheses for each child. Each contingency table was constructed to reflect if–then statements that indicated the relationship between the target behaviors and the controlling variables. For Child 1, the hypothesis was positive reinforcement, and the contingency table reflected the relationship between problem behavior and attention from teachers and aides. For Child 2, the hypothesis was negative reinforcement (he was trying to escape activities in which he had to make active responses), and the contingency table reflected the relationship between problem behavior and types of activities. For Child 3, there were two hypotheses: stimulation and positive reinforcement. For the stimulation hypothesis, the contingency table presented the relationship between problem behavior and the activity level of the task. For the positive reinforcement hypothesis, the table presented the relationship between problem behavior and types of attention from teachers and aides.

Table 4 shows the results of baseline and treatment data expressed in contingency tables containing conditional probabilities (if–then relationships) for environmental variables and child behaviors. These if–then relationships suggest whether the behavior is maintained by positive reinforcement, negative reinforcement, stimulation, or a combination of two hypotheses. Next, we describe interventions that were based on the baseline data arranged in the contingency tables.

Child 1's problem behaviors, which occurred primarily during group activities, included screaming, throwing objects, spitting, mouthing objects, rocking, biting, pinching, or scratching staff. Our hypothesis was positive

TABLE 2
Classroom Inventory to Identify Potential Environmental Variables for Functional Assessment

Variable	Variable opposite
Biobehavioral state	
Medication	Hunger
Seizures	Diet
Allergies	Sleep cycles
Injury	Activity level
Other medical complications	Mood
Physical environment	
Small area	Large area
Low density	High density
Barren	Enriched
Restricted	Accessible
Noisy	Noisy
Low visual stimulation	High visual stimulation
Predictable	Unpredictable
Activities	
Individual	Large group
Preferred	Nonpreferred
Free choice	Assigned
Easy	Difficult
Boring	Novel
Attractive materials	Unattractive materials
Individual trials	Massed trials
No opportunity to respond	Numerous opportunities to respond
Slow pace of presentation	Rapid pace of presentation
Lengthy transitions	Short transitions
Staff	
Unfamiliar	Familiar
Nonpreferred	Preferred
Not proximate	Proximate
No interaction	Frequent interaction
Negative interaction	Positive interaction
Peers	
Unfamiliar	Familiar
Preferred	Nonpreferred
No interaction	Frequent interaction
Inappropriate behavior	Appropriate behavior
Consequences for appropriate behavior	
No reinforcement	Frequent reinforcement
Artificial reinforcers	Natural reinforcers
Tokens	Assessed reinforcers
Contingent reinforcement	Noncontingent reinforcement
Consequences for inappropriate behavior	
Staff reprimand	No staff reprimand
Staff restraint	No staff restraint
Peer attention	No peer attention
Staff removal of task	Staff follow-through on task
No time-out	Frequent or lengthy time-out

TABLE 3
Variables

Student 1
  Behaviors: screaming, biting, pinching, throwing objects, mouthing, spitting, rocking, adaptive behavior.
  Environmental variables: attention to appropriate behavior, no attention to appropriate behavior, attention to problem behavior, no attention to problem behavior, individual instruction, other instruction.
Student 2
  Behaviors: tantrum, property destruction, appropriate behavior, neutral behavior.
  Environmental variables: preferred activities, nonpreferred activities, no activity, prompting procedure, contingency statement.
Student 3
  Behaviors: problem behavior, unprompted appropriate behavior, neutral behavior, no motor movement.
  Environmental variables: active task, passive task, attention to problem behavior, no attention to inappropriate behavior, attention to appropriate behavior, no attention to inappropriate behavior, prompting procedure.

---

reinforcement, a hypothesis that concerned the relationship between behavior and a consequence (attention) rather than between behavior and an antecedent (e.g., the type of task within a group activity). During baseline, appropriate behavior was followed by attention 46% of the time, whereas inappropriate behavior was followed by attention 66% of the time. Therefore, the intervention consisted of changing the relationship between attention and both appropriate and inappropriate behaviors. The overall rationale for a hypothesis-based intervention is that (a) the inappropriate behavior should be prevented from continuing to produce its same function (generating attention in this case); (b) the appropriate behavior should produce the same function that inappropriate behavior had been producing (i.e., generating attention); and (c) the appropriate behavior should produce that function more efficiently and with less effort.

This intervention, then, consisted of several procedures. When an inappropriate behavior occurred, the teacher or aide disrupted its function by ignoring the behavior while providing no eye contact, physical contact, or words other than "J.T., if you want a turn, say, 'I want a turn.' " Because problem behavior no longer gained the same type of attention it had been producing, we wanted to maximize the extent to which appropriate behaviors would provide the same function. Three procedures were used for this purpose. The first was to differentially reinforce J.T. at prescribed intervals when he was engaged in appropriate behavior. Because the data collection system indicated he was gaining attention through inappropriate behavior every 8 s on average in baseline, staff provided attention every 5 s for appropriate behavior during the first 3 days of intervention. Then, as

TABLE 4
Probability Relationship Between Behavior and Antecedents or Consequences During Baseline and Last Phase of Intervention

Child 1 (J.T.)
(Positive reinforcement hypothesis)

	Problem behavior		Appropriate behavior	
	Baseline	Intervention	Baseline	Intervention
Attention	.66	.05	.46	.79
No attention	.34	.95	.54	.21

Child 2 (David)
(Negative reinforcement hypothesis)

	Activity requiring active response		Activity not requiring active response	
	Baseline	Intervention	Baseline	Intervention
Appropriate behavior	.34	.96	1.00	1.00
Tantrums	.54	.04	.00	.00
Property destruction	.12	.00	.00	.00

Child 3 (Henry)
(Stimulation hypothesis)

	Active task		Passive task	
	Baseline	Intervention	Baseline	Intervention
Appropriate behavior	.66	.99	.08	.98
Problem behavior	.34	.01	.83	.02
No motor movement	.00	.00	.09	.00

Child 3 (Henry)
(Positive reinforcement hypothesis)

	Appropriate behavior		Inappropriate behavior	
	Baseline	Intervention	Baseline	Intervention
Attention (as consequence)	.28	.12	.58	.00
Attention (as prompt)	.12	.04	.03	.00
No attention	.60	.84	.39	1.00

the behavior decreased, that interval was increased first to 15 s, then to 30 s, then to a variable interval ranging from 30 s to 2 min that was more natural to the teaching situation. Other procedures intended to maximize attention included increasing the opportunities for J.T. to respond during activities and prompting him to say "I want a turn." For the latter, the teacher praised him for his statement and either gave him a turn immediately or shortly thereafter in the natural teaching sequence. In this way, we were increasing the opportunities for J.T. to gain attention through appropriate behaviors.

Problem behaviors for David, the second child, included tantrums (falling to the floor, kicking or hitting the teacher or aides, throwing things) and property destruction (pushing or knocking over furniture, tearing or ripping things). Our hypothesis was negative reinforcement as the baseline data showed the following relationship between types of tasks and behaviors. During activities not requiring active responses, appropriate behavior occurred 100% of time; tantrums, 0%; and property destruction, 0%. During activities requiring active responses, appropriate behavior occurred 34% of the time; tantrums, 54%; and property destruction, 12%.

The negative reinforcement hypothesis concerned the relationship between an antecedent (type of task) and behavior rather than between behavior and a consequence such as attention, so the intervention consisted of manipulating antecedents. During intervention, we provided immediate reinforcement for task completion. Our first step was to categorize tasks that were and were not associated with problem behaviors. Those that were associated with problem behaviors included group instruction, vocational activities, and any task that required the manipulation of materials. Those that were not associated with problem behavior included passive activities such as listening to music, watching TV, observing peers and staff, and eating a snack. The second step was to assemble a set of photographs that depicted the activities during which problem behaviors both occurred and did not occur. At the beginning of an activity that produced problem behavior, the teacher or aide presented a photograph of the individual or group activity and said, "David, it is time for _____." A photograph of a preferred activity was immediately presented and the teacher said, "When you are finished with _____, you may do this" (showing the picture of the preferred activity). The teacher or aide placed the photograph of the preferred activity next to her, and with each correct response she praised David and moved the photograph closer to him. By the time the task was completed, the photograph had reached David, who was allowed to pick it up and immediately engage in the activity represented by the photograph for approximately 2 min. At the beginning of the intervention, David was given brief tasks and was required to work for only 2 min. The length of the tasks was gradually increased until it resembled the length of the natural activities in the classroom. When the inappropriate behavior occurred, the teacher ignored the behavior and prompted or physically guided the appropriate response. Next, the contingent activity was delayed rather than being delivered immediately following task completion. David then had to wait until the normally scheduled time for that activity.

Problem behaviors for the third child, Henry, included running from the classroom; climbing on furniture; opening cupboards and drawers; throwing objects; and kicking, biting, or scratching teachers or aides. Baseline data suggested that problem behaviors could be explained by two hypotheses: stimulation and positive reinforcement. The contingency table for the stimulation hypothesis showed the following relationships between tasks and behaviors. During active tasks, appropriate behavior occurred 66% of the time; problem behavior, 34%; and no motor movement, 0%.

During passive tasks, appropriate behavior occurred 8% of the time; problem behavior, 83%; and no motor movement, 9%.

The intervention addressing this hypothesis consisted of changing the ratio of active to passive tasks throughout the day. This objective was met in the following ways. During baseline, 64% of the tasks were passive and 36% were active. During intervention, a set of active tasks was identified that Henry could do independently, and pictures of these activities were put in a booklet. Then, throughout the day, an aide or teacher provided one-to-one instruction in those tasks that allowed a high rate of activity on his part. In this phase, 25% of the tasks were passive and 75% were active; all activities involved gross motor movement. We have used this same approach to develop hypotheses-based interventions for many other individuals with developmental disabilities who exhibit problem behaviors. The components of the naturalistic assessment approach are summarized in Figure 1 and depict the relationships among problem behaviors and setting events, antecedent events, consequences, and hypotheses for the function of the problem behaviors.

CONCLUSION

Historically, interventions for problem behaviors were not based on a hypothesis of the function of the behavior. Their selection relied on the skill with which the clinician could choose among procedures, some of which included aversive procedures that were less acceptable to many researchers, practitioners, and advocates. Controversy over the acceptability of interventions led to interest in procedures for developing hypotheses for problem behaviors on which treatment could be based. To date, hypothesis-based interventions have proved to be primarily nonaversive and effective for reducing serious problem behaviors.

Three hypotheses for environmentally dependent problem behaviors have emerged in research with individuals with developmental disabilities: positive reinforcement, negative reinforcement, and stimulation. Although variation in terminology exists among some researchers and practitioners, these three hypotheses have been validated by the effectiveness of interventions that were based on the hypotheses.

Methods for determining which hypothesis describes the functional relationship between environmental conditions (e.g., difficult task) and problem behaviors (e.g., tantrums) have been described as indirect, analogue, and naturalistic assessment. Advantages of naturalistic functional assessment include the following: (a) Conditions designed to produce the behavior intentionally are not presented; (b) conditions affecting behavior during assessment are the same as those that are present during and after intervention, improving the validity of the assessment; (c) staff are not

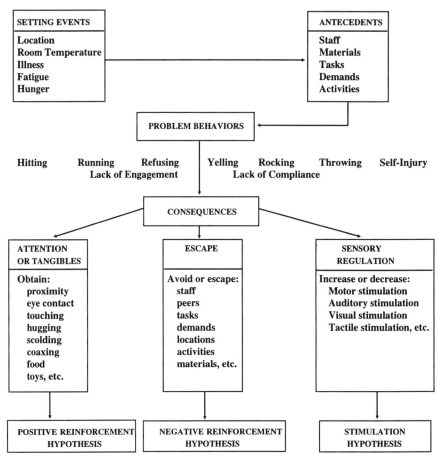

Figure 1. Examples of a schema for the relationship of problem behaviors to environmental variables and hypotheses for problem behavior.

required to change their routine or manipulate the environment; and (d) conditions in the natural setting that produce more adaptive behavior and less problem behavior are identified during the assessment.

We have used naturalistic functional assessment to develop hypothesis-based interventions for many individuals, three of whom we have described in this chapter. Because hypothesis-based interventions are derived from baseline data collected in the natural setting, the indicated interventions typically involve environmental changes that are easily implemented by teachers, direct-care staff, and parents.

Although procedures for selecting hypothesis-based interventions have been developed in the context of interventions for problem behaviors of persons with developmental disabilities, there is no aspect of these procedures that limits their use to this population. We anticipate extending our research to other individuals, such as children with behavior disorders or nondisabled children in regular-education classrooms. In addition to expanding the number of individuals with whom hypothesis-based interventions are implemented, we also anticipate expanding the number of persons trained to implement the procedures we have described.

We suggest that the following areas of study are necessary for the further development of procedures for identifying and implementing hypothesis-based interventions:

1. research on the interactions among setting events (e.g., diet), antecedent events (e.g., tasks requiring sustained attention), and behavior (e.g., listening to a story and responding to a series of questions);
2. determining the extent to which a single response, or a class of responses, may serve different functions at different times or in different settings and therefore be described under different hypotheses; and
3. further the refinement of the hypotheses for environmentally dependent problem behaviors.

In summary, interventions that are based on a hypothesis of the function of problem behavior have been shown to be nonaversive and educative in nature and effective for reducing problem behavior. We have presented a technology for analyzing behavior in the natural setting and for deriving an assessment-based intervention that can be implemented by professionals or paraprofessionals. In the future, we hope that we, as well as other researchers, can continue to expand the development and use of these techniques for improving the quality of life for a variety of individuals.

REFERENCES

Bachman, J. E., & Fuqua, R. W. (1983). Management of inappropriate behaviors of trainable mentally impaired students using antecedent exercise. *Journal of Applied Behavior Analysis, 16,* 477–484.

Berkson, G., & Mason, W. A. (1965). Stereotyped movements of mental defectives: IV. The effects of toys and the character of the acts. *American Journal of Mental Deficiency, 68,* 511–524.

Bijou, S. W. (1963). Theory and research in mental retardation. *Psychological Record, 13,* 95–110.

Bijou, S. W., & Baer, D. M. (1961). *Child development: A systematic and empirical theory* (Vol. 1). New York: Appleton-Century-Crofts.

Bijou, S. W., & Baer, D. M. (1963). Some methodological contributions from a functional analysis of child development. In L. P. Lipsitt & C. S. Spiker

(Eds.), *Advances in child development and behavior* (pp. 197–231). San Diego, CA: Academic Press.

Bijou, S. W., & Orlando, R. (1961). Rapid development of multiple schedule performances with retarded children. *Journal of the Experimental Analysis of the Behavior, 4,* 7–16.

Borthwick, S. A., Meyers, C. E., & Eyman, R. K. (1981). A comparison of adaptive and maladaptive behavior of mentally retarded clients of five residential settings in three western states. In R. H. Bruininks, C. E. Meyers, B. B. Sigford, & K. C. Lakin (Eds.), *Deinstitutionalization and community adjustment of mentally retarded people* (Monograph No. 4, pp. 351–359). Washington, DC: American Association on Mental Deficiency.

Carr, E. G. (1977). The motivation of self-injurious behavior: A review of some hypotheses. *Psychological Bulletin, 84,* 800–816.

Carr, E. G., & Durand, V. M. (1985). Reducing behavior problems through functional communication training. *Journal of Applied Behavior Analysis, 18,* 111–126.

Carr, E. G., & Newsom, C. (1985). Demand-related tantrums. *Behavior Modification, 9,* 403–426.

Carr, E. G., Newsom, C. D., & Binkoff, J. A. (1980). Escape as a factor in the aggressive behavior of two retarded children. *Journal of Applied Behavior Analysis, 13,* 101–117.

Carr, E. G., Robinson, S., & Palumbo, L. W. (1990). The wrong issue: Aversive versus nonaversive treatment. The right issue: Functional versus nonfunctional treatment. In A. C. Repp & N. N. Singh (Eds.), *Perspectives on the use of nonaversive and aversive interventions for persons with developmental disabilities* (pp. 361–379). Sycamore, IL: Sycamore Publishing.

Carr, E. G., Robinson, S., Taylor, J. C., & Carlson, J. I. (1990). *Positive approaches to the treatment of severe behavior problems in persons with developmental disabilities: A review and analysis of reinforcement and stimulus-based procedures* (Monograph No. 4). Washington, DC: Association for Persons with Severe Handicaps.

Crawford, J., Brockel, B., Schauss, S., & Miltenberger, R. G. (1992). A comparison of methods for the functional assessment of stereotypic behavior. *Journal of the Association for Persons with Severe Handicaps, 17,* 77–86.

Corbett, J. A., & Campbell, H. J. (1981). Causes of self-injurious behavior. In P. Mittler (Ed.), *Frontiers of knowledge in mental retardation: Vol. 2. Biomedical aspects* (pp. 285–292). Baltimore: University Park Press.

Day, R. M., Rea, J. A., Schussler, N. G., Larsen, S. E., & Johnson, W. L. (1988). A functionally based approach to the treatment of self-injurious behavior. *Behavior Modification, 12,* 565–589.

Derby, K. M., Wacker, D., Sasso, G., Steege, M., Northup, J., Cigrand, K., & Asmus, J. (1992). Brief functional assessment techniques to evaluate aberrant behavior in an outpatient setting: A summary of 79 cases. *Journal of Applied Behavior Analysis, 25,* 713–722.

Dunlap, G., Kern-Dunlap, L., Clarke, S., & Robbins, F. R. (1991). Functional assessment, curricular revision, and severe behavior problems. *Journal of Applied Behavior Analysis, 24*, 387–397.

Durand, V. M., & Carr, E. G. (1987). Social influences on "self-stimulatory" behavior: Analysis and treatment application. *Journal of Applied Behaviour Analysis, 20*, 119–132.

Durand, V. M., & Crimmins, D. B. (1988). Identifying the variables maintaining self-injurious behavior. *Journal of Autism and Developmental Disorders, 18*, 99–117.

Durand, V. M., & Kishi, G. (1987). Reducing severe behavior problems among persons with dual sensory impairments: An evaluation of a technical assistance model. *Journal of the Association for Persons with Severe Handicaps, 12*, 2–10.

Edelson, S. M., Taubman, M. T., & Lovaas, O. I. (1983). Some social contexts of self-destructive behavior. *Journal of Abnormal Child Psychology, 11*, 299–312.

Eyman, R. K., & Call, T. (1977). Maladaptive behavior and community placement of mentally retarded persons. *American Journal of Mental Deficiency, 82*, 137–144.

Favell, J. E., McGimsey, J. F., & Schell, R. M. (1982). Treatment of self-injury by providing alternate sensory activities. *Analysis and Intervention in Developmental Disabilities, 2*, 83–104.

Flannery, K. B., & Horner, R. H. (in press). The relationship between predictability and problem behavior for students with severe disabilities. *Journal of Behavioral Education.*

Gorman-Smith, D., & Matson, J. L. (1985). A review of treatment research for self-injurious and stereotyped responding. *Journal of Mental Deficiency Research, 29*, 295–308.

Griffen, J. C., Williams, D. E., Stark, M. T., Altmeyer, B. K., & Mason, M. (1986). Self-injurious behavior: A statewide prevalence survey of the extent and circumstances. *Applied Research in Mental Retardation, 7*, 105–116.

Horner, R. D. (1980). The effects of an environmental "enrichment" program on the behavior of institutionalized profoundly retarded children. *Journal of Applied Behavior Analysis, 13*, 473–491.

Iwata, B., Dorsey, M., Slifer, K., Bauman, K., & Richman, G. (1982). Toward a functional analysis of self-injury. *Analysis and Intervention in Developmental Disabilities, 2*, 3–20.

Iwata, B., Pace, G., Kalsher, M., Cowdery, G., & Cataldo, M. (1990). Experimental analysis and extinction of self-injurious escape behavior. *Journal of Applied Behavior Analysis, 23*, 11–27.

Iwata, B. A., Vollmer, T. R., & Zarcone, J. H. (1990). The experimental (functional) analysis of behavior disorders: Methodology, applications, and limitations. In A. C. Repp & N. N. Singh (Eds.), *Perspectives on the use of nonaversive and aversive interventions for persons with developmental disabilities* (pp. 301–330). Sycamore, IL: Sycamore Publishing.

Jacobson, J. W. (1982). Problem behavior and psychiatric impairment within a developmentally disabled population: 1. Behavior frequency. *Applied Research in Mental Retardation, 3,* 121–139.

Karsh, K. G., & Repp, A. C. (1994). *Hypothesis-based interventions for students with developmental disabilities engaging in severe problem behaviors.* Manuscript submitted for publication.

Karsh, K. G., Repp, A. C., Dahlquist, C. M., & Munk, D. (in press). A functional analysis of noncompliance and associated behaviors of students with developmental disabilities. *Journal of Behavioral Education.*

Kennedy, C. H., & Itkonen, T. (1993). Effects of setting events on the problem behavior of students with severe disabilities. *Journal of Applied Behavior Analysis, 26,* 321–327.

Kern, L., Childs, K. E., Dunlap, G., Clarke, S., & Falk, G. D. (1994). Using assessment-based curricular intervention to improve the classroom of a student with emotional and behavioral challenges. *Journal of Applied Behavior Analysis, 27,* 7–19.

Kern, L., Koegel, R. L., & Dunlap, G. (1984). The influence of vigorous versus mild exercise on autistic stereotyped behaviors. *Journal of Autism and Developmental Disorders, 14,* 57–67.

La Grow, S. J., & Repp, A. C. (1984). Stereotypic responding: A review of intervention research. *American Journal of Mental Deficiency, 88,* 595–609.

Lalli, J. S., Browder, D. M., Mace, C. F., & Brown, D. K. (1993). Teacher use of descriptive analysis to implement interventions to decrease students' problem behaviors. *Journal of Applied Behavior Analysis, 26,* 227–238.

Lundervold, D., & Bourland, G. (1988). Quantitative analysis of treatment of aggression, self-injury, and property destruction. *Behavior Modification, 12,* 590–617.

Matson, J. L., & Gorman-Smith, D. (1986). A review of treatment research for aggressive and disruptive behavior in the mentally retarded. *Applied Research in Mental Retardation, 7,* 95–103.

Matson, J. L., & Taras, M. E. (1989). A 20 year review of punishment and alternative methods to treat problem behaviors in developmentally delayed persons. *Research in Developmental Disabilities, 10,* 85–104.

Moseley, A., Faust, M., & Reardon, D. M. (1970). Effects of social and nonsocial stimuli on the stereotyped behaviors of retarded children. *American Journal of Mental Deficiency, 74,* 809–811.

Munk, D., & Repp, A. C. (1994). Behavioral assessment of feeding problems of children with severe disabilities. *Journal of Applied Behavior Analysis, 27,* 241–250.

National Institutes of Health. (1989, September). *Consensus Development Conference statement: Treatment of destructive behaviors in persons with developmental disabilities.* Rockville, MD: Author.

Northup, J., Wacker, D., Sasso, G., Steege, M., Cigrand, K., Cook, J., & DeRaad, A. (1991). A brief functional analysis of aggressive and alternative behavior in an out-clinic setting. *Journal of Applied Behavior Analysis, 24,* 509–522.

O'Brien, S., & Repp, A. C. (1990). Reinforcement-based reductive procedures: A 20-year review of their use with persons with severe handicaps. *Journal of the Association for Persons with Severe Handicaps, 15,* 148–159.

Oliver, C., Murphy, G. H., & Corbett, J. A. (1987). Self-injurious behavior in people with mental handicap: A total population study. *Journal of Mental Deficiency Research, 31,* 147–162.

O'Neill, R. E., Horner, R. H., Albin, R. W., Storey, K., & Sprague, J. R. (1990). *Functional analysis of problem behavior: A practical assessment guide.* Sycamore, IL: Sycamore Publishing.

Repp, A. C. (1983). *Teaching the mentally retarded.* Englewood Cliffs, NJ: Prentice Hall.

Repp, A. C., & Barton, L. E. (1980). Naturalistic observations of retarded persons: A comparison of licensure decisions and behavioral observations. *Journal of Applied Behavior Analysis, 13,* 333–341.

Repp, A. C., Felce, D., & Barton, L. G. (1988). Basing the treatment of stereotypic and self-injurious behaviors on hypotheses of their causes. *Journal of Applied Behavior Analysis, 21,* 281–289.

Repp, A. C., & Karsh, K. G. (1992). An analysis of a group teaching procedure for persons with developmental disabilities. *Journal of Applied Behavior Analysis, 25,* 701–712.

Repp, A. C., & Karsh, K. G. (1994). Hypothesis-based interventions for tantrum behaviors of persons with developmental disabilities in school settings. *Journal of Applied Behavior Analysis, 27,* 21–31.

Repp, A. C., Karsh, K. G., & Dahlquist, C. M. (1994). *Hypothesis-based interventions in the functional analysis of problem behaviors of persons with developmental disabilities.* Manuscript submitted for publication.

Repp, A. C., Karsh, K. G., Deitz, D. E. D., & Singh, N. N. (1992). A study of the homeostatic level of stereotypy and other motor movements of persons with mental handicaps. *Journal of Intellectual Disability Research, 36,* 61–75

Repp, A. C., & Singh, N. N. (1990). *Perspectives on the use of nonaversive and aversive interventions for persons with developmental disabilities.* Sycamore, IL: Sycamore.

Rincover, A. (1978). Sensory extinction: A procedure for eliminating self-stimulatory behavior in developmentally disabled children. *Journal of Abnormal Child Psychology, 6,* 299–310.

Singh, N. N., Donatelli, L. S., Best, A., Williams, D. E., Barrera, F. J., Lenz, M. W., Landrum, T. J., Ellis, C. R., & Moe, T. L. (1993). Factor structure of the Motivation Assessment Scale. *Journal of Intellectual Disability Research, 37,* 65–74.

Singh, N. N., Lloyd, J. W., & Kendall, K. A. (1990). Nonaversive and aversive interventions: Issues. In A. C. Repp & N. N. Singh (Eds.), *Perspectives on the use of nonaversive and aversive interventions for persons with developmental disabilities* (pp. 3–16). Sycamore, IL: Sycamore.

Steege, M. W., Wacker, D. P., Berg, W. K., Cigrand, K. K., & Cooper, L. (1989). The use of behavioral assessment to prescribe and evaluate treatments for severely handicapped children. *Journal of Applied Behavior Analysis, 22,* 23–33.

Weeks, M., & Gaylord-Ross, R. (1981). Task difficulty and aberrant behavior in severely handicapped students. *Journal of Applied Behavior Analysis, 14,* 449–463.

Winterling, V., Dunlap, G., & O'Neill, R. E. (1987). The influence of task variation on the aberrant behaviors of autistic students. *Education and Treatment of Children, 10,* 105–119.

Zarcone, J. R., Rodgers, T. A., Iwata, B. A., Rourke, D. A., & Dorsey, M. F. (1991). Reliability analysis of the Motivation Assessment Scale: A failure to replicate. *Research in Developmental Disabilities, 12,* 349–360.

22

INTERBEHAVIORAL PSYCHOLOGY: CRITICAL, SYSTEMATIC, AND INTEGRATIVE APPROACH TO CLINICAL SERVICES

DENNIS J. DELPRATO

An interbehavioral approach, above all else, aims to provide a coherent and systematic science and practice of psychology "from the ground up." The interbehavioral perspective considers it essential for a psychological practice, authentically based on science, to have a completely naturalistic approach to both science itself and psychology in general. With this in view, I will first cover historical developments and basic orienting assumptions pertaining to science itself. I will then set forth some fundamentals for psychology as a completely naturalistic science. Finally, I will present several assumptions for clinical services themselves, along with practices recommended by them.

I thank P. A. Holmes, F. D. McGlynn, P. T. Mountjoy, and N. W. Smith for their helpful comments on an earlier version of this chapter.

J. R. Kantor and Interbehaviorism

J. R. Kantor (1888–1984) originated the interbehavioral psychology (and philosophy) literature. Kantor did doctoral work in biology, psychology, and philosophy at the University of Chicago, ultimately completing the requirements for his doctoral degree in 1916. Kantor's career suggests that he was well prepared to profit from the functional and behavioral atmosphere that was underway at Chicago by the turn of the 20th century. The major message that theorists were beginning to formulate and support was that the fundamental subject matter of psychology was not mentality, mind, consciousness, or experience but adaptive behavior (Leahey, 1987). It was this thinking that led many to what became identified as *behaviorism*. By the mid-1930s, numerous versions of behaviorism had appeared. Although Kantor was sympathetic to the behavioral movement, he has been an enigma to those who find it important to place individuals and literatures into conventional categories.

Kantor took on the ambitious task of developing a coherent philosophy and psychology that centered on scientific understanding of human psychological behavior as the basis of all disciplines, whether conventionally taken as sciences or humanities. I am struck by how far Kantor's work goes toward accomplishing one of the earliest aims of the behavior therapy movement: clinical theory and practice as fundamentally continuous and harmonious with basic science and theory. This chapter aims to highlight the systematic advantages of the interbehavioral framework for the behavioral clinician.

At the heart of Kantor's thinking were his early leanings toward, and, later, explicit advocacy of, field theory. Kantor (1969) argued that despite the many advances associated with behaviorism, its lack of a field character left it open to further emendation. After trying various terms to refer to the approach he favored, Kantor ended up with *interbehaviorism*. He added "inter" to "behaviorism" to communicate that behavior must always be described in field terms. But what does this mean? At a basic level, Kantor used the prefix "inter" to denote that psychologically, the organism's actions are always coordinated with specific conditions (e.g., the behaviorists' *stimuli*) such that the two sides are always mutual or reciprocally related (i.e., neither stimulus → response nor response → stimulus, but response ↔ stimulus). Although it is possible for analysts to isolate response or stimulus factors, the actions of reciprocally related stimulus and response factors constitute a single psychological unit. When I expand on the nature of the psychological event-field below, one can find that the mutuality of response and stimulus makes response–function and stimulus–function the relevant constructions for psychologists. These abstractions, although related to physiological and physical factors, are not to be confused with them. At this point, Kantor applies a fundamental feature of field theory: the substitution of interdependence among constituents of events in place of independent (causes) and dependent (effects) variables. To understand further Kantor's field theory, it is useful to examine changes in how thinkers have approached the world over the centuries. One finds that they end up with field and system constructions.

From Lineal Mechanics to Fields/Systems

Several authoritative historical analyses (Dewey & Bentley, 1949; Einstein & Infeld, 1938; Handy & Harwood, 1973; Kantor, 1946, 1969) agreed on three general stages in the evolution of thinking about the world.[1] Thinkers first assumed that natural events acted under self-contained powers, and they postulated various weightless substances (imponderables) with unique, inherent properties to account for heat (caloric), combustion (phlogiston), biological functioning (vital force, entelechy), and human psychological behavior (soul, spirit, mind). Thus, this initial stage is referred to as the *substance theory* (Einstein & Infeld, 1938), the *substance-property* stage (Kantor, 1946, 1969), and the *self-actional* stage (Dewey & Bentley, 1949).

Lineal Mechanics

The *mechanical view* (Einstein & Infeld, 1938), *statistical-correlational* stage (Kantor, 1946, 1969), or *interactional* stage (Dewey & Bentley, 1949), is marked by the work of Galileo and associated with the advent of modern science. This second general scientific approach retained substances, but now thinkers interpreted natural phenomena in terms of attractive and repulsive forces that acted between unalterable objects (or particles) and that were dependent only on distance. According to Einstein and Infeld (1938), Newton's gravitational laws connecting the motion of the earth with the action of the distant sun exemplify the second stage: "The earth and the sun, though so far apart, are both actors in the play of forces" (p. 152). Biologists incorporated mechanisms by reducing integrated biological activity to hypothetical physicochemical causal chains. This second stage of scientific thinking was the era of the world machine, materialism, causal

---

[1]The authors just cited have expanded on and placed into historical perspective the well-known transition from mechanistic, materialistic science and its world view to modern science. In physics, where the transition first occurred, authorities use the terms *classical* (or *old* or *Newtonian*) physics (or mechanics) to designate the former and *new* (or *modern* or *quantum*) physics (or mechanics) to refer to the radically different way of going about understanding the world (e.g., Davies, 1989; Furth, 1970; Hirosige, 1976; Mehra & Rechenberg, 1982; Taylor, 1972). In summarizing what is distinctive about the new physics, one commentator recently noted that "relativistic quantum field theory [is the] jewel in the crown of [it]" (Davies, 1989, p. 2).

determinism, and reductionism. The fundamental descriptive and explanatory model was cause → effect. This stage in the evolution of thinking about the world that served science well for such a long time is aptly named *lineal mechanism.*

Although the physical sciences, and to some extent biology, have abandoned lineal mechanism, mainstream contemporary psychology has not.[2] The classic experimental model whereby causes are identified with independent variables, and effects with dependent variables, continues to reign supreme. We are encouraged to identify biological, environmental, and cognitive causes of behavior from the standpoint of stimulus → response, stimulus → cognition → response, input → information processing → behavioral output, past environmental consequences of behavior → emitted behavior, or some equivalent framework. Few psychologists endorse blatantly mechanistic claims. However, subtle forms of mechanistic thinking abound in behavioral science. We are operating from the standpoint of lineal mechanism anytime we impute independent causal status to actual or supposed variables such as heredity, brain processes, reinforcement schedule, reinforcement history, anger, frustration, central pattern generators, expectancies, thoughts, images, feedback, and so on.

Field Constructions

Physical scientists gradually abandoned mechanism (Frank, 1955), although it is not completely without influence today (Holton, 1973). Einstein and Infeld (1938) suggested that the transition from classical mechanics (e.g., Newton's gravitational laws) to Maxwell's equations was a critical development in the evolution of a third stage of thinking in physics. Now there were no material actors; the mathematical equations "do not connect two widely separated events; they do not connect the happenings *here* [or now] with the conditions *there* [or then]" (Einstein & Infeld, 1938, pp. 152–153). The mechanical theorist attempted "to describe the action of two electric charges only by concepts referring to the two charges, . . . [but] in the new field language it is the description of the field between the two charges, and not the charges themselves, which is essential for an understanding of their action" (Einstein & Infeld, 1938, p. 157). The field construct has taken physics far away from mechanistic thinking, with its bifurcations of nature (e.g., mass and energy, matter and

---

[2]In his much-cited *World Hypotheses*, Pepper (1942) was very clear that he detected physical scientists' movement from lineal mechanism (which he called "discrete mechanism") to field theory (which he called "consolidated mechanism"). Pepper viewed the lever as the "root metaphor" for the former, but the electromagnetic field as the basis of the latter, which "is not a dream, but is the most plausible theory of the nature of the world so far as physical evidence goes" (p. 214). Pepper's analysis is important insofar as several authors in psychology have promoted Pepper's "world hypothesis" theory but have totally ignored his explicit identification of movement from lineal mechanism to field theory (see Delprato, 1993).

force, gravitational mass and inertial mass), to the inertial-energy concept and the equivalence of mass–energy and gravitational-inertial mass.

Although the biological and psychological sciences lagged behind physics in progression through the three stages, field thinking definitely is found in contemporary psychology. Kantor (1941) noted several early versions of field theory, including that of the gestaltists. However, the first attempts to take a field perspective in psychology were not sufficiently advanced over earlier lineal mechanical approaches especially because of their continued adherence to internal principles and dualisms (Kantor, 1941, 1969). One example of this is the tendency of some gestaltists to take the field construct of behavior space as merely experiential. The gestalists particularly erred by borrowing the field conception from physics and treating psychological events as merely analogous to physical ones, as exemplified by their attempts to apply the perfectly acceptable physical concept of field-forces (Kantor, 1971).

No one has done more than Kantor (1959, 1969) to develop the modern field concept in psychology. According to Kantor (1969), the psychological field is

> the entire system of things and conditions operating in any event taken in its available totality. It is only the entire system of factors which will provide proper descriptive and explanatory materials for the handling of events. It is not the reacting organism alone which makes up the event but also the stimulating things and conditions, as well as the setting factors. (p. 371)

Field thinking directed explanatory efforts in physics away from mechanism and the search for ultimate causes. Modern physical scientists no longer approach their science from the cause–effect framework (e.g., Feigl, 1953; Holton, 1973; Russell, 1953). According to Feigl (1953), the field alternative to the terms *cause* and *effect* in ordinary language "is the entire *set* of conditions [event-field]" (p. 410), and this set represents the cause of an event. Kantor (1959) further clarified the field construct and made the same point in discussing the field alternative to conventional causal constructions:

> All creative agencies, all powers and forces, are rejected. An event is regarded as a field of factors all of which are equally necessary, or, more properly speaking, equal participants in the event. In fact, events are scientifically described by analyzing these participating factors and finding how they are related. (p. 90)

I noted above that Kantor adopted the prefix "inter" to communicate that psychological events are always composed of interdependent factors. Thus, a minimum of two variables is always involved, one pertaining to actions of organisms, the other to actions of at least one set of conditions with which the organism's actions are coordinated. However, a more complete conceptual description of psychological event (PE)-fields requires more factors; Kantor (1959) used the "equation" PE = C(k, sf, rf, hi, st, md). In this formulation, k symbolizes that all psychological events are unique, sf represents stimulus–function, rf stands for response–function, hi is the historical process through which the correlated sf and rf developed, st recognizes that particular sf–rf coordinations always take place in immediate ecological and organic settings, md represents a class of setting factor given separate status as the medium by which the organism contacts the physiological and physical correlates of sf (e.g., light is a medium of contact for visual interactions), and C communicates that the PE consists of an entire system of interdependent factors.

Kantor's field conception of psychological events helps us capture their complexity without the necessity of invoking anything fictitious. I find it difficult to imagine any effective clinician who does not take at least a minimal field perspective. This point is nicely illustrated by one of the classic cases of psychological analysis (and treatment). Ellenberger (1970, pp. 361–364) relates Pierre Janet's account of the recalcitrant case of Marie that Janet published in 1889. One component of Marie's plight was depressive and violent episodes marked by sudden termination of menstruation 20 hours after the beginning, a great tremor of the entire body, reports of severe pain ascending slowly from the abdomen to the throat, violent bodily contortions, and other symptoms. If Janet's reconstruction of Marie's history is accurate, from today's perspective it appears that a self-initiated classical conditioning interaction (conditional stimulus = menstruation at 20 hr, unconditional stimulus = cold water, unconditional response = vasoconstriction, shivering, and sequela) was a critical contributor to Marie's condition.[3] Upon her first menstruation at the age of 13, Marie interpreted it as shameful and tried to stop the flow by plunging herself into a large bucket of ice water approximately 20 hours after the onset of menstruation. She was successful. Menstruation suddenly stopped, and Marie returned home shivering violently. For several days after the episode, Marie was ill and delirious. She experienced no menstruation until five years later, at which time the presenting symptoms appeared.

At the risk of oversimplifying and relying on incomplete assessment, it is easy to apply the interbehavioral conception of the fundamental event-field to two important event-fields in the case of Marie. First, at the time of Marie's initial menstruation, sf–rf corresponds to menstruation-as-shameful/undesirable/aversive/to be avoided as a result of one or more historical (hi) episodes in which others directly or indirectly communicated this about a perfectly normal bodily process. Prominent setting factors (st)

---

[3]From the standpoint of interbehavioral psychology, Pavlov's classical conditioning is one way by which new sf–rf coordinations are built up in the organism's history. However, conditioning contingencies are field factors and never independent causes.

include distinctive organic conditions concurrent with menstruation and a bucket of cold water. Media of contact (md) for menstrual flow are light for visual contact and the more intimate tactual medium. All named factors are interdependent participants (C) in the field that is uniquely and only (k) Marie's at a particular point in time. A second important event-field in this case occurs 20 hours into a particular episode of the adult Marie's menstruation several years later. The earlier (hi) self-imposed adjustment of Marie to her first menstruation has contributed to the establishment of an sf–rf coordination whereby vasoconstriction, shivering, and so on is called forth by conditions 20 hours into menstruation. Setting factors (st) again include distinctive organic conditions concurrent with menstruation, and media of contact (md) are light and tactual. All factors in this unique (k) event-field are interdependent (C).

Systems

One hears little about fields in the sense described here in psychology today other than from those impressed with the Kantorian interbehavioral literature. However, although few have recognized it, field theory is healthy as found in the form of "system" constructs. Many of those advocating a system approach (e.g., Bertalanffy, 1972; Marmor, 1983; Rapoport, 1968) maintain that lineal cause → effect mechanisms must be replaced by dynamic systems (or fields) comprising interdependent components. Rapoport (1968), for example, suggested that in the study of living processes, vitalism (substance theory of the first stage of science) and mechanism, physicalism, and reductionism (second stage of scientific thinking) can be replaced with the concept of a system, that is, "a whole which functions as whole by virtue of the interdependence of its parts" (p. xvii).

Marmor (1983) discussed psychiatry from a system perspective after acknowledging that Lewin's (1951) field theory was at the same time a system theory, and it seems clear that movement to the integrated-field stage of science underlies the views of theorists who have argued for the relevance of system theory for behavioral development (e.g., Delprato, 1987; Sameroff, 1983). Researchers and theorists who have concluded that field and system constructs are fundamentally the same have found promise in the integrated-field/system perspective for behavioral methodology (Ray & Delprato, 1989), pedagogy (Hawkins & Sharpe, 1992), family therapy (Wahler & Hann, 1987), and clinical psychology in general (see Ruben & Delprato, 1987).

It is undeniable that today's behavioral science literature said to be based on system theory is not uniformly sufficiently advanced to the point of Kantor's thinking. However, Kantor supplied no research tools for investigating fields. On the other hand, behavioral systems researchers have developed strategies and tactics that yield data on psychological fields/

systems. Ray and Delprato (1989) described a comprehensive research methodology based on interbehavioral psychology and systems research. Behavioral systems analysis of psychological fields, especially, involves describing the organization of fields by tracking concurrently operating multiple factors across time. The behavioral systems researcher uses some techniques long known to psychologists but not particularly prominent in mainstream practices (e.g., multivariate techniques such as factor analysis and time-series analyses). Roger Ray's (e.g., Ray & Delprato, 1989) creative extensions of interbehavioral theory and systems research are important in that they go far toward addressing a serious limitation of interbehavioral psychology à la Kantor (i.e., absence of data-generating methodology). The future is promising if Hawkins and Sharpe's (1992) monograph on their applications of Ray's behavioral field systems analysis to sport pedagogy is any indication of what is possible.

Historicocritical Analysis

The field/system nature of interbehavioral theorizing is but one of its distinguishing marks. Despite Kantor's sometimes ambiguous status in a narrowly defined behavioral psychology, his macrohistorical and historicocritical analysis of the scientific evolution of psychology leaves no doubt that he viewed interbehaviorism as the culmination of the behavioral movement. *The Scientific Evolution of Psychology* (Kantor, 1963, 1969) documented two major developments in Western thought that get at the heart of nonbehavioral and behavioral approaches to psychology. The first, involving departure from naturalistic Hellenic thinking and the invention of a nonspatiotemporal world, underlies non- or antibehavioral psychologies. Historical events, themselves well known among historians, corroborate thinkers' gradual escapist verbal creation of a world without time and space, under the harsh living conditions of a decaying, crumbling society. The new nonspatiotemporal world was verbally placed in opposition to the world in which people live—the natural world. The venerable spiritual–material dualism developed, and we see Aristotelian naturalistic soul transformed into supernaturalistic soul-spirit. Spiritual–material dualism became institutionalized in the form of the Church, and the sacred view of the world reigned supreme for centuries. People were encouraged to give little heed to the spatiotemporal events of the world, including those of human behavior.

Supernaturalism, based on the idea of an invisible nonspatiotemporal world, made humans the repository in the natural world of a part of the verbally created spiritual realm said to be confirmed with certainty only by an alleged new way of knowing, revelation. What amounted to a synonym for "life" with purely naturalistic referents was transformed to where the construct—Aristotelian soul—was given supernaturalistic referents and placed inside humans. In the case of humans, spiritual–material dualism is exhibited in the soul–body and mental–behavior distinction that continues up to the present to haunt those who attempt take a scientific—that is, naturalistic or behavioral—approach to psychological events.

The second major development in Western thought consists of society's gradual transition from extreme supernaturalism to ever more naturalistic thinking, as exemplified in psychology first by psychodynamic theories and shortly after by the behaviorisms. A new era of our civilization began around the 11th century C.E. as living conditions began to change away from those that fed the invention and maintenance of sacred spirit. The secularization of society accompanied social, economic, and political conditions that became more similar to those of Hellenic civilization. Thinkers began to reject medieval culture and sought to return to classical Greek and Roman culture. As part of the gradual change from sacred to secular orientations, thinkers transformed supernaturalistic soul to mind, consciousness, and experience; the soul construct became less theological. Critical thinkers gradually altered the definition of the soul to the point where psychological functions were attributed to secular processes. Eventually, a point was reached when the soul became part of a new science, a science that was given an impossible task: It was asked to take a radically different (that is, naturalistic) approach to the soul and, at the same time, remain the repository of centuries of cultural tradition in the form of insubstantial, spaceless, and timeless soul.

The movement from soul to mind, consciousness, experience, and, later, behavior, has been a naturalistic one, but progress in the renaturalization process has been excruciatingly slow. There have been dynamic psychiatry, behaviorism, and phenomenology, but these movements often remained close to the material–spiritual cultural tradition, as exhibited by remnants of the mental–physical dualism in some modern varieties of each of these movements. Furthermore, no science can completely step outside of the cultural matrix that permits its origins and development. With the aid of historicocritical analysis of psychology over the centuries, interbehavioral thinkers have plunged forthrightly into radical naturalism that opts for the thorough renaturalization of humans and the rejection of all vestiges of mental–physical dualism, to complete the final step of the secularization of society and psychology.

One important consequence of a completely naturalistic approach to any aspect of the world is the discovery of the field/system nature of its subject matter (Kantor, 1963, 1969). Thus, the interbehavioral theorist thinks of psychological behavior as interbehavior—a field phenomenon. Interbehaviorists argue that only by taking the fundamental psychological event as an integrated field of simultaneous, participating factors (organismic, ecological, and historical) can we naturalistically describe and explain the full range of psychological events without excluding those posing great difficulties for behaviorisms such as attending, perceiving, imagining, feeling, thinking, and knowing.

Systematics

Critical analysis of the history of a science is one valuable way of advancing knowledge, in particular by removing cultural obstacles. For example, Mach (1883/1942) revealed the observations on which influential concepts were based and the source of superfluous interpretations workers placed on the outcomes of observational activities in mechanics; Kantor (1963, 1969) did the same for psychology. The interbehavioral perspective adds to historicocritical analysis the broad area of scientific systematics. The argument is that we must examine the logic (or systematics) of a science to clear away impediments to sound knowledge and to most efficiently develop new knowledge. To do this, we have to identify the fundamental assumptions that underlie the work we are analyzing. All intellectual enterprises are based on premises or postulates whether or not we explicitly identify them. Assumptions deleterious to understanding are most likely to impede progress when they are not made explicit and thus remain unexamined.

In brief, interbehavioral systematics involve identifying and organizing postulates so that they are (a) open to critical examination and (b) available to serve as guides for workers and students. The most effective practice shows that postulates are not offered a priori as unalterable principles but are derived from workers interbehaving with their subject matter and altering them as work proceeds. The remainder of this chapter is organized around statements of fundamental interbehavioral assumptions at the levels of basic science, psychology as a science, and the clinical practice of psychology. Given that the ultimate aspiration of the interbehavioral perspective is simply scientific understanding of psychological events and that psychologists have pursued this goal for some time, one would expect to find several familiar points and recommendations. Indeed from a global point of view, perhaps the only novel feature of the interbehavioral approach is the organizing framework it provides. When all remnants of nonscientific (i.e., nonnaturalistic) thinking have vanished from how we approach human behavior, interbehaviorism will no longer be necessary, because what it offers (e.g., a field/system perspective) will have been incorporated into psychology itself.

Scientific Fundamentals

Essential. Work said to be scientific or based on science must take observation as paramount. Judgments for acceptability of claims at a particular point are to be made with respect to their status from the standpoint of observation and observational inference, not authority, tradition, or logic.

Primary concern. Scientific work is above all else concerned with the nature and operation of events. A major task of basic scientists and practitioners of science is to guard against any received practice, assumption, or behavior on their part that impedes their descriptions and interpretations of events. The goals and motives of scientists and practitioners of science are fundamentally different from those of people who work in areas such as politics, commerce, law, and entertainment. It is scientific training that better prepares individuals to describe what happened, how it happened, and the attendant conditions to the happening.

Science as behavior-in-culture. Science is inseparable from the behavior of scientists, and scientific enterprises evolve in cultural situations, making very difficult the autonomous practice of science within a cultural complex.

Locus of events. Science finds no justification for the culturally transmitted assumption of a double world—one in which we live, experience, and find things, and another world beyond the boundaries of space–time. Events, be they astronomical, geological, physiological, microphysical (e.g., quantum), or psychological, occur only in a spatiotemporal frame. Any position that promotes the ancient tradition that psychological events such as perceiving, knowing, reasoning, judging, and thinking are uniquely different from seemingly more knowable events only because of the latter's locus in the spatiotemporal world is to be guarded against.

Constructs. Science requires constructs (descriptions, interpretations) that are (a) products that must be derived from interbehaving with events and not imposed on events from sources such as cultural presuppositions, (b) not to be confused with events, and (c) not all equal. As behavioral products, numbers recorded as a result of carpenters', physicists', or psychologists' measuring operations are constructs, as are parents' verbal accounts of their children's destructive behavior, individuals' verbal and motoric activity when asked to describe their feelings, and the many formal and informal diagnostic categories used in clinical psychology. In all cases, the constructions are as good as the operations by which they were derived and are never independent of such operations. To fail to distinguish between constructs and events is to run the risk of imposing the products of contacts with events on the original events, as when the scientist of old imbued combustion processes with heat substances or when the psychologist permits "attention-deficit disorder" to obscure children's interactions with their world.

Procedures and postulates. A common class of event in basic and applied science consists of the expert interacting with events, as when experimenters arrange for a particular thing to follow occurrences of a given movement of a subject, or when clinicians pose a particular question to a client and note their reply. Manipulative procedures are events and are not to be confused with constructs such as descriptions and interpretations that observers use to talk about their procedures or about results deriving from procedures. Furthermore, one should distinguish between procedures and the stated or unstated hypotheses and assumptions, called postulates, that contribute to the institution of one procedure instead of another or to particular interpretative remarks.

Knowing and the known. To one who has not explicitly thought of the issue, the concern with knowing and the known may appear an esoteric largess of philosophy. However, the central (so-called epistemological) issue is readily apparent once one realizes the status of events relative to anyone's knowledge of them. Events are spatially and temporally extended. Our knowledge of an event is not the event itself. Cultural tradition passed on formally by philosophers takes knowing as fundamentally different from things known (i.e., nonspatiotemporal). This has led to many ways of attempting to account for how we have the feeling of knowing events—idealism, realism, positivism, empiricism, logical empiricism, conceptualism, constructionism, and phenomenalism. Practitioners of science have no need for any of these. Instead, they take knowing as belonging to the same (spatiotemporal) framework as the things and events known. The scientist's knowing behavior is not to be confused with the known. It never reveals a "reality" behind the knowing activities, never reveals "reality" in mental states called experience, never yields absolute "truth," and is always personal in the sense that knowing is continuous with the knower's current circumstances, cultural background, and unique long-term and short-term developmental history.

Objectivity and subjectivity. As the above discussion implies, to distinguish between objective and subjective knowledge is unjustified and perpetuates the view that experiencing, perceiving, thinking, imagining, feeling, reasoning, judging, and knowing are nonspatiotemporal and "unreal" and only legitimized for science by making these psychological activities analogous to familiar physical and physiological events. The result of this artificial transforming process is that psychological events are described and interpreted in ways unrepresentative of them, as when perceiving is taken to be analogous to telecommunications systems circa 1920 or to today's electronic computing machines.

Criteria for valid knowledge. Thinkers have offered various criteria for evaluating knowledge claims. These include intersubjective agreement, correspondence with immediate experience, coherence with an assemblage of statements, and pragmatisms (e.g., workability). None of these alternatives is necessary once we identify and act on the above fundamentals. Taken together, they guide us in making decisions on the soundness of particular claims and sets of claims. The fundamentals presented here assist workers to maximize their knowledge of things and events with the assistance of whatever resources they have available, leading to the further behavior of prediction, if desired. That we reach this perhaps surprising solution to one of the most recalcitrant of epistemological problems may speak to the advantages of specifying the basics of science, as is attempted in this chapter.

INTERBEHAVIORAL PSYCHOLOGY AS SCIENCE

Field/System as Analytic Unit

The subject matter of psychology consists of the interactions of organisms with other organisms, objects, and events under the auspices of particular settings, contact media, and historical circumstances. Thus, all psychological events comprise multifactor, integrated fields or systems. One part of the field does not cause either other parts or the event-field itself. Multiple field factors simultaneously participate in the psychological event. Field factors are not related by way of independence and dependence, but rather by mutual implication or interdependence.

The Nature of Participating Field Factors

Physical, chemical, biological, ecological, and sociocultural factors participate in psychological events. Although in no way properly thought of as causes of psychological events, these factors studied by other specialists are always involved, and to ignore them is to risk incomplete description and understanding.

The Organism as Participant

The psychological event is never centered in the organism. It is not located in or at the organism. The organism is a participant in a field of other factors. Psychological events are systemic, not restricted to parts of fields. Neither is the organism's participation confined to one of its parts such as an organ (e.g., the brain) or system (e.g., hormonal). One component (e.g., cerebral) of the organism does not control other parts. Thus, the organism's participation cannot be adequately explained by citing neural or mental causes. In short, the entire organism participates in all performances, albeit with varying degrees of gradation.

Event Evolution: Inorganic and Biological

All psychological events are the outcome of prior evolutions: inorganic (e.g., chemical elements, planets, earth) and biological. Biological evolution has two major phases: phylogenetic (e.g., plants, animals, species) and ontogenetic (which begins with the union of the gametes and involves the embryological and biological development of the individual organism). All psychological behavior has bioecological roots, although sociocultural factors take increasing prominence as psychological development proceeds. Nonetheless, all psychological events are at the same time biological ones. Although psychological events require specific biological characteristics, this does not imply that the latter are sufficient or determining factors.

Event Evolution: Psychological

All psychological event-fields are the outcome of prior psychological evolution. After biological ontogenetic evolution reaches a certain point (before birth in humans) at which the requisite biological foundation is available, psychological evolution begins and is ongoing. Thus, all psychological events are developmental and dynamic. Although one must avoid improper analogies between physical and psychological fields (one of the downfalls of early attempts to take a field approach in psychology), Einstein and Infeld (1938) nicely captured the temporal continuity of all event-fields, as well as how to think about the "cause" of fields: "The field *here* and *now* depends on the field in the *immediate neighborhood* at a time *just past*" (p. 153).

Event Continuity

As the outcome of a long series of evolutions (inorganic, phylogenetic, ontogenetic, and psychological), psychological events are not unique because of the operation of nonspatiotemporal processes, as cultural tradition implies. There is no break in event continuity from particle impacts to biological activity to cognitive events such as knowing behavior. At no point do any other than naturalistic processes occur. Thus, "cognitive" and "mental" cannot and do not refer to occult or nonspatiotemporal events in whole or in part. They do refer to distinctive configurations of field factors.

Distinguishing Characteristics of Psychological Events

If psychological events are not distinguished from physical and biological ones by their mental (as nonspatiotemporal) make-up, then what, if anything, does make them unique? Clearly, to suggest that psychology takes behavior as its subject matter and that this distinguishes it from other disciplines is erroneous because all sciences take behavior as a fundamental construct (e.g., thermodynamic behavior, behavior of gas molecules, behavior of Golgi cells). However, the prevalence of the behavior construct throughout science is consistent with the interbehavioral position that behavior pertains to all events and that events are classified as physical, biological, and so on according to their behavioral characteristics. Psychological behavior is not as it is frequently thought of in behavioral, cognitive, and other writings. That is, psychological behavior is not movement in space, glandular and/or muscular, overt (public), or hidden from observers (private). Psychological behavior has other distinguishing marks and is not yet well classified.

The most striking aspect of psychological behavior is that it is never directly seen. Behavior of concern to the psychologist must always be inferred; it is an abstraction. What the person is doing psychologically is never available to direct observation. We find this when the operant is defined in terms of future orientation (purpose). For example, we observe someone allowing water to pass over the hands, applying soap to the hands, and so forth. What have we observed from a psychological perspective—hand washing, stimulating the body, avoiding work? The operant can only be inferred from a functional analysis that provides information on "controlling variables."

Given that psychological behavior is not directly observed, its status is that of a construct that must be inferred from events. The interbehaviorist argues that when theorists use the construct *mental* to typify the central concern of psychology, it is often possible to identify characteristics of the events from which they derive the construct. Psychological interactions are adjustive (or adaptive), as when the participating organism anticipates and avoids harmful conditions or seeks out circumstances that facilitate its adjustments to the world. Psychological adjustments are historical, specific, integrative, variable, and modifiable. Furthermore, an important class of psychological interaction found with humans is when self-reflection is involved. In contrast with rocks falling down a cliff, persons exhibiting the same physical trajectory may think of their plight; humans have a point of view concerning participating field factors.

CLINICAL PRACTICE

Integrative and Eclectic

The radically naturalistic interbehavioral perspective rules out no procedure a priori but does not countenance nonnaturalistic postulates. Given the firm distinction between events and procedures, on the one hand, and constructs and postulates, on the other, clinical practice has two major divisions. First, there is what the clinician does, what the identified client does, and what others may do, with specific spatial and temporal relationships among the participating factors, all at the event level. Second, there are the postulates clinicians use to guide their work and the interpretations clients, clinicians, and others make of the events. Therapists with the most supernatural postulates imaginable cannot institute nonspatiotemporal procedures, although procedures derived from nonnaturalistic presuppositions may very well be inept. Indeed, given that interbehavioral psychology offers no unique procedures because it is not a theory in the conventional sense, it would be disconfirmed only by evidence that procedures based on nonnaturalistic postulates are superior to those based on naturalistic postulates.

Implicit in the interbehavioral position is Kantor's (1963, 1969) macro- and historicocritical analysis demonstrating that the behavioral movement, above all else, represents an increasing tendency for researchers to treat psychological events as completely based in the natural (spatiotemporal) world. From this it follows that what is distinctive about behavior therapy is that this class of clinical work is expected to follow postulates that are more naturalistic (scientific) than earlier approaches, and because the postulates are closer to relevant events, stand a better chance of effectively handling real-world problems (events). Thus, the interbehavioral perspective does not require that behavior therapy interventions be based only on principles of conditioning and learning, for example.

The interbehavioral orientation promotes an integrative and eclectic clinical practice. However, the eclecticism is far removed from most of what passes for the very socially acceptable brands found today. Despite Thorne's (1973) advocacy of a complete system of clinical services based on a thoroughgoing eclectic orientation, and detailed development of it, one does not find his work much appreciated in the modern eclectic psychotherapy literature. I have been unable to find Thorne's explicit recognition of interbehavioral work; however, this leading eclectic systematist put forth an approach to clinical services that is very consistent with interbehavioral thinking. In contrast to the emphases of mainstream eclectic psychotherapies, Thorne and the interbehavioral perspective stress basic science as fundamental, are sensitive to the distinction between postulates and procedures, promote operational analysis and classification, take behavior modification as a fundamental construct, praise behavior therapy interventions as valuable, find no need for any alternative to naturalistic methods, take field and system constructions as central, and consider that all clinical problems are behavior-centered. One additional, striking point on which Thorne agrees with the interbehavioral perspective pertains to Kantor's (1963, 1969) historicocritical analysis of the scientific evolution of psychology. Kantor noted that when disciplines have not developed to the point at which there is substantial agreement that their subject matter is completely naturalistic, room is open for indefinite variation in basic postulate systems. Thus, there will continue to be competing schools, systems, or cults in psychology until such time that researchers show widespread agreement that its fundamental events contain no nonspatiotemporal factors whatsoever. Consistent with the interbehavioral viewpoint, Thorne argued that clinical specialties that split into competing schools must necessarily be in a prescientific stage of evolution. Clearly, from the interbehavioral and Thorne's point of view, eclectic psychotherapy is nothing but the systematic practice of radically naturalistic basic biobehavioral science. All postulate systems (theories) are not acceptable, and promoting practice on the basis of "what works best," irrespective of basic science knowledge, is to encourage a practice of psychology equivalent to the discredited empiric medicine (quackery) of bygone days.

Interdisciplinary

In view of the integrated participation in psychological events of nonpsychological factors, clinical services must always allow for interdisciplinary cooperation. The field/system nature of psychological events does not justify the common practice of many interdisciplinary "teams" in which a biomedical speciality is placed in a position of ultimate authority partly on the basis of the reductionistic assumption that biological factors are underlying causes of psychological behavior. Modern behavioral medicine is perhaps a dim recognition of the advantages of a field conception of psychological and biological events (Delprato & McGlynn, 1986). However, too often the biopsychosocial alternative to the blatantly lineal mechanical and reductionistic molecular biology model for medicine (cf. Engle, 1977) amounts to little more than a change in superficial verbovocal behavior.

Fundamental to Problem Resolutions: Modification of Field Factors

The field/system nature of psychological events requires that basic to all problem resolutions is the modification of field factors, including biological, ecological, social, domestic, economic, educational, vocational, and interpersonal conditions, as well as psychological ones. Unfortunately, the notion that field/system descriptions apply as much to psychological as to other natural events has been so little appreciated that there are relatively few principles available to follow for adjusting the factors in interbehavioral fields. However, given that nominally nonpsychological factors are not independent of psychological ones, we need not rely solely on conventional psychological principles. There are some established, if not overly dependable, principles for changing stimulus functions (e.g., respondent conditioning operations), altering response functions (e.g., operant procedures), and adjusting cognitive factors (e.g., verbovocal procedures).

Nonpsychological Sources of Problems and Solutions

Because criteria for psychological problems are always extrascientific and extrapsychological (Kantor, 1959), and because nonpsychological factors participate at all times in psychological event-fields, the clinician is advised to explore nonpsychological solutions to problems. Unless careful, interbehaviorally influenced practitioners can appear to be shunning their responsibilities as psychologists when they offer conventionally nonpsychological recommendations (e.g., making fragile items less accessible to a child labeled "hyperactive, emotionally impaired, and destructive" whose only known symptoms have been that he broke housewares in the normal course of moving about a cluttered residence). However, a growing appreciation for interdisciplinary approaches to social problems is helping in this area.

All Psychological Problems Require a Complainant

It is not to trivialize psychological complaints to recognize that no problem is found in the absence of a complainant, whether the identified client is the sole complainant or not. In many cases, the first task of the clinician is to explore the conditions surrounding the complaint: who, when, where, and consequences. Social factors contribute far more to psychological complaints than is the case with medical disorders, and this is the basic source of most, perhaps all, complaints, even those seemingly restricted to the identified client. Before considering more radical solutions, the clinician should take steps to ensure that targeting and modifying complaints would not result in a satisfactory resolution. Even when acceptable outcomes do not result from modifying the complaint itself, few, if any, problems will be adequately handled without addressing the complaining component.

De-emphasis of Intervention/Treatment

The field/system nature of psychological events, their continuity with other classes of events, interdependencies among participating factors, and the continuity of psychological event-fields call for a de-emphasis of conventional intervention and treatment solutions and avoidance of the overprofessionalization of what are largely social and moral issues. No doubt any referral, arriving by whatever means to a psychologist, is serious and calls for the exercise of professional skills. However, the greatest skills may be those that resolve problems as quickly as possible by making use of resources already available in the everyday life of the individual or group. One should more critically examine for their efficacy highly ritualized psychological services ranging from schedules of three 50-min meetings per week to elaborate treatment plans specifying precise locations in which to place children when they perform certain movements. However, only if such procedures are demonstrably more effective than more economical ones must they be used.

The emphasis on minimal services has serious economic implications, such as those for third-party payment for psychological services. However, because of the nature of event-fields, the interbehavioral perspective predicts that more ecologically representative interventions will be more generally effective.

One of the problems of highly artificial interventions that the principle of minimal (formal) services helps with is that referred to as the "generalization of treatment effects." This problem is partly captured by an important learning principle known as *generalization decrement* (Kimble, 1961). This refers to deleterious effects on behavior learned in one set of conditions when the conditions change. From the field/system perspective, behavior across time and situations is not a matter of conventional mediation, be it mental or biological. Following the principle that the present field is a function of the field at a time just past, "generalization," "memory," and psychological behavior in general are the outcomes of continuous evolution in which present actions of the organism are inseparable from the field as presently configured. Therefore, behavior will not henceforth be functionally similar to earlier behavior, given radical departures in participating field factors.

This thinking highlights the "artificiality dilemma." The fact that someone complains about something means that the way things are now (not artificial) is unsatisfactory and that some form of intrusion (artificiality) is called for. Yet to solve problems in highly artificial ways (e.g., physical restraint, contrived reinforcers) is to make transition to everyday life (not artificial) difficult. Two guidelines to address are as follows: make the initial phase of services as minimally artificial as possible and fade out artificiality as quickly as possible.

Clients Are Always "Identified Clients"

Given that organisms are only participants in psychological event-fields, problems are never centered in individuals. Thus, even when individuals other than the presenting client are not obviously participants in the client's problem field, one should think of the client as the identified client.

Psychological Evolution: Developmental Interactions

Behavior therapy took an important step by placing more emphasis than most alternative therapies on clients' contemporary circumstances relative to their histories. Nonetheless, behavioral ontogeny cannot be ignored, and one would expect clinical practice aspiring to scientific foundations to articulate a sound etiological theory. The interbehavioral suggestion here is a thoroughgoing developmental perspective that follows from the fundamental field view that the field at a given instance is a function of the field at a time just past. Like all natural events, psychological behavior fields are naturalistic outcomes of a continuous evolutional process. Delprato (1987) used the term *developmental interactionism* in referring to this view to recognize the interdependencies in interbehavioral fields. Developmental interactionism is far removed from earlier theories of development (e.g., environmentalism, hereditarianism). It is especially to be distinguished from currently popular heredity × environment interactionisms that posit one form or another of "interaction" between hereditary (biological) and environmental independent variables with biological factors as causes of psychological behavior. The interbehavioral approach to behavioral ontogeny is compatible with the field/system and nonreductionistic thinking of Schneirla (1966), Kuo (1967), and others. Given the origins of the behavior therapy movement and current uncertainty concerning the relevance of conditioning and learning, it is noteworthy that developmental interactionism seems to shed light on this issue. Basically, the events of conditioning and learning are retained as classes of organism–environment developmental interaction, but interpretations of outcomes of such interactions never depart from field/system postulates, thus in contrast with earlier mentalistic and mechanistic descriptions.

A Fundamental Goal: Actualization of Potentialities

Clarification of the potential and actual phases of event evolution is always important to maintain naturalistic interpretations (Kantor, 1983). Potentiality refers to the "what" of development: the evolution of structures and functions, but in the absence of other factors needed for actualization of another unique event-field. Potentiality and actualization handle the events forming the justification for distinctions between learning and performance, respectively, without the need for hypothetical mental, dualistic (e.g., learning as mental and performance as behavior = physical), or mechanistic assumptions. Naturalistically, potentialities evolve and, when coupled with other particular components, form a new event-field. For example, the developmental history of the physician prepares the specialist to participate in a specific event-field upon arrival of a particular patient. From this perspective, one finds that clinical complaints require a developmental history establishing potentiality and other factors that allow actualization of the complaint or complained-about events. At the level of problem solution, the basic goal of the therapist is to assist in the actualization of potentialities that may require development of new potentialities.

The Person as Self-Regulatory System

The movement in scientific thinking from lineal mechanism to field/ system constructions is of great import for how we view the regulation or control of behavior. Theorists as seemingly diverse as Freud and Watson looked to classical science and adhered to lineal mechanism, according to which control is a sequential process involving two mutually exclusive constructs: cause → effect. Mainstream psychology has yet to depart from conceptualizing behavior as an effect that is controlled (caused) by one or another antecedent variable in the external environment (e.g., stimuli, social circumstances) or inside the organism (e.g., brain processes, mental activity, unconscious processes, cognitive structures). Current disdain for stimulus → response psychology is rarely accompanied by promotion of a truly different way of describing how behavior is controlled. It is not a departure from lineal mechanism to simply invoke hypothetical mental mediators in a one-way causal chain consisting of environment → cognitive mediators → behavior.

The evolution of field/system thinking was a radical development in large part because it approached causality in terms of integrated event-fields instead of causal chains. The double-headed arrow (e.g., organism ↔ object), representing simultaneity of participating factors, replaced the single-headed arrow and temporal separation of causal factors from effects. Now there is no conventional directionality to causality. Behavior is no longer only an effect implied by its traditional role as a dependent variable. What this means for psychology is that the organism is a self-regulating system. The double-headed arrow of response ↔ stimulus, for example, describes the simplest version of a closed-loop feedback-control system (Delprato, 1989; Powers, 1988), according to which behavioral control is centered neither outside nor inside the behaving organism (system). Previous nonsystemic views of control stress extrasystemic (external) sources of control, either environmental or mental/cognitive, neither of which is closed-loop feedback control (i.e., "true" self-control).

Behavior therapy, in fact, has for some time exhibited a transition from external factors to self-control. However, even the most recent attempts to take into account behavior as fundamentally self-controlled, although speaking of "reciprocal determinism" (Bandura, 1986) and closed-loop feedback control (Kanfer & Schefft, 1988), fail when "reciprocal" refers to a series of one-way relationships over brief time spans (Bandura, 1986) and external control is juxtaposed with self-control and the latter is said to be active only when externally controlled responses are interrupted or ineffective (Kanfer & Schefft, 1988). The interbehavioral perspective rejects all mechanistic, one-way, external control in favor of closed-loop, cybernetic self-regulation, which allows self-control but without an autonomous organism because the psychological organism is never separate from its surroundings (Powers, 1973; Smith, 1987).

There are numerous implications of the conception of the individual as always a self-regulating system. Despite behavior therapy's less than complete conceptual development of the inherently self-regulatory nature of human behavior, many behavior therapists have emphasized the importance of a self-management model of clinical services and have used various procedures to increase identified clients' active involvement in therapy (e.g., self-monitoring, homework assignments). One general way of making clinical services more likely to take into account the self-regulatory nature of all behavior is to make them as participative as possible. This includes what seems to be common behavior therapy practices such as helping clients identify goals and negotiated contracting of various types, as well as perhaps less common practices such as including identified clients in clinical case conferences (so that they are not talked *about* but *with*), participative management practices (when the behavior therapist serves as a consultant to, or supervisor of, others), and applying Fischer's (1970) "testee as co-evaluator" model to cases in which psychological testing is used.

Responses are Interdependent (Patterned)

By now it should be clear that the interbehavioral perspective does not find the psychological event centered either inside the organism or in the organism's actions. Although one is not examining behavior when one focuses solely on responses, the response component of behavioral fields must be effectively dealt with. Given what appears to be the field/system nature of all natural events of whatever magnitude (Dewey & Bentley, 1949; Einstein & Infeld, 1938; Handy & Harwood, 1973; Kantor, 1969), it is not surprising that when researchers removed methodological blinders inherited from lineal mechanism, they found that responses are field phenomena (i.e., interdependent or patterned; Delprato, 1986; Delprato & McGlynn, 1988; Henton & Iversen, 1978; Ray & Brown, 1975). This means that responses are not independent of one another and are not therefore dependent on, and organized by, external forces such as environmental stimuli, biological states and processes, and hypothetical cognitive structures. Rather, we find response patterns or nonrandom interrelationships when two or more responses are measured over the same time period (concurrent patterns) or over different time periods (sequential patterns).

The patterned nature of responses recommends several strategies and tactics to the clinician, including routine use of multiple-response assessment and incorporation of pattern identification methods such as sequential analytic techniques. The bases of analyzing sequential response patterns are event-transition (conditional) probabilities and correlational analyses on time-ordered scores from a single subject (Delprato, 1986). One of the most useful type of data that sequential response pattern analysis can provide to the clinician is illustrated by a portion of Zlutnick, Mayville, and Moffat's (1975) findings that one seemingly innocuous response (i.e., a distinctive postural movement) reliably predicted a clinically significant one (i.e., a major seizure).

In terms of interventions, response patterning places the indirect modification of responses in a fresh light. If two responses, one of which is problematic, covary, there is no reason why field alterations such as therapeutic contingencies and other factors must always directly contact problematic responses (see Wahler & Hann, 1987). Voeltz and Evans (1982) went far toward formulating a response-pattern approach, including identification of another noteworthy implication. These authors recognized that so-called "symptom substitution" is consistent with the patterned nature of responses. For example, it is not surprising that when a response is deleted from the flow of behavior, as by some form of restraint, it will be replaced by another response that itself may be the target of complaining.

One of the most important approaches to clinical assessment and intervention that the interbehavioral system, and especially response patterns, calls for is the constructional model of service delivery. Simply put, Goldiamond (1974) distinguished between eliminative and constructional models. Eliminative approaches encourage coercive interventions, tend to treat the target of complaints as pathological, focus on eliminating behaviors, and do not explicitly identify and develop socially acceptable behaviors. Constructional approaches do not have these characteristics; instead, consistent with the fundamental goal of actualizing potentialities discussed earlier, the focus is on the construction of behaviors. Explicit identification of, and concerted attempts to foster, behaviors is crucial if responses are patterned. In the absence of this strategy, symptom-substitution effects are possible and the development of alternatives to eliminated responses is left to chance rather than to professional guidance.

Assessment: Behavioral Systems Methodology

The interbehavioral perspective's strong commitment to events makes it favorably disposed to behavioral assessment and functional analysis. The field/system nature of psychological events calls for further development of behavioral assessment methodologies even beyond the important ideal of assessing at "three levels": overt motoric, physiological, and self-description. Methodology must take into account the temporal continuity of event-fields, multiple classes of participating field factors within each of many domains, interdependencies among participating factors, and varying interbehavioral settings in which event interactions occur. As already mentioned, Ray and Delprato (1989) presented a comprehensive framework for description and analysis of any interbehavioral field/system. Behavioral systems methodology is complex and at present difficult to routinely implement even in basic research settings. However, clinicians have already taken steps toward more completely describing clinical systems by using various forms of sequential analysis to assess cases such as eating disorders (Schlundt, Johnson, & Jarrell, 1985), psychotic linguistic acts (Lyons & Williamson, 1989), and marital conflict (Gottman, Markman, & Notarius, 1977). Furthermore, a few researchers have undertaken more complete behavior-system analyses with bruxism (Wruble, 1988) and the applied area of pedagogy (Hawkins & Sharpe, 1992). In addition, Q methodology, which Stephenson (1953) based on interbehavioral psychology, shows promise as a tool to classify experiences in the phenomenal (subjective) domain (Stephenson, 1987; Taylor, Delprato, & Knapp, 1994).

CONCLUSION

In one sense, interbehavioral work is not for students of psychology who are satisfied with the status quo. This little-known approach calls for several new ways of thinking and of providing clinical services. It asks us (a) to adjust the science of psychology to recognize the field/system nature of all natural events per the evolution of scientific thinking in general, (b) to confront historical evidence and to agree that authentic scientific psychology can never, and need not, accommodate any version of material–spiritual or behavior–mental dualism and assumptions of events other than spatiotemporal ones, (c) to identify and to examine fundamental assumptions, (d) to maintain harmonious relations between postulates and procedures and among postulates at various levels, from what it means to know through the provision of clinical services, and (e) to accept some rather unusual considerations at the clinical level, such as attending first to complaining, deemphasizing psychological and intervention/treatment solutions, and regarding all psychological behavior as self-regulated (but not autonomous). Despite interbehavioral psychology's radical posture when viewed from many conventional points of view, I submit that those who have developed even moderate skills at approaching the world from the standpoint of what science is virtually uniformly taken as "all about" (i.e., observation and rejection of authority) will find considerable food for thought in the interbehavioral perspective. In essence, interbehavioral psychology is merely a continuation of the idea that psychological events are completely capable of being understood scientifically. It is this feature that makes interbehavioral psychology conventional and integrative rather than just yet another theory or system.

REFERENCES

Bandura, A. (1986). *Social foundations of thought and action.* Englewood Cliffs, NJ: Prentice-Hall.

Bertalanffy, L. V. (1972). The history and status of general systems theory. In G. J. Klir (Ed.), *Trends in general systems theory* (pp. 21–41). New York: Wiley.

Davies, P. (1989). *The new physics.* Cambridge, England: Cambridge University Press.

Delprato, D. J. (1986). Response patterns. In H. W. Reese & L. J. Parrott (Eds.), *Behavior science: Philosophical, methodological, and empirical advances* (pp. 61–113). Hillsdale, NJ: Erlbaum.

Delprato, D. J. (1987). Developmental interactionism: An integrative framework for behavior therapy. *Advances in Behaviour Research and Therapy, 9,* 173–205.

Delprato, D. J. (1989). A paradigm shift in behavior therapy: From external control to self-control. In W. A. Hershberger (Ed.), *Volitional action: Conation and control* (pp. 449–467). New York: Elsevier.

Delprato, D. J. (1993). Behavior analysis and S. C. Pepper's other mechanism. *The Behavior Analyst, 16,* 51–53.

Delprato, D. J., & McGlynn, F. D. (1986). Innovations in behavioral medicine. In *Progress in behavior modification* (Vol. 20, pp. 67–122). Orlando, FL: Academic Press.

Delprato, D. J., & McGlynn, F. D. (1988). Interactions of response patterns and their implications for behavior therapy. *Journal of Behavior Therapy and Experimental Psychiatry, 19,* 199–205.

Dewey, J., & Bentley, A. F. (1949). *Knowing and the known.* Boston: Beacon Press.

Einstein, A., & Infeld, L. (1938). *The evolution of physics.* New York: Simon & Schuster.

Ellenberger, H. F. (1970). *The discovery of the unconsciousness: The history and evolution of dynamic psychiatry.* New York: Basic Books.

Engle, G. L. (1977). The need for a new medical model: A challenge for biomedicine. *Science, 196,* 129–136.

Feigl, H. (1953). Notes on causality. In H. Feigl & M. Brodbeck (Eds.), *Readings in the philosophy of science* (pp. 408–418). New York: Appleton-Century-Crofts.

Fischer, C. T. (1970). The testee as co-evaluator. *Journal of Counseling Psychology, 17,* 70–76.

Frank, P. (1955). Foundations of physics. In O. Neurath, R. Carnap, & C. Morris (Eds.), *Foundations of the unity of science* (Vol. 1, pp. 423–504). Chicago: University of Chicago Press.

Furth, R. H. (1970). *Fundamental principles of modern theoretical physics.* New York: Pergamon Press.

Goldiamond, I. (1974). Toward a constructional approach to social problems. *Behaviorism, 2,* 1–84.

Gottman, J., Markman, H., & Notarius, C. (1977). The topography of marital conflict: A sequential analysis of verbal and nonverbal behavior. *Journal of Marriage and the Family, 39,* 461–477.

Handy, R., & Harwood, E. C. (1973). *A current appraisal of the behavioral sciences* (Rev. ed.). Great Barrington, MA: Behavioral Research Council.

Hawkins, A., & Sharpe, T. (Eds.). (1992). Field systems analysis: An alternative for the study of teaching expertise [Monograph issue]. *Journal of Teaching in Physical Education, 12*(1).

Henton, W. W., & Iversen, I. H. (1978). *Classical conditioning and operant conditioning: A response pattern analysis.* New York: Springer.

Hirosige, T. (1976). The ether problem, the mechanistic worldview, and the origins of the theory of relativity. In R. McCormmach (Ed.), *Historical studies in the physical sciences* (Vol. 7, pp. 3–82). Princeton, NJ: Princeton University Press.

Holton, G. (1973). *Introduction to concepts and theories in physical science* (2nd ed.). Reading, MA: Addison-Wesley.

Kanfer, F. H., & Schefft, B. K. (1988). *Guiding the process of therapeutic change.* Champaign, IL: Research Press.

Kantor, J. R. (1941). Current trends in psychological theory. *Psychological Bulletin, 38,* 29–65.

Kantor, J. R. (1946). The aim and progress of psychology. *American Scientist, 34,* 251–263.

Kantor, J. R. (1959). *Interbehavioral psychology* (2nd ed.). Granville, OH: Principia Press.

Kantor, J. R. (1963). *The scientific evolution of psychology* (Vol. 1). Chicago, IL: Principia Press.

Kantor, J. R. (1969). *The scientific evolution of psychology* (Vol. 2). Chicago, IL: Principia Press.

Kantor, J. R. (1971). *The aim and progress of psychology and other sciences.* Chicago, IL: Principia Press.

Kantor, J. R. (1983). *Tragedy and the event continuum.* Chicago, IL: Principia Press.

Kimble, G. A. (1961). *Hilgard and Marquis' conditioning and learning* (2nd ed.). New York: Appleton-Century-Crofts.

Kuo, Z. Y. (1967). *The dynamics of behavior development: An epigenetic view.* New York: Random House.

Leahey, T. D. (1987). *A history of psychology: Main currents in psychological thought* (2nd ed.). Englewood Cliffs, NJ: Prentice-Hall.

Lewin, K. (1951). *Field theory in social science.* New York: Harper.

Lyons, C. A., & Williamson, P. N. (1989, May). *Analysis of sequential dependencies in psychotic language.* Paper presented at the meeting of the Association for Behavior Analysis, Milwaukee, WI.

Mach, E. (1942). *The science of mechanics: A critical and historical account of its development* (2nd Eng. ed.; T. J. McCormack, Trans.). LaSalle, IL: Open Court Publishing. (Original work published 1883)

Marmor, J. (1983). Systems thinking in psychiatry: Some theoretical and clinical implications. *American Journal of Psychiatry, 140,* 833–838.

Mehra, J., & Rechenberg, H. (1982). *The historical development of quantum theory: Vol. 2. The discovery of quantum mechanics, 1925.* New York: Springer-Verlag.

Pepper, S. C. (1942). *World hypotheses: A study in evidence.* Berkeley, CA: University of California Press.

Powers, W. T. (1973). *Behavior: The control of perception.* Chicago: Aldine.

Powers, W. T. (1988). Comments from the standpoint of control system theory. *The Interbehaviorist, 16,* 22.

Rapoport, A. (1968). Foreword. In W. Buckley (Ed.), *Modern systems research for the behavioral scientist* (pp. xiii–xxv). Chicago: Aldine.

Ray, R. D., & Brown, D. A. (1975). A systems approach to behavior. *Psychological Record, 25,* 459–478.

Ray, R. D., & Delprato, D. J. (1989). Behavioral systems analysis: Methodological strategies and tactics. *Behavioral Science, 34,* 81–127.

Ruben, D. H., & Delprato, D. J. (Eds.). (1987). *New ideas in therapy.* Westport, CT: Greenwood Press.

Russell, B. (1953). On the notion of cause, with applications to the free-will problem. In H. Feigl & M. Brodbeck (Eds.), *Readings in the philosophy of science* (pp. 387–407). New York: Appleton-Century-Crofts.

Sameroff, A. J. (1983). Developmental systems: Contexts and evolution. In W. Kessen (Ed.), *Handbook of child psychology: History, theory, and methods* (Vol. 1, pp. 237–294). New York: Wiley.

Schlundt, D. G., Johnson, W. G., & Jarrell, M. P. (1985). A naturalistic functional analysis of eating behavior in bulimia and obesity. *Advances in Behaviour Research and Therapy, 7,* 149–162.

Schneirla, T. C. (1966). Behavioral development and comparative psychology. *Quarterly Review of Biology, 41,* 283–302.

Smith, K. U. (1987). *Behavioral–physiological foundation of human development.* Burnaby, British Columbia: Simon Fraser Centre for Distance Education.

Stephenson, W. (1953). *The study of behavior: Q-technique and its methodology.* Chicago: University of Chicago Press.

Stephenson, W. (1987). Q methodology: Interbehavioral and quantum theoretical connections in clinical psychology. In D. H. Ruben & D. J. Delprato (Eds.), *New ideas in therapy* (pp. 95–106). Westport, CT: Greenwood Press.

Taylor, J. G. (1972). *The new physics.* New York: Basic Books.

Taylor, P., Delprato, D. J., & Knapp, J. R. (1994). Q-methodology in the study of child phenomenology. *Psychological Record, 44,* 155–169.

Thorne, F. C. (1973). Eclectic psychotherapy. In R. Corsini (Ed.), *Current psychotherapies* (pp. 445–486). Itasca, IL: Peacock.

Voeltz, L. M., & Evans, I. M. (1982). The assessment of behavioral interrelationships in child behavior therapy. *Behavioral Assessment, 4,* 131–165.

Wahler, R. G., & Hann, D. H. (1987). An interbehavioral approach to clinical child psychology: Toward an understanding of troubled families. In D. H.

Ruben & D. J. Delprato (Eds.), *New ideas in therapy* (pp. 53–78). Westport, CT: Greenwood Press.

Wruble, M. K. (1988). *Sleep posture and sleep-related bruxism.* Unpublished master's thesis, University of Florida, Gainesville.

Zlutnick, S., Mayville, W. J., & Moffat, S. (1975). Modifications of seizure disorders: The interruption of behavioral chains. *Journal of Applied Behavior Analysis, 8,* 1–12.

23

FUNCTIONAL ANALYTIC PSYCHOTHERAPY: A BEHAVIORAL APPROACH TO INTENSIVE TREATMENT

ROBERT J. KOHLENBERG and MAVIS TSAI

It is well known that the therapeutic relationship known as transference/countertransference forms the core theoretical construct of psychodynamically oriented psychotherapy. In contrast, for behavior therapists (with the notable exceptions of Goldfried, 1982; Jacobson, 1989; and Linehan, 1993), the notion has usually been ignored or at best been added as an afterthought (R. J. Kohlenberg, Tsai, & B. S. Kohlenberg, in press). In this chapter, we will describe a behavioral theory of therapeutic change for outpatient adult psychotherapy clients in which the client–therapist relationship is at the very heart of the change process. This theory, known as Functional Analytic Psychotherapy (FAP; Kohlenberg & Tsai, 1991), is based on Skinner's radical behaviorism (Skinner, 1953, 1974) and was built from a ground-up behavioral analysis of the outpatient psychotherapy environment.

In this age of integrationism, managed health care and emphasis on brief, effective treatments, we believe that the theories and techniques of FAP can "supercharge" a traditional behavior therapy treatment by giving it more depth and intensity and can better help clients, typically those who suffer from long-standing personality disorders of the type described in *DSM–IV* (American Psychiatric Association, 1994) who are not responding to traditional behavior therapy techniques. For the generalist who is interested in psychotherapy integration, FAP is an all-encompassing theory that can account for and include the best of all therapies, yet be able to explain different techniques under one conceptual umbrella (Kohlenberg & Tsai, 1994).

Many behavior therapists[1] react against the term *radical behaviorism*, and we want to address briefly the most common misconceptions about it before proceeding further. These misconceptions are that radical behaviorism is simplistic, mechanistic, and manipulative and that it deals only with what can be publicly seen, ignoring the unconscious, creativity, the self, the client–therapist relationship, and feelings and thoughts. One reason such widespread misunderstanding exists is that radical behaviorism is based on unusual philosophical assumptions that modify the meaning of many key terms, making communication with others difficult (Hayes & Hayes, 1992). We hope to prove these conceptions false with descriptions of FAP, a treatment approach that not only capitalizes on the precision and clarity of radical behaviorism but also shows how it leads to a focus on sensitive, caring client–therapist relationships as the foundation for emotional healing.

We will first establish the theoretical foundations of FAP, then discuss its guidelines and show how these concepts are applied clinically, both in individual and marital therapy. To further illustrate the concepts of FAP, we provide a verbatim transcript of an individual FAP case. We conclude with a discussion of the relevant factors in designing research on FAP.

THE THEORETICAL FOUNDATIONS OF FAP

FAP theory is deceptively simple: All people act (do, think, feel, see, know, follow instructions, etc.) because of the contingencies of reinforcement they have experienced in past relationships. This does not mean that cognitions, defined as thinking, planning, believing, and so forth, do not play a role in treatment—they clearly do. It does mean, however, that the

---

[1]We use the term *behavior therapist* in its most generic sense, which includes the use of both cognitive and behavioral techniques.

deeper, more fundamental, and yes, unconscious motivations are best viewed as the result of past contingencies.[2]

This point of view leads to a therapeutic emphasis on the interrelated concepts of within-session contingencies, context, functional similarity, natural reinforcement, and shaping. We will discuss each in turn.

Within-Session Contingencies

A well-known aspect of reinforcement is that the closer in time and place the behavior is to its consequences, the greater will be the effect of those consequences. It follows, then, that treatment effects will be stronger if clients' problem behaviors and improvements occur during the session, where they are closest in time and place to the available reinforcement. For example, if a female client states that she has difficulty trusting others, the therapy will be much more powerful if her distrust actually manifests itself in the therapeutic relationship as opposed to being relegated only to individuals in her daily life. Thus, from this viewpoint, significant therapeutic change results from the contingencies that occur during the therapy session within the client–therapist relationship.

Context

Radical behaviorism questions the existence of a fixed, knowable reality, and instead asserts that reality does not exist independent of perceiving. Perceiving, in turn, is a behavior that is shaped by the individual's experiences from birth to the present. Thus, reality, and even the notion of reality, reflects experiential histories. In this contextualistic approach to understanding people, a client's reinforcement history, environment, and circumstances help to give a total picture of the meaning of a particular behavior. If something is taken out of context, it becomes meaningless. In order to clarify this point, let us contrast a client change in expressing feelings brought about by social skills training (involving therapist instruction, role playing, and home practice) with that brought about by contingencies in the session.

An approach emphasizing contingencies leads the therapist to notice any naturally occurring instance of the client expressing feelings (to therapist or partner during marital therapy) during the session and to immediately respond to this improvement in a naturally reinforcing way (see the next section for a more detailed discussion of natural reinforcement). In contrast, the social skills approach would involve the therapist instructing,

---

[2]For a more complete discussion of the radical behavior view of the unconscious, see R. J. Kohlenberg and Tsai (1991).

coaching, and role playing with the client to demonstrate how to express feelings. Because the role playing occurs in a contrived condition and does not involve the direct observation of the context in which it may be used, it is almost impossible for a therapist to describe the specific form and components of "expressing feeling" that is appropriate for a particular client (Ciminero, Calhoun, & Adams, 1977; Conger & Conger, 1982). This approach epitomizes the underlying structuralistic assumption of present-day behavior therapy that behavior has meaning independent of context. This assumption is in direct contrast to the functionalistic assumption underlying the focus on contingencies, and we question the idea that a client can learn to express feelings independent of the time and place for which it is appropriate (R. J. Kohlenberg, Tsai, & Dougher, 1993). A problem engendered by the failure to take context into account was alluded to in a review of the literature on the generalization of social skills training by Scott, Himadi, and Keane (1983). They concluded that lack of demonstrable generalization is responsible for the limited acceptability as a viable treatment of social skills training.

Functional Similarity

The FAP focus on client daily life problems that also occurs during the session naturally leads to generalization of treatment effects to daily life. Generalization from one setting to another occurs on the basis of the functional similarity of the settings. In our earlier discussion on the limited generalizability of social skills training, our explanation was that there is a lack of functional similarity between the training and natural environments. That is, behavior acquired through coaching, modeling, role playing, and behavioral rehearsal during the session is functionally different from the behavior that occurs in context, even though it may look the same.

Although it might appear that the therapy session does not resemble the natural milieu, the occurrence of daily life problems in the session is evidence for its functional similarity to daily life. That is, rather than looking at physical characteristics in order to determine if therapy and daily life environments are similar, the environments are compared on the basis of the behavior they evoke. If they evoke the same behavior, then they are functionally similar. For example, a man whose presenting problem is hostility in close relationships would show that the therapy context is functionally similar to his daily environment if he becomes hostile toward the therapist as their relationship develops. Furthermore, if the client experiences within-session contingencies that strengthen nonhostile ways to relate to his therapist, the same functional similarity would mediate generalization of improvements to daily life.

The within-session contingencies that are the basis of FAP treatment consist of the actions and reactions of the therapist, and in the case of couples therapy, also include the actions and reactions of the partners to each other. If the clients' daily life problems do not actually occur during the session, however, then no opportunity exists for the contingencies present in the session to have a therapeutic effect.

Natural Reinforcement

We have emphasized the importance of contingencies of reinforcement in the change process. There are, however, many misconceptions about the nature of the contingencies of reinforcement and particularly how they enter into in the change process in adult outpatient treatment. The distinction between natural and contrived reinforcement is especially important (Ferster, 1967; Skinner, 1982).

Natural reinforcers are typical and reliable in the natural environment, whereas contrived ones generally are not. For example, giving a child candy for putting on his coat is contrived, whereas being chilled for being coatless is natural. Similarly, fining a client a nickel for not making eye contact is contrived, whereas the spontaneous wandering of the therapist's attention is natural.

Contrived reinforcers can be highly effective in treating clients who are restricted in movement or who live in controllable environments such as schools, hospitals, or prisons. In these settings, contrived reinforcers can be used consistently and not just in a brief therapeutic interaction.

Contrived reinforcement can fall short, however, when the changed behavior is expected to generalize into daily life. Consider, for example, a client for whom expressing anger is a problem. Let us say that the client actually expresses anger during the therapy session about the therapist's inflexibility regarding payment terms. A therapist who then smiles and says, "I'm glad you expressed your anger toward me" is probably delivering contrived reinforcement. Such a consequence is unlikely to occur in the natural environment, and clients who learn to express anger because it was followed by a smile would not be prepared to express anger during daily life. A natural reinforcer probably would consist of the therapist's taking the client seriously, discussing, and perhaps altering the payment policy. Any changes produced by these consequences would be more likely to carry over into daily life.

Unfortunately, even the deliberate use of natural reinforcers can become contrived and "phony" and lose its effectiveness (Ferster, 1972). This problem was alluded to by Wachtel (1977), who observed that behavior therapists were often overly exuberant in their use of praise, thereby diminishing its effectiveness. Furthermore, deliberate use of consequences can be viewed as manipulative or aversive by clients and can induce efforts to reduce or alter therapeutic change efforts—what Skinner (1953) would call "countercontrol."

The use of reinforcement in psychotherapy thus presents a major dilemma. On the one hand, natural reinforcement that is contingent on the goal behavior is a primary change agent available in the therapeutic situation. On the other hand, if the therapist attempts to purposely "use" the extant natural reinforcers, they may lose their effectiveness, induce countercontrol, and, in the process, produce a manipulative, chauvinistic treatment.

The dilemma is obviated, however, when the therapy is structured so that the genuine reactions of the therapist to client behavior naturally reinforce improvements as they happen. More specifically, because the dominant aspect of psychotherapy is interactional, the immediate natural reinforcement of client improvements is most likely when the client–therapist relationship naturally evokes the client's presenting problems. For example, an intense and emotional therapist–client relationship may evoke withdrawal in a client seeking help for intimacy problems. If so, the necessary precondition has been met, and a sensitive and genuine therapist may naturally reinforce improvements as they occur.

Shaping

The concept of shaping implies that there is a large response class of client behaviors for the therapist to reinforce. Shaping is contextual in that it takes into account a client's learning history and the behaviors present and absent from the client's repertoire. The same behavior may be considered to be a problem for one client but an improvement for another. For instance, let us take a male client who pounds on his armrest and yells at the therapist, "You just don't understand me!" If this behavior came from a client who came into therapy unable to express his feelings, it would constitute an improvement, and the therapist's openness to this outburst would be important. If, however, outbursts like this were typical, the therapist might want to suggest an alternative way to express feelings of displeasure that did not involve aggressive physical demonstrations.

THE CLINICAL APPLICATION OF FAP

The core guideline for doing FAP is that a therapist should watch for clinically relevant behavior (CRB): in-session instances and improvements of the client's daily life problematic behavior. This suggestion for therapists has far-reaching implications and is much more difficult to implement than it might appear. We refer to this guideline as Rule 1 and to within-session instances of the client's problematic behavior as clinically relevant behavior type 1 (CRB1). Within session improvements in the client's problematic behavior are referred to as CRB2. Because CRB1s and Rule 1 capture the essence of the FAP, we first will explore them in detail. In all, however, there are five guidelines and three types of clinically relevant behavior. A complete description of these are given later.

Given that contingencies are the primary means of change in FAP, it might appear inconsistent that there is no mention of contingencies or reinforcement in Rule 1. Instead, this guideline merely calls for "watching" on the part of the behavior therapist, a private behavior. As behaviorists, we do not believe that watching per se will cause change in the client. We do contend, however, that "watching for CRB" will raise the behavior therapist's awareness level of CRB and automatically lead him or her to reinforce improvements naturally as they occur. Furthermore, we argue that therapists who are unaware of CRB—that is, do not follow Rule 1—might inadvertently block therapeutic gains and punish client improvements.

For example, consider Betty, who was in treatment with the first author for speech anxiety, panic, and lack of assertiveness with male authorities, such as supervisors and executives, at her work place. Her assertiveness problems were even greater if she knew the male authority and had an ongoing relationship with him. During the session, she asked the therapist to call her physician and request a refill of her prescription for tranquilizers because her doctor was resistant and she didn't want to confront him. The therapist had several strong, covert, negative reactions. First, he did not like the idea because he was inclined to discourage medication use in favor of behavioral methods. Second, he thought that getting a prescription refilled was Betty's responsibility, not his. Third, he considered this as a chance for Betty to practice being assertive with her doctor. Fourth, calling her physician was an unpleasant task for him, and he considered it an intrusion on his time. On the other hand, because of Rule 1, he was aware that this request itself was a CRB2, a clear-cut within-session assertive response with a male authority, which previously was absent from Betty's repertoire. Given his awareness, he consented to call her doctor and complimented Betty on her forthrightness in making this request. In a subsequent session, Betty described the trepidation she experienced and the considerable fear she had to overcome before making the request. She felt that interaction was a turning point in her willingness to assert herself with the therapist, and most importantly, with other authority figures in her daily life. In contrast to this good outcome, a lack of awareness on the part of the therapist that a CRB2 was occurring at the time she made the request could have led to an inadvertent punishment of her assertive behavior by his refusal to call her physician.

In order to enhance the application of Rule 1, we next will illustrate how CRB1s can arise in both individual and couples therapy.

CRB1s in Individual Therapy

Much of what clients complain about in outside relationships have in-session representations with their therapists. Some examples follow:

1. A woman whose problem is that she has no friends and "does not know how to make friends" exhibits these behaviors in session: She avoids eye contact, answers questions by talking at length in an unfocused and tangential manner, has one "crisis" after another and demands to be taken care of, gets angry at the therapist for not having all the answers, and frequently complains that the world "shits" on her and that she gets an unfair deal.
2. A man whose main problem is that he avoids getting into love relationships always decides ahead of time what he is going to talk about during the therapy hour, watches the clock during the session so that he can end precisely on time, states that he can come to therapy only every other week because of tight finances (he makes a relatively large income), and cancels the next session after making an important self-disclosure.
3. A woman who has a pattern of getting into relationships with unattainable men develops a crush on her therapist.

CRB1s in Couples Therapy

The contextualistic nature of FAP and its focus on client behaviors within the session make it particularly well suited for couples work. In their article on targeting sex-role and power issues in joint therapy, Rabin, Tsai, and R. J. Kohlenberg (in press) describe gendered behaviors that are potentially clinically relevant in daily life and their analogues in marital therapy:

1. *Unequal access to or control over finances.* Does one partner have primary control or responsibility over money in a way that does not feel good to both partners? Are their financial issues evident in the therapy in terms of who makes the financial arrangements with the therapist and who pays the fees?
2. *Unequal sharing of household chores and parenting demands.* Men often do not assume responsibility for the "bookkeeping" aspects of the marital therapy such as setting up appointments, keeping track of homework assignments, arranging baby-sit-

ting for children during the sessions, and taking the initiative in giving feedback about the progress of therapy.

3. *Unequal influence on making of decisions.* Outside of therapy, the major decisions (e.g., whether to take a job in a different city) are usually male-dominated, whereas the minor decisions (e.g., where to go on vacation) are usually female-dominated. How does this unequal influencing of decisions manifest itself in therapy? For instance, who decided to begin therapy? Who decides the problems to be worked on and the issues to be discussed? If the therapy comes to a premature ending, whose decision was it to stop coming? Which of these questions are considered major versus minor decisions?

4. *Unequal sharing of kinship and friendship obligations.* The wife often takes responsibility for nurturing family relationships and friendships by remembering birthdays and special occasions and initiating or maintaining contact either in person, on the phone, or by mail. Does this interpersonal caring behavior extend to the therapist, that is, does she do special things to nurture the relationship with the therapist such as bringing gifts, complimenting the therapist, asking how she or he is or how his or her vacation went?

5. *Unequal responsibility for relationship issues.* Men often do not actively participate in the therapy process. They may be passive and defer to their partner or the therapist for direction. They may view relationship problems in "you" terms, as in "you always want more from me"—time, attention, affection, and so on. In other words, they think the marriage would be fine if only the wife would stop complaining so much.

   On the other hand, women may overfunction during the sessions by taking too much responsibility for bringing up issues, expressing feelings, drawing the partner out, and maintaining the contact.

6. *Different patterns of communication and conflict resolution.* Men tend to demonstrate reduced self-disclosure, intimacy behaviors, and support and to send unclear messages about their own emotional states. They often are loath to admit weakness, vulnerability, and negative feeling states other than anger. They may withdraw during conflict or stressful interactions. They may have difficulty disclosing their feelings, and instead of responding with empathy to the expression of feelings by his partner, a man may withdraw or be detached and intellectual.

OVERVIEW OF CLINICALLY RELEVANT BEHAVIORS AND THERAPIST GUIDELINES

As mentioned previously, FAP focuses on three types of client behavior and involves five guidelines for therapists. The complete listing that follows includes CRB1s, CRB2s, and Rule 1, all of which have already been discussed. The list also introduces CRB3 and Rules 2, 3, 4, and 5.

Clinically Relevant Behaviors (CRBs)

As stated earlier, the types of client problems that are suitable for FAP occur during the therapy session. Three CRBs of particular relevance are problems, improvements, and interpretations of clients' own behavior. Each will be discussed in turn.

CRB1: Client problems that occur in session. CRB1s are related to the client's presenting problems and should decrease in frequency during therapy. In addition to the types of client problems discussed previously, CRB1s can also involve thinking, perceiving, feeling, seeing, and remembering that occur during the session. For example, problems known as "disturbances of the self," such as "not knowing who the real me is" and multiple personality disorder are translated into behavioral terms (e.g., problems with stimulus control of the response "I") and conceptualized as CRB1 (see R. J. Kohlenberg & Tsai, 1991, chap. 6, for a detailed discussion on how such disturbances are acquired and treated).

CRB2: Client improvements that occur in session. In the early stages of treatment, these behaviors typically are not observed or are of low strength. For example, consider a male client who withdraws and feels worthless when "people don't pay attention" to him during conversations. This client may show similar withdrawal when interrupted by his therapist. Possible CRB2s for this situation include (a) being assertive and directing the therapist back to what the client was saying or (b) discerning the therapist's waning interest in what was being said before the therapist actually interrupted.

CRB3: Client interpretations of behavior. CRB3 refers to clients' talking about their own behavior and what seems to cause it. It includes "reason giving" (Hayes, 1987; Zettle & Hayes, 1982) and "interpretations" (R. J. Kohlenberg & Tsai, 1991). The best CRB3s involve the observation and description of one's own behavior and its associated reinforcing, discriminative, and eliciting stimuli. Learning to describe functional connections can help in obtaining reinforcement in daily life. CRB3 includes descriptions of functional equivalence that indicate similarities between what happens in session and what happens in daily life. For example, Esther, age 41, had not been sexually intimate with anyone for more than 15 years. After a course of FAP with Dr. Tsai, Esther became the lover of a man she met through church. Her CRB3 was, "The reason I'm in that intimate relationship is because you had been there for me. It's such a phenomenal change. If not for you, I wouldn't be there. With you it was the first safe place I had to talk about what I feel, to find reasons why it's desirable to be sexual. There was a period of time that I was more overtly attracted to you, and you were accepting of my feelings. I learned that it was better to be whole and feel my sexuality than to be armored and empty, and I practiced learning how to be direct with you."

Guidelines for Therapists

The FAP therapist is urged to follow five strategic rules or guidelines of therapeutic technique: (a) Watch for CRBs, (b) evoke CRBs, (c) reinforce CRB2s, (d) observe the potentially reinforcing effects of therapist behavior in relation to client CRBs, and (e) give interpretations of variables that affect client CRB. Following are descriptions of each rule.

Rule 1: Watch for CRBs. As we have already underscored, this rule forms the core of FAP—the more proficient a therapist is at observing CRBs, the client daily life problems that also occur during the session, the better will be the outcome of therapy.

From a theoretical viewpoint, the importance of Rule 1 cannot be overemphasized, because it alone should promote a positive outcome. In other words, a therapist who is skilled at observing instances of clinically relevant behavior as they occur is also more likely to react naturally to these instances. Thus, a therapist following Rule 1 is more likely to naturally reinforce, punish, and extinguish client behaviors in ways that foster the development of behavior useful in daily life. Any technique that helps the therapist in the detection of CRB1 has a place in FAP. For example, FAP therapists interpret latent content of what the client says as a means to detect CRB, although these interpretations are based on the principles of verbal behavior and not on unconscious drives (R. J. Kohlenberg & Tsai, 1993). Thus, a therapist following Rule 1 is more likely to naturally reinforce, punish, and extinguish client behaviors in ways that foster the development of behavior useful in daily life.

Rule 2: Evoke CRBs. Ideally, therapy should evoke CRB1s and provide for the development of CRB2s. The degree to which this ideal is met depends, of course, on the nature of the client's daily life problems. Couples therapy easily provides such an ideal environment because the interactions between the spouses occur right in the session (as opposed to a partner working on marital issues in individual therapy who is able only to talk about the problems rather than to demonstrate them). Even for clients working on relationship issues in individual therapy, CRBs occur without the therapist's having to take special measures. This happens because the typical structure of the therapy relationship involves contradictory elements such as the encouragement of trust, closeness, and open expression of feelings versus a time limit of 50 min, a fee for service, and clear boundaries. Such a structure often evokes clients' conflicts and difficulties in forming and sustaining intimate relationships.

Of course, a therapist can aid in evoking CRBs by focusing on the client's present-moment feelings and relationship issues between the client and the therapist (see R. J. Kohlenberg & Tsai, 1991, chap. 3, for a more complete discussion of the behavioral principles underlying the relevance of "here and now" stimulus control to the evocation of CRB). The beginning, middle, and termination phases of therapy all provide stimuli that often evoke different types of CRBs.

In the beginning phase of therapy, a therapist can quickly evoke clinically relevant behavior by exploring the following questions:

1. How did you go about picking me as a therapist? How does this relate to your style of decision making and risk taking?
2. What are you like when you begin a new relationship or activity? Are you shy, cautious, and slow to trust, or do you jump in and ignore your reservations? How important is it for you to make a good impression? Do you quickly get critical of what is going on? Do you lose interest easily? Are you worried about feeling trapped? Do you start out with high hopes and get disappointed easily?
3. What are the similarities and differences between your usual style of beginning a relationship and how you are beginning therapy?
4. How can you increase the likelihood of a good beginning for your therapy?
5. What do and do you not like about therapy so far?

In the middle phase of therapy, CRB1 can be evoked regarding: closeness, expressions of closeness, progress and recognition of progress, feelings and expressions of feelings that have been difficult, such as appreciation, affection, desires for things to be different, or negative reactions. The following sentence completion questions that can be given orally in session, adapted from Bruckner-Gordon, Gangi, and Wallman (1988), can help evoke and identify target clinically relevant behavior:

Recognition of progress:
    I am pleased about my progress in
    I recognize I am changing because
    I no longer feel
    For the first time I
    It is getting easier for me to

Improving the therapy:

    I wish I had made more progress in

    I'm interested in changing my therapy to include

    You could improve our relationship by

    I could improve our relationship by

Reactions to the therapist:

    It seemed you were insensitive to me when

    I felt hurt or angry when you

    What bothers me about you is

    I feel closest to you when

    I'm most likely to push you away when

    Your policies are hard for me when

    You are a lot like

    My reactions to you remind me of

Difficult topics:

    It would be difficult for me to face

    It's hard for me to tell you about

    It's difficult for me to manage my feelings during therapy sessions when

    It has been hard to cope with my feelings in between sessions when

Reactions to the therapy:

    The beginning of a session is hard for me when

    When the therapy session ends, I often

    It has been painful for me to discover

In the termination phase, CRB1s often come up regarding self-reliance, independence, and grief about previous losses, separations, and deaths. It is a chance for the client to learn to say good-bye properly by expressing the range of feelings engendered by the ending of a special but transitional relationship (for a more complete discussion of the behavioral view of feelings and the expression of feelings, see R. J. Kohlenberg & Tsai, 1991, chap. 4). Exploring the following questions can evoke clients' CRBs about endings:

1. What are memorable losses in your life, stemming back to your childhood? How did you react to these losses?
2. What do relationship endings bring up for you?
3. How do you usually handle saying good-bye to someone?
4. How would you like our good-bye to be similar/different?
5. What have you appreciated about me? about this therapy?
6. What regrets do you have about this therapy?
7. What unfinished business do you still have regarding our relationship? What have you not yet said to me that is important for you to tell me?

Rule 3: Reinforce CRB2s. Given the contrived versus natural reinforcement issues, it is generally advisable to avoid procedures that attempt to specify the form of therapist reaction in advance. Such specification seems to happen whenever one attempts to conjure up a reinforcing reaction (e.g., phrases such as "that's terrific" or "great") without relating it to the specific client–therapist history. These specific forms of response can be contrived because they were thought of outside the context of the client–therapist environment at the moment of reinforcer delivery.

The ways that therapists can be more naturally reinforcing are examined in detail by R. J. Kohlenberg and Tsai (1991). One such way is for therapists to observe their spontaneous private reactions to client behavior and to describe these private reactions. Such private reactions are accompanied by dispositions to act in ways that are naturally reinforcing.

For example, consider a client who has intimacy concerns and lacks friends. Suppose that at some point in therapy, this client behaves in a way that evokes the following private, spontaneous reactions in the therapist: (a) dispositions to act in intimate and caring ways and (b) private reactions that correspond to "feeling close." Because these responses probably are not apparent to the client, the therapist could describe the private reactions by saying, "I feel especially close to you right now." Without such amplification, these important basic reactions would have little or no reinforcing effects on the client's behavior that evoked them (CRB2).

Rule 4: Observe the potentially reinforcing effects of therapist behavior in relation to client CRBs. Rule 4 is directly derived from behavior–analytic principles that stress the importance of the effects of the consequences of behavior on the future probabilities of that behavior. If therapists have been emitting behavior that they think is reinforcing, it would be important for them actually to observe whether they are in fact increasing, decreasing, or having no effect on a particular client behavior.

The therapist's observation of the reinforcing effects of his or her reactions on the client's behavior can help in giving interpretations (Rule 5) and in developing similar behaviors in the client—CRB3. The most obvious way this occurs is when the therapist tells the client about the self-observation: "I've noticed that each time you started talking about your spiritual beliefs, I've changed the topic, and you no longer bring it up." Thus, the therapist models making a statement of a functional relationship for the client.

Rule 4 can also lead the therapist to search for ways of enhancing the effects of reactions that could be reinforcing of CRB but that are not noticed by the client. For example, consider a male client who has had trouble expressing feelings because of a history of being ridiculed or criticized when he did so. He did not increase these behaviors, even though his therapist listened intently with empathic facial reactions and softly spoken comments each time the client expressed a feeling. Inquiries led to the discovery that the therapist's reactions were not discerned by the client because the act of expressing feelings evoked such intense emotions (collateral private respondents) that outside stimulation was not noticed. After the therapist amplified the empathic reaction by speaking loudly and clearly, the client's rate of feeling expression appeared to increase.

Rule 5: Give interpretations of variables that affect client behavior. As a general strategy, the therapist can interpret client behavior in terms of learning histories and functional relationships. Giving interpretations or reasons for behavior can affect the client in two ways.

First, the reason can lead to a prescription, instruction, or rule. The interpretation, "You are acting toward your wife like you did toward your mother" can easily be taken as a prescription or rule that the client hears as, "Don't be so unfair to your wife; treat her differently, since she obviously is not your mother. And if you treat her fairly, your marital relationship will improve." Whether or not the rule or instruction helps depends on how well it corresponds to the natural environment. For example, consider two reasons that might be given by a little girl who took a cookie when she was not supposed to. One reason might be, "The devil made me take the cookie." This reason does not correspond to environmental conditions that affected her cookie taking. On the other hand, the reason, "I took it because I haven't had a cookie in over a week" corresponds to environmental events. The latter reason suggests possible interventions (e.g., allowing her to have cookies more often) that could affect cookie stealing.

Second, a reason can enhance the salience of (increase contact with) controlling variables and increase positive and negative reinforcement density (Ferster, 1979). For example, a female client learns during FAP that the reason she feels rejected at times during the session is a function of the therapist's attentiveness, and, furthermore, this attentiveness is related to how harried or rushed the therapist appears at the beginning of the session. This interpretation could increase the client's noticing the therapist's mood at the beginning of the session and significantly affect the client's experience of a lapse in the therapist's attention. As a result, the client is in better contact (she notices how harried the therapist is) and then experiences less aversiveness when he is inattentive.

CASE EXAMPLE

Karen, age 24, presented a broad spectrum of complaints, including difficulties in forming and maintaining satisfying, romantic relationships; "low self-esteem"; anxiety; and depression. At first, treatment was a typical cognitive–behavioral therapy. This approach was only minimally effective. Dramatic improvements occurred, however, after the intervention was enhanced with FAP techniques as will be illustrated. Additional data on

Karen's presenting problems, improvement, and FAP case formulation are described by Cordova and Koerner (1993).

As part of her presenting problems, Karen described a frequently occurring interpersonal situation that made her anxious. She felt she was completely responsible for keeping conversations going when interacting with someone she cared about. In this situation, she sometimes had difficulty in coming up with interesting material or comments, and her anxiety would increase. She then would try even harder to come up with something to say, would have flights of ideas, would become confused and then experience even more anxiety—an unavoidable spiral. As part of this pattern, she did not let the other person assume responsibility for keeping the conversation going, and she never admitted that she was having difficulty with the interaction. Karen related this pattern to her low self-esteem. That is, she felt that she was intrinsically worthless and that if she relaxed and did not try harder, her true worthless, uninteresting self would be revealed, and she would be rejected and devalued.

In prior sessions, treatment consisted of a cognitive approach aimed at her assumptions regarding worthlessness, low self-esteem, and rejection, along with homework assignments designed to test her assumptions. Even though she seemed to understand the basic idea of this treatment and embraced more functional cognitions, she still became anxious and confused in the interpersonal situation described earlier. The following case material is from a session that occurred about 4 months after beginning treatment:

C: Hi.

T: Hi, how are you doing?

C: Fine. I'm having one of those situations where you say, I don't know what I'm going to say when I get here.

[Following Rule 1, the therapist is considering the possibility that CRBs are occurring at this time. First, in terms of CRB1, Karen is describing the present situation in the session in a way that resembles the daily life problem of being particularly anxious in interpersonal situations when she can't come up with interesting conversation. Because this is the kind of behavior that she attributes to low self-esteem, it is also likely that she is "having" the low self-esteem problem at this moment. There is also an improvement in comparison to past sessions at this moment. The CRB2 is her telling the therapist about the problem rather than attempting to cover it up and becoming diffuse in her efforts to say something interesting. Given the occurrence of a CRB2, Rule 3 suggests that this behavior should be reinforced. As evidenced below, the therapist is active and takes over responsibility for keeping the session going. This was probably a natural reinforcer for her revelations about the difficulty she is having with the interaction (CRB2). A passive therapeutic response at

this point (such as silence or "tell me more") is not advised at this point as it might punish the improvement.]

T: Uh, and—and you feel kind of a responsibility to say something?
[Therapist is both offering an interpretation and checking to see if this is an instance of CRB1.]

C: Uhumm. I should have liked an itinerary of topics or something.

T: Now, this is actually related to what we were talking about last week, in the sense that uhumm, you're not—you're not giving me much— you're not making me responsible for making sure we have things to talk about.
[This is an interpretation of behavior as suggested by Rule 5. Consistent with the FAP emphasis on within-session behavior, the interpretation refers to behaviors occurring in the present session and the previous one.]

C: I can't remember what we were talking about last week. I did, I remember it was something along that line.

T: It had . . . one of the general things we talked about last week, uh, was what you expect from people, what you could expect from a relationship. And, uh, basically how I thought maybe you didn't expect enough and that you didn't want to expect. . . . I think that's a better way to put it. You didn't know what you were entitled to expect and, uh, so this is a little bit related to that in the sense that here you come in and you're kind of worried about what you're going to say and I assume that you kind of feel like it's you're responsibility—you're not going to look good or. . . . Right?
[This is an elaboration of the interpretation in paragraph 6. It relates the behavior occurring in the session to daily life problems.]

C: Right. Well uhumm, I kind of feel like it's—it's final, I'm in therapy, and related to therapy . . . (unintelligible) and you lay out your problems. You know, in a sense of what I'm saying?

T: Uhumm. Well, I think it's one thing to say you're supposed to be able to give your problems and another thing to feel like responsibility for the topics that are talked about or somehow. . . . Now, am I misreading you, that you feel like it's a responsibility on your part to kind of get the ball rolling and to . . . ?

C: Yeah, I think so. And, be able to—define things. I don't know, it's hard to say. I once said that I sometimes have so many things in my mind that I can't—I couldn't possibly, you know, verbalize them; and that's kind of the situation I get into, and I'm just worried that it's gonna— I'll come off like that.

T: Uhumm. Now why, what is stopping you from walking in here and just feeling like, well, it's part of Kohlenberg's responsibility to get things going, and if I don't have anything to say, let him come up with something?

[This is prompting, a commonly used behavior therapy technique. Consistent with the FAP position that interventions are more effective in the here and now, prompting CRB2 is desirable.]

C: But I don't. I don't know why I don't, but I just don't. It's intriguing to think like that but I could never imagine myself doing that. I was—I've always been like too worried about that in a lot of situations. Uhumm, when you're going to be in a one-on-one situation, I'd wonder what I was going to talk about. I've felt like that a lot.

[Karen is providing some support for the notion that she is engaging in CRB— that is, that she is reacting to the therapist in ways that are similar to relationships in daily life.]

T: Uhumm.

T: Well . . . I . . . I . . . um . . . I think it's an important . . . I think it's important. That is, I think it's important that you can't walk in here and feel comfortable without anything to say. So.

C: Should I try to . . . [laughs]? That would be really uncomfortable. . . . Mmm.

One month after this interaction, Karen began a session without a plan about what she was going to say and looked to the therapist to start the session. Furthermore, she was relaxed and did not nervously attempt to keep the conversation going. She also reported related improvements in her interactions with other significant persons.

RESEARCH AND EVALUATION

Although FAP is informed by an abundance of data from laboratory studies on such basic concepts as reinforcement, avoidance, stimulus control, and rules, with the exception of Kohlenberg and Tsai (in press) there have not yet been any studies on its effectiveness. We are, however, currently in the process of collecting data and designing research to test the hypotheses and outcome of FAP. We will briefly describe some of the factors that are being considered in designing and conducting FAP research.

Our research efforts are guided by the answer to the question, "What is the purpose of clinical research?" Ostensibly, the main reason clinical researchers do what they do is to discover improved methods of treatment that are integrated into clinical practice. Thus, the practicing clinician is the consumer of clinical research. Whether or not the researcher's products are used by the practitioner is the ultimate reinforcer that supposedly maintains the researcher's activities.

What is supposed to be and what actually happens, however, are not necessarily the same thing. According to Barlow, a distinguished clinical researcher, "Clinical research has little or no influence on clinical practice"

(1981, p. 147). This is true, even for practicing behavioral clinicians. How can this be? Our discipline has had the goal of integrating science and practice for the past 30 years, and untold millions of dollars have been spent on the research. The root of the problem, according to Barlow, lies in the limitations of traditional research strategies involving group comparison research. The subject selection requirements as well as limiting outcome measurement to quantitative variables often preclude the possibility that practicing clinicians can use the obtained results (see Kohlenberg & Tsai, 1991 for a more complete discussion of these issues).

In a seminal article on the topic, Cordova and Koerner (1993) view the problem as resulting from the differences in the "persuasion criteria" (p. 317) for two different audiences: researchers and practitioners. Researchers are interested primarily in internal validity issues, whereas clinicians are interested in clinical utility. As a solution to the problem, they propose that researchers collect both types of data. Both Cordova and Koerner (1993) and Barlow (1981) point to case studies as having promise for addressing the concerns of clinicians. For example, Kohlenberg and Tsai (in press) used both qualitative and quantitative data in a case study of using FAP to enhance the cognitive therapy treatment of a depressed male.

Personal clinical experience is probably near the top of every therapist's list in terms of what influences his or her clinical behavior. Joseph Matarazzo, a prominent clinical researcher, stated that "even after 15 years, few of my research findings affect my practice. Psychological science per se doesn't guide me one bit. I still read avidly, but this is of little direct practical help. My *clinical experience is the only thing that has helped me in my practice to date*" (cited in Bergin & Strupp, 1972, p. 340; italics added).

Intensive local observation, proposed by Cronbach (1975), was suggested by Barlow (1981) as an alternative to traditional research strategies. This method has obvious features in common with both personal experience and influential case studies. Of intensive local observation, Cronbach said:

> An observer collecting data in one particular situation is in a position to appraise a practice or proposition in that setting, observing effects in context. In trying to describe and account for what happened, he will give attention to whatever variables were controlled. But he will give equal attention to uncontrolled conditions, to personal characteristics, and to events that occurred during treatment and measurement. (pp. 124–125)

Returning now to data collection in FAP, we are following two different strategies. One strategy emerges from the fact that FAP is in its early stages of development. Our therapeutic system must be further developed so that additional guidance can be given to therapists to detect and appropriately reinforce CRB. Thus, we call for data that have characteristics that emulate personal experience, such as those found in influential case studies and in intensive local observation. These data would have descriptions of what actually happened in the therapeutic interaction and as much contextual information as possible. Along these lines, we have presented verbatim transcribed material in this paper and elsewhere (R. J. Kohlenberg & Tsai, 1991, 1993). These excerpts are close to the raw data and give the consumer a sense of what actually happened. Such data can also be used to test a major hypothesis of FAP—that CRB occur.

Following the persuasion criteria approach, we are also proposing research that involves a more traditional design. For example, we are planning to use quantitative outcome measures and a comparison group design to evaluate our hypothesis that FAP can enhance the outcome of other cognitive–behavioral approaches. This experiment would compare the addition of a within-session focus and use of the client–therapist relationship with a standard cognitive therapy for depression.

The theory and methods of FAP along with verbatim transcriptions from Karen's sessions suggest the following: First, and perhaps foremost, the client–therapist relationship is extremely important in the therapeutic change process. Second, the centrality of the therapeutic relationship is theoretically consistent with and, in fact, is called for by a behavioral analysis of the change process. Finally, FAP offers guidelines to help therapists use the therapeutic relationship more effectively in an ongoing way.

REFERENCES

American Psychiatric Association (1994). *Diagnostic and statistical manual of mental disorders* (4th ed.). Washington, DC: Author.

Barlow, D. H. (1981). On the relation of clinical research to clinical practice. *Journal of Consulting and Clinical Psychology, 49*, 147–155.

Bergin, A. S., & Strupp, H. (1972). *Changing frontiers in the science of psychotherapy.* Chicago: Aldine-Atherton.

Bruckner-Gordon, F., Gangi, B. K., & Wallman, G. U. (1988). *Making therapy work.* New York: Harper & Row.

Ciminero, A. R., Calhoun, S. K., & Adams, H. E. (1977). *Handbook of behavioral assessment.* New York: Wiley.

Conger, J. C., & Conger, A. J. (1982). Components of heterosocial competence. In J. P. Curran & P. M. Monti (Eds.), *Social skills training* (pp. 313–347). New York: Guilford Press.

Cordova, J. V., & Koerner, K. (1993). Persuasion criteria in research and practice: Gathering more meaningful psychotherapy data. *The Behavior Analyst, 16*, 317–330.

Cronbach, L. J. (1975). Beyond the two disciplines of scientific psychology. *American Psychologist, 30,* 116–127.

Ferster, C. B. (1967). Arbitrary and natural reinforcement. *Psychological Record, 22,* 1–16.

Ferster, C. B. (1972). Clinical reinforcement. *Seminars in Psychiatry, 4,* 101–111.

Ferster, C. B. (1979). A laboratory model of psychotherapy. In P. Sjoden (Ed.), *Trends in behavior therapy,* San Diego, CA: Academic Press.

Goldfried, M. R. (1982). Resistance and clinical behavior therapy. In P. L. Wachtel (Ed.), *Resistance: Psychodynamic and behavioral approaches* (pp. 95–113). New York: Plenum Press.

Hayes, S. C. (1987). A contextual approach to therapeutic change. In N. S. Jacobson (Ed.), *Psychotherapists in clinical practice: Cognitive and behavioral perspectives* (pp. 327–387). New York: Guilford Press.

Hayes, S. C., & Hayes, L. J. (1992). Some clinical implications of contextualistic behaviorism: The example of cognition. *Behavior Therapy, 23,* 225–249.

Jacobson, N. S. (1989). The therapist–client relationship in cognitive behavior therapy: Implications for treating depression. *Journal of Cognitive Psychotherapy, 3,* 85–96.

Kohlenberg, R. J., & Tsai, M. (1991). *Functional analytic psychotherapy: Creating intense and curative therapeutic relationships.* New York: Plenum Press.

Kohlenberg, R. J., & Tsai, M. (1993). Hidden meaning: A behavioral approach. *The Behavior Therapist, 16,* 80–82.

Kohlenberg, R. J., & Tsai, M. (1994). Functional analytic psychotherapy: A radical behavioral approach to treatment and integration. *Journal of Psychotherapy Integration, 4,* 175–201.

Kohlenberg, R. J., & Tsai, M. (in press). Improving cognitive therapy for depression with functional analytic psychotherapy: Theory and case study. *The Behaviour Analyst.*

Kohlenberg, R. J., Tsai, M., & Dougher, M. J. (1993). The dimensions of clinical behavior analysis. *The Behavior Analyst, 16,* 271–282.

Kohlenberg, R. J., Tsai, M., & Kohlenberg, B. S. (in press). Functional analysis in behavior therapy. In M. Herson, R. M. Eisler, & P. M. Miller, (Eds.), *Progress in behavior modification.* Newbury Park, CA: Sage Publications.

Linehan, M. (1993). *Cognitive behavioral treatment of borderline personality disorder: The dialectics of effective treatment.* New York: Guilford Press.

Rabin, C., Tsai, M., & Kohlenberg, R. J. (in press). Targeting sex-role and power issues with a functional analytic approach: Gender patterns in behavioral marital therapy. *Journal of Feminist Family Therapy.*

Scott, R., Himadi, W., & Keane, T. (1983). Generalization of social skills. In M. Hersen, R. Eisler, & P. Miller (Eds.), *Progress in behavior modification* (Vol. 15; pp. 114–172). San Diego, CA: Academic Press.

Skinner, B. F. (1953). *Science and human behavior.* New York: Macmillan.

Skinner, B. F. (1974). *About behaviorism*. New York: Knopf.

Skinner, B. F. (1982). Contrived reinforcement. *The Behavior Analyst, 5,* 3–8.

Wachtel, P. L. (1977). *Psychoanalysis and behavior therapy: Toward an integration.* New York: Basic Books.

Zettle, R. D., & Hayes, S. C. (1982). Rule-governed behavior: A potential theoretical framework for cognitive–behavioral therapy. In P. C. Kendall (Ed.), *Advances in cognitive behavioral research and therapy* (Vol. 1, pp. 73–118). New York: Academic Press.

24

PARADIGMATIC BEHAVIORISM AND PARADIGMATIC BEHAVIOR THERAPY

ARTHUR W. STAATS

The purpose of this chapter is to characterize the general behaviorism that I have been developing over the past four decades—variously called social behaviorism, paradigmatic behaviorism (PB), and most recently, psychological behaviorism (Tryon, 1990)—and the paradigmatic behavior therapy that is part of this behaviorism. I will begin with a few words about the origin of this behaviorism, in the context of describing the early development of the modern behavioral movement.

BEHAVIOR THERAPY AND BEHAVIORISM

I became a behaviorist as a graduate student in the early 1950s, completing my training in clinical psychology, including a Veterans Administration (VA) internship, but also studying general experimental psychology (learning), the field in which I took my PhD. My goal was to use conditioning principles as an approach to the comprehensive study of human behavior, which was why I selected broad training. My doctoral dissertation at UCLA was entitled A *Behavioristic Study of Verbal and Instrumental Re-*

sponse Hierarchies and Their Relationship to Human Problem Solving (Staats, 1956). The study involved how verbal behavior could mediate problem solving and how the verbal behavior was affected by reinforcement (see Staats, 1957b). At that time, there were few if any behavioristic studies of human behavior in a quasinaturalistic situation, let alone in work with human problems. This was the first formal study in my ongoing program of work in constructing a new, general behaviorism.

Unlike that of the second-generation behaviorists, the focus of my interests was in functional human behavior, in the naturalistic situation as well as in experimental study. In fact, some time before beginning my formal experimental work, I began applying conditioning principles to the change of behavior in the openly naturalistic situation. My first subject was a pet cat, which I classically conditioned to have an emotional response to a word (for studies with human subjects, see Staats & Staats, 1957, 1958; Staats, Staats, & Crawford, 1962) and I used reinforcement procedures to train the cat to make motor responses to different words (which also served as the foundation for later human studies). Another example of my analyses is that in the mid 1950s, I organized several friends (including Jack Michael) to positively reinforce fluent speech in a hesitant speaker in our group, which resulted in evident change in behavior. That experience contributed to my first published behavior modification analysis (Staats, 1957a); the subject was a schizophrenic patient with an abnormal speech symptom that was being reinforced by the psychiatrists interviewing the patient. The analysis made explicit how the patient's speech symptom was learned and could be treated by extinction and by reinforcing normal speech. Jack Michael and his student Ted Ayllon (Ayllon & Michael, 1959) supported these behavior modification principles in work with various patients in a psychiatric hospital. The principles that I developed— reinforcement of desirable behaviors and extinction of undesirable behaviors in the naturalistic situation—became core items in the development of the field of behavior modification.[1]

There were, of course, various contributors to our beginning development of modern behavioral psychology (e.g., Dollard & Miller, 1950; Eysenck, 1960; Krasner, 1955; Krasner & Ullmann, 1965; Shoben, 1949; Staats, 1957a, 1963b [especially chaps. 10 & 11]; Ullmann & Krasner, 1965; Wolpe, 1958), and they came from different backgrounds with re-

---

[1] This was also true of other principles, methods, and procedures that emerged from the early PB work with children, such as the token-reinforcer system and time-out. PB called for extension of behavior principles and procedures generally to children with developmental disabilities, including autism and mental retardation (Staats, Finley, Minke, & Wolf, 1964), to be used by various professionals (e.g., social workers, prison officials, and special education teachers) and subprofessionals, in various settings (e.g., schools and homes for juvenile delinquents, and prisons; see Staats, 1963a; Staats & Butterfield, 1965). This formulation, which was not available in the other behaviorisms, outlined the form that the field of developmental disabilities was to take in behavior analysis.

spect to the specific behaviorism they used. For example, Wolpe (1958) used Hull's learning theory in his early work; the English behavior therapists (Eysenck, 1960) did not use Skinner's work, and at the time I visited there in 1961, they were unfamiliar with the behavior modification work some of us had begun in the United States. Others were interested in verbal conditioning within the Skinnerian theory framework (see Kanfer, 1958; Krasner, 1958). Skinner's own program, not generally understood, was that of applying his experimental analysis of behavior (EAB) laboratory generally to human behavior (see Azrin & Lindsley, 1956; Bijou, 1955; Lindsley, 1956).

However, despite the broad nature of its beginnings, as the new human behavioral field developed, it came to be "housed" more and more deeply within the radical behaviorism approach of Skinner (1938, 1953, 1957). That framework, however, carried with it certain features. As one example, Skinner's program of extending experimental analysis of behavior to human study constituted a binding methodological approach that placed a heavy value on the use of rate of response, reinforcement, cumulative recording, and free operant responding. In the early 1960s, an editor of a Skinnerian journal first wanted to reject a study of mine, of a child learning to read, because my use of learning "trials" did not seem like free operant responding. (That study and others in this program—see Staats, Finley, Minke, & Wolf, 1964—were later considered to be the foundation of the behavior–analytic field dealing with developmental disorders such as dyslexia; see O'Leary & Drabman, 1971.) The reluctance of proponents of radical behaviorism (RB) to use non-EAB methods still continues in behavior analysis. In contrast to such restrictions, my own approach was stated clearly. "[A] combination of naturalistic [and clinical] observations with the principles based upon experimental observations . . . a combination of methods . . . is necessary in understanding and dealing with human problems, [so] it is suggested that . . . psychology cannot restrict itself to the laboratory"[2] (Staats, 1963a, pp. 282–283).

Even though some radical behaviorists began using such liberalizations, and experimental analysis of behavior was changed to include use of reinforcement in the natural situation, the RB tradition generally continued to be restrictive in its methodology, in its language, and in the principles and literature used. For example, RB, like Eysenck (1960) rejected

---

[2]One of the central aspects of my work was its systemization of naturalistic research. In 1960, when my first child was born, for example, I began to apply learning principles systematically to produce and study her behavior development—in language-cognitive, emotional-motivational, and sensorimotor areas. This methodology, called experimental-longitudinal research (see Staats, Brewer, & Gross, 1970) studied the behavior development of complex repertoires over long periods of time. The work is the basis for various analyses, concepts, and principles (e.g., in Staats, 1963a, 1963b, 1968, 1971a, 1975) that formally and informally found their way into the general behavioral framework. The experimental-longitudinal methodology is still not exploited, however, although that type of research is centrally needed for developing our field.

talk therapy, along with rejection of psychodynamic psychotherapy. The verbal conditioning studies were important in showing that verbal behavior could be manipulated through reinforcement. In these studies, however, verbal behavior was not changed in order to change behavior. Language was not recognized as a general tool by which the behavioral psychologist could change behavior. Within this framework, also, there was no interest in how the individual's own language could affect the individual's behavior. Direct reinforcement of behavior is what counts within the Skinnerian framework.

That was not my view, as my works indicated in various ways (see Staats, 1963a), beginning with my dissertation. For example, my early study and analysis of the manner in which the individual's verbal responses to problem-solving objects affected the individual's problem-solving ability specified how language behavior determined overt behavior (see Staats, 1956, 1963b). Another example is that an extended series of studies showed how words that the individual has already learned can *function* to produce new emotional conditioning in the individual (see Staats & Staats, 1958). This PB study gave rise to a host of experiments by others that showed how overt behavior was affected (see Berkowitz & Knurek, 1969; Early, 1968; Hekmat & Vanian, 1971). How words can be used to condition new motor responses was indicated (Staats, 1966) and supported in research (see Herry, 1984). Having developed these principles (with supporting research), I finally wrote a specific article to criticize the RB restriction of treatment to the reinforcement of behavior. This analysis stated that the emotional and motor behavior of clients could be changed through language, by what the therapist and client say to each other (Staats, 1972). PB had shown that changes in the individual's language (i.e., reasoning, thinking, planning) can have behavioral effects. (The process was called both language behavior therapy and cognitive–behavioral therapy.) RB contained no such principles or research.

Others elaborated the PB position and shared the dissatisfaction with behavior modification's restriction to direct reinforcement procedures (see Hekmat, 1972; Meichenbaum & Goodman, 1971), and various cognitive–behavioral approaches began to emerge and become very influential. The language behavior therapy approach and the cognitive–behavioral therapies shared the view that verbal "psychotherapy" can be used to treat problems of behavior, one of the elements indicative of a third-generation behavioral approach. An RB interest only developed much later (Hamilton, 1988).

BEHAVIORISM, THEORY, AND BEHAVIOR THERAPY

The basic principles and experimental approach that were the foundations for the beginnings of behavior therapy derived from the *tradition* of behaviorism. This tradition, in its second generation, constituted a framework of principles, concepts, and methods as well as a general orientation. In more recent times, there has been confusion concerning the definition of behavior therapy. Some have considered it a development of behaviorism, others as simply an empirical methodology. I am suggesting that the emergence of behavior therapy, although it involved methodological and empirical components, was based on theory development—theory involving the analysis of behavior problems in terms of conditioning principles. The principles of classical and instrumental (operant) conditioning are actually common to each of the second-generation behaviorisms and to the behaviorisms of today. Although many believe that behavior therapy studies support Skinner's RB, the fact is that the use of conditioning principles derives from and supports all of the behaviorisms.

I suggest, moreover, that the further development of behavior therapy will rest upon theory developments that depend upon the nature of the behaviorism that is used. That is, despite a core of commonality, the behaviorisms have fundamental differences and have different implications for the development of behavior therapy. Fundamental differences appear in such things as philosophy of science, general theory, methodological position, distinctive empirical works, and a slate of problems that are considered important to confront. A general behaviorism provides a foundation for specific as well as general directions for work and fulfills various heuristic roles. In addition to providing the basic conditioning principles and general experimental methodology, a general behaviorism also provides analyses (theories) of different areas of human behavior, such as language, emotion, reading, imitation, problem sovlving, sensory–motor skills, arithmetic, attitudes, and so on. Different behaviorisms, however, differ in the number of such theories that they contain and in their heuristic value. (For example, several behavior analysts—such as MacPherson, Bonem, Green, & Osborne, 1984—have noted the lack of heuristic value of Skinner's 1957 *Verbal Behavior*.)

In addition, a behaviorism also provides an instrument for tapping into the many elements of knowledge of psychology (including behaviorism). These many elements are presented in different theory languages. There is thus a question concerning which elements are important and which are not. How can the elements be translated to a common language so that they can be understood and joined with other unrelated elements? The behaviorism that is used is the instrument that performs these functions, and the behaviorisms differ widely in their ability to serve such purposes, although this is not well understood.

The behaviorism employed also provides a *general* conception of behavior for the behavior therapist in confronting the varied problems of the clinic. That is, although many problems can be dealt with in terms of specific treatment techniques involving the principles of conditioning, there are many cases that have not been analyzed behaviorally. Some demand complex analyses. There are cases, for example, in which the individual's life circumstances, as well as the general characteristics of the individual, need to be analyzed and understood before changes, which may also be complex, can be suggested. In many cases, a central item is the behavior therapist's conception of child development, human relations, personality, intelligence, social attitudes, psychological measurement, how psychotherapy works, language development, parent–child relationships, the various behavior disorders, how changing emotions changes or does not change behavior, and so on. The behavior therapist then depends on the behaviorism that is employed to supply the necessary elements for use in analysis.

Most centrally, the behaviorism will serve as a heuristic framework with respect to research and other new developments. There are various features of this heuristic ability. For example, the greater the number of areas developed in the behaviorism that are relevant to behavior therapy, the greater the heuristic potentiality of the behaviorism, for this constitutes an agenda for the development of research. The explicitness of the behaviorism in its analysis of different areas will also be important here. As an example, consider the analysis of language, which is basic to the study of various specific and general topics in behavior therapy (including why and how verbal psychotherapy works). It is one thing to say that language is learned. That is a very general statement and provides little specific guidance for working with problems of language (and cognition). It is another thing to specify not only the principles involved but also the learning conditions that result in the learning of language. The specificity of the behavior therapist's analysis of a case of a deficit in language learning—as in childhood autism—will ordinarily depend on how specifically the behaviorism used has analyzed and researched the area. Skinner's *Verbal Behavior* dealt very little with the *learning* of language, popular belief to the contrary, and did not guide research in this direction.

The general point here is that there are different behaviorisms— Hull's behaviorism (sometimes called methodological behaviorism), Skinner's RB, PB, social learning/cognitive behaviorism, interbehaviorism, and others—and their different characteristics make them differentially able to fulfill the various uses the field of behavior therapy needs for its operation and advancement. For instance, PB and RB differ widely in terms of how they serve as instruments by which to understand and translate elements of knowledge within psychology so that they can be incorporated into behavior therapy. For example, RB rejects psychological testing. PB, in contrast, provides a means by which to understand and use psychological tests (see Fernandez-Ballesteros & Staats, 1992; Staats, 1975, 1986). Moreover, PB projects a large area of behavioral research on psychological tests (see Staats & Burns, 1981, 1982; Staats, Gross, Guay, & Carlson, 1973) that is lacking in RB.

RADICAL BEHAVIORISM
AND PSYCHOLOGICAL BEHAVIORISM

This by no means exhausts the need to compare behaviorisms with respect to their features in serving the role of overarching theories for behavior therapy. The point is that the field of behavior therapy must take such analysis and evaluation as an important task. This cannot be done in this chapter, but a few additional items can be added as a context for considering paradigmatic behavior therapy.

The Rejectionism of Radical Behaviorism, and Psychological Behaviorism's Behaviorizing of Psychology

One of the important differences between PB and RB concerns the relationship of behaviorism and psychology. The traditional goal of RB, beginning with Watson, has been to discredit and replace traditional psychology. Skinner led and institutionalized this position in the second generation, through the way he conducted his program as well as through the specific content of the program. With respect to the latter, there is almost no use of psychological concepts, methods, or findings in Skinner's (see 1953, 1957) works. Ignoring other works in a field constitutes a method that serves as a model for Skinnerians to follow. I have called this characteristic of RB "rejectionism." In this approach the aim is the defeat of psychology and its replacement by behaviorism.

It is interesting to note, however, that the major behaviorists all made analyses of things that were first studied in traditional psychology. Watson (1930), for example, analyzed emotions, talking and thinking, and personality in behavioral terms. Skinner in his *Science and Human Behavior* (1953) analyzed such topics as the self, personality, thinking, and education. Such analyses were not done to build bridges to traditional psychology, however, or to indicate that work in psychology could have some value. Rather, they were done to show how traditional psychology was defective and how behaviorism could replace it and do a better job, even on the things that traditional psychology had studied. Thus, radical behaviorism never systematically recognized that traditional psychology had valuable materials that should be addressed, even in the face of examples that such materials could be used as the "jumping-off" place for behavioristic analyses.

In contrast, the PB position is that psychology has a purview of important problems and has partially developed the study of many of those problems. However, psychology's research typically contains weaknesses and errors, and it suffers from neglecting the study of important things that fall within the purview of behaviorism. Behaviorism has great things to offer in the study of those problems that psychology does not have. What this calls for is a complementarity—not opposition. What has not been realized is that the foundation for behavior therapy (including behavior modification, behavioral assessment, and behavior analysis) was born through a *unification* of behaviorism and traditional psychology. As one example I described the early PB case involving the analysis of the opposite speech of a schizophrenic patient in terms of conditioning principles (Staats, 1957a). This analysis can be seen to constitute a theory bridge; it accepts as valuable a phenomenon that had been observed in traditional clinical work, on the one hand, and joined this with principles established in behaviorism. PB calls such a work "behaviorizing psychology"—it turns deficient (mentalistic) knowledge into solidly based behavioral knowledge. The heuristic value of such bridging theory developments can be seen in the example given, where the principles involved became basic in the general field of behavior therapy, beginning with Ayllon and Michael (1959). PB's position is that behavior therapy needs to have the behaviorizing of psychology established as a general goal for a new generation of development. This must also be done for behaviorism generally (see Staats, 1992, 1993a) if it is to become important in psychology.

PB, in making its behavior analyses, retains the *traditional* name of the topic involved: attitudes, intelligence, depression, reading, personality, schizophrenia, and so forth. The translation is done to effect a unification of behaviorism and psychology. In contrast, Skinner, seemingly in the interest of constructing a separate approach, generally avoided the names used by others: he renamed reading "texting," concept formation "abstraction," classical conditioning "respondent conditioning," and so on. Some behavior analysts (see Ulman, 1990) have confused PB's use of traditional terms with the use of intervening variables (methodological behaviorism) or mentalistic concepts, which is not the case. PB's terms are behaviorally defined, strictly, closely, specifically; its methodology is more stringent than in some of RB's concepts, such as private events and rule-governed behavior.

I described my dissertation (Staats, 1956) to indicate that PB began with a goal of behaviorizing traditional psychology problems. This has been a prominent part of the PB approach ever since, involving behavior analyses of word meaning, reasoning, thinking, communication, depression, emotion, creativity, mathematics, attitudes, religious values, intelligence, factor analytic personality traits, depression, developmental reading disorder, walking development, toilet training, the self-concept, attraction, talk therapy, catharsis, transference, rapport, and many more (see Staats, 1963b, 1968, 1971a, 1971b, 1975, 1988). PB's definition of the term *behavior anal-*

ysis, when it introduced this term (see Staats, 1963b), constituted a method for behaviorizing psychology (see also Staats, 1965).

PB now advances generally the program of behaviorizing psychology. In contrast to rejecting psychology PB, on the basis of its extensive experience, says that psychology has begun the study of many important phenomena and in doing so has formulated important methods of study and has produced important findings, concepts, and principles. Ordinarily, traditional psychological knowledge (including the cognitive–behavioral therapies) is incomplete, contains errors, includes mentalistic definitions, and is eclectic precisely because that knowledge lacks the necessary behavioral analysis. That is what the behaviorizing program of PB proposes to add. The approach calls for a huge program, because psychologists have done much—which means much behavioral analysis is needed. The products of that endeavor, however, will be a greatly expanded behaviorism and behavior therapy, unified with psychology. The fact is that when behaviorism shows interest in psychology's problems, works on them, and succeeds through behaviorizing to add valuable elements to the study, then psychology will begin to see behaviorism as important. Behavior therapy needs a behaviorism that can relate to psychology and that in doing so commands more of psychology's resources.

Radical Behaviorism and Framework Theory Strategies

Another difference between RB and PB concerns theory-construction methodology. RB, like traditional psychology generally, has followed a faulty methodology in constructing its grand theory, which is intended to be comprehensive and unifying. The methodology is to conduct systematic study in a specialized area of psychology, construct a set of principles thereby, and assume that these principles are sufficient for the explanation of all behavioral phenomena of interest to psychology. Thus, Freud studied a delimited set of phenomena (the verbalizations of his patients in the psychoanalytic situation), as did Piaget (the success of children of various ages solving certain problems) as well as the behaviorists (the animal conditioning phenomena). Although each of these theories involved systematic study of only a special part of psychology, they were considered to apply to the whole. Because the elements of the whole were never considered, the part-to-whole strategy also involved rejectionism, the wholesale rejection of all that was not studied. This strategy in behaviorism produces a two-level theory, in which the elementary conditioning principles constitute the basic level, complete and sufficient, and human behavior phenomena generally are lumped into that which is to be explained (the other level) on the basis of the principles.

When this strategy is analyzed, it becomes clear why all of the "classic grand theories in psychology have failed" (Staats, 1993c, p. 46). They did not even *consider* the vast knowledge that had to be confronted to constitute a grand theory. But, one may ask, how can any theory confront all there is in psychology—the task is too vast for any one person, in any one lifetime? Central in the PB approach is a different theory—construction methodology by which to make the task manageable, without blindly rejecting most of psychology's knowledge elements. PB's methodology introduces the concept of the "framework theory" (see Staats, 1981, 1988). This methodology simplifies, not by rejection without due process, but by dealing with psychology's complexity *progressively*, not all at once. That is, the framework theory methodology is to construct a theoretical *skeleton*, not a completed theory. This unified framework theory is applied to the analysis of the psychology's fields, to include features (concepts, principles, findings) of each field. The framework theory for each field does not address each element of knowledge that has been produced in the field. Rather, it samples those elements in a systematic way, attempting to deal first with some of the centrally significant elements in each field for the purpose of constructing a unified theory of the field. Moreover, this is done in each case to demonstrate the general theory's relevance for the field—suggesting that the theory should be extended more broadly (and deeply). Most of the elements, however, cannot be dealt with in any of the fields, at least at first. It is important, though, that the program of the framework theory is eventually to consider everything, to assess each element with respect to inclusion or exclusion. The grand framework theory, then, is composed of the several field theories along with the necessary conception that overarches the fields (see Staats, 1975, 1988).

Thus, the framework theory is an incomplete theory—but not incomplete in the sense that it is loose, that it leaves out or rejects large areas without systematic consideration, or that it is eclectic. Rather, it is incomplete by rational plan because, although it aims to treat the wide range of psychology's interests, it does not in its first formulation (and only progressively) treat them all. However, what it does do is completely consistent, developed in a systematic manner, with a planned program. All of the elements included in the framework theory must be made consistent with the basic principles, as those principles are elaborated through use of materials in the several fields. Moreover, the framework theory is a true theory, connected to the phenomena studied in the usual operational manner—and the theory in each field must show its heuristic properties.

Because psychology contains a number of major fields, there is the general task of indicating their relationships. Is one of the fields basic, containing the elementary principles for the other fields? Are all the other fields on the same level? The latter assumption has been implicit in behaviorism, part of its two-level strategy that considers conditioning principles as basic, and the rest is to be explained. In PB position, in contrast, is that each of the fields has concepts and principles to contribute and that the different fields are related to each other in a hierarchical manner, with some being basic to others.

The previous behaviorisms did not address such considerations. PB's position is that although the conditioning principles are basic, they have to be developed by adding concepts and principles through the several levels (fields) of psychology in the task of constructing a very general framework theory with which to embrace all the phenomena of human behavior. PB also takes the position that there is a rough dimension—from basic to advanced—that goes from the basic learning theory field (level) through human learning, developmental, personality, personality measurement, social, abnormal, clinical, educational, and occupational psychology. Thus, the major fields in psychology are seen to constitute connected levels of study. Each of the levels of study has principles, concepts, methods, and findings to add to the overarching theory. A field like personality, for example, has more basic fields to which it must be related, such as learning, as well as more "advanced" fields, such as personality measurement and abnormal psychology, to which *it* is basic. Moreover, PB recognizes that more advanced (and applied) levels may contribute elements of value to more basic levels—that there is a bidirectional relationship rather than one that is purely reductionistic (see Staats, 1983, 1991).

The theory construction task, it should be indicated, is complex. Each field is a very complex body of knowledge, and it is necessary in each case to pick and choose and reconstitute elements, as well as to generate necessary elements, by which to construct a framework theory of the field. Moreover, this framework theory must connect to the framework theories of the adjacent fields and thus become part of the whole. I will also add that there may be theories within each level. Thus, the PB human learning level contains a theory of emotion, of language, and so on. The PB abnormal psychology level, for another example, contains theories of the different behavior disorders (Staats, 1989).

PB, the general approach, is composed of the level-theories, such as its theory of the basic principles of developmental psychology, personality, and abnormal psychology, as well as its sublevel-theories of emotion, language, intelligence, attitudes, interests, values, reading, writing, number concept learning, depression, the anxiety disorders, dyslexia, and so on. Some of these treatments are more specific and may be considered analyses or minitheories, such as analyses of walking development, toilet training, communication, concepts, problem solving, the self-concept, number concept learning, and so on. These theories and analyses (see Staats, 1963b, 1968, 1971a, 1975), along with their empirical support, are woven together as part of the theory-construction task to constitute the framework theory (see Staats, 1975) that binds the whole together. Thus, although the framework theory is in general a skeleton, it must contain full, heuristic theories (with empirical–methodological development) at selected spots in its purview. There are many elements of the PB framework, of varying sizes and degrees of completion. There are also many empty spaces of various sizes that need to be filled in by theoretical, methodological, and empirical analyses. This will take the work of various behaviorists, a number whom have already contributed and are contributing important works.

PB is thus a large framework theory—a multilevel theory—that weaves together the more specific framework theories in a closely constructed, consistent manner. It is not possible to reduce the content of PB and its works to a single chapter. However, its range of interests, and the outline of its structure, is summarized in Exhibit 1. The table indicates the levels and their relationships, in a general way, and indicates also some of the specific interests in the areas and some of PB's concepts and principles for dealing with those interests.

CHARACTERIZATION OF PSYCHOLOGICAL BEHAVIORISM

The areas addressed by the multilevel theory are presented in the left column of Table 1. The right-hand column characterizes some of the principles, concepts, and purposes of each level. In pursuit of a characterization of PB and paradigmatic behavior therapy (PBT), I will present a few words about several of PB's levels and how PBT's characteristics derive from being anchored in this framework.

The Basic Principles Level

The behaviorisms in the second generation—those of Skinner (1938), Hull (1943), Tolman (1932), and so on—arose in the context of the animal research conducted within the two research traditions begun by Pavlov and Thorndike. The second-generation behaviorists' central tasks were to systematize (construct theories of) the many studies of the principles of conditioning, to extend their systems through additional research, and (although this was less well understood) to advance behaviorism conceptually, methodologically, and philosophically. As must be the case, the behaviorisms concentrated on their own problems of development. These behaviorisms did not in their formulation have as a context the human-level experimentation that developed later. PB is a third-generation behaviorism in part because, in addition to the first two generations of behaviorism, it had a richer human research context, some of which it produced. Of particular importance is that it took that human context into account in the construction of its basic theory. I will illustrate the difference in some detail with respect to one important issue, the *relationship* of classical conditioning and operant conditioning—a central problem for the second-generation

(text continues on page 675)

EXHIBIT 1
The Multilevel Theory of Paradigmatic Behaviorism

Levels (and Content-Area Examples)	Principles, Concepts, and Phenomena

1. Biological mechanisms of learning
  a. Sensory psychology
  b. Brain and central nervous system
  c. Response systems
  d. Evolution of learning mechanisms
	The neurophysiology of learning. The central purpose of this level of theory is to unify the biological study of organisms with their behavioral study, making the two mutually heuristic, and removing and schism that separates so much of psychology along "nature–nurture" lines. The basic bridge relates the biological concepts of sensory, response, and association organs with the behavioral concepts of stimuli, responses, and learning.

2. Basic-learning theory
  a. Elementary study: conditioning principles
  b. Generalizing study: types of stimuli, responses, and species to which principles apply
  c. Motivation principles
	Three-function learning theory. Stimuli that elicit an emotional response will because of this be reinforcing stimuli. Both functions (emotion elicitation and reinforcement) are transferred in classical conditioning. Moreover, organisms generally learn to approach positive emotional (and reinforcing) stimuli and to avoid negative emotional (and punishing) stimuli. As a consequence, emotional stimuli direct (are incentives for) behavior. This learning theory makes the study of the various forms of the classical conditioning of emotions to be a central concern in explaining behavior, giving new directions for animal and human research.

3. Human-learning principles
  a. Complex stimulus-response learning (e.g., response sequences, response hierarchies, and multiple controlling stimuli)
  b. Response repertoires
  c. Cumulative–hierarchical learning principles and others unique to humans
	Complex stimulus-response mechanisms, internal responses and stimuli, basic behavioral repertoires, and cumulative–hierarchical learning. The basic learning theory states the behavioral principles in elemental simplicity. Human skills and general characteristics are composed of exceedingly complex combinations of the basic principles. The field of human learning must study such complex combinations and the manner in which complex, interrelated sets of responses (repertoires) are learned. Centrally, complex human skills are complex repertoires that can only be acquired if the individual has already learned necessary prior repertoires (e.g., reading can only be learned after prior language repertoires are learned). These principles of cumulative–hierarchical learning require systematic, basic study.
	(exhibit continues)

EXHIBIT 1 (Continued)

Levels (and Content-Area Examples)	Principles, Concepts, and Phenomena
4. Personality a. Personality concept b. The three personality systems: language–cognitive, emotional–motivational, and sensorimotor c. Personality and environment interaction	*Personality is composed of basic behavioral repertoires.* From birth the child begins to learn complex systems of "skills" in the three general areas. These are learned in advancing complexity. There are subrepertoires that additional learning combines together (as language is composed of separately learned subrepertoires), and there are repertoires that are basic to the later learning of more advanced repertoires (as algebra skills rest on the prior learning of arithmetic operations). The three repertoires constitute personality. In interaction with the environment they determine the individual's experience, learning, and behavior. This theory makes many conceptual unifications possible in psychology and opens many new avenues of research.
5. Child development a. Language–cognitive development b. Sensorimotor development, including modeling skills c. Emotional–motivational development	*Cumulative–hierarchical learning and development.* Traditional developmental psychologists have studied many aspects of the child's development. But there has been little analysis of this development in terms of its complex learning. Paradigmatic behaviorism calls for this systematic analysis, provides exemplary theoretical–empirical analyses of language–cognitive, emotional–motivational, and sensorimotor development through learning, and calls for various new types of theory and research.
6. The social-personality level of study a. Attitudes and social cognition b. Interpersonal relations and group processes c. Personality processes, individual and group differences, and cross-cultural psychology	*Interactions among individuals and groups.* The three-function learning principles are basic. Attitudes are emotional responses to social stimuli. Thus, such stimuli have reinforcing and incentive (directive) power, depending on their emotion elicitation. Social phenomena such as group cohesion, attraction, persuasion, prejudice, and intergroup relations function by these principles. In addition to the emotional response individuals have for each other, the language-cognitive and sensorimotor personality repertoires of interactors are determinants of their social behavior. Group character and social role phenomena also operate according to the basic principles and personality principles.

(exhibit continues)

EXHIBIT 1 (Continued)

Levels (and Content-Area Examples)	Principles, Concepts, and Phenomena

7. Personality measurement
  a. Theory relating behavior principles, the concept of personality, and personality measurement and behavioral assessment
  b. Application of theory to tests and their uses (clinical, etc.)
  c. Applications to test construction and assessment: Paradigmatic behavioral assessment
	Unifying theory for a behavioral psychometrics. The personality theory provides a conceptual framework within which the personality concepts, methods, and instruments of the traditional field of psychometrics can be analyzed in a manner compatible with behaviorism. Personality tests measure aspects of the basic behavioral repertoires, which accounts for their ability to predict behavior. For example, intelligence tests heavily measure language repertoires and sensory-motor skills, and interest tests measure aspects of the emotional-motivational repertoire. The theory explains why verbal tests provide knowledge of nonverbal behavior and emotional states—because the three personality repertoires are interconnected and covary—helping resolve the behaviorism/psychometrics schism. The theory is heuristic for basic research and test construction.

8. Abnormal psychology
  a. The personality repertoires as basic determinants of abnormal behavior
  b. Diagnostic categories as deficient and inappropriate personality repertoires
  c. Personality and environment interaction in abnormal behavior
	Paradigmatic behaviorism's theory of abnormal behavior. The individual learns personality repertoires that interact with his life situation in determining his behavior. The personality repertoires may be rich and adaptive or sparse and inappropriate. In the latter case, the individual's behavior will be abnormal in certain situations. Life situations that are not normal may also produce abnormal behavior. Biological conditions can directly affect the personality repertoires and produce abnormal behavior. Using this theory, a unified analysis can be made of the various diagnostic categories. For example, schizophrenia involves disturbances especially in the language–cognitive and emotional–motivational repertoires, phobias involve only a part of the latter repertoire, and the various subtypes of depression differ in the repertoires, life events, or biological conditions involved.

9. Clinical psychology a. Behavior modification of simple problems, behavior therapy, and the psychodynamics/conditioning schism	*Paradigmatic behavior therapy.* The various levels of paradigmatic behaviorism are applied to clinical problems involving various methods of treatment. *(exhibit continues)*

EXHIBIT 1 (Continued)

Levels (and Content-Area Examples)	Principles, Concepts, and Phenomena
b. Paradigmatic behavior therapy c. Personality change and personality measurement d. Language–cognitive methods of treatment	The basic learning principles can be employed to directly treat simple problems. Sometimes personality or social-environmental problems are involved and assessment instruments and personality measurement may be needed, as well as complex social-environmental changes and learning programs. The language–cognitive level of theory indicates how behavior and personality can be changed by various verbal methods of therapy. Paradigmatic behavior therapy has been in development since the 1950s, has yielded seminal contributions to behavior therapy, and now projects new avenues for development.
10. Educational psychology a. Paradigmatic behaviorism's theories of school subjects b. Intelligence, learning readiness, retardation, and learning disability c. Treating problems of school learning	*Education and paradigmatic behaviorism.* Reading (like writing and number-concept skills) is explicated in theory and research; considered in specific terms as complex language–cognitive repertoires, learned in a cumulative–hierarchical manner, based on earlier-acquired language repertoires. Theory and research yield a conception of intelligence as composed of learned and trainable repertoires. Learning readiness, retardation, and learning disability, which are typically inferred to result from biological conditions can be better explained within a unified learning–biological theory that stipulates the repertoires involved, with directives for problem resolution. The approach provides new ways for treating and researching educational problems.
11. Organizational psychology a. Personnel selection b. Motivation in organizational settings c. Behavioral analysis of jobs d. Organizational conditions and problems	*Applying paradigmatic behaviorism to tasks in organizations.* Paradigmatic behaviorism's various levels of theory provide a richer conceptual framework than usual for analysis of organizations and their characteristics and problems. For example, the emotional–motivational theory specifies that individuals and institutions have "emotional–motivational systems" and that individual-institutional adjustment depends on harmony between the two. Because of the personality and psychological measurement levels of theory the approach can link more harmoniously with traditional knowledge in such areas as personnel selection, job analysis, and job training.

behaviorists. The first question was whether there is only one type of learning or two. Guthrie (1935) took the position that there is only learning through contiguity; Hull (1943) agreed that there is only one type of learning but said that it was through reinforcement. Skinner (1938) recognized two types of response and two types of conditioning. He continued on, however, to emphasize that they were separate, that emotions did not determine behavior, being only collateral processes (see also Skinner, 1975). This conception, its methods, and its empirical work separated emotion and behavior and provided no impetus or means for studying classical conditioning, how it occurs in uniquely human ways, or how emotions affect behavior. Thus, the field of behavior analysis, having hardly studied these questions, has a woeful weakness.

The RB basic theory, as a consequence, serves poorly for behavior therapy. It does not make sense of a therapy such as systematic desensitization, which changes behavior by changing emotions. It cannot make sense of verbal therapies—cognitive, cognitive–behavioral, and PB theories—that change behavior by changing emotions. Moreover, RB's basic theory is no help in designing methods for changing behavior by changing emotions or in conducting research on such topics, and it has been unproductive for understanding and dealing with emotion and its behavioral effects, which are very general concerns. One reason for the basic-applied separation in behavior therapy lies in this theory inadequacy.

PB's basic learning theory (see Staats, 1970, 1975, 1991) is quite different in how it treats emotion and classical conditioning and their relationship to behavior and operant conditioning. Rather than being collateral (insignificant to behavior), as in Skinner's theory, in PB, the emotional value of a stimulus is seen to determine the reinforcement value of the stimulus. When through classical conditioning the individual learns an emotional response to a stimulus, the stimulus becomes a reinforcer (see Staats, 1975; Staats & Eifert, 1990). Thus, classical conditioning determines what will be positively reinforcing and negatively reinforcing for the individual. This is central, because the number of stimuli that become emotion-elicitors, and hence reinforcers, is distinctive for humans, and very important individual differences are involved. How classical conditioning of emotions occurs, and can be produced, *in humans*, must be a central concern of behavior therapy.

It is also the case that a third function—the "incentive" value of a stimulus—depends upon the emotional response that the stimulus elicits. By way of defining incentive (or directive) value, let me say that we all learn to approach positive emotion-eliciting stimuli and to avoid negative emotion-eliciting stimuli. This principle has great significance for understanding and treating human behavior. It explains why, when we change the person's emotional response to a stimulus, we change the person's approach or avoidance to the stimulus. For example, when the phobic person's emotional response to a snake-stimulus is made less negative, the person will avoid the snake less (see Hekmat & Vanian, 1971).

The PB learning theory stipulates the importance of classical conditioning in human behavior, because it has studied how the classical conditioning of emotions takes place in humans, which is different than that demonstrated in the laboratory with animals. For one thing, much of human emotional conditioning takes place through language, and PB has researched that process (see Staats & Hammond, 1972; Staats & Staats, 1958; Staats, Staats, & Crawford, 1962). Hekmat has applied this study to treating phobias and pain (Hekmat, 1972, 1992; Hekmat & Vanian, 1971). The important point here is that the nature of the basic learning theory used affects all the human considerations made in behavior therapy. RB's and PB's learning theories differ markedly in this area.

I also wish to add that PB's treatment of emotions is a good example of what is meant by behaviorizing psychology. As Skinner (1975) recognized, traditional psychology has mentalistically used the concept of emotion as a determinant of behavior. Despite the mentalism, however, how emotional responding affects the individual's behavior involves general and important phenomena that have been studied in psychology (such as attitudes, interests, values, preferences, and paraphilias). These and many other important phenomena are not studied in RB because of Skinner's basic theory. When the phenomena are analyzed and researched in a PB framework, there is a heuristic basis for dealing with such topics of interest for both behaviorism and psychology.

Human Learning Theory

In the laboratory tradition of our discipline, the fundamental conditioning principles are established in the simplest situation possible—using simple stimuli, simple responses, and so on—because that is how the elementary, lawful relationships can clearly be isolated. Human life situations, of course, are infinitely more complex, involving constellations of stimuli of different kinds and responses of different kinds, with complex interrelationships. That is why the laboratory is needed, because it is difficult to see the action of fundamental principles within such complex constellations.

That means, of course, that having obtained the fundamental principles, the task then is to work back in the other direction, that is, to show how those principles explain the complex human events. There are many cases of human behavior that can be straightforwardly analyzed in terms of the elementary conditioning principles. There are many other human behavioral events, however, that do not lend themselves to simple analysis in terms of the elementary principles. Later in this chapter, I will describe an analysis of intelligence that is completely behavioral. The task involves several levels of theory beyond the elementary learning principles. The reason that RB has not made that analysis, it is suggested, is that it has not developed itself through the different levels of study that are demanded. I suggest that, in general, there are many phenomena that have been partially described by traditional psychology that remain untreated within RB, because there are missing levels of analysis that have to be filled in before it can be seen that the elementary principles of conditioning are relevant, but not sufficient. There are additional principles to be drawn from the different levels of analysis that are necessary for dealing with various important types of human behavior.

Over the years, PB's work revealed that those levels of study had to be developed in a systematic manner, within a framework that recognizes how they tie together to provide a means of analyzing all the forms of complex human behavior. PB's program of extension of the elementary conditioning principles begins with the human learning level of study, involving the investigation of more complex stimulus and response events (in classical and operant conditioning) than are considered in isolating basic principles. It should be understood that although the various behaviorists did not have a systematic program for this study, as part of a multilevel theory development, they nevertheless did make first steps in the study of such things. For example, Skinner and the other major behaviorists included principles of, or studied, such concepts as chains (sequences) of responses, response classes, response hierarchies, habit families, higher order conditioning, word associations, successive approximation, abstraction, semantic generalization, response mediation and, more recently, autoshaping, stimulus equivalence, and rule-governed behavior.

Such principles and concepts are not basic (elementary); rather, they involve workings of the basic principles in more complex circumstances. The PB position, therefore, is that these derived combinations add essentially to the behaviorist's theory, providing principles and concepts with which to make analyses of functional human behaviors too complex to deal with solely in terms of the elementary conditioning principles. Many applied behavior therapists are handicapped because they only know and use the principles of reinforcement in their analyses of human behavior. That is a limitation that shortchanges the value of the behavioral approach. To be able to analyze complex human behavior generally, the behavior therapist needs a rich fund of principles and concepts.

In contrast to Skinner's RB, which concentrated its basic work at the animal level, PB began in the early 1950s to investigate the complex principles of human learning within the study of language behaviors (Staats, 1956, 1957a, 1957b; Staats & Staats, 1957)—prior to Skinner's 1957 *Verbal Behavior*, which did not include empirical work. PB's program produced many studies and analyses of different aspects of language behavior (see Staats, 1963b, 1968, 1971a, 1971b, 1975; Staats & Butterfield, 1965; Staats

& Burns, 1981, 1982; Staats, Finley, Minke, & Wolf, 1964). That included language development through learning (see Staats & Staats, 1958; Staats, Staats, & Crawford, 1962). Moreover, the basic three-function learning principles have been demonstrated, showing that words serve to elicit emotions (Staats & Hammond, 1972), transfer them through conditioning, serve as reinforcers (Finley & Staats, 1967; Harms & Staats, 1978), and serve as incentives (see Staats & Warren, 1974). Behavior analysts (see Augustson & Dougher, 1992) are only beginning to study such things (see Burns & Staats, 1992). PB has also dealt with the functions of complex language in communication, problem solving, and response mediation generally. Behavior therapists need to know and use those principles and concepts. The important point here is PB's position that there is need for a stipulated field that is devoted to this general area of study—a field with a systematic, broad purview. PB's research suggests we need to study, for example, how both emotional and behavior conditioning can take place via language mechanisms in uniquely human ways (see Herry, 1984; Staats & Staats, 1958). Also needed is general study of how language processes—involving both classical (see Berkowitz & Knurek, 1969; Hekmat & Vanian, 1971) and operant conditioning (see Staats, 1963b, 1968, 1975)—can affect behavior.

One outgrowth of this work was the realization that systematic study is needed of how humans learn *repertoires*, a concept that usually has only an informal definition. Based on its study, PB set forth the conception that complex human "skills," "abilities," or "talents" involve complex repertoires. If we want to understand skills and abilities, we must study those repertoires. PB in such study derived its human learning principles of cumulative–hierarchical learning, which describe how learning one repertoire can provide the basis for learning another repertoire, which in turn provides the basis for learning yet another repertoire (see Staats, Brewer, & Gross, 1970). Typically, all complex human performances involve such cumulative–hierarchical learning of sequentially acquired repertoires. This work also produced the definition of the *basic behavioral repertoire* (BBR) as a repertoire that is necessary for later learning. Systematic study of these new principles and concepts has also generated new findings (Staats, Brewer, & Gross, 1970; Staats & Burns, 1981). For example, there is a learning acceleration phenomenon produced by cumulative–hierarchical learning. This research found that a child learning to read required progressively fewer reinforced trials as the repertoires were learned.

PB's position is that the various types of study exemplified here provide principles and concepts that add to the elementary conditioning principles and enrich the ability of clinicians and researchers to analyze cases of complex human behavior. This development—empirical, methodological, and theoretical—projects a systematic field that opens broad vistas of research on topics presently only adventitiously sampled, in an unrelated manner. This level, and its new developments—such as the concept of the BBR and the principles of cumulative–hierarchical learning—provide the basis for the more advanced levels of study. The next level—that of developmental psychology—derives in important part from these developments. As Exhibit 1 indicates, the developmental psychology of PB asks for the study of the manner in which the BBRs are learned in children. However, it is not possible to consider developmental psychology specifically here (see Staats, 1963b, 1975). I will go on to personality, which is also based on the "bridging theory constructions" of cumulative–hierarchical learning principles and the basic behavioral repertoire concept.

Personality Theory

Traditional psychology very generally employs a concept of "personality" (or various analogous terms), as an internal process or structure that determines behavior. Watson (see 1930) rejected that mentalistic concept of determination, saying in essence that personality could only be conceived of as behavior itself. Behaviorism (including PB, see Staats, 1963a) has generally recognized and rejected the circularity of inferring personality *from* behavior and then using the concept to "explain" behavior. Much of the separation of behaviorism and traditional psychology comes from these antagonistic positions. RB has rejected personality tests, for example, because they are based on the mentalistic concept of personality, and traditional psychology rejects behaviorism in good part because it does not deal with personality. It is a great disadvantage to behavior therapists, who need to use personality tests, to have a theory that provides no help in understanding or contributing to that use.

PB began its work in the context of this traditional separation, not with the goal of constructing a theory of personality, but rather with the goal of analyzing (behaviorizing) human behavior phenomena of progressively greater complexity. That work, however, ended up providing a foundation for a concept of personality that was completely behavioral (and not circular) but that also fulfills traditional psychology's concern with personality as a causal process. To elaborate, PB began with the study of complex repertoires, such as those that compose the individual's language. However, PB went beyond interpreting language in behavioral terms (see Skinner, 1957) to concern with how language repertoires are *learned* and how they *function* as determinants of the individual's further learning and behavior. The language repertoires, for example, function in most types of school learning, in tasks such as learning reading and math (see Staats, 1968), in directing the individual's behavior in problem solving and reasoning and planning, (see Staats, 1956, 1963b) in communication, and so on (Staats, 1963a, 1963b). In pursuing this type of analysis, it became increasingly clear that individual differences in learning basic behavioral repetoires, such as language, accounted for individual differences in later behavior, in the "ability" to learn, and in what the individual experiences. Such individual differences in the behavior compose the phenomena from which the concept of personality is inferred (see Staats, 1975, 1986, 1993a).

Based on its analysis of, and research on, the basic behavioral repertoires (BBRs), PB began its systematic, long-term development of a behavioral concept of personality as a "causative process," thus dealing with the concern of traditional psychology. For example, certain personality tests were analyzed in terms of the language BBRs. As one example, items on the Stanford–Binet (Terman & Merrill, 1937) could be clearly seen to measure whether the child had a verbal-labeling repertoire, verbal-motor repertoire, and so on (see Burns & Staats, 1992; Staats, 1963b, 1971a, 1975). It was also found that training children in certain language repertoires led to increases in intelligence measures in preschool children (see Staats, 1968; Staats, Brewer, & Gross, 1970). A more general theory of intelligence was formulated (Staats, 1971a), and this provided the basis for new empirical analyses. One study trained children to read letters, write letters, and use numbers—using token-reinforcer training procedures previously developed in PB to prepare deprived 4-year-old children for school. Acquisition of these BBRs produced increased intelligence test measures in explicitly predictable ways, unexpected in traditional theory (Staats & Burns, 1981). These developments meant that the PB theory of intelligence was not circular—intelligence consisted of explicit basic behavioral repertoires, whose learning (in the cases dealt with) had been analyzed. Moreover, *the knowledge produced by the approach provided the basis for manipulating intelligence.*

This is a new type of theory of personality (see Staats & Burns, 1992; Staats, 1993a, 1993b), which PB has carried into other areas (see Staats & Burns, 1982; Staats, Gross, Guay, & Carlson, 1973). As schematized in Figure 1, S_1 stands for the individual's learning environment up to the present, and *BBR* for the basic behavioral repertoires that have resulted, which constitute the individual's personality. S_2 stands for the current situation. The individual's behavior (and experience and learning)—*B* in the figure—is a function of both S_2 and the BBRs.

This personality theory calls for stipulation of each of these variables (S_1, *BBR*, S_2, and *B*) and their relationships. I emphasize that behavior principles operate throughout, both in the learning of the BBRs and in their operation, when the individual confronts the current situation. However, the individual's behavior is not explained solely by knowledge of the current situation; explanation depends also on knowledge of the individual's BBRs. This framework theory involves stipulation of what personality is in a behavioral sense, how and by what principles it is formed, and how and by what principles it has its effects on behavior. Neither traditional

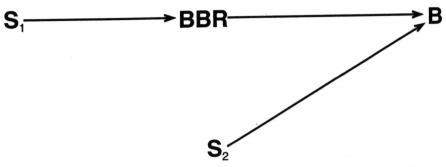

Figure 1. S_1 stands for the original environment, the environment up to the present time that has been responsible for the individual's learning her basic behavioral repertoires, *BBR*s. The present environmental situation in which the individual finds herself is depicted as S_2. The individual's behavior, *B*, in that situation will be determined by the conditions of S_2 and the *BBR*s that the individual "brings" to that situation. *B* is a function of both S_1 and *BBR*, in interaction. *B* represents overt behavior as well as the experience (emotional or ideational) that the individual has and the learning that results. *B* can affect environmental conditions, for example, the responses of others, which act back on the individual and have the effect of producing additional development of the *BBR*s. So there is a continuing interaction of *B* and the *BBR*s.

psychology nor behaviorism has provided these essential developments. PB, in contrast, provides prototypical analyses and research. This framework of theory, methodology, and findings opens the way for a huge amount of research in the task of behaviorizing the large fields of personality and personality measurement (see Fernandez-Ballesteros & Staats, 1992; Staats, 1975, 1986, 1993a, 1993b; Staats & Fernandez-Ballesteros, 1987; Staats & Burns, 1992) and making them explanatory, basic for other fields that aim to change personality in order to change behavior. It must be seen how important behaviorism would become in traditional psychology by carrying out such an agenda of development: taking major fields of traditional psychology, making them experimental science, in a manner that would make them much more powerful. Moreover, an explanatory theory is essential for applied behavior analysts and behavior therapists—in constructing and using psychological tests (enabling them to avoid today's widespread eclecticism; see Fernandez-Ballesteros & Staats, 1992; Haynes & O'Brian, 1990) and in planning treatment programs.

I will add another point here. Plaud (1992), on superficial analysis, concluded that PB offers nothing not in Skinner's RB. As one example, there is a huge difference in this area. PB's theory of personality includes systematic research, methods, concepts, and literature that are new and quite different from anything in RB (see Staats, 1993a, 1993b), where interests in such things is just beginning. Moreover, all this in PB is completely behavioral, harmonious with behaviorism, and brings new perspectives and important research directions in various areas to behavior therapy.

Abnormal Behavior Theory

PB presented the first behavioral taxonomy of abnormal behavior (Staats, 1963b), which played a heuristic role in the early fields of behavior modification and behavioral assessment (see Goldfried, 1976; Goldfried & Sprafkin, 1974; O'Leary & Drabman, 1971; Silva, 1993). PB, however, was intended as a framework theory, to be developed in successive stages, as has occurred. For example, PB's research on the BBRs, plus its analysis of personality tests in terms of the BBRs, provided a more advanced conceptual framework for a PB analysis of abnormal behavior (Staats, 1975). This new framework was first schematized (Staats, 1979) without considering the biological aspects of abnormal behavior, as shown in Figure 2. What the model says is that the individual's original environmental learning conditions, S_1, may be deficit or inappropriate and thus produce (through learning) deficit or inappropriate basic behavioral repertoires in the individual. Those abnormal BBRs, in turn, will cause the individual's experience, learning, and behavior—B in the figure—to be deficit or inappropriate in the later situations that are encountered, S_2. For example, a child with severe deficits in the BBRs of language—as in mental retardation—will not experience things like other children. Thus, a teacher's stories will be like nonsense syllables, eliciting no previously learned responses in the child. The language-deficit child, as a consequence, will not learn normally in school, home, or peer interactions. To continue, the individual with severely inappropriate language BBRs—as in schizophrenia—cannot learn well, reason well, or communicate well with others and will behave in ways considered abnormal (see Staats, 1975). In addition to the BBRs, S_2 also

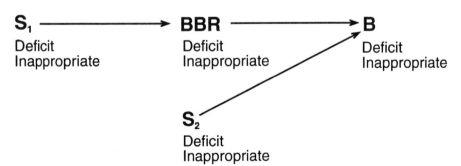

Figure 2. S_1 stands for the past environment. Deficit or inappropriate conditions in the environment will produce deficit or inappropriate BBRs in the individual, which will produce deficit or inappropriate behavior in the individual, even though the environmental situations encountered later, S_2, are normal. However, S_2 may also be deficit or inappropriate and produce deficit or inappropriate behavior in the individual, even though the the individual's BBRs are normal. Deficits and inappropriate conditions in S_2 and the BBRs interact in producing abnormal (deficit and inappropriate) behavior.

can be deficit or inappropriate and, in interaction with the *BBRs*, produce abnormal behavior.

There are various features of this theory of abnormal behavior that have heuristic implications. For example, there is a strong developmental perspective, that is, a concern with making behavior analyses of the manner in which the BBRs, and hence abnormal as well as normal behavior, are learned. This contrasts with the general behavioral position that the original determinants of abnormal behavior are irrelevant, treating behavior as that which counts (see Eysenck, 1960; Lovaas, 1966).

Some behavioral models of behavior problems have included a variable O in order to avoid the "black box" criticism (Goldfried & Sprafkin, 1974; Kanfer & Phillips, 1970). What the organism variable consists of, however, as well as what the relationship of O is to the behavioral variables, has been left unspecified. PB, in contrast, has described biological variables in stipulated ways in its general treatments (see Staats, 1963a; 1975), requiring stipulation of the principles by which biological and behavioral variables connect. Thus, the O variable in its model stipulates relationships to its behavioral variables (Fernandez-Ballesteros & Staats, 1992; Staats, 1989, 1990, 1993a). Very briefly, the position is that biological variables can play an important role in producing abnormal behavior at any of the sites of causation already described, as shown in Figure 3. At the time of original learning, abnormal biological conditions (O_1) can yield deficit or inappropriate BBR development. Down syndrome is an example of biological deficit that restricts learning of the BBRs. At a later time, *after* the BBRs have been learned, abnormal biological conditions (O_2) have a different effect. Such conditions, for example, can remove already learned BBRs, as in brain damage. Unless the BBRs are relearned, behavior is permanently affected. Finally, abnormal biological conditions acting at O_3 may also affect the way the individual can sense the present environment, as when the individual loses visual or auditory acuity in old age. (O_1, O_2, or O_3 effects can involve conditions that are temporary, as with drug use, as well as permanent.) Again, this PB model makes more explicit the several ways and times in which biological variables can in a *behavioral manner* produce abnormal behavior, analytically providing a basis for unifying and researching biological and behavioral variables.

I add only that the general PB framework has already been exemplified in preliminary analyses of various behavior disorders (Staats, 1975). Such analyses require elaboration in special theories of the particular behavior disorders. The first specialized theory—other than PB's theory of developmental disorders, including dyslexia (see Burns & Kondrick, 1992; Leduc, 1984, 1988; Staats, 1963b, 1975; Staats & Butterfield, 1965)—deals with depression (Staats & Heiby, 1985). This theory is already serving as the foundation for an extensive series of research studies, especially by Elaine Heiby (see Heiby, 1986) and others (see Rose & Staats, 1988).

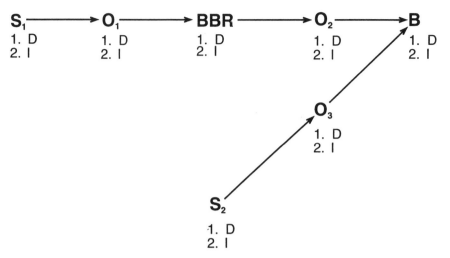

Figure 3. Organic conditions are introduced at each site of causation. S_1, *BBR*, or S_2 may be deficit (D) or inappropriate (I). But even when they are normal, organic conditions may be deficit or inappropriate for the individual during original learning (S_1), which will result in the *BBRs'* being deficit or inappropriate. Moreover, even though the *BBRs* are normal, organic conditions at a later time, O_2, may be deficit or inappropriate which will make the individual's behavior, *B*, deficit or inappropriate. Moreover, deficit or inappropriate organic conditions may make it so the individual cannot perceive (sense) a later environment, S_2, normally and thus may produce deficit or inappropriate behavior.

Theories of other behavior disorders have already been drafted (see Staats, 1989) as part of the PB general, unified theory of abnormal behavior. For example, the PB theory of the anxiety disorders (Staats, 1989) analyzes the individual anxiety disorders, indicates their commonalities and differences, and introduces new principles by which to do this. Disseminated in 1989, this particular theory is already being systematically researched by Leonard Burns (see Sternberger & Burns, 1991) and extended in more detailed treatments of the specific anxiety disorders that include more of the general literature in the field (see Eifert, Evans, & McKendrick, 1990). Each of PB's theories of the specific behavior disorders (Staats, 1989) has such heuristic potentialities.

PARADIGMATIC (PSYCHOLOGICAL) BEHAVIOR THERAPY

PBT is the behavioral approach to clinical psychology that is based upon paradigmatic behaviorism. In the brief space that is available I will attempt to characterize the PBT level.

The PBT approach, reflecting the general PB position, is that all of psychology is potentially important for the practice and study of clinical psychology. Thus, the PBT position is that all of PB's levels of study are important for clinical psychology. What this means can be seen by comparison. For example, our original behavioral works involved the application only of the basic level of study, that is, the basic conditioning principles and the model of animal training procedures. There are those who still feel that this should be the heart of a behavioral clinical psychology.

In contrast, we see also approaches that deal only with the clinical level of study. In essence, the cognitive–behavioral approaches take this position; their connections to the behavioral level, for example, are very tenous, involving at most the use of a few behavior principles. The same is true on the cognitive side; cognitive–behavioral approaches really make no use of basic cognitive psychology (see Staats, in press-a). In fact, there really is no program for relating systematically, derivatively, to either level of study, or to any others. The use of terminology—like common-sense cognitive concepts—is only a pretense of a relationship.

I will exemplify the PBT framework. It recognizes that there are important benefits to be gained from the straightforward application of basic behavior principles to problems of human behavior. That is what PB first did in applying conditioning principles to the analysis of the opposite speech of the schizophrenic patient and to the treatment recommendations of extinction for the abnormal symptom and of reinforcement of normal speech (Staats, 1957a). PB has introduced various other direct applications of conditioning principles to problems of human behavior. I also add that the many studies done by other behavior therapists that directly employ conditioning principles all fit into and support PBT's first level of study; in this respect, PBT is very consonant with traditional behavior therapy and behavior analysis.

However, I will exemplify how PB considers the human learning level of study to be just as relevant. PB's analysis of developmental reading disorder (see Staats et al., 1964; Staats, Staats, Schutz, & Wolf, 1962; Staats & Staats, 1962) was the basis for developing a treatment methodology (see Staats & Butterfield, 1965) that was basic to many studies of developmental disorders in behavior analysis. This PB development, it should be noted, was based on the analysis of the various basic behavioral repertoires that compose reading that emerged from the human learning level study of language.

Another example is that the personality and personality measurement levels of study have been developed also in PB for application to clinical problems. As has been described, for example, PB has analyzed intelligence (Staats, 1971a) as composed of BBRs, largely the language repertoires, and related those repertoires to intelligence as specified on tests. The extension to this level of study provided a foundation for working out how to train children to be more intelligent, as measured by IQ tests (Staats & Burns, 1981). This prototypical study, then, provides a basis for more detailed study that would yield methods by which to generally train children to be intelligent. More generally, PBT states that human problems can require change in personality (BBRs), not just in specific responses. This is a call for development of large new directions of research in behavior therapy, including research on the BBRs that existing psychological tests measure, as well as the design of new tests based on such analyses, and research on the therapies for BBR change.

I will add that PB's levels of study, and the theory derived from that study, provide a new conceptual basis for the consideration of therapies other than the use of the direct application of conditioning principles. That is, the theory of the language repertoires—and how these repertoires function for the individual in reasoning, planning, and problem solving, plus the theory of how language can be used to change emotions—provide the basis for a language behavior therapy, a psychotherapy whose basic principles are stipulated and can be researched. Thus, Hamid Hekmat (see Hekmat, 1973, 1992; Hekmat & Vanian, 1971) has conducted a series of studies showing how phobias and chronic pain can be treated using language conditioning methods. PB's outline of language behavior therapy (in conjunction with the other PB levels of study) opens a large field of study in the analysis of the changes that can occur in verbal therapy and how to produce them in analyses that are stipulated, not vague in the way typical of cognitive–behavioral approaches.

Additional extensions of PB to problems of behavior therapy have been described in the book *Unifying Behavior Therapy: Contributions of Paradigmatic Behaviorism*, edited by Eifert and Evans (1990). The various potentialities for PBT development, however, have not been touched. The point of this mention is to indicate that those developments can be expected to result from the use of the various levels of study of the parent behaviorism.

CONCLUSION

Our original introduction of the modern behavioral movement involved the extension of the conditioning principles—taken from the first- and second-generation developments of behaviorism—to specific problems of human behavior. This was an important development and provided the basis for doing a large number of studies and extensions. The potential power, however, of the behaviorism tradition cannot be exploited within a second-generation behaviorism that cuts behaviorism off from the rest of psychology (see Coleman & Mehlman, 1992; Fraley & Vargas, 1986; Skinner, 1988; Staats, 1993a, 1993b), including the study of personality and its measurement. That would prevent behaviorism from dealing with much of its natural subject matter.

A central conclusion to be drawn from these considerations is that behavior therapy cannot restrict itself only to the clinical level of study and remain an applied field that rests only on the basic principles of conditioning spliced with commonsense cognitive concepts. Behavior therapy, likewise, cannot advance far on the basis of separated theories of specific disorders and therapies. Although there is much to be contributed by works, that is not all that is needed. Human behavior is very complex. The learning that goes into human behavior is vast, and vastly complex. Understanding and dealing with human behavior demands a general conception of human behavior, and that conception must enable the field to confront that complexity. Training for behavior therapists that provides knowledge of basic principles of conditioning, and a smattering of cognitive terms, along with applications, is inadequate. There are no shortcuts, no easy ways out.

The several behaviorisms are different in their ability to confront the complexity of human behavior systematically and to connect to productive works that have been done in psychology. The several behaviorisms thus vary in terms of how they serve as a platform for constructing a behavior therapy for dealing broadly and deeply with human problems. For this reason, it is important that the field of behavior therapy invest in the study of its behaviorisms. By and large, our textbooks in behavior therapy do not make this investment (see Staats, 1994, in press-a). The present book—in presenting a number of behavior therapy theories ranging from specific therapies to overarching behaviorisms—is important for the manner in which it provides a step in that direction (as is the case with Fishman, Rotgers, & Franks, 1988).

The field of behavior therapy will stagnate unless its conceptual basis—its behaviorism paradigm—continues to advance. The most common conceptual foundation used today in behavior therapy is a combination of Skinner's basic theory, the principle of modeling, and common-sense cognitive concepts (see Craighead, Craighead, Kazdin, & Mahoney, 1994). The field of behavior analysis still uses only Skinner's theory works as its basic foundation. Neither will take behavior therapy and behavioral psychology into the next generation (see Staats, 1994, in press-a). The continued growth of behavior therapy depends upon the behaviorism that is used as its foundation. Thus, it is necessary that behavior therapy systematically consider what is involved.

REFERENCES

Augustson, E., & Dougher, M. (1992). *Transfer of respondent functions and avoidance behavior via stimulus equivalence.* Paper presented at the 18th annual convention of the Association for Behavior Analysis, San Francisco, CA.

Ayllon, T., & Michael, J. (1959). The psychiatric nurse as a behavioral engineer. *Journal of the Experimental Analysis of Behavior, 2*, 323–334.

Azrin, N. H., & Lindsley, O. R. (1956). The reinforcement of cooperation between children. *Journal of Abnormal and Social Psychology, 52*, 100–102.

Berkowitz, L., & Knurek, D. A. (1969). A label mediated hostility generalization. *Journal of Personality and Social Psychology, 13*, 200–206.

Bijou, S. W. (1955). A systematic approach to an experimental analysis of young children. *Child Development, 26*, 161–168.

Burns, G. L., & Kondrick, P. A. (1992). *Analysis and treatment of developmental reading disorder (dyslexia).* Symposium paper presented at the 18th annual meeting of the International Association for Behavior Analysis, San Francisco.

Burns, G. L., & Staats, A. W. (1992). Rule-governed behavior: Unifying radical and paradigmatic behaviorism. *Journal of Verbal Behavior, 9*, 127–143.

Coleman, S. R., & Mehlman, S. E. (1992). An empirical update (1969–1989) of D. L. Krantz's thesis that the experimental analysis of behavior is isolated. *The Behavior Analyst, 15*, 43–49.

Dollard, J., & Miller, N. E. (1950). *Personality and psychotherapy.* New York: Mc-Graw-Hill.

Early, J. C. (1968). Attitudinal learning in children. *Journal of Educational Psychology, 59*, 176–180.

Eifert, G. H., & Evans, I. M. (1990). *Unifying behavior therapy: Contributions of paradigmatic behaviorism.* New York: Springer.

Eifert, G. H., Evans, I. M., & McKendrick, V. (1990). Matching treatments to client problems not diagnostic labels: A case for paradigmatic behavior therapy. *Journal of Behavior Therapy and Experimental Psychiatry, 21*, 245–253.

Eysenck, H. J. (Ed.). (1960). *Behavior therapy and the neuroses.* London: Pergamon Press.

Fernandez-Ballesteros, R., & Staats, A. W. (1992). Paradigmatic behavioral assessment, treatment and evaluation: Answering the crisis in behavioral assessment. *Advances in Behavior Research and Therapy, 14*, 1–28.

Finley, J. R., & Staats, A. W. (1967). Evaluative meaning words as reinforcing stimuli. *Journal of Verbal Learning and Verbal Behavior, 6*, 193–197.

Fishman, D. B., Rotgers, F., & Franks, C. M. (1988). *Paradigms in behavior therapy.* New York: Springer.

Fraley, L. E., & Vargas, E. A. (1986). Separate disciplines: The study of behavior and the study of the psyche. *The Behavior Analyst, 9*, 47–59.

Goldfried, M. R. (1976). Behavioral assessment. In I. B. Weiner (Ed.), *Clinical methods in psychology* (pp. 281–330). New York: Wiley.

Goldfried, M. R., & Sprafkin, J. (1974). *Behavioral personality assessment.* Morristown, NJ: General Learning Press.

Guthrie, E. R. (1935). *The psychology of learning.* New York: Harper.

Hamilton, S. A. (1988). Behavioral formulation of verbal behavior in psychotherapy. *Clinical Psychology Review*, 8, 181–194.

Harms, J. Y., & Staats, A. W. (1978). Food deprivation and conditioned reinforcing value of food words: Interaction of Pavlovian and instrumental conditioning. *Bulletin of the Psychonomic Society*, 12, 294–296.

Haynes, S. N., & O'Brian, W. H. (1990). Functional analysis in behavior therapy. *Clinical Psychology Review*, 649–668.

Heiby, E. M. (1986). Social and self-reinforcement deficits in four cases of depression. *Behavior Therapy*, 17, 158–169.

Hekmat, H. (1972). The role of imagination in semantic desensitization. *Behavior Therapy*, 3, 223–231.

Hekmat, H. (1973). Systematic versus semantic desensitization and implosive therapy. *Journal of Consulting and Clinical Psychology*, 40, 202–209.

Hekmat, H. (1992). Paradigmatic behaviorism's theory and management of human pain reactions. Symposium paper presented at the 18th annual convention of the Association for Behavior Analysis, San Francisco.

Hekmat, H., & Vanian, D. (1971). Behavior modification through covert semantic desensitization. *Journal of Consulting and Clinical Psychology*, 36, 248–251.

Herry, M. (1984). Le principe du conditionnement instrumental d'ordre superieur [The principle of higher-order instrumental conditioning]. In A. Leduc (Ed.), *Recherches surle behaviorisme paradigmatique ou social* (pp. 31–42). Brossard, Quebec: Behaviora.

Hull, C. L. (1943). *Principles of behavior*. New York: Appleton-Century.

Kanfer, F. H. (1958). Verbal conditioning: Reinforcement schedules and experimenter influence. *Psychological Reports*, 4, 443–452.

Kanfer, F. H., & Phillips, J. S. (1970). *Learning foundations of behavior therapy*. New York: Wiley.

Krasner, L. (1958). Studies of the conditioning of verbal behavior. The use of generalized reinforcers in psychotherapy research. *Psychological Bulletin*, 55, 148–170.

Krasner, L., & Ullmann, L. P. (1965). *Research in behavior modification*. New York: Holt, Rinehart & Winston.

Leduc, A. (1984). *Recherches sur le behaviorisme paradigmatique ou social [Research in paradigmatic or social behaviorism]*. Brossard, Quebec: Behaviora.

Leduc, A. (1988). A paradigmatic behavioral approach to the treatment of a "wild" child. *Child and Family Behavior Therapy*, 9, 1–16.

Lindsley, O. R. (1956). Operant conditioning methods applied to research in chronic schizophrenia. *Psychiatric Research Reports*, 5, 140–153.

Lovaas, O. I. (1966). A behavior therapy approach to the treatment of childhood schizophrenia. In J. P. Hill (Ed.), *Minnesota symposium on child psychology* (Vol. 1; pp. 108–159). Minneapolis: University of Minnesota Press.

MacPherson, A., Bonem, M., Green, G., & Osborne, J. G. (1984). A citation analysis of the influence on research of Skinner's *Verbal Behavior*. *The Behavior Analyst, 7*, 158–167.

Meichenbaum, D. H., & Goodman, J. (1971). Training impulsive children to talk to themselves. *Journal of Abnormal Psychology, 77*, 115–120.

O'Leary, K. D., & Drabman, R. (1971). Token reinforcement programs in the classroom: A review. *Psychological Bulletin, 75*, 379–398.

Plaud, J. J. (1992). Should we take the "radical" out of "behaviorism"?: Some comments about behavior therapy and philosophy. *The Behavior Therapist, 15*, 121–122.

Rose, G. D., & Staats, A. W. (1988). Depression and frequency and strength of pleasant events: Exploration of the Staats-Heiby theory. *Behavior Therapy, 26*, 489–494.

Shoben, E. (1949). Psychotherapy as a problem in learning theory. *Psychological Bulletin, 46*, 366–392.

Silva, F. (1993). *Psychometric foundations of behavioral assessment.* Newbury Park, CA: Sage.

Skinner, B. F. (1938). *The behavior of organisms.* New York: Appleton.

Skinner, B. F. (1953). *Science and human behavior.* New York: Macmillan.

Skinner, B. F. (1957). *Verbal behavior.* New York: Appleton-Century-Crofts.

Skinner, B. F. (1975). The steep and thorny way to a science of behavior. *American Psychologist, 30*, 42–49.

Skinner, B. F. (1988). The cuckoos. *The ABA Newsletter, 11*, 9–10.

Staats, A. W. (1956). *A behavioristic study of verbal and instrumental response hierarchies and their relationship to human problem solving.* Unpublished doctoral dissertation, University of California, Los Angeles.

Staats, A. W. (1957a). Learning theory and "opposite speech." *Journal of Abnormal and Social Psychology, 55*, 268–269.

Staats, A. W. (1957b). Verbal and instrumental response hierarchies and their relationship to problem solving. *American Journal of Psychology, 70*, 442–446.

Staats, A. W. (1963a). Comments on Professor Russell's paper. In C. N. Cofer & B. S. Musgrave (Eds.), *Verbal behavior and learning* (pp. 271–290). New York: McGraw-Hill.

Staats, A. W. (1963b). (with contributions by C. K. Staats). *Complex human behavior.* New York: Holt, Rinehart & Winston.

Staats, A. W. (1965). A case in and a strategy for the extension of learning principles to complex human behavior. In L. Krasner, & L. P. Ulman (Eds.), *Research in Behavior Modification* (pp. 27–55). New York: Holt, Rinehart & Winston.

Staats, A. W. (1966). An integrated-functional learning approach to complex human behavior. In B. Kleinmuntz (Ed.), *Problem: Research, method, and theory* (pp. 223–284). New York: Wiley.

Staats, A. W. (1968). *Learning, language, and cognition*. New York: Holt, Rinehart & Winston.

Staats, A. W. (1970). A learning-behavior theory: A basis for unity in behavioral–social science. In A. R. Gilgen (Ed.), *Contemporary scientific psychology* (pp. 183–239). San Diego, CA: Academic Press.

Staats, A. W. (1971a). *Child learning, intelligence and personality*. New York: Harper & Row.

Staats, A. W. (1971b). Linguistic–mentalistic theory versus an explanatory S–R learning theory of language development. In D. I. Slobin (Ed.), *The ontogenesis of grammar* (pp. 103–150). New York: Academic Press.

Staats, A. W. (1972). Language behavior therapy: A derivation of social behaviorism. *Behavior Therapy*, 3, 165–192.

Staats, A. W. (1975). *Social behaviorism*. Homewood, IL: Dorsey.

Staats, A. W. (1979). El conductismo social: Un fundamento de la modificacion del comportamiento [*Social behaviorism: A foundation for behavior modification.*]. *Revista Latinoamericana de psicologia*, 11, 9–46.

Staats, A. W. (1981). Paradigmatic behaviorism, unified theory, unified theory construction methods, and the zeitgeist of separatism. *American Psychologist*, 26, 239–256.

Staats, A. W. (1983). *Psychology's crisis of disunity: Philosophy and method for a unified science*. New York: Praeger.

Staats, A. W. (1986). Behaviorism with a personality: The paradigmatic behavioral assessment approach. In R. O. Nelson & S. C. Hayes (Eds.), *Conceptual foundations of behavioral assessment* (pp. 244–296). New York: Guilford Press.

Staats, A. W. (1988). Skinner's theory and the emotion–behavior relationship: Incipient change with major implications. *American Psychologist*, 43, 747–748.

Staats, A. W. (1989). *Personality and abnormal behavior*. Unpublished manuscript.

Staats, A. W. (1990). Paradigmatic behavior therapy: A unified framework for theory, research, and practice. In G. H. Eifert & I. M. Evans (Eds.), *Unifying behavior therapy: Contributions of paradigmatic behaviorism* (pp. 14–54). New York: Springer.

Staats, A. W. (1991). Emotion and behavior. Invited address presented at the 17th annual convention of the Association for Behavior Analysis in Atlanta, GA.

Staats, A. W. (1992). Behaviorizing psychology: A fundamental program in paradigmatic behaviorism. Symposium paper presented at the 18th annual convention of the Association for Behavior Analysis, San Francisco.

Staats, A. W. (1993a). Personality theory, abnormal psychology, and psychological measurement: A psychological behaviorism. *Behavior Modification*, 17, 8–42.

Staats, A. W. (1993b). Why do we need another behaviorism (such as paradigmatic behaviorism)? *The Behavior Therapist*, 16, 64–68.

Staats, A. W. (1993c). Psychological behaviorism: An overarching theory and a theory–construction methodology. *The General Psychologist*, 29, 46–60.

Staats, A. W. (1994). Psychological behaviorism and behaviorizing psychology. *The Behavior Analyst, 17,* 93–114.

Staats, A. W. (in press-a). Good news and bad news in behavior therapy. *Child and Family Behavior Therapy.*

Staats, A. W. (in press-b). *Personality and behavior.* New York: Springer.

Staats, A. W., Brewer, B. A., & Gross, M. C. (1970). Learning and cognitive development: Representative samples, cumulative–hierarchical learning, and experimental–longitudinal methods. *Monographs of the Society for Research in Child Development, 35* (8, Whole No. 141), 1–85.

Staats, A. W., & Burns, G. L. (1981). Intelligence and child development: What intelligence is and how it is learned and functions. *Genetic Psychology Monographs, 104,* 237–301.

Staats, A. W., & Burns, G. L. (1982). Emotional personality repertoire as cause of behavior: Specification of personality and interaction principles. *Journal of Personality and Social Psychology, 43,* 873–881.

Staats, A. W., & Burns, G. L. (1992). The psychological behaviorism theory of personality. In G-V. Caprara and G. L. Van Heck (Eds.), *Modern personality theory* (pp. 161–199). New York: Harvester Wheatsheaf.

Staats, A. W., & Butterfield, W. H. (1965). Treatment of nonreading in a culturally deprived juvenile delinquent: An application of reinforcement principles. *Child Development, 36,* 925–942.

Staats, A. W., & Eifert, G. H. (1990). A paradigmatic behaviorism theory of emotions: A basis for unification. *Clinical Psychology Review, 10,* 1–40.

Staats, A. W., & Fernandez-Ballesteros, R. (1987). The self-report in personality measurement: A paradigmatic behaviorism approach to psychodiagnostics. *Evaluación Psicológica/Psychological Measurement, 3,* 151–190.

Staats, A. W., Finley, J. R., Minke, K. A., & Wolf, M. M. (1964). Reinforcement variables in the control of unit reading responses. *Journal of the Experimental Analysis of Behavior, 7,* 139–149.

Staats, A. W., Gross, M. C., Guay, P. F., & Carlson, C. G. (1973). Personality and social systems and attitude-reinforcer-discriminative theory: Interest (attitude) formation, function, and measurement. *Journal of Personality and Social Psychology, 26,* 251–261.

Staats, A. W., & Hammond, O. R. (1972). Natural words as physiological conditioned stimuli: Food-word-elicited salivation and deprivation effects. *Journal of Experimental Psychology, 96,* 206–208.

Staats, A. W., & Heiby, E. M. (1985). Paradigmatic behaviorism's theory of depression: Unified, explanatory, and heuristic. In S. Reiss & R. R. Bootzin (Eds.), *Theoretical issues in behavior therapy* (pp. 279–330). New York: Academic Press.

Staats, C. K., & Staats, A. W. (1957). Meaning established by classical conditioning. *Journal of Experimental Psychology, 54,* 74–80.

Staats, A. W., & Staats, C. K. (1958). Attitudes established by classical conditioning. *Journal of Abnormal and Social Psychology, 57,* 37–40.

Staats, A. W., & Staats, C. K. (1962). A comparison of the development of speech and reading behaviors with implications for research. *Child Development, 33,* 830–846.

Staats, A. W., Staats, C. K., & Crawford, H. L. (1962). First-order conditioning of a GSR and the parallel conditioning of meaning. *Journal of General Psychology, 67,* 159–167.

Staats, A. W., Staats, C. K., Schutz, R. E., & Wolf, M. M. (1962). The conditioning of reading responses using "extrinsic" reinforcers. *Journal of the Experimental Analysis of Behavior, 5,* 33–40.

Staats, A. W., & Warren, D. R. (1974). Motivation and three-function learning: Deprivation-satiation and approach-avoidance to food words. *Journal of Experimental Psychology, 103,* 1191–1199.

Sternberger, L. G., & Burns, G. L. (1991). Obsessions and compulsions in a college sample: Distinction between symptoms and diagnoses. *Behavior Therapy, 22,* 569–576.

Terman, L. M., & Merrill, M. A. (1937). *Measuring intelligence.* New York: Houghton-Mifflin.

Tolman, E. C. (1932). *Purposive behavior in animals and men.* New York: Century.

Tryon, W. W. (1990). Why paradigmatic behaviorism should be retitled psychological behaviorism. *The Behavior Therapist, 13,* 127–128.

Ullman, L. P., & Krasner, L. (1965). *Case studies in behavior modification.* New York: Holt, Rinehart & Winston.

Ulman, J. D. (1990). Paradigmatic behaviorism: Hierarchically schematized eclecticism. *TIBA Newsletter, 2,* 6.

Watson, J. (1930). *Behaviorism.* Chicago: University of Chicago Press.

Wolpe, J. (1958). *Psychotherapy by reciprocal inhibition.* Stanford, CA: Stanford University Press.

25

THEORIES OF BEHAVIOR THERAPY AND SCIENTIFIC PROGRESS

WILLIAM O'DONOHUE and LEONARD KRASNER

What are the roles of theories in the growth of behavior therapy? To address this question we first address the more general question of the roles of theory in the progress of any science, because we believe that much of the general case applies to the particular case of behavior therapy. We then discuss possible ways in which theories in behavior therapy may deviate from the general case.

THEORIES AND THE PROGRESS OF SCIENCE

The progress of a scientific field may be limited by a number of factors. The simplest reason may be the complexity and impenetrability of nature. This can result in a failure to discover a science-starting first paradigm (Kuhn, 1970) or may hinder progress at some subsequent point. However, there are a number of other reasons that can limit progress of science, among them scarcity of funding, level of talent in the field, ethical limitations on what can be investigated, and practical barriers to research. A

695

reason that we address in this chapter is that the lack of proper theory testing in experimentation can also contribute to slow progress.

A starting point for this discussion is the claim that observations alone have little significance. Their significance is created through their relationships with other claims, particularly more general claims. For example, an observation of a severed human limb regenerating, per se, has little significance. This same observation in the context of theories and beliefs about human physiology, however, has enormous significance because it would cast doubt on many firmly held beliefs.

Much research in behavior therapy has not been theory testing, but rather hypothesis testing, in which the embeddedness of these hypotheses in a larger framework is unclear. One cost of this focus may be that corroborated hypotheses in behavior therapy fail to point to a larger framework that may be pregnant with information. Another cost may be that falsified hypotheses do not carry critical implications to these more general beliefs or claims.

Theory testing places the theory at risk of falsification. Popper (1963) has argued, as a philosopher of science, that a search for empirical consequences that are not in keeping with a scientific theory is the essence of the critical, scientific point of view. According to Popper, the process of science should proceed as follows: A theory should be developed so that it is clear which states of affairs are compatible with it and which are not. For example, the hopelessness theory of depression is incompatible with the state of affairs in which individuals who, in the presence of negative life events, make stable and global attributions will not experience a hopelessness subtype of depression (see Metalsky et al., chapter 14, this volume). Testing a theory involves investigating whether the particular states of affairs that the theory rules out actually obtain. Thus, a good test of the hopelessness theory would involve following individuals who hold such cognitions in the presence of negative life events and assessing if they experience a depressive episode in a reasonably immediate period. If they do not experience such an episode, according to Popper, the theory would be considered falsified, and it would need to be revised in a non-ad hoc manner and tested again.

At times, psychologists have beat the drum of empiricism a bit too hard. This probably has been the result of trying to spur on colleagues who failed to expose their empirical claims to empirical test—a phenomenon that unfortunately is not only of historical interest. This emphasis has caused an important misunderstanding of the relationship between observational claims and theoretical claims. Dustbowl empiricism—the blind collection of observations—is not the best way to advance science. Popper (1963) argued that this view of science was not correct:

The belief that we can start with pure observations alone, without anything in the nature of a theory is absurd. . . . Twenty five years ago I tried to bring home the same point to a group of physics students in Vienna by beginning a lecture with the following instructions: "Take pencil and paper; carefully observe, and write down what you have observed." They asked of course, *what* I wanted them to observe. . . . Observation is always selection. It needs a chosen object, a definite task, an interest, a point of view, a problem. (Popper, 1963, p. 46)

Observation must take place in the context of argumentation. (By *argumentation* we do not mean a dispute, but a set of logically connected claims.) A theory provides a coherence, a meaning that allows the deduction (and, thus, at least a partial explanation) of a variety of observational claims. We now address some of the major considerations involved in theory testing that best result in progress in behavior therapy.

THEORY SPECIFICATION

A first step is the elucidation of the theory. Introductions to empirical articles rarely provide a detailed description of the theory in which the hypothesis is embedded, and therefore, introductions fail to explicate the larger relevance of the particular observations contained in the article. It is more typical for some broad "sense" of the larger ideas to be involved in the testing, but this "sense" does not clearly describe the full significance and connectedness of the hypothesis or the observations.

Hull (1943) probably did the best job in psychology of explicating a theory. He clearly explicated undefined terms, derived terms, postulates, theorems, corollaries, intervening variables, and operational definitions. Our point is not that Hull's particular theory is true, but rather that in it Hull did a superlative job of specifying the content of this theory. In Hull's theory one can clearly see (a) the theory in its entirety, (b) the interconnections of different aspects of the theory, and (c) the implications of the theory. Thus, a clear elucidation of a theory is important not only in itself but also as a first step to test the theory adequately.

UNDERSTANDING LOGICAL RELATIONSHIPS

After a theory has been fully and accurately elucidated, the next step is to understand the logical relationships between the different claims in the theory. Observational claims can be "tests" of theoretical claims if and only if there is a logical connection between the observational claim and the theoretical claim. Popper (1963) thought that the logical inference rule of *modus tollens* was necessary for theory testing:

Modus tollens

1. If A then B
2. Not B

3. Therefore not A

Modus tollens in theory testing

1. If theory then observational claim
2. Not observational claim

3. Therefore not theory

Modus tollens in hypothesis testing

1. If theory, then hypothesis
2. If hypothesis, then observational claim
3. Not observational claim

Therefore, not theory

Note not only that the logical inference rule of *modus tollens* is used in theory testing but also that there are important logical connections in the first premise (e.g., if theory, then observational claim). All empirical testing must involve a premise that draws out the empirical entailments or implications of the theory. These may be simple or may involve a chain of inferences. A fairly direct, simple implication is as follows: If all males are aggressive and Bob is a male, then Bob will behave aggressively. A more complex chain of logic is contained in this theory: If all males are aggressive and if aggression always leads to harm to others, then males will harm others.

As another example, deductions can be made from certain kinds of statements. For example, from the universal claim that "all men are aggressive," it can be deduced that "if x is a man then x is aggressive." If there is an x such that x is a man and x is not aggressive, then the original claim is falsified.

Note that all collections of statements do not have logical relations. For example, consider the following set of claims:

1. Depression can be caused by negative life events.
2. Women present more frequently with depression than do men.
3. Men may drink alcohol excessively to self-medicate their depression.
4. Overeating or undereating may be one symptom of depression.

Although these statements are "related" in that they all deal with depression, they are not logically related, at least not clearly. Because of their lack of logical interconnectedness, these statements make a very poor theoretical account of depression.

Logical relations are important because they tell us what empirical consequences a theory has. Deducing the empirical consequences of a theory is an essential second step for testing the theory.

SEVERE TESTS AND THE QUINE–DUHEM THESIS

So far, the specification of the theory and the logical connections between its various claims tell us much about the theory but little about the truth or falsity of the theory. Empirically testing a theory involves comparing the empirical consequences deduced from the theory (which, to reemphasize, requires a specification of the theory and an accurate understanding of the logical relations) with relevant observations.

Every good theory should divide the set of all statements derivable from it into two subsets. One set contains observation statements that are consistent with the theory. This set is uninteresting from the point of view of theory testing. However, the complementary set, which for every scientific theory should be nonempty, is the set of potential falsifiers. Rigorous scientific testing consists of efficient and ardent attempts to see if one of these potential states of affairs actually obtains. The larger the sample size, the more precise the measurement, the more precise the prediction, and the more varied the sample domain—the more efficient the test as means of finding counterexamples.

Popper (1963) pointed out that theories can differ on the degree to which they are potentially falsifiable. Theories that make point predictions are extremely falsifiable, because their sets of falsifiers include as elements all points except the particular point predicted by the theory in this instance. In general, the more precise the statement is, the more falsifiable the statement is. Furthermore, the statement "all humans are aggressive" is more falsifiable than the statement "all women are aggressive" because it excludes states of affairs (unaggressive men) that the second statement does not. In general, the more general the statement, the more falsifiable it is.

Popper (1963) noted that there is an inverse relationship between what he calls the *logical probability* of a statement and its *degree of falsifiability*. That is, tautologies such as "all brown dogs are brown" have a logical probability of 1 (they are necessarily true), but these tautologies have a 0 degree of falsifiability because they exclude no observable states of affairs. Conversely, highly falsifiable theories have a low logical probability: Because they exclude many possible states of affairs, it is logically probable that they will be refuted. Another way of saying this is that tautologies have no empirical content and that highly falsifiable statements have high empirical content. Popper values severe testing in which the scientists attempt to deduce the most improbable consequences of their theories and check whether these obtain. The general notion is that if one wants to falsify the claim that "priests don't swear," it is better to observe them on the golf course than in the pulpit.

However, the logic of research is actually more complicated. Because there are multiple premises included in any test, an anomalous observation does not indicate which particular premise is false. This difficulty is known as the *Duhem–Quine thesis*, named after the French physicist Pierre Duhem and the prominent American philosopher Wilfred Van Orman Quine (1961). Both of these individuals stressed that because of the number of what may be regarded as auxiliary propositions that are involved in research, the actual logic of research is as follows:

1. If theory and aux_1 and aux_2 and aux_3 . . . aux_n, then observation
2. Not observation
3. Therefore, not (theory and aux_1 and aux_2 and aux_3 . . . aux_n)
4. Therefore, not theory or not aux_1 or not aux_2 or not aux_3 . . . or not aux_n

This is a valid, logical argument. Notice, however, that the ultimate conclusion is ambiguous. Instead of having the arrows of *modus tollens* decisively falsify the theory under test, the conclusion simply states that some proposition involved in the deduction is false. But it does not tell us which. Logic can no longer be the guide. We are logically free to attribute blame to any one or to any set of propositions.

This is an extremely dangerous state of affairs to the whole notion of "testing" because it can defeat the very purpose of testing: criticism. We can always "save" our theory by simply attributing blame for a prediction failure to one of these auxiliary statements. Quine (1961) argued that this logical ambiguity suggested that the statements of science could not be tested one by one. Rather Quine asserted that "the unit of empirical significance is the whole of science" (p. 42). Furthermore,

> the totality of our so-called knowledge or beliefs, from most casual matters of geography and history to the profoundest laws of atomic physics or even of pure mathematics and logic, is a man-made fabric which impinges on experience only along the edges. Or, to change the figure, total science is like a field of force whose boundary conditions are experience. A conflict with experience at the periphery occasions readjustments in the interior of the field. Truth values have to be redistributed over some of our statements. Reevaluation of some statements entails reevaluation of others, because of their logical intercon-

nections—the logical laws being in turn simply certain further statements of the system, certain further elements of the field. Having reevaluated one statement we must reevaluate some others, which may be statements logically connected with the first or may be the statements of logical connections themselves. But the total field is so underdetermined by its boundary conditions, experience, that there is much latitude of choice as to what statements to reevaluate in the light of any single contrary experience. (pp. 42–43)

Thus, although the first requirement of severe or risky tests is to look for the most improbable consequences of a theory, this is not sufficient. The second requirement is that the researcher must design the test in a manner such that all the auxiliary premises are not in doubt. The researcher must make an epistemic commitment that in the case of an anomalous result it will be the theory (or hypothesis derived from the theory) under test that is considered falsified.

O'Donohue and Krasner (1988) provided an example of these points in behavior therapy. Pierce and Epling (1980) reviewed research published in the *Journal of Applied Behavior Analysis* (*JABA*) and said this about the law of effect:

> This principle is demonstrated on numerous and diverse behaviors, in different settings and with different subject populations. These articles, taken together, seem to state "the law of effect works." One can imagine an equivalent development in the science of physics. If Galileo had started an applied journal there may have been numerous articles that demonstrated the law of gravity held for a) various angles of inclined planes, b) inclined planes composed of different substances, and c) diverse balls varying in size and mass. The journal could have been called the Journal of Applied Gravities as the current JABA could be redesignated the Journal of Applied Law of Effects. (p. 6)

However, can these articles really be interpreted as providing evidence that "the law of effect works"? That is, has the law of effect in these studies actually been exposed to the risk of falsification? Let us cite a typical research investigation to examine this question.

A behavior therapist is given the task of increasing the frequency of quiet studying on the part of a child. To achieve this goal, the therapist, by whatever means, predicts that cookies will function as reinforcers for studying for this child. The law of effect states that if the child is given a positive reinforcer contingent on studying, then the frequency of studying will increase. After operationally defining *quiet studying*, the therapist gives the child a cookie if and only if the child studies quietly.

What happens if after delivery of a number of cookies, the therapist discovers that there has been no change in the child's studying? Logically, the research can be depicted as follows:

1. If x is a reinforcer, then x will increase the rate of responding (the law of effect).
2. Cookies are reinforcers for studying.
3. Cookies did not increase response rate.
---
4. Therefore, either cookies are not reinforcers in this case, or the law of effect is false.

This is a logically valid argument. However, the behavior therapist is now confronted with the Duhem–Quine thesis that was previously discussed. By *modus tollens*, the behavior therapist knows that the law of effect and the claim that cookies are reinforcers in this case cannot both be true. Logic can no longer be the guide. However, the previous points regarding proper ways of handling the Duhemian problem must be kept in mind. Namely, a test of a theory is a real test if and only if one is ready to attribute blame for a prediction failure to that proposition. Thus, the law of effect is tested in this research if and only if were the test to result in a prediction failure, the law of effect would be considered falsified.

Thus, questions can be raised regarding the extent to which the law of effect has actually been tested in applied behavioral research. The design of past research is not such that it allows one to plausibly conclude that the law of effect is false, given no observed change in response rate. It appears that researchers have, often reasonably, resolved the Duhem–Quine problem by blaming a prediction failure on the other disjunct, that is, that the predicted reinforcer really is not a reinforcer. Furthermore, if in these studies there is no outcome that could have plausibly been interpreted as a disconfirmation of the law of effect, then none of the outcomes of these studies involving the law of effect can be considered to support it. Journals that catalog the alleged "successes" of the law of effect are as meaningful as pieces of evidence as the temple pictures in the following anecdote of Francis Bacon:

> It was a good answer that was made by one who, when they showed him hanging in a temple a picture of those who had paid their vows as having escaped shipwreck, and would have him say whether he did not know acknowledge the power of the gods—"Aye," asked he again, "but where are they painted that were drowned after their vows?" And such is the way of all superstition. (*The New Organon*, bk. 1, Aphorism, LXVI)

We suggest that behavior therapists need to be more systematic in their method of reinforcement selection (see Timberlake, chapter 3, this volume). The arrows of *modus tollens* can perhaps be legitimately pointed to these methods, and science can be advanced by this criticism. Science is not advanced by behavior therapists concluding that their informal guesses about what would function as reinforcers were wrong.

THEORY REVISION—THE ESSENCE OF SCIENTIFIC PROGRESS

Magee (1973) asserted the following:

> It is not truisms which science unveils. Rather, it is part of the greatness and beauty of science that we can learn, through our own critical investigations, that the world is utterly different from what we ever imagined—until our imagination was fired by the refutations of our earlier theories. (p. 37)

Prominent philosophers of science have suggested that the optimal epistemic strategy of theory testing should not be to "prove" the truth of the theory, but rather to learn in what aspects we were mistaken: "The wrong view of science betrays itself in the craving to be right" (Popper, 1972, p. 281). A more useful strategy in theory testing is to attempt to discover and eliminate as much error as possible by exposing the theory to maximum criticism. Science grows not by accumulating evidence that some theory was initially correct, but by correcting the errors of the original theory (e.g., when Newtonian mechanics were shown to be in error and were augmented by the more general case of relativity). Severe testing as described in the previous section provides an efficient means for rooting out error.

It is important to realize that not only do we learn where errors are, but also we learn how to learn (i.e., we learn how to better criticize and more efficiently eliminate error). This is a reason that glib comments about "the scientific method" are problematic. Method in science is not ossified. As Brown (1988) stated, "modern studies of the history of science indicate that science is not just a process of learning about the world, it is also a process of learning how to learn about the world" (p. 7).

As we discussed in our first chapter in this volume, the worth of a theory is to a large extent determined by comparison with its rivals. Worth does not consist of "justifying" the theory by finding that it is in keeping with empirical evidence. Radnitzky (1988) drew a nice contrast between the critical fallibilist account described here and a justificational account:

> The justificationist asks: When is it rational to accept a particular theory?; and he suggests an answer on the lines: When it has been verified or probabilified to a sufficient degree. In the critical context the key question is: When is it *rational* (fallibly) to prefer a particular position (statement, view, standard, etc.) over its rival(s)? The answer suggested is along the lines: "It is *rational* (fallibly) to prefer a position over its rivals if and only if it has so far withstood criticism—the criticism relevant for the sort of position at stake—better than did its rivals." (p. 288)

Thus, an important part of legitimate theory appraisal is that alternatives receive a fair hearing and that all competitors are considered on their own merits without consideration of factors such as previous attachment to the theory.

Lakatos (1970) actually defined scientific progress as a certain kind of change that occurs in the revision of theories that is spurred by new, anomalous findings. A series of theory revisions is considered to be scientifically progressive if subsequent theories in the series have excess empirical content (i.e., they predict some novel observations) and some of these new observations are corroborated. If either of these criteria is not met, then the series of theories is considered to be degenerating.

Thus, to escape the criticism that a theory is being illegitimately saved by ad hoc strategies, the theory must predict new facts. For example, in the beginning of behavior therapy, psychoanalysts claimed that "successful" behavioral interventions resulted in symptom substitution: The treatment of the behavior "symptom" would, because the underlying dynamic pathology was ignored, cause a more severe behavior problem to surface. When this was not found to be the case, psychoanalysts claimed that the symptoms would be "diffuse" or "subtle." This strategy was clearly ad hoc because it predicted fewer observations than did the original claim. (The original claim predicted both subtle and nonsubtle problems.) This view is clearly degenerating because none of these claims were corroborated.

INFLUENCE OF EXPERIMENTAL PSYCHOLOGY

Lakatos (1970) also claimed that research programs are animated by certain core ideas (what he called the research program's "hard core"). These ideas provide a general template for new research ideas and give suggestions for ways that the theory can be modified in the light of anomalous findings.

The hard core of behavior therapy has traditionally come from experimental psychology, particularly animal conditioning. However, over the years, the relationship between behavior therapy and experimental psychology has weakened. We believe that the potential for progress in behavior therapy has been seriously undercut by this separation.

Too much of what passes for contemporary behavior therapy is not based on contemporary experimental psychology. Far too often, behavior therapists are still applying learning results from the 1950s or 1960s that have been superseded or at least refined by more recent research. Reinforcer selection is a case in point. Behavior therapists are still too influenced by Skinner's empirical definition and have been only minimally influenced by contemporary accounts such as response deprivation (see Timberlake, chapter 3, this volume).

It is not clear if the more cognitively inclined behavior therapists are doing any better. Much of what passes for cognitive behavior therapy has more to do with Norman Vincent Peale than with Donald Norman. Cognitive behavior therapy has very tenuous relations with contemporary experimental cognitive psychology.

This separation is serious because of two factors: (a) There are many examples of applied sciences progressing well because of their close association with basic sciences. The diverse fields of engineering and medicine are cases in point. How successful would cardiology be now if cardiologists were still enthralled with Harvey's original accounts of the circulation of blood? (b) Although in forming theories and hypotheses to solve certain applied problems, the researcher can legitimately be influenced by a variety of sources, borrowing from the results of a basic science is a great way to "hedge one's bets," because this information has already been put to the test and has survived some criticism. This does not guarantee its truth or usefulness in the applied context, but it often has better epistemic credentials than does information from other sources. Experimental psychology has come a long way since the birth of behavior therapy, and we believe it has much to offer applied behavioral theory, research, and practice that has largely been untapped.

INTEGRATION VERSUS MICROCOMMUNITY STRUCTURE OF SCIENCE

Finally, we briefly discuss the possibility of the integration of the theories of behavior therapy. That is, can some set of the disparate theories of behavior therapy contained in this volume be unified? Our position on this issue is agnostic. Discovering a unifying theory that points to deeper regularities underlying several seemingly disparate theories would undoubtedly be desirable, because it would explicate more fundamental regularities. Whether there are such fundamental regularities is currently an open question. However, we also caution against the position that a lack of such an integrative, unifying theory suggests that something is amiss with contemporary behavior therapy. In his more recent writings, Kuhn (e.g., 1977) suggested that as some sciences advance, they begin to develop a microcommunity structure. Because different scientists within some broad field are working on different subproblems, they develop somewhat unique methodologies and theories. Behavior therapists are working on a diverse set of problems; thus, behavior therapy is likely to continue to have a microcommunity structure. Finally, note that experimental psychology is not integrated and is not unified by some grand theory. To the extent that behavior therapy can be influenced by disparate parts of experimental psychology, it is likely again to evolve into microcommunities.

In summary, because theories have numerous legitimate functions in science (see O'Donohue & Krasner, chapter 1, this volume), we believe that the progress of behavior therapy depends on the progress of its theories. This progress, in turn, depends on theory specification, delineation of logical relationships, severe testing, and proper theory revision. The theories and research of contemporary experimental psychology provide important resources for advances in the theories of behavior therapy. Finally, the diversity of the theories of behavior therapy reflects the diverse problems that behavior therapists address and the diverse influences on the behavior therapist.

REFERENCES

Brown, H. I. (1988). *Rationality*. London: Routledge & Kegan Paul.

Hull, C. L. (1943). *Principles of behavior*. New York: Appleton-Century-Crofts.

Kuhn, T. S. (1970). *The structure of scientific revolutions* (2nd ed.). Chicago: University of Chicago Press.

Kuhn, T. S. (1977). *The essential tension*. Chicago: University of Chicago Press.

Lakatos, I. (1970). Falsification and the methodology of scientific research programmes. In I. Lakatos & A. Musgrave (Eds.), *Criticism and the growth of knowledge*. Cambridge, England: University of Cambridge Press.

Magee, B. (1973). *Popper*. London: Fontana.

O'Donohue, W., & Krasner, L. (1988). The logic of research and the scientific status of the law of effect. *The Psychological Record, 38*, 157–174.

Pierce, W. D., & Epling, W. F. (1980). What happened to analyses in applied behavior analyses? *The Behavior Analyst*, 1–9.

Popper, K. R. (1963). *Conjectures and refutations*. London: Routledge & Kegan Paul.

Popper, K. R. (1972). *The logic of scientific discovery*. London: Hutchinson.

Quine, W. V. O. (1961). Two dogmas of empiricism. In *From a logical point of view*. New York: Harper & Row.

Radnitzky, G. (1988). In defense of self-applicable critical rationalism. In G. Radnitzky & W. W. Bartley (Eds.), *Evolutionary epistemology, rationality, and the sociology of knowledge* (pp. 279–312). LaSalle, IL: Open Court.

NAME INDEX

Page references in italics refer to listings in reference sections.

Abel, G. G., 416n, 428, 435, 436
Abel, M., 361, 374
Abelson, R. P., 419, 420, 442
Abramovitz, A., 38, 52
Abrams, D., 246, 256
Abrams, J., 39, 57
Abramson, L. Y., 370, 371, 373, 390, 392, 394, 395, 396, 397, 398, 399, 403, 406, 409, 411
Achenbach, T. M., 296, 306
Ackil, J., 156, 169
Adams, H. E., 640, 656
Adams, N. E., 48, 49, 353, 355, 357, 359, 360, 366, 373, 374, 391, 407
Adelman, H. M., 149, 166
Adler, C. M., 210, 218, 225
Aeschleman, S. R., 118, 119, 123
Agras, S. W., 49
Agras, W. S., 45, 364, 381
Ahrens, A. H., 357, 373
Ainsworth, M. D. S., 297, 304, 306
Aitchison, R. A., 420n, 443
Aitken, R., 554, 579
Ajzen, I., 399, 406
Alberti, R. E., 458, 470
Albin, R. W., 593, 607
Alden, L., 353, 373, 391, 406
Alexander, R. D., 78, 90
Alfred, M., 133, 142
Allen, F. C. L., 519, 524
Allen, G. J., 416n, 435
Allen, J. D., 106, 126
Allen, V. L., 292, 293, 309
Allison, J., 63, 67, 90, 95, 100, 101, 103, 105, 106, 108, 109, 110, 111, 112, 114, 115, 119, 123, 124, 125, 127, 128
Allison, P. D., 139, 142, 300, 306
Allmon, D., 553, 582
Alloy, L. B., 370, 372, 390, 392, 395, 396, 397, 406
Altman, B., 243, 256
Altmeyer, B. K., 587, 605
Amatruda, C. S., 296, 308

American Psychiatric Association, 38, 49, 194, 202, 212, 225, 238, 242, 243, 250, 251, 638, 656
Ames, L. B., 296, 308
Amies, P., 42, 50
Amsel, A., 49, 49, 148, 159, 164, 165, 177, 202
Ancis, J., 213, 227
Anderson, C. A., 392, 395, 406
Anderson, T., 416n, 439
Andrews, D., 392, 395, 398, 409
Andrews, G., 43, 49, 467, 470
Andrews, G. R., 390, 394, 406
Anger, D., 160, 165
Antaki, C., 402, 406
Anthony, W. A., 416n, 435
Antony, M. A., 224, 225
Applebaum, A., 44, 52
Appleman, A. J., 394, 406
Arazie, R., 106, 126
Archer, D., 419n, 425, 438, 442
Archer, J., 503, 524
Argyle, M., 419n, 425n, 435, 442
Arkin, R. M., 394, 406
Arkwitz, H., 416n, 435
Armstrong, H. E., 553, 582
Arnold, M. B., 32, 49
Arnoult, L. H., 392, 406
Arntz, A., 241, 253
Arps, K., 364, 382
Arthur, J., 323, 344
Asher, S. R., 304, 310, 416n, 441
Asmus, J., 594, 604
Auerbach, S. M., 371, 380
Augustson, E., 678, 688
Australian Bureau of Statistics (ABS), 517, 522, 524
Avard, J., 364, 374
Ax, A. F., 32, 49
Ayllon, T., 14, 20, 660, 666, 688
Azrin, N., 79, 90
Azrin, N. H., 14, 20, 40, 49, 64, 90, 661, 688

Baars, B. J., 262, 280, 419, 435

707

Bertalanffy, L. V., 615, 633
Best, A., 593, 607
Betz, N. E., 352, 360, 364, 374
Beyer, J., 355, 357, 360, 366, 373
Bhaskar, R., 539n, 549
Biglan, A., 323, 344
Bijou, S. W., 19, 20, 586, 603, 604, 661, 688
Binkoff, J. A., 594, 604
Biran, M., 354, 371, 375
Birnbaum, D., 369, 380
Bitterman, M. E., 164, 165
Blaauw, E., 447, 467, 470
Black, A. H., 42, 50
Blanchard, E. B., 242, 252, 256, 416n, 428, 435, 436
Blanchard, E. D., 47, 49
Blehar, M., 297, 304, 306
Bless, H., 355, 381
Bloch, M., 540, 549
Block, L., 508, 525
Bloom, L., 515, 524
Bloom, L. J., 244, 257
Boice, R., 230, 253, 257
Boland, T., 416n, 442
Bolles, R. C., 80, 90
Bonem, M., 663, 690
Boone, S. E., 420, 420n, 437, 443
Booth, C. L., 303, 304, 307
Bootzin, R., 54
Bootzin, R. R., 36, 388, 407
Boozer, G., 429, 436
Bopp, M. J., 554, 580
Borden, J. W., 352, 375
Boren, J. J., 179, 206
Borgeat, F., 41, 50
Borkovec, T. D., 34, 50, 152, 154, 162, 165, 357, 370, 375, 382, 388, 412, 416n, 424, 436
Borrelli, B., 357, 360, 365, 375
Borthwick, S. A., 586, 604
Bosma, J. F., 26, 50
Boudewyns, P. A., 190, 202, 203, 206
Boulenger, J. P., 214, 228
Boulougouris, J., 238, 255
Bourdieu, P., 516, 525
Bourland, G., 587, 606
Bower, G. H., 355, 363, 369, 378
Bowlby, J., 289, 307, 498, 502, 519, 525
Boyd, T. L., 44, 53, 163, 167, 181, 182, 185, 186, 190, 203, 205

Bradbury, T. N., 401, 402, 403, 404, 407, 408, 409
Bradley, M. M., 229n, 232, 234, 239, 240, 242, 250, 251, 252, 253, 254, 256
Bradshaw, C. M., 133, 135, 137, 138, 139, 142
Brady, J. V., 87, 90
Branch, L. G., 446, 470
Brant, D. H., 81, 90
Brasted, W. S., 569, 580
Braswell, L., 276, 282
Braun, C., 251, 255
Breland, K., 63, 74, 90, 488, 493
Breland, M., 63, 74, 90, 488, 493
Bretherton, I., 304, 307
Brewer, B. A., 661n, 678, 680, 692
Bricker, W., 321, 346
Brickman, P., 353, 378
Brockel, B., 593, 604
Brodt, S. E., 388, 407
Brody, S., 251, 255
Bronfenbrenner, U., 323, 337, 342
Brooks, C. I., 151, 168
Brouillard, M. E., 353, 373
Browder, D. M., 595, 606
Brown, D. A., 630, 635
Brown, D. K., 595, 606
Brown, H. I., 703, 706
Brown, I., Jr., 354, 375
Brown, J. S., 152, 162, 165, 166, 177, 203
Brown, K., 317, 321, 347
Brown, M., 420n, 437
Brown, T. A., 213, 225, 467, 470
Brownell, K. D., 279, 280
Brownlee, S., 245, 252
Bruckner-Gordon, F., 648, 656
Bruner, J., 261, 280
Bruner, J. S., 399, 407
Brunetti, D. G., 244, 255
Brush, F. R., 182, 203
Bryant, B., 419n, 425n, 442
Buchsbaum, K., 420n, 437
Buckenbam, K., 77, 94
Budzinski, T. H., 37, 50
Buehler, R. E., 328, 342
Buie, S. E., 553, 579
Bukist, W. F., 133, 142
Burch-Vernon, A., 156, 169
Burdick, C. A., 418, 441
Burger, J. M., 394, 406

Burish, T. G., 279, *283*
Burke, M., 139, *144*
Burkhard, B., 106, 107, *124, 127*
Burns, G. L., 665, 678, 680, 681, 683, 684, 686, 688, 692, 693
Burnstein, E., 44, *52*
Burton, S. M., 246, *252*
Bush, E. S., 397, *408*
Bush, M. A., 296, 299, 303, *307*
Buss, D. M., 483, 484, 485, 489, *493*
Butcher, R. H. J., 24, *52*
Butler, G., 42, *50*
Butterfield, W. H., 660n, 676, 683, 692
Buxton, A., 114, 115, *123*

Cacciola, J., 395, 400, 401, *412*
Cacioppo, J. T., 554, *580*
Cairns, B. D., 317, 318, 328, 337, *342*
Cairns, R. B., 317, 318, 322, 328, 334, 337, *342*
Calhoun, S. K., 640, *656*
Call, T., 586, *605*
Callahan, E. J., 569, *580*
Cameron, K. N., 532, 533, *549*
Cameron, R., 459, *472*
Campbell, D. T., 478, *493*
Campbell, H. J., 586, *604*
Camper, P., 567, *582*
Cannon, W. B., 211, *225*
Cantor, N., 271, 280, 357, 361, 365, 375, 398, 399, *407*
Capaldi, D., 328, *346*
Carey, C. H., 455, *470*
Carling, A., 541n, *549*
Carlson, C. G., 665, 680, *692*
Carlson, J. I., 587, 592n, *604*
Carlson, P. M., 416n, *439*
Carr, E. G., 134, *142*, 587, 589, 590, 591, 592n, 594, 604, *605*
Carroll, D., 239, *252*
Carson, R., 210, *225*
Carter, M. M., 210, *225*
Carver, C. S., 266, 267, 268, 269, *280*
Cash, T. F., 213, *225*
Caspi, A., 298, *307*, 352, *375*
Castellon, C., 395, 400, 401, *412*
Castro, F., 544, *549*
Cataldo, M., 594, 595, *605*
Catania, A. C., 64, 90, 106, 108, *124*
Cautela, J. R., 274, 280, 284, 455, *470*
Center for Psychophysiological Study of Emotion and Attention, 251, *252*

Cerny, J. A., 212, 220, 225, 368, 369, *374*
Cervone, D., 351, 352, 355, 356, 357, 358, 359, 360, 361, 362, 363, 365, 369, 370, *373, 375, 376, 377, 380, 381, 382*
Chaffin, R., 234, *253*
Chaiken, S., 354, *376*
Chamberlain, P. C., 314, 331, 332, 333, *342, 343, 346*
Chambless, D. L., 362, *376*
Chambliss, C., 388, *407*
Chandler, M. J., 290, *311*
Chandler, T., 515, *525*
Chaney, E. F., 416n, 436, 458, *470*
Chapin, M., 398, *407*
Chaplin, W., 416n, 425, *439*
Charney, D. S., 210, *225*
Check, J., 431, *440*
Chellsen, J., 135, *143*
Chesler, P., 501, *525*
Chesney, M. A., 37, *50*
Chess, S., 292, 300, *311*
Chila, A. G., 359, *377*
Childs, K. E., 595, *606*
Chiles, H. A., 567, *582*
Christiansen, K. O., 337, *343*
Cicchetti, D., 288, 293, 296, 299, 303, *307*
Cigrand, K., 594, 604, 607, *608*
Ciminero, A. R., 640, *656*
Cioffi, D., 353, *373*
Claiborn, J. M., 243, *256*
Clark, D. M., 210, 224, *226*
Clarke, S., 590, 595, 605, *606*
Clarkin, J., 574, *581*
Cleckley, H., 241, *252*
Cloninger, C. R., 337, *343*
Clum, G. A., 352, *375*
Coates, T. J., 265, *284*
Cobb, J. A., 316, *346*
Coburn, K., 515, *524*
Cockburn, C., 518, *525*
Cody, R., 510, *525*
Coehlo, R. J., 393, *408*
Cohen, D., 31, *56*
Cohen, G. A., 541n
Cohen, R., 301, 302, *307, 310, 311*
Coie, J. D., 297, *307*, 416, 418, 420n, 421, 436, *441*
Coleman, E. M., 416n, 428, 436, *441*
Coleman, S. R., 687, *688*
Collier, G., 88, 90, 106, *124, 125*
Collins, J. L., 358, *376*

Colwill, R. M., 77, *91*

Comer, R., 571, *583*

Compas, B. E., 300, *307*

Comte, A., 19, *21*

Condiotte, M. M., 360, *376*

Conger, A. J., 416, 417, 419n, 436, 640, 656

Conger, J. C., 416, 417, 419n, 425, 436, 437, 640, 656

Conger, R. E., 330, *346*

Connor, W. H., 33, *50*

Connors, G. J., 279, *280*

Constantine, J. A., 241, *257*

Conviser, J. H., 279, *282*

Cook, B., 515, *525*

Cook, E. W., 236, 237, 238, 239, 240, 244, 247, *252, 255*

Cook, J., 594, *607*

Cook, M., 153, 162, 164, *166*, 419n, *435*

Cooper, J. O., 136, *142*

Cooper, L., 594, *608*

Cooper, M. L., 351, *379*

Cooper, S. H., 567, *583*

Coopersmith, S., 350, 351, *376*

Coppotelli, H., 297, *307*

Corbett, J. A, 587, *607*

Corbett, J. A., 586, *604*

Corbit, J. D., 153, *170*

Cordova, J. V., 651, 655, *656*

Cornforth, M., 537, 539, 540, *549*

Corrigan, P. W., 416n, 417, 418, 420n, *436*

Cosmides, L., 78, *91*, 483, 484, *494*

Costello, E. J., 296, *307*

Costner, B. M., 296, *308*

Cowan, P. A., 287, *307*

Cowdery, G., 594, 595, *605*

Cox, B. J., 213, *227*

Coyne, J. C., 394, *410*, 425, *442*

Coyne, L., 44, *52*

Cozzarelli, C., 351, *379*

Craighead, L. W., 295, 300, *308*

Craighead, W. E., 239, *251*, 272, 280, 288, 295, 300, *308, 309*

Craske, M. G., 44, *57*, 210, 218, 220, 221, *225, 226*

Crawford, H. L., 660, 676, 678, *693*

Crawford, J., 593, *604*

Crehan, K., 361, *381*

Cressy, D. R., 336, *348*

Crimmins, D. B., 593, *605*

Critelli, J. W., 393, *413*

Cronbach, L. J., 655, *656*

Crosby, L., 328, 329, *346*

Crowe, R. R., 214, *226*

Crowell, C. R., 69, 70, 92, 117, 118, *125*

Cruce, J. A. F., 106, 110, *125*

Cullen, C., 139, *142*

Cullington, A., 42, *50*

Cumming, G. F., 447, 449, 467, 468, *472*

Curran, J. P., 416n, 420, *436*

Curtis, R., 269, *281*

Cuthbert, B. N., 229n, 232, 234, 236, 237, 238, 239, 240, 241, 243, 244, 250, 252, 253, 254, 255, 256, 257

Cutrona, C. E., 353, *376*

Dahlquist, C. M., 595, 606, *607*

Damer, D., 467, *470*

Darwin, C., 476, 477, 480, 491, *493*

Davidson, W., 398, *408*

Davies, P., 611n, *633*

Davis, F. W., 361, *376*

Davis, M., 241, *252*

Davis, T. L., 240, *252*

Davison, G. C., 385, 389, *408*

Davison, M., 134, 137, 138, *142*

Dawes, R. M., 317, *346*

Day, D. M., 447, 449, 458, 463, 464, 467, 468, *471, 472*

Day, R. M., 594, 595, *604*

de Jong, J. B., 243, *256*

de Jong, P. J., 241, *253*

de Villiers, P. A., 137, 138, *142*

Deagle, E. A., 213, *225*

Dean, S. J., 158, *166*

DeBaryshe, B. D., 325, *346*

Debus, R. L., 390, 394, *406*

Deitz, D. E. D., 591, *607*

Deitz, S. M., 559, *580*

DeKay, W. T., 483, *493*

Delprato, D. J., 306, *308*, 612n, 615, 616, 625, 628, 629, 630, 631, 632, 633, 635

Dember, W. N., 419, *436*

Dembo, T., 350, *379*

Demouse, L., 192, *203*

Dennehey, D. M., 352, 358, *374*

Denny, M. R., 149, 153, 154, *166*

DePaulo, B. M., 419n, *436*, 441

DeRaad, A., 594, *607*

Derby, K. M., 594, *604*

Derryberry, D., 554, *580*

Devins, G. M., 362, 363, *376*

Dewey, J., 544, 545, *549*, 611, 630, *633*

Gaelick-Buys, L., 265, 277, *281*
Gaffney, L. R., 416n, *437*
Galanter, E., 365, *379*
Galef, B. G., 72, *91*
Galef, B. G., Jr., 164, *166*
Gallistel, C. R., 63, 76, *91*
Gangi, B. K., 648, *656*
Gannon, K. N., 68, *91*, 113, 114, 115, *127*
Gantt, W. H., 28, *51*
Garber, J., 296, *308*
Garcia, J., 71, *91*, 488, *493*
Garcia y Robertson, R., 71, *91*
Gardner, B. T., 73, 87, *91*
Gardner, R. A., 73, 87, *91*
Garfield, S. L., 41, 43, *51*
Gariepy, J. L., 328, *342*
Garmezy, N., 416n, *438*
Gattinger, E., 388, *411*
Gauthier, B., 41, *50*
Gauthier, J., 570, *580*
Gawley, D., 77, 95, *96*
Gawley, D. J., 66, 67, 84, 88, *91*, 93, 113, 115, 116, *125*, *128*
Gaylord-Ross, R., 590, *608*
Geer, J. H., 489, *494*
Gelder, M., 42, *50*
Gelder, M. G., 214, 215, *227*
Gellhorn, E., 26, *50*, *51*
Gengerelli, J., 425n, *442*
George, W. H., 447, 450, 451, 452, 453, 455, 456, 457, 458, 459, 467, *470*
Geraci, M. P., 214, *228*
Gerard, R., 425n, *442*
Gerardi, R. J., 242, *252*
Gershman, L., 39, *51*
Gessell, A., 296, *308*
Gest, S. D., 328, *342*
Gibbons, R., 352, 363, 369, *378*
Gilbert, F. S., 416n, *436*
Gilbertini, M., 351, 364, *376*
Gillespie, J. F., 296, 299, 303, *307*
Gilmore, J., 507, *527*
Gilmore, S. K., 331, *348*
Gilovich, T., 369, *377*
Gino, A., 153, 163, *169*
Girodo, M., 388, *407*
Glaros, A. G., 385, 389, *408*
Glasgow, R. E., 279, *283*
Glass, G. V., 43, *55*
Glasser, W., 453, *470*
Gleeson, S., 77, *92*
Glenn, S. S., 535, *549*

Glenwick, D. S., 302, *308*
Glynn, S. M., 351, *377*
Goetz, R. R., 210, *226*
Goldberg, J., 36, *51*
Goldfried, M., 393, 409, 416, 417, *438*
Goldfried, M. R., xi, *xviii*, 302, 308, 368, 371, *377*, 418, *437*, 637, 657, 682, 683, *689*
Goldiamond, I., 277, *281*, 631, *633*
Goldman, J. A., 151, *168*
Goldsmith, J., 416n, *438*
Goldstein, A. J., 39, *51*
Goldstein, A. P., 416n, *438*
Goldstein, D. N., 31, *56*
Goldstein, M., 246, *256*
Goldstein-Fodor, I., 514, 515, 516, *525*
Golin, S., 392, *409*
Gollwitzer, P. M., 270, *281*
Gonso, J., 416n, 425, *438*
Goodman, J., 276, 283, 662, *690*
Goodman, W. K., 210, *225*
Gordon, B. N., 296, *311*
Gordon, J., 368, *379*
Gordon, J. R., 268, 275, 278, *283*, 393, *411*, 416n, 440, 446, 449, 468, *471*
Gorman, J. M., 210, *226*
Gorman-Smith, D., 587, 605, *606*
Gossette, R. L., 46, *51*
Gotestam, K. G., 40, *56*
Gottesman, I. I., 337, *343*
Gottman, J., 632, *633*
Gottman, J. M., 136, 139, *142*, *143*, 316, 335, 339, *343*, *344*, 416n, 420, 425, 427, *438*, *439*
Gould, D., 352, 359, *382*
Gould, S. J., 477, *493*
Gracely, E. J., 362, *376*
Granados, J. L., 569, *580*
Gray, J. A., 43, *51*, 180, 203, 224, 226, 337, 339, *344*
Grayson, H., 425n, *442*
Green, C., 663, *690*
Green, J. A., 322, *342*
Green, L., 71, 87, *91*, 94, 107, *127*
Green, S. M., 337, *344*
Greenberg, L. S., 571, *581*
Greenblatt, D., 37, *56*
Greene, D., 86, *91*
Greenwald, D., 416n, *442*
Greenwald, M., 416n, *442*
Greenwald, M. K., 251, *252*
Greenwood, M. R. C., 106, 110, *125*

Herman, C. P., 388, 407
Heron, T. E., 136, 142
Herrmann, D. J., 234, 253
Herrnstein, R., 179, 203
Herrnstein, R. J., 70, 71, 92, 130, 132, 137, 138, 140, 143, 159, 167, 319, 344
Herry, M., 662, 678, 689
Hersen, M., 136, 142, 296, 310, 416n, 417, 419n, 424, 436, 438
Herz, L. R., 243, 256
Herz, R. S., 77, 94
Hess, L. E., 288, 298, 299, 309
Heth, C. D., 101, 109, 118, 125
Heward, W. L., 136, 142
Hewstone, M., 509, 526
Hibbert, G. A., 211, 226
Hickerson, S. C., 553, 579
Hickman, C., 135, 143
Higgins, E. T., 357, 377
Higgins, J., 425n, 438
Hilgard, E. R., 27, 52, 160, 167, 178, 204
Hill, G. J., 366, 377
Himadi, W. G., 230, 253, 640, 657
Hineline, P. N., 160, 167
Hines, P., 416n, 435
Hirai, H., 239, 253
Hirosige, T., 611n, 634
Hirota, A., 239, 253
Hirsch, E., 106, 124, 125
Hirsch, J., 106, 110, 125
Hirt, M. L., 301, 308
Hoberman, H. M., 371, 379
Hobsbawm, E., 534, 549
Hodgson, R., 42, 52
Hodgson, R. I., 230, 253
Hoehn-Hyde, D., 419n, 438
Hoehn-Saric, R., 388, 409
Hoekstra, C. S., 31, 56
Hogan, J. A., 77, 92
Holden, G., 367, 377
Holden, G. W., 298, 308
Holdroyd, K. A., 359, 377, 388, 409
Holland, J. G., 544, 550
Holland, P. C., 164, 169
Hollingsworth, A. S., 553, 579
Hollis, K. L., 84, 92
Hollon, S. D., 210, 225, 279, 283, 356, 378, 380, 400, 401, 409, 510, 527
Holm, J. E., 359, 377

Holmbeck, G. N., 288, 302, 306, 308
Holmes, D. S., 416n, 435
Holstein, S. B., 100, 125
Holton, A., 317, 321, 347
Holton, G., 612, 613, 634
Holtzworth-Munroe, A., 405, 410
Holzman, A. D., 148, 167, 178, 204
Hoon, E. F., 387, 410
Hoon, P. W., 387, 410
Hops, H., 323, 344
Horne, P. J., 137, 143
Horner, R. D., 591, 605
Horner, R. H., 593, 594, 605, 607
Horney, K., 502, 526
Horowitz, H. A., 288, 289, 290, 291, 295, 306, 310
Horowitz, L. H., 44, 52
Horowitz, L. M., 392, 395, 406
Houk, J. L., 132, 133, 134, 135, 136, 138, 139, 143
Houts, A. C., 2, 19, 21, 562n, 580
Howells, G. N., 366, 373, 391, 407
Hudson, S. M., 449, 472
Huesmann, L. R., 324, 344
Hugdahl, K., 45, 54, 161, 162, 169
Hughes, H. H., 393, 413
Hull, C. L., 80, 92, 148, 167, 670, 675, 689, 697, 706
Hundt, A., 109, 127
Hundt, A. G., 100, 125
Hunsley, J., 305, 310
Hunt, A., 100, 125
Hunt, R. R., 339, 343
Hunt, W. A., 446, 470
Hunter, G. F., 416n, 438
Huntley, D., 324, 348
Hurry, J., 503, 528
Hursey, K. G., 359, 377
Hurwitz, D., 106, 109, 110, 124
Huson, J., 238, 255
Huthwaite, M., 39, 55
Hyland, M. E., 269, 281

Ickes, W., 352, 382, 385, 395, 410
Ilg, F. L., 296, 308
Imber, S., 388, 409
Infeld, L., 611, 612, 622, 630, 633
Ingram, R., 368, 369, 377, 378
Ingram, R. E., 370
Inouye, D. K., 354, 375

Isaac, J. C., 537, 548, *550*
Itkonen, T., 591, 594, *606*
Iversen, I. H., 630, *634*
Iwata, B. A., 589, 593, 594, 595, 605, *608*
Izard, C. E., 425n, *437*, 554, 571, *581*

Jacklin, C., 503, 512, *526*
Jackson, A., 352, 359, 382, 393, *413*
Jackson, K., 530, 531, 535, 544, *550*
Jackson, P., 453, 458, 463, *472*
Jacobs, A., 177, *203*
Jacobs, B., 359, 361, 378, *381*
Jacobs, M. A., 416n, *439*
Jacobsen, L., 351, *379*
Jacobsen, E., 33, *52*
Jacobson, J. W., 587, *606*
Jacobson, N., 467, *473*
Jacobson, N. S., 404, 405, 407, 408, *410*, 637, *657*
Jaeger, M. E., 558, *581*
Jaffe, L. B., *425*
Jaffe, P. G., 416n, *439*
Jakubowski, P., 458, 471, 514, *526*
James, J., 504, *526*
James, J. H., 150, *166*
James, W., 1, *21*, 562, *581*
Janke, W., 388, *408*
Janoff-Bullman, R., 353, 378, *402*
Jansson, L., 230, *256*
Janz, N., 509, *526*
Jarrell, M. P., 632, *635*
Jaspars, J., 509, *526*
Jaspars, J. M., 402, *409*
Jeffrey, R. W., 367, *374*
Jenkins-Hall, K. D., 454, 456, 470, *471*
Jensen, M. P., 361, *378*
Jerremalm, A., 230, 231, *256*
Jiwani, N., 351, 358, 360, *375*
Johansson, J., 231, *256*
Johansson, S., 318, *344*
Johnson, H. J., 236, *253*
Johnson, M. R., 69, 92, 117, *125*
Johnson, P. R., 106, 110, *125*
Johnson, S. M., 318, *344*
Johnson, V. E., 38, *53*
Johnson, W. G., 632, *635*
Johnson, W. L., 594, 595, *604*
Johnson-Laird, P. N., 234, *253*, 271, *281*
Johnston, D. W., 214, 215, *227*
Johnston, J. C., 159, *170*, 179, 180, 182, *206*

Joiner, T. E., Jr., 396, 403, 404, *410*, *411*
Jones, G. E., 236, *253*
Jones, J. C., 247, *253*
Jones, M. C., xiii, *xviii*, 31, 35, *52*
Jones, R. R., 330, *346*

Kagan, J., 300, *309*, 554, *581*
Kagel, J., 71, *94*
Kagel, J. H., 107, *127*
Kahn, M., 416n, 419n, *439*
Kahneman, D., 350, 354, 355, 378, 382, 399, *410*
Kalish, H. I., 177, *203*, 204, 263, *281*
Kaloupek, D. G., 40, *52*, 416n, 424, *436*
Kalsher, M., 594, 595, *605*
Kamil, A. C., 77, *90*
Kamin, L. J., 181, 182, *206*
Kaminstein, D. S., 554, 555, *581*
Kane, M., 265, *282*
Kanfer, F. H., xiv, *xix*, 14, 18, *21*, 260, 261, 265, 267, 268, 274, 275, 277, *281*, *282*, 284, 629, *634*, 661, 683, *689*
Kanfer, R., 391, *410*
Kantor, J. R., xiii, *xix*, 610, 611, 613, 614, 616, 617, 618, 624, 625, 628, 630, *634*
Kaplan, G., 513, 518, 521, *526*
Kaplan, H. S., 38, *52*
Karas, A. Y., 38, *54*
Karnatz, T., 467, *472*
Karoly, P., 261, 264, 265, 266, 267, 268, 270, 271, 274, 275, 277, 278, *281*, *282*
Karpman, M., 100, 101, 112, *124*
Karsh, K. G., 591, 594, 595, *606*, *607*
Kastenbaum, R. J., 569, *581*
Kauffman, M. B., 287, *309*
Kavanagh, D. J., 355, 363, 369, *378*
Kavanau, J. L., 81, *90*
Kazdin, A., 387, *410*
Kazdin, A. E., 25, 47, *52*, 59, 60, 63, 92, 96, 98, *125*, 139, 140, *143*, 278, 279, *282*, 299, *309*, 331, *344*, 362, *378*
Keane, T., 640, *657*
Keane, T. M., 40, *52*
Keaney, F., 446, 447, 448, 449, 450, 451, 452, 453, 454, 455, 456, 457, 458, 459, 460, 461, 468, 469, *473*
Kelley, H. H., 350, *378*, 390, 392, 395, 398, *410*

Kellogg, R., 388, *410*
Kelly, M. L., 60, *92*
Kelly, S. Q., 135, 136, *143*
Kelsey, J. E., 106, 110, 115, *125*
Kendall, K. A., 588n, *608*
Kendall, P. C., 265, 276, 279, 282, 288, 300, 301, 302, 306, 308, 309, 356, 369, 370, 377, 378, 401, 409
Kendon, A., 419n, *439*
Kendrick, D. C., *51*
Kennedy, C. H., 591, 594, *606*
Kennedy, T. D., 388, *412*
Kenny, D. A., 365, *374*
Kent, G., 352, 362, 369, *378*
Kern, L., 591, 595, *606*
Kern-Dunlap, L., 590, *605*
Kernberg, O., 44, *52*
Kernberg, O. F., 574, *581*
Kerr, M., 369, *377*
Kettlewell, H. B. D., 477, *493*
Kiesler, D. J., 487, *493*
Kihlstrom, J. F., 357, 361, 365, *375*, 398, 399, *407*
Kilgore, K., 317, 321, *347*
Kimble, G. A., 177, *204*, 627, *634*
King, D., 73, 85, *96*
King, N. J., 297, *310*
Kinney, P. J., 360, 361, 362, *383*
Kirsch, I., 47, *52*, 356, 361, 362, *373*, *378*
Kirschenbaum, D. S., 279, *282*
Kishi, G., 593, *605*
Kitchener, R., 9, *21*
Kleck, R. E., 418, *439*
Kleifield, E., 356, 362, 367, *383*
Klein, D. F., 210, *226*
Klein, D. J., 554, *580*
Klein, E., 496, 498, 499, 522, *526*
Kleinfeld, E., 391, *413*
Kleinknecht, R. A., 39, *52*
Kloek, J., 447, 467, *470*
Klorman, R., 571, *584*
Kloss, J., 416n, *442*
Klumpp, G., 355, *381*
Knapp, J. R., 632, *635*
Knight, R. P., 44, *52*
Kniskern, D. P., 404, *409*
Knurek, D. A., 662, 678, *688*
Kobak, R. R., 554, *581*
Koegel, R. L., 591, *606*
Koelling, R., 71, *91*
Koelling, R. A., 488, *493*
Koenigsberg, H. W., 574, *581*

Koerner, K., 651, 655, *656*
Koertge, N., 5, *21*
Kohl, M. L., 37, *54*
Kohlenberg, B. S., 637, *657*
Kohlenberg, R. J., 564, *581*, 637, 638, 639n, 640, 644, 646, 647, 648, 649, 650, 654, 655, *657*
Kolb, L. C., 242, *252*, *256*
Konarski, E. A., Jr., 69, 70, 92, 117, 118, 119, *124*, *125*
Kondrick, P. A., 683, *688*
Konorski, J., 85, *92*, 239, *253*
Kopp, D. A., 351, *375*
Koss, M. P., 429, *439*
Kovacs, M., 510, *527*
Kovaleski, M., 416n, *442*
Kozak, M. J., 235, 236, 243, 244, 246, 247, 248, *253*, *254*, *255*
Kraditor, A., 496, 497, *526*
Kraeling, D., 176, *205*
Kramer, D. A., 560, *581*
Kramer, J. A., 416n, *440*
Krantz, P. J., 60, *93*
Krasner, L., xiii, xiv, *xix*, 2, 14, 15, 18, 19, *21*, 22, 660, 661, 689, 693, 701, *706*
Krasnoff, J., 107, *127*
Krebs, J. R., 77, 88, 92, *95*
Kuhl, J., 270, *283*
Kuhn, T. S., 12, 13, *22*, 399, *410*, 695, 705, *706*
Kukla, A., 390, 393, 394, 395, *413*
Kuo, Z. Y., 628, *634*

Laatsch, L., 279, *282*
Lader, M. H., 45, *52*, 387, *410*, *412*
LaGreca, A. M., 300, *309*
LaGrow, S. J., 587, *606*
Laird, J. D., 571, 580, *581*
Lakatos, I., 6, 7, *22*, 704, *706*
Lakoff, R., 519, 521, *526*
Laljee, M., 419n, *435*
Lalli, J. S., 595, *606*
Lamal, P. A., 535, *550*
Lamarck, J. B., 478, 479, *493*
Lamb, M., 304, *309*
Lambert, M. J., 40, 41, *50*
Lampman, C., 301, *308*
Landrum, T. J., 593, *607*
Lang, P. J., 229, 230, 231, 232, 235, 236, 237, 238, 239, 240, 241, 242, 243,

244, 246, 247, 250, 251, *252*, *254*, *255, 256, 257*
Lange, A. J., 458, *471*
Lange, K., 562, *581*
Lanzetta, J. T., 418, *439*
Larcouche, L. M., 41, *50*
Larrance, D., 571, *584*
Larsen, S. E., 594, 595, *604*
Lasko, N. B., 243, *256*
Lassiter, G. D., 419n, *436*
Last, C. G., 214, 215, *226*
Latahm, G. P., 365
Latham, G. P., 350, 351, *379*
Latimer, P. R., 46, *52*
Lattal, K. A., 77, 92, *93*
Laudan, L., 7, 8, *22*
Lavelle, T. L., 394, *410*
Laws, D. R., 416n, *439*
Lawson, J. E., 553, *579*
Layden, M. A., 385, 395, *410*
Lazarte, A., 34, *53*
Lazarus, A., 503, 505, 506, 510, *526*
Lazarus, A. A., 17, *22*, 24, 38, *52*, 459, *471*
Lazarus, R. S., 353, *378*, *381*, 562, 563, 571, *583*
Lazovik, A. D., 231, *255*
Leahey, T., 504, *526*
Leahey, T. D., 610, *634*
Learner, M., 548, *550*
Leduc, A., 683, *689*
Lee, C., 356, 361, *378*, *379*, 510, 512, *525*, *526*
Lee, C. L., 323, *344*
Lefkowitz, M. M., 324, *344*
Leggett, E. L., 357, 370, *376*
Legros, D., 536, *550*
Lemanski, K. M., 367, *379*
Lenins, V. I., 543, *550*
Lennane, J., 517, 522, *526*
Lent, R. W., 352, *379*
Lenz, M. W., 593, *607*
Leonard, K. E., 429, *439*
Lepper, M. R., 86, *91*, 335, *344*
Lerer, B. E., 72, 85, *93*
Lerman, D., 394, *413*
Lerman, H., 502, *526*
Lerner, H., 522, *526*
Lerner, J. V., 292, *309*
Lerner, R. M., 287, 288, 289, 292, 298, 299, 300, 308, *309*
Lester, G. W., 405, *407*
Lester, L. S., 72, 81, *91*

Lett, J., 536, 537, *550*
Levenson, R., 554, *580*
Levenson, R. W., 339, *344*, 420, 426, 427, *438*, *440*
Leventhal, H., 245, *252*
Levin, D. N., 235, 236, 243, 244, 246, 247, *254, 255*
Levine, A., 541n, 546, *552*
Levine, G. A., 42, *55*
Levine, J., 416n, *424*, *443*
Levins, R., 539n, *550*, 555, 557, *582*
Levis, D. J., 44, *53*, *55*, 148, 149, 151, 153, 159, 163, *167*, 168, *170*, 174, 175, 176, 177, 178, 179, 180, 182, 183, 185, 186, 188, 190, 191, 192, 193, *198*, *202*, *203*, *204*, *205*, *206*, *207*
Levy, L., 425n, *439*
Lewin, K., 350, *379*, 615, *634*
Lewinsohn, P. M., 371, *379*, 416n, 425, *439*, *440*
Lewis, J., 499, *526*
Lewis, M., 290, 292, *310*
Lewontin, R., 539n, *550*, 555, 557, *582*
Ley, R., 211, 224, *226*
Leyhausen, P., 77, *93*
Liberman, A., 354, *376*
Liberman, B., 388, *409*
Liberman, R. P., 416n, 417, 418, 420, *436*, *437*, *439*
Libet, J. M., 416n, *440*
Lichtenstein, E., 279, *283*, 360, *376*, 416n, *435*
Liddell, H. S., 28, *53*
Lieberman, A. F., 303, 304, *309*
Liebowitz, M. R., 210, *226*
Liker, J. K., 139, *142*
Lindquist, C. V., 416n, *440*
Lindsley, O. R., 16, 17, *22*, 661, 688, *689*
Linehan, M., 637, *657*
Linehan, M. M., 553, 554, 560, 561, 562, 564, 566, 567, 568, 569, 571, 574, 575, 576, 577, 578, *581*, *582*
Lipton, D., 420, *441*
Lipton, D. N., 416n, 429, *440*
Litt, M. D., 359, *379*
Little, B. R., 271, *283*
Little, L. M., 416n, *436*
Littman, R. A., 321, *346*
Litwin, E. M., 215, *227*
Lloyd, B., 503, *524*
Lloyd, J. W., 588n, *608*
Lloyd, K. E., 535, *550*

Maslow, A. H., 174, 191, *205*
Mason, M., 587, *605*
Mason, W. A., 591, *603*
Massel, H. K., 416n, *439*
Masserman, J. H., 28, 29, 44, *53*
Masters, J. C., 279, 283, 466, *472*
Masters, W. H., 38, *53*
Mathews, A. M., 45, *52*, 214, 215, *227*
Matjak, M., 251, *255*
Matson, J., 416n, *440*
Matson, J. L., 587, *605*, 606
Matthews, T. J., 72, 85, *93*
Mattick, R. P., 368, *379*
Maxwell, R. D. H., 37, *53*
May, J. R., 236, 239, *255*
Mayer, J., 111, *129*
Mayr, E., 476, 477, 478, 479, 480, 481, 482, 487, 493, 494
Mayville, W. J., 630, 636
Mazur, J. E., 109, 110, *126*
McAllister, D. E., 148, 149, 150, 151, 152, 153, 155, 159, 162, 163, *168*, 176, 178, 179, 181, *205*
McAllister, W. R., 148, 149, 150, 151, 152, 153, 155, 159, 162, 163, *168*, 176, 178, 179, 181, *205*
McAuley, E., 351, 353, 358, *379*
McCann, D. L., 39, *53*
McCarthy, D., 134, 137, 138, *142*
McCartney, K., 294, *311*, 561, *583*
McClannahan, L. E., 60, *93*
McClasky, C., 420, *437*
McClelland, J. L., 234, *255*
McDonel, E. C., 416, 416n, 418, 420, 421, 426, 427, 429, 430, 431, 432, 433, 440, *441*
McDowell, J. J., 70, *93*, 132, 133, 134, 138, 139, *142*, *143*
McElroy, M., 353, *379*
McFall, R., 416n, *438*
McFall, R. M., 70, 96, 416, 416n, 417, 418, 420, 421, 426, 427, 429, 430, 432, 433, *437*, 440, *441*, *442*, 459, *472*
McGee, G. G., 60, *93*
McGimsey, J. F., 590, *605*
McGlynn, F. D., 34, *53*, 625, 630, *633*
McGovern, K., 416n, *435*
McGrath, R. A., 416n, *440*
McGrath, R. J., 455, *470*
McGraw, K., 317, 321, *347*
McGuigan, F. J., 234, *255*

McGuire, T. R., 554, *582*
McKelvie, M., xi, *xix*
McKendrick, V., 684, *688*
McLean, A., 236, *255*
McLean, A., Jr., 235, 244, *254*
Mclean, A., Jr., 246, 247
McMahon, R. J., 331, 332, *345*
McMichael, A., 504, *527*
McMillin, W. P., 387, *411*
McNally, R. J., 47, 55, 163, 164, *168*, 217, 227, 239, 257
McNeil, D. W., 237, 238, 239, 244, 252, 255
McWilliams-Tullberg, R., 497, *527*
Medland, M. B., 60, *93*
Mednick, M. T., 157, *169*
Mednick, S. A., 425n, *438*
Medvec, V. H., 369, *377*
Meehl, P. E., 8, 22, 61, *93*, 97, 98, *126*, 192, *205*
Mefford, I. N., 353, 359, *374*
Mehlman, S. E., 687, *688*
Mehra, J., 611n, *635*
Meichenbaum, D., 276, 283, 369, *379*, 387, *411*, 459, *472*, 507, 520, *527*
Meichenbaum, D. H., 662, *690*
Melamed, B., 244, *254*
Melamed, B. G., 231, 237, 238, 239, 252, 255
Melchior, J., 560, *581*
Melnick, W. T., 40, *50*
Menlove, F., 47, 49
Mepham, J., 539n, *550*
Mercandante, B., 361, *381*
Merckelbach, H., 241, *253*
Merian, S., 239, 252
Mermelstein, R., 357, 360, 365, *375*
Mermelstein, R. J., 467, *472*
Merrill, M. A., 680, *693*
Metalsky, G. I., 370, 372, 390, 392, 394, 395, 396, 397, 398, 399, 403, 404, 406, 409, 410, *411*
Metzger, B., 77, *93*
Meuller, P. S., 121, *126*
Meyer, A., xiii, *xix*
Meyer, V., 35, 42, *54*
Meyers, A., 302, *311*
Meyers, A. W., 295, 300, 301, 307, 308, 310
Meyers, C. E., 586, *604*
Michael, J., 61, 64, 80, *93*, 660, 666, *688*
Michael, J. L., 141, *143*

Michael, R. L., 120, *124*
Michelson, L., 230, 231, *255*
Miller, C. L., 418, *441*
Miller, D. T., 350, *378*
Miller, G. A., 235, 236, 243, 244, 246, 247, *254, 255,* 365, *379*
Miller, G. E., 299, 300, *310*
Miller, H. C., 388, *412*
Miller, H. L., 116, *128,* 133, *142*
Miller, M., 105, 106, 109, 111, 112, *124*
Miller, N. E., xiii, *xviii,* 147, 148, 149, 151, 153, 154, 157, *166, 169,* 176, 177, *179, 203, 205,* 660, *688*
Miller, P. A., 425, *437*
Miller, P. H., 287, *310*
Miller, R. E., 37, *54*
Miller, S. M., 566, *582*
Miller, T. I., 43, *55*
Miller, W. R., 451, 463, *472*
Millett, K., 499, 501, 502, *527*
Millon, T., 561, 567, *582*
Miltenberger, R. G., 593, *604*
Miltner, W., 251, *255*
Mineka, S., 150, 153, 159, 162, 163, 164, *166, 169, 170*
Miner, M. H., 447, 449, 458, 463, 464, 467, 468, *471, 472*
Minke, K. A., *660n,* 661, 678, 685, *692*
Mirsky, I. A., 37, *54*
Mischel, W., xiv, *xix,* 274, *283,* 351, 357, *360n,* 361, *379, 380, 383,* 416n, 418, 419, *419n,* 425, *439, 441,* 567, *583*
Mittleman, B., 174, 191, *205*
Mock, L. A., 151, *170,* 185, *206*
Moe, T. L., 593, *607*
Moffat, S., 630, *636*
Monod, J., 536, *550*
Moore, K. E., 110, 114, 115, 119, *123, 124*
Moore, P. M., 34, *53*
Moot, S., 80, *90*
Morgan, C. L., 61, *93*
Morgan, M., 87, *93*
Morgan, M. P., 39, *52*
Morisset, C. E., 303, 304, *307*
Morris, E. K., 79, *93*
Morrison, R. L., *419n,* 425, *441*
Morse, E., 245, 246, *251*
Moseley, A., 591, *606*
Mosher, D. L., *416n, 435*

Mosk, M. D., *416n, 439*
Mowrer, O. H., *xix,* 146, 147, 148, 149, 157, 158, 159, 160, *169,* 175, 176, 177, 178, 179, 180, *205, 206,* 216, *227,* 266, *283*
Mowrer, W. M., xiii, *xix*
Mrosovsky, N., 81, *93*
Muehlenhard, C. L., 418, *441*
Mueller, P. M., 351, *379*
Mueser, K. T., *416n, 439*
Muller, J. J., *416n, 439*
Munby, M., 42, *50*
Munk, D., 595, *606*
Murphy, G. H., 587, *607*
Murphy, I. C., 36, *54*
Murphy, J. V., 37, *54*
Murphy, R. M., *420n, 437*
Murphy, W. D., *416n,* 428, 436, *441*
Murray, E. J., 388, *407*
Myerson, J., 129, *143*

Nafpaktitis, M. K., 458, 464, *472*
Napalkov, A. V., 38, *54,* 570, *583*
Narrow, W. E., 213, *227*
Nasby, W., *419n, 441*
Nathan, S., 241, *256*
National Institutes of Health, 587, *606*
Navarick, D. J., 135, *143*
Neckerman, H. J., 328, *342*
Nedelmann, M., 133, *142*
Needles, D. J., 396, *411*
Nelson, C., 447, 449, 453, 458, 463, 467, 468, *471, 472*
Nelson, C. J., *420n, 443*
Nelson, G., 403, *409*
Nelson, S., 398, *408*
Nemec, P. B., *416n, 435*
Newman, J. P., 241, *256, 420n,* 425, *437*
Newsom, C., 135, *143*
Newsom, C. D., 594, *604*
Newsom, J., 498, *527*
Nezworski, M. T., 295, 300, *310*
Niaura, R., 246, *256*
Nicassio, P., 36, *54,* 388, *407*
Nisbett, R. E., 385, 388, *412*
Nitz, K., 288, 298, 299, *309,* 337, *347*
Noll, J. P., 137, *144*
Noonan, K. M., 476, 477, 480, *494*
Norcross, J. C., xi, *xviii*
Northup, J., 594, *604, 607*

Pitman, R. K., 243, *256*
Pittman, C. M., 158, *166*
Platt, J. J., 418, *441*, *442*
Plaud, J. J., 119, *126*, 159, *169*, 681, 690
Plomin, R., 337, *347*
Plummer, I. L., 274, *284*
Popper, K., 25, *54*, 696, 697, 699, 703, 706
Popper, K. R., 4, 5, *22*
Porter, J. H., 106, *126*
Post, R. M., 214, *228*
Postman, L., 97, *126*, 399, *407*
Powers, W. T., 266, 267, 269, *283*, 629, 635
Premack, D., 67, 69, 93, 94, 98, 99, 100, 109, 118, 122, *125*, *126*, *127*
Prentice-Dunn, S., 359, 361, *378*, *381*
Pretzer, J. L., 404, *408*
Pribram, K. H., 365, *379*
Prinz, R. J., 299, 300, *310*
Prochaska, J. O., 351, 364, *376*
Puk, G., *54*
Pullin, J., 446, 447, 448, 449, 450, 451, 452, 453, 454, 455, 456, 457, 458, 459, 460, 461, 468, 469, *473*
Pusch, D., 506, 508, *525*

Qualls, P. J., 37, *54*
Quartermain, D., 106, 110, *125*
Quay, D. C., 337, 339, *347*
Quine, W. V. O., 700, 706

Rabin, C., 644, *657*
Rachlin, H., 102, 106, 107, 119, *124*, *127*, 263, *284*
Rachlin, H. C., 71, 94, 138, *142*
Rachman, S., 17, 19, *22*, 42, 52, 161, 162, 164, *169*, 180, 206, 248, 349, *380*
Rachman, S. J., 216, *227*, 230, 253, *256*
Radbill, S., 200, *206*
Radnitzy, G., 703, *706*
Rae, D. S., 213, *227*
Rainey, C. A., 42, *54*
Ramsey, E., 317, 325, 346, *347*
Rapee, R., 213, *227*
Rapee, R. M., 210, 215, *227*
Rapoport, A., 615, *635*
Rappoport, A., 362, *383*
Rashotte, M. E., 68, *94*
Rasmussen, B., 416n, 425, *438*
Rave, E., 502, *527*
Ray, R. D., 615, 616, 630, 631, *635*
Rayner, P., 31, *56*

Rayner, R., xiii, *xix*, *22*
Razran, G., 216, 217, *227*
Rea, J. A., 594, 595, *604*
Reading, C., 239, *256*
Reardon, D. M., 591, *606*
Rechenberg, H., 611n, *635*
Reed, L., 390, 393, 394, 395, *413*
Reede, L., 359
Reese, H. W., 287, 288, 289, 290, 291, 293, 295, 306, 306, *310*, 555, 556, 557, 558, 559, 560, 565, 574, 575, *581*, *583*
Reese, L., 48, *49*, 353, 374, 391, *407*
Regier, D. A., 213, *227*
Rehm, L., 520, 521, *527*
Rehm, L. P., 357, 380, 392, *411*
Reich, T., 337, *343*
Reichman, S., 467, *472*
Reid, A. K., 116, 117, *125*
Reid, J. B., 314, 315, 317, 318, 324, 325, 326, 327, 328, 329, 330, 331, 332, 333, 338, *343*, 346, *347*, *348*
Reinking, R. H., 37, *54*
Reisenzein, R., 386, 387, 388, 390, *411*
Reiss, S., 47, *54*, 55, 362, *380*
Remy, P., 499, 500, 509, 511, 512, 514, 516, *528*
Repp, A. C., 586, 587, 588, 591, 594, 595, *606*, *607*
Repucci, N. D., 397, *408*
Rescorla, R. A., 77, *91*, 164, *169*, 184, 206, 216, *227*
Resick, P. A., 459, *472*
Rest, S., 390, 393, 394, 395, *413*
Revusky, S. H., 72, *94*
Reyna, L. J., 17, *22*, 44, *57*
Reynolds, D. J., 231, *255*
Reynolds, G. S., 106, 108, *124*
Rhodes, L., 213, *227*
Rhodewalt, F., 571, *583*
Rhyne, L. L., 416n, *440*
Ribich, F., 388, *409*
Riccio, D. C., 148, 154, 156, *166*, *169*, *170*
Richards, C. S., 274, *283*
Richardson, R., 148, 156, *170*
Richman, G., 594, *605*
Riegel, K. F., 287, 291, *310*
Riegel, K. R., 555, 560, *583*
Rimm, D. C., 279, *283*, 388, *412*, 466, *472*
Rincover, A., 141, *143*, 590, *607*
Risley, T. R., 60, *92*
Ritt, L., 496, *524*

Rittenauer-Schatka, H., 355, *381*
Ritter, B., 47, *49*
Robbins, F. R., 590, *605*
Robins, C., 393, *409*
Robins, C. J., 370, *380*
Robinson, A., 239, *256*
Robinson, E. A., 319, 335, *347*
Robinson, S., 587, 589, 592n, *604*
Rodgers, T. A., 593, *608*
Rodick, J. D., 302, *311*
Rodin, J., 362, 380, 386, 388, *412*
Rogers, C. R., xii, *xix*, 554, *583*
Rogers, L., 359, *377*
Rogers, P., 419n, *438*
Rogers, P. L., 419n, 425, *442*
Rogers, R. W., 359, 361, 378, *381*
Roitblat, 63, 76, *94*
Rokke, P., 520, 521, *527*
Rollick, S., 451, *472*
Rollnick, S., *463*
Romanczyk, R. G., 278, *284*
Romano, J. M., 361, *378*
Romano, S. J., 192, *202*
Ronbinson, S., *591*
Rose, G. D., 683, *690*
Rose, M. P., 34, *53*
Rosen, H., 290, *311*
Rosenbaum, M., 16, *21*, 271, *284*, 507, 509, 519, *527*
Rosenbaum, R. M., 390, 393, 394, 395, *413*
Rosenberg, N., 533, 534, *551*
Rosendahl, E. H., 279, *282*
Rosenthal, D., 47, *55*
Rosenthal, L., 416n, 437, 520, *527*
Rosenthal, R., 419n, 425, 438, *442*
Rosenthal, T. L., 354, 367, *380*
Rosenzweig, S., 425n, *439*
Rosewater, L., 501, 502, 511, *527*
Rosnow, R. L., 558, *581*
Ross, D., 210, *226*
Ross, L., 386, 388, 398, 399, *412*
Rotgers, F., 687, *688*
Rothbart, M. K., 554, *580*
Rothenberg, B. B., 416n, 425, *442*
Rotter, J. B., 351, 362, 363, *380*
Rourke, D. A., 593, *608*
Rousso, P., 100, *127*
Routh, D. K., 337, 339, *347*
Rowe, D. C., 337, *347*
Roy, A. K., 136, 139, *143*
Roy-Byrne, P. P., 214, *228*

Rozin, P., 71, 94, 109, *127*
Ruben, D., 539n, *550*
Ruben, D. H., 615, *635*
Rubin, M., 39, *55*
Ruderman, A. J., 351, 365, *377*
Rudestam, K. E., 278, *284*
Ruehlman, L. S., 270, 271, *282*
Rugh, J. D., 60, *92*
Rumelhart, D. E., 234, *255*
Runck, B., 279, *284*
Rush, A., 419n, 438, 510, 521, 524, *527*
Rush, A. J., 368, 369, 370, 371, 374, 385, 392, 399, 400, *407*
Russell, B., 613, *635*
Russell, D., 394, 411, *413*
Rutter, M., 288, 292, 294, 295, 296, 297, 303, 306, *311*
Ryan, P., 242, *252*
Rybarczyk, B. D., 371, *380*

Safran, J. D., 571, *581*
Sajwaj, T., 139, *144*
Salmon, P. G., 352, *375*
Salovey, P., 354, 369, 380, *382*
Salter, A., 17, 22, 32, *55*
Sameroff, A. J., 290, *311*, 615, *635*
Sandberg, G. G., 452, 453, *472*
Sanderson, W. C., 210, *227*
Santostefano, S., 294, 302, *311*
Sappington, A. A., 262, *284*
Sarah, E., 513, *527*
Sarason, B. R., 352, *381*
Sarason, I. G., 352, *381*
Saslow, G., iv, *ix*
Sasso, G., 594, 604, *607*
Sattler, J. M., 296, *311*
Sayers, S., 401, *407*
Scarr, S., 292, 294, *311*, 561, *583*
Schachter, D. L., 77, *94*
Schachter, S., 386, 387, 388, 389, 390, *412*
Schade, M. L., 416n, 417, 418, 420n, *436*
Schaeffer, R. W., 100, 109, *127*
Schallow, J. R., 274, *284*
Schank, R. C., 419, 420, *442*
Schaumann, L., 351, *375*
Schauss, S., 593, *604*
Schefft, B. K., 265, 274, 275, 282, 629, *634*
Scheier, M. F., 266, 267, 268, 269, *280*
Schell, R. M., 590, *605*
Schleifer, M., 402, *412*
Schleser, R., 302, *311*

Stouthamer-Loeber, M., 337, *344*
Stoyva, J. M., 37, *50*
Strack, F., 355, *381*
Strack, S., 425, *442*
Strauss, C. C., 250, *252*
Strelau, J., 554, *583*
Strieber, S., 317, *347*
Strosahl, K., 567, *582*
Strupp, H., 43, *55*, 655, *656*
Stunkard, A. J., 352, 363, *380*
Suarez, A., 553, *582*
Suinn, R. M., 244, *257*
Sullivan, H. S., xiii, *xix*
Summers, A., 497, 498, *528*
Sutherland, E. H., 336, *348*
Swann, J. M., 80, *95*
Sweet, A. A., 46, 52, *56*
Symons, D., 483, 490, *494*
Szabadi, E., 133, 135, 137, 138, 139, *142*

Tablada, C., 544, *551*
Taft, R., 425, *442*
Tagiuri, R., 425, *442*
Tallman, J. F., 37, *56*
Tapert, S. F., 446, 462, *471*
Taplin, P. S., 318, 333, *348*
Taras, M. E., 587, *606*
Tarbox, A. R., 279, *280*
Taub, E., 41, *56*
Taubman, M. T., 590, *605*
Taylor, C. B., 353, 359, *373, 374*
Taylor, J. C., 587, 592n, *604*
Taylor, J. G., 40, *56*, 611n, *635*
Taylor, P., 632, *635*
Taylor, S. E., 271, *284*, 421, *437*
Tchida, G. R., 388, *412*
Teasdale, J., 554, *580*
Teasdale, J. D., 362, 371, 373, *382*, 390, 395, 396, *406*
Teitelbaum, H. A., 31, *56*
Teitelbaum, P., 109, *127*
Tennant, C., 503, *528*
Terdal, L. G., 296, 297, 298, 299, *310*
Terhune, W. S., 35, *56*
Teri, L., 371, *379*
Terman, L. M., 680, *693*
Terrell, F., 392, *409*
Testa, M., 351, *379*
Tharp, R. G., 274, *284*
Thomas, A. T., 292, 300, *311*
Thomas, D. R., 156, *170*
Thomas, G., 519, *528*

Thompson, H., 296, *308*
Thompson, R. E., 425n, *438*
Thompson, T. N., 560, *583*
Thoresen, C. E., 265, 275, *284*
Thoreson, C., 507, 519, 526, *528*
Thoreson, R. W., 507, *528*
Thorndike, E. L., xiii, *xix*, 71, 73, *95*
Thorne, F. C., 624, *635*
Tierney, K. J., 68, *91*, 113, 114, 115, 121, 126, *127*
Tiffany, S. T., 246, 247, 252, 253, *257*
Timberlake, W., 59, 60, 61, 63, 65, 66, 67, 69, 70, 71, 72, 73, 74, 77, 79, 80, 81, 82, 83, 84, 85, 88, 89, 90, *91*, 93, 100, 101, 102, 104, 105, 107, 108, 109, 112, 113, 115, 116, *124, 125, 127*, 128, 139, *144*
Tobin, D. L., 359, *377*
Tolman, E. C., 130, *144*, 670, *693*
Tooby, J., 78, *91*, 483, 484, *494*
Torgersen, S., 214, *227*
Toth, S. L., 296, 299, 303, *307*
Trattner, J., 100, 101, 112, *124*
Trivers, R. L., 490, *494*
Trotsky, L., 545, *551*
Troutman, B. R., 353, *376*
Trower, P., 416, 417, 419, 419n, 420, 425n, *442*
Truax, C. B., 554, *583*
Truax, P., 467, *473*
Trumble, D., 153, *166*
Tsai, M., 564, *581*, 637, 638, 639n, 640, 644, 646, 647, 648, 649, 650, 654, 655, *657*
Tsujimoto, R. N., 385, 389, *408*
Tuckman, B. W., 358, 361, *381*
Turk, D. C., 354, *382*
Turner, D. C., 77, *96*
Turner, J. A., 361, *378*
Turner, J. R., 243, *257*
Turner, S. M., 362, 383, 416n, *436*
Tutek, D., 553, *582*
Tversky, A., 354, 355, *382*, 399, *410*
Twardosz, S., 139, *144*
Twentyman, C., 416n, 427, *442*
Tyrer, P., 387, *410, 412*
Tyron, W. W., 659, *693*

Uhde, T. W., 214, *228*
Ullmann, L. P., xiii, xiv, *xix*, 14, 15, 18, 19, *21*, 660, 689, *693*

Wilcoxon, L. A., 25, 47, *52*
Wilder, J., 40, *56*
Williams, B., 319, *348*
Williams, D. E., 587, 593, *605, 607*
Williams, J. M. G., 569, *584*
Williams, L. S., 391, *413*
Williams, M. L., 118, 119, *123*
Williams, R. N., 261, *285*
Williams, R. W., 163, *170,* 181, *207*
Williams, S. L., 353, 354, 356, 357, 358n, 359, 360, 361, 362, 366, 367, 368, 371, *374, 376, 382, 383*
Williamson, P. N., 632, *634*
Wilson, G. T., 129, *144,* 151, *170,* 349, 354, 368, 369, 371, *375, 383*
Wilson, P. H., 446, 467, 469, *473*
Wiltz, N. A., 331, *348*
Wincze, J. P., 387, *410*
Wine, J., 352, *383*
Wing, L., 45, *52*
Wing, R. R., 279, *285*
Winterling, V., 590, *608*
Wisocki, P., 455, *473*
Wittgenstein, L., xv, xvi, *xix*
Wolf, M. M., 660n, 661, 678, 685, 692, 693
Wolf, N., 500, *528*
Wollstonecraft, M., 495, *528*
Wolpe, J., xiii, *xix.* 17, *22,* 24, 28, 29, 32, 33, 34, 38, 39, 40, 44, 45, 46, *56, 57,* 153, 159, *171,* 177, *207,* 216, 228, 231, *257,* 357, 358n, *383,* 504, 505, 507, 510, 513, 528, 661, 693
Wong, S. E., 416n, *439*
Wood, R., 351, 352, 358, 359, 360, 364, 370, *374, 375, 382, 383*
Woods, J. H., 109, *124*

Woods, R. M., 31, *56*
Woods, S. W., 210, *225*
Worell, J., 499, 500, 509, 511, 514, 516, *528*
Worrell, J., 512
Wozny, M., 104, 105, 106, 109, 111, 112, *124, 128*
Wright, C. L., 367, *374*
Wright, E. O., 541n, 546, *552*
Wright, J., 351, *383*
Wright, T. L., 361, *379*
Wruble, M. K., 632, *636*
Wuesthoff, A., 451, *471*
Wynne, C. K., 77, *94*
Wynne, L. C., 181, 182, 183, *206*

Yates, A. J., 25, *57*
Yates, B. T., 361, *376*
Yeomans, F., 574, *581*
Yoerger, K., 328, *347*
Yukelson, D., 352, *382*

Zack, J., 251, *252*
Zajonc, R. B., 554, 562, 563, *581, 584*
Zanarini, M. C., 569, *581*
Zander, J. R., 239, *257*
Zarcone, J. H., 589, 593, *605*
Zarcone, J. R., 593, *608*
Zeiss, A. M., 391, *410*
Zettle, R. D., 646, *658*
Zibung-Hoffman, P., 416n, *442*
Zigler, E., 416n, 424, *443*
Zillman, P., 388, *413*
Zimbardo, P. G., 386, 388, *407, 412*
Zirkel, S., 271, *280*
Zlutnick, S., 630, *636*
Zuckerman, M., 571, *584*
Zuriff, G. E., 261, *285*
Zuroff, D. C., 364, *382*

SUBJECT INDEX

731

in 24-hr environment, 87–88, 155
in unbaited maze, 77, 81, 83
vicious-circle behavior, 157–158
Anticipation, 80–81
Anxiety/anxiety disorders
alarm theory, 222–224
as maladaptive learned behavior, 23
attributional styles in, 394
behavior therapy techniques for, 23
cognitive errors in, 370
conservation of, 181–182, 183–185
in experimental neurosis, 28–29, 30
expression of affect and, 32
extinction procedures for, 44–45
eye movement desensitization in treatment of, 39
hierarchy of fear responses, 33
identification of precipitating events, 161–163
manipulating physiological arousal in, 387
memory network coherence in, 238
panic and, 218–222
panic vs., 224
pharmacological inhibition, 37
predisposing factors, 222–223
in psychological behaviorism, 684
reciprocal inhibition, 24, 30, 48–49
relaxation-based treatment, 33
self-efficacy strategies for, 369, 370–371, 391–392
self-efficacy vs. anticipatory fear, 367–368
sexual arousal in inhibition of, 37–38
systematic desensitization in treatment of, 34–35
verbally induced inhibition, 38–39
Apparently irrelevant decisions, 448
Appetitive systems
avoidance behavior vs., 178–179
in bioinformational theory–research, 239, 245–247, 250
in motivational–emotional organization, 239
Assertiveness, in functional analytic psychotherapy, 643
Assertiveness training
as feminist therapy, 513–516, 523–524
criticism of, 514–515
outcome research, 514, 516
reciprocal inhibition in, 32

in relapse prevention, 458
therapeutic goals, 32
Assessment
action identification, 363–364
analogue studies, 594–595
anxiety-precipitating events, 161–163
assertiveness, 514–515
attributional style, 403
of decoding skills, in social competence model, 424–433
developmental perspective, 295–299
diagnostic classification issues, 173–174, 250–251
emotional processing, 248
environmental, 298
functional analytic psychotherapy with couples, 644–645
goal systems, 271, 276
in hypothesis-based interventions, 592–601
in implosive therapy, 187–190
in interbehavioral psychology, 626, 631–632
marital distress, 403
matching law, 133–136, 138–139
microprocess modeling, 272
of molar regulatory models, 112
in natural settings, 595–601
obstacles to instrument development, 434
paired baseline, 66–68, 70, 113–114
in psychological behaviorism, 685–686
in relapse prevention theory, 451, 453, 458
in response-based reinforcement, 111
self-efficacy, 355–356, 360, 364–365
sequential response patterns, 630–631
social competence of rapists, 428–433
social competency, 417–419, 421
socialization processes, 322, 338
startle reflex, 240–241, 250
in three-systems view of fear, 230–231
in validation of social competence model, 423–424
verbal estimates of baseline responding, 120
watching for clinically relevant behaviors, 643, 647
Attachment theory, 304
Attributional Style Questionnaire, 403

Attributional styles
    abstinence violation effect, 460
    assessment, 403
    conceptual development, 395–396
    control theory, 268
    in depression, 396, 400–401
    diathesis-stress reasoning in, 396, 403
    environmental factors, 398–399
    gender differences in, 521–522
    gender differences in helplessness orientation, 397–398
    hopelessness theory, 396–397, 403–404
    internal schemas in, 399–400
    in marital distress, 403–404
    outcome research, 400–401
    reattribution training for, 397, 398
Attribution theory
    attributional styles in, 395–401
    clinical applications, 385–386
    in couples work, 401–405
    misattribution training, 386–390
    outcome research, 405
    reattribution training, 386, 390–401
    responsibility judgments, 402–403
    sequence of arousal states, 387–388
    two-factor theory of emotion, 386, 387, 388
Autism, 586
Automatic reinforcement, 36, 589, 590
Automatic thoughts, 46, 246
Autonomic responding
    as avoidance behavior, 177–178
    in desensitization treatment, 34
    feedback-based conditioning of, 60
    in posttraumatic stress disorder, 243
    in psychopathy, 241–242
    reciprocal inhibition in, 26–27
Avoidance behaviors
    in anxiety, 221
    bioinformational theory–research, 241–245
    in borderline personality disorder, 570
    conservation of anxiety hypothesis, 181–182, 183–185
    in criminal psychopathy, 241–242
    fear in, 159
    human vs. animal, 159–161
    in motivational–emotional organization, 239
    neurotic paradox, 179–181
    partial irreversibility theory, 182

in posttraumatic stress disorder, 242–243
    reward in, 146–147
    Sidman avoidance task, 160
    strength of, in fear theory, 153
    in stress, 243–244
    two-factor theory, 147, 176–179
Baseline assessment, 66–68, 113–114
Basic behavioral repertoire, 678, 680, 682, 683, 685–686
Behavior
    definition, 14
    environmental model, 13
    medical model, 13
Behavioral contracting, 60
Behavior change. *See also* Therapeutic change
    adaptation to experimental settings in, 81–82
    allocation of, 130
    assertiveness training in, 32
    capacity for, 13
    in causal-system model, 64–65, 78–80, 89–90
    changing behavior systems in, 85–86
    in children, 305
    conditioning modes in, 85
    deprivation schedules in, 80–81
    in developmental perspective, 287
    human vs. animal, 159–161
    presentation of significant stimuli for, 84–87
    response-contingent reinforcement in, 59–60
    system approach, 69–70, 73
    in 24-hr environment, 87–88
    verbal processes in, 662, 664
Behavior influence, 15
Behaviorism, 12, 17–18
    as heuristic, 664
    behavior therapy and, 662–664, 687
    conceptual development, 504–506, 610, 659–662, 670, 686–687
    feminist thought and, 505, 506
    personality concepts in, 679
Behavior modification
    clinical application, 506–507
    conceptual development, 14–16
    first reference, 14
Behavior therapy
    as paradigm shift, 17–19

behaviorism and, 662–664, 687
bioinformational theory, 248–249
choice behavior in, 129–130
class distinctions in practice of, 546–547
conceptual development, iv–v, 12–14, 12–20, 24–25, 662–663, 687, 705–706
control theory concepts, 273, 628–630
core ideas, ii–iii, 6, 466
cultural analysis in, 530
cultural materialism and, 535
definition, v–vi, 129
developmental perspective, 295, 305–306
earliest references, 16–17
early theorists, 18–19
evolutionary theory and, 485–489
experimental research and, 704–705
feminist therapy and, 511–513
interdisciplinary approaches, 625
Marxist thought and, 531, 535, 544–548
mechanism of change in, 141
outcome research, 43–44, 506–507
reciprocal inhibition theory, 43–44
relapse prevention theory, 466
scientific method in, 475–476, 505, 696–697, 701–702
self-control approaches, 260–261, 272–278
social context of, 13–14, 17–18, 529–531, 537
systems theory, 615–616
theoretical basis, 2
therapeutic relationship in, 507
types of, iv–v, 18
Belongingness, 71
Benzodiazepines, 36
Biofeedback
as relaxation technique, 37
therapist-related factors in, 41
Bioinformational theory
aversive system research, 241–245
in behavior therapy, 248–249
chronic stress in, 243–244
conceptual development, 229, 241
criminal psychopathy in, 241–242
emotion–memory networks in, 233–234
goals of, 232

imagery research in, 234–237
motivational–emotional organization in, 239–241
pain and illness states in, 244–245
physiological responding in imagery procedures, 231, 234–235, 236, 237, 239, 247
posttraumatic stress disorder in, 242–243
research needs, 250–251
sexual functioning in, 247
substance abuse in, 245–247
therapeutic change in, 248–249
Biosocial learning theory, 554, 560–561
Black box variables, 353, 504, 683
Blame, 402–403
Borchelt, Peter, 86
Borderline personality disorder
active passivity vs. apparent competence in, 566–569
affect dysregulation in, 570–573
biosocial theory, 554, 560–561
blocking emotional responding in, 571–572
dialectical behavioral therapy, 553, 560–562, 574–577
dialectical dilemmas in, 566, 568, 570
emotional vulnerability vs. self-invalidation in, 562–566
etiology, 560–561
expectations in, 563–564
invalidating environment in, 561, 564–565
learned helplessness in, 566–567
masking of negative emotion in, 567–568
patterns of behavior in, 562
therapist dilemmas in, 566, 568–569, 570
unrelenting crises vs. inhibited grieving in, 569–570
Brown, Judson, 157

Change. See Behavior change; Therapeutic change
Changeover delay, 137–138
Child abuse, 149
brain decoding of trauma in, 195–197
implosive therapy, 192–195
incidence, 192
Child behavior, in coercion theory, 315
Child therapy

activity–goal directedness in, 300–302
age-appropriate behavior, 296
assessment, 295–299
child cognitive abilities and, 300–302
coercion theory, 329–337
developmental perspective, 288, 295, 305–306
holistic perspective, 299–300
parent-training interventions, 299–300
pathogenesis, 300
problem-solving strategies, 302–303
resolution of early developmental tasks in, 303–305
social competence theories, 416
Chlorpromazine, 37
Choice behavior
all behavior as, 141
applied research, 133–136
as function of relative reinforcement rates, 133
changeover delay effects in, 137–138
child problem-solving strategies, 303
creation of meaning in, 263–264
decision skills in social competency, 421–423
matching law model, 70–71, 130–132
operant research in, 129–130
perceived self-efficacy in, 352
in reinforcement of aggressive behavior, 319–321
in self-control theory, 262–263
Circadian effects, 80–81
Classical conditioning, 145–146, 148–149, 165, 176. *See also* Conditioning
evolution and, 163, 488
indirect acquisition of phobias and, 162
operant conditioning and, 670–675
phobias in, 162, 163, 216
reciprocal inhibition in, 27
responses amenable to, 146, 147
two-factor, two-process theory, 145–146
two-factor theory, 145, 176
Clinically relevant behaviors (CRBs)
application, 644
case examples, 643, 651–654
in couples therapy, 644–645
evoking, 647–649
interpretation of, 651
reinforcement of, 649–651

types of, 642–643, 646–647
watching for, 643, 647
Coercion theory
affective processes in, 339
antisocial trait in, 324
cognitive processes in, 339
competing theories, 334–337
conceptual basis, v, 313–314
contributions of, 338, 339–340, 341–342
developmental course, 314, 315, 323
developmental model, 324–328
family interactions in, 323–324
goals, 313
integration of microsocial–macrosocial processes, 341
macrosocial analysis in, 314, 322–323
macrosocial research in, 329
microsocial analysis in, 314, 322–323
microsocial paradigm, 314–316
organismic perspective in, 340
outcome research, 331–333
parent training in, 325–326, 329–331, 330–331, 332
patterns of interaction in, 315–318
reciprocal interactions in, 315
reinforcement in, 314–315, 318–322, 338
research needs, 338–341
socialization processes in, 314, 315, 322–323
therapeutic change in, 330, 333–334
Cognitive–behavioral chain, 445–446, 453, 455, 463–464
Cognitive–behavior theory/therapy
as feminist therapy, 500, 511–512, 523
with children, 301
clinical focus of, 685
cognitive component, 509–510
conceptual basis, 508
conceptual development, 19–20, 272–273
criticisms of, 510
in depression, 392
experimental research and, 705
graded task assignments in, 392
individual differences in, 523
in marital therapy, 404–405
mechanistic perspective in, 295
psychoanalytic theory and, 508
psychopathology in, 508

relapse model, 447–449
self-efficacy strategies in, 368–371
self-management techniques, 273, 521–522, 524
social competence research and, 419–420
social context, 263
technique, 508–509
therapeutic change in, 45–46, 445–446, 507–508, 510
Cognitive correction, 23
indications for, 32, 45
misapplication of, 34–35
Cognitive processes
in adaptation, 262
in appetitive systems in drug use, 246
in avoidance behaviors, 177–178
in coercion theory, 339
control theory, 266–269
in developmental psychopathology, 294–295
dialectical thinking in, 560
feedback processes in, 266–267
feed-forward function in, 266, 267
goal structuring, 269–271
historical evolution of scientific thinking, 611–616
hypervigilants, 245
negative self-talk, 520
in panic, 210–211, 217, 218
in perceived self-efficacy, 350–353, 354–355, 364
volition in, 262–263
Cognitive restructuring, 515
Common sense, 10
Community psychology, vii
Competition
as evolutionary concept, 476–477
in capitalist economies, 542
Conditioned stimulus. *See also* Stimuli
as warning signal, 160–161
in classical conditioning, 145–146
in fear theory, 148–149, 151, 159
human vs. animal avoidance behavior, 159–161
in implosive theory, 183–186
relaxation in counterconditioning of fear, 153–154
safety signals as, 150
symptom maintenance, 183–185

in two-factor theory, 176
Conditioning. *See also* Classical conditioning; Operant conditioning
in acquisition of psychological disorders, 161–162
behavior therapy and, 17
evolutionary theory and, 487–489
implosive therapy assessment, 189
language in, 678
in naturalistic settings, 660
in psychological behaviorism, 669
reconditioning effect, 153, 184–185
selectivity of association in, 164
Conditioning therapy, 17
Consciousness raising, 503, 508, 522
Conservation of anxiety, 181–182, 183–185
Constraints on learning, 71–72
Continuity assumption, 264–265
Control theory, 266–269, 273. *See also* Self-control theory
Coping imagery procedure, 387
Countertransference, 637
Couples work, 401–405, 416, 492
in functional analytic psychotherapy, 644–645
Criminal behavior, 241–242
Cuba, 543–544
Cultural analysis, 530
Cultural factors, 73, 74
Cultural materialism, 535–537

Decision matrix, 454, 457
Defense mechanisms
in brain decoding of trauma, 195–197
in relapse, 455–456
Denial, 455–456
Depression–depressive disorders
as reasonable response, 512
attributional style in, 396, 400–401
cognitive errors in, 370, 371
conditioned stimulus extinction in, 186
hopelessness theory, 395, 396
implosive therapy, 190
maladaptive anxiety in, 46
in psychological behaviorism, 683–684
reattribution training, 400–401
self-efficacy theory, 368, 369, 370, 371, 392

social competence theories, 415–416

Deprivation schedules, 80–81, 100–101

Desensitization. *See also* Systematic desensitization
pharmacologic relaxation for, 36
relaxation and, 25
in vivo, 35–36

Desiprimine, 121

Developmental disabilities
aversive interventions, 588–589
clinical approaches to, evolution of,
586
self-injurious behaviors (SIBs) in,
586, 590, 593, 594
stereotypic behavior, 591

Developmental perspective
as dialectic process, 291, 560
assessment in, 295–299
clinical application, 288, 295, 305–
306
coercion theory, 314, 315, 317, 323,
324–328
conceptual basis, 288–295
constructivism in, 290
differentiation of goals and modes in,
294, 302–303
directedness in, 294, 300–302
discontinuities in, 291
environmental assessment, 298
focus of, 287
goodness-of-fit models in, 292
holism in, 289–290, 294, 295–300
individual differences in, 292–293
interactional model, 290–291, 292–
293
in interbehavioral psychology, 627–
628
invalidating environment, 564–565
levels of causation in, 291
mechanistic models, 288–289, 295
mobility of behavioral functioning,
294–295, 303–305
obstacles to clinical integration, 288
organismic model, 288–292
parent-training interventions, 299–
300
psychological behaviorism theory,
683
psychological theory in, 287–288
qualitative assessment, 297

structure-function relationship in,
290
targets of intervention, 299
timing of experience in, 292–293
treatment goals, 299

Developmental psychopathology, 288,
293–295

Dialectical behavioral therapy
affective processes in, 562–563, 570–
573
borderline personality disorder in,
560–570
clinical application, 553
cognitive processes in, 563–564
concept of acceptance in, 554, 573–
574
conceptual basis, 553–554
conceptual development, 578–579
consultation for therapist in, 577–578
dialectic philosophy in, 554–561
emotional regulation training in,
576–577
in groups, 574–575, 577
mindfulness training, 575–576
modes of treatment, 574
outcome research, 553
therapeutic change in, 573–574
therapeutic course, 572–573
therapeutic relationship in, 578

Dialectical materialism, 537–539, 556, 558

Dialectical philosophy
praxis in, 557–558
principles of, 555–559
psychology and, 560
therapeutic implications, 557–559

Diathesis–stress reasoning, 396, 403, 560

Differential association theory, 336

Differential reinforcement, 133

Dissociation, 196

Dramatic acting, 27

Eating disorders, 365, 500

Educational settings
analogue assessments in, 595
attributional styles in helplessness orientation, 397–398
molar regulatory theory in, 117–119
naturalistic assessment in, 595–601
women's access, 496–497, 498–499

Electromyographic feedback, 41

Emotion
    affect management techniques, 278
    affect-startle effect, 240
    as action disposition, 233–234
    in bioinformational theory, 233–234, 239–241
    in borderline personality disorder, 562–566, 567–568, 569, 571–573
    classical conditioning of, 675–676
    coercion theory, 339
    control theory, 267–268
    in criminal psychopathy, 241–242
    decoding social information, 425
    in developmental model of aggression, 335
    facial expression and, 571
    in gender role enforcement, 519
    manipulating physiological arousal in, 386–387
    in memory networks, 233–234
    motivation and, 239–241
    regulation of, skills training for, 576–577
    self-efficacy theory, 353
    in therapeutic change, 248–249
    two-factor theory, 386, 387, 388
Emotive imagery technique, 38
Empirical methodology, 3–4, 6–8, 11, 696–697
Epistemology
    Marxist, 538
    in radical behaviorism, 639
    scientific approach, 620–621
Escape, 147, 150, 160, 161
    flooding and, 152
Evolutionary psychology
    individual differences in, 484–485
    mating strategies in, 484
    theoretical basis, 483–484
Evolutionary theory
    adaptation in, 71–72, 477, 479
    behavioral processes and, 480–484
    behavior therapy and, 485–489
    clinical relevance, 492–493
    competition in, 476–477, 480
    criticisms of, 480
    evolution of vision in, 478–479
    fear responses, 211–212
    genetic programs in, 482–483
    gradualist view in, 477, 478–479

    human sexuality and, 489–492
    inheritance of acquired characteristics, 478, 479–480
    mutation in, 476
    natural selection in, 476–477
    prepared learning, 163, 216
    principle concepts, 476–480
    relevance of, 475–476
    saltationist view in, 477, 478
    specialization in, 71–72
Excitation transfer, 388
Expectancy theory, 47
Expectations
    in borderline personality disorder, 563–564
    perceived self-efficacy vs., 351–352, 361–363
Exposure theory, 45
Exposure therapy, 41, 151
Extinction theory, 44–45, 174
Eyeblink response, 240, 242
Eye movement desensitization
    mechanism of change in, 42–43
    research needs, 40
    technique, 39–40
    therapeutic applications, 39

Facial expression, 571
False-memory syndrome, 199, 200–201
Falsifiability test, 5–6, 696, 699–702
    of reciprocal inhibition principle, 25, 43
Families
    contexts of coercive interaction in, 323–324
    patterns of aggressive interaction in, 315–318
    reinforcement of aggressive behavior in, 318–319, 322
Fear
    alarm theory, 211
    as maladaptive learned behavior, 23
    as response to relaxation, 154
    in classical conditioning, 165
    classical conditioning of, 145–146, 148–149
    elimination of, in fear theory, 151–154
    generalization of, with time, 154–156
    imagery research, 237–239

implosive theory, 174
in instrumental learning, 149–151
of predation, feeding vs., 88
reciprocal inhibition of, 24
reconditioning, 153, 184–185
stimuli produced by, 148
symbolic processes in, 156–157, 176–177
symptomatic behavior and, 152–153
three-systems view, 230–231
two-factor theory, 146, 147, 177
vicious-circle behavior in, 157–158
Fear theory
avoidance behavior in, 153, 181–182
clinical application, 151–154
controlled stimulus in, 148–149
criticisms of, 158–165
frustration theory and, 148, 162–163
generalizability of animal research, 159–161
meaning of, 147
prepared learning theory and, 164–165
Feedback
in causal-system model of reinforcement, 65, 66
in cognition, 266–267
conditioning of autonomic responses, 60
in educable mentally retarded, 118
electromyography, 41
in implosive therapy imagery procedure, 187
in instrumental learning based on fear, 149–150
in model of anxiety, 218–219
molar features of reinforcement schedules as, 116–117
Feed-forward function, 266, 267
Feeding behaviors
in deconditioning human behavior, 30–31
deprivation schedules in, 80–81
pharmacologic effects on, in molar regulatory model, 120–122
in postindustrial humans, system model of, 74–76
proximity of reward in reinforcement, 72–73, 74–76, 85
reciprocal inhibition in, 28–30

in 24-hr studies, 88
Feminist thought
affective processes in, 512
assertiveness training, 513–516, 523–524
behaviorism and, 505, 506
cognitive–behavior theory/techniques in, 511–512, 523
conceptual development, 499–501
feminist therapy, 511–513
gender-based social inequity in, 516–517, 518, 522
health behavior model and, 510
micropolitics of sexism, 516–519
political history, 495–499
process of exclusion of women, 518–519
psychology and, 501–502
social learning theory and, 503–504
therapeutic goals, 519–524
women's inequality in household, 522–523
women's inequality in workforce, 516–517, 519, 522
Field theory, 610–611, 612–615
Flooding, 23
efficacy, 41–42
exposure effects in, 45, 151–152
implosion and, 175
mechanism of change in, 42–43
misapplication of, 34–35
for social fears, 35
technical development, 41
theoretical basis, 151, 152
therapeutic applications, 42
Forgetting, reciprocal inhibition in, 28
Framework theory, 667–670
Frustration, fear and, 162–163
Frustration theory, 148
Frustrative nonreward theory, 49
Functional analytic psychotherapy
case example, 651–654
change mechanism in, 637
clinical application, 642–645
contextual meaning of behavior in, 639–640
contributions of, 638
couples therapy, 644–645
generalization of session effects, 640–641

interpretation in, 651
natural reinforcement in, 641–642
practice guidelines, 647–651
research, 654–656
shaping in, 642
theoretical foundations, 638–642
types of clinically relevant behaviors, 642–643, 646–647
within-session contingencies in, 639

Gating, 77
Gender differences
in assertive behavior, 514–515
in attributional styles, 521–522
in classical psychoanalytic theory, 502
in couples work, 644–645
in helplessness orientation, 397–398
in reproductive strategies, 490–492
social role stereotyping, 512–513, 513–514
Generalizability theopry, vii
Generalization of stimulus, 154–156
Genetic factors
in development of aggressive behavior, 337
inheritance of acquired characteristics, 479
predisposition to panic, 214
Gestalt psychology, 613
Goal orientation, in social competence theories, 420
Goal setting
assessment of, 271, 275–276
in depression therapy, 392
developmental perspective, 294, 302–303
in invalidating environment, 565
perceived self-efficacy and, 365
perceived self-efficacy vs., 351
in self-control theory, 269–271
Goal systems analysis, 270–271
Goal Systems Assessment Battery (GSAB), 271, 275–276
Goodness of fit, 72, 292
Grief processes, 569–570
Group therapies
dialectical behavioral therapy in, 574–575, 577
reattribution training in, 400
Guided mastery, 367
Guided participation, 47–48

Habit, 61
Habit reversal, 40
Habituation effects, 45
Harm reduction, 462–463
Hegelian dialectics, 554–556
Helplessness theory, 395, 397–398
Herrnstein's hyperbola, 132–133, 135
Heterosocial Perception Survey, 430
Hopelessness theory, 396–398, 403–404
Hypervigilance, 245
Hypnosis, 39
Hypochondriasis, 190
Hypothesis-based interventions
analogue assessments in, 592, 594–595
categorization of, 591–593
clinical application, 586, 602–603
conceptual approach in, 585, 603
for developmental disabilities, 586
environmentally dependent behaviors in, 590–591
hypotheses for problem behavior, 589–591, 601
impetus for, 588
indirect assessment in, 592, 593–594
naturalistic functional assessment in, 592, 595–602
research opportunities, 603
setting events in, 590–591
stimulation in, 591
Hysteria, 190

Illness, 244–245
Imagery procedures
addictive behaviors, 245–247
in bioinformational research, 234–237
in chronic stress, 243–244
coping imagery procedure, 387
in criminal psychopathy, 241–242
emotional prompts in, 251
in fear research, 237–239
in implosive therapy, 183, 186–187, 191
individual differences in, 236
pain and illness processes in, 244–245
physiological responding in, 231, 234–235, 236, 237, 239, 247
in posttraumatic stress disorder, 242–243
self-initiated processing in, 236–237
sexual response in, 247

technique, 234, 235–236
Implosive theory–therapy, v, 152
    assessment in, 187
    brain decoding of trauma in, 195–197
    classification of avoided-stimulus cues, 188–190
    clinical applications, 190
    enhancement of memorial reactivation, 190–195
    imagery procedures in, 183, 186–187, 191
    stages of memory recovery in, 198–199
    symptomatic behavior in, 178
    symptom maintenance in, 183–185
    theoretical basis, 152, 174–175, 185
    therapeutic change in, 185–186, 199–200, 202
    therapeutic goals, 186
    validation of research in, 200–202
Incidental learning, 60
Incidental teaching, 69–70
Information processing. See also Bioinformation theory
    coercion theory, 339
    in cognitive–behavioral therapy, 508
    control theory, 266–269
    social competence model, 421–423
    social competence theories, 418–420, 434–435
Initial conditions, in behavior systems, 65, 66, 71–76
Insomnia, autogenic training for, 36
Instigation therapy, 18
Insulin injections, 31
Integrative theory-practice
    aggression, 335–336, 340–341
    developmental perspective, 27
    goals of, 173–174
    in interbehavioral psychology, 623–625
Intelligence testing, 685–686
Intentionality, 270
Interactive therapy, 18
Interbehavioral psychology
    as integrative practice, 623–625
    as organizing principle, 618
    assessment in, 626, 631–632
    conceptual basis, 609, 610–611, 613–615, 632
    developmental considerations in, 627–628

field factors in, 621, 625
field theory in, 610–611
in historicocritical analysis, 616–618
interdependence of responses in, 630–631
nature of psychological events in, 621–623
nonpsychological factors in, 625–626
organism as participant in, 621
origins, 610–611
principle of minimum services, 626–627
scientific fundamentals in, 618–623
self-regulation in, 629–630
systems approaches and, 615–616
therapeutic goals in, 628
unit of analysis in, 621
Internal cues, 148–149
    in alarm theory of panic, 216–217
    in implosive theory, 188–189
Interoceptive conditioning, 216–217
Interpretation, 651
Intervention therapy, 18

Janet, P., 614–615

Kantor, J. R., 610–611, 613–614
Knee-jerk response, 25–26
Kuhn, T. S., 12–13

Lakatos, I., 6–7, 11
Lamarck, J. B., 478, 479
Language
    as behavioral research topic, 662, 664, 677
    in behavior therapy, 686
    in coercion theory, 339
    in conditioning, 678
    in describing change processes, 559
    emotional responding, 678
    gender-influenced communications styles, 518–519
    goal specification, 269–270
    in image procedures, 233, 236–237
    in invalidating environment, 561
    psychological behaviorism research, 677–678
    reciprocal inhibition in, 26
    regulation in schizophrenia, 119
    in shaping behavior, 662
    symbolic processes in elicitation of fear, 156–157

verbally induced inhibition of anxiety, 38–39
Laudan, L., 7–8, 11–12
Law of effect, 97, 98–99
Learned helplessness, 395, 508
    in borderline personality disorder, 566–567
Learned resourcefulness, 271
Learning
    in avoidance, 146–147, 159
    based on fear, 149–151
    basic behavioral repertoire for, 678, 682, 683, 685–686
    constraints on, 71–72
    in fear theory, 147–148
    indirect acquisition of phobias, 162
    in panic etiology, 216–218
    preparedness model, 163–165, 216
    in psychological behaviorism, 675, 676–679
    psychopathology as, 23–24
    reciprocal inhibition in, 27–28
    stimulus generalization in, 154
    temporal effects in stimulus generalization, 155–156
    two-factor, two-process theory, 145–146
    in two-factor theory of avoidance, 176, 177, 178–179
    types of, in behavioral theories, 675
Learning theory
    behavior modification as, 15
    early behavior therapy in, 19
Logical positivism, 2–4, 11
    criticism of, 4–5

Marital Attributional Style Questionnaire, 403
Marital therapy, 401–405, 416, 492
Markov process, 334–335
Marxist thought
    as scientific thought, 533–535, 538–539
    behavior therapy and, 531, 535, 544–548
    capitalist economies in, 534, 541–543
    class conflict in, 540–541, 545–547
    cultural materialism vs., 535–537
    dialectical materialism in, 537–539
    dialectic philosophy in, 554, 556

epistemology of, 538
historical materialism in, 536, 539–541
origins of, 531–533
social application, 543–544
Mass communications, 500
Matching law, 70
    applied research, 133–136
    clinical application, 136–137, 141
    coupled regulation model and, 71
    future research, 139–141
    Herrnstein's hyperbola, 132–133, 135
    limitations of, in applied settings, 137–139
    models, 130–132
    in reinforcement of aggressive behavior, 319–321, 338
    response covariation and, 140–141
    self-control theory and, 263
    symptom substitution and, 139–140
Meditative practices, 575, 576
Memory
    in causal-system model of behavior, 76–78
    decoding of trauma, 195–197
    in emotion networks, 233–234
    false/implanted, 199, 200–201
    phobia-specific networks, 237–238
    reactivation in implosive therapy, 190–195
    species differences, 77
    stages of recovery, in implosive therapy, 198–199
Mental retardation, 117–118, 586
Meprobamate, 37
Misattribution training
    drug-induced arousal, 388
    perceived self-efficacy and, 389
    pharmacotherapy in, 387
    reattribution training vs., 390
    research, 386–390
    theoretical basis, 386
    therapeutic efficacy, 389
    therapeutic goals, 386
Modeling, 47–48, 366
    in relapse prevention, 459
    in socialization process, 504
Modus tollens, 5–6, 697–698
Molar regulatory models of reinforcement
    baseline data collection for, 120

baseline maintenance in, 113–114
clinical application, 112, 119
conservation model, 108–111, 112, 119
coupled regulation model, 71, 102, 107–108
drug effects on feeding and, 120–122
in educational settings, 117–119
future developments, 122–123
limitations of, 113, 123
minimum distance model, 102, 105–106
optimality models, 102–104
quantitative prediction in, 104
relative response deprivation model, 102, 104–105, 112
sensitivity to molar variables in, 116–117
subject preferences in, 114–115
theoretical basis, 102, 111–113
time frames in, 115–116
value maximizing model, 102, 106–107
Motivation
action theory, 270
appetitive systems in, 245–247
attributional theory, 393–394
bioinformational theory, 239–241, 245–247
conditioning of, 85
culturally specific modes, 74
dialectical behavioral model, 573
in early-phase therapy, 275–276
effect of reinforcement on, 86–87
goal structuring, 269–271
intention vs., 270
in response-contingent reinforcement, 72–73
Motivation Assessment Scale, 593
Multimodal therapy, vii
Multiple personality disorder, 190
Muscle relaxation, 33, 36–37

Natural selection, 476–477
Skinner on, 487–488
Neurophysiology
anger–anxiety inhibitory centers in, 32
in panic, 210
of reciprocal inhibition, 25–26

Neuroses
as maladaptive learned behavior, 23
conceptual development, 23–24
reciprocal inhibition in treatment of, 28–31
vicious-circle behavior, 157–158
Neurotic paradox, 175, 179–181, 183
Nonspecific effects, 40–41, 46

Obesity, 393
Object relations theory, 304
Obsessive–compulsive disorders, 188
flooding in treatment of, 42
implosive therapy for, 190
memory network coherence in, 238
Operant conditioning. See also Conditioning
of causal attributions, 394–395
classical conditioning and, 670–675
in development of behavior therapy, 14, 16–17
evolution and, 487–488
fear theory and, 147, 149–151
reciprocal inhibition in, 28
simple-causal model, 61
Organismic theory
causality in, 291
coercion theory and, 340
constructivism in, 290
in developmental conceptualizations, 288–289, 292
developmental discontinuities in, 291
dialectic processes in development, 291
holism in, 289–290
reciprocal influences in, 290–291
structure–function relationship in, 290
Orthogenetic principle, 294
Outcome research
assertiveness training, 514, 516
attributional style, 400–401
attribution theory, 405
behavior therapy, 43–44, 506–507
child cognitive abilities in, 301
coercion theory interventions, 331–334
cognitive–behavioral therapy, 510
cognitive interventions in marital distress, 404–405

cognitive therapy, 46
dialectical behavioral therapy, 553
early relational interventions, 304–305
equivalence of therapies in, 40–41
eye movement desensitization, 40
functional analytic psychotherapy, 654–655, 656
hypothesis-based interventions, 589
misattribution training, 389
multidimensional fear measurement in, 231–232
perception of self-efficacy in, 47–48
rational-emotive therapy, 46
relapse prevention, 464, 468–469
role of, ii, 654–655
self-control interventions, 278–279
self-efficacy expectancies, 391
startle reflex assessment in, 241, 250

Pain, 244–245
Panic
alarm theory, 211–212, 221–222
anxiety vs., 224
anxious apprehension and, 218–220, 221–222
biological model, 210
biopsychosocial model, 211, 215, 218, 221, 224
cognitive model, 210–211
conceptual development, 209
etiology, 213–214
future alarms, 220–221
genetic risk, 214
learned alarms in, 216–218
memory network coherence in, 238
prevalence, 212–213
research needs, 224–225
stress and, 214–216
symptoms, 212
Paradigmatic behaviorism. See Psychological behaviorism
Paradigmatic thinking, 1, 12–13, 17–18
Parent-training interventions, 299–300
in coercion theory, 325–326, 330–331, 332
Partial irreversibility, 182
Patterns of interaction, 315–318, 561
Peer interactions, in development of aggression, 317–318, 321–322, 327–328
Perceptual filters, 77

Personality theory, 679–681
Pharmacotherapy
antidepressant effects on feeding behavior, 121–122
to diminish unpleasant affect, 386–387
induced panic, 210
in inhibition of anxiety, 37
insulin treatment for anxiety, 31
in misattribution training, 387
in relaxation for desensitization, 36
Phobia(s). See also specific phobia
conditioning processes in, 216
desensitization in vivo for, 35–36
evolutionary predisposition, 163
fear theory research, 159–160
feeding behaviors in deconditioning of, 31
flooding in treatment of, 42
guided mastery for, 367
hierarchy of fear responses, 33
imagery procedures with, 235–236, 237–238
implosive therapy for, 190
phobia-specific responding, 237–238
precipitating events, 161–163
prepared learning in, 163
self-efficacy assessment in, 48, 391
startle reflex in, 241
systematic desensitization for, 34
Piaget, J., 289–291
Play behaviors, 174
Popper, K. R., 4–6, 11, 696–698, 699
Pornography, 431–432, 433, 492
Positivism, 19
Posttraumatic stress disorder
in bioinformational theory, 242–243
eye movement desensitization for, 39, 40
implosive therapy for, 190
memory network coherence in, 238, 242
self-control issues in, 521
startle response in, 243, 250
Praise, 641
Predictability hypothesis, 334
Predispositions, 71–72
Premack, D., 67, 98–100
Prepared learning, 163–165, 216
Probability differential hypothesis, 98–100
Problem-solving strategies, 302–303
for controlling family aggression, 326

verbal processes in, 662
Psychoanalytic theory
    cognitive-behavioral therapy and, 508
    developmental, 304
    development of, i–ii
    feminist thought and, 501–502
    neuroses in, 23–24
Psychodynamic therapies
    equivalence of therapies, 40–41
    outcome research, 43–44
    transference–countertransference in, 637
Psychological behaviorism, 659
    abnormal behavior theory, 682–684
    assessment in, 685–686
    basic behavioral repertoire, 678, 680, 682, 683, 685–686
    basic principles, 670–676
    clinical application, 684–686
    conditioning in, 669, 675
    developmental perspective in, 683
    emotional response to stimulus in, 675–676
    goals of, 666–667
    learning theory, 675, 676–679
    personality theory, 679–681
    radical behaviorism and, 664–670
    reinforcement in, 675–676
    theory construction in, 667–670
Psychopathology
    anxiety vs. panic disorders, 224
    as classical conditioning, 146, 148–149
    as cognitive misconception, 32, 45–46
    as maladaptive learning, 23–24, 46
    assessment of child disorders, 296–297
    bioinformational theory, 241–245
    cognitive–behavioral theory, 508
    decoding social information in, 425
    developmental perspective, 300
    diagnostic classification, 173–174, 250–251
    gender role stereotyping and, 503–504
    identification of anxiety-precipitating events, 161–163
    implosive theory, 174, 175, 190
    neurotic paradox, 179–181, 183
    in nonpsychotic depression, 46

origins of panic, 210–211
    in psychological behaviorism, 682–684
    relapse prevention theory, 449
    social competence theories, 416
    symptomatic behavior in, 152–153
Psychosomatic disorders, 190
Public speaking, 520–521

Radical behaviorism
    behavioral model, 504, 505
    behavior therapy and, 663
    contextualism and, 639
    emotional responding in, 676
    experimental analysis of behavior method, 661–662
    functional analytic psychotherapy, 637, 638
    language processes in, 662
    limitations of, 675, 677
    Marxism and, 548
    mediation of learning and, 159
    misconceptions about, 638
    personality theory in, 681
    psychological behaviorism and, 664–670
    self-control in, 263
    terminology, 666
    theory construction in, 667
    values analysis in, 547
Raised expectations of self-efficacy, 47–48
Rational–emotive therapy, 46
Rationalization, 455–456
Reattribution training
    achievement motivation and, 393–394
    in behavioral marital therapy, 405
    to change attributional style, 397, 398
    collaborative empiricism and, 400
    in depression, 400–401
    misattribution training vs., 390
    self-efficacy theory and, 390–393
    theoretical basis, 390
    therapeutic goals, 386, 390
Reciprocal inhibition
    in autonomic processes, 26–27
    in behavior therapy, 43–44
    conceptual development, 17, 24–25
    definition, 25
    experimental observation, 24
    frustrative nonreward theory and, 49
    in habit reversal therapy, 40

in language processes, 26
in learning processes, 27–28
neurophysiological basis, 25–26
nonspecific effects as, 41
in therapeutic change, 24, 25, 48–49
in therapeutic relationship, 25
therapeutic techniques mediated by, 32–40
in treatment of neuroses, 28–31, 48
Reciprocal innervation, 26
Reconditioning, 153, 184–185
Reframing, 460–461
Reinforcement, 111. *See also* Molar regulatory models of reinforcement
absence of unconditioned stimulus in, 178–179
as adaptation to schedule constraints, 102
assessment of, 592–601
in behavioral change, 59–60, 78–80
causal-system model, 64–69, 70, 89–90
changeover delay in, 137–138
in choice situations, 70–71, 129–130
of clinically relevant behaviors, 649–650
coercion theory, 314–315, 318–322, 338
in complex environments, 87–88
conceptual development, 60, 97–99
conservation model, 108–111, 112
contingency schedule in causal-system model, 65, 66–69, 70
coupled regulation model, 71, 102, 107–108
deprivation schedules in, 61, 80–81
differential reinforcement of incompatible behavior, 133
differential reinforcement of other behavior, 133
experimental development, 661–662
experimental vs. practice application, 79–80
Herrnstein's hyperbola, 132–133
in human behavior, 73–76
in hypothesis-based interventions, 589–590
identification of reinforcers, 138–139
individual differences in, 98
initial conditions in causal-system model, 65, 66, 71–76, 77
interrelationships of systems in, 73

intrinsic motivation and, 86–87
known reinforcers in, 97–98
law of effect in, 97, 98–99
limitations of traditional model, 60, 63–64
manipulation of experimental conditions, 82–83
matching law in, 130–132
memory in, 76–78
minimum distance model, 102, 105–106
model of human feeding behaviors, 74–76
motivational mode in, 72–73
in naturalistic settings, 660
optimality models, 102–104
paired baseline assessment, 66–67, 70, 112, 113–114
predictive capacity of models, 63, 64, 66–67, 104
probability differential hypothesis vs., 98–100
proximity of reward in, 72–73, 74–76, 77–78, 85, 639
reciprocal inhibition in, 27–28
regulation of behavior in causal-system model, 66–71
reinforcer value in, 69
relative rate of, 141
relative response deprivation model, 102, 104–105, 112
response covariation, 140–141
response deprivation condition in, 100–101, 102, 117–118, 119
response satiation condition in, 101–102
safety signals in, 150
settling point in, 66–67
simple-causal model, 61–64, 88
stimulus processing in causal system, 65, 76–78
systems approach, 69–70, 73
therapeutic implications, 639, 641–642
transituational reinforcers, 97–99
value maximizing model, 102, 106–107
Relapse fantasies, 452, 453
Relapse prevention
clinical application, 446
conceptual development, 445–446
self-control theory and, 278

Relapse prevention theory
  abstinence violation effect, 448–449, 460–461, 464–465
  assessment in, 451, 453, 458
  as theory, 465, 467, 468
  in behavior therapy, 466
  clinical applications, 449–450, 467–469
  cognitive-behavioral chain in, 445–446, 453, 455, 463–464
  cognitive distortions in, 454–455
  concept of lapse in, 451–452
  conceptual basis, 447, 450, 465
  conceptual development, 462–465
  contracts in, 461
  coping responses in, 448
  harm reduction concept in, 462–463
  lifestyle imbalance in, 452–453
  maladaptive behavior in, 450–451
  in managing high-risk situation, 457–459
  model of relapse, 447–449
  outcome indicators, 464, 469
  precursors to relapse, 453–454, 464
  reframing technique, 460–461
  relapse roadmap, 456–457
  seemingly irrelevant decisions in, 448, 456–457
  self-monitoring activities in, 454, 457
  stepped care in, 451, 463
  support system, 461–462
  therapeutic change in, 451
  urges and cravings, 454
  urges coping strategies, 455
Relaxation
  as reduction of fear, 149–150
  desensitization and, 25
  fear response to, 154
Relaxation-based treatment
  autogenic training as, 36
  biofeedback as, 37
  coping imagery procedure in, 387
  counterconditioning of fear by, 153–154
  pharmacologic, 36, 37
  reciprocal inhibition in, 33–35
  in systematic desensitization, 33–34
  transcendental meditation as, 36
Religion–spirituality, 576
Replication therapy, 18
Repression, 24
Response covariation, 140–141

Response deprivation condition, 100–101, 102, 117–118, 119
Response processing, 65
Response satiation condition, 101–102
Reward
  in avoidance, 146–147
  temporal proximity, 72–73, 74–76, 77–78, 85, 639
Rituals, 42

Safety signals, 150
Salivation response, 250
Schedule constraints
  animal studies, 116–117
  baseline maintenance, 113–114
  clinical relevance, 69–70, 112, 119
  conservation theory, 108–111
  individual differences in repsonse to, 114–115
  minimum distance model, 105–106
  molar regulatory models, 111–112
  optimality models, 102–107, 104, 105
  programmed vs. realized, 68
  quantitative predictions, 104
  in regulation of behavior, 67–69
  response deprivation–satiation, 100–102, 104–105
  in systems model of reinforcement, 65, 107–108
  time frame of responding, 115–116
  value maximizing model, 106–107
Schizophrenia, 119, 416
Scientific method
  in behavioral research, 676–677, 696, 701–702
  in behavior modification research, 15–16
  in behavior therapy, 475, 505
  clinical cases in, 192
  dialectics in, 565
  Duhem–Quine thesis, 700–702
  empirical science in, 3–4, 6–8, 11, 696–697
  falsifiability test in, 5–6, 25, 696, 699–702
  field theory in, 612–615
  historical evolution of scientific thinking, 611–616
  in historicocritical analysis, 616–618
  in interbehavioral psychology, 618–621
  lineal mechanism in, 611–612

therapeutic manipulation of, 277–278
Skinner, B. F., 661. *See also Name Index*
  on definition of behavior, 14
  on environmental factors, 13
  on natural selection, 487–488
  on role of theory, 8–10
Sleep disorders, 388, 389
Smoking, 246–247, 367, 393
Social anxiety, 34–35
Social Anxiety and Distress Scale, 427, 428
Social behaviorism. *See* Psychological behaviorism
Social cognitive theory, 335
  conceptual basis, 356
  self-efficacy theory in, 356–357
Social competence
  aggregated skill assessment, 434
  assessment goals, 421
  assessment methodology, 417–419
  behavior-analytic approach, 417–418
  clinical relevance, 415–416, 423
  component social skills, 416–417
  conceptual development, 416–420
  decoding–encoding in, 421–423
  decoding skills, assessment of, 424–433
  definition, 421
  information-processing concepts in, 418–420, 434–435
  information-processing model of, 421–423
  information-processing skills in, 421–422
  personal attractiveness in measures of, 427, 428
  physiological response in measures of, 427–428
  process skills, 417
  self-monitoring, 423
  of sex offenders, 428–433
  situation specific, 418
  skill building in relapse prevention, 459
  social skills in, 421
  theoretical basis, 416
  topographic behavior model, 417
  validation of information-processing model, 423–424
Socialization processes
  coercion theory, 314, 316–318, 322–323

gender role stereotyping in, 503–504, 512–513
  micropolitics of sexism in, 517–518
Social learning theory
  in behavior, 14, 19
  feminist thought and, 503–504
Social planning, 19
Social Situations Questionnaire, 427, 428
SORKC model, 297
Specialization, 71–72
Startle response, 240–241, 242, 243, 250, 251
Stimuli
  in avoidance maintenance, 183–185
  changeover delay studies, 137–138
  classical conditioning model, 145–146, 176, 675
  conditioning of motivational modes and, 85
  in desensitization procedures, 33–36
  in emotion-memory networks, 233–234
  in experimentally induced neuroses, 28–29
  experimental presentation, 84–86
  in experimental vs. natural settings, 149
  in extinction of fear, 151–154
  in fear theory, 148–149
  in fear vs. frustration, 148
  feedback stimulus, 149–150
  filters, 71, 77
  generalization of fear, 154–156
  in hypothesis-based interventions, 589, 590, 591
  in instrumental learning based on fear, 149–151
  in law of effect, 97–99
  in molar regulatory models, 111–112
  processing styles in reinforcement, 76–78
  in reciprocal inhibition principle, 24
  in response-contingent reinforcement, 97
  response produced, 72, 148
  sequence effects, 72–73, 114–115, 149, 151–152, 183, 184, 387–388
  in simple-causal model of reinforcement, 61
  for standardized assessment, 251
  symbolic evocation, 156–157, 176–177

in systems model of reinforcement, 65, 76–78
in two-factor theory of avoidance, 176–179
unconditional, sudden change and, 85–86
weakening of response through exposure, 44–45
Strain theory, 336
Stress
    in bioinformational model, 243–244
    in borderline personality disorder, 569
    in coercive interactions in families, 323–324
    panic disorders and, 214–216
    physiological risk in, 244
    predisposition, 243–244
    type A behavior, 244
Stuttering, 40
Substance abuse
    bioinformational theory, 245–247
    development of relapse prevention, 446
    dialectical behavioral therapy for, 553
Substance theory, 611
Suicide/suicidal behavior
    as dialectical challenge, 556
    dialectical behavioral therapy for, 553
Surplus powerlessness, 548
Survey of Heterosexual Interactions, 427, 428
Symbolic modeling, 47
Symbolic processes, 156–157, 176–177
Symptom substitution, 139–140, 631
Systematic desensitization, 23
    automated, 231–232
    coping imagery procedure in, 387
    efficacy, 34
    habituation effects in, 45
    multidimensional fear measurement in outcomes, 231–232
    perceived self-efficacy and, 366
    in radical behavioral theory, 675
    technique, 33–34
    therapeutic applications, 34–35
Systematics, 618
Systems theory, 615–616
    application of, 64
    reinforcement in, 64–65

Termination of therapy, 649

Test of Reading Affective Cues (TRAC)
    design, 426–427
    development of, 426, 434–435
    Validation Study I, 427–428
    Validation Study II, 428–429
    Validation Study III, 429–430
    Validation Study IV, 431–432
    Validation Study S, 432–433
Theory. *See also specific theory*
    in behavior therapy, evolution of, 12–20, 24–25, 663–664, 695, 696, 705–706
    causal-system model of reinforcement, 64–65
    developmental psychology, 287–288
    framework construction methodology, 667–670
    Lakatos on, 6–7
    Laudan on, 7–8
    in logical positivism, 2–4
    logical relationships in, 697–699
    Popper on, 4–6, 696–698, 699
    psychotherapy development, i–iii
    revision of, 703–704
    scientific role of, 1–12, 20, 695–697
    Skinner on, 8–10
    testing of, 697–702
Therapeutic change. *See also* Behavior change; Outcome research
    as unlearning maladaptive behavior, 23–24
    in behavior therapy, 141
    bioinformational theory, 248–249
    in borderline personality disorder, 566, 568–569, 570
    client acceptance in, 553–554
    coercion theory, 330, 333–334
    in cognitive–behavioral therapy, 445–446, 507–508, 510
    cognitive theories, 45–46
    contingency scheduling in behavior systems, 70
    developmental issues in, 288
    in dialectical behavioral therapy, 573–574
    dialectical praxis in, 557–559
    early-phase motivation for, 275–276
    in early relational interventions, 304–305
    emotional processing in, 248–249

expectancy theory, 47
in exposure flooding, 152
exposure theory, 45
extinction theory, 44–45
in eye movement desensitization, 40, 42–43
fear theory, 151–154
feeding strategies in, 30–31
feminist goals in, 519–524
in flooding therapy, 42–43
in functional analytic psychotherapy, 643
generalization of session effects, 640
implosive theory, 185–186
in implosive therapy, 174–175, 199–200, 202
in learning-based approaches, 259–260
matching law in, 136–137
in misattribution training, 389
molar regulatory theory, 119
nonspecific effects in, 40–41, 46
persistence of, 447
psychoanalytic theory, 23–24
radical behaviorism and, 675
raised expectations of self-efficacy in, 47–48
reattribution training, 395
reciprocal inhibition in, 24, 25
reinforcement concepts in, 639, 641–642
relapse prevention goals, 445–446
relapse prevention theory, 451
relaxation in counterconditioning of fear, 153–154
self-efficacy theory, 365–368
social context of, 529–531
symptom substitution in, 139–140, 631
systematic desensitization, 33–34
technical-theoretical integration, 173–174
therapeutic relationship in, 637
transmarginal inhibition in, 43
treatment generalization in, 139–140, 627
verbal processes in, 686
Therapeutic contracts, 461
Therapeutic relationship
as nonspecific effect, 41, 46

in behavior therapy, 507
in cognitive–behavioral therapy, 508
contradictory elements in, 647–648
in dialectical behavioral therapy, 578
in dialectical behavioral therapy with borderline disorder, 572, 573–574
in flooding therapy outcomes, 42–43
in implosive therapy, 19
reciprocal inhibition of fear in, 25
in therapeutic change, 637
Therapeutic technique
affect management, 278
for anxiety disorders, 23
aversive debate, 588–589
in behavior therapy, 18, 506–507
categorization, 587–588
child cognitive ability and, 300–302
in coercion theory, 329–331
in cognitive–behavioral therapy, 508–509
cognitive interventions in marital distress, 404–405
cognitive restructuring, 457
constructional vs. eliminative approaches, 631
in dialectical behavioral therapy with borderline disorder, 572–573, 575–577
drug-induced arousal, 388
in fear theory, 151–152
feminist therapy, 511
in functional analytic psychotherapy, 639–642, 647–651
graded task assignments in depression, 392
guided mastery, 367
holistic developmental perspective, 299–300
identifying cognitive errors, 370–371
in implosive therapy, 174, 186–187, 190–195
in interbehavioral psychology, 631
manipulation of environmental cues, 277–278
misattribution training, 386–390
modeling in, 47–48
natural vs. contrived reinforcement, 641–642
principle of minimum services, 626–627

problem-solving strategies, 302–303
reattribution training, 386, 390–401, 393, 394–395, 399–400
reciprocal inhibition in, 32–40
reinforcement based, 59–60
relapse prevention, 451, 453, 454–455, 455, 456–457, 458–459, 460–461, 468
resolution of early developmental tasks, 303–305
selection of, 35
self-control theory, 260, 273–278
self-efficacy education, 369–370
self-managed, 519–520, 521–522, 524
self-monitoring skills, 277
sexual arousal as, 37–38
shaping, 642
social skills approach, 639–640
termination phase, 649
therapist-evoked responses, 40–41
three-system assessment for, 231
urge coping, 455
within-session contingencies, 639–640
Three-systems view
of fear, 230–231
urge systems in drug abuse, 245–246
Token economies, 60
Topographic behavior model, 417
Trait factors
in coercive interactions in families, 323, 324
in development of aggressive behavior, 336–337
in social competency models, 418

Tranquilizers, 37
Transcendental meditation, 36
Transference, 637
Transmarginal inhibition, 43
Treatment generalization, 139–140, 627
Tricyclic antidepressants, 121–122
Twenty-four-hour environments, 87–88, 155
Two-factor theory of avoidance. *See also* Fear theory
conservation of anxiety hypothesis and, 181–182
criticism of, 160, 180
in implosive theory, 175–179
partial irreversibility principle in, 182
principles of, 145–147
resistance to extinction of avoidance, 180–181
vicious-circle behavior and, 158
Two-factor theory of emotion, 386, 387, 388
Two-factor theory of fear, 147–148
Two-process theory, 145
Type A behavior, 244

Unconditioned stimulus. *See also* Stimuli
absence of, in reinforcement, 178–179
animal vs. human response, 159–161
in classical conditioning, 146
in two-factor theory, 176

Vicious-circle behavior, 157–158
Volition, 262–263

Zen philosophy, 554, 575

ABOUT THE EDITORS

William O'Donohue is an assistant professor of psychology at Northern Illinois University. He received a doctorate in clinical psychology from the State University of New York at Stony Brook and a master's degree in philosophy from Indiana University. He has coedited several books, including *Theories of Human Sexuality*, *The Sexual Abuse of Children*, and *The Handbook of the Sexual Dysfunctions* (all with J. H. Geer) and *Handbook of Psychological Skills Training* (with Leonard Krasner). He has published in the areas of human sexuality and its problems, cognitive behavior therapy, clinical decision making, and the philosophy of psychology.

Leonard Krasner received his doctorate from Columbia University. He is a licensed clinical psychologist (California and New York) and has been involved in training clinical psychologists as scientists–practitioners in various academic and hospital settings. He has authored, coauthored, edited, or coedited numerous books and articles. He is currently clinical professor, Department of Psychiatry and Behavioral Sciences, Stanford University.